GAAP GUIDE, VOLUME I

Restatement and Analysis of
Current FASB Standards and Other Current FASB, EITF,
and AICPA Announcements

JAN R. WILLIAMS, Ph.D., CPA

JOSEPH V. CARCELLO, Ph.D., CPA, CMA, CIA

TERRY L. NEAL, Ph.D., CPA

JUDITH WEISS, CPA

Editorial Staff

Editor .... Elizabeth Murphy
Production .... Kavitha Seheran; Linda Kalteux

This publication is designed to provide accurate and authoritative information in regard to the subject matter covered. It is sold with the understanding that the publisher is not engaged in rendering legal, accounting, or other professional services. If legal advice or other professional assistance is required, the services of a competent professional person should be sought.

—From a *Declaration of Principles* jointly adopted by a Committee of the American Bar Association and a Committee of Publishers and Associations

ISBN: 978-0-8080-3549-7 (Set)
ISBN: 978-0-8080-3546-6 (Vol. I)
ISBN: 970-0-8080-3548-0 (Vol. II)

© 2013 CCH Incorporated. All Rights Reserved.
4025 W. Peterson Avenue
Chicago, IL 60646-6085
800 248 3248
CCHGroup.com

No claim is made to original government works; however, within this Product or Publication, the following are subject to CCH Incorporated's copyright: (1) the gathering, compilation, and arrangement of such government materials; (2) the magnetic translation and digital conversion of data, if applicable; (3) the historical, statutory and other notes and references; and (4) the commentary and other materials.

Portions of this work were published in a previous edition.

Printed in the United States of America

GAAP Guide, Volumes I & II

By Jan R. Williams, Joseph V. Carcello, Terry L. Neal, and Judith Weiss

Highlights

The 2014 CCH *GAAP Guide* analyzes financial reporting standards contained in the FASB's Accounting Standards Codification™ (ASC). The authoritative literature is organized in a manner consistent with the ASC and uses the numbering system in the ASC. As applicable, each chapter is separated into two sections: (1) General Guidance, and (2) Interpretive Guidance to assist users of the *GAAP Guide* in understanding and applying GAAP for a particular transaction or financial reporting situation.

2014 Edition

This edition of the *GAAP Guide* includes new and expanded coverage for the following subjects:

- Chapter 2 covering ASC 205 (Presentation of Financial Statements) has been revised to include ASU 2013-07, *Presentation of Financial Statements: Liquidation Basis of Accounting.*

- Chapter 3 covering ASC 210 (Balance Sheet) has been revised to include ASU 2013-01, *Clarifying the Scope of Disclosures about Offsetting Assets and Liabilities.*

- Chapter 7 covering ASC 230 (Statement of Cash Flows) has been revised to include ASU 2012-05, *Not-for-Profit Entities: Classification of the Sale of Proceeds of Donated Financial Assets in the Statement of Cash Flows.*

- Chapter 26 covering ASC 405 (Liabilities) has been revised to include ASU 2013-04, *Obligations Resulting from Joint and Several Liability Agreements for Which the Total Amount of the Obligation is Fixed at the Reporting Date.*

- Chapter 44 covering ASC 740 (Income Taxes) has been revised to include ASU 2013-11, *Presentation of an Unrecognized Tax Benefit When a Net Operating Loss Carryforward, a Similar Tax Loss, or a Tax Credit Carryforward Exists.*

- Chapter 45 covering ASC 805 (Business Combinations) has been revised to include ASU 2012-06, *Subsequent Accounting for an Indemnification Asset Recognized at the Acquisition Date as a Result of a Government-Assisted Acquisition of a Financial Institution.*

- Chapter 48 covering ASC 815 (Derivatives and Hedging) has been revised to include ASU 2013-10, *Inclusion of the Fed Funds Effective Swap Rate (or Overnight Index Swap Rate) as a Benchmark Interest Rate for Hedge Accounting Purposes.*

- Chapter 50 covering ASC 825 (Financial Instruments) has been revised to include ASU 2013-03, *Financial Instruments.*

- Chapter 51 covering ASC 830 (Foreign Currency Matters) has been revised to include ASU 2013-05, *Foreign Currency Matters: Parent's Accounting for the Cumulative Translation Adjustment for Derecognition of Certain Subsidiaries or Groups of Assets within a Foreign Entity or of an Investment in a Foreign Entity.*
- Appendix C covering ASC 92X (Entertainment) has been revised to add general guidance coverage of major entertainment industries: broadcasters, cable television companies, casinos, films, and music. It has also been revised to include ASU 2012-07, *Accounting for Fair Value Information that Arises after the Measurement Date and its Inclusion in the Impairment Analysis of Unamortized Film Costs.*
- Appendix H covering ASC 958 (Not-for-Profit Entities) has been revised to include ASU 2013-06, *Services Received from Personnel of an Affiliate.*

Important Notices regarding Exposure Drafts of Accounting Standards Updates that are outstanding at the time the 2014 CCH *GAAP Guide* goes to press are included, as follows:

- Chapter 18 (Receivables), *Reclassification of Collateralized Mortgage Loans upon a Troubled Debt Restructuring.*
- Chapter 24 (Intangibles—Goodwill and Others), *Intangibles—Goodwill and Other.*
- Chapter 36 (Revenue Recognition), *Revenue Recognition from Contracts and Customers.*
- Chapter 45 (Business Combinations), *Business Combinations.*
- Chapter 47 (Consolidations), *Measuring the Financial Liabilities of a Consolidated Collateralized Financing Entity.*
- Chapter 48 (Derivatives and Hedging), *Derivatives and Hedging.*
- Chapter 50 (Financial Instruments), *Disclosures about Liquidity Risk and Interest Rate Risk* and *Credit Losses* and *Recognition and Measurement of Financial Assets and Liabilities* (three Exposure Drafts).
- Chapter 52 (Insurance Contracts), *Insurance Contracts.*
- Chapter 54 (Leases), *Leases.*
- Chapter 58 (Accounting for Service Concession Arrangements), *Service Concession Arrangements.*
- Chapter 60 (Transfers and Servicing), *Transfers and Servicing.*

CCH Learning Center

CCH's goal is to provide you with the clearest, most concise, and up-to-date accounting and auditing information to help further your professional development, as well as a convenient method to help you satisfy your continuing professional education requirements. The CCH Learning Center* offers a com-

---

* CCH is registered with the National Association of State Boards of Accountancy (NASBA) as a sponsor of continuing professional education on the National Registry of CPE Sponsors. State boards of accountancy have final authority on the acceptance of indi-

plete line of self-study courses covering complex and constantly evolving accounting and auditing issues. We are continually adding new courses to the library to help you stay current on all the latest developments. The CCH Learning Center courses are available 24 hours a day, seven days a week. You'll get immediate exam results and certification. To view our complete accounting and auditing course catalog, go to: **cch.learningcenter.com**.

Accounting Research Manager®

Accounting Research Manager is the most comprehensive, up-to-date, and objective online database of financial reporting literature. It includes all authoritative and proposed accounting, auditing, and SEC literature, plus independent, expert-written interpretive guidance.

Our Weekly Summary e-mail newsletter highlights the key developments of the week, giving you the assurance that you have the most current information. It provides links to new FASB, AICPA, SEC, PCAOB, EITF, and IASB authoritative and proposal-stage literature, plus insightful guidance from financial reporting experts.

Our outstanding team of content experts takes pride in updating the system on a daily basis, so you stay as current as possible. You'll learn of newly released literature and deliberations of current financial reporting projects as soon as they occur! Plus, you benefit from their easy-to-understand technical translations.

With **Accounting Research Manager**, you maximize the efficiency of your research time, while enhancing your results. Learn more about our content, our experts and how you can request a FREE trial by visiting us at **accountingresearchmanager.com**.

11/13

© 2013 CCH Incorporated. All Rights Reserved.

(Footnote Continued)

vidual courses for CPE credit. Complaints regarding registered sponsors may be addressed to the National Registry of CPE Sponsors, 150 Fourth Avenue North, Nashville, TN 37219-2417. Telephone: 615-880-4200.

* CCH is registered with the National Association of State Boards of Accountancy as a Quality Assurance Service (QAS) sponsor of continuing professional education. Participating state boards of accountancy have final authority on the acceptance of individual courses for CPE credit. Complaints regarding QAS program sponsors may be addressed to NASBA, 150 Fourth Avenue North, Suite 700, Nashville, TN 37219-2417. Telephone: 615-880-4200.

Contents

Our Peer Review Policy	xi
Peer Review Statement	xiii
Preface	xv
About the Authors	xvii
About the Accounting Standards Codification and the Former GAAP Hierarchy	xix

VOLUME I
Generally Accepted Accounting Principles

Chapter 1	ASC 105—Generally Accepted Accounting Principles	1001
Chapter 2	ASC 205—Presentation of Financial Statements	2001
Chapter 3	ASC 210—Balance Sheet	3001
Chapter 4	ASC 215—Statement of Shareholder Equity	4001
Chapter 5	ASC 220—Comprehensive Income	5001
Chapter 6	ASC 225—Income Statement	6001
Chapter 7	ASC 230—Statement of Cash Flows	7001
Chapter 8	ASC 235—Accounting Policies and Standards	8001
Chapter 9	ASC 250—Accounting Changes and Error Corrections	9001
Chapter 10	ASC 255—Changing Prices	10,001
Chapter 11	ASC 260—Earnings Per Share	11,001
Chapter 12	ASC 270—Interim Reporting	12,001
Chapter 13	ASC 272—Limited Liability Entities	13,001
Chapter 14	ASC 274—Personal Financial Statements	14,001
Chapter 15	ASC 275—Risks and Uncertainties	15,001
Chapter 16	ASC 280—Segment Reporting	16,001
Chapter 17	ASC 305—Cash and Cash Equivalents	17,001
Chapter 18	ASC 310—Receivables	18,001
Chapter 19	ASC 320—Investments—Debt and Equity Securities	19,001
Chapter 20	ASC 323—Investments—Equity Method and Joint Ventures	20,001
Chapter 21	ASC 325—Investments—Other	21,001
Chapter 22	ASC 330—Inventory	22,001
Chapter 23	ASC 340—Deferred Costs and Other Assets	23,001
Chapter 24	ASC 350—Intangibles—Goodwill and Other	24,001

Chapter 25	ASC 360—Property, Plant, and Equipment	25,001
Chapter 26	ASC 405—Liabilities	26,001
Chapter 27	ASC 410—Asset Retirement and Environmental Obligations	27,001
Chapter 28	ASC 420—Exit or Disposal Cost Obligations	28,001
Chapter 29	ASC 430—Deferred Revenue	29,001
Chapter 30	ASC 440—Commitments	30,001
Chapter 31	ASC 450—Contingencies	31,001
Chapter 32	ASC 460—Guarantees	32,001
Chapter 33	ASC 470—Debt	33,001
Chapter 34	ASC 480—Distinguishing Liabilities From Equity	34,001
Chapter 35	ASC 505—Equity	35,001
Chapter 36	ASC 605—Revenue Recognition	36,001
Chapter 37	ASC 705—Cost of Sales and Services	37,001
Chapter 38	ASC 710—Compensation—General	38,001
Chapter 39	ASC 712—Compensation—Nonretirement Postemployment Benefits	39,001
Chapter 40	ASC 715—Compensation—Retirement Benefits	40,001

VOLUME II

Chapter 41	ASC 718—Compensation—Stock Compensation	41,001
Chapter 42	ASC 720—Other Expenses	42,001
Chapter 43	ASC 730—Research and Development	43,001
Chapter 44	ASC 740—Income Taxes	44,001
Chapter 45	ASC 805—Business Combinations	45,001
Chapter 46	ASC 808—Collaborative Arrangements	46,001
Chapter 47	ASC 810—Consolidation	47,001
Chapter 48	ASC 815—Derivatives and Hedging	48,001
Chapter 49	ASC 820—Fair Value Measurement	49,001
Chapter 50	ASC 825—Financial Instruments	50,001
Chapter 51	ASC 830—Foreign Currency Matters	51,001
Chapter 52	ASC 834—Insurance Contracts	52,001
Chapter 53	ASC 835—Interest	53,001
Chapter 54	ASC 840—Leases	54,001
Chapter 55	ASC 845—Nonmonetary Transactions	55,001
Chapter 56	ASC 850—Related Party Disclosures	56,001
Chapter 57	ASC 852—Reorganizations	57,001
Chapter 58	ASC 853—Accounting for Service Concession Arrangements	58,001
Chapter 59	ASC 855—Subsequent Events	59,001
Chapter 60	ASC 860—Transfers and Servicing	60,001

Appendices

Appendix A	ASC 912—Contractors—Federal Government	61,001
Appendix B	ASC 915—Development Stage Entities	62,001
Appendix C	ASC 92X—Entertainment	63,001
Appendix D	ASC 93X—Extractive Activities	64,001
Appendix E	ASC 94X—Financial Services	65,001
Appendix F	ASC 952—Franchisors	66,001
Appendix G	ASC 954—Health Care Entities	67,001
Appendix H	ASC 958—Not-For-Profit Entities	68,001
Appendix I	ASC 962—Plan Accounting	69,001
Appendix J	ASC 970—Real Estate—General	70,001
Appendix K	ASC 976—Real Estate—Retail Land	71,001
Appendix L	ASC 980—Regulated Operations	72,001
Appendix M	ASC 985—Software	73,001

Accounting Resources on the Web   74,001
Index   75,001

For the most recent activities of the FASB and the AICPA, refer to the *GAAP Update Service* **and the** *GAAP Library* **(CCHGroup.com).**

Our Peer Review Policy

Thank you for ordering the 2014 *GAAP Guide*. Each year we bring you the best accounting and auditing reference guides. To confirm the technical accuracy and quality control of our materials, CCH voluntarily submitted to a peer review of our publishing system and our publications (see the Peer Review Report on the following page).

In addition to peer review, our publications undergo strict technical and content reviews by qualified practitioners. This ensures that our books meet "real-world" standards and applicability.

Our publications are reviewed every step of the way—from conception to production—to ensure that we bring you the finest guides on the market.

Updated annually, peer reviewed, technically accurate, convenient, and practical—the 2014 *GAAP Guide* shows our commitment to creating books and practice aids you can trust.

Note that the most recent Peer Review Statement will be included in our next edition and is available upon request by emailing elizabeth.murphy@wolterskluwer.com.

Peer Review Statement

Caldwell, Becker, Dervin, Petrick & Co., L.L.P.
CERTIFIED PUBLIC ACCOUNTANTS

Quality Control Materials Review Report

November 12, 2009

Executive Board
CCH, a Wolters Kluwer business
and the National Peer Review Committee

We have reviewed the system of quality control for the development and maintenance of GAAP Guide (2010 Edition) (hereafter referred to as *materials*) of CCH, a Wolters Kluwer business (the organization) and the resultant materials in effect at October 31, 2009. Our quality control materials peer review was conducted in accordance with the Standards for Performing and Reporting on Peer Reviews established by the Peer Review Board of the American Institute of Certified Public Accountants. The organization is responsible for designing a system of quality control and complying with it to provide users of the materials with reasonable assurance that the materials are reliable aids to assist them in conforming with those professional standards that the materials purport to encompass. Our responsibility is to express an opinion on the design of the system and the organization's compliance with that system based on our review. The nature, objectives, scope, limitations of, and the procedures performed in a Quality Control Materials Review are described in the standards at www.aicpa.org/prsummary.

In our opinion, the system of quality control for the development and maintenance of the quality control materials of CCH, a Wolters Kluwer business was suitably designed and was being complied with during the year ended October 31, 2009, to provide users of the materials with reasonable assurance that the materials are reliable aids to assist them in conforming with those professional standards the materials purport to encompass. Also, in our opinion, the quality control materials referred to above are reliable aids at October 31, 2009. Organizations can receive a rating of *pass*, *pass with deficiency(ies)*, or *fail*. CCH, a Wolters Kluwer business has received a peer review rating of *pass*.

CALDWELL, BECKER, DERVIN, PETRICK & CO., LLP.
CALDWELL, BECKER, DERVIN, PETRICK & CO., L.L.P.

20750 Ventura Boulevard, Suite 140 • Woodland Hills, CA 91364
(818) 704-1040 • FAX (818) 704-5536

Preface

The 2014 *GAAP Guide* explains and analyzes promulgated accounting standards in use today as reflected in the FASB Accounting Standards Codification™ (ASC). This edition is current through the issuance of Accounting Standards Update 2013-11 and assists users by including citations to the ASC throughout.

New Accounting Standards Updates and Outstanding Exposure Drafts

- ASU 2012-05 — Statement of Cash Flows: Not-for-Profit Entities: Classification of the Sale of Proceeds of Donated Financial Assets in the Statement of Cash Flows
- ASU 2012-06 — Business Combinations: Subsequent Accounting for an Indemnification Asset Recognized at the Acquisition Date as a Result of a Government-Assisted Acquisition of a Financial Institution
- ASU 2012-07 — Entertainment—Films: Accounting for Fair Value Information That Arises after the Measurement Date and Its Inclusion in the Impairment Analysis of Unamortized Film costs
- ASU 2013-01 — Balance Sheet: Clarifying the Scope of Disclosures about Offsetting Assets and Liabilities
- ASU 2013-03 — Financial Instruments: Clarifying the Scope and Applicability of a Particular Disclosure to Nonpublic Entities
- ASU 2013-04 — Liabilities: Obligations Resulting from Joint and Several Liability Agreements for which the Total Amount of the Obligation is Fixed at the Reporting Date
- ASU 2013-05 — Foreign Currency Matters: Parent's Accounting for the Cumulative Translation Adjustment for Derecognition of Certain Subsidiaries or Groups of Assets within a Foreign Entity or of an Investment in a Foreign Entity
- ASU 2013-06 — Not-for-Profit Entities: Services Received from Personnel of an Affiliate
- ASU 2013-07 — Presentation of Financial Statements: Liquidation Basis of Accounting
- ASU 2013-10 — Derivatives and Hedging: Inclusion of the Fed Funds Effective Swap Rate (or Overnight Index Swap Rate) as a Benchmark Interest Rate for Hedge Accounting Purposes
- ASU 2013-11 — Income Taxes: Presentation of an Unrecognized Tax Benefit When a Net Operating Loss Carryforward, Similar Tax Loss, or Tax Credit Forward Exists

- ASU Exposure Draft Reclassification of Collateralized Mortgage Loans Upon a Troubled Debt Restructuring
- ASU Exposure Draft Intangibles—Goodwill and Others
- ASU Exposure Draft Revenue Recognition from Contracts and Customers
- ASU Exposure Draft Business Combinations
- ASU Exposure Draft Measuring the Financial Liabilities of a Consolidated Collateralized Financing Entity
- ASU Exposure Draft Derivatives and Hedging
- ASU Exposure Draft Disclosures about Liquidity Risk and Interest Rate Risk
- ASU Exposure Draft Service Concession Arrangements
- ASU Exposure Draft Credit Losses
- ASU Exposure Draft Recognition and Measurement of Financial Assets and Liabilities
- ASU Exposure Draft Insurance Contracts
- ASU Exposure Draft Leases
- ASU Exposure Draft Transfers and Servicing

How to Use the 2014 *GAAP Guide*

The 2014 *GAAP Guide* organizes accounting pronouncements around the major sections of the FASB Accounting Standards Codification™. The Codification brings together in a single location all GAAP for a particular transaction or other financial reporting situation.

The complete *GAAP Guide* is available on CD-ROM and as an eBook. Researching the *GAAP Guide* is now easier than ever.

The *GAAP Guide* is written in clear, comprehensible language. Each section of the Codification covered in the 2014 *GAAP Guide* is discussed in a comprehensive format that makes it easy to understand and apply. Practical illustrations and examples demonstrate and clarify specific accounting principles.

The **Practice Pointers** throughout this edition do just that: they point out in plain English how to apply the standards just discussed.

The **Practice Notes** enrich the discussion by presenting interesting aspects of GAAP.

To facilitate research, the *GAAP Guide* includes extensive codification references to pertinent paragraphs of the original pronouncements.

The 2014 *GAAP Guide* meets accounting industry standards overseen by the peer review system. A document covering the peer review of this book is reprinted for your reference.

About the Authors

Jan R. Williams, Ph.D., CPA, is Dean and Professor Emeritus of the College of Business Administration at the University of Tennessee, Knoxville, where he has been on the faculty since 1977. Formerly, he was on the faculties of the University of Georgia and Texas Tech University. He received a Ph.D. in business administration from the University of Arkansas and is a CPA licensed in Arkansas (inactive) and Tennessee (license to practice).

Dr. Williams has, for many years, been actively involved in the American Institute of Certified Public Accountants, the Tennessee Society of Certified Public Accountants, and several other professional accounting organizations. Throughout his career, he has taught continuing professional education for CPAs. In 1994, Dr. Williams received the Outstanding Accounting Educator Award from both the Tennessee Society of CPAs and the AICPA. He was president of the American Accounting Association in 1999–2000 and has authored or co-authored five books and more than 70 articles and other publications on issues related to financial reporting and accounting education. Dr. Williams is the past chair of the Board of Directors of the AACSB (Association to Advance Collegiate Schools of Business) International, the largest accreditation organization for business schools in the world. He retired from the University of Tennessee in 2013 and continues his involvement in several academic and professional organizations.

Joseph V. Carcello, Ph.D., CPA, CMA, CIA, is the Ernst & Young Professor in the Department of Accounting and Information Management at the University of Tennessee. Dr. Carcello also is co-founder and Director of Research for the University's Corporate Governance Center. He has taught continuing professional education courses for two of the Big 4 accounting firms, the AICPA, the Institute of Internal Auditors, the Institute of Management Accountants, and the Tennessee and Florida Societies of CPAs. He has provided consulting services to public companies on revenue recognition and on Section 404 of the Sarbanes-Oxley Act. Dr. Carcello has served the Securities and Exchange Commission as an expert witness.

Dr. Carcello is the co-author of CCH's *GAAS Guide.* He is also the co-author of funded research studies by the Committee of Sponsoring Organizations (COSO) of the Treadway Commission that examines fraudulent financial reporting between 1987 and 2007. Dr. Carcello also is the co-author of a monograph published by the AICPA entitled, *Fraud-Related SEC Enforcement Actions Against Auditors: 1987-1997.* Dr. Carcello serves a member of the Public Company Accounting Oversight Board's (PCAOB) Investor Advisory Group and Standing Advisory Group. He formerly served on COSO's Small Business Controls Guidance Task Force.

Terry L. Neal, Ph.D., CPA, is the Dennis Hendrix Professor in Accounting in the Department of Accounting and Information Management at the University of Tennessee. He also is a Research Fellow at the University of Tennessee's Corporate Governance Center. Dr. Neal currently teaches a graduate course in advanced financial accounting topics, an undergraduate intermediate accounting course, and has also taught undergraduate auditing. He has also taught continuing professional education courses for one of the Big 4 accounting firms for several years. Dr. Neal serves as the director of the Ph.D. program in Accounting and teaches a doctoral seminar in empirical/archival research, with an emphasis on auditing and corporate governance issues. Dr. Neal also serves as a research fellow of the ERM Initiative at North Carolina State University.

Dr. Neal received a B.S. in accounting from Tennessee Technological University (1988) and a Ph.D. from the University of Tennessee (1998). Prior to joining the faculty at the University of Tennessee, Dr. Neal was on the faculty of the Douglas J. Von Allmen School of Accountancy at the University of Kentucky.

Judith Weiss, CPA, has an M.S. in Accounting from Long Island University, Greenvale, New York, and an M.S. in Education from Queens College, Flushing, New York. After several years in public accounting and private industry, she worked as a technical manager in the AICPA's Accounting Standards Division, where she helped industry committees to develop Audit and Accounting Guides and Statements of Position. As a senior manager in the national offices of Deloitte & Touche LLP and Grant Thornton LLP, she was involved in projects related to standard-setting by the FASB and the AICPA. Ms. Weiss has followed the work of the EITF since its inception and has attended its meetings in person or through the internet regularly since 1991.

Since 1993, Ms. Weiss has combined her extensive experience in the development and implementation of accounting and auditing standards with her technical writing background in writing projects related to accounting standards. She has contributed to several books in the area of accounting and auditing. She also has coauthored articles on accounting standards for several publications, including the *Journal of Accountancy, The CPA Journal, The Journal of Real Estate Accounting and Taxation,* and the *Journal of Corporate Accounting and Finance.* Ms. Weiss is also the author of the *GAAP Update Service.*

Acknowledgments

Judith Weiss gives thanks to the late Thomas W. McRae and to Paul Rosenfield, formerly of the AICPA, who taught her about writing and the accounting standards-setting process; former colleagues and friends who helped to make the Guide a reality; and four very important CPAs: her husband, Carl, sons, Daniel and Jonathan, and daughter-in-law, Robyn, for their interest and tireless encouragement in this project.

About the Accounting Standards Codification and the Former GAAP Hierarchy

For many years, generally accepted accounting principles comprised standards that were issued by different standard-setting bodies and professional organizations.

In June of 2009, after an extended period of preparation, experimentation, and testing, the FASB issued the FASB Accounting Standards Codification™ (ASC) and replaced all standards by establishing and codifying a single source of authoritative nongovernmental U.S. GAAP. The ASC organizes the large number of U.S. GAAP pronouncements into approximately 90 accounting topics, placing them in a consistent structure that includes relevant Securities and Exchange Commission guidance for public companies. The Codification did not change GAAP but, rather, introduced a new structure that is described by the FASB as easily accessible and user-friendly. The FASB expects the codification to assist in researching accounting topics. The improved usability of the authoritative literature and accessibility of updates to standards are expected to mitigate the risk of noncompliance.

The Codification was generally effective for financial statements issued for interim and annual periods ending after September 15, 2009, with limited exceptions. At that time, all non-SEC accounting and reporting standards were superseded, with limited exceptions. Additional coverage of the Codification is found in Chapter 2 of CCH's 2014 *GAAP Guide, Volume I.*

Generally Accepted Accounting Principles

CHAPTER 1
ASC 105—GENERALLY ACCEPTED ACCOUNTING PRINCIPLES

General Guidance	1001
ASC 105-10: Overall	1001
GAAP Hierarchy and the Accounting Standards Codification	1001

GENERAL GUIDANCE

ASC 105-10: OVERALL

GAAP HIERARCHY AND THE ACCOUNTING STANDARDS CODIFICATION

The meaning of the term *generally accepted accounting principles* (GAAP) has varied over time. Originally, GAAP referred to accounting policies and procedures that were widely used in practice. As standard-setting bodies and professional organizations became more involved in establishing required or preferred practices, the term came to refer more to the pronouncements issued by particular accounting bodies. Today, the term "GAAP" is defined by the FASB's Accounting Standards Codification (ASC). The ASC is now the single source of authoritative accounting principles recognized by the FASB to be applied by nongovernmental entities in the preparation of financial statements in accordance with generally accepted accounting principles. Rules and interpretative releases of the Securities and Exchange Commission under the authority of federal law are also sources of authoritative GAAP for SEC registrants (ASC 105-10-5-1).

Prior to the issuance of the Codification, the FASB established what is commonly referred to as the GAAP hierarchy. The purpose of the GAAP hierarchy was to instruct financial statement preparers, auditors, and users of financial statements concerning the relative priority of the different sources of GAAP used by auditors to judge the fairness of presentation in financial statements. Since the issuance of the Codification, which superseded the GAAP hierarchy, all authoritative sources of GAAP included in the Codification carry the same level of authority.

If the guidance for a transaction or event is not specified in the ASC, the entity shall first consider accounting principles for similar transactions or events that exists within the ASC. Next the entity is to consider nonauthoritative guidance from other sources, including FASB Concepts Statements, AICPA Issue Papers, International Financial Reporting Standards, pronouncements of professional associations or regulatory agencies, Technical Information Services Inquiries and Replies included in AICPA Technical Practice Aids, and accounting textbooks (ASC 105-10-5-2, 3).

The Codification excludes governmental standards and codifies the following standards:

- FASB Standards
  - Statements
  - Interpretations
  - Technical Bulletins
  - Staff Positions
  - Staff Implementation Guides
- Emerging Issues Task Force
  - Abstracts
  - Appendix D Topics
  - Staff Implementation Guides
- Derivative Implementation Issues
- Accounting Principles Board Opinions
- Accounting Research Bulletins
- Accounting Interpretations
- AICPA
  - Statements of Position
  - Audit and Accounting Guides
  - Practice Bulletins
  - Technical Inquiry Services

PRACTICE POINTER: The ASC can be accessed through the FASB's web site at www.fasb.org. An opportunity is available for limited use of the ASC for those who are not familiar with it. This is a good way to explore the ASC, test its capabilities and functionality, and make an informed decision regarding a subscription options.

CHAPTER 2
ASC 205—PRESENTATION OF FINANCIAL STATEMENTS

Part I: General Guidance	2001
ASC 205-10: Overall	2001
Overview	2001
Background	2001
Comparative Financial Statements	2002
ASC 205-20: Discontinued Operations	2002
Discontinued Operations	2002
Illustration of Presentation of Net Income	2003
Assets to Be Disposed Of	2003
Illustration of Presentation of Discontinued Operations	2004
ASC 205-30: Liquidation Basis of Accounting	2005
Important Notice for 2014	2006
Part II: Interpretive Guidance	2007
ASC 205-20: Discontinued Operations	2007
ASC 205-20-45-6 through 45-69; S50-1; S99-3	
Allocation of Interest to Discontinued Operations	2007
Illustration of Allocation of Interest to Discontinued Operations	
ASC 205-20-50-4, 50-6; 55-4 through 55-26, 55-35, 55-37 through 55-40, 55-49 through 55-58, 55-60 through 55-65, 55-67 through 55-79	
Applying the Conditions in Paragraph 42 of FASB Statement No. 144, *Accounting for the Impairment or Disposal of Long-Lived Assets,* in Determining Whether to Report Discontinued Operations	2009

PART I: GENERAL GUIDANCE

ASC 205-10: OVERALL

OVERVIEW

Reporting the results of operations, primarily determining and presenting net income and comprehensive income, is one of the most important aspects of financial reporting. GAAP provide specific guidance concerning how certain items should be presented in the income statement.

BACKGROUND

For many years, there were differences of opinion in the accounting profession as to what should be included in net income. Proponents of the *all-inclusive concept* (sometimes called "clean surplus") believed that all items affecting net increases in owners' equity, except dividends and capital transactions, should be included in computing net income. Alternatively, proponents of the *current operating performance concept* (sometimes called "dirty surplus") advocated limiting the determination of net income to normal, recurring items of profit and loss that relate only to the current period and recognizing other items by direct charges and credits to retained earnings. Differences between the two concepts are seen most clearly in the treatment of the following items:

- Unusual or infrequent items
- Extraordinary items
- Changes in accounting principles
- Discontinued operations
- Prior period adjustments
- Certain items that are required by GAAP to be recognized directly in stockholders' equity rather than in net income

Current GAAP generally requires the presentation of income in a manner that generally is consistent with the all inclusive concept. Net income includes all items of revenue, expense, gain, and loss during a reporting period, except prior period adjustments, dividends, and capital transactions, and a limited number of items that are required to be recognized directly in equity. Examples of items treated in this manner are certain foreign currency adjustments and certain changes in the value of debt and equity investments.

COMPARATIVE FINANCIAL STATEMENTS

Comparative financial statements reveal more information than noncomparative statements and furnish useful data about differences in the results of operations for the periods involved or in the financial position at the comparison dates (ASC 205-10-45-1).

Consistency is a major factor in creating comparability. Prior-year amounts and classifications must be comparable with the current period presented, and exceptions must be disclosed clearly (ASC 205-10-45-2, 4).

ASC 205-20: DISCONTINUED OPERATIONS

DISCONTINUED OPERATIONS

ASC 205 provides guidance with regard to reporting of discontinued operations. For purposes of applying ASC 205, a component of an entity comprises operations and cash flows that can be clearly distinguished, operationally and for financial reporting purposes, from the rest of the entity. A component may be a reportable segment or an operating segment as those terms are defined in ASC 280 (Segment Reporting), a subsidiary, or an asset group (ASC Glossary).

The results of operations of a component that has been disposed of or is classified as held for sale are reported in discontinued operations if both of the following conditions are met: (1) the operations and cash flows of the component have been, or will be, eliminated from the ongoing operations of the entity as a result of the disposal, and (2) the entity will have no significant continuing involvement in the operations of the component after the disposal transaction (ASC 205-20-45-1).

ASC 205—Presentation of Financial Statements

In a period in which a component of an entity either has been disposed of or is classified as held for sale, the income statement of a business enterprise (statement of activities for a not-for-profit organization) shall report the results of operations of the component, including any gain or loss recognized on the initial or subsequent write-down to fair value of the component, in discontinued operations. Discontinued operations are reported as a separate component, before extraordinary items. Any gain or loss recognized on the disposal that is part of the discontinued operations element shall be separately disclosed (ASC 205-20-45-3).

The following information is required to be disclosed in conjunction with discontinued operations (ASC 205-20-50-1):

- A description of the facts and circumstances leading to the disposal and, if not separately presented on the face of the income statement, the carrying amount(s) of the major classes of assets and liabilities included in the disposal.

- The gain or loss recognized on the initial or subsequent writedown to fair value and, if not separately disclosed on the income statement, the line item where it is included.

- If applicable, the amounts of revenue and pretax profit or loss reported in discontinued operations.

- If applicable, the segment in which the long-lived asset (asset group) is reported under ASC 280.

Illustration of Presentation of Net Income

The following illustrates the presentation of income in accordance with GAAP:

Income (loss) from continuing operations before provision for income taxes	$400,000	
Provision for income taxes	(136,000)	
Income (loss) from continuing operations		$264,000
Discontinued operations (Note: _____)		
Income (loss) from operations of discontinued component A (less applicable income taxes $34,000)	$(66,000)	
Loss (gain) on disposal of component A (less applicable income taxes of $17,000)	(33,000)	
Net income (loss) from discontinued operations		(99,000)
Net income (loss) before extraordinary items		$165,000
Extraordinary gain (or loss) (Note: _____) (less applicable income taxes of $41,000)		79,000
Net income		$244,000

Assets to Be Disposed Of

The results of operations of a component of an entity that has either been disposed of or is classified as held for sale is reported in discontinued operations if both of the following conditions are met: (1) The operations and cash flows of the component have been eliminated from the ongoing operations of the entity as a result of the disposal transaction and (2) the entity will have no significant continuing involvement in the operations of the component after the disposal transaction. Discontinued Operations is presented in the income statement following the caption, Income from Continuing Operations (ASC 205-20-45-1).

Illustration of Presentation of Discontinued Operations

Note: This illustration uses assumed numbers (in thousands of dollars) for purposes of illustrating how discontinued operations are presented in the income statement.

Income from continuing operations before income taxes		$10,000
Income taxes		3,500
Income from continuing operations		6,500
Discontinued operations (Note X)		
Loss from operations of discontinued component ABC, including loss on disposal	3,000	
Income tax benefit*	1,050	
Loss on discontinued operations		1,950
Net income		$ 4,550

* Separate disclosure of a gain or loss on disposal is required, either on the face of the income statement or in a related note (ASC 205-20-45-3).

Adjustments to amounts previously reported in discontinued operations that are directly related to the disposal of a component of an entity in a period are classified in the current period as discontinued operations. The nature and amount of such adjustment shall be disclosed (ASC 205-20-45-4).

A gain or loss recognized on the sale of a long-lived asset that is not a component of an entity is included in income from continuing operations before income taxes in the income statement of a business enterprise and in income from continuing operations of a not-for-profit organization (ASC 360-10-45-5).

The following information is required in notes to the financial statements when a long-lived asset has been sold or is classified as held for sale (ASC 205-20-50-1):

- Description of the facts and circumstances leading to the expected disposal, the expected manner and timing of that disposal, and the carrying amount(s) of the major classes of assets and liabilities included as part of the disposal group.
- The gain or loss recognized on the initial, or subsequent, write-down to fair value and, if not separately presented on the face of the income statement, the location in the income statement of the gain or loss.

- If applicable, the amounts of revenue and pretax profit or loss reported in discontinued operations.
- If applicable, the segment in which the long-lived asset is reported under ASC 280.

ASC 205-30: LIQUIDATION BASIS OF ACCOUNTING

An entity is required to prepare financial statements in accordance with the liquidation basis of accounting when liquidation is imminent. Liquidation is considered imminent when either of the following occurs:

- A plan for liquidation has been approved by the person or persons with the authority to make such a plan effective, and the likelihood is remote that any of the following will occur:
  — Execution of the plan will be blocked by other parties (e.g., shareholders with certain rights).
  — The entity will return from liquidation.
- A plan for liquidation is imposed by other forces (e.g., involuntary bankruptcy) and the likelihood is remote that the entity will return from liquidation. (ASC 205-30-25-2)

Liquidation is defined as the process by which an entity converts its assets to cash or other assets and settles its obligations with creditors in anticipation of the entity ceasing all activities. Upon cessation of the entity's activities, any remaining cash or other assets are distributed to the entity's investors or other claimants. Liquidation may be compulsory or voluntary. Dissolution of an entity as a result of that entity being acquired by another entity or merged into another entity in its entirety and with the expectation of continuing its business does not qualify as liquidation. (ASC Glossary)

Following are several principles applicable to the liquidation basis of accounting:

- When applying the liquidation basis of accounting, an entity shall recognize other items that it previously had not recognized (e.g., trademarks) but that it expects to either sell in liquidation or use to settle liabilities.
- The entity shall recognize liabilities in accordance with the recognition provisions that would otherwise apply to those liabilities.
- The entity shall accrue estimated costs to dispose of assets or other items that it expects to sell in liquidation and present those costs in the aggregate separately from those assets or items. Discounting provisions in measuring the accrual for estimated disposal costs shall not be used.
- The entity shall accrue costs and income that it expects to incur or earn through the end of its liquidation and when it has a reasonable basis for estimation.
- The entity shall measure assets to reflect the estimated amount of cash or other consideration that it expects to collect in settling or disposing of those assets in carrying out its liquidation plan.

- The entity shall measure liabilities in accordance with the measurement provisions that would otherwise be applied except as noted above for the accrual of estimated disposal costs and expected income and expenses related to liquidation.
- At each reporting date, the entity shall remeasure its assets and other items it expects to sell that it has not previously recognized, liabilities, and the accruals of disposal or other costs or income to reflect the actual or estimated change in carrying value since the previous reporting date. (ASC 205-30-25-1 through 35-1)

At a minimum, the entity applying the liquidation basis shall prepare a statement of net assets in liquidation and a statement of changes in net assets in liquidation. The liquidation basis shall be applied prospectively from the date that the liquidation becomes imminent.

All of the following are required to be disclosed:

- That the financial statements are prepared by the liquidation basis, including the facts and circumstances surrounding the adoption of the liquidation basis.
- A description of the entity's plan for liquidation, including a description of:
  — The manner in which it expects to dispose of its assets and other items.
  — The manner by which it expects to settle its liabilities.
  — The expected date by which it expects to complete its liquidation.
- The methods and significant assumptions used to measure assets and liabilities, including any subsequent changes to those methods and assumptions.
- The type and amount of costs and income accrued in the statement of net assets in liquidation for the period over which those costs are expected to be paid or income earned. (ASC 205-30-50-2)

PRESENTATION OF FINANCIAL STATEMENTS

IMPORTANT NOTICE FOR 2014

As CCH's 2014 *GAAP Guide* goes to press, the FASB has outstanding a proposed Accounting Standards Update that will affect the presentation of financial statements in the future. This proposed update deals with the disclosure of uncertainties about an entity's going concern assumption.

An inherent assumption underlying financial statements is that the entity will continue as a going concern unless and until that entity's liquidation is imminent. There is no guidance in U.S. GAAP about when and how going concern uncertainties should be disclosed in an entity's financial statement notes. This proposed update would require an entity to assess all relevant information about conditions and events to determine their potential effect on the entity's potential inability to meet its obligations within 24 months after the financial statement date. Specifically, the entity would consider information about sources of liquidity and availability of credit, funds necessary to maintain operations, and conditional and unconditional obligations due or anticipated within 24 months after the financial statement date.

When there is substantial doubt about an entity's ability to continue as a going concern, the following information would be required to be disclosed:

- Principal conditions and events that give rise to the entity's potential inability to meet its obligations.
- The possible effects those conditions and events could have on the entity.
- Management's evaluation of the significance of those conditions and events.
- Mitigating conditions and events.
- Management's plans to address the entity's potential inability to meet its obligations.

Disclosures may be less extensive in the early stages of an entity's inability to meet its obligations and would expect to become more extensive as additional information becomes available.

The current FASB technical plan does not include a projected date for issuance of a final Accounting Standards Update.

PART II: INTERPRETIVE GUIDANCE

ASC 205-20: DISCONTINUED OPERATIONS

ASC 205-20-45-6 through 45-69; S50-1; S99-3 Allocation of Interest to Discontinued Operations

OVERVIEW

A company selling a business segment (or line of business) reports the sale separately as a discontinued operation. The company has debt on its balance sheet.

ACCOUNTING ISSUES

- Can interest expense be allocated to discontinued operations based on the debt's principal amount that will or could be paid with proceeds from the sale of operations?
- If so, how should such interest be allocated?
- Can general overhead expenses be allocated to discontinued operations?

ACCOUNTING GUIDANCE

1. Allocation of interest to discontinued operations is permitted but not required. (See the subsequent development section below.)
2. The following method should be used if allocation of interest to discontinued operations is elected:
    a. Allocate other consolidated interest not attributable to the entity's other operations based on a ratio of net assets to be sold or discontinued less debt required to be paid due to the disposal transaction to

the sum of the consolidated entity's total net assets plus consolidated debt *other than:*

   (1) Debt of the discontinued operation that will be assumed by the buyer,
   (2) Debt required to be paid due to the disposal transaction, and
   (3) Debt that can be directly attributed to the entity's other operations.

  b. A uniform consolidated debt-to-equity ratio for all operations is assumed. If that is not the case because the assets being sold are atypical, as in a finance company, a normal debt-to-equity ratio for that type of business can be used.
  c. Allocate interest to discontinued operations based on debt that can be identified as specifically related to those operations, if allocation based on net assets would not provide meaningful results.

 3. General and corporate overhead should not be allocated to discontinued operations.

SUBSEQUENT DEVELOPMENT

Under the guidance in this Issue, which was based on the framework of the AICPA Accounting Principles Board Opinion No. 30 (APB-30), an entity has been permitted to, but not required to, allocate interest expense related to discontinued operations based on the principal amount of debt that will or could be paid with proceeds received on the sale of discontinued operations. The EITF's consensus has also limited the maximum amount of interest that could be allocated and has provided guidance on the appropriate allocation method. Although ASC 360 and the guidance in ASC 205-10 supersedes the guidance in APB-30 regarding discontinued operations, the requirement that discontinued operations be reported separately in the income statement from continuing operations has been retained.

In June 2002, the EITF reached a consensus requiring that interest on debt that will be assumed by a buyer and debt that must be repaid when the disposal of discontinued operations occurs be allocated to discontinued operations. This consensus modifies the original consensus in Issue 1, but it does *not* affect the allocation of other consolidated interest to discontinued operations, which has been permitted but not required.

SEC STAFF COMMENT

The SEC Observer stated that registrants that elect to allocate interest in accordance with the consensus will be expected to clearly disclose their accounting policy, including the method of allocation, and the amount allocated to and included in discontinued operations for all periods presented.

Illustration of Allocation of Interest to Discontinued Operations

Assets	
Assets of discontinued operations	$ 400,000
Other assets	800,000
Total assets	$1,200,000

Liabilities and Equity

Trade payables and other noninterest-bearing debt	$ 250,000
Debt related to discontinued operations to be assumed by the buyer	100,000
Debt required to be paid due to disposal	150,000
Debt related to other operations	150,000
Debt unrelated to other operations	250,000
Deferred taxes	50,000
Total liabilities	$ 950,000
Stockholders' equity	250,000
Total liabilities and equity	$1,200,000

The consensus applies to the income statement presentation of both continuing and discontinued operations and including presentation of the gain or loss on disposal of a component of an enterprise. The decision whether to allocate interest should be applied consistently to all discontinued operations.

Total interest expense (10% average interest rate × $650,000 interest-bearing debt) = $65,000

Allocation of interest on consolidated interest not attributable to other operations is computed as follows:

$$\frac{\text{Net assets to be discontinued less debt required to be paid due to disposal}}{\text{Sum of consolidated net assets* plus debt unrelated to other operations}} = \frac{\$400,000 - \$100,000 - \$150,000}{\$250,000 + \$250,000} = .3$$

* ($1,200,000 - $950,000 = $250,000)

Interest on debt unrelated to other operations	= $250,000 ×.10
	= $25,000 × .3
	= $7,500
Interest on debt assumed by buyer	= $100,000 ×.10
	= $10,000
Interest allocated to discontinued operations	= $7,500 + $10,000
	= $17,500

DISCUSSION

This Issue was raised by the FASB staff, who noted that practice is varied. The allocation approach chosen by the Task Force is based on the rationale that interest is a cost that should be associated with the assets financed with the debt. The Task Force favored an allocation approach based on the amount of debt that will be repaid with the proceeds of the sale of discontinued operations. However, they decided to limit that amount to debt that will be assumed by the buyer and other debt unrelated to operations, such as general corporate debt.

ASC 205-20-50-4, 50-6; 55-4 through 55-26, 55-35, 55-37 through 55-40, 55-49 through 55-58, 55-60 through 55-65, 55-67 through 55-79 Applying the

Conditions in Paragraph 42 of FASB Statement No. 144, *Accounting for the Impairment or Disposal of Long-Lived Assets*, in Determining Whether to Report Discontinued Operations

OVERVIEW

ASC 205-20-45-1, which provides guidance on whether the results of operations of a component of an entity that has been disposed of or that is classified as held for sale should be reported in discontinued operations, requires that both of the following two criteria be met: (1) the component's operations and cash flows have been or will be eliminated from the ongoing entity's operations as a result of the disposal transaction and (2) the ongoing entity should have no significant continuing involvement in the disposed of component's operations after a disposal transaction has occurred. This Issue was raised because the FASB had received questions as to whether a disposed of component can have any continuing cash flows that have gone through the ongoing entity's operations.

ACCOUNTING ISSUES

1. How should an ongoing entity evaluate whether operations and cash flows of a component that it has disposed of have been or will be eliminated from the ongoing entity's operations?

2. What types of continuing involvement represent a significant continuing involvement in the operations of a component that has been disposed of?

ACCOUNTING GUIDANCE

The EITF reached the following consensus positions on an approach for determining whether an ongoing entity that has *eliminated* from its ongoing operations the operations and cash flows of a component it has disposed of has met the criteria in ASC 205-20-45-1 for presentation in discontinued operations of the results of operations of a component that has been disposed of or one being held for sale:

1. The process of evaluating whether the operations and cash flows of a disposed of component have been or will be eliminated from an entity's ongoing operations requires a determination of whether the ongoing entity expects to continue generating *direct* or *indirect* cash flows from activities related to that component. Direct and indirect cash flows are distinguished based on their *nature* and *significance* in accordance with management's expectations and the best available information. Generating *direct* cash flows from a disposed of component is an indicator that an entity has *not* eliminated the component from its operations and, therefore, should *not* present the component in discontinued operations; however, the requirement in ASC 205-20-45-1, the purpose of which is to determine whether an entity continues a disposed of component's revenue-producing or cost-generating activities after a disposal has occurred, would be met and the component would qualify for presentation in discontinued operations if continuing cash flows are *indirect*.

2. A component's continuing revenue-producing and cost-generating activities are considered to be *direct* cash inflows or outflows if the ongoing entity expects to:

   a. Recognize significant cash inflows and outflows as a result of *migration*, which is the sale of similar commodities or services to specific customers of the disposed of component, *or*

   b. Recognize significant cash inflows and outflows as a result of the continuation of revenue-producing or cost-generating activities with the disposed of component.

Activities That Generate Continuing Cash Flows

An ongoing entity's cash flows after disposal of a component would be considered to be *direct* cash flows if:

- It is likely that revenues and costs being generated by the entity would have been generated by the disposed of component had the disposal not occurred (*migration*), or

- The ongoing entity's revenues and costs are generated as a result of an active involvement with the disposed of component (*continuation of activities*).

If an ongoing entity is generating cash flows as a result of a migration or continuation of activities, the entity should determine whether the cash flows are significant. Although the significance of continuing cash flows generated as a result of other factors need not be determined, an ongoing entity should evaluate the criteria in ASC 205-20-45-1 to determine whether its continuing involvement in the disposed of component's operations is significant. Interest earned on financing provided by a seller, contingent consideration in a business combination, dividends on an investment, and passive royalty interests in the operations of a component that has been disposed of are examples of continuing cash flows that would *not* be direct.

Significance of Continuing Cash Flows

Judgment is required to determine the significance of continuing cash flows as a result of migration or continuation of activities between an ongoing entity and the disposed of component. The continuing cash flows that an ongoing entity expects to generate after a disposal of a component should be compared to the cash flows that an entity would have expected if the disposal had not occurred. The latter cash flows should include cash flows from transactions with third parties and from intercompany transactions, which should be determined as if they had occurred between the component and a third party. Continuing cash inflows and outflows should be considered separately, regardless of how they are presented in the income statement (gross or net). If it is determined that cash inflows are *direct* cash flows, it is not necessary to evaluate cash outflows.

Significant Continuing Involvement

An ongoing entity that eliminates the operations and cash flows of a disposed of component from its ongoing operations due to a disposal transaction should evaluate whether it will have a significant continuing involvement in the component's operations *after* the transaction has occurred.

The EITF reached a consensus that a continuing involvement in a disposed of component's operations enables the ongoing entity to influence that component's operating and financial policies. An evaluation of whether an ongoing entity has that ability should consider whether the entity retains any risks or is able to obtain benefits from the disposed of component's ongoing operations. Risk retention or the ability to obtain benefits, however, is not by itself an indicator of an ongoing entity's ability to influence a disposed of component's operating and financial policies. Rather, to determine whether an ongoing entity has a continuing involvement with a disposed of component, it is necessary to evaluate the existence of an interest in the disposed of component or a contractual or other type of arrangement with that component, if any.

Qualitative and quantitative factors from the perspective of the disposed of component should be considered in determining whether a continuing involvement is significant. All types of continuing involvement should be considered individually and in total. The following are some factors that should be considered when determining whether an ongoing entity has a *significant* continuing involvement in a disposed of component:

- The entity has retained a sufficiently large interest in a disposed of component that enables it to significantly influence the disposed of component's operating and financial policies. Interests other than common stock or in-substance common stock may provide such influence, but a cost method investment in common stock or in-substance common stock would *not* be considered a significant continuing involvement.
- The ongoing entity and the buyer or the disposed of component have entered into a contractual agreement that provides the previous owner with significant influence over the disposed of component's operating and financial policies. Determining whether a contract or other arrangement provides the ongoing entity with significant continuing involvement requires judgment and consideration of all available information. The following factors, which are *not* individually presumptive or determinative, should be considered:
  — The contract's significance to the disposed of component's overall operations
  — The extent of an ongoing entity's involvement in a disposed of component's operations
  — Each party's rights under the contract
  — The contract or arrangement's pricing terms

Period of Assessment

The EITF reached a consensus that the *assessment period* should include the point when the component initially meets the criteria to be classified as held for sale or is disposed of and should last for one year after the component is actually disposed of. The assessment should be based on all the facts and circumstances including the intent and ability of the ongoing entity's management:

- To eliminate the disposed of component from its operations, and
- To avoid a continuing involvement with the disposed of component's operations.

If during the year following the disposal, significant events or circumstances occur that may change the ongoing entity's current assessment, the entity should reassess whether it expects to meet the criteria in (ASC 205-20-45-1. The component's operations should *not* be presented in discontinued operations if such an event occurs and causes the ongoing entity to expect that the criteria in ASC 205-20-45-1 will *not* be met by the end of the assessment period. If it is expected that those criteria in will be met by the end of the assessment period, however, presentation in discontinued operations is permitted. The occurrence of such events may result in the reclassification of a disposed of component into and out of discontinued operations for all periods during the assessment period.

If as a result of circumstances beyond an ongoing entity's control, eliminating a disposed-of component's cash flows from its operations or eliminating its significant involvement in a disposed of component's operations requires more than one year from the actual date of disposal, the assessment period may be extended if the ongoing entity takes the necessary actions to resolve the situation and expects that the disposed of component's direct cash flows and its continuing involvement will be eliminated.

If a component is either disposed of or classified as held for sale at the balance sheet date, significant events or circumstances that occur *after* the balance sheet date but *before* the financial statements are issued should be included in determining whether the criteria in (ASC 205-20-45-1 are expected to be met so that discontinued operations will be presented in accordance with that paragraph.

Disclosure

An ongoing entity should disclose in the notes to its financial statements the following information about each discontinued operation that generates continuing cash flows:

- The nature of activities generating continuing cash flows
- The period of time over which continuing cash flows are expected to be generated
- The primary factors causing the entity to conclude that expected continuing cash flows are *not* direct cash flows of the disposed-of component
- Intercompany revenues and expenses for all periods presented before the disposal of components (*a*) with which the ongoing entity is involved in *continuation of activities* after their disposal and (*b*) for which the ongoing entity presents in continuing operations after their disposal revenues and expenses that had been accounted for as intercompany transactions before the disposal of those components. In the period in which operations are initially classified as discontinued, the types of continuing involvement, if any, that the ongoing entity will have after a disposal transaction.
- In the period in which operations are initially classified as discontinued, the types of continuing involvement, if any, that the ongoing entity will have after a disposal transaction.

CHAPTER 3
ASC 210—BALANCE SHEET

CONTENTS

Part I: General Guidance	3002
ASC 210-10: Overall	3002
Overview	3002
Background	3002
Basic Definitions	3002
Current Assets	3002
Cash	3003
Cash Equivalents	3003
Secondary Cash Resources	3003
Receivables	3003
Inventories	3003
Prepaid Expenses	3003
Current Liabilities	3003
Payables from Operations	3004
Debt Maturities	3004
Revenue Received in Advance	3004
Other Accruals	3004
Working Capital and Related Ratios	3004
Changes in Each Element of Working Capital	3004
Illustration of Determining Working Capital	3004
Illustration of Current Ratio	3005
Illustration of Acid-Test Ratio	3005
Receivables	3005
Direct Write-Off Method	3006
Allowance Method	3006
Illustration of Accounting for Uncollectible Accounts by the Allowance Method	3007
Discounted Notes Receivable	3008
Illustration of Discounted Notes Receivable	3008
Factoring	3008
Pledging	3008
Cash Surrender Value of Life Insurance	3009
Insurable Interest	3009
Illustration of Insurable Interest	3009
Liability Classification Issues	3009
Current Obligations Expected to Be Refinanced	3010
Callable Obligations	3010
Compensated Absences	3010
ASC 210-20: Offsetting	3010
Offsetting Assets and Liabilities—General	3010
Illustration of Offsetting Assets and Liabilities	3011

Offsetting of Derivatives, Repurchase and Repurchase Agreements, and Securities Lending Transactions	3012
Disclosure Standards	3014
Part II: Interpretive Guidance	3015
ASC 210-20: Offsetting	3015
ASC 210-20-45-9	
Assurance That a Right of Setoff Is Enforceable in a Bankruptcy under FASB Interpretation No. 39	3015

PART I: GENERAL GUIDANCE

ASC 210-10: OVERALL

OVERVIEW

The distinction between current and noncurrent assets and liabilities in a classified balance sheet is an important feature of financial reporting. There is considerable interest in the liquidity of the reporting enterprise, and the separate classification of current assets and liabilities is an important part of liquidity analysis.

BACKGROUND

In the ordinary course of business, there is a continuing circulation of capital within the current assets. For example, a manufacturer expends cash for materials, labor, and factory overhead that are converted into finished inventory. After being sold, inventory usually is converted into trade receivables and, on collection of receivables, is converted back to cash. The average time elapsing between expending of cash and receiving the cash back from the collection of the trade receivable is called the *operating cycle*. One year is used as a basis for segregating current assets when more than one operating cycle occurs within a year. When the operating cycle is longer than one year, as with the lumber, tobacco, and distillery businesses, the operating cycle is used for segregating current assets. *In the event that a business clearly has no operating cycle, the one-year rule is used* (ASC 210-10-45-3).

Frequently, businesses have a *natural business year*, at the end of which the company's activity, inventory, and trade receivables are at their lowest point. This is often the point in time selected as the end of the entity's accounting period for financial reporting purposes.

BASIC DEFINITIONS

Current Assets

Resources that are expected to be realized in cash, sold, or consumed during the next year (or longer operating cycle) are classified as current assets. Current assets are sometimes called circulating or working assets; cash that is restricted as to withdrawal or use for other than current operations is not classified as a current asset (ASC 210-10-45-4).

The basic types of current assets are cash, cash equivalents, secondary cash resources, receivables, inventories, and prepaid expenses (ASC 210-10-45-1).

Cash

Includes money in any form, for example, cash on deposit, cash awaiting deposit, and cash funds available for use.

Cash Equivalents

Short-term, highly liquid investments that are (*a*) readily convertible to known amounts of cash and (*b*) so near their maturities that they present insignificant risk of changes in value because of changes in interest rates.

Secondary Cash Resources

The most common type of secondary cash resources is marketable securities.

Receivables

Include accounts receivable, notes receivable, and receivables from officers and employees.

Inventories

Include merchandise, raw materials, work in process, finished goods, operating supplies, and ordinary maintenance material and parts.

Prepaid Expenses

Include prepaid insurance, interest, rents, taxes, advertising, and operating supplies. Prepaid expenses, unlike other current assets, are not expected to be converted into cash; but, if they had not been paid in advance, they would require the use of current assets during the operating cycle.

Current Liabilities

Current liabilities are obligations for which repayment is expected to require the use of current assets or the creation of other current liabilities.

> **PRACTICE POINTER:** The definition of current liabilities is based on the asset category from which the liability is expected to be retired rather than on a specific period of time. As a practical matter, most current liabilities are those that are expected to be retired during the period of time encompassed by the definition of current assets. Care should be taken, however, to identify instances where liabilities that are due in the near future should be classified as noncurrent because they will not require the use of current assets. Examples are short-term obligations expected to be refinanced, and noncurrent liabilities that are near their maturity but that will be paid from noncurrent assets (e.g., bond sinking funds).

ASC 210—Balance Sheet

There are several basic types of current liabilities (ASC 210-10-45-8):

Payables from Operations

Include items that have entered the operating cycle, which include trade payables and accrued liabilities such as wages and taxes.

Debt Maturities

Include amounts expected to be liquidated during the current operating cycle, such as short-term notes and the currently maturing portion of long-term debt.

Revenue Received in Advance

Includes collections received in advance of services, for example, prepaid subscriptions and other deferred revenues. This type of current liability is typically liquidated by means other than the payment of cash.

Other Accruals

Include estimates of accrued amounts that are expected to be required to cover expenditures within the year for known obligations (a), when the amount can be determined only approximately (provision for accrued bonuses payable) or (b) when the specific person(s) to whom payment will be made is (are) unascertainable (provision for warranty of a product) (ASC 210-10-45-6).

Working Capital and Related Ratios

Working capital is the excess of current assets over current liabilities, and it is often used as a measure of the liquidity of an enterprise (ASC 210-10-05-5).

Changes in Each Element of Working Capital

The changes in each element of working capital are the increases or decreases in each current asset and current liability over the amounts in the preceding year.

Illustration of Determining Working Capital

	20X8	20X9	Working Capital Increase or (Decrease)
Current Assets:			
Cash	$10,000	$15,000	$5,000
Accounts receivable, net	25,000	35,000	10,000
Inventory	50,000	60,000	10,000
Prepaid expenses	1,000	500	(500)
Total current assets	$86,000	$110,500	$24,500
Current Liabilities:			
Accounts payable	$10,000	$15,000	$(5,000)
Notes payable-current	20,000	15,000	5,000
Accrued expenses	1,000	1,500	(500)
Total current liabilities	$31,000	$31,500	$(500)

	20X8	20X9	Working Capital Increase or (Decrease)
Net working capital	$55,000	$79,000	
Increase in working capital			$24,000

The *current ratio,* or *working capital ratio,* is a measure of current position and is useful in analyzing short-term credit. The current ratio is computed by dividing the total current assets by the total current liabilities.

Illustration of Current Ratio

	20X8	20X9
Current assets	$86,000	$110,500
Current liabilities	(31,000)	(31,500)
Working capital	$55,000	$79,000
Current ratio (86 ÷ 31), (110.5 ÷ 31.5)	2.8:1	3.5:1

The *acid-test ratio* (also called the *quick ratio*) is determined by dividing those assets typically closest to cash by total current liabilities. The assets used to calculate this ratio consist of only the most liquid assets, typically cash, receivables, and marketable securities.

PRACTICE POINTER: Only receivables and securities *convertible into cash* are included; restricted cash and securities are excluded.

Illustration of Acid-Test Ratio

	20X8	20X9
Cash	$10,000	$15,000
Receivables, net	25,000	35,000
Total *quick* assets	$35,000	$50,000
Total current liabilities	$31,000	$31,500
Acid-test ratio (35 ÷ 31), (50 ÷ 31.5)	1.1:1	1.6:1

RECEIVABLES

Accounts receivable are reported in the financial statements at net realizable value. Net realizable value is equal to the gross amount of receivables less an estimated allowance for uncollectible accounts.

Two common procedures of accounting for uncollectible accounts are (1) the direct write-off method and (2) the allowance method.

Direct Write-Off Method

This method recognizes a bad debt expense only when a specific account is determined to be uncollectible. The conceptual weaknesses of the direct write-off method are:

- Bad debt expense is not *matched* with the related sales.

- Accounts receivable are overstated, because no attempt is made to account for the unknown bad debts included therein.

Ordinarily, the direct write-off method is not considered GAAP, because it results in a mismatching of revenues and expenses (i.e., expenses are recognized in a later period than the revenue to which they relate) and overstates the amount of assets. The method may be acceptable in situations where uncollectible accounts are immaterial in amount.

Allowance Method

The allowance method recognizes an estimate of uncollectible accounts each period, even though the specific individual accounts that will not be collected cannot be identified at that time. Estimates of uncollectible accounts usually are made as a percentage of credit sales or ending receivables. This method is consistent with ASC 450 (Contingencies), as explained below.

Under ASC 450, a contingency exists if, at the date of the financial statements, an enterprise does not expect to collect the full amount of its accounts receivable. Under this circumstance, an accrual for a loss contingency must be recognized, if both of the following conditions exist:

- It is *probable* that as of the date of the financial statements an asset has been impaired or a liability incurred, based on information available before the issuance of the financial statements.

- The amount of the loss can be *estimated reasonably*.

If both of the above conditions are met, an accrual for the estimated amount of uncollectible receivables is made even if the specific uncollectible receivables cannot be identified at the time of the accrual. An enterprise may base its estimate of uncollectible receivables on its prior experience, the experience of other enterprises in the same industry, the debtor's ability to pay, or an appraisal of current economic conditions. Significant uncertainty may exist in the ultimate collection of receivables if an enterprise is unable to estimate reasonably the amount that is uncollectible. If a significant uncertainty exists in the ultimate collection of the receivables, the installment sales method, cost-recovery method, or some other method of revenue recognition should be used. In the event that both of the above conditions for accrual are not met and a loss contingency is at least *reasonably possible*, certain financial statement disclosures are required by ASC 450.

Illustration of Accounting for Uncollectible Accounts by the Allowance Method

AMB Co. estimates uncollectible accounts at 1% of credit sales. For the current year, credit sales totaled $1,000,000. The year-end balances in accounts receivable and the unadjusted allowance for uncollectible accounts are $250,000 and $15,000, respectively.

The entry to record uncollectible accounts ($1,000,000 × 1% = $10,000) is as follows:

Bad debt expense	10,000	
Allowance for uncollectible accounts		10,000

The balance sheet will include accounts receivable of $250,000, allowance for uncollectible accounts of $25,000 ($15,000 + $10,000), and net accounts receivable of $225,000 ($250,000 - $25,000).

When a specific uncollectible account is written off (e.g., $2,100), the following entry is required:

Allowance for uncollectible accounts	2,100	
Accounts receivable (specific account)		2,100

This entry has no effect on the amount of net accounts receivable, because both the receivables balance and the allowance balance are reduced by the same amount.

If the estimate of uncollectibles is based on the ending balance of accounts receivable, the same procedure is followed, except that the existing balance in the allowance would require consideration. For example, if uncollectible accounts were estimated at 9% of the ending balance in accounts receivable, the bad debt expense for the year would be $7,500, computed as follows:

Required allowance ($250,000 × 9%)	$22,500
Balance before adjustment	(15,000)
Required adjustment	$ 7,500

The balance sheet includes accounts receivable of $250,000, an allowance of $22,500, and a net receivables amount of $227,500.

A variation on the previous method is to "age" accounts receivable, a procedure that provides for recognizing an increasing percentage as uncollectible as accounts become increasingly delinquent. For example, applying this procedure to the $250,000 receivables balance above might result in the following:

	Within 30 Days	30 Days Overdue	60 Days Overdue	Past 60 Days Overdue
Accounts receivable balance	$120,000	$50,000	$50,000	$30,000
Uncollectible %	2%	7%	12%	25%
Uncollectible balance	$2,400	$3,500	$6,000	$7,500

The total uncollectible balance is $19,400, ($2,400 + $3,500 + $6,000 + $7,500), resulting in the recognition of bad debt expense of $4,400, assuming a previous allowance balance of $15,000 ($19,400 - $15,000 = $4,400).

Discounted Notes Receivable

Discounted notes receivable arise when the holder endorses the note (with or without recourse) to a third party and receives a sum of cash. The difference between the amount of cash received by the holder and the maturity value of the note is called the discount. If the note is discounted with recourse, the assignor remains contingently liable for the ultimate payment of the note when it becomes due. If the note is discounted without recourse, the assignor assumes no further liability.

The account "discounted notes receivable" is a contra account, which is deducted from the related receivables for financial statement purposes. The following is the procedure for computing the proceeds of a discounted note:

1. Compute the total maturity value of the note, including interest due at maturity.

2. Compute the discount amount (the maturity value of the note multiplied by the discount rate for the time involved).

3. The difference between the two amounts (1, less 2) equals the proceeds of the note.

Illustration of Discounted Notes Receivable

A $1,000 90-day 10% note is discounted at a bank at 8% when 60 days are remaining to maturity.

Maturity—$1,000 + ($1,000 × .10 × 90/360)	$1,025.00
Discount—$1,025 × .08 × 60/360	(13.67)
Proceeds of note	$1,011.33

Factoring

Factoring is a process by which a company converts its receivables into immediate cash by assigning them to a factor either with or without recourse. *With recourse* means that the assignee can return the receivable to the company and get back the funds paid if the receivable is uncollectible. *Without recourse* means that the assignee assumes the risk of losses on collections. Under factoring arrangements, the customer may or may not be notified.

Pledging

Pledging is the process whereby the company uses existing accounts receivable as collateral for a loan. The company retains title to the receivables but pledges that it will use the proceeds to pay the loan.

CASH SURRENDER VALUE OF LIFE INSURANCE

The proceeds of a life insurance policy usually provide some degree of financial security to one or more beneficiaries named in the policy. Upon death of the insured, the insurance company pays the beneficiary the face amount of the policy, less any outstanding indebtedness.

Insurable Interest

An owner of an insurance interest in life insurance need only exist at the time the policy is issued, while an insurable interest in property insurance must exist at the time of a loss. An insurable interest is a test of financial relationship. A husband may insure the life of his wife, an employer the life of an employee, a creditor the life of a debtor, and a partner the life of a copartner.

An investment in a life insurance policy is accounted for at the amount that can be realized by the owner of the policy as of the date of its statement of financial position. Generally, the amount that can be realized from a life insurance policy is the amount of its *cash surrender value*. The increase in the cash surrender value of an insurance policy for a particular period is recorded by the owner of the policy and the cash surrender value is included as an asset in its statement of financial position. The insurance expense for the same period is the difference between the total amount of premium paid and the amount of increase in the cash surrender value of the policy.

Illustration of Insurable Interest

An enterprise is the owner and sole beneficiary of a $200,000 life insurance policy on its president. The annual premium is $16,000. The policy is starting its fourth year, and the schedule of cash values indicates that at the end of the fourth year the cash value increases $25 per thousand. The enterprise pays the $16,000 premium, and the journal entry to record the transaction is as follows:

Life insurance expense—officers	11,000	
Cash surrender value—life insurance policy (200 × $25)	5,000	
Cash		16,000

The cash surrender value of a life insurance policy is classified either as a current or noncurrent asset in the policy owner's statement of financial position, depending upon the intentions of the policy owner. If the policy owner intends to surrender the policy to the insurer for its cash value within its normal operating cycle, the cash surrender value is classified as a current asset in the statement of financial position. If there is no intention of collecting the policy's cash value within the normal operating cycle of the policy owner, the cash surrender value is classified as a noncurrent asset in the statement of financial position.

LIABILITY CLASSIFICATION ISSUES

ASC 480 more clearly defines the distinction between liabilities and equity. ASC 480 also establishes standards for issuers of financial instruments with characteristics of both liabilities and equity related to the classification and measurement of those instruments.

Current Obligations Expected to Be Refinanced

ASC 210 establishes GAAP for classifying a short-term obligation that is expected to be refinanced into a long-term liability or stockholders' equity. ASC 210 applies only to those companies that issue classified balance sheets (ASC 210-10-15-3). ASC 470 provides guidance on when a short-term obligation can be excluded from current liabilities and reclassified as non-current.

Callable Obligations

ASC 470 establishes GAAP for the current/noncurrent classification in the debtor's balance sheet of obligations that are payable on demand or callable by the creditor.

Compensated Absences

For guidance regarding the proper accrual of the liability for employees' compensated absences, see ASC 420.

ASC 210-20: OFFSETTING

OFFSETTING ASSETS AND LIABILITIES—GENERAL

Offsetting is the display of a recognized asset and a recognized liability as one net amount in a financial statement. If the amount of the recognized asset is the same as the amount of the recognized liability, then the net or combined amount of both is zero, and, as a result, no amount would appear in the financial statement. If the two amounts are not the same, the net amount of the two items that have been offset is presented in the financial statement and classified in the manner of the larger item.

ASC 210 discusses the general principle of offsetting in the balance sheet in the context of income tax amounts. ASC 210 includes the following guidance:

- Offsetting assets and liabilities in the balance sheet is improper except where a right of setoff exists.
- This includes offsetting cash or other assets against a tax liability or other amounts owed to governments that are not, by their terms, designated specifically for the payment of taxes.
- The only exception to this general principle occurs when it is clear that a purchase of securities that are acceptable for the payment of taxes is in substance an advance payment of taxes that are payable in the relatively near future.

The general principle of financial reporting, which holds that offsetting assets and liabilities is improper except where a right of setoff exists, usually is considered in the context of unconditional receivables from and payables to another party. ASC 210 extends this general principle to *conditional* amounts recognized for contracts under which the amounts to be received or paid or the items to be exchanged depend on future interest rates, future exchange rates, future commodity prices, or other factors.

ASC 210 specifies four criteria that must be met for the right of setoff to exist (ASC 210-20-45-1):

1. Each party owes the other party specific amounts.
2. The reporting party has the right to set off the amount payable, by contract or other agreement, with the amount receivable from the other party.
3. The reporting party intends to set off.
4. The right of setoff is enforceable at law.

OBSERVATIONS: The importance of managerial intent is apparent in the third criterion, which states that the reporting party *intends* to set off its payable and receivable. When all of these conditions are met, the reporting entity has a valid right of setoff and may present the net amount of the payable or receivable in the balance sheet.

Generally, debts may be set off if they exist between mutual debtors, each acting in its capacity as both debtor and creditor. State laws and the U.S. Bankruptcy Code may impose restrictions on or prohibitions against the right of set off in bankruptcy under certain circumstances.

Illustration of Offsetting Assets and Liabilities

The offsetting of assets and liabilities is an important issue to consider when determining financial statement presentation of current assets and current liabilities. Any time items are set off, information that would otherwise be available is lost. In addition, important financial statement relationships may be altered when assets and liabilities are set off. Consider the following example:

	Current Assets	
Receivable from M Co.		$100
Other assets		400
		$500
	Current Liabilities	
Payable to M Co.		$ 75
Other liabilities		175
		$250
Current ratio (500/250)		2:1

Now, consider the same situation, except the $75 payable to M Co. is offset against the $100 receivable from M Co.:

	Current Assets	
Net receivable from M Co. ($100 - $75)		$25
Other assets		400
		$425

	Current Liabilities	
Other liabilities		$175
Current ratio (425/175)		2.4:1

When offsetting is applied, the individual amounts of the receivable and payable are not presented, and only the net amount of $25 is present in the balance sheet. Further, the current ratio is significantly altered by the offsetting activity. This is a simple example, but it illustrates the impact of offsetting, and thus its importance as a financial statement reporting issue.

An exception to the general offsetting rule exists for derivative contracts executed with the same counterparty under a master netting agreement. A master netting agreement is a contractual agreement entered into by two parties to multiple contracts that provides for the net settlement of all contracts covered by the agreement in the event of default under any one contract. For such derivative contracts, assets and liabilities may be offset and presented as a net amount even if the reporting entity does not meet the requirement in ASC 210 that the reporting entity has the intent to net settle. Offsetting derivative assets and liabilities under this exception is an election and the reporting entity must apply the election consistently.

Many sources of authoritative accounting standards specify accounting treatments that result in offsetting or in a balance sheet presentation that has an effect similar to offsetting. ASC 210 is not intended to modify the accounting treatment in any of those particular circumstances.

OFFSETTING OF DERIVATIVES, PURCHASE AND REPURCHASE AGREEMENTS, AND SECURITIES LENDING TRANSACTIONS

ASC 210 provides specific guidance as to when payables under repurchase agreements can be offset with receivables under reverse repurchase agreements. These criteria are (ASC 210-20-45-11):

1. The agreements are executed with the same counterparty.
2. The agreements have the same settlement date, set forth at inception.
3. The agreements are executed in accordance with a master netting arrangement.
4. The securities under the agreements exist in "book entry" form and can be transferred only by means of entries in the records of the transfer system operator or securities custodian.
5. The agreements will be settled on a securities transfer system that operates in the manner described below, and the enterprise must have associated banking arrangements in place as described below. Cash settlements for securities transferred are made under established banking arrangements that provide that the enterprise will need available cash on deposit only for any net amounts that are due at the end of the business day. It must be *probable* that the associated banking arrange-

ments will provide sufficient *daylight overdraft or other intraday credit* at the settlement date for each of the parties.

6. The enterprise intends to use the same account at the clearing bank (or other financial institution) to settle its receivable (i.e., cash inflow from the reverse purchasing agreement) and its payable (i.e., cash outflow to settle the offsetting repurchase agreement).

If these six criteria are met, the enterprise has the option to offset. That choice must be applied consistently.

The third criterion refers to a "master netting arrangement." A master netting arrangement exists if the reporting entity has multiple contracts, whether for the same type of conditional or exchange contract or for different types of contracts, with a single counterparty that are subject to a contractual agreement that provides for the net settlement of all contracts through a single payment in a single currency in the event of default on or termination of any one contract (ASC 210).

The fourth criterion refers to "book entry" form. ASC 210 considers this a key element because it provides control over the securities. The controlling record for a "book entry" security is maintained by the transfer system operator. A securities custodian that has a security account with the transfer system operation may maintain "subsidiary" records of "book entry" securities and may transfer the securities within its subsidiary records; however, a security cannot be traded from the account of that custodian to a new custodian without a "book entry" transfer of the security over the securities transfer system. This form of accounting record facilitates repurchase and reverse repurchase agreement transactions on securities transfer systems.

For a transfer system for repurchase and reverse repurchase agreements to meet the fifth criterion, cash transfers must be initiated by the owner of record of the securities notifying its securities custodian to transfer those securities to the counterparty to the arrangement. Under associated banking arrangements, each party to a same-day settlement of both a repurchase agreement and a reverse repurchase agreement would be obligated to pay a gross amount of cash for the securities transferred from its counterparty, but the party would be able to reduce that gross obligation by notifying its securities custodian to transfer other securities to that counterparty the same day (ASC 210-20-45-14).

In the fifth criterion, the term *probable* has the same definition as in ASC 450, meaning that a transaction or event is more likely to occur than not. The phrase "daylight overdraft or other intraday credit" refers to the feature of the banking arrangement that permits transactions to be completed during the day when insufficient cash is on deposit, provided there is sufficient cash to cover the net cash requirement at the end of the day.

ASC 210 requirements apply to recognized derivatives accounted for in accordance with Topic 815, including bifurcated embedded derivatives, repurchase agreements and reverse repurchase agreements, and securities borrowing and securities lending transactions that are offset in accordance with either Topics 210 or 815. These requirements are also applicable for recognized derivative instruments accounted for in accordance with Topic 815 that are subject to an enforceable master netting arrangement or similar agreement, irrespective of whether they are offset in accordance with Topic 210 or 815 (ASC 210-250-2).

DISCLOSURE STANDARDS

Current assets and current liabilities must be identified clearly in the financial statements, and the basis for determining the stated amounts must be disclosed fully (ASC 210-10-05-5). The following are the common disclosures that are required for current assets and current liabilities in the financial statements or in notes thereto:

- Classification of inventories and the method used (e.g., FIFO, LIFO, average cost)
- Restrictions on current assets
- Current portions of long-term obligations
- Description of accounting policies relating to current assets and current liabilities

Accounts receivable and notes receivable from officers, employees, or affiliated companies, if material, must be reported separately in the financial statements (ASC 310-10-45-13).

The above disclosure requirements apply to both of the following:
  a. Recognized financial instruments and derivative instruments that are offset.
  b. Recognized financial instruments and derivative instruments that are subject to an enforceable master netting arrangement or similar agreement. (ASC 210-20-50-1)

Disclosure is required of information to enable users of an entity's financial statements to evaluate the effect or potential effect of netting arrangements on its financial position. This includes the effort or potential effect of rights of offset associated with the entity's recognized assets and liabilities. (ASC 210-20-50-2) To meet this objective, the entity must disclose at the end of the reporting period the following quantitative information:
  a. The gross amounts of those recognized assets and liabilities.
  b. The amounts offset to determine the net amounts presented in the statement of financial position.
  c. The net amounts presented in the statement of financial position.
  d. The amounts subject to an enforceable master netting arrangement or similar arrangement:
    1. The amounts related to recognized financial instruments and other derivative instruments that either management makes a policy election not to offset or do not meet some of the guidance in ASC 210-20-45 or 815-10-45.
    2. The amounts related to financial collateral, including cash collateral.
  e. The net amounts after deducting the amounts in (d) from the amounts in (c). (ASC 210-20-50-3)

The above information is required in a tabular form, separately for assets and liabilities unless another format is more appropriate. (ASC 210-20-50-4) A description of the rights of offset associated with an entity's recognized assets and liabilities subject to an enforceable master netting arrangement or similar agreement is required. (ASC 210-20-50-5) If the information above is presented in more than one note to the financial statements, cross-references between notes is required. (ASC 210-20-50-6)

PART II: INTERPRETIVE GUIDANCE

ASC 210-20: OFFSETTING

ASC 210-20-45-9—Assurance That a Right of Setoff Is Enforceable in a Bankruptcy under FASB Interpretation No. 39

At the November 1994 meeting of the EITF, the FASB staff clarified the meaning of the phrase "the right of setoff is enforceable at law," which is one of the conditions for offsetting in ASC 210-20-45.

Some have questioned whether the right of setoff is effective if a debtor is in bankruptcy. Two opposing views were suggested about the relationship between ASC 210-20-45-8, which states that "legal constraints should be considered to determine whether the right of setoff is enforceable," and paragraph 48 of FASB Interpretation No. 39 (FIN-39) (not in ASC), which stated that "this Interpretation does not include a separate requirement for protection in bankruptcy." Some believed that the effectiveness of the right of setoff in bankruptcy needs to be proved, while others believed that it is unnecessary to consider bankruptcy in financial statements that are prepared under the going-concern concept.

The FASB staff's views about the amount of certainty needed to determine whether the right of setoff should be upheld in bankruptcy straddles those two views. They believe that because the phrase "enforceable at law" includes the concept that the right of setoff should be recognized in bankruptcy, FIN-39 does not include a requirement for protection in bankruptcy. To assert in financial statements that the right of setoff is enforceable at law requires support that depends on cost-benefit constraints, and facts and circumstances. Amounts should be offset only if—based on all available positive and negative information about the ability to legally enforce the setoff—"there is reasonable assurance that the right of setoff would be upheld in bankruptcy."

CHAPTER 4
ASC 215—STATEMENT OF SHAREHOLDER EQUITY

ASC 215 does not provide any unique guidance but rather only provides a link to guidance on shareholders' equity in other ASC subtopics.

CHAPTER 5
ASC 220—COMPREHENSIVE INCOME

CONTENTS

General Guidance	5001
ASC 220-10: Overall	5001
Overview	5001
Background	5001
Reporting Comprehensive Income	5002
Objectives of Presenting Comprehensive Income	5002
Display Alternatives	5003
Components of Net Income	5004
Components of Other Comprehensive Income	5004
Presentation of Income Tax Effects	5005
Reclassification Adjustments	5005
Illustration of Reclassification Adjustment	5005
Illustration of Alternative Presentations of Comprehensive Income	5006
Reporting Accumulated Other Comprehensive Income	5007
Equity Section of the Statement of Financial Position	5007

GENERAL GUIDANCE

ASC 220-10: OVERALL

OVERVIEW

Reporting the results of operations, including comprehensive income, is one of the most important aspects of financial reporting. GAAP provide specific guidance concerning how comprehensive income should be presented. For discussion of the guidance concerning how net income should be determined and presented, see the Chapter 2, *ASC 205—Presentation of Financial Statements*, and Chapter 6, *ASC 225—Income Statement*.

BACKGROUND

The FASB first introduced the term "comprehensive income" in its conceptual framework, CON-3 (Elements of Financial Statements), which was replaced subsequently by CON-6 of the same title. *Comprehensive income* is the change in equity of a business enterprise from transactions, other events, and circumstances from nonowner sources during a period. It includes all changes in equity during a period except those resulting from investments by owners and distributions to owners. CON-5 (Recognition and Measurement in Financial Statements of Business Enterprises) concluded that comprehensive income and its components should be reported as part of a full set of financial statements for a period and that earnings (i.e., net income) is a more narrow measurement of performance and, therefore, is a part of comprehensive income. ASC 220 requires the presentation of comprehensive income and its components in the financial statements.

REPORTING COMPREHENSIVE INCOME

Several accounting standards currently require that certain items that qualify as part of comprehensive income be reported directly in the equity section of the statement of financial position without having been recognized in the determination of net income.

ASC 220 applies to all enterprises that provide a full set of financial statements reporting financial position, results of operations, and cash flows. It does *not* apply to (ASC 220-10-15-2, 3):

- Enterprises that have no items of other comprehensive income in any period presented.
- Not-for-profit organizations that must follow ASC 958 (Not-for-Profit Entities).

ASC 220 deals with the presentation and display of comprehensive income, but it does not specify when to recognize or how to measure the components of comprehensive income. Those subjects are covered in other current standards or will be covered in future standards (ASC 220-10-05-1).

Objectives of Presenting Comprehensive Income

Comprehensive income is presented to report a measure of all changes in equity of an entity that result from recognized transactions and other economic events of the period other than transactions with owners in their capacity as owners. (ASC 220-10-10-1) When used in conjunction with related disclosures and other information in the financial statements, comprehensive income assists investors, creditors, and others in assessing the entity's activities and future cash flows. (ASC 220-10-10-2)

The term *comprehensive income,* as used in ASC 220, includes net income plus all other components of comprehensive income. The term *other comprehensive income* denotes revenues, expenses, gains, and losses that are included in comprehensive income but not in net income in accordance with GAAP. While the terms *comprehensive income* and *other comprehensive income* are used throughout ASC 220, those precise terms are not required to be used in an enterprise's financial statements (ASC 220-10-15-4; ASC Glossary).

PRACTICE NOTE: Before ASC 220, some elements of comprehensive income were presented in the income statement and others were reported directly in the equity section of the statement of financial position. However, all elements were *not* required to be brought together in a single amount of comprehensive income.

The FASB believes that information an enterprise provides by reporting comprehensive income—along with related disclosures and other information in the financial statements—helps investors, creditors, and others to assess the enterprise's activities and the timing and magnitude of its future cash flows. Given the diverse nature of the components of other comprehensive income, the FASB indicates that detailed information about each component is important. In fact, the FASB states that information about the components of comprehensive income may be more important than the total of comprehensive income, and the required disclosures are intended to support this stance (ASC 220-10-10-2, 3).

If a company has no components of comprehensive income other than net income, it is not required to report comprehensive income.

> **PRACTICE NOTE:** Apparently, the FASB believes that in a situation in which there are no elements of other comprehensive income, to designate a single amount as both net income and comprehensive income is potentially confusing to financial statement users. In this situation, the amount is comparable with net income of an enterprise that presents both net income and comprehensive income, so the FASB determined that no reporting of comprehensive income is appropriate. This should limit the applicability of ASC 220 considerably, because many enterprises do not have transactions that would create a difference between net income and comprehensive income.

Display Alternatives

Presenting comprehensive income applies to all entities, including (1) entities that provide a full set of financial statements that report financial position, results of operations, and cash flows, and (2) investment companies, defined benefit pension plans, and other employment plans that are exempt from the presentation of a statement of cash flows. (ASC 220-10-15-2)

Entities are required to report comprehensive income either in a single continuous financial statement or in two separate but consecutive financial statements. If presented in a single continuous financial statements, the following information is required:

- A total amount of net income together with the components that make up net income.
- A total amount for other comprehensive income together with the components that make up other comprehensive income.
- Total comprehensive income. (ASC 220-10-45-1A)

When an entity reports comprehensive income in two separate consecutive financial statements, the following information is required:

- Components of and the total of net income in the statement of net income.
- Components and the total for other comprehensive income as well as a total for comprehensive income in the statement of other comprehensive income presented immediately after the statement of net income. (ASC 220-10-45-1B)

> **PRACTICE NOTE:** The previous practice of presenting the components of other comprehensive income as a part of the statement of changes in stockholders' equity (or other similar title) is no longer acceptable. When this alternative was available, it was the most commonly-used method of presenting comprehensive income.

Components of Net Income

Components of net income are presented in various components, including income from continuing operations, discontinued operations, and extraordinary items. (ASC 220-10-45-7)

Components of Other Comprehensive Income

Following are items of other comprehensive income:

- Foreign currency translation adjustments.
- Gains and losses on foreign currency transactions that are designated as economic hedges of a net investment in a foreign entity.
- Gains and losses on intra-entity foreign currency transactions that are of a long-term-investment nature when the entities to the transactions are consolidated, combined, or accounting for by the equity method.
- Gains and losses on derivative instruments that are designated and qualify as cash flow hedges.
- Unrealized holding gains and losses on available-for-sale securities.
- Unrealized holding gains and losses that result from a debt security being transferred into the available-for-sale and held-to-maturity category from the held-to-maturity category.
- Amounts recognized in other comprehensive income for debt securities classified as available-for-sale and held-to-maturity related to an other-than-temporary impairment if the impairment is not recognized in earnings.
- Subsequent decreases or increases in the fair value of available-for-sale securities previously written down as impaired.
- Gains or losses associated with pension and other postretirement benefits that are not recognized immediately as a component of net periodic income.
- Prior service costs or credits associated with pension or other postretirement benefits.
- Transition assets or obligations associated with pension or other postretirement benefits that are not recognized immediately as a component of net periodic benefit cost.

Presentation of Income Tax Effects

An entity shall present the amount of income tax expense or benefit allocated to each component of other comprehensive income, including reclassification adjustments, in the statement in which those components are presented or disclose it in notes to the financial statements. (ASC 220-10-45-12)

Reclassification Adjustments

Items recognized in other comprehensive income that are later recognized in net income require a reclassification adjustment in order to prevent double counting of transactions in the determination of comprehensive income. An example of these transactions is accumulated gains or losses on available-for-sale investment securities that are accumulated in stockholders' equity under ASC 320 until the securities are sold. At the time of the sale, any previously recognized gains or losses that were accumulated in stockholders' equity (i.e., an element of other comprehensive income) are reversed in other comprehensive income and then recognized as an element of net income. The reversal of the previous recognition in other comprehensive income offsets the recognition from the previous period and effectively moves the recognition from other comprehensive income to net income when the gain or loss is actually realized in a sale (ASC 220-10-45-15).

PRACTICE POINTER: Reclassification adjustments may be displayed on the face of the financial statement in which comprehensive income is reported, or they may be disclosed in notes to the financial statements. For all reclassification adjustments, an enterprise may use either a gross display on the face of the financial statement or a net display on the face of the financial statement or in notes to the financial statements.

Illustration of Reclassification Adjustment

A company accounts for its available-for-sale investments in debt and equity securities at fair value in accordance with ASC 320. Information on these investments prior to 20X5—the year in which the investment was sold—is as follows (all numbers in thousands):

	20X3	20X4
Purchase	$100	$125
Market value	$120	$260

In 20X3, $20 ($120 - $100) would be recognized by increasing the investment and recording an accumulated unrecognized gain in stockholders' equity. In 20X4, a gain of $15 [$260 - ($125 + $120)] would be recognized in a similar fashion.

Assuming the investments are sold in 20X5 for $260, the accumulated unrecognized gain of $35 ($20 + $15) is offset by the recognition of a $35 reclassification loss in other comprehensive income, and a $35 realized gain is recognized in net income. This transaction results in the following presentation over the three-year period:

	20X3	20X4	20X5
Net income	None	None	$35
Other comprehensive income	$20	$15	($35)
Comprehensive income	$20	$15	None

If the reclassification of ($35) had not been recognized in other comprehensive income in 20X4, a $35 gain would have been recognized in comprehensive income *twice*—once as an element of other comprehensive income and once as an element of net income.

Illustration of Alternative Presentations of Comprehensive Income

Warner, Inc. has revenues of $1,559,231, expenses of $790,000, and two components of other comprehensive income, as follows:

- Accumulated gains of $100,000 on available-for-sale investments
- Foreign currency translation adjustments (losses) of $25,000

Net income is $500,000 for 20X5, the current year. Warner's income tax rate is 35%.

Format 1—One Income-Statement Format

Warner, Inc.
Statement of Income and Comprehensive Income for Year 20X5

Revenues		$1,559,231
Expenses		790,000
Income before income tax		$769,231
Income tax		269,231
Net income		$500,000
Other comprehensive income, net of income tax:		
Unrealized holding gains [$100,000 × (1−.35)]	$65,000	
Foreign currency translation [$25,000 × (1−.35)]	(16,250)	48,750
Comprehensive income		$548,750

Format 2—Two Income-Statement Format

Warner, Inc.
Statement of Comprehensive Income for Year 20X5*

Net income		$500,000
Other comprehensive income, net of income tax:		
Unrealized holding gains	$65,000	
Foreign currency translation	(16,250)	48,750
Comprehensive income		$548,750

* Statement ending in "net income" unchanged by ASC 220.

Reporting Accumulated Other Comprehensive Income

The amount of total accumulated other comprehensive income shall be presented as a component of equity that is separate from the amount of retained earnings and additional paid-in capital. A descriptive title, such as accumulated other comprehensive income, shall be used for that component of equity. (ASC 220-10-4-14)

Either on the face of the financial statements or in a separate note disclosure, the changes in the accumulated balances for each component of other comprehensive income included in that separate component of equity shall be presented. In addition to the presentation of changes in accumulated balances for each component of other comprehensive income, current period reclassifications out of accumulated other comprehensive income and other amounts of current-period other comprehensive income is required. (ASC 220-10-45-14A)

An entity shall separately provide information about the effects on net income of significant amounts reclassified out of each component of accumulated other comprehensive income if those amounts all are required to be reclassified to income in the same reporting period. This information may be presented either on the face of the statement where net income is presented or in as separate disclosure in notes to the financial statements. (ASC 220-10-45-17)

Equity Section of the Statement of Financial Position

At the end of the reporting period, the total of other comprehensive income is transferred to a separate stockholders' equity account, much like net income is transferred to retained earnings. This separate stockholders' equity account should have an appropriate descriptive title, such as *Accumulated Other Comprehensive Income*. Disclosure of the accumulated balances for each classification of that separate component of equity shall be made on the face of the statement of financial position, in a statement of changes in stockholders' equity, or in notes to the financial statements (ASC 220-10-45-14).

The classifications used in the disclosure of the balances of individual components of other comprehensive income must correspond to the classifications used elsewhere in the same financial statements (ASC 220-10-45-14).

CHAPTER 6
ASC 225—INCOME STATEMENT

CONTENTS

Part I: General Guidance	6001
ASC 225-10: Overall	6001
Overview	6001
Background	6001
ASC 225-20: Extraordinary and Unusual Items	6002
Irregular Items Reported in Net Income	6002
Extraordinary Items	6002
Unusual or Infrequent Items	6002
Part II: Interpretive Guidance	6003
ASC 225: Income Statement	6003
ASC 225-20: Extraordinary and Unusual Items	6003
ASC 225-20-55-4	
Reporting the Results of Operations: Unofficial Accounting Interpretations of APB Opinion No. 9	6003
ASC 225-20-55-3 through 55-4	
Reporting the Results of Operations: Accounting Interpretations of APB Opinion No. 30	6004
ASC 225-30: Business Interruption Insurance	6004
ASC 225-30-05-2, 45-1, 50-1; ASC 450-30-60-2 through 60-3	
Income Statement Display of Business Interruption Insurance Recoveries	6004

PART I: GENERAL GUIDANCE

ASC 225-10: OVERALL

OVERVIEW

Reporting the results of operations, primarily determining and presenting net income and comprehensive income, is one of the most important aspects of financial reporting. GAAP provide specific guidance concerning how certain items should be presented in the income statement.

BACKGROUND

For many years, there were differences of opinion in the accounting profession as to what should be included in net income. Proponents of the *all-inclusive concept* (sometimes called "clean surplus") believed that all items affecting net increases in owners' equity, except dividends and capital transactions, should be included in determining net income. Alternatively, proponents of the *current operating performance concept* (sometimes called "dirty surplus") advocated limiting the determination of net income to normal, recurring items of profit and loss that relate only to the current period and recognizing other items directly in retained earnings. Differences between the two concepts are seen most clearly in the treatment of the following items:

- Unusual or infrequent items
- Extraordinary items
- Changes in accounting principles
- Discontinued operations
- Prior period adjustments
- Certain items that are required by GAAP to be recognized directly in stockholders' equity rather than in net income

Current GAAP generally require the presentation of income in a manner that generally is consistent with the all inclusive concept. Net income includes all items of revenue, expense, gain, and loss during a reporting period, except prior period adjustments, dividends, and capital transactions, and a limited number of items that are required to be recognized directly in equity. Examples of items treated in this manner are certain foreign currency adjustments and certain changes in the value of debt and equity investments.

ASC 225-20: EXTRAORDINARY AND UNUSUAL ITEMS

IRREGULAR ITEMS REPORTED IN NET INCOME

Extraordinary Items

Extraordinary items are transactions and other events that are (*a*) material in nature, (*b*) unusual in nature, and (*c*) infrequent in occurrence (ASC Glossary). Extraordinary items are disclosed separately in the income statement, net of any related income tax effect (ASC 225-20-45-10). EPS for extraordinary items must be presented on the face of the income statement or in the notes.

Identifying extraordinary items requires informed professional judgment, taking into consideration all the facts involved in a particular situation. Some areas of promulgated GAAP, however, require that an item be treated as extraordinary. The following are the more common items that, if material, should be reported as extraordinary items if they are determined to be unusual in nature, and infrequent in occurrence:

- Most expropriations of property (ASC 225-20-45-5)
- Gains or losses that are the direct result of a major casualty (ASC 225-20-45-54)
- Losses resulting from prohibition under a newly enacted law or regulation (ASC 225-20-45-5)

Unusual or Infrequent Items

If professional judgment dictates individual treatment of a material event or transaction that does not qualify as an extraordinary item (e.g., unusual or infrequent, but not both), it may be reported separately as a component of income from continuing operations with appropriate footnote disclosure. In this event, however, the separately identified item should not be reported net of its related tax effects or in a manner that implies that the item is an extraordinary item (ASC 225-20-45-16).

PRACTICE POINTER: The FASB does not state precisely what should *not* be done in the presentation of an unusual or infrequent item in order for it to *not* be confused with an extraordinary item. In the presentation of unusual or infrequent items, avoid the following, which are characteristics of the presentation of extraordinary items:
- Net-of-tax presentation
- Presentation of earnings per share on the item
- Presentation of income before and after the item

PART II: INTERPRETIVE GUIDANCE

ASC 225: INCOME STATEMENT

ASC 225-20: EXTRAORDINARY AND UNUSUAL ITEMS

ASC 225-20-55-4 Reporting the Results of Operations: Unofficial Accounting Interpretations of APB Opinion No. 9

BACKGROUND

ASC 225-20-55-4 addresses whether a regulatory-agency requirement to recognize a particular write-off as an extraordinary loss applies in reports to shareholders.

ACCOUNTING GUIDANCE

Question: The Interstate Commerce Commission has ruled that railroads must write off certain receivables from other railroads as extraordinary losses. Is this accounting treatment appropriate for annual reports to shareholders and for annual reports of entities other than railroads?

Answer: No. Regulatory authorities often rule on the accounting treatment of companies under their jurisdiction. Despite the appropriateness of this practice for regulatory reporting purposes, ASC 225-20-55-4, as amended by ASC 225-20-45-1 through 45-6, 45-8, 45-10 through 45-14, 45-16, 45-19, 15-2; 55-1 through 55-3 specifies that, regardless of size, losses from receivables do not constitute extraordinary losses. Treatment of uncollectible receivables as an extraordinary item in the financial statements should result in a qualified audit opinion.

ASC 225-20-55-3 through 55-4 Reporting the Results of Operations: Accounting Interpretations of APB Opinion No. 30

BACKGROUND

ASC 225-20-55-3 through 55-4 presents three issues that pertain to the application of the guidance in ASC 225-20-45-1 through 45-6, 45-8, 45-10 through 45-14, 45-16, 45-19, 15-2, 55-1 through 55-3

ACCOUNTING GUIDANCE

Question 1: What factors should be considered in determining whether a particular event or transaction (*a*) is an extraordinary item or (*b*) should otherwise be set forth in the income statement? How are these factors applied in practice?

Answer: The unusual nature and the infrequency of occurrence of events and transactions should be considered when determining whether a transaction qualifies for treatment as an extraordinary item.) The relationship of those two criteria to the environment in which an entity conducts its business is discussed in ASC 225-20-45-1. Gains and losses that meet those criteria and therefore are reported in the financial statements as extraordinary items should result directly from a major casualty, an expropriation, or a prohibition under a newly enacted law or regulation. Four examples are presented in ASC 225-20-55-3 through 55-4, each of transactions that do and do not meet the criteria. For example, if a large portion of a tobacco manufacturer's crops are destroyed by a hail storm in a locality where hail storms are rare, the criterion for extraordinary classification would be met. On the other hand, if a citrus grower's Florida crop is damaged by frost and experience indicates that frost damage occurs every three or four years, the criterion of infrequent occurrence is not met and the loss would not be presented as extraordinary.

ASC 225-30: BUSINESS INTERRUPTION INSURANCE

ASC 225-30-05-2, 45-1, 50-1; ASC 450-30-60-2 through 60-3 Income Statement Display of Business Interruption Insurance Recoveries

BACKGROUND

Business interruption (BI) insurance is discussed in: ASC 605-40-05-1 through 05-2; 25-1 through 25-4; 30-1; 45-1; 55-66; 60-1, ASC 450-10-60-4 and in ASC 410-30-05-1 through 05-3, 05-5 through 05-25; 10-1; 15-1 through 15-3; 25-1 through 25-15, 25-17, 25-20 through 25-23; 30-1 through 30-19; 35-1 through 35-5, 35-7 through 35-12, 35-12A; 45-1 through 45-5; 50-1 through 50-17; 55-1 through 55-6, 55-14 through 55-17, 55-27 through 55-51; 60-3, 60-8.

ASC 605-40-05-1 through 05-2; 25-1 through 25-4; 30-1; 45-1; 55-66; and 60-1, and ASC 450-10-60-4 provides broad guidance on the recognition, measurement, and classification of insurance recoveries related to property and equipment. Under the Interpretation, gains or losses on involuntary conversions of property and equipment into insurance proceeds should be measured as the difference between the carrying amount of the property or equipment and the insurance proceeds received. Such recoveries are reported in the financial statements on the same line as a reduction of the related loss.

The guidance in ASC 410-30-05-1 through 05-3, 05-5 through 05-25; 10-1; 15-1 through 15-3; 25-1 through 25-15, 25-17, 25-20 through 25-23; 30-1 through 30-19; 35-1 through 35-5, 35-7 through 35-12, 35-12A; 45-1 through 45-5; 50-1 through

50-17; 55-1 through 55-6, 55-14 through 55-17, 55-27 through 55-51; and 60-3, 60-8, which applies to insurance recoveries for environmental remediation costs, requires that expenses related to environmental remediation be reported in *operating* income in financial statements that classify items as operating or nonoperating. Credits from recoveries of such expenses should be reported on the same income statement line as a reduction of the expense.

BI insurance differs from the types of insurance discussed above, because it protects an insured entity's future earnings or profits if its operations are suspended because of a loss of use of equipment and property as a result of a covered event. Such insurance usually reimburses the insured entity for certain costs and losses incurred during a reasonable period in which the entity rebuilds, repairs, or replaces the damaged property. Covered losses include costs related to gross margin not earned because normal operations have been halted, a portion of fixed charges and expenses related to a loss of gross margin, and other expenses such as the rental of temporary facilities and equipment.

ACCOUNTING ISSUE

How should recoveries of business interruption insurance be displayed in the income statement?

ACCOUNTING GUIDANCE

Entities are permitted to decide how to present recoveries from business interruption insurance in their financial statements as long as the presentation is acceptable under current GAAP. In addition, the following disclosures should be made in the period in which such recoveries are reported:

- The nature of the event that caused losses due to business interruption.
- The total amount of recoveries from business interruption insurance reported during the period and the income statement line items in which recoveries are reported (including amounts reported as extraordinary items under the guidance in ASC 225-20-45-1 through 45-6, 45-8, 45-10 through 45-14, 45-16, 45-19; 15-2; and 55-1 through 55-3.

CHAPTER 7
ASC 230—STATEMENT OF CASH FLOWS

CONTENTS

Part I: General Guidance	7001
ASC 230-10: Overall	7001
Overview	7001
Background	7002
Statement of Cash Flows—General	7002
Cash Equivalents	7003
Gross and Net Cash Flows	7003
Classification of Cash Receipts and Cash Payments	7003
Foreign Currency Cash Flows	7006
Exemption for Certain Investment Companies	7007
Content and Form of Statement of Cash Flows	7007
Direct Method	7008
Indirect Method	7009
Reconciliation of Net Income to Net Cash Flow	7009
Noncash Investing and Financing Activities	7010
Cash Flow per Share	7010
Financial Institutions	7010
Illustration of Procedures for Preparing a Statement of Cash Flows	7011
Part II: Interpretive Guidance	7019
ASC 230-10: Overall	7019
ASC 230-10-45-12, 21A, 65-1; ASC 958-230-55-3	
Not-for-Profit Entities: Classification of the Sale of Donated Financial Assets in the Statement of Cash Flows	7019
ASC 230-10-45-15	
Classification of Debt Issue Costs in the Statement of Cash Flows	7020
ASC 230-10-45-17; ASC 410-20-45-3	
Classification in the Statement of Cash Flows of Payments Made to Settle an Asset Retirement Obligation within the Scope of FASB Statement No. 143, *Accounting for Asset Retirement Obligations*	7021

PART I: GENERAL GUIDANCE

ASC 230-10: OVERALL

OVERVIEW

A statement of cash flows is required as part of a complete set of financial statements prepared in conformity with GAAP for all business enterprises. Within that statement, cash receipts and payments are classified as operating, investing, and financing activities, which are presented in a manner to reconcile the change in cash from the beginning to the end of the period.

BACKGROUND

Information in a statement of cash flows, when used in conjunction with information available in other financial statements and related disclosures, is expected to be helpful to investors, creditors, and other users to:

- Assess the enterprise's ability to generate positive future net cash flows

- Assess the enterprise's ability to meet its obligations, pay dividends, and satisfy its needs for external financing

- Assess the reasons for differences between net income and associated cash receipts and payments

- Assess the effects on an enterprise's financial position of both its cash and noncash investing and financing transactions

ASC 230 (Statement of Cash Flows) requires that a *statement of cash flows* be included as part of a full set of general financial statements that are externally issued by any business enterprise. All business enterprises are required to comply with the provision of ASC 230.

There are certain exemptions from the requirements in ASC 230. That is, ASC 230 does not apply to: (*a*) certain employee benefit plans and (*b*) highly liquid investment companies that meet certain conditions (ASC 230-10-15-4). Also, cash receipts and cash payments resulting from transactions in certain securities, other assets, and loans acquired specifically for resale must be classified as *operating cash flows* in a statement of cash flows (ASC 230-10-45-20, 21). In addition, banks, savings institutions, and credit unions can report net cash flows from certain transactions instead of gross cash flows (ASC 230-10-45-8). Finally, an enterprise that meets certain conditions can classify the cash flow of a hedging transaction and the cash flow of its related hedged item in the same category of cash flow (operating activity, investing activity, or financing activity).

STATEMENT OF CASH FLOWS—GENERAL

A statement of cash flows specifies the amount of net cash provided or used by an enterprise during a period from (*a*) operating activities, (*b*) investing activities, and (*c*) financing activities. The statement of cash flows indicates the net effect of these cash flows on the enterprise's cash and cash equivalents. A reconciliation of beginning and ending cash and cash equivalents is required in the statement of cash flows. ASC 230 also requires that the statement of cash flows contain separate related disclosures about all investing and financing activities of an enterprise that affect its financial position, but do not directly affect its cash flows during the period (ASC 230-10-45-2). Descriptive terms such as *cash* or *cash and cash equivalents* are required in the statement of cash flows, whereas ambiguous terms such as *funds* are inappropriate (ASC 230-10-45-4).

Cash Equivalents

Under ASC 230, cash equivalents are short-term, highly liquid investments that are (*a*) readily convertible to known amounts of cash and (*b*) so near their maturities that they present insignificant risk of changes in value because of changes in interest rates. As a general rule, only investments with *original maturities* of three months or less qualify as cash equivalents (ASC Glossary). Examples of items commonly considered to be cash equivalents include Treasury bills, commercial paper, money market funds, and federal funds that are sold (ASC Glossary).

> **PRACTICE POINTER:** An enterprise must disclose its policy for determining which items are treated as cash equivalents. Any change in that policy is accounted for as a change in accounting principle by restating financial statements of earlier years that are presented for comparative purposes (ASC 230-10-50-1). ASC 230 does not specify the accounting treatment of amounts in bank accounts that are unavailable for immediate withdrawal, such as compensating balances in the bank account of a borrower. Logically, these amounts should be treated as cash, with disclosure of any material restrictions on withdrawal.

Gross and Net Cash Flows

As a general rule, ASC 230 requires an enterprise to report the gross amounts of its cash receipts and cash payments in the statement of cash flows. For example, outlays for acquisitions of property, plant, and equipment are reported separately from proceeds from the sale of these assets. Similarly, proceeds from borrowing are reported separately from repayments. The gross amounts of cash receipts and cash payments usually are presumed to be more relevant than net amounts. It may be sufficient in some circumstances, however, to report the net amounts of certain assets and liabilities instead of their gross amounts (ASC 230-10-45-7).

The net changes during a period may be reported for those assets and liabilities in which turnover is quick, amounts are large, and maturities are short (ASC 230-10-45-8). These include cash receipts and cash payments pertaining to (*a*) investments (other than cash equivalents), (*b*) loans receivable, and (*c*) debt, provided the original maturity of the asset or liability is three months or less (ASC 230-10-45-9).

ASC 230 permits banks, savings institutions, and credit unions to report net amounts for (*a*) deposits placed with other financial institutions and withdrawals of deposits, (*b*) time deposits accepted and repayments of deposits, and (*c*) loans made to customers and principal collections of loans.

Classification of Cash Receipts and Cash Payments

Under ASC 230, an enterprise is required to classify its cash receipts and cash payments into operating activities, investing activities, or financing activities (ASC 230-10-45-10).

Operating Activities include all transactions and other events that are not defined as investing or financing activities. Operating activities generally involve producing and delivering goods and providing services (i.e., transactions that enter into the determination of net income) (ASC Glossary).

Cash inflows:

- Cash receipts from sales of goods or services, including receipts from collection or sale of accounts receivable and short-term and long-term notes arising from such sales
- Cash receipts from returns on loans, other debt instruments of other entities, and equity securities
- All other cash receipts not classified as investing or financing activities

Cash outflows:

- Cash payments for materials for manufacture or goods for resale, including principal payments on accounts payable and short-term and long-term notes to suppliers
- Cash payments to other suppliers and employers for other goods and services
- Cash payments to governments for taxes, duties, fines, and other fees or penalties
- Cash payments to lenders and others for interest
- All other cash payments not classified as investing or financing activities

Investing Activities include making and collecting loans and acquiring and disposing of debt or equity instruments and property, plant, and equipment and other productive assets; that is, assets held for or used in the production of goods or services by the enterprise (other than materials that are part of the enterprise's inventory) (ASC Glossary). Acquiring and disposing of certain loans or other debt or equity instruments that are acquired specifically for resale are excluded from investing activities (ASC Glossary).

Cash inflows:

- Receipts from collections or sales of loans and of others' debt instruments
- Receipts from sales of equity instruments of other enterprises and from returns of investments in those instruments
- Receipts from sales of property, plant, and equipment and other productive assets

Cash outflows:

- Payments for loans made by the enterprise and to acquire debt instruments of other entities
- Payments to acquire equity instruments in other enterprises
- Payments at the time of purchase or soon thereafter to acquire property, plant, and equipment and other productive assets

PRACTICE POINTER: Receipts from sales of equity instruments of other entities, are generally classified as cash inflows from investing activities. Certain donated equity instruments received by NFP organizations are an exception. Cash receipts resulting from the sale of donated financial assets by NFPs that upon receipt were directed without any NFP-imposed limitations for sale and were converted nearly immediately into cash are classified as operating cash flows. If, however, the donor restricted the use of the contributed resource to a long-term purpose, those cash receipts meeting stated criteria are classified as financing activities.

Financing Activities include obtaining resources from owners and providing them with a return on, and return of, their investment; borrowing money and repaying amounts borrowed, or otherwise settling the obligation; and obtaining and paying for other resources obtained from creditors on long-term credit (ASC Glossary).

Cash inflows:

- Proceeds from issuing equity instruments
- Proceeds from issuing bonds, mortgages, notes, and other short-term or long-term borrowing

Cash outflows:

- Payments of dividends or other distributions to owners, including outlays to reacquire the enterprise's equity instruments
- Repayments of amounts borrowed
- Other principal payments to creditors that have extended long-term credit

---

PRACTICE POINTER: Classify cash received from sales of inventory to customers is presented as cash from operating activities, whether received at the time of sale or collected at some other time, on open account or on a note (short-term, long-term, or installment). Similarly, cash paid to suppliers for inventory is presented as cash used for operating activities, whether paid at the time of purchase or paid at some other time, on open account or on a note (short-term, long-term, or installment).

A cash receipt or a cash payment that can qualify for more than one cash flow activity is appropriately classified as the activity that is likely to be the predominant source of cash flows for that item. For example, the acquisition and sale of equipment used by an enterprise or rented to others generally are investing activities. If the intention of an enterprise is to use or rent the equipment for a short period of time and then sell it, however, the cash receipts and cash payments associated with the acquisition or production of the equipment and the subsequent sale are considered cash flows from operating activities (ASC 230-10-45-22).

> **PRACTICE POINTER:** Care should be taken in classifying certain cash flows. The FASB has indicated how to classify certain items that might fit logically in more than one of the major categories of the statement of cash flows. Following are examples of these items:
>
> *Interest paid:* Presented as an operating activity, despite their close association with financing activities and the fact that dividends paid are presented as a financing activity.
>
> *Interest and dividends received:* Presented as an operating activity, despite their close association with other activities presented as investing activities.
>
> *Gains and losses on asset and liability transactions* (e.g., sale of plant assets, extinguishment of debt): Presented as investing and financing activities, although the gain/loss was included in net income.
>
> *Income taxes:* Presented entirely as an operating activity, despite the fact that some gains and losses that may affect income taxes are presented as investing and financing activities.

As a general rule, each cash receipt or cash payment is required to be classified according to its source (operating, investing, or financing) without regard to whether it arose as a hedge of another item. However, ASC 230 indicates that the cash flows from derivative instruments that are accounted for as fair-value or cash-flow hedges under ASC 815 may be classified in the same category as the cash flow of the related hedged item, provided that the enterprise (*a*) discloses this accounting policy and (*b*) reports the gain or loss on the hedging instrument in the same accounting period as the offsetting gain or loss on the hedged item.

ASC 230 provides that cash receipts and cash payments must be classified as operating cash flows in a statement of cash flows when such cash receipts and cash payments result from the acquisition or sale of (*a*) securities and other assets that are acquired specifically for resale and carried at market value in a trading account and (*b*) loans that are acquired specifically for resale and carried at market value or the lower of cost or market value (ASC 230-10-45-20, 21). The cash receipts and cash payments from the sale of loans originally acquired as investments, however, are classified as investing cash flows in a statement of cash flows, regardless of any subsequent change in the purpose of holding those loans (ASC 230-10-45-12).

Foreign Currency Cash Flows

An enterprise with foreign currency translations or foreign operations shall report, in its statement of cash flows, the reporting currency equivalent of foreign currency cash flows using the exchange rates in effect at the time of the cash flows. An appropriately weighted average exchange rate for the period may be used in lieu of the actual currency rates at the dates of the cash flows, provided that the results are substantially the same. The effect of exchange rate changes on cash balances held in foreign currencies is reported in the statement of cash flows as a separate part of the reconciliation of the change in cash and cash equivalents during the period (ASC 830-230-45-1).

Exemption for Certain Investment Companies

Investment-type entities that meet certain conditions are not required to include a statement of cash flows as part of their complete financial presentation in accordance with GAAP. The entities entitled to this exemption are as follows (ASC 230-10-15-4):

- Investment companies that are subject to the registration and regulatory requirements of the Investment Company Act of 1940 (1940 Act)
- Investment enterprises that have essentially the same characteristics as investment companies subject to the 1940 Act
- Common trust funds, variable annuity accounts, or similar funds maintained by a bank, insurance company, or other enterprise in its capacity as a trustee, administrator, or guardian for the collective investment and reinvestment of moneys

The investment-type entities specified above are not required to include a statement of cash flows in their financial presentations, provided that they meet all of the following conditions (ASC 230-10-15-4):

- Substantially all investments owned by the enterprise were highly liquid during the period covered by the financial statements (highly liquid investments include, but are not limited to, marketable securities and other assets that can be sold through existing markets).
- Substantially all of the investments owned by the enterprise are carried at market value including securities for which market value is calculated by the use of matrix pricing techniques (described in the AICPA Industry Audit and Accounting Guide titled Audits of Investment Companies). Securities that do not meet this condition are those for which (a) market value is not readily ascertainable and (b) fair value must be determined in good faith by the board of directors of the enterprise.
- Based on average debt outstanding during the period, the enterprise had little or no debt in relation to average total assets. For these purposes, average debt outstanding generally may exclude obligations from (a) redemption of shares by the enterprise, (b) unsettled purchases of securities or similar assets, or (c) written covered options.
- The enterprise provides a statement of changes in net assets.

CONTENT AND FORM OF STATEMENT OF CASH FLOWS

A statement of cash flows shall disclose separately the amount of net cash provided or used during a period from an enterprise's (*a*) operating activities, (*b*) investing activities, and (*c*) financing activities. The effect of the total amount of net cash provided or used during a period from all sources (operating, investing, and financing) on an enterprise's cash and cash equivalents shall be clearly disclosed in a manner that reconciles beginning and ending cash and cash equivalents (ASC 230-10-45-24).

In reporting cash flows from *operating activities* in the statement of cash flows, ASC 230 encourages but does not require an enterprise to use the *direct method* (ASC 230-10-45-25). Enterprises that do not use the direct method to report their cash flows from operating activities may use the *indirect method* (also referred to as the reconciliation method). The amount of cash flows from operating activities is the same whether calculated and presented by the direct or indirect method. There is no difference in reporting the cash flows from investing and financing activities, regardless of whether the direct or indirect method is used to report cash flows from operations.

Direct Method

A presentation of a statement of cash flows by the direct method reflects the gross amounts of the principal components of cash receipts and cash payments from operating activities, such as cash received from customers and cash paid to suppliers and employees. Using the direct method, the amount of net cash provided by or used in operating activities during the period is equal to the difference between the total amount of gross cash receipts and the total amount of gross cash payments arising from operating activities.

ASC 230 requires enterprises using the direct method of reporting the amount of net cash flow provided from or used by operating activities to present separately, at a minimum, in their statement of cash flows, the following principal components of operating cash receipts and operating cash payments (ASC 230-10-45-25):

- Cash collected from customers, including lessees, licensees, and other similar receipts
- Interest and dividends received
- Any other operating cash receipts
- Cash paid to employees and other suppliers of goods or services including suppliers of insurance, advertising, and other similar cash payments
- Any other operating cash payments, including interest paid, income taxes paid, and other similar cash payments

---

PRACTICE POINTER: An enterprise may use an alternate method of computation to arrive at the amounts shown in a statement of cash flows. For example, when preparing a direct method statement of cash flows, an enterprise may make an alternate computation to determine the amount of cash received from customers; i.e., it may start with total sales for the period and adjust that figure for the difference between beginning and ending accounts receivable.

The provisions of ASC 230 encourage, but do not require, an enterprise to include in its statement of cash flows other meaningful details pertaining to its cash receipts and cash payments from operating activities. For example, a retailer or manufacturer might decide to subdivide cash paid to employees and suppliers into cash payments for costs of inventory and cash payments for selling, general, and administrative expenses (ASC 230-10-45-25).

> **PRACTICE NOTE:** The use of the direct method is encouraged by ASC 230 because it reflects the gross amounts of the principal components of cash receipts and cash payments from operating activities, while the indirect method does not. This presentation is more compatible with the manner of presenting cash flows from financing and investing activities than is the indirect method. Despite the FASB's preference for the direct method, the predominant method used in practice is the indirect method.

Indirect Method

Enterprises that choose not to provide information about major classes of operating cash receipts and cash payments by the direct method, as encouraged by ASC 230, can indirectly determine and report the same amount of net cash flow from operating activities by reconciling net income to net cash flow from operating activities (the indirect or reconciliation method). The adjustments necessary to reconcile net income to net cash flow are made to net income to remove (*a*) the effects of all deferrals of past operating cash receipts and cash payments, such as changes during the period in inventory and deferred income, (*b*) the effects of all accruals of expected future operating cash receipts and cash payments, such as changes during the period in receivables and payables, and (*c*) the effects of all items classified as investing or financing cash flows, such as gains or losses on sales of property, plant, and equipment and discontinued operations (investing activities), and gains or losses on extinguishment of debt (financing activities) (ASC 230-10-45-28).

Reconciliation of Net Income to Net Cash Flow

Regardless of whether an enterprise uses the direct or indirect method of reporting net cash flow from *operating* activities, ASC 230 requires that a reconciliation of net income to net cash flow be provided in conjunction with the statement of cash flows. The reconciliation of net income to net cash flow from operating activities provides information about the net effects of operating transactions and other events that affect net income and operating cash flows in different periods. This reconciliation separately reflects all major classes of reconciling items. For example, major classes of deferrals of past operating cash receipts and payments and accruals of expected future operating cash receipts and payments, including at a minimum changes during the period in receivables and payables pertaining to *operating* activities, are reported separately. Enterprises are encouraged to further break down those categories they consider meaningful. For example, changes in trade receivables for an enterprise's sale of goods or services might be reported separately from changes in other operating receivables (ASC 230-10-45-29).

If an enterprise uses the direct method, the reconciliation of net income to net cash flow from operating activities is provided in a separate schedule accompanying the statement of cash flows (ASC 230-10-45-30).

If an enterprise uses the indirect method, the reconciliation may be *either* included within and as part of the statement of cash flows *or* provided in a separate schedule, with the statement of cash flows reporting only the net cash flow from operating activities. If the reconciliation is included within and as part of the statement of cash flows, all adjustments to net income to determine net cash flow from operating activities must be clearly identified as reconciling items (ASC 230-10-45-31, 32).

> **PRACTICE NOTE:** The fact that a reconciliation of net income to net cash flows from operating activities is required if a company uses the direct method may explain why the majority of companies use the indirect method. Companies report that developing the additional information required to use the direct method may also explain the popularity of the indirect method.

Regardless of whether the direct or the indirect method is used to report net cash flow from operating activities, ASC 230 requires the separate disclosure of the amounts of interest paid (net of amounts capitalized) and income taxes paid during the period (ASC 230-10-45-29). These disclosures usually are in the operating activities section of the statement if the direct method is used and in a note if the indirect method is used.

Noncash Investing and Financing Activities

Disclosures in conjunction with the statement of cash flows must contain information about all investing and financing activities of an enterprise during a period that affect recognized assets or liabilities but that do not result in cash receipts or cash payments. These disclosures may be either narrative or summarized in a schedule, and they shall clearly relate the cash and noncash aspects of transactions involving similar items. Examples of noncash investing and financing transactions include:

- Converting debt to equity
- Acquiring assets by assuming directly related liabilities (e.g., capital leases, purchasing a building by incurring a mortgage to the seller)
- Exchanging noncash assets or liabilities for other noncash assets or liabilities

Only the cash portion of a part-cash, part-noncash transaction is reported in the body of the statement of cash flows (ASC 230-10-50-4).

Cash Flow per Share

An enterprise is prohibited from reporting any amount representing cash flow per share in its financial statements (ASC 230-10-45-3).

FINANCIAL INSTITUTIONS

There are different requirements for the statement of cash flows for financial institutions. Cash receipts and payments associated with securities that are carried in *trading accounts* by banks, brokers, and dealers in securities are classified as cash flows from operating activities. In addition, cash inflows and outflows associated with securities classified as trading securities (see ASC 320

(Investments—Debt and Equity Securities)) must be shown as operating cash flows. On the other hand, if securities are acquired for investment purposes, the related cash receipts and cash payments are classified as cash flows from investing activities. Loans are given similar treatment. The cash receipts and cash payments associated with mortgage loans that are held for resale by a bank or mortgage broker are classified as cash flows from operating activities. If the mortgage loans are held for investment purposes, however, the related cash receipts and cash payments are classified as cash flows from investing activities (ASC 230-10-45-12, 21).

Instead of reporting gross amounts of cash flows in their statements of cash flows, as would be required by ASC 230, banks, savings institutions, and credit unions are permitted to report *net* amounts of cash flows that result from (*a*) deposits and deposit withdrawals with other financial institutions, (*b*) time deposits accepted and repayments of deposits, and (*c*) loans to customers and principal collections of loans. Financial institutions have the following choices in reporting cash flows in its statement of cash flows:

- To report the gross amount of all cash receipts and disbursements
- To report the net cash flows in the limited situations allowed by ASC 230, such as loans with maturities of three months or less, and to report gross amounts for all other transactions
- If the enterprise is a bank, savings institution, or credit union, to report net cash flows in the limited situations allowed by GAAP, such as time deposits, and to report gross amounts for all other transactions
- If the enterprise is a bank, savings institution, or credit union, to report net cash flows in the situations allowed by ASC 230, and to report gross amounts for all other transactions

If a consolidated enterprise includes a bank, savings institution, or credit union that uses net cash reporting as allowed by ASC 230, the statement of cash flows of the consolidated enterprise must report separately (*a*) the net cash flows of the financial institution and (*b*) the gross cash receipts and cash payments of other members of the consolidated enterprise, including subsidiaries of a financial institution that are not themselves financial institutions.

Illustration of Procedures for Preparing a Statement of Cash Flows

Following are Holcomb Company's balance sheets for the year ending December 31, 20X8 and the quarter ending March 31, 20X9, as well as the income statement for the three months ending March 31, 20X9.

ASC 230—Statement of Cash Flows

Balance Sheet

	December 31, 20X8	March 31, 20X9
Cash	$ 25,300	$ 87,400
Marketable securities	16,500	7,300
Accounts receivable, net	24,320	49,320
Inventory	31,090	48,590
Total current assets	97,210	192,610
Land	40,000	18,700
Building	250,000	250,000
Equipment	—	81,500
Accumulated depreciation	(15,000)	(16,250)
Investment in 30% owned company	61,220	67,100
Other assets	15,100	15,100
Total	$448,530	$608,760
Accounts payable	$ 21,220	$ 17,330
Dividend payable	—	8,000
Income taxes payable	—	34,616
Total current liabilities	21,220	59,946
Other liabilities	186,000	186,000
Bonds payable	50,000	115,000
Discount on bonds payable	(2,300)	(2,150)
Deferred income taxes	510	846
Preferred stock ($2 par)	30,000	—
Common stock ($1 par)	80,000	110,000
Dividends declared	—	(8,000)
Retained earnings	83,100	147,118
Total	$448,530	$608,760

Income Statement
For the Three Months Ended March 31, 20X9

Sales	$242,807
Gain on sale of marketable investments	2,400
Equity in earnings of 30% owned company	5,880
Gain on condemnation of land	10,700
Total revenues and gains	261,787
Cost of sales	138,407
General and administrative expenses	22,010
Depreciation	1,250
Interest expense	1,150
Income taxes	34,952
	197,769
Net income	$ 64,018

The following information has been identified:

(1) In January 20X9, the company sold marketable securities for cash of $11,600. These securities had been held for several months.
(2) The preferred stock is convertible into common stock at a rate of one share of preferred for three shares of common.
(3) In February 20X9, land was condemned. An award of $32,000 in cash was received in March.
(4) During February 20X9, the company purchased equipment for cash.
(5) During March 20X9, bonds were issued by the company at par for cash.
(6) The investment in the 30% owned company included $3,220 attributable to goodwill at December 31, 20X8.

Worksheet for Preparing the Statement of Cash Flows for the Quarter Ended March 31, 20X9

Real Accounts	Balances 12/31/X8	Changes Debit	Changes Credit	Balances 3/31/X9
Debits:				
Cash	$ 25,300	(n) $62,100		$87,400
Marketable Securities	16,500		(f) 9,200	7,300
Accounts Receivable, Net	24,320	(a) 25,000		49,320
Inventory	31,090	(b) 17,500		48,590
Land	40,000		(g) 21,300	18,700
Building	250,000			250,000

ASC 230—Statement of Cash Flows

Real Accounts	Balances 12/31/X8	Changes Debit			Changes Credit		Balances 3/31/X9
Equipment	0	(h)	81,500				81,500
Investment in 30% Owned Company	61,220	(j)	5,880				67,100
Other Assets	15,100						15,100
Discount on Bonds Payable	2,300			(e)		150	2,150
Dividends Declared	0	(m)	8,000				8,000
	465,830						635,160
Credits:							
Accumulated Depreciation	15,000			(d)		1,250	16,250
Accounts Payable	21,220	(b)	3,890				17,330
Dividend Payable	0			(m)		8,000	8,000
Income Taxes Payable	0			(i)		34,616	34,616
Other Liabilities	186,000						186,000
Bonds Payable	50,000			(k)		65,000	115,000
Deferred Income Taxes	510			(i)		336	846
Preferred Stock	30,000	(l)	30,000				0
Common Stock	80,000			(l)		30,000	110,000
Retained Earnings	83,100					64,018⟵	147,118
	465,830		233,870			233,870	635,160

Nominal Accounts

Sales				(a)	242,807	
Gain on Sale of Marketable Securities				(f)	2,400	
Equity in Earnings of 30% Owned Company				(j)	5,880	
Gain on Condemnation of Land				(g)	10,700	
Cost of Sales	(b)	138,407				
General and Administrative Expenses	(c)	22,010				
Depreciation	(d)	1,250				
Interest Expense	(e)	1,150				
Income Taxes	(i)	34,952				
		197,769			261,787	
		64,018				
		261,787			261,787	

ASC 230—Statement of Cash Flows **7015**

	Balances 12/31/X8	Changes Debit	Changes Credit	Balances 3/31/X9
Cash Flow Categories				
Operating Activities:				
Cash Collected from Customers		(a) 217,807		
Cash Paid for Goods to Be Sold			(b) 159,797	
Cash Flow Categories				
Cash Paid for General and Administrative Expenses			(c) 22,010	
Cash Paid for Interest			(e) 1,000	
Investing Activities				
Cash Received from Sale of Marketable Securities		(f) 11,600		
Cash Received from Land Condemnation		(g) 32,000		
Cash Paid for Purchase of Equipment			(h) 81,500	
Financing Activities				
Cash Received from Sale of Bonds Payable		(k) 65,000		
		326,407	264,307	
Increase in Cash			(n) 62,100	
		326,407	326,407	

Explanation of Worksheet Entries

(a)	Sales	$242,807
	Less increase in receivables	(25,000)
	Cash collected from customers	$217,807
(b)	Cost of sales	$138,407
	Plus increase in inventory	17,500
	Plus decrease in accounts payable	3,890
	Cash paid for goods to be sold	$159,797
(c)	G&A expenses	$ 22,010
	No adjustments	—
	Cash paid for G&A expenses	$ 22,010

(d) $1,250 reconciliation of depreciation expense and change in accumulated depreciation. No statement of cash flow effects.

(e) Interest expense $ 1,150
    Less decrease in discount on bonds payable (150)
    Cash paid for interest $ 1,000

(f) Decrease in marketable securities $ 9,200
    Plus gain on sale of marketable securities 2,400
    Cash received from sale of marketable securities $ 11,600

(g) Decrease in land $ 21,300
    Plus gain on condemnation of land 10,700
    Cash received from land condemnation $ 32,000

(h) Increase in equipment account ($81,500) also cash paid for equipment.

(i) Reconciliation of income tax expense ($34,952) to income tax payable ($34,616) and increase in deferred income tax ($336). No statement of cash flow effect.

(j) Reconciliation of $5,880 equity in earnings of 30% owned company (income statement) to change in inventory in 30% owned company. No statement of cash flow effects.

(k) Increase in bonds payable account $ 65,000
    No adjustment —
    Cash received from sale of bonds payable $ 65,000

(l) Noncash transaction to record retirement of preferred stock and issuance of common stock at $30,000. No statement of cash flow effects, but disclosure is required.

(m) Reconciliation of $8,000 dividends declared to increase in dividends payable. No statement of cash flow effects but disclosure is required.

(n) Reconciliation of $62,100 increase in cash to net of all sources (increases) and uses (decreases) in cash.

Holcomb Company
Statement of Cash Flows (Direct Method)
for the Three Months Ended March 31, 20X9

Cash Flows from Operating Activities
    Cash Received from
      Customers $217,807
    Cash Paid for Goods
      to be Sold $ 159,797
    Cash Paid for General
      and Administrative Expenses 22,010
    Cash Paid for Interest 1,000
    Cash Disbursed for
      Operating Activities 182,807
    Net Cash Provided by
      Operating Activities $ 35,000

Cash Flows from Investing Activities
  Proceeds from Sale of
    Marketable Securities $ 11,600
  Proceeds from
    Condemnation of Land   32,000
  Purchases of Equipment   (81,500)
  Net Cash Used in Investing
    Activities   (37,900)
Cash Flows from Financing Activities
  Proceeds of Long-Term Debt   65,000
  Net Increase in Cash $ 62,100
Cash, January 1, 20X9   25,300
Cash, March 31, 20X9 $ 87,400

Reconciliation of Net Income to
Net Cash Provided by
Operating Activities:
  Net Income $64,018
  Adjustments to Reconcile Net
    Income to Net Cash Provided
    by Operating Activities:
    Depreciation Expense   1,250
    Bond Discount Amortization   150
    Increase in Deferred Income
      Tax   336
    Gain on Sale of Marketable
      Securities   (2,400)
    Equity in Earnings of
      Investee   (5,880)
    Gain on Sale of Land   (10,700)
    Accounts Receivable Increase   (25,000)
    Inventory Increase   (17,500)
    Accounts Payable Decrease   (3,890)
    Income Taxes Payable
      Increase   34,616
  Net Cash Provided by Operating
    Activities $ 35,000

Schedule of Noncash Financing Activities

Retirement of Preferred Stock by Conversion to
  Common Stock $ 30,000

Declaration of Cash Dividends to be Paid $ 8,000

Holcomb Company
Statement of Cash Flows (Indirect Method)
for the Three Months Ended March 31, 20X9

Cash Flows from Operating Activities		
Net Income		$64,018
Adjustments to Reconcile Net Income to Net Cash Provided by Operating Activities:		
Depreciation Expense		1,250
Bond Discount Amortization		150
Increase in Deferred Income Tax		336
Gain on Sale of Marketable Securities		(2,400)
Equity in Earnings of Investee		(5,880)
Gain on Sale of Land		(10,700)
Accounts Receivable Increase		(25,000)
Inventory Increase		(17,500)
Accounts Payable Decrease		(3,890)
Income Taxes Payable Increase		34,616
Net Cash Provided by Operating Activities		$ 35,000
Cash Flows from Investing Activities		
Proceeds from Sale of Marketable Securities	$ 11,600	
Proceeds from Condemnation of Land	32,000	
Purchases of Equipment	(81,500)	
Net Cash Used in Investing Activities		(37,900)
Cash Flows from Financing Activities		
Proceeds of Long-Term Debt		65,000
Net Increase in Cash		$ 62,100
Cash, January 1, 20X9		25,300
Cash, March 31, 20X9		$ 87,400

Schedule of Noncash Financing Activities

Retirement of Preferred Stock by Conversion to Common Stock	$ 30,000
Declaration of Cash Dividends to be Paid	$ 8,000

PART II: INTERPRETIVE GUIDANCE

ASC 230-10: OVERALL

ASC 230-10-45-12, 21A, 65-1; ASC 958-230-55-3 Not-for-Profit Entities: Classification of the Sale of Donated Financial Assets in the Statement of Cash Flows

BACKGROUND

Not-for-profit entities (NFPs) usually receive donations in the form of cash, but to accommodate donors, some NFPs accept donations in the form of financial instruments, which are most often immediately sold and converted into cash to comply with those entities' operating policies. The EITF discussed this issue because of diversity in the way NFPs classified cash receipts from the sale of donated securities in their statements of cash flows. Cash receipts from the sale of donated securities were being presented in the statement of cash flows as investing, financing, or operating cash flows.

Under the guidance in FASB Accounting Standards Codification™ (ASC) 230, *Statement of Cash Flows*, an entity may classify cash receipts as operating, investing, or financing activities. Under the guidance in ASC 230-10-45-11 through 45-12, cash flows from a sale of available-for-sale securities and most receipts from sales of other debt and equity instruments should be classified as investing activities. However, under the guidance in ASC 230-10-45-20, cash receipts from assets that were acquired for resale and held in a trading account for a short time should be classified as operating cash flows. According to the guidance in ASC 230-10-45-22, cash flows with features of more than one classification should be classified based on the primary source of the cash flows.

ACCOUNTING ISSUE

How should NFP entities that account for their transactions under the guidance in ASC 958, *Not-for-Profit Entities*, account for donations received in the form of debt or equity instruments?

ACCOUNTING GUIDANCE

ASC 230-10-45-21A provides the following guidance for the classification of donated debt and equity instruments in the cash flow statements of NFPs accounted for under the guidance in ASC 958, *Not-for-Profit Entities*:

- Classify as "operating" cash flows, cash received from the sale of donated debt or equity instruments that were sold with no limitations imposed by the NFP entity and were converted to cash almost immediately after they were received.
- Classify as a "financing" activity, cash received from the sale of donated debt or equity instruments, which meets the conditions in ASC 230-10-45-21A, but the use of which has been restricted by a *donor* to a long-term purpose described in ASC 230-10-45-14(c) as intended for "the purposes of acquiring, constructing, or improving, property, plant, equipment, or other long-lived assets or establishing or increasing a permanent endowment or term endowment."

7020 ASC 230—Statement of Cash Flows

The guidance in ASC 230-10-45-12(a) and 45-12(b) has been amended to exclude certain donated debt and equity instruments discussed in ASC 230-10-45-21A from classification as "investing" activities.

A reference to the guidance in ASC 230-10-45-21A has been added to the implementation guidance in ASC 958-230-55-3, which is related to the accounting for cash received with a donor restriction that limits the use of that cash to a long-term purpose.

TRANSITION

ASC 230-10-65-1 provides the following transition guidance:

- The guidance should be applied prospectively to cash receipts from the sale of donated financial assets on or after the date the guidance is adopted for fiscal years, and interim periods within those years that begin after June 15, 2013.
- Retrospective application to all prior periods presented on the adoption date is permitted, but not required.
- Early adoption of the guidance is permitted from the beginning of the fiscal year in which the guidance is adopted. Early adoption for fiscal years that began before October 22, 2012, is permitted only if an NFP's financial statements for the fiscal years and interim periods within those years are not yet available for issuance.
- The disclosures in ASC 250-10-50-1 through 50-3 should be provided in the period the guidance is adopted.

ASC 230-10-45-15 Classification of Debt Issue Costs in the Statement of Cash Flows

BACKGROUND

Entities incur certain costs in connection with issuing debt securities or other short-term or long-term borrowings. Such costs, which include underwriting, accounting, legal fees, and printing, generally are subtracted by the underwriter or lender from the proceeds of the debt or are paid by the borrower directly to the service providers.

Debt issue costs, which are required to be reported in the balance sheet as deferred charges, in accordance with FASB Accounting Standards Codification™ (ASC) 835-30-45-3, generally are reported as assets and amortized over the term of the debt.

There has been diversity in practice in the cash flow statement classification of debt issue costs paid directly by a borrower—some have associated such costs with an entity's financing activities while others have associated them with an entity's operating activities. In an informal survey conducted by the FASB staff, debt issue costs were most often classified as a financing activity.

ACCOUNTING ISSUE

How should a borrower's cash payments for debt issue costs be classified in the statement of cash flows?

ACCOUNTING GUIDANCE

A borrower's cash payments for debt issue costs should be classified as a financing activity in the statement of cash flows.

DISCUSSION

The following arguments support classification of debt issue costs as a financing activity:

- There is a direct relationship between the debt issue and the debt issue costs.
- It is inconsistent to classify such costs as an operating activity, because according to the guidance in ASC 230-10-45-17, cash from operations includes activities that are *other* than financing or investing activities. Also, according to the guidance in ASC 230-10-45-22, classification depends on the "predominant source of cash flows for the item."
- Additions to property, plant, and equipment, which are subsequently depreciated, are not included in operating cash flows. Likewise, even though the asset is subsequently amortized, it is not meaningful to include payments for debt issue costs in the operating activity classification.

ASC 230-10-45-17; ASC 410-20-45-3 Classification in the Statement of Cash Flows of Payments Made to Settle an Asset Retirement Obligation within the Scope of FASB Statement No. 143, *Accounting for Asset Retirement Obligations*

BACKGROUND

The guidance in ASC 410-20 applies to *legal* obligations related to the retirement of tangible long-lived assets that result from the acquisition, construction, or development and the normal operation of those assets. Asset retirement obligations under the scope of ASC 410-20 must be recognized at the fair value of the liability in the period incurred. The associated costs should be capitalized as part of a long-lived asset's carrying amount and amortized to expense using a systematic and rational method over the asset's useful life. A liability must be recognized on the acquisition date for an existing retirement obligation related to acquired tangible long-lived assets as if the obligation had been incurred on that date. The guidance in this Issue does *not* apply to obligations under the scope of ASC 410-20, which are related to the treatment of environmental contamination that occurs after its guidance has been adopted.

Although under the guidance in ASC 230 cash receipts and payments should be classified as operating, investing, or financing activities, neither ASC 230 nor ASC 410-20 provide guidance for the classification of cash paid for obligations associated with the retirement of tangible long-lived assets and associated retirement costs.

ACCOUNTING ISSUE

How should cash paid to settle an asset retirement obligation be classified in the cash flow statement?

ACCOUNTING GUIDANCE

A cash payment made to settle an asset retirement obligation should be classified in the statement of cash flows as an *operating* activity.

CHAPTER 8
ASC 235—ACCOUNTING POLICIES AND STANDARDS

CONTENTS

General Guidance	8001
ASC 235-10: Overall	8001
Overview	8001
Background	8001
Disclosure of Significant Accounting Policies	8001
Illustration of Disclosure of Significant Accounting Policies	8002

GENERAL GUIDANCE

ASC 235-10: OVERALL

OVERVIEW

Accounting policies are important considerations in understanding the content of financial statements. FASB standards require the disclosure of accounting policies as an integral part of financial statements when those statements are intended to present financial position, cash flows, and results of operations in conformity with GAAP.

BACKGROUND

Generally accepted accounting principles have been developed gradually over a period of approximately 60 years. For many years the hierarchy of generally accepted accounting principles established the relative authority of the various pronouncements that had been issued over time. That hierarchy has been replaced by the FASB Codification of GAAP. ASC 105 contains further discussion of the GAAP hierarchy and Accounting Standards Codification.

All financial statements that present financial position, cash flows, and results of operations in accordance with GAAP must include disclosure of significant accounting policies. This includes financial statements of not-for-profit entities. Unaudited interim financial statements that do not include changes in accounting policies since the end of the preceding year are not required to disclose accounting policies in those interim statements (ASC 235-10-50-1, 2).

DISCLOSURE OF SIGNIFICANT ACCOUNTING POLICIES

GAAP require a description of all significant accounting policies of a reporting entity as an integral part of the financial statements. The preferable presentation of disclosing accounting policies is in the first note of the financial statements, under the caption "Summary of Significant Accounting Policies." ASC 235 specifically states this preference, but recognizes the need for flexibility in the matter of formats (ASC 235-10-50-6).

Examples of areas of accounting for which policies are required to be disclosed are (ASC 235-10-50-4):

- Basis of consolidation
- Depreciation methods
- Inventory methods
- Amortization of intangibles
- Recognition of profit on long-term construction contracts
- Recognition of revenue from franchising and leasing operations

Accounting principles and methods of applying them should be disclosed. Informed professional judgment is necessary to select for disclosure those principles that materially affect financial position, cash flows, and results of operations. Accounting principles and their method of application in the following areas are considered particularly important (ASC 235-10-50-3):

- A selection from existing acceptable alternatives
- The areas peculiar to a specific industry in which the entity functions
- Unusual and innovative applications of GAAP

Disclosure of accounting policies should not duplicate information presented elsewhere in the financial statements. In disclosing accounting policies, it may become necessary to refer to items presented elsewhere in the report, such as in the case of a change in an accounting principle that requires specific treatment (ASC 235-10-50-5).

PRACTICE POINTER: Many pronouncements require disclosure of information about accounting policies. For example, ASC 230 (Statement of Cash Flows) requires disclosure of the accounting policy for defining the term *cash equivalents*. Because there are so many requirements of this type embedded in the authoritative accounting literature, a financial statement disclosure checklist is a very useful tool to guard against the inadvertent omission of required information.

Illustration of Disclosure of Significant Accounting Policies

Principles of consolidation The consolidated financial statements include the assets, liabilities, revenues, and expenses of all significant subsidiaries. All significant intercompany transactions have been eliminated in consolidation. Investments in significant companies that are 20% to 50% owned are accounted for by the equity method, which requires the corporation's share of earnings to be included in income. All other investments are carried at market value or amortized cost in conformity with ASC 320 (Investments—Debt and Equity Securities).

Cash equivalents Securities with maturities of three months or less when purchased are treated as cash equivalents in presenting the statement of cash flows.

Accounts receivable The company grants trade credit to its customers. Receivables are valued at management's estimate of the amount that will ultimately be collected. The allowance for doubtful accounts is based on specific identification of uncollectible accounts and the company's historical collection experience.

Plant assets and depreciation Plant assets are carried at cost, less accumulated depreciation. Expenditures for replacements are capitalized, and the replaced items are retired. Maintenance and repairs are charged to operations. Gains and losses from the sale of plant assets are included in income. Depreciation is calculated on a straight-line basis utilizing the assets' estimated useful lives. The corporation and its subsidiaries use accelerated depreciation methods (generally accelerated) for tax purposes where appropriate.

Inventories Inventories are stated at the lower of cost or market using the last-in, first-out (LIFO) method for substantially all qualifying domestic inventories and the average cost method for other inventories.

Patents, trademarks, and goodwill Amounts paid for purchased patents and trademarks and for securities of newly acquired subsidiaries in excess of the fair value of the net assets of such subsidiaries are charged to patents, trademarks, and goodwill, respectively. Intangible assets with finite useful lives are amortized over those useful lives. Intangible assets with indefinite useful lives are not amortized, but these assets are evaluated, at least annually, for impairment.

Earnings per share Earnings per share is based on the weighted-average number of shares of common stock outstanding in each year. There would have been no material dilutive effect on net income per share for 20X2 or 20X3 if convertible securities had been converted and if outstanding stock options had been exercised.

Pension plans The company has pension plans that cover substantially all salaried employees. Benefits are based primarily on each employee's years of service and average compensation during the last five years of employment. Company policy is to fund annual periodic pension cost to the maximum allowable for federal income tax purposes.

Income taxes Income taxes are accounted for by the asset/liability approach in accordance with ASC 740 (Income Taxes). Deferred taxes represent the expected future tax consequences when the reported amounts of assets and liabilities are recovered or paid. They arise from differences between the financial reporting and tax bases of assets and liabilities and are adjusted for changes in tax laws and tax rates when those changes are enacted. The provision for income taxes represents the total of income taxes paid or payable for the current year, plus the change in deferred taxes during the year.

Interest costs Interest related to construction of qualifying assets is capitalized as part of construction costs in accordance with ASC835 (Capitalization of Interest Cost).

Revenue recognition on long-term contracts The company recognizes revenue on long-term contracts by the percentage-of-completion method of accounting. In accordance with that method, revenue is estimated during each financial reporting period encompassed by the contract based on the degree of completion.

PRACTICE POINTER: ASC 235 states a preference for all accounting policies to be presented together, and for that presentation to be between the financial statements and their notes or as the first note. In meeting this requirement, some companies present detailed information in the policy statement that is not directly related to accounting policy. For example, in addition to stating the inventory cost method used, a company also may indicate the dollar breakdown of raw materials, work-in-process, and finished goods. In the author's opinion, this tends to obscure the accounting policy information. A preferable approach is to limit disclosure in the policy statement to information about accounting policy and to present other information in other notes, possibly with cross-references. For example, in the section of the policy statement that states inventory policy, a cross-reference to another note covering in detail information about the amount of various types of inventory may be appropriate.

CHAPTER 9
ASC 250—ACCOUNTING CHANGES AND ERROR CORRECTIONS

CONTENTS

General Guidance	9001
ASC 250-10: Overall	9001
Overview	9001
Background	9002
Changes in Accounting Principle	9003
Illustration of the Application of ASC 250—Change in Accounting Principle	9005
Disclosure	9008
Changes in Accounting Estimate	9009
Illustration of Current and Prospective Method	9010
Disclosure	9010
Changes in Reporting Entity	9011
Disclosure	9011
Corrections of Errors in Previously Issued Financial Statements	9011
Illustration of Correction of Error in Previously Issued Financial Statements	9012
Disclosure	9014
Interim Period Adjustments	9014

GENERAL GUIDANCE

ASC 250-10: OVERALL

OVERVIEW

Accounting changes are broadly classified as (*a*) changes in an accounting principle, (*b*) changes in an accounting estimate, and (*c*) changes in the reporting entity (ASC Glossary). *Corrections of errors in previously issued financial statements are not accounting changes but are covered in the same accounting literature because of their similarity* (ASC 250-10-05-4).

Two different accounting methods are used within GAAP to account for accounting changes and corrections of errors: (1) current and prospective method, and (2) retroactive restatement method.

> **PRACTICE POINTER:** These methods are not alternatives for the same type of accounting change or correction of an error. The authoritative literature clearly identifies the situations in which each is to be applied.

BACKGROUND

Changes in accounting principle, estimate, and entity are described in the authoritative literature as follows:

- *Change in accounting principle*—Results from the adoption of a generally accepted accounting principle different from the one used previously for financial reporting purposes. The term *principle* includes not only principles and practices, but also methods of applying them (ASC Glossary).
- *Change in accounting estimate*—Necessary consequence of periodic presentations of financial statements and the many estimates and assumptions that underlie those statements. A change in estimate results in a change in the carrying amount of an existing asset or liability or a change in the future accounting treatment of an existing asset or liability (ASC Glossary).
- *Change in accounting entity*—A special type of change in accounting principle that results when the reporting entity is different from that of previous periods. This type of change is characterized by (*a*) presenting consolidated or combined financial statements in place of individual company statements, (*b*) changing specific subsidiaries that make up the group of companies for which consolidated financial statements are presented, and (*c*) changing the companies included in combined financial statements (ASC Glossary).

Corrections of errors are not accounting changes. They are sufficiently similar, however, that the authoritative literature discusses them with accounting changes (ASC 250-10-05-4). Errors in financial statements result from mathematical mistakes, mistakes in the application of accounting principles, and the oversight or misuse of facts that existed at the time financial statements were prepared. A change from an unacceptable accounting principle or method to an acceptable one is also considered a correction of an error (ASC Glossary).

Two approaches for dealing with accounting changes and corrections of errors are included in ASC 250: (1) the current and prospective method, and (2) the retroactive restatement method. In the current and prospective method, the impact of the change is reflected in current and future financial statements without adjustment to prior years. In the retroactive restatement method, prior years' financial statements are restated to include the effect of the change.

The following areas are not considered changes in an accounting principle (ASC 250-10-45-1):

- A principle, practice, or method adopted for the first time on new or previously immaterial events or transactions
- A principle, practice, or method adopted or modified because of events or transactions that are clearly different in substance

PRACTICE POINTER: A situation that is not mentioned in ASC 250, but generally is not considered a change in accounting principle, is changing from an accelerated depreciation method to the straight-line method at a point in the life of the asset, provided the change is planned at the time the accelerated method is adopted and the policy is applied consistently (ASC 250-10-45-20).

A change in the composition of the elements of cost (material, labor, and overhead) included in inventory is an accounting change that must be justified based on the rule of preferability (ASC 250-10-55-1).

The primary source of GAAP for accounting changes and error corrections is ASC 250. ASC 250 applies to all voluntary changes in accounting principle and to changes required by an accounting pronouncement in the unusual instance that the pronouncement does not indicate a specific transition method (ASC 250-10-05-2). ASC 250 requires the retrospective application of the new accounting principle to prior periods' financial statements. Retrospective application is defined as the application of a different accounting principle to prior accounting periods as if that principle had always been used or as the adjustment of previously issued financial statements to reflect a change in the reporting entity (ASC Glossary). Any voluntary change in accounting principle must be justified on the basis of its preferability (ASC 250-10-45-2).

ASC 250 establishes retrospective application as the required method for reporting a change in accounting principle in the absence of explicit transition requirements specified in a newly adopted accounting standard. The standard provides guidance on when retrospective application is impracticable and for reporting a change in accounting principle in that circumstance. Error corrections are to be reported by restating previously issued financial statements (ASC 250-10-05-4). ASC 250 applies to financial statements of business enterprises and not-for-profit organizations. It also applies to financial summaries of information based on primary financial statements that include an accounting period in which an accounting change or error correction is reflected (ASC 250-10-15-3).

ASC 250 provides standards of accounting and reporting, followed by specific disclosure requirements, for four situations: changes in accounting principle, changes in accounting estimate, changes in reporting entity, and corrections of errors in previously issued financial statements.

CHANGES IN ACCOUNTING PRINCIPLE

The following are some common changes in accounting principle:

- A change in the method of pricing inventory, such as LIFO to FIFO or FIFO to LIFO
- A change in the method of accounting for long-term construction-type contracts
- A change in the method of accounting for software development costs.

Financial reporting standards presume that an accounting principle, once adopted, will not be changed in accounting for events and transactions of the same type. Consistent use of accounting principles from period to period is an important dimension of high-value financial statements that facilitate analysis and enhance comparability (ASC 250-10-45-1). A reporting entity shall change an accounting principle only if the change is required by a newly issued accounting pronouncement or the entity can justify the use of a different allowable accounting principle on the basis that it is preferable (ASC 250-10-45-2).

> **PRACTICE NOTE:** Justifying a change in accounting principle on the basis of preferability is difficult. One commonly-accepted rationale for changing an accounting principle is to align the company's accounting with generally accepted industry practice.

An entity making a change in accounting principle will report that change by retrospective application of the new principle to all periods, unless it is impracticable to do so. Retrospective application requires the following three steps (ASC 250-10-45-5):

Step 1. The cumulative effect of the change to the new principle on periods prior to those presented shall be reflected in the carrying amount of assets and liabilities as of the beginning of the first period presented.

Step 2. An offsetting adjustment, if any, shall be made to the opening balance of retained earnings for that period.

Step 3. Financial statements for each individual prior period presented are adjusted to reflect the period-specific effects of applying the new principle.

The term "impracticable," as used in ASC 250, means that at least one of the following applies (ASC 250-10-45-9):

- After making every reasonable effort to do so, the entity is unable to apply the requirement.
- Retrospective application requires assumptions about management's intent in a prior period that cannot be independently substantiated.
- Retrospective application requires significant estimates, and it is impossible to develop objective information about those estimates that provide evidence of circumstances that existed on the date(s) at which those amounts would be recognized, measured, or disclosed under retrospective application and would have been available when the financial statements for that period were issued.

If the cumulative effect of applying a change in accounting principle to all prior periods can be determined, but it is impracticable to determine the period-specific effects of that change on all prior periods presented, the cumulative effect of the change should be applied to the carrying amounts of assets and liabilities as of the beginning of the earliest period to which the new accounting principle can be applied. The offsetting adjustment, if any, is to the opening balance of retained earnings for that period (ASC 250-10-45-6).

If it is impracticable to determine the cumulative effect of applying a change in accounting principle to any prior period, the new principle is applied as if the change was made prospectively as of the earliest date practicable. A change from the first-in, first-out (FIFO) inventory method to the last-in, first-out (LIFO) inventory method when the effects of having been on LIFO in the past cannot be determined is an example of such a situation (ASC 250-10-45-7).

Changing an accounting principle must be supported by a justification on the basis of preferability. The issuance of an accounting pronouncement may require the use of a new accounting principle, interpreting an existing principle, expressing a preference for an accounting principle, or rejecting a specific principle. Any of these may require an entity to change an accounting principle. Such a requirement is sufficient justification for making a change in an accounting principle. The burden of justifying other changes in accounting principle rests with the reporting entity making the change (ASC 250-10-45-13).

Retrospective application shall ordinarily include only the direct effects of a change in accounting principle, including the income tax effects. If indirect effects are actually incurred and recognized, they shall be reported in the period in which the accounting change is made (ASC 250-10-45-8).

A change in accounting principle made in an interim period shall be reported by retrospective application. However, the impracticability exception stated above may not be applied to prechange interim periods of the fiscal year in which the change is made. When retrospective application to prechange interim periods is impractical, the desired change may only be made as of the beginning of a subsequent fiscal year (ASC 250-10-45-14).

Publicly traded companies that do not issue separate fourth-quarter reports must disclose in a note to their annual reports any effect of an accounting change made during the fourth quarter (ASC 250-10-45-15).

Illustration of the Application of ASC 250—Change in Accounting Principle

Universal Technologies Inc. changes from the LIFO method of inventory valuation to the FIFO method at January 1, 20X7. Universal Technologies had used the LIFO method since its inception on January 1, 20X4. The change in inventory method is preferable.

Sales are $15,000 for each year from 20X4 through 20X7 and selling, general, and administrative expenses are $5,000 in each year. Universal Technologies' effective income tax rate is 30 percent in each year and it has no temporary or permanent income tax differences. Income taxes accrued at the end of each year are paid in cash at the beginning of the next year. Universal Technologies' annual report to shareholders includes three years of income statements and statements of cash flows and two years of balance sheets. (Earnings per share computations are ignored.)

Universal Technologies has determined that the effect of changing from LIFO inventory valuation to FIFO inventory valuation has the following effects on inventory and cost of goods sold for each year from 20X4 through 20X7:

Date	Inventory Determined by		Cost of Sales Determined by	
	LIFO Method	FIFO Method	LIFO Method	FIFO Method
1/1/20X4	0	0	0	0
12/31/20X4	600	400	4,800	5,000
12/31/20X5	1,000	1,440	5,000	4,360
12/31/20X6	1,200	1,100	5,200	5,740
12/31/20X7	1,600	2,340	5,000	4,160

9006 ASC 250—Accounting Changes and Error Corrections

Universal Technologies' originally reported income statements for 20X4 through 20X6 (using the LIFO inventory method) are:

Income Statement (as originally reported)

	20X6	20X5	20X4
Sales	$15,000	$15,000	$15,000
Cost of goods sold	5,200	5,000	4,800
Selling, general, and administrative expenses	5,000	5,000	5,000
Income before income taxes	4,800	5,000	5,200
Income taxes	1,440	1,500	1,560
Net income	$ 3,360	$ 3,500	$ 3,640

Universal Technologies' income statements showing the retrospective application of the FIFO inventory method (from the LIFO method) are:

Income Statement

	20X7	20X6 As Adjusted (Note A)	20X5 As Adjusted (Note A)
Sales	$15,000	$15,000	$15,000
Cost of goods sold	4,160	5,740	4,360
Selling, general, and administrative expenses	5,000	5,000	5,000
Income before income taxes	5,840	4,260	5,640
Income taxes	1,752	1,278	1,692
Net income	$ 4,088	$ 2,982	$ 3,948

NOTE A: Change in Method of Inventory Valuation On January 1, 20X7, Universal Technologies Inc. changed from the LIFO inventory valuation method to the FIFO inventory valuation method. The FIFO inventory valuation method was adopted [provide justification for why the FIFO method is preferable to the LIFO method] and the comparative financial statements for 20X6 and 20X5 have been adjusted to apply the FIFO method on a retrospective basis. The following financial statement line items for fiscal years 20X7, 20X6, and 20X5 were affected by the change in accounting principle.

Income Statement—20X7

	As Computed Under LIFO	As Reported Under FIFO	Effect of Change
Cost of goods sold	$5,000	$4,160	$(840)
Income before taxes	$5,000	$5,840	$ 840
Income tax expense	$1,500	$1,752	$ 252
Net income	$3,500	$4,088	$ 588

Income Statement—20X6

	As Originally Reported	As Adjusted	Effect of Change
Cost of goods sold	$5,200	$5,740	$540
Income before taxes	$4,800	$4,260	$(540)
Income tax expense	$1,440	$1,278	$(162)
Net income	$3,360	$2,982	$(378)

Income Statement—20X5

	As Originally Reported	As Adjusted	Effect of Change
Cost of goods sold	$5,000	$4,360	$(640)
Income before taxes	$5,000	$5,640	$640
Income tax expense	$1,500	$1,692	$192
Net income	$3,500	$3,948	$448

Balance Sheet—12/31/X7

	As Computed Under FIFO	As Reported Under FIFO	Effect of Change
Cash	$113,900	$113,930	$30
Inventory	$1,600	$2,340	$740
Total assets	$115,500	$116,270	$770
Income tax liability	$1,500	$1,752	$252
Retained earnings	$14,000	$14,518	$518

Balance Sheet—12/31/X6

	As Originally Reported	As Adjusted	Effect of Change
Cash	$10,740	$110,608	$(132)
Inventory	$1,200	$1,100	$(100)
Total assets	$111,940	$111,708	$(232)
Income tax liability	$1,440	$1,278	$(162)
Retained earnings	$10,500	$10,430	$(70)

Balance Sheet—12/31/X5

	As Originally Reported	As Adjusted	Effect of Change
Cash	$107,640	$107,700	$60
Inventory	$1,000	$1,440	$440
Total assets	$108,640	$109,140	$500
Income tax liability	$1,500	$1,692	$192
Retained earnings	$7,140	$7,448	$308

As a result of the accounting change, retained earnings as of January 1, 20X5 decreased from $3,640, as originally reported using the LIFO method, to $3,500 using the FIFO method.

Statement of Cash Flows—20X7

	As Computed Under LIFO	As Reported Under FIFO	Effect of Change
Net income	$3,500	$ 4,088	$ 588
(Increase) decrease in inventory	$ (400)	$ (1,240)	$ (840)
Increase (decrease) in income tax liability	$ 60	$ 474	$ 414
Net cash provided by operating activities	$3,160	$ 3,322	$ 162
Change in cash	$3,160	$ 3,322	$ 162

Statement of Cash Flows—20X6

	As Originally Reported	As Adjusted	Effect of Change
Net income	$3,360	$2,982	$(378)
(Increase) decrease in inventory	$ (200)	$ 340	$ 540
Increase (decrease) in income tax liability	$ (60)	$ (414)	$(354)
Net cash provided by operating activities	$3,100	$2,908	$(192)
Change in cash	$3,100	$2,908	$(192)

Statement of Cash Flow—20X5

	As Originally Reported	As Adjusted	Effect of Change
Net income	$ 3,500	$ 3,948	$ 448
(Increase) decrease in inventory	$ (400)	$ (1,040)	$ (640)
Increase (decrease) in income tax liability	$ (60)	$ 192	$ 252
Net cash provided by operating activities	$ 3,040	$ 3,100	$ 60
Change in cash	$ 3,040	$ 3,100	$ 60

Disclosure

The following items are required disclosures in the period during which the change in accounting principle is made (ASC 250-10-50-1):

- The nature of and reason for the change in principle, including an explanation of why the new principle is preferable.

- The method of applying the change, and:
  - A description of the prior-period information that has been retrospectively adjusted, if any.
  - The effect of the change on income from continuing operations, net income, any other affected financial statement item, and any affected per-share amounts for the current period and any prior periods retrospectively adjusted.
  - The cumulative effect of the change on retained earnings (or other components of equity or net assets in the statement of financial position) as of the beginning of the earliest period presented.
  - If retrospective application to all periods is impracticable, the reasons therefore and a description of the alternative method used to report the change.
- If indirect effects of a change in accounting principle are recognized:
  - A description of the indirect effects, including the amounts that have been recognized in the current period and the related per-share amounts, if applicable.
  - Unless impracticable, the amount of the total recognized indirect effects of the accounting change and the related per-share amounts, if applicable, that are attributable to each prior period presented.

In the fiscal year in which a new accounting principle is adopted, financial information reported for interim periods after the date of adoption will disclose the effect of the change in income from continuing operations, net income, and related per-share amounts, if applicable, for the post-change interim periods (ASC 250-10-50-3).

CHANGES IN ACCOUNTING ESTIMATE

A change in accounting estimate is accounted for in the period of change if the change affects only that period, or is accounted for in the period of change and future periods if the change affects both. A change in accounting estimate is not accounted for by restating or retrospectively adjusting amounts reported in financial statements of prior periods or by reporting pro forma amounts for prior periods (ASC 250-10-45-17).

Distinguishing between a change in accounting principle and a change in accounting estimate may be difficult. In some cases, a change in estimate is effected by a change in accounting principle, such as when a depreciation method is changed to reflect a change in the estimated future benefits of the asset or the pattern of consumption of those benefits. The change in principle cannot be separated from the effect of the change in accounting estimate. Changes of this type are considered changes in estimate (ASC 250-10-45-17). Similar to other changes in accounting principle, a change in accounting estimate that is effected by a change in accounting principle is appropriate only if the new principle is justifiable on the basis that it is preferable (ASC 250-10-45-18).

Illustration of Current and Prospective Method

In 20X6, Martin Co. paid $150,000 for a building that was expected to have a ten-year life with an estimated value at the end of that period of $25,000. Straight-line depreciation was used through 20X9. In 20Y0, management's reassessment of the useful lives of all assets resulted in a decision that the useful life would be 15 years from the time of purchase, at which time the estimated value would be approximately $10,000.

The book value of the asset at the time of the change is computed as follows:

Cost	$150,000
Accumulated depreciation [($150,000 - $25,000)/10] × 4	(50,000)
	$100,000

Depreciation for 20Y0 and each of the next 11 years (15 years total - 4 years depreciated to date) is computed and recorded as follows:

Book value at time of change		$100,000
Estimated residual value		(10,000)
Depreciable cost		$90,000
Depreciation per year ($90,000/11)		$8,182
Entry: Depreciation Expense	8,182	
Accumulated Depreciation		8,182

No cumulative effect is recorded. Disclosure is required of the nature of the change and the impact on income ($12,500 - $8,182 = $4,318) as follows:

During 20Y0, management determined that the useful life of the building was longer than originally expected. A change in accounting estimate was recognized to reflect this decision, resulting in an increase in net income of $4,318.

Disclosure

The effect on income from continuing operations, net income, and any related per-share amounts of the current period must be disclosed for a change in estimate that affects several future periods. Disclosure of those effects is not necessary for estimates made each period in the ordinary course of accounting for items, such as uncollectible accounts or inventory obsolescence. Effects of such a change in estimate must be disclosed, however, if the effect is material (ASC 250-10-50-4).

When an entity effects a change in estimate by changing an accounting principle, the disclosures required for a change in accounting principles (stated above) are required. If a change in estimate does not have a material effect in the period of change, but is reasonably certain to have a material effect in later periods, a description of the change is required whenever the financial statements of the period of the change are presented (ASC 250-10-50-4).

CHANGES IN REPORTING ENTITY

ASC 250 specifies that an accounting change that results in financial statements that are, in effect, those of a different reporting entity must be retrospectively applied so that the specific entities that comprise the reporting entity in the current period are comparable to the specific entities that comprised the reporting entity in previous years. Previously issued interim financial information shall be presented on a retrospective basis with the following exception: the amount of interest cost previously capitalized on investments accounted for by the equity method will not be changed when retrospectively applying the accounting change to the financial statements of prior periods (ASC 250-10-45-21).

Disclosure

When there has been a change in reporting entity, the financial statements of the period of change must include a description of the nature of the change and the reason for the change. The effect of the change on income before extraordinary items, net income, other comprehensive income, and any related per-share amounts must be disclosed for all periods presented (ASC 250-10-50-6).

CORRECTIONS OF ERRORS IN PREVIOUSLY ISSUED FINANCIAL STATEMENTS

An error in financial statements of prior periods that is discovered after those statements are issued is reported as a prior-period adjustment by restating the prior period financial statements. This requires the following three steps (ASC 250-10-45-23):

Step 1. The cumulative effect of the error on periods prior to the period in which the error is discovered and corrected is reflected in the carrying amounts of assets and liabilities as of the beginning of that period.

Step 2. An offsetting adjustment, if any, is made to the opening balance of retained earnings (or other component of equity or net assets in the statement of financial position) for that period.

Step 3. Financial statements for each individual prior period presented are adjusted to reflect correction of the period-specific effects of the error.

PRACTICE POINTER: Distinguishing between a *change in accounting estimate* and the *correction of an error* may be difficult and may require significant professional judgment. In the final analysis, the difference comes down to the timing of the availability of the information upon which the change or correction is made. If the information is newly available, the adjustment is a change in accounting estimate. If the information was previously available, but was not used or was incorrectly used, the adjustment is a correction of an error. This classification is important because the change in estimate is accounted for prospectively while the correction of an error requires restatement of previously issued financial statements.

Illustration of Correction of Error in Previously Issued Financial Statements

In 20X7 and 20X8, Warren, Inc., inappropriately capitalized $100,000 of period costs as fixed assets in each year. This intentional misstatement was discovered and corrected in 20X9. The period costs inappropriately capitalized as fixed assets were being depreciated on a straight-line basis (with no salvage value) over 10 years. Warren, Inc. accounted for the $100,000 of period costs correctly in 20X9. Warren, Inc.'s effective tax rate is 30 percent, and all income taxes due are paid in full during the year in which they are incurred. Warren, Inc.'s income statements, balance sheets, and statements of retained earnings as originally filed are as follows:

Income Statements (as originally presented)

	20X8	20X7
Revenues	$500,000	$500,000
Cost of goods sold	250,000	250,000
Other expenses (excluding depreciation)	100,000	100,000
Depreciation expense	20,000	10,000
Income before taxes	130,000	140,000
Income tax expense (at 30%)	39,000	42,000
Net income	$ 91,000	$ 98,000

Balance Sheets (as originally presented)

	20X8	20X7
Cash	$119,000	$100,000
Receivables	80,000	60,000
Inventories	80,000	108,000
Income tax refund receivable	—	—
Fixed assets (net)	170,000	90,000
Total assets	$449,000	$358,000
Accounts payable	$ 20,000	$ 20,000
Long-term liabilities	40,000	40,000
Total liabilities	60,000	60,000
Paid-in capital	200,000	200,000
Retained earnings	189,000	98,000
Total stockholders' equity	389,000	298,000
Total liabilities and stockholders' equity	$449,000	$358,000

Statements of Retained Earnings (as originally presented)

	20X8	20X7
Balance, January 1	$98,000	$ —
Net income	91,000	98,000
Balance, December 31	$189,000	$ 98,000

The entry to record the correction of this error in 20X9 is as follows:

Accumulated depreciation	30,000	
Retained earnings [($200,000 - $30,000) × .7]	119,000	
Income tax refund receivable	51,000	
Fixed assets		200,000

In 20X9, Warren, Inc. presents income statements and statements of retained earnings for 20X9 and 20X8 and a balance sheet for 20X9. (Warren, Inc.'s statement of cash flows and required disclosures are not presented.)

Income Statements

	20X9	20X9 (as restated)
Revenues	$500,000	$500,000
Cost of goods sold	250,000	250,000
Other expenses (excluding depreciation)	200,000	200,000
Depreciation expense		
Income before taxes	50,000	50,000
Income tax expense (at 30%)	15,000	15,000
Net income	$ 35,000	$ 35,000

Statements of Retained Earnings

	20X9	20X8 (as restated)
Balance, January 1	$ 70,000	$ 98,000
Adjustment to correct the error of improper capitalization of period expenses (net of tax)		(63,000)*
Adjusted balance, January 1	70,000	35,000
Net income	35,000	35,000
Balance, December 31	$105,000	$70,000

* ($10,000-$100,000) × (1-.3)

Balance Sheet

	20X9
Cash	$110,000
Receivables	94,000
Inventories	110,000
Income tax refund receivable	51,000
Fixed assets (net)	-0-
Total assets	$365,000
Accounts payable	$20,000
Long-term liabilities	40,000
Total liabilities	60,000

	20X9
Paid-in capital	200,000
Retained earnings	105,000
Total stockholders' equity	305,000
Total liabilities and stockholders' equity	$365,000

Disclosure

When financial statements have been restated for the correction of an error, the entity must disclose the nature of the error and the fact that previously issued financial statements have been restated. Prior period adjustments are excluded from the determination of net income (ASC 250-10-45-22). All other items of profit and loss (including accruals for loss contingencies) shall be included in the determination of net income for the period. The entity must disclose (ASC 250-10-50-7, ASC 250-10-50-9):

- The effect of the correction on each financial statement line item and any per-share amounts affected for each prior period presented.
- The gross and net effect (of related income taxes) of prior period adjustments on net income should be disclosed in the year of adjustment and all years presented.
- The cumulative effect of the change on retained earnings or other appropriate components of equity (or net assets in the statement of financial position) as of the beginning of the earliest period presented.

INTERIM PERIOD ADJUSTMENTS

An adjustment of prior interim periods of a current fiscal year can include any of the following settlements (ASC 250-10-45-25):

1. Litigation or similar claims
2. Income taxes
3. Renegotiation
4. Utility revenues governed by rate-making processes

In adjusting interim periods of the current year, any adjustment of prior periods is made to the first interim period of the current year. Adjustments to the other interim periods of the current year are related to the interim period affected (ASC 250-10-45-26).

The effects (*a*) on income from continuous operations, (*b*) on net income, and (*c*) on earnings per share of an adjustment to a current interim period must be disclosed fully (ASC 250-10-50-11).

CHAPTER 10
ASC 255—CHANGING PRICES

CONTENTS

Part I: General Guidance	10,002
ASC 255-10: Overall	10,002
Overview	10,002
Background	10,002
Reporting under ASC 255	10,002
Net Monetary Position	10,002
Current Cost Accounting	10,003
Determining Current Costs	10,004
Depreciation Methods	10,004
Recoverable Amounts	10,004
Net Realizable Value	10,005
Value in Use	10,005
Income Tax Expense	10,005
Minimum Supplementary Information under ASC 255	10,005
Net Sales and Other Operating Revenue	10,006
Income from Continuing Operations on a Current Cost Basis	10,006
Purchasing Power Gain or Loss on Net Monetary Items	10,007
Increase or Decrease in Inventory, Property, Plant, and Equipment at Current Costs	10,007
Aggregate Foreign Currency Translation Adjustment (if Applicable)	10,007
Net Assets at End of Each Fiscal Year	10,007
Income per Common Share from Continuing Operations on a Current Cost Basis	10,008
Cash Dividends Declared per Common Share	10,008
Market Price per Common Share at Year-End	10,008
Average Level of CPI-U	10,008
Explanatory Disclosures	10,008
Additional Disclosures for the Current Year	10,008
Specialized Assets	10,010
Timber Assets	10,010
Mineral Resource Assets	10,010
Part II: Interpretive Guidance	10,012
ASC 255: Overall	10,012
ASC 255-10-15-2, 255-15-45-2 through 45-4	
Rescission of Accounting Principles Board Statements	10,012

PART I: GENERAL GUIDANCE

ASC 255-10: OVERALL

OVERVIEW

Financial statements prepared in conformity with GAAP are based on the assumption of a stable monetary unit. That is, the assumption is made that the monetary unit used to convert all financial statement items into a common denominator (i.e., dollars) does not vary sufficiently over time so that distortions in the financial statements are material. In addition, financial statements prepared in conformity with GAAP are primarily based on historical cost (i.e., the characteristic of most financial statement items that is measured and presented is the historical cost of the item).

Over the years, two approaches have been proposed and procedures developed to compensate for changes in the monetary unit and changes in the value of assets and liabilities after their acquisition—current value accounting and general price-level accounting. Current value accounting substitutes a measure of current value for historical cost as the primary measurement upon which the elements of financial statements are based. General price-level accounting adheres to historical cost but substitutes a current value of the dollar for historical dollars through the use of price indexes. Neither current value accounting nor general price-level accounting is required at the present time, although specific applications of current or fair value are gradually being incorporated into GAAP. In ASC 255, the FASB has developed disclosure standards that are optional for dealing with the problem of the impact of changing prices on financial statements.

BACKGROUND

Guidance related to financial reporting and changing prices, issued in 1979, required certain large enterprises to disclose the effects of changing prices via a series of supplemental disclosures. These disclosures are now encouraged, but are no longer required (ASC 255-10-50-1).

REPORTING UNDER ASC 255

Net Monetary Position

Assets and liabilities are identified as monetary items if their amounts are fixed or determinable without reference to future prices of specific goods and services. Cash, accounts and notes receivable in cash, and accounts and notes payable in cash are examples of monetary items (ASC Glossary).

Monetary items lose or gain general purchasing power during inflation or deflation as a result of changes in the general price-level index (ASC 255-10-50-51). For example, a holder of a $10,000 promissory note executed ten years ago and due today will receive exactly $10,000 today, in spite of the fact that $10,000 in cash today is worth less than $10,000 was worth ten years ago.

Assets and liabilities that are not fixed in terms of the monetary unit are called nonmonetary items. Inventories, investment in common stocks, property, plant, and equipment, and deferred charges are examples of nonmonetary items (ASC 255-10-50-51). A nonmonetary asset or liability is affected (*a*) by the rise or fall of the general price-level index and (*b*) by the increase or decrease of the fair value of the nonmonetary item. Holders of nonmonetary items lose or gain with the rise or fall of the general price-level index if the nonmonetary item does not rise or fall in proportion to the change in the price-level index. For example, the purchaser of 10,000 shares of common stock ten years ago was subject (*a*) to the decrease in purchasing power of the dollar and (*b*) to the change in the fair value of the stock. Only if the decrease in purchasing power exactly offsets an increase in the price of the stock is the purchaser in the same economic position today as ten years ago.

The difference between monetary assets and monetary liabilities at any specific date is the net monetary position. The net monetary position may be either positive (monetary assets exceed monetary liabilities) or negative (monetary liabilities exceed monetary assets).

In periods in which the general price level is rising (inflation), it is advantageous for a business to maintain a net negative (liability) monetary position. The opposite is true during periods in which the general price level is falling (deflation). In periods of inflation, a business that has a net negative monetary position will experience general price-level gains, because it can pay its liabilities in a fixed number of dollars that are declining in value over time. In contrast, in periods of inflation, a business that has a net positive (asset) monetary position will experience general price-level losses because it holds more monetary assets than liabilities and the value of the dollar is declining.

PRACTICE POINTER: Some assets and liabilities have characteristics of both monetary and nonmonetary items. Convertible debt, for example, is monetary in terms of its fixed obligation, but nonmonetary in terms of its conversion feature. Whether an item is monetary or nonmonetary is determined as of the balance sheet date. Therefore, if convertible debt has not been converted as of that date, classify it as a monetary item. Additionally, classify a bond receivable held for speculation as nonmonetary, because the amount that will be received when the bond is sold is no longer fixed in amount, as it would be if the same bond were held to maturity. ASC 255-10-55-1 contains a table that reflects the monetary/nonmonetary classification of most assets and liabilities.

Current Cost Accounting

Current cost accounting is a method of measuring and reporting assets and expenses associated with the use or sale of assets at their current cost or lower recoverable amount at the balance sheet date or at the date of use or sale. Current cost/constant purchasing power accounting is a method of accounting based on measures of current cost of lower recoverable amounts in units of currency that each have the same general purchasing power. For operations for which the U.S. dollar is the functional currency, the general purchasing power of the dollar is used. For operations for which the functional currency is other than the U.S. dollar, the general purchasing power of either (a) the dollar or (b) the functional currency is used (ASC Glossary).

Determining Current Costs

Current cost is the current cost to purchase or reproduce a specific asset. Current reproduction cost must contain an allocation for current overhead costs (direct costing is not permitted).

The current cost of inventory owned by an enterprise is the current cost to purchase or reproduce that specific inventory. The current cost of property, plant, and equipment owned by an enterprise is the current cost of acquiring an asset that will perform or produce in a manner similar to the owned asset (ASC 255-10-50-21, 22).

An enterprise may obtain its current cost information internally or externally, including independent appraisals, and may apply the information to a single item or to groups of items. An enterprise is expected to select the types of current cost information that are most appropriate for its particular circumstances. The following types and sources of current cost information may be utilized by an enterprise (ASC 255-10-50-23):

- Current invoice prices
- Vendor firms' price lists, quotations, or estimates
- Standard manufacturing costs that reflect current costs
- Unit pricing, which is a method of determining current cost for assets, such as buildings, by applying a unit price per square foot of space to the total square footage in the building
- Revision of historical cost by the use of indexation, based on:
  — Externally generated price indexes for the goods or services being restated, or
  — Internally generated indexes for the goods or services being restated

Depreciation Methods

Depreciation methods, useful lives, and salvage values used for current cost purposes are generally the same as those used for historical cost purposes. If historical cost computations already include an allowance for changing prices, then a different method may be used for current cost purposes. However, any material differences shall be disclosed in the explanatory notes to the supplementary information (ASC 255-10-50-29).

Recoverable Amounts

Recoverable amounts may be determined by reference to net realizable values or values in use. They reflect write-downs during a current period, from the current cost amount to a lower recoverable amount. These reductions reflect a permanent decline in the value of inventory, or property, plant, and equipment.

Net Realizable Value

Net realizable value is the expected amount of net cash or other net equivalent to be received from the sale of an asset in the regular course of business. Net realizable value is used only if the specific asset is about to be sold (ASC 255-10-50-36).

Value in Use

Value in use is the total present value of all future cash inflows that are expected to be received from the use of an asset. Value in use is used only if there is no immediate intention to sell or otherwise dispose of the asset. Value in use is estimated by taking into consideration an appropriate discount rate that includes an allowance for the risk involved in the circumstances (ASC Glossary).

Income Tax Expense

Income tax expense and the provision for deferred taxes, if any, are not restated in terms of current cost and are presented in the supplementary information at their historical cost. Disclosure is required in the supplementary information to the effect that income tax expense for the current period is presented at its historical cost.

Minimum Supplementary Information under ASC 255

Under ASC 255, an enterprise is encouraged to disclose certain minimum supplementary information for each of its five most recent years. In addition, if income from continuing operations as shown in the primary financial statements differs significantly from income from continuing operations determined on a current cost/constant purchasing power basis, certain additional disclosures relating to the components of income from continuing operations for the current year also should be disclosed (ASC 255-10-50-11).

The minimum supplementary information encouraged by ASC 255 is disclosed in average-for-the-year units of constant purchasing power. The Consumer Price Index for All Urban Consumers (CPI-U) is used to restate the current cost of an item in average-for-the-year units of constant purchasing power. Alternatively, an enterprise may disclose the minimum supplementary information in dollars having a purchasing power equal to that of dollars of the base period used in calculating the CPI-U. The level of the CPI-U used for each of the five most recent years should be disclosed (ASC 255-10-50-7, 8).

An enterprise is encouraged to disclose the following minimum supplementary information for the five most recent years (ASC 255-10-50-3):

- Net sales and other operating revenue
- Income from continuing operations on a current cost basis
- Purchasing power gain or loss on net monetary items
- Increase or decrease in the current cost or lower recoverable amount of inventory and property, plant, and equipment, net of inflation
- Aggregate foreign currency translation adjustment on a current cost basis, if applicable

- Net assets at the end of each fiscal year on a current cost basis
- Income per common share from continuing operations on a current cost basis
- Cash dividends declared per common share
- Market price per common share at year-end
- Average level of the CPI-U for each year

Each of the above disclosures included in the five-year summary of selected financial data is discussed below.

Net Sales and Other Operating Revenue

Net sales and other operating revenue for each of the five most recent years is restated in average-for-the-year units of constant purchasing power using the CPI-U.

Income from Continuing Operations on a Current Cost Basis

Income from continuing operations on a current cost basis for each of the five most recent years is computed in accordance with ASC 255 and then restated in average-for-the-year units of constant purchasing power using the CPI-U. For purposes of the minimum supplementary information, only certain items that are included in income from continuing operations in the primary financial statements have to be adjusted to compute income from continuing operations on a current cost basis. Under ASC 255, these items are adjusted to compare income from continuing operations on a current basis (ASC 255-10-50-39):

- *Cost of goods sold* Determined on a current cost basis or lower recoverable amount at the date of a sale or at the date on which resources are used on or committed to a specific contract
- *Depreciation, depletion, and amortization* Determined based on the average current cost of the assets' service potentials or lower recoverable amounts during the period of use
- *Gain or loss on the sale, retirement, or write-down of inventory, property, plant, and equipment* Equal to the difference between the value of the consideration received or the written-down amount and the current cost or lower recoverable amount of the item prior to its sale, retirement, or write-down

All other revenue, expenses, gains, and losses that are included in the primary financial statements are not adjusted in computing income from continuing operations on a current cost basis.

Income tax expense that is included in the primary financial statements is not adjusted in computing income from continuing operations on a current cost basis (ASC 255-10-50-41). Disclosure must be made in the minimum supplementary information to the effect that income tax expense for the current period is presented at its historical cost.

Purchasing Power Gain or Loss on Net Monetary Items

The purchasing power gain or loss on net monetary items for each of the five most recent years is computed and then restated in average-for-the-year units of constant purchasing power using the CPI-U. The purchasing power gain or loss on net monetary items is determined by restating in units of constant purchasing power the opening and closing balances of, and transactions in, monetary assets and monetary liabilities (ASC 255-10-50-50).

Increase or Decrease in Inventory, Property, Plant, and Equipment at Current Costs

The increase or decrease in current costs for inventory and property, plant, and equipment for each of the five most recent years must be restated in average-for-the-year units of constant purchasing power using the CPI-U. The increase or decrease in the current cost amounts represents the difference between the measures of the assets at their entry dates for the year and at their exit dates for the year. The entry date is the beginning of the year or the date of acquisition, whichever is applicable. The exit date is the end of the year or the date of use, sale, or commitment to a specific contract, whichever is applicable (ASC 255-10-50-42).

The increase or decrease in the current cost amounts of inventory, property, plant, and equipment for the five-year summary is reported after the effects of each year's general inflation. The increase or decrease in the current cost amounts for the current year is reported both before and after the effects of general inflation (ASC 255-10-50-43).

Aggregate Foreign Currency Translation Adjustment (if Applicable)

The aggregate foreign currency translation adjustment (if applicable) for each of the five most recent years is computed on a current cost basis and then restated in average-for-the-year units of constant purchasing power using the CPI-U.

Current cost information for operations measured in a foreign functional currency is measured either (*a*) after translation and based on the CPI-U (the translate-restate method) or (*b*) before translation and based on a broad measure of the change in the general purchasing power of the functional currency (the restate-translate method). In this event, the same method must be used for all operations measured in foreign functional currencies and for all periods presented. ASC 255-10-55-66, 67-70 and ASC 255-10-55-78, 79-80 contain illustrative calculations of current cost/constant purchasing power information (ASC 255-10-50-45, 46).

Net Assets at End of Each Fiscal Year

For purposes of the minimum supplementary information required by ASC 255, net assets at the end of each fiscal year are equal to all of the net assets appearing in the basic historical cost financial statements except that inventories, property, plant, and equipment are included at their current costs or at a lower recoverable amount. (Total net assets at historical cost less inventories, property, plant, and equipment at historical cost, plus inventories, property, plant, and equipment at current costs or lower recoverable amounts, equals net assets as encouraged by

ASC 255.) The amount computed for net assets at end of each fiscal year is then restated in average-for-the-year units of constant purchasing power using the CPI-U (ASC 255-10-50-34).

When comprehensive restatement of financial statements is made in lieu of the minimum supplementary information, net assets for the five-year summary of selected financial data may be reported at the same amount shown in the comprehensive restated financial statements (ASC 255-10-50-35).

Income per Common Share from Continuing Operations on a Current Cost Basis

Income per common share from continuing operations for each of the five most recent years is computed and then restated in average-for-the-year units of constant purchasing power using the CPI-U. Income per common share from continuing operations on a current cost basis is found by dividing the outstanding number of shares of common stock into the total restated income from continuing operations on a current cost basis.

Cash Dividends Declared per Common Share

Cash dividends declared per common share for each of the five most recent years are restated in average-for-the-year units of constant purchasing power using the CPI-U.

Market Price per Common Share at Year-End

Market price per common share at year-end for each of the five most recent years is restated in average-for-the-year units of constant purchasing power using the CPI-U.

Average Level of CPI-U

The average level of CPI-U for each of the five most recent years is disclosed in a note to the minimum supplementary information. If an enterprise presents comprehensive current cost/constant purchasing power financial statements measured in year-end units of purchasing power, the year-end level of the CPI-U for each of the five most recent years is disclosed (ASC 255-10-50-8).

Explanatory Disclosures

An enterprise shall provide an explanation of the disclosures encouraged by ASC 255 and a discussion of their significance in the circumstances of the enterprise. These explanatory statements should be detailed sufficiently so that a user who possesses reasonable business acumen will be able to understand the information presented (ASC 255-10-50-10).

Additional Disclosures for the Current Year

If income from continuing operations as shown in the primary financial statements differs significantly from income from continuing operations determined on a current cost/constant purchasing power basis, certain other disclosures for the current year are encouraged by ASC 255 in addition to the minimum supplementary information.

Income from continuing operations for the current year on a current cost basis is computed in accordance with ASC 255 and then restated in average-for-the-year units of constant purchasing power using the CPI-U. The information for income from continuing operations for the current year on a current cost basis is presented in either a *statement format* or a *reconciliation format*, which discloses all adjustments between the supplementary information and the basic historical cost financial statements (see illustrations in ASC 255-10-55-14, 15-21). The same categories of revenue and expense that appear in the basic historical cost financial statements are used for the presentation of income from continuing operations for the current year on a current cost basis. Account classifications may be combined if they are not individually significant for restating purposes, or if the restated amounts are approximately the same as the historical cost amounts (ASC 255-10-50-12).

Income from continuing operations for the current year on a current cost basis does not include (*a*) the purchasing power gain or loss on net monetary items; (*b*) the increase or decrease in the current cost or lower recoverable amount of inventory and property, plant, and equipment, net of inflation; and (*c*) the translation adjustment (if applicable). However, an enterprise may include this information after the presentation of income from continuing operations for the current year on a current cost basis (ASC 255-10-50-14).

Only certain items that are included in income from continuing operations in the primary financial statements have to be adjusted to compute income from continuing operations for the current year on a current cost basis. Under ASC 255, these items are (ASC 255-10-50-39):

- *Cost of goods sold* Determined on a current cost basis or lower recoverable amount at the date of sale or at the date on which resources are used on or committed to a specific contract

- *Depreciation, depletion, and amortization* Determined based on the average current cost of the assets' service potentials or lower recoverable amounts during the period of use

- *Gain or loss on the sale, retirement, or write-down of inventory, property, plant, and equipment* Equal to the difference between the value of the consideration received or the written down amount and the current cost or lower recoverable amount of the item prior to its sale, retirement, or write-down

Other revenues, expenses, gains, and losses that are included in the primary financial statements are not adjusted and may be measured at amounts included in those statements.

Income tax expense that is included in the primary financial statements is not adjusted in computing income from continuing operations for the current year on a current cost basis (ASC 255-10-50-41). Disclosure must be made in the minimum supplementary information to the effect that income tax expense for the current period is presented at its historical cost.

Disclosure must also include (ASC 255-10-50-16):

- Separate amounts for the current cost or lower recoverable amount at the end of the current year of (*a*) inventory and (*b*) property, plant, and equipment.
- The increase or decrease in current cost or lower recoverable amount before and after adjusting for the effects of inflation of (*a*) inventory and (*b*) property, plant, and equipment.
- The principal types and sources of information used to calculate current costs for the current year.
- The differences, if any, in depreciation methods, useful lives, and salvage values used in (*a*) the primary financial statements and (*b*) the disclosure of current cost information for the current year.

Specialized Assets

Timberlands, growing timber, mineral ore bodies, proved oil and gas reserves, income-producing real estate, and motion picture films are classified as specialized assets. Specialized assets are considered unique, and the determination of their current costs frequently is difficult, if not impossible. For example, the current cost of an existing oil field may be difficult to determine because the oil field is one of a kind and cannot be duplicated. Yet, the definition of current cost is the current cost to purchase or reproduce the specific asset, and the current cost of property that is owned is the current cost of acquiring an asset that will perform or produce in a manner similar to that of the owned property.

ASC 255 provides special rules for determining the current costs of specialized assets. As a substitute for the current cost amounts and related expenses, the historical cost amounts of specialized assets may be adjusted for changes in specific prices by the use of a broad index of general purchasing power (ASC 255-10-50-32).

> **PRACTICE NOTE:** ASC 255 provides additional guidance on reporting the effects of changing prices on timber assets and mineral resource assets, but does not provide similar guidance for other types of specialized assets.

Timber Assets

In the event an enterprise estimates the current cost of growing timber and timber harvested by adjusting historical costs for changes in specific prices, the historical costs may include either (*a*) only costs that are capitalized in the primary financial statements or (*b*) all direct costs of reforestation and forest management, even if such costs are not capitalized in the primary financial statements. Reforestation and forest management costs include planting, fertilization, fire protection, property taxes, and nursery stock (ASC 255-10-50-33).

Mineral Resource Assets

The requirements for determining the current cost amounts for mineral resource assets are flexible because there is no generally accepted approach for measuring the current cost of finding mineral reserves. In determining the current cost amounts of mineral resource assets, ASC 255 permits the use of specific price indexes applied to historical costs, market buying prices, and other statistical data to determine current replacement costs. ASC 255 encourages the disclosure of the types of data or information that are used to determine current cost amounts (ASC 255-10-50-30).

ASC 255 contains the following definition for mineral resource assets (ASC Glossary):

> **Mineral resource assets** Assets that are directly associated with and derive value from all minerals extracted from the earth. Such minerals include oil and gas, ores containing ferrous and nonferrous metals, coal, shale, geothermal steam, sulphur, salt, stone, phosphate, sand, and gravel. Mineral resource assets include mineral interests in properties, completed and uncompleted wells, and related equipment and facilities, and other facilities required for purposes of extraction. The definition does not cover support equipment, because that equipment is included in the property, plant, and equipment for which current cost measurements are required.

For enterprises that own significant mineral reserves, the following information on owned mineral reserves, excluding oil and gas, is encouraged to be disclosed for each of the five most recent years (ASC 255-10-50-17):

- The estimated amount of proved or of proved and probable mineral reserves on hand at the end of the year. A date during the year may be used, but the date must be disclosed.
- The estimated quantity of each significant mineral product that is commercially recoverable from the mineral reserves in (1) above. The estimated quantity may be expressed in percentages or in physical units.
- The quantities of each significant mineral produced during the year. The quantity of each significant mineral produced by milling or similar processes also must be disclosed.
- The quantity of mineral reserves (proved or proved and probable) purchased or sold in place during the year.
- The average market price of each significant mineral product. If transferred within the enterprise, the equivalent market price prior to further use should be disclosed.

In classifying and detailing the above information, current industry practices should prevail.

The following procedures shall be used in determining the quantities of mineral reserves that should be reported (ASC 255-10-50-18):

- In consolidated financial statements, 100 percent of the quantities of mineral reserves attributable to both the parent company and all consolidated subsidiaries shall be reported regardless of whether a subsidiary is partially or wholly owned.
- In a proportionately consolidated investment, an investor shall include only its proportionate share of the investor's mineral reserves.
- Mineral reserve quantities attributable to an investment accounted for by the equity method shall not be included at all. If significant, however, the mineral reserve quantities should be reported separately by the investor.

PART II: INTERPRETIVE GUIDANCE

ASC 255: OVERALL

ASC 255-10-15-2, 255-15-45-2 through 45-4 Rescission of Accounting Principles Board Statements

BACKGROUND

The Accounting Standards Executive Committee (AcSEC) was a senior technical body of the AICPA authorized to represent the AICPA on matters related to industry specific accounting and financial reporting guidance, which AcSEC issued in Statements of Position (SOPs) that represented the views of at least two-thirds of the committee's members. AcSEC is no longer authorized to issue authoritative accounting guidance. Since 2009, it has been known as the Financial Reporting Standards Executive Committee (FRSEC).

The FASB's predecessor, the Accounting Principles Board (APB), had issued 31 Opinions and four Statements between its inception in 1959 and the formation of the FASB 1973. APB Opinions that had not been superseded by an FASB Statement were part of the authoritative accounting literature encompassed by Rule 203 of the AICPA's Code of Professional Conduct.

The APB's *Statements* never were considered to be rules or standards that AICPA members had to follow (i.e., they were not encompassed by the Code of Professional Conduct). Before the FASB's issuance of the Accounting Standards Codification™ (ASC) on July 1, 2009, which considers that guidance to be nonauthoritative, practitioners were permitted to choose to follow items included in that category, but they were not required to do so. Even though APB Statements never represented a source of authoritative guidance, some practitioners erroneously viewed APB Statements as authoritative. The following guidance (formerly, SOP 93-3) was issued to rectify that situation.

ACCOUNTING GUIDANCE

This guidance rescinds Statements 1 through 4, which were issued by the APB. AcSEC took that action to eliminate any confusion as to whether APB Statements represent a source of authoritative accounting literature. Also, each of the four APB Statements have been effectively superseded by FASB pronouncements. The following APB Statements were rescinded:

- APB Statement No. 1 (Statement by the Accounting Principles Board)
- APB Statement No. 2 (Disclosure of Supplemental Financial Information by Diversified Companies)—effectively superseded by FAS-14, which was superseded by FAS-131
- APB Statement No. 3 (Financial Statements Restated for General Price-Level Changes)—partially superseded by FAS-89
- APB Statement No. 4 (Basic Concepts and Accounting Principles Underlying Financial Statements of Business Enterprises)—effectively superseded by the various FASB Statements of Financial Accounting Concepts

APB Statement No. 3 (Financial Statements Restated for General Price-Level Changes) provided guidance for a comprehensive application of price-level adjusted financial statements. ASC 255 has effectively superseded a portion of APB-3. However, the provisions of ASC 255-10-50-1, 50-3, 50-5, 50-7 through 50-55, 55-1 through 55-89 provide guidance for the presentation of partial price-level data only. Although APB Statement No. 3 was rescinded by SOP 93-3, entities are not precluded from following its guidance in preparing a comprehensive set of price-level adjusted financial statements (assuming those statements are not inconsistent with the guidance in ASC 255 regarding historical cost/constant purchasing power accounting, such as the classification of assets and liabilities as monetary or nonmonetary).

CHAPTER 11
ASC 260—EARNINGS PER SHARE

CONTENTS

Part I: General Guidance	11,002
ASC 260-10: Overall	11,002
Overview	11,002
Background	11,002
Simple and Complex Capital Structures	11,003
Simple Capital Structures	11,003
Complex Capital Structures	11,004
Calculating EPS	11,004
Objectives and General Guidance	11,004
Table 11-1: Basic EPS vs. Diluted EPS	11,005
Illustration of Determining Weighted-Average Shares	11,006
Antidilution	11,007
Illustration of Antidilution	11,007
Options and Warrants	11,008
Figure 11-1: Control Income Figure for Judging Dilution	11,009
Illustration of Application of the Treasury Stock Method	11,009
Illustration of Computation of Incremental Shares for Stock Options and Similar Instruments	11,010
Share-Based Payment Arrangements and Awards of Share Options and Nonvested Shares	11,011
Illustration of Application of Treasury Stock Method to a Share-Based Payment Arrangement	11,011
Written Put Options and Purchased Options	11,013
Illustration of the Reverse Treasury Stock Method	11,013
Convertible Securities	11,014
Illustration of the If-Converted Method	11,015
Contracts Subject to Settlement in Stock or Cash	11,015
Contingently Issuable Shares	11,016
Income Statement Presentation and Disclosure	11,016
Including Antidilution	11,018
Excluding Dilution	11,018
Illustration of Basic and Diluted EPS	11,019
Part II: Interpretive Guidance	11,020
ASC 260-10: Overall	11,020
ASC 260-10-45-61A, 45-68B, 55-76A through 55-76D, 65-2	
Determining Whether Instruments Granted in Share-Based Transactions Are Participating Securities	11,020
ASC 260-10-45-60, 45-60A through 45-68; 55-24 through 55-30, 55-71 through 55-75	
Participating Securities and the Two-Class Method under FASB Statement No. 128, *Earnings per Share*	11,021

11,002   ASC 260—Earnings Per Share

ASC 260-10-45-43 through 45-44; 55-78 through 55-79, 55-81 through 55-82, 55-84 through 55-84B
    The Effect of Contingently Convertible Instruments on Diluted Earnings per Share   **11,024**

ASC 260-10-05-3 through 05-5; 15-5; 45-72 through 45-73; 55-103 through 55-110
    Application of the Two-Class Method under FASB Statement No. 128, *Earnings per Share*, to Master Limited Partnerships   **11,025**

ASC 260-10-99S-2
    The Effect on the Calculation of Earnings per Share for a Period that Includes for the Redemption or Induced Conversion of Preferred Stock   **11,028**

ASC 260-10-S99-3
    Computation of Earnings per Share for a Period That Includes a Redemption or an Induced Conversion of a Portion of a Class of Preferred Stock   **11,030**

ASC 260-10-55-3A, 55-3B, 55-85 through 55-87
    Computing Year-to-Date Diluted Earnings per Share under FASB Statement No. 128   **11,030**
        Illustration of Quarterly and Year-to-Date Calculation

ASC 260-10-55-32, 55-34, 55-36, 55-36A; 45-22
    Effect of Contracts That May Be Settled in Stock or Cash on the Computation of Diluted Earnings per Share   **11,032**

ASC 260-10-45-11, 45-12
    Effect of Preferred Stock Dividends Payable in Common Shares on Computation of Income Available to Common Stockholders   **11,034**

PART I: GENERAL GUIDANCE

ASC 260-10: OVERALL

OVERVIEW

Earnings per share (EPS) is an important measure of corporate performance for investors and other users of financial statements. EPS figures are required to be presented in the income statement of publicly held companies and are presented in a manner consistent with the captions included in the income statement. Certain securities, such as convertible bonds, preferred stock, and stock options, permit their holders to become common stockholders or add to the number of shares of common stock already held. When potential reduction, called *dilution*, of EPS figures is inherent in a company's capital structure, a dual presentation of EPS is required—basic and diluted EPS.

BACKGROUND

EPS figures are used to evaluate the past operating performance of a business in evaluating its potential and in making investment decisions. EPS figures are commonly presented in prospectuses, proxy material, and financial reports to shareholders. They are also used in the compilation of business earnings data for the press, statistical services, and other publications. EPS figures are believed to be of value to investors in weighing the significance of a corporation's current net income and of changes in its net income from period to period in relation to the shares the investor holds or may acquire.

The U.S. guidance on EPS codified in ASC 260 was issued at the same time as IASC-33 (Earnings per Share) and includes provisions that are substantially the same. ASC 260 applies to entities with publicly held common stock or potential common stock (e.g., financial instruments or contracts that could result in the issuance of additional shares). It simplified existing standards for computing EPS by replacing primary earnings per share with basic EPS and by altering the calculation of diluted EPS, which replaced fully diluted EPS.

SIMPLE AND COMPLEX CAPITAL STRUCTURES

ASC 260 applies to all entities that have issued common stock or potential common stock that trades in a public market (i.e., in a stock exchange or in an over-the-counter market, including securities that trade only locally or regionally). *Potential common stock* consists of other securities and contractual arrangements that may result in the issuance of common stock in the future, such as (ASC 260-10-15-2):

- Options
- Warrants
- Convertible securities
- Contingent stock agreements

Additional guidance on the applicability of ASC 260 includes the following (ASC 260-10-15-3):

- The standard applies in situations in which an entity has made a filing, or is in the process of making a filing, with a regulatory agency in anticipation of selling securities in the future.
- The standard does *not* require the presentation of EPS by investment companies or in financial statements of wholly owned subsidiaries.
- The standard applies to entities that are not required to present EPS but choose to do so.

For purposes of presenting earnings per share, a distinction is made between enterprises with a simple capital structure and those with a complex capital structure.

Simple Capital Structures

A simple capital structure is one that consists of capital stock and includes no potential for dilution via conversions, exercise of options, or other arrangements that would increase the number of shares outstanding. For organizations with simple capital structures, the presentation of EPS using assumed income numbers and 50,000 shares of common stock outstanding in the income statement would appear as follows:

	20X9	20X8
Income before extraordinary item	$175,000	$160,000
Extraordinary item (describe)	15,000	—
Net income	$190,000	$160,000
Earnings per common share:		
Income before extraordinary item (175 ÷ 50), (160 ÷ 50)	$3.50	$3.20
Extraordinary item	.30	—
Net income per share (190 ÷ 50), (160 ÷ 50)	$3.80	$3.20

Complex Capital Structures

For organizations with complex capital structures, two EPS figures are presented with equal prominence on the face of the income statement. The captions for the two EPS figures are "Earnings per common share" and "Earnings per common share—assuming dilution" (or other similar descriptions).

The first of these captions is often referred to as *basic EPS* and the second as *diluted EPS*. The difference between basic EPS and diluted EPS is that basic EPS considers only outstanding common stock, whereas diluted EPS incorporates the potential dilution from all potentially dilutive securities that would have reduced EPS.

Based on the information presented in the previous section and assuming 60,000 shares of stock outstanding for basic EPS and 75,000 for diluted EPS, EPS for a complex capital structure might appear as follows:

	20X9	20X8
Earnings per common share		
Income before extraordinary item	$ 2.92	$ 2.67
Extraordinary item	.25	—
Net income	$ 3.17	$ 2.67
Earnings per share assuming dilution		
Income before extraordinary item	$ 2.33	$ 2.13
Extraordinary item	.20	—
Net income	$ 2.53	$ 2.13

CALCULATING EPS

Objectives and General Guidance

The objectives and general approach for measuring basic and diluted EPS are presented in Table 11-1:

Table 11-1: Basic EPS vs. Diluted EPS

	Basic EPS	Diluted EPS
Objective	To measure the performance of an entity over the reporting period based on its outstanding common stock	To measure the performance of an entity over the reporting period based on its outstanding common stock and after giving effect to all dilutive potential common shares that were outstanding during the period
Computation	Income attributable to common stock ÷ Weighted average number of common shares outstanding	(Income attributable to common stock + Adjustments for changes in income [loss] that are consistent with the issuance of dilutive potential common shares) ÷ (Weighted average number of common shares outstanding + Dilutive potential common shares)

Additional guidelines for determining *basic EPS* are as follows (ASC 260-10-45-10, 11, 12, 13):

- Shares issued and acquired (e.g., treasury stock) during the period are weighted for the portion of the period they were outstanding.

- The amount of income (or loss) attributable to common stock is reduced (or increased) by dividends declared on preferred stock (whether or not paid) and by dividends on cumulative preferred stock (whether or not declared or paid).

- Contingently issuable shares (i.e., shares that are issuable for little or no cash consideration upon the satisfaction of certain conditions) are treated as outstanding and included in computing basic EPS as of the date that the conditions required for their issuance have been satisfied.

Additional guidelines for computing *diluted EPS* are as follows (ASC 260-10-45-16, 21):

- The denominator is similar to that for basic EPS, except that dilutive potential common shares are added.

- Numerator adjustments are required that are consistent with the assumed issuance of dilutive potential common shares. For example, if shares issuable upon conversion of a convertible bond are added to the denominator, the after-tax interest savings is added to the numerator.

- The denominator of diluted EPS is based on the most advantageous conversion rate or exercise price from the standpoint of the security holder (i.e., the maximum number of shares that would be issued).

- Once EPS figures have been published, they are not retroactively restated for subsequent conversions or changes in the market price of the common stock.

11,006 ASC 260—Earnings Per Share

When computing both basic and diluted EPS in consolidated financial statements, if one or more less-than-wholly-owned subsidiaries are included in the consolidated group, the income attributable to the noncontrolling interest is excluded from income from continuing operations and net income (ASC 260-10-45-11A).

Illustration of Determining Weighted-Average Shares

Common stock outstanding, 1/1/20X9	200,000 shares
Preferred stock (convertible into 2 shares of common stock) outstanding, 1/1/20X9	50,000 shares
Convertible debentures (convertible into 100 shares of common stock for each $1,000 bond)	$100,000

On March 31, ABC reacquired 5,000 shares of its own common stock.

On May 1, 20,000 shares of ABC preferred stock were converted into common stock.

On July 1, $50,000 of ABC convertible debentures was converted into common stock.

On September 30, ABC reacquired 5,000 shares of its common stock.

Computation of Weighted-Average Shares

1.	Common stock outstanding, 1/1/X9	200,000
2.	Common stock reacquired, 3/31/X9 (5,000 × 9/12)	(3,750)
3.	Conversion of preferred stock on 5/1/X9 (20,000 × 2 × 8/12)	26,667
4.	Conversion of convertible debentures on 7/1/X9 (50 × 100 × 6/12)	2,500
5.	Common stock reacquired on 9/30/X9 (5,000 × 3/12)	(1,250)
	Total weighted average shares, 20X9	224,167

1. **Common stock outstanding** Because the 200,000 shares of common stock were outstanding for the entire year, all the shares are included in the weighted average shares.

2. **Common stock reacquired** On March 31, 20X9, 5,000 shares were reacquired, which means that 9/12 of the year they were not outstanding. Since the 5,000 shares are already included in the 200,000 shares (1. above), that portion which was not outstanding during the full year is deducted. 9/12 of the 5,000 shares, or 3,750 shares, are excluded from the computations, which means that only 196,250 of the 200,000 shares were outstanding for the full year.

3. **Conversion of preferred** On May 1, 20X9, 20,000 shares of the preferred were converted into common stock. Since the conversion rate is 2 for 1, an additional 40,000 shares were outstanding from May 1 to the end of the year. 8/12 of the 40,000 shares, or 26,667 shares, are included in the weighted average shares outstanding for the year.

4. **Conversion of convertible debentures** On July 1, 20X9, $50,000 of the convertible debentures were converted into common stock. The conversion rate is 100 shares for each $1,000 bond, which means that

the $50,000 converted consisted of fifty $1,000 bonds, or 5,000 shares of common stock. Since the conversion was on July 1, only 6/12 of the 5,000 shares, or 2,500 shares, are included in the weighted average shares outstanding for the year.

5. **Common stock reacquired** 5,000 additional shares out of the 200,000 shares outstanding at the beginning of the year were reacquired on September 30, which means that for 3/12 of the year they were not outstanding. 3/12 of 5,000 shares, or 1,250 shares, are excluded from the computation of weighted average shares outstanding for the year.

Stock splits or stock dividends (or reverse splits or dividends) are retroactively recognized in all periods presented in the financial statements. A stock split or stock dividend is recognized if it occurs after the close of the period but before issuance of the financial statements. If this situation occurs, it must be disclosed in the statements. Also, the dividends per share must be reported in terms of the equivalent number of shares outstanding at the time the dividend is declared.

Antidilution

The term *antidilution* refers to increases in EPS or decreases in loss per share. Diluted EPS computed in accordance with ASC 260 is intended to be a conservative measure of performance and, accordingly, is intended to reflect the potential reduction in EPS resulting from issuance of additional common shares. Thus, potential issuances that would increase EPS or reduce loss per share generally are excluded from the calculation.

Illustration of Antidilution

A company reports net income of $100,000 and has 50,000 shares of outstanding common stock. Basic EPS is $2.00 ($100,000/50,000 shares). The same company has 15,000 shares of potential common stock.

Situation 1

Assume the numerator adjustment for the potential common shares is +$15,000. Including these potential common shares, EPS is computed as follows:

$$\frac{\$100,000 + \$15,000}{50,000 + 15,000} = \frac{\$115,000}{65,000} = \$1.77 \text{ per share}$$

In this situation, the potential common shares are *dilutive* (i.e., they reduce EPS), and diluted EPS is $1.77.

Situation 2

Assume the numerator adjustment for the potential common shares is +$50,000. Including these potential common shares, EPS is computed as follows:

$$\frac{\$100,000 + \$50,000}{50,000 + 15,000} = \frac{\$150,000}{65,000} = \$2.31 \text{ per share}$$

In this situation, the potential common shares are *antidilutive* (i.e., they increase EPS), and would not be included in diluted EPS.

In applying the antidilution provisions of ASC 260, the following guidelines are important (ASC 260-10-45-17, 18):

- In determining whether potential common shares are dilutive or antidilutive, each issue or series of issues of potential common shares is considered separately.

- In cases in which multiple issuances of potential common shares exist, one may be dilutive on its own but antidilutive when combined with other potential common shares. To reflect maximum dilution, each issue or series of issues of potential common shares is considered in sequence, starting with the most dilutive and moving to the least dilutive.

- An entity may report more than one income figure in its income statement (e.g., income from continuing operations, income before extraordinary item or income before accounting change, as well as net income). For purposes of determining whether potential common stock is dilutive, the diagram in Figure 11-1 shows which income figure should be used.

Once an issue or series of issues of potential common shares is determined to be *dilutive* using the appropriate income figure in Exhibit I, that issue or series of issues is considered to be outstanding in computing diluted EPS on all income amounts, even if it is antidilutive in one or more of those amounts. Similarly, once an issue or series of issues of potential common shares is determined to be *antidilutive* using the appropriate income figure in Figure 11-1, that issue or series of issues is omitted in computing diluted EPS on all income amounts, even if it would have been dilutive in one or more of those amounts.

Options and Warrants

The dilutive effect of options and warrants generally is determined by the *treasury stock method* (ASC 260-10-45-23). That method involves three interrelated steps, as follows:

Step 1: Exercise is assumed to have taken place and common shares are assumed to have been issued.

Step 2: The proceeds from the issuance of common stock are assumed to have been used to purchase treasury stock at the average market price for the period.

Step 3: The incremental shares issued (i.e., shares sold in Step 1 reduced by share repurchased in Step 2) are added to the denominator of the diluted EPS computation.

Figure 11-1: Control Income Figure for Judging Dilution

```
           ┌─────────────────────┐
           │ Does income statement│
           │ include both net income│ ──Yes──┐
           │ and income from     │          │
           │ continuing operations?│         │
           └──────────┬──────────┘          │
                      │ No                  │
           ┌──────────┴──────────┐          │
           │ Does income statement│          │
           │ include both net income│──Yes──┐│
           │ and income before   │         ││
           │ extraordinary item? │         ││
           └──────────┬──────────┘         ││
                      │ No                 ││
                      ▼                    ▼▼
Income to use as control   Net       Income before    Income from
figure for judging dilution: income   extraordinary   continuing
                                      item            operations
```

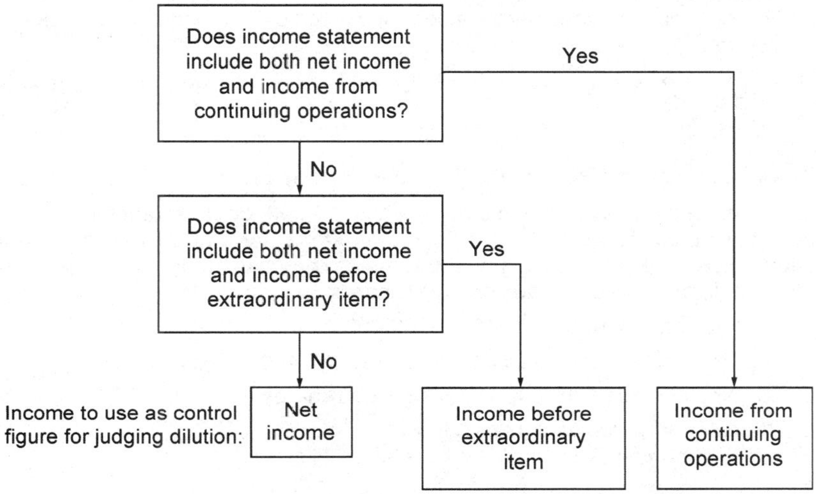

Illustration of Application of the Treasury Stock Method

By dividing its $100,000 net income by 100,000 shares of outstanding common stock, a company determines its basic EPS to be $1. In addition, options are outstanding that permit the purchase of 10,000 shares of common stock at $25. The average market price of the stock is $40. The treasury stock method is applied as follows:

Step 1:   10,000 shares sold at $25: 10,000 × $25 = $250,000 in proceeds

Step 2: $250,000 used to purchase treasury stock at $40: $250,000 / $40 = 6,250

Step 3:   Net increase in outstanding shares: 10,000 − 6,250 = 3,750

Diluted EPS is computed as follows:

$$\frac{\$100{,}000}{100{,}000 + 3{,}750} = \$.96$$

Under this method, options and warrants will have a dilutive effect on EPS when the average market price of the stock (used for assumed repurchase in Step 2) exceeds the issuance price (used for assumed sale in Step 1), because of an assumed net increase in the number of outstanding shares. In this situation, options and warrants are described as "in the money." When options and warrants are outstanding for only part of the period, the amount determined by applying the treasury stock method is weighted for the part of the period the options and warrants were outstanding.

The rationale behind the treasury stock method is that any number of shares of common stock that could have been purchased on the open market with the exercised price funds from the options or similar instruments are not additional outstanding stock and have no dilutive effect on EPS.

PRACTICE POINTER: A shortcut method of calculating the net increase in the number of outstanding shares of common stock by the treasury stock method is as follows:

$$\text{Incremental shares outstanding} = \frac{M - E}{M} \times \text{Number of shares obtainable}$$

where M = the market price and E = the exercise price

For example, assume a company has 10,000 options outstanding that permit the purchase of 1 share of common stock each at $16. The average market price is $25. Applying the three-step process of the treasury stock method indicates a net increase of 3,600 shares:

1. Proceeds = 10,000 × $16 = $160,000
2. Repurchase of shares = $160,000/25 = 6,400 shares
3. Net increase = 10,000 - 6,400 = 3,600 shares

The short-cut calculation is as follows:

$$\frac{\$25 - \$16}{\$25} \times \$10,000 = 3,600$$

When the market price of common stock rises significantly during the year, computation of the weighted average on a quarterly basis is preferred.

Illustration of Computation of Incremental Shares for Stock Options and Similar Instruments

A company has 10,000 stock options outstanding, which are exercisable at $60 each. Given the following market prices, determine the incremental shares by quarters, and the number of shares that are included in diluted EPS.

	Quarters			
	1	2	3	4
Average market price	56	64	70	68
Ending market price	60	68	72	64

Determining the incremental shares by quarters for diluted EPS follows:

1st quarter: no calculation*	=	0
2nd quarter: $10,000 - \left[\dfrac{10,000 \times \$60}{\$64}\right]$	=	625
3nd quarter: $10,000 - \left[\dfrac{10,000 \times \$60}{\$70}\right]$	=	1,429
4th quarter: $10,000 - \left[\dfrac{10,000 \times \$60}{\$68}\right]$	=	1,176
Total incremental shares	=	3,230
Divided by 4 quarters (3,230 ÷ 4)	=	808

* The exercise price of $60 is higher than the average market price.

The total is divided by four quarters because four quarters entered into the computation. The 808 shares are included in the computation of diluted EPS.

Share-Based Payment Arrangements and Awards of Share Options and Nonvested Shares

Fixed awards and nonvested stock to be issued to an employee under a stock-based compensation plan are considered options for purposes of computing diluted EPS. Guidelines for including these arrangements in diluted EPS are (ASC 260-10-45-15):

- They are considered to be outstanding as of the grant date, even though their exercise may be contingent upon vesting.

- They are included even if the employee may not receive the stock until some future date.

- Their impact is determined by applying the treasury stock method, and they are included only if their impact is dilutive.

In applying the treasury stock method, an important determination is the amount of proceeds due the issuing entity. ASC 260 identifies three components of the amount of proceeds from stock-based compensation arrangements:

1. The amount, if any, the employee must pay

2. The amount of compensation cost attributed to future services and not yet recognized

3. The amount of current and deferred tax benefits, if any, that would be credited to additional paid-in capital upon exercise of the options

These paragraphs make several other important observations. First, if stock-based compensation arrangements are payable in common stock or in cash at the discretion of either the employee or the employer, the determination of whether they are potential common shares is based on the guidance in ASC 260-10-45-45 (covered below). Second, if the plan permits the employee to choose between types of equity instruments, diluted EPS is computed based on the terms used in the computation of compensation expense for the period. Finally, performance awards and targeted stock price options are subject to ASC 260's provisions on contingently issuable shares (covered below).

Illustration of Application of Treasury Stock Method to a Share-Based Payment Arrangement

Entity H adopted a share option plan on January 1, 20X8, and granted 500,000 at-the-money share options with an exercise price of $25. On that date, the fair value of each share option granted was $16.33. All share options vest at the end of five years (cliff vesting). At the grant date, Entity H assumes an annual forfeiture rate of 2% and therefore expects to receive the requisite service for 451,960 [500,000 × $(.98^5)$] share options. Employees forfeited 8,000 stock options ratably during 20X8. Thus, the weighted average number of share options outstanding in 20X8 equaled 496,000 [(500,000 + 492,000)/2]. The average stock price during 20X8 is $40, and there are 15,000,000 weighted-average common shares outstanding for the year. Net income for the period is $50,000,000 (inclusive of share-based compensation). Entity H's tax rate is 35%.

Entity H has sufficient previously recognized excess tax benefits in additional paid-in capital from prior share-based payment arrangements to offset any write-off of deferred tax assets associated with its grant of share options on January 1, 20X8. All share options are the type that upon exercise give rise to deductible compensation cost for income tax purposes.

Computation of Basic EPS for the Year Ended 12/31/20X8:

Net income	$50,000,000
Weighted-average common shares outstanding	15,000,000
Basic earnings per share	$ 3.33

Computation of average unrecognized compensation cost in 20X8:

Beginning of period:

Unrecognized compensation cost (500,000 × $16.33)		$8,165,000
End of period:		
Beginning unrecognized compensation cost	$8,165,000	
Annual compensation cost recognized during 20X8, based on estimated forfeitures [(451,960 × $16.33) / 3]	(2,460,169)	
Annual compensation cost not recognized during the period related to outstanding options at 12/31/20X8, for which service is not expected to be rendered [(492,000 - 451,960) × $16.33) / 3]	(217,951)	
Total compensation cost of actual forfeited options (8,000 × $16.33)	(130,640)	
Total unrecognized compensation cost at end of period, based on actual forfeitures		5,356,240
Average total unrecognized compensation, based on actual forfeitures [(8,165,000 + 5,356,240) / 2]		$6,760,620

Computation of tax benefit:

Total compensation cost of average outstanding options (496,000 × $16.33)	$8,099,680
Intrinsic value of average outstanding options for the year ended 12/31/20X8 [496,000 × ($40 - $25)]	(7,440,000)
Excess of total compensation cost over estimated tax deduction	659,680
Tax benefit deficiency ($659,680 × .35)	$ 230,888

Computation of assumed proceeds for diluted earnings per share:

Amount employees would pay if the weighted-average number of options outstanding were exercised using the average exercise price (496,000 × $25)	$12,400,000
Average unrecognized compensation cost in 20X8 (see above calculation)	6,760,620
Tax benefit deficiency that would be offset in paid-in capital (see above calculation)	(230,888)
Assumed proceeds	$18,929,732

Assumed repurchase of shares:

Repurchase shares at average market price during the year ($18,929,732 ÷ $40)		473,243
Incremental shares (496,000 - 473,243)		22,757

Computation of Diluted EPS for the Year Ended 12/31/20X8:

Net income		$50,000,000
Weighted-average common shares outstanding	15,000,000	
Incremental shares	22,757	
Total shares outstanding		15,022,757
Diluted earnings per share ($50,000,000 ÷ 15,022,757)		$ 3.328

Written Put Options and Purchased Options

Certain contracts may require an entity to repurchase its own stock. Examples are written put options and forward purchase contracts other than forward purchase contracts accounted for as a liability according to ASC 480, *Distinguishing Liabilities from Equity*. These contracts are reflected in the calculation of diluted EPS if their effect is dilutive when the *reverse treasury stock method* is applied. As the name implies, that method is the reverse of the treasury stock method for requirements to repurchase, rather than issue, shares of common stock in stock option plans (ASC 260-10-45-35).

The steps in the reverse treasury stock method are analogous to those in the treasury stock method:

Step 1: Assume that enough common shares were issued at the average market price to raise enough proceeds to satisfy the contract.

Step 2: The proceeds are assumed to be used to buy back the shares required in the contract.

Step 3: The increase in number of shares (i.e., shares sold in Step 1 reduced by the shares purchased in Step 2) is added to the denominator of the diluted EPS computation.

Applying the reverse treasury stock method results in dilution of EPS if the options are "in the money" (i.e., the exercise price is above the average market price).

Illustration of the Reverse Treasury Stock Method

Ranalli's Lawn Service International (RLSI) has sold 10,000 put options at an exercise price of $40 per option. The average market price of RLSI's common stock during 20X8 is $25 per share. RLSI would apply the reverse treasury stock method as follows:

Step 1: RLSI needs to raise $400,000 (10,000 × $40) to satisfy its obligation under the put contract. In order to raise $400,000, RLSI must sell 16,000 shares of common stock, given the average market price per share of its stock during 20X8 ($400,000 ÷ $25 = 16,000 shares).

Step 2: It is assumed that the $400,000 will be used to buy back the 10,000 shares, at $40 per share, per the terms of the put options written by RLSI.

Step 3: The 6,000 increase in the number of shares outstanding (16,000 shares issued from Step 1 minus the 10,000 shares repurchased from Step 2) are added to the denominator in calculating diluted EPS.

Contracts held by an entity on its own stock (e.g., purchased put options and purchased call options) are not included in the determination of diluted EPS, because to do so would be antidilutive due to the reduced number of outstanding shares (ASC 260-10-45-37).

Convertible Securities

Incorporating the dilutive effect of convertible securities into EPS figures requires application of the *if-converted method* (ASC 260-10-45-40). The method derives its name from the underlying assumption that both the numerator and the denominator of the EPS calculation are restated to what they would have been if the convertible security had already been converted into common stock for the period. This usually requires the numerator to be adjusted for the amount of the preferred dividend (convertible preferred stock) or the interest expense (convertible debt instrument).

Specific guidelines for applying the if-converted method are as follows:

- For convertible preferred stock, the amount of the preferred dividend deducted in determining income attributable to common stockholders is added back in the numerator.
- For convertible debt securities, the numerator is adjusted for the following:
  — Interest charges applicable to the security are added back to the numerator.
  — To the extent nondiscretionary adjustments based on income would have been computed differently if the interest on convertible debt had never been recognized, the numerator is adjusted appropriately (e.g., for profit-sharing and royalty arrangements).
  — The above adjustments are made net-of-tax.
- Convertible preferred stock and convertible debt are treated as having been converted at the beginning of the period or at the time of issuance, if later.
- Conversion is not assumed if the effect is antidilutive. (This effect occurs when the preferred dividend per common share or the interest net of tax and nondiscretionary adjustments per common share exceeds basic EPS.)

Illustration of the If-Converted Method

A company had $100,000 of net income for the year and 100,000 shares of common stock outstanding. Consider the following two independent situations:

Situation 1

25,000 shares of 6%, $10 par-value convertible preferred stock are outstanding, and are convertible into 25,000 shares of common stock.

Basic EPS: $\dfrac{\$100,000 - \$15,000^*}{\$100,000 \text{ shares}} = \dfrac{\$85,000}{100,000} = \$.85$

* Preferred dividend = 25,000 shares × $10 par × .06.

Diluted EPS: $\dfrac{\$100,000 + \$15,000 - \$15,000}{100,000 + 25,000 \text{ shares}} = \dfrac{\$100,000}{125,000} = \$.80$

Explanation: The $15,000 preferred dividend is deducted to determine basic EPS. To determine diluted EPS, the preferred dividend is added back to the numerator, and the 25,000 equivalent common shares are added to the denominator. This reduces EPS from $.85 to $.80.

Situation 2

100 convertible bonds, 10%, 1,000 par value, are outstanding, and each is convertible into 150 shares of common stock. The income tax rate is 35%, and interest already has been deducted in determining net income.

Basic EPS: $\dfrac{\$100,000}{\$100,000 \text{ shares}} = \$1.00$

Diluted EPS: $\dfrac{\$100,000 + \$6,500^*}{100,000 + (100 \times 150) \text{ shares}} = \dfrac{\$106,500}{115,000} = \$.93$

* After-tax interest: (100 bonds × $1,000 par × .10) × (1 - .35).

Explanation: Basic EPS is calculated based on $100,000 of net income and 100,000 shares of common stock outstanding. To include the dilutive effect of the convertible bonds in diluted EPS, the after-tax effect of the interest is added to the numerator (i.e., interest that would have been avoided and the accompanying increase in income taxes), and the equivalent number of common shares (150 per bond × 100 bonds = 15,000) is added to the denominator. The impact is a reduction in EPS from $1.00 to $.93.

Contracts Subject to Settlement in Stock or Cash

Entities may issue a contract that allows either the entity or the holder to elect settlement in either common stock or cash. The impact of this type of arrangement on EPS is determined on the basis of the facts available each period. Usually it will be assumed that the contract will be settled in common stock if the effect of that assumption is more dilutive than an assumption that the contract will be settled in cash. If past experience or stated policy provides a reasonable basis for assuming that the contract will be settled in cash, however, the assumption that it will be settled in common stock may be overcome.

A contract that is reported as an asset or liability in the financial statements may require an adjustment to the numerator for any change in income or loss that would have taken place if the contract had been reported as an equity instrument. This is similar to the numerator adjustment for a convertible security presented earlier (i.e., the if-converted method) (ASC 260-10-45-45).

Contingently Issuable Shares

Contingently issuable shares are shares that must be issued upon the satisfaction of certain conditions. They are considered outstanding and are included in diluted EPS as follows (ASC 260-10-45-48):

- *All conditions for issuance satisfied by the end of the period*—Contingently issuable shares are included as of the beginning of the period in which the conditions were satisfied, or as of the date of the contingent stock agreement, if later.
- *All conditions for issuance not satisfied by the end of the period*—The number of contingently issuable shares included in diluted EPS is based on the number of shares, if any, that would be issuable if the end of the reporting period were the end of the contingency period.

In applying these procedures, the following guidance is provided (ASC 260-10-45-51, 52, 53, 54, 55):

Condition for Issuance of Stock	Treatment of Contingent Issuance in Diluted EPS, If Dilutive
Attainment or maintenance of a specified level of earnings, and that amount has been attained	Additional shares that would be issued, based on current earnings, are included in diluted EPS.
Future market price of stock	Additional shares that would be issued, based on the current market price, are included in diluted EPS.
Future earnings and market price of stock	Additional shares that would be issued, based on both current earnings and current market price of stock, are included in diluted EPS only if both conditions are met.
Condition other than earnings and/or market price of stock	Additional shares that would be issued under an assumption that the current status will remain unchanged are included in diluted EPS.
Other contingently issuable potential common shares (e.g., contingently issuable convertible securities)	Additional shares that would be issuable under current conditions based on appropriate sections of ASC 260 for options and warrants, convertible securities, and contracts that may be settled in stock or cash are included in diluted EPS.

INCOME STATEMENT PRESENTATION AND DISCLOSURE

Entities with simple capital structures (i.e., without potential common shares) and entities with complex capital structures (i.e., with potential common shares) are required to present EPS on the face of the income statement as follows (ASC 260-10-45-2):

- *Simple capital structure*—basic EPS on income from continuing operations (or income before extraordinary item and/or change in accounting) and net income
- *Complex capital structure*—basic and diluted EPS (with equal prominence) on income from continuing operations (or income before extraordinary item and/or change in accounting) and net income

An entity that reports discontinued operations, an extraordinary item, or a cumulative effect of an accounting change shall include basic and diluted EPS on these items either on the face of the income statement or in related notes. If an entity chooses to present EPS figures on other items, those figures must be in notes to the financial statements, along with an indication of whether the EPS figures are pretax or net-of-tax (ASC 260-10-45-3, 5).

Several other guidelines for the presentation of EPS figures are as follows (ASC 260-10-45-4, 7):

- EPS figures are required for all periods for which an income statement (or summary of earnings) is presented.
- If diluted EPS is presented for one period, it must be presented for all periods presented, even if it is the same as basic EPS for one or more periods.
- The terms "basic EPS" and "diluted EPS" are used in ASC 260, but are not required to be used in financial statements. Alternative titles, such as "earnings per common share" and "earnings per common share—assuming dilution" are acceptable.

In addition to specifying the EPS content on the face of the financial statement, ASC 260 also requires the following disclosures (ASC 260-10-50-1):

- A reconciliation of the numerators and denominators used to compute basic and diluted EPS for income from continuing operations or income before extraordinary item or net income, as appropriate.
- The amount of preferred dividend deducted in arriving at the amount of income attributable to common stockholders.
- Potential common stock that was not included in the calculation of diluted EPS because it is antidilutive in the current period.
- Description of any transaction that occurred after the end of the most recent period that would have materially affected the number of common shares outstanding or potential common shares if the transaction had occurred before the end of the reporting period.

PRACTICE POINTER: Normally, antidilutive potential common stock is omitted in determining diluted EPS. In applying the specific provisions of ASC 260, however, there are some instances in which potential common stock that is antidilutive is required to be included. There are also instances in which potential common stock that appears to be dilutive must be excluded. Take care to include or exclude the potential common stock in determining diluted EPS, even though doing this may seem counter-intuitive to the assumptions and intent underlying diluted EPS.

Including Antidilution

If the income statement includes more than one income figure [e.g., income (loss) from continuing operations, income (loss) before extraordinary item, net income (loss)], the one that appears first in the income statement is the benchmark number for determining whether potential common stock is included. If the potential diluter dilutes that income figure, it is included in determining diluted EPS for both or all three income figures, even though it may be antidilutive in the second or third income figure presented. For example, a company may report income as follows:

Income before extraordinary item	$100,000
Extraordinary loss	(125,000)
Net loss	($25,000)

Stock options that would dilute EPS on income before extraordinary item are outstanding. Because the market price of the stock exceeds the exercise price of the options, these options are dilutive and are included in computing earnings per share.

In this case, the stock options are considered to be potential common stock in determining earnings (loss) per share on *both* income before extraordinary item and net loss, even though they are dilutive in the first figure and antidilutive in the second.

Excluding Dilution

Where multiple convertible securities exist, test them for dilution in their order of dilutive effect, beginning with the most dilutive and proceeding to the least dilutive. EPS adjusted for previously considered convertible securities becomes the basis for judging the potential of each convertible security in the order considered.

For example, assume a company has basic EPS of $1.00 and has two convertible bond issues outstanding. These two convertibles have ratios of numerator adjustment (interest net of tax) to denominator adjustment (number of shares) as follows:

Bonds A	$.90
Bonds B	$.95

Bonds A are more dilutive than Bonds B ($.90 is less than $.95), so they are considered first. Assume that including Bonds A reduces EPS from $1.00 to $.97. The $.95 figure for Bonds B is compared with $.97, determined to be further dilutive, and included in determining diluted EPS. On the other hand, if including Bonds A had reduced EPS from $1.00 to $.85, Bonds B would have been judged antidilutive and excluded from the determination of diluted EPS, even though they would have been dilutive if considered alone.

Illustration of Basic and Diluted EPS

In 20X8, Stahl, Inc., a calendar-year public company, had 52,500 shares of common stock outstanding at January 1, sold 10,500 shares on March 1, and repurchased 2,000 shares on November 1. Net income for the year was $375,000, and the appropriate income tax rate was 35%. Stahl's common stock sold for an average of $25 during the year and ended the year at $28.

Other financial instruments in the company's capital structure are as follows:

- Preferred stock—10,000 shares outstanding, $50 par, 6% dividend (cumulative)
- Stock options—15,000 options to purchase one share each of common stock stock at $20 each
- Convertible bonds—$200,000 par, 10%, convertible into 20 shares of common stock per $1,000 bond

Basic and diluted EPS are determined as follows:

Preliminary Calculations

Weighted-average number of common shares outstanding

Jan. 1	52,500	× 2 months	= 105,000
	10,500		
March 1	63,000	× 8 months	= 504,000
	(2000)		= 122,000
Nov. 1	61,000	× 2 months	731,000
	731,000 / 12 months	=	60,917

Alternatively, the weighted-average can be calculated as follows:

Jan. 1	Outstanding	=	52,500
March 1	10,500 × 10/12	=	8,750
Nov. 1	2,000 × 2/12	=	(333)
			60,917

Preferred dividend

10,000 shares × $50 par value × .06 = $30,000

Treasury stock method applied to stock options

Sale of common stock	15,000 shares × $20	=	$300,000
Repurchase of common stock	$300,000 / $25	=	12,000
Net increase in outstanding shares	15,000 - 12,000	=	3,000

Alternatively, the effect of applying the treasury stock method may be computed as follows:

(25 - 20) / 25 × 15,000 = 3,000

If-converted method applied to convertible bonds

Numerator increase	$200,000 × .10 × (1 - .35)	=	$13,000
Denominator increase	20 shares × 200 bonds	=	4,000
Dilutive effect	$13,000 / 4,000 shares	=	3.25

Basic and Diluted EPS

Numerator	Net income	$375,000	
	Preferred income	(30,000)	
		$345,000	Basic
	Impact of potential common shares:		
	Convertible bonds	13,000	
		$358,000	Diluted
Denominator	Weighted-average outstanding shares	60,917	Basic
	Impact of potential common shares:		
	Convertible bonds	4,000	
	Stock options	3,000	
		67,917	Diluted
Basic EPS		$345,000/60,917 = $5.66	
Diluted EPS		$358,000/67,917 = $5.27	

PART II: INTERPRETIVE GUIDANCE

ASC 260-10: OVERALL

ASC 260-10-45-61A, 45-68B, 55-76A through 55-76D, 65-2 Determining Whether Instruments Granted in Share-Based Transactions Are Participating Securities

BACKGROUND

Participating securities are defined in ASC 260-10-45-59A as:

> Securities that may participate in dividends with common stocks according to a predetermined formula (for example, two for one) with, at times, an upper limit on participation (for example, up to, but not beyond a specified amount per share).

Further, under the guidance in ASC 260, entities that have participating securities or multiple classes of securities with a different dividend rate for each class of security are required to compute their earnings per share by the two-class method.

The guidance on issue 2 of ASC 260-10-45-60, 45-60A through 45-68; 55-24 through 55-30, 55-71 through 55-75 (Participating Securities and the Two-Class Method under FASB Statement No. 128) (discussed below), provides that a participating security is one that may participate in undistributed earnings with common stock in its current form, regardless of whether or not participation depends on the occurrence of a specific event. However, that guidance applies *only* to share-based payment awards that are *fully* vested and ASC 260-10-45-60, 45-60A through 45-68; 55-24 through 55-30, 55-71 through 55-75 does *not* address whether unvested share-based payment awards are participating securities.

ACCOUNTING ISSUE

Can instruments granted in share-based payment transactions be participating securities before the required service has been rendered?

ACCOUNTING GUIDANCE

The computation of basic earnings per share under the two-class method should include *unvested* share-based payment awards, which include *nonforefeitable* rights to paid or unpaid dividends or dividend equivalents, because securities that include such rights are considered to be participating securities. A share-based payment award that includes a right to receive a dividend that is *not* forfeited regardless of whether the award becomes vested or remains unvested is a participating right, because it is *not* contingent on the performance of additional services after the dividend has been declared. However, an award under which the right to dividends would be forfeited if the award does *not* vest would *not* be treated as a participating right, because it does not meet the definition of a participating security. In addition, an award whose exercise price would be reduced by amounts equivalent to distributions to common shareholders would *not* be treated as a participating right; the transfer of value to the holder of the award is not a nonforfeitable right, because it would occur only if the award is exercised.

Under the guidance in ASC 718-10-55-45, nonrefundable dividends or dividend equivalents paid on awards for which the required service has *not* been or is *not* expected to be rendered and therefore do *not* vest must be recognized as additional compensation cost and dividends or dividend equivalents paid on awards for which the required service has been or is expected to be performed must be recognized in retained earnings. Consequently, dividends or dividend equivalents recognized as compensation cost on unvested share-based payment awards that are *not* expected to or do *not* vest should *not* be included in the earnings allocation for the computation of earnings per share because doing so would result in a double reduction of earnings available to common shareholders—as compensation cost and as a distribution of earnings. However, *undistributed* earnings should be allocated to all outstanding share-based payment awards, including those for which the required service is *not* expected to be performed. For the purpose of calculating EPS under the guidance in this FSP, the estimated number of awards for which it is expected that the required service will *not* be performed should be consistent with an entity's estimate used to recognize compensation cost under the guidance in ASC 718. A change in estimate of the number of awards for which the required service is *not* expected to be performed should be applied in the period in which the change in estimate occurs. Although that change in estimate will affect an entity's current period income, an entity's change in the current period of its expected forfeiture rate would *not* affect its EPS calculations in prior periods.

ASC 260-10-45-60, 45-60A through 45-68; 55-24 through 55-30, 55-71 through 55-75 Participating Securities and the Two-Class Method under FASB Statement No. 128, *Earnings* **per** *Share*

BACKGROUND

Under the guidance in ASC 260, entities that have issued participating securities, which are defined in ASC 260-10-45-59A as securities that may participate in dividends with common stock according to a prescribed formula, are required to compute earnings per share (EPS) by the two-class method. ASC 260-10-45-60B states further that the two-class method should be used for securities that are *not* convertible into a class of common stock.

In Topic D-95 (Effect of Participating Convertible Securities on the Computation of Basic Earnings per Share) (nullified by this Issue), the FASB staff clarified that participating securities convertible into common stock should be included in the computation of basic EPS if the effect of doing so is dilutive. In addition, the FASB staff stated that the decision whether basic EPS should be computed by the if-converted or the two-class method is an accounting policy. The if-converted method should *not* be used to compute basic EPS, however, if the result would be *less* dilutive than if the security were not convertible to common stock and basic EPS were computed by the two-class method. This Issue addresses questions about the application of the two-class method and its interaction with the guidance in Topic D-95.

ACCOUNTING ISSUES

1. Does the two-class method require the presentation of basic and diluted EPS for all participating securities?

1a. When should basic and diluted EPS be presented if the two-class method does not require the presentation of basic and diluted EPS for all participating securities?

2. How should a participating security requiring the application of ASC 260-10-45-60B be defined?

2a. Should all potential common shares, that is, securities or other contracts that may entitle their holders to obtain common stock (such as options, warrants, forwards, convertible debt, and convertible preferred stock), be participating securities?

2b. Do dividends or dividend equivalents paid to the holder of a convertible participating security that are applied to either reduce the conversion price or increase the conversion ratio of the security represent participation rights?

3. How should undistributed earnings be allocated to a participating security?

4. Would an entity that allocated undistributed earnings to a nonconvertible participating security continue to do so in a period of net loss if the effect is anti-dilutive?

5. Would a convertible participating security be excluded from the computation of basic EPS if an entity has a net loss from continuing operations?

6. How should a convertible participating security be included in the computation of diluted EPS?

ACCOUNTING GUIDANCE

The EITF reached the following consensus positions:

1. Under the two-class method, presentation of basic and diluted earnings per share is *not* required for all participating securities.

2. For the purpose of applying the requirements in ASC 260-10-45-59A, 45-60B, a participating security is defined as one that may participate with common stocks in undistributed earnings without considering (*a*) the form of participation and (*b*) whether participation depends on the occurrence of a specific event.

3. Dividends or dividend equivalents transferred to a holder of a convertible security in the form of a reduction of the conversion price or an increase in the security's conversion ratio are not participation rights. This consensus would also apply to other contracts or securities to issue an entity's common stock if the exercise price would be adjusted as a result of an issuer's declaration of dividends. However, this guidance does *not* apply to forward contracts to issue an entity's own equity shares because forward contracts are participating securities.

4. An issuer should consider whether a dividend or dividend equivalent applied to reduce the conversion price or increase the conversion ratio of a convertible security in its financial statements is a contingent beneficial conversion feature. That decision should be made in accordance with the guidance in ASC 470-20-05-7, 05-8; 25-4 through 6; 30-3, 30-6, 30-8, 30-10, 30-11, 30-15; 35-2, 35-7; 40-2, 40-3; 55-30 through 55-33, 55-35 through 55-38, 55-40 through 55-43, 55-45 through 55-48, 55-50 through 55-54, 55-54A, 55-56 through 55-60, 55-60A, 55-62 through 55-66, 55-69; 505-10-50-8 (See "Accounting for Convertible Securities with Beneficial Conversion Features or Contingently Adjustable Conversion Ratios") and "Application of Issue No. 98-5 to Certain Convertible Instruments" in Chapter 33, "ASC 470—Debt")

5. Undistributed earnings for a period should be allocated based on a security's contractual participation rights to share in current earnings as if all of the earnings for the period had been distributed. Undistributed earnings should *not* be allocated based on arbitrary assumptions if the participating security's terms do *not* state objectively determinable, nondiscretionary participation rights. This consensus is based on the guidance in ASC 260-10-45-60B which states that under the two-class method, "the remaining earnings shall be allocated to common stock and participating securities to the extent that each security may share in earnings as if all the earnings for the period had been distributed," even though this is a pro forma allocation and may not represent the economic probabilities of actual distributions to the holders of the participating securities.

6. An entity should allocate losses to a nonconvertible participating security in a period in which the entity has a net loss if the security's contractual terms provide that, in addition to the right to participate in the issuer's earnings, the security also has an obligation to share in the issuer's losses on an objectively determinable basis. A holder of a nonconvertible participating security has an obligation to share in the issuer's losses if either of the following conditions exists:

   a. The holder has an obligation to commit assets in addition to the initial investment to fund the issuing entity's losses without increasing the holder's investment interest in the entity.

b. The participating security's contractual principal or mandatory redemption amount is reduced by the issuing entity's incurred losses.

7. The basis for the guidance in item 6 (above) also applies to the inclusion of convertible securities in basic EPS when an issuer has a net loss and the security's contractual terms provide that the participating security has an obligation to share in the issuer's losses on an objectively determinable basis. The existence of an obligation to share in an issuer's losses should be determined in the applicable reporting period based on the security's contractual rights and obligations.

8. The computation of basic EPS using the two-class method should include participating securities.

9. All securities that meet the definition of a participating security in item 2 (above) should be included in the computation of basic EPS under the two-class method, regardless of whether they are convertible, nonconvertible, or potential common stock securities.

10. Until options or shares are fully vested, the guidance in this Issue does not apply to stock-based compensation, accounted for under the provisions of ASC 718 (FAS-123(R), Share-Based Payments), such as options and nonvested stock that include a right to receive dividends declared on an issuer's common stock.

ASC 260-10-45-43 through 45-44; 55-78 through 55-79, 55-81 through 55-82, 55-84 through 55-84B The Effect of Contingently Convertible Instruments on Diluted Earnings per Share

BACKGROUND

This issue addresses the question of when to include the dilutive effect of contingently convertible debt instruments (Co-Cos) in diluted earnings per share (EPS). Co-Cos are convertible debt instruments that include a contingent feature and are generally convertible into an issuer's common shares after the stock price of the issuer's common stock exceeds a predetermined amount for a specified period of time, known as the market price trigger. A Co-Co's conversion price usually is higher than the underlying stock's market price when the Co-Co is issued and its market price trigger usually is higher than the conversion price. Because the market price trigger is higher than the conversion price, a Co-Co is less likely to be converted than is a convertible debt instrument without a market price trigger.

The Issue was discussed because some issuers were accounting for Co-Cos differently than for convertible debt without a market price trigger. That is, most issuers of Co-Cos are not including the instrument's dilutive effect in diluted EPS until the market price trigger has been reached. Some issuers, however, are including the dilutive effect of convertible debt without a market price trigger in diluted EPS as of the instrument's issue date.

ACCOUNTING ISSUE

When should the dilutive effect of a contingently convertible instrument be included in diluted earnings per share calculations?

ACCOUNTING GUIDANCE

All financial instruments with embedded contingent conversion features, such as contingently convertible debt and contingently preferred stock should be included in the calculation of diluted earnings per share, if dilutive, without considering whether the market conditions for conversion have been met, because the economics of such instruments do not differ from conventional convertible debt with a market price conversion premium. Instruments with more than one contingency also should be included if at least one of the instrument's contingencies requires the occurrence of a market condition that would trigger conversion, regardless of whether a non-market condition, such as a change in control, has been met. Instruments requiring that both a market trigger *and* a substantive nonmarket-based contingency be met for conversion to occur, however, are *not* included under the scope of this Issue until the non-market-based contingency has occurred.

ASC 260-10-05-3 through 05-5; 15-5; 45-72 through 45-73; 55-103 through 55-110 Application of the Two-Class Method under FASB Statement No. 128, *Earnings per Share*, **to Master Limited Partnerships**

BACKGROUND

Master limited partnerships (MLPs) that are publicly traded may issue several classes of securities with the right to participate in a partnership's distributions based on a formula that is specified in the partnership agreement. Generally, an MLP's capital structure is composed of publicly traded "common units" that are held by its limited partners (LPs), a general partner (GP) interest, and holders of incentive distribution rights (IDRs), which may be a separate class of non-voting LP interests depending on the MLP's capital structure. In some cases, IDRs may initially be held by a GP that may transfer or sell them separately from its general interest, but sometimes IDRs are embedded in a GP's interest so that they cannot be detached and sold separately from the GP's interest in the MLP.

In accordance with the provisions of a partnership agreement, a GP usually is required to distribute 100% of an MLP's "available cash" (as defined in the partnership agreement) to the GP and the LPs at the end of each reporting period. That distribution is based on a schedule referred to as a "waterfall," which stipulates the distributions at each threshold. As certain thresholds are met, available cash is distributed further to holders of IDRs or to a GP whose IDRs are embedded in the GP's interest in the MLP. The timing of a distribution after the end of a reporting period is stipulated in an MLP's contract. "Available cash" is defined as all cash on hand at the end of each reporting period *less* cash retained by the partnership as capital to: (1) operate the business; (2) meet debt obligations and other legal obligations; and (3) provide funds for distribution to the holders of common units, the GP, and the IDR holders for one or more of the following reporting periods. After considering priority income allocations as a result of incentive distributions, a partnership's net income or loss is distributed to its GP's and LPs' capital accounts based on their respective sharing of income and losses stated in the partnership agreement.

Because of their capital structure, MLPs must compute earnings per unit (EPU) under the provisions for the two-class method discussed in ASC 260, which requires that undistributed earnings be allocated to common units and participating securities as if all of the period's earnings had been distributed. However, under the guidance in Issue 3 of "Participating Securities and the Two-Class Method under FASB Statement No. 128" (discussed above), a reporting period's undistributed earnings are allocated to a participating security based on its contractual participation rights to share in the current period's earnings as if *all* of that period's earnings had been distributed. Consequently, the FASB received requests for guidance on the effect of IDRs on the computation of EPU when the two-class method is applied to the interests of an MLP's LPs and its GP.

ACCOUNTING GUIDANCE

The following conclusions were reached:

- *Scope.* The guidance in this Issue applies to MLPs making incentive distributions that are treated as equity distributions when certain thresholds are met. This Issue does *not* provide guidance for determining whether an incentive distribution should be accounted for as an equity distribution or as compensation cost.

- *IDRs that are a separate class of LP interest.* IDRs that are held separately are participating securities because they are entitled to participate in earnings with common equity holders. Consequently, an MLP's earnings for a reporting period should be allocated to the GP, LPs, and IDR holders using the two-class method in ASC 260 to calculate EPU as follows:

    — When the two-class method is used to calculate an MLP's EPU, the current period's net income (or loss) should be reduced (or increased) by the amount of available cash that has been or will be distributed for that period to the GP, LPs, and IDR holders. For example, under the XYZ MLP's partnership agreement, its GP is required to distribute available cash within 60 days after the end of each fiscal quarter. Because XYZ must file its financial statements with a regulatory agency within 45 days after the end of each fiscal quarter, the amount of available cash that will be distributed to the GP, LPs, and IDR holders must be determined in order to calculate the MLP's EPU for the first quarter. Further, XYZ's income or loss must be reduced (or increased) by the amount of available cash to be distributed in order to compute the *undistributed* earnings that must be allocated to the GP, LPs, and IDR holders in the computation of the first quarter's EPU.

    — *Undistributed earnings*, if any, should be distributed to the GP, LPs, and IDR holders based on the terms of the partnership agreement. Although available cash must be distributed for the period presented based on the distribution waterfall specified in the partnership agreement, undistributed earning must be distributed to IDR holders based on an IDR's *contractual participation rights* to share in the current period's earnings. However, if a partnership agreement includes a "specified threshold" for the distribution of undistributed earnings (e.g., 5% of earnings), as discussed in ASC 260-10-55-24, undistributed earnings should *not* be distributed to an IDR holder beyond that specified threshold.

— To determine whether there is a specified threshold for distributions to IDR holders, it is necessary to evaluate whether such distributions are contractually limited to available cash, as defined in the partnership agreement, if all of a period's earnings have been distributed. In that case, an IDR holder that has received a distribution of available cash up to its specific threshold would *not* be eligible to share *in undistributed* earnings. However, if a partnership agreement's provisions do *not* specifically limit distributions to IDR holders to available cash, undistributed earnings should be distributed to IDR holders based on the partnership agreement's distribution waterfall for available cash.

— If cash distributions *exceed* current-period earnings, such excess distributions over earnings should be allocated to the GP and LPs based on the partnership agreement's provisions for the allocation of losses to the respective partners' capital accounts. If IDR holders do *not* have a contractual obligation to share in an MLP's losses, *no* portion of an excess distribution over earnings would be allocated to them. However, if IDR holders have a contractual obligation to share in an MLP's losses on an objectively determined basis, excess distributions, if any, would be allocated to the GP, LPs, and IDR holders based on the partnership agreement's provisions for their respective sharing of losses.

- *IDRs embedded in a GP's interest.* Although IDRs embedded in a GP's interest are not separate participating securities, the two-class method should be used to calculate EPU for the GP's and LPs' interests because those interests are separate classes of equity:

  — When an MLP's EPU is calculated under the two-class method, the current period's net income (or loss) should be reduced (or increased) by the amount of available cash that has been or will be distributed for that period to the GP (including the embedded IDR's distribution rights) and LPs. For example, under the XYZ MLP's partnership agreement, its GP is required to distribute available cash within 60 days after the end of each fiscal quarter. Because XYZ must file financial statements with a regulatory agency within 45 days after the end of each fiscal quarter, the amount of available cash that will be distributed to the GP and LPs must be determined in order to calculate the MLP's EPU for the first quarter. Furthermore, XYZ's income or loss should be reduced (or increased) by the amount of available cash to be distributed in order to compute the *undistributed* earnings that must be allocated to the GP and LPs in the computation of the first quarter's EPU.

- *Undistributed earnings.* Undistributed earnings, if any, should be distributed to the GP (including the embedded IDR's distribution rights) and LPs based on the terms of the partnership agreement. Although *available cash* must be distributed for the period presented based on the distribution waterfall specified in the partnership agreement, undistributed earnings should be distributed to the GP based on an embedded IDR's *contractual participation rights* to share in the current period's earnings. However, if a partnership agreement includes a specified threshold for the distribution of undistributed earnings (e.g., 5% of earnings), as discussed in ASC 260-10-55-24, undistributed earnings should *not* be distributed to the GP for the embedded IDR's distribution rights beyond that specified threshold:
    — To determine whether there is a specified threshold for distributions to a GP for the embedded IDR's distribution rights, it is necessary to evaluate whether such distributions are contractually limited to available cash, as defined in the partnership agreement, if all of a period's earnings have been distributed. In that case, a GP that has received a distribution of available cash up to its specific threshold for the embedded IDR's distribution rights would *not* be eligible to share in undistributed earnings. However, if a partnership agreement's provisions do *not* specifically limit distributions to a GP for the distribution rights of embedded IDRs to available cash, undistributed earnings should be distributed to the GP for the distribution rights of embedded IDRs based on the partnership agreement's distribution waterfall for available cash.
    — If cash distributions *exceed* current-period earnings, such excess distributions over earnings would be allocated to the GP and LPs based on the partnership agreement's provisions for their respective sharing of losses for the period.

ASC 260-10-99S-2 The Effect on the Calculation of Earnings per Share for a Period that Includes the Redemption or Induced Conversion of Preferred Stock

The SEC staff's guidance in this announcement has been amended by ASU 2009-8.

The SEC staff's guidance applies to redemptions and induced conversions of preferred stock instruments that are classified in equity. Such transactions should be accounted for as follows:

- An exchange or modification of preferred stock instruments is considered a redemption if the transaction is accounted for as an extinguishment and results in a new basis of accounting for the modified or exchanged preferred stock.

- The guidance in this pronouncement applies to redemptions and induced conversions of preferred stock classified in temporary equity under the guidance in ASR 268 and ASC 480-10-S99-3A (Topic D-98), which are considered to be classified in equity.
- A subsequent reclassification of an equity security to a liability based on guidance in other GAAP (e.g., if a preferred share becomes mandatorily redeemable under the guidance in ASC 480-10) is considered to be a redemption of equity by means of issuing a debt instrument.

This announcement does not affect the accounting for conversions of preferred stock into other securities classified as equity as a result of conversion privileges included under the terms of instruments at issuance.

The SEC staff believes that on such redemptions or conversions, the difference between the fair value of the consideration transferred to the preferred stockholders and the carrying amount of the preferred stock in the registrant's balance sheet (net of issuance costs) should be subtracted from or added to net income for the calculation of income available to common stockholders used in computing earnings per share. The SEC staff believes that the difference between the fair value of the consideration transferred to the preferred stockholders and the carrying amount of the preferred stock in the registrant's balance sheet represents a return to the preferred shareholder that should be treated similarly to dividends paid on preferred stock whether or not the embedded conversion feature is "in the money" or "out of the money" at redemption. If a redemption includes the reacquisition of a beneficial conversion feature in a convertible preferred stock that had previously been recognized, the fair value of the consideration transferred should be reduced by the intrinsic value of the conversion option at the commitment date.

The SEC Staff believes that if the fair value of securities and other consideration transferred by a registrant to the holders of convertible preferred stock as a result of an offer inducing conversion exceeds the fair value of the securities that would have been issued based on the original conversion terms, the difference should be subtracted from net earnings used to calculate net earnings available to common shareholders in the earnings per share calculation. Registrants should follow the guidance in ASC 470-20-05-10; 40-13 through 40-17; 45-2; 55-2 through 55-9 to determine whether conversion occurred as a result of an inducement offer.

SEC OBSERVER COMMENT

Subsequently, the SEC Observer responded to a question about the accounting for redemption of convertible preferred stock that has appreciated since issuance. He reiterated that the guidance stated above applies to all classes of preferred stock and that the entire redemption amount that exceeds the *carrying amount* of the preferred stock should be deducted from earnings available to common shareholders. (See below in ASC 260-10-S99 and the discussion in ASC 470-20-40-13, "Determining Whether Certain Conversions of Convertible Debt to Equity Securities Are within the Scope of FASB Statement No. 84, *Induced Conversions of Convertible Debt*" in Chapter 33, "ASC 470—Debt.")

ASC 260-10-S99-3 Computation of Earnings per Share for a Period That Includes a Redemption or an Induced Conversion of a Portion of a Class of Preferred Stock

If only a portion of the outstanding securities of a class of preferred stock is redeemed or converted as a result of an induced conversion, the SEC staff believes that to determine whether the "if converted" method is dilutive for the period, those shares should be considered separately from other shares of the same class that have not been redeemed or converted. The staff also believes that preferred securities with different effective dividend yields should not be combined in testing whether the "if converted" method is dilutive.

To illustrate, a registrant has 100 shares of convertible preferred stock outstanding at the beginning of the period and redeems 20 convertible preferred shares during the period.

FACTS:

Fair value at issuance: $10 per share

Par value: $10 per share

Stated dividend: 5 percent

Dividend for the period: $0.125

Conversion ratio: 1 share of convertible preferred into 1 share of common stock

Redemption premium: $2

The SEC staff believes that the registrant should determine whether the conversion is dilutive:

4. For the 80 preferred shares not redeemed—Apply the "if converted" method from the beginning of the period to the end of the period using the stated 5 percent dividend

5. For the 20 preferred shares redeemed—Apply the "if converted" method from the beginning of the period to the date of redemption using the stated 5 percent dividend and the $2 redemption premium per share.

CALCULATION:

- To determine whether the 20 redeemed shares are dilutive, compare the effect of $2 plus $0.125 = $2.125 per share if the shares were converted into 20 shares of common stock to the effect if they had not been converted, weighted for the period for which were outstanding.
- The "if converted" effect of the 80 shares should be determined separately from the redeemed shares by comparing the EPS effect of the $0.125 dividend per share to the effect of those 80 shares if they had been converted into 80 shares of common stock.

ASC 260-10-55-3A, 55-3B, 55-85 through 55-87 Computing Year-to-Date Diluted Earnings per Share under FASB Statement No. 128

BACKGROUND

A member of the FASB staff discussed their view on the computation of a company's year-to-date diluted EPS if it has a year-to-date loss from continuing operations but has had income from continuing operations in one or more quarters. The question was raised because the guidance in ASC 260-10-45-17; 260-10-55-3 seems to conflict when a company has a year-to-date loss for a period of more than three months but has had income in some quarters during the year. ASC 260-10-55-3 provides the following computational guidance for applying the treasury stock method; the number of incremental shares that will be included in the denominator is determined by computing the year-to-date weighted average of incremental shares included in each quarterly computation of diluted EPS, however, the antidilution rule in ASC 260-10-45-19 states that the conversion, exercise, or contingent issuance of securities should not be assumed if the effect on EPS is antidilutive.

ACCOUNTING GUIDANCE

The FASB staff believes that the guidance in ASC 260-10-45-17 should be followed; therefore, no potential common shares (incremental shares) should be included in the computation of diluted EPS if the result is antidilutive.

Illustration of Quarterly and Year-to-Date Calculation

ABC Company has:

- 20,000 common shares outstanding
- 2,000 shares of preferred stock convertible into 4,000 common shares
- Quarterly income (loss) (same as income from continuing operations) as follows:

	Q1:	Q2:	Q3:	Q4:
	$20,000	($30,000)	($8,000)	$10,000

Quarterly EPS

	Q1	Q2	Q3	Q4
Income	$20,000	$(30,000)	($8,000)	$10,000
Common shares	20,000	20,000	20,000	20,000
Incremental shares	4,000	0*	0*	4,000
Basic EPS	$1.00	($1.50)	($.40)	$.50
Diluted EPS	$.83	($1.50)	($.40)	$.42

Year-to-date EPS

	Q1	Q2	Q3	Q4
Income	$20,000	($10,000)	($18,000)	$(8,000)
Common shares	20,000	20,000	20,000	20,000
Incremental shares	4,000	0*	0*	0*
Basic EPS	$1.00	($.50)	($.90)	($.40)
Diluted EPS	$.83	($.50)	($.90)	($.40)

* Incremental shares are not included because they are antidilutive.

ASC 260-10-55-32, 55-34, 55-36, 55-36A; 45-22 Effect of Contracts That May Be Settled in Stock or Cash on the Computation of Diluted Earnings per Share

> **OBSERVATION:** The requirements for calculating earnings per share (EPS) in this announcement and for mandatorily redeemable financial instruments and forward contracts requiring physical settlement by repurchasing a fixed number of shares in exchange for cash are partially nullified by the guidance in ASC 480-10-05-1 through 05-6; 10-1; 15-3 through 15-5, 15-7 through 15-10; 25-1 through 25-2, 25-4 through 25-15; 30-1 through 30-7; 35-3 through 35-5; 45-1 through 45-4; 50-1 through 50-4; 55-1 through 55-12, 55-14 through 55-28, 55-34 through 55-41, 55-64; 835-10-60-13. ASC 260-10-45-70A (FAS-150) requires that such instruments be classified as liabilities. Consequently, ASC 480-10-45-4 requires that common shares redeemed or repurchased be excluded from the calculation of basic and diluted earnings per share. Amounts, if any, related to such shares that have not been recognized as interest cost, such as participation rights, should be deducted from the numerator in the calculation, which is income available to common shareholders. This treatment is consistent with the "two-class" method discussed in ASC 260-10-45-60B. The guidance in this announcement continues to apply to other financial instruments, including those that are recognized as liabilities under the provisions of ASC 480, Distinguishing Liabilities and Equity.

A FASB staff representative announced the staff's view on the effect on a company's computation of diluted EPS for contracts indexed to and potentially settled in the company's own stock.

The guidance in ASC 815-40, Contracts in an Entity's Own Equity, states that freestanding contracts that must be settled in net cash generally should be recognized as assets or liabilities and contracts that must be settled in shares should be recognized as equity instruments. It is assumed that contracts that permit a *company* to choose whether to settle in net cash or in net shares are settled in net shares. Similarly, it is assumed that contracts that permit the *counterparty* to choose whether to settle in net cash or in net shares are settled in net cash.

ASC 260-10-45-45 through 45-46 provides guidance on the effect of such contracts on the issuer's calculation of EPS. It provides that if the issuer or the counterparty can choose the method of settling a contract, it is presumed that the contract will be settled in shares and the potential common shares should be included in diluted EPS, if the effect is dilutive. That presumption may be overcome, however, if it is reasonable to believe that the contract will be settled in cash based on the company's stated policy on the settlement method or past practice.

That guidance is inconsistent with the guidance in ASC 815-40, Contracts in an Entity's Own Equity, because under that guidance, initial balance sheet recognition of such contracts does not consider a company's stated policy on the settlement method or past experience. Nevertheless, ASC 260-10-45-45 through 45-46 addresses the effect of that inconsistency on the computation of diluted earnings per share for contracts classified as assets or liabilities according to the guidance in ASC 815-40. It states that the numerator of contracts reported as assets or liabilities for accounting purposes may need to be adjusted for the difference between the reported income or loss, if any, and the amount that would have been reported had the contracts been accounted for as equity instruments during the reporting period.

Likewise, the FASB staff believes that the numerator should be adjusted for contracts accounted for as equity instruments under the guidance ASC 460-10-60-14; 480-10-55-63; 505-10-60-5; 815-10-15-78; 55-52; 815-15-25-15; 815-40-05-1 through 05-4, 05-10 through 05-12; 25-1 through 25-5, 25-7 through 25-20, 25-22 through 25-24, 25-26 through 25-35; 25-37 through 25-40; 30-1; 35-1, 35-2, 35-4 through 35-6, 35-8 through 35-13; 40-1, 40-2; 50-1 through 50-5; 55-1 through 55-18 (formerly Issue 00-19), if it is reasonable to believe that those contracts will be settled partially or wholly in cash based on the company's stated policy or past practice. The numerator for such contracts may need to be adjusted for the difference between the reported income or loss, if any, and the amount that would have been reported had the contracts been accounted for as assets or liabilities during the reporting period. In addition, the denominator would not include potential dilutive shares. The FASB staff noted that such adjustments to the numerator for the purpose of computing diluted earnings per share should be made only for contracts that qualify to be accounted for based on the guidance in Issue 00-19 (see ASC references above), because net income would be affected differently by the classification of the contract as an asset or liability or as an equity instrument. The guidance in ASC 260-10-45-45 through 45-46 (formerly paragraph 29 of FAS-128) should be used to determine whether shares issued for stock-based compensation arrangements that are payable in common stock or in cash at the election of the entity or the employee should be included in the denominator in computing diluted EPS. In those situations, the numerator is not adjusted.

The FASB staff clarified that under the guidance in ASC 260-10-45-45 through 45-46, it is assumed that the company will settle the contract in shares if the company can choose the settlement method under the contract. This presumption can be overcome based on the company's past practice or policy. However, if the counterparty chooses the settlement method, the company's past practice or policy would not affect the accounting. In that case, the company should use the more dilutive settlement method in its EPS calculation.

Under certain circumstances, it may be necessary to adjust the numerator in year-to-date diluted EPS calculations. If, for example, the counterparty can choose the settlement method and a settlement in shares would have a more dilutive effect, the numerator would be adjusted for the effect on earnings of the asset or liability's change in fair value recognized during the year-to-date period in accordance with the guidance in ASC 815-40. The number of additional shares included in the denominator in that example is calculated by determining the number of shares necessary to settle the contract at the average price per share during the year-to-date period.

The staff noted that the calculation of diluted earnings per share should exclude antidilutive contracts such as purchased put options and purchased call options.

The FASB staff summarized the interaction between the requirements in ASC 260 and ASC 815-40 as follows:

Settlement method assumed*	Accounting method (per 96-13)	Should recorded earnings (numerator) be adjusted to compute diluted earnings per share?	Should number of shares included in denominator be adjusted?
Shares	Asset/liability	Yes (according to ASC 260-10-45-45 through 45-46)	Yes
Shares	Equity	No	Yes
Cash	Asset/liability	No	No
Cash	Equity	Yes (according to this staff announcement)	No

* For the purpose of computing EPS, it is assumed that an exchange of the full amount of cash for the full stated number of shares (physical settlement) is considered a share settlement.

ASC 260-10-45-11, 45-12 Effect of Preferred Stock Dividends Payable in Common Shares on Computation of Income Available to Common Stockholders

This announcement clarifies the accounting for preferred stock dividends that an issuer has paid or intends to pay in its own common shares when the issuer computes income available to common stockholders. The FASB staff announced that in accordance with the definition of income available to common stockholders in ASC, *Glossary*, and the guidance in ASC 260-10-45-11, issuers should adjust the amount of net income or loss for dividends on preferred stock, regardless of the method of payment. The staff noted that this approach is consistent with the accounting for common stock issued for goods and services. To apply the guidance in this announcement, issuers should restate earnings per share reported in prior periods.

CHAPTER 12
ASC 270—INTERIM REPORTING

CONTENTS

General Guidance	12,001
ASC 270-10: Overall	12,001
Overview	12,001
Background	12,001
Accounting and Reporting in Interim Periods	12,002
Summarized Interim Financial Information	12,003
Illustration of Format for Presenting Interim Financial Information	12,005

GENERAL GUIDANCE

ASC 270-10: OVERALL

OVERVIEW

Interim financial reports may be issued quarterly, monthly, or at other intervals, and may include complete financial statements or summarized information. In addition, they usually include the current interim period and a cumulative year-to-date period, or last 12 months to date, with comparative reports on the corresponding periods of the immediately preceding fiscal year.

BACKGROUND

The majority of GAAP have been developed for annual financial reporting purposes. These reporting standards generally are also applicable to interim financial reports. Some problems exist, however, in attempting to apply GAAP intended primarily for annual reporting purposes to financial reporting for shorter periods of time.

Two competing approaches explain the relationship between interim financial reports and annual financial reports. The *discrete* approach, sometimes called the *independent* approach, views an interim period in the same way as an annual period. Within this approach accounting principles for an annual period are equally appropriate for periods of differing lengths of time and are applied in the same manner. Opposite that view is the *integral* approach, sometimes called the *dependent* approach, which views an interim period as a component, or *integral* part, of the annual period rather than as a separate or discrete period. Within this approach, the purpose of interim financial reporting is to provide information over the course of the annual period that assists in anticipating annual results.

ASC 270 endorses certain aspects of both the discrete and integral approaches, but generally favors the *integral*, or *dependent*, approach to financial reporting for interim periods. Accordingly, certain procedures that are used in reporting for annual periods are modified in reporting for interim periods.

PRACTICE POINTER: Take care in preparing and reviewing interim financial information *not* to assume that GAAP appropriate for *annual* financial statements has been applied. Examples where GAAP may differ are the determination of cost of goods sold where a LIFO inventory layer has been eroded in an early interim period, accounting for income taxes on a cumulative year-to-date basis, and the determination of the materiality of items in interim financial statements.

ACCOUNTING AND REPORTING IN INTERIM PERIODS

Each interim period should generally be viewed as an integral part of the annual period. An important objective of interim reporting is for the user of the information to become progressively better informed about annual information as time passes. Accounting principles and reporting practices generally are those of the latest annual reports of the entity, with limited exceptions, such as a change in an accounting principle (ASC 270-10-45-2). A change in an accounting principle during an interim period is discussed in the chapter covering ASC 250 (Accounting Changes and Error Corrections).

Revenues are recognized as earned on the same basis as fiscal periods (ASC 270-10-45-3).

As closely as possible, product costs are determined as those for the fiscal period with some exceptions for inventory valuation, as follows (ASC 270-10-45-5, 6):

- Companies using the gross profit method to determine interim inventory costs, or other estimation methods different from those used for annual inventory valuation, should disclose the method used at the interim date and any significant adjustments that result from reconciliation(s) with the annual physical inventory.

- A liquidation of a base-period LIFO inventory at an interim date that is expected to be recovered by the end of the annual period is valued at the expected cost of replacement. Cost of sales for the interim period includes the expected cost of replacement and not the cost of the base-period LIFO inventory.

- Inventory losses from market declines are included in the interim period in which they occur, and gains in subsequent interim periods are recognized in such interim periods but cannot exceed the losses included in prior interim periods. (*Temporary* market declines that are expected to be made up by the end of the annual period need not be recognized in interim periods.)

- Inventory and product costs computed by the use of a standard cost accounting system are determined by the same procedures used at the end of a fiscal year. Variances from standard costs that are expected to be made up by the end of the fiscal year need not be included in interim-period statements.

ASC 270—Interim Reporting **12,003**

> **PRACTICE POINTER:** Although all four of these procedures are acceptable in interim financial statements, they are not considered GAAP for purposes of annual financial statements. Some may result in material differences in the amount of net income (e.g., using the replacement cost for erosion of a LIFO layer in an early interim period), and care should be taken that a similar procedure is not used in annual financial statements.

Other costs and expenses are charged or allocated to produce a fair presentation of the results of operations, cash flows, and financial position for all interim periods. The following apply in accounting for other costs and expenses:

- A general rule in preparing interim-period financial statements is that costs and expenses that clearly benefit more than one period are allocated to the periods affected. This procedure should be applied consistently (ASC 270-10-45-9).
- Companies that have material seasonal revenue variations must take care to avoid the possibility that interim-period financial statements become misleading. Disclosure of such variations should be made in the interim-period financial statements. In addition, it is desirable to disclose results for a full year, ending with the current interim period (ASC 270-10-45-11).
- Unusual and infrequent transactions that are material and not designated as extraordinary items, such as the effects of a disposal of a segment of business, are reported separately in the interim periods in which they occur (ASC 270-10-45-11A).
- All other pertinent information, such as accounting changes, contingencies, seasonal results, and business combinations, is disclosed to provide the necessary information for the proper understanding of the interim financial statements (ASC 270-10-50-5, 6).

Interim reports should not contain arbitrary amounts of costs or expenses. Estimates should be reasonable and based on all available information applied consistently from period to period (ASC 270-10-45-10). An effective tax rate is used for determining the income tax provision in interim periods, applied on a cumulative year-to-date basis (ASC 740-270-30-4, 5). Income taxes for interim-period reports are discussed in *GAAP Guide* Chapter 44, ASC 740—Income Taxes.

Material contingencies and other uncertainties that exist at an interim date are disclosed in interim reports in the same manner as that required for annual reports. These interim-date contingencies and uncertainties should be evaluated in relation to the annual report. The disclosure for such items must be repeated in every interim and annual report until the contingency is resolved or becomes immaterial (ASC 270-10-50-6).

SUMMARIZED INTERIM FINANCIAL INFORMATION

Publicly traded companies reporting summarized financial information at interim dates should include the following (ASC 270-10-50-1):

- Gross revenues, provision for income taxes, extraordinary items, effects of changes in accounting principles, and net income
- Basic and diluted earnings-per-share data
- Material seasonal variations of revenues, costs, or expenses

- Significant changes in estimates or provisions for income taxes
- Disposal of a segment of a business and extraordinary, unusual, or infrequently occurring items
- Contingent items
- Changes in accounting principles or estimates
- Significant changes in financial position
- Information about fair value recognized in the statement of position per ASC 820 (Fair Value Measurement)
- Information about derivative instruments as required by ASC 815 (Derivatives and Hedging)
- Information about the credit quality of financing receivables and the allowance for credit losses determined in accordance with ASC 310 (Receivables), including:
  — Nonaccrual and past due financing receivables

  — Allowance for credit losses related to financing receivables

  — Impaired loans

  — Credit quality information related to financing receivables

  — Modifications of financing receivables

PRACTICE POINTER: To satisfy the above disclosure requirements, companies may present abbreviated financial statements, separate information items, or both. For example, a company may present an abbreviated income statement and selected information items from the balance sheet and statement of cash flows. Another company may present abbreviated versions of all financial statements. In all approaches, companies typically omit most of the detailed note disclosures that are required in annual financial statements.

When summarized financial information is reported regularly on a quarterly basis, the above information should be furnished for the current quarter, the current year-to-date or the last twelve months to date, with comparable information for the preceding year (ASC 270-10-50-1). (The illustration at the end of this chapter suggests a format for this information.)

PRACTICE POINTER: Summarized interim financial statements based on these minimum disclosures *do not* constitute a fair presentation of financial position and results of operations in conformity with GAAP. Care should be taken that statements do not imply that interim information is in accordance with GAAP for annual financial statements unless it is (which is rarely the case).

PRACTICE POINTER: The authors favor presenting the last 12 months for comparative information rather than year-to-date information. Presenting last 12 month information is generally more useful for assessing the current interim period impact on annual results.

In the event that fourth-quarter results are not issued separately, the annual report should include disclosures for the fourth quarter on the aggregate effect of material year-end adjustments and infrequently occurring items, extraordinary items, and disposal of business segments that occurred in the fourth quarter (ASC 270-10-50-2).

Illustration of Format for Presenting Interim Financial Information

When quarterly information is regularly reported by publicly held companies, ASC 270 requires (1) minimum disclosure of specific information items for the current quarter and comparable information for the same quarter of the previous year and (2) current year-to-date or twelve-months-to-date information and comparable information for the same period of the previous year.

The following is a suggested format, using illustrative dates and numbers, for the presentation of this information:

Hypothetical Company Interim Financial Information For Quarter Ending June 30, 20X8, and Comparable Periods (in thousands)

	Current Quarter		Twelve-Months-to-Date	
	3 months ending 6/30/20X8	3 months ending 6/30/20X7	Year ending 6/30/20X8	Year ending 6/30/20X7
[Information item]	$50	$40	$425	$575

13,001

CHAPTER 13
ASC 272—LIMITED LIABILITY ENTITIES

CONTENTS

Interpretive Guidance	**13,001**
ASC 272-10: Overall	**13,001**
ASC 272-10-05-1, 05-2, 05-5, 05-6; 45-1 through 45-7; 50-1 through 50-5; ASC 850-10-60-9	
Accounting and Reporting by Limited Liability Companies and Limited Liability Partnerships	**13,001**
ASC 272-10-05-3, 05-4; ASC 323-30-35-3; 15-4	
Accounting for Investments in Limited Liability Companies	**13,003**

INTERPRETIVE GUIDANCE

ASC 272-10: OVERALL

ASC 272-10-05-1, 05-2, 05-5, 05-6; 45-1 through 45-7; 50-1 through 50-5; ASC 850-10-60-9 Accounting and Reporting by Limited Liability Companies and Limited Liability Partnerships

BACKGROUND

Limited liability companies and limited liability partnerships (referred to hereafter as LLCs) are formed under the laws of individual states and therefore have characteristics that are not uniform. Generally, however, they have the following characteristics:

- They are unincorporated associations of two or more persons.
- Their members have limited personal liability for the obligations of the LLC.
- They are treated as partnerships for federal income tax purposes.
- At least two of the following corporate characteristics are lacking:
  — Limited liability
  — Free transferability of interests
  — Centralized management
  — Continuity of life

PB-14 provides guidance for U.S. LLCs that prepare financial statements in accordance with generally accepted accounting principles.

ACCOUNTING GUIDANCE

LLCs that are subject to U.S. federal, foreign, state, or local taxes (including franchise taxes) must account for those taxes in accordance with the guidance in ASC 740 (Income Taxes), including accounting for a change in tax status.

Financial Statement Display

- A complete set of financial statements must include the following:
  — Statement of financial position
  — Statement of operations
  — Statement of cash flows
  — Notes to financial statements
- Disclosure is required of changes in members' equity for the period, either in a separate statement or in notes to the financial statements.
- The equity section of the statement of financial position is referred to as "members' equity." Information about the different classes of members' equity is required, including the amount of each class, stated separately, either in the financial statements (preferable) or in notes to the financial statements (acceptable).
- If the members' equity is less than zero, the deficit should be reported, even though the members' liability may be limited.
- If an LLC maintains separate accounts for components of members' equity (e.g., undistributed earnings, earnings available for withdrawal, unallocated capital), disclosure of these accounts is required in the financial statements or notes.
- If an LLC records amounts due from members for capital contributions, such amounts receivable should generally be presented as deductions from members' equity, with the very limited exception of instances where there is substantial evidence of ability and intent to pay within a reasonably short period.
- Comparative financial statements are encouraged, but not required. Any exceptions to comparability must be disclosed in the notes to the financial statements.
- If the formation of an LLC results in a new reporting entity, the guidance in ASC 250-10-45-21 for a change in reporting entity should be followed. In accordance with an amendment in Accounting Standards Update (ASU) 2010-8, a change should be applied retrospectively to prior periods presented to show financial information for the new reporting entity for those periods.

Disclosures

- The following information should be disclosed:
  — Description of any limitation of members' liability
  — The different classes of members' interests and the respective rights, preferences, and privileges of each class

- The amount of each class of members' equity included in the statement of financial position
- If an LLC has a limited life, the date on which the LLC will cease to exist.

ASC 272-10-05-3, 05-4; ASC 323-30-35-3; 15-4 Accounting for Investments in Limited Liability Companies

BACKGROUND

Although limited liability companies (LLCs) are similar both to corporations and to partnerships, LLCs also differ in many ways from those types of entities. LLCs are similar to corporations because their members generally are *not* personally liable for the LLC's liabilities. They differ from corporations in that owners of LLCs control the operations of those entities, whereas the operations of corporations are controlled by their Boards of Directors and their committees rather than by their common shareholders.

LLCs are *similar* to partnerships in the following ways: (*a*) the members of LLCs are taxed on their shares of the LLCs' earnings; (*b*) LLC members generally cannot assign their financial interests without the consent of *all* members; and (*c*) most LLCs are dissolved as a result of a member's death, bankruptcy, or withdrawal.

LLCs *differ* from partnerships in that (*a*) it is *not* necessary for *one* owner to be liable for the LLC's liabilities, such as the general partner in a limited partnership; (*b*) the owners of LLCs control the operations of those entities, unlike limited partnerships, whose operations are managed by the general partner; and (*c*) all partners in a general partnership have *unlimited* liability.

Although the authoritative accounting literature provides no specific guidance regarding the accounting for noncontrolling LLCs, the guidance in ASC 323 (Investments-Equity Method and Joint Ventures) currently is being applied in accounting for those entities. Under the provisions of ASC 323, the equity method should be used to account for investments in which an investor can exercise *significant influence* over an investee's operating and financial policies. It is presumed that investments of at least 20% meet that requirement. Even though that guidance does *not* specifically apply to partnerships, ASC 323-30-15-3; 25-2; 30-1 through 30-2; 35-1 through 35-2; 810-10-45-14 states that many of the provisions would be "appropriate in accounting" for partnerships.

ASC 970-323 states that noncontrolling interests in limited partnerships should be accounted for under the equity method, unless a limited partner's interest is "so minor that the limited partner may have virtually no influence over partnership operating and financial policies." The cost method should be used under those circumstances. Another source of guidance is ASC 323-30-S99-1; S55-1, in which the SEC staff clarifies what percentage is considered minor. It states that investments in limited partnerships of *more* than 3%-5% should be accounted for by the equity method, because they are more than minor investments.

ASC 272—Limited Liability Entities

ACCOUNTING ISSUE

To determine whether a *noncontrolling* investment in an LLC should be accounted for by the cost method or by the equity method, should an LLC be considered to be similar to a corporation or to a partnership?

ACCOUNTING GUIDANCE

The following guidance applies when determining how to account for a noncontrolling investment in an LLC:

- The guidance in this Issue does *not* apply to:
- Investments in LLCs that must be accounted for as debt securities under the guidance in ASC 860-20-35-2 (Accounting for Transfers and Servicing of Financial Assets and Extinguishments of Liabilities);
- Equity interests in LLCs that must be accounted for under the guidance in ASC 325-40-05-1 through 05-2, 15-2 through 15-9, 25-1 through 25-3, 30-1 through 30-3, 35-1 through 35-10A, 35-13, 35-16, 45-1, 55-1 through 55-2; ASC 310-20-60-1 through 60-2; ASC 310-30-15-5, 60-1; ASC 320-10-35-38, 55-2; ASC 835-10-60-7 (Recognition of Interest Income and Impairment on Purchased and Retained Beneficial Interests in Securitized Financial Assets) and
- LLCs that must be accounted for under the guidance in ASC 810-10-15-10, 25-1 through 25-8, 25-10 through 25-14, 55-1 (Investor's Accounting for an Investee When the Investor Has a Majority of the Voting Interest but the Noncontrolling Shareholder or Shareholders Have Certain Approval or Veto Rights) (see Chapter 47, ASC 810—Consolidations).

An LLC that maintains a "specific ownership account" for each investor in the LLC is treating its investors in a manner similar to the way partnership capital accounts are structured. Consequently, investments treated in that manner should be considered to be similar to limited partnerships (LPs) when determining the appropriate accounting. Such LLCs should be accounted for under the guidance in ASC 970-323 and the guidance in the SEC's announcement in ASC 323-30-S99-1, S55-1, which is discussed in Chapter 20, ASC 323—Investments—Equity Method and Joint Ventures. It was noted that specific ownership accounts may exist in entities organized in another form. The characteristics of those organizations were not considered, but some suggested that it may be appropriate for such entities to analogize to the guidance in this Issue.

CHAPTER 14
ASC 274—PERSONAL FINANCIAL STATEMENTS

CONTENTS

Interpretive Guidance	14,001
ASC 274-10: Overall	14,001
ASC 274-10-05-1 through 05-3; 15-1, 15-2; 25-1; 35-1 through 35-15; 45-1 through 45-13; 50-1, 50-2; 55-1 through 55-7, 55-9 through 55-14	
Accounting and Financial Reporting for Personal Financial Statements	14,001

INTERPRETIVE GUIDANCE

ASC 274-10: OVERALL

ASC 274-10-05-1 through 05-3; 15-1, 15-2; 25-1; 35-1 through 35-15; 45-1 through 45-13; 50-1, 50-2; 55-1 through 55-7, 55-9 through 55-14 Accounting and Financial Reporting for Personal Financial Statements

BACKGROUND

The guidance in ASC 274 addresses the preparation and presentation of personal financial statements for individuals or groups of related individuals (e.g., a husband and wife, a family).

    The primary focus of personal financial statements is on an individual's assets and liabilities. Users of personal financial statements normally consider estimated current value information to be more relevant to their decision-making than historical cost information. The guidance in ASC 274 explains how the estimated current amounts of assets and liabilities should be determined and applied in a presentation of personal financial statements.

ACCOUNTING GUIDANCE

Form of the Statements

Personal financial statements consist of the following:

- *Statement of financial condition* Presents the estimated current values of assets, estimated current amounts of liabilities, estimated income taxes on the differences between the estimated current values of assets and the estimated current amounts of liabilities and their tax bases, and net worth as of a specified date.

   The term *net worth* is used to designate the difference between total assets and total liabilities, after deduction of estimated income taxes on the differences between the current amounts of those items and their tax bases.

- *Statement of changes in net worth* Presents the major sources of increases and decreases in net worth (e.g., income or (loss)), changes in the estimated current values of assets, changes in the estimated amounts of liabilities, changes in the estimated income tax on the differences between the estimated current value of assets and the estimated current amount of liabilities and their related tax bases).
- *Comparative financial statements* Presents information about the current period and one or more prior periods (optional).

Methods of Presentation

Assets and liabilities should be recognized on the accrual basis rather than on the cash basis. The most useful presentation of assets and liabilities is in their order of liquidity and maturity, respectively, without classification as current and noncurrent.

In personal financial statements for one of a group of joint owners of assets, the statements should include only that individual's interest as a beneficial owner. Business interests that constitute a large part of an individual's total assets should be shown separately from other investments. The estimated current value of an investment in a separate entity should be shown in one amount as an investment if the entity is marketable as a going concern. Assets and liabilities of the separate entity should not be combined with similar personal items.

The estimated current values of assets and the estimated current amounts of liabilities of limited business activities not conducted in a separate business entity (e.g., investment in real estate and a related mortgage) should be presented as separate amounts, particularly if a large portion of the liabilities may be satisfied with funds from sources unrelated to the investment.

Guidelines for Determining Current Values and Amounts

The estimated current value of an asset in personal financial statements is the amount at which the item could be exchanged between a buyer and a seller, each of whom is well informed and willing, and neither of whom is compelled to buy or sell. Costs of disposal should be considered in estimating current values. Recent transactions involving similar assets and liabilities in similar circumstances ordinarily provide a reasonable basis for determining the current value of an asset and the estimated current amount of a liability. In the absence of recent similar transactions, adjustments of historical cost for changes in a specific price index, appraisals, and discounted amounts of projected cash receipts and payments may be appropriate.

Receivables

Receivables should be presented at the amounts of estimated cash that will be collected, using appropriate interest rates at the date of the financial statements.

Marketable Securities

The value of marketable securities should be based on quoted market prices, if available, based on their closing prices on the date of the financial statements if the securities were traded on that date. Bid-and-ask quotations may be used to estimate the current value of securities. An adjustment to market price may be required if an investor owns sufficient amounts of securities that if sold would influence the market price.

Options

If published prices of options are unavailable, their current value should be determined on the basis of the values of the underlying assets, taking into consideration such factors as the options' exercise price and length of the option period.

Investments in Life Insurance

The estimated current value of life insurance is the cash value of a policy less the amount of loans against it, if any. The policy's face value should be disclosed.

Investments in Closely Held Businesses

There is no one generally accepted procedure for determining the estimated current value of an investment in a closely held business. Alternative valuation procedures include the following:

- Multiple of earnings
- Liquidation value
- Reproduction value
- Appraisal
- Discounted amounts of projected cash receipts and payments
- Adjustments of book value or cost of the person's share of equity

The objective should be to approximate the amount at which an investment could be exchanged between a buyer and a seller, each of whom is well informed and willing, and neither of whom is compelled to buy or sell.

Real Estate

Investments in real estate, including leaseholds, should be presented at current value, with consideration given to information such as the following:

- Sales of similar property in similar circumstances
- The discounted amount of projected receipts and payments related to a property or a property's net realizable value, based on planned courses of action
- Appraisals based on estimates of selling prices and costs
- Appraisals used to obtain financing
- Assessed value for property taxes

Intangible Assets

Investments in intangible assets should be based on discounted amounts of projected cash receipts and payments based on the planned use or sale of the assets. A purchased intangible asset's cost may be used if no other information is available.

Future Interests and Similar Assets

Rights to receive future sums that will not be forfeited should be presented as assets at their discounted amounts if those rights have all of the following characteristics:

- The rights are for fixed or determinable amounts.
- The rights are not contingent on a holder's life expectancy or the occurrence of a particular event, such as disability or death.
- The rights do not require a holder to perform future services.

Examples of rights that may have those characteristics are guaranteed minimum portions of pensions, deferred compensation contracts, and beneficial interests in trusts.

Payables and Other Liabilities

Payables and other liabilities should be presented at their discounted amounts of cash to be paid. The discount rate should be the rate implicit in the transaction in which the debt was incurred—unless the debtor is able to discharge the debt currently at a lower amount, in which case the debt should be presented at the lower amount.

Noncancelable Commitments

Noncancelable commitments to pay future sums should be presented as liabilities at their discounted amounts if those commitments have all of the following characteristics:

- The commitments are for fixed or determinable amounts.
- The commitments are not contingent on others' life expectancies or on the occurrence of a particular event, such as disability or death.
- The commitments do not require future performance of services by others.

Income Taxes Payable

A liability for income taxes should include unpaid income taxes for completed tax years and an estimate of the amount of accrued income taxes for the elapsed portion of the financial statements' current year.

Estimated Income Taxes on the Difference between the Estimated Current Values of Assets and the Current Amounts of Liabilities and Their Tax Bases

A provision should be made for estimated income taxes on the difference between the estimated current values of assets and the estimated current amounts of liabilities and their tax bases. The estimate should include consideration of negative tax bases of tax shelters, if any. That amount should be presented between liabilities and net worth in the statement of financial condition. Methods and assumptions used to estimate income taxes should be disclosed.

Financial Statement Disclosure

Personal financial statements should include adequate information to make the statements informative. The items in the following list, which is *not* all-inclusive, indicate the nature and type of information that should be disclosed:

- The name(s) of individual(s) covered by the financial statements
- A statement that assets are presented at their estimated current values and liabilities at their estimated current amounts
- The method used to estimate current values of assets and current amounts of liabilities
- If assets are held jointly by the individual and others, the nature of the joint ownership
- If the individual's investment portfolio is material in relation to other assets and is concentrated in one or a few companies, the names of the companies or industries and the current values of the securities
- If the individual has a material investment in a closely held business:
  — The name of the company and the individual's ownership percentage
  — The nature of the business
  — Summarized financial information about the assets, liabilities and results of operations of the business
- Descriptions of intangible assets and their estimated useful lives
- Amount of life insurance
- Nonforfeitable rights (that do not have the characteristics described above)
- The following tax information:
  — The methods and assumptions used to compute the estimated income taxes on the difference between the estimated current values of assets and the estimated current amounts of liabilities and their tax bases
  — Unused operating losses and capital loss carryforwards
  — Other unused deductions and credits and their expiration dates
  — The difference between the estimated current values of major assets and the estimated current amounts of liabilities or categories of assets and liabilities and their tax bases
- Maturities, interest rates, collateral, and other details related to receivables and debt
- Noncancelable commitments (that do not have the characteristics described above)

PRACTICE POINTER: Generally accepted accounting principles other than those described in ASC 274 may apply to the preparation of personal financial statements. For example, ASC 450 and ASC 850 may provide useful guidance in preparing personal financial statements.

CHAPTER 15
ASC 275—RISKS AND UNCERTAINTIES

CONTENTS

Interpretive Guidance	15,001
ASC 275-10: Overall	15,001
ASC 275-10-05-2 through 05-8; 10-1; 15-3 through 15-6; 50-1 through 50-2, 50-4, 50-6 through 50-21, 50-23; 55-1 through 55-19; 60-3; ASC 205-20-55-80; ASC 330-10-55-8 through 55-13; ASC 814-10-30-55-8 through 55-13; ASC 450-20-50-2; 55-36 through 55-37; ASC 460-10-55-27; ASC 605-35-55-3 through 55-10; ASC 740-10-55-219 through 55-222; ASC 932-360-55-15 through 15-19; ASC 958-205-60-1; ASC 605-55-70; ASC 985-20-55-24 through 5-29	
Disclosure of Certain Significant Risks and Uncertainties	15,001

INTERPRETIVE GUIDANCE

ASC 275-10: OVERALL

ASC 275-10-05-2 through 05-8; 10-1; 15-3 through 15-6; 50-1 through 50-2, 50-4, 50-6 through 50-21, 50-23; 55-1 through 55-19; 60-3; ASC 205-20-55-80; ASC 330-10-55-8 through 55-13; ASC 814-10-30-55-8 through 55-13; ASC 450-20-50-2; 55-36 through 55-37; ASC 460-10-55-27; ASC 605-35-55-3 through 55-10; ASC 740-10-55-219 through 55-222; ASC 932-360-55-15 through 15-19; ASC 958-205-60-1; ASC 605-55-70; ASC 985-20-55-24 through 5-29 Disclosure of Certain Significant Risks and Uncertainties

BACKGROUND

Volatility and uncertainty in the business and economic environment result in the need for disclosure of information about the risks and uncertainties confronted by reporting entities. Under the guidance in this pronouncement, disclosure is required about significant risks and uncertainties that confront entities in the following areas: nature of operations, use of estimates in the preparation of financial statements, certain significant estimates, and current vulnerability due to certain concentrations.

ACCOUNTING GUIDANCE

Nature of Operations

Financial statements should include a description of the major products or services an entity sells or provides and its principal markets and locations of those markets. Entities that operate in more than one market must indicate the relative importance of their operations in each market. Disclosures concerning the nature of operations are not required to be quantified, and relative importance may be described by terms such as *predominantly, about equally, major,* and *other.*

Illustration of a Nature of Operations Note for a Pharmaceutical Company

Geneca Inc. is a research-driven pharmaceutical company that discovers, develops, manufactures, and markets a broad range of human, animal, and agricultural health products. Human health products include therapeutic and preventive agents, generally sold by prescription, for the treatment of human disorders.

PRACTICE POINTER: Entities that operate in more than one market are required to indicate the relative importance of their operations in each market. Similar to the previous illustration, most companies do not include this disclosure in the "nature of operations" note. Rather, information on the relative importance of operations in different markets is typically found in the business segments note.

Use of Estimates

Financial statements should include a statement that they were prepared in conformity with GAAP, which requires the application of management's estimates.

Illustration of a Use of Estimates Note—Basic

We prepare our financial statements under generally accepted accounting principles, which require management to make estimates and assumptions that affect the reported amounts or certain disclosures. Actual results could differ from those estimates.

Illustration of a Use of Estimates Note—Detailed

We prepare our financial statements under generally accepted accounting principles, which require management to make estimates and assumptions that affect the reported amounts or certain disclosures. Actual results could differ from those estimates. Estimates are used when accounting for certain items such as long-term contracts, allowance for doubtful accounts, depreciation and amortization, employee benefit plans, taxes, restructuring reserves, and contingencies.

Significant Estimates

Disclosure regarding an estimate is required when *both* of the following conditions are met:

- It is at least reasonably possible that the estimate of the effect on the financial statements of a condition, situation, or set of circumstances that existed at the date of the financial statements will change in the near term due to one or more future confirming events.
- The effect of the change would have a material effect on the financial statements.

The disclosure requirements in ASC 450 for contingencies are supplemented by the following guidance:

- If an estimate requires disclosure under the guidance in ASC 450 or another pronouncement, there should be an indication that it is at least reasonably possible that a change in the estimate will occur in the near term.
- An estimate that does not require disclosure under the guidance in ASC 450 (such as estimates associated with long-term operating assets and amounts reported under profitable long-term contracts) may meet the standards described above and, if so, requires the following:
  — Disclosure of its nature
  — An indication that it is reasonably possible that a change in the estimate will occur in the near term

The following are examples of the types of situations that may require disclosure in accordance with the guidance in this pronouncement, assuming the conditions stated above are met:

- Inventory subject to rapid technological obsolescence
- Specialized equipment subject to technological obsolescence
- Valuation allowances for deferred tax assets based on future taxable income
- Capitalized motion picture film production costs
- Capitalized computer software costs
- Deferred policy acquisition costs of insurance enterprises
- Valuation allowances for commercial and real estate loans
- Environmental remediation-related obligations
- Litigation-related obligations
- Contingent liabilities for obligations of other entities
- Amounts reported for long-term obligations (e.g., pensions and other post-retirement benefits)
- Estimated net proceeds recoverable, the provisions for expected loss to be incurred, etc., on disposition of a business or assets
- Amounts reported for long-term contracts

Vulnerability from Concentrations

Vulnerability from concentrations exists because of an enterprise's greater exposure to risk than would be the case if the enterprise had mitigated its risk through diversification. Financial statements should disclose concentrations if *all* of the following conditions are met:

- The concentration existed at the date of the financial statements.
- The concentration makes the enterprise vulnerable to the risk of a near-term severe impact.
- It is reasonably possible that the events that could cause the severe impact will occur in the near term.

Information sufficient to inform financial statement users of the general nature of the risk associated with the concentration is required for the following specific concentrations:

- Concentrations in the volume of business transacted with a particular customer, supplier, lender, grantor, or contributor
- Concentrations in revenue from particular products, services, or fund-raising events
- Concentrations in the available sources of supply of materials, labor, or services, or of licenses or other rights used in the entity's operations
- Concentrations in the market or geographic area in which an entity conducts its operations

In addition, for concentrations of labor subject to collective bargaining agreements, disclosure shall include both the percentage of the labor force covered by a collective bargaining agreement and the percentage of the labor force covered by a collective bargaining agreement that will expire within one year. For concentrations of operations located outside the entity's home country, disclosure shall include the carrying amounts of net assets and the geographic areas in which they are located.

Illustration of a Note on Concentrations—No Exposure

As of December 31, 20X4, we do not have any significant concentration of business transacted with a particular customer, supplier, or lender that could, if suddenly eliminated, severely impact our operations. We also do not have a concentration of available sources of labor or services that could, if suddenly eliminated, severely impact our operations. We invest our cash with high-quality credit institutions.

Illustration of a Note on Concentrations—Customer Concentration Exposure

The company's five largest customers accounted for approximately 48% of net revenues for 20X4. At December 31, 20X4, these customers accounted for approximately 38% of net accounts receivable.

CHAPTER 16
ASC 280—SEGMENT REPORTING

CONTENTS

Part I: General Guidance	16,001
ASC 280-10: Overall	16,001
Overview	16,001
Background	16,002
Identifying Segments	16,002
Scope	16,002
Operating Segments	16,003
Reportable Segments	16,004
Quantitative Thresholds	16,004
Comparability	16,005
Disclosure of Information about Multiple Reportable Segments	16,005
General Information	16,006
Information about Segment Profit or Loss and Assets	16,006
Reconciliations	16,008
Interim Period Information	16,008
Restatement of Previously Reported Information	16,009
Disclosure of Enterprise-Wide Information	16,010
Illustration—Sample Disclosures of Segment Information	16,011
Part II: Interpretive Guidance	16,013
ASC 280-10: Overall	16,013
ASC 280-10-55-25	
Segment Reporting of Puerto Rican Operations	16,013
ASC 280-10-50-13	
Determining Whether to Aggregate Operating Segments That Do Not Meet the Quantitative Thresholds	16,013
ASC 280-10-55-12 through 55-14	
Questions Related to the Implementation of FASB Statement No. 131	16,014

PART I: GENERAL GUIDANCE

ASC 280-10: OVERALL

OVERVIEW

The term *segment reporting* refers to the presentation of information about certain parts of an enterprise, in contrast to information about the entire enterprise. The need for segment information became increasingly apparent in the 1960s and 1970s as enterprises diversified their activities into different industries and product lines, as well as into different geographic areas. Financial analysts and other groups of financial statement users insisted on the importance of disaggregated information—in order for them to assess risk and perform other types of analyses.

BACKGROUND

The objective of presenting disaggregated information about segments of a business enterprise is to produce information about the types of activities in which an enterprise is engaged in and the economic environment in which those activities are carried out. Specifically, the FASB believes that segment information assists financial statement users to (ASC 280-10-10-1):

- Understand enterprise performance
- Assess its prospects for future net cash flows
- Make informed decisions about the enterprise

PRACTICE NOTE: The FASB does not specifically discuss the objective of providing information to assist in risk assessment. Risk assessment, however, is an important dimension of financial analysis and underlies, to some extent, the need for segment information. The requirements of ASC 280 include information about products and services, information about activities in different geographic areas, and information about reliance on major customers. All relate to areas of significant risk to an enterprise and to areas where risk may vary considerably from situation to situation, including different levels associated with different products, operating in different geographic areas, and differing levels of reliance on major customers.

In 1994, the AICPA's Special Committee on Financial Reporting (the "Jenkins Committee") issued its report, which suggests that for users analyzing a company involved in diverse business segments, information about those segments may be as important as information about the company as a whole. That study suggests that standard setters should give a high priority to improving segment reporting, and that segment information should be reoriented toward the way management operates the business enterprise. In identifying operating segments, ASC 280 requires a management approach that is generally consistent with the AICPA special committee's recommendations.

IDENTIFYING SEGMENTS

Scope

ASC 280 applies to public business enterprises. Any single aspect or combination of the following identifies an enterprise as a public enterprise (ASC 280-10-15-2; Glossary):

- Has issued debt or equity securities that are traded in a public market (a domestic or foreign stock exchange or an over-the-counter market)
- Is required to file financial statements with the Securities and Exchange Commission
- Provides financial statements for the purpose of issuing securities in a public market

ASC 280 does not apply in the following situations (ASC 280-10-15-3):
- Nonpublic business enterprises
- Not-for-profit enterprises
- The separate financial statements of parents, subsidiaries, joint ventures, or equity method investees if those enterprises' separate statements are consolidated or combined and both the separate company statements and the consolidated or combined statements are included in the same financial report

Although the requirements of ASC 280 are not required for *nonpublic* business enterprises, ASC 280 encourages them to provide the same information as public business enterprises.

Operating Segments

The concept of operating segments is instrumental to understanding ASC 280. Operating segments are components of an enterprise (ASC 280-10-50-1):
- That engage in business activities from which revenues may be earned and in which expenses are incurred.
- Whose operating results are reviewed by the enterprise's chief operating decision maker for purposes of making decisions with regard to resource allocation and performance evaluation.
- For which discrete financial information is available.

ASC 280 includes several guidelines that help implement these general criteria for identifying an enterprise's operating segments, as follows:
- Having earned revenues is not a requirement for a component of a business to be an operating segment (ASC 280-10-50-3). For example, a start-up component of the business, which has yet to earn revenue, may be an operating segment.
- Not every component of an enterprise is an operating segment or part of an operating segment (ASC 280-10-50-4). For example, corporate headquarters may not be an operating segment.
- Concerning personnel involved in segments (ASC 280-10-50-5, 7, 8):
  — The term *chief operating decision maker* is intended to refer to a function, not a specific position title. The intent is to identify that person who performs two functions: (*i*) makes decisions relative to the allocation of resources and (*ii*) evaluates the performance of the segments of the enterprise. The chief operating decision maker could be an individual (e.g., chief executive officer, chief operating officer) or it may be a group of individuals.

PRACTICE NOTE: ASC 280 is careful not to use a specific position title that might mean different things in different enterprises. The term *chief operating decision maker* was developed to apply to whatever position within an enterprise that meets certain criteria. A chief operating decision maker makes decisions relative to the allocation of resources and evaluates the performance of segments of the enterprise.

- The term *segment manager* is intended to refer to the functions having direct accountability to and regular contact with the chief operating decision maker to discuss operating activities, financial results, forecasts, and similar matters. A segment manager may be responsible for more than one segment. The chief operating decision maker also may be a segment manager for one or more operating segments.

- Other factors that may be important in identifying an enterprise's operating segments are (*a*) the nature of the business activities of each component of the enterprise, (*b*) the way the business is organized in terms of managerial responsibility for components of the enterprise, and (*c*) the manner in which information is presented to the board of directors of the enterprise (ASC 280-10-50-6).

- The three primary characteristics of an operating segment may apply to two or more overlapping components of an enterprise (i.e., a matrix organization). For example, one individual may be responsible for each product and service line and another individual may be responsible for each geographic area in which those product and service lines are distributed. The chief operating decision maker may use information both based on products and services and on geographic areas to make decisions about resource allocation and segment performance. In this situation, the components based on products and services are considered operating segments (ASC 280-10-50-9)).

Reportable Segments

Reportable segments are operating segments that meet the criteria for separate reporting under ASC 280. Essentially, a reportable segment is one that accounts for a sufficient amount of an enterprise's activities to warrant disclosure of separate information.

Quantitative Thresholds

A logical starting point is the quantitative thresholds for identifying reportable segments. These criteria state that an operating segment is a reportable segment if any of the following quantitative criteria is met (ASC 280-10-50-12).

- The operating segment's total revenues (both external, such as sales to other enterprises, and intersegment, such as sales between operating segments) make up 10% or more of the combined revenue of all operating segments.

- The absolute amount of the reported profit or loss of the operating segments is 10% or more of the greater (absolute amount) of the total profit of all operating segments reporting a profit or the total loss of all operating segments reporting a loss.

- The operating segment's assets make up 10% or more of the combined assets of all operating segments.

In determining its reportable segments that meet these quantitative criteria, management may combine the activities of two or more operating segments, but only if certain similar economic characteristics are present in both (or all) operating segments. These operating segments' segment characteristics include (ASC 280-10-50-11):

- The nature of their products and services
- The nature of their production processes
- The types of their customers
- Their distribution methods
- The nature of their regulatory environment (if applicable).

Another quantitative criterion is that the identified reportable segments must constitute at least 75% of the total consolidated revenue (ASC 280-10-50-14). If the operating segments that are initially identified as reportable segments do not meet this threshold, additional operating segments must be identified, even if they do *not* meet the quantitative criteria presented earlier. Information about those operating segments for which separate information is not presented can be combined and presented in the aggregate with an appropriate description (e.g., "all other segments").

Comparability

Comparability among years is an important factor in identifying reportable segments, as evidenced by the following requirements that relate to changes in segments meeting the quantitative criteria from one year to the next (ASC 280-10-50-16, 17):

- If a prior year reportable segment fails to meet one of the quantitative criteria but management believes it to be of continuing significance, information about that segment shall continue to be presented.
- If an operating segment meets the criteria as a reportable segment for the first time in the current period, prior-year segment information that is presented for comparative purposes shall be restated to reflect the new reportable segment as a separate segment.

As a practical matter, ASC 280 indicates that ten reportable segments is probably a reasonable maximum number for purposes of disclosing separate segment information (ASC 280-10-50-18). While the maximum of ten is not stated as an absolute requirement, management is advised that when the number of reportable segments exceeds ten, consideration should be given to whether a practical limit has been reached.

DISCLOSURE OF INFORMATION ABOUT MULTIPLE REPORTABLE SEGMENTS

Segment information is required in four areas (ASC 280-10-50-20):
1. General information
2. Information about segment profit or loss and assets

3. Reconciliation of segment information to aggregate enterprise amounts
4. Interim period information

The information required by ASC 280 must be reported for each period for which an income statement is presented, including prior periods presented for comparative purposes. Reconciliation of segment balance sheet information to enterprise balance sheet amounts is only required when a balance sheet is presented (ASC 280-10-50-20).

The following sections cover the specific disclosure requirements in the four general areas identified above.

General Information

General information is necessary for financial statement users to understand the specific information about segments that is required to be disclosed. The general information logically would precede the information about segment profit or loss and assets and reconciliations, which are identified in the following two sections (ASC 280-10-50-21):

1. Factors used to identify the enterprise's reportable segments
2. Types of products and services that are the basis for revenues from each reportable segment

In identifying the enterprise's reportable segments, an explanation of the basis for organization is required. Management may have used the following organizational alternatives, for example:

- Products and services
- Geographic areas
- Regulatory environment
- Combination of factors

Information about Segment Profit or Loss and Assets

The heart of the segment reporting requirements of ASC 280 is information about segments' profit or loss and assets. A measure of profit or loss and total assets is required for each reportable segment. This amount should be based on the information reported to the chief operating decision maker for making decisions about allocating resources to segments and assessing segment performance.

If the chief operating decision maker uses only one measure of segment profit or loss and only one measure of assets, those are the measures that should be reported. On the other hand, if the chief operating decision maker uses multiple measures of segment profit or loss or segment assets in resource allocation decisions and performance evaluation, the information reported to satisfy ASC 280 should be that which management believes is determined most consistently with that used in the determination of the corresponding amounts in the enterprise's consolidated financial statements (ASC 280-10-50-28).

In presenting segment profit or loss, the following information is required for each segment if the specific amounts are included in the measure of segment profit or loss reviewed by the chief operating decision maker (ASC 280-10-50-22):

- Revenues from external customers
- Revenues from other operating segments
- Interest revenue
- Interest expense
- Depreciation, depletion, and amortization
- Unusual items
- Income recognized on equity-method investments
- Income tax expense or benefit
- Extraordinary items
- Significant noncash items other than depreciation, depletion and amortization

Following are guidelines included in ASC 280 for the determination of the information items listed above:

- In identifying unusual items, ASC 225-20 (Income Statement—Extraordinary and Unusual Items) is the primary source of authority.
- Interest revenue and expense should be presented separately (i.e., not net) unless the net amount is the figure used by the chief operating decision maker to assess performance and make resource allocation decisions.

Additional information about assets of each reportable segment is required, as follows, if these amounts are considered by the chief operating decision maker in evaluating the assets held by a segment (ASC 280-10-50-25):

- The amount of investment in equity method investees
- Total expenditures for additions to long-lived assets (except financial instruments, long-term customer relationships of a financial institution, mortgage and other servicing rights, deferred policy acquisition costs, and deferred income taxes)

In addition to the specific information items about segment profit or loss and segment assets, enterprises are required to present explanatory information that should assist users of the financial statements in better understanding the meaning of that information, as follows (ASC 280-10-50-29):

- The basis of accounting for transactions between reportable segments
- Differences in the measurement of the reportable segments' profit or loss and the enterprise's consolidated income before income taxes, extraordinary items, discontinued operations, and cumulative effect of changes in accounting principle
- Differences in the measurement of the reportable segments' assets and the enterprise's consolidated assets
- Any changes from prior years in the measurement of reported segment profit or loss, and the effect, if any, of those changes on the amount of segment profit or loss
- The nature of any asymmetrical allocations to segments

PRACTICE NOTE: In further explaining the second and third requirements above, ASC 280 points out that the required reconciliation information (explained below) may satisfy this requirement. It also indicates that enterprises should consider whether differences in accounting policies with regard to the allocation of centrally incurred costs are necessary for understanding the segment information and, if so, to explain those allocation policies. In further explaining the fifth requirement above, ASC 280 illustrates an "asymmetrical allocation" as an enterprise allocating depreciation to a segment without allocating the related depreciable asset to that segment.

Reconciliations

Reconciliations of certain segment information to the enterprise's consolidated totals are an important part of the disclosure requirements of ASC 280, as indicated in the following table (ASC 280-10-50-30):

Segment information	Reconciled to Consolidated information
1. Reportable segments' revenues	1. Consolidated revenues
2. Reportable segments' profit or loss	2. Consolidated income before income taxes, extraordinary items, discontinued operations, and cumulative effect of change in accounting principle
3. Reportable segments' assets	3. Consolidated assets
4. Reportable segments' amounts for other significant items	4. Corresponding consolidated amounts

In presenting these reconciliations, all significant reconciling items must be separately identified and described.

PRACTICE POINTER: ASC 280, like many authoritative accounting standards, establishes minimum required disclosures. In the case of segment information, the illustration in ASC 280-10-50-30d implies that a decision to disclose information beyond the minimum requirements carries with it a responsibility to provide reconciling information about that item for the segments and for the consolidated enterprise. The following wording in ASC 280-10-50-30d is important: ". . . an enterprise *may choose* to disclose liabilities for its reportable segments, *in which case the enterprise would reconcile* the total of reportable segments' liabilities for each segment to the enterprise's consolidated liabilities if segment liabilities are significant."

Interim Period Information

ASC 280 requires abbreviated segment information in interim financial statements. The following is an abbreviated categorized listing of the information required to be disclosed in condensed interim financial statements (ASC 280-10-50-32):

Revenue
> From external customers
>
> Intersegment

Segment profit or loss

Material changes from last annual report
> Total assets
>
> Basis of segmentation
>
> Basis of measuring segment profit or loss

Reconciliation of segment profit or loss to enterprise consolidated income

In meeting the reconciliation of segment profit or loss requirement, enterprises have two alternatives, depending on whether they allocate items such as income taxes and extraordinary items to segments. If they do *not* allocate these items, the reconciliation should be from reportable segments' profit or loss to enterprise consolidated income before income taxes, extraordinary items, discontinued operations, and the cumulative effect of a change in accounting principle. On the other hand, if the items indicated above are allocated to segments, the reconciliation may be from segments' profit or loss to consolidated income after those items. In either case, significant reconciling items are to be separately identified and described in that reconciliation.

PRACTICE POINTER: If an enterprise allocates items such as income taxes and extraordinary items to segments, it would be reasonable to expect fewer reconciling items between the total of the reportable segments' profit or loss and the related consolidated totals than would be the case if these same items were *not* allocated to segments and, therefore, were required to be part of the reconciliation. In other words, the more items that are allocated down to the segments in determining their profit or loss, the closer the total of the reportable segments' profit and loss will be to the consolidated enterprise's net income and the fewer the items required to meet the reconciliation requirement.

Restatement of Previously Reported Information

An enterprise may change the structure of its internal organization in a manner that causes information about its reportable segments to lack comparability with previous period information. In this situation, and where practicable, previous period information presented for comparative purposes should be restated in accordance with the revised organization. This requirement applies to both previous interim and annual periods. In addition to restating the financial information presented, an explanation of the change is required, including that previous period information has been restated (ASC 280-10-50-34).

Should restatement of previous period information not be practicable in the year of the internal organization change, disclosure is required of current period information under both the previous and the new organizational structure if it is practicable to do so (ASC 280-10-50-35).

16,010 ASC 280—Segment Reporting

DISCLOSURE OF ENTERPRISE-WIDE INFORMATION

The previous discussion has focused on disclosure of information about multiple reporting segments. An enterprise is required to report certain disaggregated information, even if it functions as a single operating unit.

Enterprise-wide information is required in the following three areas:

1. Information about products and services
2. Information about geographic areas
3. Information about major customers

Enterprises that are organized around reporting segments may have satisfied these requirements already as a result of satisfying the disclosure requirements for multiple reporting segments. If not, they are required to present the enterprise-wide information, as are enterprises that are not subject to the requirements of those enterprises with multiple reportable segments. Information required in the three areas identified above is as follows:

Products and Services (ASC 280-10-50-40)

- Revenues from external customers for each product and service or group of related products and services

Geographic Areas (ASC 280-10-50-41)

- Revenues from external customers:
  — Attributable to the enterprise's country of domicile
  — Attributed to all foreign countries in total from which revenue is derived
  — Revenues from individual foreign countries if the amounts are material
  — The basis for attributing revenues from external customers to individual countries
- Long-lived assets (not including financial instruments, long-term customer relationships of a financial institution, mortgage and other servicing rights, deferred policy of acquisition costs, and deferred income taxes:
  — Attributable to the enterprise's country of domicile
  — Attributable to all foreign countries in total where assets are held
  — Assets from individual foreign countries if the amounts are material

Major Customers (ASC 280-10-50-42)

- Revenues from a single customer that accounts for 10% or more of revenue
- The segment(s) from which sales to each major customer were made

In preparing the information about products and services and geographic areas, amounts should be based on the same information used to prepare the enterprise's general purpose-financial statements. If this is impracticable, the information is not required, but an explanation should be provided.

In preparing the information about major customers, the following additional guidance is provided:

- Neither the identity of the major customer nor the amount of revenue that each segment reports from that customer is required
- A group of entities under common control is considered a single customer.
- For purposes of identifying major *governmental* customers, the federal government, a state government, a local government, or a foreign government is considered a single customer.

Illustration—Sample Disclosures of Segment Information

ASC 280 requires the disclosure of extensive information about an enterprise's operating segments. Following are brief examples of how some of these requirements might appear in notes to the financial statements. In all cases, dollar figures (in thousands) are assumed for illustrative purposes.

Management Policy in Identifying Reportable Segments

Company A's reportable business segments are strategic business units that offer distinctive products and services that are marketed through different channels. They are managed separately because of their unique technology, marketing, and distribution requirements.

Types of Products and Services

Company B has four reportable segments: food processing, apparel manufacturing, insurance, and entertainment. Food processing is a canning operating for sales to regional grocery chains. The apparel segment produces mid-price clothing for distribution through discount department stores. The insurance segment provides primarily property insurance for heavy manufacturing enterprises. The entertainment segment includes several theme parks and multiple-screen theaters.

Segment Profit or Loss

Company C's accounting policies for segments are the same as those described in the summary of significant accounting policies. Management evaluates segment performance based on segment profit or loss before income taxes and nonrecurring gains and losses. Transfers between segments are accounted for at market value.

	Segments				Consolidated	
	A	B	C	D	Other	Totals
Revenues from external customers	$200	$200	$300	$400	$100	$1,200
Intersegment revenues		50		60		110
Interest revenue	10	15		40		65
Interest expense	20	10	40	30		100
Depreciation and amortization	50	60	100	120		330
Segment profit	40	75	80	180		375
Segment assets	$180	$220	$280	$450	$250	$1,380
Expenditures for segment assets	20	70	30	80	20	220

Reconciliation of Segment Information to Consolidated Amounts

Information for Company D's reportable segments relates to the enterprise's consolidated totals as follows:

Revenues

Total revenues for reportable segments	$1,800
Other revenues	250
Intersegment revenues	(200)
Total consolidated revenues	$1,850

Profit or Loss

Total profit or loss for reportable segments	$250
Other profit or loss	40
Intersegment profits	(35)
General corporate expenses	(50)
Income before income taxes	$205

Assets

Total assets for reportable segments	$3,000
Assets not attributed to segments	200
Elimination of intersegment receivables	(300)
General corporate assets not attributed to segments	500
Total consolidated assets	$3,400

Geographic Information

Company E attributes revenues and long-lived assets to different geographic areas on the basis of the location of the customer. Revenues and investment in long-lived assets by geographic area are as follows:

	Revenues	Long-lived Assets
United States	$1,200	$ 800
Mexico	500	400
Brazil	450	375
Taiwan	300	200
Other	800	720
Total	$3,250	$2,495

Major Customer Information

Company F has revenue from a single customer that represents $800 of the enterprise's consolidated revenue. This customer is served by the automotive parts operating segment.

PART II: INTERPRETIVE GUIDANCE

ASC 280-10: OVERALL

ASC 280-10-55-25 Segment Reporting of Puerto Rican Operations
BACKGROUND

Under the guidance in ASC 280, an entity is required to disclose certain information about its foreign operations and export sales. Further, according to the guidance, foreign operations include an entity's revenue-producing operations that are located outside its home country (e.g., the United States for U.S. enterprises).

ACCOUNTING GUIDANCE

Question: Are Puerto Rican operations and operations in other areas under U.S. sovereignty or jurisdiction (e.g., Virgin Islands, American Samoa) considered foreign for purposes of applying the guidance in ASC 280.

Answer: Puerto Rican operations, as well as those in other non-self-governing U.S. territories, should be considered domestic operations. Factors such as proximity, economic affinity, and similarities of business environments indicate this classification for these operations.

ASC 280-10-50-13 Determining Whether to Aggregate Operating Segments That Do Not Meet the Quantitative Thresholds
BACKGROUND

Under the guidance in ASC 280-10-50-10, entities are required to report separate information about each operating segment that has been identified in accordance with the guidance in ASC 280-10-50-1-9 or that has been created by combining two or more segments in accordance with the guidance in ASC 280-10-50-11 and exceeds the quantitative thresholds in ASC 280-10-50-12. Under the guidance in ASC 280-10-50-11 the combination of two or more operating segments into a single operating segment is permitted if the combination is consistent with the objective and basic principles of ASC 280, the segments have similar economic characteristics, and they are similar in each of the following areas:

- The nature of the products and services
- The nature of the production processes
- The type or class of customer for their products or services
- The methods used to distribute their products or provide their services
- The nature of the regulatory environment, for example, banking, insurance, or public utilities, if applicable.

Segments about which information must be reported separately are referred to as reportable segments.

ACCOUNTING ISSUE

How should an entity evaluate the criteria in ASC 280-10-50-11 that are used to combine two or more operating segments into a single segment when determining whether operating segments that do not meet the quantitative thresholds may be aggregated in accordance with the guidance in ASC 280-10-50-13?

ACCOUNTING GUIDANCE

Operating segments that do *not* meet the quantitative thresholds can be combined only if: (*a*) the combination is consistent with the objective and basic principles of ASC 280 (*b*) the segments have similar economic characteristics, and (*c*) the segments share a majority of the criteria for combination listed in ASC 280-10-50-11.

ASC 280-10-55-12 through 55-14 Questions Related to the Implementation of FASB Statement No. 131

The FASB staff reported on the following technical questions about ASC 280 received from constituents and the staff's responses:

Question 1: Is an entity required to disclose the amount of depreciation and amortization for each reportable segment if the entity's chief operating decision maker uses the amount of earnings before interest, taxes, depreciation, and amortization (EBITDA) to evaluate the performance of the entity's segments but management reports reviewed by the operating decision maker also include summaries of depreciation and amortization expense related to each reportable segment?

Answer: Yes. Based on the guidance in ASC 280-10-50-22 and 50-25 (paragraphs 27 and 28 of FAS-131), depreciation and amortization expense should be disclosed for each reportable segment under the above circumstances. Under the guidance in ASC 280-10-50-22, entities are required to report a measure of profit or loss for each reportable segment, and under the guidance in ASC 280-10-50-22 and 50-25 other amounts must be disclosed about each reportable segment if those amounts are *included* in the measure of profit or loss reviewed by the chief operating decision maker. The FASB staff believes that amortization and depreciation expense should be reported for each reportable segment in the circumstances stated above, even though those amounts are *not* included in the measure of segment profit and loss used by a chief operating decision maker to evaluate each business segment's performance, is based on the guidance in ASC 280-10-50-22 and 50-25, which states that "the amount of each segment item reported shall be the measure reported to the chief operating decision maker for purposes of making decisions about allocating resources to the segment and assessing its performance." The staff noted that this guidance can be applied to other amounts reported to the chief operating decision maker that are not included in the amount of segment profit or loss used to evaluate a segment's performance.

Question 2: ASC 280-10-50-12 provides a choice of three quantitative thresholds to determine whether an entity should report separate information about an operating segment. Specifically, ASC 280-10-50-12 states that separate information should be reported about an operating segment if "the absolute amount of its reported profit or loss is 10% or more of the greater, in absolute amount, of (1) the combined reported profit of all operating segments that did not report a loss or (2) the combined reported loss of all operating segments that did report a loss." If a chief operating decision maker uses different measures of profit or loss to evaluate the performance of separate segments (e.g., the performance of three of seven segments is evaluated based on operating income and the performance of the remaining four segments is evaluated based on net income), how should the quantitative threshold for segment profit or loss be applied?

Answer: The purpose of the guidance in ASC 280-10-50-12 is to identify the segments for which to report separate information. Therefore, the size of each segment's profit or loss must be compared on a consistent basis to the entity's total profit and loss, which should be similar to the amount used in the consolidated financial statements (without reconciling items), because the total amount would include segments and business activities that do not meet the criterion for a reportable segment and consequently are reported in the "all other" classification. The requirement that a reportable segment should be one that makes up 10% or more of an the entity's *total* reported profit or loss (or revenue or assets) is similar to previous guidance, which also required as in ASC 280-10-50-14, that reportable segments should account for at least 75% of an entity's total consolidated revenue from *external* sources.

If an entity's chief operating decision maker does not evaluate the performance of all segments based on the same measures of profit and loss, the criterion in ASC 280-10-50-12, nevertheless, should be applied to a consistent measure of segment profit and loss to determine the entity's reportable segments. That procedure does not affect the requirement in ASC 280-10-50-22 that the actual measure of profit or loss used by the chief operating decision maker to evaluate each reportable segment's performance be disclosed.

The staff noted that the above guidance for ASC 280-10-50-12 also applies if the criteria in ASC 280-10-50-12 are used, that is, the 10% threshold of revenue or assets should be applied to total revenues or assets, which should be similar to the amount of consolidated revenues or assets (without reconciling items).

CHAPTER 17
ASC 305—CASH AND CASH EQUIVALENTS

ASC 305 does not provide any unique accounting guidance but rather only provides implementation guidance on cash on deposit at a financial institution.

CHAPTER 18
ASC 310—RECEIVABLES

CONTENTS

Part I: General Guidance	18,003
Overview	18,003
Background	18,004
ASC 310-10: Overall	18,005
Allowance for Uncollectible Receivables	18,005
Impairment of Loans	18,005
Recognition of Impairment	18,007
Measurement of Impairment	18,007
Income Measurement	18,008
Disclosures	18,009
ASC 310-20: Nonrefundable Fees and Other Costs	18,009
ASC 310-30: Loans and Debt Securities Acquired with Deteriorated Credit Quality	18,009
ASC 310-40: Troubled Debt Restructurings by Creditors	18,009
Accounting for Troubled Debt Restructurings	18,009
Granting a Concession	18,010
Assessing Financial Difficulty	18,010
Effective Dates and Transition	18,011
Transfer of Asset(s)	18,011
Illustration of Transfer of Assets	18,012
Transfer of Equity Interest	18,012
Illustration of Transfer of Equity Interest	18,012
Modification of Terms	18,012
Illustration of Modification of Terms	18,013
Combination of Types	18,013
Related Issues	18,013
Creditor Disclosure Requirements for Troubled Debt Restructurings	18,013
Part II: Interpretive Guidance	18,014
ASC 310-10: Overall	18,014
ASC 310-10-05-9, 15-5, 25-15 through 25-30, 35-55 through 35-61, 40-3 through 40-5, 45-15; ASC 360-10-35-3, 35-9	
Purpose and Scope of AcSEC Practice Bulletins and Procedures for Their Issuance	18,014

18,002   ASC 310—Receivables

ASC 310-10-05-5, 05-7; 25-3, 25-6, 25-8; 25-13; 30-7; 35-41 through 35-43, 35-46 through 35-49; 45-2, through 45-3; 50-2 through 50-11; ASC 310-20-15-3; 50-1; ASC 460-10-35-3; 45-1; ASC 460-605-25-7; ASC 825-10-35-1 through 35-3; ASC 835-30-15-1; ASC 860-20-50-5; ASC 860-50-15-3; ASC 860-50-40-2, 40-6; ASC 860-942-15-2 through 15-3; ASC 942-210-45-1 through 45-2; ASC 942-305-05-2; 45-1; 50-1; ASC 942-310-15-2; ASC 942-320-50-4; ASC 942-325-25-1 through 25-3; 35-1 through 35-4; ASC 942-360-45-2; ASC 942-405-25-1 through 25-4; 35-1; 45-1 through 45-4; 50-1; ASC 942-470-45-1 through 45-2; 50-2 through 50-3; ASC 942-505-50-1H through 50-7; ASC 942-825-50-1 through 50-2; ASC 944-320-50-1; ASC 948-10-15-3; 50-2 through 50-5

    Accounting by Certain Entities (Including Entities with Trade Receivables) That Lend to or Finance the Activities of Others   **18,018**

ASC 310-10-25-7; 35-52

    Difference between Initial Investment and Principal Amount of Loans in a Purchased Credit Card Portfolio   **18,021**

ASC 310-10-05-9; ASC 815-15-55-9 through 55-10

    Application of the AICPA Notice to Practitioners Regarding Acquisition, Development, and Construction Arrangements to Acquisition of an Operating Property   **18,022**

ASC 310-10-50-18; ASC 310-30-05-2 through 05-3; 15-1 through 15-4, 15-6 through 15-10; 25-1; 30-1; 35-2 through 35-3, 35-5 through 35-6, 35-8 through 35-15; 40-1; 45-1; 50-1 through 50-3; 55-2, 55-5 through 55-29; 60-3

    Accounting for Certain Loans or Debt Securities in a Transfer   **18,024**

ASC 310-10-35-2, 35-4, 35-6, 35-8, 35-15, 35-19, 35-25, 35-27, 35-34 through 35-36, 35-38; 55-1 through 55-6; ASC 310-40-50-4; ASC 310-45-20-60-3

    Application of FASB Statements No. 5 and No. 114 to a Loan Portfolio   **18,028**

ASC 310-20: Nonrefundable Fees and Other Costs   **18,029**

ASC 310-20-05-3; 35-4, 35-6, 50-4

    Amortization Period for Net Deferred Credit Card Origination Costs   **18,029**

ASC 310-20-05-4; 25-18; 35-8

    Accounting for Individual Credit Card Acquisitions   **18,030**

ASC 310-20-35-11

    Creditor's Accounting for a Modification or an Exchange of Debt Instruments   **18,032**

ASC 310-30: Loans and Debt Securities Acquired with Deteriorated Credit Quality   **18,033**

ASC-310-30-35-13, 40-1 through 40-2; 310-40-15-11

    Effect of a Loan Modification When the Loan Is Part of a Pool That Is Accounted for as a Single Asset   **18,033**

ASC 310-40: Troubled Debt Restructurings by Creditors   **18,034**

ASC 310-40-40-10; 35-11; 55-13 through 55-15

    Determination of Cost Basis for Foreclosed Assets under FASB Statement No. 15, *Accounting by Debtors and Creditors for Troubled Debt Restructurings*, and the Measurement of Cumulative Losses Previously Recognized under Paragraph 37 of FASB Statement No. 144, *Accounting for the Impairment or Disposal of Long-Lived Assets*   **18,034**

ASC 310-40-40-6A, 40-7; 55-12

    Valuation of Repossessed Real Estate   **18,035**

Illustration of Valuation of Foreclosed Real Estate	18,035
ASC 310-40-15-3; 55-4; ASC 470-60-15-3; 55-15	
Classification of Debt Restructurings by Debtors and Creditors	18,037
ASC 310-40-55-6 through 55-10	
Use of Zero Coupon Bonds in a Troubled Debt Restructuring	18,037
ASC 310-40-40-1	
Substituted Debtors in a Troubled Debt Restructuring	18,038
ASC 310-40-40-8A, 40-9	
Accounting for Conversion of a Loan into a Debt Security in a Debt Restructuring	18,039
Illustration of the Conversion of a Loan into a Debt Security	18,040
ASC 310-40-50-5; S50-1; S99-1	
Applicability of the Disclosures Required by FASB Statement No. 114 When a Loan Is Restructured in a Troubled Debt Restructuring into Two (or More) Loans	18,042
Illustration of Required Disclosure Requirements When a Loan Is Restructured in a Troubled Debt Restructuring into Two (or More) Loans	18,043
Important Notice for 2014	18,044

PART I: GENERAL GUIDANCE

OVERVIEW

Accounts receivable must be reported at their net realizable value for the purposes of GAAP. Net realizable value is equal to the total amount of the receivables less an estimated allowance for uncollectible accounts. GAAP also addresses how allowances for credit losses related to certain loans should be determined, including how to recognize and measure loan impairment and how to measure income on impaired loans.

ASC 310 establishes accounting and reporting standards for nonrefundable fees and costs associated with lending, committing to lend, or purchasing a loan or group of loans. Under ASC 310, direct loan origination fees and costs, including initial direct costs incurred by a lessor in negotiating and consummating a lease, are offset against each other and the net amount is deferred and recognized over the life of the loan as an adjustment to the yield on the loan. The provisions of ASC 310 apply to all types of loans, including debt securities, and to all types of lenders, including banks, thrift institutions, insurance companies, mortgage bankers, and other financial and nonfinancial institutions. However, ASC 310 does not apply to nonrefundable fees and costs that are associated with originating or acquiring loans that are carried at market value.

Debt may be restructured for a variety of reasons. A restructuring of debt is considered a troubled debt restructuring (TDR) if the creditor, for economic or legal reasons related to the debtor's financial difficulties, grants a concession to the debtor that it would not otherwise consider. The concession may stem from an agreement between the creditor and the debtor, or it may be imposed by law or court (ASC Glossary).

A loan is impaired if, based on current information and events, it is probable that the creditor will be unable to collect all amounts due according to the contractual terms of the loan agreement, including both the contractual interest and the principal receivable. For further discussion of troubled debt restructurings from the perspective of the debtor, see the coverage of ASC 470-60 (Troubled Debt Restructurings by Debtors).

BACKGROUND

A troubled debt restructuring is one in which the creditor grants the debtor certain concessions that would not normally be considered. The concessions are made because of the debtor's financial difficulty, and the creditor's objective is to maximize recovery of its investment. Troubled debt restructurings are often the result of legal proceedings or of negotiation between the parties (ASC 310-40-15-5, 6).

Troubled debt restructurings include situations in which (ASC 310-40-15-9):

- The creditor accepts a third-party receivable or other asset(s) of the debtor, in lieu of the receivable from the debtor.
- The creditor accepts an equity interest in the debtor in lieu of the receivable. (This is not to be confused with convertible securities, which are *not* troubled debt restructurings.)
- The creditor accepts modification of the terms of the debt, including but not limited to:
  — Reduction in the stated interest
  — Extension of maturity at an interest rate below the current market rate
  — Reduction in face amount of the debt
  — Reduction in accrued interest

The reductions mentioned in the bulleted item above can be either absolute or contingent.

For the purposes of ASC 310-40, troubled debt restructurings do not include the following (ASC 310-40-15-11):

- Changes in lease agreements
- Employment-related agreements, such as deferred compensation contracts or pension plans
- A debtor's failure to pay trade accounts that do not involve a restructure agreement
- A creditor's legal action to collect accounts that do not involve a restructure agreement

A troubled debt restructuring by a debtor in bankruptcy proceedings is permitted under ASC 310 provided that the restructuring does *not* constitute a *general restatement* of the debtor's liabilities (ASC 310-40-15-10). ASC 310 requires that a creditor account for all loans that are restructured as part of a TDR involving a modification of terms as an impaired loan.

Not all debt restructuring is considered troubled, even though the debtor is in financial difficulty. Circumstances in which the restructuring is *not* troubled include (ASC 310-40-15-12):

- The debtor satisfies the debt by giving assets or equity with a fair value that at least equals either:
    — The creditor's recorded receivable, or
    — The debtor's carrying amount of the payable.
- The creditor reduces the interest rate primarily in response to changes in market rates.
- In exchange for the debtor's debt, the debtor issues new debt securities that have an effective interest rate that is at or near the current market interest rate of debt with similar maturity dates and interest rates issued by non-troubled debtors.

PRACTICE NOTE: If the debtor can obtain funds at current market rates and conditions, this provides evidence that the restructuring is not a troubled debt restructuring.

ASC 310-10: OVERALL

ALLOWANCE FOR UNCOLLECTIBLE RECEIVABLES

For the purposes of GAAP, accounts receivable must be reported at their net realizable value. Net realizable value is equal to the total amount of the receivables less an estimated allowance for uncollectible accounts.

Under ASC 450, an accrual for a loss contingency must be charged to income if both of the following conditions are met:

- It is *probable* that as of the date of the financial statements an enterprise does not expect to collect the full amount of its accounts receivable, based on information available before the actual issuance of the financial statements, and
- The amount of loss contingency (uncollectible receivables) can be *reasonably estimated*.

If both of these conditions are met, an accrual for the estimated amount of uncollectible receivables must be made even if the uncollectible receivables cannot be identified specifically (ASC 310-10-35-9). An enterprise may base its estimate of uncollectible receivables on its prior experience, the experience of other enterprises in the same industry, the debtor's ability to pay, and/or an appraisal of current economic conditions (ASC 310-10-35-10).

IMPAIRMENT OF LOANS

A *loan* is defined as "a contractual right to receive money on demand or on fixed or determinable dates that is recognized as an asset in the creditor's statement of financial position." GAAP addresses how allowances for credit losses related to certain loans should be determined (ASC Glossary).

ASC 310—Receivables

GAAP does not specify how a creditor should identify loans that are to be evaluated for collectibility. A creditor may apply its normal loan review procedures in making that judgment. Guidance for this decision is found in the AICPA's Audit Procedure Study *Auditing the Allowance for Credit Losses of Banks* and includes the following items:

- Materiality criterion
- Regulatory reports of examination
- Internally generated listings such as "watch lists," past due reports, overdraft listings, and listings of loans to insiders
- Management reports of total loan amounts by borrower
- Historical loss experience by type of loan
- Loan files lacking current financial data related to borrowers and guarantors
- Borrowers experiencing problems such as operating losses, marginal working capital, inadequate cash flow, or business interruptions
- Loans secured by collateral that is not readily marketable or that is subject to deterioration in realizable value
- Loans to borrowers in industries or countries experiencing economic instability
- Loan documentation and compliance exception reports

Direct write-downs of an impaired loan and assessment of overall adequacy of the allowance for credit losses are not covered in ASC 310.

ASC 310 applies to all impaired loans except (ASC 310-10-35-13):

- A large group of homogeneous loans with small balances where impairment is evaluated on a collective basis (e.g., home mortgage, credit card, consumer installment loans)
- Loans carried at fair value or at the lower of cost or fair value
- Leases
- Debt securities (per ASC 320)

PRACTICE NOTE: The FASB believes that accounting for impaired loans should be consistent among all creditors and types of loans, except those specifically identified above as loans to which ASC 310 does not apply. The Board was unable to identify any compelling reasons why the lending process for consumer, mortgage, commercial, and other loans—whether uncollateralized or collateralized—is fundamentally different. In addition, the Board could not identify any compelling reasons why different types of creditors should account for impaired loans differently, or why financial statement users for a particular industry or size of entity would be better served by accounting that differs from that of other creditors.

Recognition of Impairment

ASC 310 ties accounting for an impairment of a loan directly to the criteria established in ASC 450 (Contingencies) for recognizing a loss contingency. Specifically, ASC 310 indicates that a loan is impaired when it is *probable* that a creditor will be unable to collect all amounts due, including principal and interest, according to the contractual terms and schedules of the loan agreement. Normal loan review procedures are to be used in making that judgment. A loan is not considered impaired if (ASC 310-10-35-16, 17):

- There is merely an insignificant delay or shortfall in amounts of payments.
- The creditor expects to collect all amounts due, including interest accrued at the contractual interest rate for the period of the delay.

PRACTICE NOTE: Use of the term *probable* in ASC 310 is consistent with its use in ASC 450. ASC 450 indicates a range of probability that must be considered in the decision to accrue a loss contingency, including *probable*, *reasonably possible*, and *remote*. Virtual certainty is not required before a loss can be accrued. While ASC 310 changes the wording of ASC 450 as it relates to loan impairments that require accrual, it does not change the overall intent of applying the guidance in ASC 450 (ASC 310-10-35-18, 19).

Measurement of Impairment

The process of measuring impaired loans requires judgment and estimation, and the eventual outcomes may differ from the estimates. Following is guidance concerning the measurement of impaired loans under ASC 310. Measurement may be on a loan-by-loan or an aggregate basis (ASC 310-10-35-21).

- Impairment generally is based on the present value of expected future cash flows discounted at the loan's effective interest rate. As a practical matter, a creditor may measure impairment based on a loan's observable market price or on the fair value of the collateral if the loan is collateral dependent (ASC 310-10-35-22).
- A loan is considered collateral dependent when the creditor determines that foreclosure is probable or if the loan is expected to be repaid solely by the underlying collateral (ASC 310-10-35-32; ASC Glossary).
- Estimated costs to sell, on a discounted basis, may be a factor in measuring impairment if those costs are expected to reduce the cash flow available to repay or otherwise satisfy the loan (ASC 310-10-35-24).
- If the present value of expected future cash flows (or the loan's observable market price or the collateral's fair value) is less than the recorded investment in the loan (including accrued interest, net deferred loan fees or costs, and unamortized premium or discount), the creditor shall recognize the impairment by creating or adjusting a valuation allowance with a corresponding charge to bad-debt expense (ASC 310-10-35-24).

- The present value amount, based on estimated future cash flows of an impaired loan, is discounted at the loan's contractual interest rate. That rate is the rate of return implicit in the loan (ASC 310-10-35-25).

  — For a loan restructured in a troubled debt restructuring, present value is based on the original contractual rate, not on the rate specified in the restructuring agreement.

  — If the loan's contractual rate varies based on changes in an independent factor, such as an index or a rate, the loan's effective interest rate may be calculated based on the factor as it changes over the life of the loan, or it may be fixed at the rate that is in effect at the date the loan meets the impairment criteria. (The alternative chosen shall be applied consistently for all loans whose contractual interest rate varies based on subsequent changes in an independent factor.)

- In estimating expected future cash flows, all available evidence should be considered—including the estimated costs to sell if those costs are expected to reduce the cash flows available to repay or otherwise satisfy the loan. The weight given to the evidence should be commensurate with the extent to which the evidence can be objectively verified (ASC 310-10-35-26).

- After the initial measurement of impairment, any significant change in the amount or timing of an impaired loan's expected or actual future cash flows should be reflected by a recalculation of the impairment and an adjustment to the allowance account (ASC 310-10-35-37).

PRACTICE POINTER: ASC 310 requires that impairment be measured based on the loan's effective interest rate. Alternatively, impairment can be measured based on a new direct measurement of the asset, reflecting the current market rate of interest. The Board concluded that the measurement of impairment should recognize the change in the net carrying amount of the loan based on new information about expected future cash flows, rather than on other factors that may cause a change in the fair value of an impaired loan.

Income Measurement

Some accounting methods for recognizing income on an impaired loan may result in a recorded investment in an impaired loan that is less than the present value of expected future cash flows (or other basis for valuing the loan). In this case, no additional impairment would be recognized. Those accounting methods include recognition of interest income using a cost-recovery method, a cash-basis method, or some combination of those methods. The recorded investment in an impaired loan also may be less than the present value of expected future cash flows (or other basis for valuing the loan) because the creditor has charged off part of the loan (ASC 310-10-35-39).

Disclosures

GAAP requires that certain information be disclosed, by class of financing receivable, for loans that meet the definition of an impaired loan.

These disclosures include (ASC 310-10-50-15):

- For each balance sheet presented: (1) the recorded investment in impaired loans at the end of each period, broken out separately by the recorded investment where an allowance for credit losses has been recorded and the recorded investment where an allowance for credit losses has not been recorded; (2) the amount of the allowance for credit losses; and (3) the total unpaid principal balance of the impaired loans.
- The entity's policy for recognizing interest income on impaired loans, as well as how the creditor records cash receipts.
- For each income statement presented: (1) the average investment in impaired loans, (2) the amount of interest income recognized during the time within that period when loans were impaired, and (3) the amount of interest income that would have been recognized under the cash basis of accounting during the time within that period when loans were impaired (if practicable).
- The entity's policy for determining which loans to assess for impairment.
- The factors considered in determining that the loan is impaired.

ASC 310-20: NONREFUNDABLE FEES AND OTHER COSTS

Please refer to *Part II: Interpretive Guidance* in this chapter for coverage of this ASC subtopic.

ASC 310-30: LOANS AND DEBT SECURITIES ACQUIRED WITH DETERIORATED CREDIT QUALITY

Please refer to *Part II: Interpretive Guidance* in this chapter for coverage of this ASC subtopic.

ASC 310-40: TROUBLED DEBT RESTRUCTURINGS BY CREDITORS

ACCOUNTING FOR TROUBLED DEBT RESTRUCTURINGS

A restructuring is considered a troubled debt restructuring (TDR) if the creditor for economic or legal reasons related to the debtor's financial difficulties grants a concession to the debtor that it would not otherwise consider. A concession is usually granted by the creditor in an attempt to protect as much of its investment as possible. (ASC 310-40-15-5)

Generally, a debtor that can obtain funds from sources other than the existing creditor at market interest rates at or near those rates for non-troubled debt is *not* involved in a TDR. A TDR may include, but is not limited to, the following:

- Transfers from the debtor to the creditor of receivables from third parties, real estate, or other assets to satisfy fully or partially a debt.
- Issuance or other granting of an equity interest to the creditor by the debtor to satisfy fully or partially a debt unless the equity interest is granted pursuant to existing terms for converting the debt into an equity interest.
- Modification of terms of a debt, such as:
  — Reduction of the stated interest rate for the remaining original life of the debt.
  — Extension of the maturity date or dates of a stated interest rate lower than the current market rate for new debt with similar risk.
  — Reduction of the face amount or maturity amount of the debt as stated in the instrument or other agreement.
  — Reduction of accrued interest. (ASC 310-40-15-9)

In determining whether a restructuring is a TDR, the creditor must separately conclude that *both* of the following exists:

- The restructuring constitutes a concession.
- The debtor is experiencing financial difficulty.

Granting a Concession

The following additional guidance is provided to assist creditors in determining whether it has granted a concession. If the debtor does not otherwise have access to funds at a below market rate or debt with similar risk characteristics as the restructuring debt, the restructuring is considered to be at a below-market rate and may indicate that the creditor has granted a concession. In that circumstance, the creditor should consider all aspects of the restructuring to determine if it has made a concession. (ASC 310-40-15-15)

A temporary or permanent increase in the contractual interest rate as a result of a restructuring does not preclude the restructuring from being considered a concession because the new contractual interest rate on the restructured may still be below the market interest rate for new debt with similar risk characteristics. In this situation, the creditor should consider all aspects of the restructuring to determine whether a concession has been granted. (ASC 310-40-15-16)

A restructuring that results in an insignificant delay in payment is not considered a concession. The creditor should consider various factors in assessing whether a restructuring that results in a delay in payment is insignificant. (ASC 310-40-15-17)

Assessing Financial Difficulty

If a decision is made that the creditor has made a concession, a separate assessment must be made whether the debtor is experiencing financial difficulties to determine whether the restructuring constitutes a TDR.

The following should be considered in making this judgment:

- The debtor is currently in payment default on any if its debt.
- The probability that the debtor will be in payment default on any of its debt in the foreseeable future without the modification.

- The debtor has declared or is in the process of declaring bankruptcy.
- There is substantial doubt as to whether the debtor will continue to be a going concern.
- The debtor has securities that have been delisted, are in the process of being delisted, or are under threat of being delisted from an exchange.
- On the basis of estimates and projections that only encompass the debtor's current capabilities, the creditor forecasts that the debtor's entity-specific cash flows will be insufficient to service any of its debt in accordance with the contractual terms of the existing agreement for the foreseeable future.
- Without the current modification, the debtor cannot obtain funds from sources other than the existing creditors at an effective interest rate equal to the market rate for similar debt for a non-troubled debtor. (ASC 310-40-15-20)

Further guidance to assist the creditor in assessing whether a debtor is experiencing financial difficulties include the following. Payment default is not a necessary criterion for determining that a debtor is having financial difficulties. A creditor should evaluate whether it is probable that the debtor will be in payment default on any of its debt in the foreseeable future without the current modification in its debt.

Effective Dates and Transition

For public entities, the above discussions of granting a concession and assessing financial difficulty (ASU 2011-02) are effective for the first interim or annual period *beginning on or after June 15, 2011*. ASU 2011-2 is to be applied retrospectively to the beginning of the annual period of adoption. For nonpublic entities, these requirements are effective for annual periods *ending on or after December 15, 2012*, including interim periods within those annual periods. Early adoption is permitted for both public and nonpublic entities. A nonpublic entity may elect early adoption for any interim period of the fiscal year of the adoption. A nonpublic entity that elects early adoption should apply the provisions of the update retrospectively to restructurings occurring on or after the beginning of the fiscal year of adoption.

Transfer of Asset(s)

When the creditor receives assets as full settlement of a receivable, they are accounted for at their fair value at the time of the restructuring. The fair value of the receivable satisfied can be used if it is more clearly determinable than the fair value of the asset or equity acquired. In partial payments the creditor *must* use the fair value of the asset or equity received (ASC 310-40-35-6).

The excess of the recorded receivable over the fair value of the assets received (less cost to sell if a long-lived asset is received) is recognized as a loss (ASC 310-40-40-3). The creditor accounts for these assets as if they were acquired for cash (ASC 310-40-40-5).

Illustration of Transfer of Assets

A debtor owes $20,000, including accrued interest. The creditor accepts land valued at $17,000 and carried on the debtor's books at its $12,000 cost, in full payment.

Under GAAP, the debtor recognizes two gains: $5,000 ($17,000 – $12,000) on the transfer of the assets, and $3,000 ($20,000 – $17,000) on the extinguishment of debt.

The creditor recognizes a loss of $3,000 ($20,000 – $17,000).

Transfer of Equity Interest

The creditor records the receipt of an equity interest as any other asset by recording the investment at its fair value and recognizing a loss equal to the difference between the fair value of the equity interest and the amount of the receivable (ASC 310-40-40-3).

Illustration of Transfer of Equity Interest

A debtor grants an equity interest valued at $10,000, consisting of 500 shares of $15 par value stock, to retire a payable of $12,000. Given these facts, the debtor records the issuance of the stock at $10,000 ($7,500 par value and $2,500 additional paid-in capital) and a gain on the extinguishment of debt of $2,000 ($12,000 – $10,000). The creditor records an investment asset of $10,000 and an ordinary loss of $2,000 ($12,000 – $10,000) on the TDR.

PRACTICE POINTER: Determining the fair value of an equity interest of a debtor company involved in a troubled debt restructuring may be difficult. In many cases, the company's stock will not be publicly traded, and there may be no recent stock transactions that would be helpful. Even if a recent market price were available, consider whether that price reflects the financially troubled status of the company that exists at the time the troubled debt restructuring takes place.

Modification of Terms

A creditor in a TDR involving a modification of terms accounts for the restructured loan at the present value of expected future cash flows discounted at the loan's contractual interest rate, the loan's observable market price, or the fair value of collateral if the loan is collateral-dependent.

PRACTICE NOTE: A loan is impaired if it is probable that a creditor will be unable to collect all amounts due according to the contractual terms of the loan agreement. A loan whose terms are modified in a TDR will have already been identified as impaired. A loan is considered collateral-dependent if repayment is expected to be provided solely by the underlying collateral.

Illustration of Modification of Terms

A debtor has a loan to a creditor, details of which are as follows:

Principal	$10,000
Accrued interest	500
Total	$10,500

They agree on a restructuring in which the total future cash payments, both principal and interest, are $8,000. The present value of these payments is $7,500.

Under GAAP, the debtor recognizes a gain of $2,500 ($10,500 − $8,000) at the time of the restructuring, and all future payments are specified as principal payments. Under GAAP, the creditor recognizes a loss of $3,000 ($10,500 − $7,500).

Combination of Types

When a restructuring involves combinations of asset or equity transfers and modification of terms, the creditor reduces the recorded investment by the fair value of assets received less cost to sell, including an equity interest in the debtor. Thereafter, the creditor accounts for the TDR in accordance with ASC 310 (ASC 310-40-35-7).

Related Issues

Legal fees and other direct costs resulting from a TDR are expensed by the creditor when incurred (ASC 310-40-25-1).

A receivable obtained by a creditor from the sale of assets previously obtained in a TDR is accounted for in accordance with ASC 835-30 (Interest—Imputation of Interest), regardless of whether the assets were obtained in satisfaction of a receivable to which ASC 835-30 was not intended to apply (ASC 310-40-40-8).

For creditors, a troubled debt restructuring may involve substituting debt of another business enterprise, individual, or governmental unit for that of a troubled debtor. That kind of restructuring should be accounted for according to its substance (ASC 310-40-25-2).

CREDITOR DISCLOSURE REQUIREMENTS FOR TROUBLED DEBT RESTRUCTURINGS

The creditor shall disclose the following regarding troubled debt restructurings (ASC 310-40-50-1):

1. As of the date of each statement of financial position presented, the total recorded investment in the impaired loans at the end of each period, as well as (*a*) the amount of the recorded investment for which there is a related allowance for credit losses, and the amount of that allowance;

and (b) the amount of the recorded investment for which there is no related allowance for credit losses

2. The creditor's policy for recognizing interest income on impaired loans, including how cash receipts are recorded
3. For each period for which results of operations are presented, the average recorded investment in the impaired loans during each period; the related amount of interest income recognized during the time within that period that the loans were impaired; and, if practicable, the amount of interest income recognized (cash-basis method of accounting) during the time within that period that the loans were impaired
4. Amount(s) of any commitment(s) to lend additional funds to any debtor who is a party to a restructuring

PART II: INTERPRETIVE GUIDANCE

ASC 310-10: OVERALL

ASC 310-10-05-9; 15-5; 25-15 through 25-30; 35-55 through 35-61; 40-3 through 40-5; 45-15; ASC 360-10-35-3, 35-9 Purpose and Scope of AcSEC Practice Bulletins and Procedures for Their Issuance

BACKGROUND

The AICPA issued Practice Bulletins to disseminate the views of the AICPA Accounting Standards Executive Committee (AcSEC) (now known as the Financial Reporting Executive Committee) on narrow financial accounting and reporting issues. AcSEC was a senior technical body of the AICPA authorized to represent the AICPA on matters that addressed accounting and financial reporting unique to specific industries. Practice Bulletins addressed issues that were not addressed and are not expected to be addressed by either the FASB or the Governmental Accounting Standards Board (GASB).

ACCOUNTING GUIDANCE

Before 1987, when AcSEC began to issue Practice Bulletins, similar guidance was provided in "Notices to Practitioners," which were published in either *The CPA Letter* or the *Journal of Accountancy*. Unlike Notices to Practitioners, which are not numbered for retrievability, Practice Bulletins are numbered and designed to convey information that will enhance the quality and comparability of financial statements.

Drafts of proposed Practice Bulletins, which have been discussed at AcSEC open meetings, are available to the public as part of the meeting's agenda. However, Practice Bulletins have not been exposed for public comment, and their issuance is not subject to public hearings.

A Practice Bulletin is issued if both of the following conditions are met: (a) two-thirds or more of AcSEC's members vote to issue the proposed Bulletin, and (b) after reviewing the proposed Bulletin, the FASB and GASB indicate that neither plans to address the particular issue.

Most of the Notices to Practitioners that preceded the issuance of Practice Bulletins have been superseded. Three Notices to Practitioners continue to be in effect, however, and are discussed in the appendix to PB-1, "Purpose and Scope of AcSEC Practice Bulletins and Procedures for Their Issuance." The following is a brief discussion of the three Notices to Practitioners that were not superseded.

ACRS Lives and GAAP

In most cases, the number of years specified by the ACRS for recovery deductions will not bear any reasonable resemblance to the asset's useful life. In these cases, ACRS recovery deductions cannot be used as the depreciation expense amount for financial reporting purposes. Rather, depreciation for financial reporting purposes should be based on the asset's useful life.

Accounting by Colleges and Universities for Compensated Absences

Note: The following discussion pertains solely to private (nonpublic) colleges and universities.

When ASC 710, *Compensation—General*, and ASC 420, *Exit or Disposal Cost Obligations* were issued, there was some discussion as to whether the guidance in ASC 710 would apply to colleges and universities. The FASB decided *not* to exempt colleges and universities from the provisions of that standard. A Notice to Practitioners was issued to assist colleges and universities in applying that guidance. The essential conclusions of the Notice were as follows:

- In recognizing the liability, and the associated charge, for compensated absences in the current and prior years, the unrestricted current fund is to be used (use of the plant fund is specifically prohibited).

- In some cases, the liability for compensated absences might be recoverable from future state and federal grants and contracts for funded research. A receivable, and the associated revenue, can be recognized to offset a portion of the liability only in limited situations. More specifically, a receivable can be recognized only if it meets the definition of an *asset* in Statement of Financial Accounting Concepts No. 6 (Elements of Financial Statements of Business Enterprises). In evaluating the receivable, the college or university should consider the measurability and collectibility of the receivable and the institution's legal right to it.

- The reduction in the unrestricted current fund balance caused by recognizing the liability for compensated absences may be reduced by interfund transfers. These interfund transfers may be recognized only if (*a*) unrestricted assets are available for permanent transfer and (*b*) payment (or other settlement) to the unrestricted current fund is expected within a reasonable period.

ADC Arrangements

This Notice to Practitioners addresses the funding provided by financial institutions for real estate acquisition, development, and construction (ADC). In some cases, financial institutions enter into ADC agreements where the institution has essentially the same risks and rewards as an investor or a joint venture participant. In these cases, treating the ADC funding as a loan would not be appropriate.

The notice applies only to ADC arrangements in which a financial institution is expected to receive some or all of the residual profit. Expected residual profit is the amount of funds the lender is expected to receive—whether these funds are referred to as interest, as fees, or as an equity kicker—above a customary amount of interest and fees normally received for providing comparable financing.

The profit participation between the lender and the developer is not always part of the mortgage loan agreement. Therefore, the auditor should be cognizant that such side agreements may exist and should design the audit to detect such profit participation agreements between the lender and the developer.

> **PRACTICE POINTER:** A side agreement may exist to provide the lender with a profit participation in ADC loans. This side agreement may not be referred to in the mortgage agreement between the lender and the developer. The auditor should specifically ask the lender to confirm whether it is party to a profit participation agreement on a particular loan.

A number of characteristics, in addition to the sharing of the expected residual profit, indicate that the ADC arrangement is more akin to an investment or a joint venture than to a loan. These characteristics are as follows:

- The financial institution provides all, or substantially all, of the funds necessary to acquire, develop, and construct the project. The developer has title but little or no equity investment in the project.
- The financial institution rolls into the loan any commitment and/or origination fees.
- The financial institution adds to the loan balance all, or substantially all, interest and fees during the term of the loan.
- The financial institution's only security for the loan is the ADC project. There is no recourse to other assets of the borrower. Also, the borrower does not guarantee the debt.
- The financial institution recovers its investment in one of three ways: (a) the project is completed and sold to an independent third party, (b) the borrower obtains refinancing from another source, or (c) the project is completed and placed in service, and cash flows are sufficient to fund the repayment of principal and interest.
- Foreclosure during the development period due to delinquency is unlikely, because the borrower is not required to make any payments during this period.

In some cases, even though a lender is expected to participate in the residual profit from the project, the facts and circumstances of the borrowing arrangement are consistent with a loan. The following characteristics of an ADC arrangement are consistent with a loan:

- The lender's participation in the expected residual profit is less than 50%.
- The borrower has a substantial equity investment in the project, not funded by the lender. This equity investment can be either in the form of cash or in the form of the contribution of land to the project.
- Either (*a*) the lender has recourse to other substantial, tangible assets of the borrower, which have not already been pledged under other loans, or (*b*) the borrower has secured an irrevocable letter of credit from a creditworthy, independent third party for substantially all of the loan balance and for the entire term of the loan.
- A take-out commitment for the entire amount of the loan has been secured from a creditworthy, independent third party. If the take-out commitment is conditional, the conditions should be reasonable and their attainment should be probable.

Some ADC loans contain personal guarantees from the borrower or from a third party, but such guarantees are rarely sufficient to support classifying an ADC arrangement as a loan.

In evaluating the substance of a personal guarantee, the following factors should be considered: (1) the ability of the guarantor to perform under the guarantee, (2) the practicality of enforcing the guarantee in the applicable jurisdiction, and (3) a demonstrated intent on the part of the lender to enforce the guarantee. Factors that might indicate the ability to perform under the guarantee include placing liquid assets in escrow, pledging marketable securities, and obtaining irrevocable letters of credit from a creditworthy, independent third party.

In the absence of the support discussed above for a guarantee, a guarantor's financial statements should be evaluated. In evaluating a guarantor's financial statements, an auditor should consider both the guarantor's liquidity and net worth. A guarantee has little substance if it is supported only by assets already pledged as security for other debt. Also, guarantees made by a guarantor on other projects should be considered.

If a lender expects to receive more than 50% of the residual profit from a project, the lender should account for the income or loss from the arrangement as a real estate investment. The guidance in ASC 970, Real Estate-General, ASC 360, Property Plant and Equipment, and ASC 976, Real Estate-Retail Land should be followed.

If a lender expects to receive less than 50% of the residual profit from a project, an ADC arrangement should be accounted for as a loan or as a joint venture, depending on the applicable circumstances. If an ADC arrangement is classified as a loan, interest and fees accounted for as a receivable may be recognized as income if they are recoverable. In assessing the recoverability of loan amounts and accrued interest, the guidance in both ASC 974, Real Estate-Real Estate Investment Trusts, and the guidance in ASC 942 (Audit and Accounting Guide, *Banks and Savings Institutions*) might be useful. If an ADC arrangement is classified as a joint venture, the primary accounting guidance may be found in ASC 970 and in ASC 835-20, Interest-Capitalization.

For balance sheet reporting purposes, ADC arrangements classified as investments in real estate or as joint ventures should be combined and reported separately from ADC arrangements accounted for as loans.

In some cases, a lender's share of the expected residual profit is sold before a project is completed. The applicable accounting in those cases hinges on whether the ADC arrangement was treated as a loan, as an investment in real estate, or as a joint venture. If an ADC arrangement was treated as a loan, proceeds received from a sale of the expected residual profit should be recognized as additional interest income over the remaining term of the loan. If an ADC arrangement was treated as a real estate investment or a joint venture, any gain to be recognized upon sale of the expected residual profit is determined based on the guidance ASC 976.

The accounting treatment of an ADC project should be periodically reassessed. For example, an ADC arrangement originally classified as an investment or as a joint venture might subsequently be classified as a loan if a lender is not expected to receive more than 50% of the residual profit and if the risk to the lender has decreased significantly. It is important to note that a change in accounting for an ADC arrangement depends on a change in the facts that were relied upon when the ADC arrangement was initially classified. The absence of, or a reduced participation in, a residual profit is not sufficient to change the categorization of an ADC arrangement. In addition, it is possible for an ADC arrangement initially classified as a loan to be reclassified as a real estate investment or a joint venture. A lender may take on additional risks and rewards of ownership by releasing collateral to support a guarantee and by increasing its percentage of profit participation. An improvement in a project's economic prospects does not justify a change in how an ADC arrangement is categorized. A change in classification is expected to be rare and should be supported by adequate documentation.

Finally, regardless of the accounting treatment for an ADC arrangement, it is necessary to continually assess the collectibility of principal, accrued interest, and fees. Also, ADC financing often entails a heightened risk of related-party transactions. An auditor needs to design the audit accordingly.

ASC 310-10-05-5, 05-7; 25-3, 25-6, 25-8; 25-13; 30-7; 35-41 through 35-43, 35-46 through 35-49; 45-2, through 45-3; 50-2 through 50-11; ASC 310-20-15-3; 50-1; ASC 460-10-35-3; 45-1; ASC 460-605-25-7; ASC 825-10-35-1 through 35-3; ASC 835-30-15-1; ASC 860-20-50-5; ASC 860-50-15-3; ASC 860-50-40-2, 40-6; ASC 860-942-15-2 through 15-3; ASC 942-210-45-1 through 45-2; ASC 942-305-05-2; 45-1; 50-1; ASC 942-310-15-2; ASC 942-320-50-4; ASC 942-325-25-1 through 25-3; 35-1 through 35-4; ASC 942-360-45-2; ASC 942-405-25-1 through 25-4; 35-1; 45-1 through 45-4; 50-1; ASC 942-470-45-1 through 45-2; 50-2 through 50-3; ASC 942-505-50-1H through 50-7; ASC 942-825-50-1 through 50-2; ASC 944-320-50-1; ASC 948-10-15-3; 50-2 through 50-5 Accounting by Certain Entities (Including Entities with Trade Receivables) That Lend to or Finance the Activities of Others

BACKGROUND

This guidance was issued to reduce the variability among financial institutions (including entities with trade receivables) in accounting for similar transactions.

It provides accounting guidance for entities that lend to or finance the activities of other parties, including entities that simply extend normal trade credit to customers (i.e., accounts receivable). The guidance does *not* apply to entities that carry loans and trade receivables at fair value, with changes in fair value flowing through the current period's income statement. Examples of such entities include: investment companies, broker-dealers in securities, and employee benefit plans.

> **OBSERVATION:** This guidance applies to all entities that lend to or finance the activities of their customers or other parties, even if an entity is not considered to be a finance company. Therefore, the guidance on the recognition, measurement, and disclosure of loans and trade receivables, credit losses, and other items, applies to manufacturers, retailers, and other non-financial entities. Also, more specific guidance is provided for finance companies.

ACCOUNTING GUIDANCE

Recognition and Measurement

The recognition and measurement guidance applies to a number of items, including loans and trade receivables not held for sale, nonmortgage loans held for sale, sales of loans not held for sale, credit losses—including losses on off-balance-sheet instruments, standby commitments to purchase loans, delinquency fees, prepayment fees, and rebates.

An entity has a loan or trade receivable not held for sale if management has the intent and ability to hold the loan or receivable for the foreseeable future or until maturity. Such loans and receivables should be recognized at the outstanding principal adjusted for charge-offs, the allowance for loan losses (allowance for doubtful accounts), deferred fees or costs on originated loans, and unamortized premiums or discounts for purchased loans. A nonmortgage loan held for sale should be recognized at the lower of cost or fair value.

An entity may decide to sell a loan not previously classified as held for sale. Once a decision is made to sell such a loan, the loan should be transferred into the held for sale category and carried at the lower of cost or fair value.

Credit losses—whether for loans or trade receivables—should be subtracted from the related allowance account. A loan or trade receivable should be written off in the period in which the particular loan or receivable is deemed uncollectible.

> **PRACTICE POINTER:** The recognition and measurement of trade receivables should not be changed as a result of this guidance. However, it is likely that the presentation and disclosure of trade receivables will change.

An entity may have credit losses arising from off-balance-sheet exposures. If an entity has such a loss, the loss and a related liability should be recognized. A loss accrual should be recorded separately from any valuation account related to a recognized financial instrument that may exist.

Entities may enter into standby commitments to purchase loans. In return for a fee, the entity stands ready to purchase loans at a stated price. The appropriate accounting treatment depends on whether (1) the settlement date is reasonable and (2) the entity has the intent and ability to accept the loans without selling assets. An example of a reasonable settlement date is one within a normal loan commitment period. If both of those criteria are met, the loan is recorded at cost, less any standby commitment fee received, at the settlement date. If either one of the criteria is not met, the standby commitment is recorded as a written put option.

Delinquency fees should be recognized in income if the entity is allowed to charge a fee (i.e., the conditions necessary for charging delinquency fees have been met). This treatment assumes that the collection of delinquency fees is reasonably assured. Prepayment penalties should not be recognized in income until the loans are prepaid.

Borrowers are sometimes entitled to rebates of previous finance charges paid. The calculation of rebate amounts is typically governed by state law, often using the Rule of 78s, rather than reflecting an entity's internal accounting procedures, which typically follow the interest method. Any differences between rebate calculations and interest income previously recognized are treated as adjustments of previously recognized interest income. The difference should be recognized in income when loans (or receivables) are prepaid or renewed.

Presentation and Disclosure

This presentation and disclosure guidelines are related to (1) accounting policies for loans and trade receivables, (2) accounting policies for credit losses and doubtful accounts, (3) accounting policies for nonaccrual and past due loans and trade receivables, (4) sales of loans and trade receivables, (5) loans or trade receivables, (6) foreclosed or repossessed assets, (7) nonaccrual and past due loans and trade receivables, and (8) assets serving as collateral.

The following are the presentation and disclosure requirements:

- To provide a summary of the entity's significant accounting policies for loans and trade receivables, and its basis of accounting for loans, trade receivables, and lease financings must be disclosed. In addition, an entity must disclose (a) whether it uses the aggregate or individual asset basis to determine the lower of cost or fair value of nonmortgage loans held for sale; (b) the classification and method of accounting for interest-only strips, loans, other receivables, and certain retained interests in securitizations; and (c) its method of recognizing interest income on loan and trade receivables.

- To describe the entity's policies and methodology for determining the allowance for loan losses, allowance for doubtful accounts, and any liability for off-balance-sheet credit losses.

- To disclose its policy and methodology for the recognition and measurement of losses related to loans, trade receivables, and other credit exposures.
- To provide disclosures about its policies for nonaccrual and past due loans and trade receivables.
- To describe its policy for placing loans (or trade receivables) on nonaccrual status, and how payments received on nonaccrual loans (or trade receivables) are treated.
- To disclose its policy for restoring loans (or receivables) to accrual status.
- To disclose its policy for writing off loans and trade receivables as uncollectible.
- To describe whether it evaluates past due (or delinquency) status based on when the most recent payment was received or based on contractual terms.
- To separately disclose its aggregate gains or losses from sales of loans or trade receivables.
- To present major categories of loans and trade receivables separately, either in the financial statements or in the notes.
- To present receivables held for sale as a separate category on the balance sheet.
- To present foreclosed or repossessed assets as a separate line item on the balance sheet or as part of other assets with disclosure of the amounts related to foreclosed or repossessed assets in the notes.
- For nonaccrual and past due loans and receivables, to disclose in the notes to the financial statements (a) the entity's recorded investment in nonaccrual loans and trade receivables as of each balance sheet date, and (b) its recorded investment in loans (or receivables) that are still accruing interest even though they are past due 90 days or more.
- To disclose the carrying amounts of loans, receivables, securities, and financial instruments that are serving as collateral for borrowings.

ASC 310-10-25-7; 35-52 Difference between Initial Investment and Principal Amount of Loans in a Purchased Credit Card Portfolio

BACKGROUND

An entity has purchased a credit card portfolio for an amount of cash that exceeds the balance of the credit card receivables.

The guidance in ASC 310-20-35-15; 25-22 states that the difference between the amount paid to acquire a loan (initial investment) and the loan's principal amount at acquisition should be recognized over the life of the loan as a yield adjustment. The financial institution should defer and amortize the premium on a straight-line basis over the period the cardholders are entitled to use their cards.

This Issue was addressed because of diversity in practice.

ACCOUNTING ISSUES

- Should the difference (premium) between the amount an entity pays to purchase credit card loans and the sum of the balances of the receivables at the date of purchase be allocated between the loans acquired and identifiable intangible assets acquired, if any?
- Over what period should an entity amortize amounts allocated to loans and identifiable intangible assets acquired?

ACCOUNTING GUIDANCE

The following guidance should be followed:

- The difference (premium) between the amount an entity pays to purchase a credit card portfolio, including the cardholder relationships, and the sum of the balances of the credit card loans at the date of purchase should be allocated between the credit cardholder relationships acquired and loans acquired. (See Effect of ASC 860 below)
- The portion of a premium related to credit cardholder relationships is an identifiable intangible asset and should be amortized over the period of estimated benefit under the provisions of ASC 350. The portion allocated to the loans should be amortized over the life of the loans in accordance with the guidance in ASC 310, Receivables. A determination of the life of a credit card loan should consider whether the terms of the agreement permit the loan's repayment period to continue after the expiration date of the credit card if the card is not renewed.

OBSERVATION: Under the guidance in ASC 350, intangible assets should be amortized over their useful lives, unless the life of the intangible asset is considered to be indefinite.

EFFECT OF ASC 860

Under the guidance in ASC 860, Transfers and Servicing, the consensus position in Issue 1, that the difference between the amount paid to purchase credit card loans and the sum of the balances of the receivables at the purchase date should be allocated between the credit cardholder relationships and the loans acquired, is unaffected if the conditions for treatment as a sale in ASC 860-10-40-4 through 40-5 and 55-68A exist. ASC 860-20-30-1 provides that assets obtained and liabilities incurred by a transferee should be measured and recognized at fair value. The subsequent measurement issues discussed in Issue 2 are not addressed in ASC 860 and therefore do not affect the guidance on the amortization of credit cardholder relationships.

ASC 310-10-05-9; ASC 815-15-55-9, 55-10 Application of the AICPA Notice to Practitioners Regarding Acquisition, Development, and Construction Arrangements to Acquisition of an Operating Property

BACKGROUND

Company A, not necessarily a financial institution, makes a 10- to 15-year loan to Company B to acquire an operating property. In addition to paying a market interest rate and fees, Company B agrees that upon sale or refinancing of the loan, it will share with Company A a certain percentage of the property's appreciation, which is calculated as the difference between the original loan balance and the net proceeds from the sale of the property or the property's appraised value. Company B may discontinue paying a portion of accrued interest during the term of the loan but will pay that interest at maturity.

ACCOUNTING ISSUES

- Does ASC 310-10-5-9; 15-5; 25-15 through 25-30; 45-15; 40-3 40-5; 310-35-55-61 apply to financing of acquisitions of operating properties?
- If yes, how should its guidance be applied?

ACCOUNTING GUIDANCE

- The guidance in ASC 310-10-5-9; 15-5; 25-15 through 25-30; 45-15; 40-3 40-5; and ASC 310-35-55-61 should be considered by preparers and auditors in accounting for shared appreciation mortgages, loans on operating real estate properties, and real estate acquisition, development, and construction (ADC) arrangements entered into by entities that are not financial institutions, even though the third Notice discussed only ADC arrangements of financial institutions.
- The nature of expected residual profit should be determined based on the guidance in ASC 310-10-25-15 through 25-17, which discuss various profit-sharing arrangements, such as a specific percentage of the borrower's profit on a sale.
- The guidance in ASC 310-10-5-9; 15-5; 25-15 through 25-30; 45-15; 40-3 40-5; and ASC 310-35-55-61 is the best guidance available to preparers and auditors on this subject.

OBSERVATION: The guidance in ASC 810 requires the consolidation of variable interest entities by an entity that absorbs a majority of a variable entity's expected losses or has the right to receive a greater part of the variable entity's expected residual returns or both.

EFFECT OF ASC 815

The embedded equity kicker discussed in this Issue should be analyzed to determine whether it is a separate derivative under the definition in ASC 815. If not, the guidance above continues to apply.

SEC OBSERVER COMMENT

The SEC Observer stated that *all* SEC registrants are expected to follow the guidance in ASC 310-10-5-9; 15-5; 25-15 through 25-30; 45-15; 40-3 40-5; and ASC 310-35-55-61 for existing and future real estate ADC arrangements.

SUBSEQUENT DEVELOPMENTS

The following events occurred after this guidance was issued:

- The SEC staff issued SAB-71, which incorporates the guidance in ASC 310-10-5-9; 15-5; 25-15 through 25-30; 45-15; 40-3 40-5; and ASC 310-35-55-61 in its discussion of mortgage loans having the economics of a real estate investment or joint venture instead of a loan. The SAB also refers to the guidance in this Issue and was supplemented by SAB-71A.

- The Federal Home Loan Bank Board (FHLBB) issued a notice that requires all financial institutions insured by the Federal Savings and Loan Insurance Corporation (FSLIC) or its affiliates to follow the principles in ASC 310-10-5-9; 15-5; 25-15 through 25-30; 45-15; 40-3 40-5; and ASC 310-35-55-61 in classifying and accounting for ADC arrangements in reports or financial statements filed with the FSLIC and the FHLBB.

ASC 310-10-50-18; 30-05-2 through 05-3; 15-1 through 15-4, 15-6 through 15-10; 25-1; 30-1; 35-2 through 35-3, 35-5 through 35-6, 35-8 through 35-15; 40-1; 45-1; 50-1 through 50-3; 55-2, 55-5 through 55-29; 60-3 Accounting for Certain Loans or Debt Securities in a Transfer

SCOPE

The guidance in this pronouncement applies to all nongovernmental entities that acquire loans, including not-for-profit organizations. Loans under its scope: (1) have had a deterioration in credit quality since origination; (2) have been acquired in a transfer that (*a*) meets the conditions in ASC 860-10-40-4 through 40-5 to be accounted for as a sale or purchase, (*b*) is a business combination, (*c*) is made to a newly created subsidiary if the investor wrote down the loan to its fair value with the intent of transferring the subsidiary's stock as a dividend to the parent company's shareholders, or (*d*) is a contribution receivable or a transfer in satisfaction of a prior promise to give; and (3) it is probable at acquisition, as defined in ASC 860-10-35-3, that all contractually required payments receivable will not be collected, with the following exceptions:

- Loans measured at fair value with all changes in fair value included in earnings or, for not-for-profit organizations, loans measured at fair value with all changes in fair value included in the statement of activities and included in the performance indicator, if one is presented

- Mortgage loans classified as held for sale under the guidance in ASC 948-310-35-1

- Leases defined in ASC 840

- Loans acquired in a business combination accounted for at historical cost

- Loans held by liquidating banks

- Revolving credit agreements (e.g., credit cards and home equity loans), if the borrower has revolving privileges at the acquisition date

- Loans that are retained interests

Loans that are derivative instruments accounted for under the provisions of ASC 815 Accounting for also are excluded from the scope. However, if a loan that would normally come under the scope of this guidance has an embedded derivative accounted for under the provisions of ASC 815, the host instrument would be accounted for under the scope of this guidance if it meets the scope requirements.

Recognition, Measurement, and Display

A loan loss allowance should *not* be established at acquisition for loans acquired in a transfer. Loans acquired in a business combination should be initially recognized at the present value of amounts expected to be received. A valuation allowance should be established only for incurred losses at the present value of cash flows that were expected at acquisition but not received.

Income recognition should be based on a reasonable expectation about the timing and amount of cash flows to be collected. If after acquisition, an investor is unable to calculate a yield on a loan because of a lack of information necessary to reasonably estimate the cash flows expected to be collected, the investor is permitted to place the loan on a nonaccrual status and recognize income by the cost recovery method or on a cash basis. If, however, the timing and amount of cash flows expected to be collected, for example, from a sale of a loan into the secondary market or a sale of loan collateral, is reasonably estimable, the cash flows should be used to apply the interest method under the guidance in this pronouncement. Interest income should *not* be recognized if it would cause the net investment in the loan to exceed the payoff amount. Income should *not* be accrued on loans acquired primarily for the rewards of owning the underlying collateral, such as for the use of the collateral in the entity's operations or to improve it for resale.

Changes in Cash Flows Expected to Be Collected

Investors should account for changes in cash flows expected to be collected as follows:

1. For loans accounted for as debt securities, cash flows expected to be collected over the life of a loan should continue to be estimated, unless a subsequent evaluation reveals that:

    a. The debt security's fair value is *less* than its amortized cost basis. In that case, it should be determined whether the decline is other than temporary and the guidance on impairment of securities in ASC 320-20-45-9 should be applied. The timing and amount of cash flows expected to be collected should be considered in determining the probability of collecting all cash flows that were expected to be collected at acquisition as well as additional cash flows as a result of changes in estimates made after acquisition.

    b. It is probable, based on current information and events, that cash flows previously expected to be collected have significantly increased or actual cash flows significantly exceed previously expected cash flows. The amount of the accretable yield for the loan should be recalculated as the excess of the revised cash flows expected to be collected over the sum of (i) the initial investment *less* (ii) cash collected *less* (iii) other-than-temporary impairments *plus* (iv) the yield accreted to date. The amount of accretable yield should be adjusted by reclassifying amounts from the nonaccretable difference.

This adjustment should be accounted for as a change in estimate in accordance with the guidance in ASC 250. The amount of periodic accretion should be adjusted over the remaining life of the loan.

2. For loans *not* accounted for as debt securities, cash flows expected to be collected over the life of a loan should continue to be estimated, unless a subsequent evaluation reveals that:

   a. It is probable, based on current information and events, that all cash flows originally expected to be collected and additional cash flows expected to be collected as a result of changes in estimates after acquisition will *not* be collected, in which case, the condition in ASC 450-20-25-2 is met. Therefore, the loan should be considered impaired when applying the measurement and other provisions of ASC 450 or the provisions of ASC 310, if applicable.

   b. It is probable based on current information and events that cash flows originally expected to be collected have increased significantly or actual cash flows significantly exceed cash flows previously expected to be collected. In that case:

      (1) The remaining valuation allowance or allowance for loan losses established after the loan's acquisition should be reduced by the increase in the present value of cash flows expected to be collected; *and*

      (2) The amount of the loan's accretable yield should be recalculated as the excess of revised cash flows expected to be collected over the sum of (1) the initial investment *less* (2) cash collected *less* (3) write-downs *plus* (4) the yield accreted to date. The amount of accretable yield should be adjusted by reclassifying the nonaccretable difference. This adjustment should be accounted for as a change in estimate in accordance with the guidance in ASC 250. The amount of periodic accretion should be adjusted over the remaining life of the loan.

Prepayments

The treatment of expected prepayments should be consistent in accounting for cash flows expected to be collected and for projections of contractual cash flows so that the nonaccretable difference will *not* be affected. The nonaccretable difference also should *not* be affected if actual prepayments differ from expected prepayments.

Restructured or Refinanced Loan

A loan that is refinanced or restructured subsequent to acquisition, other than by a troubled debt restructuring, should *not* be accounted for as a new loan. The provisions of this pronouncement, including those related to changes in cash flows expected to be collected, continue to apply.

Variable Rate Loans

Contractually required payments receivable on a loan with a contractual interest rate that varies based on subsequent changes in an independent factor, for example, the prime rate, should be based on the factor as it changes over the life of the loan. The loan's effective interest rate or cash flows expected to be collected should *not* be based on projections of future changes in that factor. At acquisition, the amount of cash flows expected to be collected should be calculated based on the rate in effect at the acquisition date. Increases in cash flows expected to be collected should be accounted for according to the guidance in 1(b) and 2(b), above, in the discussion of changes in cash flows expected to be collected. The amount of cash flows originally expected to be collected and the accretable yield should be reduced if cash flows expected to be collected decrease as a direct result of a change in the contractual interest rate. This change should be accounted for according to the guidance in 1(a) and 2(a), above, in the discussion of changes in cash flows originally expected to be collected and recognized prospectively as a change in accounting estimate according to the guidance in ASC 250. In this case, *no* loss will be recognized, but the future yield will be reduced.

Multiple Loans Accounted for as a Single Asset

Investors are permitted to recognize, measure, and disclose information about loans *not* accounted for as debt securities as a similar single asset if the loans were acquired in the same fiscal year and have similar credit risks or risk ratings, and have one or more common major characteristic, such as financial asset type, collateral type, size, interest rate, date of origination, term, or geographic location, so that a composite interest rate and expectation of cash flows to be collected for the pool can be used. However, each individual loan should meet the scope criteria discussed above. The total cost of the acquired assets should be allocated to the individual assets based on their relative fair values at the acquisition date. The amount by which contractually required payments receivable exceed an investor's initial investment for a specific loan or a pool of loans with common risk characteristics should not be used to offset changes in cash flows expected to be collected from another loan or another pool of loans with different risk characteristics.

Once aggregated, the carrying amounts of individual loans should *not* be removed from the pool unless the investor sells, forecloses, writes off, or pays off the loan in another manner. The percentage yield calculation used to recognize accretable yield on a pool of loans should *not* be affected by the difference between a loan's carrying amount and the fair value of the collateral or other assets received.

Disclosures

The notes to the financial statements should include the following information about loans that meet the scope criteria in this SOP:

1. How prepayments are considered in determining contractual cash flows and cash flows expected to be collected
2. Disclosures required in ASC 310-10-50-12 through 50-13 and 35-34, if the condition in ASC 320-20-45-9 or ASC 450-20-25-2 related to the discussion of changes in cash flows expected to be collected is met
3. Separate information about loans accounted for as debt securities and those that are *not*, including:

(a) The outstanding balance, which consists of the undiscounted sum of all amounts, including amounts considered to be principal, interest, fees, penalties, and other amounts under the loan owed to the investor at the reporting date, except for amounts irrevocably forgiven in a debt restructuring; amounts legally discharged and interest, fees, penalties, and other amounts that would be accrued after the reporting date for loans with a net carrying amount; and the related carrying amount at the beginning and end of the period.

(b) The accretable yield at the beginning and at the end of the period, reconciled for additions, accretion, disposals of loans, and reclassifications to or from the nonaccretable difference during the period.

(c) Contractually required payments receivable, cash flows expected to be collected, and the fair value at the acquisition date of loans acquired during the period.

(d) The carrying amount at the acquisition date of loans under the scope of this guidance not accounted for in accordance with the income recognition model in this pronouncement that are acquired during the period and the carrying amount of all such loans at the end of the period.

4. The following disclosures are required only for loans *not* accounted for as debt securities:

(a) For each period for which an income statement is presented, the amount of (*a*) expenses, if any, recognized in accordance with the guidance in 2(a) of the section on changes in cash flows expected to be collected and (*b*) reductions of the allowance recognized in accordance with the guidance in 2(b)(1) of the section on changes in cash flows expected to be collected.

(b) The amount of the allowance for uncollectible accounts at the beginning and end of the period.

ASC 310-10-35-2, 35-4, 35-6, 35-8, 35-15, 35-19, 35-25, 35-27, 35-34 through 35-36, 35-38; 55-1 through 55-6; 310-40-50-4; 310-45-20-60-3 Application of FASB Statements No. 5 and No. 114 to a Loan Portfolio

The SEC staff issued this announcement in response to inquiries regarding the transition required for companies that change their application of generally accepted accounting principles as a result of the guidance in the FASB staff's Viewpoints article, "Application of FASB Statements 5 and 114 to a Loan Portfolio," which was published in the FASB's April 12, 1999, *Status Report*. The SEC staff noted that the guidance in that article is part of generally accepted accounting principles and should be followed by *all* creditors.

According to the SEC staff, if an SEC registrant's application of the guidance in the Viewpoints article results in a material adjustment, the change should be reported and disclosed in the first quarter ending after May 20, 1999, like a cumulative effect of a change in accounting principles in accordance with the guidance in ASC 250-10-45-5. The SEC staff reported that a March 10, 1999, letter to financial institutions—which was issued jointly by the SEC, Federal Deposit Insurance Corporation, Federal Reserve Board, Office of the Controller of the Currency, and Office of Thrift Supervision (the Agencies)—encourages the FASB and its staff to issue additional guidance on accounting for loan losses. In addition, the letter states that the Agencies support the work of the AICPA's Allowance for Loan Losses Task Force in its effort to develop specific guidance on the measurement of credit losses and how to distinguish probable losses inherent in a portfolio at the balance sheet date from possible or future losses that are not inherent in the balance sheet at that date. The Agencies require that allowances be reported for probable losses. The letter also states that the senior staff of the Agencies are working jointly on guidance for (*a*) documentation to support the allowance in addition to that provided in the SEC Financial Reporting Release No. 28 (Accounting for Loan Losses by Registrants Engaged in Lending Activities) under the heading *Procedural Discipline in Determining the Allowance and Provision for Loan Losses to be Reported* and (*b*) improved disclosures about allowances for credit losses.

The EITF asked that the Viewpoints article and a May 21, 1999, letter from the Board of Governors of the Federal Reserve System, which provides guidance to supervisors and bankers regarding the Viewpoints article, be attached to the announcement. The SEC staff supports that guidance.

ASC 310-20: NONREFUNDABLE FEES AND OTHER COSTS

ASC 310-20-05-3; 35-4, 35-6, 50-4 Amortization Period for Net Deferred Credit Card Origination Costs

BACKGROUND

A credit card issuer normally charges annual fees to its cardholders. Sometimes, as part of a promotion designed to attract new customers, the issuer waives the annual fee or charges no fee. The issuer incurs certain direct costs of issuing credit cards. In addition, the credit card agreement entered into as part of the promotion generally provides the cardholder with an extended period to repay the outstanding balance on the credit card in the event of cancellation or nonrenewal. If a cardholder does not renew the card after a one-year period, for example, the agreement may allow the cardholder to repay the outstanding balance over an additional period, such as two or three years.

The guidance in ASC 310 does not specifically address the amortization of costs associated with credit card originations. The Statement requires that direct loan origination costs be offset against origination fees, with the net amount deferred and recognized as an adjustment to the loan yield.

The Issue applies to the amortization of deferred origination costs on credit cards with fees, without fees, or if fees have been waived for a limited period of time. It does not apply, however, to origination costs for private label credit cards, which are issued by, or on behalf of, an entity for purchases only of that entity's goods or services.

ACCOUNTING ISSUE

Over what period of time should direct credit card origination costs be amortized when the credit card arrangement provides for no fees?

ACCOUNTING GUIDANCE

- Based on the definition of *Direct Loan Origination Costs* in the ASC *Master Glossary*, a credit card issuer should net credit card origination costs that qualify for deferral against the related credit card fee, if any, and should amortize the net amount on a straight-line basis over the privilege period. If a significant fee is charged, the privilege period is the period over which the cardholder is entitled to use the card. If no significant fee is charged, the privilege period is one year. The significance of the fee should be evaluated based on the relationship of the fee and related costs.
- An entity should disclose its accounting policy, the net amount capitalized at the balance sheet date, and the amortization period of credit card fees and costs for purchased and originated cards.

This guidance applies only to originated credit card accounts, not accounts purchased from third parties. The amortization of a premium, if any, paid on purchases of credit card portfolios is discussed in ASC 310-10-25-7 and 35-52.

SUBSEQUENT DEVELOPMENT

In a discussion of the guidance in ASC 310-20-05-4, 25-18 and 35-8, which is discussed below, a conclusion was reached that credit card accounts acquired individually should be accounted for as originations under the guidance in this Issue.

DISCUSSION

Three approaches for amortization of direct loan origination costs were proposed: (*a*) over the privilege period, or one year; (*b*) over the repayment period, which may extend beyond the privilege period; or (*c*) over the relationship period, which includes renewal periods.

The guidance is based on the first approach. It is consistent with the guidance in ASC 310-20-25-15; 310-20-35-5, which states that "fees that are periodically charged to cardholders shall be deferred and recognized on a straight-line basis over the period the fee entitles the cardholder to use the card." It is also consistent with the guidance in ASC 310-20-35-6 through 35-7 and 25-16 through 25-17, in which the FASB staff repeated the guidance in ASC 310-20-25-15; 35-5 and stated further that "[r]elated origination costs eligible for deferral should be amortized over the same period on a straight-line basis." Proponents of this approach argued that credit card fees and related costs should be netted and amortized over the same period. Additional arguments for amortization of initiation costs over the privilege period included the fact that this approach is simple, conservative, and it enhances comparability among credit card issuers.

ASC 310-20-05-4; 25-18; 35-8 Accounting for Individual Credit Card Acquisitions

BACKGROUND

A credit card issuer can obtain new customer accounts by (*a*) purchasing a portfolio of existing credit card accounts, (*b*) originating the credit card relationship, or (*c*) purchasing individual credit card accounts through a third party. The accounts normally have no outstanding receivable balances at acquisition. The accounting for the cost associated with a bulk purchase of a credit card portfolio was addressed in ASC 310-10-25-7 and 35-52 and internal credit card origination in ASC 310-20-05-3; 35-4, 35-6; and 50-4, both of which were discussed above. However, neither provided guidance for situations in which credit card accounts are purchased individually.

Individual credit card accounts can be obtained three ways:

- *Direct marketing specialist* The credit card issuer hires a marketing company to solicit new credit card customers and usually pays the specialist a fee for each approved credit card agreement.
- *Affinity group* The credit card issuer enters into an arrangement with a company or an organization to solicit credit card accounts from their customers or members. This third-party entity is responsible for the solicitation and related costs and sells the approved credit card accounts to the issuer for a fee.
- *Co-branding* Co-branding is a variation of an affinity group, in which the name of the third party is included on the credit card. The co-branding third party provides additional products and services, such as extended warranties and discounts. In this type of arrangement, the credit card issuer and the third party benefit from increased card usage, an extended cardholder relationship period, and increased sales of the third party's products or services. Whatever the method of acquisition, the credit card issuer incurs a cost in obtaining new accounts.

ACCOUNTING ISSUE

Should a credit card issuer account for acquisitions of individual credit card accounts as purchases in accordance with the guidance in ASC 310-10-25-7 and 35-52 or as self-originations, in accordance with the guidance in ASC 310 and ASC 310-20-05-3; 35-4, 35-6, and 50-4?

ACCOUNTING GUIDANCE

A credit card issuer should:

- Account for credit card accounts acquired individually as self-originations, in accordance with the guidance in ASC 310 and ASC 310-20-05-3; 35-4, 35-6; and 50-4.
- Defer amounts paid to third parties to acquire individual credit card accounts, net those amounts against any related credit card fees, and amortize the net amount on a straight-line basis over the privilege period.

The privilege period is the period during which a cardholder is entitled to use the card, if the credit cardholder is charged a significant fee. The privilege period is one year, if there is no significant fee. The significance of the fee is based on the relationship of its amount to the card's acquisition cost.

DISCUSSION

Alternative methods of accounting for purchases of individual credit card accounts were considered and different criteria to distinguish purchases from self-originations were discussed. Proponents of the final guidance noted that the definition of *Direct Loan Origination Costs* in the ASC *Master Glossary* addresses this third-party activity as follows: "Direct loan origination costs of a completed loan shall include only (*a*) incremental direct costs of loan origination incurred in transactions with independent third parties for that loan and (*b*) certain costs directly related to specified activities performed by the lender for that loan." Further, it was noted that the third-party relationship in this situation is merely a marketing tool in which a credit card issuer is outsourcing its solicitation and origination activities. The risks and costs are still borne, however, by the credit card issuer. Proponents supported their contention that these credit card accounts are self-originations rather than purchases by arguing that the third party only solicits accounts and acts as an agent for the issuer, and the customer cannot use the credit card until it is issued by the issuer. They also argued that purchases of individual credit card accounts are unlike bulk purchases of existing credit card accounts that may have outstanding balances. In the latter transactions, the credit card issuer must accept the account and issue a credit card.

ASC 310-20-35-11 Creditor's Accounting for a Modification or an Exchange of Debt Instruments

BACKGROUND

The authoritative accounting literature provides different guidance to creditors and debtors as to how to determine whether a modification or exchange of a debt instrument should be accounted for as an extinguishment of a debt instrument and its replacement with a new debt instrument or as a continuation of a debt instrument that has been modified. ASC 310 provides such guidance for creditors and ASC 470-50-05-4, 15-3, 40-6 through 40-14, 40-17 through 40-20, 55-1 through 55-9 (EITF Issue 96-19), provides such guidance for debtors. Under the guidance in that Issue, which is discussed below, a debtor is required to account for a modification or exchange of debt as new debt if it is *substantially different* from the original debt. Whereas, under the guidance in ASC 310 (FAS-91), a creditor is not permitted to account for an original debt instrument that has been modified as a new instrument unless the modification is *more than minor*. However, ASC 310 (FAS-91) provides no guidance on how to evaluate what is more than a minor modification.

ACCOUNTING ISSUE

How should a creditor evaluate whether a modification of a debt instrument's terms as a result of a refinancing or restructuring (other than in a troubled debt restructuring) should be considered to be more than *minor* in applying the guidance in ASC 310-20-35-10?

ACCOUNTING GUIDANCE

The following guidance is provided:
- When applying the guidance in ASC 310-20-35-10, a modification or an exchange of debt instruments should be considered *more than minor* if the present value of the cash flows under the new debt instrument differs by at least *10%* from the present value of the remaining cash flows under the terms of the original debt instrument.
- If the difference between the present value of the cash flows of a new and an existing debt instrument differs by *less than* 10%, the creditor should evaluate whether a modification or exchange of debt instruments is *more*

than minor based on the facts and circumstances and other relevant information related to the modification.

- Creditors should apply the guidance in ASC 470-50-05-4, 15-3, 40-6 through 40-14, 40-17 through 40-20, 55-1 through 55-9 to calculate a debt instrument's present value of cash flows when applying the 10% test.

ASC 310-30: LOANS AND DEBT SECURITIES ACQUIRED WITH DETERIORATED CREDIT QUALITY

ASC-310-30-35-13, 40-1 through 40-2; ASC 310-40-15-11 Effect of a Loan Modification When the Loan Is Part of a Pool That Is Accounted for as a Single Asset

BACKGROUND

Under the guidance in ASC 310-30-15-6, an entity is permitted to account for acquired assets with "common risk characteristics" in a pool of assets, which becomes a unit of accounting when it is established. Because the purchase discount for loans accounted for in a pool is not allocated to the individual loans, all the loans in a pool are accreted at a rate based on the cash flow projection for the pool. Also, impairment is tested on the total pool and not on the individual loans.

Guidance for evaluating whether a loan modification should be classified as a troubled debt restructuring (TDR) is provided in ASC 310-40-15-4, which states that a restructuring of debt represents a TDR if a creditor grants a concession to the debtor as a result of the debtor's financial difficulties. Questions have been raised about whether TDR accounting applies if acquired loans with credit deterioration are accounted for in a pool. If so, some believe that the troubled loan should be removed from the pool or that the whole pool should be accounted for as a TDR. A loan that is removed from a pool would no longer be accounted for under the guidance in ASC 310-30. However, others believe that such loans should not be removed from the pool.

SCOPE

The guidance in this Issue applies to modifications of loans accounted for as a pool that is established under the provisions of ASC 310-30-15-6. The guidance in this Issue does *not* apply to loans accounted for individually under the guidance in ASC 310-30 or those not under the scope of that guidance.

ACCOUNTING GUIDANCE

TDR accounting should *not* be applied to loans accounted for as a pool under the guidance in ASC 310-30 if those loans had deteriorating credit when they were acquired. The Additional disclosures are not required, because it is expected that as part of its project on loan loss disclosures, the FASB will consider whether additional disclosures should be required about loan modifications, including for loans accounted for within a pool under the guidance in ASC 310-30.

ASC 310-40: TROUBLED DEBT RESTRUCTURINGS BY CREDITORS

ASC 310-40-40-10; 35-11; 55-13 through 55-15 Determination of Cost Basis for Foreclosed Assets under FASB Statement No. 15, *Accounting by Debtors and Creditors for Troubled Debt Restructurings*, and the Measurement of Cumulative Losses Previously Recognized under Paragraph 37 of FASB Statement No. 144, *Accounting for the Impairment or Disposal of Long-Lived Assets*

Question: When a long-lived asset is accounted for under the guidance in ASC 360 and ASC 840 after foreclosure, should a valuation allowance related to the loan that was collateralized by that long-lived asset be carried over as a separate element of the asset's cost basis?

Answer: No. When a loan is foreclosed, the lender receives the long-lived asset collateralizing the loan in full satisfaction of the receivable. As required in ASC 310-40-40-3, the asset that collateralized the loan must be measured at its fair value less selling costs, with the amount of that measurement becoming the asset's new cost basis. After foreclosure, when the asset is accounted for under the provisions of ASC 360, the valuation allowance related to the loan before foreclosure should *not* be carried over to the long-lived asset's cost basis because under the guidance in ASC 360-10-35-40 and 40-5, the amount of gain that can be recognized on a long-lived asset is limited to the amount of cumulative impairment losses recognized and measured under the guidance in ASC 360, Property, Plant, and Equipment, previously measured and recognized under the guidance in ASC 450, Contingencies, and ASC 310, Receivables, do *not* enter into the calculation of the impairment of an asset's value under the guidance in ASC 360.

For example, a lender has a $100,000 loan receivable, which is collateralized by a long-lived asset with a fair value of $80,000 and estimated selling costs of $6,000 at the date on which the lender determines that foreclosure is probable. One month later, when the asset is foreclosed, the fair value of the collateral is unchanged. Based on the guidance in ASC 310-40-05-8 and ASC 310-10-35-16 through 35-17, the lender's *loan impairment* loss at the foreclosure date is measured at $26,000, based on the difference between the loan receivable ($100,000) and the fair value of the collateral ($80,000) less selling costs ($6,000). At that date, the new cost basis of the long-lived asset received in full satisfaction of the receivable also is measured at $74,000 under the guidance in ASC 310). Three months later when the asset is tested for impairment under the guidance in ASC 360 its value has declined to $70,000 with estimated selling costs of $4,000. Under the provisions of ASC 360, the lender recognizes an $8,000 asset impairment loss [($80,000–$6,000)–($70,000–$4,000)]. When the asset is sold six months later, its fair value has increased to $84,000, less $7,000 in selling costs. Although the asset's fair value has increased by $11,000 [($84,000–$7,000)–($70,000–$4,000)], the lender can recognize a gain of only $8,000, which is the amount of the asset's impairment loss previously recognized under the guidance in ASC 360. The

$26,000 loan impairment loss on foreclosure is *not* included in measuring the cumulative losses recognized under the guidance in ASC 360.

ASC 310-40-40-6A, 40-7; 55-12 Valuation of Repossessed Real Estate

BACKGROUND

A seller finances a sale of real estate. Although the buyer's initial investment is insufficient for full accrual profit recognition under the guidance in ASC 360, the transaction qualifies for sales recognition, with profit deferred and recognized on the installment or cost recovery methods. Some time after the sale, the buyer defaults on the seller's mortgage, and the seller forecloses the property. The property's fair value at foreclosure is less than the seller's gross receivable, which includes the cost of the property and deferred profit, but is greater than the net receivable, which consists of principal and interest receivable reduced by deferred profit and related allowances.

ACCOUNTING ISSUE

At what amount should a seller recognize the foreclosed property?

ACCOUNTING GUIDANCE

A seller should recognize a foreclosed property at the lower of the net receivable or the property's fair value. This guidance assumes that under the circumstances, it is appropriate under the circumstances to include any accrued interest income on the financing in the net receivable. It was noted that the guidance in ASC 470, Debt, does *not* apply in this situation, because deferred profit is not considered a valuation allowance account, as contemplated in ASC 470. However, the guidance in ASC 470 would apply, if profit had been recognized on the full accrual method, with recognition of the property at fair value, if appropriate.

OBSERVATION: ASC 360 provides guidance on accounting for long-lived assets held for sale as well as specific criteria on how to determine when a long-lived asset should be classified as held for sale. Under that guidance, a newly acquired foreclosed asset classified as held for sale should be recognized at the lower of its carrying amount or fair value less selling costs.

Illustration of Valuation of Foreclosed Real Estate

	Installment Method	Cost Recovery Method
Sales transaction:		
Seller's financing	$475,000	$475,000
Buyer's initial investment	25,000	25,000
Sales value	$500,000	$500,000
Sales value	$500,000	$500,000
Cost	350,000	
Gain	150,000	150,000
Amount recognized	(7,500)	0
Deferred profit	$142,500	$150,000

ASC 310—Receivables

	Installment Method	Cost Recovery Method
Foreclosure at end of first year:		
Original principal balance	$475,000	$475,000
Accrued interest in first year at 8%	38,000	38,000
Gross receivable at foreclosure	513,000	513,000
Less: Deferred profit	(142,500)	(150,000)
Net receivable	$370,500	$363,000
Property's fair value at foreclosure	$430,000	$430,000

Under the guidance in this Issue, the foreclosed property would be recognized at $370,500 under the installment method or at $363,000 under the cost recovery method.

DISCUSSION

As stated above, it was noted that the guidance in ASC 470 does not apply in this transaction, because deferred profit is not considered a valuation allowance under the guidance in ASC 470. That comment is based on the guidance in ASC 470-60-15-12, which states that a foreclosure is not considered a troubled debt restructuring if the fair value of the receivable is at least equal to the "recorded investment in the receivable." The primary focus of the guidance in ASC 470 is on transactions that would result in a loss. In the case of a sale on which profit has been deferred—as in the transaction in this Issue—the net receivable, not the gross receivable, should be considered the seller's recorded investment in the receivable and compared to fair value, because it does not include deferred profit on a sale. If profit had been recognized on the full accrual method, the gross receivable would have been compared to fair value.

Recognition of foreclosed real estate at the net receivable amount results in no gain or loss on foreclosure. The original cost of the property is increased or decreased by gains and interest income recognized in prior periods and cash collected on the sale and financing. More cash may be received than recognized as gains and interest income under the installment method if the gain is a small percentage of the sales price. The same may occur under the cost recovery method, because no gain is recognized until the cost has been recovered. In those situations, the property would be recognized at less than its original cost because of the excess cash. In the above Illustration, a $3 gain was recognized on the sale, $15 of interest income was accrued, and $10 cash was received on the down payment. When the property is recognized at foreclosure, the original cost of $140 would be increased by $8 (3 + 15 − 10) to $148, which also equals the $205 receivable less deferred profit of $57.

The journal entry to recognize the foreclosed property would be as follows:
Property	$370,500	
Deferred profit	142,500	
Receivable		$513,000

ASC 310-40-15-3; 55-4; 470-60-15-3; 55-15 Classification of Debt Restructurings by Debtors and Creditors

BACKGROUND

A *troubled debt restructuring* is defined in ASC 310-40-15-3 through 15-12; 35-2, 35-5 through 35-7; 40-2, 40-5 through 40-6, 40-8; 25-1 through 25-2; 50-1; 55-2; 10-1 through 10-2; and ASC 470-60-15-3 through 15-12; 55-3; 35 through 35-12; 45-1 through 45-2; 50-1 through 50-2; 10-1 through 10-2; and ASC 450-20-60-12 as a restructuring in which a creditor, for economic or legal reasons related to a debtor's financial difficulties, grants a concession to the debtor that the creditor otherwise would *not* consider.

ACCOUNTING GUIDANCE

Question: In applying the guidance in ASC 310-40-15-3 through 15-12; 35-2; 35-5 through 35-7; 40-2, 40-5 through 40-6, 40-8; 25-1 through 25-2; 50-1; 55-2; 10-1 through 10-2; ASC 470-60-15-3 through 15-12; 55-3, 35 through 35-12, 45-1 through 45-2, 50-1 through 50-2, 10-1 through 10-2; and ASC 450-20-60-12, can a debt restructuring be a troubled debt restructuring (TDR) for a debtor but not for a creditor?

Answer: Yes, a debtor may have a TDR even though the creditor does not have a TDR. A debtor and a creditor apply that guidance individually based on their specific facts and circumstances to determine whether a particular restructuring constitutes a TDR. The guidance in ASC 310-40-15-8, 15-12 is especially helpful to creditors in determining whether a particular restructuring is a TDR for debtors or creditors. The guidance in ASC 310-40-15-3 through 15-12, 35-2, 35-5 through 35-7, 40-2, 40-5 through 40-6, 40-8, 25-1 through 25-2, 50-1, 55-2, 10-1 through 10-2; ASC 470-60-15-3 through 15-12, 55-3, 35 through 35-12, 45-1 through 45-2, 50-1 through 50-2, 10-1 through 10-2; and ASC 450-20-60-12 establishes tests for applicability that are not necessarily symmetrical between a debtor and a creditor, especially if a debtor's carrying amount and a creditor's recorded investment differ.

ASC 310-40-55-6 through 55-10 Use of Zero Coupon Bonds in a Troubled Debt Restructuring

BACKGROUND

A creditor agrees to a troubled debt restructuring on a collateralized loan. Under the terms of the agreement, the debtor liquidates some of the collateral and repays a portion of the loan. The remainder of the loan is restructured. The debtor then liquidates the remainder of the collateral, with the creditor's approval, and invests the proceeds in a series of zero coupon bonds that will mature each year at a value equal to the yearly debt service requirement under the restructured loan. The creditor holds the zero coupon bonds as the only collateral for the restructured loan.

ACCOUNTING ISSUE

Is the sale of collateral and a creditor's receipt of zero coupon bonds with a fair value that is lower than the creditor's net investment in the loan, a debt settlement that requires the creditor to recognize a loss?

ACCOUNTING GUIDANCE

Because the loan is settled with zero coupon bonds, the creditor should recognize (*a*) a loss on the difference between the fair value of the zero coupon bonds and the net investment in the loan and (*b*) an asset for the fair value of the zero coupon bonds.

> **OBSERVATION:** Under the guidance in ASC 310-40-40-3 creditors are required to account for long-lived assets received from a debtor in full satisfaction of a receivable at fair value less cost to sell. A loss should be recognized if the recorded investment in the receivable exceeds the fair value of the assets less selling costs. Such losses are included in the creditor's income for the period, unless all or a part of the loss is offset against the allowance for uncollectible accounts or other valuation accounts.

EFFECT OF ASC 860

ASC 860-30-05-2 through 05-3 provides guidance to debtors and creditors on the accounting for collateral based on whether the secured party has the right to sell or pledge the collateral. Under the circumstances in this Issue, the debtor would reclassify the zero coupon bond held by the creditor as an encumbered asset and report it in the balance sheet separately from other assets that are not encumbered in that manner. That guidance was not reconsidered in ASC 860. Under the guidance ASC 860-50-50-4 a creditor would report the fair value of the collateral and any portion that has been sold or repledged, if the creditor has the right to sell or pledge the collateral. If a creditor does not have that right, the *debtor* should report information about that collateral.

DISCUSSION

The guidance in ASC 310-40-40-6 provides that a creditor must have physical possession of the collateral, regardless of whether it has been legally foreclosed, to account for a loan as in-substance foreclosed and to recognize the fair value of the asset. That is, a creditor should continue to account for a loan for which foreclosure is probable as a loan until the creditor has possession of the collateral.

Although in this Issue, the creditor did not legally foreclose on the loan, the debtor's obligation on the restructured loan was settled with the zero coupon bonds because the creditor had possession of the bonds and was collecting annual payments. The creditor should therefore recognize a loss on that transaction. Under the guidance in ASC 310-40-40-6, this transaction qualifies for accounting as an in-substance foreclosure and would be accounted for under the accounting guidance in this Issue.

ASC 310-40-40-1 Substituted Debtors in a Troubled Debt Restructuring

BACKGROUND

A creditor and a debtor agree to a troubled debt restructuring on a mortgage loan receivable under which the debtor will make payments to the creditor for the next 30 years. With the creditor's permission, the debtor sells the house, collateralizing the loan on a contract for deed to a third party for less than the creditor's net investment in the loan. The debtor retains title to the house and the creditor retains a lien on the property. The debtor finances the sale of the house to the third party so that the monthly principal and interest payments equal the debtor's required payments on the restructured loan. The third party makes the monthly payments directly to the creditor.

ACCOUNTING ISSUE

Should the sale of the collateral and subsequent payments by the third party to the creditor be considered a settlement of the restructured loan, thus requiring the creditor to recognize a loss for the difference between the carrying amount of the net investment in the restructured loan and the fair value of the payments to be received from the third party purchaser?

ACCOUNTING GUIDANCE

The creditor should recognize an asset for the fair value of the payments to be received from the third-party purchaser and a loss on the settlement of the restructured loan that is measured based on the difference between the creditor's net investment in the loan and the fair value of the asset received to satisfy the loan in accordance with the guidance in ASC 310-40-40-3.

ASC 310-40-40-8A, 40-9 Accounting for Conversion of a Loan into a Debt Security in a Debt Restructuring

BACKGROUND

A creditor receives a debt security issued by a debtor in a debt restructuring. The fair value of the debt security differs from the creditor's basis in the loan on the date the debt is restructured because (*a*) there has been a direct write-off against the loan, so the fair value of the security exceeds the basis of the loan, or (*b*) there has been no direct write-off against the loan, so the basis of the loan exceeds the fair value of the security.

ASC 310-35-13 through 35-14, 35-16 through 35-26, 35-28, 35-29, 35-34, 35-37, 35-39; 45-5 through 45-6; 50-15, 50-19; ASC 310-30-30-2; ASC 310-40-35-8, 35-12; 50-2 through 50-3, 50-12 through 50-13 provides guidance to creditors on accounting for impaired loans, while ASC 320-10-05-2; 50-1A through 50-3, 50-5, 50-9 through 50-11; 55-3; 15-5; 30-1; 35-1 through 35-2, 35-4 through 35-5, 35-10 through 35-13, 35-18; 15-2 through 15-4, 15-7; 25-3 through 25-6, 25-9, 25-11 through 25-12, 25-14 through 25-16; 45-1 through 45-2, 45-8 through 45-11, 45-13, provides guidance on accounting for investments in marketable securities and investments in all debt securities. ASC 320-10-15-6, 55-2 states that the provisions of the latter apply to securities received in a debt restructuring.

ACCOUNTING ISSUES

1. At what amount should a creditor recognize a debt security issued by a debtor and received in a debt restructuring?
2. How should a creditor account for a difference, if any, between the creditor's basis in a loan and the fair value of a debt security issued by the debtor at the date of a restructuring?

18,040 ASC 310—Receivables

ACCOUNTING GUIDANCE

- A creditor should recognize a debt security issued by a debtor and received in a debt restructuring at the fair value of the security at the date of the restructuring.
- A creditor should account for the difference between the creditor's basis in a loan and the fair value of a debt security issued by a debtor as follows:
  - Recognize the difference as a recovery of the loan if the fair value of the debt security exceeds the net carrying amount of the loan.
  - Recognize the difference as a charge to the allowance for credit losses if the net carrying amount of the loan exceeds the fair value of the debt security.
  - After a restructuring, account for a debt security issued by the debtor in accordance with the guidance in ASC 320-10-05-2; 50-1A through 50-3, 50-5, 50-9 through 50-11; 55-3; 15-5; 30-1; 35-1 through 35-2, 35-4 through 35-5, 35-10 through 35-13, 35-18; 15-2 through 15-4, 15-7; 25-3 through 25-6, 25-9, 25-11 through 25-12, 25-14 through 25-16; 45-1 through 45-2, 45-8 through 45-11, 45-13
- If a security is received in a restructuring to settle a claim for past-due interest on a loan, the security should be measured at its fair value at the date of the restructuring and accounted for consistent with the entity's policy for recognizing cash received for past-due interest. After the restructuring, the security should be accounted for based on the guidance in ASC 320-10-05-2; 50-1A through 50-3, 50-5, 50-9 through 50-11; 55-3; 15-5; 30-1; 35-1 through 35-2, 35-4 through 35-5, 35-10 through 35-13, 35-18; 15-2 through 15-4, 15-7; 25-3 through 25-6, 25-9, 25-11 through 25-12, 25-14 through 25-16; 45-1 through 45-2, 45-8 through 45-11, 45-13.

Illustration of the Conversion of a Loan into a Debt Security
Example 1—Conversion of a Loan with a Prior Write-down into a Security

Original recorded investment in the loan		$50,000
Write-down		(5,000)
Recorded investment in the loan as adjusted		$45,000
Fair value of security at restructuring:		
Scenario 1		$47,000
Scenario 2		$45,000
Scenario 3		$40,000

Accounting for a Debt Security Classified as Available-for-Sale

Scenario 1		
Investment in debt security	$47,000	
Loan		$45,000
Allowance for credit losses—recovery		2,000
Scenario 2		
Investment in debt security	$45,000	
Loan		$45,000

Scenario 3

Investment in debt security	$40,000	
Allowance for credit losses	5,000	
Loan		$45,000

Example 2—Conversion of a Loan with a Valuation Allowance into a Security

Recorded investment in the loan	$50,000
Valuation allowance	5,000
Net carrying amount of the loan	$45,000
Fair value of security at restructuring:	
Scenario 1	$47,000
Scenario 2	$45,000
Scenario 3	$40,000

Accounting for a Debt Security Classified as Available-for-Sale

Scenario 1

Investment in debt security	$47,000	
Valuation allowance	5,000	
Loan		$50,000
Allowance for credit losses—recovery		2,000

Scenario 2

Investment in debt security	$45,000	
Valuation allowance	5,000	
Loan		$50,000

Scenario 3

Investment in debt security	$40,000	
Valuation allowance	5,000	
Allowance for credit losses	5,000	
Loan		$50,000

DISCUSSION

- Debt securities are within the scope of ASC 320-10-05-2; 50-1A through 50-3, 50-5, 50-9 through 50-11; 55-3; 15-5; 30-1; 35-1 through 35-2, 35-4 through 35-5, 35-10 through 35-13, 35-18; 15-2 through 15-4, 15-7; 25-3 through 25-6, 25-9, 25-11 through 25-12, 25-14 through 25-16; 45-1 through 45-2, 45-8 through 45-11, 45-13, and must be recognized at fair value, if they are classified as trading or available-for-sale.
- Two alternative approaches were discussed. Under one approach, the difference, if any, between a creditor's basis in a loan and the fair value of the debt security at the date of the restructuring would be accounted for as a fair value adjustment under the guidance in ASC 320.

  The other approach—the one adopted—is that of settlement accounting. Proponents of this approach argued that assets carried at fair value are excluded by the modification-of-terms provisions in ASC 310-40-15-3 through 15-12; 35-2, 35-5 through 35-7; 40-2, 40-5 through 40-6, 40-8; 25-1 through 25-2; 50-1; 55-2; 10-1 through 10-2; ASC 470-60-15-3 through 15-12; 55-3; 35 through 35-12; 45-1 through 45-2; 50-1 through 50-2; 10-1 through 10-2; ASC 450-20-60-12 (FAS-15) as well as from the scope of ASC 310-35-13 through 35-14, 35-16 through 35-26, 35-28, 35-29, 35-34, 35-37, 35-39; 45-5 through 45-6; 50-15, 50-19; ASC 310-30-30-2; ASC 310-40-35-8, 35-12; 50-2 through 50-3, 50-12 through 50-13, because modification-of-terms accounting and allowance for loan losses are unnecessary when an asset is accounted for at fair value. Proponents of this view believed that accounting for a debt security at fair value provides an embedded gain or loss that should be accounted for as a recovery, if there is a gain, or as a write-off, if there is a loss. They noted that recovery accounting is an established practice that measures historical loan loss experience. The gain is a function of the market's evaluation of collectability based on credit considerations instead of market interest rates. Proponents of this view also argued that a gain should not be considered a holding gain, because the gain in that case occurred before the restructuring, whereas here the asset was a loan and it would be misleading to recognize it as a gain on the security. An adjustment of bad debt expense for the loan would therefore best present the economics of the transaction.

- The accounting guidance is based on the notion that a gain on securities received in payment for past-due interest that was never recognized on the balance sheet should be recognized as income, as if those claims were sold for cash.

ASC 310-40-50-5; S50-1; S99-1 Applicability of the Disclosures Required by FASB Statement No. 114 When a Loan Is Restructured in a Troubled Debt Restructuring into Two (or More) Loans

BACKGROUND

Under the provisions of ASC 310-35-13 through 35-14, 35-16 through 35-26, 35-28, 35-29, 35-34, 35-37, 35-39; 45-5 through 45-6; 50-15, 50-19; ASC 310-30-30-2; ASC 310-40-35-8, 35-12; 50-2 through 50-3, 50-12 through 50-13, as amended by ASC 310-10-35-40; 50-16 through 50-17, 50-20; ASC 310-40-35-10; 50-6, creditors must disclose information about their investments in impaired loans and related allowances for credit losses. Creditors need not make those disclosures in years subsequent to the year in which a loan is restructured in a troubled debt restructuring that involves a modification of terms if the following two criteria are met: (*a*) the interest rate provided for in the restructuring agreement at least equals the rate the creditor was willing to accept for a new loan with comparable risk at the time the loan was restructured and (*b*) the loan is not impaired under the terms of the restructuring agreement.

Because it was expected that the above criteria would be applied to a single loan resulting from a loan restructuring, some have questioned whether loans resulting from a loan restructuring that involves a loan-splitting or other multiple-loan structure—in which the original loan is restructured into two or more loans—should be considered separately or together for the purpose of impairment disclosures. For example, a lender may restructure a loan by splitting it into two loans: Loan A, which meets the criteria for exemption from the disclosures after the year of the restructuring, and Loan B, which includes the remaining cash flows under the original loan that are not expected to be collected and have been charged off. Here, Loan B does not meet the criteria for exemption from disclosure. Loan B may be forgiven when Loan A is paid off, or the debtor may be required to make payments on Loan B only if its results of operations exceed certain sales levels.

ACCOUNTING ISSUE

Should two or more restructured loans that result from a troubled debt restructuring be considered independently or collectively when assessing whether the disclosures required in ASC 310-10-50-12 through 13, 35-34, apply?

ACCOUNTING GUIDANCE

Two or more loan agreements resulting from a troubled debt restructuring, as defined in ASC 310-40-15-3 through 15-12; 35-2, 35-5 through 35-7; 40-2, 40-5 through 40-6, 40-8; 25-1 through 25-2; 50-1; 55-2; 10-1 through 10-2; ASC 470-60-15-3 through 50-12; 55-3; 35 through 35-12; 45-1 through 45-2; 50-1 through 50-2; 10-1 through 10-2; ASC 450-20-60-12 , should be considered separately when assessing whether the disclosures in ASC 310-10-50-12 through 13, 35-34, should be made in years subsequent to the year of the restructuring, because the loans are legally distinct from the original loan. Nevertheless, a creditor should continue measuring a loan's impairment based on the contractual terms of the *original* loan agreement, in accordance with the guidance in ASC 310-10-35-20 through 35-22, 35-24 through 35-27, 35-32, 35-37; ASC 310-40-35-12; ASC 310-30-30-2.

SEC OBSERVER COMMENT

The SEC Observer stated the staff's concern that disclosures about impaired loans after the loans have been restructured into multiple loans in a troubled debt restructuring may imply under some circumstances that the quality of the loan portfolio has improved merely as result of a troubled debt restructuring. Consequently, the staff believes that registrants should inform users clearly about how multiple loan structures affect the disclosures about impaired loans.

Illustration of Required Disclosure Requirements When a Loan Is Restructured in a Troubled Debt Restructuring into Two (or More) Loans

MHR Corp. restructures a loan into two loans in a troubled debt restructuring. Loan A represents the portion of the contractual cash flows expected to be collected and meets the criteria for exemption from disclosure in the years following the restructuring. Loan B represents the portion of the contractual cash flows *not* expected to be collected and that will be written off.

MHR should disclose information about Loan B in years subsequent to the restructuring in conformity with the requirements of ASC 310-35-13 through 35-14, 35-16 through 35-26, 35-28, 35-29, 35-34, 35-37, 35-39; 45-5 through 45-6; 50-15, 50-19; ASC 310-30-30-2; ASC 310-40-35-8, 35-12; 50-2 through 50-3, 50-12 through 50-13, because the recorded investment in that loan and the related allowance for credit losses would be zero.

DISCUSSION

Loans resulting from a troubled debt restructuring are legally separate loans that should, therefore, be considered separately when assessing whether they should be exempted from disclosure. Although the combined loans meet the definition of an impaired loan and must be measured for impairment purposes based on the terms of the original loan agreement, the loans should be considered new loans for disclosure purposes, because the criteria for exemption from disclosure are based on the terms specified in the restructuring agreement—not on those stated in the original loan agreement.

TROUBLED DEBT RESTRUCTURINGS BY CREDITORS

IMPORTANT NOTICE FOR 2014

As CCH's 2014 *GAAP Guide* goes to press, the FASB has outstanding an Exposure Draft of an Accounting Standards Update (ASU) (Reclassifications of Collateralized Mortgage Loans upon a Troubled Debt Restructuring (EITF Issue No. 13-E)), that may affect the preparation of future financial statements.

The Emerging Issues Task Force (EITF) was asked address this issue because of the large number of residential real estate properties held by lenders as a result of the economic downturn and weakness in the real estate market, which has resulted in many foreclosures. Lenders refer to such holdings as other real estate owned (OREO), which are not related to a lender's operations. Under the existing guidance in the FASB Accounting Standards Codification™ (ASC) 310 (Receivables) (ASC 310-40-40-6), which applies to troubled debt restructurings, a creditor is required to derecognize a receivable for a loan and recognize the collateral in "a troubled debt restructuring that is in substance a repossession or foreclosure by the creditor, that is, the creditor receives physical possession of the debtor's assets regardless of whether formal foreclosure proceedings take place . . . ." As a result of the extended timeline of the foreclosure process, some creditors have been applying that guidance to residential real estate consumer mortgage loans. That practice has caused diversity in the reporting for foreclosed residential real estate because the terms "in substance repossession or foreclosure" and "physical possession" have not been defined in the accounting literature. Therefore, creditors have had difficulty in determining when an "in substance repossession" of residential real estate property occurs.

The proposed guidance would clarify how that guidance applies to the accounting for consumer mortgage loans collateralized by residential real estate properties. ASC 310-40 would be amended by the addition of ASC 310-40-55-10A, which would permit a creditor to consider that physical possession of residential real estate property collateralizing a consumer mortgage loan has been received if one of the following two conditions has been met:

1. The creditor has received legal title to the residential real estate property.
2. The borrower satisfied the loan by conveying all interest in the residential real estate property to the creditor in a deed in lieu of foreclosure or a similar legal agreement, after the borrower and the creditor have satisfied agreed terms and conditions, even if legal title may not yet have been passed.

In addition, ASC 310-10-50-11 would be amended to require an entity that has received "physical possession," as discussed in ASC 310-40-40-6 and ASC 310 40-55-10A, of a residential real estate property collateralizing a consumer mortgage loan to provide a reconciliation of the beginning and ending balances related to those foreclosed real estate properties for each interim and annual reporting period presented, with separate presentation of the changes during the period as a result of:

- Additions from foreclosures of residential real estate properties collateralizing consumer mortgage loans;
- Reductions for sales or transfers of foreclosed residential real estate properties;
- Adjustments made to foreclosed residential real estate properties at the lower of their carrying amounts or fair value less selling costs; and
- Other adjustments (including explanation of significant amounts, if the nature of an adjustment is not clear from the caption used for other adjustments).

Disclosures about loans in the process of foreclosure would be required. Proposed ASC 310-10-50-35 would be added to require an entity to disclose at the end of each interim and annual reporting period presented information about its recorded investment in consumer mortgage loans secured by residential real estate for which formal foreclosure proceedings are in process according to the applicable local jurisdiction's requirements.

The guidance would be effective for fiscal years and interim periods within those years that begin on a date to be determined after comments on the proposal have been considered. Early adoption of the guidance would be permitted.

CHAPTER 19
ASC 320—INVESTMENTS—DEBT AND EQUITY SECURITIES

CONTENTS

Part I: General Guidance	**19,002**
ASC 320-10: Overall	**19,002**
Overview	**19,002**
Background	**19,003**
Debt Security	**19,003**
Equity Security	**19,003**
Accounting for Investments	**19,004**
Scope	**19,004**
Classifications of Debt and Equity Securities	**19,004**
Held-to-Maturity Securities	**19,005**
Trading Securities	**19,006**
Available-for-Sale Securities	**19,006**
Standards of Accounting and Reporting Subsequent to Classification	**19,006**
Reporting Changes in Fair Value	**19,006**
Transfers between Categories	**19,007**
Impairment of Securities	**19,007**
Financial Statement Presentation and Disclosures	**19,008**
Illustration of General Application of ASC 320	**19,011**
Part II: Interpretive Guidance	**19,015**
ASC 320-10: Overall	**19,015**
ASC 320-10-25-19 through 25-20, 40-3, 55-14 through 55-15, 55-21	
Structured Notes Acquired for a Specified Investment Strategy	**19,015**
ASC 320-10-35-38 through 35-43, 55-10 through 55-12, 55-16 through 55-19; ASC 835-10-60-6	
Recognition of Interest Income and Balance Sheet Classification of Structured Notes	**19,016**
ASC 320-10-15-7, 35-17, 35-20, through 35-30, 35-32A through 35-35A, 35-45, 35-8A through 35-9A, 50-6 through 50-8B, 55-22 through 55-23	
The Meaning of Other-Than-Temporary Impairment and Its Application to Certain Investments	**19,020**
ASC 320-10-25-18	
Impact of Certain Transactions on the Held-to-Maturity Classification under FASB Statement No. 115	**19,024**
ASC 320-10-S35-1, S99-2	
Adjustments in Assets and Liabilities for Holding Gains and Losses as Related to the Implementation of FASB Statement No. 115	**19,025**
ASC 320-10-25-18; ASC 860-10-55-34, 55-74	
The Applicability of FASB Statement No. 115 to Desecuritizations of Financial Assets	**19,026**

19,002 ASC 320—Investments—Debt and Equity Securities

ASC 320-10-15-2, 15-5, 25-1, 25-5, 25 through 25-8, 25-10, 25-12 through 25-13, 25-16 through 25-18, 30-3 through 30-4, 35-6 through 35-9, 35-13, 35-15 through 35-16, 35-18, 35-32 through 35-33, 40-1 through 40-2, 45-3 through 45-7, 45-12, 50-12 through 50-14, 55-2 through 55-6, 55-8 through 55-9, 55-24 through 55-25; ASC 323-30-60-2; ASC 958-320-15-4, 15-6, 55-2 through 55-3, 60-1

A Guide to Implementation of Statement 115 on Accounting for Certain Investments in Debt and Equity Securities	19,027
Illustration of Sale of Available-for-Sale Securities	19,035
Illustration of Transferring a Security from Available-for-Sale to Held-to-Maturity	19,036
Illustration of Disclosing Unrealized Gains and Losses	19,038
ASC 320-10-15-6, 55-2	
Application of Statement 115 to Debt Securities Restructured in a Troubled Debt Restructuring	19,039

PART I: GENERAL GUIDANCE

ASC 320-10: OVERALL

OVERVIEW

The primary issue in accounting and reporting for debt and equity investments is the appropriate use of market value. ASC 320 addresses accounting and reporting for (*a*) investments in equity securities that have readily determinable fair values and (*b*) all investments in debt securities. It requires that these securities be classified in three categories and given specific accounting treatments, as follows:

Classification	Accounting Treatment
Held-to-maturity Debt securities with the intent and ability to hold to maturity	Amortized cost
Trading securities Debt and equity securities bought and held primarily for sale in the near term	Fair value, with unrealized holding gains and losses included in earnings
Available-for-sale Debt and equity securities not classified as held-to-maturity or trading	Fair value, with unrealized holding gains and losses excluded from earnings and reported as a separate component of shareholders' equity

PRACTICE POINTER: Guidance in ASC 825 (Financial Instruments) permits companies to account for a variety of financial instruments by the fair value method. To the extent to which an entity selects the fair value method for investments that would otherwise have been accounted for under ASC 320, the following applies: An enterprise shall report its investments in available-for-sale securities and trading securities separately from similar assets that are subsequently measured using another measurement attribute on the face of the statement of financial position. Two options are available for presenting this information: (1) the aggregate of those measured by fair value and those measured by non-fair-value amounts are presented in the same line item and the amount of fair value included in the aggregate amount is parenthetically disclosed; (2) two separate line items are presented, one for the fair value amount and one for the non-fair-value amount. For further discussion of fair value, see Chapter 20, ASC 820—Fair Value Measurement.

BACKGROUND

ASC 320 defines *debt securities* and *equity securities* as follows:

Debt Security

A *debt security* is any security that represents a creditor relationship with an enterprise. It includes preferred stock that must be redeemed by the issuing enterprise or that is redeemable at the option of the investor. It also includes a collateralized mortgage obligation that is issued in equity form but is required to be accounted for as a nonequity instrument, regardless of how that instrument is classified in the issuer's statement of financial position. Other examples of debt securities are the following:

- U.S. Treasury securities
- U.S. government agency securities
- Municipal securities
- Corporate bonds
- Convertible debt
- Commercial paper
- All securitized debt instruments, such as collateralized mortgage obligations and real estate mortgage investment conduits
- Interest-only and principal-only strips

The following items are *not* debt securities:

- Option contracts
- Financial futures contracts
- Forward contracts
- Lease contracts
- Trade accounts receivable arising from sales on credit by industrial or commercial enterprises
- Loans receivable arising from consumer, commercial, and real estate lending activities of financial institutions

These last two items are examples of receivables that do not meet the definition of *security* unless they have been securitized, in which case they *do* meet the definition.

Equity Security

An *equity security* is any security representing an ownership interest in an enterprise (e.g., common, preferred, or other capital stock) or the right to acquire or dispose of an ownership interest in an enterprise at fixed or determinable prices (e.g., warrants, rights, call options, and put options).

ACCOUNTING FOR INVESTMENTS

Scope

ASC 320 establishes standards of financial accounting and reporting for (*a*) investments in equity securities that have readily determinable fair values and (*b*) all investments in debt securities. Following are guidelines for the determination of fair value (ASC 320-10-15-5):

- Fair value of an equity security is readily determinable if sales prices and bid-and-asked quotations are currently available on a securities exchange registered with the Securities and Exchange Commission or in the over-the-counter market, assuming the over-the-counter securities are publicly reported by the National Association of Securities Dealers Automated Quotations system or by Pink Sheets LLC. This also applies to restricted stock if the restriction terminates within one year.
- Fair value of an equity security traded only on a foreign market is considered readily determinable if that foreign market is of a breadth and scope comparable to one of the U.S. markets referred to above.
- Fair value of an investment in a mutual fund is readily determinable if the fair value per share is determined and published and is the basis for current transactions.

ASC 320 does not apply to the following (ASC 320-10-15-7):

- Investments in equity securities that, absent the election of the fair value option under ASC 825 (Financial Instruments), are required to be accounted for by the equity method.
- Investments in consolidated subsidiaries.
- Enterprises whose specialized accounting practices include accounting for substantially all investments in debt and equity securities at market or fair value, with changes in value recognized in earnings or in the change in net assets.
- Investments in derivative instruments subject to the guidance in ASC 815 (Derivatives and Hedging). If a derivative instrument is embedded into an investment security, the host instrument (i.e., the investment security itself) remains subject to ASC 320.
- Not-for-profit organizations; guidance on accounting for investments for not-for-profit organizations is provided in ASC 958 (Not-for-Profit Entities).

Classifications of Debt and Equity Securities

ASC 320 requires that an enterprise classify all debt securities and selected equity securities into one of three categories: (1) held-to-maturity, (2) trading, or (3) available-for-sale. The enterprise should reassess the classification at each reporting date (ASC 320-10-25-1).

> **PRACTICE POINTER:** ASC 320 provides little guidance on how management should determine the appropriate classification of debt and equity investments. Classification is based primarily on management's intent for holding a particular investment:

- Trading securities (both debt and equity) provide a source of ready cash when needed, with the hope of gain from holding the investment for a short period of time.
- Held-to-maturity investments (debt only) are positively intended to be retained until maturity.
- Available-for-sale investments (both debt and equity) rest somewhere between these extremes.

  Management's past patterns of practices with regard to securities are an important consideration in determining appropriate classification, as are projections of cash requirements that may imply a need to liquidate investments.

Held-to-Maturity Securities

The *held-to-maturity* category is limited to debt securities. They are measured at amortized cost in the statement of financial position only if the reporting enterprise has the intent and ability to hold them to maturity (ASC 320-10-35-1). In certain circumstances, a company may change its intent concerning securities originally classified as held-to-maturity, resulting in their sale or reclassification, without calling into question the company's intent to hold other securities to maturity. ASC 320 identifies the following circumstances in which the sale or transfer of held-to-maturity investments is not considered to be inconsistent with their original classification (ASC 320-10-25-6):

- Significant deterioration in the issuer's creditworthiness
- Change in tax law that eliminates or reduces the tax-exempt status of interest on the debt security
- A major business combination or major disposition that necessitates the sale or transfer of the security to maintain the enterprise's existing interest rate risk position or credit risk policy
- A change in statutory or regulatory requirements significantly modifying either what constitutes a permissible investment or the maximum level of investments in certain kinds of securities
- A significant increase by the regulator in the industry's capital requirements that causes a need to downsize by selling held-to-maturity securities
- A significant increase in the risk weights of debt securities used for regulatory risk-based capital purposes
- Other events that are isolated, nonrecurring, and unusual and that could not have been reasonably anticipated by the enterprise

A debt security is not classified as held-to-maturity if the investing enterprise intends to hold the security for only an indefinite period. A debt security is not appropriately classified as held-to-maturity, for example, if it is available for sale in response to the following circumstances (ASC 320-10-25-4):

- Changes in market interest rates and related changes in the security's prepayment risk
- Need for liquidity
- Changes in the availability of and the yield on alternative investments
- Changes in funding sources and terms
- Changes in foreign currency risk

ASC 825 (Financial Instruments) includes certain options to record held-to-maturity securities at fair value. Doing so does not challenge the intent to hold to maturity (see the chapter in this *Guide* discussing ASC 820 (Fair Value Measurement)).

Trading Securities

The *trading securities* category includes both debt securities and equity securities with readily determinable fair values. They are measured at fair value in the statement of financial position. Trading securities (ASC 320-10-25-1):

- Are bought and held primarily for purposes of selling them in the near term.
- Reflect active and frequent buying and selling.
- Generally are used with the objective of generating profits on short-term differences in price.

Available-for-Sale Securities

The *available-for-sale* category of debt securities includes those debt securities that are not classified in either the held-to-maturity category or the trading category (ASC 320-10-25-1).

Standards of Accounting and Reporting Subsequent to Classification

After debt and equity investments are classified as held-to-maturity, trading, and available-for-sale, three important accounting issues must be addressed: (1) reporting changes in fair value, (2) transfers between categories, and (3) impairment of securities.

Reporting Changes in Fair Value

Investments in debt and equity securities classified as trading and available-for-sale are required to be carried at fair value in the statement of financial position. Unrealized holding gains and losses represent the net change in fair value of a security, *excluding*:

- Dividend or interest income recognized but not yet received.
- Any write-downs for permanent impairment.

Unrealized holding gains and losses are accounted for as follows (ASC 320-10-35-1):

- *Trading*—included in earnings.
- *Available-for-sale*—excluded from earnings and reported in other comprehensive income until realized.

> **PRACTICE POINTER:** The accumulated amount of unrealized holding gains and losses on available-for-sale investments that is included in stockholders' equity is *not* a direct adjustment to retained earnings. It is a separate component of stockholders' equity—a positive amount (credit balance) for accumulated unrealized gains and a negative amount (debit balance) for accumulated unrealized losses. Adjust this account each time the portfolio of available-for-sale investments is revalued (e.g., at the end of each accounting period) as an element of other comprehensive income. Recognize the accumulated unrealized gain or loss for a particular security as an element of net income when that security is sold and recognize it in income at that time.

Dividend and interest income, including amortization of premium and discount arising at acquisition, are included in earnings for all three categories of investments. Also, realized gains and losses for securities classified as available-for-sale and held-to-maturity are reported in earnings (ASC 320-10-35-4).

Transfers between Categories

Transfers of securities between categories of investments are accounted for at fair value with an unrealized holding gain or loss treated as indicated in the following summarization (ASC 320-10-35-10):

From	Transfer* To	Accounting Treatment
T	A or H	Unrealized holding gain or loss was already recognized in earnings during prior period(s) and is not reversed.
A or H	T	Unrealized holding gain or loss at the date of transfer is immediately recognized in earnings.
H	A	Unrealized holding gain or loss at the date of transfer is reported in other comprehensive income.
A	H	Unrealized holding gain or loss continues to be reported in a separate component of shareholders' equity and is amortized over the remaining life of the security as an adjustment of yield.

* T = Trading; A = Available-for-sale; H = Held-to-maturity

Given the criteria for classification of debt securities in the held-to-maturity category, transfers from that category should be rare. Also, because of the securities' nature, transfers to or from trading are rare (ASC 320-10-35-11, 12).

Impairment of Securities

For individual securities classified as either available-for-sale or held-to-maturity, when fair value declines below amortized cost an enterprise should determine whether the decline is temporary or permanent. If the decline in fair value is other than temporary, the following standards apply (ASC 320-10-35-18):

- The cost basis of the individual security is written down to fair value as a new cost basis.
- The amount of the write-down is included in current earnings (i.e., accounted for as a realized loss).
- The new cost basis is not changed for subsequent recoveries in fair value; subsequent increases in fair value of available-for sale securities are included in other comprehensive income; any subsequent decreases in fair value, if temporary, are also included in other comprehensive income.

PRACTICE POINTER: Professional judgment is required to determine whether a decline in fair value of an available-for-sale investment is temporary or other than temporary. A starting point is to judge whether the decline in value results from company specific events, industry developments, general economic conditions, or other reasons. Once the general reason for the decline is identified, further judgments are required as to whether those causal events are likely to reverse and, if so, whether that reversal is likely to result in a recovery of the fair value of the investment. To help make these judgments, consider how similar circumstances have affected other debt and equity securities.

Financial Statement Presentation and Disclosures

Financial statement presentation of debt and equity investment activities subject to ASC 320 is summarized as follows:

- In the statement of financial position (ASC 320-10-45-1, 2):
  - *Trading securities, held-to-maturity, and available-for-sale securities*—Current or noncurrent, as defined in the ASC Glossary
  - Investments in available-for-sale securities and trading securities that are measured at fair value and non-fair value amounts are reported separately, either as two line items or via parenthetical disclosure of the fair value amount.
- In the statement of cash flows (ASC 320-10-45-11):
  - *Trading securities*—Cash flows from purchases, sales, and maturities classified based on the nature and purpose for which the securities were purchased
  - *Held-to-maturity and available-for-sale*—Cash flows from purchases, sales, and maturities classified as investing activities and reported gross for each classification

---

PRACTICE POINTER: For available-for-sale and held-to-maturity investments, the usual classification in the statement of financial position would be noncurrent, since securities that are held primarily for *liquidity purposes* should be in the trading category. In certain circumstances, however, these investments may qualify for inclusion among current assets. For example, when held-to-maturity (debt) investments are within one year of maturity, they are expected to provide near-term cash and would be classified appropriately as current assets. Similarly, management intent concerning available-for-sale securities that have been held for a period of time may qualify those securities for classification as current, whereas in the past they would have been considered noncurrent.

Treating cash flows from trading securities in the operating category in the statement of cash flows is consistent with the fact that trading securities involve active and frequent buying and selling, and are used generally with the objective of generating profits. Classifying cash flows from held-to-maturity and available-for-sale securities as investing cash flows is consistent with the longer-term nature of those investments.

ASC 320 disclosure requirements are as follows:

Required disclosures, by major security type at the date of each statement of financial position presented, for available-for-sale securities are as follows (ASC 320-10-50-2):

- Aggregate fair value
- Total gains for securities with net gains in accumulated other comprehensive income
- Total losses for securities with net losses in accumulated other comprehensive income

Required disclosures, by major security type at the date of each statement of financial position presented, for held-to-maturity securities are as follows (ASC 320-10-50-5):

- Aggregate fair value
- Gross unrecognized holding gains
- Gross unrecognized holding losses
- Net carrying amount
- Gross gains and losses in accumulated other comprehensive income for derivatives that hedged the forecasted acquisition of held-to-maturity securities

In complying with this requirement, financial institutions shall include the following major types of securities, although additional types may also be included as appropriate:

— Equity securities
— Debt securities issued by the U.S. Treasury and other U.S. government corporations and agencies
— Debt securities issued by states of the United States and political subdivisions of the states
— Debt securities issued by foreign governments
— Corporate debt securities
— Mortgage-backed securities
— Other debt securities (ASC 942-320-50-2)

- Contractual maturities as of the date of the most recent statement of financial position (ASC 942-320-50-3). [In complying with this requirement, financial institutions shall disclose the fair value and amortized cost of debt securities in at least four maturity groupings:
  — Within one year
  — One to five years
  — Five to ten years
  — After ten years]

For each period for which the results of operations are presented, the following disclosures are required (ASC 320-10-50-9):

- Proceeds from the sale of available-for-sale securities and the gross realized gains and losses included in earnings
- The basis on which cost of a security sold or the amount reclassified out of accumulated other comprehensive income into earnings was determined (i.e., specific identification, average cost, or other)
- Gross gains and losses from transfers of securities from the available-for-sale category to the trading category that are included in earnings
- Amount of the net unrealized holding gain or loss on available-for-sale securities for the period that has been included in accumulated other comprehensive income, and the amount of gains and losses reclassified out of accumulated other comprehensive income during the period
- Portion of trading gains and losses for the period pertaining to those trading securities still held at the balance sheet date

For each period for which results of operations are presented, the following information is required for held-to-maturity securities that are sold or transferred into another category (ASC 320-10-50-10):

- The net carrying amount of the sold or transferred security
- The net gain or loss in accumulated other comprehensive income for any derivative that hedged the forecasted acquisition of the held-to-maturity security
- The related realized or unrealized gain or loss
- The circumstances leading to the decision to sell or transfer the security

---

PRACTICE POINTER: If a company has more than one category of debt and equity investments, an efficient way to make many of the required disclosures is to prepare a table: Use columns for investment type (e.g., trading, available-for-sale, and/or held-to-maturity) and rows for the specific information items (e.g., aggregate fair value, unrealized holding gains and losses). This approach not only saves space, but also is relatively easy for users of the financial statements to read and understand. If a company has only one category of investments, presentation of information may be more efficient in paragraph form.

Illustration of General Application of ASC 320

To illustrate the general application of ASC 320, consider the case of Marble Co., which invests in two securities on January 1, 20X5, as follows:

> **Debt investment**—$100,000 par value, 9% Paper Co. bonds priced to yield 10%, maturity date 12/31/X9
>
> **Equity investment**—5,000 shares of Plastic Co. $1 par value common stock at $30 per share

ASC 320 is applied to each investment from the date of purchase. Assume that the debt investment pays interest annually and matures five years from purchase. The purchase price of the two securities is as follows:

Paper Co. bonds:

Present value of interest payments ($100,000 × 9% × 3.79079*)	$ 34,117
Present value of maturity value ($100,000 × .62092**)	62,092
	$ 96,209

Plastic Co. common stock:

5,000 shares @ $30 per share	$150,000
Total	$246,209

* Present value of annuity at 10%, compounded annually, five periods.
** Present value of one at 10%, five periods.

The discount on the Paper Co. bonds is amortized over the five-year period to maturity by the effective-interest method, as follows:

	(A) Interest Income	(B) Cash Rec'd	(C) Discount Amortization	(D) Remaining Discount	(E) Carrying Amount
1/1/X5	—	—	—	$3,791	$96,209
12/31/X5	$9,621	$9,000	$621	3,170	96,830
12/31/X6	9,683	9,000	683	2,487	97,513
12/31/X7	9,751	9,000	751	1,736	98,264
12/31/X8	9,826	9,000	826	910	99,090
12/31/X9	9,910	9,000	910	—	100,000

(A) Previous carrying amount (E) × 10%
(B) $100,000 × 9%
(C) [(A) - (B)]
(D) [Previous-year (D)] - [Current-year (C)]
(E) $100,000 - (D)

Market values for the investments are as follows:

	12/31/X5	12/31/X6
Paper Co. bond	$ 98,000	$ 97,500
Plastic Co. common	155,000	152,000
	$253,000	$249,500

ASC 320—Investments—Debt and Equity Securities

Trading Securities

Assume that Marble Co. classifies the investments described above as trading securities. The securities are initially recorded at cost when they are purchased; discount is amortized on the bond investments to state interest income properly; interest and dividend income are recorded as they are received; and the securities are adjusted to market value at the end of the year with the unrealized gain or loss recognized in income. Assuming dividends of $4 per share are received on October 31, 20X5, on the Plastic Co. common, entries to record all events for 20X5 are as follows:

1/1/X5	Investments (trading)	96,209	
	Cash		96,209
	Purchase of bonds as trading investment.		
1/1/X5	Investments (trading)	150,000	
	Cash		150,000
	Purchase of common as trading investment.		
10/31/X5	Cash (5,000 shares @ $4)	20,000	
	Dividend income		20,000
	Dividends received on common stock investment.		
12/31/X5	Investments (trading)	621	
	Cash	9,000	
	Interest income		9,621
	Interest received and amortization of discount on bond investment.		
12/31/X5	Investments (trading)	6,170	
	Unrealized gain on investments		6,170
	Market value adjustment for trading investments.		

The $6,170 unrealized gain is determined as follows:

Market value of trading securities at 12/31/X5 ($98,000 + $155,000)	$253,000
Carrying amount of trading securities at 12/31/X5 ($96,830 + $150,000)	(246,830)
Unrealized gain	$ 6,170

ASC 320 requires the presentation of trading securities in the balance sheet as current assets and cash flows from trading securities to be classified as operating activities in the statement of cash flows. Those presentations are illustrated later in this example.

Continuing the example into 20X6, assume that the Plastic Co. common pays a $3 per share dividend on October 31. Entries for 20X6 are as follows:

10/31/X6	Cash (5,000 × $3)	15,000	
	Dividend income		15,000
	Dividend received on trading investment.		
12/31/X6	Investments (trading)	683	
	Cash	9,000	
	Interest income		9,683
	Interest and amortization of discount on bond investment.		

12/31/X6 Unrealized loss on investments	4,183	
Investments (trading)		4,183
Market value adjustment for trading investments.		

The market value adjustment is determined as follows:

Market value at 12/31/X6 ($97,500 + $152,000)	$249,500
Carrying amount at 12/31/X6 ($98,683 + $155,000)	(253,683)
Unrealized loss	$ 4,183

    The carrying amount of the bond investment is the 12/31/X5 market value, adjusted for the discount amortization ($98,000 + $683).

    The financial statement presentation for 20X5 and 20X6 for the trading securities is illustrated as follows:

	20X5	20X6
Balance Sheet:		
Current assets: Trading investments	$253,000	$249,500
Income Statement:		
Interest income	$ 9,621	$ 9,683
Dividend income	20,000	15,000
Unrealized gain (loss) on investments	6,170	(4,183)
Statement of Cash Flows:		
Operating activities:		
Dividends	$ 20,000	$ 15,000
Interest	9,000	9,000
Purchase of investment	246,209	—

Available-for-Sale

Now assume that these same investments are classified by management as available-for-sale. All entries for 20X5 and 20X6 are the same, except as follows:

- The investments account is subtitled "available-for-sale" rather than "trading."
- The year-end market value adjustment is not recognized in income, but rather is accumulated and presented in other comprehensive income.

The final entries for 20X5 and 20X6 are as follows:

12/31/X5 Investments (available-for-sale)	6,170	
Accumulated unrealized gains/losses on investments		6,170
Market value adjustment for available-for-sale investments.		
12/31/X6 Accumulated unrealized gains/losses on investments	4,183	
Investments (available-for-sale)		4,183
Market value adjustment for available-for-sale investments.		

    In 20X6, the accumulated unrealized gains/losses on investments account is used to accumulate the net unrealized gains and losses over the two years. That

19,014 ASC 320—Investments—Debt and Equity Securities

account has a positive (credit) balance of $6,170 at the end of 20X5; it has a positive (credit) balance of $1,987 ($6,170 - $4,183) at the end of 20X6. ASC 320 indicates that available-for-sale securities may be classified in the balance sheet as either current or noncurrent. Assuming currently marketable investments, that decision would be made primarily on the basis of managerial intent. Cash flows from the purchase and sale of available-for-sale securities are classified in the statement of cash flows as investing activities.

The financial statement presentation for 20X5 and 20X6 for the available-for-sale securities is as follows:

	20X5	20X6
Balance Sheet:		
Assets: Available-for-sale investments	$253,000	$249,500
Stockholders' equity: Other comprehensive income	6,170	1,987
Income Statement:		
Interest income	9,621	9,683
Dividend income	20,000	15,000
Statement of Cash Flows:		
Operating activities:		
Dividends	$ 20,000	$ 15,000
Interest	9,000	9,000
Investing activities:		
Purchase of investments	$246,209	—

Held-to-Maturity

Now assume that the bond investment used in the previous illustrations is classified as held-to-maturity. (The stock investment is not included in the continuation of the illustration, because the held-to-maturity classification is available for debt investments only.)

The entries relative to the purchase of the bond investment and the receipt of interest and amortization of discount are also appropriate for the held-to-maturity classification, assuming the investment account is properly identified as held-to-maturity. No entry is made, however, to recognize the change in market value of the investment at the end of each year, because the method of accounting for the held-to-maturity securities is amortized cost. Held-to-maturity investments ordinarily would be classified in the balance sheet as noncurrent, except when the maturity date is within the period used to identify current assets (e.g., one year). Cash flows from transactions involving held-to-maturity investments are classified as investing activities in the statement of cash flows.

The financial statement presentation for the held-to-maturity investment for 20X5 and 20X6 is as follows:

	20X5	20X6
Balance Sheet:		
Assets: Held-to-maturity investments	$96,830	$97,513
Income Statement:		
Interest income	$ 9,621	$9,683

	20X5	20X6
Statement of Cash Flows:		
Operating activities:		
Interest	$ 9,000	$9,000
Investing activities:		
Purchase of investments	$96,209	—

PART II: INTERPRETIVE GUIDANCE

ASC 320-10: OVERALL

ASC 320-10-25-19 through 25-20, 40-3, 55-14 through 55-15, 55-21 Structured Notes Acquired for a Specified Investment Strategy

BACKGROUND

Structured notes are securities that are issued combined with other structured note securities as a unit or a pair to accomplish a strategic investment result for an investor. Under one strategy, two structured notes with opposite reset positions are purchased. (For example, one month after issuance, the interest rate on Bond A resets from 8% to 1% if ten-year Treasury bond rates decreased by one basis point since the Bond's issuance or to 15% if Treasury rates increased by one basis point. The interest rate on Bond B would reset in the opposite direction.) Each structured note's coupon rate or maturity date is determined shortly after issuance based on the movement of market rates. Although the yields on the two structured notes move in opposite directions after the reset date, the average yield of the two securities generally represents the market yield of the combined instruments at issuance.

ACCOUNTING ISSUE

Should an investor account separately for each structured note security or account for the two securities as a unit?

ACCOUNTING GUIDANCE

An investor who purchases structured notes for a specific investment strategy should account for the two structured notes as a unit until one of the securities is sold. Thereafter, the remaining security would be accounted for in accordance with the guidance in Accounting Standards Update No. 2009-16 (*Transfers and Servicing, Topic 860, Accounting for Transfers of Financial Assets*).

In making a judgment as to whether the securities were purchased for a specified investment strategy (not all the indicators are required for the securities to be accounted for under the consensus), the Task Force stated that the following indicators should be used:

1. The securities are related because their fair values will move in opposite directions in response to changes in interest rates on a specified date or after a specified period following issuance. Their fair values may change because of changes in their coupon interest rates or changes in their maturities.

2. The securities are issued simultaneously or they are issued separately but the terms for their remaining lives are as discussed in (1) above.
3. The securities are issued by the same counterparty and/or the same issuer. They may also be issued by different issuers but are structured through an intermediary.
4. The investor's *only* reason for purchasing the two securities is to achieve a specific accounting result, because there would be no valid business purpose for entering into the transactions individually. The investor would not purchase the securities otherwise.

The Task Force noted that the substance of the investment strategy in these transactions is that the investor has purchased one market-based security that results in no gain or loss when the interest rate resets and should be accounted for as such. However, the unit's fair value may change as a result of a change in credit ratings or a change in market rates.

OBSERVATION: ASC 860 was amended in 2009 to require that transfers of structured notes that meet the conditions for sale accounting in ASC 860 be accounted for in accordance with the guidance in ASC 860-20-30-1.

ASC 320-10-35-38 through 35-43, 55-10 through 55-12, 55-16 through 55-19; ASC 835-10-60-6 Recognition of Interest Income and Balance Sheet Classification of Structured Notes

BACKGROUND

The guidance in ASC 320 on accounting for debt securities also applies to *structured notes*, which are debt instruments whose cash flows are linked to the movement in one or more indices, interest rates, foreign exchange rates, commodities prices, prepayment rates, or other market variables. Such instruments are issued by enterprises sponsored by the U.S. government, multilateral development banks, municipalities, and private corporations. Interest payments on structured notes may be based on formulas related to the investor's preference for risk and return, and principal payments may be indexed to movements in an underlying market. Structured notes normally include forward or option components, such as caps, calls, and floors, which are not separable or detachable. Consequently, investors that use structured notes to manage financial risks and enhance yield often prefer those debt instruments for administrative reasons over debt securities with fixed interest rates, which may require entering into separate derivatives.

In general, interest income on structured notes is comprised of a stated or coupon interest, acquisition premium or discount amortization, if any, and possible adjustments of the principal based on an index or formula. The following is a list of some common forms of structured notes that are within the scope of this Issue:

- *Index amortizing notes* Principal is repaid based on a predetermined amortization schedule, which is linked to movements in a specific mortgage-backed security or index. Although the investor receives the total principal by the maturity date, it is uncertain when principal payments will be received, because the note's maturity is extended in relation to increasing market interest rates or decreasing prepayment rates. An above-market interest rate is paid on such notes.

- *Inverse floating-rate notes* The coupon rate on such notes changes in an inverse relationship to a specified interest rate level or index.
- *Range bonds* The interest rate on such bonds depends on the number of days a reference rate is between predetermined levels at issuance. No interest or a below-market interest rate is earned when the reference rate is not within the range.
- *Dual index notes* The coupon rate on these notes often is fixed for a short period (the first year) and becomes variable for a longer period. It generally is determined by the spread between two market indices, usually the Constant Maturity Treasury rate and LIBOR.
- *Inflation bonds* The bond's contractual principal is indexed to the inflation rate and its coupon rate is below that for traditional bonds with similar maturity.
- *Equity-linked bear notes* These notes have a fixed coupon rate that is lower than traditional debt. Their principal is guaranteed but may exceed the initial investment based on a decrease in the S&P index.

ACCOUNTING ISSUES

- How should investors in structured notes estimate cash flows that will be received?
- How should changes in cash flow estimates be recognized and measured in interest income?
- Is a held-to-maturity classification permitted for investments in structured notes under the provisions of ASC 320?

ACCOUNTING GUIDANCE

Income on structured note securities that are classified as debt securities under the available-for-sale or held-to-maturity categories of ASC 310 should be measured using the *retrospective interest method*.

Income for a reporting period is measured under the retrospective interest method as the sum of (1) the difference between a security's amortized cost at the end of the period and its amortized cost at the beginning of the period and (2) cash received during the period. A security's amortized cost is based on the present value of estimated future cash flows at an effective yield (the internal rate of return) that equates all past actual and current estimated cash flow streams to the initial investment. If the sum of newly estimated undiscounted cash flows is less than the security's amortized cost, the effective yield is negative. In that case, a zero effective yield is used to compute amortized cost.

All estimates of future cash flows used to determine the effective yield for income recognition under the retrospective interest method either should be based on quoted forward market rates or prices in active markets, if available or should be based on spot rates or prices as of the reporting date if market-based prices are unavailable.

The impairment guidance in ASC 320 continues to apply to *host contracts* from which embedded derivatives have been separated based on the guidance in ASC 310-20-35-9, 35-10 and should be accounted for at fair value.

- Structured notes for which income is recognized using the retrospective method must meet at least one of the following conditions:
  — The note's contractual principal that will be paid at maturity or the original investment is at risk (other than due to a borrower's failure to pay the contractual amounts due). Principal-indexed notes whose principal repayment is based on movements in the S&P 500 index or notes whose principal repayment is linked to certain events or circumstances are examples of these instruments.
  — The note's return on investment varies (other than due to changes in a borrower's credit rating) because either:
    (1) The coupon rate is not stated or a stated coupon rate is not fixed or pre-specified, *and* the variation in coupon rate or the return on investment is not a constant percentage of, or does not move in the same direction as, changes in market-based interest rates or interest rate indices, such as LIBOR or the Treasury Bill Index, or
    (2) A variable or fixed coupon rate is below market interest rates for traditional notes with comparable maturities and a portion of the potential yield depends on the occurrence of future events or circumstances. Inverse floating-rate notes, dual index notes, and equity-linked bear notes are examples of these instruments.
  — The note's contractual maturity is based on a specific index or on the occurrence of specific events or circumstances that cannot be controlled by the parties to the transaction, except for the passage of time or events that cause normal covenant violations. Index amortizing notes and notes whose contractual maturity is based on the price of oil are examples of these instruments.
- The following financial instruments are *not* within the scope of the guidance in this Issue:
  — Mortgage loans or similar debt instruments that are not securities under the guidance in ASC 320; traditional bonds convertible into the issuer's stock; multicurrency debt securities; debt securities classified as trading; debt securities that participate directly in an issuer's operations, such as participating mortgages; reverse mortgages;
  — Structured notes that are accounted for as trading securities under the guidance in ASC 320, because based on their terms it is reasonably possible that an investor could lose all or substantially all of the investment (other than if a borrower fails to pay all amounts due).
- Entities should determine, based on the provisions of ASC 320, whether the value of an individual structured note has experienced an other-than-temporary decline below amortized cost and should include the change in earnings.

It was noted that after recognizing an other-than-temporary impairment on a structured note, an entity should consider its collectibility in estimating future cash flows for the purpose of determining the effective yield used in the retrospective interest method calculation of income to be recognized on the note. That is, the entity would no longer assume that the contractual interest and the note's principal would be repaid. For example, if an investor has recognized a $30 other-than-temporary loss on a $100 investment whose fair value has decreased to $70, and the investor expects to collect no more than $80 of the principal at maturity, only $80 of principal should be used in estimating future cash flows for the effective yield calculation.

EFFECT OF ASC 815

The impairment guidance in ASC 320 continues to apply to *host contracts* from which embedded derivatives have been separated based on the guidance in ASC 815-15-25-1, 25-14, 25-26 through 25-29 and should be accounted for at fair value.

The guidance on the second Issue is partially nullified by ASC 815, which requires the separation of certain embedded derivatives from the host contract under the conditions discussed in ASC 815-15-25-1. Those derivatives should be accounted for at fair value under the guidance in ASC 815. Although they may not be designated as hedging instruments, contracts with embedded derivatives that cannot be reliably identified for separation from their host contracts should be measured at fair value in their entirety. However, the guidance in this Issue should continue to apply to (1) embedded derivatives that are *not* required to be separated under the guidance in this Issue, and (2) host contracts that meet any of the three conditions above, even though their embedded derivatives have been separated under the guidance in ASC 815. The calculation of the effective yield is not addressed in the Statement.

SUBSEQUENT DEVELOPMENT

In its discussion of the guidance in ASC 310-20-60-1, 60-2; ASC 310-30-15-5; ASC 320-10-35-38; 55-2; ASC 325-40-05-1, 05-2; 15-2 through 15-9; 25-1 through 25-3; 30-1 through 30-3; 35-1 through 35-13, 35-15 through 35-16; 45-1; 55-1 through 55-25; 60-7 (see Chapter 60, *ASC 860—Transfers and Servicing*) at the July 2000 meeting, the Emerging Issues Task Force (EITF) agreed that the guidance in this Issue should apply to the recognition of interest income from beneficial interests in a securitization structure that holds common stocks, because the guidance in ASC 310-20-60-1 through 60-2; ASC 310-30-15-5; ASC 320-10-35-38; 55-2, ASC 325-40-05-1, 05-2; 15-2 through 15-9, 25-1 through 25-3, 30-1 through 30-3, 35-1 through 35-13, 35-15, 35-16, 45-1, 55-1 through 55-25, 60-7 applies only to securitized financial assets with contractual cash flows, for example, loans, receivables, and guaranteed lease residuals.

DISCUSSION

- The retrospective method is based on the interest method discussed in ASC 310-20-35-26. It was recommended that this method be used to calculate income on structured notes, whose contractual cash flows are volatile, because the effects of differences between actual cash flows and previously estimated cash flows in each reporting period are recognized. Proponents believed that the volatility in income caused by this method represents the inherent risks of investing in structured notes.

The effective yield, which initially is calculated for the life of an instrument, is recalculated either from the date of acquisition of a structured note or from the most recent date on which an impairment was recognized under the guidance in ASC 320, if actual cash flows at a reporting date are different from anticipated amounts or if estimates for anticipated future cash flows have been revised. A structured note's amortized cost is recalculated based on the newly calculated effective yield—just as if that yield had been used from inception. The change in amortized cost is reported in that period's earnings.

If the recalculated effective yield is less than zero—because actual past and anticipated future earnings will be insufficient to recover the initial net investment—a *temporary* loss is recognized and an allowance is established. Additional losses or recoveries of previous losses in future periods are charged or credited to the allowance. The allowance should not be reduced to a negative amount, however. It is reduced, but not below zero, for an other-than-temporary impairment loss, and a new cost basis is established.

Under the accounting guidance, a structured note's amortized cost is written down to fair value if an impairment is other than temporary, in accordance with the provisions of ASC 320. The amount of the writedown is recognized in earnings, except for amounts previously recognized in the allowance. Subsequent recoveries in fair value are not recognized.

- The Issue's scope limitations were influenced by the SEC Observer's concerns that some might apply the recommended treatment to financial instruments that should be accounted for as trading securities—whose changes in fair value are recognized in income. Structured notes that are similar or identical to variable debt instruments accounted for under the guidance in ASC 310 are outside this Issue's scope.

ASC 320-10-15-7, 35-17, 35-20, through 35-30, 35-32A through 35-35A, 35-45, 35-45, 35-8A through 35-9A, 50-6 through 50-8B, 55-22 through 55-23 The Meaning of Other-Than-Temporary Impairment and Its Application to Certain Investments

BACKGROUND

The following discussion provides guidance on how to determine when an investment is considered to be impaired, whether the impairment is other than temporary, and how to measure an impairment loss. It also provides guidance on accounting considerations after another-than-temporary impairment has been recognized and requires certain disclosures about unrealized losses that have not been recognized as other-than-temporary impairments. As a result of the issuance of this guidance, certain provisions of ASC 320, ASC 958-320, and ASC 323 are amended.

SCOPE

The following guidance applies to investments in:

- Debt and equity securities under the scope of ASC 320.
  - The guidance applies to all equity securities held by insurance companies, because those securities must be reported at fair value.
  - An investment should be evaluated for impairment based on its form (e.g., a mutual fund that primarily invests in debt securities should be evaluated for impairment as an equity security).
  - Investments that meet the criteria in ASC 815-15-25-1, which should be bifurcated so that the host instrument and the embedded derivative are accounted for separately. The guidance should be applied to host instruments that meet the scope of this guidance.
- Debt and equity securities under the scope of ASC 958-320 held by investors that report a "performance indicator" as defined in ASC 954.
- Equity securities *not* under the scope of ASC 320 and ASC 958-320 and not accounted for under the equity method in ASC 323 and related interpretations (i.e., cost-method investments).

ACCOUNTING GUIDANCE

Step 1: Determining Whether an Investment is Impaired

Each security (investment) should be evaluated for impairment individually. An investment is impaired if its fair value is less than its amortized cost at the balance sheet reporting date. That evaluation should be made in each reporting period, including interim periods for entities that issue such reports, except as discussed for cost-method investments below.

Separate contracts, such as a debt security and a guarantee or other credit enhancement, should not be combined for the determination of a debt security's impairment or whether the debt security can be contractually prepaid or settled in manner that would prevent an investor from recovering substantially all of its cost.

Proceed to step 2 if the fair value of an investment, other than a cost-method investment, is less than its amortized cost.

Cost-method investments. An investment accounted for on the cost method should be evaluated as follows because the fair value of such investments is not easy to determine:

If the fair value of a cost-method investment has been estimated, an investor should use that estimate to determine whether the investment is impaired for the reporting period in which the investor has estimated fair value. Proceed to step 2 if the fair value of an investment is less than its cost.

In reporting periods in which the fair value of a cost-method investment has not been estimated, an investor should evaluate whether an impairment indicator has occurred in that reporting period, i.e., an event or a change in circumstances that would adversely affect an investment's fair value. The following are some impairment indicators among others:

- A significant deterioration in an investee's earnings performance, credit rating, asset quality, or business prospects;
- A significant adverse change in an investee's regulatory, economic, or technological environment;
- A significant adverse change in the general market condition of the geographic area or industry in which an investee operates;
- A solicited or unsolicited bona fide purchase offer, an investee's offer to sell, or a completed auction process for the same or a similar security at less than the investment's original cost;
- Factors raising significant concerns about an investee's ability to continue as a going concern, such as negative operating cash flows, working capital deficiencies, or noncompliance with statutory capital requirements or debt covenants.

For investments that were previously tested for impairment under Step 2 and were determined not to be other-than-temporarily impaired, an investor should continue to estimate their fair value in each subsequent reporting period until (a) an investment recovers its fair value up to or above its cost, or (b) an other-than-temporary impairment is recognized.

An investment's fair value should be estimated if there is an impairment indicator and should be evaluated under Step 2 if its fair value is less than its amortized cost.

Step 2: Evaluating Whether an Impairment is Other Than Temporary

An investment's impairment is either temporary or other than temporary if the investment's fair value is less than its amortized cost at the balance sheet date of the reporting period in which the evaluation was made. Other guidance may also be used to determine whether an impairment is other than temporary, such as the guidance in ASC 320-10-35-18, 45-9; ASC 323-10-35; ASC 325-20-05-7, 25-1 through 25-2, 30-1, 35-1 through 35-2, 35-5, 35-31; ASC 958-320-810-60-1 and ASC 310-20-60-1 through 60-2; ASC 310-30-15-5; ASC 320-10-35-38, 55-2; ASC 325-40-05-1 through 05-2, 15-2 through 15-9, 25-1 through 25-3, 30-1 through 30-3, 35-1 through 35-13, 35-15 through 35-16, 45-1, 55-1 through 55-25, 60-7; and ASC 325-40-35, if applicable.

If an investor decides to sell an available-for-sale security that is impaired and does not expect that the security's fair value will be fully recovered before the expected time of the sale, the security should be considered to be other-than-temporarily impaired in the period in which the investor has decided to sell the security An impairment loss should be recognized when the security's impairment is considered to be other-than-temporary, even if the investor has decided not to sell the security.

Step 3: Recognizing an Impairment Loss Equal to the Difference Between the Cost of an Investment and its Fair Value If an Impairment is Other Than Temporary

An impairment loss equal to the difference between an investment's cost and its fair value at the balance sheet date of the reporting period in which the evaluation was made should be recognized in earnings if it is determined in Step 2 that the security's impairment is other-than-temporary. Partial recoveries after the balance sheet date should not be included in the measurement of impairment. The investment's fair value would become its new cost basis, which should not be adjusted if the investment's fair value recovers thereafter.

Accounting for Debt Securities After Recognition of an Other-Than-Temporary Impairment

An investor should account for a debt security after an other-than-temporary impairment has been recognized as if the debt security had been purchased on the measurement date of the other-than-temporary impairment. A discount or reduced premium recorded for the debt security based on the new cost basis should be amortized *prospectively* over the debt security's remaining life based on the amount and timing of future estimated cash flows.

Disclosures

An investor should disclose the following information in its annual financial statements about all investments whose costs exceed their fair value (unrealized loss position), including those disclosed under the guidance in ASC 310-30-15-5; ASC 320-10-35-38, 55-2; ASC 325-40-05-1 through 05-2, 15-2 through 15-9, 25-1 through 25-3, 30-1 through 30-3, 35-1 through 35-13, 35-15 through 35-16, 45-1, 55-1 through 55-25, 60-7, for which other-than-temporary impairments have *not* been recognized:

- Quantitative information about the items in (a) and (b) below should be presented in a table, as of each date on which a balance sheet is presented, by category of investment as required under the guidance in ASC 320 and ASC 958-320 and cost method investments:

    a. The total fair value of investments with unrealized losses;

    b. The total amount of unrealized losses.

    That information should be reported separately for investments that have been continuously in an unrealized loss position for *less* than 12 months and those that have been in that position for twelve months or *longer*. To determine how long an investment has been in a continuous unrealized loss position, the balance sheet date of the reporting period in which an impairment has been identified is used as the reference point. The annual balance sheet date of the period in which an impairment is identified should be used as the reference point by entities that do not prepare interim financial information. A continuous unrealized loss position ends in the period in which (a) an other-than-temporary impairment is recognized or (b) an investment's fair value has been recovered up to or beyond its cost.

- Additional information in a narrative format as of the most recent balance date to help users of the financial statements to understand the quantitative disclosures as well as the rationale for the conclusion that unrealized losses are not other than temporary impairments. Those disclosures may be presented by combined investment categories, but significant unreal-

ized losses should be presented separately. The following information could include:
— The nature of the investments;
— The causes of impairments;
— The number of investment positions in an unrealized position;
— Other evidence that an investor considered to reach the conclusion that an investment is not other-than-temporarily impaired, for example, reports of industry analysts, sector credit ratings, the volatility of a security's fair value, and other information considered to be relevant.

The following additional information, if applicable, should be disclosed for investments accounted for on the cost method, as of each date for which a balance sheet is presented in annual financial statements:

- The total carrying amount of all cost-method investments;
- The total carrying amount of cost-method investments that were not evaluated for impairment;
- The fact that the fair value of a cost-method investment is not estimated if no events or changes in circumstances that may have a significant effect on the investment's fair value were identified, and
  — The investor determined that in accordance with the guidance in ASC 825-10-50-16 through 23 and ASC 958-320-50-4 that it is not practicable to estimate the investment's fair value, or
  — The investor is exempt from estimating fair value under the guidance in ASC 825.

ASC 320-10-25-18 Impact of Certain Transactions on the Held-to-Maturity Classification under FASB Statement No. 115

BACKGROUND

Under current guidance sales recognition is required if control of a security has been transferred to another entity, unless a concurrent contract to repurchase the security exists. Wash sales and certain bond swaps that do not involve the issuer are accounted for as sales, therefore, under guidance in ASC 860.

Although the guidance in ASC 320 lists changes in circumstances that would result in a change of intent to hold a security to maturity without calling into question the entity's intent to hold other debt securities to maturity, it does not discuss the effect of exchanges not accounted for as sales.

ACCOUNTING ISSUE

Are certain transactions related to held-to-maturity securities that are not accounted for as sales (such as wash sales and bond swaps) inconsistent with an entity's previously stated intent to hold those securities to maturity, and do such transactions therefore call into question the entity's intent to hold other debt securities to maturity?

ACCOUNTING GUIDANCE

If a transaction, such as a wash sale or bond swap, involving held-to-maturity securities is *not accounted for as a sale*, the transaction is not inconsistent with the entity's previously stated intent to hold the security to maturity and, therefore, would *not* call into question the entity's intent to hold other debt securities to maturity.

> **OBSERVATION:** ASC 860-10-40-5 which requires that a wash sale or swap be accounted for as a sale, partially nullifies the guidance in this Issue. Unless there is a concurrent contract to repurchase or redeem the transferred financial assets from the transferee, the transferor does not continue to have effective control over the transferred assets. However, the guidance would apply to other transactions not accounted for as sales under ASC 860, such as the desecuritization of securities discussed in ASC 320-10-25-18; ASC 860-10-55-34, 55-74 below. This Issue was not reconsidered in ASC 860. Additional guidance on wash sales may be found in ASC 860-10-55-57.

It was noted, however, that an entity's intent to hold other debt securities to maturity would be called into question if the entity does not hold to maturity the debt instrument received or retained as a result of the transaction.

DISCUSSION

The guidance is based on the view that a transaction that is not accounted for as a sale should not be considered a sale when applying the provisions of ASC 320 Proponents of this view argued that a sale has not occurred because the entity is in the same economic position as before the wash sale or swap occurred; the risks and benefits of ownership are not transferred when an entity receives substantially the same security as the security transferred.

ASC 320-10-S35-1, S99-2 Adjustments in Assets and Liabilities for Holding Gains and Losses as Related to the Implementation of FASB Statement No. 115

The SEC staff has been asked about the adjustment of certain assets and liabilities, such as noncontrolling interests, certain life insurance policyholder liabilities, deferred acquisition costs, amortized using the gross-profits method, or and intangible assets acquired in business combination with a corresponding adjustment to other comprehensive income when unrealized holding gains and losses from securities held as available-for-sale are recognized in comprehensive income. In other words, whether an entity should adjust the carrying amounts of those assets and liabilities to the amount at which they would have been reported if those unrealized gains and losses had been realized.

The SEC observer analogized to the guidance in ASC 740-20-45-11, which discusses the classification of deferred tax effects of unrealized holding gains and losses reported in comprehensive income. Under that guidance, entities are required to report the tax effects of those gains and losses as charges or credits to other comprehensive income. In other words, by recognizing unrealized holding gains and losses in equity, temporary differences may be created. Deferred differences would be recognized for those temporary differences and their effect would be reported in accumulated other comprehensive income with the related unrealized holding gains and losses. Consequently, deferred tax assets and liabilities must be recognized for temporary differences related to unrealized holding gains and losses, but their corresponding charges or credits are reported in other comprehensive income as charges or credits to income in the income statement.

By analogy to the guidance in ASC 740-20-45-11, the SEC staff believes that registrants should adjust certain assets and liabilities, such as noncontrolling interests, certain life insurance policyholder liabilities, deferred acquisition costs amortized using the gross-profits method, and intangible assets related to the acquisition of insurance contracts in a business combination that are amortized using the gross-profits method for unrealized holding gains or losses from securities classified as available-for-sale if such adjustments would have been made had the gains or losses actually been realized. Corresponding credits or charges should be made to other comprehensive income. Assets should be adjusted at subsequent balance sheet dates through valuation allowances.

Liabilities, such as certain policyholder liabilities should be adjusted if an insurance policy requires the holder to be charged or credited for a portion or all of the realized gains or losses of specific securities classified as available-for-sale. In addition, assets that are amortized using the gross-profits method, such as deferred acquisition costs accounted for under the guidance in ASC 944-30-35-4 and certain intangible assets as a result of insurance contracts acquired in a business combination should be adjusted to show the effects that would have been recognized if unrealized gains or losses had actually been realized. However, capitalized acquisition costs related to such insurance contracts under the scope of ASC 944-30-35-4 should not be adjusted for unrealized gains or losses unless there would have been a "premium deficiency" if the gain or loss had been realized.

The guidance in this SEC staff announcement should not affect reported net income.

ASC 320-10-25-18; ASC 860-10-55-34, 55-74 The Applicability of FASB Statement No. 115 to Desecuritizations of Financial Assets

The FASB staff made the following announcements about the applicability of ASC 320 to the accounting for the desecuritization of financial assets: the process by which securities are broken down into their underlying loans or other financial assets.

- The FASB staff addressed the accounting for desecuritizations by analogizing to ASC 860-10-40-5, which addressed the accounting for the securitization of financial assets. The paragraph states that a transfer of financial assets over which the transferor surrenders control should be accounted for as a sale if consideration (other than a beneficial interest in the transferred assets) has been received. (In contrast, sales accounting is not appropriate for a transaction transferring securities or a beneficial interest in a securitized pool of financial assets in which the only consideration received by the transferor is the financial assets underlying the securities or the beneficial interest in the transferred securities.) The FASB agreed that this approach should be used for desecuritizations in general.

- The FASB staff believes that the guidance in ASC 320-10-25-18 on the effect of the held-to-maturity classification of wash sales and bond swaps also should apply to desecuritizations that are not accounted for as sales. The guidance in ASC 320-10-25-18 provides that an entity's intent to hold other debt securities to maturity under the guidance in ASC 320 is not called into question if the entity holds to maturity securities received or retained in a wash sale or bond swap transaction not accounted for as a sale. Similarly, the FASB staff believes that an entity's intent to hold other debt securities to maturity should not be called into question if an entity that transfers beneficial interests classified as held-to-maturity in a desecuritization transaction not accounted for as a sale holds to maturity the financial assets received or retained in the desecuritization.

ASC 320-10-15-2, 15-5, 25-1, 25-5, 25 through 25-8, 25-10, 25-12 through 25-13, 25-16 through 25-18, 30-3 through 30-4, 35-6 through 35-9, 35-13, 35-15 through 35-16, 35-18, 35-32 through 35-33, 40-1 through 40-2, 45-3 through 45-7, 45-12, 50-12 through 50-14, 55-2 through 55-6, 55-8 through 55-9, 55-24 through 55-25; ASC 323-30-60-2; ASC 958-320-15-4, 15-6, 55-2 through 55-3, 60-1 A Guide to Implementation of Statement 115 on Accounting for Certain Investments in Debt and Equity Securities

BACKGROUND

The guidance in this section, includes responses to 60 specific questions regarding the application of ASC 320.

STANDARDS

Scope

Question 1: Does the guidance in ASC 320 apply to a loan that has been insured, such as a loan insured by the Federal Housing Administration, or to a conforming mortgage loan?

Answer: No. The guidance in ASC 320 applies only to debt securities, including debt instruments that have been securitized. A loan is not a debt security until it has been securitized.

Question 2: For a loan that was restructured in a troubled debt restructuring involving a modification of terms, does the guidance in ASC 320 apply to the accounting by the creditor (i.e., investor) if the restructured loan meets the definition of a *security* in ASC 320?

Answer: Yes. The guidance in ASC 320 applies to all debt securities. See ASC 860; ASC 320-10-15-6; 55-2; and ASC 310-40-40-8A, 40-9 for further guidance on this general topic.

Question 3: Are options on securities covered by ASC 320?

Answer: In some cases. An investment in an option on an equity interest is covered by the guidance in ASC 320 if the option has a fair value that is "currently available on a securities exchange." An equity interest includes any security that gives the holder the right to acquire (e.g., warrants, rights, calls) or to sell (e.g., puts) an ownership interest in an enterprise at a fixed or determinable price. The guidance in ASC 320 does not cover written options, cash-settled options on equity securities, options on equity-based indexes, or options on debt securities.

Question 4: What accounting literature addresses the accounting for equity securities that do not have readily determinable fair values?

Answer: ASC 323 provides guidance in accounting for equity securities that do not have readily determinable fair values. If the investment does not qualify for treatment under the equity method (i.e., typically less than a 20% ownership stake), the investment is accounted for using the cost method. Investments accounted for using the cost method are to be adjusted to reflect other-than temporary declines in fair value. [There is an exception to this general requirement for investments made by insurance companies—see ASC 944]. There is currently no authoritative guidance as to the accounting for options and warrants in the absence of a readily determinable fair value.

Question 5: An entity invests in a limited partnership interest (or a venture capital company) that meets the definition of an *equity security* but does not have a readily determinable fair value. However, substantially all of the partnership's assets consist of investments in debt securities or equity securities that have readily determinable fair values. Is it appropriate to "look through" the form of an investment to determine whether the guidance in ASC 320 applies?

Answer: No, an entity should not "look through" its investment to the nature of the securities held by an investee. Therefore, given the lack of a readily determinable market value in this case, the guidance in ASC 320 would not apply. Guidance on accounting for limited partnership investments is provided in ASC 323-30.

Securities Classified as Held-to-Maturity

Question 6: Does ASC 320 apply to certificates of deposit (CDs) or guaranteed investment contracts (GICs)?

Answer: It depends on whether the CD or GIC meets the definition of a *security*. The definition of a *security* in ASC 320 was modeled after the Uniform Commercial Code definition. Most CDs and GICs would not be classified as securities under this definition; however, certain jumbo CDs and GICs might qualify as securities.

Question 7: Are short sales of securities (sales of securities that the seller does not own at the time of the sale) under the scope of ASC 320?

Answer: No. A short sale gives rise to an obligation to deliver securities. Short sales are not investments and therefore do not fall under the scope of ASC 320. Various AICPA Industry Audit Guides require obligations due to short sales to be periodically adjusted to market value. Changes in the underlying obligation are reflected in earnings as they occur.

Question 8: Not discussed in the Codification.

Question 9: Does the guidance in ASC 320 apply to preferred stock that is convertible into marketable common stock?

Answer: If the convertible preferred stock is redeemable (either on a fixed date or at the option of the holder), it would be classified as a debt security. Therefore, the guidance in ASC 320 would apply even if the preferred stock did not have a readily determinable fair value. A convertible preferred stock that is not redeemable would be subject to the provisions of ASC 320 only if the preferred stock (now treated as an equity security) has a readily determinable fair value.

Question 10: Does the guidance in ASC 320 apply to financial statements issued by a trust?

Answer: It depends. ASC 320 applies if the trust does not report all of its investments at fair value. Some trusts record all investments at fair or market value, with any resulting changes reflected in income or in the change in net assets. ASC 320 does not apply in such cases.

Question 11: ASC 320-20-35-5 states, "At each reporting date, the appropriateness of the [security's] classification shall be reassessed." If the guidance in ASC 320-20-35-5 requires an enterprise to reassess its classification of securities, why do transfers or sales of held-to-maturity securities for reasons other than those specified in ASC 320-10-25-6, 25-9, and 25-14 call into question ("taint") an enterprise's intent to hold other debt securities to maturity in the future?

Answer: The point of ASC 320-20-35-5 is primarily to require a periodic evaluation of an entity's ability to hold a security to maturity. An enterprise's intent to hold a security to maturity should not change; however, the ability of the enterprise to hold the security to maturity may change. Also, while an entity may initially classify a debt security as available-for-sale, subsequent developments may indicate that the entity has the ability to hold the securities to maturity. Assuming management intends to hold the debt securities to maturity, the investment would be reclassified from the available-for-sale portfolio to the held-to-maturity portfolio.

Question 12: What are the consequences of a sale or transfer of held-to-maturity securities for a reason other than those specified in ASC 320-10-25-6, 25-9, and 25-14? In other words, what does it mean to "call into question [the entity's] intent to hold other debt securities to maturity in the future"?

Answer: A sale or transfer of held-to-maturity securities for a reason other than those specified in ASC 320-10-25-6, 25-9, and 25-14 calls into question the appropriateness of continuing to classify any debt securities as held-to-maturity. If the sale represents a material contradiction of the entity's stated intent to hold securities to maturity, any remaining securities classified as held-to-maturity would need to be reclassified as available-for-sale. Also, if a pattern of sales of held-to-maturity securities has occurred, any remaining securities classified as held-to-maturity would need to be reclassified. The reclassification would occur in the reporting period in which the sale occurred.

Question 13: If a sale or transfer of a security classified as held-to-maturity occurs for a reason other than those specified in ASC 320-10-25-6, 25-9, and 25-14, does the sale or transfer call into question ("taint") the enterprise's intent about only the same type of securities (e.g., municipal bonds) that were sold or transferred, or about all securities that remain in the held-to-maturity category?

Answer: All securities that remain in the held-to-maturity category would be tainted.

Question 14: If held-to-maturity securities are reclassified to available-for-sale because sales occurred for reasons other than those specified in ASC 320-10-25-6, 25-9, and 25-14, what amount of time must pass before the enterprise can again classify securities as held-to-maturity?

Answer: This is a matter of judgment. The key issue is whether circumstances have changed sufficiently for management to assert with a greater degree of credibility that it has the intent and ability to hold the debt securities to maturity.

> **PRACTICE POINTER:** No specific guidance is provided on the length of time that must pass before an entity can again classify securities as held-to-maturity when it had previously sold held-to-maturity securities for reasons other than those specified in ASC 320-10-25-6, 25-9, and 25-14. At a minimum, the reasons why management previously sold held-to-maturity securities must have changed. For example, if management previously sold held-to-maturity securities due to a cash shortage brought about by the enterprise's deteriorating financial condition, the financial condition and cash position of the enterprise must have substantially improved. Or, if held-to-maturity securities were sold in the past due to a shortage of capital, the enterprise must have obtained or have ready access to the capital it is likely to need in the future.
>
> In addition, it would seem reasonable for at least one year to pass before an enterprise could again classify securities as held-to-maturity when it had previously sold held-to-maturity securities for reasons other than those specified in ASC 320-10-25-6, 25-9, and 25-14. Finally, a change in top management—particularly financial management—may allow management to credibly assert that it has the intent to hold debt securities to maturity. The ability of the entity to hold such securities to maturity even after new management is hired would still need to be assessed.

Question 15: Is it consistent with the guidance in ASC 320 to have a documented policy to initially classify all debt securities as held-to-maturity but then automatically transfer every security to available-for-sale when it reaches a predetermined point before maturity (e.g., every held-to-maturity security will be transferred to available-for-sale 24 months before its stated maturity) so that an entity has the flexibility to sell securities?

Answer: No. Such a policy would suggest that the entity does not have the intent and ability to hold the security to maturity.

Question 16: May securities classified as held-to-maturity be pledged as collateral?

Answer: Yes. However, the entity must believe that it will be able to satisfy the liability and thereby recover unrestricted access to the debt security that is serving as collateral for the borrowing. However, if sale accounting is used according to the guidance in ASC 860, the securities pledged may not be treated as held-to-maturity.

Question 17: May held-to-maturity securities be subject to a repurchase agreement (or a securities lending agreement)?

Answer: Yes, if the repurchase agreement is accounted for as a secured borrowing. The entity must intend and expect to repay the borrowing and thereby recover unrestricted access to the debt security that is serving as collateral for the borrowing.

Question 18: May convertible debt securities be classified as held-to-maturity?

Answer: Although such treatment is not specifically prohibited, classifying convertible debt securities as held-to-maturity generally would be inappropriate. Convertible debt securities generally carry a lower interest rate than standard debt securities. However, the holder of a debt security stands to profit from the conversion feature if the common stock of the entity issuing the convertible security rises in value. It is implausible to suggest that an entity would not avail itself of such a profit opportunity because it characterized securities as held-to-maturity. If an entity exercises a conversion feature on a security being treated as held-to-maturity, it will call into question the appropriateness of classifying any other securities as held-to-maturity.

Question 19: May a callable debt security be classified as held-to-maturity?

Answer: Yes. The debt instrument's maturity date is viewed as being accelerated if an issuer exercises its call provision. The issuer's exercise of a call feature in no way invalidates the holder's treatment of the security as held-to-maturity. However, per ASC 860, some callable debt securities may not qualify for treatment as held-to-maturity securities. More specifically, this limitation applies to a callable debt security purchased at a significant premium if that security can be prepaid or otherwise settled in such a way that the holder would not recover its full investment.

Question 20: May a puttable debt security be classified as held-to-maturity?

Answer: Yes, if the entity has the intent and ability to hold the puttable debt security to maturity. If the entity exercises the put feature, it will call into question the appropriateness of classifying any other debt securities as held-to-maturity. In addition, some puttable debt securities may not qualify for held-to-maturity treatment per ASC 860-20-35-2.

Question 21 Not included in the Codification.

Question 22: May a mortgage-backed interest-only certificate be classified as held-to-maturity?

Answer: No. ASC 860 amends the guidance in ASC 320 to prohibit held-to-maturity accounting for interest-only strips.

Question 23: If an enterprise holds a debt security classified as held-to-maturity, and that security is downgraded by a rating agency, would a sale or transfer of that security call into question the entity's intent to hold other debt securities to maturity in the future?

ASC 320—Investments—Debt and Equity Securities

Answer: No. A downgrade by a rating agency is an example of a significant deterioration in the issuer's creditworthiness. A sale or transfer that results from such a deterioration does not "taint" the remaining held-to-maturity portfolio (see ASC 320-10-25-6).

Question 24: What constitutes a "major" business combination or a "major" disposition under the guidance in ASC 320-10-25-6.

Answer: A sale or transfer of held-to-maturity securities is permitted under the guidance in ASC 320-10-25-6 as part of a "major" business combination or "major" disposition if necessary to maintain an entity's existing interest rate risk position or credit risk policy. However, the guidance in ASC 320 does not define what constitutes a "major" business combination or disposition. The Statement does state that the sale of a component of an entity qualifies as a major disposition. The purchase or sale of a large pool of financial assets or liabilities would not constitute a major business combination or disposition. In addition, the sale of held-to-maturity securities to fund a business combination is not permitted.

Question 25: Not included in the Codification.

Question 26: May securities classified as held-to-maturity be sold under the exception provided in ASC 320-10-25-6 in anticipation of or otherwise prior to a major business combination or disposition without calling into question the enterprise's intent to hold other debt securities to maturity in the future?

Answer: No. Any such transfers or sales should occur at the same time as or after the business combination or disposition.

Question 27: The guidance in ASC 320-10-25-12 provides that "necessary transfers or sales should occur concurrent with or shortly after the business combination or disposition." How long is *shortly*?

Answer: The term *shortly* is not defined in ASC 320. However, as time elapses it becomes increasingly difficult to justify that any sale or transfer of held-to-maturity securities was necessitated by the combination or disposition, and not by other events and circumstances.

Question 28: If a regulator directs a particular institution (rather than all institutions supervised by that regulator) to sell or transfer held-to-maturity securities (e.g., to increase liquid assets), are those sales or transfers consistent with ASC 320-10-25-6?

Answer: No. The exception provided in ASC 320-10-25-6 pertains only to a change in regulations affecting all entities affected by the legislation or regulator. However, this type of sale does not necessarily "taint" the remainder of the held-to-maturity portfolio. A forced sale by a regulator may qualify as an event that is isolated, nonrecurring, and unusual, and that could not have been reasonably anticipated (see ASC 320-10-25-6).

Question 29: Is a sale of held-to-maturity securities in response to an unsolicited tender offer from the issuer consistent with the guidance in ASC 320-10-25-6?

Answer: No. Such a sale does not fall under one of the specific exceptions outlined in ASC 320-10-25-6. It also does not qualify as an event that is isolated, nonrecurring, and unusual, and that could not have been reasonably anticipated.

Therefore, if held-to-maturity securities are sold in response to the tender offer, the remaining held-to-maturity portfolio is tainted.

Question 30: Is it consistent with the guidance in ASC 320 for an insurance company or other regulated enterprise to classify securities as held-to-maturity and also indicate to regulators that those securities could be sold to meet liquidity needs in a defined interest rate scenario whose likelihood of occurrence is reasonably possible but not probable?

Answer: No. Stating that held-to-maturity securities could be sold if a particular interest-rate environment developed is inconsistent with management's intent and ability to hold these securities to maturity.

Question 31: Is it ever appropriate to apply the exceptions in ASC 320-10-25-6 to situations that are similar, but not the same?

Answer: No. The exceptions outlined in ASC 320-10-25-6 are quite specific by design. They should not be extended to similar fact patterns. The guidance in ASC 320-10-25-6 does permit a general exception to the requirement for holding held-to-maturity securities to maturity. That is, held-to-maturity securities can be sold in response to an event that is isolated, nonrecurring, and unusual, and that could not have been reasonably anticipated.

Question 32: What constitutes an event that is "isolated, nonrecurring, and unusual-that could not have been reasonably anticipated" as described in ASC 320-10-25-6?

Answer: This general exception provision involves four elements. Three of these elements are as follows: (1) Was the event isolated? (2) Was the event nonrecurring? (3) Was the event unusual? The fourth element pertains to the extent that the event could have been reasonably anticipated. Very few events will meet all four of these conditions. In general, the types of events that would qualify are extremely remote disaster scenarios. For example, a run on a bank or on an insurance company would qualify.

Question 33: The guidance in ASC 320-10-25-14 allows a sale of a held-to-maturity security to be considered a maturity when the enterprise has collected a substantial portion (at least 85%) of the principal outstanding at acquisition due to scheduled payments on a debt security payable in equal installments (that comprise both principal and interest) over its term. What types of securities would typically qualify or not qualify for this exception?

Answer: This exception applies to (*a*) debt securities that are payable in equal installments, comprising both principal and interest, and (*b*) variable rate debt securities that would be payable in equal installments if there were no change in interest rates. It does not apply to debt securities for which the principal payment is level and the interest amount is based on the outstanding principal balance.

Securities Classified as Trading and as Available-for-Sale

Question 34: How often must sales occur for an activity to be considered "trading"?

Answer: Under the guidance in ASC 320, trading securities are described as securities that will be held for only a short period of time or that will be sold in the near term. Securities that management intends to hold for only hours or days must be classified as trading securities. However, securities that will be held for a longer period of time are not precluded from being classified as trading securities.

Question 35: If an enterprise acquires a security without intending to sell it in the near term, may the enterprise classify the security in the trading category?

Answer: Yes. In general, securities classified as trading will be held for a short period of time or will be sold in the near term. This general requirement is not an absolute. However, the decision to classify a security as trading is to be made at the time the security is acquired. Transfers of securities into or out of the trading category should be rare.

Question 36: If an enterprise decides to sell a security that has been classified as available-for-sale, should the security be transferred to trading?

Answer: No. Securities that will mature within one year or that management intends to sell within one year should not automatically be transferred into the trading category. Similarly, if an entity decides to sell a held-to-maturity security (in response to one of the conditions outlined in ASC 320-10-25-6, such security should not be reclassified as available-for-sale or trading. Refer to ASC 320-10-50-9 and 50-10 for mandated disclosures relating to the sale.

Question 37: What should be the initial carrying amount under ASC 320 of a previously nonmarketable equity security that becomes marketable (i.e., due to a change in circumstances, it now has a fair value that is readily determinable)?

Answer: In general, the basis for applying the provisions of ASC 320 should be the security's cost. However, if the change in marketability provides evidence that an other-than-temporary impairment has occurred, the impairment loss should be recognized and the writedown recorded prior to applying ASC 320. This treatment assumes that the nonmarketable security had not been accounted for using the equity method.)

Question 38: What should be the initial carrying amount under ASC 320 of a marketable equity security that should no longer be accounted for under the equity method (e.g., due to a decrease in the level of ownership)?

Answer: The initial carrying amount of the security should be the previous carrying amount of the investment.

Changes in Fair Value—Reporting

Question 39: How is a sale of an available-for-sale security recorded?

Answer: In general, cash or a receivable account should be debited for the amount of the proceeds, and the investment account should be credited for its fair value (i.e., its selling price). Any unrealized gain or loss relating to the investment being sold (recorded in comprehensive income) is reversed into earnings. Deferred tax accounts that relate to any unrealized gain or loss are also adjusted. This general procedure needs to be modified if the entity has not yet recorded all changes in the value of the security being sold (some entities record these changes only at reporting dates), or if a write-down for an other-than-temporary impairment has already been recorded.

Illustration of Sale of Available-for-Sale Securities

Pluto Enterprises purchases 1000 shares of Venus, Inc., common stock for $10 per share on April 1, 20X5. Pluto accounts for these securities as available-for-sale securities. The fair value of Venus' stock at December 31, 20X5, is $12 per share. Therefore, in Pluto's December 31, 20X5, balance sheet, its investment in the Venus securities would be recorded at $12,000. A $2,000 unrealized gain would be recorded in the stockholders' equity section of Pluto. Pluto's effective tax rate is 34%. Pluto sells these shares on June 30, 20X6, at $7 per share. Pluto adjusts the carrying value of securities only at year-end. The journal entry to record the sale would be as follows:

Cash (1,000 shares × $7 per share)	$7,000	
Unrealized gain	2,000	
Deferred tax liability ($2000 × 34%)	680	
Loss on sale of securities	3,000	
Available-for-sale securities		$12,000
Income tax expense		680

Question 40: How is a sale of a trading security recorded?

Answer: For trading securities, changes in fair value are recorded as they occur. Therefore, in most cases, the entry is to debit cash (or a receivables account) for the proceeds received, and to credit the trading securities account for the fair value of the securities sold (i.e., the selling price of the securities). This procedure must be modified if, for example, changes in the fair value of securities are recorded at the end of the day. Also, for those entities not taxed on a marked-to-market basis, the deferred tax accounts would be adjusted.

Questions 41 and 42 Not discussed in the Codification.

Transfer of Securities between Category Type

Question 43: When securities are transferred from available-for-sale to held-to-maturity or vice versa, is the subsequent amortization of a premium or discount based on the amortized cost of the security or on its fair value at the date of transfer?

Answer: The answer to this question depends on whether the transfer is from the available-for-sale category to the held-to-maturity category, or vice versa.

In the case of *transfer from available-for-sale to held-to-maturity*, the difference between the par value of the debt security that is transferred and its fair value on the date of transfer is accounted for as a yield adjustment in accordance with the provisions of ASC 310. The fair value of the debt security on the date of transfer, adjusted for subsequent amortization, serves as the security's amortized cost basis for required disclosures.

In the case of *transfer from held-to-maturity to available-for-sale*, the amortized cost of the security in the held-to-maturity portfolio is transferred to the available-for-sale portfolio for purposes of determining future amortization. In addition, the amortized cost of the security is used for comparing the cost of the security with its fair value (for the purpose of computing unrealized gain or loss) and for disclosure purposes.

Question 44: It is indicated in ASC 320-10-35-10 and 35-12 that for transfers involving the trading category, the unrealized holding gain or loss should be recognized in earnings. How should the gain or loss be classified on the income statement?

Answer: Unrealized gains or losses that have accumulated before the transfer date should be recognized in the income statement when securities are transferred into the trading category. Such gains or losses are recognized in a manner consistent with how realized gains and losses for the category from which the security being transferred are treated.

Question 45: How is a transfer from available-for-sale to held-to-maturity accounted for?

Answer: The following are some of the salient points in transferring a security from available-for-sale to held-to-maturity:

- Any unrealized holding gain or loss is combined with any unamortized premium or discount. This aggregate figure serves as the "adjusted" discount or premium, which is the amount that is amortized against income in the future. The net effect is to state the security at its fair value on the date of transfer.

- The adjusted discount or premium is amortized to income over the remaining life of the debt security.

- Any unrealized holding gain or loss (reflected in stockholders' equity) on the transfer date is amortized to income over the remaining life of the debt security.

- The net effect of steps 2 and 3 is that only the unamortized discount or premium (on the transfer date) from the original par value of the debt security is reflected in income over the remaining life of the debt security.

- Future changes in the fair value of the debt security are ignored, because the security is now classified as held-to-maturity.

Illustration of Transferring a Security from Available-for-Sale to Held-to-Maturity

Sonic, Inc., has a $1,000 par value bond that it acquired at $1,100 on January 1, 20X4. The bond has a ten-year life. During 20X4, $10 of the bond premium would be amortized. The bond is originally accounted for as available-for-sale. On December 31, 20X4, the fair value of the bond is $1,180. Therefore, at December 31, 20X4, Sonic would have $90 of unrealized gain in stockholders' equity. The $90 of unrealized gain plus the $90 of unamortized premium has the effect of stating the bond at its fair value, $1,180.

On January 1, 20X5, Sonic transfers this debt security into its held-to-maturity category. On the date of transfer, the adjusted bond premium is $180 ($90 of original unamortized premium and the $90 unrealized gain). The remaining life of the debt security is nine years. Each year for the next nine years, Sonic will amortize $20 of the bond investment premium. This has the effect of reducing income. Sonic also will amortize the unrealized gain that existed on the date of transfer at the rate of $10 per year ($90/9 years). This has the effect of increasing income. The net effect of both amortization entries is a reduction in Sonic's income of $10 per year for the next nine years (the remaining life of the bond). This amount, $10, is equal to what would be amortized based on the original unamortized bond premium.

Impairment

Question 46 Not discussed in the Codification

Question 47: Should an enterprise recognize an other-than-temporary impairment when it decides to sell a specific available-for-sale debt security at a loss shortly after the balance sheet date?

Answer: In most cases, yes. A loss should be recognized if the enterprise does not expect the fair value of the security to recover before the planned sale date. The loss resulting from an other-than-temporary impairment is to be recorded in the period in which the decision to sell the security was made, not in the period when the actual sale occurs.

Question 48: May a valuation allowance be used to recognize impairment on securities subject to ASC 320?

Answer: No. A general allowance for unidentified impairments in an overall portfolio is inappropriate. Other-than-temporary impairments are to be evaluated on a security-by-security basis. When such an impairment is identified, the related security is to be written down to this reduced value, which serves as the security's cost basis going forward. Such a write-down is recognized in earnings when it occurs.

Questions 49 and 50 Not discussed in the Codification

Presentation of Financial Statements and Disclosure

Question 51: Must the statement of cash flows show purchases, sales, and maturities of securities reported as cash equivalents?

Answer: No. The guidance in ASC 320 does not change the portion of the guidance in ASC 230 that permits showing cash equivalents as a net change within the statement of cash flows. However, ASC 320 does require the disclosure of the amortized cost and fair values of cash equivalents, shown separately by major security type. In addition, a note should explain what portion of each category of securities is shown as cash equivalents in the statement of financial position and the statement of cash flows.

Question 52: Must the disclosures required in ASC 320-10-50-1 through 50-3, 50-5, 50-9 through 50-10 be included in interim financial statements?

Answer: Only if a complete set of financial statements is presented at an interim-period date. If the interim financial statements are limited to summary financial information, per the requirements of APB-28 (Interim Financial Reporting), the above-mentioned disclosure requirements of ASC 320 are not required.

Question 53: ASC 320-10-50-9 requires disclosure of the change in the net unrealized holding gain or loss on trading securities that has been included in earnings during the period. How is that amount calculated?

Answer: ASC 320-10-50-9 requires the disclosure of gains or losses recognized in income during the period that resulted from trading securities still held at the end of the period.

Illustration of Disclosing Unrealized Gains and Losses

Rutledge, Inc., reports $100,000 of net gains and losses from trading securities in its 20X5 income statement. Of this amount, $80,000 resulted from securities that were sold during 20X5. Therefore, to satisfy the disclosure requirement of ASC 320-10-50-9, Rutledge would disclose that $20,000 of gains recognized during 20X5 pertain to trading securities still held at December 31, 20X5.

Deferred Tax Implications

Question 54: If an enterprise recognizes a deferred tax asset relating only to a net unrealized loss on available-for-sale securities and at the same time concludes that it is more likely than not that some or all of that deferred tax asset will not be realized, is the offsetting entry to the valuation allowance reported in other comprehensive income related to the unrealized loss under ASC 320 or as an item in determining income from continuing operations?

Answer: The offsetting entry to the valuation allowance would be reported as a component of other comprehensive income. This is because the valuation allowance is directly related to the unrealized loss on the available-for-sale securities.

Question 55: An enterprise has recognized a deferred tax asset relating to other deductible temporary differences in a previous fiscal year and at the same time has concluded that no valuation allowance was warranted. If in the current year the enterprise recognizes a deferred tax asset relating to a net unrealized loss on available-for-sale securities that arose in the current year and at the same time concludes that a valuation allowance is warranted, is the offsetting entry reported in the ASC 320 component of other comprehensive income or as an item in determining income from continuing operations?

Answer: Management needs to determine the extent to which the valuation allowance directly pertains to the unrealized loss on available-for-sale securities. The offsetting entry is reported in the ASC 320 component of other comprehensive income only to the extent that the valuation allowance pertains to the available-for-sale securities.

Question 56: If an enterprise does not need to recognize a valuation allowance at the same time that it establishes a deferred tax asset relating to a net unrealized loss on available-for-sale securities, but in a subsequent fiscal year concludes that it is more likely than not that some or all of that deferred tax asset will not be realized, is the offsetting entry to the valuation allowance reported in the ASC 320 component of other comprehensive income or as an item in determining income from continuing operations?

Answer: The offsetting entry should be included as an item in determining income from continuing operations.

Question 57: An enterprise recognizes a deferred tax asset relating to a net unrealized loss on available-for-sale securities and at the same time concludes that a valuation allowance is warranted. In a subsequent fiscal year the enterprise makes a change in judgment about the level of future years' taxable income such that all or a portion of that valuation allowance is no longer warranted. Is the offsetting entry reported in the ASC 320 component of other comprehensive income or as an item in determining income from continuing operations?

Answer: The entry to record the reversal in the valuation allowance account should be recorded as an item in determining income from continuing operations. This is the case even though the original entry was to the ASC 320 component of other comprehensive income. However, if the entity generates taxable income in the current year that can utilize the benefit of the deferred tax asset (rather than a change in judgment about future years' taxable income), the reduction of the valuation allowance account is allocated to that taxable income. See ASC 740-10-45-20; ASC 740-20-45-20; ASC 225-20-60-2; ASC 740-20-45-2 through 45-3, 45-5, 45-8, 45-11 through 45-12, and 45-14; and ASC 740-20-05-2 for additional information.

Questions 58 through 60: Not included in the Codification.

ASC 320-10-15-6, 55-2 Application of Statement 115 to Debt Securities Restructured in a Troubled Debt Restructuring

BACKGROUND

This guidance was issued to clarify a perceived inconsistency between ASC 310-10-35-13 through 35-14, 35-16 through 35-26, 35-28, 35-29, 35-34, 35-37, 35-39, 45-5 through 45-6, 50-15, 50-19; ASC 310-30-30-2; ASC 310-40-35-8, 35-12, 50-2 through 50-3, 50-12 through 50-13 and ASC 320-10-05-2, 50-1A through 50-3, 50-5, 50-9 through 50-11, 55-3, 15-5, 30-1, 35-1 through 35-2, 35-4 through 35-5, 35-10 through 35-13, 35-18, 15-2 through 15-4, 15-7; 25-3 through 25-6, 25-9, 25-11 through 25-12, 25-14 through 25-16, 45-1 through 45-2, 45-8 through 45-11, 45-13. This problem came to light during the FASB's discussion of the applicability of the guidance in ASC 320 to Brady bonds that were received in a troubled debt restructuring (TDR). The term *Brady bonds* refers to bonds issued to financial institutions by foreign governments under a program designed by Treasury Secretary Nicholas Brady in the late 1980s to help developing countries refinance their debt to those institutions.

If the guidance in ASC 320 did not apply to a debt security that was restructured in a TDR involving a modification of terms before the effective date of the guidance in ASC 310-10-35-13 through 35-14, 35-16 through 35-26, 35-28, 35-29, 35-34, 35-37, 35-39; 45-5 through 45-6, 50-15, 50-19; ASC 310-30-30-2; ASC 310-40-35-8, 35-12; 50-2 through 50-3, 50-12 through 50-13, the provisions related to impairment under that guidance and the guidance in ASC 320 would not apply. Consequently, such a debt security would be accounted for in accordance with the guidance in ASC 310-40-15-3 through 15-12, 35-2, 35-5 through 35-7, 40-2, 40-5 through 40-6, 40-8, 25-1 through 25-2, 50-1, 55-2, 10-1 through 10-2;

ASC 470-60-15-3 through 15-12, 55-3, 35-11 through 35-12, 45-1 through 45-2, 50-1 through 50-2, 10-1 through 10-2; ASC 450-20-60-12, which would not require the recognition of the time value of money or the security's fair value.

STANDARDS

Question: For a loan that was restructured in a TDR involving a modification of terms, does the guidance in ASC 320 apply to the accounting by a creditor if the restructured loan meets the definition of a *security* in ASC 320?

Answer: The guidance in ASC 320-10-05-2, 50-1A through 50-3, 50-5, 50-9 through 50-11, 55-3, 15-5, 30-1, 35-1 through 35-2, 35-4 through 35-5, 35-10 through 35-13, 35-18, 15-2 through 15-4, 15-7, 25-3 through 25-6, 25-9, 25-11 through 25-12, 25-14 through 25-16, 45-1 through 45-2, 45-8 through 45-11, 45-13 applies to all loans that meet the definition of the term of a *security* under that guidance. Therefore, any loan that was restructured in a TDR involving a modification of terms, including loans restructured before the effective date of the guidance in ASC 310-10-35-13 through 35-14, 35-16 through 35-26, 35-28, 35-29, 35-34, 35-37, 35-39, 45-5 through 45-6, 50-15, 50-19; ASC 310-30-30-2; ASC 310-40-35-8, 35-12; 50-2 through 50-3, 50-12 through 50-13, are subject to the requirements under the guidance in ASC 320-10-05-2, 50-1A through 50-3, 50-5, 50-9 through 50-11, 55-3, 15-5, 30-1; 35-1 through 35-2, 35-4 through 35-5, 35-10 through 35-13, 35-18, 15-2 through 15-4, 15-7, 25-3 through 25-6, 25-9, 25-11 through 25-12, 25-14 through 25-16, 45-1 through 45-2, 45-8 through 45-11, 45-13.

CHAPTER 20
ASC 323—INVESTMENTS—EQUITY METHOD AND JOINT VENTURES

CONTENTS

Part I: General Guidance	20,002
ASC 323-10: Overall	20,002
Overview	20,002
Background	20,002
Presumption of Significant Influence	20,003
Change in Significant Influence	20,005
Applying the Equity Method	20,006
Illustration of Equity Method	20,007
Illustration of Step Acquisition	20,008
Joint Ventures	20,009
Income Taxes	20,009
Intercompany Profits and Losses	20,009
Illustration of Elimination of Intercompany Profits	20,010
Disclosure Standards	20,010
Part II: Interpretive Guidance	20,011
ASC 323-10: Overall	20,011
ASC 323-10-15-3 through 15-5, 15-13 through 15-18, 55-1 through 55-18	
Whether an Investor Should Apply the Equity Method of Accounting to Investments Other than Common Stock	20,011
ASC 323-10-25-2A, 30-2A through 30-2B, 35-14A, 35-32A, 40-1	
Equity Method Investment Accounting Considerations	20,013
ASC 323-10-25-3 through 25-5, 30-3, S45-1, S99-4, 55-19 through 55-20; ASC 718-10-S60-1	
Accounting by an Investor for Stock-Based Compensation Granted to Employees of an Equity Method Investee	20,014
ASC 323-10-35-7 through 11, 55-27 through 55-29, 15-5; ASC 323-30-15-3, 25-2, 35-1 through 35-2; ASC 810-10-45-14	
The Equity Method of Accounting for Investments in Common Stock: Accounting Interpretations of APB Opinion No. 18	20,015
Illustration of Upstream Intercompany Profit Elimination	20,016
ASC 323-10-35-19	
Accounting by an Equity Method Investor for Investee Losses When the Investor Has Loans to and Investments in Other Securities of an Investee	20,017
ASC 323-10-35-23 through 35-26, 55-30 through 55-32, 55-34 through 55-47; ASC 320-10-35-3	
Accounting by an Equity Method Investor for Investee Losses When the Investor Has Loans to and Investments in Other Securities of the Investee	20,018

20,002 ASC 323—Investments—Equity Method and Joint Ventures

Illustration of the Application of the Guidance to Equity Method Investments and Other Investments in an Investee	20,021
ASC 323-10-35-27 and 28, 55-49 through 57	
Percentage Used to Determine the Amount of Equity Method Losses	20,024
ASC 323-10-35-29, 35-30	
Accounting for Subsequent Investments in an Investee after Suspension of Equity Method Loss Recognition	20,025
ASC 323-10-35-37 through 35-39; ASC 323-30-35-4	
Accounting by an Investor for Its Proportionate Share of Accumulated Other Comprehensive Income of an Investee Accounted for under the Equity Method in Accordance with APB Opinion No. 18 upon a Loss of Significant Influence	20,027
ASC 323-30: Partnerships, Joint Ventures, and Limited Liability Companies	20,027
ASC 323-30-25-1; ASC 910-810-45-1; ASC 810-1-45-14; ASC 930-810-45-1; ASC 932-810-45-1	
Investor Balance Sheet and Income Statement Display under the Equity Method for Investments in Certain Partnerships and Other Ventures	20,027
ASC 323-30-S99-1, S55-1	
Accounting for Limited Partnership Investments	20,029
ASC 323-740: Investments-Income Taxes	20,029
ASC 323-740-05-3, S25-1, 25-1 through 25-5, 35-2, 45-2, 55-2 through 55-10, S99-2; ASC325-20-35-5, 35-6	
Accounting for Tax Benefits Resulting from Investments in Affordable Housing Projects	20,029

PART I: GENERAL GUIDANCE

ASC 323-10: OVERALL

OVERVIEW

The equity method of accounting for investments in common stock is appropriate if an investment enables the investor to influence the operating or financial decisions of the investee. In these circumstances, the investor has a degree of responsibility for the return on its investment, and it is appropriate to include in the investor's results of operations its share of the earnings or losses of the investee. The equity method is not intended as a substitute for consolidated financial statements when the conditions for consolidation are present.

BACKGROUND

Domestic and foreign investments in common stock and corporate joint ventures shall be presented in financial statements on the *equity basis* by an investor whose investment in the voting stock and other factors give it the ability to *exercise significant influence over the operating and financial policies* of the investment.

Under the equity method of accounting for investments in common stock, net income during a period includes the investor's proportionate share of the net income reported by the investee for the periods subsequent to acquisition. *The* effect of this treatment is that net income for the period and stockholders' equity at the end of the period are the same as if the companies had been consolidated. Any dividends received are treated as adjustments of the amount of the investment under the equity basis.

When appropriate, investors use the equity method to account for investments in common stock, corporate joint ventures, and in other common stock investments (domestic and foreign) in which ownership is less than a majority interest. Generally an investor should measure an investment in the common stock of an investee, including a joint venture, initially at cost in accordance with the guidance in ASC 805-50-30. An exception is that an investor shall initially measure at fair value a retained investment in the common stock of an investee, including a joint venture, in a deconsolidation transaction in accordance with ASC 810-10-40-3A through 40-5.

PRESUMPTION OF SIGNIFICANT INFLUENCE

Evidence that the investor has significant influence over the investee includes the following (ASC 323-10-15-6):

- Investor has representation on the board of directors of the investee.
- Investor participates in the policy-making process of the investee.
- Material intercompany transactions occur between the investor and the investee.
- There is an interchange of managerial personnel between the investor and the investee.
- Technological dependency of the investee on the investor exists.
- There exists significant extent of ownership of the investor in relation to the concentration of other shareholders.

Absent evidence to the contrary, an investment (directly or indirectly) of less than 20% of the voting stock of an investee is presumed to indicate lack of significant influence, and the use of the equity method or consolidated statements is not required.

Absent evidence to the contrary, *an investment (directly or indirectly) of 20% or more of the voting stock of an investee is presumed to indicate the ability to exercise significant influence, and the equity method is required for a fair presentation* (ASC 323-10-15-3).

PRACTICE POINTER: There is a presumption that significant influence does not exist in an investment of less than 20%. However, this presumption may be overcome by evidence to the contrary. Thus, significant influence over the operating and financial policies of an investment of less than 20% can occur. The 20% cut-off is intended to be a guideline, subject to individual judgment, rather than a rigid rule.

For example, an investor might own only 15% of the voting common stock of an investee, be responsible for a substantial amount of the sales of the investee, and be represented on the investee's board of directors. In this case, the equity method may be the appropriate method of accounting by the investor, even though the investor holds only 15% of the voting stock.

Even with an investment of 20% or more, evidence may exist to demonstrate that the investor cannot exercise significant influence over the operating and financial policies of the investee. Thus, the presumption of significant influence in investments of 20% or more may be overcome by sufficient evidence.

The 20% ownership is based on current outstanding securities that have voting privilege. Potential ownership and potential voting privileges should be disregarded (ASC 323-10-15-9).

The following conditions may indicate that an investor is *unable* to exercise significant influence over the operating and financial policies of an investee:

- The investee opposes the investment (e.g., files a lawsuit, complains to government regulatory authorities), challenging the ability of the investee to exercise significant influence (ASC 323-10-15-10).
- An agreement is executed between the investee and the investor that indicates that significant influence does not exist (ASC 323-10-15-10).

PRACTICE POINTER: These types of agreements generally are referred to as *standstill agreements* and frequently are used to settle disputes between an investor and an investee. They may contain information as to whether the investor can or cannot exercise significant influence over the investee. The following are some typical provisions of a standstill agreement:

- The investee agrees to use its best efforts to obtain representation for the investor on its board of directors.
- The investor agrees not to seek representation on the investee's board of directors.
- The investee may agree to cooperate with the investor.
- The investor may agree to limit its ownership in the investee.
- The investor may agree not to exercise its significant influence over the investee.
- The investee may acknowledge or refute the investor's ability to exercise significant influence.

If a standstill agreement contains provisions indicating that the investor has given up some significant rights as a shareholder, the agreement is regarded, under ASC 323, as a factor in determining that the equity method should not be used.

- Significant influence is exercised by a small group of shareholders other than the investor representing majority ownership of the investee (ASC 323-10-15-10).
- The investor attempts, but cannot obtain, the financial information that is necessary to apply the equity method (ASC 323-10-15-10).

> **PRACTICE POINTER:** The *Codification of Statements on Auditing Standards* (AU 332.57(f)(3)) states "Management's inability to obtain information from an investee may suggest that it does not have the ability to significantly influence the investee."

- The investor attempts and fails to obtain representation on the investee's board of directors (ASC 323-10-15-10).

> **PRACTICE POINTER:** ASC 323 implies that the investor must actually try to obtain financial information or representation on the investee's board. It seems logical that the same effect should result in the event that the investor had prior knowledge that it would fail in these attempts and, therefore, did not even attempt them.

Many other factors, not listed above, may affect an investor's ability to exercise significant influence over the operating and financial policies of an investee. An investor must evaluate all existing circumstances to determine whether factors exist that overcome the presumption of significant influence in an investment of 20% or more of an investee.

> **PRACTICE POINTER:** On the other hand, an investor must also evaluate existing circumstances in an investment of less than 20% of an investee. The presumption that significant influence does not exist in an investment of less than 20% may be overcome by factors that indicate that significant influence does exist.
>
> If there is not enough evidence to reach a definitive conclusion at the time that the investment is made, it may be advisable to wait until more evidence becomes available.

Change in Significant Influence

Because of the purchase or sale of investment shares, and for other reasons that may affect the assessment of the ability to significantly influence the investee, an investor may be required to change to or from the equity method. The following procedures are applied in the following circumstances (ASC 323-10-35-33, 36):

- If an investment in voting stock falls below the 20% level, or other factors indicate that the investor can no longer exercise significant influence, the presumption is that the investor has lost the ability to exercise significant influence and control, in which case the equity method should be discontinued. The carrying amount at the date of discontinuance becomes the cost of the investment. Subsequent dividends are accounted for in current income from the date the equity method was discontinued.
- An investor who, because of other factors, obtains significant influence or who acquires more than 20% ownership in an investee after having had less than 20% *must retroactively adjust its accounts* as if the equity method

had been in effect during all previous periods in which the investment was held. In this event, at the date of each step in the acquisition, the carrying value of the investment is compared with the underlying net assets of the investee to determine the existence of differences between investment cost and the underlying book value of the investee's net assets. Such differential is amortized as an addition to or a deduction from investment income.

PRACTICE POINTER: In applying the equity method on a step-by-step basis, use the actual percentage of common stock owned in past periods, even if at that time the investment did *not* qualify for equity-method accounting. For example, assume that a company owned 10% of the common stock of an investee in 20X8 and 20X9, increased its ownership to 15% for 20Y0, and again increased its ownership to 24% in 20Y1, at which time the company adopted the equity method. The step-by-step restatement would include 10% of income for 20X8 and 20X9 and 15% of income for 20Y0, even though those ownership percentages did not justify the use of the equity method during those years.

APPLYING THE EQUITY METHOD

Under the equity method, the original investment is recorded at cost and is adjusted periodically to recognize the investor's share of earnings or losses after the date of acquisition. *Dividends received reduce the basis of the investment.* Continuing operating losses from the investment may indicate the need for an adjustment in the basis of the investment in excess of those recognized by the application of the equity method.

An investor's share of earnings or losses from its investment usually is shown as a *single amount* (called a *one-line consolidation*) in the income statement. The following procedures are appropriate in applying the equity method (ASC 323-10-35-5, 6, 8, 16):

1. Intercompany profits and losses are eliminated by reducing the investment balance and the income from investee for the investor's share of the unrealized intercompany profits and losses.

2. The investment is shown in the investor's balance sheet as a single amount and earnings or losses are shown as a single amount (one-line consolidation) in the income statement, *except for the investor's share of (a) extraordinary items and (b) prior-period adjustments, which are shown separately.*

3. Capital transactions of the investee that affect the investor's share of stockholders' equity are accounted for on a step-by-step basis.

4. Gain or loss is recognized when an investor sells the common stock investment, *equal to the difference between the selling price and the carrying amount of the investment at the time of sale.*

5. If the investee's financial reports are not timely enough for an investor to apply the equity method currently, the investor may use the most recent

available financial statements, and the lag in time created should be consistent from period to period.

6. Other than temporary declines, a loss in value of an investment should be recognized in the books of the investor.

7. When the investee has losses, applying the equity method decreases the basis of the investment. The investment account generally is not reduced below zero, at which point the use of the equity method is discontinued, unless the investor has guaranteed obligations of the investee or is committed to provide financial support. The investor resumes the equity method when the investee subsequently reports net income and the net income exceeds the investor's share of any net losses that were not recognized during the period of discontinuance.

8. Dividends for cumulative preferred stock of the investee are deducted before the investor's share of earnings or losses is computed, whether the dividend was declared or not.

9. The investor's shares of earnings or losses from an investment accounted for by the equity method are based on the outstanding shares of the investee without regard to common stock equivalents (ASC 323-10-35-19).

PRACTICE POINTER: As a result of ASC 350 (Intangibles - Goodwill and Other) any difference between the underlying equity in net assets of the investee and the cost of the investment is *no longer amortized*. However, equity method goodwill is tested for impairment, no less frequently than on an annual basis. Moreover, an impairment in the value of an equity method investment that is other than temporary should be recognized currently in income (ASC 350-20-35-58, 59).

Illustration of Equity Method

On December 31, 20X8, LKM Corporation acquired a 30% interest in Nerox Company for $260,000. Total stockholders' equity on the date of acquisition consisted of capital stock (common $1 par) of $500,000 and retained earnings of $250,000. During 20X9, Nerox Company had net income of $90,000 and paid a $40,000 dividend. LKM has an income tax rate of 35%.

Entries to record the investment, the dividends and net income of the investee are as follows:

Investment in Nerox	260,000	
Cash		260,000
Cash ($40,000 × 30%)	12,000	
Investment in Nerox		12,000
Investment in Nerox	27,000	
Income from investee		27,000
Income tax expense	5,250	
Deferred income taxes		5,250

20,008 ASC 323—Investments—Equity Method and Joint Ventures

The deferred income tax is determined as follows:

$$(\$27{,}000 - \$12{,}000) \times 35\% = \$5{,}250$$

On December 31, 20X9, the investment account on the balance sheet would show $275,000 ($260,000 − $12,000 + $27,000) and the income statement would show $27,000 as income from investee. Income tax expense and deferred income tax liability would increase by $5,250. Also, at December 31, 20X9, LKM Corporation would have to test the equity method goodwill for impairment using the ASC 350 guidance (see Chapter 24, *ASC 350—Intangibles—Goodwill and Other*, in this *Guide*). The equity method goodwill at acquisition is determined as follows:

$$(\$260{,}000 - 30\%\,(\$500{,}000 + \$250{,}000)) = \$35{,}000$$

Assume that the equity method goodwill is not impaired as of December 31, 20X9.

The balance in the investment account equals the investment percentage multiplied by the stockholders' equity of the investee, adjusted for any unamortized goodwill. This reconciliation for the above example is as follows:

Stockholders' equity, beginning of 20X9	$750,000
Add: 20X9 net income	90,000
Deduct: 20X9 dividends	(40,000)
Stockholders' equity, end of 20X9	$800,000
Ownership percentage	30%
Pro rata share of stockholders' equity	$240,000
Investment balance, end of 20X9	$275,000
Less: Equity method goodwill	(35,000)
Investment balance adjusted for equity method goodwill	$240,000

Illustration of Step Acquisition

Roper, Inc. owned common stock in Purple Tiger Co. from 20X8 to 20Y1 as follows: 20X8 and 20X9—10%; 20Y0—17%; 20Y1—25%. Purple Tiger has no preferred stock outstanding. Roper, Inc. carries the investment at cost, which approximates market value.

As part of the audit of the 20Y1 financial statements, the decision was made to change to the equity method for the investment in Purple Tiger Co. The net income and dividends paid by Purple Tiger Co. from 20X8 to 20Y1 were as follows:

	Net Income	Dividends Paid
20X8	$72,500	$30,000
20X9	65,000	35,000
20Y0	68,800	38,000
20Y1	85,000	40,000

Dividends received have been properly recorded for 20X8-20Y1 as dividend revenue. All investments were made in amounts approximating the underlying book value acquired.

The general journal entry to record Roper, Inc.'s change from the cost to the equity method, ignoring income taxes, is as follows:

Dividend income	10,000	
Investment in Purple Tiger, Co. ($46,696 − 22,960)	23,736	
Equity in income of Purple Tiger Co.		21,250
Retained earnings ($25,446 − 12,960)		12,486

Analysis of net income and dividends:

	Net Income	Roper Share	Dividends	Roper Share
20X8	$72,500 × 10% =	$7,250	$30,000 × 10% =	$3,000
20X9	65,000 × 10% =	6,500	35,000 × 10% =	3,500
20Y0	68,800 × 17% =	11,696	38,000 × 17% =	6,460
		25,446		12,960
20Y1	85,000 × 25% =	21,250	40,000 × 25% =	10,000
		$46,696		$22,960

Joint Ventures

A *joint venture* is an entity that is owned, operated, and jointly controlled by a group of investors. A joint venture might be organized as a partnership or a corporation, or be unincorporated (each investor holding an undivided interest).

Technically, ASC 323 applies only to corporate joint ventures. If the criteria for applying the equity method are met, investments in corporate joint ventures must use the equity method. In 1979, the AICPA Accounting Standards Executive Committee (AcSEC) published an Issues Paper titled *Joint Venture Accounting,* which made several recommendations regarding accounting for joint ventures:

- The equity method should be applied to investments in unincorporated joint ventures subject to joint control.
- Majority interests in unincorporated joint ventures should be consolidated.
- Investments in joint ventures not subject to joint control should be accounted for by proportionate consolidation.
- Additional supplementary disclosures regarding the assets, liabilities, and results of operations are required for all material investments in unincorporated joint ventures.

Income Taxes

Applying the equity method results in the recognition of income based on the undistributed earnings of the investee. If the investee is not an S corporation, the investor has no tax liability for equity method income until those earnings are distributed. Thus, application of the equity method gives rise to temporary differences that should be considered when deferred tax assets and liabilities are measured.

ASC 323—Investments—Equity Method and Joint Ventures

Intercompany Profits and Losses

Intra-entity profits and losses are eliminated until realized by the investor or investee as if the investee were consolidated. Intra-entity profits or losses on assets remaining with an investor or investee shall be eliminated, giving effect to any income taxes on the intra-entity transactions, except for both of the following:

1. A transaction with an investee, including a joint venture investee, that is accounted for as a deconsolidation of a subsidiary or a derecognition of a group of assets in accordance with ASC 810-10-40-3A through 40-5.
2. A transaction with an investee, including a joint venture investee, that is accounted for as a change in ownership transaction in accordance with paragraphs 810-10-45-21A through 45-24.

Illustration of Elimination of Intercompany Profits

An equity method investor sells inventory "downstream" to an investee. At the end of the year, $50,000 of profit remains in inventory from intercompany sales. The investor has a 40% interest in the voting stock of the investee, and the income tax rate is 30%. The entry for the elimination of intercompany profits is made as follows:

Income from investee ($50,000 × 40%)	20,000	
Deferred tax asset ($20,000 × 30%)	6,000	
Investment in investee		20,000
Income tax expense		6,000

If the intercompany sales were "upstream" (i.e., from the investee to the investor), the elimination entry would be as follows:

Income from investee [$20,000 × (1 − .30)]	14,000	
Deferred tax asset	6,000	
Inventory		20,000

DISCLOSURE STANDARDS

Disclosure must be made for investments accounted for by the equity method and include (ASC 323-10-50-3):

- The name of the investment
- The percentage of ownership
- The accounting policies of the investor in accounting for the investment
- The difference between the carrying value of the investment and the underlying equity in the net assets, and the accounting treatment of such difference
- The quoted market price of the investment, except if it is a subsidiary
- If material, a summary of the assets, liabilities, and results of operations presented as a footnote or as separate statements
- The material effect on the investor of any convertible securities of the investee

If the equity method is not used for an investment of 20% or more of the voting stock, disclosure of the reason is required. Conversely, if the equity method is used for an investment of less than 20%, disclosure of the reason is required.

> **PRACTICE POINTER:** In evaluating the extent of disclosure, the investor must weigh the significance of the investment in relation to its financial position and results of operations.

PART II: INTERPRETIVE GUIDANCE

ASC 323-10: OVERALL

ASC 323-10-15-3 through 15-5, 15-13 through 15-18, 55-1 through 55-18 Whether an Investor Should Apply the Equity Method of Accounting to Investments Other than Common Stock

BACKGROUND

According to the guidance in ASC 323-10-15-3, 15-4, 15-6 through 15-8, the guidance in ASC 323 applies only to an interest in a business entity's voting *common stock*. However, investments in such vehicles as convertible debt, preferred equity securities, options, warrants, interests in unincorporated entities, complex licensing and management arrangements, and other types of financial instruments have been giving investors rights, privileges, or preferences that previously had been limited to investors in common stock. Rights, privileges, or preferences—such as (*a*) the right to vote with common stockholders, (*b*) the right to appoint directors to the company's board, (*c*) important participating and protective rights as discussed in ASC 810-10-15-10, 25-1 through 25-8, 25-10 through 25-14, and 55-1, (*d*) the right to cumulative and participating dividends, and (*e*) liquidation preferences—may enable investors in such financial instruments to exercise significant influence over an investee's operating and financial policies even though they do not own the company's voting common stock.

ACCOUNTING ISSUE

Should an investor who exercises significant influence over an investee by means other than an ownership of the investee's voting common stock account for the investee by the equity method of accounting?

ACCOUNTING GUIDANCE

The following guidance should be applied:

- Investors that have significant influence over their investees' operating and financial policies should apply the equity method of accounting as discussed in ASC 323 only if those investments are in common stock or in-substance common stock.
- The risk and reward characteristics of an entity's in-substance common stock must be substantially the same as those of the entity's common stock. An investment in an entity is *not* in-substance common stock if one

of the following characteristics indicates it is *not* substantially similar to an investment in that entity's common stock:

— *Subordination* An investment's subordination characteristics must be substantially similar to those of the entity's common stock. If an investment has a substantive liquidation preference over common stock, it is not substantially similar to the common stock.

— *Risks and rewards of ownership* An investment's risk and reward of ownership characteristics must be substantially similar to those of the entity's common stock. For example, an investment that is not expected to participate in an entity's earnings and losses and capital appreciation and depreciation in substantially the same manner as common stock is not substantially similar to common stock. In contrast, if an investment participates in an investee's dividend payments in a manner that is substantially similar to the participation of common stock in such dividend payments, the investment is substantially the same as common stock. It was noted that the right to convert certain investments to common stock would indicate that those investments can participate in the investee's earnings and losses and in capital appreciation and depreciation in a substantially similar manner as common stock.

— *Obligation to transfer value* Obligation to transfer value If an investee is obligated to transfer substantive value to an investor, but the entity's common stockholders do not participate in the same manner, the investment is not substantially similar to common stock. An example is an investment's substantive redemption provision, such as a mandatory redemption provision or a put option at other than fair value, which is not offered to common shareholders.

An investment is in-substance common stock if its subordination and risk and reward characteristics are substantially similar to an investee's common stock and the investee is *not* required to transfer value to the investor in a manner that differs from the participation of common shareholders. If, based on the characteristics discussed previously, an investor is unable to determine whether an investment in an entity is substantially similar to the entity's common stock, the investor should determine whether it is expected that there will be a high correlation between future changes in the investment's fair value and changes in the fair value of the common stock. The investment is not in-substance common stock if that high correlation is not expected to exist.

An investor that has significant influence over an investee's operating and financial policies should determine whether an investment is substantially similar to common stock on the date on which the investor makes the investment. That determination should be reconsidered if one or more of the following circumstances occur:

- An investment's contractual terms change so that there is a change in any of the characteristics previously discussed.
- The investee's capital structure changes significantly, including the receipt of additional subordinated financing.
- The amount of an existing interest has increased. Consequently, the investor's method of accounting for its cumulative interest should be based on the characteristics of the investment on which the additional investment was made so that one method will be used by the investor to account for the cumulative interest in an investment of the same issuance.

An investee's losses, however, should not cause an investor to reconsider the determination of whether an investment is substantially similar to common stock.

An investor that gains the ability to exercise significant influence over an investee's operating and financial policies after the date on which the investment in the entity was made should determine whether the investment is substantially similar to common stock by considering the characteristics previously discussed and the relevant information existing on the date the investor obtained significant influence.

Investments other than common stock that have a "readily determinable fair value" under the guidance in ASC 320-10-15-5, 35-2 and 30-1 should be accounted for in accordance with the guidance in ASC 320 rather than based on this guidance. It was noted that the equity method of accounting should be applied in all cases under the scope of this guidance if an investor has significant influence over an investee's operating and financial policies and owns an investee's common stock or in-substance common stock.

ASC 323-10-25-2A, 30-2A through 30-2B, 35-14A, 35-32A, 40-1 Equity Method Investment Accounting Considerations

BACKGROUND

The project in which the FASB and the International Accounting Standards Board (IASB) collaborated to converge the guidance on accounting for business combinations and that on accounting and reporting for noncontrolling interests resulted in the issuance of revised guidance in ASC 805 and ASC 810-10-65-1 whose principles are based on the premise that a reporting entity has gained or lost control of a business or a subsidiary. Although it was not the objective of that project to reconsider the accounting for equity method investments, the issuance of that guidance has affected the application of the equity method. Consequently, some constituents asked whether all of the provisions of the revised guidance must be applied when accounting for an equity method investment because an entity's ability to control an investee differs substantially from its ability to exert significant influence on an investee's activities.

SCOPE

The following guidance applies to all investments accounted for under the equity method.

ACCOUNTING GUIDANCE

The accounting guidance is as follows:

Initial measurement. An equity-method investment's initial carrying value should be measured based on the cost accumulation model discussed in ASC 805-50-25-1, 30-1 through 30-3, 35-1 for asset acquisitions. The initial measurement of an equity method investment should include contingent consideration only if doing so is required in specific authoritative guidance other than ASC 805. Nevertheless, if there is an arrangement for contingent consideration in an agreement in which the fair value of an investor's share of an investee's net assets exceeds the investor's initial cost, the entity should recognize a liability for one of the following amounts, whichever is less:

- The maximum amount of consideration not otherwise recognized; or
- The amount by which the investor's share of an investee's net assets exceeds the initial cost measurement that includes contingent consideration otherwise recognized.

If a contingency related to a liability recognized based on the guidance above is resolved and the consideration is issued or becomes issuable, the amount by which the fair value of the contingent consideration exceeds the amount of the recognized liability should be added to the cost of the investment. However, the cost of an investment should be reduced if the recognized liability exceeds the fair value of the consideration.

Decrease in the value of an investment. In accordance with the guidance in ASC 323-10-35-32, an equity method investor should recognize other-than-temporary impairments related to an equity method investment. Although that investor should not perform a separate impairment test of an investee's asset, the investor should recognize its share of an impairment, if any, that is recognized by an investee in accordance with the guidance in ASC 323-10-35-7, 35-13 and should consider how the impairment, if any, affects the investor's basis difference in the assets that caused the investee to recognize an impairment.

Change in level of ownership or degree of influence. An equity method investor should account for an investee's issuance of shares as if the investor had sold a proportionate share of its investment with a gain or loss recognized in earnings.

ASC 323-10-25-3 through 25-5, 30-3, S45-1, S99-4, 55-19 through 55-20; ASC 718-10-S60-1 Accounting by an Investor for Stock-Based Compensation Granted to Employees of an Equity Method Investee

BACKGROUND

ASC 323 provides guidance to investors on the accounting for gains or losses on investments accounted for under the equity method. It does not, however, provide guidance to investors on how they should account for unreimbursed costs incurred on behalf of an investee, such as the cost of stock-based compensation granted to an investee's employees. Under the circumstances considered in this Issue, the entity's other investors do not contribute a proportionate amount and the investor's relative ownership percentage of the investee does not increase. It is assumed in this Issue that the grant of stock-based compensation to the investee's employees did not occur as a result of the investor's agreement to acquire an interest in the investee.

ACCOUNTING ISSUES

1. Should a contributing investor and an equity method investee capitalize or expense stock-based compensation costs incurred by the investor on behalf of the investee and when should the investee and the contributing investor account for those costs?
2. How should noncontributing equity method investors in an investee account for stock-based compensation costs incurred by a contributing equity method investor on behalf of the investee if they do not fund a proportionate amount of those costs?

ACCOUNTING GUIDANCE

- A contributing investor that incurs stock-based compensation cost on behalf of an equity method investee should expense those costs as incurred (i.e., in the same period in which the investee recognizes those costs) in so far as the investor's claim on the investee's book value does not increase.

  An investee should recognize an expense and a corresponding capital contribution for the costs of stock-based compensation incurred on its behalf by a contributing investor as the investor incurs those costs, as if the investor had paid cash to the investee's employees according to the guidance in ASC 505-50-25-4 and 25-9..

- Noncontributing investors should recognize income for an amount that corresponds to their increased interest in the investee's net book value (i.e., their proportionate share of the increase in the investee's contributed capital) because of the contributing investor's funding of stock-based compensation for the investee's employees. They also should recognize their percentage share of the investee's gains or losses, which would include the expense recognized for the cost of stock-based compensation incurred by the contributing investor on the investee's behalf.

SEC OBSERVER COMMENT

The SEC Observer stated that registrants should classify income or expense, if any, as a result of the consensus in this Issue under the same income statement caption that includes the registrant's equity in the investee's earnings.

ASC 323-10-35-7 through 11, 55-27 through 55-29, 15-5; ASC 323-30-15-3, 25-2, 35-1 through 35-2; ASC 810-10-45-14 The Equity Method of Accounting for Investments in Common Stock: Accounting Interpretations of APB Opinion No. 18

BACKGROUND

The following is the guidance for two implementation issues associated with ASC 323: (1) elimination of intercompany profit or loss and (2) its applicability to partnerships and joint ventures.

ACCOUNTING GUIDANCE

Question 1: Under the guidance in ASC 323 and ASC 810, intercompany profits or losses on assets still remaining with an investor or an investee at a reporting date must be eliminated. Should all of the intercompany profit or loss be eliminated, or should only the portion related to the investor's common stock interest in the investee be eliminated?

Answer: The extent of intercompany profits or losses, all or a proportionate amount, that should be eliminated under the equity method depends on the relationship between an investor and its investee. Under certain relationships between an investor and its investee, the investor would recognize no intercompany profits or losses until they have been realized through transactions with third parties. The following are examples of situations in which this accounting treatment would apply:

- An investor owns a majority of an investee's voting shares and enters into a transaction with the investee that is not on an arm's-length basis.

- An investee is established with the investor's cooperation and the investor controls the investee by guarantying the investee's debt, extending credit and making other special arrangements for the benefit of the investee, or through the investor's ownership of warrants or convertible securities issued by the investee. This type of arrangement exists if an investee is established for the purpose of financing and operating or leasing property sold by an investor to an investee.

In other cases, an investor would eliminate intercompany profit based on its percentage ownership of an investee. If so, the percentage of intercompany profit eliminated would be the same regardless of whether the transaction is "downstream" (the investor sells to its investee) or "upstream" (the investee sells to the investor). Intercompany profit should be eliminated on a net-of-tax basis.

Illustration of Upstream Intercompany Profit Elimination

At year-end, an investor that owns 40% of its investee's outstanding common stock holds $800,000 of inventory purchased from the investee during the year. The investee's gross profit rate on sales of inventory is 25%. Thus, at year-end, the investor holds inventory for which the investee recognized $200,000 of gross profit ($800,000 × 25%). Both the investor and the investee are subject to a 36% tax rate.

To compute its equity "pickup", the investor (a) deducts $128,000 [$200,000 less 36% income tax] from the investee's net income and (b) eliminates $51,200 ($128,000 × 40%), its share of the intercompany after-tax gross profit, from its equity income. The investor's offsetting entry of $51,200 would be made either to its investment account (the most common approach) or to its inventory account.

Question 2: Do the provisions of ASC 323 apply to investments in partnerships and joint ventures?

Answer: Not directly, because the guidance in ASC 323-10 applies only to common stock investments in corporations. It does not pertain to partnerships and unincorporated joint ventures. However, many of the provisions would apply in accounting for investments in unincorporated ventures. For example, partnership profits and losses accrued by investor-partners are generally reflected in their financial statements at a single amount. In addition, and consistent with the guidance in ASC 323-30, the following additional provisions would apply to a partnership: (1) the elimination of intercompany profits and losses, and (2) the accrual of income taxes on the profits accrued by investor-partners regardless of the tax basis used in the partnership return.

Generally, the preceding discussion regarding the applicability of the guidance in ASC 323-10 to partnerships would also apply to unincorporated joint ventures. However, under the guidance in ASC 810-10-45-14, if it is established industry practice, an investor-venturer may present its pro rata share of a venture's assets, liabilities, revenues, and expenses in its financial statements, except in the construction and extractive industries.

> **OBSERVATION:** The G4+1 (standard setters representing Australia, Canada, New Zealand, the United Kingdom, the United States, and the International Accounting Standards Committee (IASC)) released a Special Report titled *Reporting Interests in Joint Ventures and Similar Arrangements*. The Special Report recommends the use of the equity method in accounting for joint ventures. In addition, the Special Report rejects the notion that joint venture participants should depart from the equity method by recognizing their pro rata share of the assets, liabilities, revenues, and expenses of the venture.

ASC 323-10-35-19 Accounting by an Equity Method Investor for Investee Losses When the Investor Has Loans to and Investments in Other Securities of an Investee

This guidance is intended to clarify the guidance in ASC 323-10-35-3 through 35-4, 35-6 through 35-7, 35-13, 35-15 through 35-16, 35-19 through 35-22, 35-20, 35-32 through 35-33 through 35-36, 45-1 through 45-2, 45-12; ASC 225-20-60-1; ASC 250-10-60-2; ASC 460-10-60-1 regarding whether an investor in an investee's common or other voting stock should provide for the investee's operating losses if its common stock investment has been reduced to zero, but in addition, the investor: (*a*) owns the investee's debt securities, which may include mandatorily redeemable preferred stock, (*b*) owns the investee's preferred stock, or (*c*) has made loans to the investee.

The FASB staff believes that the carrying amount of an equity method investor's *total* investment includes additional support committed to or made by the investor in the form of capital contributions, investments in additional common or preferred stock, loans, debt securities, or advances. The investee's losses, therefore, should be reported up to the *total* investment.

The staff believes that this position is consistent with the provisions of ASC 970-323-35-34, 35-5, 35-12. It provides the following examples of circumstances in which an investor would reduce its equity in a real estate venture for losses that exceed the investment:

- The investor is legally obligated because of its position as guarantor or general partner.
- The investor's commitment to provide additional support is implied based on considerations such as the investor's business reputation, in-

tercompany relationships, or the investor's credit standing. A commitment may also be implied by an investor's previous support to the investee or the investor's statements to other investors or third parties about its intentions.

ASC 323-10-35-23 through 35-26, 55-30 through 55-32, 55-34 through 55-47; ASC 320-10-35-3 Accounting by an Equity Method Investor for Investee Losses When the Investor Has Loans to and Investments in Other Securities of the Investee

BACKGROUND

In ASC 323-10-35-19, which is discussed above, the FASB staff clarified the guidance in ASC 323-10-35-23 through 35-28 regarding how an equity method investor in an investee's common or other voting stock should account for the investee's operating losses when the investment has been reduced to zero *and* the investor also has one or more of the following: (*a*) the investee's debt securities, which include mandatory redeemable preferred stock; (*b*) the investee's preferred stock; or (*c*) loans to the investee.

The FASB staff believes that the guidance in ASC 323-10-35-19 indicates that an equity method investor's *total* investment in an investee includes, in addition to its investment in the investee's common stock or other voting stock, the investor's additional support committed to or made to the investee in the form of capital contributions, investments in additional common or preferred stock, loans, debt securities, or advances. The investor should, therefore, report an investee's losses up to the amount of the *total* investment.

This Issue is a follow-up to the FASB staff's guidance in ASC 323-10-35-19. It is intended to clarify the relationship among the guidance in ASC 323, the guidance on impaired loans in ASC 310-10-30-2, 35-13 through 35-14, 35-16 through 35-22, 35-24 through 35-29, 35-32, 35-34, 35-37, 35-39, 45-5 through 45-6, 50-12 through 50-13, 50-15, 50-19; ASC 310-40-35-8 through 35-9, 35-12; 50-2 through 50-3 and that in ASC 320-10 in accounting for an equity method investor's *total* investment in an investee.

ACCOUNTING ISSUE

If the carrying value of an equity method investee's common stock has been reduced to zero, how does the investor's accounting under the guidance in ASC 323 interact with the investor's accounting for its investments in the investee's other securities?

ACCOUNTING GUIDANCE

1. An investor should continue to report its share of equity method losses in an investee in the income statement up to the balance of and as an adjustment of the adjusted basis of the investor's other investments in the investee—such as preferred stock, debt securities, and loans—if (*a*) the investor is not required to advance additional funds to the investee and (*b*) the investment in the investee's common stock has been reduced to zero.

OBSERVATION: See the guidance in ASC 323-10-35-27 and 28, 55-49 through 57.

Equity method losses should be distributed to those other investments according to their order of seniority (that is, priority in liquidation). In each period, an investor should first charge the adjusted basis of other investments with equity method losses incurred during the period, and then should apply the provisions of ASC 310-10-30-2, 35-13 through 35-14, 35-16 through 35-22, 35-24 through 35-29, 35-32, 35-34, 35-37, 35-39, 45-5 through 45-6, 50-12 through 50-13, 50-15, 50-19; ASC 310-40-35-8 through 35-9, 35-12; 50-2 through 50-3 and those in ASC 320-10 to those investments, as appropriate.

The *cost basis* of the other investments as defined under this guidance is their original cost, which has been adjusted for other-than-temporary write-downs and amortization of a discount or premium, if any, on debt securities and loans. The *adjusted basis* of the other investments is the cost basis adjusted for a valuation allowance under the guidance in ASC 310-10-30-2, 35-13 through 35-14, 35-16 through 35-22, 35-24 through 35-29, 35-32, 35-34, 35-37, 35-39, 45-5 through 45-6, 50-12 through 50-13, 50-15, 50-19 and ASC 310-40-35-8 through 35-9, 35-12; 50-2 through 50-3 for loans to an investee and the cumulative amount of losses under the equity method that have been charged to the other investments. Subsequent income earned on the equity method investment should be attributed to the adjusted basis of the other investments in reverse of the order in which losses were attributed to those other investments.

2. To determine the amount of a loss on the equity method that should be reported at the end of the period, an investor that holds an investee's securities and debt under the scope of the guidance in ASC 310-10-30-2, 35-13 through 35-14, 35-16 through 35-22, 35-24 through 35-29, 35-32, 35-34, 35-37, 35-39, 45-5 through 45-6, 50-12 through 50-13, 50-15, 50-19; ASC 310-40-35-8 through 35-9, 35-12, 50-2 through 50-3 and the guidance in ASC 320-10 should perform the following tasks:

   a. Determine the maximum amount of equity method losses under the provisions of ASC 323.

   b. Account for equity method losses as follows:

      (1) If the adjusted basis of the other investments in the investee is positive, adjust the balance of the other investment for the amount of the loss on the equity method based on that investment's seniority. The adjusted basis of an investment accounted for in accordance with the guidance in ASC 320-10 becomes the security's basis used to measure subsequent fair value changes.

      (2) If the adjusted basis of the other investment is zero, further losses on the equity method investment should *not* be reported. However, an investor, should continue to keep track of unrecorded equity method losses in order to apply the guidance in ASC 323-10-35-19. If one of the other investments is sold when

its carrying amount is greater than its adjusted basis, the difference between the investment's cost basis and its adjusted basis on sale equals the equity method losses that were attributed to that other investment and that difference should be reversed when the asset is sold. Such amounts are considered unreported equity losses that should be tracked before the investor can report future income on the equity method investment.

c. The provisions in ASC 310-10-30-2, 35-13 through 35-14, 35-16 through 35-22, 35-24 through 35-29, 35-32, 35-34, 35-37, 35-39, 45-5 through 45-6, 50-12 through 50-13, 50-15, 50-19; ASC 310-40-35-8 through 35-9, 35-12; 50-2 through 50-3 and those in ASC 320-10 should be applied to the adjusted basis of the other investments in the investee, if appropriate, after the provisions of ASC 323 have been applied. Other generally accepted accounting principles not within the scope of the guidance in ASC 310-10-30-2, 35-13 through 35-14, 35-16 through 35-22, 35-24 through 35-29, 35-32, 35-34, 35-37, 35-39, 45-5 through 45-6, 50-12 through 50-13, 50-15, 50-19; ASC 310-40-35-8 through 35-9, 35-12; 50-2 through 50-3 and in ASC 320-10 should also be applied to other investments, if appropriate.

OBSERVATION: An entity that has an interest in a variable interest entity and is required to absorb the majority of that entity's expected losses or is entitled to receive most of the entity's expected residual returns, or both, must consolidate that entity in accordance with the guidance in ASC 323-10-45-4; ASC 810-10-05-8 through 05-13, 15-12, 15-13B, 15-14, 15-15 through 15-17, 25-37 through 25-47, 25-55 through 25-57, 30-1 through 30-4, 30-7 through 30-9, 35-3 through 35-5, 45-25, 50-2 through 50-4 through 50-7, 50-9 through 50-10, 55-16 through 55-49, 55-93 through 55-181, 55-183 through 55-205; ASC 860-10-60-2; ASC 954-810-15-3, 45-2; ASC 958-810-15-4; ASC 715-60-60-3; ASC 715-30-60-7; ASC 712-10-60-2; and ASC 460-10-60-13, as amended by the guidance in ASC 810-10-65-2, and 30-7 through 30-9, which also provides guidance on the consolidation of some corporations that investors previously may have accounted for under the equity method.

OBSERVATION: When applying the guidance in ASC 323, the term "common stock" also applies to "in-substance common stock," as defined under the guidance in ASC 323-10-15-3 through 15-5, 15-13 through 15-18, 55-1 through 55-18. Consequently, investors that have significant influence over their investees' operating and financial policies should apply the guidance in ASC 323-10-35-23 through 35-26, 55-30 through 55-32, 55-34 through 55-47; and ASC 320-10-35-3 only to investments in common stock or in-substance common stock.

Illustration of the Application of the Guidance to Equity Method Investments and Other Investments in an Investee

At the beginning of 20X9, Company A has a 45% equity method investment in Company B's common stock, which has been reduced to zero as a result of losses in previous years. On that date, the carrying amounts of Company A's other investments in Company B are as follows:

- Preferred stock at $35,000, which constitutes 45% of Company B's outstanding preferred stock.
- A $60,000 loan, which constitutes 45% of Company B's loan indebtedness.

Company A has no obligation to fund Company B's additional losses.

It is assumed in this illustration that all of Company B's operating income and losses discussed below have been adjusted for intercompany interest on the loan and dividends received on the preferred stock in accordance with ASC 323-10-35-19.

The table on the following pages summarizes the following information about Company A's accounting for income or loss on its equity method investment in Company B and for changes in the value of its other investments in Company B after its common stock investment in Company B has been reduced to zero:

1. *12/31/X9*—Company B has a loss of $50,000. The fair value of the preferred stock is $30,000 and the carrying value of the loan is $54,000.
2. *12/31/Y0*—Company B has a loss of $150,000. The fair value of the preferred stock is $15,000 and the carrying value of the loan is $45,000.
3. *12/31/Y1*—Company B has no income. The fair value of the preferred stock is $29,000 and the carrying value of the loan is $40,000.
4. *12/31/Y2*—Company B has $200,000 income. The fair value of the preferred stock is $30,000 and carrying value of the loan is $55,000.
5. *12/31/Y3*—Company B has no income. The fair value of the preferred stock is $32,000 and the carrying value of the loan is $58,000.
6. *12/31/Y4*—Company B has income of $100,000. Company A sells the preferred stock for $33,000. The carrying value of the loan is $60,000.

Summary of Transactions (Amounts are in thousands)

Year	Inc/Loss (Equity Loss)	Preferred Stock Fair Value	Preferred Stock Adjusted Basis	Loan	Common Stock	Investment in Company B Carrying Amount	Investment in Company B Adjusted Basis	OCI	P&L	Cash	Unrecognized Loss
1/1/X9		35.0	35.0	60.0	0.00	95.0	95.0				
20×9	(22.5)	(22.5)	(22.5)			(22.5)	(22.5)		(22.5)		
		17.5[a]				17.5		17.5			
20×0	(67.5)	30.0	12.5	(6.0)		(6.0)	(6.0)		(6.0)		
		(12.5)	(12.5)	54.0		84.0	66.5	17.5	28.5		
		(2.5)		(54.0)		(66.5)	(66.5)[b]		(66.5)		(1.0)[c]
		15.0	0.0	0.0		(2.5)		(2.5)	(66.5)		
						15.0	0.0	15.0	0.0		
20×1	0.0										(1.0)
20×2	72.0	14.0				14.0		14.0			
		29.0				29.0		29.0			
		17.0	17.0	54.0		71.0	71.0		71.0[d]		
		(16.0)				(16.0)		(16.0)			1.0
20×3	0.0	30.0	17.0	1.0		1.0	1.0				
				55.0		85.0	72.0	13.0	71.0		
		2.0				2.0		2.0	0.0		
				3.0		3.0	3.0		3.0		
20×4	45.0	32.0	17.0	58.0	27.0	90.0	75.0	15.0	3.0		
						27.0	27.0		27.0[e]		
		(32.0)	(17.0)			(32.0)	(17.0)	(15.0)	15.0	32.0	
				2.0		2.0	2.0		2.0		
		0.0	0.0	60.0	27.0	87.0	87.0	0.0	44.0	32.0	0.0

(a) Because the carrying amount of the preferred stock was reduced to $12,500 when Company B's $22,500 equity method loss was applied against the balance of the preferred stock investment in Company B, an unrealized gain of $17,500 is recognized to adjust the preferred stock to its fair value of $30,000.

(b) A portion of the $67,500 loss is recognized by reducing the $12,500 adjusted cost basis of the preferred stock investment to zero. The $54,000 adjusted basis of the loan is then reduced to zero. Because the equity method loss is limited to Company A's total adjusted basis of its total investments in Company B, the remaining $1,000 of equity method loss is unrecognized but should be tracked.

(c) Because the loan has been reduced to zero, no additional reduction in the value of the loan would be recognized.

(d) In accordance with the guidance in ASC 323, the equity method income of $72,000 must be reduced by the unrecognized $1,000 loss in 20×0 when the preferred stock investment and the loan were reduced to zero. The adjusted cost bases of the other investments are reinstated in reverse of the order in which the equity method loss was applied. That is, the loan is reinstated first to its adjusted amount of $54,000 and the remaining $17,000 is allocated to the preferred stock.

(e) During the previous years, Company A recognized $18,000 in losses related to its investment in Company B's preferred stock ($35,000 cost less $17,000 adjusted basis). Although the $15,000 gain recognized on the sale of the preferred stock investment reverses some of those losses, Company A actually incurred a $3,000 loss on the sale of the investment ($35,000 cost basis less $32,000 proceeds). Therefore, only $27,000 of the equity method income should be recognized ($45,000 less $18,000 losses on the preferred stock). That amount is used to reinstate a portion of the common stock investment in Company B.

ASC 323—Investments—Equity Method and Joint Ventures

ASC 323-10-35-27 and 28, 55-49 through 57 Percentage Used to Determine the Amount of Equity Method Losses

BACKGROUND

Under the guidance in ASC 323, an investor that is not obligated to provide additional financing after its common stock investment in an equity method investee has been reduced to zero must apply subsequent equity method losses—such as debt securities, preferred stock, and loans—to its other investments in the investee.

ACCOUNTING ISSUE

How should an investor who is *not* obligated to provide additional financing after its common stock investment in an equity method investee has been reduced to zero measure and recognize subsequent equity method losses applied to its other investments in the investee?

ACCOUNTING GUIDANCE

The following example was used in the discussion:

> An investor owns 40% of an investee's outstanding common stock, 50% of the investee's outstanding preferred stock, and has extended loans that represent 60% of the investee's outstanding loans. The investor's common stock investment has been reduced to zero and the investor is not obligated to provide additional funds.

The following accounting guidance applies under the circumstances:

- An investor should *not* recognize equity method losses based exclusively on the investor's percentage ownership of the investee's common stock.

- In a discussion of whether equity method losses should be recognized based on (*a*) the specific ownership percentage of the investment to which the equity method losses are applied or (*b*) the change in the investor's claim on the investee's book value. Although the results were the same under both approaches for the above example, it was not clear whether the results might differ in other situations. It was noted that both approaches would be acceptable and that other approaches not discussed also may be acceptable. However, once the guidance in ASC 323-10-35-23 through 35-26, 55-30 through 55-32, 55-34 through 55-47; ASC 320-10-35-3 has been applied to the other investments, no additional adjustments would be necessary.

- Entities should choose one approach that should be applied entity-wide to distribute equity method losses to the other investments after the common stock investment has been reduced to zero as a result of previous losses. The policy should be disclosed in the notes to the financial statements.

SUBSEQUENT DEVELOPMENT

A conclusion was reached in ASC 323-10-15-3 through 15-5, 15-13 through 15-18, 55-1 through 55-18 (Whether an Investor Should Apply the Equity Method of Accounting to Investments Other Than Common Stock), that when the guidance in ASC 323 is applied, the term "common stock" also applies to "in-substance common stock," as defined under that guidance. Consequently, investors that have significant influence over their investees' operating and financial policies should apply the guidance in ASC 323-10-35-23 through 35-26, 55-30 through 55-32, 55-34 through 55-47; ASC 320-10-35-3 only to investments in common stock or in-substance common stock.

ASC 323-10-35-29, 35-30 Accounting for Subsequent Investments in an Investee after Suspension of Equity Method Loss Recognition

BACKGROUND

According to the guidance in ASC 323-10-35-20 an investor should discontinue applying the equity method of accounting when an investment (and net advances) equal zero. Further, an investor should recognize losses only if the investor has guaranteed an investee's obligations or is committed to provide financial support to an investee. Even after an investee has resumed recognition of net income, an investor should *not* resume applying the equity method until the investor's share of net income equals the amount of net losses not recognized after application of the equity method was suspended.

Although the following guidance applies to related matters, none addresses the question discussed in this Issue:

- In ASC 323-10-35-19, Accounting by an Equity Method Investor for Investee Losses When the Investor Has Loans to and Investments in Other Securities of an Investee, (see above), the FASB staff stated that an equity method investor should report its losses in an investee up to its *total* investment in the investee, which in the staff's view includes additional support to an investee in the form of capital contributions, investments in additional common or preferred stock, loans, debt securities, or advances.

- The guidance in ASC 323-10-35-23 through 35-26, 55-30 through 55-32, 55-34 through 55-47; ASC 320-10-35-3, Accounting by an Equity Method Investor for Investee Losses When the Investor Has Loans to and Investments in Other Securities of the Investee, addresses the interaction of an investor's accounting for an investee under the guidance in ASC 323 with the investor's accounting for its investments in an investee's other securities in accordance with the guidance in ASC 310-10-35, Accounting by Creditors for Impairment of a Loan—An Amendment of FASB Statements Nos. 5 and 15, and ASC 320-10. Under that guidance, an investor should continue reporting its share of equity method losses in an investee up to the balance of and as an adjustment of the adjusted basis of an investor's other investments in an investee, such as preferred stock, debt securities, and loans, if (a) the investor is *not* required to advance additional funds to the investee and (b) the investment in the investee's common stock has been reduced to zero.

- The guidance in ASC 323-10-35-27 and 28; 55-49 through 57, Percentage Used to Determine the Amount of Equity Method Losses, addresses how an investor that is *not* obligated to provide additional support to an equity method investee after its common stock investment has been reduced to zero should measure and recognize subsequent equity method losses applied to its other investments in an investee. Under that guidance, an investor should *not* recognize equity method losses based exclusively on its percentage ownership of the investee's common stock. Two methods of recognizing equity method losses were discussed: (1) based on an investor's specific ownership percentage of an investment to which the equity method losses are applied or (2) based on a change in an investor's claim on an investee's book value.

ACCOUNTING ISSUE

If an investor that has suspended equity method loss recognition in an investee in accordance with the guidance in ASC 323-10-35-19 and that in ASC 323-10-35-23 through 35-26, 55-30 through 55-32, 55-34 through 55-47; and ASC 320-10-35-3 (see above) subsequently makes an additional investment in an investee but *does not* increase its ownership from significant influence to one of control, should that investor (*a*) account for the transaction as a step acquisition, or (*b*) recognize a loss in the amount of previously suspended losses?

ACCOUNTING GUIDANCE

The EITF reached the following consensus positions on the issues:

- If all or part of an additional investment made by an investor who has appropriately suspended recognition of equity method losses in accordance with the guidance in ASC 323-10-35-19 and in ASC 323-10-35-23 through 35-26, 55-30 through 55-32, 55-34 through 55-47; and ASC 320-10-35-3 is in substance funding earlier losses, the investor should recognize its previously suspended losses only up to the amount that the additional investment is considered to be a funding of earlier losses discussed in (*b*) below.

- Whether the additional investment should be considered to be a funding of previous losses depends on the facts and circumstances of the investment and requires judgment.

The following factors should be considered in making that determination, but no one factor alone should be considered presumptive or determinative:

— *The source of the investment, a third party or the investee* If an investor purchases an additional investment in an investee from a third party and neither the investor nor the third party provide additional funds to the investee, it is unlikely that prior losses are being funded.

— *Whether the amount paid to acquire an additional investment in an investee represents the fair value of the additional ownership interest received* A payment that exceeds the fair value of an additional investment in an investee would indicate that the excess paid over fair value is intended to fund prior losses.

— *Whether an additional investment in an investee increases the investor's ownership percentage of the investee* If an investment is made directly with an investee, the form of the investment should be considered and whether other investors are also making investments proportionate to their interests in the investee. It may be an indication that prior losses are being funded if (*a*) an additional investment in an investee does not increase the investor's ownership or other interests in the investee, or (*b*) if all other existing investors are also making additional pro rata equity investments in the investee.

— *Seniority of an additional investment* If an investor's additional investment in an investee has a *lower* seniority than the investor's existing investment in the investee, it may be an indication that an additional investment is funding previous losses.

It was noted that an investor making an additional investment in an investee should also consider whether as a result of the additional investment the investor becomes "otherwise committed" to provide financial support to the investee as a result of the additional investment.

ASC 323-10-35-37 through 35-39; ASC 323-30-35-4 Accounting by an Investor for Its Proportionate Share of Accumulated Other Comprehensive Income of an Investee Accounted for under the Equity Method in Accordance with APB Opinion No. 18 upon a Loss of Significant Influence

BACKGROUND

Under the guidance in ASC 323-10-35-18, an investor is required to recognize its proportionate share of an investee's equity adjustments in other comprehensive income, such as unrealized gains and losses on available-for-sale securities, minimum pension liability adjustments, and foreign currency items, as increases or decreases in the investment account with corresponding adjustments to equity in accordance with the guidance in ASC 323-10-35-15. Constituents have asked the question below.

Question: How should an investor account for its proportionate share of an investee's adjustments of other comprehensive income (OCI) if the investor has lost significant influence in the investee?

ACCOUNTING GUIDANCE

When an investor loses significant influence over an investee, the investor should offset its proportionate share of the investee's equity adjustments of OCI against the investment's carrying value. However, if the offset amount would reduce the investment's carrying value to *less than* zero, the investor should (*a*) reduce the carrying value to zero, and (*b*) recognize the remaining amount in income.

ASC 323-30: PARTNERSHIPS, JOINT VENTURES, AND LIMITED LIABILITY COMPANIES

ASC 323-30-25-1; ASC 910-810-45-1; ASC 810-1-45-14; ASC 930-810-45-1; ASC 932-810-45-1 Investor Balance Sheet and Income Statement Display under the Equity Method for Investments in Certain Partnerships and Other Ventures

BACKGROUND

Although the guidance in ASC 323-10 applies only to corporate entities, partnerships and other unincorporated entities have analogized to that guidance and applied the equity method when accounting for investments in investees over which they can exercise significant influence. Generally, such investments are reported as a single amount in the balance sheet with the investor's share of the investee's earnings or losses displayed as a single amount in the income statement. Even though the guidance in ASC 323-10 does not apply to situations in which an investor has an undivided interest in each asset and a proportionate obligation for the liabilities of a partnership or other venture, which is not a separate legal entity, it has been the practice of companies in some industries (e.g., oil and gas, mining, and construction) to report their investments in other entities by the equity method on a proportionate gross basis. Those entities present a proportionate share of an investee's revenues and expenses under each major revenue and expense category in their income statement and may present their proportionate share of the investee's assets and liabilities separately under each related major caption in the balance sheet.

The pro rata consolidation method is discussed in several pronouncements of the authoritative accounting literature. The guidance in ASC 323-30-15-3, 25-2, 35-1 through 35-2 and ASC 810-10-45-14 provides that in industries in which it is established industry practice, an investor-venturer in an unincorporated joint venture who owns an undivided interest in each asset and is proportionately liable for its share of each liability may account in its financial statements for a pro rata share of the venture's assets, liabilities, revenues, and expenses.

The guidance in ASC 970-323, which is sometimes applied by analogy to non-real estate ventures, also provides guidance on pro rata consolidation. The guidance in ASC 970-810-45-1 provides that an investor/venturer may present its undivided interest in a venture's assets, liabilities, revenues, and expenses if (*a*) decisions related to the venture's financing, development, sale, or operations can be made without the approval of two or more of the owners, (*b*) each investor/venturer is only entitled to its share of the income, (*c*) each is responsible only for its pro rata share of the venture's expenses, and (*d*) each is liable only for liabilities incurred for its proportionate interest in the entity.

Real estate entities under the scope of ASC 970-323 are required to apply the guidance in ASC 970-810-45-1. That is, real property owned by undivided interests that is under joint control should be presented under the equity method, like investments in noncontrolled partnerships.

ACCOUNTING ISSUE

Are there circumstances under the equity method in which it is appropriate to use a proportionate gross presentation in the financial statements of a legal entity?

ACCOUNTING GUIDANCE

- A proportionate gross financial statement presentation may *not* be used to report on investments in unincorporated *legal* entities, which are normally accounted for on the equity method, except by entities in the construction industry or the extractive industries, because that type of reporting has been a longstanding practice in those industries. Under this guidance, entities are considered to be in the extractive industries only if their activities are limited to the extraction of mineral resources, such as those involved in oil and gas exploration and production. This guidance does *not* apply to entities involved in refining, marketing, or transporting extracted mineral resources.

- The guidance in ASC 323-10 applies to common stock investments of *all* corporate entities in which an investor has significant influence over the investee. Consequently, the guidance in ASC 323-10-35-19, which requires the display of a single amount for such investments, should be applied. This guidance does not affect the accounting for undivided interests under the circumstances discussed in the Background section above..

SEC OBSERVER COMMENT

The SEC Observer indicated that the SEC staff expects corporate entities to follow the provisions of ASC 323-10 if an investor has significant influence over its investee. Further, the use of pro rata consolidation by such entities is not acceptable in SEC filings even if under an agreement, the benefits and risks are attributed to the owners as if they held undivided interests in the entity.

ASC 323-30-S99-1, S55-1 Accounting for Limited Partnership Investments

The Acting Chief Accountant of the SEC announced at the May 1995 meeting of the Emerging Issues Task Force that the SEC staff will no longer accept cost method accounting for an investment in a limited partnership, even though the partner has an interest of 20% or less and has no significant influence over an investee. The staff now believes that investors in limited partnerships should follow the guidance in ASC 970-323-25-6 through 25-7 under which limited partners are required to use the equity method to account for such investments, unless their interest is so minor that they have virtually no influence over the partnership's operating and financial policies. According to the SEC staff, investments of more than 3%-5% generally have been considered to be more than minor in practice. The announcement applies to all investments in limited partnerships made after May 18, 1995, not just to those holding real estate.

ASC 323-740: INVESTMENTS-INCOME TAXES

ASC 323-740-05-3, S25-1, 25-1 through 25-5, 35-2, 45-2, 55-2 through 55-10, S99-2; ASC 325-20-35-5, 35-6 Accounting for Tax Benefits Resulting from Investments in Affordable Housing Projects

BACKGROUND

The affordable housing credit, which had expired after June 30, 1992, is a tax benefit that was retroactively extended and made permanent under the Revenue Reconciliation Act of 1993. Investors commonly receive such tax benefits by purchasing interests in limited partnerships that operate qualified affordable housing projects; the tax benefits are passed through to the limited partners. Credits are available if a sufficient number of units are rented to qualifying tenants at a rental that does not exceed statutory amounts. For example, a housing project with 20% or more residential units that are rent-restricted and occupied by individuals whose income is 50% or less of the community's median gross income qualifies for the credit. The affordable housing credit may be taken on the tax return each year for ten years and is subject to recapture over 15 years, beginning with the first year tax credits are earned.

ACCOUNTING ISSUE

How should investors in qualified affordable housing project limited partnerships account for their investments?

ACCOUNTING GUIDANCE

- A receivable for tax benefits to be received over the term of an investment should *not* be recognized at the time an investment in a qualified affordable housing project is purchased.
- Income from affordable housing credits should *not* be recognized for financial reporting purposes before they are reported for tax purposes.
- Limited partnership investments in qualified affordable housing projects should be reviewed periodically for impairment.
- A liability should be recognized for (*a*) unconditional and legally binding delayed equity contributions and for (*b*) equity contributions contingent on a future event when it becomes probable.

The Task Force observed that additional guidance on accounting for delayed equity contributions may be found in ASC 450, ASC 840-30-55-15, 55-16, and Statement of Financial Accounting Concepts No. 6 (not in the ASC). Limited partnership investments in affordable housing projects should be accounted for as follows.

Effective yield method

a. The effective yield method should be elected if a limited partnership investment in an affordable housing project meets *all* of the following conditions:

  (1) A creditworthy entity guarantees the availability of tax credits to the investor by a letter of credit, a tax indemnity agreement, or a similar arrangement.

  (2) A positive yield is expected on the investment, based only on cash flows from guaranteed tax credits.

  (3) The investor's partnership interest is limited for legal and tax purposes with liability limited to the capital investment.

b. The effective yield method should be applied as follows:

  (1) Tax credits are recognized as they are allocated.

  (2) The initial cost of an investment is amortized so that it results in a constant effective yield over the period tax credits are received. (The effective yield is the investor's internal rate of return on the investment, determined by the cost of the investment and guaranteed tax credits.)

  (3) Any expected residual value is excluded from the effective yield calculation.

(4) Income for cash received from the limited partnership's operations or sale of the property is recognized when it is realized or realizable.

(5) The investor's share of the tax credit, net of amortization of the investment in the limited partnership, is presented in the income statement as a component of income taxes related to continuing operations.

(6) Other tax benefits received are accounted for in accordance with the guidance in ASC 740.

It was noted that the effective yield method should not be applied whenever an individual investment meets the required conditions, but rather because it is the entity's accounting policy to do so. In addition, the SEC Observer stated that the SEC staff believes that the effective yield method should not be used in analogous situations.

Equity method

For investments not accounted for on the effective yield method or the cost method, the guidance in ASC 970-323 and ASC 323 and guidance not related to the effective yield method should be followed.

Under the guidance in ASC 970-323 and ASC 323, application of the equity method is generally required to account for limited partnership investments in real estate ventures, unless the limited partner has only a minor interest with practically no influence over the partnership's operating and financial policies.

OBSERVATION: The equity method may be used to account for investments in limited partnerships even if an ownership interest does not meet the 20% presumption of significant influence. See the discussion of the SEC staff's position on the use of the equity method to account for limited partnership investments in ASC 323-30-S99-1, S55-1 above.

Cost method

a. The cost method should be used only if an investment is so minor that there is virtually no influence over operating and financial policies.

b. The difference between the carrying amount of an investment and its estimated residual value should be amortized during the periods in which an investor receives allocated tax credits.

(1) The estimated residual value is the value of the investment at the end of the last period in which tax credits are allocated to the investor without considering anticipated inflation.

(2) Annual amortization is calculated based on the ratio of tax credits received in the current year to total estimated tax credits that will be allocated to the investor.

> **OBSERVATION:** Under the guidance in ASC 810, an entity that absorbs a majority of a variable entity's expected losses or has the right to receive a greater part of the variable entity's expected residual returns or both is required to consolidate the variable interest entity.

DISCUSSION

The decision to limit the use of the effective yield method to situations in which specific conditions are met reflects an effort to differentiate between investments in limited partnerships that are purchased for tax purposes and those that are real estate investments. Use of the effective yield method is limited to investments entered into for the purpose of realizing tax benefits if there is assurance that the tax benefits will be realized to mitigate the risks of the real estate business. In addition, lack of control over a limited partnership's operations and limited liability provide assurance that an investor's cash flows will not be negative in future periods and is another indicator that the intent of the investment is to realize tax benefits.

21,001

CHAPTER 21
ASC 325—INVESTMENTS—OTHER

CONTENTS

Interpretive Guidance	21,001
ASC 325-20: Cost Method Investments	21,001
ASC 325-20-30-2 through 30-6	
Nonmonetary Exchange of Cost-Method Investments	21,001
Illustration of the Accounting Guidance	21,003
ASC 325-30: Investments in Insurance Contracts	21,003
ASC 325-30-05-3 through 05-5, 15-2 through 15-3, 25-1, 35-1 through 35-2	
Accounting for Purchases of Life Insurance	21,003
Illustration of the Accounting for a Life Insurance Contract	21,004
ASC 325-30-05-2, 05-6 through 05-9, 15-4, 30-1, 35-3 through 35-7, 50-1, 55-2 through 55-4	
Accounting for Purchases of Life Insurance—Determining the Amount That Could Be Realized in Accordance with FASB Technical Bulletin No. 85-4	21,004
ASC 325-30-05-59A, 25-1A, 30-1B, 40-1	
Accounting for Stock Received from the Demutualization of a Mutual Insurance Company	21,006
ASC 325-30-15-6, 25-2; 30-1C through 30-2, 35-8 through 35-12, 40-1A, 45-1 through 45-5, 50-2 through 50-10	
Accounting for Life Settlement Contracts by Third-Party Providers	21,007
ASC 325-30-35-1 Recognition of Insurance Death Benefits	21,010
ASC 325-40: Beneficial Interests in Securitized Financial Assets	21,011
ASC 325-40-05-1 through 05-2, 15-2 through 15-9, 25-1 through 25-3, 30-1 through 30-3, 35-1 through 35-13, 35-15 through 35-16, 45-1, 55-1 through 55-25, 60-7; ASC 310-20-60-1 through 60-2; ASC 310-30-15-5; ASC 320-10-35-38, 55-2	
Recognition of Interest Income and Impairment on Purchased Beneficial Interests and Transferor's Beneficial Interests in Securitized Financial Assets Obtained in a Transfer Accounted for as a Sale	21,011

INTERPRETIVE GUIDANCE

ASC 325-20: COST METHOD INVESTMENTS

ASC 325-20-30-2 through 30-6 Nonmonetary Exchange of Cost-Method Investments

BACKGROUND

A cost-method investor has an investment in the common stock of a company, which is involved in a business combination. The investor will receive either new stock that represents an ownership interest in the combined entity, or the shares currently held by the investor will represent an ownership interest in the combined entity. According to the provisions of ASC 805-10-25-5 the company that will hold a majority interest in the combined entity is considered to be the acquirer. The combined company will continue to be publicly traded.

ACCOUNTING ISSUES

1. Should an investor that uses the cost method to account for an investment in shares of Company B (the *acquiree*) account for an exchange of those shares in a business combination at fair value, thus recognizing a new accounting basis in the investment and a *realized* gain or loss to the extent fair value differs from the investor's cost basis?
2. Should an investor in Company A, which is considered to be the *acquirer* in a business combination, account for a cost-method investment in the same manner as the investor in Issue 1?
3. Would an agreement on Issues 1 and 2 change if before the business combination, an investor in either company also held an investment in the other company that is a party to the transaction?

ACCOUNTING GUIDANCE

1. A cost-method investor in a company considered to be the acquiree should recognize the investment at fair value.

> **OBSERVATION:** Under the guidance in ASC 320-10, entities report investments in marketable equity securities at fair value. *Realized* gains on securities available for sale (not trading securities) are reported in the financial statements in income. *Unrealized* holding gains and losses are reported in the financial statements in other comprehensive income in accordance with the guidance in ASC 220-10, which amends the guidance in ASC 320, but the total amount of accumulated unrealized gains and losses should continue to be reported in a separate component of shareholders' equity until those amounts are realized. Accordingly, under the guidance on Issue 1, an investor would recognize a new cost basis in the securities of Company B exchanged for securities in the combined entity and report a realized gain or loss in income.

2. A cost-method investor in a company considered to be the acquirer should continue to carry the investment at historical cost.

> **OBSERVATION:** Although an investor would continue carrying the investment at its historical cost, under the provisions of ASC 320, as amended (see Observation above), an investor is required to report the fair value of the investment in its financial statements and to report *unrealized* holding gains or losses in comprehensive income.

> **OBSERVATION:** ASC 805-10-25-5 provides guidance for identifying the acquirer in a business combination, but has no effect on the guidance provided in this issue.

3. The conclusion in Issues 1 and 2 would not change if an investor in either company also held an investment in the other company before the merger.

Illustration of the Accounting Guidance

Company Z has an investment in 1,000 shares of Company T, which it carries at cost ($35,000), and an investment in 1,000 shares of Company A, which it also carries at cost ($50,000). Company T enters into a business combination with Company A. Shareholders of Company T receive 0.5 shares of stock in Company A for each share of Company T. Company A accounts for the transaction as a pooling of interests. After the combination, 1,000,000 shares of the combined entity are outstanding, of which 550,000 (or 55%) are owned by former shareholders in Company A and 450,000 shares are owned by former shareholders in Company T. The fair value of a share in the combined entity is $80.

As a result of the transaction, Company Z would own 1,500 shares of the combined entity (1,000 × .5 shares of Company T plus 1,000 shares of Company A). Based on the consensus in Issue 1, Company Z would change its basis in the 500 shares of Company A received for its stake in Company T to $40,000 (500 × $80) and would realize a gain of $5,000. Under the consensus in Issue 2, Company Z would continue carrying its investment in the combined entity at $50,000, which is the cost basis of its investment in Company A.

DISCUSSION

The underlying question in this Issue is whether the investor's exchange of shares of one entity for shares in the combined entity is an event that culminates the earnings process. That depends on whether the original investment is in the company whose shareholders receive the greater interest in the shares of the combined entity (the acquirer) or in the company whose shareholders receive the lesser interest (the acquiree). The accounting guidance reflects the view that the exchange of shares by the acquiree's shareholders results in the culmination of the earnings process. Those shareholders actually disposed of their investment in Company T (see Illustration) in exchange for shares in the combined entity in which they will not have a controlling interest.

ASC 325-30: INVESTMENTS IN INSURANCE CONTRACTS

ASC 325-30-05-3 through 05-5, 15-2 through 15-3, 25-1, 35-1 through 35-2
Accounting for Purchases of Life Insurance

BACKGROUND

The premium paid by a purchaser of life insurance serves several purposes. Part of it pays the insurer for assumption of mortality risk and provides for recovery of the insurer's contract acquisition, initiation, and maintenance costs. Part of the premium contributes to the accumulated contract value. The relative amounts of premium payment credited to various contract attributes change over time as the age of the insured person increases and as earnings are credited to previous contract values. An insurance contract is significantly different from other investment agreements. The various attributes of the policy could be obtained separately through term insurance and the purchase of separate investments, but the combination of benefits and contract values typically could not be acquired without the insurance contract.

ACCOUNTING GUIDANCE

Question: How should an entity account for an investment in life insurance?

Answer: The amount that could be realized under the contract at the date of the financial statements (i.e., the contract's cash surrender value) should be reported as an asset. The change in that value during the period is an adjustment to the amount of premium paid in recognizing expense or income for that period.

Illustration of the Accounting for a Life Insurance Contract

Roth Enterprises carries a "key-person" life insurance policy on its CEO, Susan Ray. The face value of the policy is $1 million. The cash surrender value of the policy was $50,000 at 1/1/20X4. During 20X4 Roth Enterprises paid premiums of $10,000, and the cash surrender value of the policy was $55,000 at 12/31/20X4. The cash surrender value at 12/31/20X4, $55,000, would be included as an asset on the balance sheet of Roth Enterprises. The insurance premium expense recognized on the income statement, $5,000, is the net of premiums paid, $10,000, and the increase in the policy's cash surrender value, $5,000 [$55,000–$50,000].

ASC 325-30-05-2, 05-6 through 05-9, 15-4, 30-1, 35-3 through 35-7, 50-1, 55-2 through 55-4 Accounting for Purchases of Life Insurance—Determining the Amount That Could Be Realized in Accordance with FASB Technical Bulletin No. 85-4

BACKGROUND

Some entities purchase insurance policies—corporate-owned life insurance (COLI) or bank-owned life insurance (BOLI)—to fund the cost of providing employee benefits; others do so to protect the entity against the loss of "key" employees. COLI and BOLI may be structured as:

- *Individual-life policies*, which have a contract value component and may include a surrender charge and a cash surrender value that represents the amount that could be realized if the policy is surrendered.
- *Multiple individual-life policies*, which are individual-life policies on which an employer has taken a rider at an additional cost so that the surrender charges on individual policies would be waived if all of the individual policies are surrendered at once.
- *Group life policies*, which are legal contracts with an insurance company that enables an employer to cover multiple employees with individual-life insurance. Although separate certificates are issued to the covered individuals, the group policy contract is the controlling document. Under a group life policy, a policyholder receives the full cash surrender value if an individual policy is surrendered separately.

Many policies include provisions to make them more attractive to a policyholder, such as a provision that allows the policyholder to recover certain costs. However, the policies may also include provisions, such as a prohibition against a change of control or a restructuring that occurs within the last 24 months, a prohibition against a planned restructuring within the prior 12 months, or a limit on a policyholder operating a loss carryforward position, that would limit the amount that an entity may be able to recover in cash. Additionally, a policy may require that a policyholder meet certain criteria to recover any amount. Further, the amount due to the policyholder may be received over an extended period after the insurance policy or certificate has been surrendered.

There has been diversity in practice in the calculation of the amount that would be realized on multiple individual policies with a separate group-level rider agreement, multiple individual policies with a contractual requirement in each individual policy referring to the other policies as a group, or a group life policy with multiple certificates in the form of individual life insurance for multiple employees. The issues addressed here are related to an interpretation of the phrase "the amount that could be realized under an insurance contract" in ASC 325-30, which requires that this amount be reported in the balance sheet as an asset. To calculate that amount, it is necessary to assume how the contracts are settled and whether they are surrendered individually or as a group.

ACCOUNTING ISSUES

1. Should a policyholder consider any additional amounts included in an insurance policy's contractual terms, other than its cash surrender value, when calculating the amount of cash into which an insurance policy could be converted under the guidance in ASC 325-30?

2. Should a policyholder consider its contractual ability to surrender all of the individual life insurance policies or certificates in a group policy at once when calculating the amount of cash into which the insurance policy could be converted under the guidance ASC 325-30?

ACCOUNTING GUIDANCE

- In determining the "amount that could be realized under the life insurance contract," policy holders should to take into account any contractual amounts that are included in addition to the policy's cash surrender value. Contractual limitations also should be considered when realizable amounts are determined if it is probable that those terms would limit the amounts that could be realized under an insurance contract. Amounts recoverable at an insurance company's discretion should be *excluded* from the computation of the amount that could be realized under an insurance contract. Amounts that policyholders can recover more than one year after a policy has been surrendered should be discounted based on the guidance in ASC 835-30-15.

- Policyholders should determine the "amount that could be realized under the life insurance contract" by assuming that individual life insurance contracts and individual certificates in group policies will be surrendered individually. In addition, the amount that a policyholder would ultimately realize, if any, on an assumed surrender of a final policy or a final certificate in a group policy should be included in the computation.

- If a policyholder who has made a request to surrender a policy with contractual limitations on the holder's ability to surrender the policy continues to participate in changes in the policy's cash surrender value in the same manner as before making the request, the policyholder should *not* discount the cash surrender value component of the amount that could be realized under the insurance contract. However, a future amount that could be realized under an insurance contract should be discounted under the guidance in ASC 835-30-15 if the policyholder is not permitted to participate in changes to the policy's cash surrender value because of the policy's contractual restrictions. It was noted that Internal Revenue Code Section 1035 exchanges (Sec. 1035 exchanges) do *not* represent a cash surrender as intended in ASC 325-30. A policyholder should determine the amount that could be realized under an insurance contract on a group basis if a group of individual life policies or a group policy only permit that all individual-life policies or certificates be surrendered as a group.

DISCLOSURE

Policyholders should disclose the existence of contractual restrictions on the ability to surrender a policy.

ASC 325-30-05-59A, 25-1A, 30-1B, 40-1 Accounting for Stock Received from the Demutualization of a Mutual Insurance Company

BACKGROUND

A mutual insurance company is not owned by stockholders, but by its policyholders who are members with rights by virtue of their insurance contract, the corporation's bylaws and charter, or its articles of incorporation and various laws. Such rights may include sharing in the mutual's excess capital, participating in corporate governance, receiving the corporation's remaining value on liquidation, and the expectation that the corporation will be operated to benefit the members.

Although policyholders' membership interests in a mutual differ significantly for a number of reasons from stockholders' ownership interests in a corporation, their rights are important when a mutual insurance company is demutualized and there are changes to a corporation owned by its stockholders. In that situation, the mutual entity values each policyholder's membership rights and distributes those amounts to the policyholders in stock, cash, policy enhancements, or in combination. The members' rights are extinguished in a demutualization—the members become customers and perhaps stockholders as well.

GAAP does not permit policyholders in a mutual insurance company to recognize their membership interests as an asset, because the members receive no information as to the value of those interests. Further, those interests are forfeited if the policy lapses.

ACCOUNTING ISSUE

How should a policyholder account for stock received in a demutualization of a mutual insurance company?

ACCOUNTING GUIDANCE

A member receiving stock in a demutualization of an insurance company should determine the fair value of the stock and recognize it in income as a gain from continuing operations.

ASC 325-30-15-6, 25-2; 30-1C through 30-2, 35-8 through 35-12, 40-1A, 45-1 through 45-5, 50-2 through 50-10 Accounting for Life Settlement Contracts by Third-Party Providers

BACKGROUND

The following is guidance for the initial and subsequent measurement, financial presentation, and disclosure of third-party investors' investments in life settlement contracts, which for the purpose of this guidance are contracts between owners of life insurance policies and third-party investors with the following features:

- The investor does not have the insurable interest (i.e., an interest in the insured's survival) necessary to issue an insurance policy.
- Consideration given by an investor to the policy's owner exceeds the policy's current cash surrender value.
- Under the contract, the investor will be paid the face value of the insurance policy when the insured dies.

Investments in such contracts had been accounted under the guidance in ASC 325-30-15-2 through 15-3, 35-1 through 35-2, 25-1, 05-3 through 05-5 under which investors reported the amount that could be realized on such insurance contracts as assets. As a result, investors recognized the excess of the purchase price of a life settlement contract over the cash surrender value of the underlying insurance policy as an expense.

Owners of life insurance policies enter into life settlement contracts for various reasons, such as for estate planning, compensation arrangements, and for the purpose of investing. Some have questioned whether the guidance in ASC 325-30-15-2 through 15-3, 35-1 through 35-2, 25-1, 05-3 through 05-5 should apply to life settlement contracts entered for investing purposes, because they believe that a policy's cash surrender value does *not* present the economic substance of the investing activity.

The following guidance applies to transactions in which a broker assists in the settlement transaction between a policy owner and an investor and to those that occur without a broker's assistance.

Certain provisions of ASC 325-30-15-2 through 15-3, 35-1 through 35-2, 25-1, 05-3 through 05-5 and of ASC 815 are amended by the following guidance.

ACCOUNTING GUIDANCE

Under this guidance, investors may elect to account for investments in life settlement contracts by the investment method or the fair value method. That election, which is irrevocable, should be made based on the facts of the specific contract and should be supported by contemporaneous documentation or a documented policy permitting an automatic election.

Investment Method

Under the investment method, an investor should account for an investment in a life settlement contract as follows:

- The initial investment is recognized at the price of the transaction plus all initial direct external costs.
- Continuing costs, such as policy premiums and direct external costs, if any, to keep the policy in force should be capitalized.
- No gain should be recognized until the insured has died.
- When an insured has died, an investor should recognize in earnings, or other performance indicators if an entity does not report earnings, the difference between a life settlement contract's carrying amount and the proceeds received from the underlying life insurance policy.
- An investment in a life settlement contract should be tested for impairment whenever an investor becomes aware of new or updated information indicating that, when the insured dies, the carrying amount of the investment plus expected undiscounted future premiums and capitalizable direct external costs, if any, will exceed the expected proceeds from the insurance policy. That information includes, but is not limited to, a change in expected mortality and in the creditworthiness of the underlying insurance policy's issuer. Testing a life settlement contract for impairment is *not* necessary if only a change in interest rates occurs.
- An impairment loss should be recognized if expected undiscounted cash inflows (generally, the insurance proceeds) are less than an investment's carrying amount plus expected undiscounted future premiums and capitalizable direct external costs, if any. If there are expected discounted future premiums and capitalizable direct external costs, the investment should be written down to fair value.
- Current interest rates should be considered in the fair value measurement.

Fair Value Method

Under the fair value measurement method, an investor should account for an investment in a life settlement contract as follows:

- An initial investment in a life settlement contract should be accounted for at its transaction price.
- In subsequent periods, the entire investment should be remeasured at fair value at each reporting period and changes in the investment's fair value should be recognized in earnings in the period in which they occur or by other performance indicators if an entity does not report earnings.
- Premiums paid and life insurance proceeds received should be reported on the same financial reporting line in which changes in fair value are reported.

Financial Statement Presentation

1. *Balance sheet presentation*

Investments that are remeasured at fair value should be reported on the face of the balance sheet separately from investments reported under the investment method. Investors may elect to use one of the following presentation alternatives:
   a. Display the carrying amounts of investments accounted for under the fair value method on a separate line from those accounted for under the investment method.
   b. Display the total carrying amount of investments accounted for under the fair value method and those accounted for under the investment method and parenthetically disclose separate information about the carrying amounts of the investments accounted for under each method.

2. *Income statement presentation*

Investment income from investments in life settlement contracts that are remeasured at fair value should be presented separately on the face of the income statement from investment income on such investments accounted for under the investment method. Investors may elect one of the following presentation alternatives:
   a. Display income from investments in life settlement contracts accounted for under the fair value method and income from such investments accounted for under the investment method as separate line items.
   b. Display the total amount of investment income from investments in life settlement contracts accounted for under the fair value method with the investment income from such contracts accounted for under the investment method and parenthetically disclose separate information about the investment income from investments accounted for under each method.

3. *Statement of cash flows presentation*

Cash receipts and cash payments related to life settlement contracts under the guidance in ASC 230 should be classified based on the nature and purpose for which the life settlement contracts were acquired.

4. *Disclosures*

Investors should disclose the following information:
   a. The accounting policy for life settlement contracts, including the classification of cash receipts and disbursements in the statement of cash flows.
   b. The disclosures required in other U.S. pronouncements of generally accepted accounting principles, including other disclosure requirements regarding the use of fair value.
   c. Life settlement contracts accounted for under the investment method:
      (1) Based on the remaining life expectancy for each of the first five succeeding years from the balance-sheet date and thereafter, as well as the total, the number of life settlement contracts, the carrying values, and the death benefits of the underlying insurance policies.

(2) The nature of new or updated information that causes a change in an investor's expectations on the timing of realization of proceeds from investments in life settlement contracts, including the information in item (1) above. However, investors are *not* required to seek out such information to update the assumptions used to determine the remaining life expectancy of their life settlement contracts.
d. Life settlement contracts accounted for under the fair value method:
  (1) The methods and significant assumptions used to estimate the fair value of investments in life settlement contracts, including mortality assumptions, if any.
  (2) Based on the remaining life expectancy for each of the first five succeeding years from the balance-sheet date and thereafter, the total number of life settlement contracts, the carrying values, and the death benefits of the underlying insurance policies.
  (3) Reasons for changes in the expectation of the timing of realization of investments in life settlement contracts, including significant changes to amounts disclosed in item (2) above.
e. For each period reported in the income statement:
  (1) Gains and losses recognized during the period on investments sold during the period.
  (2) Unrecognized gains or losses recognized during the period on investments still held at the balance sheet date.

ASC 325-30-35-1 Recognition of Insurance Death Benefits

BACKGROUND

Some companies purchase life insurance policies to cover the lives of certain employees, with the company as the beneficiary. Such policies, referred to as corporate-owned life insurance (COLI) policies, are used for various purposes: (*a*) to protect the company if a key employee dies; (*b*) to accumulate funds to finance a shareholder/partner buy/sell agreement in case a shareholder/partner dies or leaves the company; or (*c*) to fund the employer's obligations to certain employee benefit plans, such as pension plans, by borrowing against the policy.

In the past, companies have recognized income on COLI policies when proceeds were received upon the death of an employee. Because companies were taking out policies on certain groups of employees, it was suggested that income from death benefits on COLI policies could be recognized over the estimated period of the employees' lives on an actuarially projected basis.

ACCOUNTING ISSUES

1. Should an entity recognize income on death benefits from COLI policies on an actuarially projected basis or upon the death of the insured?
2. If a company intends to retain COLI policies in force until the death of the insured and to borrow against them, should the company recognize the policy as an asset at the policy's net loan value, which is the maximum amount that the entity can contractually borrow against the policy, or at its cash surrender value?

ACCOUNTING GUIDANCE

1. A purchaser of life insurance should not recognize income from death benefits based on actuarial projections. Under the guidance in ASC 325-30-15-2 through 15-3, 35-1 through 35-2, 25-1, 05-3 through 05-5, a purchaser is required to recognize an asset for the amount at which the policy could be realized on the date of the financial statements. Because a death benefit may not be realized before the insured's actual death, recognition of death benefits on an actuarially projected basis is an inappropriate means of measuring the asset.

2. It was noted that the guidance in ASC 325-30-15-2 through 15-3, 35-1 through 35-2, 25-1, 05-3 through 05-5, specifies that the asset should be measured at its cash surrender value and that changes in that value be used to adjust policy premiums. The issue whether it is appropriate to recognize the difference between the cash surrender value and premiums paid as a temporary difference has been resolved by the guidance in ASC 740-10-25-30, which states that "[t]hat excess is a temporary difference if the cash surrender value is expected to be recovered by surrendering the policy, but it is not a temporary difference if the asset is expected to be recovered without tax consequences upon the death of the insured (there will be no taxable amount if the insurance policy is held until the death of the insured)."

ASC 325-40: BENEFICIAL INTERESTS IN SECURITIZED FINANCIAL ASSETS

ASC 325-40-05-1 through 05-2, 15-2 through 15-9, 25-1 through 25-3, 30-1 through 30-3, 35-1 through 35-13, 35-15 through 35-16, 45-1, 55-1 through 55-25, 60-7; ASC 310-20-60-1 through 60-2; ASC 310-30-15-5; ASC 320-10-35-38, 55-2 Recognition of Interest Income and Impairment on Purchased Beneficial Interests and Transferor's Beneficial Interests in Securitized Financial Assets Obtained in a Transfer Accounted for as a Sale

BACKGROUND

OBSERVATION: In June 2009, the FASB issued the guidance in ASC 860-10-35-4, 35-6, 05-8; ASC 860-20-25-5, 55-46 through 55-48; ASC 460-10-60-35; ASC 860-50-05-2 through 05-4, 30-1 through 30-2, 35-1A, 35-3, 35-9 through 35-11, 25-2 through 25-3, 25-6, 50-5, which has amended the guidance discussed below.

Scope

This guidance applies to beneficial interests that a transferor *acquires as proceeds* in securitization transactions accounted for as sales under the guidance in ASC 860 as amended by ASC 860-10-35-4, 35-6, 05-8; 860-20-25-5, 55-46 through 55-48; 460-10-60-35; 860-50-05-2 through 05-4, 30-1, 30-2, 35-1A, 35-3, 35-9 through 35-11,

25-2 through 25-3, 25-6, 50-5 and to *purchased* beneficial interests in securitized financial assets. This guidance also applies to beneficial interests that are:

- Debt securities accounted for under the guidance in ASC 310 or required to be accounted for like debt securities in accordance with the guidance in ASC 860-20-35-2; ASC 320-35-45, as amended by the guidance in ASC 860-10-35-4, 35-6, 05-8; ASC 860-20-25-5, 55-46 through 55-48; ASC 460-10-60-35; 860-50-05-2 through 05-4, 30-1 through 30-2, 35-1A, 35-3, 35-9 through 35-11; 25-2, 25-3, 25-6, 50-5.

- Securitized financial assets that have contractual cash flows, such as loans, receivables, and guaranteed lease residuals (The guidance in ASC 320-10-35-38 through 35-43, 55-10 through 55-12, 55-16 through 55-19; ASC 835-10-60-6 applies to securitized financial assets that do not involve contractual cash flows, such as common stock equity securities.)

- Financial instruments that do not cause an entity holding the beneficial interests to consolidate the entity that issued the beneficial interests (e.g., a special purpose entity).

- Not included under the scope of AICPA Practice Bulletin 6 (not in ASC), as amended by ASC 310-10-35-12 through 35-14, 35-16 through 35-26, 35-28 through 35-29, 35-32, 35-34, 35-37, 35-39; 45-5 through 45-6, 50-13, 50-15, 50-19; ASC 310-30-30-2; ASC 310-40-35-8 through 45-9, 45-12; ASC 310-40-50-2 through 50-3, 50-12 and ASC 320-10-05-2, 15-2 through 15-5, 15-7, 25-1, 25-3 through 25-6, 25-9, 25-12, 25-14 through 25-16, 25-18, 30-1, 35-1 through 35-2, 35-4 through 35-5, 35-10 through 35-13, 35-18, 45-1 through 45-2, 45-8 through 45-11, 45-13, 50-1A through 50-3, 50-5, 50-9 through 50-11, 55-3; ASC 942-320-50-1 through 50-3 and ASC 310-30-05-2 through 05-3, 15-1 through 15-4, 15-6 through 15-10, 25-1, 30-1, 35-2 through 35-3, 35-6, 35-8 through 35-15, 40-1, 45-1, 50-1 through 50-3, 50-18, 55-5, 55-29; ASC 835-10-60-3.

- (a) Not beneficial interests in securitized financial assets with high credit quality (e.g., guaranteed by the U.S. government) so that the possibility of credit loss is remote and (b) do not permit a debtor to prepay or settle the obligation so that the holder would not recover substantially all of its recorded investment. Interest income on such beneficial interests should be recognized in accordance with the guidance in ASC 310-20. The guidance in ASC 320-10-35-38 through 35-43; 55-10 through 55-12, 55-16 through 55-19; ASC 835-10-60-6, ASC 320, SEC Staff Bulletin 59, and Statement of Auditing Standards 92, should be followed to determine whether an other-than-temporary impairment of such beneficial assets exists.

- Issued in equity form but meet the definition of a "debt security" in the ASC, Glossary, such as (a) a right to receive a future stream of cash flows under specified terms and conditions or (b) that must be redeemed by the issuer or must be redeemable at the investor's option.

- Classified as trading securities under the guidance in ASC 320, because under GAAP, entities in certain industries, such as banks and investment companies, are required to report investment income as a separate item in the income statement even though those entities report their investments at fair value and report changes in value in earnings. The fact that beneficial interests are classified as held-to-maturity, available-for-sale, or trading should not affect the recognition and measurement of interest income on those instruments.

- The portions of hybrid beneficial interests referred to as host contracts, if they meet the scope requirements. A host contract must be separated from a hybrid instrument's embedded derivative, which must be accounted for separately according to the guidance in ASC 815-15-05-1, 35-2A, 25-1, 25-14, 25-26 through 25-29; ASC 815-10-15-72 through 15-73. Hybrid beneficial interests measured at fair value in accordance with the guidance in ASC 815-15-30-1 are not included under the scope if a transferor does not report interest income from those instruments as a separate item in the income statement.

ACCOUNTING ISSUE

How should a transferor that retains an interest in securitized financial assets or an entity that purchases a beneficial interest in securitized financial assets account for income and impairment?

ACCOUNTING GUIDANCE

1. The holder of a beneficial interest should estimate at the date the beneficial interest is acquired (the transaction date) the amount by which all cash flows that will be received from the beneficial interest will exceed the initial investment (the accretable yield). The holder should use the effective yield method to recognize that amount as interest income over the life of the beneficial interest. The initial investment is the fair value of the beneficial interest as of the transfer date if the holder also is the transferor as required under the guidance in ASC 860, as amended by the guidance in ASC 860-10-35-4, 35-6, 05-8; ASC 860-20-25-5, 55-46 through 55-48; ASC 460-10-60-35; 860-50-05-2 through 05-4, 30-1 through 30-2, 35-1A, 35-3, 35-9 through 35-11, 25-2 through 25-3, 25-6; 50-5. The accretable yield should not be presented in the balance sheet.

2. The estimated cash flows should be adjusted over the life of the beneficial interest if:

    a. Based on the estimated fair value of the beneficial interest, using current information and events, it is probable that estimated cash flows will be more or less than the previous projection. An investor should recalculate the amount of the accretable yield for the beneficial interest on that date as the excess of estimated cash flows over the sum of (*a*) the initial investment *less* (*b*) cash received to date *less* (*c*) other-than-temporary impairment recognized to date *plus* (*d*) the yield accreted to date. The adjustment should be recognized prospectively as a change in estimate in accordance with the guidance in ASC 250 and the periodic accretion should be adjusted over the life of the beneficial interest. Based on cash flows, interest income may be recognized on a beneficial interest, even if accretion of the net investment in the beneficial interest results in an amount that exceeds the amount at which the beneficial interest could be settled if the entire amount were prepaid immediately.

b. A beneficial interest's fair value is less than its reference amount. The guidance on impairment of securities in ASC 320-10-45-9 should be applied to determine whether a decline is other-than-temporary. If based on the holder's best estimate of cash flows, all of the cash flows estimated in accordance with paragraph 2a above will not be collected, an other-than-temporary impairment has occurred and the beneficial interest should be written down to fair value. The change in value should be included in income. However, an other-than-temporary impairment need not be recognized if a change in the interest rate of a *plain vanilla* variable rate beneficial interest occurs without other indicators of impairment. To determine whether a favorable or adverse change in estimated cash flows from the amount previously projected (based on the timing and amount of estimated cash flows) has occurred, the present value of the remaining cash flows estimated at the initial transaction date, or the last date on which the amount was previously revised, should be compared to the present value of estimated cash flows at the current financial reporting date. Cash flows should be discounted at a rate that equals the current yield used to accrete the beneficial interest. A change is considered to be favorable—that is, an other-than-temporary impairment has *not* occurred—if the present value of the current estimated cash flows exceeds the present value of the estimated cash flows at the initial transaction date or the last date at which the amount was previously revised. A change is considered to be adverse—that is, an other-than-temporary impairment has occurred—if the present value of the current estimated cash flows is less than the present value of estimated cash flows at the initial transaction date or the last date at which the amount was previously revised.

3. At the transaction date, estimated cash flows are defined as the estimate of the amount and timing of future cash flows of principal and interest used to determine the purchase price or the holder's fair value for gain or loss recognition under the guidance in ASC 860. Thereafter, estimated cash flows are defined as the holder's estimate of the amount and timing of estimated cash flows from principal and interest payments, based on the holder's best assessment of current information and events a market participant would use to determine the current fair value of a beneficial interest. A favorable or adverse change in estimated cash flows is considered in terms of the timing and amount of estimated cash flows.

4. An entity that intends to sell a retained interest classified as available-for-sale should recognize a loss on an other-than-temporary impairment at the time a decision to sell is made, if the retained interest will be sold at a loss shortly after the balance sheet date, its fair value is less than its carrying amount, and it is not expected to recover before the date of an

expected sale. The guidance in SAB-59, SAS-81, and ASC 860 should also be considered in determining whether an other-than-temporary impairment exists.

5. The cost recovery method should be used if a beneficial interest is placed on nonaccrual status or if a holder cannot reliably estimate the security's cash flows.

OBSERVATION: Under the guidance in ASC 810, an entity that absorbs a majority of a variable entity's expected losses or has the right to receive a greater part of a variable entity's expected residual returns or both is required to consolidate that variable interest entity.

OBSERVATION: The guidance in ASC 815 is amended by the guidance in ASC 815-15-25-4 through 25-5, which provides an election for the fair value measurement of certain hybrid financial instruments with embedded derivatives that otherwise would have to be bifurcated. If an entity elects to account for an entire hybrid financial instrument at fair value, that financial instrument should not be used as a hedging instrument in a hedging relationship under the guidance in ASC 815.

OBSERVATION: Although the guidance in ASC 860-50-35-3, 35-6 through 35-7, 50-5 amends the accounting guidance in ASC 860 for separately recognized servicing assets and servicing liabilities, it does not affect the guidance herein. The guidance in ASC 325-40-05-1 through 05-2, 15-2 through 15-9, 25-1 through 25-3, 30-1 through 30-3, 35-1 through 35-13, 35-15 through 35-16, 45-1, 55-1 through 55-25, 60-7; ASC 310-20-60-1 through 60-2; ASC 310-30-15-5; ASC 320-10-35-38, 55-2 represents the FASB's decision in ASC 860-50-35-3, 35-6 through 35-7, 50-5 to replace the term "retained interests" with "interests that continue to be held by a transferor".

OBSERVATION: The guidance in ASC 860-10-35-4, 35-6, 05-8; ASC 860-20-25-5, 55-46 through 55-48; ASC 460-10-60-35; ASC 860-50-05-2 through 05-4, 30-1 through 30-2, 35-1A, 35-3, 35-9 through 35-11, 25-2 through 25-3, 25-6, 50-5 amends the previous guidance in ASC 860 by eliminating the concept of a special-purpose entity and the scope exception that exempted special-purpose entities from following the guidance in ASC 810. Under the guidance in ASC 810, derecognition provisions should be applied to a transfer of an entire financial asset, a group of entire financial assets, or a participating interest in an entire financial asset. In addition, interests acquired by a transferor on completion of a transfer of an entire financial asset or an entire group of financial assets that meet the conditions to be accounted for as a sale should be recognized and measured initially at fair value. The term "interests that continue to be held by a transferor" as it is used In ASC 860, applies only if a transferor retains participating interests on completion of a transfer of participating rights in a transaction that meets the conditions to be accounted for as a sale. Under the guidance in ASC 860-10-35-4, 35-6, 05-8; ASC 860-20-25-5, 55-46 through 55-48; ASC 460-10-60-35; ASC 860-50-05-2 through 05-4, 30-1 through 30-2, 35-1A, 35-3, 35-9 through 35-11, 25-2 through 25-3, 25-6, 50-5, that term should be used only for such retained participation rights.

CHAPTER 22
ASC 330—INVENTORY

CONTENTS

Part I: General Guidance	22,002
ASC 330-10: Overall	22,002
Overview	22,002
Background	22,002
Inventory Systems	22,003
Periodic System	22,003
Perpetual System	22,003
Lower of Cost or Market	22,003
Illustration of How Maximum and Minimum Constraints Impact Lower-of-Cost-or-Market Determination	22,004
Inventory Cost Methods	22,005
First-In, First-Out Method (FIFO)	22,005
Last-In, First-Out Method (LIFO)	22,005
Weighted-Average Method	22,006
Illustration of Application of FIFO, LIFO, and the Weighted-Average Methods of Inventory Valuation	22,006
Moving-Average Method	22,008
Illustration of Moving-Average Method	22,008
Dollar-Value LIFO Method	22,009
Illustration of Dollar-Value LIFO Method	22,009
Retail Inventory Method	22,009
Illustration of Basic Retail Inventory Method	22,010
Illustration of Markups and Markdowns	22,010
Lower-of-Cost-or-Market Application	22,012
Illustration of Retail Method/Lower-of-Cost-or-Market Application	22,013
LIFO Application	22,014
Illustration of Retail Method/LIFO Application	22,014
Miscellaneous Inventory Issues	22,015
Title to Goods	22,015
Abnormal Facility and Other Costs	22,016
Standard Costs	22,017
Relative Sales Value Costing	22,017
Illustration of Relative Sales Value Costing	22,017
Firm Purchase Commitments	22,018
Discontinued Operations	22,018
Interim Financial Reporting	22,018
Terminated Contracts	22,019
Research and Development	22,019
Intercompany Profits	22,020
Long-Term Construction-Type Contracts	22,020
Income Taxes	22,020

22,002 ASC 330—Inventory

Accounting Change	22,020
Nonmonetary Exchanges	22,020
Inventory Profits	22,020
Disclosure	22,021
Part II: Interpretive Guidance	22,021
ASC 330-10: Overall	22,021
ASC 330-10-55-2	
Recognition of Inventory Market Declines at Interim Reporting Dates	22,021
ASC 330-10-55-3 through 55-4	
Uniform Capitalization Rules for Inventory under the Tax Reform Act of 1986	22,022
ASC 330-10-S35-2; ASC 420-10-S45-2, S99-3	
Classification of Inventory Markdowns and Other Costs Associated with a Restructuring	22,022

PART I: GENERAL GUIDANCE

ASC 330-10: OVERALL

OVERVIEW

The preparation of financial statements requires careful determination of an appropriate dollar amount of inventory. Usually, that amount is presented as a current asset in the balance sheet and is a direct determinant of cost of goods sold in the income statement; as such, it has a significant impact on the amount of net income. When the matching principle is applied in determining net income, the valuation of inventories is of primary importance.

BACKGROUND

Inventories of goods must periodically be compiled, measured, and recorded in the books of accounts of a business. Inventory usually is classified as (*a*) finished goods, (*b*) work in process, or (*c*) raw materials (ASC Glossary). Inventories exclude long-term assets that are subject to depreciation.

PRACTICE POINTER: Inventories are normally classified as current assets. However, when there are excessive quantities that may not reasonably be expected to be used or sold within the normal operating cycle of a business, we believe that excess inventory should be classified as noncurrent.

The basis of accounting for inventories is cost, which is the price paid or consideration given to acquire the asset. In inventory accounting, cost is the sum of the expenditures and charges, direct and indirect, in bringing goods to their existing condition or location (ASC 330-10-30-1).

While the principle of measuring inventory at cost can be easily stated, the application of the principle, particularly to work-in-process items and finished goods, is difficult because of the problem involved in allocating various costs and charges. For example, idle factory expense, excessive spoilage, double freight, and rehandling costs can be so abnormal that they may have to be charged to the current period, rather than be treated as elements of inventory cost. Selling expenses are not part of inventory costs. *The exclusion of all overhead from inventory costs* (direct or variable costing) *is an unacceptable accounting procedure* (ASC 330-10-30-2, 8).

INVENTORY SYSTEMS

Periodic System

Inventory is determined by a physical count as of a specific date. As long as the count is made frequently enough for reporting purposes, it is not necessary to maintain extensive inventory records. The inventory shown in the balance sheet is determined by the physical count and is priced in accordance with the inventory costing method used. The net change between the beginning and ending inventories enters into the computation of the cost of goods sold.

Perpetual System

In a perpetual system, inventory records are maintained and updated continuously as items are purchased and sold. The system has the advantage of providing inventory information on a timely basis but requires the maintenance of a full set of inventory records. Theoretically, physical counts are not necessary, but they are normally taken to verify the inventory records. GAAP require that a physical check of perpetual inventory records be made periodically.

LOWER OF COST OR MARKET

When the utility of the goods in the ordinary course of business is no longer as great as their cost, a departure from the cost principle of measuring the inventory is required. Whether the cause is obsolescence, physical deterioration, changes in price levels, or any other, the difference should be recognized by a charge to income in the current period. This usually is accomplished by stating the goods at a lower level designated as market (lower of cost or market principle) (ASC 330-10-35-1).

In the phrase *lower of cost or market*, the term *market* means current replacement cost, whether by purchase or by reproduction, *but is limited to the following maximum and minimum amounts* (ASC Glossary):

- *Maximum:* the estimated selling price less any costs of completion and disposal, referred to as net realizable value
- *Minimum:* net realizable value, less an allowance for normal profit

The purpose of reducing inventory to the lower of cost or market is to reflect fairly the income of the period. When market is lower than cost, the purposes of the maximum and minimum limitations are:

- The maximum prevents a loss in future periods by at least valuing the inventory at its estimated selling price less costs of completion and disposal.
- The minimum prevents any future periods from realizing any more than a normal profit.

Illustration of How Maximum and Minimum Constraints Impact Lower-of-Cost-or-Market Determination

Item	Cost	Replacement Cost	(1) Selling Price	(2) Cost of Completion	(1 – 2) Maximum*	(3) Normal Profit	[(1 – 2) – 3] Minimum
1	$ 20.50	$ 19.00	$ 25.00	$ 1.00	$ 24.00	$ 6.00	$ 18.00
2	26.00	20.00	30.00	2.00	28.00	7.00	21.00
3	10.00	12.00	15.00	1.00	14.00	3.00	11.00
4	40.00	55.00	60.00	6.00	54.00	4.00	50.00
	$96.50	$106.00	$130.00	$10.00	$120.00	$20.00	$100.00

* The maximum is equal to the realizable value.

Applying the lower of cost or market to the above four items individually results in the following amounts:

Item 1	$19.00	Item 3	$10.00
Item 2	$21.00	Item 4	$40.00

The lower of cost or market principle may be applied to a single item, a category, or the total inventory, provided that the method most clearly reflects periodic income (ASC 330-10-35-8). The basic principle of consistency must be applied in the valuation of inventory, and the method should be disclosed in the financial statements (ASC 330-10-50-1).

The write-down of inventory to market usually is reflected in cost of goods sold, unless the amount is unusually material, in which case the loss should be identified separately in the income statement (ASC 330-10-50-2).

In the event that a significant change occurs in the measurement of inventory, disclosure of the nature of the change and, if material, the effect on income should be made in the financial statements.

Exceptional cases, such as precious metals having a fixed determinable monetary value with no substantial cost of marketing, may be stated at such monetary value. When inventory is stated at a value in excess of cost, this fact should be disclosed fully in the financial statements (ASC 330-10-50-3).

To apply this exception to other types of inventory, there must be: (*a*) immediate marketability at quoted prices, (*b*) inability to determine approximate costs, and (*c*) interchangeability of units.

> **PRACTICE NOTE:** ASC 815 (Derivatives and Hedging) states that if inventory has been the hedged item in a fair value hedge, the inventory's cost basis used in determining the lower-of-cost-or-market shall include the effects of adjusting its carrying amount as a result of recording the gain or loss on the hedged item. For further coverage of this topic, see the chapter of this *Guide* discussing ASC 815.

INVENTORY COST METHODS

For inventory purposes, cost may be determined by specific identification or by the association of the flow of cost factors—first-in, first out (FIFO), last-in, first-out (LIFO), and average cost.

In selecting an inventory cost method, an important objective is the selection of the method that under the circumstances most clearly reflects periodic income. When similar goods are purchased at different times, it may not be possible or practical to identify and match the specific costs of the item sold. Frequently, the identity of goods and their specific related costs are lost between the time of acquisition and the time of use or sale. This has resulted in the general acceptance of several assumptions with respect to the flow of cost factors to provide practical bases for the measurement of periodic income (ASC 330-10-30-9).

First-In, First-Out Method (FIFO)

The FIFO method of identifying inventory is based on the assumption that costs are charged against revenue in the order in which they occur. The inventory remaining on hand is presumed to consist of the most recent costs.

Theoretically, FIFO approximates the results that would be obtained by the specific identification method if items were sold in the order in which they were purchased.

Last-In, First-Out Method (LIFO)

The LIFO method matches the most recent costs incurred with current revenue, leaving the first cost incurred to be included as inventory. LIFO requires that records be maintained as to the base-year layer and additional layers that may be created or used up. An additional LIFO layer is created in any year in which the quantity of ending inventory is more than the beginning inventory and is priced at the earliest or average costs of the year in which it was created.

When the quantity of ending inventory is less than the beginning inventory, one or more LIFO layers may be used up. Once a LIFO layer is used up, any future new LIFO layer is priced at the cost of the year in which it is created, and not by reinstating a prior LIFO layer cost.

In addition to the disclosure of significant accounting policies required by ASC 235 (Notes to Financial Statements) and of composition of inventories (ASC 330-10-50-1), a business using the LIFO method of reporting inventory must disclose the following, if it reports to the SEC:

- Current replacement value of the LIFO inventories at each balance sheet date presented
- The effect on the results of operations for any reduction of a LIFO layer

> **PRACTICE POINTER:** Although using the LIFO inventory method is sometimes justified on the basis of a superior matching of current revenues and current costs, the primary catalysts for using it are its acceptance for income tax purposes and the lower taxable income that it produces. Income tax law requires a company that uses LIFO for tax purposes to also use LIFO for financial reporting purposes. In changing from another inventory cost method to the LIFO method for financial reporting purposes, the company must present a justification. Changing an accounting method for financial reporting purposes because of its preferability for tax purposes generally is not acceptable. Therefore, changing to LIFO usually is justified by reasons such as higher quality earnings that result from matching current revenues with current costs, and bringing the company into conformity with normal industry practice.

Weighted-Average Method

The weighted-average method of inventory valuation assumes that costs are charged against revenue based on an average of the number of units acquired at each price level. The resulting average price is applied to the ending inventory to find the total ending inventory value. The weighted average is determined by dividing the total costs of the inventory available, including any beginning inventory, by the total number of units.

Illustration of Application of FIFO, LIFO, and the Weighted-Average Methods of Inventory Valuation

Assume the following facts:

Date	Units Purchased During the Year		
	Units	Cost per Unit	Total Cost
January 15	10,000	$5.10	$ 51,000
March 20	20,000	5.20	104,000
May 10	50,000	5.00	250,000
June 8	30,000	5.40	162,000
October 12	5,000	5.30	26,500
December 21	5,000	5.50	27,500
Totals	120,000		$621,000

Beginning inventory consisted of 10,000 units at $5.

Ending inventory consisted of 14,000 units.

Under *FIFO*, the first units in stock are the first units out, which means that the ending inventory is of the units purchased last. Since the ending inventory is 14,000 units and December purchases were only 5,000 units, go back to October purchases for another 5,000 units and to June purchases for another 4,000 units, as follows:

December purchases	5,000 units @	$5.50	=	$27,500
October purchases	5,000 units @	5.30	=	26,500
From June purchases	4,000 units @	5.40	=	21,600
Ending inventory using FIFO	14,000 units			$75,600

Under *LIFO*, the last units in stock are the first units out, which means that the ending inventory is composed of the units purchased first. Using LIFO, go back to the earliest inventory to start the calculations. The earliest inventory available is the *beginning inventory* of 10,000 units at $5, but the ending inventory is 14,000 units. Thus, go to the next earliest purchase, which is January, and use 4,000 units at the January price to complete the ending inventory valuation, as follows:

Beginning inventory	10,000 units @	$5.00	=	$50,000
From January purchase	4,000 units @	5.10	=	20,400
Ending inventory using LIFO	14,000 units			$70,400

Under the *weighted-average* method, multiply the weighted-average cost per unit by the 14,000 units in the ending inventory, thus:

	Units	Cost per Unit	Total Cost
Beginning inventory	10,000	$5.00	$50,000
Purchases:			
January 15	10,000	5.10	51,000
March 20	20,000	5.20	104,000
May 10	50,000	5.00	250,000
June 8	30,000	5.40	162,000

22,008 ASC 330—Inventory

	Units	Cost per Unit	Total Cost
October 12	5,000	5.30	26,500
December 21	5,000	5.50	27,500
Totals	130,000		$671,000

Weighted average	=	Total costs divided by total units
	=	$671,000 divided by 130,000
	=	$5.1615 per unit
Ending inventory	=	14,000 × $5.1615 per unit = $72,261

Comparison of the Three Methods

Ending inventory, FIFO	$75,600
Ending inventory, LIFO	70,400
Ending inventory, weighted average	72,261

In periods of inflation, the FIFO method produces the highest ending inventory, resulting in the lowest cost of goods sold and the highest gross profit. LIFO produces the lowest ending inventory, resulting in the highest cost of goods sold and the lowest gross profit. The weighted-average method yields results between those of LIFO and FIFO.

Moving-Average Method

The moving-average method can be used only with a perpetual inventory. The cost per unit is recomputed after every addition to the inventory.

Illustration of Moving-Average Method

	Total Units	Total Cost	Unit Cost
Beginning inventory	1,000	$ 5,000	$5.00
Sales of 200 units	800	4,000	5.00
Purchase of 1,200 @ $6	2,000	11,200*	5.60
Sales of 1,000 units	1,000	5,600	5.60
Purchase of 1,000 @ $5	2,000	10,600**	5.30

Note: Only purchases change the unit price; sales are taken out at the prior moving-average unit cost.

* $4,000+(1,200 @ $6)=$11,200; $11,200/2,000 units =$5.60/unit
** $5,600+(1,000 @ $5)=$10,600; $10,600/2,000 units =$5.30/unit

Under the moving-average method, the ending inventory is costed at the last moving-average unit cost for the period.

Dollar-Value LIFO Method

A variation of the conventional LIFO method is the dollar-value LIFO method. Under the regular LIFO method, units of inventory are priced at unit prices. Under the dollar-value LIFO method, the base-year inventory is priced in dollars; for inventories of all subsequent years, price indices are used, with the base year as 100.

Illustration of Dollar-Value LIFO Method

Year	Inventory at Base-Year Prices	Price Index	LIFO Inventory Amount
1	$100,000	100	$100,000
2	20,000	105	21,000
3	10,000	110	11,000
4	20,000	120	24,000
5	20,000	125	25,000
Totals	$170,000		$181,000

Retail Inventory Method

Because of the great variety and quantity of inventory in some types of businesses, the reversed markup procedure of inventory pricing, such as the retail inventory method, may be both practical and appropriate.

The retail inventory method requires the maintenance of records of purchases at both cost and selling price. A ratio of cost to retail is calculated and applied to the ending inventory at retail to compute the approximate cost.

Illustration of Basic Retail Inventory Method

	Cost	Retail
Inventory, at beginning of period	$100,000	$150,000
Purchases during the period	1,100,000	1,850,000
Totals (ratio of cost to retail 60%)	$1,200,000	$2,000,000
Sales during the period		(1,800,000)
Estimated ending inventory at retail		$200,000
Estimated ending inventory at cost (60% × $200,000)		$120,000

Physical inventories measured by the retail method should be taken periodically as a check on the accuracy of the estimated inventories.

Original selling prices may be modified, thus necessitating an understanding of the following terminology:

- *Original retail*—the first selling price at which goods are offered for sale
- *Markup*—the selling price raised above the original selling price
- *Markdown*—the selling price lowered below the original selling price
- *Markup cancellation*—markup selling price decreased, but not below the original selling price
- *Markdown cancellation*—markdown selling price increased, but not above the original selling price
- *Net markup*—markup less markup cancellation
- *Net markdown*—markdown less markdown cancellation
- *Markon*—difference between the cost and the original selling price, plus any net markups

Illustration of Markups and Markdowns

Original cost	$100
Original selling price ($50 markon)	$150
Markup	50

Original selling price plus markup	200
Markup cancellation	(25)
Original selling price plus net markup	175
Markdown (consists of $25 markup cancellation and a $25 markdown)	(50)
Original selling price less markdown	125
Markdown	(25)
Original selling price less markdown	100
Markdown cancellation	25
Original selling price less net markdown	125
Markup (consists of a $25 markdown cancellation and a $25 markup)	50
Original selling price plus net markup	$175

Theoretically, the last selling price consists of:

$50	markup
(25)	markup cancellation
(25)	markup cancellation
(25)	markdown
(25)	markdown
25	markdown cancellation
25	markdown cancellation
25	markup
$25	net plus change

Now the goods are priced at the original selling price plus a net markup of $25, or a total of $175.

The purpose of the conventional retail inventory method is to produce an inventory valuation closely approximating what would be obtained by taking a physical inventory and pricing the goods at the lower of cost or market.

The basic assumption of the retail inventory method is that there exists an equal distribution of goods (high-cost ratio and low-cost ratio) between sales, beginning inventory, and ending inventory. In instances in which this basic premise does not prevail, cost ratios should be determined by departments or small units. This requires keeping separate sales, purchases, markups, markdowns, and beginning and ending inventories by departments.

Lower-of-Cost-or-Market Application

To approximate the lower of cost or market in the computations, *markdowns and markdown cancellations are excluded in calculating the ratio of cost to retail and are added to the retail inventory after the ratio is determined.*

In calculating the cost-to-retail ratio, any adjustment to the retail value will necessarily affect the ratio and the resulting cost figure. Adjustments that decrease the denominator of the ratio increase the ratio and the value for ending inventory at cost, increasing gross profit. In the interest of conservatism, as well as for other reasons, adjustments that decrease the retail figure should be avoided. Markups, which increase the denominator, however, are included *net* of cancellations.

Net markdowns (markdowns less markdown cancellations) are an example of adjustments that decrease the denominator. Including them in the retail figure violates the lower-of-cost-or-market rule. As shown below, net markdowns are not included in the calculation of the ratio but *are* included in the determination of ending inventory after computing the ratio. The rationale for this is that the cost-to-retail ratio is presumed to be based on normal conditions, and markdown is not a normal condition. When *applying* the ratio, however, to conform to the lower-of-cost-or-market rule, the retail value must be reduced by the amount of the markdowns.

Employee discounts apply only to goods sold, not those remaining on hand. A sale at less than normal retail price to an employee does not represent a valid reduction to lower of cost or market, nor does it represent a valid adjustment of the cost-to-retail ratio or the value of the ending inventory. Therefore, employee discounts should not enter into any of the calculations, but are deducted from retail in the same way as markdowns after the computation of the cost-to-retail ratio.

Inventory spoilage and shrinkage affect the ending inventory figure but do not enter into the cost-to-retail ratio calculation. When arriving at the final figure for inventory at cost, the amount of shrinkage is deducted either at cost or at retail depending upon whether shrinkage is stated at cost or at retail.

Illustration of Retail Method/Lower-of-Cost-or-Market Application

	Cost	Retail
Inventory, at beginning of period	$ 200,000	$ 300,000
Purchases	550,000	800,000
Transportation-in	50,000	
Markups		100,000
Markup cancellations		20,000
Markdowns		70,000
Markdown cancellations		10,000

The calculations are as follows:

	Cost	Retail
Inventory, at beginning of period	$200,000	$ 300,000
Purchases	550,000	800,000
Transportation-in	50,000	
Markups		100,000
Markup cancellations		(20,000)
Totals (ratio of cost to retail 67.8%)	$800,000	$1,180,000
Markdowns		(70,000)
Markdown cancellations		10,000
Total goods at retail		$1,120,000

	Cost	Retail
Less: Sales during the period		(860,000)
Inventory, ending (at retail)		$ 260,000
Inventory, ending (67.8% × $260,000)*		$ 176,280
At estimated lower cost or market		

LIFO Application

The LIFO method of evaluating inventory can be estimated via the retail inventory method by using procedures somewhat different from the conventional retail method. Basically, two differences have to be taken into consideration:

1. Because the LIFO method produces a valuation approximating cost, and the conventional retail method produces a valuation approximating the lower of cost or market, to apply the LIFO concept to the conventional retail method it is necessary to include all markdowns as well as markups in determining the ratio of cost to retail.
2. With the LIFO method, the quantity of inventory on hand is from the earliest purchases during the year or from prior years' LIFO layers. The cost-to-retail ratio considers the current relationship between cost and selling price. Therefore, the beginning inventory is omitted from the cost-to-retail ratio, because it may cause a distortion.

Illustration of Retail Method/LIFO Application

Information from the previous example is restated on a LIFO basis, as follows:

	Cost	Retail
Inventory, beginning of period	omitted	omitted
Purchases	$550,000	$ 800,000
Transportation-in	50,000	
Markups		100,000
Markup cancellations		(20,000)
Markdowns		(70,000)
Markdown cancellations		10,000
Totals (ratio of cost to retail 73.2%)	$600,000	$ 820,000

	Cost	Retail
Add: Inventory, beginning of period		300,000
Total goods at retail		$1,120,000
Less: Sales during period		(860,000)
Inventory, ending of period (at retail)		$ 260,000

Because the $260,000 ending LIFO inventory (at retail) is less than the $300,000 beginning LIFO inventory (at retail), a prior LIFO layer was partially depleted:

	Retail
Beginning inventory	$300,000
Ending inventory	(260,000)
LIFO layer depleted	$ 40,000

The $40,000 difference is multiplied by the beginning inventory cost-to-retail ratio ($200,000/$300,000 = 66.7%) and then subtracted from the beginning inventory at cost, as follows:

	Cost
Beginning inventory	$200,000
$40,000 × 66.7%	(26,680)
Ending inventory (at cost)	$173,320

If the ending LIFO inventory (at retail) had been greater than the beginning LIFO inventory (at retail), a new LIFO layer would have been created which would have been costed at the new cost-to-retail ratio (73.2%).

MISCELLANEOUS INVENTORY ISSUES

Title to Goods

Legal title to merchandise usually determines whether or not it is included in the inventory of an enterprise. Title to goods passes from the seller to the buyer in any manner and on any conditions explicitly agreed on by the parties. If no conditions are explicitly agreed on, title to goods passes from the seller to the buyer at the time and place at which the seller completes its performance with reference to the physical delivery of the goods. Title passes to the buyer at the time and place of shipment if the seller is required only to send the goods. If the contract requires delivery at destination, however, title passes when the goods are tendered at the destination.

Commonly encountered terms are *F.O.B. (free on board) Destination* and *F.O.B. Shipping Point*. In the former case, the seller is responsible for the goods during shipment; title passes when the goods are received by the buyer. In the latter case, the buyer is responsible for the goods during shipment; title passes when the goods leave the seller's location.

Abnormal Facility and Other Costs

ASC 330 also provides guidance in accounting for abnormal amounts of idle facility expense, freight, handling costs, and spoilage. The basic principle for accounting for inventory is that inventories are to be accounted for at cost, meaning acquisition and production costs. Although this principle may be easily stated, it is difficult to apply because of the variety of considerations inherent in the allocation of costs and charges. Guidelines for applying these principles can be summarized as follows:

- Variable production overhead costs are allocated to each unit of production on the basis of the actual use of the production facilities.
- The allocation of fixed production overheads to the costs of conversion is based on the normal capacity of the production facilities.
- "Normal capacity" refers to a range of production levels and is the production expected to be achieved over a number of periods or seasons under normal circumstances, taking into account the loss of capacity resulting from planned maintenance.
- Some variation in production levels from period to period is expected and establishes the range of normal production. This range will vary based on business-related and industry-related factors.
- Judgment is required to determine when a production level is abnormally low (i.e., outside the range of expected variation in production).
- Examples of factors that might be anticipated to cause an abnormally low production level include significantly reduced demand, labor and materials shortages, and unplanned facilities or equipment downtime.
- The actual level of production may be used if it approximates normal capacity.
- In periods of abnormally high production, the amount of fixed overhead allocated to each unit of production is decreased so that inventories are not measured above cost. The amount of fixed overhead allocated to each unit of production is not increased as a consequence of abnormally low production or an idle plant.

Unallocated overhead costs are recognized as an expense in the period in which they are incurred. Other costs, such as abnormal handling costs, are treated as a current period expense, as are general and administrative costs, except for the portion that clearly relates to production and constitutes a part of inventory costs. Selling expenses are not included in inventory costs. The exclusion of all overhead costs from inventory costs is not an accepted accounting procedure.

> **PRACTICE POINTER:** The exercise of judgment in individual situations involves a consideration of the adequacy of the procedures of the cost accounting system in use, the soundness of the principles on which that system is based, and the consistency of the application of those principles.

Standard Costs

The use of standard costs is a management tool that identifies favorable or unfavorable variances from predetermined estimates established by past performance or time and motion studies. Inventory valuation by the use of standard costs is acceptable, if adjusted at reasonable intervals to reflect the approximate costs computed under one of the recognized methods, and adequate disclosure is made in the financial statements.

At the end of the reporting period, the physical inventory is costed at LIFO, FIFO, or some other generally accepted method. Any variation between this result and the carrying value of the inventory at standard cost must be closed out to cost of goods sold and ending inventory such that the reported figure represents that which the generally accepted method would yield.

Relative Sales Value Costing

Determining the relative sales cost of inventory items is used when costs cannot be determined individually. Joint products, lump-sum purchase of assets (basket purchase), and large assets that are subdivided (real estate tracts) are examples of items that would be costed by their relative sales value.

Illustration of Relative Sales Value Costing

ABC Company purchases inventory consisting of four large pieces of machinery for $100,000. At the time of purchase, an appraisal discloses the following fair values:

Machine #1	$ 12,000
Machine #2	28,000
Machine #3	40,000
Machine #4	30,000
Total	$110,000

The cost of each machine is an allocated amount, based on relative fair values, as follows:

Machine #1	12/110 × $100,000	=	$ 10,909
Machine #2	28/110 × $100,000	=	25,455
Machine #3	40/110 × $100,000	=	36,364
Machine #4	30/110 × $100,000	=	27,272
	Total cost allocated		$100,000

Alternatively, a percentage of total cost to the appraised value can be computed: $100,000/$110,000 = 90.91%. That percentage is then applied to the value of each item to determine its cost. For example, cost for Machine #1 is $12,000 × 90.91% = $10,909.

Firm Purchase Commitments

Losses on firm purchase commitments for inventory goods are measured in the same manner as inventory losses and, if material, recognized in the accounts and disclosed separately in the income statement (ASC 330-10-50-5).

The recognition of losses, which are expected to arise from firm, noncancelable commitments and which arise from the decline in the utility of a cost expenditure, should be disclosed in the current period income statement. In addition, all significant firm purchase commitments must be disclosed in the financial statements or in footnotes, whether or not any losses are recognized.

Discontinued Operations

Inventories used in a component of a business entity should be written down to their fair value less cost to sell and the amount of write-down included as part of the gain or loss recognized on the disposal of the component of the business entity (ASC 360-10-35-40). Such a write-down, however, should not be attributable to any inventory adjustment that should have been recognized prior to the measurement date of the loss on disposal. In this event, the loss on the write down is included in the operating results of the component of the business entity in accordance with ASC 205-20 (Presentation of Financial Statements—Discontinued Operations) (ASC 205-20-45-3).

Interim Financial Reporting

Generally, the same principles and methods are used to value inventories for interim financial statements as are used for annual reports. For practical purposes, however, ASC 270 specifies certain exceptions (ASC 270-10-45-6):

- An estimated gross profit frequently is used to determine the cost of goods sold during an interim period. This is acceptable for GAAP, as long as periodic physical inventories are taken to adjust the gross profit percentage used. Companies using the gross profit method for interim financial statements should disclose that fact and any significant adjustments that may occur in amounts determined by a physical count.

- When the LIFO method is used for interim financial statements and a LIFO layer is depleted, in part or in whole, that is expected to be replaced before the end of the fiscal period, it is acceptable to use the expected cost of replacement for the depleted LIFO inventory in determining cost of goods sold for the interim period.

- Inventory losses from market declines, other than those expected to be recovered before the end of the fiscal year, are included in the results of operations of the interim period in which the loss occurs. Subsequent gains from market price recovery in later interim periods are included in the results of operation in which the gain occurs, but only to the extent of the previously recognized losses.

- Standard costs are acceptable in determining inventory valuations for interim financial reporting. Unplanned or unanticipated purchase price, volume, or capacity variances should be included in the results of operations of the interim period in which they occur. Anticipated and planned purchase price, volume, or capacity variances that are expected to be recovered by the end of the fiscal year are deferred at interim dates. In general, the same procedures for standard costs used at the end of the fiscal year should be used for interim financial reporting.

PRACTICE POINTER: Although all four of these procedures are acceptable in interim financial statements, they are not considered GAAP for purposes of annual financial statements. Some may result in material differences in the amount of net income (e.g., using the replacement cost for erosion of a LIFO layer in an early interim period), and care should be taken that a similar procedure is not used in annual financial statements.

Terminated Contracts

When inventory is acquired for a specific customer contract that is subsequently terminated for any purpose, the carrying value of such inventory should be adjusted to reflect any loss in value.

Research and Development

ASC 730 (Research and Development) contains GAAP relevant to inventory expense allocation. Inventories of supplies used in research and development activities are charged to expense unless they clearly have an alternative use or can be used in future research and development projects.

When research and development activities consume goods, supplies, or materials from other sources within an organization, the carrying value of such inventory is charged to research and development expense. Goods produced by research and development activities that may be used in the regular inventory of the organization may be transferred physically to regular inventory, at which time a credit in the amount of the costs assigned to the goods should be made to research and development.

Intercompany Profits

Regardless of any noncontrolling interest, all intercompany profits in inventory are eliminated for consolidated financial statements and investments in common stocks accounted for by the equity method.

Long-Term Construction-Type Contracts

The construction in progress account used in both the completed contract and percentage-of-completion methods of accounting for long-term construction-type contracts is an inventory account.

Income Taxes

Inventories accounted differently for financial accounting and tax purposes may create temporary differences for which the recognition of deferred taxes may be necessary.

Accounting Change

An accounting change involving inventories in interim or annual reports necessitates accounting for the cumulative effect of the change and/or restatement of prior-period reports, including certain required pro forma information in accordance with ASC 250 (Accounting Changes and Error Corrections).

Nonmonetary Exchanges

A nonmonetary exchange of inventory held for sale in the ordinary course of business for similar property to be held for the same purpose does not complete the earnings process and no gain or loss is recognized. The inventory received in the nonmonetary exchange should be recorded at the book value of the inventory surrendered, unless cash is also involved in the transaction, in accordance with ASC 845 (Nonmonetary Transactions).

Inventory Profits

Profits from the sale of inventory, whose cost and selling price have increased significantly since acquisition, may include *ghost profits* or *inventory profits*. These profits are abnormal, because the cost to replace the inventory has increased significantly and the normal gross profit on the inventory is considerably less than the gross profit containing the ghost or inventory profits.

During periods of rapid inflation, a significant portion of reported net income of a business may actually be ghost or inventory profits. The use of the LIFO method for pricing inventories may offset part or all of any ghost or inventory profits, because current purchases or production costs are matched against current revenue, leaving the earliest inventory on hand.

Certain publicly held companies are encouraged by the SEC to disclose in a supplemental statement the current replacement cost for cost of goods sold, inventories, and resulting ghost or inventory profits.

DISCLOSURE

The general disclosure requirements for inventories are:

- A description of accounting principles used and the methods of applying those principles (ASC 235-10-50-3).
- Any accounting principles or methods that are peculiar to a particular industry (ASC 235-10-50-3).
- Classification of inventories (ASC 330-10-50-1).
- Basis of pricing inventories (ASC 330-10-50-1).

Businesses that depend on a limited number of sources for raw material or inventory or upon precarious sources (labor problems, foreign governments, etc.) should disclose the pertinent facts in their financial statements or footnotes thereto.

PART II: INTERPRETIVE GUIDANCE

ASC 330-10: OVERALL

ASC 330-10-55-2 Recognition of Inventory Market Declines at Interim Reporting Dates

BACKGROUND

A company has inventory whose market price has declined below its cost in an interim period. Although economic projections indicate that prices will not recover in the near term, there is considerable uncertainty about the accuracy of such projections.

ACCOUNTING ISSUE

Should a company account for a decline in the market price of its inventory below cost during an interim period if it is uncertain whether the market price will recover in the near term?

ACCOUNTING GUIDANCE

Under the provisions of ASC 270, the value of inventory should be reduced to the lower of cost or market during an interim period unless (1) there is strong evidence that market prices will recover before the inventory is sold or that (2) inventory accounted for by the LIFO method will regain its value by year-end unless a decline in market prices is the result of seasonal price fluctuations, the value of the inventory generally should be reduced.

DISCUSSION

This Issue was raised in an attempt to clarify the language in ASC 270-20-45-6 related to the recognition of market declines in interim periods if there is a *reasonable* expectation that prices will recover in the fiscal year. It states that "*[t]emporary* market declines need not be recognized at the interim date since no loss is expected to be incurred in the fiscal year." This referred to SEC SAB-59 (Views on Accounting for Noncurrent Marketable Equity Securities), which states that the SEC staff does not believe that the term *other than temporary*, as used in the guidance in ASC 320 should be interpreted to mean *permanent impairment* as used elsewhere in accounting practice. The conclusion on this Issue appears to indicate that the Emerging Issues Task Force was unwilling to interpret the language in ASC 270 to mean anything other than what it says, and that positive evidence of recovery is necessary to avoid a write-down rather than uncertainty that the decline will be permanent

ASC 330-10-55-3 through 55-4 Uniform Capitalization Rules for Inventory under the Tax Reform Act of 1986

BACKGROUND

Under the Tax Reform Act of 1986, manufacturers of products and wholesalers and retailers of goods for resale are required to capitalize certain direct costs and a portion of indirect costs related to the inventory produced or acquired for resale. Examples of such costs are excess tax depreciation over depreciation for financial reporting purposes, warehousing costs, insurance premiums, certain personnel costs, and costs related to accounting and data services operations for inventory. Previously, such costs were charged to expense for financial reporting and tax purposes.

ACCOUNTING ISSUES

- Are the types of costs required to be allocated to inventories for tax purposes capitalizable for financial reporting purposes under generally accepted accounting principles?
- If so, would a new costing method be a preferable method for justifying a change in accounting method?

ACCOUNTING GUIDANCE

It may not be preferable or appropriate to capitalize costs for reporting purposes that are capitalizable for tax purposes. However, some costs capitalized for tax purposes also may qualify to be capitalized for financial reporting purposes, depending on such factors as the nature of an entity's operations and industry practice. An entity should decide whether to capitalize or expense such costs based on an analysis of the individual facts and circumstances.

ASC 330-10-S35-2; ASC 420-10-S45-2, S99-3 Classification of Inventory Markdowns and Other Costs Associated with a Restructuring

BACKGROUND

A previous pronouncement, which was superseded by ASC 420 provided guidance on the timing of liability recognition related to exit or restructuring costs. It also provided guidance on the types of costs that could be accrued when an exit or restructuring plan is adopted. It did not specifically address asset impairments that might result from an exit plan, nor did it provide guidance as to whether a liability for such costs should be presented in the income statement with restructuring charges.

ACCOUNTING ISSUE

Should inventory markdowns associated with an exit plan or a restructuring activity be classified in the income statement as a cost of goods sold or as an exit or restructuring cost?

ACCOUNTING GUIDANCE

Although no guidance was provided on this Issue, it was noted that disclosure of the amount of inventory markdowns related to an exit plan or restructuring activity may be appropriate, regardless of how the inventory markdowns are classified.

SEC OBSERVER COMMENT

During the discussion of this Issue, the SEC Observer stated that the SEC staff prefers classification of such inventory markdowns as a cost of goods sold in the income statement. Subsequently, the SEC Observer reiterated that the staff's preference is based on the view that (a) it is difficult to distinguish inventory markdowns due to a decision to restructure a business or to exit an activity from markdowns caused by external market conditions that are independent of that decision, and (b) decisions about the timing, method, and pricing of inventory dispositions are normal recurring activities related to the management of an ongoing business.

CHAPTER 23
ASC 340—DEFERRED COSTS AND OTHER ASSETS

CONTENTS

Interpretive Guidance	23,001
ASC 340-10: Overall	23,001
ASC 340-10-05-6, 25-1 through 3, S50-1, 55-2 through 55-5, S99-3; ASC 460-10-60-2; ASC 730-10-60-1	
Accounting for Pre-Production Costs Related to Long-Term Supply Arrangements	23,001
ASC 340-20: Capitalized Advertising Costs	23,003
ASC 340-20-05-2, 15-3 through 15-4, 25-1 through 25-4, 25-6, 25-8 through 25-16, 30-2, 35-1 through 35-6, 45-1, 50-1, 55-1; ASC 720-35-05-1 through 05-5, 15-2 through 15-4; 25-1 through 25-6, 35-1, 50-1, 55-1; ASC 958-720-25-5	
Reporting on Advertising Costs	23,003
ASC 340-20-25-17 through 25-18, 35-7	
Direct-Response Advertising and Probable Future Benefits	23,008

INTERPRETIVE GUIDANCE

ASC 340-10: OVERALL

ASC 340-10-05-6, 25-1 through 3, S50-1, 55-2 through 55-5, S99-3; ASC 460-10-60-2; ASC 730-10-60-1 Accounting for Pre-Production Costs Related to Long-Term Supply Arrangements

BACKGROUND

Manufacturers that supply parts to original equipment manufacturers (OEMs), such as manufacturers of automobiles, often incur pre-production costs associated with the design and development of products they will manufacture for their customers. They incur pre-production engineering costs—for example, in designing, developing, and building molds, dies, and other tools—which will be used in manufacturing parts such as seats and instrument panels for automobiles. Those costs are referred to in the Issue as *tooling costs*.

Eligibility to be awarded a contract to supply *production parts* to the automotive industry includes the capability to produce the tooling used to manufacture the parts. Although suppliers begin pre-production activities and incur tooling costs several years before actual production begins, they do so only after they have been awarded a contract to produce specific parts for a specific car or model, approximately two to five years before production begins.

Suppliers recover tooling costs in several ways. An OEM may be contractually obligated to pay the supplier a guaranteed amount for tooling costs, which is included in the price of each part purchased; the OEM may agree to pay the supplier a lump sum for those costs; or if there is no specific agreement for reimbursement, the supplier may include those costs in the price of each part. Even if there is no contractual reimbursement arrangement, OEMs have historically compensated their suppliers for tooling costs if a program terminates early or the number of units purchased is less than expected.

Although this Issue is discussed in terms of the automotive industry, a consensus would also apply to other industries with similar production arrangements.

ACCOUNTING ISSUES

1. How should an entity account for costs incurred to design and develop products sold under long-term supply arrangements?
2. How should an entity account for costs incurred to design and develop molds, dies, and other tools used in producing products sold under long-term supply arrangements?
3. Should customer reimbursement for design and development costs affect the supplier's accounting for such costs?

ACCOUNTING GUIDANCE

1. Suppliers should expense design and development costs for products sold under long-term supply contracts as they are incurred.
2. Design and development costs for molds, dies, and other tools used in producing products under long-term supply contracts should be accounted for as follows:
    a. Capitalize as part of the cost of molds, dies, and other tools (subject to the impairment test in ASC 360-10), that are *owned* by the supplier and will be used to produce products under long-term supply arrangements.
    b. Capitalize as part of the cost of molds, dies, and other tools (subject to impairment test in ASC 360-10) that are *not owned* by the supplier and will be used to produce products under long-term supply arrangements if the supplier has a *noncancelable* right under the arrangement (as long as the supplier is performing under the terms of the arrangement) to use the molds, dies, and other tools during the supply arrangement.
    c. Expense design and development costs of *nonowned* molds, dies, and other tools as incurred if the supplier does *not* have a noncancelable right to use the molds, dies, and other tools during the supply arrangement.
    d. Expense as incurred in accordance with the guidance in ASC 730-10-05-1, 05-25, 05-50. 05-55 if design and development costs are for owned or not owned molds, dies, and other tools that involve new technology.

3. Recognize design and development costs as assets as incurred if the supplier has a *contractual guarantee* for reimbursement of those costs. That is, the guarantee is included in a legally enforceable supply arrangement that provides criteria (e.g., a maximum total amount or a specific amount per part) for the objective measurement and verification of the reimbursement.

ASC 340-20: CAPITALIZED ADVERTISING COSTS

ASC 340-20-05-2, 15-3 through 15-4, 25-1 through 25-4, 25-6, 25-8 through 25-16, 30-2, 35-1 through 35-6, 45-1, 50-1, 55-1; ASC 720-35-05-1 through 05-5, 15-2 through 15-4; 25-1 through 25-6, 35-1, 50-1, 55-1; ASC 958-720-25-5 Reporting on Advertising Costs

BACKGROUND

Before the issuance of the guidance in ASC 340, there was no broad authoritative guidance on the treatment of advertising costs. Entities accounted for these costs in diverse ways. Some entities charged advertising expenditures to expense as incurred. Other entities, believing that advertising created a probable future economic benefit that was sufficiently measurable, capitalized these costs and amortized them against future revenues.

Advertising is defined as the promotion of an industry, company, brand, product name, or specific product or service for the purpose of improving an entity's image and/or increasing future revenues. Advertising is typically distributed via one or more media outlets (e.g., television, radio, magazines, direct mail).

ACCOUNTING GUIDANCE

In most cases, the costs of advertising should be expensed as incurred or the first time the advertisement appears. There are two exceptions to this general rule. First, entities are to capitalize certain direct-response advertising. Second, expenditures for advertising costs that are made subsequent to the recognition of revenues related to those costs are to be capitalized and charged to expense when the related revenues are recognized. For example, some entities enter into an arrangement whereby they are responsible for reimbursing some or all of their customers' advertising costs. In most cases, revenues related to the transactions creating these obligations are earned before the reimbursements are made. The entity responsible for reimbursing advertising expenditures would recognize a liability and the related advertising expense concurrently with the recognition of revenue.

There are two general types of advertising costs: the costs of producing advertisements and the costs of communicating them. Costs of communicating advertisements should not be expensed until the dissemination service has been received. For example, the costs of purchasing television or radio airtime should not be expensed until the advertisement is aired (the costs of communicating certain direct-response advertisements will be charged to expense as the advertising benefit is received).

Illustration of Expensing Advertising Costs

Ace Motor Company plans to introduce a series of new cars (the A series). Ace Motor agrees to reimburse dealerships for advertising costs they incur during January of 20X5 to promote this new series of cars. The reimbursement rate is set at 20% of the value of orders placed by the dealership for cars in the A series (up to 50% of the advertising costs incurred by the dealership). Russell Ace, a dealership in Waterbury, Connecticut, incurs $100,000 of advertising costs during January 20X5 and places $300,000 of orders for cars from the A series during that month. When the automobiles are shipped, Ace Motor will record $300,000 of revenue. Concurrently with recognizing the revenue, Ace Motor is to record a liability and a charge to advertising expense for $50,000 (Ace's reimbursement obligation to the Russell Ace dealership).

Direct-Response Advertising

Direct-response advertising must meet two conditions in order to be capitalized. First, the primary purpose of the advertising must be to generate sales, and these sales must be capable of being traced specifically to the advertising. Second, the direct-response advertising must result in probable future economic benefits.

Generation of Sales and Traceability to Direct-Response Advertising

In order for the costs of direct-response advertising to be capitalized, sales derived therefrom must be traceable directly to the advertising. The entity must maintain records that identify customers making purchases and the advertisement that customers responded to. Acceptable documentation includes the following examples:

4. Files indicating customer names and the applicable direct-response advertisement

5. A coded order form, coupon, or response card, included with an advertisement that includes the customer name

6. A log of customers placing phone orders in response to a number appearing in an advertisement, linking those calls to the advertisement

Illustration of Direct-Response Advertising

Fantastic Systems, Inc., has developed a new product—an aerobic exercise machine called the Air Flyer. In order to elicit sales of this product, Fantastic Systems produces a 30-minute infomercial. Fantastic Systems has obtained a unique toll-free telephone number to facilitate sales that result from the airing of this infomercial. This toll-free number is displayed frequently throughout the infomercial. Assuming this infomercial results in probable future economic benefits to Fantastic Systems (discussed below in the section titled "Probable Future Economic Benefits of Direct-Response Advertising"), the cost of producing and airing this infomercial would be capitalizable as direct-response advertising. Given the targeted toll-free number used, the resultant sales and the customer names can be traced to a specific advertisement (i.e., the infomercial).

Certain advertising costs may be related to a direct-response advertising campaign and yet still not be capitalizable. If the subsequent sale cannot be traced to the direct-response advertising, the related advertising costs cannot be capitalized.

Illustration of Advertising Costs Not Capitalized

Fleet Foot, Inc., a large athletic-shoe manufacturer, incurs costs to produce and air a television advertisement for a new running shoe. The commercial states that order forms, with discount coupons, will soon be distributed to certain consumers (this is the direct-response advertisement). The costs of producing and airing the television commercial are not capitalizable, since there is no link between subsequent sales and the television commercial. However, the cost of producing and distributing the order forms would be capitalizable (assuming this direct-response advertisement provided Fleet Foot with future economic benefits).

Probable Future Economic Benefits of Direct-Response Advertising

Probable future economic benefits are expected future revenues from direct-response advertising minus the costs to be incurred in generating those revenues. In order for the costs of direct-response advertising to be capitalized, there must be *persuasive evidence* that the effect of the current advertising campaign will be similar to that of previous advertising campaigns that generated future economic benefits. In terms of probable future benefits, attributes to consider in evaluating the similarity between the current direct-response advertising campaign and prior campaigns include audience demographics, the advertising method, the product, and economic conditions.

A specific entity needs to base its decision about whether to capitalize direct-response advertising costs on its past results with other direct-response advertising campaigns. In the absence of prior experience with direct-response advertising, an entity cannot rely on industry statistics as support for capitalizing advertising costs. The most persuasive type of evidence in support of the capitalization of direct-response advertising costs is a prior history of similar advertising for similar products that resulted in future economic benefits. Although an entity may not have a prior history of advertising a similar product, it may have used direct-response advertising to promote a related product or service. An entity may be able to support the capitalization of direct-response advertising for the new product or service if it can document that the results from a prior advertising campaign for a related product or service are likely to be highly correlated with the current advertising campaign. Test market results may suggest that the reaction of prospective consumers to the advertising campaign for a new product or service is likely to be similar to consumer reaction to a similar campaign for a different product or service.

PRACTICE POINTER: In the absence of a high degree of correlation between a current campaign and previous advertising campaigns for other products, a success rate based on the historical ratio of successful products or services to total products or services introduced to the marketplace would not be sufficient to support capitalization.

Illustration of Capitalizing Costs of Subsequent Products

As discussed in a previous illustration, Fantastic Systems, Inc., marketed a new fitness product, the Air Flyer, via a direct-response television campaign. This product was introduced in 20X4, and the costs of the campaign were capitalized as direct-response advertising. Fantastic Systems plans to introduce a new product, the Magic Club, in 20X5. The Magic Club, which is a new type of golf club, clearly represents a different product than the Air Flyer. On the basis of test market results, however, Fantastic Systems believes that there will be a high degree of correlation between the response of consumers to the ads for the Air Flyer and the response to the ads for the Magic Club. Therefore, Fantastic Systems can capitalize the costs of producing and distributing an infomercial for the Magic Club.

Direct-response advertising that is not capitalized, because future economic benefits are uncertain, should not be retroactively capitalized if future results indicate that the advertisement did produce economic benefits.

Measurement of the Costs of Direct-Response Advertising

Each separate direct-response advertising campaign that meets the capitalization criteria represents a *separate stand-alone cost pool*.

The costs of direct-response advertising that should be capitalized include both of the following:

- Incremental direct costs of direct-response advertising incurred in transactions with independent third parties (e.g., idea development, writing advertising copy, artwork, printing, magazine space, and mailing).

- Payroll and payroll-related costs for the direct-response advertising activities of employees who are directly associated with and devote time to the advertising reported as assets (e.g., idea development, writing advertising copy, artwork, printing, and mailing). The costs of payroll and fringe benefits for these employees should be capitalized only to the extent of the time spent working on the particular advertising project (i.e., if 10% of an employee's time is spent working on a direct-response advertising campaign that is subject to capitalization, 10% of that employee's compensation and fringe benefit costs would be included among the costs to be capitalized).

If the criteria for capitalization are met, the entire cost of the direct-response campaign, not just a pro rata share of the cost based on the expected response rate of consumers to the campaign, is capitalizable. For example, an entity distributes one million order forms and coupons to target customers and expects to receive 10,000 orders as a result of this mailing. In this case, orders can be directly traced to the advertisement. If this advertising campaign is likely to generate future economic benefits, the cost of the entire mailing campaign should be capitalized (not just the cost of mailing to the 10,000 individuals who are likely to place an order).

Amortization of Capitalized Advertising Costs

Amortization of direct-response advertising costs for a particular cost pool is as follows: Current Period Revenues Attributable to the Direct-Response Advertising Cost Pool/(Current Period Revenues Attributable to the Direct-Response Advertising Cost Pool + Estimated Future Revenues Attributable to the Direct-Response Advertising Cost Pool). Estimated future revenues may change over time, and the amortization ratio is to be recalculated each period.

Direct-response advertising costs are typically amortized over a period of not more than one year or one operating cycle. This suggests that future revenues attributable to the advertisement are limited to those likely to result within the next year (or within the next operating cycle). This recommendation is based on the view that the reliability of future revenue estimates decreases as the length of time for which such estimates are made increases. However, a possible exception to this general recommendation is illustrated below.

Illustration of Amortizing Advertising Costs

An entity undertakes a direct-response advertising campaign, via a series of television commercials and a dedicated toll-free number, to sell classic works of literature (e.g., *Moby Dick* and *A Tale of Two Cities*). Because sales can be tied directly to the advertisement, the costs of this campaign will be capitalized if the campaign is likely to generate probable future economic benefits. For this entity such benefits exist. Customers who buy the first book are sent a response card on a monthly basis thereafter, asking them if they would like to order another book in the set (there are 24 books in the collection). These future advertising efforts (mailing the response card on a monthly basis) are viewed as minimal. The entity also knows that a certain percentage of the customers who buy the first book will buy a quantifiable percentage of the remaining books. In this case, the amortization ratio used will include total revenues expected from all sales, including an estimate of future book sales. If a significant advertising effort was necessary for each book sold, however, each of these advertising efforts would be treated separately—in terms of both initial capitalization and subsequent amortization.

Assessment of Realizability of Capitalized Advertising Costs

The realizability of capitalized direct-response advertising costs should be evaluated at each reporting date on a cost-pool-by-cost-pool basis. The unamortized direct-response advertising costs are to be compared to probable future *net revenues* that are expected to be generated directly from such advertising. *Net revenues* are gross revenues less costs to be incurred in generating those revenues, excluding the amortization of advertising costs. Examples of costs to be included in making this evaluation are cost of goods sold, sales commissions, and payroll and payroll-related costs.

ASC 340—Deferred Costs and Other Assets

If the carrying amount of unamortized direct-response advertising exceeds probable future net revenues, the difference should be charged to advertising expense in the current period.

Illustration of Write-Off of Unamortized Advertising Costs

MMX Enterprises has $400,000 of unamortized direct-response advertising costs at December 31, 20X5; probable future net revenues are $300,000. This difference—$100,000—would be reported as advertising expense in 20X5.

Any later-period increase in probable future net revenue cannot be used to increase the carrying amount of the unamortized advertising costs (i.e., the write-down cannot be reversed on the basis of a subsequent increase in probable net revenues).

Miscellaneous Issues

Certain tangible assets (e.g., blimps and billboards) may be used in a number of different advertising campaigns. These tangible assets should be capitalized and depreciated over their estimated useful lives. The related depreciation charge is a cost of advertising to the extent that the tangible asset has been used for an advertising-related purpose.

Costs to produce a film, audio, or a video that is used as a vehicle for an advertisement do not constitute tangible assets under this guidance. Sales materials, such as brochures and catalogs, should be classified as prepaid supplies until they are no longer owned or expected to be used. At that point, the related cost would be considered a cost of advertising.

Disclosures

The notes to the financial statements should contain the following disclosures:

- The accounting policy selected for non-direct-response advertising costs. The two choices are to (a) expense these costs as incurred or (b) expense them the first time the advertising takes place.
- A description of the direct-response advertising reported as assets (if any), the related accounting policy, and the amortization period.
- The total amount charged to advertising expense for each income statement presented, with a separate disclosure (if any) of amounts representing a write-down to net realizable value.
- The total amount of advertising expenditures reported as an asset for each balance sheet presented.

ASC 340-20-25-17 through 25-18, 35-7 Direct-Response Advertising and Probable Future Benefits

BACKGROUND

Under the provisions of ASC 340 and ASC 720, a direct-response advertisement must provide an entity with probable future economic benefits in order for the related advertising costs to be capitalized. In determining whether an advertisement provides an entity with probable future economic benefits, an entity estimates future revenues (derived from the advertisement) less costs incurred in generating those revenues. There has been diversity in practice as to which revenues are considered in making this determination.

Some entities have limited their consideration of future revenues to primary revenues, that is, revenues derived from sales to customers receiving and responding to a direct-response advertisement. Other entities have taken a more expansive view of the appropriate revenues to consider. Those entities consider both primary and secondary revenues in evaluating whether an advertisement provides probable future economic benefits. Secondary revenues are revenues other than those derived from sales to customers receiving and responding to a direct-response advertisement. For example, revenues that publishers receive from magazine subscriptions are considered primary revenues. Revenues resulting from advertisements placed in the magazine are considered secondary revenues.

ACCOUNTING GUIDANCE

In determining probable future revenues, an entity should consider only primary revenues—that is, revenues expected from customers who receive and respond to a direct-response advertisement. In addition, only primary revenues should be considered for the purpose of amortizing capitalized direct-response advertising costs and for assessing whether those costs, which are reported as assets, will be realized.

CHAPTER 24
ASC 350—INTANGIBLES—GOODWILL AND OTHER

CONTENTS

Part I: General Guidance	24,002
ASC 350-10: Overall	24,002
Overview	24,002
Background	24,002
Identifiability	24,003
Manner of Acquisition	24,003
Determinate or Indeterminate Life	24,003
Transferability	24,003
Cost of Intangibles	24,003
Scope	24,003
Not-for-Profit Enterprises	24,004
ASC 350-20: Goodwill	24,005
Accounting for Goodwill	24,005
Fair Value Measurements	24,005
Testing for Impairment	24,005
Assigning Assets and Liabilities to Reporting Units	24,007
Assigning Goodwill to Reporting Units	24,007
Subsidiary Goodwill	24,007
Disposal of a Reporting Unit	24,008
Testing for Impairment and Disposal of a Reporting Unit When the Reporting Unit Is Less than Wholly Owned	24,008
Financial Statement Presentation and Disclosure of Goodwill	24,008
ASC 350-30: General Intangibles Other Than Goodwill	24,009
Accounting for Intangible Assets Other Than Goodwill	24,009
Initial Recognition and Measurement	24,009
Accounting Subsequent to Acquisition	24,009
Intangible Assets Subject to Amortization	24,009
Intangible Assets Not Subject to Amortization	24,009
Financial Statement Presentation and Disclosure	24,012
Important Notice for 2014	24,014
Part II: Interpretive Guidance	24,014
ASC 350-20: Goodwill	24,014
ASC 350-20-35-7, 35-25 through 35-26, 35-20, 35-21, 55-10 through 55-16, 55-18 through 55-23	
Deferred Income Tax Considerations in Applying the Goodwill Impairment Test in ASC 350, Intangibles—Goodwill and Other	24,014
ASC 350-20-35-6, 35-8A, 35-30; ASC 350-10-65-2	
When to Perform Step 2 of the Goodwill Impairment Test for Reporting Units with Zero or Negative Carrying Amounts	24,016

ASC 350-20-55-1 through 55-9
   Clarification of Reporting Unit Guidance in ASC 350-20-35-34 through 35-35 24,017
ASC 350-30: General Intangibles Other Than Goodwill 24,018
ASC 350-30-15-5, 25-5, 35-5A through 35-5B, 55-1 through 55-1B, 55-28H through 55-28I, 55-28K through 55-28L, 65-2
   Accounting for Defensive Intangible Assets 24,018
ASC 350-30-35-21 through 35-28, 35-30 through 35-32, 35-34 through 35-35, 35-37 through 35-38
   Unit of Accounting for Testing Impairment of Indefinite-Lived Intangible Assets 24,019
ASC 350-30-50-4 through 50-5, 55-1(c), 65-1; ASC 275-10-50-15A
   Determination of the Useful Life of Intangible Assets 24,021
ASC 350-40: Internal-Use Software 24,023
ASC 350-10-05-6, 40-05-2 through 05-6, 05-8, 05-9, 15-2 through 15-7, 25-1 through 25-16, 30-1 through 30-4, 35-1 through 35-10, 50-1, 55-1 through 55-4; ASC 730-10-60-2; 985-20-60-1
   Accounting for Costs of Computer Software Developed or Obtained for Internal Use 24,023
ASC 350-50: Website Development Costs 24,026
ASC 350-10-05-7; ASC 350-50-15-2 through 15-3, 25-2 through 25-17, 55-2 through 55-9
   Accounting for Web Site Development Costs 24,026

PART I: GENERAL GUIDANCE

ASC 350-10: OVERALL

OVERVIEW

Intangible assets are long-lived assets used in the production of goods and services. They are similar to property, plant, and equipment except for their lack of physical properties. Examples of intangible assets include copyrights, patents, trademarks, and goodwill. Intangible assets with finite lives are subject to amortization over their estimated useful lives. Assets with indefinite useful lives are not amortized. Each period these assets are tested annually for impairment and also to determine whether the assumption of an indefinite useful life is still valid. If the asset's life is determined to have become limited, it is amortized prospectively over its remaining useful life.

BACKGROUND

The term *intangible asset* refers to non-financial assets that lack physical substance and that provide the entity with various benefits. Intangible assets differ considerably in their characteristics, useful lives, and relationship to operations of an enterprise.

ASC 350 requires the separation of intangible assets into two categories—those with finite useful lives, which are amortized, and those with indefinite useful lives, which are not amortized.

The following are some of the basic principles upon which accounting for intangible assets in accordance with ASC 350 is based.

Identifiability

Patents, copyrights, franchises, trademarks, and other similar intangible assets can be specifically identified with reasonably descriptive names. Other types of intangible assets lack specific identification, the most common being goodwill.

Manner of Acquisition

Intangible assets may be purchased or developed internally and may be acquired singly, in groups, or in business combinations.

Determinate or Indeterminate Life

Patents, copyrights, and most franchises are examples of intangible assets with determinate lives, established by law or by contract. Other intangible assets, such as secret processes and goodwill, have no established term of existence, and the expected period of benefit may be indeterminate at the time of acquisition.

Transferability

The rights to a patent, copyright, or franchise can be identified separately and bought or sold. Goodwill, on the other hand, is inseparable from a business and is transferable only as an inseparable intangible asset of an enterprise.

Cost of Intangibles

A company records as assets the costs of intangible assets acquired from other enterprises or individuals. The cost of an intangible asset is measured by (*a*) the amount of cash disbursed or the fair value of other assets distributed, (*b*) the present value of amounts to be paid for liabilities incurred, and (*c*) the fair value of consideration received for stock issued.

Scope

ASC 350 covers the following aspects of accounting and reporting for intangible assets:

- Intangible assets acquired individually or with a group of assets other than in a business combination
- Intangible assets, including goodwill recognized in accordance with ASC 805 (Business Combinations) or ASC 958 (Not-for-Profit Entities), subsequent to their acquisition (ASC 350-30-15-3)

Intangible assets acquired in a business combination are covered in ASC 805. ASC 350 does not change accounting that is prescribed in the following pronouncements (ASC 350-10-15-4):

- ASC 730 (Research and Development)
- ASC 740 (Income Taxes)
- ASC 860 (Transfers and Servicing)
- ASC 920 (Entertainment—Broadcasters)
- ASC 928 (Entertainment—Music)
- ASC 932 (Extractive Industries—Oil and Gas)
- ASC 950 (Financial Services—Title Plant)
- ASC 980 (Regulated Operations)
- ASC 985 (Software)

NOT-FOR-PROFIT ENTERPRISES

ASC 350 shall be applied to previously recognized goodwill and intangible assets acquired in a combination between not-for-profit organizations or arising from the acquisition of a for-profit business by a not-for-profit organization as of the beginning of the initial or first annual reporting period beginning on or after December 15, 2009.

A NFP entity that is predominantly supported by contributions and returns on investments shall write off previously recognized goodwill by a separate charge in the statement of activities as the effect of the accounting change (net of tax) (ASC 350-10-65-1).

A NFP that is not predominantly supported by contributions and returns on investments shall establish its reporting units based on the guidance provided in ASC 350. The entity's recognized net assets, including previously recognized goodwill, shall be assigned to these reporting units (ASC 350-10-65-1). After the entity establishes its reporting units, the entity needs to test whether the recognized goodwill amount is impaired at transition using the ASC 350 guidance. Any goodwill impairment recognized is reflected as a change in accounting principle (net of tax) and displayed on the statement of activities between extraordinary items and change in net assets (ASC 350-10-65-1). A transitional goodwill impairment loss is not to be included within a performance indicator (ASC 350-10-65-1). In addition, a transitional goodwill impairment loss is to be presented in the first interim period even if the impairment loss is determined in a later period (i.e., early interim periods would be restated) (ASC 350-10-65-1).

In addition to evaluating previously recognized goodwill for impairment, the entity should also evaluate any previously recognized intangible assets that were recorded using previously effective accounting guidance. In some cases, the useful life of an intangible asset might be longer than the 40-year maximum permitted by previously effective accounting guidance and, as such, the carrying value of the asset should be adjusted to reflect the new useful life. In addition, the entity should evaluate whether any previously recognized intangible asset is impaired. Any impairment loss is displayed in the same manner as a transitional goodwill impairment loss (ASC 350-10-65-1).

ASC 350-20: GOODWILL

ACCOUNTING FOR GOODWILL

The costs of intangible assets that are developed internally as well as the costs of maintaining or restoring intangible assets that have indeterminate lives or that are inherent in a continuing business or nonprofit activity and related to the entity as a whole, are expensed as incurred (ASC 350-20-25-3).

Goodwill is not amortized and is tested for impairment at a level of reporting referred to as a reporting unit (ASC 350-20-35-1). A reporting unit is an operating segment or one level below an operating segment (referred to as a component) as defined in ASC 280 (Segment Reporting). A component of an operating segment is a reporting unit if the component constitutes a business or nonprofit activity for which discrete financial information is available and segment management regularly reviews the operating results of that component. Two or more components of an operating segment shall be aggregated and treated as a single reporting unit if the components have similar operating characteristics. An operating segment is deemed to be a reporting unit if (1) all of its components are similar, (2) none of its components is a reporting unit, or (3) if it comprises only a single component (ASC 350-20-35-34, 35, 36).

Fair Value Measurements

The fair value of an asset or liability is the amount at which that asset or liability could be bought or incurred, or sold or settled, in a current transaction—other than a forced liquidation—between willing parties. Quoted market prices are the best evidence of fair value. If quoted market prices are not available, an estimate of fair value should be based on the best information available. This may involve prices of similar assets and liabilities and the use of other valuation techniques, such as a present value technique. An estimate of fair value may be based on multiples of earnings or revenue or another similar performance measure if that technique is consistent with the objectives of measuring fair value (ASC 350-20-35-22, 24).

Testing for Impairment

Goodwill is tested for impairment on an annual basis, or more frequently if events and circumstances change (ASC 350-20-35-28). An entity should use a two-step impairment test to identify potential goodwill impairment. However, before applying the two-step impairment test, an entity may first consider qualitative factors to determine if the two-step test is even necessary (ASC 350-20-35-3). This optional qualitative assessment is used to determine whether it is more likely than not (i.e., a likelihood of more than 50 percent) that the fair value of a reporting unit is less than its carrying amount, including goodwill. In making this determination, an entity must assess relevant events and circumstances including, but not limited to, the following (ASC 350-20-35-3C):

1. Macroeconomic conditions
   a. Deterioration in general economic conditions
   b. Limitations on accessing capital
   c. Fluctuations in foreign exchange rates
   d. Other developments in equity and credit markets

2. Industry and market considerations
    a. Deterioration in the environment in which an entity operates
    b. Increased competitive environment
    c. Decline in market-dependent multiples or metrics
    d. Change in the market for an entity's products or services
    e. Regulatory or political development
3. Cost factors such as increases in raw materials, labor, or other costs that have a negative effect on earnings or cash flows
4. Overall financial performance
    a. Negative or declining cash flows
    b. Decline in actual or planned revenue or earnings
5. Other relevant entity-specific events
    a. Changes in management, key personnel, strategy, or customers
    b. Contemplation of bankruptcy
    c. Litigation
6. Events affecting a reporting unit
    a. Change in the composition or carrying amount of its net assets
    b. A more-likely-than-not expectation of selling or disposing all, or a portion, of a reporting unit
    c. Testing for recoverability of a significant asset group within a reporting unit
    d. Recognition of a goodwill impairment loss in the financial statements of a subsidiary that is a component of a reporting unit
7. If applicable, a sustained decrease in share price

These examples of events to be considered are not all-inclusive and an entity must consider the extent to which each of the adverse events identified could affect the comparison of a reporting unit's fair value with its carrying amount. An entity should also consider positive and mitigating events that may affect the determination of whether it is more likely than not that an impairment exists (ASC 350-20-35-3F).

If, after considering the totality of the events and circumstances such as those listed above, an entity determines that it is not more likely than not that the fair value of a reporting unit is less than its carrying amount, then the two-step impairment test is not necessary. However, if an entity determines that it is more likely than not that the fair value of the reporting entity is less than its carrying amount, the entity must perform the two-step impairment test as follows (ASC 350-20-35-4, 9):

Step 1: Identify potential impairment by comparing the fair value of a reporting unit with its carrying amount, including goodwill.

Step 2: Measure the amount of goodwill loss by comparing the implied fair value of the reporting unit goodwill with the carrying amount of that goodwill and recognize a loss by the excess of the latter over the former.

The implied fair value of goodwill is determined in the same way that goodwill is recognized in a business combination or in an acquisition involving a not-for-profit entity. The entity assigns the fair value of a reporting unit to all the assets and liabilities of that unit as if the reporting unit had been acquired in a business combination or in an acquisition involving a not-for-profit entity. The excess of the fair value of the unit over the amounts assigned to its other assets and its liabilities is the implied fair value of goodwill. That process is performed only for purposes of testing goodwill for impairment. The entity shall neither write up nor write down a recognized asset or liability, nor should it recognize a previously unrecognized intangible asset as a result of the allocation process (ASC 350-20-35-14, 17).

If the determination of the amount of loss due to the impairment of goodwill is not complete when the financial statements are issued and a goodwill impairment loss is considered probable and can be reasonably estimated, the best estimate of that loss shall be recognized in the financial statements (ASC 350-20-35-18).

Assigning Assets and Liabilities to Reporting Units

For purposes of testing goodwill impairment, acquired assets and assumed liabilities are assigned to a reporting unit if both of the following criteria are met:

- The asset will be employed in, or the liability relates to, the operations of a reporting unit.

- The asset or liability will be considered in determining the fair value of the reporting unit.

Assets and liabilities may be employed in the operations of more than one reporting unit. The method used to determine the amount of such assets and liabilities to be assigned to a reporting unit must be reasonable and supported, and applied consistently (ASC 350-20-35-39, 40).

Assigning Goodwill to Reporting Units

For purposes of testing goodwill for impairment, all goodwill that is acquired in a business combination or in an acquisition involving a not-for-profit entity must be assigned to one or more reporting units as of the acquisition date. Goodwill is assigned to reporting units on the basis of expected benefits from the synergies of the combination, even though other assets or liabilities of the acquired entity may not be assigned to those reporting units. Goodwill may be divided among multiple reporting units, and the method of allocating goodwill must be reasonable and supportable, and applied consistently (ASC 350-20-35-41).

Subsidiary Goodwill

Goodwill recognized by a public or nonpublic subsidiary in its separate financial statements prepared in accordance with GAAP shall be accounted for in accordance with ASC 350. Such subsidiary goodwill shall be tested for impairment in accordance with ASC 350 using the subsidiary's reporting unit. If a goodwill impairment loss is recognized at the subsidiary level, goodwill of the reporting unit(s), at which the subsidiary resides, must be tested for impairment if the event that gave rise to the loss at the subsidiary level would more likely than not reduce the fair value of the reporting unit below its carrying amount (ASC 350-20-35-48).

Disposal of a Reporting Unit

When a reporting unit is to be disposed of in its entirety, goodwill of that unit shall be included in the carrying amount of the reporting unit in determining any gain or loss on disposal. When a portion of a reporting unit that constitutes a business or nonprofit activity is to be disposed of, goodwill associated with that business or nonprofit activity shall be included in the carrying amount of the business or nonprofit activity in determining the gain or loss on disposal. The amount of goodwill included is based on the relative fair value of the business or nonprofit activity to be disposed of and the portion of the reporting unit that will be retained (ASC 350-20-35-51, 52, 53).

Testing for Impairment and Disposal of a Reporting Unit When the Reporting Unit Is Less than Wholly Owned

If a reporting unit is less than wholly owned, any impairment loss shall be attributed to the parent and the noncontrolling interest on a rational basis. Similarly, when all or a portion of a less-than-wholly-owned reporting unit is disposed of, the gain or loss on disposal shall be attributed to both the parent and the noncontrolling interest (ASC 350-20-35-57, A).

Financial Statement Presentation and Disclosure of Goodwill

The aggregate amount of goodwill shall be presented as a separate line item in the statement of financial position. The aggregate amount of goodwill impairment losses shall be presented as a separate line item in the income statement (statement of activities) before the amount of income from continuing operations, unless the goodwill impairment is associated with discontinued operations, in which case the impairment loss is presented within discontinued operations (ASC 350-20-45-1, 2, 3).

For each goodwill impairment loss recognized, the following information is required to be disclosed (ASC 350-20-50-2):

- A description of the facts and circumstances leading to the impairment
- The amount of the impairment loss and the method of determining the fair value of the associated reporting unit
- If a recognized impairment loss is an estimate that has not yet been finalized, that fact and the reasons therefore and, in subsequent years, the nature and amount of any significant adjustments made to the initial estimate of the impairment loss

The quantitative disclosures about Level 3 unobservable inputs used in fair value measurements, which are required by ASC 820-10-50-2(bbb), are not required for fair value measurements related to financial accounting and reporting for goodwill after its initial recognition in a business combination (ASC 350-20-50-3).

ASC 350-30: GENERAL INTANGIBLES OTHER THAN GOODWILL

ACCOUNTING FOR INTANGIBLE ASSETS OTHER THAN GOODWILL

Initial Recognition and Measurement

Intangible assets that are acquired individually or as part of a group of assets are initially recorded at their fair value. The cost of a group of assets acquired in a transaction is allocated to the individual assets based on their relative fair values. Goodwill does not arise in such a transaction. Intangible assets, including related goodwill, that are acquired in a business combination are accounted for in accordance with ASC 805 (ASC 350-30-25-1, 2), and goodwill arising in connection with an acquisition of a nonprofit activity by a not-for-profit entity is accounted for in accordance with ASC 958 (ASC 350-30-05-1).

Accounting Subsequent to Acquisition

Intangible Assets Subject to Amortization

Intangible assets with finite useful lives are amortized over those lives. Intangible assets with indefinite useful lives are not amortized. Guidelines for determining the useful lives of intangible assets are:

- The expected use of the asset by the entity
- The expected useful life of another asset or group of assets to which the useful life of the asset in question may relate
- Legal, regulatory, or contractual provisions that may limit the asset's useful life
- Legal, regulatory, or contractual provisions that enable renewal or extension of the useful life without significant cost
- The effects of obsolescence, demand, competition, and other economic factors
- The level of maintenance expenditures required to obtain the expected future cash flows from the asset (ASC 350-30-35-3)

As asset for which no legal, regulatory, contractual, competitive, economic, or other factors limit the useful life is considered to have an indefinite, but not infinite, useful life (ASC 350-30-35-4).

The cost of a recognized intangible asset, less its residual value to the reporting entity, should be amortized over its useful life unless that life is determined to be indefinite.

The remaining amortization period, for those assets being amortized, should be reviewed at each reporting period (ASC 350-30-35-9). If the life is finite, but the precise length of that life is not known, the best estimate of the asset's useful life shall be used for amortization purposes. The method of amortization shall be the pattern in which the economic benefits are consumed or otherwise used up. If that pattern cannot be reliably determined, the straight-line method shall be used. An intangible asset should not be written off in the period of acquisition unless it is determined to be impaired during that period (ASC 350-30-35-6, 7).

An intangible asset that is subject to amortization shall be reviewed for impairment in accordance with the guidance in ASC 360.

> **PRACTICE POINTER:** An entity acquires a copyright that has a remaining legal life of 40 years. The entity expects to receive cash flows from the copyright for the next 20 years. The copyright will be amortized over the next 20 years, in a manner consistent with the benefits received from the copyright. The copyright will be reviewed for impairment using the provisions of ASC 360.

Intangible Assets Not Subject to Amortization

If an intangible asset is determined to have an indefinite useful life, it shall not be amortized until its useful life is determined to be no longer indefinite. An assessment of the useful life of an intangible asset that is not being amortized is required each reporting period to determine whether events and circumstances continue to support an indefinite useful life. If such an asset is determined to have a finite useful life, the asset shall be tested for impairment in accordance with ASC 350-30-35-18, 19. Intangible assets acquired in a business combination or in an acquisition involving a not-for-profit entity that are used in research and development activities shall be considered to have an indefinite life until the related research and development efforts end (ASC 350-30-35-15, 16, 17).

All intangible assets not subject to amortization (those with indefinite useful lives) shall be tested for impairment annually, and more frequently if events and circumstances indicate that it is more likely than not that the asset may be impaired.

However, before conducting a quantitative impairment test, an entity may first consider qualitative factors to determine if the quantitative test is even necessary. This optional qualitative assessment is used to determine whether it is more likely than not (i.e., a likelihood of more than 50 percent) that an indefinite-lived intangible asset is impaired (ASC 350-30-35-18). In making this determination, an entity must assess relevant events and circumstances including, but not limited to, the following (ASC 350-30-35-18B):

1. Cost factors such as increases in raw materials, labor, or other costs that have a negative effect on earnings or cash flows
2. Overall financial performance
    a. Negative or declining cash flows
    b. Decline in actual or planned revenue or earnings
3. Legal, regulatory, contractual, political, business, or other factors, including asset-specific factors

4. Other relevant entity-specific events
   a. Changes in management, key personnel, strategy, or customers
   b. Contemplation of bankruptcy
   c. Litigation
5. Industry and market considerations
   a. Deterioration in the environment in which an entity operates
   b. Increased competitive environment
   c. Decline in market-dependent multiples or metrics
   d. Change in the market for an entity's products or services
6. Macroeconomic conditions
   a. Deterioration in general economic conditions
   b. Limitations on accessing capital
   c. Fluctuations in foreign exchange rates
   d. Other developments in equity and credit markets

These examples of events to be considered are not all-inclusive and an entity must consider other relevant events and circumstances that could affect significant inputs used to determine the fair value of the indefinite-lived intangible asset. An entity should also consider the following to determine whether it is more likely than not that the indefinite-lived intangible asset is impaired (ASC 350-30-35-18C):

1. Positive and mitigating events and circumstances that could affect the significant inputs
2. If an entity has made a recent fair value calculation for an indefinite-lived intangible asset, the difference between that fair value and the then carrying amount
3. Whether there have been any changes to the carrying amount of the indefinite-lived intangible asset.

If, after considering the totality of events and circumstances such as those listed above, an entity determines that it is not more likely than not that the indefinite-lived asset is impaired, then the entity does not need to calculate the fair value of the asset and conduct the quantitative impairment test. However, if an entity determines that it is more likely than not that the indefinite-lived asset is impaired, the entity must calculate the fair value and conduct the quantitative impairment test (ASC 350-30-35-18E, F).

If impaired, an impairment loss is recognized in an amount equal to the excess of the asset's carrying value over its fair value. After such a loss is recognized, the adjusted carrying amount of the asset is its new accounting basis. Subsequent reversal of a previously recognized impairment loss is prohibited (ASC 350-30-35-19, 20).

PRACTICE POINTER: The remaining useful life of an intangible asset subject to amortization is reviewed each reporting period, as is the continuing status of intangible assets viewed to have an indefinite life. Conversely, unless certain events or circumstances suggest otherwise, the impairment status of intangible assets are only tested on an annual basis.

PRACTICE POINTER: Assume an entity has the rights to a broadcast license that can be renewed indefinitely. Based on a review of the relevant facts and circumstances, it appears likely that the entity will continue to renew its license for the foreseeable future and that the license will continue to have economic value and will generate positive cash flows for the entity holding the license. The cost of the broadcast license will not be amortized because the expected useful life of the license is indefinite. The broadcast license will be reviewed for impairment using the guidance in ASC 350 (ASC 350-30-35-18, 19).

PRACTICE POINTER: An entity acquired a trademark associated with a product in 20X8. At acquisition, based on the relevant facts and circumstances, the trademarked product appeared to have an indefinite life. Therefore, the cost of the trademark was not amortized. In 20Y1, the entity decided to phase out production of the trademarked product over a period of five years. The entity would first evaluate whether the trademark is impaired using the guidance in ASC 350. The carrying amount of the trademark, after any necessary impairment-related adjustment, would be amortized over the next five years. During each of the next five years, the trademark would be reviewed for impairment using the provisions of ASC 360 (since the intangible asset is now subject to periodic amortization).

Financial Statement Presentation and Disclosure

At a minimum, all intangible assets shall be combined and presented as a separate line item in the statement of financial position (balance sheet). This is not intended to preclude separate presentation of individual intangible assets or classes of intangible assets. Amortization expense and impairment losses on intangible assets are required to be presented in the income statement (statement of activities) as separate items within continuing operations (or a similar caption). An impairment loss is not recognized as a change in accounting principle (ASC 350-30-45-1, 2, 3).

In the period of acquisition, the following information is required for intangible assets acquired, whether acquired individually or as part of a group of assets (ASC 350-30-50-1):

- For intangible assets subject to amortization:
    — The total amount assigned and the amount assigned to any major intangible asset class
    — The amount of any significant residual value, in total and by major intangible asset class
    — The weighted-average amortization period in total and by major intangible asset class

- For intangible assets not subject to amortization, the total amount assigned and the amount assigned to any major intangible asset class.
- The amount of research and development assets acquired in a transaction other than a business combination and written off in the period, and the line item in the income statement in which the amounts written off are aggregated.

The following information is required in the financial statements or related notes for each period for which a statement of financial position (balance sheet) is presented (ASC 350-30-50-2):

- The gross carrying amount and accumulated amortization, in total and by major intangible asset class
- The aggregate amortization expense for the period
- The estimated aggregate amortization expense for each of the five succeeding years
- For intangible assets not subject to amortization, the total carrying amount and the carrying amount for each major intangible asset class
- Changes in the carrying amount of goodwill during the period showing separately (ASC 350-20-50-1):
    — The gross amount and accumulated impairment losses at the beginning of the period
    — Additional goodwill recognized during the period
    — Adjustments resulting from the subsequent recognition of deferred tax assets
    — Goodwill included in a disposal group classified as held for sale
    — Impairment losses recognized during the period
    — Net exchange differences recognized during the period in accordance with ASC 830 (Foreign Currency Matters)
    — Any other changes in the carrying amounts during the period
    — The gross amount and accumulated impairment losses at the end of the period

For each impairment loss recognized related to an intangible asset, the following information is required to be disclosed (ASC 350-30-50-3):

- A description of the impaired intangible asset, and the facts and circumstances leading to the impairment
- The amount of the impairment loss and the method of determining fair value
- The caption in the income statement (or the statement of activities) in which the impairment loss is aggregated
- The segment in which the impaired intangible asset is reported under ASC 280, if applicable

INTANGIBLES—GOODWILL AND OTHER

IMPORTANT NOTICE FOR 2014

As CCH's 2014 *GAAP Guide* goes to press, the FASB has outstanding an Exposure Draft of an Accounting Standards Update (ASU) (Accounting for Goodwill) that may have an important impact on the preparation of financial statements in the future. This exposure draft represents a proposal of the Private Company Council and provides alternative guidance for private companies. This alternative guidance for private companies was provided in response to concerns expressed about the recurring costs and complexity of the current goodwill impairment test.

Under the proposed guidance, a private company that elects to apply the alternative guidance would amortize goodwill on a straight-line basis over the useful life of the primary asset acquired in a business combination, not to exceed 10 years. A primary asset is the long-lived asset that is the most significant asset of the acquired entity. Testing for impairment of goodwill would only be required when a triggering event occurs that would indicate that the fair value of the entity is below its carrying amount. In addition, the impairment testing would be performed at the entity-wide level rather than the reporting unit level.

The effective date for this proposed ASU will be determined when the final ASU is issued. The accounting alternative for goodwill would be applied prospectively for all existing goodwill and for all new goodwill generated in business combinations after the effective date.

PART II: INTERPRETIVE GUIDANCE

ASC 350-20: GOODWILL

ASC 350-20-35-7, 35-25 through 35-26, 35-20, 35-21, 55-10 through 55-16, 55-18 through 55-23 Deferred Income Tax Considerations in Applying the Goodwill Impairment Test in ASC 350, *Intangibles—Goodwill and Other*

OVERVIEW

As a result of the guidance in ASC 350, there has been a drastic change in the way that companies account for goodwill acquired in a business combination. Under that guidance, an entity must allocate goodwill acquired in a business combination to one or more reporting units. In addition, corporate assets and liabilities also must be allocated to reporting units if (*a*) an asset is employed or a liability is related to a reporting unit's operations, and (*b*) the asset or liability will be taken into account in determining the reporting unit's fair value.

Under the guidance in ASC 350, goodwill must be tested for impairment at the reporting level at least annually using the following procedure: (1) a reporting unit's fair value is compared to its carrying amount to determine whether the carrying amount exceeds its fair value (an excess, if any, may be a goodwill impairment), and (2) the *implied* fair value of goodwill, which is determined in the same way as the measurement of goodwill in a business combination under the provisions of ASC 805, Business Combinations, an acquisition of a business, or a nonprofit activity acquired by a not-for-profit entity under the guidance in ASC 958-805, which is compared with the carrying amount of goodwill.

ACCOUNTING ISSUES

- In estimating a reporting unit's fair value, should it be assumed that it would be bought or sold in a *nontaxable* rather than in a *taxable* transaction?
- Should deferred income taxes be included in a reporting unit's carrying amount when comparing the reporting unit's fair value to its carrying amount?
- When measuring deferred tax assets and liabilities for the purpose of determining the implied fair value of a reporting unit's goodwill for the ASC 350 goodwill impairment test, should an entity use the existing income tax bases or assume new income tax bases for a reporting unit's assets and liabilities?

ACCOUNTING GUIDANCE

The following guidance was provided:

- Judgment based on the relevant facts and circumstances should be used in determining whether the fair value of a reporting unit should be estimated based on the assumption that the reporting unit could be bought or sold in a nontaxable transaction rather than in a taxable transaction. That decision should be made on a case-by-case basis by considering whether (*a*) the assumption is consistent with those that others in the marketplace would include in fair value estimates, (*b*) the assumed structure is practicable, and (*c*) the assumed structure provides a seller with the highest and best use and would provide the maximum value for the reporting unit, including consideration of related tax implications. Members noted that in determining whether a nontaxable transaction is practicable, an entity should consider whether the reporting unit could be sold in a nontaxable transaction; and whether the entity's ability to treat a sale as a nontaxable transaction would be impeded by income tax laws and regulations or corporate governance requirements.
- Deferred income taxes should be included in a reporting unit's carrying amount for Step 1 of the goodwill impairment test, regardless of the tax structure (taxable or nontaxable) on which the reporting unit's fair value will be determined based on an assumption that it would be bought or sold in a taxable or nontaxable transaction.
- The income tax bases of a reporting unit's assets and liabilities inherent in the tax structure (taxable or nontaxable) assumed in an entity's estimate of the reporting unit's fair value in Step 1 of the impairment test should be used in determining the implied fair value of the reporting unit's goodwill in Step 2 of the impairment test. If a *nontaxable* transaction is assumed, the entity's existing income tax bases should be used. New income tax bases should be used if a *taxable* transaction is assumed. It was noted that in Step 2 of the test, the implied fair value of a reporting entity's goodwill is determined in the same way as the amount of good-

will recognized in a business combination under the guidance in ASC 805-30-30-5. This method is also used to determine the amount of goodwill recognized in an acquisition of a business or the acquisition of a nonprofit activity by a not-for-profit entity under the guidance in ASC 958-805.

The income tax bases of a reporting unit's assets and liabilities inherent in the tax structure (taxable or nontaxable) assumed in an entity's estimate of the reporting unit's fair value in Step 1 of the impairment test should be used in determining the implied fair value of the reporting unit's goodwill in Step 2 of the impairment test. If a *nontaxable* transaction is assumed, the entity's existing income tax bases should be used. *New* income tax bases should be used if a *taxable* transaction is assumed. It was noted that in Step 2 of the test, the implied fair value of a reporting entity's goodwill is determined in the same way as the amount of goodwill recognized in a business combination under the guidance in ASC 805-30-30-5. This method is also used to determine the amount of goodwill recognized in an acquisition of a business or the acquisition of a nonprofit activity by a not-for-profit entity under the guidance in ASC 958-805.

ASC 350-20-35-6, 35-8A, 35-30; ASC 350-10-65-2 When to Perform Step 2 of the Goodwill Impairment Test for Reporting Units with Zero or Negative Carrying Amounts

BACKGROUND

Under the two-step goodwill impairment test, a reporting unit's fair value is compared to its carrying amount, which includes goodwill. The second step of this test, which measures the amount of impairment, must be performed only if a reporting unit's carrying amount exceeds its fair value. As a result of practice issues, such as reporting units with zero or negative carrying values, and significant differences in the fair value of debt as compared to its par value, some are questioning whether the carrying amount of a reporting unit should be based on an "Enterprise Premise" or an "Equity Premise."

SCOPE

This guidance applies to reporting entities that are required to test goodwill for impairment and have one or more reporting units with a carrying amount that is zero or negative for the purpose of performing Step 1 of the goodwill impairment test.

ACCOUNTING GUIDANCE

If a reporting unit's carrying amount is zero or negative in Step 1 of the goodwill impairment test, regardless of the method used to calculate the reporting unit's carrying value, Step 2 of the goodwill impairment test must be performed to determine the amount of an impairment loss, if any, if it is more likely than not (i.e., more than a 50 percent likelihood) that a goodwill impairment exists. Consideration of the likelihood that a goodwill impairment exists should be conducted using the process discussed in ASC 350-20-35-3(F) through 3(G) to evaluate the existence of adverse qualitative factors, including the examples of events and circumstances discussed in ASC 350-20-35-3C(a) through 35-3C(g).

That evaluation should consider whether the carrying amount and the estimated fair value of the entity's assets and liabilities differs significantly and whether significant unrecognized intangible assets exist. Although a method for determining the amount of a reporting unit's carrying value was not recommended, it was noted that a reporting unit's fair value should be determined on a basis that is consistent with the manner in which the reporting unit's assets and liabilities are included in determining the reporting unit's carrying amount.

In addition, the goodwill of a reporting unit with a zero or negative carrying amount should be tested for impairment annually or on an interim basis if an event occurs or based on circumstances indicating that it is more likely than not that a goodwill impairment exists. Examples of such events and circumstances are discussed in ASC 350-20-35-3C(a) through 35-3C(g). Additional factors to consider if a reporting unit's carrying amount is zero or negative are discussed in ASC 350-20-35-8A.

TRANSITION METHOD, TRANSITION DISCLOSURES, AND EFFECTIVE DATE

A reporting unit with a zero or negative carrying amount at the date that this guidance is adopted must perform Step 2 of the goodwill impairment test if it is more likely than not that goodwill is impaired as of that date. In addition, a goodwill impairment, if any, recognized on adoption of this guidance should be presented as a cumulative-effect adjustment to beginning retained earnings of the period of adoption as a result of a change in accounting principle.

Amendments to the Codification as a result of this guidance are effective for interim and annual reporting periods in fiscal years that begin after December 15, 2011.

ASC 350-20-55-1 through 55-9 Clarification of Reporting Unit Guidance in ASC 350-20-35-33 through 35-35

To clarify the guidance in ASC 350-20-35-33 through 35-35, the FASB staff has provided the following guidance on how to determine whether a component of an operating segment is a reporting unit:

- Judgment should be used based on the specific facts and circumstances related to the entity.
- No single characteristic or factor among those listed in ASC 350-20-35-33 through 35-35 is determinative.

The way an entity's operations are managed and the way it has integrated an acquired entity with its own operations are significant.

The guidance in ASC 350-20-35-33 through 35-35 states that "[a] component of an operating segment is a reporting unit if the component constitutes a business for which discrete financial information is available and segment management regularly review the operating results of the component." Judgment based on the specific facts and circumstances is necessary to determine whether a component is a business. The guidance in ASC 805, Business Combinations, should be used to determine whether a group of assets represents a business.

This pronouncement has been amended by the guidance in ASC 958-805, which states that any references to a "business or businesses" likewise refer to a "nonprofit activity" and "nonprofit activities," respectively.

ASC 350-30: GENERAL INTANGIBLES OTHER THAN GOODWILL

ASC 350-30-15-5, 25-5, 35-5A through 35-5B, 55-1 through 55-1B, 55-28H through 55-28I, 55-28K through 55-28L, 65-2 Accounting for Defensive Intangible Assets

BACKGROUND

A "defensive asset" or "locked-up asset" is an intangible asset that has been acquired in a business combination or in an asset acquisition that an entity does *not* intend to actively use but intends to keep others from using it. Although the entity does not actively use the asset, its existence probably increases the value of other assets owned by the acquiring entity. In the past, entities have attributed little or no value to acquired intangible assets that they did not intend to actively use, regardless of whether they might have been actively used by another acquirer.

However, as a result of the issuance of ASC 805 and ASC 820, Fair Value Measurement, intangible assets must be recognized at a value that represents an asset's *highest and best use* based on assumptions about other entities in the market. When those Statements become effective, entities will generally assign a greater value to defensive intangible assets than they previously would have assigned under the guidance in ASC 805. Consequently, constituents have asked how defensive assets should be accounted for after their acquisition, including the assignment of an estimated useful life.

SCOPE

This guidance applies to all acquired intangible assets that an entity does *not* intend to use actively but intends to hold to keep competitors from gaining access to those assets, except if an intangible asset is used in research and development activities, which are accounted for in accordance with the guidance in ASC 350-30-35-15 through 35-17A. Whether an asset is a defensive asset depends on the entity's intentions for its use. The accounting for such assets may change if an entity decides to begin to actively use the asset.

The identification of market participants, market participants' assumptions, or valuation issues related to defensive intangible assets are not discussed in this Issue.

ACCOUNTING GUIDANCE

The following guidance applies:

Recognition. A defensive intangible asset should be accounted for as a separate unit of accounting and should not be included in the cost of an entity's existing intangible assets because defensive intangible assets are identified separately.

Subsequent measurement. A defensive asset's benefit to an entity that holds it is represented by the direct or indirect cash flows that result from preventing others from realizing value from that asset. The useful life assigned to a defensive intangible asset, in accordance with the guidance in ASC 350-30-35-1 through 35-3 should represent an entity's consumption of the expected benefits related to the asset by estimating the period over which the asset's fair value will diminish. That period is a surrogate for the period over which an entity expects that the defensive asset will contribute indirectly to the entity's future cash flows.

Defensive intangible assets rarely have an indefinite useful life because their fair value generally diminishes over time due to a lack of market exposure or as a result of competitive or other factors. In addition, an acquired intangible asset that meets the definition of a defensive intangible asset cannot be considered as immediately abandoned.

ASC 350-30-35-21 through 35-28, 35-30 through 35-32, 35-34 through 35-35, 35-37 through 35-38 Unit of Accounting for Testing Impairment of Indefinite-Lived Intangible Assets

BACKGROUND

Under the provisions of ASC 350, intangible assets that are not required to be amortized must be evaluated for impairment at least annually. If an intangible asset's carrying amount exceeds its fair value, an impairment loss should be recognized. Recognized losses should not be restored in the future.

Constituents asked for guidance regarding the unit of accounting to be used when evaluating the impairment of intangible assets with indefinite lives. That is, (*a*) whether identical or similar indefinite-lived intangible assets may be combined for the purpose of testing impairment, for example, contiguous easements that were purchased in separate transactions but that are used as one asset, and (*b*) whether different indefinite-lived intangible assets, for example, a trade name and an easement, may be tested for impairment on a combined basis.

ACCOUNTING ISSUE

What unit of accounting should be used when testing indefinite-lived intangible assets for impairment under the guidance in ASC 350-30-35-18 through 35-20?

ACCOUNTING GUIDANCE

Acquired or internally developed *intangible* assets with indefinite lives that have been separately recognized and are inseparable from each other because they are operated as a single unit should be combined in one accounting unit when testing impairment. Judgment, depending on the relevant facts and circumstances, is required to determine whether several such intangible assets are inseparable. Although the indicators discussed below should be considered in making that determination, they should not be considered to be presumptive or determinative.

Indicators that two or more indefinite-lived intangible assets should be combined as a single unit of accounting when testing for impairment

- The assets were purchased to construct or improve a single asset and will be used together.
- The assets would have been recognized as one asset if they had been acquired at the same time.
- The assets represent the highest and best use when considered as a group, because (a) it is unlikely that a substantial portion of the assets would be sold separately or (b) if a substantial portion of the assets were sold individually, the fair value of the remaining assets as a group would be significantly lower.
- An entity's marketing or branding strategy indicates that the assets are complementary, as that term is used in ASC 805-20-55-18.

Indicators that two or more indefinite-lived intangible assets should not be combined as a single unit of accounting for impairment testing purposes

- The assets generate cash flows independently of one another.
- Each asset is likely to be sold separately. Previous separate sales of such assets are an indicator that combining them is not appropriate.
- The entity has a plan or is considering one to dispose of one or more of those assets separately.
- The assets are used exclusively by different asset groups referred to in ASC 360.
- Economic and other factors that might limit the useful economic life of one of the assets would not necessarily be the same for other assets combined in the unit of accounting.

The following was noted about the unit of accounting used to test indefinite-lived intangible assets for impairment:

- Indefinite-lived intangible assets should be in a separate unit of accounting, not tested with goodwill or finite-lived assets.
- A unit of accounting cannot consist of indefinite-lived assets that together represent a business.
- A unit of accounting may consist of indefinite-lived intangible assets presented in the separate financial statements of consolidated subsidiaries. Consequently, a loss recognized in consolidated financial statements may differ from total impairment losses, if any, recognized in the subsidiaries' separate financial statements.
- A unit of accounting and associated fair value used to test impairment of indefinite-lived intangible assets contained in a single reporting unit also should be used to measure a goodwill impairment loss in accordance with the guidance in ASC 350-20-35-9 through 13.
- If, because of a change in the way its intangible assets are used, a company combines those assets with assets that were previously tested separately for impairment to constitute a unit of accounting for the purpose of testing for impairment, the assets that were accounted for

separately should be tested for impairment in accordance with the guidance in ASC 350-30-35-18 through 20 before they are combined as a unit of accounting.

ASC 350-30-50-4 through 50-5, 55-1(c), 65-1; ASC 275-10-50-15A Determination of the Useful Life of Intangible Assets

BACKGROUND

Under the guidance in ASC 350-30-35-3, the "legal, regulatory, or contractual provisions that enable renewal or extension of the asset's legal or contractual life without substantial cost" must be considered, but only if renewal or extension of an asset's useful life is supported by evidence and can be achieved without "material modifications of the existing terms and conditions."

The problem is that the useful life of an intangible asset recognized under the guidance in ASC 350 frequently differs from the period of expected cash flows used to measure an asset's fair value under the guidance in ASC 805, Business Combinations, if the underlying arrangement includes terms related to the renewal or extension of the asset's useful life (i.e., the useful life of an asset accounted for under the guidance in ASC 350 is usually shorter than the expected period of cash flows under the guidance in ASC 805). That difference may occur, especially if material modifications are required for renewal or extension of a long-lived intangible asset's useful life, even though the likelihood of renewal or extension is high. The FASB was asked to consider whether the difference between an intangible asset's useful life and the period of expected cash flows used to measure its fair value is justified. This following guidance does *not* address the *initial measurement* of recognized intangible assets, the *amortization method* to be used, and the accounting for costs incurred to renew or extend a recognized intangible asset's term.

ACCOUNTING GUIDANCE

This guidance applies to recognized intangible assets accounted for under the guidance in ASC 350, regardless of how they were acquired.

Subsequent Measurement—Determining Useful Life

To determine the useful life of a recognized intangible asset, an entity is required to develop assumptions about the renewal or extension of an arrangement based on its own historical experience related to the renewal or extension of similar arrangements, which should be adjusted for entity-specific factors discussed in ASC 350-30-35-3. An entity that has no historical experience should consider assumptions that other participants in the market would use about an arrangement's renewal or extension that are (1) consistent with the asset's highest and best use and (2) adjusted for factors in ASC 350-30-35-3 that specifically apply to the entity.

Before this discussion, the guidance in ASC 350-30-35-3 did not permit an entity to base its assumptions on its own past experience related to the renewal or extension of an arrangement if it was likely that doing so would require incurring a substantial cost or making material modifications to an arrangement, because of a concern that entities might lengthen the useful lives of intangible assets inappropriately. The FASB staff believes that the guidance related to the fair value measurement of intangible assets and the requirement to test intangible assets for impairment along with the disclosure requirements would reduce that concern. As a result of this amendment of the guidance in ASC 350-30-35-3, an entity is permitted to base its assumptions on its *own* past experience even if it would result in a substantial cost or would require material modifications to an arrangement.

Entities that measure a recognized intangible asset's fair value by the *income approach* should determine the asset's useful life for amortization purposes by considering the period of expected cash flows used to measure the intangible asset's fair value adjusted for the entity's specific circumstances in accordance with the guidance in ASC 350-30-35-3. Those factors include, but are not limited to, an entity's expected use for the asset and its past experience in renewals and extensions of such arrangements.

If the useful life of a recognized intangible asset differs from the expected cash flows used to measure the asset's fair value, it is usually because the assumptions used by the entity to measure the asset's fair value are specific to the entity and thus differ from those used by other entities in the market to determine the asset's price. In that case, the entity should use its own assumptions because its amortization of a recognized intangible asset should be based on the period over which the asset will contribute, directly or indirectly, to the entity's future cash flows.

DISCLOSURES

Entities are required to disclose information about recognized intangible assets that would help users of financial statements to determine how the entity's intent or ability to renew or extend an arrangement affects the entity's expected cash flows associated with the asset.

Disclosure of the following information is required, if applicable, in addition to the disclosures required in ASC 350-20-50-1 through 50-2:

- The entity's accounting policy for costs incurred to renew or extend a recognized intangible asset's term;
- For each class of major intangible assets, the weighted-average period at acquisition or renewal before the next explicit or implicit renewal or extension;
- If renewal or extension costs are capitalized, the total cost incurred to renew or extend the term of a recognized intangible asset disclosed by major class of intangible assets for each period for which a balance sheet is presented.

The criterion in ASC 275-10-50-8, which provides guidance on when an entity should disclose information about an estimate, has been met if the effect of a change in either an intangible asset's (a) useful life, or (b) the expected likelihood of its renewal or extension would be material to the financial statements, either individually or in total by major class of intangible assets.

… ASC 350—Intangibles—Goodwill and Other 24,023

ASC 350-40: INTERNAL-USE SOFTWARE

ASC 350-10-05-6, ASC 350-40-05-2 through 05-6, 05-8, 05-9, 15-2 through 15-7, 25-1 through 25-16, 30-1 through 30-4, 35-1 through 35-10, 50-1, 55-1 through 55-4; ASC 730-10-60-2; ASC 985-20-60-1 Accounting for Costs of Computer Software Developed or Obtained for Internal Use

BACKGROUND

This guidance has been provided as a result of diversity in practice in accounting for costs associated with software purchased for internal use. Some entities have been capitalizing the costs of software purchased for internal use, while other entities have been expensing those costs if the software was developed internally.

ACCOUNTING GUIDANCE

Internal-use software has the following characteristics: (1) the software is acquired, internally developed, or modified solely to meet an entity's internal requirements; or (2) the entity has no substantive plan to externally market internally developed or modified software. If an entity has a history of developing software internally and marketing it externally, there is a rebuttable presumption that any software developed by that entity is intended for sale, lease, or other marketing. ASC 986-20 provides the applicable authoritative guidance.

Software that becomes part of a product or a process that is sold (e.g., software designed for and embedded in a semiconductor chip) should be accounted for under the provisions of ASC 986-20, not under the guidance in this pronouncement. However, software used in the production of a product or the provision of a service but not acquired by the customer (e.g., software embedded in a switch used by a telecommunications company to provide telephone service) should be accounted for under the guidance in this pronouncement.

Stages of Computer Software Development

The three stages of computer software development are (1) preliminary project stage, (2) application development stage, and (3) post-implementation/operation stage. The preliminary project stage includes the conceptual formulation of alternatives, evaluation of alternatives, determination of the existence of needed technology, and the final selection of alternatives. The application development stage includes the design of chosen paths, including software configuration and software interfaces, coding, installation of hardware, and testing (including the parallel processing phase). The post-implementation/operation stage includes training and application maintenance.

Internal-Use Computer Software Costs as R&D

Internal-use computer software costs may be incurred for research and development purposes. Such costs, which are accounted for in accordance with the guidance in ASC 730-20, include the following:

- Purchased or leased computer software used in R&D activities if the software does not have alternative future uses.
- All internally developed internal-use computer software if (*a*) the software developed represents a pilot project or (*b*) the software is used in a particular R&D project, regardless of whether the software has alternative future uses.

Capitalizing or Expensing Internal Computer Software Costs

The accounting treatment of internal-use computer software costs (i.e., capitalize or expense) largely depends on the nature of the cost incurred. Internal and external costs incurred during the preliminary project stage should be expensed as incurred. Internal and external costs incurred during the application development stage should be capitalized. Software costs that allow for access or conversion of old data by new systems also should be capitalized. Internal and external training costs and maintenance costs should be expensed as incurred.

Upgrades and Enhancements

Upgrades and enhancements are defined as modifications to existing internal-use software that result in additional functionality (e.g., modifications to enable software to perform tasks that it was previously incapable of performing). In order for the costs of upgrades or enhancements to be capitalized, it must be probable that these expenditures will result in additional software functionality. Internal costs of upgrades or enhancements should be expensed if the activity relates to the preliminary project stage or the post-implementation/operation stage; costs incurred during the application development stage are to be capitalized. External costs of upgrades or enhancements should be expensed if the activity relates to the preliminary project stage or the post-implementation/operation stage; costs incurred during the application development stage are to be capitalized.

Applying the Capitalization Criteria

Capitalization of costs should begin when both of the following occur:

- The preliminary project stage is complete.
- Management with applicable authority authorizes, implicitly or explicitly, the project's funding, and it is probable that the project will be completed and the software will be used to perform the intended function.

Capitalization should cease no later than when the software project is substantially complete and ready for its intended use. The software is ready for its intended use after all substantial testing is completed.

The development of new software that is intended to replace existing internal-use software affects the accounting for any unamortized costs. First, the remaining useful lives of software that is to be replaced should be reconsidered. Second, when new software that is replacing the existing software is ready for its intended use, the unamortized cost of the software that is being replaced should be charged to expense.

The following types of costs, incurred during the application development stage, are eligible for capitalization:

- External direct costs of materials and services consumed in developing or obtaining the software (e.g., fees paid to third-party developers, costs incurred to obtain software from third parties, and travel expenses in-

curred by employees in their duties directly associated with developing software)
- Payroll and payroll-related costs (e.g., employee benefits) for employees who are directly associated with and who devote time to the internal-use computer software project, to the extent of time spent directly on the project
- Interest costs incurred while developing internal-use computer software (see ASC 835-20).

General and administrative costs and overhead costs should *not* be capitalized.

Software Purchased for Internal Use with Multiple Elements

In some cases, the purchase price of a software package includes multiple elements. For example, a software product may be purchased from an external vendor for a lump sum that includes the software itself, training, a maintenance agreement, data conversion services, reengineering, and rights to future upgrades and enhancements. The total purchase price should be allocated among all individual elements based on objective evidence of the fair values of the contract components. Such fair values may differ from prices stated within the contract for each element.

Impairment

Impairment of internal-use computer software costs should be recognized and measured in accordance with the provisions of ASC 360. If it is no longer probable that the software being developed will be completed and placed in service, the asset should be reported at the lower of its carrying amount or its fair value less costs to sell. The rebuttable presumption is that such uncompleted software has a fair value of zero. Indications that the software may not be completed and placed in service include the following:

- A lack of expenditures budgeted or incurred for the project
- Programming difficulties that cannot be resolved on a timely basis
- Significant cost overruns
- Management plans to purchase third-party software rather than completing the internally developed software; costs of internally developed software will significantly exceed the cost of comparable software from a third-party vendor
- Management plans to purchase third-party software rather than completing the internally developed software; third-party software has more advanced features
- The business segment or unit to which the software relates is unprofitable or has been or will be discontinued

Amortization

The costs of software developed for internal use are to be amortized. Amortization is on a straight-line basis unless another systematic and rational basis is more representative of the software's use. The amortization period should be relatively short.

External Marketing of Internal-Use Computer Software

In some cases, the entity decides to market software developed for internal use to external parties. Proceeds received from the sale of such software, net of direct incremental costs of marketing, should be applied against the carrying amount of the internal use software. Direct incremental costs of marketing include commissions, software reproduction costs, warranty and service obligations, and installation costs. No profit should be recognized until the proceeds received from the sale of the internal use software and amortization charges reduce the carrying amount of the software to zero. Subsequent proceeds should be recognized in revenue as earned.

ASC 350-50: WEBSITE DEVELOPMENT COSTS

ASC 350-10-05-7; ASC 350-50-15-2 through 15-3, 25-2 through 25-17, 55-2 through 55-9 Accounting for Web Site Development Costs

BACKGROUND

Web sites are developed by different kinds of companies. Many are "brick and mortar" companies; others are start-up companies that will be conducting their business operations only on the Internet. There are three broad categories of Internet web sites: (1) sites that provide information only, (2) sites that provide information and a service, and (3) sites that provide information and enter into transactions with customers over the Internet. In addition, Internet web sites can be accessed by the general public, extranet sites can be accessed only by subscribers, and intranet sites can be accessed only by individuals within a specific company.

The stages of web site development include (*a*) planning, (*b*) web application and infrastructure development, (*c*) graphics and content, and (*d*) production. Because there is no specific guidance on the accounting for web site development costs, the accounting for those costs has been diverse.

This Issue does not apply to costs of hardware, such as servers, necessary to support a web site. It also does not apply to costs incurred under web site development contracts for others. Such costs are accounted for under contract accounting.

ACCOUNTING ISSUE

How should an entity account for costs incurred to develop a web site?

ACCOUNTING GUIDANCE

Planning Stage Activities

All costs of web site planning activities should be expensed, regardless of whether they are related to software. Those costs include, but are not limited to, a business plan, a project plan, or both; identification of specific goals; determining the web site's functions (e.g., order placement, shipment tracking); identifying necessary hardware and web applications; determining whether the technology necessary to achieve the site's intended functions exists; alternative means of achieving the site's functions; identifying software tools; and legal costs to address copyright issues.

Web Site Application and Infrastructure Development Stage

During the web site application and infrastructure development stage, the necessary hardware is acquired and software is developed. This guidance does *not* apply to costs of hardware acquired. It is assumed that all costs related to software development are incurred for the purpose of operating the web site (internal-use software). Those costs should be accounted for according to the guidance in ASC 350-10-05-6; ASC 350-40-05-2 through 05-6, 05-8, 05-9, 15-2 through 15-7, 25-1 through 25-16, 30-1 through 30-4, 35-1 through 35-10, 50-1, 55-1 through 55-4; ASC 730-10-60-2; ASC 985-20-60-1. That is, the costs generally should be *capitalized* under the guidance in ASC 350-40-25-2 through 25-15, 05-8 through 5-9, 15-2, 30-1 An entity that has a plan or is developing a plan to market the software to others should account for those costs under the guidance in ASC 985-20-05-1 through 05-2, 15-2 through 15-4, 25-1 through 25-4, 25-6 through 25-11, 35-1 through 35-4, 50-1 through 50-2; ASC 985-330-40-1; ASC 730-10-60-4, 55-1. Costs of obtaining or registering an Internet name would be capitalized in accordance with the guidance in ASC 350. In addition, fees paid periodically to an Internet service provider for hosting a web site on its servers, generally, should be *expensed* over the benefit period.

Graphics Development Costs

Graphics involve the design of a web page and do not change with content. Because they are part of the software, they should be *capitalized* according to the guidance in ASC 350-40-25-2 through 25-4 for internal-use software. If those costs are related to software to be sold to others, they should be accounted for based on the provisions of ASC 985-20-05-1 through 05-2, 15-2 through 15-4, 25-1 through 25-4, 25-6 through 25-11, 35-1 through 35-4, 50-1 through 50-2; ASC 985-330-40-1; ASC 730-10-60-4, 55-1. Changes to a web site's graphics after the site has been launched may be related to web site maintenance or enhancements. The accounting for such changes is discussed in 5(b) below.

Content Development Costs

A web site's content may consist of articles, pictures, maps, and so forth and may be presented as text or in graphical form. (The graphics discussed above are not included here.) The accounting is not addressed here, because the accounting guidance for costs of web site content, which may be acquired from others or developed internally, may not be limited to forms of content found only on web sites.

Costs Incurred to Operate a Web Site

Costs incurred to operate a web site should be accounted for as follows:
- *Costs with no future benefit.* Expense operating costs with no future benefit as incurred (e.g., training, administration, maintenance, and other web site operating costs) because the costs of operating a web site should be accounted for in the same way as the costs of operating other kinds of entities.
- *Costs with a future benefit.* Costs incurred to develop upgrades and enhancements that increase the functions of web site software should be accounted for in the same way as the costs of developing new software

according to the guidance in ASC 350-10-05-6; ASC 350-40-05-2 through 05-6, 05-8, 05-9, 15-2 through 15-7, 25-1 through 25-16, 30-1 through 30-4, 35-1 through 35-10, 50-1; 55-1 through 55-4; ASC 730-10-60-2; ASC 985-20-60-1. Similar costs incurred for upgrades or enhancements to software to be sold to others should be accounted for based on the guidance for product enhancements in ASC 985-20-05-1 through 05-2, 15-2 through 15-4, 25-1 through 25-4, 25-6 through 25-11, 35-1 through 35-4, 50-1 through 50-2; ASC 985-330-40-1; ASC 730-10-60-4; 55-1. Determining whether a change to web site software is an upgrade or enhancement (product enhancement) or maintenance requires judgment based on the specific facts and circumstances. In addition, it was noted that the guidance in ASC 350-10-05-6; ASC 350-40-05-2 through 05-6, 05-8 through 05-9, 15-2 through 15-7, 25-1 through 25-16, 30-1 through 30-4, 35-1 through 35-10, 50-1; 55-1 through 55-4; ASC 730-10-60-2; ASC 985-20-60-1 provides that if it is not cost-effective to separate internal costs incurred for maintenance from those incurred for minor upgrades and enhancements, the total amount should be expensed as incurred.

CHAPTER 25
ASC 360—PROPERTY, PLANT, AND EQUIPMENT

CONTENTS

Part I: General Guidance	25,003
Overview	25,003
Background	25,004
ASC 360-10: Overall	25,006
Principles of Accounting for Depreciable Assets	25,006
Asset Cost	25,006
Salvage Value	25,006
Estimated Useful Life	25,006
Valuation of Assets	25,006
Historical Cost	25,006
Replacement Cost	25,006
Fair Market Value	25,006
Present Value	25,007
General Price-Level Restatement	25,007
Leasehold Improvements	25,007
Self-Constructed Depreciable Assets	25,008
Illustration of Self-Constructed Depreciable Assets	25,008
Improvement of Depreciable Assets	25,008
Illustration of Improvement of Depreciable Assets	25,009
Depreciation	25,009
Types of Depreciation	25,009
Depreciation Methods	25,009
Straight-Line Method	25,009
Illustration of Straight-Line Method of Depreciation	25,010
Units-of-Production Method	25,010
Illustration of Units-of-Production Method of Depreciation	25,010
Sum-of-the-Years'-Digits Method	25,010
Illustration of Sum-of-the-Years'-Digits Method of Depreciation	25,011
Declining-Balance Methods	25,011
Illustration of Double-Declining-Balance Method of Depreciation	25,012
Partial-Year Depreciation	25,012
Illustration of Partial-Year Depreciation	25,013
Other Types of Depreciation	25,013
Replacement Depreciation	25,013
Retirement Depreciation	25,014
Present-Value Depreciation	25,014
Impairment	25,014
Long-Lived Assets to Be Held and Used	25,014
Testing Assets for Recoverability	25,014

ASC 360—Property, Plant, and Equipment

Grouping Assets	25,015
New Cost Basis	25,016
Estimating Future Cash Flows	25,017
Fair Value	25,017
Illustration of Recognizing an Impairment Loss on Assets to Be Held and Used	25,017
Long-Lived Assets to Be Disposed Of	25,018
Disposal by Sale	25,018
Figure 25-1: Impairment of Assets Held and Used	25,020
Illustration of Impairment of Asset to Be Disposed Of	25,021
Changes in a Plan to Sell	25,021
Depletion	25,021
Disclosure	25,022
ASC 360-20: Real Estate Sales	25,023
Recognition of Sales	25,023
Real Estate Sales (Except Retail Land Sales)	25,023
When a Real Estate Sale Is Consummated	25,024
Buyer's Initial and Continuing Investment	25,024
Illustration of Computation of Sales Value	25,025
Illustration of Determination of Buyer's Minimum Initial Investment	25,028
Release Provisions	25,029
Future Subordination	25,029
Nontransfer of Ownership and Seller's Continued Involvement	25,030
Profit Recognition Other Than Full Accrual Basis	25,030
Deposit Accounting	25,031
Cost Recovery Method	25,031
Installment Sales Method	25,032
Illustration of Installment Sales Method	25,032
Reduced Profit Method	25,033
Change to Full Accrual Method	25,033
Profit Recognition When Sale Is Not Consummated	25,034
Profit Recognition When Buyer's Investment Is Inadequate	25,035
Profit Recognition—Subordinated Receivable	25,035
Profit Recognition—Seller's Continued Involvement	25,035
Initiating and Supporting Operations	25,036
Services without Compensation	25,037
Sale of Real Estate Options	25,037
Sales of Partial Interests in Property	25,037
Disclosures	25,038
Retail Land Sales	25,038
Part II: Interpretive Guidance	25,039
ASC 360-10: Overall	25,039
ASC 360-10-25-2 through 25-4, 30-3, 30-4, 30-13 through 30-14; ASC 840-30-35-21, 35-53	
Accounting for an Interest in the Residual Value of a Leased Asset	25,039
ASC 360-10-25-5, 45-1; ASC 340-10-25-5; ASC 908-360-45-2	
Accounting for Planned Major Maintenance Activities	25,040

ASC 360—Property, Plant, and Equipment   **25,003**

ASC 360-20: Real Estate Sales	25,041
ASC 360-20-15-3	
Accounting for Transfers of Investments That Are in Substance Real Estate	25,041
ASC 360-20-15-3(f), 55-68 through 55-77, 65-2; ASC 810-10-40-3B	
Derecognition of In-Substance Real Estate—a Scope Clarification	25,042
ASC 360-20-15-4 through 15-8 55-58 through 55-59	
Determining Whether Equipment Is "Integral Equipment" Subject to ASC 360	25,043
ASC 360-20-40-11 through 40-12, 55-3	
Profit Recognition on Sales of Real Estate with Insured Mortgages or Surety Bonds	25,044
ASC 360-20-40-14 through 40-17, 40-32; 55-55 through 55-56	
Effect of Various Forms of Financing under ASC 360	25,046
Illustration of Profit Recognition When Buyer's Initial Investment Is Inadequate	25,047
ASC 360-20-40-35	
Profit Recognition on Sales of Real Estate with Graduated Payment Mortgages or Insured Mortgages	25,048
ASC 360-20-40-39	
Antispeculation Clauses in Real Estate Sales Contracts	25,049
ASC 360-20-40-50-55	
Applicability of the Assessment of a Buyer's Continuing Investment under ASC 360 for Sales of Condominiums	25,050
ASC 360-20-55-66 through 55-67	
Transfer of Ownership Interest as Part of Down Payment under ASC 360	25,052
ASC 360-20-60-1; 55-2 through 55-6, 55-8, 55-13 through 55-18	
The Treatment of Certain Site Restoration/Environmental Exit Costs When Testing a Long-Lived Asset for Impairment	25,052

PART I: GENERAL GUIDANCE

OVERVIEW

Among the issues addressed in ASC 360 are the acquisition and depreciation of property, plant, and equipment. In addition, guidance in recognizing and measuring the impairment of fixed assets is included in this section. Finally, ASC 360 provides guidance in accounting for certain real estate sales.

Recognition of depreciation is required in general-purpose financial statements that present financial position, cash flows, and results of operations. Depreciation is an area where a variety of methods are available in practice.

Impairment of a long-lived asset exists when the asset's fair value is less than its carrying amount, which is defined as cost less accumulated depreciation and is often referred to as book value. Recognition of an impairment loss is required in this circumstance, because the carrying amount will not be recovered in the future. This general principle underlies accounting for impairment losses of all long-lived assets, but it is applied differently for those assets that are expected to be held and used and for assets to be disposed of by sale or otherwise.

A significant financial reporting issue encountered in accounting for real estate transactions is the timing of revenue recognition. Promulgated GAAP address this important issue by classifying real estate transactions into the following three categories:

1. Real estate sales, except retail land sales
2. Sale-leasebacks involving real estate
3. Retail land sales

ASC 360 addresses real estate sales and retail land sales. ASC 840 (Leases) addresses sale-leasebacks involving real estate.

BACKGROUND

Fixed assets, also referred to as *property, plant, and equipment,* or *plant assets,* are used in production, distribution, and services by all enterprises. Examples include land, buildings, furniture, fixtures, machinery, equipment, and vehicles. The nature of the assets employed by a particular enterprise is determined by the nature of its activities.

Fixed assets have two primary characteristics:

1. They are acquired for use in operations and enter into the revenue-generating stream indirectly. They are held primarily for use, not for sale.
2. They have relatively long lives.

GAAP generally require fixed assets to be recorded at their cost, which is subsequently reduced by depreciation or amortization as the asset's cost is gradually transferred to the income statement in a manner that allocates the cost as an expense over the useful life of the asset. Commonly used depreciation methods include straight-line, units of production, sum-of-the-years'-digits, and declining balance, although other methods may meet the criteria of *systematic* and *rational.* This process is commonly referred to as "matching," and is an important element in the determination of periodic net income. This process focuses primarily on the determination of income rather than the valuation of the asset. In fact, the resulting carrying amount or book value of the asset, which is included in the balance sheet, is not intended to represent the current or fair value of the asset, but is best thought of as that portion of the historical cost of the asset that is awaiting allocation to income in future periods.

Historically, the practice of systematically allocating the cost of a long-lived asset to expense as a part of determining net income was modified in some circumstances in which the value of the asset was believed to be impaired, and was generally defined as its future value being less than its carrying amount. A loss was recognized for the amount of this excess, although this practice was not consistently followed.

ASC 360 applies to long-lived assets (i.e., plant or fixed assets), to intangible assets being amortized, and to long-lived assets to be disposed of. ASC 360's scope includes capital leases of lessees, long-lived assets of lessors under operating leases, proved oil and gas properties accounted for under the successful efforts method, and long-term prepaid assets (ASC 360-10-15-4). ASC 360 applies to all entities. It does not apply to the following types of assets (ASC 360-10-15-5):

1. Goodwill
2. Intangible assets not being amortized that are to be held and used
3. Financial instruments, including cost- or equity-method investments
4. Deferred policy acquisition costs
5. Deferred tax assets
6. Unproved oil and gas properties under the successful efforts method

Certain sections of the Codification establish separate standards of accounting for specific long-lived assets in specialized situations. Specifically, assets whose accounting is prescribed in other sections of the Codification are (ASC 360-10-15-5):

1. ASC 928 (Entertainment—Music)
2. ASC 920 (Entertainment—Broadcasters)
3. ASC 985 (Software)
4. ASC 980 (Regulated Operations)

GAAP require that the realization of revenue be recognized in the accounting period in which the earning process is substantially completed and an exchange has taken place. If revenue is deferred to a future period, the associated costs of that revenue are also deferred. Frequently, it may be necessary to estimate revenue and/or costs to achieve a proper matching.

In addition, revenue usually is recognized at the amount established by the parties to the exchange, except for transactions in which collection of the receivable is not reasonably assured. In the event that collection of the receivable is not reasonably assured, the installment method or cost-recovery method may be used. Alternatively, collections may be recorded properly as deposits in the event that considerable uncertainty exists as to their eventual collectibility.

ASC 360 addresses the recognition of revenue from real estate sales and contains specialized accounting and reporting principles and practices.

ASC 360 establishes GAAP for the recognition of revenue on all real estate transactions for any type of accounting entity. It provides separate criteria for the recognition of revenue on (*a*) all real estate transactions except retail land sales and (*b*) retail land sales. The following items are expressly excluded from the provisions of ASC 360:

1. Exchanges of real estate for other real estate
2. Sales and leasebacks

ASC 360-10: OVERALL

PRINCIPLES OF ACCOUNTING FOR DEPRECIABLE ASSETS

Asset Cost

The basis of accounting for depreciable fixed assets is cost, and all normal expenditures of readying an asset for use are capitalized. However, unnecessary expenditures that do not add to the utility of the asset are charged to expense. For example, an expenditure for repairing a piece of equipment that was damaged during shipment should be charged to expense.

Razing and removal costs (less salvage value) of structures located on land purchased as a building site are added to the cost of the land. Land itself is never depreciated.

Salvage Value

Salvage or *residual value* is an estimate of the amount that will be realized at the end of the useful life of a depreciable asset through sale or other disposal. Frequently, depreciable assets have little or no salvage value at the end of their estimated useful life and, if immaterial, the amount(s) may be ignored.

Estimated Useful Life

The *estimated useful life* of a depreciable asset is the period over which services are expected to be rendered by the asset (ASC 360-10-35-4). An asset's estimated useful life may differ from company to company or industry to industry. A company's maintenance policy may affect the longevity of a depreciable asset.

PRACTICE NOTE: Total utility of an asset, expressed in time, is called the *physical life*. The utility of an asset to a specific owner, expressed in time, is called the *service life*.

Valuation of Assets

Under specific circumstances, assets may be valued in the following ways:

Historical Cost

The amount paid at the date of acquisition, including all normal expenditures of readying an asset for use.

Replacement Cost

The amount that it would cost to replace an asset. Frequently, replacement cost is the same as fair value.

Fair Market Value

The price at which a willing seller would sell to a willing buyer, neither of them being under any compulsion to buy or to sell.

Present Value

The value today of something due in the future.

General Price-Level Restatement

The value of an asset restated in terms of current purchasing power.

Leasehold Improvements

Leased assets may provide the lessee (i.e., party acquiring use of the assets) with many of the benefits of ownership. The lessee may invest in improvements on leased assets to enhance their usefulness. These investments are referred to as *leasehold improvements*.

Leasehold improvements frequently are made to property for which the lease extends over a relatively long period. For example, improvements to a leased building might range from relatively inexpensive improvements to extensive remodeling to prepare the leased asset for the intended use of the lessee.

Leasehold improvements are established in a separate account at cost and amortized over the shorter of the life of the improvement or the length of the lease. Amortization or depreciation policy is usually the same as similar expenditures for owned assets. If no similar assets are owned, amortization or depreciation must employ a method that is systematic and rational (as discussed above) and based on reasonable assumptions.

PRACTICE POINTER: Leasehold improvements generally should be depreciated over the estimated useful lives of the improvements or the remaining lease term, whichever is less. For example, if the lessee constructs a street, curbs, and lighting on land leased for 15 years, those improvements should be depreciated over their estimated useful lives or 15 years, whichever is less. The method of depreciation (most likely straight-line) should generally be that of similar assets (i.e., streets, curbs, lighting) that the company has installed on owned land. Because improvements will revert to the lessor at the end of the lease term, the period of depreciation should not exceed the term of the lease.

Some leases contain renewal options, and a number of entities (particularly retailers) have depreciated leasehold improvements over the remaining lease term plus the term of the renewal period (assuming that this period is less than the estimated economic life of the leasehold improvement). The SEC addressed the appropriateness of this accounting treatment in a letter from the Chief Accountant's office to the AICPA in February 2005. Leasehold improvements should only be depreciated over a term that includes the renewal option period when the exercise of the renewal option is "reasonably assured." A renewal option is only "reasonably assured" if the rent available at renewal is sufficiently less than the property's fair rental value as to reasonably assure that the renewal option will be exercised. Many public companies were routinely including the renewal option period in determining the depreciable live of the leasehold improvement, even if the renewal rental amount was not below fair value. In addition, companies should disclose the depreciation (amortization) period of material leasehold improvements and the relationship of this period to the initial lease term.

Some lessors provide incentives or allowances under operating leases to fund leasehold improvements. These incentives or allowances are to be accounted for as leasehold improvements and depreciated as discussed above. The proper accounting treatment for incentives or allowances received from lessors is discussed in Chapter 54, *ASC 840—Leases*.

Self-Constructed Depreciable Assets

When a business constructs a depreciable asset for its own use, the following procedure is appropriate:

1. All *direct costs* are included in the total cost of the asset.
2. *Fixed overhead costs* are not included unless they are increased by the construction of the asset.
3. *Interest costs* may or may not be capitalized as part of construction cost of the fixed assets.

PRACTICE POINTER: Interest costs that are material must be capitalized on certain qualifying assets under the provisions of ASC 835.

Illustration of Self-Constructed Depreciable Assets

A company takes advantage of excess capacity to construct its own machinery. Costs associated with the construction are as follows:

Direct material	$100,000
Direct labor	50,000
Overhead—Variable	25,000
—Fixed	35,000
	$210,000

The machinery has an estimated useful life of five years, with an expected salvage value of 10% of its cost.

The cost of the machine is $175,000, which includes all of the scheduled costs above except fixed overhead. Because fixed overhead is unaffected by the construction of the machinery, to capitalize fixed overhead as part of the cost would relieve operations of expenses that should be charged to them.

The amount subject to depreciation is computed as follows:

$$\$175,000 - .10\,(\$175,000) = \$157,500$$

Improvement of Depreciable Assets

Expenditures that increase the capacity or operating efficiency or extend the useful life of an asset, if they are substantial, are capitalized. Minor expenditures usually are treated as period costs even though they may have the characteristics of capital expenditures. When the cost of improvements is substantial or when there is a change in the estimated useful life of an asset, depreciation charges for future periods are revised based on the new book value and the new estimated remaining useful life.

The revision of an asset's estimated useful life is measured prospectively and accounted for in the current and future periods. No adjustment is made to prior depreciation.

Illustration of Improvement of Depreciable Assets

A machine that originally cost $100,000 was being depreciated (no salvage value) over ten years, using the straight-line method. At the beginning of the fifth year, $20,000 was expended, which improved the operating efficiency of the machine and extended its useful life two years.

Original cost	$100,000
Less: Four years' depreciation	(40,000)
Book value	$ 60,000
New expenditures	20,000
New depreciable base	$ 80,000
Divided by: Useful life (6 + 2) in years	8
Amount of annual depreciation	$ 10,000

DEPRECIATION

Types of Depreciation

Physical depreciation is related to a depreciable asset's wear and deterioration over a period.

Functional depreciation arises from obsolescence or inadequacy of the asset to perform efficiently. Obsolescence may arise when there is no further demand for the product that the depreciable asset produces or from the availability of a new depreciable asset that can perform the same function for substantially less cost.

Depreciation Methods

The goal of depreciation methods is to provide for a reasonable, consistent matching of revenue and expense by allocating the cost of the depreciable asset systematically over its estimated useful life.

The accumulation of depreciation in the books is accomplished by using a contra account, called accumulated depreciation or allowance for depreciation.

The amount subject to depreciation—*depreciable base*—is the difference between cost and estimate of residual or salvage value.

Straight-Line Method

Straight-line depreciation is determined by the formula:

$$\frac{\text{Cost less salvage value}}{\text{Estimated useful life in years}}$$

25,010   ASC 360—Property, Plant, and Equipment

The straight-line method of depreciation is appropriate when the asset use is expected to be relatively even over its estimated useful life or there is no discernible pattern of decline in service potential.

Illustration of Straight-Line Method of Depreciation

A machine with an invoice price of $500,000 has an expected useful life of eight years. Costs to transport, install, and test the machine were $25,000. The salvage value of the machine at the end of its eight-year life is estimated to be $50,000.

Straight-line depreciation is the same each year. It is computed by adding the $25,000 costs to prepare the asset for its intended use to the $500,000 invoice price, reducing that amount by the estimated salvage value of $50,000, and dividing by the estimated years of useful life:

$$\frac{(\$500{,}000 + \$25{,}000) - \$50{,}000}{8 \text{ years}} = \$59{,}375$$

Units-of-Production Method

The *units-of-production method* relates depreciation to the estimated production capability of an asset and is expressed in a rate per unit or hour. The formula is:

$$\frac{\text{Cost less salvage value}}{\text{Estimated units or hours}}$$

Illustration of Units-of-Production Method of Depreciation

A machine is purchased at a cost of $850,000 and has a salvage value of $100,000. It is estimated that the machine has a useful life of 75,000 hours.

$$\frac{\$850{,}000 - \$100{,}000}{75{,}000} = \$10 \text{ per hour depreciation}$$

In an accounting period during which the machine was used 12,500 hours, depreciation would be $125,000 (12,500 × $10).

The units-of-production method is used in situations in which the usage of the depreciable asset varies considerably from period to period, and in those circumstances in which the service life is more a function of use than passage of time.

Sum-of-the-Years'-Digits Method

The *sum-of-the-years'-digits method* is an accelerated method of depreciation that provides higher depreciation expense in the early years and lower charges in later years.

To find the sum of the years' digits, the digit of each year is progressively numbered and then added up. For example, the sum of the years' digits for a five-year life would be:

$$5 + 4 + 3 + 2 + 1 = 15$$

The sum of the years' digits becomes the denominator, and the digit of the highest year becomes the first numerator. For example, the first year's depreciation for a five-year life would be 5/15 of the depreciable base of the asset, the second year's depreciation would be 4/15, and so on.

When dealing with an asset with a long life, it is helpful to use the following formula for finding the sum of the years' digits, S, where N is the number of years in the asset's life.

$$S = \frac{N(N+1)}{2}$$

To find the sum of the years' digits for an asset with a 50-year life:

$$S = \frac{50(50+1)}{2}$$

$$S = 50(25\ 1/2)$$

$$S = 1{,}275$$

Illustration of Sum-of-the-Years'-Digits Method of Depreciation

Assume that an asset costing $11,000 has a salvage value of $1,000 and an estimated useful life of four years.

The first step is to determine the depreciable base:

Cost of asset	$11,000
Less: Salvage value	1,000
Depreciable base	$10,000

The sum of the years' digits for four years is: 4 + 3 + 2 + 1 = 10

The first year's depreciation is 4/10, the second year's 3/10, the third year's 2/10, and the fourth year's 1/10, as follows:

4/10 of $10,000	=	$ 4,000
3/10 of $10,000	=	3,000
2/10 of $10,000	=	2,000
1/10 of $10,000	=	1,000
Total depreciation		$10,000

Declining-Balance Methods

A frequently used accelerated method is the *double-declining-balance method*, although other alternative (lower than double) methods are acceptable. Under double-declining balance, depreciation is computed at double the straight-line rate and this percentage is applied to the remaining book value. No allowance is made for salvage until the book value (cost less accumulated depreciation) reaches estimated salvage value. At that time, depreciation recognition ceases.

Illustration of Double-Declining-Balance Method of Depreciation

An asset costing $10,000 has an estimated useful life of ten years. Using the double-declining-balance method, depreciation expense is computed as follows.

First, the regular straight-line method percentage is determined, which in this case is 10% (ten-year life). This amount is doubled to 20% and applied each year to the remaining book value, as follows:

Year	Percentage	Remaining book value	Depreciation expense
1	20	$10,000	$2,000
2	20	8,000	1,600
3	20	6,400	1,280
4	20	5,120	1,024
5	20	4,096	819
6	20	3,277	655
7	20	2,622	524
8	20	2,098	420
9	20	1,678	336
10	20	1,342	268
Salvage value		1,074	

In this example, a book value (i.e., portion of cost not depreciated) of $1,074 remains after recognizing ten years of depreciation. Should the asset remain in service, depreciation would continue to be recognized until the asset is no longer used or the book value approaches zero. Should the salvage value be a greater amount (e.g., $1,500), depreciation would cease to be recognized when a total of $8,500 is reached ($10,000 cost − $8,500 accumulated depreciation = $1,500 book value). In the above example, under this assumption, only $178 of depreciation would be recognized in the ninth year, leaving a book value of $1,500. No depreciation would be recognized in the tenth year.

Had the preceding illustration been 150% of declining balance, the rate would have been 15% of the remaining book value (i.e., 150% of 10%). The declining-balance method meets the requirements of being systematic and rational. If the expected productivity or revenue-earning power of the asset is relatively greater during the early years of its life, or where maintenance charges tend to increase during later years, the declining-balance method may provide the most satisfactory allocation of cost.

Partial-Year Depreciation

When an asset is placed in service during the year, the depreciation expense is taken only for the portion of the year that the asset is used. For example, if an asset (of a company on a calendar-year basis) is placed in service on July 1, only six months' depreciation is taken.

Alternatively, a company may adopt a simplifying assumption concerning partial-year depreciation which, applied consistently, usually is considered a reasonable approximation of depreciation computed to the nearest month. For example, the following policies are sometimes encountered:

- A half year of depreciation in the year of purchase and in the year of disposal
- A full year of depreciation taken in the year of purchase and none taken in the year of sale (or the opposite)

These policies are particularly appropriate when a large number of fixed assets are placed in service and removed from service on a constant basis.

Illustration of Partial-Year Depreciation

A calendar-year company purchased a machine on March 7. The machine cost $64,000, and at the end of its expected five-year life it will have a salvage value of $10,000.

Depreciation on a yearly basis is calculated as follows:

$$\frac{\$64,000 - \$10,000}{5 \text{ years}} = \$10,800$$

Depreciation for the year of purchase under three different policies is as follows:

$$\frac{\$10,800}{12 \text{ months}} = \$900 \text{ per month}$$

Policy	Depreciation for Year of Purchase
Computed to nearest full month	10 months × $900 = $9,000
Full year's depreciation in year of purchase; none in last year of asset's useful life	$10,800
Half year's depreciation in first and last years of asset's life	$10,800 × 1/2 = $5,400

Other Types of Depreciation

GAAP require that depreciation be determined in a manner that systematically and rationally allocates the cost of an asset over its estimated useful life. Straight-line, units-of-production, sum-of-theyears'-digits, and declining-depreciation methods are considered acceptable, provided they are based on reasonable estimates of useful life and salvage value. Other methods that are used less frequently are:

Replacement Depreciation

The original cost is carried on the books, and the replacement cost is charged to expense in the period the replacement occurs.

Retirement Depreciation

The cost of the asset is charged to expense in the period it is retired.

Present-Value Depreciation

Depreciation is computed so that the return on the investment of the asset remains constant over the period involved.

PRACTICE POINTER: For financial accounting purposes, companies should not use depreciation guidelines or other tax regulations issued by the IRS, but should estimate useful lives and calculate depreciation expense according to generally accepted accounting procedures. Only when the difference between a GAAP depreciation method and a tax depreciation method is immaterial is the latter acceptable in financial statements. When fixed asset write-offs for tax purposes differ from depreciation for financial accounting purposes, deferred income taxes are recognized.

In periods of inflation, depreciation charges based on historical cost of the original fixed asset may not reflect current price levels, and hence may not be an appropriate matching of revenues and expenses for the current period. In 1953, promulgated GAAP took the position that it was acceptable to provide an appropriation of retained earnings for replacement of fixed assets, but not acceptable to depart from the traditional cost method in the treatment of depreciation, because a radical departure from the generally accepted procedures would create too much confusion in the minds of the users of financial statements. Although inflation has become quite serious from time to time, depreciation based on historical cost remains the official, promulgated accounting principle.

IMPAIRMENT

Long-Lived Assets to Be Held and Used

Impairment is defined in ASC 360 as the condition that exists when the carrying amount of a long-lived asset exceeds its fair value. An impairment loss is recognized only if the carrying amount of a long-lived asset is not recoverable and exceeds its fair value. This circumstance exits if the carrying amount of the asset in question exceeds the sum of the undiscounted cash flows expected to result from the use and eventual disposition of the asset. The impairment loss is measured as the amount by which the carrying amount of a long-lived asset exceeds its fair value (ASC 360-10-35-17).

Testing Assets for Recoverability

A long-lived asset must be tested for recoverability when events or changes in circumstances indicate that the carrying amount of the asset may not be recoverable. Examples of such events or changes in circumstances are (ASC 360-10-35-21):

- A significant decrease in the market price of a long-lived asset.
- A significant adverse change in the extent or manner in which a long-lived asset is used, or in its physical condition.

- A significant adverse change in legal factors or in the business climate that could affect the value of a long-lived asset.

- An accumulation of costs significantly in excess of the amount originally expected for the acquisition or construction of a long-lived asset.

- A current period operating or cash flow loss, combined with a history of operating or cash flow losses or a projection or forecast that demonstrates continuing losses associated with the use of a long-lived asset.

- A current expectation that it is more likely than not that a long-lived asset will be sold or otherwise disposed of significantly before the end of its previously estimated useful life.

Testing a long-lived asset for recoverability may require a review of depreciation estimates and method as required by ASC 250 (Accounting Changes and Error Corrections) or the amortization period required by ASC 350 (Intangibles—Goodwill and Other). Any revision in the remaining useful life of a long-lived asset resulting from that review shall be considered in developing the estimates of future cash flows that are used to test the asset for recoverability (ASC 360-10-35-22).

> **PRACTICE NOTE:** The approach identified in ASC 360 requires the investigation of potential impairments on an **exception basis.** The requirement to compare undiscounted future cash flows with the carrying amount of the asset represents a "trigger mechanism" to assist in identifying those assets that require further analysis. In explaining its conclusions, the FASB states that an asset must be tested for recoverability only if there is reason to believe that the asset is impaired.

Grouping Assets

For purposes of recognizing and measuring an impairment loss, a long-lived asset shall be grouped with other assets and liabilities at the lowest level for which identifiable cash flows are largely independent of the cash flows of other assets and liabilities. In limited circumstances, a long-lived asset may not have identifiable cash flows that are largely independent of the cash flows of other assets and liabilities. In this situation, the asset group for the long-lived asset that is being evaluated for an impairment loss includes all assets and liabilities of the entity. An example of this circumstance is a corporate headquarters facility (ASC 360-10-35-22, 23).

When fair value is estimated on the basis of the present value of expected future cash flows, assets should be grouped at the lowest level for which there are identifiable cash flows that are largely independent of the cash flows of other groups of assets. For example, assume a company has four long-lived assets identified as A, B, C, and D. Evidence suggests that the value of Asset A is impaired. If the cash flows of the four assets can be separately identified, those associated with Asset A alone are used to measure the fair value of that asset. On the other hand, if the cash flows of Assets A and B are intermingled such that separate identification of cash flows of each asset is impossible, the joint cash flows of these two assets must be considered in measuring the fair value of Assets A and B combined, even though evidence does not suggest that the value of Asset B is impaired.

PRACTICE POINTER: As the level of aggregation of assets in applying ASC 360 goes up, the likelihood that a loss will be recognized goes down. This is because when assets are aggregated, the impairment loss that may exist within one asset is offset by the excess of fair value over carrying amount for the other assets that are part of the aggregation. For example, if impairment appears to exist for Asset A, and if Asset A can be valued independently, a loss is recognized. On the other hand, if the fair value of Asset A cannot be determined independently of Assets B and C, the excess of fair value over carrying amount of these two assets must be overcome by the impairment loss of Asset A before a loss is recognized. When assets are aggregated in applying ASC 360, it is reasonable to conclude that some—perhaps many—impairment losses are never recognized, because they are offset against the fair value in excess of carrying amount of other assets.

Goodwill is included in an asset group to be tested for impairment under ASC 360 only if the asset group is or includes a reporting unit. A reporting unit is defined in ASC 350 as one level below an operating segment. ASC 350 requires goodwill to be tested for impairment at the reporting unit level. Goodwill shall not be included in a lower level asset group that includes only part of a reporting unit. Estimates of future cash flows used to test that lower-level asset group for recoverability shall not be adjusted for the effect of excluding goodwill from the group (ASC 360-10-35-26).

Other than goodwill, the carrying amounts of any assets and liabilities not covered by ASC 360 that are included in an asset group shall be adjusted in accordance with other applicable generally accepted accounting principles prior to testing the asset group for recoverability (ASC 360-10-35-27).

An impairment loss for an asset group reduces only the carrying amounts of a long-lived asset or assets of the group. The loss is allocated to the long-lived assets of the group on a pro rata basis using the relative carrying amounts of the assets, except that the loss allocated to an individual long-lived asset of the group shall not reduce the carrying amount of that asset below its fair value whenever that fair value is determinable without undue cost and effort (ASC 360-10-35-28).

New Cost Basis

When an impairment loss is recognized, the adjusted carrying amount of the long-lived asset becomes its new cost basis. This basis is used to depreciate the asset over its remaining useful life. Restoration of previously recognized impairment losses is prohibited, even though circumstances subsequent to the loss recognition indicate that the earlier carrying amount of the asset is recoverable (ASC 360-10-35-20).

ASC 360—Property, Plant, and Equipment 25,017

Estimating Future Cash Flows

Estimates of future cash flows used to test the recoverability of a long-lived asset shall include only the future cash flows that are directly associated with, and that are expected to arise, as a direct result of using and eventually disposing of the asset. Estimates of future cash flows used to test recoverability shall incorporate the entity's own assumptions about its use of the asset and shall consider all available evidence (ASC 360-10-35-29, 30).

Estimates of future cash flows used to test recoverability shall be made for the remaining useful life of the asset to the entity. The remaining useful life, where recoverability is evaluated at an asset group level, is based on the remaining useful life of the primary asset in the group. The primary asset is the asset group's most significant cash-flow-generating tangible asset being depreciated or intangible asset being amortized. These estimates are based on the existing service potential of the asset to the entity. Estimates of future cash flows used to test the recoverability of a long-lived asset that is in use, including a long-lived asset for which development is substantially complete, are based on the existing service potential of the asset at the date it is tested. This encompasses its remaining useful life, cash flow generating capacity and, for tangible assets, physical output capacity. Those estimates include cash flows associated with future expenditures necessary to maintain the existing service potential of a long-lived asset, including those that replace the service potential of a component part of a long-lived asset. Those estimates exclude cash flows associated with future capital expenditures that would increase the potential of a long-lived asset (ASC 360-10-35-31, 32, 33).

Estimates of future cash flows used to test the recoverability of a long-lived asset that is under development shall be based on the expected service potential of the asset when it is substantially complete, including cash flows associated with all future expenditures necessary to develop a long-lived asset and including interest payments that will be capitalized as part of the cost of the asset (ASC 360-10-35-34).

Fair Value

Fair value is best estimated using an expected present value technique. This is especially true when the long-lived assets have uncertainties as to both timing and amount.

Illustration of Recognizing an Impairment Loss on Assets to Be Held and Used

Zeta Company has machinery for which circumstances indicate a potential impairment in value. The machinery cost $100,000 and has accumulated depreciation of $35,000, resulting in a carrying amount of $65,000. The first step is to determine how the undiscounted future cash flows compare with $65,000. Assuming that those cash flows are estimated to be $50,000, an impairment loss is evident. The next step is to determine the fair value of the asset by the appropriate method (i.e., quoted market price, estimate based on similar assets, estimate based on an appropriate valuation technique). If the fair value is determined to be $40,000, the result is an impairment loss of $25,000, computed as follows:

Asset cost	$100,000
Less: Accumulated depreciation	35,000
Carrying amount	$ 65,000
Less: Fair value	40,000
Impairment loss	$ 25,000

An impairment loss of $25,000 is recognized, and $40,000 is now considered the cost of the asset for future accounting and depreciation purposes. Notice that the undiscounted future cash flow of $50,000 is used only to identify the need to measure the amount of the impairment loss. That amount is not used directly to determine the amount of the loss, although it may be useful if the fair value is determined by estimating the present value of future cash flows.

Long-Lived Assets to Be Disposed Of

In addition to covering assets to be held and used, ASC 360 also specifies accounting standards for assets to be disposed of. Assets to be disposed of other than by sale (e.g., by abandonment or in an exchange for a similar productive asset) shall continue to be classified as held and used until disposition. An asset to be abandoned is considered disposed of when it ceases to be used. If an entity commits to a plan to abandon a long-lived asset before the end of its estimated useful life, depreciation estimates shall be revised in accordance with ASC 250 to reflect the use of the asset over a shorter useful life than originally expected. A temporarily idle asset is not considered abandoned. An asset to be exchanged for a similar productive asset is considered disposed of when it is exchanged. Similarly, an asset that is to be distributed to owners in a spin-off is considered to have been disposed of when it is distributed (ASC 360-10-45-15; 360-10-35-47).

Disposal by Sale

A long-lived asset to be sold is classified as held for sale in the period in which all of the following criteria are met (ASC 360-10-45-9):

- Management commits to a plan to sell the asset or asset group.
- The asset (asset group) is available for immediate sale in its present condition.
- An active program to locate a buyer has been initiated.
- The sale of the asset (asset group) is probable, and transfer of the asset (asset group) is expected to qualify for recognition as a completed sale within one year. ASC 360 provides certain exceptions to this one-year requirement (ASC 360-10-45-11)).

- The asset (asset group) is being actively marketed for sale at a price that is reasonable in relation to its fair value.

- Actions required to complete the plan indicate that it is unlikely that significant changes in the plan will be made or that the plan will be withdrawn.

A long-lived asset (asset group) that is newly acquired and that will be held for sale rather than for use should be classified as held for sale as of the acquisition date only if the sale is expected within one year and the other requirements stated in the previous paragraph that are not met are probable of being met within a short period from the acquisition date (ASC 360-10-45-12).

PRACTICE POINTER: ASC 360 indicates that in applying this requirement, the term "short period" should be interpreted as within three months.

If the criteria for considering an asset as held for sale are met after the financial statement date, but before the financial statements are issued, that asset shall be treated as held and used in the financial statements. Information concerning the intent to sell the asset is required to be presented in notes to the financial statements (ASC 360-10-45-13).

A long-lived asset (asset group) classified as held for sale shall be measured at the lower of its carrying amount or fair value less cost to sell. If the asset (asset group) is newly acquired, the carrying amount of the asset (asset group) shall be based on its fair value less cost to sell at the acquisition date. A long-lived asset shall not be depreciated once it is classified as held for sale (ASC 360-10-35-43).

Costs to sell are the incremental direct costs to transact a sale. These are the costs that result directly from and are essential to a sale transaction and that would not have been incurred if the decision to sell had not been made. These costs include:

1. Broker commissions
2. Legal and title transfer fees
3. Closing costs that must be incurred before legal title can be transferred

These costs exclude expected future losses associated with the operations of the asset (asset group) while it is classified as held for sale (ASC 360-10-35-38).

A loss shall be recognized for any initial or subsequent write-down to fair value less cost to sell. A gain shall be recognized for any subsequent increase in fair value less cost to sell, but not in excess of the cumulative loss previously recognized. The loss or gain shall adjust only the carrying amount of a long-lived asset, whether classified as held for sale individually, or as part of a disposal group (ASC 360-10-35-40).

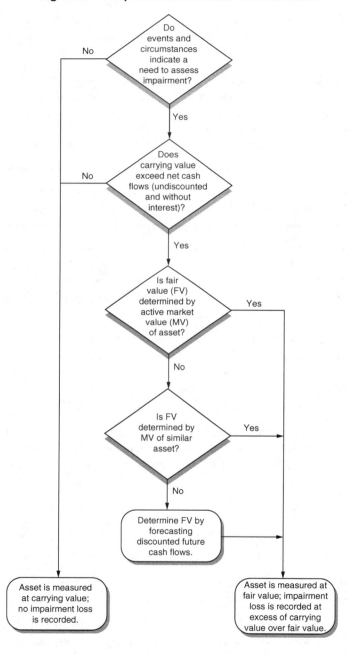

Figure 25-1: Impairment of Assets Held and Used

Illustration of Impairment of Asset to Be Disposed Of

Wampler, Inc. has a piece of specialized machinery that is no longer efficiently usable for its operations as a result of technological advances that require replacement. The machine cost Wampler $500,000 and has an accumulated depreciation (based on double-declining balance) of $275,000. Estimates of the selling price and the cost to sell, including solicitation and execution of a sales agreement, are $185,000 and $25,000, respectively. Wampler should record an impairment loss in the current period, as follows:

Asset cost		$500,000
Accumulated depreciation		(275,000)
Asset carrying amount		$225,000
Less: Estimated selling price	$185,000	
Cost to sell	(25,000)	(160,000)
Impairment loss		$ 65,000

Changes in a Plan to Sell

Circumstances may arise that cause an entity to decide not to sell a long-lived asset (asset group) that was previously classified as held for sale. In this instance the asset (asset group) should be reclassified as to be held and used. An asset (asset group) that is so reclassified should be measured individually at the lower of (1) its carrying amount before the asset (asset group) was classified as held for sale, adjusted for any depreciation or amortization expense that would have been recognized had the asset (asset group) been continuously classified as held and used, or (2) the fair value at the date of the decision not to sell the asset (ASC 360-10-35-44). Any adjustment required by this process is included as an element of income from continuing operations in the period of the decision to not sell the asset (ASC 360-10-45-7).

DEPLETION

Depletion is the process of allocating the cost of a natural resource over its estimated useful life in a manner similar to depreciation. An estimate is made of the amount of natural resources to be extracted, in units or tons, barrels, or any other measurement. The estimate of total recoverable units is then divided into the total cost of the depletable asset, to arrive at a depletion rate per unit. Estimated costs to restore the property should be added, and estimated residual value should be subtracted. The annual depletion expense is the rate per unit times the number of units extracted during the fiscal year. If at any time there is a revision of the estimated number of units that are expected to be extracted, a new unit rate is computed. The cost of the natural resource property is reduced each year by the amount of the depletion expense for the year. This process is similar to the units-of-production depreciation method explained earlier.

DISCLOSURE

Accumulated depreciation and depletion are deducted from the assets to which they relate. The following disclosures of depreciable assets and depreciation are required in the financial statements or notes thereto (ASC 360-10-50-1).

- Depreciation expense for the period
- Balances of major classes of depreciable assets by nature or function
- Accumulated depreciation allowances by classes or in total
- The methods used, by major classes, in computing depreciation

PRACTICE NOTE: Practice varies on whether these disclosures are made in the aggregate for all categories of depreciable assets or separately for each category. Presentation in the aggregate seems to be the dominant practice, despite the fact that separate disclosure provides more useful information.

PRACTICE POINTER: ASC 360-10-50-1 requires that the above disclosures be made in the financial statements or in the notes. In addition, ASC 250 (Accounting Changes and Error Corrections) requires disclosure of the effect of a change from one depreciation method to another (ASC 250-10-50-4).

Reporting on impairment losses depends on whether the assets are to be held and used or disposed of. An impairment loss on long-lived assets to be held and used shall be included in income from continuing operations before income taxes in the income statement of a business enterprise and in income from continuing operations in the statement of activities of a not-for-profit organization (ASC 360-10-45-4).

The following information shall be disclosed in the period in which an impairment loss on an asset to be held and used is recognized (ASC 360-10-50-2):

- Description of the impaired long-lived asset and the facts and circumstances leading to the impairment.
- The amount of the impairment loss and the caption of the income statement or statement of activities that includes the loss.
- The method(s) of determining fair value.
- If applicable, the segment in which the impaired long-lived asset is reported under ASC 280 (Segment Reporting).

For coverage of the reporting requirements for assets to be disposed of, see the discussion in Chapter 2, *ASC 205—Presentation of Financial Statements*.

ASC 360-20: REAL ESTATE SALES

RECOGNITION OF SALES

Real Estate Sales (Except Retail Land Sales)

In a real estate sale, a significant portion of the sales price usually is represented by a long-term receivable, which is not backed by the full faith and credit of the buyer. Usually, the seller can recover the property only in the event of default by the buyer. Another unusual facet of real estate sales is the seller's possible continuing involvement in the property. For instance, the seller may be legally bound to make certain improvements to the property or to adjacent property.

To ensure the collection of the long-term receivable, which usually is part of a real estate transaction, ASC 360 requires minimum down payments for all real estate sales before a seller is permitted to recognize a profit. ASC 360 emphasizes the timing of the recognition of profits but does not cover other aspects of real estate accounting.

Real estate transactions that are *not* considered "retail land sales" include the following:

1. Sales of homes, buildings, and parcels of land
2. Sales of lots to builders
3. Sales of corporate stock or a partnership interest in which the substance of the transaction is actually a sale of real estate
4. Sales of options to acquire real estate
5. Sales of time-sharing interests in real estate

As stated above, sales of time-sharing interests in real estate are to be accounted for as nonretail land sales. For a seller to report the total profit on a sale of real estate (other than a retail land sale) by the full accrual method, ASC 360 requires that the transaction meet specific criteria, as follows (ASC 360-20-40-5):

- A sale must be completed (consummated).
- The buyer's initial and continuing payments (investment) must be adequate.
- The seller's receivable is not subject to future subordination, except to (*a*) a primary lien on the property existing at the date of sale or (*b*) a future loan or an existing permanent loan commitment the proceeds of which must first be applied to the payment of the seller's receivable.
- All of the benefits and risks of ownership in the property are substantially transferred to the buyer by the seller.
- The seller does not have a substantial continued involvement with the property after the sale.

If a sale of real estate, other than a retail land sale, meets all of the above criteria, the seller must recognize the entire profit on the sale in accordance with the full accrual method of accounting. If a real estate sale fails to meet all of the above criteria, profit on the sale is recognized by (*a*) the deposit method, (*b*) the installment sales method, (*c*) the cost-recovery method, (*d*) the reduced profit method, or (*e*) the percentage-of-completion method. The method that is used is determined by the specific circumstances of each real estate sale.

> **PRACTICE NOTE:** For sale-leaseback transactions, the sale portion of such a transaction involving real estate is accounted for as a sale only if it qualifies as a sale under the provisions of ASC 360. In addition, ASC 840 prohibits a lease involving real estate from being classified as a sales-type lease unless the lease agreement provides for the title of the leased property to be transferred to the lessee at or shortly after the end of the lease term. Additional coverage of the accounting for sale-leaseback transactions can be found in our discussion of ASC 840 (Leases).

When a Real Estate Sale Is Consummated

ASC 360 contains four criteria that must be met for a sale of real estate to be considered "consummated" (ASC 360-20-40-7):

1. The contracting parties are legally bound by the contract.
2. All consideration required by the terms of the contract has been paid.
3. If the seller is responsible by the terms of the contract to obtain permanent financing for the buyer, the seller must have arranged for such financing.
4. The seller has performed all of the acts required by the contract to earn the revenue.

As a general rule, the above criteria are met at the time of, or after, the closing of the real estate sale. These criteria rarely are met before closing or at the time a sales agreement is executed.

An exception to the "consummation rule" may occur if, after the date of sale, the seller has continued involvement with the property to construct office buildings, condominiums, shopping centers, or other similar improvements on the land that take a long time to complete. As will be discussed later, ASC 360 permits some profit recognition under certain circumstances even if the seller has this type of substantial continued involvement with the property.

Buyer's Initial and Continuing Investment

In determining whether the buyer's minimum initial investment is adequate under the provisions of ASC 360, the *sales value* of the property—not the stated sales price in the contract—is used. The *sales value* is defined as the stated sales price of the property, increased or decreased for other considerations included in the sale that clearly represent greater or smaller proceeds to the seller on the sale. Thus, any payments made by the buyer that are not included in the stated sales price in the contract and that represent additional proceeds to the seller are included as part of the buyer's minimum investment. These additional proceeds enter into the determination of both the buyer's minimum investment and the sales value of the property. Examples of additional proceeds to the seller are (*a*) the exercise price of a real estate option to purchase the property, (*b*) management fees, (*c*) points to obtain financing, (*d*) prepaid interest and principal payments, (*e*) payments by the buyer to third parties that reduce previously existing indebtedness on the property, and (*f*) any payments made by the buyer to the seller that will be applied at a future date against amounts due the seller (ASC 360-20-40-8). However, payments by the buyer to third parties for improvements to the property or payments that are not verifiable are not considered as additional proceeds to the seller (ASC 360-20-40-13). See ASC 970 for a discussion of other real estate costs a buyer or seller may incur such as preacquisition costs, postacquisition costs, and costs to sell or rent real estate.

Decreases in the stated sales price that are necessary to arrive at the sales value of the property may include, but are not limited to, the following (ASC 360-20-40-8):

- The amount of discount, if any, necessary to reduce the receivable from the buyer to its present value. Thus, if the buyer's receivable does not bear interest or if the rate of interest is less than the prevailing rate, a discount would be required to reduce it to its present value.
- The present value of services that the seller agrees to perform without compensation or, if the seller agrees to perform services at less than prevailing rates, the difference between (a) the present value of the services at prevailing rates and (b) the present value of the agreed-upon compensation.

Illustration of Computation of Sales Value

XYZ, Inc. agrees to build improvements for ABC Company for a total price of $1,750,000. The improvements are to be built on land leased by ABC from a third party. The payments on the land lease are $18,000 per year, payable monthly in advance, and the lease term is for 45 years. ABC Company will pay for the improvements as follows:

Cash down payment	$ 250,000
10% unsecured note payable in five annual payments of $20,000 plus interest	100,000
Primary loan from insurance company secured by improvements to the property, payable in equal monthly payments over 28 years at 8 1/2% interest	1,400,000
Total stated sales price of improvements	$1,750,000

The computation of the *sales value*, as required by ASC 360, is as follows:

Present value of land lease payments for 28 years, payable $1,500 monthly, discounted at 8 1/2% interest	$ 193,361
Primary loan from insurance company	1,400,000
Total equivalent primary debt	$1,593,361
Unsecured note from buyer to seller	100,000
Cash down payment	250,000
Sales value*	$1,943,361

---

* The adequacy of the buyer's minimum initial investment in the property is based on the *sales value* of the property and not on the stated sales price.

As indicated in the previous illustration, the effects of an underlying land lease must also be included in computing the sales value of the property. If a seller sells a buyer improvements that are to be built on property subject to an underlying land lease, the present value of the lease payments must be included in the sales value of the property. The present value of the lease payments is computed over the actual term of the primary indebtedness of the improvements, if any, or over the usual term of primary indebtedness for the type of improvements involved. The present value of the land lease payments is tantamount to additional indebtedness on the property. If the land lease is not subordinated, the discount rate to determine the present value of the land lease payments should be comparable to interest rates on primary debt of the same nature. If the land lease is subordinated, however, a higher discount rate comparable to secondary debt of the same nature should be used.

If a land lease exists between the buyer and a third party, its effects on the sales value of the property are used only to determine the adequacy of the buyer's initial investment. When the seller of the improvements is also the lessor of the land lease, however, the computation of the profit on the sale of the improvements is also affected. Because it is impossible to separate the profits on the improvements from the profits on the underlying lease, ASC 360 requires a special computation limiting the amount of profit that can be recognized. The amount of profit that can be recognized on the improvements is equal to the sales value of the property, less the cost of improvements and the cost of the land. However, the present value of the lease payments in the sales value may not exceed the actual cost of the land (ASC 360-20-40-57).

The result of limiting the amount of profit that can be recognized on the sale of improvements is to defer any residual profit on the land from being recognized until the land is sold or the future rental payments actually are received (ASC 360-20-40-59).

If a land lease between a buyer and a seller of improvements on the land is for a term of less than 20 years or does not substantially cover the economic life of the improvements being made to the property, the transaction should be accounted for as a single lease of land and improvements (ASC 360-20-40-56).

The buyer's minimum initial investment must be made in cash or cash equivalency at or before the time of sale. A buyer's note does not qualify for the minimum initial investment unless payment of the note is unconditionally guaranteed by an irrevocable letter of credit from an established unrelated lending institution. A permanent loan commitment by an independent third party to replace a loan made by the seller is not included in the buyer's initial investment. Any funds that have been loaned or will be loaned, directly or indirectly, to the buyer by the seller are deducted from the buyer's initial investment (down payment) to determine whether the required minimum has been met. For the purposes of this provision, the seller must be exposed to a potential loss as a result of the funds loaned to the buyer. For example, if a buyer made an initial cash investment of $200,000 in a real estate transaction, $25,000 of which was a loan from the seller, the buyer's minimum initial investment under the provisions of ASC 360 would be $175,000. However, if an unrelated banking institution unconditionally guaranteed the timely repayment of the $25,000 to the seller, the entire $200,000 would be eligible as the buyer's initial investment (ASC 360-20-40-10, 13).

A direct relationship exists between the amount of a buyer's first investment (down payment) and the probability that the seller eventually will collect the balance due. The larger the down payment, the more likely it is that the buyer will pay the balance due. A reasonable basis for establishing the amount of a buyer's initial investment is the prevailing practices of independent lending institutions. Thus, the difference between the amount of primary mortgage an independent lending institution would lend on a particular parcel of real estate and the sales value of the property is a realistic guide to figure the amount of the buyer's initial investment (ASC 360-20-40-18).

To apply the full accrual method of accounting to a real estate transaction (other than a retail land sale), ASC 360 provides that the minimum initial investment (down payment) of the buyer should be the *greater* of 1 or 2 below:

1. The percentage of the sales value of the property as indicated in the following (ASC 360-20-55-1):

	Minimum Down Payment (% of Sales Value)
Land:	
Held for commercial, industrial, or residential development to commence within two years after sale	20%
Held for commercial, industrial, or residential development after two years	25%
Commercial and Industrial Property:	
Office and industrial buildings, shopping centers, etc.:	
Properties subject to lease on a long-term lease basis to parties having satisfactory credit rating; cash flow currently sufficient to service all indebtedness	10%
Single tenancy properties sold to a user having a satisfactory credit rating	15%
All other	20%
Other Income-Producing Properties (hotels, motels, marinas, mobile home parks, etc.):	
Cash flow currently sufficient to service all indebtedness	15%
Start-up situations or current deficiencies in cash flow	25%
Multi-Family Residential Property:	
Primary residence:	
Cash flow currently sufficient to service all indebtedness	10%
Start-up situations or current deficiencies in cash flow	15%
Secondary or recreational residence:	
Cash flow currently sufficient to service all indebtedness	15%

	Minimum Down Payment (% of Sales Value)
Start-up situations or current deficiencies in cash flow	25%
Single Family Residential Property (including condominium or cooperative housing):	
Primary residence of the buyer	5%*
Secondary or recreational residence	10%*

* If collectibility of the remaining portion of the sales price cannot be supported by reliable evidence of collection experience, a higher down payment is called for and should not be less than 60% of the difference between the sales value and the financing available from loans guaranteed by regulatory bodies, such as FHA or VA, or from independent financial institutions. This 60% test applies when independent first-mortgage financing is not utilized and the seller takes a receivable from the buyer for the difference between the sales value and the initial investment. When independent first-mortgage financing is utilized, the adequacy of the initial investment on sales of single-family residential property should be determined in accordance with ASC 360.

2. The *lesser* of the following (ASC 360-20-55-1):

   a. The difference between the sales value of the property and 115% of the maximum permanent mortgage loan or commitment on the property recently obtained from a primary independent lending institution, or

   b. Twenty-five percent (25%) of the sales value of the property

---

Illustration of Determination of Buyer's Minimum Initial Investment

The sales value of property being sold is $200,000, and the maximum permanent mortgage loan recently placed on the property from an independent lending institution is $150,000. The property being sold is commercial land, which will be developed by the buyer within two years after the date of sale. For the full accrual method of accounting to be applied to this real estate transaction, ASC 360 provides that the minimum initial investment (down payment) of the buyer should be the greater of (1) or (2) below:

1. The percentage of the sales value of the property as indicated on the table is $40,000 (20% of $200,000).

2. a. The difference between the sales value of the property and 115% of the recently placed permanent mortgage loan is $27,500 (115% of $150,000 = $172,500 and the difference between $200,000 [sales value] and $172,500 is $27,500).

   b. 25% of the sales value ($200,000) is $50,000.

   The lesser of 2a ($27,500) and 2b ($50,000) = $27,500.

   The greater of 2a ($27,500) and 1 ($40,000) = $40,000.

   Thus, the minimum down payment of the buyer is $40,000.

PRACTICE POINTER: Even if the buyer makes the required minimum initial investment, make a separate assessment to determine the collectibility of the receivable. In other words, there must be reasonable assurance that the receivable will be collected after the seller receives the minimum initial investment; if there is not, do not record the sale by the full accrual method. The buyer must make the minimum initial investment, and the seller must be reasonably assured that the balance of the sales price will be collected, before the real estate sale is recorded and any profits are recognized. The assessment of the receivable by the seller should include credit reports on the buyer and an evaluation of the adequacy of the cash flow from the property.

In addition to an adequate initial investment, ASC 360 requires that the buyer maintain a continuing investment in the property by increasing his or her investment each year. The buyer's total indebtedness for the purchase price of the property must be reduced each year in equal amounts, which will extinguish the entire indebtedness (interest and principal) over a specified maximum period. The specified maximum period for land transactions is 20 years. The specified maximum period for all other real estate transactions is no more than that offered by independent financial institutions at the time of sale for first mortgages (ASC 360-20-40-19).

The buyer's commitment to pay the full amount of his or her indebtedness to the seller becomes doubtful if the total indebtedness is not to be paid within the specified maximum period.

A buyer's payments on his or her indebtedness must be in cash or cash equivalency. Funds provided directly or indirectly by the seller cannot be considered in determining the buyer's continuing investment in the property (ASC 360-20-40-20).

Release Provisions

Real estate agreements involving land frequently provide for the periodic release of part of the land to the buyer. The buyer obtains the released land free of any liens. The conditions for the release usually require the buyer to have previously paid sufficient funds to cover the sales price of the released land, and often an additional sum is required to effectuate the release. In these types of transactions involving released land, the requirements for a buyer's initial and continuing investment must be determined based on the sales value of property not released or not subject to release (ASC 360-20-40-21). In other words, for a seller to recognize profit at the time of sale, a buyer's investment must be enough to pay any amounts for the release of land and still meet the specified initial and continued investment required by the provisions of ASC 360 (ASC 360-20-40-22). If the buyer's initial and continuing investment is not sufficient, then each release of land should be treated as a separate sale and profit recognized at that time (ASC 360-20-40-23).

Future Subordination

If, at the time of sale, a seller's receivable is subject to future subordination, other than (*a*) to a primary (first mortgage) lien on the property existing at the date of sale or (*b*) to a future loan or existing permanent loan commitment the proceeds of which must first be applied to the payment of the seller's receivable, no profit should be recognized, because the effect of future subordination on the collectibility of a receivable cannot be evaluated reasonably. The cost-recovery method should be used to recognize profit at the time of sale if the seller's receivable is subject to future subordination, other than the exceptions (*a*) and (*b*) noted above (ASC 360-20-40-25).

Nontransfer of Ownership and Seller's Continued Involvement

Real estate transactions must be analyzed carefully to determine their economic substance. Frequently, the economic substance of a real estate sale is no more than a management fee arrangement or an indication that the risks and benefits of ownership have not really been transferred in the agreement. Accounting for a real estate transaction can become quite complicated because of the many types of continuing relations that can exist between a buyer and a seller. The substance of the real estate transaction should dictate the accounting method that should be used.

PRACTICE POINTER: As a general rule, before a profit is recognized, a sale must occur, collectibility of the receivable must be reasonably assured, and the seller must perform all of the acts required by the contract to earn the revenue. Profit also may be recognized—at the time of the sale—on contracts that provide for the continued involvement of the seller if the maximum potential loss of the seller is expressly limited and defined by the terms of the contract. In this event, recognize the total profit on the sale, less the maximum potential loss that could occur because of the seller's involvement, at the time of the sale.

Two important factors in evaluating the economic substance of a real estate sale are (1) the transfer of the usual risks and rewards of ownership in the property and (2) the full performance by the seller of all acts required by the contract to earn the revenue. Generally, both of these factors must be accomplished before full profit can be recognized on the sale of real estate. The more common types of real estate transactions and how they should be accounted for are discussed in the following paragraphs.

Profit Recognition Other Than Full Accrual Basis

If a sale of real estate, other than a retail land sale, meets all of the ASC 360 criteria discussed earlier, the seller must recognize the entire profit on the sale in accordance with the full accrual basis of accounting.

When one (or more) of the ASC 360 criteria is not met in a real estate sale, an alternative method of recognizing revenue from the sale must be used. The alternative method selected may be required by ASC 360 or may be a matter of professional judgment. The four accounting methods recommended by ASC 360 are (1) the deposit method, (2) the cost-recovery method, (3) the installment sales method, and (4) the reduced profit method.

Deposit Accounting

The uncertainty about the collectibility of the sales price in a real estate transaction may be so great that the effective date of the sale is deferred and any cash received by the seller is accounted for as a deposit. However, cash received that is designated by contract as nonrefundable interest may be applied as an offset to existing carrying charges on the property, such as property taxes and interest, instead of being accounted for as a deposit.

All cash received, except that appropriately used as an offset to the carrying charges of the property, must be reflected in the seller's balance sheet as a liability (deposit on a contract for the sale of real estate). No change is made in accounting for the property subject to the contract and its related mortgage debt, if any. However, the seller's financial statements should disclose that these items are subject to a sales contract. Depreciation expense should continue as a period cost, in spite of the fact that the property has been sold legally. Until the requirements of ASC 360 are met for profit recognition, the seller does not report a sale and continues to report all cash received (including interest received) either as a deposit or, in the case of nonrefundable interest, as an offset to the carrying charges of the property involved (ASC 360-20-55-17). If the buyer forfeits a nonrefundable deposit, or defaults on the contract, the seller should reduce the deposit account appropriately and include such amounts in income of the period (ASC 360-20-55-19).

Cost-Recovery Method

If a seller's receivable is subject to subordination that cannot be reasonably evaluated, or if uncertainty exists as to the recovery of the seller's cost on default by the buyer, the cost recovery method should be used. Even if cost has been recovered by the seller but additional collections are highly doubtful, the cost-recovery method is appropriate. Frequently, the cost recovery method is used initially for transactions that would also qualify for the installment sales method.

PRACTICE NOTE: Both the cost recovery method and the installment sales method defer the recognition of profit on the sale until collections actually are received.

Under the cost recovery method, all collections (including interest received) are applied first to the recovery of the cost of the property; only after full cost has been received is any profit recognized (ASC Glossary). The only expenses remaining to be charged against the profit are those relating to the collection process. When the cost recovery method is used, the total sales value is included in the income statement for the period in which the sale is made (ASC 360-20-55-14). From the total sales value in the income statement, the total cost of the sale and the deferred gross profit on the sale are deducted. On the balance sheet, the deferred gross profit is reflected as a reduction of the related receivable. Until full cost is recovered, principal payments received are applied to reduce the related receivable, and interest payments received are added to the deferred gross profit. At any given time, the related receivable, less the deferred gross profit, equals the remaining cost that must be recovered. After all cost is recovered, subsequent collections reduce the deferred gross profit and appear as a separate item of revenue on the income statement.

Installment Sales Method

Promulgated GAAP prohibit accounting for sales by installment accounting except under exceptional circumstances in which collectibility cannot be assured or estimated reasonably. Collectibility can be in doubt because of the length of an extended collection period or because no basis of estimation can be established.

PRACTICE NOTE: The installment sales method frequently is more appropriate for real estate transactions in which collectibility of the receivable from the buyer cannot be reasonably assured because defaults on loans secured by real estate usually result in the recovery of the property sold.

Under the installment sales method of accounting, each payment collected consists of part recovery of cost and part recovery of gross profit, in the same ratio that these two elements existed in the original sale. In a real estate transaction, the original sale is equal to the sales value of the property. Thus, under the installment sales method, profit is recognized on cash payments made by the buyer to the holder of the primary debt assumed and on cash payments to the seller. The profit recognized on the cash payments is based on the percentage of total profit to total sales value (ASC 360-20-55-7).

Illustration of Installment Sales Method

Jones Company sells real property to Smith for $2,000,000. Smith will assume an existing $1,200,000 first mortgage and pay $300,000 in cash as a down payment. The $500,000 balance will be in the form of a 12% second mortgage to Jones Company payable in equal payments of principal and interest over a ten-year period. The cost of the property to Jones is $1,200,000.

Computation of Sales Value and Gross Profit

Cash	$ 300,000
Second mortgage	500,000
First mortgage	1,200,000
Total sales value (which is the same as the stated sales price)	$2,000,000
Less: Cost of property sold	1,200,000
Total gross profit on sale	$ 800,000
Gross profit percentage ($800,000/$2,000,000)	40.0%
Profit to be recognized on down payment (40% of $300,000)	$ 120,000

Assuming that the $300,000 down payment is not sufficient to meet the requirements of full profit recognition on the sale, Jones recognizes $120,000 gross profit at the time of sale. Several months later Smith makes a cash payment of $100,000 on the first mortgage and $50,000 on the second mortgage. The amount of gross profit that Jones recognizes on these payments would be as follows:

Payment on first mortgage	$100,000
Payment on second mortgage	50,000
Total cash payments	$150,000
Gross profit realized (40% of $150,000)	$ 60,000

Even though Jones does not receive any cash on Smith's payment on the first mortgage, gross profit is still realized because the gross profit percentage was based on the total sales value, which included the first mortgage liability.

When the installment sales method is used, the total sales value is included in the income statement of the period in which the sale is made. From the total sales value in the income statement, the total cost of the sale and the deferred gross profit are deducted (ASC 360-20-55-10). On the balance sheet, the deferred gross profit on the sale is deducted from the related receivable. As cash payments are received, the portion allocated to realized gross profit is presented as a separate item of revenue on the income statement and deferred gross profit is reduced by the same amount. At any given time, the related receivable, less the deferred gross profit, represents the remaining cost of the property sold (ASC 360-20-55-9). Since realized gross profit is recognized as a portion of each cash collection, a percentage relationship will always exist between the long-term receivable and its related deferred gross profit. This percentage relationship will be the same as the gross profit ratio on the initial sales value.

Reduced Profit Method

The buyer's receivable is discounted to the present value of the lowest level of annual payments required by the sales contract. The discount period is the maximum allowed under the provisions of ASC 360, and all lump-sum payments are excluded in the calculation. The discount rate cannot be less than that stated in the sales contract, if any, or than the prevailing interest rate in accordance with existing GAAP. The buyer's receivable discounted as described above is used in determining the profit on the sale of real estate and usually results in a "reduced profit" from that which would be obtained under normal accounting procedures. Lump sum and other payments are recognized as profit when the seller receives them (ASC 360-20-55-16).

Change to Full Accrual Method

After the cost-recovery method or the installment sales method is adopted for a real estate transaction, the receivable should be evaluated periodically for collectibility. When it becomes apparent that the seller's receivable is reasonably assured of being collected, the seller should change to the full accrual accounting method. The change is a change in accounting estimate. When the change to the full accrual accounting method is made, any remaining deferred gross profit is recognized in full in the period in which the change is made (ASC 360-20-55-12,

15). If the change creates a material effect on the seller's financial statements, full disclosure of the effects and the reason for the change should be appropriately made in the financial statements or notes thereto.

Profit Recognition When Sale Is Not Consummated

If a real estate sale has not been consummated in accordance with the provisions of ASC 360, the deposit method of accounting is used until the sale is consummated (ASC 360-20-40-28).

As mentioned previously, an exception to the "consummation rule" occurs if the terms of the contract require the seller to sell a parcel of land and also construct on the same parcel a building that takes an extended period to complete. In other words, the seller is still involved with the property after the sale because he or she must construct the building. In most jurisdictions a "certificate of occupancy" must be obtained, indicating that the building or other structure has been constructed in accordance with the local building regulations and is ready for occupancy. Thus, a certificate of occupancy usually is necessary to consummate the real estate transaction. However, ASC 360 contains a special provision for profit recognition when a sale of real estate requires the seller to develop the property in the future. If the seller has contracted (*a*) for future development of the land; (*b*) to construct buildings, amenities, or other facilities on the land; or (*c*) to provide offsite improvements, partial recognition of profit may be made if future costs of development can be estimated reasonably at the time of sale (ASC 360-20-40-28). In this event, profit can be recognized for any work performed and finished by the seller when (*a*) the sale of the land is consummated and (*b*) the initial and continuing investments of the buyer are adequate. In other words, if the sale of the land meets the first two criteria for the use of the full accrual method of accounting, any profit allocable to (*a*) the work performed before the sale of the land and (*b*) the sale of the land can be recognized by the percentage of-completion method. Thus, the total profit on the sale may be allocated to work performed before the sale of the land and before future construction and development work. The allocation of the total profit is based on the estimated costs for each activity using a uniform rate of gross profit for all activities. If significant uncertainties exist or if costs and profits cannot be reasonably estimated, however, the completed contract method should be used (ASC 360-20-40-62, 63).

If a buyer has the right to defer until completion payments due for developmental and construction work, or if the buyer is financially unable to pay these amounts as they come due, care should be exercised in recognizing any profits until completion or satisfactory payment.

The terms of a real estate transaction accounted for by the deposit method may indicate that the carrying amount of the property involved is more than the sales value in the contract and that a loss has been incurred. Because the seller is using the deposit method, no sale is recorded and thus no loss. However, the information indicates an impairment of an asset that should be appropriately recorded by the seller in the period of discovery by a charge to income and the creation of a valuation allowance account for the property involved (ASC 360-20-40-29).

Profit Recognition When Buyer's Investment Is Inadequate

If all of the criteria for the full accrual method of accounting are met except that the buyer's initial investment is inadequate, the seller accounts for the sale by the installment sales method, provided the seller is reasonably assured of recovering the cost of the property if the buyer defaults. If the seller is not reasonably assured of recovering the cost of the property, or if cost recovery has been made but future collections are uncertain, the seller uses the cost-recovery method or the deposit method to account for the sale (ASC 360-20-40-31).

If all of the criteria for the full accrual method of accounting are met except that the buyer's continuing investment is inadequate, the seller shall account for the sale by the reduced profit method, provided the buyer's periodic payments cover both of the following items (ASC 360-20-40-33):

- Amortization of principal and interest based on the maximum primary mortgage that could be obtained on the property
- Interest, at an appropriate rate, on the excess amount, if any, of the total actual debt on the property over the maximum primary mortgage that could be obtained on the property

If both of the above conditions are not met, the seller shall not use the reduced profit method. Instead, the seller should account for the sale by either the installment sales method or the cost-recovery method, whichever is more appropriate under the specific circumstances (ASC 360-20-40-34).

Profit Recognition—Subordinated Receivable

As mentioned previously, the cost-recovery method is used to recognize profit at the time of sale if the seller's receivable is subject to future subordination (ASC 360-20-40-26).

This restriction does not apply in the following circumstances (ASC 360-20-40-25):

- A receivable is subordinate to a first mortgage on the property existing at the time of sale.
- A future loan, including an existing permanent loan commitment, is provided for by the terms of the sale, and the proceeds of the loan will be applied first to the payment of the seller's receivable.

Profit Recognition—Seller's Continued Involvement

In some real estate transactions the seller does not transfer the benefits and risks of ownership to the buyer, or the seller maintains a substantial continued involvement with the property after the date of sale. These types of real estate transactions require careful examination to determine the appropriate method of accounting to be applied.

In legal form a real estate transaction may be a sale, but if in substance the contract is a profit sharing, financing, or leasing arrangement, no sale or profit is recognized. If a real estate contract contains any of the following provisions, it should be accounted for as a profit sharing, financing, or leasing arrangement:

- The return of the buyer's investment in the property is guaranteed by the seller (ASC 360-20-40-41).
- The buyer can compel the seller to repurchase the property (ASC 360-20-40-38).
- An option or obligation exists for the seller to repurchase the property (ASC 360-20-40-38).
- The seller is required to operate the property at its own risk for an extended period (ASC 360-20-40-42).
- The seller, as general partner, holds a receivable from the limited partnership as a result of a real estate sale. The collection of the receivable depends on the successful operation of the limited partnership by the general partner, who is also the seller and holder of the receivable (ASC 360-20-40-40).
- The seller guarantees a specific return on the buyer's investment for an extended period of time (ASC 360-20-40-41).
- The sale includes a leaseback to the seller of all or part of the property.

In real estate transactions in which the seller guarantees for a limited period (*a*) to return the buyer's investment or (*b*) to give the buyer a specific rate of return, the seller shall account for the sale by the deposit method of accounting. After the operations of the property become profitable, the seller may recognize profit based on performance. After the limited period has expired and all of the criteria for the full accrual method of accounting are met in accordance with ASC 360, the seller may recognize in full any remaining profit on the sale of real estate.

Initiating and Supporting Operations

As part of a real estate transaction, the seller may be required to initiate or support the operations of the property for a stated period of time or until a certain level of operations has been achieved. In other words, the seller may agree to operate the property for a certain period or until a certain level of rental income has been reached.

Even if there is no agreement, there is a presumption that a seller has an obligation to initiate and support operations of the property he or she has sold in any of the following circumstances (ASC 360-20-40-40):

- The seller sells to a limited partnership an interest in property in which he or she is a general partner.
- The seller retains an equity interest in the property sold by the seller.
- A management contract between the buyer and seller provides for compensation that is significantly higher or lower than comparable prevailing rates and that cannot be terminated by either the buyer or the seller.
- The collection of the receivable from the sale held by the seller is dependent on the operations of the property and represents a significant portion of the sales price. A *significant receivable* is defined as one in excess of 15%

of the maximum primary financing that could have been obtained from an established lending institution.

If the seller has agreed to the initiating and supporting operations for a limited period, the seller may recognize profit on the sale based on the performance of the required services. The measurement of performance shall be related to the cost incurred to date and the total estimated costs to be incurred for the services. However, profit recognition may not start until there is reasonable assurance that estimated future rent receipts will cover (*a*) all operating costs, (*b*) debt service, and (*c*) any payments due the seller under the terms of the contract. For this purpose, the estimated future rental receipts shall not exceed the greater of (*a*) leases actually executed or (*b*) two-thirds of the estimated future rent receipts. The difference between the estimated future rent receipts and the greater of (*a*) or (*b*) shall be reserved as a safety factor (ASC 360-20-40-44).

If the sales contract does not specify the period for which the seller must initiate and support operations of the property, a two-year period shall be presumed. The two-year period shall commence at the time of initial rental, unless rental receipts cover all operating cost, debt service, and other commitments before the end of the two-year period (ASC 360-20-40-43).

Services without Compensation

As part of the contract for the sale of real estate, the seller may be required to perform services related to the property sold without compensation or at a reduced rate. In determining profit to be recognized at the time of sale, a value should be placed on such services at the prevailing rates and deducted from the sales price of the property sold. The value of the compensation should then be recognized over the period in which the services are to be performed by the seller (ASC 360-20-40-43).

Sale of Real Estate Options

Proceeds from the sale of real estate options shall be accounted for by the deposit method. If the option is not exercised by its expiration date, the seller of the option shall recognize profit at that time. If an option is sold by the owner of the land and subsequently exercised, the proceeds from the sale of the option are included in determining the sales value of the property sold (ASC 360-20-40-45).

Sales of Partial Interests in Property

A seller may continue to be involved in property sold by retaining an interest in the property and by giving the buyer preference as to profits, cash flow, return on investment, or some other similar arrangement. In this event, if the transaction is in substance a sale, the seller shall recognize profit to the extent that the sale proceeds, including receivables, exceed the seller's total cost in the property (ASC 360-20-40-49).

A seller may retain a partial interest in the property sold, such as an undivided interest or some other form of equity. If a seller sells a partial interest in real estate property and the sale meets all of the criteria for the full accrual method, except for the seller's continued involvement related to the partial interest in the property, the seller shall recognize the proportionate share of the profit that is attributable to the outside interests in the property. If the seller controls the buyer, however, profit on the sale shall not be recognized until realized from transactions with outside individuals, or through the sale of the property to outside parties (ASC 360-20-40-47).

A seller may sell single-family units or time-sharing interests in a condominium project. If the units or interests are sold individually, the seller shall recognize profit on the sales by the percentage-of-completion method, provided all of the following conditions are met (ASC 360-20-40-50):

- Construction has progressed beyond the preliminary stage, which means that the engineering and design work, execution of construction contracts, site clearance and preparation, and excavation or completion of the building foundation have all been completed.
- The buyer cannot obtain a refund, except for nondelivery.
- The property will not revert to rental property, as evidenced by the number of units or interests that have been sold. In determining the sufficiency of the number of units or interests sold, reference shall be made to local and state laws, the provisions of the condominium or time-sharing contract, and the terms of the financing agreements.
- Total sales and costs can be estimated reasonably in accordance with the percentage-of-completion method of accounting.
- Sales prices are collectible.

Until all of the above conditions are met, the seller shall account for the sales proceeds from the single-family units or time-sharing interests by the deposit method of accounting (ASC 360-20-40-50).

Disclosures

ASC 360 does not contain any specific disclosure requirements for the sale of real estate, other than retail land sales. However, professional judgment may require that a significant sale of real estate be disclosed appropriately in the financial statements.

If interest is imputed on a receivable arising out of a real estate sale, certain disclosures are required by ASC 835 (Interest). In addition, if commitments or contingencies arise in a real estate sale, disclosure may be required by ASC 450 (Contingencies).

Retail Land Sales

The development of a large tract of land, usually over several years, is typical for a company in the retail land sales industry. Master plans are drawn for the improvement of the property, which may include amenities, and all necessary regulatory approvals are obtained. Large advertising campaigns are held at an early stage, frequently resulting in substantial sales before significant development of the property. In most retail land sales, a substantial portion of the sales price is financed by the seller in the form of a long-term receivable secured by the property. Interest and principal are paid by the buyer over an extended number of years. In the event of default, the buyer usually loses his or her entire equity and the property reverts back to the seller. Frequently, the retail land sales contract or existing state law provides for a period in which the purchaser may receive a refund of all or part of any payments made. In addition, the seller may be unable to obtain a deficiency judgment against the buyer because of operation of the law. Finally, many project-wide improvements and amenities are deferred until the later stages of development, when the seller may be faced with financial difficulties.

Because of small down payments, frequent cancellations and refunds, and the possibility that the retail land sales company may not be financially able to complete the project, certain specific conditions must be met before a sale can be recognized. ASC 976 (Real Estate - Retail Land) provides guidance regarding profit recognition for retail land sales.

PART II: INTERPRETIVE GUIDANCE

ASC 360-10: OVERALL

ASC 360-10-25-2 through 25-4, 30-3, 30-4, 30-13 through 30-14; ASC 840-30-35-21, 35-53 Accounting for an Interest in the Residual Value of a Leased Asset

BACKGROUND

This guidance responds to five questions related to accounting for the residual value of a leased asset.

ACCOUNTING GUIDANCE

Question 1: How should an entity account for (a) the acquisition from a lessor of an unconditional right to own and possess, at the end of a lease term, an asset subject to the lease; and (b) the acquisition of a right to receive all or a portion of the proceeds from the sale of a leased asset at the end of the lease?

Answer: At the date the rights are acquired, both transactions involve a right to receive, at the end of the lease term, all or a portion of the future benefit included in a leased asset. That right should be accounted for as the acquisition of an asset.

Question 2: How should an entity acquiring an interest in the residual value of a leased asset determine the cost at acquisition?

Answer: The cost is the amount of cash disbursed, the fair value of other consideration given (which could include noncash assets or services rendered), and the present value of liabilities assumed. The fair value of the interest in the residual value at the date of the agreement should be used to measure the cost of the interest if that fair value is more clearly evident than the fair value of the assets surrendered, services rendered, or liabilities assumed.

Question 3: How does an entity that acquires an interest in the residual value of a leased asset account for that asset during the lease term?

Answer: An entity that acquires an interest in the residual value of a leased asset should not recognize increases in the asset's estimated value over the remaining term of the lease. The asset should be reported at no more than its acquisition cost until sale or disposition. If the value of the asset declines below its carrying amount and that decline is considered other than temporary, the asset should be written down to fair value and the amount of the write-down should be recognized as a loss. Subsequent increases in fair value before sale or disposition should not be recorded.

Question 4: Do the provisions indicated in the answer to Question 3 apply to lease brokers?

Answer: Yes.

Question 5: If a lessor sells substantially all of the minimum rental payments associated with a sales-type, direct financing, or leveraged lease and retains an interest in the residual value of the leased asset, how should the lessor account for that asset over the remaining lease term?

Answer: The lessor should not recognize increases in the leased asset's residual value over the remaining lease term. However, if the fair value of the residual declines, that decline should be recognized as a loss if the decline is considered other than temporary. Subsequent recoveries in fair value should not be recorded.

ASC 360-10-25-5, 45-1; ASC 340-10-25-5; ASC 908-360-45-2 Accounting for Planned Major Maintenance Activities

BACKGROUND

ASC 908 provides guidance regarding the accounting for planned major maintenance activities in the airline industry that is also followed by entities in other industries. Under the guidance in ASC 908, the following four alternative methods of accounting for planned major maintenance activities are permitted: (1) direct expense; (2) built-in overhaul; (3) deferral; and (4) accrual in advance. The FASB believes that liabilities for planned major maintenance activities recognized under the accrual-in-advance method do *not* meet the definition of a liability in FASB Concepts Statement No. 6 (Elements of Financial Statements (not in ASC), because an expense is recognized in a period before a transaction or event obligating the entity has occurred. Future costs to be incurred for maintenance to improve an asset's operating efficiency, comply with regulatory operating guidelines, or extend an asset's useful life do *not* represent an entity's current duty or responsibility before an obligating transaction or event has occurred. Therefore, the guidance in ASC 908 regarding the accounting for planned major maintenance activities is being amended by the guidance in this FSP, which applies to *all* industries.

ACCOUNTING GUIDANCE

Application of the accrual-in-advance method to account for planned major maintenance activities is prohibited in annual and interim financial reporting periods. Major maintenance activities should be accounted for based on the direct expense, built-in overhaul, or deferral method, which should be applied in the same manner in annual and interim financial reporting periods.

ASC 360-20: REAL ESTATE SALES

ASC 360-20-15-3 Accounting for Transfers of Investments That Are in Substance Real Estate

BACKGROUND

The guidance in ASC 860 on accounting for transfers of financial assets differs substantially from the guidance in ASC 360 on the accounting for sales of real estate. This Issue was raised because some believe that sales or exchanges of financial assets, such as corporate stock of enterprises with substantial real estate assets, partnership interests, and time-sharing interests, that are in substance real estate should be accounted for under the guidance in ASC 360, not under the guidance in ASC 860 (FAS-140).

Under the guidance in ASC 860, a transfer of financial assets is accounted for as a sale if it meets the criteria in ASC 860-10-40-4, 40-5. The requirements for profit recognition on sales of real estate assets are discussed in ASC 360-20-40-5. Although both pronouncements require a transferor to relinquish control over the asset by prohibiting a transferor from maintaining a continuing involvement with the asset, the requirements for sales recognition and for subsequent accounting for transactions that do not meet their respective criteria are different.

ACCOUNTING ISSUE

Should sales or transfers of financial assets that are in substance real estate be accounted for under the provisions of ASC 360 or the provisions of ASC 860?

ACCOUNTING GUIDANCE

Sales or transfers of investments in the form of financial assets that are in substance real estate should be accounted for under the provisions of ASC 360.

It was noted that the guidance would apply to transfers of acquisition, development, and construction loans (ADC loans), which are considered to be investments that are in substance real estate according to ASC 810-10-25-59. However, this guidance would not apply to marketable investments in real estate investment trusts (REITs) accounted for under the provisions of ASC 320, because they are not considered to be investments that are in substance real estate. Sales or exchanges of such investments should be accounted for under the guidance in ASC 860.

> **OBSERVATION:** The guidance in ASC 860-10-15-4 provides that transfers of ownership interests that are in substance real estate are not under its scope. Such transactions should be accounted for under the guidance in ASC 360. That provision affirms the above guidance.

DISCUSSION

Proponents of the view that the guidance in ASC 360 should apply to transfers of assets that are in substance real estate believe that the substance of an investment is more important than its form. They argued that it would be unacceptable to change the revenue recognition model for real estate by changing the form of the investment. In addition, they noted that ASC 976-10-15-4 cites corporate stock of entities with substantial real estate, sales of interests in a partnership that was formed for the purpose of acquiring real estate directly from third parties, and sales of time-sharing interests in real estate properties as examples of financial assets that are in substance real estate. They suggested that ASC 976-10-15-4 should be consulted to determine which financial assets should be accounted for under the guidance in ASC 360.

ASC 360-20-15-3(f), 55-68 through 55-77, 65-2; ASC 810-10-40-3B Derecognition of In-Substance Real Estate—a Scope Clarification

BACKGROUND

During 2010, the FASB issued Accounting Standards Update (ASU) 2010-2, *Consolidation (Topic 810): Accounting and Reporting for Decreases in Ownership of a Subsidiary—a Scope Clarification*. That guidance, which has been incorporated in the Codification in ASC 810-10-40-3A, 40-4 through 40-5, 45-21A, 50-1B, 65-3; ASC 845-10-15-20, 30-22, 30-25 through 25A; ASC 323-10-30-2, 35-7; and ASC 805-10-50-2 requires an entity that gives up control of a subsidiary to deconsolidate the subsidiary and to recognize a profit or a loss under the transaction. However, if an entity reduces its ownership interest in a subsidiary but there is no change in control, the transaction is accounted for as a change in the entity's equity in the subsidiary. In addition, that guidance applies only if such transactions are consummated by a business entity or a nonprofit activity.

That guidance does *not* apply to sales of in substance real estate, which should be accounted for under the guidance in ASC 360, *Property, Plant, and Equipment* (ASC 360-20). A subsidiary that is in substance real estate is an entity that has been established by an investor (parent) for the sole purpose of purchasing real estate that is capitalized with nonrecourse debt. There has been diversity in practice because some practitioners have questioned whether the criteria in ASC 360-20 related to continuing involvement must be met for a parent to deconsolidate a subsidiary that is in substance real estate. Others have expressed concern that the guidance in ASC 810, *Consolidation* (ASC 810-10), would apply if the derecognition is not due to a sale of the real estate, but rather occurs because the subsidiary has defaulted on its nonrecoursedebt.

ACCOUNTING ISSUE

Does the accounting guidance in ASC 360-20 apply to a parent (reporting entity) that no longer has a controlling financial interest in an substance real estate subsidiary?

SCOPE

The following guidance applies only to situations in which has lost its controlling financial interest (as discussed in ASC 810-10) in a wholly owned in substance real estate subsidiary as a result of the subsidiary's default on its nonrecourse debt.

ACCOUNTING GUIDANCE

A parent should apply the guidance in ASC 360 to determine whether an in substance real estate subsidiary should be derecognized. That is, if a parent of an in-substance real estate subsidiary no longer has a controlling financial interest in the subsidiary, as discussed in ASC 810-10, because the subsidiary has defaulted on its nonrecourse debt, the reporting entity should apply the guidance in ASC 360-20-40-5 to determine whether it should derecognize real estate owned by its in-substance real estate subsidiary. In addition:

- The requirements for derecognition in ASC 360-20-40-5 apply regardless of whether a reporting entity owns the real estate directly or indirectly through its in-substance real estate subsidiary;
- A two-step impairment approach required under the guidance in ASC 360-20 does not permit the consideration of nonrecourse debt when a real estate asset is evaluated for impairment; and
- It would be inappropriate for a parent to derecognize the substance subsidiary's nonrecourse debt until it has been legally released from that obligation by the lender.

TRANSITION AND EFFECTIVE DATE

The guidance discussed above should be applied as follows:

- The guidance is effective as follows:
  - For public entities, the guidance is effective for fiscal years and interim periods within those years that begin on or after June 15, 2012.
  - For nonpublic entities, the guidance is effective for fiscal years that end after December 15, 2013, and interim and annual periods that follow.
- Earlier application of the guidance is permitted.
- A parent should apply the guidance prospectively to a deconsolidation as a result of an in substance subsidiary's default of its nonrecourse debt, which occurs on or after the effective date. Prior periods should not be adjusted even if the parent has a continuing involvement with previously derecognized in substance real estate entities.
- The disclosures in ASC 250-10-50-1 through 50-3 should be provided in the period in which the parent adopts the guidance.

ASC 360-20-15-4 through 15-8; 55-58 through 55-59 Determining Whether Equipment Is "Integral Equipment" Subject to ASC 360

BACKGROUND

The guidance in ASC 360-20-15-2 through 15-3, 15-10, 55-4 through 55-5, which concludes that sales of "integral equipment" should be accounted for under the guidance in ASC 360, defines that term as ". . . any physical structure or equipment attached to the real estate that cannot be removed and used separately without incurring significant cost." An office building, a manufacturing facility, a power plant, and a refinery are cited as examples. Some are concerned that in applying the provisions of ASC 840 and ASC 360 there will be diversity in determining which assets are considered "integral equipment," because the accounting literature on real estate sales and leasing transactions does not provide guidance on how to interpret the phrase "...cannot be removed and used separately without incurring significant cost."

ACCOUNTING ISSUE

How should entities determine whether equipment is "integral equipment"?

ACCOUNTING GUIDANCE

- The phrase "cannot be removed and used separately without incurring significant cost" raises the following two questions: (a) whether the equipment can be removed without incurring significant cost and (b) whether the equipment can be moved to another location to be used by another entity without significantly diminishing its fair value or usefulness.

- To determine whether an asset should be considered to be integral equipment, it is necessary to know (a) the significance of the cost of removing the equipment from its existing location, including the cost of repairing damage caused by its removal, and (b) the diminution in the equipment's fair value due to its removal. The cost of shipping and reinstalling equipment at a new location should be considered the minimum amount of diminution in the fair value of equipment due to its removal. To determine whether there is additional diminution in fair value, it is necessary to consider the nature of the equipment and its likely use by other potential users.

- Equipment should be considered to be "integral equipment" if the combined cost of removal and the equipment's decrease in value exceeds 10% of the fair value of the installed equipment. For leasing transactions, estimates of the costs of removal, the decrease in the equipment's value, as well as its fair value should be based on information as of the inception of the lease.

ASC 360-20-40-11 through 40-12 and 55-3 Profit Recognition on Sales of Real Estate with Insured Mortgages or Surety Bonds

BACKGROUND

Sellers financing residential or other properties may require mortgage insurance on a portion of the loan. They often accept surety bonds instead of letters of credit to support the buyer's notes. Under the guidance in ASC 360-20-40-10, one of the conditions for a buyer's initial investment under the full accrual method is that the buyer's notes be accompanied by a letter of credit from an independent lending institution.

ACCOUNTING ISSUES

1. Can a financial instrument, such as a surety bond, that meets the following conditions be considered equivalent to an irrevocable letter of credit in determining whether a buyer's notes should be included in the buyer's initial investment, so profit can be recognized on the full accrual method, if

a. The seller has the same rights of collection as under an irrevocable letter of credit;

b. The surety has the same obligation to the seller as under an irrevocable letter of credit;

c. The surety has the same recourse to the buyer in the case of default as under an irrevocable letter of credit?

2. Can government or private insurance covering part of the balance of a mortgage be considered equivalent to an irrevocable letter of credit and included in a buyer's initial and continuing investment, in determining whether to recognize profit on a sale using the full accrual method?

3. Do the minimum down payment percentages stated in ASC 360-20-55-1, 55-2 apply, or should the loan limits in governmental programs be used if a buyer of a single-family residential property qualifies for a loan from the Federal Housing Administration (FHA) or Veterans Administration (VA), which insure or guarantee a part or the full amount of the mortgage, but require no down payments or down payments of less than 5%?

ACCOUNTING GUIDANCE

- A seller may consider an irrevocable financial instrument, such as a surety bond from an independent insurer that meets the conditions stated in Issue 1 above, to be equivalent to an irrevocable letter of credit that can be used to support a buyer's notes, which are included in the buyer's initial investment in determining whether profit can be recognized under the full accrual method. The buyer's commitment to pay is an important criterion in ASC 360 that must be met for full profit recognition.

- Mortgage insurance is not considered equivalent to an irrevocable letter of credit in determining whether the full accrual method is appropriate, because purchasing mortgage insurance does not demonstrate the buyer's commitment to meet the obligation to pay for the property.

- The normal down payment requirements or loan limits under FHA or VA government-insured programs may be used by a seller for sales of owner-occupied single-family homes financed under those programs instead of the minimum initial investment percentages stated in paragraphs 53 and 54 of ASC 360-20-55-1 through 55-2 to determine whether a seller may recognize profit on the full accrual method if the mortgage receivable is insured under the FHA or VA program. All loans insured by the VA or FHA qualify for full accrual profit recognition, but this guidance does not apply to private mortgage insurance, because government insurance transfers the risk on the mortgage receivable to the governmental agency.

DISCUSSION

1. A surety bond differs from mortgage insurance, because the bond exposes the buyer to the same risk of loss as under an irrevocable letter of credit. If a buyer defaults on the notes, the surety has recourse to the buyer's general assets for the amount of the bond. Those who believed that a surety bond is equivalent to an irrevocable letter of credit and should therefore qualify under the requirements of the guidance in ASC 360 argued that it (*a*) demonstrates the buyer's commitment to pay for

the property and (b) increases the likelihood that the seller will collect the receivable supported by the bond.
2. Mortgage insurance should not be considered equivalent to an irrevocable letter of credit, because it does not demonstrate the buyer's commitment to pay for the property—a requirement of ASC 360 even though it increases the likelihood that the sales price will be collected.

ASC 360-20-40-14 through 40-17, 40-32; 55-55 through 55-56 Effect of Various Forms of Financing under ASC 360

BACKGROUND

Real estate sales are financed in various ways. The financing may be provided by independent third parties, by the seller, or both. Also, the financing may be nonrecourse to the buyer; that is, the lender's only recourse in the event the buyer defaults is to foreclose on the property. The financing also may involve the buyer's assumption of the seller's preexisting recourse or nonrecourse mortgage obligations.

The guidance in ASC 360 establishes accounting standards for recognizing profit or loss on sales of real estate. It is unclear, however, as to how various forms of financing affect a seller's profit recognition.

The guidance in ASC 360-20-40-3 states that a seller recognizes profit on the full accrual method if *both* of the following conditions are met:

1. The profit can be determined; there is reasonable assurance that the sales price is collectible; and it is possible to estimate the amount that will not be collectible.
2. The earnings process is essentially complete; the seller has no obligation to perform significant activities after the sale.

In applying condition 1, collectibility is demonstrated by a buyer's initial and continuing investments, which must be adequate to demonstrate a commitment to pay for the real estate. A sufficient investment puts the buyer at risk of loss through default and motivates the buyer to pay on the debt. Unless both conditions are met, the seller must defer all or a part of the profit. Deferred profit would be recognized in the future on the installment, cost-recovery, or the reduced-profit method.

ACCOUNTING ISSUE

How should profit be recognized on sales of real estate that involve various forms of financing?

ACCOUNTING GUIDANCE

- The initial and continuing investment requirements of ASC 360 apply. However, a seller can recognize profit on the full accrual method if consideration received by the seller for the *full* sales value of the property consists of the following:
  — Cash, as long as the seller has no contingent liability on debt the buyer might incur or assume
  — The seller's existing nonrecourse debt on the property is assumed by the buyer

- Recourse debt on the property is assumed by the buyer with the seller's *complete release* from those obligations
- Any combination of the above

- In determining the adequacy of a buyer's initial investment for purposes of recognizing profit by the full accrual method, *neither* of the following forms of financing should be included as part of a buyer's initial investment:
  - Debt secured by the property, whether borrowed directly from the seller or others or indirectly by the buyer's assumption of the seller's existing debt
  - Payments to the seller from the proceeds of debt secured by the property.

  The buyer's commitment to pay for the property is demonstrated only by the payment of a sufficient amount of cash or other qualifying form of investment, not by a borrowing secured by the property. Items included or excluded from the initial investment are discussed in ASC 360-20-40-10 and 40-13.

- Neither of the following should be considered a buyer's cash payments in the seller's computation of the amount of profit that can be recognized initially under the installment, cost recovery, or reduced-profit method:
  - A buyer's debt secured by the property, either incurred directly from the seller or others or indirectly by assuming the seller's existing debt
  - Cash paid to the seller from the proceeds of a buyer's debt secured by the property.

  A seller may, however, recognize as income deferred profit in excess of the total amount of (*a*) the seller's financing and (*b*) the buyer's outstanding debt secured by the property for which the seller is contingently liable.

Illustration of Profit Recognition When Buyer's Initial Investment Is Inadequate

Assumptions

Sales price		$250,000
Seller's basis in property sold		$187,500
Seller's profit		$62,500
Initial investment requirement		20%
Continuing investment test is met.		
a.	Buyer's initial cash investment	0
	Seller's recourse mortgage assumed*	$250,000
	No profit recognized	
b.	Buyer's initial cash investment	0
	Seller financing	$250,000
	No profit recognized	
c.	Buyer's initial cash investment	0
	Seller financing	$50,000

	Seller's recourse mortgage assumed*	$200,000
	No profit recognized	
d.	Buyer's initial cash investment	0
	First mortgage from independent lender	$200,000
	Seller financing	$50,000
	Profit recognized on cost recovery or installment method on excess over seller financing	$12,500
e.	Buyer's initial cash investment	$25,000
	Seller financing	$225,000
	Profit recognized on the installment method ($25,000 × .25)	$ 6,250
f.	Buyer's initial cash investment	$25,000
	Seller's recourse mortgage assumed*	$225,000
	Profit recognized on the installment method ($25,000 ×.25)	$6,250
g.	Buyer's initial cash investment	$25,000
	First mortgage from independent lender	$200,000
	Seller financing	$25,000
	Profit recognized on cost recovery or installment method on excess of seller financing ($62,500 — $25,000)	$37,500
h.	Buyer's initial cash investment	$25,000
	Seller's nonrecourse mortgage assumed	$200,000
	Seller financing	$25,000
	Profit recognized on cost recovery or installment method on excess of seller financing	$37,500
i.	Buyer's initial cash investment	$25,000
	Seller's recourse mortgage assumed*	$200,000
	Seller financing	$25,000
	Profit recognized on the installment method ($25,000 × .25)	$6,250

* The seller remains contingently liable on the mortgage.

ASC 360-20-40-35 Profit Recognition on Sales of Real Estate with Graduated Payment Mortgages or Insured Mortgages

BACKGROUND

A sale of real estate is financed by a graduated payment mortgage. Such mortgages may have negative amortization of principal in the early years and may be partially or fully insured.

ACCOUNTING ISSUES

- Do graduated payment mortgages meet the requirements for the buyer's initial and continuing investment under the full accrual method?

- Can government or private mortgage insurance be considered part of the buyer's initial and continuing investment?

ACCOUNTING GUIDANCE

- A graduated payment mortgage with negative amortization of principal does not meet the continuing investment test in ASC 360. Therefore, profit should not be recognized based on the full accrual method.
- See the guidance in ASC 360-20-40-11 through 40-12 and 55-3, Profit Recognition on Sales of Real Estate with Insured Mortgages or Surety Bonds, above.

DISCUSSION

The guidance ASC 360 is based on AICPA accounting guides that were issued in the 1970s to curb profit recognition abuses in the real estate industry. The purpose of the buyer's initial and continuing investment requirements is to demonstrate that the buyer has an economic commitment to the property. Under the guidance in ASC 360-20-40-10, 40-19 through 40-20, which provide guidance on those requirements, a buyer must be contractually obligated to make sufficient annual payments to *reduce* the indebtedness on the property. In contrast, a negative amortization mortgage *increases* the buyer's indebtedness, because the balance of the loan increases.

ASC 360-20-40-39 Antispeculation Clauses in Real Estate Sales Contracts

BACKGROUND

An antispeculation clause is included in some land sales contracts to assure that a buyer develops the land according to a master plan. Under such contracts, the buyer is required to develop the land within a specified period of time and may be prohibited from developing it for certain uses. If the buyer does not comply with the contract, the seller has the right, but not the obligation, to repurchase the property, which represents a potential penalty to the buyer for not complying with the sales contract. The buyer does not, however, have the right to put the property back to the seller.

According to the guidance in ASC 360-20-40-38, a seller should not recognize profit on a sale on the full accrual method, if a sales contract includes a repurchase option. Such a transaction should be accounted for as a financing, leasing, or profit-sharing arrangement instead of as a sale.

ACCOUNTING ISSUE

Is a seller precluded from recognizing a sale if a real estate sales contract includes an antispeculation clause?

ACCOUNTING GUIDANCE

A seller is not precluded from recognizing a sale if there is only a *remote probability* that the buyer will not comply with a sales contract's antispeculation clause.

However, a probability test is not appropriate if a seller has an option to repurchase the property that is not contingent on the buyer's compliance with a specific requirement.

DISCUSSION

The following factors that would indicate that there is only a remote probability that the buyer will not comply with the contract's antispeculation clause were discussed:

- The buyer has the ability and intent to follow the provisions of the sales contract. If the buyer is a substantive party and the seller does not expect to have a right to repurchase the property, no option exists on sale.
- The risks and rewards of ownership have been transferred to the buyer. The buyer will benefit from the appreciation of the property if it is developed according to the contract, while the seller has no obligation and would have no incentive to repurchase the property if its value depreciates. The seller does not share in the appreciation or depreciation of the property.
- There are business reasons for the option. The seller includes the antispeculation clause in the contract only to enforce the buyer's promise to develop the property as agreed in the contract. The clause is more like a restriction in a deed than a repurchase option. In practice, deed restrictions in retail land sales that limit the type of home that can be built on a property do not preclude full accrual profit recognition.

ASC 360-20-40-50-55 Applicability of the Assessment of a Buyer's Continuing Investment under ASC 360 for Sales of Condominiums

BACKGROUND

Developers of condominium units usually sell individual units during a project's construction phase. Under the guidance in ASC 360-20-40-5 on accounting for real estate sales, one of the requirements for the seller to recognize profit under the full accrual method is that the buyer must demonstrate a commitment to pay by having an adequate continuing investment in the property. However, that requirement may not be met during a condominium's construction phase, because of the length of time it takes to complete such a project. In addition, because the risks and rewards of ownership have *not* been transferred to the buyer during the construction phase, the developer's continuing involvement is discussed further in ASC 360-20-40-50.

Under the guidance in ASC 360-20-40-50, a developer may recognize profit on individual condominium units using the percentage-of-completion method during a project's construction phase, if certain criteria are met. One of those criteria is the collectibility of the sales price. ASC 360-20-40-4 states that a buyer that makes a substantial initial and continuing investment in a property demonstrates a commitment to pay the remainder of the sales price, because the buyer will not want to lose that investment through a default. Additional factors to consider in an evaluation of collectibility are the buyer's credit standing, the property's age and location, and the adequacy of cash flow from the property. Some have questioned whether a developer needs to apply the continuing investment test discussed in ASC 360-2-40-19 through 40-20 in order to conclude that the sales price is collectible and profit may be recognized on the percentage-of-completion method.

ACCOUNTING ISSUES

1. Does an entity that recognizes profit on the percentage-of-completion method need to evaluate the adequacy of a buyer's continuing investment under the guidance in ASC 360-20-40-19, 40-20?

2. When the criteria in ASC 360-20-40-50 are applied to reassess whether profit may be recognized on the percentage-of-completion method, should the initial and continuing investment tests be applied on a cumulative basis (*a*) from the date the seller and the buyer entered into a contract or (*b*) prospectively from the date on which a reassessment is made to determine whether profit may be recognized on the percentage-of-completion method on a transaction that previously did *not* meet the criteria in ASC 360-20-40-50 for profit recognition on that method?

ACCOUNTING GUIDANCE

1. When evaluating the collectibility of the sales price of an individual condominium unit under the guidance in paragraph ASC 360-20-40-50, a seller's conclusion should be based on whether the buyer's initial and continuing investment is adequate. It was noted that just as for other types of real estate sales, a buyer's initial and continuing investment should be made in the form required in ASC 360-20-40-10 and that only the nonrefundable portion of such investments should be counted toward the buyer's initial and continuing investment. The continuing investment criterion in ASC 360-20-40-19 through 40-20 has been met if a buyer is required to either (1) pay additional amounts during the construction term that are at least equal to the level annual payments required to fund principal and interest on an amortizing customary mortgage for the property's remaining purchase price, which is the difference between the purchase price and the buyer's initial investment; or (2) increase the minimum initial investment by an equivalent total amount. The remaining purchase price is calculated based on the property's sales price. This test should be performed by using a hypothetical loan between a seller and a buyer for the amount of the purchase price *less* the buyer's initial investment. Using the remaining purchase price is consistent with the guidance in ASC 360-20-40-19 through 40-20, because it refers to a buyer's "debt for the purchase price of the property."

2. The deposit method discussed in ASC 360-20-55-17, 55-19 through 55-20 should be used until a buyer's payments meet the criteria in ASC 360-20-40-50, including an assessment of collectibility using the initial and continuing investment tests discussed in ASC 360-20-40-9, 40-10, 40-13, 40-18 40-20. When an entity reevaluates whether profit should be recognized under the percentage-of-completion method, all of the criteria in ASC 360-20-40-50 should be reevaluated.

3. The initial and continuing investment tests should be applied *prospectively* from the date on which the collectibility of the sales price is reevaluated, as if the deposit was received on that date.

ASC 360-20-55-66 through 55-67 Transfer of Ownership Interest as Part of Down Payment under ASC 360

BACKGROUND

An income-producing property is owned in a partnership by two parties. One of the parties, which holds a 75% interest in the property, sells its interest to the party holding a 25% interest in the property. The seller receives a 10% down payment and a note for the balance secured by 100% of the property, which has no outstanding debt. ASC 360-20-55- specifies a minimum initial investment of 15% of the sales value of the property as an initial investment for this type of transaction.

ACCOUNTING ISSUES

- Does the buyer's pledge of 100% of the purchased property as security for a note meet the requirements for the buyer's initial investment in determining whether profit may be recognized on the full accrual method?
- If yes, can a note collateralized by assets other than the purchased property, such as other real estate or marketable securities, be included as part of the buyer's initial investment in determining whether profit can be recognized on the full accrual method?

ACCOUNTING GUIDANCE

Under the provisions of ASC 360 full accrual profit recognition is not permitted for this transaction, because the buyer's initial investment should not include the purchased property or other assets pledged as security for a note.

DISCUSSION

Under the criteria stated in ASC 360-20-40-10, only a buyer's cash down payment in this transaction qualifies to be included in the buyer's initial investment. A note would have to be supported by an irrevocable letter of credit from an independent lending institution. Under the guidance in ASC 360-20-40-11 through 40-12 and 55-3, which is discussed above, a surety bond meeting certain conditions could be substituted for an irrevocable letter of credit, but mortgage insurance is not acceptable because it does not demonstrate a buyer's commitment to pay for the property. Under a strict interpretation of ASC 360-20-40-10, a note collateralized by the property or other assets would not qualify.

In addition, this transaction would not qualify for full accrual profit recognition, because the 10% down payment does not meet the minimum down payment required in ASC 360-20-55-2 for an income-producing property, which is 15% of the sales value.

ASC 360-20-60-1; 55-2 through 55-6, 55-8, 55-13 through 55-18 The Treatment of Certain Site Restoration/Environmental Exit Costs When Testing a Long-Lived Asset for Impairment

BACKGROUND

This Issue addresses the accounting for environmental exit costs that have not been recognized for accounting purposes and that are incurred when operations cease (even if the asset is retained) or if the asset is sold or abandoned. Such costs can include an environmental audit or assessment; a feasibility study or other assessment; actual remediation and/or site restoration; monitoring activities; legal costs; costs to change permits or licenses; costs related to equipment shutdown; and fines and penalties. An entity may incur environmental exit costs if certain assets are sold, abandoned, or cease operations. Funds for such costs may not be expended for some time if the costs are not incurred until the end of the asset's life or if the costs are deferred indefinitely, because the asset has not been sold or abandoned.

Under the provisions of ASC 360, future cash flows from using or eventually disposing of an asset must be estimated when the recovery of the asset's carrying amount is reviewed because events or changes in circumstances suggest that it may be impaired. An impairment loss is recognized based on the asset's fair value if its carrying amount exceeds the sum of the asset's expected undiscounted future cash flows, excluding interest charges.

The environmental exit costs considered generally are not accrued over the life of an asset, and it is unclear whether those costs should be included in undiscounted future cash flows used in the impairment calculation. Because such costs might not be incurred for many years, the amount would be small on a discounted basis but might be very large on an undiscounted basis. Consequently, including such costs in the undiscounted cash flow test would result in more frequent measurement of asset impairment and asset revaluation to fair value. (See the Subsequent Development section.)

ACCOUNTING ISSUE

Should undiscounted expected future cash flows used to test the recoverability of the carrying amount of a long-lived asset under the guidance in ASC 360 include exit costs related to environmental matters that may be incurred if a long-lived asset is sold, abandoned, or ceases operations?

ACCOUNTING GUIDANCE

> **OBSERVATION:** ASC 410 provides guidance for the initial recognition and measurement of asset retirement obligations and subsequent accounting for such obligations. It applies to all *legal* obligations related to the retirement of tangible long-lived assets and requires that the fair value, if estimable, of such obligations be recognized in the period in which the liability is incurred. If the fair value is not estimable at that time, recognition is required when a reasonable estimate of fair value can be made. Previous guidance in this Issue related to liabilities that have not been recognized has been partially nullified by the guidance in ASC 410.

Previous guidance reached in this Issue based on the guidance in (*a*) ASC 360 and (*b*) ASC 410, has been modified as follows:

- The guidance in ASC 410 nullifies the original guidance that future cash flows for environmental exit costs that have been *recognized* as a liability be excluded from undiscounted expected future cash flows used to test an asset's recoverability under the guidance in ASC 360 even though under the guidance in ASC 410 future cash flows for a liability that has been recognized for an asset's retirement obligation should be excluded from undiscounted cash flows used to test the asset for recoverability.

- The guidance in ASC 360 affects the guidance regarding management's intent for an asset by requiring that the likelihood of possible outcomes be considered if (*a*) a range of possible future cash flows is estimated or (*b*) management intends to recover an asset's carrying amount by alternative means instead of by selling or abandoning the asset, or ceasing its operations.

The FASB staff developed examples of situations in which environmental exit costs either would be included in or excluded from undiscounted cash flows, based on management's intent for the asset. Environmental exit costs would be *included* in the ASC 360 recoverability test in the following situations:

- The asset's useful life is expected to be limited because of actual or expected technological advances, contractual provisions, or regulatory restrictions, and management intends to sell, abandon, or close the asset at the end of its useful life and will incur environmental exit costs in doing so.

- Although management expects the asset to become profitable in the future, the asset has a negative cash flow from operations in the current period, and a forecast or projection anticipates continuing losses. Management is uncertain whether it can continue funding future cash outflows until the asset begins generating net cash inflows. Under a forced liquidation, management would have to sell, abandon, or close the asset and would incur environmental exit costs.

- Management's intent to sell or abandon the asset in the future will result in remediation costs to conform with applicable laws or regulations.

Environmental exit costs would be *excluded* from undiscounted expected future cash flows in the following situations:

- The asset has an indefinite useful life; management intends to operate the asset indefinitely and has the ability to do so; and based on all available information the asset will continue to be profitable. Expected future cash flows for repair, maintenance, and capital expenditures required to obtain future cash flows would be included in the recoverability test under the guidance in ASC 360, however.

- Management intends to operate the asset at least during its remaining depreciable life. Total undiscounted future cash flows expected from operating the asset during that period exceed its carrying amount, including related goodwill, and there is no reason for management to believe that disposal of the asset would result in a net cash outflow.

- Environmental exit costs related to an asset that has a finite life would be incurred only if it is sold or abandoned. To avoid the cost of remediating the asset, management intends to close the asset permanently at the end of its useful life or to idle it by reducing production to a minimal level. The recoverability test should consider the entity's assumptions for the use of the asset. Expected future cash flows required to (*a*) maintain or protect the asset after it has been closed or (*b*) to fund losses incurred after the asset has been idled should nevertheless be included in the recoverability test under the guidance in ASC 360.

- Management expects to sell the asset in the future without incurring environmental exit costs. The effect of environmental exit costs on the asset's fair value should be considered in estimating net proceeds from a future sale to be used in the recoverability test under the guidance in ASC 360

DISCUSSION

The accounting guidance is based on the premise that the environmental exit costs discussed in this Issue generally are not accrued over the life of the asset, either because they are considered avoidable or because in some jurisdictions, they are considered deferrable indefinitely as long as the asset is in operation or is not sold or abandoned, even if its operations cease. It was agreed that the trigger should be based on management's plans for the asset. However, management's intention to operate an asset indefinitely or to idle it, but not sell or abandon it, would have to be supported by cash flow estimates demonstrating an entity's ability to do so.

The FASB staff's scenarios—under which exit costs would be included or excluded from the calculation under the provisions of ASC 360 are intended to provide facts and circumstances for the application of the consensus, but they also provide some specific guidance. For example, the second and fourth situations—under which environmental exit costs would *not* be included in undiscounted cash flows—nevertheless specify certain costs that *would be included* in the recoverability test under the guidance in ASC 360.

CHAPTER 26
ASC 405—LIABILITIES

CONTENTS

Part I: General Guidance	26,001
ASC 405-10: Overall	26,001
ASC 405-20: Extinguishments of Liabilities	26,001
Background	26,001
Derecognition	26,001
Part II: Interpretive Guidance	26,002
ASC 405-40: Obligations Resulting from Joint and Several Liability Arrangements	26,002
ASC 405-40-50-1 through 50-2, 30-1 through 30-2, 15-1, 25-1 through 25-2, 05-1, 35-1, 65-1 Obligations Resulting from Joint and Several Liability Arrangements for Which the Total Amount of the Obligation is Fixed at the Reporting Date	26,002

PART I: GENERAL GUIDANCE

ASC 405-10: OVERALL

ASC 405-10 does not provide any accounting guidance but rather only provides a link to guidance on liabilities in other ASC subtopics.

ASC 405-20: EXTINGUISHMENTS OF LIABILITIES

BACKGROUND

Liabilities may be settled by either transferring assets to the creditor or by otherwise obtaining an unconditional release from the creditor. Alternatively, an entity may choose to set aside certain assets dedicated to the eventual settlement of a liability. However, this alternative approach of setting aside assets dedicated for eventual settlement has raised issues about when a liability should be considered extinguished. This subtopic provides guidance for resolving those issues. The guidance in this subtopic applies to the extinguishment of all liabilities, including both financial and nonfinancial liabilities.

DERECOGNITION

A liability must be derecognized only if it has been extinguished. A liability has been extinguished if either of the following conditions is met (ASC 405-20-40-1):

1. The debtor pays the creditor and is relieved of its obligation for the liability.
2. The debtor is legally released from being the primary obligor under the liability, either by the courts or by the creditor.

If a debtor is released by the creditor from being the primary obligor for a liability under the condition that a third party assumes the role of primary obligor and the original debtor becomes secondarily liable, that release is considered to have extinguished the original debtor's liability. However, in such a case, the original debtor would become a guarantor, and must recognize a guarantor obligation. The guarantor obligation must be initially measured at fair value and that amount would reduce the gain or increase the loss that the debtor recognized on the extinguishment of the original liability (ASC 405-20-40-2).

PART II: INTERPRETIVE GUIDANCE

ASC 405-40: OBLIGATIONS RESULTING FROM JOINT AND SEVERAL LIABILITY ARRANGEMENTS

ASC 405-40-50-1 through 50-2, 30-1 through 30-2, 15-1, 25-1 through 25-2, 05-1, 35-1, 65-1 Obligations Resulting from Joint and Several Liability Arrangements for Which the Total Amount of the Obligation is Fixed at the Reporting Date

BACKGROUND

There has been diversity in practice in accounting for obligations that result from joint and several liability obligations that have a fixed amount at the reporting date because U.S. generally accepted accounting principles (GAAP) has provided no accounting guidance for the recognition, measurement, and disclosure of such obligations. The scope of this ASU includes debt arrangements, other contractual obligations, settled litigation, and judicial rulings. Some entities have been recording the total amounts under such arrangements based on the existing guidance for liability extinguishment in Financial Accounting Standards Board (FASB) Accounting Standards Codification™ (ASC) 405, *Liabilities* (ASC 405-20), while others have been following the guidance for contingent liabilities in ASC 450, *Contingencies* (ASC 450-20), or ASC 410, *Asset Retirement and Environmental Obligations* (ASC 410-30), by recognizing a lower amount that may be based on an allocation, an amount equal to proceeds received, or the portion of an obligation that an entity has agreed to pay as a co-obligor.

ACCOUNTING GUIDANCE

ASC 405-40 has been added to ASC 405 to address the recognition, measurement, and disclosure of obligations incurred in joint and several liability arrangements that have a fixed amount at the reporting date. That guidance is as follows:

- *ASC 405-40-15-1* provides the *scope* of the guidance in ASC 405-40, which applies to obligations incurred in joint and several liability arrangements for which the total amount under the arrangement is fixed at the reporting date, except for obligations accounted for under the guidance in: (1) ASC 410 for asset retirements; (2) ASC 450 for contingencies; (3) ASC 460 for guarantees; (4) ASC 715 for compensation—retirement benefits; and (5) ASC 740 for income taxes. The amount of an obligation may be considered to be fixed at the reporting date only if there is no measurement uncertainty about its total amount. However, the total amount may differ in subsequent reporting periods as a result of factors other than an uncertainty about an obligation's measurement (e.g., because an additional amount was borrowed under a line of credit or due to a change in an arrangement's interest rate).

- *ASC 405-40-25-1 and 25-2* provide *recognition* guidance for obligations as a result of joint and several liability arrangements under the scope of ASC 405. For example, the guidance applies at the inception of debt arrangements, but it applies to other arrangements after their inception, such as when an obligation's total amount becomes fixed after an arrangement's inception. Corresponding entries should depend on an obligation's facts and circumstances. The following are examples of corresponding entries:

  — Cash for proceeds from a debt arrangement;

  — An expense for a legal settlement;

  — A receivable (that is assessed for impairment) for a contractual right; or

  — An equity transaction with an entity under common control.

- *ASC 405-30-1 and 30-2* provide *initial measurement* guidance for such liability arrangements, which would initially be measured as the sum of the following:

  — The amount a reporting entity agreed to pay based on an arrangement among its co-obligors; and

  — An additional amount that a reporting entity expects to pay on behalf of its co-obligors. If a reporting entity believes that a certain amount within a range that it expects to pay is a better estimate than other amounts within the range, it should include it as the additional amount in the obligation's measurement. The minimum amount in a range should be included as the additional amount in measuring an obligation if no other amount within a range is a better estimate. The corresponding entry or entries should be based on the facts and circumstances.

- *ASC 405-40-35-1* provides that the *subsequent* measurement of obligations as a result of joint and several liability arrangements under the scope of ASC 405 should be based on the guidance in ASC 405-40-30.

- *ASC 405-40-50-1 and 50-2* provide the following guidance for the required *disclosures* about each obligation, or each group of similar obligations, as a result of joint and several liability arrangements:

  — The nature of an arrangement, including how the liability was incurred, the entity's relationship with the co-obligors, and the arrangement's terms and conditions;

  — An arrangement's total outstanding amount, which should not be reduced by the effect of amounts, if any, that may be recovered from other entities;

- An entity's carrying amount of a liability, if any, and the carrying amount of a recognized receivable, if any;
- The nature of recourse provisions, if any, that would enable the entity to recover from other entities amounts that it paid, including limitations, if any, on the amounts that may be recovered; and
- In the period in which an entity first recognizes and measures the liability or in a period in which the liability changes significantly, the corresponding entry and its location in the financial statements.

The disclosures discussed above should be made in addition to the required disclosures about related parties in ASC 850, *Related Party Disclosures*.

TRANSITION AND EFFECTIVE DATE

The following is the effective date and transition guidance in ASC 405-40-65-1:

- For public entities, the guidance in ASU 2013-04 is effective for fiscal years, and interim periods within those years, that begin after December 15, 2013. Nonpublic entities are required to begin applying the guidance in this ASU for fiscal years that end after December 15, 2014, and for interim and annual periods thereafter.
- The guidance in ASU 2013-04 should be applied retrospectively to all prior periods presented for obligations that arise from joint and several liability arrangements that exist at the beginning of an entity's fiscal year in which the guidance is adopted.
- An entity that changes its accounting as a result of the adoption of the guidance in ASU 2013-04 may elect to use hindsight for comparative periods presented in the year in which the guidance is adopted and should disclose that it has done so.
- Early adoption of the guidance is permitted.
- Disclosure of the information in ASC 250, *Accounting Changes and Error Corrections* (250-10-50-1 through 50-3), is required in the period in which the guidance is adopted.

CHAPTER 27
ASC 410—ASSET RETIREMENT AND ENVIRONMENTAL OBLIGATIONS

CONTENTS

Part I: General Guidance	27,001
ASC 410-10: Overall	27,001
ASC 410-20: Asset Retirement Obligations	27,002
Overview	27,002
Asset Retirement Obligations	27,002
Initial Recognition and Measurement	27,002
Accounting Subsequent to Initial Recognition	27,003
Illustration of Accounting for an Asset Retirement Obligation—Obligation Incurred in a Single Reporting Period	27,004
Illustration of Accounting for an Asset Retirement Obligation—Obligation Incurred over Multiple Reporting Periods	27,006
Conditional Asset Retirement Obligations	27,008
Interpretive Guidance	27,009
Illustration of Accounting for a Conditional Asset Retirement Obligation	27,010
Disclosure	27,010
Part II: Interpretive Guidance	27,011
ASC 410-30: Environmental Obligations	27,011
ASC 410-30-05-1 through 3, 05-5 through 05-25; 10-1; 15-1 through 15-3; 25-1 through 25-15, 25-17, 25-20 through 25-23; 30-1 through 30-19; 35-1 through 35-5, 35-7 through 35-12, 35-12A; 45-1 through 45-5; 50-1 through 50-17; 55-1 through 55-6, 55-14 through 55-17, 55-27 through 55-51; 60-3, 60-8	
Environmental Remediation Liabilities	27,011
Illustration of Estimating an Environmental Remediation Liability	27,013
Illustration of Accounting Policy Note	27,019
Illustration of Disclosures for Loss Contingencies	27,020
ASC 410-30-15-3, 25-16, 25-18, 25-19, 35-14, 55-19 through 55-26; ASC 410-20-15-2	
Capitalization of Costs to Treat Environmental Contamination	27,021
ASC 410-30-45-6; ASC 410-20-15-3	
Accounting for the Cost of Asbestos Removal	27,022

PART I: GENERAL GUIDANCE

ASC 410-10: OVERALL

The sole purpose of ASC 410-10 is to differentiate between asset retirement obligations and environmental obligations. (ASC 410-10-05-1). ASC 410-20 provides guidance on accounting for asset retirement obligations, including asset retirement costs, including environmental remediation liabilities resulting from the normal use of a long-lived asset (ASC 410-10-05-2). ASC 410-30 provides guidance on accounting for environmental remediation liabilities (ASC 410-10-05-2).

ASC 410-20: ASSET RETIREMENT OBLIGATIONS

OVERVIEW

ASC 410 requires accounting recognition and measurement of a liability for an asset retirement obligation and associated asset retirement costs. It was issued to narrow areas of differences in the way that companies previously accounted for obligations related to the retirement of long-lived assets, some of which recognized liabilities as they were incurred, while others did not recognize liabilities until the asset was retired. Also, practices varied in terms of how asset retirement obligations were measured and presented in financial statements.

ASC 410 applies to all entities, including rate-regulated entities that meet the criteria for applying ASC 980 (Regulated Operations). It applies to all legal obligations associated with the retirement of tangible long-lived assets that result from an acquisition, construction, or development. A legal obligation is defined as an obligation that a party is required to settle as a result of an existing or enacted law, statue, ordinance, or written or oral contract, or by legal construction of a contract under the doctrine of promissory estoppel (ASC 410-20-15-1).

ASC 410 does not apply to obligations that arise solely from a plan to dispose of a long-lived asset as defined in ASC 360. ASC 410 does not apply to obligations of a lessee in connection with leased property (ASC 410-20-15-3).

ASSET RETIREMENT OBLIGATIONS

Initial Recognition and Measurement

Recognition of a liability for the fair value of an asset retirement obligation is required in the period in which it is incurred, if a reasonable estimate of fair value can be made. If such an estimate cannot be made in the period the obligation is incurred, the liability shall be recognized when a reasonable estimate of fair value can be made.

PRACTICE NOTE: The FASB indicates that this requirement is consistent with the definition of a liability in CON-6 (Elements of Financial Statements), which states that liabilities are probable future sacrifices of economic benefits arising from present obligations of a particular entity to transfer assets or provide services to other entities in the future as a result of past transactions or events. The term "probable," in CON-5 (Recognition and Measurement in Financial Statements of Business Enterprises), is used with its general meaning and refers to that which can be reasonably expected or believed on the basis of available evidence or logic, but is neither certain nor proved. It is intended to reflect the fact that business and other economic activities occur in an environment in which few outcomes are certain. This is in contrast to the use of the word "probable" in ASC 450 (Contingencies), which requires a high degree of expectation.

ASC 410—Asset Retirement and Environmental Obligations

The fair value of a liability for an asset retirement obligation will typically be determined using an expected present value technique. Cash flows shall be discounted using a credit-adjusted risk-free rate. This results in the effect of an entity's credit standing affecting the discount rate rather than affecting expected cash flows.

The obligation may be incurred over more than one financial reporting period if the events that lead to the obligation occur over more than one period. An incremental liability incurred in a subsequent reporting period shall be considered an additional layer of the original liability, with each layer measured at fair value and combined with the original layer(s) (ASC 410-20-35-1).

Accounting Subsequent to Initial Recognition

When the initial liability is recognized, the asset cost is increased by the amount equal to the same amount as the liability. That cost shall subsequently be allocated to expense using a systematic and rational method over the asset's useful life. This process does not preclude the entity from capitalizing an amount of asset retirement cost and allocating an equal amount to expense in the same accounting period (ASC 410-20-35-2).

In applying the provisions of ASC 360 in asset impairment situations, the carrying amount of the asset being tested for impairment shall include the amounts of capitalized asset retirement costs. Estimates of future cash flows related to the liability for an asset retirement obligation that has been recognized in the financial statements shall be excluded from the undiscounted cash flows used to test the asset for recoverability and from the discounted cash flows used to measure the asset's fair value. If the fair value of the asset is based on a quoted market price and that price considers the costs that will be incurred in retiring the asset, the quoted market price shall be increased by the fair value of the asset retirement obligation when measuring the amount of impairment (ASC 360-10-35-18, 19).

In subsequent periods, changes in the liability for an asset retirement obligation resulting from the passage of time and revisions to either the timing or amount of the original estimate of undiscounted cash flows shall be recognized. In so doing, changes due to the passage of time shall first be incorporated before measuring changes resulting from a revision of either the timing or the amount of estimated cash flows (ASC 410-20-35-3, 4). Changes in the liability due to the passage of time shall be measured by applying an interest method of allocation to the liability at the beginning of the period using the credit-adjusted risk-free interest rate that existed when the liability was initially measured. That amount shall be recognized as an increase in the carrying amount of the liability and the expense shown as an operating item in the income statement (referred to as accretion expense) (ASC 410-20-35-5). Changes resulting from revisions in the amount and/or timing of the original estimate of undiscounted cash flows shall be recognized as an increase or decrease in the carrying amount of the liability

27,004 ASC 410—Asset Retirement and Environmental Obligations

and the related asset retirement cost capitalized. Upward revisions shall be discounted using the current credit-adjusted risk-free rate. Downward revisions shall be discounted using the credit-adjusted risk-free rate that existed when the original liability was recognized. When the asset cost changes as a result of revisions to estimated cash flows, the amount of the asset retirement cost allocated to expense in the period of change and subsequent periods, as appropriate, shall be adjusted (ASC 410-20-35-8).

Illustration of Accounting for an Asset Retirement Obligation—Obligation Incurred in a Single Reporting Period

This example illustrates (a) initial measurement of a liability for an asset retirement obligation using an expected present value technique, (b) subsequent measurement assuming that there are no changes in expected cash flows, and (c) settlement of the asset retirement obligation (ARO liability) at the end of its term.

Ocaxet Inc. completes construction of and places into service an offshore oil platform on January 1, 20X8. The entity is legally required to dismantle and remove the platform at the end of its useful life, which is estimated to be five years. Ocaxet Inc. develops the following estimates of costs to dismantle and remove the platform.

Labor costs are based on current, relevant marketplace wages and Ocaxet Inc. estimates the probability of a range of cash flow estimates as follows:

Cash Flow Estimate	Estimated Probability	Expected Cash Flows
$ 125,000	20%	$ 25,000
150,000	60	90,000
200,000	20	40,000
		$ 155,000

Ocaxet Inc. estimates allocated overhead and equipment charges to be 70% of labor costs.

Ocaxet Inc. understands that the contractor typically adds a markup on labor and allocated internal costs to provide a profit margin on the job and estimates this markup rate to be 15%. Ocaxet Inc. also estimates the market risk premium to be 5% of the estimated inflation-adjusted cash flows. The risk-free rate of interest is 4%, and Ocaxet Inc. adjusts that rate by 3% to reflect the effect of its credit standing. Thus, the credit-adjusted risk-free rate used to compute expected present value is 7%. Ocaxet Inc. also assumes an annual inflation rate of 3.5% annually over the five-year period.

Initial measurement of the ARO liability at January 1, 20X8:

	Expected Cash Flows
Expected labor costs	$ 155,000
Allocated overhead and equipment charges (.70 × $155,000)	108,500
Contractor's markup [.15 × ($155,000 + $108,500)]	39,525
Expected cash outflows before inflation adjustment	303,025
Inflation factor (1.035^5)	1.1877

	Expected Cash Flows
Expected cash flows adjusted for inflation	359,903
Market-risk premium (.05 × $359,903)	17,995
Expected cash flows adjusted for market risk	$377,898
Expected Present value using credit-adjusted risk-free rate of 7% for 5 years [(1/(1 + .07^5) × $377,898]	$269,436

On December 31, 20Y2, Ocaxet Inc. settles its asset retirement obligation by using its internal workforce at a cost of $357,000. Assuming no changes during the five-year period in the cash flows used to estimate the obligation, the entity would recognize a gain of $20,898 on settlement of the obligation:

Labor	$210,000
Allocated overhead and equipment charges (70% of labor)	147,000
Total costs incurred	357,000
ARO liability	377,898
Gain on settlement of obligation	$ 20,898

Interest Method of Allocation

Year	Liability Balance 1/1	Accretion (7%)	Liability Balance 12/31
20X8	269,436	18,861	288,297
20X9	288,297	20,181	308,478
20Y0	308,478	21,593	330,071
20Y1	330,071	23,105	353,176
20Y2	353,176	24,722	377,898

Schedule of Expenses

Year-End	Accretion Expense	Depreciation Expense*	Total Expense
20X8	18,861	53,887	72,748
20X9	20,181	53,887	74,068
20Y0	21,593	53,887	75,480
20Y1	23,105	53,887	76,992
20Y2	24,722	53,887	78,609

* Assume straight-line deprecation ($269,436/5)

27,006 ASC 410—Asset Retirement and Environmental Obligations

Journal Entries:

January 1, 20X8:
    Long-lived asset (asset retirement cost)   269,436
        ARO liability   269,436
    To record the initial fair value of the ARO liability

December 31, 20X8-20Y2:
    Depreciation expense (asset retirement cost)   53,887
        Accumulated depreciation   53,887
    To record straight-line depreciation on the asset retirement cost
    Accretion expense   Per schedule
        ARO liability   Per schedule
    To record accretion expense on the ARO liability

December 31, 20Y2:
    ARO liability   377,898
        Wages payable   210,000
        Allocated overhead and equipment charges   147,000
        Gain on settlement of ARO liability   20,898
    To record settlement of the ARO liability

Illustration of Accounting for an Asset Retirement Obligation—Obligation Incurred over Multiple Reporting Periods

This example highlights the recognition and measurement provisions for an ARO liability that is incurred over more than one reporting period.

Asem Inc. places a nuclear utility plant into service on December 31, 20X8. The entity is legally required to decommission the plant at the end of its useful life, which is estimated to be ten years.

The following schedule reflects the expected cash flows and respective credit-adjusted risk-free rates used to measure each portion of the liability through December 31, 20Y0, at which time the plant is 90% contaminated:

Date	Expected Cash Flows	Credit-Adjusted Risk-Free Rate
12/31/X8	$30,000	8.0%
12/31/X9	2,250	7.3
12/31/Y0	2,775	7.7

On December 31, 20Y0, Asem Inc. increases by 10% its estimate of expected cash flows that were used to measure those portions of the liability recognized on December 31, 20X8, and December 31, 20X9. Because the change results in an upward revision to the expected cash flows, the incremental estimated cash flow is discounted at the current credit-adjusted risk-free rate of 7.7%. As a

ASC 410—Asset Retirement and Environmental Obligations 27,007

result, the total incremental cash flows of $6,000 [($30,000 + $2,250) × 10%) + $2,775] are discounted at the then current credit-adjusted risk-free rate of 7.7% and recorded as a liability on December 31, 20Y0.

	Date Incurred		
	12/31/X8	12/31/X9	12/31/Y0
Initial measurement of the ARO liability:			
Expected labor cost	$30,000	$2,250	$2,775
Credit-adjusted risk-free rate	8.0%	7.3%	7.7%
Discount period in years	10	9	8
Expected present value	$13,896	$1,193	$1,533

Measurement of incremental expected cash flows occurring on 12/31/Y0:

Increase in expected cash flows of 10% [($30,000 + 2,250) × 10%]	$3,225
Credit-adjusted risk-free rate at December 31, 2010	7.7%
Discount period remaining in years	8
Expected present value [$3,225 × (1/(1.077^8)]	$1,782

Carrying Amount of Liability Incurred in 20X8

Year	Liability Balance 1/1	Accretion (8.0%)	New Liability	Liability Balance 12/31
20X8			13,896	13,896
20X9	13,896	1,112		15,008
20Y0	15,008	1,201		16,209

Carrying Amount of Liability Incurred in 20X9

Year	Liability Balance 1/1	Accretion (7.3%)	New Liability	Liability Balance 12/31
20X9			$1,193	$1,193
20Y0	$1,193	$87		1,280

Carrying Amount of Liability Incurred in 20Y0 Plus Effect of Change in Expected Cash Flows

Year	Liability Balance 1/1	Accretion (7.7%)	Change in Cash Flow Estimate	New Liability	Liability Balance 12/31
20Y0			$1,782	$1,533	$3,315

Carrying Amount of Total Liability

Year	Liability Balance 1/1	Accretion	Change in Cash Flow Estimate	New Liability	Liability Balance 12/31
20X8				$13,896	$13,896
20X9	$13,896	$1,112		1,193	16,201
20Y0	16,201	1,288	$1,782	1,533	20,804

Journal Entries:

December 31, 20X8:

Long-lived asset (asset retirement cost)	13,896	
ARO liability		13,896
To record the initial fair value of the ARO liability incurred in this period		

December 31, 20X9:

Depreciation expense ($13,896/10)	1,390	
Accumulated depreciation		1,390
To record straight-line depreciation on the asset retirement cost		
Accretion expense	1,112	
ARO liability		1,112
To record accretion expense on the ARO liability		
Long-lived asset (asset retirement cost)	1,193	
ARO liability		1,193
To record the initial fair value of the ARO liability incurred in this period		

December 31, 20Y0:

Depreciation expense [($13,896/10) + ($1,193/9)]	1,523	
Accumulated depreciation		1,523
To record straight-line depreciation on the asset retirement cost		
Accretion expense	1,288	
ARO liability		1,288
To record accretion expense on the ARO liability		
Long-lived asset (asset retirement cost)	1,782	
ARO liability		1,782
To record the change in liability resulting from a revision in expected cash flows		
Long-lived asset (asset retirement cost)	1,533	
ARO liability		1,533
To record the initial fair value of the ARO liability incurred in this period		

CONDITIONAL ASSET RETIREMENT OBLIGATIONS

ASC 410 provides guidance on measuring the liability associated with an asset retirement obligation when there is uncertainty associated with the timing or method of the asset retirement. Although ASC 410 requires entities to recognize the fair value of an asset retirement obligation in the period in which the obligation is incurred, differences in practice have arisen because of differences in interpretation as to when a reasonable estimate of fair value can be made. In particular, although an entity may be legally required to retire a fixed asset, there may be uncertainties associated with the timing and/or method of the asset retirement. The timing and/or method may be conditional on a future event, and the entity may or may not control this future event. Some entities recognize a liability at the time the asset retirement obligation is incurred, and consider the uncertainties associated with the timing and/or method of retiring the asset in estimating the liability's fair value. Other entities only recognize a liability when the date and method of asset retirement are essentially fixed. ASC 410 is designed to reduce these differences in practice.

Interpretive Guidance

An asset can be retired by, among other ways, sale, abandonment, recycling, and disposal. A liability exists if an entity has a legal obligation to retire a fixed asset, even if the timing and/or method of retiring the asset is conditional on a future event. That is, the obligation to retire the asset is unconditional, even though the timing and/or method of retiring the asset may be uncertain. Because a liability exists, that liability should be recognized if its fair value can be reasonably estimated (ASC 410-20-25-7).

An asset retirement obligation is reasonably estimable if (1) the purchase price of the asset reflects the costs associated with the legally mandated obligation to retire the fixed asset, (2) the entity could transfer the asset retirement obligation to another party because an active market for such transfers exists, and (3) enough information exists to apply an expected present value technique (ASC 410-20-25-6). In many instances, the fair value of the asset retirement obligation will not be transparent in the purchase price, nor will an active market for the transfer of the obligation exist. Therefore, very commonly, the fair value of an asset retirement obligation is determined using an expected present value technique.

Assuming the use of an expected present value technique, the fair value of an asset retirement obligation is reasonably estimable if either of two conditions exists (ASC 410-20-25-8):

1. The settlement date and the method of settlement have been determined by the party that created the legal obligation (e.g., the legislative, executive, or private body that created the law, regulation, or contract giving rise to the legal obligation).

> **PRACTICE POINTER:** The only uncertainty remaining if the date and method of settlement have been determined is whether the entity will be required to retire the asset by the party that created the legal obligation. The entity will either be required to retire the asset or it will not. If no information exists as to which outcome is more likely, the entity is to assign a 50% probability to each outcome.

2. Information is available that enables the entity to estimate the settlement date or range of possible settlement dates, and to assign probabilities to these potential settlement dates, and estimate the settlement method or potential settlement alternatives, and to assign probabilities to these potential settlement methods. This information should be developed from the entity's past practice, industry practice, the intent of management, and the asset's economic life.

> **PRACTICE POINTER:** In some cases the entity still may be able to arrive at a reasonable estimate of the fair value of the asset retirement obligation even if the entity cannot assign probabilities to the potential settlement dates or methods of settlement. For example, the potential settlement dates may be close in time to each other and the alternative settlement methods may involve similar cash outflows. In this instance, differences in the assigned probabilities would not have a material effect on the computed fair value of the asset retirement obligation.

Notwithstanding the above guidance, there will be some instances where although a legal obligation to retire the asset exists (i.e., a liability exists), the liability will not be recognized because the entity cannot reasonably estimate the fair value of the liability. A liability must be recorded in a latter period, however, when information becomes available to estimate the fair value of the liability. And, if a liability is not recognized because it cannot be reasonably estimated, the entity must disclose that fact and must disclose the reasons the fair value of the liability cannot be reasonably estimated (ASC 410-20-25-10).

> **Illustration of Accounting for a Conditional Asset Retirement Obligation**
>
> A company constructs manufacturing, distribution, and sales facilities that contain a building material that is non-toxic in its present state, but which is toxic if disposed of without following special procedures. There is no legal requirement to dispose of the building material. If any building is destroyed or substantially remodeled, however, the entity must follow legally mandated disposal procedures for the toxic material.
>
> The company is able to estimate dates on which it is likely to destroy (raze) or substantially remodel each building, the methods that are likely to be used, and the associated probabilities. Therefore, at the date that each building is constructed, the company is able to estimate the asset retirement obligation using an expected present value technique. The recorded value of each building would be increased by the estimated present value of the asset retirement obligation, and a liability for the asset retirement obligation would be recognized as well.

DISCLOSURE

Following are disclosures required about asset retirement obligations:

- General description of the asset retirement obligation and the associated long-lived asset
- Fair value of assets that are legally restricted for purposes of settling asset retirement obligations
- A reconciliation of the beginning and ending carrying amounts of asset retirement obligations showing separately:
  — Liabilities incurred in the current period
  — Liabilities settled in the current period

- Accretion expense
- Revisions in estimated cash flows where there is a significant change in the current period

If the fair value of an asset retirement obligation cannot be reasonably estimated, that fact and the reasons should be disclosed (ASC 410-20-50-1, 2).

PART II: INTERPRETIVE GUIDANCE

ASC 410-30: ENVIRONMENTAL OBLIGATIONS

ASC 410-30-05-1 through 3, 05-5 through 05-25; 10-1; 15-1 through 15-3; 25-1 through 25-15, 25-17, 25-20 through 25-23; 30-1 through 30-19; 35-1 through 35-5, 35-7 through 35-12, 35-12A; 45-1 through 45-5; 50-1 through 50-17; 55-1 through 55-6, 55-14 through 55-17, 55-27 through 55-51; 60-3, 60-8 Environmental Remediation Liabilities

BACKGROUND

This SOP provides accounting guidance for environmental remediation liabilities that relate to pollution resulting from some past act. Generally, these liabilities result from one of the following:

- Superfund provisions
- The corrective-action provisions of the Resource Conservation and Recovery Act (RCRA)
- State and non-U.S. laws and regulations that are analogous to the RCRA

The SOP applies to all entities that prepare financial statements in conformity with generally accepted accounting principles applicable to nongovernmental entities. The provisions of SOP 96-1 are intended to be applied on a site-by-site basis.

The SOP is written in the context of operations taking place in the United States, although the guidance provided is applicable to all of a reporting entity's operations. It is *not* intended to provide guidance for the following:

- Accounting for pollution control costs with respect to current operations
- Accounting for costs of future site restoration or closure that are required upon the cessation of operations or sale of facilities
- Accounting for environmental remediation actions that are undertaken at the sole discretion of management and that are not induced by the threat of litigation or of assertion or by a claim of assessment by governments or other parties
- Recognizing liabilities of insurance companies for unpaid claims
- Asset impairment issues

PRACTICE POINTER: Guidance on the accounting for costs of future site restoration or closure that are required upon the cessation of operations or sale of facilities is provided in ASC 410-20; ASC 450-20; ASC 835-20; ASC 360-10-35; ASC 840-40 and ASC 840-10; ASC 980-410. In addition, guidance

ASC 410—Asset Retirement and Environmental Obligations

on asset impairment issues is provided in ASC 360-10; ASC 840-30; ASC 840-20; ASC 205-10, ASC 205-20; ASC 958-225-45, ASC 958-360; ASC 855-10; ASC 225-20.

The following discussion is intended to provide guidance for the accounting for "cleanup" activities rather than preventative or other activities. For example, it does not discuss situations in which remediation is required only when a property is for sale. The discussion focuses on the document's detailed guidance on accounting and disclosure for environmental remediation liabilities.

ACCOUNTING GUIDANCE

Recognition of Environmental Remediation Liabilities

The guidance for the recognition of environmental remediation liabilities is based on the recognition criteria in ASC 450 by requiring the accrual of a liability when *both* of the following conditions are met:

- Information available before the financial statements are issued or are available for issuance (as discussed in ASC 855-10-25) indicates that it is probable that an asset has been impaired or a liability has been incurred at the date of the financial statements.
- The amount of the loss can be reasonably estimated.

A liability related to environmental remediation often results over a period of time rather than as a distinct event. The underlying cause of such a liability is the past or present ownership or operation of a site, or the contribution or transportation of waste to a site, at which remedial actions must be made. To meet the criteria for recognizing a liability, the underlying cause must have occurred on or before the date of the financial statements.

Probability That a Liability Has Been Incurred

Applying the criteria in ASC 450-20-25-2 to environmental remediation liabilities requires the followingIt has been asserted (or it is probable that it will be asserted) that the entity is responsible for participating in a remediation process because of a past event. This usually means that litigation has begun, a claim or an assessment has been asserted, or commencement of litigation or assertion of a claim or assessment is considered probable.

1. Available evidence indicates that the outcome of such litigation, claim, or assessment will be unfavorable (i.e., the entity will be held responsible for participating in a remediation process because of the past event).

In recognition of the legal framework in which most environmental remediation liabilities occur, the guidance is based on a presumption that if litigation has commenced (or a claim or an assessment has been asserted or is considered probable), and the reporting entity is associated with the site, the outcome will be unfavorable for the entity.

Ability to Make a Reasonable Estimate

Developing an estimate of environmental remediation liabilities involves a consideration of many factors, such as the following:

ASC 410—Asset Retirement and Environmental Obligations

1. The extent and types of hazardous substances at the site
2. The range of technologies that can be used for remediation
3. Evolving standards of what constitutes acceptable remediation
4. The number and financial condition of other potentially responsible parties and the extent of their responsibility for the remediation

---

Illustration of Estimating an Environmental Remediation Liability

Foster, Inc., has determined that its environmental remediation obligation meets the recognition criteria in the SOP The company is in the process of estimating the amount of the obligation that will be recognized. The company has further determined that the liability consists of four components, described as follows:

Component	Description
A	Estimated at $750,000
B	Estimated to be within a range of $500,000 to $900,000, with the most likely amount at $625,000
C	Estimated to be within a range of $275,000 to $400,000, with no amount within that range more likely than any other amount
D	Unable to estimate

The environmental remediation liability that should be recognized at this time, subject to adjustment in the future as additional information becomes available, is determined as follows:

Component A	$ 750,000
Component B	625,000
Component C	275,000
Component D	None
	$1,650,000

The guidance in ASC 450-20-25-5, 30-1, 05-5, 55-23 through 55-34 is particularly important in estimating the amount of an environmental remediation liability. In the early stages of the remediation process, liabilities are not easily quantified. The range and ultimate amount of the liability will be determined as events occur over time. The range of an environmental remediation liability typically is estimated by first estimating the various components of the liability—which may themselves be in the form of a range. As suggested under the guidance in ASC 450-20-25-5, 30-1, 05-5, 55-23 through 55-34, if an amount within a range is a better estimate than any other amount within the range, that amount should be used. If no amount within a range is a more reliable estimate than any other, the minimum amount in the range should be used. Thus, the amount of an environmental remediation liability will be a combination of most likely amounts and minimum amounts of the components of the liability. Even if a range for certain components of the liability cannot be estimated, a liability still should be recognized and recorded at the appropriate amount for the components that can be estimated. A complexity that arises in estimating environmental remediation liabilities is the assignment and allocation among the various potentially responsible parties (PRPs). The final allocation may not be known until the remediation effort is substantially complete and may depend on factors such as the PRPs' willingness to negotiate a cost allocation. This fact should not preclude an entity from recognizing its best estimate of its share of a liability if the probability criterion is met. A change, if any, in estimating an environmental remediation liability, including those due to negotiations with other PRPs, is accounted for as a change in accounting estimate in accordance with the guidance in ASC 250.

Measurement of Environmental Remediation Liabilities

Once an entity determines that it is probable that an environmental remediation liability has been incurred, it must estimate the amount of that liability based on available evidence. The liability's estimate includes the allocable share of the liability for a specific site, and the share of amounts related to the site that will not be paid by other PRPs or the government.

The following four issues that must be addressed in the measurement of an entity's environmental remediation liability are identified:

- Costs that should be included in the measurement
- Whether the measurement should consider the effects of expected future events or developments
- How the measurement should be affected by the existence of other PRPs
- How the measurement should be affected by potential recoveries

Costs to Be Included

Costs to be included in the measurement of an environmental remediation liability include (a) incremental direct costs of the remediation effort and (b) costs of compensation and benefits for employees who are expected to devote a significant amount of time on the remediation effort (e.g., in-house lawyers and engineers).

The remediation effort is considered on a site-by-site basis and includes the following:

- Precleanup activities (e.g., the performance of a remedial investigation, risk assessment, or feasibility study and the preparation of remedial action plan)
- Performance of remedial actions under Superfund, corrective actions under RCRA, and analogous actions under state and non-U.S. laws
- Government oversight and enforcement activities
- Operation and maintenance of the remedy

The following are examples of incremental direct costs of a remediation effort:

- Fees paid to outside law firms for work related to remedial actions
- Costs related to completing the remedial investigation/feasibility study
- Fees to outside engineering and consulting firms for site investigations and the development of remedial action plans and designs
- Costs of contractors performing remedial actions
- Government oversight costs

- Costs of machinery and equipment related to the remedial effort that do not have alternative uses
- The PRP's assessments of the costs it incurred in dealing with a site
- Operating costs and remedial action maintenance

The costs of the following are included in the measurement of the remediation liability:

- Determining the extent of the remedial actions that are required
- Determining the types of remedial actions to be used
- Allocating the costs among PRPs

The costs of routine environmental compliance matters and litigation costs involved with potential recoveries are *not* part of the remediation effort. Further, including the cost of defense against assertions of liability in the measurement of the environmental remediation liability is not required. Practice is diverse: some include legal defense costs in the measurement of a liability under the guidance in ASC 450, while most entities treat litigation costs as period costs.

Effects of Expected Future Events or Developments

Remediation of a site may extend over several years. As a result, the laws that govern the remediation process and the technology available may change during the remediation process. Other factors that may affect estimates of costs to be incurred are the effect of inflation and productivity improvements.

Enacted laws and adopted regulations and policies should provide the basis for measuring a remediation liability. Changes in those factors should not be anticipated, and the effect of changes that are enacted or adopted should be recognized only when they occur. The remediation plan should be based on the methodology that is expected to be approved, and the liability should be based on that methodology and remediation technology, which should continue to be the basis for the liability until it is probable that a revised methodology will be accepted.

The measurement of environmental remediation liabilities should be based on the reporting entity's estimate of what it will cost to perform each of the elements of the remediation effort (identified earlier) when those elements are expected to be performed. As such, an entity should take into account productivity improvements due to experience, as well as inflation. If it is not practicable to estimate inflation, a cost estimate should include the minimum in the range of the liability until the costs can be estimated more reasonably.

If the amount and timing of cash payments is (reasonably) fixed or reliably determinable, the measurement of the liability, or a component of the liability, may be discounted to reflect the time value of money. The discount rate that should be used is that rate (*a*) that will produce an amount at which the environmental liability theoretically could be settled in an arm's-length transaction with a third party and (*b*) that does not exceed the interest rate on monetary assets that are essentially risk-free and have maturities comparable to that of the environmental liability.

ASC 410—Asset Retirement and Environmental Obligations

Allocation of the Liability Among PRPs

The environmental remediation liability recorded by an entity should be based on the entity's estimate of its allocable share of the joint and several remediation liability. This requires an identification of the PRPs for the site, an assessment of the likelihood that other PRPs will pay their share of the liability, and a determination of the portion of the liability that will be allocated to the entity.

Identification of PRPs The SOP identifies five categories of PRPs:

1. *Participating PRPs* PRPs that acknowledge their potential involvement with the site. These PRPs also are referred to as "players."

2. *Recalcitrant PRPs* PRPs that adopt an attitude of nonresponsibility, even though evidence suggests their involvement in the site. Typically, parties in this category must be sued in order for their allocable share of the remediation liability to be collected.

3. *Unproven PRPs* Parties that have been identified as PRPs by the Environmental Protection Agency (EPA) but that do not acknowledge their potential involvement because no substantive evidence currently links them to the site. These PRPs eventually will be reclassified based on evidence that is later discovered.

4. *Parties that have not been identified as PRPs* As the investigation progresses, additional PRPs may be identified. These PRPs will later be reclassified to the participating category or the recalcitrant category.

5. *PRPs that cannot be identified or have no assets* PRPs from which no contributions will be received because they are not found or have no assets. These PRPs are sometimes referred to as "orphan PRPs."

Allocation process The environmental remediation liability is allocated only among participating PRPs. There are several ways to allocate the liability among PRPs. The following are the four principal factors that are considered in a typical allocation process:

1. *Elements of fair share* Examples are the amount of waste based on volume, mass, type, and toxicity and the length of time the site was used.

2. *Classification of PRP* Examples are site operator, transporter of waste, and generator of waste.

3. *Limitations on payments* Any statutory or regulatory limitations on contributions.

4. *Degree of care* Refers to the degree of care exercised in selecting the site or in selecting a transporter.

The environmental remediation liability may be allocated according to any of the following methods: (1) PRPs may agree among themselves as to the allocation, (2) PRPs may hire an allocation consultant whose conclusions may or may not be binding, or (3) PRPs may request a nonbinding allocation of responsibility from the EPA. The allocation method or percentages may change as the project moves forward.

An entity should determine its allocable share of the remediation liability based on its estimate of the allocation method and its percentage of the amount that will ultimately be used for the entire remediation effort. Sources for this estimate should be the allocation method and the percentages that the PRPs have agreed to, the method and percentages that have been assigned by a consultant, or the method and percentages determined by the EPA, depending on the method that is chosen (as described in the preceding paragraph). If the entity's estimate of the ultimate liability differs significantly from the method or percentage from these primary sources, the entity's estimate should be based on objective, verifiable evidence, such as the following:

- Existing data about the kinds and quantities of waste at the site
- Experience with allocation approaches in comparable situations
- Reports of environmental specialists
- Internal data refuting EPA allegations about the entity's contribution of waste to the site

A consideration in estimating an entity's allocable share of the liability is the financial condition of the participating PRPs, including their ability to pay. The entity should include in its liability its share of amounts that are not expected to be paid by other PRPs or by the government.

Impact of potential recoveries Potential recoveries may come from a number of sources, such as insurers, PRPs other than participating PRPs, and government or third-party funds. The environmental remediation liability should be determined without regard to potential recoveries. An asset related to recoveries should be separately recognized only when realization is considered probable. If the claim is subject to litigation, the realization of the recovery claim is not considered probable.

The amount that may be recovered should be determined based on the available information and the specific circumstances (see ASC 410-30-30-15). The transaction costs of receiving a potential recovery also should be considered in measuring the potential amount. In addition, the time value of money should be considered in measuring the amount of a potential recovery if the time value of money has been considered in measuring the liability.

Financial Statement Presentation and Disclosure

The following are guidelines for financial statement presentation and disclosure related to environmental remediation obligations. Entities that are subject to the rules and regulations of the Securities and Exchange Commission (SEC) also are required to adhere to various SEC rules that apply to environmental matters.

Financial Statement Presentation

Several assets may result from an environmental remediation obligation, including the following:

- Receivables from other PRPs that are not providing initial funding
- Anticipated recoveries from insurers
- Anticipated recoveries from prior owners as a result of indemnification agreements

ASC 210-20, ASC 815-10 specifies that offsetting assets and liabilities is appropriate only if a right of setoff exists, which requires *all* of the following:

- Each of the two parties owes the other party a determinable amount.
- The reporting entity has the right to set off the amounts owed with the amount owed by the other party.
- The reporting entity intends to set off.
- The right of setoff is enforceable at law.

Although those conditions would apply to assets and liabilities related to an environmental remediation, it would be rare for the facts and circumstances surrounding environmental remediation liabilities and related assets to meet those conditions.

Recording an environmental remediation liability usually results in a charge to income. Such a charge does not meet the criteria of ASC 225-20-45-1 through 45-6, 45-8, 45-10 through 45-14, 45-16; 15-2; 50-2 through 50-3; 55-1 through 55-2; 830-10-45-19 for classification as an extraordinary item, because it does not result from an event that is unusual in nature and infrequent in occurrence. Furthermore, it is difficult to substantiate the classification of environmental remediation costs as a component of nonoperating expenses, because the events underlying the obligation are part of the entity's operations. Thus, environmental remediation-related expenses should be reported as a component of operating income in an income statement that separates operating and nonoperating items. Credits (i.e., gains or loss recoveries) recognized in an entity's financial statements should be presented in the income statement in the same manner. Any earnings on assets that are reflected in an entity's balance sheet and are reserved for its environmental liabilities should be reported as investment income. Environmental remediation-related expenses and recoveries that are associated with disposals of a segment of a business and accounted for in accordance with the guidance in ASC 225-20-45-1 through 45-6, 45-8, 45-10 through 45-14, 45-16, 15-2, 50-2 through 50-3, 55-1 through 55-2; ASC 830-10-45-19 should be classified as discontinued operations.

DISCLOSURE

Accounting policies ASC 235-10-05-3 through 05-4, 50-1 through 50-6 provides guidance concerning information that must be disclosed about the accounting policies used by an entity in the preparation of its financial statements. With regard to environmental remediation liabilities, that disclosure should include an indication of whether the accrual is measured on a discounted basis.

Environmental remediation liabilities are increasingly significant and involve subjective judgment. As a result, entities are encouraged, but not required, to disclose the event, situation, or set of circumstances that generally triggers recognition of loss contingencies that arise out of the entity's environmental remediation-related obligations. Entities also are encouraged to disclose their policy regarding the timing of recognition of recoveries. An example of an accounting policy note is presented in the following Illustration.

Illustration of Accounting Policy Note

Environmental remediation costs—Company X accrues losses associated with environmental remediation obligations when they are probable and reasonably estimable, which usually is no later than the time of completion of the remedial feasibility study. These accruals are adjusted as additional information is available or if circumstances change. Costs of future expenditures for environmental remediation obligations are [not] discounted to their present value. Expected recoveries of environmental remediation costs from other parties are recognized as assets when their receipt is judged to be probable.

Loss contingencies The disclosure requirements in ASC 450 and in ASC 275-10-05-2 through 05-8, 10-1, 15-3 through 15-6, 50-1 through 50-2, 50-4, 50-6 through 50-21, 50-23, 55-1 through 55-19, 60-3; ASC 205-20-55-80; ASC 330-10-55-8 through 55-13; ASC 814-10-30-55-8 through 55-13; ASC 450-20-50-2; 55-36 through 55-37; ASC 460-10-55-27; ASC 605-35-55-3 through 55-10; ASC ASC 740-10-55-219 through 5-22; ASC 932-360-55-15 through 15-19; ASC 958-205-60-1; ASC 605-55-70; ASC 985-20-55-24 through 55-29 are particularly important for environmental remediation liabilities. The guidance in ASC 450 requires that the following disclosures be made about loss contingencies:

- If accrual is possible, the nature of an accrual for a loss contingency and, in some circumstances, the amount accrued to keep financial statements from being misleading
- If no accrual is possible because the loss is either not probable or estimable, or if an exposure to loss exists in excess of the accrued amount, the reasonable possibility of loss, the nature of the loss, and an estimate of the possible range of loss, or a statement that such an estimate cannot be made

The disclosure requirements in ASC 275-10-50-6 through 50-15 that are particularly important for an environmental remediation liability are the following:

- Estimates used in determining the carrying amount of assets or liabilities or gain or loss contingencies
- Information regarding an estimate when information known before issuance of the financial statements indicates that both of the following are met:
  — It is at least reasonably possible that the estimate of the effect on the financial statements of a condition, situation, or set of circumstances that existed at the date of the financial statements will change in the near term due to one or more future confirming events.
  — The effect of the change would be material to the financial statements.
- Information regarding the nature of the uncertainty and an indication that it is at least reasonably possible that a change in the estimate will occur in the near term. (If the estimate involves a loss contingency covered by ASC 450, the disclosure also should include an estimate of the possible loss or range of loss or state that such an estimate cannot be made.)

Uncertainties associated with environmental remediation loss contingencies are pervasive and may result in wide ranges of reasonably possible loss contingencies. Those contingencies may occur over many years. As a result, additional specific disclosures related to environmental remediation loss contingencies that would contribute to a better understanding of an entity's financial statements are encouraged but are not required.

The following Illustration summarizes the disclosure requirements for loss contingencies related to environmental remediation liabilities.

Illustration of Disclosures for Loss Contingencies

Related to Recorded Accruals

1. The nature of an accrual (if required to keep financial statements from being misleading), including the total amount accrued
2. If any portion of an accrued obligation is discounted, the undiscounted amount of the obligation and the discount rate used in the present value calculation
3. If the criteria ASC 275-10-50-8 are met with respect to the accrued obligation or to any recognized asset for third-party recoveries, an indication that it is at least reasonably possible that a change in the estimate, obligation, or asset will occur in the near term

Related to Reasonably Possible Loss Contingencies

1. The nature of the reasonably possible loss contingency; also, an estimate of the possible loss exposure, or the fact that such an estimate cannot be made
2. If the criteria in ASC 275-10-50-8 regarding estimated gain or loss contingencies are met, it is an indication that it is at least reasonably possible that a change in the estimate will occur in the near term

Disclosures Encouraged But Not Required

1. The estimated time frame of disbursements for recorded amounts if expenditures are expected to continue over a long period of time
2. The estimated time frame for realization of recognized probable recoveries if those recoveries are not expected in the near term
3. If the criteria in ASC 275-10-50-8 are met regarding an accrued obligation, to any recognized asset for third-party recoveries, or to reasonably possible loss exposures or disclosed gain contingencies, the factors that cause the estimate to be sensitive to change
4. If an estimate of the probable or reasonably possible loss or range of loss cannot be made, the reasons why
5. If information about the reasonably possible loss or the recognized and additional reasonably possible loss for an environmental remediation obligation related to an individual site is relevant to an understanding of the financial statements, the following with respect to that site:
    a. The total amount accrued for the site
    b. The nature of any reasonably possible loss contingency or additional loss, and an estimate of the possible loss or the fact that such an estimate cannot be made and why
    c. Whether other PRPs are involved, and the entity's estimated share of the obligation
    d. The status of regulatory proceedings
    e. The estimated time frame for resolution of the contingency

Probable But Not Reasonably Estimable Losses

1. If the environmental remediation liability may be material, a description of the remediation obligation and the fact that a reasonable estimate cannot be made

2. Disclosure of the estimated time frame for resolution of the uncertainty about the amount of the loss (encouraged, but not required)

Unasserted Claims

1. If an entity is required by existing laws and regulations to report the release of hazardous substances and to begin a remediation study, or if assertion of a claim is considered probable, the matter represents a loss contingency subject to the disclosure requirements for unasserted claims under the guidance in ASC 450.

Environmental Remediation Costs Currently Recognized

Entities are encouraged, but not required, to disclose the following details concerning environmental remediation costs:

1. The amount recognized for environmental remediation loss contingencies for each period

2. The amount of any recovery from third parties that is credited to environmental remediation costs in each period

3. The income statement caption in which environmental remediation costs and credits are included.

ASC 410-30-15-3, 25-16, 25-18, 25-19, 35-14, 55-19 through 55-26; ASC 410-20-15-2 Capitalization of Costs to Treat Environmental Contamination

BACKGROUND

Companies may incur environmental contamination treatment costs such as removal costs, containment costs, neutralization costs, and costs to prevent current or future contamination. Examples of those costs include: costs to remove contamination (e.g., cleaning up a disposal site); costs to acquire tangible property (e.g., air pollution control equipment); costs of environmental studies; and costs of fines. Such costs may be incurred voluntarily or be required by law.

This issue does not address the following:

- When to recognize liabilities resulting from environmental contamination
- How to measure such liabilities
- Whether to report costs of treating environmental contamination as an unusual or extraordinary item

ACCOUNTING ISSUE

Should costs of treating environmental contamination be capitalized or expensed?

ACCOUNTING GUIDANCE

Environmental cleanup costs should generally be expensed as incurred. In accordance with the guidance in ASC 410-30-25-18, some costs may be capitalized if they are recoverable and meet *one* of the following criteria:

- The cost extends the life, increases the capacity, or improves the safety or efficiency of existing owned property. To determine whether this criterion has been met, the condition of the property after making the expenditure must be compared to its condition when first constructed or acquired. Its condition must be improved to qualify for capitalization.

  For example, reinforcement of an oil tanker's hull would be a qualifying expenditure. Reinforcing the hull makes the tanker safer than it was when originally acquired. Removing toxic waste from a site would not qualify under this criterion, because the expenditure only restores the property to its original condition. (See the third criterion for an exception.)

- The cost prevents or reduces future environmental contamination that may result from an entity's operations or activities (e.g., installing air scrubbers in a factory's smokestack).

- The cost is incurred to treat property currently held for sale (e.g., removing toxic waste from a site would qualify under this criterion, if the property is held for sale).

DISCUSSION

Proponents of using specific criteria to distinguish between environmental cleanup costs that should be capitalized and those that should be expensed believed that such costs generally should be expensed, but realized that under certain circumstances, it may be appropriate to capitalize those costs. They noted that by establishing specific criteria for capitalization, the predominant practice of expensing environmental cleanup costs would be retained. For example, cleaning up a gasoline station's contaminated soil does not create an asset because it does not increase the station's capacity or improve its safety or efficiency over its condition when it was first constructed. Rather, the soil is restored to its original condition.

If the criterion of improvement rather than repair is applied, some believed it would be appropriate to capitalize asbestos cleanup costs based on the premise that a building containing asbestos was unsafe even when it was built and that removal made it safer.

ASC 410-30-45-6; ASC 410-20-15-3 Accounting for the Cost of Asbestos Removal

NOTE: The original guidance in this Issue has been updated to conform with the requirements in ASC 410-30.

BACKGROUND

Many jurisdictions require that "dangerous asbestos" found in buildings be treated by removal or containment. In addition, many companies have voluntarily treated asbestos in buildings they own.

ACCOUNTING ISSUES

- Should costs incurred to treat an asbestos problem in an existing property that was identified after acquiring the property be capitalized or recognized as an expense?
- Should those costs be charged to expense, and if so, should they be reported as an extraordinary item?

ACCOUNTING GUIDANCE

- Costs incurred to treat asbestos problems in an existing property may be *capitalized* if they are recoverable and meet at least one of the following criteria in ASC 410-30-25-18:
  — The property's useful life is extended, its capacity is increased or its safety or efficiency improves. That is, the property's condition must be better than it was before the costs were incurred.
  — Incurring those costs will mitigate or prevent environmental contamination that has not yet occurred and that otherwise may occur as a result of operations and activities. The property's condition must be better than it was before the costs were incurred.
  — The costs are incurred to prepare a property currently held for sale.
- The costs of asbestos treatment generally should be treated as expenses. They do not qualify for treatment as extraordinary items in accordance with the guidance in ASC 225-20.

SEC OBSERVER COMMENT

The SEC Observer noted that registrants should discuss significant exposure to asbestos treatment costs in "Management's Discussion and Analysis" regardless of the treatment of such costs in the financial statements.

DISCUSSION

Issue 1 The threshold question in Issue 1 is whether costs of treating asbestos that are incurred while owning a building improve the property and extend its useful life, or whether they are incurred to repair the property. Those who supported capitalization argued that the nature and extent of the costs influence the decision whether to capitalize or expense the costs of asbestos treatment. They contended that treatment extends the building's useful life because it cannot continue to be occupied unless the hazardous condition was remedied.

Others noted that if the fair value of the building after asbestos treatment exceeds its book value by more than the cost of treatment, the owner has an economic incentive to incur the cost.

Issue 2 Classification as an extraordinary item requires an event or transaction to be unusual and infrequent. Some argued that although asbestos treatment may not meet both criteria for an extraordinary item, such events occur infrequently. Consequently, related costs might qualify under the guidance in ASC 225-20-45-16 to be classified as a separate component of income from continuing operations. Although it was agreed that expenses related to asbestos treatment are not extraordinary, the conclusion does not address whether such costs may be accounted for as infrequent items.

SUBSEQUENT DISCUSSION

The discussion of related issues in ASC 410-30-15-3, 25-16, 25-18, 25-19, 35-14, 55-19 through 55-26: ASC 410-20-15-2 through 15-3 (discussed below) and the conclusion on the first Issue provides additional guidance for the capitalization of asbestos treatment costs.

The guidance in ASC 410-20 applies only to *legal* obligations related to the retirement of tangible long-lived assets that result from the acquisition, construction, or development and the normal operation of those assets. That guidance does *not* apply to an obligation to remove asbestos resulting from other than the normal operation of an asset. However, the guidance in ASC 410-30-05, 05-15, 05-25, 05-30, 05-35, 05-55 (discussed below) may apply in those circumstances. Asset retirement obligations under the scope of ASC 410-20 must be recognized at the fair value of the liability in the period incurred. The associated costs should be capitalized as part of a long-lived asset's carrying amount and amortized to expense using a systematic and rational method over the asset's useful life. A liability should be recognized on the acquisition date for an existing retirement obligation related to acquired tangible long-lived assets as if the obligation had been incurred on that date.

CHAPTER 28
ASC 420—EXIT OR DISPOSAL COST OBLIGATIONS

CONTENTS

Part I: General Guidance	28,001
ASC 420-10: Overall	28,001
Overview	28,001
Background	28,001
Accounting for Costs Associated with Exit or Disposal Activities	28,002
Recognition and Measurement	28,002
Recognition and Measurement of Certain Costs	28,003
Illustration of One-Time Termination Benefits—No Future Employee Service Required	28,004
Illustration of One-Time Termination Benefits—Future Employee Service Required	28,005
Illustration of Costs to Terminate an Operating Lease	28,006
Reporting and Disclosure	28,008
Part II: Interpretive Guidance	28,009
ASC 420-10: Exit or Disposal Cost Obligations	28,009
ASC 420-10-55-1, 55-16, 55-19; ASC 715-30-60-4	
Evaluating Whether a One-Time Termination Benefit Offered in Connection with an Exit or Disposal Activity Is Essentially an Enhancement to an Ongoing Benefit Arrangement	28,009
ASC 420-10-60-3; ASC 450-10-60-7; ASC 710-10-60-4; ASC 712-10-60-1; ASC 715-60-60-2; ASC 805-20-55-50, 55-51	
Recognition of Liabilities for Contractual Termination Benefits or Changing Benefit Plan Assumptions in Anticipation of a Business Combination	28,010

PART I: GENERAL GUIDANCE

ASC 420-10: OVERALL

OVERVIEW

ASC 420 addresses financial accounting and reporting for costs associated with exit or disposal activities. The objective of this ASC Topic is to improve financial reporting by requiring that a liability for a cost related to exit or disposal activities be recognized and measured initially at fair value only when the liability is incurred.

BACKGROUND

ASC 420 applies to costs associated with an exit activity including exit activities associated with an entity newly acquired in a business combination (or in an acquisition involving a not-for-profit entity), or with a disposal activity covered by ASC 360 (Property, Plant, and Equipment). The costs covered by ASC 420 include, but are not limited to (ASC 420-10-15-3):

- Termination benefits provided to current employees that are voluntarily terminated under the terms of a benefit arrangement that is, in substance, not an ongoing benefit arrangement or an individual deferred compensation contract.
- Costs to terminate a contract that is not a capital lease.
- Costs to consolidate facilities or relocate employees.

ASC 420 does not apply to costs associated with the retirement of a long-lived asset covered by ASC 410 (Asset Retirement and Environmental Obligations) or to the following (ASC 420-10-05-4):

- Severance or termination pay
- Stock or stock options issued to employees
- Deferred compensation
- Postretirement benefits
- Group insurance, disability pay, and other long-term fringe benefits
- Certain sick pay benefits that accumulate

PRACTICE NOTE: Exit activities include, but are not limited to, restructurings. Examples of restructurings are (1) sale or termination of a line of business, (2) closing business activities in a particular location, (3) relocation of business activities, (4) change in management structure, and (5) a reorganization that fundamentally changes the entity's operating nature and focus.

ACCOUNTING FOR COSTS ASSOCIATED WITH EXIT OR DISPOSAL ACTIVITIES

Recognition and Measurement

ASC 420 requires liability recognition for a cost associated with an exit or disposal activity, measured at fair value, in the period in which the liability is incurred (with limited exceptions). In the unusual circumstance in which fair value cannot be reasonably estimated, liability recognition is delayed until such an estimate can reasonably be made (ASC 420-10-25-1).

A liability for a cost associated with an exit or disposal activity is incurred when the CON-6 (Elements of Financial Statements) definition of a liability is met:

> Liabilities are probable future sacrifices of economic benefits arising from present obligations of a particular entity to transfer assets or provide services to another entity in the future as a result of past transactions or events.

Only present obligations to others are liabilities under this definition. An obligation becomes a present obligation when a transaction or event occurs that leaves the entity little or no discretion to avoid the future transfer or use of an asset to settle the liability. An exit or disposal plan, in and of itself, does not create a present obligation, although it may lead to one in the future if the criteria for liability recognition are met (ASC 420-10-25-2).

The objective of initial measurement of a liability for a cost associated with an exit or disposal activity is fair value. A present value technique is often the best available valuation technique for estimating the fair value of a liability for a cost associated with an exit or disposal activity. For a liability that has uncertainties both in timing and amount, an expected present value technique generally is the appropriate technique.

PRACTICE POINTER: In many cases, a quoted market price for the restructuring liability will not be available and the most appropriate valuation technique will be a present value technique. An expected present value technique is generally preferred to a traditional present value technique. In an expected present value technique, the entity weighs multiple cash flow outcomes, based on their probability of occurrence, and then discounts these cash flows using a credit-adjusted (for the entity's credit standing), risk-free discount rate. The discounted cash flows are then added together to compute the expected present value of the restructuring liability. Conversely, a traditional present value technique subjectively adjusts the discount rate to reflect uncertainty in the amount and timing of the most likely cash flow pattern associated with the restructuring liability. Because a restructuring liability often has uncertainty associated with the amount and timing of the relevant cash flows, ASC 420 expresses a preference for the expected present value technique. CON-7 (Using Cash Flow Information and Present Value in Accounting Measurements) provides a detailed discussion of present value techniques available.

Once a liability for an exit or disposal activity has been recognized, in subsequent periods changes in the liability shall be measured using the credit-adjusted, risk-free rate that was used to measure the liability initially. The cumulative effect of a change resulting from a revision to either the timing or the amount of estimated cash flows shall be recognized as an adjustment to the liability in the period of the change and reported in the income statement in the same line item that was used when the related costs were recognized initially and recorded as liabilities. Changes due to the passage of time are recognized as an increase in the carrying amount of the liability and as an expense (e.g., accretion expense) (ASC 420-10-35-1, 2, 4).

PRACTICE NOTE: Accretion expense is not interest cost eligible for capitalization under the provisions of ASC 835 (Interest).

Recognition and Measurement of Certain Costs

One-time termination benefits are benefits provided to current employees who are involuntarily terminated under a one-time benefit arrangement. A one-time benefit arrangement is an arrangement established by a plan or termination that applies for a specified termination event or for a specified future period. A one-time termination benefit arrangement exists at the date the plan termination meets all of the following criteria and has been communicated to employees (ASC 420-10-25-4):

- Management commits to a plan of termination.
- The plan identifies the number of employees to be terminated, their job classifications or functions, their locations, and the expected completion date.
- The plan establishes the terms of the benefit arrangement, including the benefits that employees will receive, in sufficient detail to enable employees to determine the type and amount of benefits they will receive if they are involuntarily terminated.
- Actions required to complete the plan indicate that it is unlikely that significant changes to the plan will be made or that the plan will be withdrawn.

The timing of recognition and related measurement of a liability for one-time termination benefits depend on whether employees are required to render service until they are terminated in order to receive the termination benefits and, if so, whether employees will be retained to render services beyond a minimum retention period. The minimum retention period shall not exceed the legal notification period or, if none exists, 60 days (ASC 420-10-25-6, 7).

If employees are not required to render service until they are terminated in order to receive the termination benefits or if employees will not be retained to render services beyond the minimum retention period, a liability for the termination benefits shall be recognized (measured at fair value) at the communication date (ASC 420-10-25-8).

Illustration of One-Time Termination Benefits—No Future Employee Service Required

On May 1, 20X9, Gardial, Inc., announces plans to close its operations in Bakersfield, California. Gardial, Inc., notifies all of its 300 employees that they will be terminated within 75 days. Each employee will receive a cash payment of $10,000 when that employee ceases providing service during the 75-day period. Because no future employee service is required to receive the one-time termination benefits, Gardial, Inc., will recognize the fair value of its termination liability on the date the plan is communicated to the employees (assuming that the termination benefit plan meets the ASC 420 criteria for recognizing a liability). A liability of $3,000,000 will be recorded on the communication date (given the short discount period, the gross value of the liability is not likely to differ materially from the fair value of the liability).

If employees are required to render service until they are terminated in order to receive the termination benefits and will be retained to render service beyond the minimum retention period, a liability for the termination benefits shall be measured initially at the communication date, based on the fair value of the liability as of the termination date, but recognized ratably over the future service period (ASC 420-10-25-9). A change resulting from a revision to either the timing or the amount of estimated cash flows over the future service period shall be measured using the credit-adjusted, risk-free rate that was used initially to measure the liability, and the cumulative effect of the change shall be recognized as an adjustment to the liability in the period of change (ASC 420-10-35-3).

Illustration of One-Time Termination Benefits—Future Employee Service Required

On October 1, 20X5, Miller, Inc., announces plans to close its plant in San Antonio, Texas, in 24 months. Employees who remain with Miller until the plant closes will receive a $15,000 cash retention bonus. The bonus will be paid one year after the termination date. An employee who leaves voluntarily before the plant closes will not be eligible for any of the retention bonus.

Miller has 1,000 employees on October 1, 20X5. Miller develops a number of scenarios associated with its likely employee retention over the next 24 months. These are:

- Most likely scenario (70% probability)—600 employees stay with Miller until 9/30/X7
- Optimistic scenario (20% probability)—800 employees stay with Miller until 9/30/X7
- Pessimistic scenario (10% probability)—300 employees stay with Miller until 9/30/X7

Miller announces its restructuring and communicates the employee retention plan to its employees on October 1, 20X5 (assume that Miller meets the ASC 420 criteria for recognizing a liability).

Miller measures what the fair value of the liability will be on the *termination date* (9/30/X7) on the *communication date*. This computation is as follows:

600 employees × $15,000 × 0.70	=	$6,300,000
800 employees × $15,000 × 0.20	=	2,400,000
300 employees × $15,000 × 0.10	=	450,000
Expected payment		$9,150,000

Miller's best estimate on 10/1/X5 (the communication date) of the undiscounted amount of its liability at 9/30/X7 (the termination date) is $9,150,000. Miller's credit-adjusted, risk-free interest rate is 10%. Therefore, the expected present value of Miller's liability on the termination date is computed as follows:

$9,150,000 × .909090 (present value interest factor = $8,318,174 for $1 at 10% for 1 year)

The expected present value of Miller's termination liability, $8,318,174, is recognized ratably over the next 24 months (i.e., the future service period).

The following journal entry will be made each month for the next 24 months:

Restructuring Expense (8,318,174 / 24)   346,590.48
     Liability for Termination Benefits   346,590.58

During the 12 months from 9/30/X7 (the termination date) until 9/30/X8 (the date of payment of the retention bonus), the liability will increase due to the passage of time and accretion expense will be recognized. The following journal entry will be made each month from 10/1/X7 through 9/30/X8:

Accretion Expense [(9,150,000 - 8,318,174)/12]	69,318.83	
Liability for Termination Benefits		69,318.83

By 9/30/X8, Miller will have a balance of $9,150,000 in the "Liability for Termination Benefits" account. The following journal entry will be recorded on 9/30/X8 for the payment of the retention bonuses:

Liability for Termination Benefits	9,150,000	
Cash		9,150,000

Some termination plans offer both voluntary and involuntary benefits. A voluntary benefit, which is more than the involuntary benefit, is offered to employees who voluntarily terminate their employment. An involuntary benefit is provided to all employees losing their jobs. In this case, a liability for the involuntary benefits is recognized when the restructuring and the benefits under the termination plan are communicated to employees (ASC 420-10-25-10). A liability and an expense, for the difference between the voluntary benefit and the involuntary benefit, are recognized when the employee voluntarily resigns (i.e., at that time the employee accepts the employer's offer and a liability exists). ASC 715 (Compensation—Retirement Benefits) provides additional details on the required accounting.

A liability for costs to terminate a lease or other contract before the end of its term shall be recognized and measured at its fair value when the entity terminates the contract in accordance with the contract terms. A liability for costs that will continue to be incurred under a contract for its remaining term without economic benefit to the company shall be recognized and measured at its fair value when the entity ceases using the right conveyed by the contract (e.g., the right to used leased property). If the contract is an operating lease, the fair value of the liability at the cease-use date shall be determined based on the remaining lease rentals, reduced by estimated sublease rentals that could be reasonably obtained for the property, even if the entity does not intend to enter into a sublease. Remaining lease rentals shall not be reduced to an amount less than zero (ASC 420-10-25-11, 12, 13).

Illustration of Costs to Terminate an Operating Lease

Ladd, Rentz, and Rush (LRR) lease a facility under an operating lease for $50,000 per year for 15 years. The operating lease began on 1/1/X1. After using the facility for seven years, LRR entered into an exit plan (1/1/X8) where the leased facility will no longer be used beginning on 1/1/X9. Based on market rentals, LRR determines that it could sublease this facility at $35,000 per year for the last seven years of the operating lease. However, LRR, for competitive reasons, decides *not* to sublease this facility beginning on 1/1/X9. LRR's credit-adjusted, risk-free interest rate is 12%.

ASC 420—Exit or Disposal Cost Obligations **28,007**

The fair value of the liability at the cease-use date is computed as follows:

Yearly lease payment	$50,000
Less: Available (market-based) yearly sublease rentals (regardless of whether the property is subleased)	(35,000)
Expected yearly net cash flows	$15,000

The expected present value of LRR's liability on the cease-use date is computed as follows:

$15,000 × 5.1114 (PVIF for an ordinary annuity of = $76,761 $1 at 12% for seven years)

The following journal entry would be made on the cease-use date to record the liability:

1/1/X9
Restructuring Expense	76,671	
Liability for Restructuring Costs		76,671

The following additional journal entries would be made in years X9 through Y5:

1/1/X9 - 1/1/Y5
Restructuring Expense	35,000	
Liability for Restructuring Costs	15,000	
Cash		50,000

12/31/X9
Accretion Expense	7,401	
Liability for Restructuring Costs		7,401

12/31/Y0
Accretion Expense	6,489	
Liability for Restructuring Costs		6,489

12/31/Y1
Accretion Expense	5,467	
Liability for Restructuring Costs		5,467

12/31/Y2
Accretion Expense	4,323	
Liability for Restructuring Costs		4,323

12/31/Y3
Accretion Expense	3,042	
Liability for Restructuring Costs		3,042

ASC 420—Exit or Disposal Cost Obligations

12/31/Y4		
Accretion Expense	1,607	
Liability for Restructuring Costs		1,607

Other costs associated with an exit or disposal activity include, but are not limited to, costs to consolidate or close facilities and relocate employees. A liability for costs of this type are recognized and measured at fair value in the period in which the liability is incurred, which generally is when goods or services associated with the activity are received. The liability shall not be recognized before it is incurred, even if the costs are incremental to other operating costs and will be incurred as a direct result of a plan (ASC 420-10-25-14, 15).

PRACTICE POINTER: Note that many costs associated with a restructuring (e.g., costs of consolidating facilities, closing facilities, and relocating employees) are not recognized until the period when the cost is incurred. Generally, this is the period when the goods or services associated with the restructuring activity are received. This treatment differs from the treatment afforded one-time termination benefits and that afforded the costs associated with terminating a contract. The liability associated with one-time termination benefits is either recorded on the communication date or gradually recognized over the interval between the communication date and the termination date (see the two illustrations of one-time termination benefits, preceding). The liability associated with terminating a contract is recognized on the contract termination date or, in the case of an operating lease, on the cease-use date (see the preceding example on costs to terminate an operating lease). Note that by limiting those costs that can be recognized as a liability before the period when goods or services are received, the judgment required in establishing reserves for restructuring activity is reduced, which is designed to limit management's ability to manage income by establishing overly large restructuring reserves and then reversing these reserves in future periods with the effect of increasing income.

Reporting and Disclosure

Costs associated with an exit or disposal activity that does not involve a discontinued operation shall be included in income from continuing operations before taxes in the income statement of a business enterprise and in income from continuing operations in the statement of activities of a not-for-profit organization. If a subtotal "Income from Operations" is presented, it shall include the amounts of those costs. Costs associated with an exit or disposal activity that is presented as a discontinued operation are included in the results of discontinued operations (ASC 420-10-45-3).

If an event or circumstance occurs that discharges an entity's previously recognized liability for an exit or disposal activity, then the liability shall be reversed and the related costs reversed through the same line item in the income statement (statement of activities) used when the liability was previously recognized (ASC 420-10-40-1).

The following information shall be disclosed in notes to financial statements in the period in which an exit or disposal activity is initiated, and in future periods until the exit or disposal activity is completed (ASC 420-10-50-1):

- A description of the exit or disposal activity, including the facts and circumstances leading to the expected activity and the expected completion date
- For each major type of costs associated with the activity:
  — The total amount expected to be incurred in connection with the activity, the amount incurred in the period, and the cumulative amount incurred to date
  — A reconciliation of the beginning and ending liability balances showing separately the changes during the period attributable to costs incurred and charged to expense, costs paid or otherwise settled, and adjustments to the liability with an explanation of the reasons for those adjustments
- The line item in the income statement (statement of activities) in which the costs described above are aggregated
- For each reportable segment, the total amount of costs expected to be incurred in connection with the activity, the amount incurred in the period, and the cumulative amount incurred to date, net of any adjustments to the liability with an explanation of the reason(s) therefore
- If a liability for a cost associated with the activity is not recognized because fair value cannot be reasonably determined, that fact and the reasons therefore

PART II: INTERPRETIVE GUIDANCE

ASC 420-10: EXIT OR DISPOSAL COST OBLIGATIONS

ASC 420-10-55-1, 55-16, 55-19; ASC 715-30-60-4 Evaluating Whether a One-Time Termination Benefit Offered in Connection with an Exit or Disposal Activity Is Essentially an Enhancement to an Ongoing Benefit Arrangement

Question: Under what circumstances are additional termination benefits offered in connection with an exit or disposal activity considered, in substance (*a*) enhancements to an ongoing benefit arrangement and, therefore, subject to the provisions of ASC 715, and ASC 712, or (*b*) one-time termination benefits subject to the guidance in ASC 420?

Answer: Certain companies offer postretirement (e.g., pension and health care) and other postemployment benefits to employees under the terms of an ongoing employee benefit plan. Those types of benefit plans are accounted for under the terms discussed in ASC 715, and ASC 712. The issue is whether a one-time termination benefit should be accounted for under the terms discussed in ASC, or ASC 712 or under the terms of ASC 420. The guidance in ASC 715, or ASC 712, applies if an additional termination benefit amends the terms of an existing pension, other postretirement, or postemployment benefit arrangement. For example, if a company has an employee benefit plan providing that employees who are terminated for reasons other than cause will receive one week of salary for every year of service, the provisions of ASC 712 would apply if, as part of an exit or disposal activity, that plan is revised to provide that each involuntarily terminated employee will receive *two* weeks of salary for every year of service, and the revised terms of the employee benefit plan would apply to future exit or disposal activities. If, however, the terms of the ongoing employee benefit arrangement are *not* revised, and an additional termination benefit only applies to an exit or disposal activity that occurs in the current year, the provisions of ASC 420 would apply.

ASC 420-10-60-3; ASC 450-10-60-7; ASC 710-10-60-4; ASC 712-10-60-1; ASC 715-60-60-2; ASC 805-20-55-50, 55-51 Recognition of Liabilities for Contractual Termination Benefits or Changing Benefit Plan Assumptions in Anticipation of a Business Combination

BACKGROUND

The timing of liability recognition for termination benefits paid to involuntarily terminated employees for a plan that is governed by an *existing contractual agreement* that will be implemented only if a business combination occurs is addressed in this Issue.

The guidance applies, but is not limited to, the following types of agreements, which are referred to here as *contractual termination benefits:*

- Golden parachute employment agreements that require payment if control changes in a business combination
- Union agreements requiring payment of termination benefits for involuntary terminations when a plant closes as a result of a business combination
- Postemployment plans requiring payments for involuntary terminations due to a business combination

Curtailment losses also may be incurred as a result of the write-off of unrecognized prior service costs and a change in the projected benefit obligation from a significant reduction in the expected years of future service of current employees. Payments under the above-mentioned agreements are addressed.

Guidance on loss recognition for curtailments and liabilities is provided in ASC 450-20-25-1 to 25-7, ASC 715-30, ASC 715-20, ASC 715-60, 715-70, and ASC 712-10. To recognize a loss under ASC 450, which is the primary source of guidance on loss accruals, it must be probable before the financial statements are issued that an asset has been impaired or a liability has been incurred at the date of the financial statements and the amount of the loss is reasonably estimable. The guidance in ASC 715-30 provides that a loss and a liability should be recognized for a pension plan curtailment and for contractual termination benefits when it is probable that a curtailment will occur or that employees will be entitled to contractual benefits and the amount can be reasonably estimated. Comparable guidance for other postretirement curtailment losses is provided under the guidance in ASC 715-60. Costs related to the termination of employees under a postemployment benefit plan may result in curtailment losses or accruals for contractual termination benefits under the guidance in ASC 712-10.

In the situation addressed below, a transaction in which an entity has agreed to a business combination is discussed. The entity's management believes that the combination is probable and has developed a plan under which certain employees will be terminated if the combination is consummated. Termination benefits will be paid under a preexisting plan or contractual relationship.

ACCOUNTING ISSUE

Should a liability for contractual termination benefits and curtailment losses under an employee benefit plan that will be triggered when a business combination is consummated be recognized when it is probable that the business combination will occur or when the business combination is consummated?

ACCOUNTING GUIDANCE

An entity should recognize a liability for contractual termination benefits and curtailment losses under employee benefit plans that are triggered by a business combination only when the business combination is consummated.

DISCUSSION

The guidance is based on the view that a business combination is not merely a confirming event—it is the necessary event that triggers a contractual obligation to pay termination benefits when an entity undergoes a business combination. Proponents argued that an entity can avoid liability recognition until a business combination has been consummated. In addition, the FASB staff believes that if a business combination is considered a discrete event, a liability for contractual termination benefits should be recognized only when the business combination has been consummated, because the effects of a business combination should not be recognized until it has occurred.

CHAPTER 29
ASC 430—DEFERRED REVENUE

ASC 430 does not provide any unique guidance but rather only provides a link to guidance on deferred revenue related to vendor sales incentives in other ASC subtopics.

CHAPTER 30
ASC 440—COMMITMENTS

CONTENTS

General Guidance	30,001
ASC 440-10: Overall	30,001
Overview	30,001
Background	30,001
Purchase Obligations	30,002
Unconditional Purchase Obligations	30,002
Disclosure of Unrecorded Unconditional Purchase Obligations	30,003
Disclosure of Recognized Commitments	30,004
Illustration of Take-or-Pay, Throughput, and Similar Contracts	30,005
Illustration of Maturities and Sinking Fund Requirements	30,005
Illustration of Redemption of Capital Stock	30,006

GENERAL GUIDANCE

ASC 440-10: OVERALL

OVERVIEW

The authoritative accounting literature contains disclosure requirements for many types of long-term obligations. These include unrecorded obligations (e.g., unrecorded unconditional purchase obligations), as well as recorded obligations (e.g., recorded purchase obligations, debt maturities, required stock redemptions).

Other pronouncements cover disclosure requirements for specific types of obligations (e.g., ASC 840 (Leases)).

For unrecorded unconditional purchase obligations, ASC 440 requires disclosure of the nature and terms of the obligation, amounts of the obligation at the latest balance sheet date, and for each of the next five years, a description of any variable portion of the obligation and amounts purchased under the obligation for each period for which an income statement is presented. Similar disclosures are required for recorded obligations, including purchase obligations, debt maturities, and capital stock redemption requirements.

BACKGROUND

Enterprises and/or individuals frequently acquire assets or liabilities by written contract. A contract may contain unconditional rights and obligations or conditional rights and obligations. A right or obligation is unconditional when only the passage of time is necessary for it to mature. A conditional right or obligation is one that matures only on the occurrence of one or more events that are specified in the contract.

If a significant period elapses between the execution and subsequent performance of a contract, a problem may arise as to when, if at all, the assets and/or liabilities created by the contract should be recognized by the contracting parties. Under existing accounting practices, assets and/or liabilities that are created by a contract may not be recognized at all, or may be either recognized in the accounts or disclosed in a note to the financial statements.

Under existing accounting principles, exchanges between enterprises or individuals usually are recorded when the transfer of resources, services, and/or obligations occurs. Unfulfilled purchase commitments for the future exchange of resources, services, and/or obligations, however, are not recorded until the commitment is at least partially fulfilled by one of the contracting parties. Exceptions to the general rule for unfulfilled purchase commitments are certain leases and losses on firm noncancelable purchase commitments, which are recorded under existing accounting principles.

> **PRACTICE POINTER:** The disclosure of certain contractual rights or obligations is sometimes confused with the disclosure of a contingency. The disclosure of a contingency is necessary only when a contingent *gain* or *loss* exists in accordance with the provisions of ASC 450 (Contingencies). If there is no contingent *gain* or *loss*, disclosure is not required. On the other hand, the disclosure of information on certain contractual rights or obligations may be required by GAAP to avoid financial statements that are misleading.
>
> A situation may arise in which the disclosure of a contractual obligation is required by GAAP and—at the same time—a *loss contingency* may exist involving the same contractual obligation. In this event, disclose the information concerning both the obligation and the contingency in accordance with GAAP.

PURCHASE OBLIGATIONS

Unconditional Purchase Obligations

For the purposes of ASC 440, an *unconditional purchase obligation* is one in which one party is required to transfer funds to another party in return for future delivery of specified quantities of goods or services at specified prices.

> **PRACTICE NOTE:** In contrast, an unconditional purchase obligation to transfer assets other than funds to another party in return for specified quantities of goods or services at specified prices is not considered an unconditional obligation and, apparently, would not be covered by ASC 440.

For ASC 440 disclosure requirements to apply, an unconditional purchase obligation must be associated with the financing arrangements (*a*) for the facilities that will provide the contracted goods or services or (*b*) relating to the costs of the contracted goods or services (such as carrying costs). Unconditional purchase obligations that have a remaining term of one year or less are excluded from the provisions of ASC 440. An unconditional purchase obligation qualifies for disclosure even though it is cancelable because of (ASC 440-10-50-2):

- A remote contingency
- Permission of the other party
- A replacement agreement between the same parties
- A provision for a penalty payment in an amount that reasonably assures the continuation of the agreement

The provisions in ASC 440 dealing with unrecorded purchase obligations are primarily directed to take-or-pay contracts and throughput contracts.

PRACTICE POINTER: In a *take-or-pay contract*, a buyer agrees to pay certain periodic amounts for certain products or services. The buyer must make the specified periodic payments, even though it does not take delivery of the products or services.

In a *throughput contract*, one party agrees to pay certain periodic amounts to another party for the transportation or processing of a product. The periodic payments must be made, even though the minimum quantities specified in the agreement in each period have not been sent to the other party for transporting or processing.

In take-or-pay contracts and throughput contracts, the periodic payments are unconditional and are not dependent on the occurrence of a specified event or the fulfillment of a condition.

Disclosure of Unrecorded Unconditional Purchase Obligations

ASC 440 does not change GAAP in terms of the recording of liabilities in conjunction with unconditional purchase obligations or other similar obligations. It does, however, require disclosure of information for unrecorded unconditional purchase obligations that are (*a*) substantially noncancelable, (*b*) associated with the financing arrangements for the facilities that will provide the contracted goods or services or related to the costs of the contracted goods or services (such as carrying costs), and (*c*) for a remaining term in excess of one year. The following information is to be disclosed (ASC 440-10-50-4):

- A description of the nature and term of the obligation
- The total determinable amount of unrecorded unconditional purchase obligations as of the latest balance sheet date, and the total determinable amount of unrecorded unconditional purchase obligations for each of the five years after the latest balance sheet date
- A description of the nature of any variable component of the unrecorded unconditional purchase obligations
- For each income statement presented, the amounts actually purchased under the unconditional purchase obligations

---

PRACTICE POINTER: An unconditional obligation may consist of a determinable portion and a variable portion. The determinable portion is quantified and disclosed in accordance with item (2) above. The variable portion need not be quantified, but the nature of such amounts must be disclosed in accordance with item (3) above.

Similar or related obligations may be combined and disclosures are not required if the aggregate commitment of all unrecorded unconditional purchase obligations is immaterial.

ASC 840 (Leases) requires the disclosure of certain minimum lease payments. Minimum lease payments that are not required to be disclosed in accordance with ASC 840, however, must be disclosed if they meet the requirements for disclosure outlined in ASC 440 (ASC 440-10-50-3).

PRACTICE NOTE: Apparently, ASC 440 requires the disclosure of certain leases that were specifically excluded from ASC 840, if such leases are (a) substantially noncancelable, (b) part of the financing arrangements for the facilities that will provide specified goods or services, or related to the costs of the specified goods or services, and (c) for a remaining term in excess of one year. The following types of leases and similar agreements were expressly excluded from ASC 840 and may require disclosure under the provisions of ASC 440:

1. Natural resource leases, including oil, gas, minerals, and timber
2. Leases involving services only
3. Licensing agreements, including motion picture films, plays, manuscripts, patents, and copyrights

Furthermore, despite the similarity to take-or-pay contracts, "nuclear fuel heat supply contracts" are specifically included in ASC 840 as leases and therefore are not covered by ASC 440.

ASC 440 does not require, but does encourage, the disclosure of the present value of the total determinable amounts of unrecorded unconditional purchase obligations for each of the five years after the latest balance sheet date (item 2 above). In computing the present value of an obligation, the discount rate usually is the effective interest rate at the inception of the borrowings that (a) financed the project or (b) are associated with the unrecorded unconditional purchase obligations. If it is not practical to determine the discount rate, or if there are no borrowings associated with the obligations, the discount rate is the purchaser's incremental borrowing rate. The purchaser's incremental borrowing rate is the rate the purchaser would have incurred at the inception of the obligation to borrow funds, on similar terms, to discharge the unconditional purchase obligation (ASC 440-10-50-5).

DISCLOSURE OF RECOGNIZED COMMITMENTS

In addition to requiring disclosure of information about unrecognized commitments, ASC 440 requires disclosure of similar information for recognized commitments. A purchaser shall disclose for each of the five years following the date of the latest balance sheet presented the aggregate amount of payments for recognized unconditional purchase obligations that meet the criteria stated above for unrecognized commitments. The information to be disclosed is the same as that stated above for unrecognized commitments (ASC 440-10-50-6, 7).

PRACTICE NOTE: The requirement to disclose the payments due in each of the next five years on recorded obligations is sometimes overlooked, according to several studies of disclosure deficiencies in financial statements. This may be because ASC 440 is erroneously thought of as requiring disclosure only for unrecorded obligations. While it does cover unrecorded obligations, it also applies to recorded obligations.

Illustration of Take-or-Pay, Throughput, and Similar Contracts

During 20X5, Memphis Company entered into a long-term contract to purchase all of the widgets produced by a supplier. The contract expires in 20Y3, and Memphis Company must make minimum annual payments to the supplier, whether or not it takes delivery of the widgets. The minimum total payments for each of the five and later years succeeding December 31, 20X5, are as follows:

Year	Total Payments (in thousands)
20X6	$ 4,000
20X7	12,000
20X8	14,000
20X9	10,000
20Y0	12,000
Subsequent years	28,000
Total	80,000
Less: Imputed interest	(30,000)
Present value of payments	$50,000

Illustration of Maturities and Sinking Fund Requirements

Maturities of long-term debt and sinking fund requirements on long-term debt for each of the five years* succeeding December 31, 20X5, are as follows:

Year	Long-Term Debt and Sinking Fund Requirements
20X6	$50,000
20X7	50,000
20X8	100,000
20X9	100,000
20Y0	50,000

---

* ASC 440 does *not* require the disclosure of the above information for periods subsequent to the fifth year.

Illustration of Redemption of Capital Stock

Mandatory redemption requirements for all classes of capital stock for each of the five years* succeeding December 31, 20X5, are as follows:

Year	4% Preferred	7% Preferred
20X6	$ 200,000	$ 400,000
20X7	200,000	400,000
20X8	200,000	400,000
20X9	none	400,000
20Y0	none	400,000

PRACTICE POINTER: When disclosing unconditional obligations, much like operating leases, take care that the financial statements present both sides of the transaction. Thus, when recording an obligation, including a capital lease, both the asset (i.e., benefit) and the liability (i.e., obligation) are disclosed. Disclosure under ASC 440 applies only to the obligation side of the contract.

ASC 440 requires a statement about the nature and term of the obligation, and may be the appropriate place for an enterprise to describe the associated benefits, if any. The lack of explicit requirements to disclose associated benefits does not preclude an enterprise from describing those benefits.

PRACTICE NOTE: ASC 440 contains specific disclosure requirements for recorded and unrecorded take-or-pay and throughput contracts (ASC 440-10-50-4). Both of these types of contracts are considered unconditional obligations under the provisions of ASC 440. However, a take-or-pay or throughput contract may, in substance, be a product financing arrangement. A product financing arrangement may also require unconditional periodic payments that are not dependent on the occurrence of a specified event or the fulfillment of a specified condition. Product financing arrangements are covered in this Guide in the chapter covering ASC 470-40 (Debt—Product Financing Arrangements).

---

* ASC 440 does *not* require the disclosure of the above information for periods subsequent to the fifth year.

CHAPTER 31
ASC 450—CONTINGENCIES

CONTENTS

Part I: General Guidance	31,001
ASC 450-10: Overall	31,001
Overview	31,001
Background	31,002
ASC 450-20: Loss Contingencies	31,003
Loss Contingencies	31,003
Classification	31,003
Accounting and Reporting	31,003
Illustration of Accrued Contingent Liability	31,004
Figure 31-1: Probability That Future Event(s) Will Confirm Loss	31,004
Litigation, Claims, or Assessments	31,005
Illustration of Disclosed Loss Contingency	31,005
Allowance for Uncollectible Receivables	31,005
Product or Service Warranty Obligation	31,006
Loss Contingencies Arising after the Date of the Financial Statements	31,006
Unasserted Claims or Assessments	31,006
Disclosure of Noninsured Property	31,007
Appropriations of Retained Earnings	31,007
Acquisition Contingencies	31,007
Measurement at the Acquisition Date	31,007
Subsequent Measurement and Accounting	31,008
ASC 450-30: Gain Contingencies	31,008
Gain Contingencies	31,008
Part II: Interpretive Guidance	31,008
ASC 450-20: Loss Contingencies	31,008
ASC 450-20-S25-1, S50-2, S99-2	
Accounting for Legal Costs Expected to Be Incurred in Connection with a Loss Contingency	31,008

PART I: GENERAL GUIDANCE

ASC 450-10: OVERALL

OVERVIEW

Accounting for contingencies is an important feature of the preparation of financial statements in accordance with GAAP, because of the many uncertainties that may exist at the end of each accounting period. Standards governing accounting for loss contingencies require accrual and/or note disclosure when specified recognition and disclosure criteria are met. Gain contingencies generally are not recognized in financial statements but may be disclosed.

ASC 275 (Risks and Uncertainties) contains material that is closely related to the material on contingencies in ASC 450 and has broad applicability, particularly in four areas:

1. Nature of an entity's operations
2. Use of certain information in the preparation of financial statements
3. Certain significant estimates
4. Current vulnerability to concentrations

For coverage of ASC 275, see the Chapter 15, "Risks and Uncertainties."

BACKGROUND

A *contingency* is an existing condition, situation, or set of circumstances involving uncertainty that may, through one or more related future events, result in the acquisition or loss of an asset or the incurrence or avoidance of a liability, usually with the concurrence of a gain or loss. The resulting gain or loss is referred to as a *gain contingency* or a *loss contingency.*

The existence of a loss contingency may be established on or before the date of the financial statements, or after the date of the financial statements but prior to the issuance of the financial statements. After a loss contingency is established, the probability of its developing into an actual loss must be evaluated. Accounting for a loss contingency is based on the degree of probability that one or more future events will occur that will confirm that a loss has already occurred. Gain contingencies are ordinarily not recorded until they are actually realized, although note disclosure in the financial statements may be necessary.

Loss contingencies may arise from the risk of exposure resulting from items such as the following (ASC 450-20-05-3):

- Collectibility of receivables
- Property loss by fire, explosion, or other hazards
- Expropriation of assets
- Pending or threatened litigation, claims, or assessments
- Product warranties or defects
- Catastrophic losses of property

PRACTICE POINTER: Not all uncertainties in the accounting process are *contingencies*, as that term is used in ASC 450. Many estimates that are inherent in the financial reporting process are *not* contingencies, and the authoritative literature covered in this section does *not* apply. For example, depreciable assets have a reasonably estimated life, and depreciation expense is used to allocate the cost of the asset systematically over its estimated useful life.

> **PRACTICE NOTE:** ASC 450 does not apply to accounting for income taxes. ASC 740 addresses the uncertainty associated with income taxes.

ASC 450-20: LOSS CONTINGENCIES

LOSS CONTINGENCIES

Classification

A loss contingency develops into an actual loss only upon the occurrence of one or more future events, whose likelihood of occurring may vary significantly. The likelihood that future events will confirm a loss must be classified as (*a*) probable (likely to occur), (*b*) reasonably possible (between *probable* and *remote*), or (*c*) remote (low chance of occurring) (ASC 450-20-25-1).

The accounting treatment for loss contingencies flows logically from the three ranges of probability described in the previous paragraph. Figure 31-1 provides the general structure of accounting that is required.

Accounting and Reporting

Depending upon whether a loss contingency is classified as probable, reasonably possible, or remote, it should be (*a*) accrued as a charge to income as of the date of the financial statements, (*b*) disclosed by note to the financial statements, or (*c*) neither accrued nor disclosed.

The following two conditions must be met for a *loss contingency* to be accrued as a charge to income as of the date of the financial statements (ASC 450-20-25-2):

1. It is *probable* that as of the date of the financial statements an asset has been impaired or a liability incurred, based on information available before the actual issuance date of the financial statements. Implicit in this condition is that it is *probable* that one or more future events will occur to confirm the loss.
2. The amount of loss can be estimated reasonably.

> **PRACTICE POINTER:** If a loss contingency is classified as *probable* and only a range of possible loss (similar to a minimum-maximum) can be established, then the **minimum** amount in the range is accrued, unless some other amount within the range appears to be a better estimate (ASC 450-20-30-1). The range of possible loss must also be disclosed.

Loss contingencies that are accrued ordinarily also require note disclosure so that the financial statements are not misleading. This disclosure ordinarily consists of the nature of the contingency and, in some circumstances, the amount accrued. The term *reserve* should only be used for an amount of unidentified or unsegregated assets held for a specific purpose (ASC 450-20-50-1).

Illustration of Accrued Contingent Liability

Following is a pro forma illustration of disclosure of a loss contingency for which the probability of future events confirming a loss is high and for which an amount can be reasonably estimated:

> During 20X8, the Company became aware of past circumstances (describe nature of contingency) that management believes are likely to require recognition of a loss(es) in future year(s). While the exact amount of this (these) loss(es) is not known, a reasonable estimate, based on information currently available, is $XXX. This amount has been recognized as a loss in the current year and appears as a contingent liability (provide title) in the 20X8 statement of financial position. Recognition of this loss had the impact of reducing net income and earnings per share by $XX and $XX, respectively, in 20X8.

If one or both conditions for the accrual of a loss contingency is/are not met and the likelihood of loss is considered either *probable* or *reasonably possible*, financial statement disclosure of the loss contingency is required. The disclosure shall contain a description of the nature of the loss contingency and the range of possible loss, or include a statement that an estimate of the loss cannot be made (ASC 450-20-50-3, 4). However, these disclosures are not required for loss contingencies arising from an entity's recurring estimation of its allowance for credit losses (ASC 450-20-50-2A).

Figure 31-1: Probability That Future Event(s) Will Confirm Loss

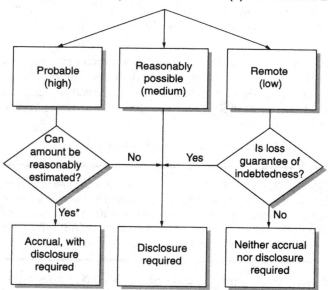

* Includes estimation of a range of loss, in which case the minimum amount is accrued and the amount of the range is disclosed.

Litigation, Claims, or Assessments

If both conditions for the accrual of a loss contingency are met, an accrual for the estimated amount of pending or threatened litigation and actual or possible claims or assessments is required. Some of the factors that should be considered in determining whether the conditions for accrual have been met are (a) the nature of the litigation, claim, or assessment, (b) progress of the case, including progress after the date of the financial statements but before the issuance date of the financial statements, (c) opinions of legal counsel, and (d) management's intended response to the litigation, claim, or assessment (ASC 450-20-55-12).

Illustration of Disclosed Loss Contingency

Following is a pro forma illustration of disclosure of a loss contingency for which the probability of future events confirming the loss is reasonably possible and for which the outcome is sufficiently uncertain that accrual is not appropriate:

> During 20X8, a suit was filed against the company by a former employee alleging that the company engaged in discriminatory employment practices. The suit requests damages of $1,000,000. Management has indicated its plans to vigorously contest this suit and believes that the loss, if any, resulting from the suit will not have a material impact on the company's financial position, results of operations, or cash flows in future years.

Allowance for Uncollectible Receivables

For the purposes of GAAP, accounts receivable must be reported at their net realizable value. Net realizable value is equal to the total amount of the receivables less an estimated allowance for uncollectible accounts.

Under ASC 450, an accrual for a loss contingency must be charged to income if both of the following conditions are met:

- It is *probable* that as of the date of the financial statements an enterprise does not expect to collect the full amount of its accounts receivable, based on information available before the actual issuance of the financial statements.

- The amount of loss contingency (uncollectible receivables) can be *reasonably estimated*.

If both of these conditions are met, an accrual for the estimated amount of uncollectible receivables must be made even if the uncollectible receivables cannot be identified specifically (ASC 310-10-35-9). An enterprise may base its estimate of uncollectible receivables on its prior experience, the experience of other enterprises in the same industry, the debtor's ability to pay, and/or an appraisal of current economic conditions (ASC 310-10-35-10).

PRACTICE POINTER: A significant uncertainty exists in the ultimate collection of accounts receivable if an enterprise is unable to estimate reasonably the amount of its uncollectible receivables. If a significant uncertainty does exist in the collection of the receivables, use the installment sales method, cost-recovery method, or some other method of revenue recognition (ASC 605-10-25-4).

Product or Service Warranty Obligation

A product or service warranty obligation is a contingency under the provisions of ASC 450, because of the potential claims that may result from the warranty. If both of the conditions for the accrual of a loss contingency are met, an accrual for the estimated amount of a warranty obligation must be made even if the warranty obligation cannot be identified specifically. An enterprise may base its estimate of a warranty obligation on its prior experience, the experience of other enterprises in the same industry, and/or an appraisal of current economic conditions. If an enterprise is unable to estimate reasonably the amount of its warranty obligation and the range of possible loss is wide, significant uncertainty exists as to whether a sale should be recorded (ASC 460-10-25-6). If a significant uncertainty does exist in estimating a warranty obligation, a sale shall not be recorded and the installment sales method, cost-recovery method, or some other method of revenue recognition shall be used (ASC 605-10-25-3).

Loss Contingencies Arising after the Date of the Financial Statements

A loss contingency that is classified as *probable* or *reasonably possible*, that occurs after the balance sheet date but before the issuance date of the financial statements, may have to be disclosed to avoid misleading financial statements. If professional judgment deems this type of disclosure necessary, the disclosure shall contain a description of the nature of the loss contingency and the range of possible loss, or include a statement that no estimate of the loss can be made. It may be desirable to disclose this type of loss contingency by supplementing the historical financial statements with pro forma statements reflecting the loss as if it occurred at the date of the financial statements (ASC 450-20-50-9).

PRACTICE POINTER: Disclosing loss contingencies that arise after the date of the financial statements may require either adjustment to the financial statements or note disclosure, depending on the nature of the loss contingency. If the subsequent event confirms or provides additional information on a condition that existed at the financial statement date, make an adjustment to the financial statements. Otherwise, disclose the loss contingency, which, in some cases, may be made best by presenting pro forma restated financial information as a part of the note disclosure.

Unasserted Claims or Assessments

An *unasserted claim* is one that has not been asserted by the claimant because the claimant has no knowledge of the existing claim or has not elected to assert the existing claim. If it is *probable* that an unasserted claim will be asserted by the claimant and it is *probable* or *reasonably possible* that an unfavorable outcome will result, the unasserted claim must be disclosed in the financial statements. If these conditions are not met, however, disclosure is not required for unasserted claims or assessments in which the potential claimant apparently has no knowledge of the claim's existence (ASC 450-20-55-14, 15).

Disclosure of Noninsured Property

An enterprise may be underinsured or not insured at all against the risk of future loss or damage to its property by fire, explosion, or other hazard. The fact that an enterprise's property is underinsured or not insured at all constitutes an existing uncertainty as defined by ASC 450. The absence of insurance does not mean, however, that an asset has been impaired or a liability incurred as of the date of the financial statements (ASC 450-20-55-5). ASC 450 does not require financial statement disclosure of noninsurance or underinsurance of possible losses, but specifically states that it does not discourage this practice (ASC 450-20-50-7).

> **PRACTICE POINTER:** The removal of insurance does not, in and of itself, mean that a loss has already been incurred and that a contingent liability should be recorded. While the uninsured enterprise assumes greater risk than an insured one, a contingent loss results from a past event and the removal of insurance does not qualify for such an event.

Appropriations of Retained Earnings

ASC 450 does not prohibit an enterprise from appropriating specific amounts of retained earnings for potential loss contingencies. The amount of appropriated retained earnings, however, must be reported within the stockholders' equity section of the balance sheet and clearly identified as an appropriation of retained earnings. In addition, the following rules must be observed (ASC 505-10-45-3):

- No costs or losses shall be charged against the appropriated retained earnings and no part of the appropriated retained earnings may be transferred to income or in any way used to affect the determination of net income for any period.
- The appropriated retained earnings shall be restored intact to retained earnings when the appropriation is no longer considered necessary.

ACQUISITION CONTINGENCIES

Measurement at the Acquisition Date

The acquirer *does not apply* the guidance in ASC 450 in determining which assets and liabilities arising from contingencies to recognize as of the acquisition date. ASC 805 provides this guidance and further details are provided in our discussion of ASC 805.

In addition, ASC 450 does not apply to contingent gains and losses that are recognized at the acquisition or merger date if the acquisition or merger involves not-for-profit entities. Guidance on the subsequent accounting for contingent gains and losses recognized at the acquisition or merger date is provided in ACC

958. However, ASC 450 does apply to contingent gains and losses that existed at the acquisition or merger date but were not recognized because they did not meet the recognition criteria in ASC 958.

Subsequent Measurement and Accounting

In general, the assets acquired, liabilities assumed or incurred, and equity instruments issued in a business combination shall be subsequently measured and accounted for by the acquirer in accordance with other applicable GAAP.

An asset or liability arising from a contingency recognized as of the acquisition date, that would be in the scope of ASC 450 if not acquired or assumed in a business combination, shall continue to be recognized by the acquirer at its acquisition-date fair value unless new information is obtained about the possible outcome of the contingency. When new information is obtained, the acquirer must evaluate that information and measure an asset at the *lower* of its acquisition-date fair value or the best estimate of its future settlement amount, while a liability is measured at the *higher* of its acquisition-date fair value or the amount that would be recognized under ASC 450. An asset or liability arising from a contingency shall only be derecognized by the acquirer when the contingency is resolved.

ASC 450-30: GAIN CONTINGENCIES

GAIN CONTINGENCIES

Gain contingencies may be disclosed in the financial statements by note, but should not be reflected in income, because doing so may result in recognizing revenue prior to its realization. Care should be exercised in disclosing gain contingencies to avoid misleading implications concerning the recognition of revenue prior to its realization (ASC 450-30-25-1; 450-30-50-1).

PART II: INTERPRETIVE GUIDANCE

ASC 450-20: LOSS CONTINGENCIES

ASC 450-20-S25-1, S50-2, S99-2 Accounting for Legal Costs Expected to Be Incurred in Connection with a Loss Contingency

The accounting for legal costs expected to be incurred in connection with a loss contingency under the guidance in ASC 450 was discussed. It was noted that practice is to expense such costs, but some suggested that accounting practice for such costs is mixed. Although the Emerging Issues Task Force decided not to discuss this matter any further, the SEC Observer stated that the SEC staff expects registrants to apply their accounting policies consistently and to disclose material accounting policies and the methods of applying those policies in accordance with the requirements in ASC 235-10-05 and 10-50.

CHAPTER 32
ASC 460—GUARANTEES

CONTENTS

Part I: General Guidance	32,001
ASC 460-10: Overall	32,001
Overview	32,001
Background	32,002
Accounting for Guarantees	32,002
Disclosure of Guarantees	32,003
Recognition of a Guarantee Liability	32,003
Indirect Guarantees	32,004
Part II: Interpretive Guidance	32,004
ASC 460-10: Overall	32,004
ASC 460-10-35-2	
Whether FASB Interpretation No. 45, *Guarantor's Accounting and Disclosure Requirements for Guarantees, Including Indirect Guarantees of Indebtedness of Others,* Provides Support for Subsequently Accounting for a Guarantor's Liability at Fair Value	32,004
ASC 460-10-55-1, 55-10 through 55-11; ASC 954-460-55-1	
Application of FASB Interpretation No. 45 in Minimum Revenue Guarantees Granted to a Business or Its Owners	32,005
ASC 460-10-55-17	
Impact of FASB Interpretation No. 45, *Guarantor's Accounting and Disclosure Requirements for Guarantees, Including Indirect Guarantees of Indebtedness of Others,* on EITF Issue No. 95-1, *Revenue Recognition on Sales with a Guaranteed Minimum Resale Value*	32,006
ASC 460-10-55-31 through 55-34	
Accounting for Intellectual Property Infringement Indemnification under FIN-45	32,007

PART I: GENERAL GUIDANCE

ASC 460-10: OVERALL

OVERVIEW

Guarantees are a relatively common business transaction. Examples include (1) the guarantee of the indebtedness of another party, (2) obligations of commercial banks under "standby letters of credit," and (3) guarantees to repurchase receivables that have been sold. The FASB observed differences in how companies interpret the need for issuers of guarantees to recognize a liability and the disclosures required by issuers of guarantees. ASC 460 intends to clarify both of these issues.

BACKGROUND

ASC 460 does not specify the subsequent accounting for guarantees that have been recognized. If a guarantee represents a derivative financial instrument, appropriate accounting is in conformity with ASC 815 (Derivatives and Hedging). If the guarantee does not qualify for derivative accounting, guidance is provided by ASC 460 (ASC 460-10-35-4).

ACCOUNTING FOR GUARANTEES

ASC 460 applies to guarantees that have any of the following characteristics:

- Contracts that contingently require the guarantor to make payments (in cash, financial instruments, other assets, shares of its stock, or provision of services) to the guaranteed party based on changes in the *underlying* that is related to an asset, liability, or an equity security of the guaranteed party (ASC 460-10-15-4).

> **PRACTICE NOTE:** ASC 815 uses the term *underlying* to denote a specified interest rate, security price, commodity price, foreign exchange rate, index of price or rate, or other variable. An underlying may be a price or rate of an asset or liability but is not the asset or liability itself.

- Contracts that require the guarantor to make payments to the guaranteed party based on another entity's failure to perform under an obligating agreement (ASC 460-10-15-4).

- Indemnification agreements that contingently require the indemnifying party to make payments to the indemnified party based on changes in an underlying that is related to an asset, liability, or equity security of the indemnified party (ASC 460-10-15-4).

- Indirect guarantees of the indebtedness of others (ASC 460-10-15-4).

Commercial letters of credit or other loan commitments that are commonly thought of as guarantees of funding are not included in the scope of ASC 460 because they do not meet the characteristics of guarantees as previously stated. Similarly, the scope of ASC 460 does not include indemnifications or guarantees based on an entity's own future performance (ASC 460-10-55-16).

The provisions of ASC 460 related to recognizing a liability do *not* apply to the following, but the disclosure requirements of ASC 460 do apply in these circumstances (ASC 460-10-25-1):

- Product warranties

- Guarantees that are accounted for as derivatives

- Guarantees that represent contingent consideration in a business combination (or an acquisition involving a not-for-profit entity)

- Guarantees for which the guarantor's obligation would be reported by an equity item (i.e., rather than a liability)

- An original lessee's guarantee of lease payments when the lessee remains secondarily liable in conjunction with being relieved from being the primary obligor under a lease restructuring
- Guarantees issued between either parents and their subsidiaries or corporations under common control
- A parent's guarantee of a subsidiary's debt to a third party, and a subsidiary's guarantee of the debt owed to a third party by either its parent or another subsidiary of the parent

Disclosure of Guarantees

ASC 460 clarified that a guarantor is required to disclose the following information (ASC 460-10-50-4):

- The nature of the guarantee, including the approximate term of the guarantee, how it arose, and the events or circumstances that would require the guarantor to perform under the guarantee
- The maximum potential amount of future payments under the guarantee
- The carrying amount of the liability, if any, for the guarantor's obligations under the guarantee
- The nature and extent of any recourse provisions or available collateral that would enable the guarantor to recover the amounts paid under the guarantee

For product warranties, the guarantor is required to disclose its accounting policy and method of determining its liability under the warranty rather than disclosing the maximum potential amount for future payments under the guarantee. In addition, a tabular reconciliation of the changes in the guarantor's product warranty liability for the reporting period is required (ASC 460-10-50-8).

Recognition of a Guarantee Liability

In addition to clarifying the disclosure required for guarantee liabilities, ASC 460 clarifies that a guarantor is required to recognize, at the inception of a guarantee, a liability for the obligations it has undertaken, including its ongoing obligations to perform under the terms of a guarantee in the event the specified triggering events or conditions occur. The initial recording of the liability should be the fair value of the guarantee at its inception (ASC 460-10-25-4; 460-10-30-2).

When a liability due to the issuance of a guarantee is recorded, the nature of the offsetting debit depends on the nature of the original transaction giving rise to the guarantee (ASC 460-10-55-23). If the guarantee is issued in a standalone transaction *for consideration*, cash or a receivable is debited. If the guarantee is issued in a standalone transaction to an unrelated party *for no consideration*, an expense is debited. If the guarantee is issued as part of a sale of assets, a product, or a business, the consideration received in the sale is allocated between the guarantee and the assets, product, or business sold. If the guarantee relates to the formation of a partially owned business or joint venture, the offsetting debit is to increase the value of the investment account. If a lessee provides a guarantee of the lease property's residual value in an operating lease, the offsetting debit is to prepaid rent.

The FASB states that some entities may not recognize liabilities for a guarantee because (1) the recognition requirements in ASC 450 related to loss contingencies have not been met at the inception of the guarantee and (2) the premium for the guarantee was not separately identified because it was embedded in purchase or sales agreements, service contracts, joint venture agreements, or other commercial agreements. ASC 460 indicates that an entity is required to record the fair value of a guarantee at inception, even if it is *not* probable that payments will be required under the guarantee (ASC 460-10-25-3). ASC 460 also indicates that where the premium for the guarantee is not separately identified, it must be estimated. The party issuing the guarantee should consider what the premium would be if the guarantee had been issued on a standalone basis in a transaction with an unrelated party as a practical expedient (ASC 460-10-30-2).

Indirect Guarantees

Indirect guarantees arise under an agreement that obligates one entity to transfer funds to a second entity upon the occurrence of specified events under conditions whereby the funds become legally available to the creditors of the second entity and those creditors may enforce the second entity's claim against the first entity under the agreement (ASC Glossary). Although the risk of loss may be remote, indirect guarantees of the indebtedness of others are required to be disclosed in the financial statements (ASC 460-10-50-2).

PART II: INTERPRETIVE GUIDANCE

ASC 460-10: OVERALL

ASC 460-10-35-2 Whether FASB Interpretation No. 45, Guarantor's Accounting and Disclosure Requirements for Guarantees, Including Indirect Guarantees of Indebtedness of Others, Provides Support for Subsequently Accounting for a Guarantor's Liability at Fair Value

Question: Is a guarantor that wishes to report its liability for obligations under a guarantee (including a seller's recourse obligations, if any, included in ASC 460-10-15-4, 25-34, 55-2, 55-5, 55-12 through 55-13 at fair value after initial recognition permitted to cite the guidance in ASC 460 to justify using that accounting method for *subsequent measurement* of the liability?

Answer: No. A guarantor may *not* cite ASC 460 to justify measuring the guarantor's liability for its obligations at fair value after a guarantee has been issued. The guidance in ASC 460 applies only to the measurement of a guarantor's liability for the guarantee when it is initially recognized.

The FASB staff has noted that although ASC 460-10-35-1 through 35-2, 35-4 discusses three methods that are used in practice to measure a liability *after* initial recognition, the discussion is *not* intended to imply that a guarantor can choose any of those methods to subsequently account for a liability. A guarantor should *not* account for a liability for its obligation under a previously issued guarantee at fair value in subsequent periods unless doing so can be justified under generally accepted accounting principles, for example, accounting for a guarantee as a derivative under the guidance in ASC 815. Subsequent to initial recognition, a guarantor that is using fair value to measure its obligations under a guarantee, other than one under the scope of ASC 815, and relying on the guidance in ASC 460 to justify that treatment should reconsider the appropriateness of that treatment.

ASC 460-10-55-1, 55-10 through 55-11; ASC 954-460-55-1 Application of FASB Interpretation No. 45 in Minimum Revenue Guarantees Granted to a Business or Its Owners

BACKGROUND

The guidance below, which has amended the guidance in ASC 460, was issued in response to questions raised by constituents regarding the applicability of the guidance in ASC 460 to a guarantee granted to a business or its owner under which the business or the owner is guaranteed a specified minimum amount of revenue for a specified period of time. For example, a not-for-profit health care facility that recruits a nonemployee physician to establish a practice in a certain area guarantees to make a payment to the physician if the physician's gross revenues do not equal or exceed a specified dollar amount during a specified period of time. In another example, a corporation that wants a daycare center to open a facility next to its plant guarantees to the daycare center that it will earn a minimum amount of revenue per month over a specified period of time (e.g., during the first 12 months). If the daycare center does not earn the guaranteed minimum amount during any month in the first 12 months, the corporation guarantees to make up the shortfall.

ACCOUNTING GUIDANCE

The guidance in ASC 460-10-15-4, 25-34, 50-2, 50-5, 50-12 through 50-13 was amended to provide the following

- Except as provided in ASC 460-10-15-7, the following provisions of apply to guarantee contracts with the following characteristics, if any:
  — Contracts under which a guarantor is contingently required to make payments (either in cash, financial instruments, other assets, shares of stock, or provision of services) to the guaranteed party based on changes in an *underlying* (as defined in ASC, *Glossary*, that is related to a *guaranteed* party's asset, liability, or equity security).
  — Contracts under which a guarantor is contingently required to make payments to a guaranteed party if another entity does not perform under an obligating agreement (a performance guarantee). Contracts under which a guarantor is contingently required to make payments (either in cash, financial instruments, other assets, shares of its stock, or provision of services) to the guaranteed party based on changes in an *underlying* (as defined in ASC, *Glossary*) that is related to an indemnified party's asset, liability, or equity security.

— Indirect guarantees of others' indebtedness, even if a payment to a guaranteed party is not based on changes related to a guaranteed party's asset, liability, or equity security.

A guarantor should recognize a liability in its balance sheet at the inception of a guarantee.

The examples in the Background discussion above are codified as an example of a financial guarantee in ASC 460-10-55-2e as follows:

A guarantee to a business or its owner(s) that revenue earned by a business (or a specific portion of the business) will be at least a specified amount for a specified period of time.

FASB BASIS FOR CONCLUSION

The FASB reached a conclusion that the guarantee discussed under this guidance meets the characteristics discussed in ASC 460-10-55-2, because the guarantee's *underlying*, which, in this case, is the gross revenues of a business or of a business owner, is related to an asset or equity security belonging to the party receiving the guarantee. A business' revenues change as result of transactions with customers. Because the gross revenues of a business are related to changes in its assets or liabilities, a guarantee made to a business meets the characteristics in ASC 460-10-55-2. In addition, a guarantee made to an owner of a business meets the characteristics in ASC 460-10-55-2, because the gross revenues of the business are related to changes in the owner's investment in the business. The FASB further believes that guarantors should account for minimum revenue guarantees under the provisions in ASC 460 because a minimum revenue guarantee granted to a business or its owners does *not* meet any of the scope exceptions in ASC 460-10-15-7, 15-9, 15-10, 25-1, and 30-1.

The FASB noted that the list of examples under the guidance in ASC 460-10-55-23 (FIN-45, paragraph 11) is not a comprehensive all-inclusive list of contracts that would meet the provisions of that paragraph. In addition, minimum revenue guarantees granted to physicians should be accounted for under the provisions of this FSP regardless of whether the physician's practice is considered to be a business under the guidance in ASC 718-10-55-85A; ASC 810-10-05-15 through 05-16, 15-19 through 15-22, 25-61 through 25-64, 25-66 through 25-72, 25-74 through 25-79, 25-81, 55-90, 55-91, and 55-92.

ASC 460-10-55-17 Impact of FASB Interpretation No. 45, *Guarantor's Accounting and Disclosure Requirements for Guarantees, Including Indirect Guarantees of Indebtedness of Others,* **on EITF Issue No. 95-1,** *Revenue Recognition on Sales with a Guaranteed Minimum Resale Value*

BACKGROUND

The guidance in ASC 460-10-55-17, 60-22; ASC 605-50-60-1; ASC 840-10-55-12 through 55-25, addresses whether a manufacturer should recognize a sale on equipment sold with a resale value guarantee. Under that guidance, a manufacturer should *not* recognize a sale on a transfer of equipment if the buyer receives a resale value guarantee. A conclusion was also reached that the transaction should be accounted for as a lease, based on the guidance in ASC 840, because the buyer has the right to use the equipment from the sales date to the date on which the manufacturer guarantees a minimum resale value for the equipment. Further, classification as a sales-type lease or an operating lease should be based on the calculation of the minimum lease payments, as defined in ASC 840-10-25-4, which would be the difference between the proceeds on the initial transfer of the equipment to the buyer (the selling price) and the manufacturer's residual value guarantee at the first date on which the buyer can exercise the guarantee.

When ASC 460 was issued, the FASB staff determined that the guidance for sales-type leases should be nullified by the guidance in ASC 460 because the guarantee would be related to an asset removed from the manufacturer's books under that type of lease. Some constituents questioned that decision, because under a sales-type lease, a manufacturer would be required to recognize two guarantees for the same asset, that is, once when a sales-type lease transaction is recorded with the amount of the residual value of the equipment remaining on the manufacturer's books and again in accordance with the requirements of ASC 460, at the fair value of the guarantee at inception.

ACCOUNTING ISSUE

How does the guidance in ASC 460 affect the conclusion in ASC 460-10-55-17, 60-22; ASC 605-50-60-1; ASC 840-10-55-12 through 55-25?

ACCOUNTING GUIDANCE

The guidance in ASC 460-10-55-17, 60-22; ASC 605-50-60-1; ASC 840-10-55-12 through 55-25 applies to a sales-type lease, under which a manufacturer guarantees the residual value of equipment transferred under the lease and continues to recognize an asset for the residual value of the guaranteed equipment. A conclusion was reached that the provisions of ASC 460 do *not* affect the guidance in ASC 460-10-55-17, 60-22; ASC 605-50-60-1; ASC 840-10-55-12 through 55-25 related to sales-type leases, because the guidance in ASC 460 does *not* apply to a guarantee for an asset related to an underlying lease recorded on a guarantor's books.

ASC 460-10-55-31 through 55-34 Accounting for Intellectual Property Infringement Indemnification under FIN-45

Question: A software vendor-licensor may include an indemnification clause in a software licensing agreement that indemnifies a licensee against liability and damages arising from any claims of patent, copyright, trademark, or trade secret infringement by the software vendor's software. Does an indemnification of that type constitute a guarantee subject to the scope of ASC 460?

Answer: Yes. An infringement indemnification arrangement requires a guarantor to make a payment to the guaranteed party if an infringement claim against the licensee results in a liability or damage, if any, related to the licensed software. However, because an infringement claim can impair a licensee's ability to use the software, the occurrence of an infringement claim is related to the licensed software's performance. Therefore, an infringement indemnification arrangement falls under the scope of ASC 460 and a liability need not be recognized at the inception of the guarantee (i.e., the product scope exception applies). The disclosure requirements of ASC 460 related to guarantees under product warranties would apply to guarantees related to infringement indemnification arrangements.

CHAPTER 33
ASC 470—DEBT

CONTENTS

Part I: General Guidance	33,004
Overview	33,004
Background	33,005
Convertible Debt	33,005
Product Financing Arrangements	33,005
Modifications and Extinguishments of Debt	33,007
Troubled Debt Restructuring	33,007
ASC 470-10: Overall	33,007
Liability Classification Issues	33,007
Current Obligations Expected to Be Refinanced	33,007
Callable Obligations	33,009
Acceleration Clauses	33,010
ASC 470-20: Debt with Conversion and Other Options	33,010
Convertible Debt	33,010
Issuance	33,010
Illustration of Convertible Bond Issuance	33,011
Conversion	33,011
Illustration of Convertible Debt Security Converted into Equity Security	33,011
Induced Conversion	33,012
Illustration of Induced Conversion	33,013
Debt with Detachable Purchase Warrants	33,014
Issuance	33,014
Illustration of Issuance of Debt with Detachable Warrants	33,014
Exercise of Warrants	33,014
Illustration of Exercise of Separate Purchase Feature	33,015
ASC 470-40: Product Financing Arrangements	33,015
Accounting for Product Financing Arrangements	33,015
Illustration of Accounting for Product Financing Arrangements	33,016
ASC 470-50: Modifications and Extinguishments	33,017
When Debt Is Extinguished	33,017
Accounting for Extinguishments of Debt	33,017
Reacquisition Price	33,018
Net Carrying Amount	33,018
Refunding of Tax-Exempt Debt	33,018
Income Statement Classification of Debt Extinguishment	33,018
Illustration of Reacquisition Loss on Extinguishment	33,019
ASC 470-60: Troubled Debt Restructurings by Debtors	33,020
Accounting for Troubled Debt Restructurings	33,020
Transfer of Asset(s)	33,020
Illustration of Transfer of Assets	33,020

33,002 ASC 470—Debt

Transfer of Equity Interest	33,021
Illustration of Transfer of Equity Interest	33,021
Modification of Terms	33,021
Illustration of Modification of Terms	33,022
Combination of Types	33,022
Related Issues	33,022
Disclosure Requirements for Troubled Debt Restructurings	33,023
Debtors	33,023
Part II: Interpretive Guidance	33,023
ASC 470-10: Overall	33,023
ASC 470-10-25-1 through 25-2, 35-3	
Sales of Future Revenues	33,023
ASC 470-10-35-1 through 35-2, 45-7 through 45-8; ASC 835-10-60-9	
Increasing-Rate Debt	33,024
ASC 470-10-45-1, 55-3 through 55-6	
Classification of Obligations When a Violation Is Waived by the Creditor	33,026
ASC 470-10-S45-1, S99-4; ASC 810-10-S45-1	
Classification of a Subsidiary's Loan Payable in Consolidated Balance Sheet When Subsidiary's and Parent's Fiscal Years Differ	33,027
ASC 470-10-45-2, 50-3	
Subjective Acceleration Clauses in Long-Term Debt Agreements	33,028
ASC 470-10-45-3 through 45-6	
Balance Sheet Classification of Borrowings Outstanding under Revolving Credit Agreements That Include both a Subjective Acceleration Clause and a Lock-Box Arrangement	33,028
ASC 470-10-45-2, 50-3	
Classifying Demand Notes with Repayment Terms	33,030
ASC 470-10-55-1	
Subjective Acceleration Clauses and Debt Classification	33,031
ASC 470-10-55-7 through 9	
Classification by the Issuer of Redeemable Instruments That Are Subject to Remarketing Agreements	33,031
ASC 470-20: Debt with Conversion and Other Options	33,032
ASC 470-20-05-1, 05-12A through 12C, 15-2, 25-1, 25-20A, 30-26A, 35-11A, 45-2A, 50-2A through 50-2C, 65-3; ASC 260-10-45-70B	
Accounting for Own-Share Lending Arrangements in Contemplation of Convertible Debt Issuance	33,032
ASC 470-20-05-7, through 05-8, 25-4 through 25-6, 30-3, 30-6, 30-8, 30-10 through 30-11, 30-15, 35-2, 35-7, 40-2 through 40-3, 55-30 through 55-33, 55-35 through 55-38, 55-40 through 55-43, 55-45 through 50-48, 55-50 through 55-54A, 55-56 through 55-60A, 55-62 through 55-66, 55-69; ASC 505-10-50-8	
Accounting for Convertible Securities with Beneficial Conversion Features or Contingently Adjustable Conversion Ratios	33,035
Illustrations of the Accounting for a Beneficial Conversion Feature of a Convertible Security	33,041
ASC 470-20-05-9, 35-11, 40-11; ASC 835-10-60-10	
Accrued Interest upon Conversion of Convertible Debt	33,044

ASC 470—Debt **33,003**

ASC 470-20-05-11; 40-4A through 40-10; 55-68
    Accounting for the Conversion of an Instrument That Becomes Convertible upon the Issuer's Exercise of a Call Option **33,044**

ASC 470-20-10-1 through 10-2, 15-2, 15-4 through 15-6, 25-21 through 25-27, 30-27 through 30-31, 35-12 through 35-20, 40-19 through 40-26, 45-3, 50-3 through 50-6, 55-70 through 55-82, 65-1; ASC 815-15-55-76A; ASC 825-10-15-5
    Accounting for Convertible Debt Instruments That May Be Settled in Cash upon Conversion (Including Partial Cash Settlement) **33,047**

ASC 470-20-25-8 through 25-9, 25-20, 30-1, 30-5, 30-7, 30-9 through 30-10, 30-12 through 30-13, 30-16 through 30-21, 35-1, 35-4, 35-7 through 35-10, 40-1, 40-4, 45-1, 55-11 through 55-12, 55-14 through 55-17, 55-19 through 55-21, 55-23 through 55-24, 55-26 through 55-27; ASC 505-10-50-7; ASC 260-10-50-1
    Application of Issue No. 98-5 to Certain Convertible Securities **33,054**

ASC 470-20-40-13
    Determining Whether Certain Conversions of Convertible Debt to Equity Securities Are within the Scope of FASB Statement No. 84, Induced Conversions of Convertible Debt **33,061**

ASC 470-20-S99-1, S25-1
    Revenue Recognition on Options to Purchase Stock of Another Entity **33,062**

ASC 470-20-05-12; 25-17 through 25-19; 30-22 through 30-26
    Accounting for a Convertible Instrument Granted or Issued to a Nonemployee for Goods or Services and Cash **33,063**

ASC 470-50: Modifications and Extinguishments **33,066**

ASC 470-50-05-1, 15-2 through 15-3, 40-3
    Early Extinguishment of Debt through Exchange for Common or Preferred Stock **33,066**

ASC 470-50-05-4, 15-3, 40-6 through 40-14, 40-17 through 40-20, 55-1 through 55-9
    Debtor's Accounting for a Substantive Modification and Exchange of Debt Securities **33,066**
        Illustrations of Debtor's Accounting for a Substantive Modification and Exchange of Debt Securities **33,071**

ASC 470-50-40-5, 15-3; ASC 470-20-40-4
    Early Extinguishment of Debt: Accounting Interpretations of APB Opinion No. 26 .... **33,074**
        Illustration of Debt Tendered to Exercise Detachable Warrants **33,074**

ASC 470-50-40-12, 40-15 through 40-16
    Debtor's Accounting for a Modification (or Exchange) of Convertible Debt Instruments **33,075**

ASC 470-50-40-21 through 40-22, 45-2, 55-11 through 55-13
    Debtor's Accounting for Changes in Line-of-Credit or Revolving-Debt Arrangements **33,076**
        Illustration of a Debtor's Accounting for Changes in a Line of Credit or Revolving Credit Arrangement **33,077**

ASC 470-60: Troubled Debt Restructurings by Debtors **33,078**

ASC 470-60-15-10, 55-1, 55-2
    Applicability of Statement 15 to Debtors in Bankruptcy Situations **33,078**

ASC 470-60-55-4 through 55-14, 15-13
  Debtor's Accounting for a Modification or an Exchange of Debt
  Instruments in Accordance with FASB Statement No. 15, Accounting by
  Debtors and Creditors for Troubled Debt Restructurings   **33,079**

PART I: GENERAL GUIDANCE

OVERVIEW

ASC 470 establishes GAAP for the current/noncurrent classification in the debtor's balance sheet of obligations that are payable on demand or callable by the creditor. This includes guidance regarding when a short-term obligation can be excluded from current liabilities. ASC 470 also addresses convertible debt, product financing, debt modifications and extinguishments, and the accounting by debtors for a troubled debt restructuring.

Debt may be issued with a conversion feature or a feature that permits the separate purchase of other securities, usually common stock of the issuing company. These "hybrid" debt/equity securities generally derive some portion of their value from the equity component (i.e., the conversion feature or the separate purchase option) that is included in the issue price. The significant accounting question that arises is the recognition, if any, of the equity feature when a hybrid security is issued. That treatment, in turn, affects the subsequent accounting when the conversion feature or separate purchase option is exercised.

A *product financing arrangement* is a transaction in which an enterprise sells and agrees to repurchase inventory at a purchase price equal to the original sale price plus carrying and financing costs, or other similar transaction. In certain circumstances, a transaction labeled a *sale* is, in substance, a product financing arrangement and should be treated as such.

An *extinguishment of debt* is the reacquisition of debt, or removal of debt from the balance sheet, prior to or at the maturity date of that debt. Gain or loss on the extinguishment is the difference between the total reacquisition cost of the debt to the debtor and the net carrying amount of the debt on the debtor's books at the date of extinguishment.

The authoritative literature carefully defines when debt has been extinguished and generally requires any gain or loss on extinguishments of debt to be included in the determination of net income in the period of the extinguishment transaction.

Debt may be restructured for a variety of reasons. A restructuring of debt is considered a troubled debt restructuring (TDR) if the creditor, for economic or legal reasons related to the debtor's financial difficulties, grants a concession to the debtor that it would not otherwise consider. The concession may stem from an agreement between the creditor and the debtor, or it may be imposed by law or court (ASC Glossary).

A loan is impaired if, based on current information and events, it is probable that the creditor will be unable to collect all amounts due according to the contractual terms of the loan agreement, including both the contractual interest and the principal receivable. For a discussion of troubled debt restructurings from the creditor's perspective, see the coverage in ASC 310-40 (Troubled Debt Restructurings by Creditors).

BACKGROUND

Convertible Debt

Convertible debt is convertible into the common stock of the issuer or an affiliated enterprise. Common characteristics of convertible debt are (ASC 470-20-25-11).

- The interest rate is lower than the interest rate on an equivalent, but not convertible, security.
- The initial conversion price is greater than the market value of the underlying security.
- The conversion price does not change (except pursuant to certain antidilutive considerations).
- The security usually is callable by the issuer.
- The debt usually is subordinate to the nonconvertible debt of the issuer.

Conversion of the convertible debt requires the holders to relinquish their status as debtholders to become stockholders.

Debt also may be issued with detachable purchase warrants that usually permit the holders to purchase shares of common stock at a set price for a specified period. The holders of the detachable warrants are not required to relinquish their status as debtholders to become stockholders.

Product Financing Arrangements

Product financing arrangements usually provide for one entity to obtain inventory or product for another entity (the sponsor), which agrees to purchase the inventory or product at specific prices over a specific period. The agreed-upon prices usually include financing and holding costs. The following are examples of common types of product financing arrangements (ASC 470-40-05-2):

- A sponsor sells inventory or product to another entity and in a related arrangement agrees to buy the inventory or product back.
- An entity agrees to purchase a product or inventory for a sponsor, who, in a related arrangement, agrees to buy the product or inventory from the first entity.
- A sponsor, by arrangement, controls the product or inventory purchased or held by another entity.

In all of the above examples of product financing arrangements, the sponsor agrees to purchase, over a specified period, the product or inventory from the other entity at prearranged prices. The substance of a product financing arrangement, regardless of its legal form, is that of a financing arrangement rather than a sale or purchase by the sponsor.

PRACTICE NOTE: Distinguishing a product financing arrangement from the outright sale of products may require careful professional judgment. Usually it will require an analysis and consideration of two related transactions rather than a single transaction. For example, if a sponsor sells inventory or product to another entity and in a separate agreement contracts to buy the inventory or product back, the initial transaction may appear to be a sale. Only when the two transactions (i.e., the "sale" and the later repurchase) are combined is the true substance of the transaction apparent. In applying GAAP for product financing arrangements, an important dimension is the follow-through analysis and understanding of the subsequent transaction.

Other factors that may be present in a product financing arrangement are (ASC 470-40-05-4):

- The entity that provides the financing arrangement to the sponsor is an existing trust, nonbusiness entity or credit grantor, or was formed for the sole purpose of providing the financing arrangement to the sponsor.
- Small quantities of the product involved in the financing arrangement may be sold by the financing entity, but most of the product is ultimately used or sold by the sponsor.
- The product is stored on the sponsor's premises.
- The sponsor guarantees the debt of the other entity.

For purposes of the guidance in ASC 470, unmined or unharvested natural resources and financial instruments are not considered products. Thus, they are not covered by the provisions of ASC 470 (ASC 470-40-15-3).

PRACTICE NOTE: No mention is made in ASC 470-40 as to how a product financing arrangement involving unmined or unharvested natural resources should be accounted for. For example, X Company enters into a financing arrangement with Y Company wherein Y Company acquires 10,000 acres of unharvested timberlands for the sole benefit of X Company. X Company guarantees the bank loan that was necessary to acquire the timberlands and agrees to purchase the processed timber from Y Company at specified prices over a specified period. The specified prices include (a) the cost of the timber, (b) processing costs, (c) interest costs on the bank loan, and (d) a handling fee. Only the standing timber was purchased and not the land.

It appears that the provisions of ASC 470-40 are appropriate for this type of transaction, but ASC 470-40 does not expressly cover this situation.

In a product financing arrangement, the specified prices that the sponsor must pay cannot be subject to change except for fluctuations because of finance and holding costs. The specified prices may be stated or determinable by reference to the substance of the arrangement, such as (a) resale price guarantees or (b) options that, in substance, compel or require the sponsor to purchase the product. In addition, the cost of the product and related costs to the other entity must be covered substantially by the specified prices that the seller must pay for the product. Related costs include interest, holding costs, and other fees charged by the other entity (ASC 470-40-15-2).

Modifications and Extinguishments of Debt

Prior to the establishment of GAAP for extinguishment of debt, differences in practice existed with regard to the recognition of gains and losses from refunding of debt issues. ASC 470 requires that gains and losses from early extinguishment of debt be included in net income of the period of extinguishment.

Troubled Debt Restructuring

A troubled debt restructuring is one in which the creditor grants the debtor certain concessions that would not normally be considered. The concessions are made because of the debtor's financial difficulty, and the creditor's objective is to maximize recovery of its investment. Troubled debt restructurings are often the result of legal proceedings or of negotiation between the parties (ASC 310-40-15-5, 6).

Troubled debt restructurings include situations in which (ASC 310-40-15-9):

- The creditor accepts a third-party receivable or other asset(s) of the debtor, in lieu of the receivable from the debtor.
- The creditor accepts an equity interest in the debtor in lieu of the receivable. (This is not to be confused with convertible securities, which are *not* troubled debt restructurings.)
- The creditor accepts modification of the terms of the debt, including but not limited to:
  — Reduction in the stated interest
  — Extension of maturity at an interest rate below the current market rate
  — Reduction in face amount of the debt
  — Reduction in accrued interest

The reductions mentioned in the bulleted item above can be either absolute or contingent.

PRACTICE NOTE: If the debtor can obtain funds at current market rates and conditions, this provides evidence that the restructuring is not a troubled debt restructuring.

ASC 470-10: OVERALL

LIABILITY CLASSIFICATION ISSUES

Current Obligations Expected to Be Refinanced

A short-term obligation can be excluded from current liabilities only if the company intends to refinance it on a long-term basis and the intent is supported by the ability to refinance that is demonstrated in one of the following ways (ASC 470-10-45-14):

- A long-term obligation or equity security whose proceeds are used to retire the short-term obligation is issued after the date of the balance sheet but before the issuance of the financial statements.
- Before the issuance of the financial statements, the company has entered into an agreement that enables it to refinance a short-term obligation on a long-term basis. The terms of the agreement must be clear and unambiguous and must contain the following provisions:
  - The agreement may not be canceled by the lender or investor, and it must extend beyond the normal operating cycle of the company.
  - At the balance sheet date and at its issuance, the company was not in violation, nor was there any information that indicated a violation, of the agreement.
  - The lender or investor is expected to be financially capable of honoring the agreement.

PRACTICE POINTER: If the company has no operating cycle or the operating cycle occurs more than once a year, then the one-year rule is used.

The amount of short-term obligation that can be reclassified as non-current cannot exceed the actual proceeds received from the issuance of the new long-term obligation or the amount of available refinancing covered by the established agreement. The amount must be adjusted for any limitations in the agreement that indicate the full amount obtainable will not be available to retire the short-term obligation. In addition, if the agreement indicates that the amount available for refinancing will fluctuate, then the most conservative estimate must be used. If no reasonable estimate can be made, then the agreement does not fulfill the necessary requirements and the full amount of current liabilities must be presented (ASC 470-10-45-18).

An enterprise may intend to seek alternative financing sources besides those in the established agreement when the short-term obligation becomes due. If alternative sources do not materialize, however, the company must intend to borrow from the source in the agreement (ASC 470-10-45-20).

PRACTICE POINTER: If the terms of the agreement allow the prospective lender or investor to set interest rates, collateral requirements, or similar conditions that are unreasonable to the company, the intent to refinance may not exist.

ASC 470 addresses the issue of a short-term obligation that is repaid and is subsequently replaced with a long-term debt obligation or equity securities. Because cash is temporarily required to retire the short-term obligation, the obligation should be classified as a current liability in the balance sheet (ASC 470-10-45-15).

Any *rollover agreements* or *revolving credit agreements* must meet the above provisions to enable a company to classify the related short-term obligations as noncurrent (ASC 470-10-45-21). The financial statements must contain a note disclosing the amount excluded from current liabilities and a full description of the financial agreement and new obligations incurred or expected to be incurred or the equity securities issued or expected to be issued (ASC 470-10-50-4).

Callable Obligations

ASC 470 establishes GAAP for the current/noncurrent classification in the debtor's balance sheet of obligations that are payable on demand or callable by the creditor.

ASC 470 is applied to a classified balance sheet to determine whether the obligation should be classified as current or noncurrent for balance sheet purposes. ASC 470 is applied to both classified and unclassified balance sheets to determine the maturity dates of obligations disclosed by notes. For example, an unclassified balance sheet may contain a note disclosure of the maturity dates of obligations, despite the fact that the obligations are not classified in the unclassified balance sheet, or may not be identified separately from other obligations in the unclassified balance sheet.

At the debtor's balance sheet date, an obligation may, by its terms, be payable on demand. This includes long-term obligations that are callable because a violation of an objective acceleration clause in a long-term debt agreement may exist at the date of the debtor's balance sheet. Such callable obligations must be classified as a current liability at the debtor's balance sheet date unless (ASC 470-10-45-11):

- The creditor has waived the right to demand payment for a period that extends beyond one year (or the debtor's normal operating cycle if longer), or
- The debtor has cured the violation after the balance sheet date, but prior to the issuance date of the financial statements, and the obligation is not callable for a period that extends beyond one year (or the debtor's normal operating cycle if longer).

A long-term debt agreement may provide for a grace period that commences after the occurrence of a violation of an objective acceleration clause. ASC 470 requires that such an obligation be classified as a current liability at the debtor's balance sheet date, unless the two criteria above are met and, in addition, the unexpired grace period extends beyond one year (or the debtor's normal operating cycle if longer) (ASC 470-10-45-11).

PRACTICE NOTE: ASC 470 requires that an obligation be classified as current or noncurrent, based solely on whether the legal terms of the loan agreement require payment within one year (or the operating cycle if longer).

A creditor may have waived the right to demand payment on a specific obligation for a period that extends beyond one year (or the operating cycle if longer). In this event, the debtor shall classify the obligation as a noncurrent liability.

Acceleration Clauses

An *objective acceleration clause* in a long-term debt agreement is one that contains objective criteria that the creditor must use as the basis for calling part or all of the loan, such as a specified minimum amount of working capital or net worth requirement.

In the event of a violation of an objective acceleration clause, most long-term obligations become immediately callable by the creditor, or become callable after a grace period that is specified in the loan agreement. When this occurs, the creditor can demand payment of part or all of the loan balance, in accordance with the terms of the debt agreement.

A subjective acceleration clause is one that permits the lender to unilaterally accelerate part or all of a long-term obligation. For example, the debt agreement might state that "if, in the opinion of the lender, the borrower experiences recurring losses or liquidity problems, the lender may at its sole discretion accelerate part or all of the loan balance . . . ."

Acceleration clauses are accounted for in the same manner as other loss contingencies. If it is *probable* that the subjective acceleration clause will be exercised by the creditor, the amount of the long-term obligation that is likely to be accelerated shall be classified as a current liability by the debtor. On the other hand, if it is only *reasonably possible* that the subjective acceleration clause will be exercised by the creditor, note disclosure may be all that is required. Finally, if the possibility of subjective acceleration is *remote*, no disclosure may be required.

ASC 470-20: DEBT WITH CONVERSION AND OTHER OPTIONS

CONVERTIBLE DEBT

Issuance

Under current GAAP, when convertible debt is issued, no portion of the proceeds is accounted for as attributable to the conversion feature. At that time, the debt issue is treated entirely as debt and no formal accounting recognition is assigned to the value inherent in the conversion feature. In reaching this conclusion, greater weight was placed on the inseparability of the debt and the conversion feature, and less weight on practical problems of valuing the conversion feature (ASC 470-20-25-12).

PRACTICE NOTE: In considering alternative methods of accounting for convertible debt, some believe that the value of the equity component (conversion feature) should be recognized at the time the convertible debt is issued; others felt that it should be given formal recognition not at that time, but later when conversion occurs. Existing GAAP concludes that the most important reason for accounting for convertible debt solely as debt at the time of issuance is the inseparability of the debt and conversion option. The holder must give up rights as a debt holder to become a stockholder. In other words, the alternatives are mutually exclusive.

Illustration of Convertible Bond Issuance

Alpha Company issues $1,000,000 of convertible bonds at 98% of par value. Each $1,000 bond is convertible into 10 shares of the company's common stock. The bond issue is recorded as if there were no conversion feature, as follows:

Cash ($1,000,000 × 98%)	980,000	
Discount on bonds payable	20,000	
Bonds payable		1,000,000

Disclosure of the features of the bond, including the conversion option, is required. The entry above, however, is the same as it would be had the bonds not been convertible.

Conversion

When a convertible debt security with an inseparable conversion feature is converted into equity securities of the debtor in accordance with the original conversion terms, the convertible debt security is surrendered by the holder and the debt is retired by the debtor. The issuer substitutes equity for debt in its balance sheet. The following is an illustration of such a transaction.

Illustration of Convertible Debt Security Converted into Equity Security

Blue Corporation has outstanding $20,000,000 of 8% convertible bonds, with an unamortized bond premium balance of $800,000. Each $1,000 bond is convertible into ten shares of Blue Corporation's $5 par value common stock. On April 1, 20X8, all of the convertible bonds were converted by the bondholders.

8% convertible bonds payable	20,000,000	
Unamortized bond premium	800,000	
Common stock ($5 par × 200,000)		1,000,000
Capital in excess of par (common stock)		19,800,000

Under current accounting practice, no gain or loss is recognized on the conversion of convertible bonds to common stock if the conversion is made in accordance with the original conversion terms.

Generally, convertible debt is issued in anticipation that it will be converted into equity securities, and that the issuer will repay the face amount of the debt at its maturity date. Although most convertible debt issues provide for the issuance of common equity shares upon conversion, the terms of a convertible debt security may provide for the issuance of preferred or other type of equity security upon conversion. When an enterprise converts debt to common equity shares, the liability for the debt is eliminated and the number of common equity shares outstanding is increased, which may affect the computation of earnings per share (EPS). When debt is converted to common equity shares, the pretax net income of the enterprise also increases by the amount of interest expense that was previously paid on the convertible debt.

> **PRACTICE POINTER:** Convertible debt generally is converted by a holder when the market value of its underlying equity securities into which the debt can be converted exceeds the face amount of the debt. If a convertible bondholder does not convert, the issuer may exercise the call provision in the debt to force conversion.

Convertible debt usually is not converted when the market value of its underlying equity securities is less than the face amount of the debt. Under this circumstance, the issuer may (a) exercise the call provision in the debt and pay the bondholders the face amount of the convertible debt, (b) offer the bondholders an inducement to convert that exceeds the original conversion terms, or (c) not pay off the debt until the scheduled maturity date (ASC 470-20-05-5).

Induced Conversion

ASC 470 applies to conversions of convertible debt in which the original conversion terms are changed by the debtor to encourage the holder of the convertible debt to convert to equity securities of the debtor. Changes in the original conversion terms may include (a) the reduction of the original conversion price to increase the number of shares of equity securities received by the bondholder, (b) the issuance of warrants or other securities, or (c) the payment of cash or some other type of consideration (ASC 470-20-40-15).

ASC 470 applies only to induced conversions that (a) are exercisable for a limited period of time and (b) include the issuance of no less than the number of shares of equity securities required by the original conversion terms for each convertible bond converted. For each convertible bond that is converted, the debtor must issue, at a minimum, the amount of equity securities required by the original conversion terms (ASC 470-20-40-13).

In an induced conversion of convertible debt, a debtor does not recognize any gain or loss on the amount of equity securities that are required to be issued under the original conversion terms for each convertible bond converted. However, the fair value of any equity securities or other consideration paid or issued by the debtor that exceeds the amount of equity securities required to be issued for each convertible bond converted under the original conversion terms is recognized as current expense on the date the inducement offer is accepted by the bondholder (ASC 470-20-40-16).

If the additional inducement consists of equity securities, the market value of such securities is credited to capital stock, and if necessary to capital in excess of par, with an offsetting debit to debt conversion expense. If the additional inducement consists of assets other than the debtor's equity securities, the market value of such assets is credited with an offsetting debit to debt conversion expense.

The fair value of the securities or other consideration is measured as of the date the inducement offer is accepted by the debtholder. This usually is the date the debtholder converts the debt into equity securities or enters into a binding agreement to do so (ASC 470-20-40-16).

PRACTICE POINTER: If individual bondholders accepted an inducement offer on many different days during the "limited period of time" allowed by existing GAAP, a separate computation of the fair value of the incremental consideration would be required if the fair value of the debtor's common stock changes from day to day.

Illustration of Induced Conversion

Black Corporation has outstanding 100 10% convertible bonds, issued at par value and due on December 31, 20X8. Each $1,000 bond is convertible into 20 shares of Black Corporation $1 par value common stock. To induce bondholders to convert to its common stock, Black Corporation increases the conversion rate from 20 shares per $1,000 bond to 25 shares per $1,000 bond. This offer was made by Black Corporation for a limited period of 60 days commencing March 1, 20X9.

On April 1, when the market price of Black's common stock was $60, one bondholder tendered a $1,000 convertible bond for conversion. Under ASC 470, the amount of incremental consideration is equal to the fair value of the additional five shares of Black Corporation's common stock on April 1. The amount of incremental consideration is $300 (5 shares × $60 per share).

The journal entry to record the transaction is:

Convertible bonds payable	1,000	
Debt conversion expense	300	
Common stock ($1 par value) ($1 × 25 shares)		25
Capital in excess of par (common stock)		1,275

The incremental consideration paid or issued by a debtor may also be calculated as the difference between (a) the fair value of the equity securities and/or other consideration required to be issued under the original terms of the conversion privilege and (b) the fair value of the equity securities and/or other consideration that is actually issued.

Market value of securities based on inducement (25 × $60)	$1,500
Market value of securities based on original terms (20 × $60)	(1,200)
Fair value of incremental consideration	$ 300

PRACTICE NOTE: There is a significant difference between extinguishment accounting and conversion accounting. As a rule, gain or loss is recognized in extinguishment accounting, while no gain or loss is recognized in conversion accounting. Extinguishment accounting results in the *extinguishment* of a debt, while conversion accounting results in the issuance of equity securities and the *retirement* of a debt.

DEBT WITH DETACHABLE PURCHASE WARRANTS

Issuance

In contrast to accounting for convertible debt, when detachable purchase warrants are issued in conjunction with debt, ASC 470 requires that separate amounts attributable to the debt and the purchase warrants be computed and accounting recognition be given to each component. The allocation to the two components of the hybrid debt/equity security is based on the relative market values of the two securities at the time of issuance (ASC 470-20-25-2). This conclusion is based primarily on the fact that the options available to the debtholder are *not* mutually exclusive—bondholders can become stockholders and retain their status as bondholders.

Illustration of Issuance of Debt with Detachable Warrants

Xeta Corporation issues 100 $100-par-value, 5% bonds with a detachable common stock warrant to purchase one share of Xeta's common stock at a specified price. At the time of issuance, the quoted market price of the bonds was $97, and the stock warrants were quoted at $2 each. The proceeds of the sale to Xeta Corporation were $9,900. The transaction is accounted for as follows:

Cash	9,900	
Discount on 5% bonds payable (100 × $3)	300	
5% bonds payable		10,000
Paid-in capital (stock warrants) (100 × $2)		200

The bonds and warrants are recorded separately at their market values:

Bonds: $10,000 × 97% = $9,700, recorded at $10,000 par value, less $300 discount

Warrants: 100 × $2 = $200

Exercise of Warrants

Once a separate purchase feature, such as a detachable stock purchase warrant, is issued, it usually is traded separately from its related convertible debt security. The separate purchase feature has its own market price, and conversion requires (*a*) the surrender of the purchase option and (*b*) the payment of any other consideration required by the terms of the warrant.

Under current accounting practice (ASC 470), when a separate purchase feature is exercised in accordance with the original purchase terms, no gain or loss is recognized on the transaction. The amount previously credited to paid-in capital for the purchase feature at issuance is eliminated, the amount of cash received, if any, is recorded, and the par value of the capital stock issued and the appropriate amount of capital stock in excess of par is recorded. The following is an illustration of such a transaction.

Illustration of Exercise of Separate Purchase Feature

Ace Corporation previously issued debt securities with detachable stock purchase warrants. A credit of $10 for each warrant was recorded in paid-in capital at the date of issuance, representing the relative market value of each warrant. There was no discount or premium on the issuance of the related debt with detachable stock purchase warrants. Each stock purchase warrant permitted the purchase of 50 shares of Ace's $1 par value common stock, upon the payment of $200 and the surrender of the warrant. Assuming that one warrant was exercised, the journal entry would be:

Cash	200	
Paid-in capital (stock warrants)	10	
Capital stock ($1 par value)		50
Capital in excess of par (common stock)		160

The conversion of a separate conversion feature, such as a detachable stock purchase warrant, is accounted for solely as an equity transaction, and no gain or loss is recorded.

PRACTICE POINTER: The accounting described in this section applies to "detachable" stock purchase warrants and other similar instruments, meaning that the stock purchase warrant can be exercised without affecting the other security from which it is detachable. Occasionally, a stock purchase warrant is encountered that is inseparable from another security (i.e., a nondetachable stock purchase warrant), and the related security must be surrendered to effect the stock purchase. In this case, although the name may imply otherwise, the stock purchase warrant effectively is part of a convertible security and should be accounted for as such.

PRACTICE NOTE: ASC 470 recognizes that it is not practical to discuss all possible types of debt with conversion features and debt issued with purchase warrants, or debt issued with a combination of the two. It states that securities not explicitly dealt with in ASC 470 should be accounted for in accordance with the substance of the transaction in a manner consistent with existing GAAP (ASC 470-20-25-13).

ASC 470-40: PRODUCT FINANCING ARRANGEMENTS

ACCOUNTING FOR PRODUCT FINANCING ARRANGEMENTS

An arrangement that contains the characteristics of a product financing arrangement is accounted for by the sponsor of the arrangement as follows (ASC 470-40-25-2):

- If an entity buys a product from a sponsor and in a related arrangement agrees to sell the product, or a processed product containing the original product, back to the sponsor, no sale is recorded and the product remains an asset on the sponsor's books. Also, the sponsor records a liability in the amount of the proceeds received from the other entity under the provisions of the product financing arrangement.

- If an entity buys a product for a sponsor's benefit and the sponsor agrees, in a related arrangement, to buy the product, or a processed product containing the original product, back from the other entity, an asset and the related liability are recorded by the sponsor at the time the other entity acquires the product.

Excluding processing costs, the difference between (a) the regular product cost the sponsor would have paid if there were no product financing arrangement and (b) the cost the sponsor actually pays under the terms of the product financing arrangement is accounted for by the sponsor as financing and holding costs. These financing and holding costs are recorded on the books of the sponsor in accordance with its regular accounting policies for such costs, even though the costs are incurred and paid directly by the other entity (ASC 470-40-25-3).

Separately identified interest costs that the sponsor pays as part of the specified prices may qualify for interest capitalization under ASC 835. If not, the separately identified interest costs actually paid by the sponsor are included in the total interest costs incurred during the period (ASC 470-40-25-4).

Illustration of Accounting for Product Financing Arrangements

Assume that each of the following situations meets the definition of a product financing arrangement (PFA) in accordance with ASC 470. In each situation, Walsh is the sponsor and Foster is the purchaser. Following are the appropriate journal entries for Walsh.

Case 1: Walsh sells inventory costing $800 to Foster for $1,000 and agrees to repurchase the same inventory for $1,050 in 30 days.

Cash (or receivable)	1,000	
Due to Foster under PFA		1,000
Inventory under PFA	800	
Inventory		800

Case 2: Walsh arranges for Foster to purchase inventory costing $1,000 from a third party and agrees to purchase that inventory from Foster for $1,050 in 30 days.

Inventory under PFA	1,000	
Due to Foster under PFA		1,000

Case 3: Walsh sells inventory costing $700 to Foster for $800 and agrees to a resale price of $1,000 to outside parties.

Cash (or receivable)	800	
Due to Foster under PFA		800
Inventory under PFA	700	
Inventory		700

Case 4: Walsh arranges for Foster to acquire inventory from an outside party for $750 and guarantees the resale price to outside parties for $850.

Inventory under PFA	750	
Due to Foster under PFA		750

ASC 470-50: MODIFICATIONS AND EXTINGUISHMENTS

WHEN DEBT IS EXTINGUISHED

Debt is extinguished and is derecognized in, or removed from, the debtor's financial statements only in the following circumstances (ASC 405-20-40-1):

- The debtor pays the creditor and is relieved of its obligations for the liability. This includes (*a*) the transfer of cash, other financial assets, goods, or services or (*b*) the debtor's reacquisition of its outstanding debt securities, whether the securities are cancelled or held as treasury bonds.

- The debtor is legally released from being the primary obligor under the liability, either judicially or by the creditor. If a third party assumes nonrecourse debt in conjunction with the sale of an asset that serves as sole collateral for that debt, the sale and related assumption effectively accomplish a legal release of the seller-debtor for purposes of applying ASC 405.

When a refunding is desired because of lower interest rates or some other reason, the old debt issue may not be callable for several years. This is the usual circumstance for an advance refunding. In an advance refunding, a new debt issue is sold to replace the old debt issue that cannot be called. The proceeds from the sale of the new debt issue are used to purchase high grade investments, which are placed in an escrow account. The earnings from the investments in the escrow account are used to pay the interest and/or principal payments on the existing debt, up to the date that the existing debt can be called. On the call date of the existing debt, whatever remains in the escrow account is used to pay the call premium, if any, and all remaining principal and interest due on the existing debt. This process is frequently referred to as an in-substance defeasance. An in-substance defeasance is *not* considered an extinguishment of debt.

ACCOUNTING FOR EXTINGUISHMENTS OF DEBT

Under ASC 470, all extinguishments of debt are basically alike, and accounting for such transactions is the same, regardless of the method used to achieve the extinguishment. Therefore, in terms of gain or loss recognition, there is no difference in accounting for an extinguishment of debt by (*a*) cash purchase, (*b*) exchange of stock for debt, (*c*) exchange of debt for debt, or (*d*) any other method.

Gain or loss on the extinguishment of debt is the difference between the reacquisition price and the net carrying amount of the debt on the date of the extinguishment (ASC 470-50-40-2).

Reacquisition Price

This is the amount paid for the extinguishment. It includes call premium and any other costs of reacquiring the portion of the debt being extinguished (ASC Glossary). When extinguishment is achieved through the exchange of securities, the reacquisition price is the total present value of the new securities being issued.

Net Carrying Amount

This is the amount due at the maturity of the debt, adjusted for any unamortized premium or discount and any other costs of issuance (legal, accounting, underwriter's fees, etc.) (ASC Glossary).

REFUNDING OF TAX-EXEMPT DEBT

If a change in a lease occurs as a result of a refunding by the lessor of tax-exempt debt and (a) the lessee receives the economic advantages of the refunding and (b) the revised lease qualifies and is classified either as a capital lease by the lessee or as a direct financing lease by the lessor, the change in the lease is accounted for on the basis of whether or not an extinguishment of debt has occurred, as follows (ASC 840-30-35-10):

- Accounted for as an extinguishment of debt:
  - The lessee adjusts the lease obligation to the present value of the future minimum lease payments under the revised agreement, using the effective interest rate of the new lease agreement. Any gain or loss shall be treated as a gain or loss on an early extinguishment of debt.
  - The lessor adjusts the balance of the minimum lease payments receivable and the gross investment in the lease (if affected) for the difference between the present values of the old and new or revised agreement. Any gain or loss shall be recognized in the current period.
- Not accounted for as an extinguishment of debt:
  - The lessee accrues any costs connected with the refunding that it is obligated to reimburse to the lessor. The interest method is used to amortize the costs over the period from the date of the refunding to the call date of the debt to be refunded.
  - The lessor recognizes as revenue any reimbursements to be received from the lessee for costs paid related to the debt to be refunded over the period from the date of the refunding to the call date of the debt to be refunded.

INCOME STATEMENT CLASSIFICATION OF DEBT EXTINGUISHMENT

ASC 470 requires that gains or losses on debt extinguishments be evaluated for proper income statement classification in the same manner as all other business transactions and events. That is, if the two criteria for extraordinary item treatment specified in ASC 225 (Income Statement) are met—the transaction or event is unusual in nature and infrequent in occurrence—the gain or loss on the debt extinguishments would be treated as an extraordinary item (ASC 470-50-45-1). If the two criteria in ASC 225 are not met, the gain or loss on debt extinguishments is included in income before discontinued operations and extraordinary items.

ASC 470—Debt 33,019

PRACTICE NOTE: The FASB recognizes that the application of ASC 225 to debt extinguishments will seldom, if ever, result in gains or losses from debt extinguishments being accounted for as extraordinary items. However, the Board pointed out that ASC 225 requires separate disclosure (not net of tax) of gains or losses from transactions that are *either* unusual in *nature or* infrequent in occurrence. Therefore, although gains or losses from debt extinguishments seldom qualify for extraordinary item treatment, and such gains or losses usually should be disclosed separately on the face of the income statement as a component of income from continuing operations (ASC 470-50-45-1).

Illustration of Reacquisition Loss on Extinguishment

On December 31, 20X8, a corporation decides to retire $500,000 of an original issue of $1,000,000 8% debentures, which were sold on December 31, 20X3, for $98 per $100 par-value bond and are callable at $101 per bond. Legal and other expenses for issuing the debentures were $30,000. Both the original discount and the issue costs are being amortized over the 10-year life of the issue by the straight-line method.

Amount of original expenses of issue	$30,000
Amount of original discount (2% of $1,000,000)	$20,000
Amount of premium paid for redemption (debentures callable at 101, 1% of $500,000)	$ 5,000
Date of issue	12/31/20X3
Date of maturity	12/31/20Y3
Date of redemption	12/31/20X8

Because that the original expenses of $30,000 are being amortized over the ten year life of the issue and five years have elapsed since the issue date, half of these expenses have been amortized, leaving a balance of $15,000 at the date of reacquisition. Only half of the outstanding debentures are being retired, however, which leaves $7,500 to account for in the computation of gain or loss.

The original discount of $20,000 (debentures sold at $98) is handled the same as the legal and other expenses. Because half of the discount has already been amortized, leaving a $10,000 balance at the date of redemption, and because only half of the issue is being reacquired, $5,000 is included into the computation of gain or loss.

Based on the above information, the loss on reacquisition is computed as follows:

Reacquisition price:		
$500,000 × 101%		$505,000
Net carrying amount:		
Face value	$500,000	
Discount	(5,000)	
Legal and other expenses	(7,500)	
		(487,500)
Loss on reacquisition		$ 17,500

The general journal entry to record the reacquisition of the bonds is as follows:

Bond payable	500,000	
Loss of retirement of bonds payable	17,500	
Discount on bonds payable		5,000
Deferred legal and other expenses		7,500
Cash		$505,000

ASC 470-60: TROUBLED DEBT RESTRUCTURINGS BY DEBTORS

ACCOUNTING FOR TROUBLED DEBT RESTRUCTURINGS

Debtors account for troubled debt restructurings by the type of restructuring. Types of restructuring include:

- Transfer of asset(s) in full settlement.
- Transfer of an equity interest in full settlement.
- Modification of terms of the debt.
- Combinations of the above three types.

Transfer of Asset(s)

The debtor recognizes a gain equal to the excess of the carrying amount of the payable (including accrued interest, premiums, etc.) over the fair value of the asset(s) given up. The difference between the fair value and the carrying amount of the asset(s) given up is the gain or loss on the transfer of asset(s), which is also included in net income in the period the transfer occurs (not presented as an extraordinary item) (ASC 470-60-35-2, 3).

> **PRACTICE POINTER:** Determine fair value either by the assets given up or by the amount payable, whichever is more clearly evident. In the case of a partial settlement, however, use the value of the asset(s) given up. This eliminates the need to allocate the fair value of the payable between the settled portion and the remaining outstanding balance.

Illustration of Transfer of Assets

A debtor owes $20,000, including accrued interest. The creditor accepts land valued at $17,000 and carried on the debtor's books at its $12,000 cost, in full payment.

Under GAAP, the debtor recognizes two gains: $5,000 ($17,000 − $12,000) on the transfer of the assets, and $3,000 ($20,000 − $17,000) on the extinguishment of debt.

The creditor recognizes a loss of $3,000 ($20,000 − $17,000).

Transfer of Equity Interest

The difference between the fair value of the equity interest and the carrying amount of the payable is recognized as a gain by the debtor (ASC 470-60-35-4).

Illustration of Transfer of Equity Interest

A debtor grants an equity interest valued at $10,000, consisting of 500 shares of $15 par value stock, to retire a payable of $12,000. Given these facts, the debtor records the issuance of the stock at $10,000 ($7,500 par value and $2,500 additional paid-in capital) and a gain on the extinguishment of debt of $2,000 ($12,000 − $10,000). The creditor records an investment asset of $10,000 and an ordinary loss of $2,000 ($12,000 − $10,000) on the TDR.

PRACTICE POINTER: Determining the fair value of an equity interest of a debtor company involved in a troubled debt restructuring may be difficult. In many cases, the company's stock will not be publicly traded, and there may be no recent stock transactions that would be helpful. Even if a recent market price were available, consider whether that price reflects the financially troubled status of the company that exists at the time the troubled debt restructuring takes place.

Modification of Terms

A restructuring that does not involve the transfer of assets or equity often involves the modification of the terms of the debt. The debtor accounts for the effects of the restructuring prospectively and does not change the carrying amount unless the carrying amount exceeds the total future cash payments specified by the new terms. The *total future cash payments* are the principal and interest, including any accrued interest at the time of the restructuring that will be payable by the new terms. *Interest expense* is computed by a method that results in a constant effective rate (such as the interest method). The new effective rate of interest is the discount rate at which the carrying amount of the debt is equal to the present value of the future cash payments (ASC 470-60-35-5).

When the total future cash payments are less than the carrying amount, the debtor reduces the carrying amount accordingly and recognizes the difference as a gain. When there are several related accounts (e.g., discount, premium), the reduction may need to be allocated among them. All cash payments after the restructuring go toward reducing the carrying amount and *no* interest expense is recognized after the date of restructure (ASC 470-60-35-6).

When there are indeterminate future payments, or any time the future payments might exceed the carrying amount, the debtor recognizes no gain. The debtor assumes that the future contingent payments will have to be made at least to the extent necessary to obviate any gain. In estimating future cash payments, it is assumed that the maximum amount of periods (and interest) is going to occur (ASC 470-60-35-7).

Illustration of Modification of Terms

A debtor has a loan to a creditor, details of which are as follows:

Principal	$10,000
Accrued interest	500
Total	$10,500

They reach an agreement to restructure the total future cash payments, both principal and interest, to $8,000. The present value of these payments is $7,500.

Under GAAP, the debtor recognizes a gain of $2,500 ($10,500 − $8,000) at the time of the restructuring, and all future payments are specified as principal payments. Under GAAP, the creditor recognizes a loss of $3,000 ($10,500 − $7,500).

Combination of Types

When a restructuring involves combinations of asset or equity transfers and modification of terms, the debtor first uses the fair value of any asset or equity to reduce the carrying amount of the payable. The difference between the fair value and the carrying amount of any asset(s) transferred is recognized as gain or loss. The remainder of the restructuring is accounted for as a modification of terms in accordance with ASC 470 (ASC 470-60-35-8).

Related Issues

Amounts contingently payable in future periods are recognized as payable and as interest expense in accordance with the treatment of other contingencies. The criteria for recognizing a loss contingency are the following:

- It is probable that the liability has been incurred.
- The amount can be reasonably estimable.

If any contingently payable amounts were included in the total future cash payments, they must now be deducted from the carrying amount of the restructured payable to the extent they originally prevented recognition of a gain at the time of the restructuring (ASC 470-60-35-10).

In estimating future payments subject to fluctuation, estimates are based on the interest rate in effect at the time of restructure. A change in future rates is treated as a change in accounting estimate. The accounting for these fluctuations cannot result in an immediate gain. Rather, the future payments will reduce the carrying amount, and any residual value is considered gain (ASC 470-60-35-11).

Legal fees and other direct costs that a debtor incurs in granting an equity interest to a creditor reduce the amount otherwise recorded for that equity interest. All other direct costs that a debtor incurs to effect a TDR are deducted in measuring the gain on restructuring of payables or are included in expense for the period, if no gain on restructuring is recognized (ASC 470-60-35-12).

DISCLOSURE REQUIREMENTS FOR TROUBLED DEBT RESTRUCTURINGS

Debtors

The debtor must disclose the following regarding any debt restructuring during a period (ASC 470-60-50-1):

- Description of the terms of each restructuring
- Aggregate gain on the restructuring
- Aggregate net gain or loss on asset transfer
- Per share amount of aggregate gain on the restructuring

The debtor should disclose contingently payable amounts included in the carrying amount of restructured payables and the total of contingently payable amounts and the conditions under which the amounts become payable or are forgiven (ASC 470-60-50-2).

PART II: INTERPRETIVE GUIDANCE

ASC 470-10: OVERALL

ASC 470-10-25-1 through 25-2, 35-3 Sales of Future Revenues

BACKGROUND

Company G enters into an agreement with Company H (an investor) to receive a sum of cash in exchange for a specified percentage or amount of Company G's future revenues or another measure of income, such as gross margin or operating income, for a particular product line, business segment, trademark, patent, or contractual right, for a specified period. The future revenue or income may be from a foreign contract, transaction, or operation denominated in a foreign currency.

ACCOUNTING ISSUES

- Assuming the proceeds received from a sale of future revenues are appropriately accounted for as a liability, should the liability be characterized as debt or deferred income?
- How should debt or deferred income be amortized? How should foreign currency effects, if any, be recognized?

OBSERVATION: The distinction between recognizing a liability as debt or as deferred income is significant, because (1) liabilities characterized as deferred income are generally ignored in the calculation of the debt-to-equity ratio and (2) under the provisions of ASC 830, Foreign Currency Matters, the effects on debt of changes in foreign currency exchange rates are accounted for differently from the effects of such changes on deferred income.

ACCOUNTING GUIDANCE

- A liability's characterization depends on the specific facts and circumstances of the underlying transaction.
- The existence of any one of the following factors would result in a rebuttable presumption that a liability should be characterized as debt:
  - Based on its form, the transaction is intended as a borrowing, not a sale.
  - The company has a significant, continuing involvement in generating cash flows that will be paid to an investor.
  - The company or an investor may cancel the transaction, with the company paying a lump sum of cash or transferring other assets to the investor.
  - The terms of the transaction implicitly or explicitly limit an investor's return. (The limitation may be stated explicitly; for example, a rate of return not to exceed 10%. Or the limitation may be implicit in the agreement; for example, if revenues for a particular period do not meet certain expectations, the payment to the investor is calculated in an alternate manner that limits the investor's return.)
  - An investor's rate of return is not significantly affected by variations in the company's measure of performance on which the transaction is based.
  - The investor has recourse to the company for payments due.
- If the proceeds are classified as debt, they should be amortized under the interest method.
- If the proceeds are recognized as revenue, they should be amortized under the units-of-revenue method.
- Amortization for a period under the units-of-revenue method is calculated based on the ratio of the proceeds received from an investor to the total payments expected to be made to the investor over the term of the agreement. That ratio is applied to the cash payment for the period.

ASC 470-10-35-1 through 35-2, 45-7 through 45-8; ASC 835-10-60-9 Increasing-Rate Debt

BACKGROUND

Increasing-rate debt is a financial instrument consisting of notes that mature three months from the original issue date, for example, and that can be extended at the issuer's option for another period of the same duration at each maturity date. The interest rate on the notes increases each time their maturity is extended.

Whether to classify increasing-rate debt as a current or long-term liability is a secondary issue in this discussion, which addresses primarily how to determine interest expense on such debt.

ACCOUNTING ISSUE

- How should an issuer determine interest expense on increasing-rate debt, and what maturity date should be used in that determination?

- How should an issuer account for an excess interest accrual if interest expense is determined by the interest method and the debt is paid earlier than estimated, and should any of it be classified as extraordinary?
- How should the note be classified in the balance sheet?

ACCOUNTING GUIDANCE

- An issuer should determine periodic interest expense on increasing-rate debt by the interest method based on an estimate of the outstanding term of the debt. That estimate should consider the issuer's plans, ability, and intent to service the debt.
- If an issuer repays increasing-rate debt at par before its estimated maturity date, interest expense should be adjusted for excess accrued interest, if any. Such an adjustment should not be considered an extraordinary item.
- Increasing-rate debt should be classified as current or noncurrent based on whether the borrower anticipates repaying the notes with current assets or noncurrent assets. For example, the debt would be classified as current if repayment were from current assets or from a new short-term borrowing. It would be classified as long-term if repayment were financed by a long-term financing arrangement or from the issuance of equity securities.

EFFECT OF ASC 815

Provisions that extend the term of a debt instrument should be analyzed to determine whether they represent a derivative that should be accounted for separately under the guidance in ASC 815.

> **OBSERVATION:** The guidance in ASC 815 has been amended by the guidance in ASC 815-15-25-4 through 25-5, which permits an entity to elect to measure at their fair value certain hybrid financial instruments with embedded derivatives that otherwise would have to be bifurcated. If an entity elects to measure an entire hybrid instrument at its fair value, that financial instrument *cannot* be used as a hedging instrument in hedging relationship under the guidance in ASC 815.

SUBSEQUENT DEVELOPMENT

ASC 340-10-S99-2 states the view of the SEC staff that the above guidance should be followed in accounting for "bridge financing" that consists of increasing-rate debt.

DISCUSSION

The above guidance is consistent with the guidance in ASC 310-45-13; ASC 505-10-25-1; ASC 605-10-25-1, 25-3, 25-5; ASC 850-10-50-2 (which states that liabilities that are expected to be satisfied with current assets should be classified as current liabilities. Based on the provisions of ASC 470 however, if an entity intends to repay a short-term obligation scheduled to mature within one year of the balance sheet date with (1) proceeds from a long-term obligation, (2) the issuance of equity securities, or (3) by renewing, extending, or replacing it with short-term obligations for an uninterrupted period extending beyond one year (or the operating cycle) from the balance sheet date, the obligation should be classified as a long-term liability, subject to certain criteria.

ASC 470-10-45-1, 55-3 through 55-6 Classification of Obligations When a Violation Is Waived by the Creditor

BACKGROUND

Under Company F's loan agreement with a financial institution, the company must comply with certain covenants that, for example, require maintaining a minimum current ratio or debt-to-equity ratio on a quarterly basis. If Company F violates a covenant at specified dates, quarterly or semiannually, the lender may call the loan. However, the lender may waive the right to call the loan for longer than one year while retaining the right to require the company to comply with the covenant requirement during that period.

ACCOUNTING ISSUE

Under such circumstances, can Company F continue to classify the debt as a noncurrent liability or should the debt be reclassified as a current liability?

ACCOUNTING GUIDANCE

Unless the facts and circumstances indicate otherwise (e.g., the borrower violates a covenant after the balance sheet date but before the financial statements are issued), noncurrent classification is appropriate unless:

- A covenant was violated at the balance sheet date or would have been violated without a loan modification, and
- It is probable that the borrower will not be able to comply with a loan covenant on measurement dates within the next 12 months.

Further, borrowers that classify debt as noncurrent should disclose the negative effects of probable future noncompliance with debt covenants.

DISCUSSION

Resolving how to classify debt when a lender has waived the right to call the debt, but has retained the right to require compliance with debt covenants at interim dates, involves a determination of whether the lender's waiver of the right to call the debt can be considered a grace period as contemplated in ASC 470-10-45-12. Under that guidance in a grace period is a specified period of time during which a lender has waived the right to call the debt, giving the borrower time to cure the violation. For example, if an agreement provides that a borrower who has violated a covenant at the balance sheet date has a three-month grace period to cure a violation, the lender does not have the right to call the debt at the balance sheet date. The guidance in ASC 470-10-45-12 provides that the debt can continue to be classified as noncurrent if it is probable (as defined in ASC 450) at the balance sheet date that the borrower can comply with the covenant within the grace period, thus preventing the lender from calling the debt. If the concept of a grace period in ASC 470-10-45-12 is extended to this issue, it would be necessary to assess the probability that the borrower can comply with the covenant by the next measurement date.

The following five scenarios were discussed:
1. The debt covenants apply only after the balance sheet date, and it is probable that the borrower will not be able to comply with the covenants as required three months after the balance sheet date.
2. The borrower complies with the debt covenants at the balance sheet date, but it is probable that the borrower will fail the requirements three months after the balance sheet date.
3. The borrower complies with the debt covenants at the balance sheet date, but it is probable that the borrower will not meet a more restrictive covenant three months later at the next compliance date.
4. On the compliance date, which occurred three months before the balance sheet date, the borrower had complied with the loan covenants. Before the balance sheet date, the borrower negotiates with the lender to modify the loan agreement by eliminating a compliance requirement at the balance sheet date or by modifying a requirement that the borrower would otherwise fail. The borrower must, however, meet the same requirement or a more restrictive requirement three months later at the next compliance date, and it is probable that the borrower will fail the requirement at that time.
5. The borrower has violated the covenant at the balance sheet date, but obtained a waiver from the lender before issuing the financial statements. The borrower must, however, meet the same or a more restrictive covenant three months later. It is probable that the borrower will not meet the requirement at that date.

Applying the accounting guidance above to those five scenarios, it appears that the debt classification should be based on existing circumstances at the balance sheet date rather than based on expectations. Thus, the debt in scenarios 1, 2, and 3 can continue to be classified as noncurrent, because in each case the borrower complied with the loan covenants at the balance sheet date. In scenarios 4 and 5, however, in which the borrower failed to comply at the balance sheet date, current classification would be required even though the borrower negotiated a waiver in both cases. Noncurrent classification would, nevertheless, be permitted if the borrower expects to repay the debt with noncurrent assets and meets the conditions in ASC 470.

> **OBSERVATION:** Although it is not stated specifically, the presumption is that the waiver of the lender's right to call the debt while retaining the right to require compliance with the debt covenants is, in substance, a grace period, because the the probability test in in ASC 470-10-45-12 is applied.

ASC 470-10-S45-1, S99-4; ASC 810-10-S45-1 Classification of a Subsidiary's Loan Payable in Consolidated Balance Sheet When Subsidiary's and Parent's Fiscal Years Differ

BACKGROUND

Company A, which has a February 28, 20X5, year-end, issues consolidated financial statements that include its subsidiary, Company B, which has a December 31, 20X0, year-end. Company B has a material loan payable with a January 31, 20X6, maturity.

Under the guidance in ASC 810-10-45-12, a parent company is permitted to consolidate a subsidiary's financial statements if the difference between their year-ends is no more than three months.

ACCOUNTING ISSUE

How should Company A classify Company B's loan payable in its February 28, 20X5, consolidated financial statements?

SEC STAFF COMMENT

The SEC Observer stated that the SEC staff would expect registrants to classify the loan as current under those circumstances.

ASC 470-10-45-2, 50-3 Subjective Acceleration Clauses in Long-Term Debt Agreements

ACCOUNTING GUIDANCE

Question: Should long-term debt that includes a subjective acceleration clause be classified as a current liability?

Answer: The classification of debt as long-term or current depends on the circumstances. If a borrower has recurring losses or liquidity problems, long-term debt should be classified as current. Otherwise, only disclosure of the acceleration clause would be required. If the likelihood that the debt's due date will be accelerated is remote, neither reclassification nor disclosure would be required.

ASC 470-10-45-3 through 45-6 Balance Sheet Classification of Borrowings Outstanding under Revolving Credit Agreements That Include both a Subjective Acceleration Clause and a Lock-Box Arrangement

BACKGROUND

An entity has a revolving credit agreement with a note due in three years. The borrowing, which is collateralized, includes a subjective acceleration clause and is evidenced by a note signed on entering into the agreement. Under the agreement, the borrower is *required* to maintain a lock-box with the lender, to which the borrower's customers must remit their payments. The lender applies the outstanding payments to reduce the debt.

The effect of an acceleration clause on balance sheet classification for long-term obligations is determined based on the guidance in ASC 470-10-45-2 and 50-3. However, if a borrowing considered to be a short-term obligation has a subjective acceleration clause, it has been classified in the balance sheet as a current liability, under the guidance in ASC 470-10-05-4, 15-2 through 15-3, 45-5, 45-12A through 45-14, 45-16 through 45-21, 50-4, 55-14 through 55-32. The following accounting guidance does not apply if maintaining a lock-box is at a borrower's discretion.

The following guidance also addresses the balance sheet classification of a borrowing with a subjective acceleration clause and a "springing" lock-box arrangement under which amounts paid by a borrower's customers are deposited in the *borrower's* general bank account and are not used by the bank to reduce the debt without the lender's activation of a subjective acceleration clause. However, if a lender exercises the subjective acceleration clause, the lender has the right to redirect all of the lock-box's receipts to the lender's loan account and to apply them against the outstanding debt.

ACCOUNTING ISSUES

1. Should a borrowing under a revolving credit agreement be considered a short-term borrowing if it includes a subjective acceleration clause and requires the borrower to maintain a lock-box with the lender so that customers' payments are remitted directly to the lender and applied to reduce the outstanding debt?
2. Does the answer to question (1) apply to a revolving credit arrangement with a springing lock and a subjective acceleration clause?

ACCOUNTING GUIDANCE

A revolving credit agreement under which borrowings are due at the end of a specified period, such as at the end of three years, not when short-term notes under that agreement roll over, for example, every 90 days, may be classified as long-term debt.

The effect of a subjective acceleration clause on a revolving-credit agreement that is classified as long term debt should be determined based on the guidance in ASC 470-10-45-2. That is, the classification of a revolving credit agreement as long-term or current under those circumstances depends on the circumstances. If a borrower has recurring losses or liquidity problems, long-term debt should be reclassified as current. Otherwise, only disclosure of a subjective acceleration clause would be required. However, neither reclassification nor disclosure would be required if the likelihood that the lender will accelerate the debt's due date is remote.

Some lenders require borrowers with revolving credit agreements to maintain a lock box with the lender to which customers remit their payments. A revolving credit agreement should be classified as a short-term borrowing if it includes *both* a subjective acceleration clause and a requirement for the borrower to maintain a lock-box with the lender to which customers remit payments that are used to reduce the debt.

The balance sheet classification of debt that includes a subjective acceleration clause should be based on the guidance in ASC 470-10-05-4, 15-2 through 15-3, 45-5, 45-12A through 45-14, 45-16 through 45-21, 50-4, 55-14 through 55-32 or that in ASC 470-10-05-4, 15-2 through 15-3, 45-5, 45-12A through 45-14, 45-16 through 45-21, 50-4, and 55-14 through 55-32, which requires short-term debt with an acceleration clause to be classified as a current liability. An obligation may be classified as a long-term obligation, however, if it is refinanced after the balance sheet date on a long-term basis, thus meeting the conditions in ASC 470-10-45-14, based on an agreement other than a revolving credit agreement.

The term *lock-box arrangement* as it is used in this guidance applies to situations in which a debt agreement requires that a borrower's cash receipts be used in the ordinary course of business to repay the debt without the occurrence of another event. Therefore, because a borrower has no alternative but to use working capital to repay the obligation, under those circumstances a revolving credit agreement should be classified as a *short-term* obligation.

Debt in an arrangement with a springing lock box should be classified as a *long-term* obligation, because the customers' payments are *not* used automatically to reduce the debt unless another event has occurred. Because the debt is classified as a long-term obligation, the guidance in ASC 470-10-45-2 (discussed above) should be used to determine the effect of a subjective acceleration clause on the classification of the arrangement discussed.

DISCUSSION

The deciding factor in the first conclusion—the borrowing is a short-term obligation—was the fact that the agreement requires the borrower to maintain a lock-box, enabling the lender to use the proceeds to repay the borrowing and then lend the money back to the borrower under the revolving credit agreement, which results in a new borrowing. Those who supported this view argued that because of the lock-box requirement, the borrowing is repaid with current assets.

ASC 470-10-45-9 through 45-10 Classifying Demand Notes with Repayment Terms

BACKGROUND

In addition to specifying repayment terms, some loan agreements also may include language that enables a creditor to call a loan on demand. For example, an agreement may state that "the term note shall mature in monthly installments as set forth therein *or on demand, whichever is earlier,*" or "principal and interest shall be due *on demand, or if no demand is made,* in quarterly installments beginning on . . . ."

ACCOUNTING ISSUES

- How should a loan agreement that allows a creditor to demand payment at the creditor's discretion be classified in a classified balance sheet?
- What disclosures should be made about maturities of a long-term obligation that includes such a clause?

ACCOUNTING GUIDANCE

Debt under an agreement that enables the creditor to demand payment at the creditor's discretion should be classified as a current liability, in accordance with the guidance in ASC 470-10-45-10. A demand provision is not the same as a subjective acceleration clause, which is discussed in ASC 470-10-45-2; ASC 470-10-50-3.

DISCUSSION

The guidance in ASC 470-10-45-10 deals specifically with the classification of an obligation that by its terms can be called by a lender on demand within one year from the balance sheet date (or operating cycle, if longer). It provides that such an obligation should be classified as a current liability, even if the obligation is not expected to be liquidated during that period unless (*a*) the creditor has waived or lost the right to call the debt or (*b*) it is probable that the debtor will cure the violation during the grace period. This issue was addressed, because some had been treating the "due on demand clause" as a subjective acceleration clause under the guidance in ASC 470-10-45-2, 50-3.

ASC 470-10-55-1 Subjective Acceleration Clauses and Debt Classification

The FASB staff discussed its response to an inquiry as to whether the treatment of subjective acceleration clauses under the guidance in (a) ASC 470-10-45-2, 50-3 and that in (b) ASC 470-10-45-13 through 45-20 is inconsistent. Under the guidance in (b), short-term obligations can be classified as noncurrent if an entity has the ability and intent to refinance the obligation on a long-term basis. That ability can be demonstrated by an existing financial agreement. However, under that guidance, an agreement would only qualify if it has no subjective acceleration clauses that enable the lender to accelerate the debt. Conversely, under the guidance in (a), as long as acceleration of the due date is remote, there is no need to reclassify a noncurrent liability and disclose the existence of a subjective acceleration clause.

The FASB staff explained that the circumstances discussed in the two pronouncements differ. The guidance in (a) deals with loans made initially on a long-term basis; thus, continuing that classification requires a judgment about the likelihood that the loan's due date will be accelerated. Conversely, the guidance in (b) deals with circumstances under which a short-term obligation may be excluded from classification as a current liability by getting a new loan or refinancing the debt with long-term debt based on conditions at date refinancing date. The FASB staff justified the higher standard required in (b) because it deals with a refinancing of a short-term obligation as long-term rather than with the likelihood that existing long-term debt will be accelerated.

ASC 470-10-55-7 through 9 Classification by the Issuer of Redeemable Instruments That Are Subject to Remarketing Agreements

The FASB staff reported that it received inquiries about the balance sheet classification of debt instruments with the following characteristics:

- The debt has a long maturity (e.g., 30 to 40 years).
- The debt can be put to the issuer for redemption on short notice (within 7 to 30 days).
- The issuer has a remarketing agreement with an agent who agrees to resell redeemed bonds on a best efforts basis under which the agent is required to buy only securities that the agent can sell to the public. The issuer must pay off any debt the agent is unable to resell.
- A short-term letter of credit is used to secure the debt to protect the holder if the redeemed debt cannot be remarketed. The issuer of the redeemable debt must repay the issuer of the letter of credit for amounts drawn down on the same day.

According to the guidance in ASC 470-10-45-10, obligations that are due on demand within one year of the balance sheet should be classified as current liabilities, even if they will not be repaid during that period. The following two conditions are specified in ASC 470-10-45-14 for a short-term liability to be classified as noncurrent if a debtor intends to refinance the liability:

1. The liability will be refinanced on a long-term basis.
2. Either of the following two events occurs before the issuance of the balance sheet to confirm the debtor's ability to refinance short-debt debt on a long-term basis:
   a. A long-term obligation or equity securities have been issued.
   b. The debtor entered into a *financing agreement* based on readily determinable terms meeting all of the following conditions:
      (1) The agreement does not expire within one year (or the entity's operating cycle) from the balance sheet date and cannot be canceled by the lender or investor (obligations incurred cannot be called) during the period except if the debtor violates a provision with which compliance can be determined or measured objectively.
      (2) The debtor had not violated any of the provisions at the balance sheet date and there is no indication that any violations occurred after that date but before the balance sheet was issued. Alternatively, the lender has waived any violation that had occurred at the balance sheet date or before the balance sheet was issued.
      (3) The lender or investor is expected to be financially viable to honor the agreement.

The FASB Staff believes that, in accordance with the guidance in ASC 470-1-45-12 issuers should classify as current liabilities debt instruments that can be redeemed by the holder on demand or within one year, even if a best efforts remarketing agreement exists. In that situation, classification as a long-term liability would be acceptable only if a letter-of-credit arrangement meets the requirements in ASC 470-10-45-14 for a financing agreement, as discussed above.

ASC 470-20: DEBT WITH CONVERSION AND OTHER OPTIONS

ASC 470-20-05-1, 05-12A through 12C, 15-2, 25-1, 25-20A, 30-26A, 35-11A, 45-2A, 50-2A through 50-2C, 65-3; ASC 260-10-45-70B Accounting for Own-Share Lending Arrangements in Contemplation of Convertible Debt Issuance

BACKGROUND

Under certain market conditions, entities that need financing find it easier to place convertible debt rather than straight debt; issuing such debt may also be more attractive to the issuer because it has a lower interest rate. Investors that purchase convertible debt frequently use a hedging technique called "delta neutral" hedging to hedge changes in the value of an option to buy shares, such as the one embedded in convertible debt, with a "short" position on the shares.

By using a hedge, an investor offsets gains on the conversion option if the price of the stock increases and offsets losses on the conversion option if the stock's price decreases.

Many issuers of convertible debt have also been entering into separate arrangements with the investment bank that underwrites their offering under which the entity issues legally outstanding shares of its own common stock and lends those shares to the investment bank in exchange for a loan processing fee that usually equals the par value of the common stock. Even though the holders of the shares are legally entitled to receive dividends and to vote, such arrangements require that during the period that the shares are loaned to the investment bank, it must reimburse the issuer for dividends paid on the shares even if those shares have been sold in the market. In addition, as long as the investment bank is the owner of record, it is precluded from voting on matters submitted to the issuer's shareholders for a vote. Some agreements include a provision requiring the investment bank to post collateral during the loan term. However, issuers usually do not enforce that requirement.

Investment banks use those shares to enter into equity derivative contracts, such as options, forwards, and total return swaps, on their own behalf with investors in the issuers' convertible debt instruments. Those equity derivative contracts enable the investors to hedge the long position in the issuer's stock that they hold through the convertible debt's embedded conversion option. The investment bank may also sell the loaned shares in equity markets.

Investment banks enter into share loan arrangements, which create a short position, to hedge their own market risk related to their long position as a result of the equity derivative contracts entered into with the investors. By borrowing issuers' shares and the sale of derivatives to investors, investment banks eliminate their own exposure to changes in the issuers' stock prices and create a short position that hedges the investors' conversion option in the convertible debt instruments.

When the convertible debt matures, the investment bank generally must return the loaned shares to the issuer without additional consideration. An issuer may be entitled to a cash payment for the fair value of its common stock if an investment bank does not return the loaned shares.

SCOPE

This guidance applies to an equity-classified share-lending arrangement on an entity's own shares that is executed in contemplation of a convertible debt offering or other financing.

ACCOUNTING GUIDANCE

- *Measurement.* An entity that plans to issue convertible debt instruments or other financing should: (1) measure a share-lending arrangement of its own shares at the fair value of the shares at the date of issuance; and (2) recognize the arrangement in its financial statements as an issuance cost with an offset to additional paid-in capital.
- *Subsequent measurement.* If the default of a counterparty to a share-lending arrangement becomes probable, the issuer of the share-lending arrange-

ment should recognize an expense that equals the then fair value of the unreturned shares, net of the fair value of probable recoveries, with an offset to additional paid-in capital. An issuer of a share-lending arrangement should remeasure the fair value of unreturned shares each reporting period through earnings until consideration on the arrangement payable by the counterparty becomes fixed. Subsequent changes in the amount of probable recoveries also should be recognized in earnings.

- *Earnings per share presentation.* Loaned shares should be excluded from the basic and diluted earnings-per-share calculations unless there is a default of the share-lending arrangement. In that case, the loaned shares would be included in the calculation of basic and diluted earnings per share. If dividends on the loaned shares are not reimbursed to the entity, amounts, if any, including contractual (accumulated) dividends and participation rights in undistributed earnings that may be attributed to the loaned shares should be deducted in the computation of income available to common shareholders, as required in the "two-class" method discussed in ASC 260-10-45-60B.

DISCLOSURE

The following disclosures should be made by entities that enter into a share-lending arrangement on their own shares in contemplation of a convertible debt offering or other financing arrangement. The information should be disclosed in the interim and annual financial statements, in any period in which a share-lending arrangement is outstanding:

- A description of outstanding share-lending arrangements, if any, on an entity's own stock and all significant terms of such arrangements, including the number of shares, the term, the circumstances under which cash settlement would be required, and requirements, if any, for the counterparty to provide collateral.
- The entity's reason for entering into a share-lending arrangement.
- The fair value of outstanding loaned shares as of the balance sheet date.
- How the share-lending arrangement is treated in the earnings per share calculation.
- The unamortized amount and classification of issuance costs related to the share-lending arrangement at the balance sheet date.
- The amount of interest cost recognized in conjunction with the amortization of the issuance costs related to the share-lending arrangement for the reporting period.
- The amounts of dividends, if any, paid for loaned shares that will not be reimbursed.

The disclosures required ASC 470-10-50-5; ASC 505-10-15-1, 50-3 through 50-5, 50-11 apply to entities that enter into share lending arrangements on their own shares in contemplation of a convertible debt offering or other financing and should disclose:

- The amount of expense reported in the income statement that is related to a default in the period the entity concludes that it is probable that a counterparty to its share-lending arrangement will default.
- In any subsequent period, material changes, if any, in the amount of expense as a result of changes in the fair value of the entity's shares or the probable recoveries.
- If a default is probable but has not yet occurred, the number of shares related to a share-lending arrangement that will be shown in basic and diluted earnings per share when the counterparty's default occurs.

ASC 470-20-05-7 through 05-8, 25-4 through 25-6, 30-3, 30-6, 30-8, 30-10 through 30-11, 30-15, 35-2, 35-7, 40-2 through 40-3, 55-30 through 55-33, 55-35 through 55-38, 55-40 through 55-43, 55-45 through 50-48, 55-50 through 55-54A, 55-56 through 55-60A, 55-62 through 55-66, 55-69; ASC 505-10-50-8 Accounting for Convertible Securities with Beneficial Conversion Features or Contingently Adjustable Conversion Ratios

BACKGROUND

This Issue was addressed because some entities were issuing convertible debt securities and convertible preferred stock with a nondetachable conversion feature that are in-the-money at the commitment date a beneficial conversion feature), which is the date on which there is an agreement on the terms of the transaction and an investor has committed to purchase the convertible securities based on those terms. The securities may be converted into common stock at a conversion rate that is fixed on the commitment date or at a fixed discount from the common stock's market price at the conversion date, whichever is lower. The conversion price of some convertible securities may vary based on future events—for example, subsequent financing at a lower price than the original conversion price, the company's liquidation or a change of control, or an initial public offering that has a lower price per share than the agreed upon amount.

This guidance applies to convertible debt securities with beneficial conversion features that must be settled in stock and convertible shares with beneficial conversion features that allow an issuer to choose whether to satisfy the obligation in stock or in cash. It also applies to instruments in which the beneficial conversion features are convertible into more than one instrument, such as convertible preferred stock that can be converted into common stock and detachable warrants. The guidance does *not* apply to instruments under the scope of ASC 470-20-10-1 through 10-2, 15-2, 15-4 through 15-6, 25-21 through 25-27, 30-27 through 30-31, 35-12 through 35-20, 40-19 through 40-26, 45-3, 50-3 through 50-6, 55-70 through 55-82, 65-1; ASC 815-15-55-76A; ASC 825-10-15-5.

ACCOUNTING ISSUES

1. Should a beneficial conversion feature embedded in a convertible security be valued separately at the commitment date?
2. If an embedded beneficial conversion feature should be valued separately, how should it be recognized and measured?
3. How should convertible securities issued with conversion ratios that are adjusted as a result of the occurrence of future events be accounted for?

ACCOUNTING GUIDANCE

Beneficial conversion features embedded in convertible securities should be valued *separately* at the commitment date. (See "Effect of ASC 815," below.)

> **OBSERVATION:** See the guidance on Issue 5 in ASC 470-20-25-8 through 25-9, 25-20, 30-1, 30-5, 30-7, 30-9 through 30-10, 30-12 through 30-13, 30-16 through 30-21, 35-1, 35-4, 35-7 through 35-10, 40-1, 40-4, 45-1, 55-11 through 55-12, 55-14 through 55-17, 55-19 through 55-21, 55-23 through 55-24, 55-26 through 55-27; ASC 505-10-50-7; ASC 260-10-50-1, Application of Issue No. 98-5 to Certain Convertible Instruments, below for a revised definition of *a commitment date*

1. The *commitment* date is defined here as the date on which an entity has reached an agreement with an unrelated party that is binding on both parties and is usually legally enforceable. The agreement has the following two features:

    - It includes specific information about all significant terms, including the quantity to be exchanged, a fixed price, and the timing of the transaction. The price may be stated as a specific amount of an entity's functional currency or of a foreign currency. In addition, a specified interest rate or specified effective yield may be stated.

    - It includes a disincentive for nonperformance that is large enough to make performance probable. For the purpose of applying the definition of a firm commitment, the existence of statutory rights in the legal jurisdiction governing the agreement, such as remedies for default that equal the damages suffered by the counterparty to the agreement, would be a sufficiently large disincentive for nonperformance that makes performance probable.

    It was noted that the commitment date of an agreement that includes subjective provisions permitting either party to rescind its commitment to consummate the transaction should *not* occur until the provisions expire or the convertible instrument is issued, whichever occurs first. For example, an investor may be allowed to rescind its commitment to purchase a convertible instrument if a material adverse change occurs in the issuer's operations or financial condition, or the commitment is conditional on customary due diligence or shareholder approval.

    If the securities are purchased by several investors, such as a group of lenders that participate in a syndicate, the commitment date is the latest commitment date for the group or the issuance date for each individual security, whichever comes first.

2. Embedded beneficial conversion features should be *recognized* and *measured* as follows:

    a. Allocate a portion of the proceeds equal to the intrinsic value of the embedded beneficial conversion feature to additional paid-in capital at the commitment date. The intrinsic value is calculated as the difference between the *conversion price* and the *fair value* of the common stock or other securities into which the security can be converted multiplied by the *number* of shares into which the security can be converted. Fair value is determined at the market price, if available, or at the best estimate of fair value, without adjustments for transferability restrictions, large block factors, avoided underwriter's fees, or time value discounts. To allocate an amount to the beneficial conversion feature of convertible securities issued with detachable warrants or with another security, such as common stock, the proceeds are first allocated between the convertible instruments and the detachable warrants based on the relative fair value method in ASC 470-20-05-2 through 05-6, 25-2 through 25-3, 25-10 through 25-13, 30-1 through 30-2; ASC 505-10-60-3.

b. If the *intrinsic value* of the beneficial conversion feature is *greater* than the proceeds from the sale of the convertible instrument, the discount assigned to the beneficial conversion feature should *not* exceed the amount of the proceeds allocated to the convertible instrument. (This guidance has been partially nullified by the guidance in ASC 815.)

A discount as a result of the recognition of a beneficial conversion option of a convertible instrument that has a stated redemption date should be amortized from the issuance date to the convertible instrument's stated redemption date regardless of when the instrument's earliest conversion date occurs. However, a discount as a result of the recognition of a beneficial conversion option of a convertible instrument with *no* stated redemption date, such as perpetual preferred stock, should be amortized from the issuance date to the earliest conversion date. (Updated based on the guidance on issue 6 of ASC 470-20-25-8 through 25-9, 25-20, 30-1, 30-5, 30-7, 30-9 through 30-10, 30-12 through 30-13, 30-16 through 30-21, 35-1, 35-4, 35-7 through 35-10, 40-1, 40-4, 45-1, 55-11 through 55-12, 55-14 through 55-17, 55-19 through 55-21, 55-23 through 55-24, 55-26 through 55-27; ASC 505-10-50-7; ASC 260-10-50-1 Application of Issue No. 98-5 to Certain Convertible Securities. Also see the Subsequent Development section.) SEC registrants should account for other discounts on perpetual preferred stock with no stated redemption date but with the requirement that it be redeemed upon the occurrence of a future event outside the issuer's control (such as a change in control) based on the guidance in ASC 480-10-S99.

The issuer should disclose the terms of the transaction in the notes to the financial statements in accordance with the guidance in ASC 470-10-50-5; ASC 505-10-15-1, 50-3 through 50-5, 50-11. That disclosure also should include information about the amount in excess of the instruments' total fair value to be received by the holder at conversion over the proceeds received by the issuer and the amortization period of the discount.

A discount on convertible *preferred* securities resulting from the allocation of proceeds to a beneficial conversion feature is analogous to a *dividend*, which should be recognized as a return to the preferred shareholders by the effective yield method. (Updated based on the guidance on issue 6 of ASC 470-20-25-8 through 25-9, 25-20, 30-1, 30-5, 30-7, 30-9 through 30-10, 30-12 through 30-13, 30-16 through 30-21, 35-1, 35-4, 35-7 through 35-10, 40-1, 40-4, 45-1, 55-11 through 55-12, 55-14 through 55-17, 55-19 through 55-21, 55-23 through 55-24, 55-26 through 55-27; ASC 505-10-50-7; ASC 260-10-50-1, Application of Issue No. 98-5 to Certain Convertible Securities. Also see the Subsequent Development section.) A discount on convertible *debt* securities as a result of the allocation of proceeds to the beneficial conversion feature should be recognized as *interest expense* using the effective yield method. (Updated based on the guidance on issue 6 of ASC 470-20-25-8 through 25-9, 25-20, 30-1, 30-5, 30-7, 30-9 through 30-10, 30-12 through 30-13, 30-16 through 30-21, 35-1, 35-4, 35-7 through 35-10, 40-1, 40-4, 45-1, 55-11 through 55-12, 55-14 through 55-17, 55-19 through 55-21, 55-23 through 55-24, 55-26 through 55-27; ASC 505-10-50-7; ASC 260-10-50-1 Application of Issue No. 98-5 to Certain Convertible Instruments. See discussion of the effect of that guidance.)

c. The basic accounting model is modified if an instrument has a multiple-step discount to the market price that increases over time (e.g., 10% at three months, 15% at six months, 20% at nine months, and 25% at one year). The beneficial conversion feature's intrinsic value should be calculated based on the conversion terms that are most beneficial to an *investor*. The resulting discount is amortized over the shortest period during which an investor can recognize that return (e.g., in the above example, 25% over one year).

A discount on a convertible instrument with a stated redemption date should be amortized from the instrument's issuance date to its stated redemption date, regardless of when the earliest conversion date occurs. In the example above, the discount would be 25% and the amortization period would be from the issuance date to the redemption date. (Updated based on the guidance in Issue 6 of ASC 470-20-25-8 through 25-9, 25-20, 30-1, 30-5, 30-7, 30-9 through 30-10, 30-12 through 30-13, 30-16 through 30-21, 35-1, 35-4, 35-7 through 35-10, 40-1, 40-4, 45-1, 55-11 through 55-12, 55-14 through 55-17, 55-19 through 55-21, 55-23 through 55-24, 55-26 through 55-27; ASC 505-10-50-7; ASC 260-10-50-1, Application of Issue No. 98-5 to Certain Convertible Instruments. Also see the Subsequent Development section.)

A discount on a convertible instrument that has *no* stated redemption date should be amortized over the minimum period in which the investor can recognize that return. In the example above, the discount would be 25% and the amortization period would be one year. (Updated based on the guidance in issue 6 of ASC 470-20-25-8 through 25-9, 25-20, 30-1, 30-5, 30-7, 30-9 through 30-10, 30-12 through 30-13, 30-16 through 30-21, 35-1, 35-4, 35-7 through 35-10, 40-1, 40-4, 45-1, 55-11 through 55-12, 55-14 through 55-17, 55-19 through 55-21, 55-23 through 55-24, 55-26 through 55-27; ASC 505-10-50-7; ASC 260-10-50-1 (Application of Issue No. 98-5 to Certain Convertible Instruments). Also see the Subsequent Development section.) However, the amortized portion of the discount may have to be adjusted so that, at any point in time, the discount at least equals the amount the investor could obtain if the security were converted at that date. In the example above, a discount of at least 10% should have been recognized at the end of three months. Under this method, the cumulative amortization should equal the *greater of* (a) the amount obtained by using the effective yield method based on the conversion terms most beneficial to an investor or (b) the amount of discount that an investor can realize at that interim date.

If the instrument is converted *before* the discount has been fully amortized, the unamortized portion of the discount at the conversion date should be recognized immediately as interest expense or as a dividend, whichever is appropriate. If the remaining amount of the unamortized discount is recognize as an expense because the convertible instrument was in the form of debt, that expense should *not* be classified as extraordinary. (Updated based on the guidance in issue 6 of ASC 470-20-25-8 through 25-9, 25-20, 30-1, 30-5, 30-7, 30-9 through 30-10, 30-12 through 30-13, 30-16 through 30-21, 35-1, 35-4, 35-7 through 35-10, 40-1, 40-4, 45-1, 55-11 through 55-12, 55-14 through 55-17, 55-19 through 55-21, 55-23 through 55-24, 55-26 through 55-27; ASC 505-10-50-7; ASC 260-10-50-1 (Application of Issue No. 98-5 to Certain Convertible Instruments). Also see the Subsequent Development section.) However, no adjustment should be made to amounts previously amortized if the amortized discount is greater than the amount realized by the holder because the instrument was converted at an earlier date. The portion of the discount already amortized need not be adjusted, however, if that amount exceeds the amount the holder realized on an early conversion.

d. If an instrument with an embedded beneficial conversion feature is extinguished before its conversion, a portion of the price to reacquire the security includes a repurchase of the beneficial conversion feature. The amount of the price that is allocated to the beneficial conversion feature should be measured based on the intrinsic value of the beneficial conversion feature at the date of extinguishment. An excess, if any, is allocated to the convertible security. A gain or loss on the extinguishment of *debt* should be classified in accordance with the guidance in ASC 470-50-45-1 through 45-2. A gain or loss on a *preferred security* should be accounted for based on the guidance in ASC 260-10-S99-2 and ASC 260-10-S99-3.

The guidance in ASC 470-50 and in ASC 470-20-05-9, 35-11, 40-11; ASC 835-10-60-10, which provide that a convertible debt's carrying amount, including an unamortized premium or discount, if any, should be credited to equity on conversion, continues to apply to convertible debt that does not include a beneficial conversion option.

> **OBSERVATION:** Although ASC 470-50-45-1 supersedes FAS-4, which required that gains and losses on extinguishments of debt be classified as extraordinary items, that guidance does *not* prohibit using that classification for extinguished debt that meets the criteria in ASC 225-20-45-10 through 45-16, 45-1 through 45-6, 45-8, 15-2, 55-1 through 55-2; 50-2 through 50-3; ASC 830-10-45-19 (APB-30).

3. A *contingent* beneficial conversion feature of a security that (*a*) becomes convertible only if a future event not under the holder's control occurs and (*b*) is convertible from inception with conversion terms that change if a future event occurs is *measured* at the stock price on the commitment date, but *recognized* in earnings only when the contingency is *resolved*.

EFFECT OF ASC 815

The guidance in ASC 815 partially nullifies the consensus Issue 1. An issuer and a holder of a security with an embedded conversion feature should analyze the terms of the entire embedded conversion feature to determine whether the guidance in ASC 815-15-25-1 from the host contract for separation and accounting of embedded derivatives applies. Although instruments that meet the criteria under ASC 815-10-15-74 may not be considered derivatives for the purpose of the issuer's accounting and, therefore, would be exempted from the requirements in ASC 815, this exemption does not apply to a holder's accounting for a security that is convertible into an issuer's stock. In addition, a holder will generally find that the conversion feature can be separated from the instrument if it meets the requirement for separation in ASC 815-15-25-1—that is, its economic characteristics and risks are not clearly and closely related to those of the host contract.

Under the guidance in ASC 815-15-25-4 through 25-5, which amends the guidance in ASC 815 entities are permitted to measure at fair value certain hybrid financial instruments with embedded derivatives that otherwise would have to be separated. A hybrid financial instrument that is accounted for entirely at fair value cannot be used as a hedging instrument in a hedging relationship under the guidance in ASC 815. During the discussion of this Issue, some stated that an issuer of such securities would usually be unable to make a reliable measurement of the fair value of an embedded conversion feature. Similarly, that also would apply to the holder of such securities. Under the guidance in ASC 815-15-25-52, however, it would be unusual for an entity to conclude that it cannot reliably separate an embedded derivative from its host contract.

EFFECT OF ASC 480

ASC 480-10-05-1 through 05-6, 10-1, 15-3 through 15-5, 15-7 through 15-10, 25-1 through 25-2, 25-4 through 25-15, 30-1 through 30-7, 35-3 through 35-5, 45-1 through 45-4, 50-1 through 50-4, 55-1 through 55-12, 55-14 through 55-28, 55-34 through 55-41, 55-64; ASC 835-10-60-13; ASC 260-10-45-70A establishes classification and measurement guidance for certain financial instruments that have the characteristics of both liabilities and equity. An issuer is required to classify a financial instrument under the scope of that guidance as a liability or as an asset in some circumstances.

SUBSEQUENT DEVELOPMENT

If the commitment date defined under this guidance did not occur before November 16, 2000, the guidance in ASC 470-20-25-8 through 25-9, 25-20, 30-1, 30-5, 30-7, 30-9 through 30-10, 30-12 through 30-13, 30-16 through 30-21, 35-1, 35-4, 35-7 through 35-10, 40-1, 40-4, 45-1, 55-11 through 55-12, 55-14 through 55-17, 55-19 through 55-21, 55-23 through 55-24, 55-26 through 55-27; ASC 505-10-50-7. ASC 260-10-50-1 (Formerly Issue 00-27, Application of Issue 98-5 to Certain Convertible Instruments) (discussed below) should be applied to all instruments issued after that date. See that guidance for the SEC Observer's comments, which provide specific guidance for SEC registrants.

Illustrations of the Accounting for a Beneficial Conversion Feature of a Convertible Security

Example 1—Instruments that are convertible at issuance

A. *Fixed dollar conversion terms*—Convertible debt issued at a $600,000 face value is convertible at issuance into the issuer's common stock at $20 a share. The redemption date is on the fifth anniversary of issuance. The fair value of each share is $25 on the commitment date. The accounting for such instruments is as follows:

1. Calculate the number of shares into which the debt will be converted at the conversion price: $600,000/$20 = 30,000 shares.

2. Calculate the intrinsic value of the beneficial conversion feature at the commitment date: fair value of $25 − $20 conversion price at the commitment date = $5 × 30,000 shares = $150,000.

3. The debt is recognized at $600,000, with the $150,000 intrinsic value of the debt credited to additional paid-in capital.

4. The debt discount should be amortized over a period of five years from the issuance date to the redemption date, because the debt has a stated redemption on the fifth anniversary of the issuance date.

5. Entry at issuance date:

Cash	$600,000	
Debt discount	150,000	
Debt		$600,000
Additional paid-in capital		150,000

(Examples B and C were deleted because they were superseded by later guidance.)

ASC 470—Debt

D. *Instrument with fixed terms that change when a future event occurs*—Convertible debt issued at a $600,000 face value is convertible at issuance and redeemable on the fifth anniversary of issuance. The instrument is convertible into the issuer's common stock at $24, 80% of the stock's $30 fair value at the commitment date. However, if the company has an IPO, the convertible debt can be converted at 80% of the fair value of the IPO price or the fair value on the commitment date, whichever is less. Such debt instruments should be accounted for as follows:

1. The instrument includes a "basic" beneficial conversion feature that does not depend at issuance on the occurrence of a future event; its intrinsic value is calculated as follows: (600,000/24) = 25,000 × (30−24) = $150,000, which is calculated at the commitment date and recognized at the issuance date. The debt discount (equal to the intrinsic value of the beneficial conversion feature) should be amortized over a five year period from the issuance date to the stated redemption date. (For guidance on recognition and measurement of the contingent beneficial conversion feature, see the guidance on issues 3 and 7 of ASC 470-20-25-8 through 25-9, 25-20, 30-1, 30-5, 30-7, 30-9 through 30-10, 30-12 through 30-13, 30-16 through 30-21, 35-1, 35-4, 35-7 through 35-10, 40-1, 40-4, 45-1, 55-11 through 55-12, 55-14 through 55-17, 55-19 through 55-21, 55-23 through 55-24, 55-26 through 55-27; ASC 505-10-50-7. ASC 260-10-50-1, Application of Issue No. 98-5 to Certain Convertible Instruments.)

2. The accounting entry at issuance date:

Cash	$600,000	
Debt discount	150,000	
Debt		$600,000
Additional Paid-in Capital		150,000

Under the terms of the convertible debt instrument, a calculation of the number of shares that would be received on conversion if an IPO occurs is not permitted at the commitment date.

E. *Instrument with variable terms that depend on the occurrence of a future event*—Convertible debt issued at $600,000 face value is redeemable on the fifth anniversary of the issuance date. The instrument is convertible at issuance into the issuer's common stock at 80% of the $30 stock price at the commitment date. However, if the price of each common share has increased by at least 20% one year after an IPO, the debt can be converted at 60% of the stock price. Such instruments should be accounted for as follows:

1. The intrinsic value of the beneficial conversion feature is measured based on the terms at issuance. Calculated at the commitment date, it equals $150,000 (calculated in the same manner as in example D above) and is recognized at issuance. The debt discount is amortized over the five-year redemption period.

2. The accounting entry is the same as the one in example D above.

3. Under the terms of the convertible debt instrument, a calculation of the number of shares that would be received on conversion if an IPO occurs is not permitted at the commitment date. (For guidance on recognition and measurement of the contingent beneficial conversion feature, see the guidance on issues 3 and 7 of ASC 470-20-25-8

through 25-9, 25-20, 30-1, 30-5, 30-7, 30-9 through 30-10, 30-12 through 30-13, 30-16 through 30-21, 35-1, 35-4, 35-7 through 35-10, 40-1, 40-4, 45-1, 55-11 through 55-12, 55-14 through 55-17, 55-19 through 55-21, 55-23 through 55-24, 55-26 through 55-27; ASC 505-10-50-7; ASC 260-10-50-1 Application of Issue No. 98-5 to Certain Convertible Instruments)

(Example F has been superseded by subsequent guidance.)

Example 2—Instruments that are *not* convertible at issuance

A. *Fixed dollar conversion terms*—(This Example, formerly Example A, has been modified as a result of the guidance in ASC 470-20-25-8 through 25-9, 25-20, 30-1, 30-5, 30-7, 30-9 through 30-10, 30-12 through 30-13, 30-16 through 30-21, 35-1, 35-4, 35-7 through 35-10, 40-1, 40-4, 45-1, 55-11 through 55-12, 55-14 through 55-17, 55-19 through 55-21, 55-23 through 55-24, 55-26 through 55-27; ASC 505-10-50-7; ASC 260-10-50-1, Application of Issue No. 98-5 to Certain Convertible Instruments.)

Convertible debt with a $600,000 face value redeemable on the fifth anniversary of issuance is convertible any time after one year into the issuer's common stock at $24 per share. The fair value of each share is $30 at the commitment date. The accounting for such instruments is as follows:

1. Calculate the intrinsic value of the beneficial conversion feature as in the previous examples.
2. A portion of the proceeds from the issuance of the convertible debt, equal to the intrinsic value is allocated to additional paid-in capital.
3. The debt discount should be amortized over the five-year redemption period.
4. The accounting entry is the same as above.

(Example B has been superseded by subsequent guidance.)

Example 3—Extinguishment of convertible debt with a beneficial conversion feature before conversion

(This example has been modified as a result of the guidance in ASC 470-20-25-8 through 25-9, 25-20, 30-1, 30-5, 30-7, 30-9 through 30-10, 30-12 through 30-13, 30-16 through 30-21, 35-1, 35-4, 35-7 through 35-10, 40-1, 40-4, 45-1, 55-11 through 55-12, 55-14 through 55-17, 55-19 through 55-21, 55-23 through 55-24, 55-26 through 55-27; ASC 505-10-50-7; ASC 260-10-50-1, Application of Issue No. 98-5 to Certain Convertible Instruments.)

Proceeds from the issuance of zero coupon debt	$600,000
The intrinsic value of the beneficial conversion feature	$540,000

The issuer recognizes $540,000 at the commitment date as a discount on the debt. The offsetting entry is a credit to additional paid-in capital. The remaining $60,000 is recognized as debt and is accreted to its full face value of $600,000 over the five-year redemption period of the debt. The debt is extinguished one year after the issuance date.

Facts at the extinguishment date:

Reacquisition price	$700,000
Intrinsic value of beneficial conversion feature	432,000
Carrying value of debt	140,000

At the extinguishment date, the proceeds from the extinguishment first should be allocated to the beneficial conversion feature ($432,000) with the remainder allocated to the extinguishment of the convertible debt security.

The accounting entry to record the extinguishment is as follows:

*Debt	$140,000	
Additional paid-in capital	432,000	
Loss on extinguishment	128,000	
Cash		$700,000

* The net carrying amount of the debt one year after issuance is calculated using the effective interest method to amortize the debt discount over the five-year redemption period.

OBSERVATION: See ASC 505, Equity, for a discussion of ASC 505-10-15-2, 50-6, 50-8A, 50-9 through 50-10; ASC 470-10-60-2, Disclosure of Information about Capital Structure Relating to Contingently Convertible Securities).

ASC 470-20-05-9, 35-11, 40-11; ASC 835-10-60-10 Accrued Interest upon Conversion of Convertible Debt

BACKGROUND

The conversion terms of some convertible debt instruments provide that former debt holders will forfeit interest accrued but unpaid at the conversion date if they convert zero coupon bonds, which do not pay interest, or other convertible debt securities into the issuer's equity securities between interest payment dates.

ACCOUNTING ISSUES

1. Should interest expense be accrued or imputed on such debt instruments to the date of conversion when it is forfeited?
2. If interest should be accrued to the date of conversion, how should it be recognized when the debt is converted into common stock?

ACCOUNTING GUIDANCE

1. Accrue or impute interest to the date the debt instrument is converted to equity securities.
2. Interest accrued from the last payment date, if applicable, to the date of conversion should be charged to interest expense and credited to capital as part of the cost of securities issued, net of related income tax effects, the same as the converted debt principal and unamortized issue discount or premium on the debt, if any.

ASC 470-20-05-11; 40-4A through 40-10; 55-68 Accounting for the Conversion of an Instrument That Becomes Convertible upon the Issuer's Exercise of a Call Option

BACKGROUND

Contingently convertible debt instruments (CoCos), which were discussed in ASC 260-10-45-43 through 45-44, 55-78 through 55-79, 55-81 through 55-82, 55-84 through 55-84B (, The Effect of Contingently Convertible Instruments on Diluted

Earnings per Share), are convertible debt instruments that include a contingent feature and generally are convertible into an issuer's common shares after the stock price of the issuer's common stock exceeds a predetermined amount, known as a market price trigger, for a specified period of time. A CoCo's conversion price usually is higher than the underlying stock's market price when the CoCo is issued and its market price trigger usually is higher than the conversion price.

Since the issuance of the guidance in ASC 260-10-45-43 through 45-44, 55-78 through 55-79, 55-81 through 55-82, 55-84 through 55-84B, some have asked whether CoCos also may include embedded call options under which issuers can call such debt instruments when they would not be otherwise convertible. Holders would have the option to receive cash for the call price or a specified number of shares of the issuer's stock. For example, a CoCo with a $1,000 par amount matures on September 30, 2012. The holder can convert the debt to the issuer's securities if the price of the debt security exceeds $1,500. The issuer has the option to call the debt between 2008 and the debt's maturity date. The holder may choose to receive cash for the call amount or a fixed number of shares, regardless of whether the price trigger of $1,500 has been met.

SCOPE

This guidance applies only to the accounting for the issuance of equity securities to settle a debt instrument that has become convertible because the issuer has exercised a call option included in the original terms of the debt instrument and that otherwise would *not* have been convertible at the conversion date. Conversions based on terms that include changes made by a debtor to conversion privileges under the terms of the debt at issuance in order to encourage conversion are accounted for according to the guidance in ASC 470-20-05-10, 40-13 through 40-17, 45-2, 55-2 through 55-9, and guidance for modifications to embedded conversion options is discussed in ASC 470-50-40-12, 40-15 through 40-16 (Debtor's Accounting for a Modification (or exchange) of Convertible Debt). This guidance does *not* apply to convertible debt instruments accounted for under the scope of ASC 470-20-10-1 through 10-2, 15-2, 15-4 through 15-6, 25-21 through 25-27, 30-27 through 30-31, 35-12 through 35-20, 40-19 through 40-26, 45-3, 50-3 through 50-6, 55-70 through 55-82, 65-1; ASC 815-15-55-76A; ASC 825-10-15-5 (Accounting for Convertible Debt Instruments That May Be Settled in Cash upon Conversion (Including Partial Cash Settlement)).

ACCOUNTING ISSUE

How should an issuer account for the conversion of a debt instrument that becomes convertible when the issuer exercises its call option under the original terms of the debt instrument?

ACCOUNTING GUIDANCE

- Equity securities issued on the conversion of a debt instrument that include a *substantive* conversion feature at the issuance date should be accounted for as a *conversion* if the debt instrument becomes convertible because the issuer has exercised a call option based on the debt instrument's original conversion terms. *No* gain or loss should be recognized on the issuance of equity securities to settle the debt instrument.

- Equity securities issued on the conversion of a debt instrument that does *not* include a *substantive* conversion feature at the issuance date should be accounted for as a *debt extinguishment* if the debt instrument becomes convertible because the issuer has exercised a call option based on the debt instrument's original conversion terms. In that case, the equity securities' fair value should be considered a part of the price of reacquiring the debt.

- A convertible debt instrument's issuance date is its *commitment* date, as defined in Issue 4 of ASC 470-20-25-8 through 25-9, 25-20, 30-1, 30-5, 30-7, 30-9 through 30-10, 30-12 through 30-13, 30-16 through 30-21, 35-1, 35-4, 35-7 through 35-10, 40-1, 40-4, 45-1, 55-11 through 55-12, 55-14 through 55-17, 55-19 through 55-21, 55-23 through 55-24, 55-26 through 55-27; ASC 505-10-50-7; ASC 260-10-50-1 (Application of EITF Issue 98-5, "Accounting for Convertible Securities with Beneficial Conversion Features or Contingently Adjustable Conversion Ratios," to Certain Convertible Instruments). The determination as to whether a conversion feature is substantive should be based on the assumptions, considerations, and information about the marketplace available as of the issuance date, although that determination may be made *after* the issuance date.

The guidance above should be applied as follows:

- A conversion feature is considered to be *substantive* if it is at least *reasonably possible*, as defined in ASC 450, that the conversion feature will be exercisable in the future without the issuer's exercise of its call option. The holder's intent need not be evaluated to make such a determination.

- It was noted that for the purpose of this guidance, a conversion feature would *not* be considered to be substantive if the debt instrument's conversion price at issuance is so high that it would *not* be regarded at least *reasonably possible* at the date of issuance that a conversion would occur—even if the instrument includes a feature that would permit conversion *before* the maturity date. Further, a debt instrument does *not* include a substantive conversion feature if a conversion can only occur if the issuer exercises its call option.

- The determination as to whether a debt instrument's conversion feature is *substantive* should be based solely on assumptions, considerations, and marketplace information that were available as of the instrument's *issuance* date, even though that determination may be made *after* the debt instrument has been issued.

The following guidance, which is *not* all inclusive, may be useful in determining whether a conversion feature is substantive—that is, that it is at least reasonably possible that the conversion feature will exercised in the future:

- Compare the fair value of the conversion feature to the fair value of the debt instrument.
- Compare the effective annual interest rate based on the terms of the debt instrument to the estimated effective annual rate that an issuer estimates it could get on a similar nonconvertible debt instrument with an equivalent expected term and credit risk.
- Compare the fair value of the debt instrument to the fair value of an identical convertible instrument that has a *noncontingent* conversion option to determine the effect of a contingency. Similarity in the fair value of the two instruments may indicate that the conversion feature is substantive. To use this approach, it must be clear that the conversion feature, without considering the contingencies, is substantive.
- Consider the nature of the conditions required for the instrument to become convertible by a qualitative evaluation of the conversion provisions. For example, if it is likely that a contingent event will occur *before* an instrument's maturity date, it may indicate that a conversion feature is substantive. To use this approach, it must be clear that the conversion feature, without considering the contingencies, is substantive.

It was noted that guidance on this Issue does *not* address the accounting for a contingently convertible debt instrument when the guidance in ASC 260, Earnings per Share, and related interpretive guidance, including the guidance in ASC 260-10-45-43 through 45-44, 55-78 through 55-79, 55-81 through 55-82, 55-84 through 55-84B (The Effect of Contingently Convertible Instruments on Diluted Earnings per Share), is applied.

ASC 470-20-10-1 through 10-2, 15-2, 15-4 through 15-6, 25-21 through 25-27, 30-27 through 30-31, 35-12 through 35-20, 40-19 through 40-26, 45-3, 50-3 through 50-6, 55-70 through 55-82, 65-1; ASC 815-15-55-76A; ASC 825-10-15-5 Accounting for Convertible Debt Instruments That May Be Settled in Cash upon Conversion (Including Partial Cash Settlement)

BACKGROUND

The type of convertible debt instruments discussed below are settled (a) in cash on conversion for the accreted value of the obligation, and (2) in cash or stock for the conversion spread, which is the excess conversion value over the accreted value. Those debt instruments have been accounted for as a convertible debt instruments in accordance with the guidance in ASC 470-20-05-2 through 05-6, 25-2 through 25-3, 25-11 through 25-13, 30-1 through 30-2; ASC 505-10-60-3. Diluted earnings per share on such instruments have been calculated in the same manner as debt issued with detachable warrants. Because the accounting for those instruments has a less dilutive effect on the calculation of diluted earnings per share than convertible debt instruments for which earnings per share must be calculated by the if-converted method, the issuance of such convertible debt instruments has become very popular and has caused some practitioners to question whether the accounting for those debt instruments properly represents their economic effects. In addition, the FASB staff believes that the accounting for those debt instruments results in an inappropriate expansion of the guidance in

ASC 470-20-25-12 which initially did not apply to convertible debt instruments settled in cash or partial cash, and that the manner in which those debt instruments are accounted for misleads investors.

ACCOUNTING GUIDANCE

Scope

The convertible debt instruments under the scope of this guidance are *not* discussed in ASC 470-20-25-12. This guidance applies only to convertible debt instruments that, in accordance with their terms, must be settled at conversion in cash or partially in cash, unless an instrument includes an embedded conversion option that must be accounted for separately as a derivative under the provisions of ASC 815. In addition, mandatorily convertible preferred shares classified as liabilities under the provisions of ASC 480-10-05-1 through 05-6, 10-1, 15-3 through 15-5, 15-7 through 15-10, 25-1 through 25-2, 25-4 through 25-15, 30-1 through 30-7, 35-3 through 35-5, 45-1 through 45-4, 50-1 through 50-4, 55-1 through 55-12, 55-14 through 55-28, 55-34 through 55-41, 55-64; ASC 835-10-60-13; and ASC 260-10-45-70A, which include an unconditional obligation requiring an issuer to settle the face amount of the instruments in cash at a specified date are considered to be convertible debt instruments for the purpose of determining whether the instruments should be accounted for under the scope of this guidance. However, convertible preferred shares accounted for as equity or as temporary equity are *not* included under the scope of this guidance.

The following guidance also does *not* apply to convertible debt instruments that:

- Require or permit settlement in cash or other assets on conversion only if the holders of the underlying shares receive the same form of consideration in exchange for their shares.
- Require issuers to settle their obligations for fractional shares on conversion in cash, but otherwise do *not* require or permit settlement on conversion in cash or other assets.

Recognition

The underlying principle of the approach of this guidance is that interest costs related to convertible debt instruments recognized in periods *after* their initial recognition should represent the borrowing rate an entity would have incurred had it issued a comparable debt instrument *without* the embedded conversion option. That goal is accomplished by requiring issuers to separately account for the liability and equity components of convertible debt instruments.

Initial Measurement

Issuers should apply the following guidance for the *initial* measurement of convertible debt:

- First, determine the carrying amount of an instrument's liability component based on a fair value measurement of a similar liability (including embedded features, if any, other than the conversion option) that has *no* related equity component.

- Next, determine the carrying amount of the instrument's equity component corresponding to the embedded conversion option by deducting the liability component's fair value from the initial proceeds attributed to the total convertible debt instrument.
- For the purpose of the determinations made in the two bullets above and for the purpose of subsequent measurement, evaluate in the context of a total convertible debt instrument whether its embedded features, other than the conversion option (including an embedded prepayment feature) are *substantive* at the issuance date. If, at issuance, an entity has concluded that it is *probable* that a convertible instrument's embedded feature will *not* be exercised, that embedded feature is deemed to be *nonsubstantive* and would *not* affect the initial measurement of an instrument's liability component.
- Attribute a portion of the initial proceeds of a convertible debt instrument to additional unstated (or stated) rights or privileges, if any, included in the transaction based on guidance in other applicable U.S. generally accepted accounting principles (GAAP).
- Apply the guidance in ASC 815 first if embedded features *other* than the conversion option (e.g., prepayment options) are embedded in a convertible debt instrument accounted for under this guidance to determine whether any of those features should be accounted for separately from the liability component as derivative instruments under the guidance in ASC 815 and its related interpretations. As stated above, this guidance does *not* apply if *no* equity component exists because the conversion option is accounted for separately as a derivative under the guidance in ASC 815 The following steps provide guidance to issuers of convertible debt instruments on how to apply the guidance in ASC 815 and its related interpretations to the accounting for embedded derivatives:

    Step 1: Identify the embedded features, other than the embedded conversion option, that should be evaluated under the guidance in ASC 815 and its related interpretations.

    Step 2: Apply the guidance in ASC 815 and its related interpretations to determine whether any of the embedded features identified in Step 1 should be accounted for separately as derivative instruments. This guidance does *not* affect the determination of whether an embedded feature needs to be accounted for separately as a derivative.

    Step 3: Apply the guidance in the first two bullets above to separate the liability component, including embedded features, if any, other than the conversion option, from the equity component.

    Step 4: If applicable, split embedded features, if any, which must be accounted for separately as derivates based on the evaluation in Step 2, from the convertible debt instrument's liability component in accordance with the guidance in ASC 815 and its related interpretations. An embedded derivative's separation from the liability component would *not* affect the accounting for the equity component.

Transaction costs incurred with third parties other than the investors that are directly related to the issuance of convertible debt instruments accounted for under this guidance should be allocated to the liability and equity components in the same proportion as the allocation of proceeds and accounted for as costs of issuing debt and equity, respectively.

Because of the separate recognition of a liability component and an equity component for convertible debt instruments accounted for under this guidance, a temporary basis difference related to the liability component may occur when the provisions of ASC are applied. Additional paid-in capital should be adjusted when deferred taxes are initially recognized for the tax effect of that temporary difference.

The fair value option under the scope exception in ASC 825-10-15-5 does *not* apply to convertible debt instruments under the scope of this guidance.

Subsequent Measurement

Under this guidance, the excess of the principal amount of the liability component *over* its initial fair value must be amortized to interest cost based on the interest method discussed in ASC 835-30-35-2. In accordance with the interest method, debt discounts must be amortized over the expected life of a similar liability that does *not* have a related equity component (considering the effects of embedded features other than the conversion option). An issuer that initially measured the fair value of the liability component based on a valuation technique consistent with an income approach is required to consider the periods of cash flows used initially to determine the appropriate period over which to amortize the debt discount.

A liability component's expected life is *no*t affected by embedded features that were determined to be *nonsubstantive* at the time the convertible debt instrument is issued. The third bullet under the discussion related to initial measurement above provides guidance for determining whether or not an embedded feature, other than the conversion option, is substantive.

An equity component that continues to meet the conditions for equity classification in ASC 460-10-60-14; ASC 480-10-55-63; ASC 505-10-60-5; ASC 815-10-15-78, 55-52; ASC 815-15-25-15; ASC 815-40-05-1 through 50-4, 05-10 through 05-12, 25-1 through 25-5, 25-7 through 25-20, 25-22 through 25-24, 25-26 through 25-35. 25-37 through 25-40, 30-1, 35-1 through 35-2, 35-4 through 35-6, 35-8 through 35-13, 40-1 through 40-2, 50-1 through 50-5, 55-1 through 55-18, Accounting for Derivative Financial Instruments Indexed to, and Potentially Settled in, a Company's Own Stock, need *not* be remeasured in subsequent periods. If in accordance with the provisions of that guidance a conversion option must be reclassified from stockholders' equity to a liability measured at fair value, the difference between the amount that had been recognized in equity and the fair value of the conversion option at the reclassification date should be accounted for as an adjustment to stockholders' equity. However, if a conversion option that had been accounted for in stockholders' equity is reclassified as a liability, gains or losses recognized to account for that conversion option at fair value while classified as a liability should *not* be reversed if subsequently the conversion option is reclassified back to stockholders' equity. Reclassifications of a conversion option do *not* affect the accounting for the liability component.

ASC 470—Debt **33,051**

Derecognition

An issuer that derecognizes an instrument under this guidance should allocate the consideration transferred and the related transaction costs incurred to the extinguishment of the liability component and the reacquisition of the equity component.

Instruments accounted for under this guidance should be derecognized as follows, regardless of the form of consideration transferred at settlement, which may include cash or other assets, stock, or any combination of the two:

- Measure the fair value of the consideration transferred to the holder. In the case of a modification or exchange that results in the original instrument's derecognition, measure the new instrument at fair value (including both the liability and equity components if the new instrument also is accounted for under the provisions of this guidance).
- Allocate the fair value of the consideration transferred to the holder between the liability and equity components of the original debt instrument as follows:
    1. Allocate a portion of the settlement consideration to the liability component's extinguishment at its fair value immediately *before* the extinguishment. Recognize a gain or loss on debt extinguishment in the income statement for a difference, if any, between consideration allocated to the liability component and the sum of (a) the net carrying amount of the liability component, and (b) unamortized debt issuance costs, if any.
    2. Allocate the remaining settlement consideration to the equity component's reacquisition and recognize that amount as a reduction of stockholders' equity.

Allocate a portion of the settlement consideration to other unstated (or stated) rights or privileges, if any, included in the derecognition transaction in addition to the settlement of the convertible debt instrument based on guidance in other applicable U.S. GAAP.

Allocate to the liability and equity components transaction costs incurred with third parties other than the investor(s) that are directly related to the settlement of a convertible debt instrument accounted for under this guidance in proportion to the allocation of consideration transferred at settlement and accounted for as debt extinguishment costs and equity reacquisition costs, respectively.

Modifications and Exchanges

To determine whether a modification or an exchange of an original instrument accounted for under the scope of this guidance should be accounted for as an extinguishment of that instrument or as a modification to the original instrument's terms, an issuer should apply the guidance in ASC 470-50-40-12, 40-15, 40-16 (Debtor's Accounting for a Modification (or Exchange) of Convertible Debt Instruments) and ASC 470-50-05-4, 15-3, 40-6 through 40-14, 40-17 through 40-20, 55-1 through 55-9 (Debtor's Accounting for a Modification or Exchange of Debt Instruments). An issuer of an original instrument that is a modified or exchanged instrument, but *not* derecognized, should reevaluate the liability component's expected life under the section for subsequent measurement in this guidance, and determine a new effective interest rate for the liability component in accordance with the guidance in ASC 470-50-40-12, 40-15, 40-16 and ASC 470-50-05-4, 15-3, 40-6 through 40-14, 40-17 through 40-20, 55-1 through 55-9.

The components of an instrument under the scope of this guidance that has been modified to no longer require or permit cash settlement on conversion should continue to be accounted for separately, unless the original instrument must be derecognized under the guidance in ASC 470-50-40-12, 40-15, 40-16 and ASC 470-50-05-4, 15-3, 40-6 through 40-14, 40-17 through 40-20, 55-1 through 55-9. Accounting in accordance with *other* GAAP (e.g., ASC 470-20-25-12, not this guidance, is required for a new convertible debt instrument that was issued after the original convertible debt instrument was derecognized under the guidance in ASC 470-50-40-12, 40-15, 40-16 and ASC 470-50-05-4, 15-3, 40-6 through 40-14, 40-17 through 40-20, 55-1 through 55-9 and that may *not* be settled in cash on conversion.

An issuer should apply the guidance in ASC 470-50-40-12, 40-15, 40-16 and ASC 470-50-05-4, 15-3, 40-6 through 40-14, 40-17 through 40-20, 55-1 through 55-9. to determine whether extinguishment accounting is required if a convertible debt instrument *not* originally under the scope of this guidance is modified so that it qualifies to be accounted for under the scope of this guidance. If the modification is *not* accounted for as an extinguishment, the guidance discussed above should be applied *prospectively* from the date of the modification and the liability component should be measured at its fair value as of the date of the modification. The fair value of the liability component should be deducted from the total carrying amount of the convertible debt instrument to determine the carrying amount of the equity component represented by the embedded conversion option. A portion of the unamortized debt issuance costs, if any, should be reclassified at the modification date and accounted for as equity issuance costs based on the proportion of the overall carrying amount of the convertible debt instrument allocated to the equity component.

Induced Conversions

The terms of an instrument under the scope of this guidance may be amended to bring about early conversion (e.g., by offering a more favorable conversion ratio or paying an additional amount for conversions that occur *before* a specific date). In that case, an issuer should recognize a loss equal to the fair value of all securities and other amounts transferred in the transaction that exceed the fair value of the consideration that would have been issued under the instrument's original conversion terms. The instruments would be derecognized based on this guidance for derecognition using the fair value of the consideration that would have been issued in accordance with the instrument's original conversion terms. This guidance does *not* apply if the holder does not exercise the embedded conversion option.

Balance Sheet Classification of the Liability Component

An issuer's determination whether to classify the liability component as a current or a long-term liability is *not* affected by this guidance. All of a convertible debt instrument's terms (including the equity component) should be considered in making that determination by applying other applicable U.S. GAAP. The liability component's balance sheet classification also has *no* effect on that component's measurement in accordance with this measurement guidance.

Disclosure

The objective of the disclosure requirements under this guidance is to provide information to financial statement users about the terms of convertible debt instruments within the scope of those financial statements and how information about those debt instruments is presented in an issuer's balance sheet and income statement. In addition to the disclosures required in other applicable GAAP, entities should provide the following information in their annual financial statements about convertible debt instruments under the scope of this guidance that were outstanding during any of the periods presented.

An entity should disclose the following information as of each date for which a balance sheet is presented:

    a. The carrying amount of the equity component

    b. The principal amount of the liability component, its amortized discount, and its net carrying amount.

The following information should be disclosed as of the most recent balance sheet presented:

    a. The remaining period over which a discount on the liability component, if any, will be amortized

    b. The conversion price and the number of shares used to determine the total consideration to be delivered on conversion

    c. The amount by which the instrument's if-converted value exceeds its principal amount, regardless of whether the instrument is currently convertible. This disclosure is required only for public entities, as defined in ASC, *Glossary*

    d. Information about derivative transactions entered into in connection with the issuance of instruments within the scope of this guidance, including the terms of those derivative transactions, how they relate to the instruments under the scope of this guidance, the number of shares underlying the derivative transactions, and the reasons for entering into those derivative transactions. The purchase of call options that are expected to substantially offset changes in the conversion option's fair value is an example of a derivative transaction entered into in connection with the issuance of an instrument under the scope of this guidance. That disclosure is required regardless of whether the related derivative transactions are accounted for as assets, liabilities, or equity instruments.

An entity should disclose the following information for each period for which an income statement is presented:

    a. The effective interest rate on the liability component for the period

    b. The amount of interest cost related to both the contractual interest coupon and amortization of the discount on the liability component recognized for the period.

ASC 470-20-25-8 through 25-9, 25-20, 30-1, 30-5, 30-7, 30-9 through 30-10, 30-12 through 30-13, 30-16 through 30-21, 35-1, 35-4, 35-7 through 35-10, 40-1, 40-4, 45-1, 55-11 through 55-12, 55-14 through 55-17, 55-19 through 55-21, 55-23 through 55-24, 55-26 through 55-27; ASC 505-10-50-7; ASC 260-10-50-1 Application of Issue No. 98-5 to Certain Convertible Securities

BACKGROUND

Under the guidance in ASC 470-20-05-7 through 05-8, 25-4 through 25-6, 30-3, 30-6, 30-8, 30-10 through 30-11, 30-15, 35-2, 35-7, 40-2 through 40-3, 55-30 through 55-33, 55-35 through 55-38, 55-40 through 55-43, 55-45 through 50-48, 55-50 through 55-54A, 55-56 through 55-60A, 55-62 through 55-66, 55-69; ASC 505-10-50-8 (formerly EITF Issue 98-5, which is discussed above) an in-the-money nondetachable beneficial conversion features embedded in convertible securities should be valued separately at the issue date. Under that guidance, embedded beneficial conversion features are recognized and measured based on their intrinsic value at the commitment date. Guidance is also provided on the measurement and recognition of beneficial conversion features *contingent* on future events. That guidance has been reconsidered because certain practice questions have been raised about the application of that guidance.

> **OBSERVATION:** See ASC 740, Income Taxes, for a discussion of ASC 470-10-55-51 (Income Tax Consequences of Issuing Convertible Debt with a Beneficial Conversion Feature).

ACCOUNTING ISSUES

1. Is the intrinsic value model discussed in ASC 470-20-05-7 through 05-8, 25-4 through 25-6, 30-3, 30-6, 30-8, 30-10 through 30-11, 30-15, 35-2, 35-7, 40-2 through 40-3, 55-30 through 55-33, 55-35 through 55-38, 55-40 through 55-43, 55-45 through 50-48, 55-50 through 55-54A, 55-56 through 55-60A, 55-62 through 55-66, 55-69; ASC 505-10-50-8 sufficiently operational to address practice Issues or should embedded beneficial conversion options be measured based on a fair value method?

2. If the intrinsic value model is retained, in determining whether an instrument includes a beneficial conversion feature, should an issuer calculate the intrinsic value of a conversion option based on (*a*) a conversion price specified in the instrument or (*b*) an effective conversion price based on the proceeds received for or allocated to the convertible instrument?

3. Under the guidance in the ASC references in Issue 1, above, if a convertible instrument includes an embedded *contingent* conversion option, the intrinsic value of the contingent conversion option is measured based on the fair value of the underlying stock at the commitment date, but that amount is not recognized unless an event occurs that causes the contin-

ASC 470—Debt **33,055**

gency to be resolved. In applying the model under that guidance, which conversion option should be considered an "initial" conversion option and which should be considered a "contingent" conversion option?

4. Is a contingent conversion feature that will reduce the conversion price if the fair value of the underlying stock declines after the commitment date to or below a specified price that is lower than the fair value of the underlying stock at the commitment date, a beneficial conversion option even under both of the following conditions: (*a*) the initial active conversion price equals or exceeds the fair value of the underlying stock at the commitment date; and (*b*) at the future date on which the adjustment of the conversion price is triggered, the *contingent* conversion price exceeds the fair value of the underlying stock at the commitment date?

5. When does a commitment date occur for the purpose of determining the fair value of an issuer's common stock used to measure an embedded conversion option's fair value?

6. Should the commitment date, as defined in Issue 5 above, also be the date on which the assumptions, including the fair value of an issuer's stock, are determined for the purpose of allocating the proceeds, in accordance with the guidance in ASC 470-20-05-2 through 05-6, 25-2 through 25-3, 25-10 through 25-13, 30-1 through 30-2; ASC 505-10-60-3 on a relative fair value basis to separate instruments in a financing transaction that includes a convertible instrument with an embedded conversion feature?

7. Is it appropriate to accrete (*a*) a discount that results from an allocation of proceeds on a relative fair value basis to a transaction's separate instruments over the convertible instrument's life and (*b*) a discount from recording a beneficial conversion option under the guidance in the ASC references in Issue 1 above over the period to the first date the convertible instrument may be converted?

8. How should an issuer apply the guidance in the ASC references in Issue 1 above if a contingent conversion option's terms do not permit calculation at the commitment date of the number of shares a holder would receive when the price is adjusted on the occurrence of a contingent event until the contingent event actually occurs?

9. How should the guidance in the ASC references in Issue 1 above be applied if a beneficial conversion option terminates after a specified period of time and the instrument is mandatorily redeemable at a premium at that date?

10. How should a convertible instrument issued to a provider of goods or services be accounted for?

11. Is a commitment date for convertible instruments issued as paid-in-kind (PIK) interest or dividends (*a*) the commitment date of the original convertible instrument to which the PIK issuance relates or (*b*) the date on which interest is recognized as a liability or a dividend is declared?

12. How should an issuer account for the issuance of a convertible instrument to repay its debt on a nonconvertible instrument when the nonconvertible instrument's matures, including whether the model under the

guidance in the ASC references in Issue 1 above applies to the embedded conversion option in the instrument issued as payment of the matured debt?

ACCOUNTING GUIDANCE

1. The intrinsic value model in ASC 470-20-05-7 through 05-8, 25-4 through 25-6, 30-3, 30-6, 30-8, 30-10 through 30-11, 30-15, 35-2, 35-7, 40-2 through 40-3, 55-30 through 55-33, 55-35 through 55-38, 55-40 through 55-43, 55-45 through 55-48, 55-50 through 55-54A, 55-56 through 55-60A, 55-62 through 55-66, 55-69; ASC 505-10-50-8 (Issue 98-5) should be retained.

2. The intrinsic value, if any, of an embedded conversion option should be computed using the effective conversion price based on the proceeds received for, or allocated to, the convertible instruments. Consequently, an issuer would account for a financing transaction that includes a convertible instrument as follows: (*a*) allocate the proceeds received on a fair value basis to the convertible instrument and other detachable instruments, such as detachable warrants, if any, included in the exchange, and (*b*) apply the model in ASC 470-20-05-7 through 05-8, 25-4 through 25-6, 30-3, 30-6, 30-8, 30-10 through 30-11, 30-15, 35-2, 35-7, 40-2 through 40-3, 55-30 through 55-33, 55-35 through 55-38, 55-40 through 55-43, 55-45 through 55-48, 55-50 through 55-54A, 55-56 through 55-60A, 55-62 through 55-66, 55-69; ASC 505-10-50-8 to the amount allocated to the convertible security and calculate an effective conversion price, which will be used to measure an embedded conversion option's intrinsic value, if any.

3. The intrinsic value of an embedded conversion option should be measured using the most favorable conversion price that would be in effect at the conversion date assuming that the current circumstances will not change, except for the passage of time. An issuer should account for changes to conversion terms that would be triggered by future events not under the Issuer's control as contingent conversion options of which the intrinsic value is not recognized until the triggering event occurs.

   Excess amortization should not be reversed if the amortized amount of a discount on a convertible security as a result of an initial measurement of a conversion option's intrinsic value (before the conversion option is adjusted due to the occurrence of a future event) is greater than the remeasured amount of the conversion option's intrinsic value after the conversion option has been adjusted. In contrast, a debit should be recognized in paid-in-capital to adjust an amount initially recognized inequity for the conversion option's intrinsic value if the unamortized portion of an original discount is greater than the amount required for the total discount (amortized and unamortized) to equal the adjusted conversion option's intrinsic value if the unamortized portion of an original discount is greater than the amount required for the total discount (amortized and unamortized) to equal the adjusted conversion option's intrinsic value. An adjusted unamortized discount, if any, should be amortized based on the interest method and the guidance in Issue 8 below.

4. A beneficial conversion amount must be recognized if a conversion price is reduced (reset) under the circumstances discussed in Issue 4 above as a result of a contingent conversion feature, because the holder realizes the instrument's enhanced economic value when the price is reset. A convertible instrument should be considered to be debt settled in stock if the price of the security's conversion option is continuously reset based on price increases or decreases of the underlying stock so that the value of the common stock to the holder is fixed at any conversion date. In that case, the guidance in ASC 470-20-05-7 through 05-8, 25-4 through 25-6, 30-3, 30-6, 30-8, 30-10 through 30-11, 30-15, 35-2, 35-7, 40-2 through 40-3, 55-30 through 55-33, 55-35 through 55-38, 55-40 through 55-43, 55-45 through 55-48, 55-50 through 55-54A, 55-56 through 55-60A, 55-62 through 55-66, 55-69; ASC 505-10-50-8 would apply only to the initial accounting for the convertible security, including an initial active beneficial conversion feature, if any, but the provisions related to the contingent beneficial conversion option apply only the first time the option price is reset.

5. For consistency with the definition of a firm commitment in ASC 815 and in ASC 815-25-55-84, the definition of a commitment date in ASC 470-20-05-7 through 05-8, 25-4 through 25-6, 30-3, 30-6, 30-8, 30-10 through 30-11, 30-15, 35-2, 35-7, 40-2 through 40-3, 55-30 through 55-33, 55-35 through 55-38, 55-40 through 55-43, 55-45 through 55-48, 55-50 through 55-54A, 55-56 through 55-60A, 55-62 through 55-66, 55-69; ASC 505-10-50-8 is replaced by the following definition:

   A legally enforceable agreement reached with an unrelated party that is binding on both parties has the following characteristics:

   a. All significant terms are specified, including the quantity to be exchanged in the transaction, a fixed price in the entity's functional currency or a foreign currency or as a specified interest or specified effective yield, and its timing.

   b. Performance is probable because there is a sufficiently large disincentive for nonperformance. The existence of statutory rights in the legal jurisdiction governing the agreement under which the nondefaulting party can pursue remedies equivalent to the damages suffered provides, in and of itself, a sufficiently large disincentive for nonperformance to apply the definition of a firm commitment.

   It was noted that a commitment date would *not* occur until an agreement's subjective provisions that would permit either party to rescind its commitment to consummate a transaction have expired or the convertible security has been issued, whichever occurs earlier.

6. The same measurement date should be used in applying the guidance in ASC 470-20-05-2 through 05-6, 25-2 through 25-3, 25-10 through 25-13,

30-1 through 30-2; 505-10-60-3 and in ASC 470-20-05-7 through 05-8, 25-4 through 25-6, 30-3, 30-6, 30-8, 30-10 through 30-11, 30-15, 35-2, 35-7, 40-2 through 40-3, 55-30 through 55-33, 55-35 through 55-38, 55-40 through 55-43, 55-45 through 55-48, 55-50 through 55-54A, 55-56 through 55-60A, 55-62 through 55-66, 55-69; ASC 505-10-50-8 so that (*a*) the proceeds from a transaction are allocated to the separable components and (*b*) the intrinsic value of a conversion option is measured based on measurement attributes as of the same point in time. Therefore, when the proceeds of a convertible security are allocated under the guidance in ASC 470-20-05-2 through 05-6, 25-2 through 25-3, 25-10 through 25-13, 30-1 through 30-2; ASC 505-10-60-3 to the separate securities issued together with it, the allocation should be determined based on the relative fair values of all the securities at the commitment date defined in Issue 5 above.

7. The following is guidance for the accretion of discounts:

   a. The model discussed in ASC 470-20-05-7 through 05-8, 25-4 through 25-6, 30-3, 30-6, 30-8, 30-10 through 30-11, 30-15, 35-2, 35-7, 40-2 through 40-3, 55-30 through 55-33, 55-35 through 55-38, 55-40 through 55-43, 55-45 through 50-48, 55-50 through 55-54A, 55-56 through 55-60A, 55-62 through 55-66, 55-69; ASC 505-10-50-8 should be modified to require that issuers of convertible securities that have a *stated* redemption date be required to recognize a discount when they recognize a beneficial conversion option that will be accreted from the date of issuance to the stated convertible security's redemption date, regardless of the earliest conversion date.

   b. The guidance in ASC 470-20-05-7 through 05-8, 25-4 through 25-6, 30-3, 30-6, 30-8, 30-10 through 30-11, 30-15, 35-2, 35-7, 40-2 through 40-3, 55-30 through 55-33, 55-35 through 55-38, 55-40 through 55-43, 55-45 through 50-48, 55-50 through 55-54A, 55-56 through 55-60A, 55-62 through 55-66, 55-69; ASC 505-10-50-8 should continue to apply to convertible securities without a stated redemption date.

   c. At the date of conversion, interest expense or a dividend, as appropriate, should be immediately recognized for the remaining unamortized discount due to (*a*) an allocation of proceeds under the guidance in ASC 470-20-05-2 through 05-6, 25-2 through 25-3, 25-10 through 25-13, 30-1 through 30-2; ASC 505-10-60-3 to other separable securities included in securities with beneficial conversion features and (*b*) the discount that results from the accounting for the beneficial conversion. If an expense is recognized, it should not be classified as extraordinary.

   d. The calculation of an embedded conversion option's intrinsic value is not affected by costs of issuing convertible securities. Such costs should also not be offset in the calculation of the conversion option's intrinsic value against proceeds received from the issuance. The Task Force noted that issuance costs in this consensus are limited to incremental and direct costs incurred with parties other than the investor in the convertible security. Amounts paid to an investor when the transaction is consummated should be accounted for as a reduction in the issuer's proceeds, not as issuance costs, they do affect the calculation of an embedded option's intrinsic value.

All discounts should be accounted for based on their nature, i.e., a discount that occurs as a result of the accounting for a beneficial conversion option is amortized from the date on which a security was issued to the earliest conversion date. SEC registrants should account for other discounts on perpetual preferred stock that has no redemption date but that must be redeemed upon the occurrence of a future event not under the issuer's control based on the guidance in ASC 480-10-S99.

8. If under the terms of a contingent conversion option, an issuer is not permitted to calculate the number of shares the holder would receive when the price is adjusted on the occurrence of a contingent event, the issuer should calculate the number of shares that the holder would receive based on the new conversion price. That number of shares should be compared to the number that would have been received before the contingent event occurred. The incremental intrinsic value from the resolution of the contingency and the adjustment to the conversion price, which is recognized when the contingent event occurs, equals the difference between the number of shares in the two calculations multiplied by the stock price at the commitment date. The discount would be accreted in accordance with the guidance in Issue 5 above.

OBSERVATION: This guidance applies to convertible securities with a beneficial conversion feature that ends after a specified period of time. A convertible security under the scope of this guidance that was issued in the form of equity shares and whose terms require the holder to redeem the shares if the conversion feature expires becomes a liability under the guidance in ASC 480-10-05-1 through 05-6, 10-1, 15-3 through 15-5, 15-7 through 15-10, 25-1 through 25-2, 25-4 through 25-15, 30-1 through 30-7, 35-3 through 35-5, 45-1 through 45-4, 50-1 through 50-4, 55-1 through 55-12, 55-14 through 55-28, 55-34 through 55-41, 55-64; ASC 835-10-60-13; ASC 260-10-45-70A when the conversion feature expires. Under the guidance in ASC 480-10-30-2 a security that becomes redeemable and is reclassified as a liability should be measured at its fair value. A corresponding reduction should be made to equity by adjusting paid-in capital if the fair value of the liability is different from the amount at which the convertible debt was reported. No gain or loss should be recognized. If a convertible security in the form of shares is convertible into a variable number of shares based mainly or exclusively on one of the conditions stated in ASC 480-10-25-14 but must be redeemed by transferring assets if the security is *not* converted, the convertible security becomes a liability under the guidance in ASC 480-10-25-14 because the outstanding shares represent an unconditional obligation to be redeemed. That security is no longer accounted for under the scope of this guidance.

9. If a beneficial conversion option terminates after a specified time period and the security becomes mandatorily redeemable at a premium, the

guidance in ASC 470-20-05-7 through 05-8, 25-4 through 25-6, 30-3, 30-6, 30-8, 30-10 through 30-11, 30-15, 35-2, 35-7, 40-2 through 40-3, 55-30 through 55-33, 55-35 through 55-38, 55-40 through 55-43, 55-45 through 50-48, 55-50 through 55-54A, 55-56 through 55-60A, 55-62 through 55-66, 55-69; ASC 505-10-50-8 should be applied with the discount accreted to the mandatory redemption amount, because a holder who received an in-the-money embedded conversion option is entitled to receive a premium when the instrument is redeemed.

10. See ASC 470-20-05-12, 25-17 through 25-19; ASC 470-30-22-26 below. ASC 480-10-05-1 through 05-6, 10-1, 15-3 through 15-5, 15-7 through 15-10, 25-1 through 25-2, 25-4 through 25-15, 30-1 through 30-7, 35-3 through 35-5, 45-1 through 45-4, 50-1 through 50-4, 55-1 through 55-12, 55-14 through 55-28, 55-34 through 55-41, 55-64; ASC 835-10-60-13; ASC 260-10-45-70A provides guidance to issuers on the classification and measurement of certain financial instruments with the characteristics of both liabilities and equity and requires issuers to classify financial instruments under the scope of that guidance as liabilities or as assets, under certain circumstances.

11. The original commitment date for convertible securities on which interest or dividends must be paid-in-kind (PIK) with the same convertible securities as those originally issued is the commitment date for the convertible securities issued to satisfy the agreement if the issuer or holder cannot choose another form of payment, and the holder will always receive the number of shares on conversion as if all accumulated dividends or interest have been PIK, even if the original security or a portion of it has been converted before accumulated dividends or interest were declared or accrued. If so, the fair value of the issuer's underlying stock at the commitment date for the original issuance is used to measure the intrinsic value of the embedded conversion option in the PIK securities. In other situations, the date that interest is recognized as a liability or a dividend is declared is the commitment date for convertible securities issued as PIK interest or dividends with the intrinsic value of the conversion option embedded in such PIK securities being measured based on the fair value of the issuer's underlying stock at that date.

12. The fair value of a convertible security issued to repay a nonconvertible security at maturity should be equal to the redemption amount owed on the nonconvertible debt if the old debt has matured and the Issuer's exchange of debt securities is *not* a troubled debt restructuring under the guidance in ASC 310; ASC 470. The fair value of the convertible debt should not exceed the amount at which the nonconvertible debt must be redeemed, because the issuer could have paid that amount in cash. The intrinsic value, if any, of the new debt's embedded conversion option should be measured and accounted for after the exchange under the model in ASC 470-20-05-7 through 05-8, 25-4 through 25-6, 30-3, 30-6, 30-8, 30-10 through 30-11, 30-15, 35-2, 35-7, 40-2 through 40-3, 55-30 through 55-33, 55-35 through 55-38, 55-40 through 55-43, 55-45 through 50-48, 55-50 through 55-54A, 55-56 through 55-60A, 55-62 through 55-66,

55-69; ASC 505-10-50-8 based on the fair value of the proceeds received. It was noted that the guidance in ASC 470-50-05-4, 15-3, 40-6 through 40-14, 40-17 through 40-20, 55-1 through 55-9 (Debtor's Accounting for a Modification or Exchange of Debt Securities) should be applied first if the original instrument is extinguished before its maturity.

SEC OBSERVER COMMENT

The SEC Observer stated that registrants are expected to apply the guidance in Issue 2 to all transactions accounted for under the guidance in ASC 470-20-05-7 through 05-8, 25-4 through 25-6, 30-3, 30-6, 30-8, 30-10 through 30-11, 30-15, 35-2, 35-7, 40-2 through 40-3, 55-30 through 55-33, 55-35 through 55-38, 55-40 through 55-43, 55-45 through 50-48, 55-50 through 55-54A, 55-56 through 55-60A, 55-62 through 55-66, 55-69; ASC 505-10-50-8, including those for which a commitment date occurred before November 16, 2000. Registrants should report the initial application of that guidance to all existing, terminated, and converted transactions subject to the guidance in ASC 470-20-05-7 through 05-8, 25-4 through 25-6, 30-3, 30-6, 30-8, 30-10 through 30-11, 30-15, 35-2, 35-7, 40-2 through 40-3, 55-30 through 55-33, 55-35 through 55-38, 55-40 through 55-43, 55-45 through 50-48, 55-50 through 55-54A, 55-56 through 55-60A, 55-62 through 55-66, 55-69; ASC 505-10-50-8, as of the beginning of the registrant's quarter that includes November 16, 2000, in a manner similar to a cumulative effect of a change in accounting principle in accordance with the guidance in ASC 250 (FAS-154). A cumulative effect, if any, should be recognized and accounted for in accordance with the guidance in Issue 98-5 before recognizing the effect of other consensus positions in this Issue.

ASC 470-20-40-13 Determining Whether Certain Conversions of Convertible Debt to Equity Securities Are within the Scope of FASB Statement No. 84, Induced Conversions of Convertible Debt

BACKGROUND

Under the guidance in ASC 470-50-05-1, 15-3 through 15-4, 40-2, 40-4; ASC 850-10-60-3, all extinguishments of debt were accounted for the same, regardless of how the extinguishment was accomplished. The guidance in ASC 470-20-05-10, 40-13 through 40-17, 45-2, 55-2 through 55-9, which amended the guidance in ASC 470-50-05-1, 15-3 through 15-4, 40-2, 40-4; ASC 850-10-60-3, excluded from its scope convertible debt that is converted to a debtor's equity securities based on conversion privileges that (*a*) differ from those stated in the original terms of the debt when it was originally issued, (*b*) are effective for a limited period of time, (*c*) include additional consideration, and (*d*) are intended to induce conversion. Convertible debt securities with those characteristics are covered under the scope of ASC 470-20-05-10, 40-13 through 40-17, 45-2, 55-2 through 55-9.

Some have asked whether the guidance in ASC 470-20-05-10, 40-13 through 40-17, 45-2, 55-2 through 55-9 would apply to offers to induce conversion made by a debt *holder* to a debtor in which the conversion terms of the convertible debt are increased from the original terms, for example, to include cash or an additional number of shares. In addition, such offers to induce conversion may not be extended to all debt holders, but may apply only to the debt holders making the offer to the debtor.

ACCOUNTING ISSUE

Does the guidance in ASC 470-20-05-10, 40-13 through 40-17, 45-2, 55-2 through 55-9 apply if an offer for consideration that exceeds a debt security's original terms is made by a debt *holder*, including if (*a*) a third party that purchases the debt in the open market at a significant discount from face value asks the debtor to increase the security's conversion terms, and (*b*) the offer is not made to all debt holders?

ACCOUNTING GUIDANCE

The guidance in ASC 470-20-05-10, 40-13 through 40-17, 45-2, 55-2 through 55-9 applies to *all* conversions of convertible debt if the conversion (*a*) results from changes in conversion privileges that can be exercised only for a limited time period, and (*b*) includes the issuance of all of the equity securities that can be issued for each converted debt security under the conversion privileges stated in the terms of the debt at issuance, regardless of whether the offer has been made by the issuer or the holder of the debt or whether the offer applies to all debt holders.

ASC 470-20-S99-1, S25-1 Revenue Recognition on Options to Purchase Stock of Another Entity

BACKGROUND

Normally, convertible debt or detachable warrants issued with a company's debt obligations are convertible into the issuer's own equity securities. For example, Company A issues debt securities that can be converted by a holder into the securities of Company B, which Company A holds as an investment. Company A may issue such debt in the form of convertible debt securities that must be tendered by the holder in exchange for a certain number of Company B's equity securities, or in the form of debt securities with warrants that can be detached from the debt and converted into Company B's securities at a specific price.

ACCOUNTING ISSUES

- Should the amount of a warrant issued with debt be amortized over its term or should it be credited to income only when it is exercised or has expired?
- Should debt securities that must be tendered for conversion into securities other than the issuer's be accounted for the same as convertible debt, based on the provisions in ASC 470-20-05-2 through 05-6, 25-2 through 25-3, 25-11 through 25-13, 30-1 through 30-2; ASC 505-10-60-3, or should the conversion feature be accounted for separately, as in the case of a detachable warrant?

ACCOUNTING GUIDANCE

- An issuer of debt with detachable warrants should recognize a liability for the value of a warrant that can be converted into the common stock of an

ASC 470—Debt **33,063**

entity in which the issuer has an investment, but should not amortize that amount into income until the warrant has been exercised or has expired.

> **OBSERVATION:** This consensus is partially nullified by the guidance in ASC 815. Therefore, it applies only to detachable warrants that do *not* meet the definition of a derivative in ASC 815.

- No guidance was provided on Issue 2.

> **OBSERVATION:** This Issue has been resolved by the guidance in ASC 815-15-05-1, 35-1 through 35-2A, 25-1, 25-4 through 25-6, 25-11 through 25-14, 25-26 through 25-29, 25-54, 30-1, 15-5 through 15-6, 15-8 through 15-10, 15-14; ASC 815-10-15-72 through 15-73, 15-11, 15-84; ASC 815-20-25-71.

ASC 470-20-05-12; 25-17 through 25-19; 30-22-26 Accounting for a Convertible Security Granted or Issued to a Nonemployee for Goods or Services and Cash

BACKGROUND

In addition to the FASB's guidance in ASC 470, the EITF issued the guidance on accounting for convertible securities with beneficial conversion features in ASC 470-20-05-7 through 05-8, 25-4 through 25-6, 30-3, 30-6, 30-8, 30-10 through 30-11, 30-15, 35-2, 35-7, 40-2 through 40-3, 55-30 through 55-33, 55-35 through 55-38, 55-40 through 55-43, 55-45 through 50-48, 55-50 through 55-54A, 55-56 through 55-60A, 55-62 through 55-66, 55-69; ASC 505-10-50-8 (Formerly, Issue 98-5, Accounting for Convertible Securities with Beneficial Conversion Features or Contingently Adjustable Conversion Ratios) and in ASC 470-20-25-8 through 25-9, 25-20, 30-1, 30-5, 30-7, 30-9 through 30-10, 30-12 through 30-13, 30-16 through 30-21, 35-1, 35-4, 35-7 through 35-10, 40-1, 40-4, 45-1, 55-11 through 55-12, 55-14 through 55-17, 55-19 through 55-21, 55-23 through 55-24, 55-26 through 55-27; ASC 505-10-50-7. ASC 260-10-50-1 (Formerly Issue 00-27, Application of EITF Issue 98-5 to Certain Convertible Securities (both Issues are discussed above)). In addition, ASC 718, *Compensation, Stock Compensation*, and ASC 505-50-05-3, 05-8, 15-2 through 15-3, 25-2, 25-4, 25-9, 30-2 through 30-7, 30-11 through 30-14, 30-21 through 30-23, 30-25 through 30-28, 30-30 through 30-31, 35-3, 35-5 through 35-10, 55-2 through 55-11, 55-13 through 55-17, 55-20 through 55-24, 55-28, 55-31 through 55-40; ASC 440-10-60-4 (Formerly Issue 96-18, Accounting for Equity Securities That Are Issued to Other Than Employees for Acquiring, or in Conjunction with Selling, Goods or Services) have provided guidance on accounting for equity securities (including convertible securities) that are issued in exchange for goods or services. However, neither the FASB nor the EITF has provided guidance for the recognition and measurement of transactions in which convertible securities are issued to nonemployees in exchange for goods or services or combined with cash. The convertible securities discussed below include a nondetachable conversion option that allows a holder to convert the security into the issuer's stock.

33,064 ASC 470—Debt

ACCOUNTING ISSUES

1. Should the intrinsic value of the conversion option of a convertible security issued in exchange for goods or services or combined with cash be measured under the model in ASC 470-20-05-7 through 05-8, 25-4 through 25-6, 30-3, 30-6, 30-8, 30-10 through 30-11, 30-15, 35-2, 35-7, 40-2 through 40-3, 55-30 through 55-33, 55-35 through 55-38, 55-40 through 55-43, 55-45 through 50-48, 55-50 through 55-54A, 55-56 through 55-60A, 55-62 through 55-66, 55-69; ASC 505-10-50-8 (Formerly, Issue 98-5, Accounting for Convertible Securities with Beneficial Conversion Features or Contingently Adjustable Conversion Ratios), as interpreted by ASC 470-20-25-8 through 25-9, 25-20, 30-1, 30-5, 30-7, 30-9 through 30-10, 30-12 through 30-13, 30-16 through 30-21, 35-1, 35-4, 35-7 through 35-10, 40-1, 40-4, 45-1, 55-11 through 55-12, 55-14 through 55-17, 55-19 through 55-21, 55-23 through 55-24, 55-26 through 55-27; ASC 505-10-50-7. ASC 260-10-50-1 (Formerly Issue 00-27, Application of EITF Issue 98-5 to Certain Convertible Securities, at (*a*) the security's commitment date as defined in Issue 00-27, (*b*) the measurement date under Issue 96-18, or (*c*) the later of the two dates?
2. How should the fair value of the convertible security be measured?
3. Should distributions paid or payable on such convertible securities be recognized as a financing cost (interest expense or dividend) or as a cost of the goods or services received from the counterparty?
4. Should a purchaser of a convertible security with a beneficial conversion option for cash account for goods or services provided (received) as an adjustment to the consideration for the convertible security if the purchaser also provides (receives) goods or services to (from) the issuer under a different contract?

ACCOUNTING GUIDANCE

It was noted that the existing guidance should be applied as follows:

1. To determine the fair value of a convertible equity or debt security issued in exchange for goods or services (or combined with cash) that can be converted into the issuer's equity securities, apply the guidance in ASC 718, as interpreted by ASC 505-50-05-3, 05-8, 15-2 through 15-3, 25-2, 25-4, 25-9, 30-2 through 30-7, 30-11 through 30-14, 30-21 through 30-23, 30-25 through 30-28, 30-30 through 30-31, 35-3, 35-5 through 35-10, 55-2 through 55-11, 55-13 through 55-17, 55-20 through 55-24, 55-28, 55-31 through 55-40; ASC 440-10-60-4 (Issue 96-18).
2. To determine whether a convertible security includes a beneficial conversion option, apply the requirements of Issue 98-5 and Issue 00-27 so that the fair value determined in (a) above is considered the proceeds from issuing the security.
3. To measure the intrinsic value, if any, of the conversion option under Issue 98-5, as interpreted by Issue 00-27, compare the proceeds received for the security (fair value calculated under (a) above) to the fair value of the common stock the counterparty would receive when the option is exercised.

The following guidance was provided on the Issues:
1. The fair value of a convertible security issued in exchange for goods or services and the intrinsic value, if any, of a conversion option under the guidance in ASC 470-20-05-7 through 05-8, 25-4 through 25-6, 30-3, 30-6, 30-8, 30-10 through 30-11, 30-15, 35-2, 35-7, 40-2 through 40-3, 55-30 through 55-33, 55-35 through 55-38, 55-40 through 55-43, 55-45 through 55-48, 55-50 through 55-54A, 55-56 through 55-60A, 55-62 through 55-66, 55-69, and ASC 505-10-50-8 (formerly Issue 98-5) should be determined using the *measurement date* in ASC 505-50-05-3, 05-8, 15-2 through 15-3, 25-2, 25-4, 25-9, 30-2 through 30-7, 30-11 through 30-14, 30-21 through 30-23, 30-25 through 30-28, 30-30 through 30-31, 35-3, 35-5 through 35-10, 55-2 through 55-11, 55-13 through 55-17, 55-20 through 55-24, 55-28, 55-31 through 55-40; ASC 440-10-60-4 (formerly Issue 96-18), not the commitment date in ASC 470-20-25-8 through 25-9, 25-20, 30-1, 30-5, 30-7, 30-9 through 30-10, 30-12 through 30-13, 30-16 through 30-21, 35-1, 35-4, 35-7 through 35-10, 40-1, 40-4, 45-1, 55-11 through 55-12, 55-14 through 55-17, 55-19 through 55-21, 55-23 through 55-24, 55-26 through 55-27; ASC 505-10-50-7; ASC 260-10-50-1 (formerly Issue 00-27).
2. The following guidelines should be used to determine the fair value of a convertible security:
    a. The fair value of the goods or services received should be used if that amount can be determined with reliability and the issuer has not recently issued similar convertible securities.
    b. The best evidence of a convertible security's fair value may be found in recent issuances of similar convertible securities for cash to parties having only an investor relationship with the issuer.
    c. The fair value of a convertible security should not be less than the fair value of equity shares to which it would be converted if reliable information about (a) or (b) above does not exist.
3. Distributions paid or payable under a convertible security should be accounted for as a cost of goods or services received unless the security is considered to have been issued under the guidance in ASC 718 and ASC 505-50-S25-1; S99-1 (formerly Topic D-90, Grantor Balance Sheet Presentation of Unvested, Forfeitable Equity Securities Granted to a Nonemployee), which provides that forfeitable equity securities are considered unissued until future services have been provided. Thereafter, distributions under such securities should be accounted for as financing costs. A discount on a convertible security as a result of a beneficial conversion feature should not be accreted until the securities are considered to have been issued for accounting purposes.
4. To determine whether the fair value of goods and services and that of a convertible security equal the separately stated pricing of an agreement for goods or services and of a convertible security, it is necessary to evaluate the terms of both. If the fair value and separately stated pricing are not equal, the terms of those transactions should be adjusted by recognizing the fair value of the convertible security and adjusting the

fair value of the purchase or sales price of the goods or services. To determine the fair value of a convertible security issued to a provider of goods or service that is part of a larger issuance, evidence of the fair value of that convertible security may be found in the amount paid by unrelated investors making a substantive investment in the issuance.

ASC 470-50: MODIFICATIONS AND EXTINGUISHMENTS

ASC 470-50-05-1, 15-2 through 15-3, 40-3 Early Extinguishment of Debt through Exchange for Common or Preferred Stock

BACKGROUND

Under the guidance in ASC 470-50-05-1, 15-3 through 15-4, 40-2, 40-4; ASC 850-10-60-3, a conversion of debt into common or preferred stock is not an extinguishment if the conversion represents the exercise of a conversion right contained in the terms of the debt issue. Other exchanges of common or preferred stock for debt would constitute an extinguishment.

ACCOUNTING GUIDANCE

Question: Does the guidance in ASC 470-50-05-1, 15-3 through 15-4, 40-2, 40-4; ASC 850-10-60-3, apply to extinguishments of debt effected by the issuance of common or preferred stock, including redeemable and fixed-maturity preferred stock?

Answer: All extinguishments of debt must be accounted for in accordance with the guidance in ASC 310-40-15-3 through 15-12, 10-1 through 10-2, 25-1 through 25-2, 35-2, 35-5, 35-7, 40-2 through 40-6, 40-8, 50-1 through 50-2, 55-2; ASC 470-60-15-3 through 15-12, 35-1 through 35-12, 45-1 through 45-2, 55-3, 10-1 through 10-2; ASC 450-20-60-12 as amended by the guidance in ASC 470-50-45-1. The guidance in ASC 470-50-05-1, 15-3 through 15-4, 40-2, 40-4; ASC 850-10-60-3 applies to all extinguishments except those subject to the requirements of ASC 310-40-15-3 through 15-12, 10-1 through 10-2, 25-1 through 25-2, 35-2, 35-5, 35-7, 40-2 through 40-6, 40-8, 50-1 through 50-2, 55-2; ASC 470-60-15-3 through 15-12, 35-1 through 35-12, 45-1 through 45-2, 55-3, 10-1 through 10-2; ASC 450-20-60-12, which applies to extinguishments in troubled debt restructurings. In accordance with the guidance in ASC 470-50-05-1 15-3 through 15-4 40-2, 40-4; ASC 850-10-60-3, the difference between the net carrying amount of the extinguished debt and the reacquisition price is recognized currently in income of the period of extinguishment. In this situation, the reacquisition price of the extinguished debt is the value of the common or preferred stock issued or the value of the debt, whichever is more clearly evident.

ASC 470-50-05-4, 15-3, 40-6 through 40-14, 40-17 through 40-20, 55-1 through 55-9 Debtor's Accounting for a Substantive Modification and Exchange of Debt Securities

> **OBSERVATION:** The guidance in ASC 860, which superseded the guidance in FAS-125, did not change that pronouncement's guidance on the extinguishment of liabilities. The guidance in this Issue was not reconsidered in ASC

860-10-35-4, 35-6, 05-8; ASC 860-20-25-5, 55-46 through 55-48; ASC 860-50-05-2 through 05-4, 30-1 through 30-2, 35-1A, 35-3, 35-9 through 35-11, 25-2 through 25-3, 25-6, 50-5; ASC 460-10-60-35 which amended the guidance in ASC 860.

NOTE: The guidance in this Issue has been amended by the guidance in Debtor's Accounting for a Modification (or Exchange) of Convertible Debt Securities, which is discussed below.

BACKGROUND

Under the provisions of ASC 405-20-40-1, which superseded existing guidance on extinguishment of debt, a liability is extinguished and derecognized only if one of the following two conditions exists:

- The debtor is relieved of the obligation by paying the creditor in cash, other financial assets, goods, or services, or the debtor has reacquired the outstanding debt securities, which are either canceled or held as treasury bonds, *or*
- The debtor obtains a legal release from being primarily liable on the obligation.

Exchanges of debt or modifications of debt that have a substantive effect on the amount and timing of the future cash flows of the debt securities are not treated as extinguishments under the guidance in ASC 860, which does not address the accounting for such transactions.

ACCOUNTING ISSUES

- How should a debtor account for an exchange of debt securities with substantially different terms?
- How should a debtor account for a substantial modification of terms of an existing debt agreement that is not a troubled debt restructuring?
- Should a gain or loss recognized on an exchange or modification of debt be reported as extraordinary?

ACCOUNTING GUIDANCE

- An *exchange* of debt securities with substantially different terms is accounted for as a debt extinguishment, with the liability for the existing debt derecognized in accordance with the guidance in ASC 405-20-40-1.
- A substantial modification of the terms of existing debt is accounted for and reported as an extinguishment the same as an exchange of debt with substantially different terms, because the debtor can achieve the same economic result in the two transactions.
- From a debtor's perspective, if the present value of the cash flows under the terms of a new debt security differ by at least 10% from the present value of the cash flows remaining under the original debt security, the exchange of debt securities with the creditor or the modification of debt in a nontroubled debt restructuring is achieved with substantially different debt securities. Present value is calculated based on the following guidance:

- The new debt security's cash flows include all cash flows stated in the terms of the new debt security as well as amounts paid by the debtor to the creditor less amounts received by the debtor from the creditor in the exchange or modification.
- For debt securities (original or new) that have a floating interest rate, the variable rate effective on the date of the exchange or modification is used to calculate the security's cash flows.
- For debt securities (original or new) that are callable or puttable, cash flows are analyzed separately assuming exercise and nonexercise of the put option. Cash flow assumptions that result in a smaller change are used to determine whether the 10% difference for substantially different securities is met.
- Judgment should be used to determine the appropriate cash flows of debt securities with contingent payment terms or unusual interest rate terms.
- For accounting purposes, the effective interest rate of the original debt security is used as the discount rate to calculate the present value of cash flows.
- If debt exchanged or modified within one year before the current transaction was determined not to be substantially different, the debt terms existing before that exchange are used to determine whether the current exchange or modification is substantially different.

- Changes in the amount of principal, interest rates, or maturity of the debt can affect cash flow. Fees exchanged between a debtor and a creditor for the purpose of changing any of the following features or provisions of the debt also can affect cash flows:
  - Recourse or nonrecourse features
  - Priority of the obligation
  - Collateralization (including changes in collateral) or noncollateralization features
  - A guarantor or elimination thereof
  - Option features

  Debt securities are *not* substantially different if a debt security is changed or modified as discussed above, but the effect on the present value of cash flow is less than 10%.

- New debt securities as a result of exchanges or modifications of old debt that are considered to be substantially different (the old debt is extinguished) are recognized initially at fair value. That amount is used to determine the gain or loss on extinguishment and the effective interest rate of the new debt security.

- New debt securities as a result of exchanges or modifications of old debt that are *not* considered to be substantially different are *not* accounted for as extinguishments of the old debt. A new effective interest rate is

calculated on the date of the exchange or modification based on the carrying amount of the original debt security and the revised cash flows.
- For exchanges or modifications that result in an extinguishment of the old debt and the new debt is initially recognized at fair value:
  — Fees paid by a debtor to a creditor or received by a debtor from a creditor (for example, to cancel the debtor's call option or to extend a no-call period) in the exchange or modification are associated with the extinguishment transaction and included in determining the gain loss on the extinguishment.
  — Amounts paid to third parties as a result of an exchange or modification (such as legal fees) are associated with the new or modified debt securities and amortized over the term of the new or modified debt based on the interest method similar to debt issue costs.
- For exchanges or modifications that do *not* result in an extinguishment of the old debt:
  — Fees paid by the debtor to the creditor or received by the debtor from the creditor (for example, to cancel the debtor's call option or to extend a no-call period) in the exchange or modification are associated with the new or modified debt securities and amortized with existing unamortized discount or premium to adjust interest expense over the remaining term of the new or modified debt based on the interest method.
  — Amounts paid to third parties as a result of the exchange or modification, such as legal fees, are expensed as incurred.

The following guidance applies to a transaction in which a borrower, who instead of acquiring debt securities directly, loans money to a third party to acquire the borrower's debt securities. The borrower and third party agree to offset the payments of their payables and receivables as they become due as long as the third party retains the borrower's debt. Under those circumstances, the original debt securities should not be extinguished and the securities should not be offset in the borrower's financial statements against the receivable from the third party.

Because the above guidance contemplate only single debtors and creditors and does not consider how actions taken by a third-party intermediary acting as an agent or a principal would affect a debtor's accounting, the following implementation guidance is provided:

1. A transaction in which a debtor pays cash to a creditor to extinguish its current debt and the creditor issues new debt in exchange should be accounted for as an extinguishment of the current debt only if the new debt security has substantially different terms, as defined in the Issue. This guidance does *not* apply to exchanges of cash between debtors and creditors, because such transactions already meet the requirement for debt extinguishment in ASC 405-20-40-1.

2. In determining whether there has been an exchange of debt securities or a modification of the terms of an existing debt security between a debtor

and a creditor, the actions of a third-party intermediary acting as an *agent* for a debtor should be considered in the same manner as if they had been taken by the debtor.

3. In determining whether there has been an exchange of debt securities or a modification of the terms of an existing debt security between a debtor and a creditor, the actions of a third-party intermediary acting as a *principal* should be considered to be those of a third-party creditor in the same manner as the actions of any other creditor.

4. A debtor's accounting for a debt is not affected by transactions among debt holders, because such actions do not cause a modification of the terms of the original debt or an exchange of debt securities between a debtor and the debt holders.

5. To determine whether a gain or loss should be recognized on transactions between a debtor and a third-party creditor, the guidance in ASC 405-20-40-1 and the guidance in this Issue should apply.

When applying the guidance, it may be necessary to determine whether a third-party intermediary is acting as an agent or as a principal. Legal definitions of those terms and an evaluation of the facts and circumstances related to a third-party intermediary's involvement may be useful. The following indicators should be considered:

- If an intermediary is only required to place or reacquire debt for a debtor but does not risk its own funds, it is an indicator that the third-party intermediary is acting as an *agent* for the debtor. For example, an intermediary that uses its own funds is acting as an agent if the debtor will compensate the intermediary for any incurred losses. However, an intermediary is acting as a *principal* if the intermediary risks losing its own funds.

- If an intermediary places notes issued by a debtor in accordance with a best-efforts agreement under which the intermediary agrees to buy only securities that can be sold to others and otherwise the debtor must repay the debt, it is an indicator that the intermediary is acting as an *agent* for the debtor. An intermediary can be deemed to be acting as a *principal* if the intermediary acts on a firmly committed basis and must hold debt that is not sold.

- An indicator that an intermediary is acting as an *agent* is an arrangement in which the intermediary can act only on an exchange of debt or a modification of debt terms based on the debtor's instructions. However, an intermediary that acquires debt from or exchanges debt with another debt holder in the market and the transaction exposes the intermediary to the risk of loss may be deemed to be acting as a *principal*.

- If an intermediary is paid only a specified fee to act for the debtor, it is an indicator that the intermediary is acting as an *agent*. An intermediary's ability to realize a gain on the transaction based on the value of the security issued by the debtor is an indicator that the intermediary is acting as a *principal*.

Debtors can recognize gains or losses on transactions related to a modification or exchange of debt securities only for transactions meeting the conditions in ASC 405-20-40-1 or the requirements for extinguishment under this guidance.

Illustrations of Debtor's Accounting for a Substantive Modification and Exchange of Debt Securities

Identification of Debtor and Creditor

- XYZ Bank (lead bank/creditor) makes a $10 million loan to ABC Construction Co. (debtor). The debt instrument is a contract between the bank and the debtor. Subsequently, the bank transfers a $1 million undivided interest in the debt to each of nine banks that have a participating interest in the loan, as evidenced by a certificate of participation, but are not direct creditors. The debtor would apply this guidance only if the debtor and the lead bank agree to exchange the debt or to modify its terms.

- A syndicate of ten banks (creditors) jointly funds a $10 million loan to ABC Construction Co. (debtor). In this transaction, each member of the syndicate individually loans $1 million to the debtor and issues a separate debt instrument. After one year, the debtor asks the creditors to modify the terms of the debt instruments. Six creditors agree to the modification, but four do not. Because each of the creditors has a separate right to repayment under the provisions of ASC 860-10-55-4 and ASC 310-10-25-4, the debtor accounts for the modified loans in accordance with the guidance in this Issue. The loans from creditors who would not modify the terms of the debt instruments are unaffected.

- IHT Manufacturing Corp. issues identical debt instruments to an underwriter who sells them in the form of securities to the public. Each investor (creditor) holding a security (debt instrument) is considered to be a separate creditor for the purpose of applying the guidance in this Issue. If IHT asks the holders of the securities for a modification in the terms of the debt instruments (or an exchange of debt instruments), the debtor applies the guidance only to debt instruments held by creditors that agree to an exchange or modification. Debt instruments held by the other security holders are unaffected.

Exchanges or Modifications of Debt Involving a Third-Party Intermediary

1. In the following three scenarios, the actions of an investment banker acting in the capacity of a third-party intermediary for a debtor (*agent*) are viewed as the actions of the debtor:

    a. The investment banker acquires debt instruments from holders for cash and later transfers debt instruments with the same or different terms to the same or different investors. The debtor accounts for the cash transaction as an extinguishment of the debt, because it meets the criterion in ASC 405-20-40-1.

    b. The investment banker redeems the debtor's outstanding debt instruments in exchange for new debt instruments. The debtor must account for that transaction under the guidance in this Issue. The transaction would be accounted for as an extinguishment only if the terms of the new debt are substantially different from those of the debt exchanged.

    c. The investment banker acquires debt instruments from holders for cash and at the same time issues new debt instruments for cash. This transaction is also accounted for under the guidance in this Issue; the original debt is extinguished only if the terms of the new debt are substantially different from those of the original debt.

2. In this transaction, a third-party investment banker acts as a *principal* and is treated the same as other debt holders. If the investment banker acquires debt instruments from other debt holders, the transaction does not affect the debtor's accounting. Exchanges and modifications between the investment banker and the debtor are accounted for under the guidance in this Issue based on whether the terms of the new or modified debt instrument differ substantially from those of the original debt instrument.

Transactions among Debt Holders

An investment banker intermediary acting as a *principal* for a debt holder exchanges a debt instrument for cash with another party in the marketplace. Because the funds do not pass through the debtor or its agent, the debtor's accounting is not affected by that transaction. However, if the cash exchanged by the debt holders passes through the debtor, the debtor would account for the transaction as an extinguishment.

Gain or Loss Recognition

A debtor cannot recognize a gain or loss in the following situations until the debt has been extinguished under the provisions of ASC 405-20-40-1 and the consensus in this Issue:

1. A debtor announces it intends to call a debt instrument at the first call date. (The SEC Staff Accounting Bulletin No. 94 (Recognition of a Gain or Loss on Early Extinguishment of Debt) states that the staff would object to gain or loss recognition in a period other than the period in which the debt is extinguished.)

2. A debtor places amounts equal to the principal, interest, and prepayment penalties of the debt instrument in an irrevocable trust established for the benefit of the creditor. (Under the guidance in ASC 860, debt is not extinguished in an in-substance defeasance.)

3. The debtor and a creditor agree that the debtor will redeem a debt instrument issued by the debtor from a third party.

SUBSEQUENT DEVELOPMENT

The guidance in ASC 470-50-40-12, 40-15 through 40-16 (Debtor's Accounting for a Modification (or Exchange) of Convertible Debt Instruments), which was issued in 2006, amends the guidance discussed above and provides the following guidance:

- If a debt instrument is exchanged or its terms are modified, the resulting change in the embedded conversion option's fair value should *not* be included in the cash flow test used under the guidance in this Issue to determine whether a new debt instrument's terms are *substantially* different from those in the original debt instrument. If the results of the cash flow test under the guidance in this Issue are inconclusive as to whether a *substantial* modification or an exchange has occurred, a separate analysis should be performed. Debt extinguishment accounting is required if:

- A *substantial* modification or an exchange is deemed to have occurred based on the results of a separate analysis, because the change in the embedded conversion option's fair value that is calculated as the difference between the fair value of the embedded conversion option immediately *before* and *after* a modification or exchange has occurred equals at least 10% of the carrying amount of the *original* debt instrument immediately *before* the modification or exchange occurred.

- A modification or exchange is considered to be substantial if a *substantive* conversion option is *added* or a conversion option that was substantive at the date of a modification or exchange of a convertible debt instrument is *eliminated*. To determine whether an embedded conversion option is substantive on the date it is added to or eliminated from a debt instrument, the guidance in ASC 470-20-05-11. 40-4A through 40-10. 55-68 (Accounting for Conversion of an Instrument That Became Convertible upon the Issuer's Exercise of a Call Option), which is discussed above.

- If a modification or exchange of a convertible debt instrument is *not* accounted for as a debt extinguishment, the debt instrument's carrying amount should be reduced by an *increase* in the embedded conversion option's fair value, which is calculated as the difference between the fair value immediately *before* and *after* the modification or exchange, by increasing a debt discount or reducing a debt premium. A corresponding increase should be made to additional paid-in capital. However, a decrease in an embedded conversion option's fair value should *not* be recognized. Further, if a modification or exchange of a convertible debt instrument is *not* accounted for as a debt extinguishment, the issuer should *not* recognize a beneficial conversion feature or reevaluate an existing one as a result of that transaction.

DISCUSSION

This guidance is based on a determination of whether the economics of an exchanged or modified debt instrument differ substantially from those of the original debt instrument. The decision whether to account for an exchange or modification of debt instruments as an extinguishment should be based on whether the instruments exchanged or modified are substantially different and the debtor is in a different *economic* position after an exchange or modification than before the transaction.

A cutoff of 10% rather than 5% was used to determine whether debt instruments are substantially different to compensate for using the historical effective interest rate instead of a market rate in computing the present value of cash flows. The difference in the present value of cash flows is used as the primary test. A working group suggested that negotiated fees exchanged between a debtor and a creditor to change debt terms other than the principal amount, interest rate, or maturity of the debt should be used as a surrogate for measuring the significance of the other changes.

33,074 ASC 470—Debt

ASC 470-50-40-5, 15-3; ASC 470-20-40-4 Early Extinguishment of Debt: Accounting Interpretations of APB Opinion No. 26

BACKGROUND

The guidance in ASC 470-50-40-5, 15-3; ASC 470-20-40-4 clarifies the applicability of ASC 470-50-05-1, 15-3 through 15-4, 40-2, 40-4; ASC 850-10-60-3 to debt tendered to exercise warrants.

ACCOUNTING GUIDANCE

Question: The guidance in ASC 470-50-05-1, 15-3 through 15-4, 40-2, 40-4; ASC 850-10-60-3 indicates that a gain or loss should be recognized currently in income when a debt security is reacquired by the issuer except through conversion by the holder. Does that guidance apply to debt tendered to exercise warrants that were originally issued with that debt, but which were detachable?

Answer: The guidance in ASC 470-50-05-1, 15-3 through 15-4, 40-2, 40-4; ASC 850-10-60-3 does not apply to debt tendered to exercise detachable warrants that were originally issued with that debt if the debt is permitted to be tendered toward the exercise price of the warrants under the terms of the securities at issuance. In this circumstance, the debt is considered a conversion. The guidance in ASC 470-50-05-1, 15-3 through 15-4, 40-2, 40-4; ASC 850-10-60-3 does not apply to a conversion of debt. In practice, however, the carrying amount of the debt, including any unamortized premium or discount, is transferred to capital accounts when the debt is converted. No gain or loss is recognized.

Illustration of Debt Tendered to Exercise Detachable Warrants

DeVries Chemical originally issued a $100 million bond issue at par. In addition, each bond contained two detachable warrants, enabling the holder to purchase DeVries stock at $50 per warrant. DeVries allocated $3 million of the purchase price to the detachable stock warrants. Therefore, the net carrying amount of the bonds at issuance was $97 million.

The terms of the indenture permitted holders to tender their bonds toward the exercise price of the warrants. The carrying value of the $100 million bond issue on 7/15/20X4 was $98.5 million. Given a decline in interest rates since the bonds were issued, the market price of DeVries? bonds on 7/15/20X4 had risen to $100 million.

Institutional Equities International holds 20% of the DeVries bond issue. On 7/15/20X4 Institutional Equities exercises all of its warrants, 40,000 [($20,000,000 / $1,000) × 2], by tendering bonds with a market value of $2 million (40,000 × $50). The par value of DeVries? common stock is $1 per share.

DeVries Chemical would prepare the following journal entry to record the issuance of its stock as the result of Institutional Equities exercising its warrants and tendering bonds with a market value of $2 million.

Bonds payable		2,000,000
Discount on bonds payable	30,000	
Common stock	40,000	
Additional paid-in capital	1,930,000	

ASC 470-50-40-12, 40-15 through 40-16 Debtor's Accounting for a Modification (or Exchange) of Convertible Debt Instruments

BACKGROUND

The need for the following guidance arose because of concerns about the accounting for modifications that *decrease* the value of or *eliminate* an embedded conversion option.

ACCOUNTING ISSUES

1. How should an issuer consider a modification of a debt instrument (or an exchange of debt instruments) that affects an embedded conversion option's terms in analysis to determine whether debt extinguishment accounting applies?
2. How should an issuer account for a debt instrument's modification or an exchange of debt instruments that affects an embedded conversion option's terms if extinguishment accounting does *not* apply?

SCOPE

This guidance applies to modifications and exchanges of debt instruments that (*a*) add or eliminate an embedded conversion option or (*b*) affect an existing embedded conversion option's fair value. Nob accounting guidance is provided for a modification or exchange of a debt instrument if its embedded conversion option is separately accounted for as a derivative under the guidance in ASC 815 before a modification occurs, after the modification, or in both instances.

ACCOUNTING GUIDANCE

1. If a debt instrument is exchanged or its terms are modified, the resulting change in the embedded conversion option's fair value should *not* be included in the cash flow test used under the guidance in ASC 470-50-05-4, 15-3, 40-6 through 40-14, 40-17 through 40-20, 55-1 through 55-9 to determine whether a new debt instrument's terms are substantially different from those in the original debt instrument. If the results of the cash flow test under the guidance in ASC 470-50-05-4, 15-3, 40-6 through 40-14, 40-17 through 40-20, 55-1 through 55-9 are inconclusive as to whether a *substantial* modification or an exchange has occurred, a separate analysis should be performed. Debt extinguishment accounting is required if:

    a. A *substantial* modification or an exchange is deemed to have occurred based on the results of a separate analysis, because the change in the embedded conversion option's fair value that is calculated as the difference between the fair value of the embedded conversion option immediately *before* and *after* a modification or exchange has occurred equals at least 10% of the carrying amount of the *original* debt instrument immediately *before* the modification or exchange occurred.

    b. A modification or exchange is considered to be substantial if a *substantive* conversion option is *added* or a conversion option that was substantive at the date of a modification or exchange of a convertible debt instrument is *eliminated*. To determine whether an embedded conversion option is substantive on the date it is added to or eliminated from a debt instrument, the guidance in ASC 470-20-05-11, 40-4A through 40-10, 55-68, (Accounting for the Conversion of an Instrument That Became Convertible upon the Issuer's Exercise of a Call Option) should be considered.

2. If a modification or exchange of a convertible debt instrument is *not* accounted for as a debt extinguishment, the debt instrument's carrying amount should be reduced by an *increase* in the embedded conversion option's fair value, which is calculated as the difference between the fair value immediately *before* and *after* the modification or exchange, by increasing a debt discount or reducing a debt premium. A corresponding increase should be made to additional paid-in capital. However, a decrease in an embedded conversion option's fair value should *not* be recognized. Further, if a modification or exchange of a convertible debt instrument is not accounted for as a debt extinguishment, the issuer should *not* recognize a beneficial conversion feature or reevaluate an existing one as a result of that transaction.

ASC 470-50-40-21 through 40-22, 45-2, 55-11 through 55-13 Debtor's Accounting for Changes in Line-of-Credit or Revolving-Debt Arrangements

BACKGROUND

A line-of-credit or a revolving-debt arrangement enables a debtor to borrow up to an agreed amount, to repay some of the indebtedness, and to borrow additional amounts. Such arrangements may include amounts borrowed by the debtor and a lender's commitment to make additional funds available under specified terms. Usually, a debtor incurs a cost to establish a line-of-credit or a revolving-credit arrangement. Such costs are usually deferred and amortized over the term of an arrangement. The guidance in ASC 470-50-05-4, 15-3, 40-6 through 40-14, 40-17 through 40-20, 55-1 through 55-9 did not specifically address modifications or exchanges of revolving debt arrangements or lines of credit on which amounts have been drawn. It specifically excluded those on which no funds had been drawn because of their unique characteristics.

Application of the guidance in ASC 470-50-05-4, 15-3, 40-6 through 40-14, 40-17 through 40-20, 55-1 through 55-9 to *revolving-debt* arrangements and to *lines of credit* is unclear, because of the difficulty of determining whether a change is substantial when there is an outstanding balance and a lender has committed to lend additional amounts. The guidance in ASC 470-50-40-21 through 40-22, 45-2, 55-11 through 55-13 applies to modifications and exchanges of lines-of-credit and revolving-debt arrangements.

ACCOUNTING ISSUE

How should a debtor account for modifications to or exchanges of line-of-credit or revolving-debt arrangements, including the accounting for unamortized costs at the time of the change, fees paid to or received from the creditor, and third-party costs incurred?

ACCOUNTING GUIDANCE

A modification to or exchange of a line-of-credit or a revolving debt arrangement that results in a new line-of-credit or revolving-debt arrangement or in a traditional term debt arrangement should be evaluated as follows:

> A debtor should compare the product of the remaining term and the maximum available credit of the *old* arrangement (referred to as the borrowing capacity) with the borrowing capacity under the *new* arrangement and should account for related costs in the following manner:
>
> - *Fees paid to the creditor, and third-party costs incurred, if any* Associate those costs with the *new* arrangement, regardless whether the borrowing capacity of the new arrangement is *greater* than, *equal* to, or *less* than under the old arrangement, by deferring and amortizing those costs over the term of the new arrangement.
> - *Unamortized deferred costs of the old arrangement* Account for the unamortized, deferred costs of the *old* arrangement as follows:
>   (1) *Borrowing capacity of the new arrangement is greater than or equal to the new arrangement* Amortize over the term of the *new* arrangement.
>   (2) *Borrowing capacity of the new arrangement is less than that under the old arrangement* Write off the unamortized deferred costs of the *old* arrangement at the time of the change in proportion to the decrease in borrowing capacity. Defer and amortize the remaining amount related to the *old* arrangement over the term of the *new* arrangement.
> - Charges to earnings, if any, as a result of the write-off of unamortized costs of the old arrangement under b(ii) above should *not* be classified as an extraordinary expense.

The scope of this guidance is limited to modifications of or exchanges of line-of-credit or revolving-debt arrangements in *nontroubled* situations involving a debtor and creditor who were involved in the original arrangement.

Illustration of a Debtor's Accounting for Changes in a Line of Credit or Revolving Credit Arrangement

On 1/1/X9 Company M has a revolving credit arrangement with Bank X that has a 6-year term with 4 years remaining and a $12 million commitment. The company's borrowing capacity under this arrangement is $48 million (4 years × $12 million commitment).

On 4/1/X9, the company renegotiates its credit arrangement with Bank X. At that time, $250,000 in unamortized costs relating to the company's current credit arrangement remain on its balance sheet. To change the credit arrangement, the company will have pay a $150,000 fee to the bank and will also incur $250,000 in third-party costs. The company can choose among the following changes to its current arrangement:

- **Terms** (1) Increase the amount of the bank's commitment to $18 million with the term remaining at 4 years, or (2) replace the original revolving agreement with a 4-year, $12 million term loan on which the principal is due at the end of 4 years. Thus, the loan has a $48 million borrowing capacity.

Accounting Result (1) The company's borrowing capacity increases from $48 million to $72 million. The $250,000 of unamortized costs of the original arrangement is amortized over the 4-year term of the new arrangement. The $400,000 in fees to the bank and third parties is deferred and amortized over 4 years. (2) The company's borrowing capacity is unchanged. The accounting for unamortized deferred costs of the old arrangement and costs of the new arrangement is the same as in (1).

- **Terms** Decrease the amount of the bank's commitment to $6 million and increase the term to 5 years.

  Accounting Result The company's borrowing capacity decreases from $48 million to $30 million, a reduction of 37.5%. Therefore, $93,750 ($250,000 × .375) of the unamortized costs of the original arrangement is written off. The remaining $156,250 is amortized over the 5-year term of the new arrangement. The $400,000 in fees to the bank and third parties is deferred and amortized over 5 years.

- **Terms** Replace the bank's revolving credit arrangement with a $6 million term loan on which the principal is due at the end of 3 years.

  Accounting Result The company's borrowing capacity decreases from $48 million to $18 million, a reduction of 62.5%. Therefore, $156,250 ($250,000 × .625) of the unamortized costs of the original arrangement is written off. The remaining $93,750 is amortized over the 3-year term of the new arrangement. The $400,000 in fees to the bank and third parties is deferred and amortized over 3 years.

ASC 470-60: TROUBLED DEBT RESTRUCTURINGS BY DEBTORS

ASC 470-60-15-10, 55-1, 55-2 Applicability of Statement 15 to Debtors in Bankruptcy Situations

BACKGROUND

Some confusion arose over the applicability of ASC 310-40-15-3 through 15-12, 35-2, 35-5 through 35-7, 40-2 through 40-6, 40-8, 25-1 through 25-2, 50-1, 55-2, 10-1 through 10-2; ASC 470-60-15-3 through 15-12, 55-3, 35-1 through 35-12, 45-1 through 45-2, 50-1 through 50-2, 10-1 through 10-2; ASC 450-20-60-12 to bankruptcy situations, prompting the issuance of ASC 470-60-15-10, 55-1 through 55-2. On the one hand, the guidance in ASC 310-40-15-3 through 15-12, 35-2, 35-5 through 35-7, 40-2, 40-5 through 40-6, 40-8, 25-1 through 25-2, 50-1, 55-2, 10-1 through 10-2; ASC 470-60-15-3 through 15-12, 55-3, 35-1 through 35-12, 45-1 through 45-2, 50-1 through 50-2, 10-1 through 10-2; ASC 450-20-60-12 indicates that it applies to troubled debt restructurings (TDRs) consummated under a reorganization arrangement, other provisions of the Federal Bankruptcy Act or other federal statutes. On the other hand, the guidance indicates that it does not apply to situations in which liabilities are generally restated under federal statutes, a quasi-reorganization, or corporate adjustment.

ACCOUNTING GUIDANCE

Question: Does the guidance in ASC 310-40-15-3 through 15-12, 10-1 through 10-2, 25-1 through 25-2, 35-2, 35-5, 35-7, 40-2 through 40-6, 40-8, 50-1 through 50-2, 55-2; ASC 470-60-15-3 through 15-12, 35-1 through 35-12, 45-1 through 45-2, 55-3, 10-1 through 10-2; ASC 450-20-60-12 apply to TDRs of debtors involved in bankruptcy proceedings?

Answer: That guidance does not apply to debtors who, in connection with bankruptcy proceedings, enter into a TDR that results in a general restatement of a debtor's liabilities.

ASC 470-60-55-4 through 55-14, 15-13 Debtor's Accounting for a Modification or an Exchange of Debt Instruments in accordance with FASB Statement No. 15, *Accounting by Debtors and Creditors for Troubled Debt Restructurings*

OVERVIEW

ASC 310-40-15-3 through 15-12, 10-1 through 10-2, 25-1 through 25-2, 35-2, 35-5 through 35-7, 40-2 through 40-6, 40-8, 50-1 through 50-2, 55-2; ASC 470-60-15-3 through 15-12, 35-1 through 35-12, 45-1 through 45-2, 50-1, 10-1 through 10-2; ASC 450-20-60-12 provides some guidance on determining whether a modification or exchange of debt constitutes a troubled debt restructuring. The guidance in ASC 470-60-15-9 includes a list of factors that may exist in a troubled debt restructuring and ASC 470-60-15-12 lists factors that *may* indicate that a modification or exchange of debt does *not* "necessarily" constitute a troubled debt restructuring. However, it appears that further clarification is required. For example, some question whether a reduction in the face amount of a debt instrument should always be accounted for as a troubled debt restructuring based on the guidance in ASC 470-60-15-9, and whether the guidance in ASC 310-40-15-3 through 15-12, 10-1 through 10-2, 25-1 through 25-2, 35-2, 35-5, 35-7, 40-2 through 40-6, 40-8, 50-1 through 50-2, 55-2; ASC 470-60-15-3 through 15-12, 35-1 through 35-12, 45-1 through 45-2, 50-1, 10-1 through 10-2; ASC 450-20-60-12 applies to a transaction in which a debtor exchanges its existing debt by issuing new marketable debt that meets the criterion in ASC 470-60-15-12 for a non-troubled debt restructuring. In the latter situation, the new debt's effective interest rate is based on a market price that approximates the price of debt with similar maturity dates and stated interest rates that has been issued by a nontroubled borrower.

ACCOUNTING ISSUE

Does any single characteristic or factor, taken alone, determine whether a debtor should account for a modification or exchange as a troubled debt restructuring under the guidance in ASC 310-40-15-3 through 15-12, 10-1 through 10-2, 25-1 through 25-2, 35-2, 35-5, 35-7, 40-2 through 40-6, 40-8, 50-1 through 50-2, 55-2;

ASC 470-60-15-3 through 15-12, 35-1 through 35-12, 45-1 through 45-2, 55-3, 10-1 through 10-2; ASC 450-20-60-12?

ACCOUNTING GUIDANCE

When determining whether a modification or an exchange of debt instruments is within the scope of the guidance in ASC 310-40-15-3 through 15-12, 10-1 through 10-2, 25-1 through 25-2, 35-2, 35-5, 35-7, 40-2 through 40-6, 40-8, 50-1 through 50-2, 55-2; ASC 470-60-15-3 through 15-12, 35-1 through 35-12, 45-1 through 45-2, 50-1, 10-1 through 10-2; ASC 450-20-60-12, a debtor should consider (*a*) whether the entity is experiencing financial difficulty and (*b*) whether the creditor has granted a concession to the debtor. A debtor would follow that guidance if both questions are answered affirmatively. If the answer to either question is negative, a debt modification or exchange should *not* be accounted for under that guidance.

The following factors are irrelevant in determining whether the guidance in ASC 310-40-15-3 through 15-12, 10-1 through 10-2, 25-1 through 25-2, 35-2, 35-5, 35-7, 40-2 through 40-6, 40-8, 50-1 through 50-2, 55-2; ASC 470-60-15-3 through 15-12, 35-1 through 35-12, 45-1 through 45-2, 55-3, 10-1 through 10-2; ASC 450-20-60-12 applies to a debt modification or exchange:

- The amount that current creditors had invested in the old debt.
- A comparison of the fair value of new debt at issuance to the fair value of the old debt immediately before a modification or exchange.
- Transactions among debt holders.

The length of time that current creditors have held an investment in an old debt is also irrelevant in determining whether a modification or exchange is under the scope of that guidance *unless* all the current creditors recently acquired the debt from the previous debt holders in what is, effectively, a planned refinancing.

Determining Whether a Debtor Is Experiencing Financial Difficulties

A debtor should evaluate whether it is experiencing financial difficulties if its creditworthiness has deteriorated since the debt was first issued. A debtor is experiencing financial difficulties if the following indicators exist:

- The debtor is currently in default on any of its debt.
- The debtor has declared or is declaring bankruptcy.
- Significant doubt exists whether the debtor will continue as a going concern.
- The debtor's securities have been delisted, are in the process of being delisted, or are under the threat of being delisted from an exchange.
- The debtor forecasts that based on estimates covering only its current business capabilities, the debtor's entity-specific cash flows will be insufficient to service interest and principal on the debt through maturity in accordance with the contractual terms of the existing agreement.
- The debtor cannot obtain funds from other sources at an effective interest rate that equals the current market interest rate for similar debt for a non-troubled debtor.

Despite the criteria listed above, if *both* of the following factors exist, there is determinative evidence that a debtor is *not* experiencing financial difficulties and a modification or exchange would *not* be under the scope of the guidance in ASC 310-40-15-3 through 15-12, 10-1 through 10-2, 25-1 through 25-2, 35-2, 35-5, 35-7, 40-2 through 40-6, 40-8, 50-1 through 50-2, 55-2; ASC 470-60-15-3 through 15-12, 35-1 through 35-12, 45-1 through 45-2, 55-3, 10-1 through 10-2; ASC 450-20-60-12:

- The debtor is servicing its old debt on a current basis and can obtain funds to repay the old debt from sources other than the current creditors at an effective interest rate that equals the current market interest rate for a non-troubled debtor *and*

- The creditors agree to restructure the old debt only to show a decrease in current interest rates for the debtor or positive changes in the debtor's creditworthiness since the original issuance of the debt.

Determining Whether a Creditor Granted a Concession

- A creditor has granted a concession if the debtor's effective borrowing rate on restructured debt is less than the effective borrowing rate of the old debt immediately *before* it was restructured. To calculate the effective borrowing rate of restructured debt, after considering all the terms including new or revised options or warrants, if any, and new or revised guarantees or letters of credit, if any, all cash flows under the new terms should be projected and the discount rate that equates the present value of the cash flows under the *new* terms to the debtor's current carrying amount of the *old* debt should be computed.

- Although this is rare, if persuasive evidence exists that a decrease in the borrowing rate is attributed exclusively to a factor that is not depicted in the computation, such as additional collateral, a creditor may not have granted a concession and the modification or exchange should be evaluated based on the substance of the modification.

Despite the guidance provided above, an entity that is currently restructuring its debt after having done so recently should calculate the effective borrowing rate of the restructured debt, after considering all the terms including new or revised options or warrants, if any, and new or revised guarantees or letters of credit, if any, by projecting all cash flows under the new terms and determining the debtor's previous carrying amount of the debt immediately before the previous restructuring. To determine whether the effective borrowing rate has decreased and therefore the creditor has granted a concession, the debtor should compare the new effective borrowing rate to that related to the debt immediately before the previous restructuring.

CHAPTER 34
ASC 480—DISTINGUISHING LIABILITIES FROM EQUITY

CONTENTS

Part I: General Guidance	34,002
ASC 480-10: Overall	34,002
Overview	34,002
Liabilities and Equity	34,002
Distinction between Liabilities and Equity	34,002
Required Disclosures	34,003
Deferred Effective Date	34,003
Illustration of Applying ASC 480	34,004
Part II: Interpretive Guidance	34,005
ASC 480-10: Overall	34,005
ASC 480-10-15-8	
Issuer's Accounting for Employee Stock Ownership Plans under FASB Statement No. 150, *Accounting for Certain Financial Instruments with Characteristics of both Liabilities and Equity*	34,005
ASC 480-10-25-9, 25-13, 55-33	
Issuer's Accounting under FASB Statement No. 150 for Freestanding Warrants and Other Similar Instruments on Shares That Are Redeemable	34,006
ASC 480-10-45-2A through 45-2B	
Accounting for Mandatorily Redeemable Shares Requiring Redemption by Payment of an Amount That Differs from the Book Value of Those Shares, under FASB Statement No. 150, *Accounting for Certain Financial Instruments with Characteristics of both Liabilities and Equity*	34,007
ASC 480-10-S45-5; S99-4	
Sponsor's Balance Sheet Classification of Capital Stock with a Put Option Held by an Employee Stock Ownership Plan	34,008
ASC 480-10-55-29 through 55-32, 40-42 through 40-52	
Issuer's Accounting for Freestanding Financial Instruments Composed of More Than One Option or Forward Contract Embodying Obligations under FASB Statement No. 150, *Accounting for Certain Financial Instruments with Characteristics of both Liabilities and Equity*	34,010
ASC 480-10-55-53 through 55-61; ASC 460-10-60-6	
Majority Owner's Accounting for a Transaction in the Shares of a Consolidated Subsidiary and a Derivative Indexed to the Noncontrolling Interest in That Subsidiary	34,012
ASC 480-10-S99-3A	
Classification and Measurement of Redeemable Securities	34,015

ASC 480-10-65-1
Effective Date and Transition for Mandatorily Redeemable Financial Instruments of Certain Nonpublic Entities of FASB Statement No. 150, Accounting for Certain Financial Instruments with Characteristics of both Liabilities and Equity 34,023

PART I: GENERAL GUIDANCE

ASC 480-10: OVERALL

OVERVIEW

ASC 480 more clearly defines the distinction between liabilities and equity. The approach taken is to specifically define liabilities and require that all other financial instruments be classified as equity in the balance sheet. The FASB states that ASC 480 is generally consistent with its definitions of the various elements of the statement of financial position (balance sheet), income statement, and statement of cash flows.

ASC 480 establishes standards for issuers of financial instruments with characteristics of both liabilities and equity related to the classification and measurement of those instruments. It requires the issuer to classify a financial instrument as a liability, or asset in some cases, which was previously classified as equity. The classification standards are generally consistent with the definition of liabilities in FASB Concepts Statement No. 6 and with the FASB's proposal to revise that definition to encompass certain obligations that a reporting entity can or must settle by issuing its own equity shares.

LIABILITIES AND EQUITY

Distinction between Liabilities and Equity

ASC 480 requires an issuer to classify the following instruments as liabilities, or assets in certain circumstances:

- A financial instrument issued in the form of shares that is mandatorily redeemable in that it embodies an unconditional obligation that requires the issuer to redeem the shares by transferring the entity's assets at a specified or determinable date(s) or upon an event that is certain to occur.

- A financial instrument other than an outstanding share that, at its inception, embodies an obligation to repurchase the issuer's equity shares, or is indexed to such an obligation, and that requires or may require the issuer to settle the obligation by transferring assets (ASC 480-10-25-8).

- A financial instrument other than an outstanding share that embodies an unconditional obligation that the issuer must or may settle by issuing a variable number of equity shares if, at inception, the monetary value of the obligation is based solely or predominantly on any of the following (ASC 480-10-25-14):

- A fixed monetary amount known at inception (e.g., a payable to be settled with a variable number of the issuer's equity shares).
- Variations in something other than the fair value of the issuer's equity shares (e.g., a financial instrument indexed to the S&P 500 and settleable with a variable number of the issuer's equity shares).
- Variables inversely related to changes in the fair value of the issuer's equity shares (e.g., a written put option that could be net share settled).

ASC 480 applies to issuers' classification and measurement of freestanding financial instruments, including those that comprise more than one option or forward contract. It does not apply to features that are embedded in a financial instrument that is not a derivative in its entirety. In applying the classification provisions of ASC 480, nonsubstantive or minimal features are to be disregarded.

Required Disclosures

Issuers of financial instruments are required to disclose the nature and terms of the financial instruments and the rights and obligations embodied in those instruments. That disclosure shall include information about any settlement alternatives in the contract and identify the entity that controls the settlement alternatives (ASC 480-10-50-1).

For all outstanding financial instruments within the scope of ASC 480, and the settlement alternative(s), the following information is required to be disclosed by issuers (ASC 480-10-50-2):

- The amount that would be paid, or the number of shares that would be issued and their fair value, determined under the conditions specified in the contract if the settlement were to occur at the reporting date.
- How changes in the fair value of the issuer's equity shares would affect those settlement amounts.
- The maximum amount that the issuer could be required to pay to redeem the instrument by physical settlement, if applicable.
- The maximum number of shares that could be required to be issued, if applicable.
- That a contract does not limit the amount that the issuer could be required to pay or the number of shares that the issuer could be required to issue, if applicable.
- For a forward contract or an option indexed to the issuer's equity shares, the forward price or option strike price, the number of the issuer's shares to which the contract is indexed, and the settlement date(s) of the contract.

Deferred Effective Date

The effective date of ASC 480 has been deferred for certain mandatorily redeemable financial instruments of nonpublic entities *that are not registered with the SEC*. ASC 480 is deferred indefinitely for a mandatorily redeemable financial instrument if the instrument is not due on a fixed date for a fixed amount, or if the amount due is not tied to an interest rate index, currency index, or other external index.

In addition, ASC 480's provisions for mandatorily redeemable noncontrolling interests are deferred indefinitely for both public and nonpublic entities under some circumstances. ASC 480's provisions for mandatorily redeemable noncontrolling interests are deferred indefinitely if the interest would not be classified as a liability by the subsidiary (under the "only upon liquidation" exception in ASC 480) but would be classified as a liability by the parent in the consolidated financial statements. In addition, the *measurement* provisions of ASC 480 are deferred indefinitely for mandatorily redeemable noncontrolling interests issued before November 5, 2003. This deferral applies to both the parent company and the subsidiary that issued the noncontrolling interests. The *classification* provisions of ASC 480 are *not* deferred for mandatorily redeemable noncontrolling interests issued before November 5, 2003 (ASC 480-10-65-1).

ASC 480 should be implemented by reporting the cumulative effect of a change in accounting principle for financial instruments created prior to the issuance date of the standard and still in existence at the beginning of the interim period of adoption. Restatement of prior years' financial statements is not permitted.

Illustration of Applying ASC 480

Mandatorily redeemable financial instruments. Financial instruments issued in the form of shares that embody unconditional obligations of the issuer to redeem the instruments by transferring its assets at a specified or determinable date(s) or upon an event that is certain to occur are required to be classified as liabilities. This includes certain forms of trust-preferred securities and stock that must be redeemed upon the death or termination of the individual who holds them. Although some mandatorily redeemable instruments are issued in the form of shares, those instruments are classified as liabilities under ASC 480 because of the embodied obligation on the part of the issuer to transfer its assets in the future:

Example:

Statement of Financial Position

Total assets	$5,000,000
Liabilities other than shares	$4,200,000
Shares subject to mandatory redemption	800,000
Total liabilities	$5,000,000

Notes to Financial Statements

Shares subject to mandatory redemption:	
Common stock	$600,000
Retained earnings attributed to those shares	200,000
	$800,000

Certain obligations to issue a variable number of shares. ASC 480 requires liability classification if, at inception, the monetary value of an obligation to issue a variable number of shares is based solely or predominantly on any of the following:

- A fixed monetary amount known at inception
- Variations in something other than the fair value of the issuer's equity shares
- Variations inversely related to changes in the fair value of the issuer's equity shares

Example: An entity may receive $500,000 in exchange for a promise to issue a sufficient number of shares of its own stock to be worth $525,000 at a specified future date. The number of shares to be issued to settle the obligation is variable, depending on the number required to meet the $525,000 obligation, and will be determined based on the fair value of the shares at the settlement date. The instrument is classified as a liability under ASC 480.

Freestanding financial instruments. ASC 480 requires that certain of its provisions to be applied to a freestanding instrument in its entirety:

Example: An issuer has two freestanding instruments with the same counterparty: (1) a contract that combines a written put option at one strike price and a purchased call option at another strike price on its equity shares; and (2) outstanding shares of stock. The primary requirements of ASC 480 are applied to the entire freestanding instrument that includes both a put option and a call option. It is classified as a liability and is measured at fair value. The outstanding shares of stock are not within the scope of ASC 480.

PART II: INTERPRETIVE GUIDANCE

ASC 480-10: OVERALL

ASC 480-10-15-8 Issuers' Accounting for Employee Stock Ownership Plans under FASB Statement No. 150, *Accounting for Certain Financial Instruments with Characteristics of both Liabilities and Equity*

BACKGROUND

Employee Stock Ownership Plans (ESOPs) are employee benefit plans under the Employee Retirement Income Security Act of 1974 (ERISA) and the Internal Revenue Code (IRC) of 1986. Employers that sponsor ESOPs are required by law to provide employees with a put option or another means of redeeming shares that cannot be readily traded. ESOPs often require that shares be sold back to the employer at fair value when an employee dies, retires, or reaches a certain age. Shares that must be redeemed meet the definition of mandatorily redeemable shares in ASC 480, which does *not* apply to obligations under stock-based compensation arrangements accounted for under the guidance in ASC 718-10-10-1 through 10-2, 15-3 through 15-4, 15-6 through 15-7, 25-2 through 25-4, 25-6 through 25-20, 30-2 through 30-14, 30-17 through 30-27, 35-2 through 35-8, 451 through 45-2, 50-1 through 50-2, 55-3 through 55-25, 55-27 through 55-34, 55-36 through 55-37, 55-39 through 55-42, 55-44 through 55-48, 55-51 through 55-52, 55-55 through 55-58, 55-60 through 55-79, 55-81 through 55-83, 55-87 through 55-88, 55-90 through 55-91, 55-93 through 55-96, 55-98 through 55-99, 55-102 through 55-106, 55-108 through 55-115; ASC 718-20-15-3, 35-1 through 35-9, 55-6 through 55-34, 55-36 through 55-40, 55-42 through 55-46, 55-48 through 55-50, 55-52 through 55-58; ASC 718-30-15-3, 30-1 through 30-2, 35-1 through 35-4; ASC 718-50-25-1 through 25-3; ASC 718-740-05-4, 25-2 through 25-4, 30-1

ASC 480—Distinguishing Liabilities from Equity

through 30-2, 353, 35-5. 35-7, 45-2, 45-4; ASC 505-05-9, 10-1, 15-2, 25-3, 25-6, 25-10, 30-4 through 40-6; ASC 505-60-60-1; ASC 260-10-60-1A (formerly FAS-123(R)), and ASC 718-40-05-2 through 05-4. 15-2 through 15-4, 25-2 through 25-7, 25-9 through 25-17, 25-19 through 25-21. 30-1 through 30-5, 40-2 through 40-7, 45-2 through 45-9, 50-1, 55-1 through 55-33, 55-35 through 55-38; ASC 460-10-60-11 (formerly SOP 93-6), or related guidance. However, according to ASC 480-10-15-8, the guidance in ASC 480-10-05-1 through 05-6, 10-1, 15-3 through 15-5, 15-7 through 15-8, 25-1 through 25-2. 25-4 through 25-15, 30-1 through 30-5, 30-7, 35-1, 35-3 through 35-5, 45-1 through 45-4, 50-1 through 50-4, 55-1 through 55-12, 55-14 through 55-28, 55-34 through 55-41, 55-64; ASC 835-10-60-13; ASC 26010-45-70A (formerly FAS-150) does apply to freestanding financial instruments issued under stock-based compensation arrangements that are no longer required to be accounted for the guidance referred to above.

ACCOUNTING GUIDANCE

Question: Does the guidance in ASC 480-10 apply to mandatorily redeemable ESOP shares or freestanding agreements to repurchase ESOP shares?

Answer: No. The guidance in ASC 480-10 does *not* apply to mandatorily redeemable ESOP shares or freestanding agreements to repurchase those shares, because until they are redeemed, such shares are accounted for under the provisions of ASC 718-40-05-2 through 05-4. 15-2 through 15-4, 25-2 through 25-7, 25-9 through 25-17, 25-19 through 25-21. 30-1 through 30-5, 40-2 through 40-7, 45-2 through 45-9, 50-1, 55-1 through 55-33, 55-35 through 55-38; ASC 460-10-60-11 or its related guidance, such as that in ASC 480-10-S45-5; S99-4 (formerly EITF Issue 89-11), which includes a discussion of the SEC's requirement that registrants classify amounts related to mandatorily redeemable stock outside of permanent equity in accordance with the guidance in the SEC's ASR-268 (Presentation in Financial Statements of "Redeemable Preferred Stocks").

ASC 480-10-25-9, 25-13, 55-33 Issuer's Accounting under FASB Statement No. 150 for Freestanding Warrants and Other Similar Instruments on Shares That Are Redeemable

BACKGROUND

This guidance applies to freestanding financial instruments that are *not* outstanding shares, such as warrants. They are issued with an obligation to repurchase the issuer's equity shares and require or may require settlement by a transfer of assets. Such financial instruments, therefore, are accounted for as liabilities under the guidance in ASC 480-10-25-9 through 25-12.. In ASC 480-10-55-29 through 55-32, 40-42 through 40-52, there is an example of a warrant that may be put to the issuer at a fixed price immediately after the warrant has been exercised. Constituents have raised the following question.

QUESTION

Does the timing of the redemption feature or the redemption price, which may be at fair value or a fixed amount, affect whether the guidance in ASC 480-10-25-9 through 25-12 should be applied to warrants for shares that can be put to the issuer?

ACCOUNTING GUIDANCE

Because freestanding warrants and other similar instruments on shares that are puttable or mandatorily redeemable include obligations to transfer assets, they should be accounted for as liabilities under the guidance in ASC 480-10-25-9 through 25-12) regardless of when they are redeemed or their redemption price.

The phrase "requires or may require" is used in ASC 480-10-25-9 through 25-12 to refer to financial instruments under which an issuer is conditionally or unconditionally obligated to transfer assets. For puttable shares, the issuer would be *conditionally* obligated to transfer assets if the warrant is exercised and the shares are put to the issuer. In the case of mandatorily redeemable shares, the issuer would be *conditionally* obligated to transfer assets if the holder exercises the warrant. In both cases, the warrant should be accounted for as a liability.

ASC 480-10-45-2A through 45-2B Accounting for Mandatorily Redeemable Shares Requiring Redemption by Payment of an Amount That Differs from the Book Value of Those Shares, under FASB Statement No. 150, *Accounting for Certain Financial Instruments with Characteristics of both Liabilities and Equity*

Question: Some companies have outstanding shares, all of which are subject to mandatory redemption on the occurrence of events that are certain to occur. Assume that on the date of adoption, the redemption price of the shares is more than their book value. On the date of adoption, the company would recognize a liability for the redemption price of the shares that are subject to mandatory redemption, reclassifying the amounts previously classified as equity. Any difference between the redemption price on the date of adoption and the amounts previously recognized in equity is reported in income as a cumulative effect transition adjustment loss. The redemption price may be a fixed amount or may vary based on specified conditions. How should the cumulative transition adjustment and subsequent adjustment to reflect changes in the redemption price of the shares be reported if they exceed the company's equity balance?

Answer: The cumulative adjustment amount and any subsequent adjustments to it should be reported as an excess of liabilities over assets (i.e., as a deficit). If the redemption price of the mandatorily redeemable shares is less than the book value of those shares, the excess of that book value over the liability reported for the mandatorily redeemable shares should be reported as an excess of assets over liability (i.e., as equity).

For example, assume that Company X adopts the guidance in ASC 480 when both the fair value and redemption value of the mandatorily redeemable shares is $20 million and the book value of those shares is $15 million of which $10 million is paid-in capital. On the date that guidance is adopted, the company would recognize a liability of $20 million by transferring $15 million from equity and recognizing a cumulative transition adjustment loss of $5 million. Assume further that net income attributable to the mandatorily redeemable share is $1 million for the year and the fair value of the shares at the end of the year is $21.2 million. No cash dividends are paid. The following is the presentation in the statement of financial position at the end of the year, assuming assets of $26 million and other liabilities of $10 million (all numbers in millions):

Assets	$26,000
Liabilities other than shares	$10,000
Shares subject to mandatory redemption	21,200
Total liabilities	$31,200
Excess of liabilities over assets	(5,200)
Total	$26,000

ASC 480-10-S45-5; S99-4 Sponsor's Balance Sheet Classification of Capital Stock with a Put Option Held by an Employee Stock Ownership Plan

BACKGROUND

Federal income tax regulations require employer securities held by an ESOP to have a put option, referred to as a liquidity put, allowing the employee to demand redemption if the securities are not readily marketable. The employer may have the option to satisfy the demand for redemption with cash, marketable securities, or both. Under the provisions of some ESOPs, the ESOP may substitute for the employer in redeeming the employees' shares.

Companies may also issue to their ESOPs convertible preferred stock, which is convertible into the company's common stock. Such stock is not publicly traded and therefore has a put option. The holder generally has the option of when to convert the stock, but under the terms of some convertible stock the issuer/employer is permitted to convert the shares. In some cases, the stock is converted or put to the employer when there is a takeover attempt or a merger. The convertible stock may have the following features:

- It has a "floor put" feature that guarantees the participant a minimum value, and is exercised if the convertible is "out of the money." The employer may have the option of redeeming the stock for cash, giving the participant common stock that would be issuable on conversion plus additional shares, or giving the participant common stock that would be issuable on conversion plus cash. The participant may have the option of receiving cash, common shares, or a combination of both.

- After a certain period of time, the employer may have the option to call the stock at a stipulated price. The ESOP can hold callable stock if it provides for a reasonable period of time after calling for the stock to be converted to common shares instead of cash, if participants so desire.

- The convertible stock can be held only by the ESOP and is automatically converted to common stock when distributed to participants leaving the plan. However, a floor put feature enables participants to require the trustee to put the convertible stock even before it has been distributed to participants if the convertible stock is "out of the money."

SEC Staff Accounting Series Release (ASR) 268 (Presentation in Financial Statements of "Redeemable Preferred Stocks") requires public companies to classify mandatorily redeemable preferred stock or stock whose redemption is outside the issuer's control outside of stockholders' equity.

In a leveraged ESOP, the employer records the ESOP's debt as a liability. The liability is offset by a contra-equity account referred to as "unearned ESOP shares," which is recorded as a debit in equity. (Before the issuance of ASC 718-40 (Employers' Accounting for Employee Stock Ownership Plans), such an account was referred to as *loan to ESOP or deferred* compensation.) When the employer issues stock to the ESOP, this contra-equity account is credited and there is no effect on equity.

ACCOUNTING ISSUES

- Under what circumstances should all or a portion of convertible preferred stock with put options held by an ESOP be classified outside of equity?

- If convertible preferred stock with put options issued to a leveraged ESOP is classified outside of stockholders' equity, should the contra-equity account, unearned ESOP shares, be classified in the same manner?

ACCOUNTING GUIDANCE

- Publicly held companies should classify convertible preferred stock issued to ESOPs in accordance with the provisions of ASR-268, which requires that mandatorily redeemable preferred stock be classified as a separate item between liabilities and equity, commonly referred to as the "mezzanine."

- A proportional amount of the contra-equity account in the employer's balance sheet should be similarly classified.

For example, if $7,500,000 of $10,000,000 of preferred stock issued to an ESOP is convertible and therefore is classified outside of stockholders' equity, 75% of the balance of the contra-equity account would be classified in the same manner. Thus, if the remaining ESOP debt is $8,000,000, 75% (or $6,000,000) of the contra-equity account, unearned ESOP shares, would be classified outside of stockholders' equity.

OBSERVATION: Under the guidance in ASC 460-10-55-5, a put option issued by an ESOP may be a guarantee. If a put is a guarantee that is not accounted for under the provisions of ASC 815-10-15, the ESOP sponsor's obligations under that guarantee would be reported as a liability under GAAP; the sponsor would be required to recognize a liability for the fair value of the put at its inception and provide the disclosures specified in ASC 460. The requirement in ASC 460 that a put be recognized as a liability at its inception and the requirement to disclose additional information change the sponsor's reporting and, therefore, partially nullify the guidance above.

ASC 480-10 provides guidance to issuers on the classification and measurement of financial instruments with characteristics of both liabilities and equity, except for mandatorily redeemable financial instruments of nonpublic entities. Financial instruments under the scope of ASC 480-10 should be classified as liabilities or, in some cases, as assets. Because ESOP shares with embedded repurchase features or freestanding instruments to repurchase ESOP shares are covered under the guidance in ASC 718-40 (Employers' Accounting for Employee Stock Ownership Plans) and related guidance, the guidance in

34,010 ASC 480—Distinguishing Liabilities from Equity

ASC 480-10 does not apply to those shares. However, the requirement in the SEC's ASR-268 that ESOP shares be reported in temporary equity continues to apply.

EFFECT OF ASC 815

Put options discussed in this Issue should be analyzed to determine whether they meet the definition of a derivative in ASC 815. Contracts classified in temporary equity may qualify for the exception in ASC 815-10-15-74, because temporary equity is considered to be stockholders' equity.

SEC STAFF COMMENT

The SEC Observer stated that under ASR-268, the maximum possible cash obligation related to equity securities that give a holder the option to demand redemption in cash, regardless of the probability of occurrence, should be reported outside of equity. Consequently, employers should report outside of equity all allocated and unallocated convertible preferred securities held by an ESOP that are redeemable in cash. However, if a cash obligation is related only to the market-value guarantee feature of some convertible securities, the SEC staff would not object if a registrant reports outside of equity only amounts representing the maximum cash obligation based on the market price of the underlying securities at the reporting date. The entire guaranteed amount of such securities may, nevertheless, be reported outside of equity at the registrant's option to recognize the uncertainty of the ultimate cash obligation resulting from possible declines in the market value of the underlying security.

DISCUSSION

- In this Issue, arguments for classification outside stockholders' equity focused on the fact that redemption may be outside the control of the employer as a result of the put and the employer's potential cash obligation.
- Some supported classifying all or a portion of the contra-equity account outside of equity because that account, unearned ESOP shares, resulted from a transaction in which the employer issued the securities and incurred the liability. They argued that the purpose of the contra-equity account is to offset shares that have not been paid for, as in a stock subscription. Thus, if shares not paid for are reclassified, the contra-equity account should be treated in the same manner.

ASC 480-10-55-29 through 55-32, 40-42 through 40-52 Issuer's Accounting for Freestanding Financial Instruments Composed of More Than One Option or Forward Contract Embodying Obligations under FASB Statement No. 150, *Accounting for Certain Financial Instruments with Characteristics of both Liabilities and Equity*

Question 1: How does ASC 480-10-25-8 through 25-12 apply to freestanding financial instruments composed of more than one option or forward contract embodying obligations that require or that may require settlement by transfer of assets? An example of this type of financial instrument is a puttable warrant that allows the holder to purchase a fixed number of the issuer's shares at a fixed price that also is puttable by the holder at a specified date for a fixed monetary amount that the holder could require the issuer to pay.

Answer: ASC 480-10-15-3 through 15-4 states that the guidance applies to freestanding financial instruments, including those that are composed of more than one option or forward contract. The guidance in ASC 480-10-25-4 through 25-14 applies to a freestanding financial instrument in its entirety. Under the guidance in ASC 480-10-25-8 through 25-12, if a freestanding instrument is composed of a written call option and a written put option, the existence of the call option does not affect the instrument's classification. Thus, a puttable warrant is a liability because it includes an obligation indexed to an obligation to repurchase the issuer's shares and may require a transfer of assets. It is a liability even if the repurchase feature is conditional on a defined contingency in addition to the level of the issuer's share price. The warrant is *not* an outstanding share and does *not* meet the exception for outstanding shares in ASC 480-10-25-8 through 25-12 and, unlike the application of ASC 480-10-25-14 does *not* involve making any judgments about whether it is predominant among the entity's obligations or contingencies.

For example, Company X issues a puttable warrant to Investor Y. Under the warrant's terms, Investor Y is permitted to purchase one equity share at a strike price of $10 on a specified date. The put feature permits Investor Y to put the warrant back to Company X on that date for $2 and to require settlement in cash. If the share price on the settlement date exceeds $12, Investor Y would be expected to exercise the warrant, obligating Company X to issue a fixed number of shares in exchange for a fixed amount of cash. That feature of the financial instrument does *not* result in a liability. However, if the share price is equal to or less than $12, Investor Y would be expected to put the warrant back to Company X and could choose to obligate Company X to pay $2 in cash. That feature does result in a liability, because the financial instrument includes an obligation that is indexed to an obligation to repurchase the issuer's shares and may require a transfer of assets. Therefore, under the guidance in ASC 480-10-25-8 through 25-12 , Company X would be required to classify the financial instrument as a liability.

Question 2: How does the guidance in ASC 480-10-25-14 apply to freestanding financial instruments composed of more than one option or forward contract that include obligations? For example, a puttable warrant that allows the holder to purchase a fixed number of the issuer's shares at a fixed price that also is puttable by the holder at a specified date for a fixed monetary amount to be paid, at the issuer's discretion, in cash or in a variable number of shares. Does such a financial instrument include an obligation for the issuer that is a liability in accordance with the guidance in ASC 480-10?

Answer: The answer depends on the circumstances. A financial instrument that is composed of more than one option or forward contract including obligations to issue shares must be analyzed to determine whether the obligations under any of the instrument's components have one of the characteristics discussed in ASC 480-10-25-14 and, if so, whether those obligations are predominant relative to other obligations. The analysis involves two steps.

Step 1:	Identify any component obligations that, if freestanding, would be liabilities under the guidance in ASC 480-10-25-14 and, also, identify other component obligations of the financial instrument.
Step 2:	Assess whether the monetary value of any freestanding components are collectively predominant over the collective monetary value of any other component obligations. If so, the entire financial instrument is accounted for under the guidance in ASC 480-10-25-14. If not, the financial instrument is not included under the scope of ASC 480-10.

For example, Company X issues a puttable warrant to Investor Y. The warrant allows Investor Y to purchase one equity share at a strike price of $10 at a specified date. The put feature allows Investor Y to put the warrant back to Company X on that date at $2, and can be settled in fractional shares. If the share price on the settlement date exceeds $12, Investor Y would be expected to exercise the warrant and obligate Company X to issue a fixed number of shares in exchange for a fixed amount of cash. The monetary value of the shares varies directly with changes in the share price above $12. If the share price is equal to or less than $12, Investor Y would most likely put the warrant back to Company X, obligating it to issue a variable number of shares with a fixed monetary value (known at inception) of $2. Thus, at inception, the number of shares that the puttable warrant obligates Company X to issue can vary, and the financial instrument must be examined as described previously. The facts and circumstances are used to make a judgment whether the monetary value of the obligation to issue a number of shares that varies is predominantly based on a fixed monetary amount that is known at inception and, if so, it is a liability under the guidance in ASC 480-10-25-14.

In the previous example, if Company X's share price is well below the $10 exercise price of the warrant at inception, the warrant has a short life, and Company X's stock is determined to have low volatility, the circumstances would suggest that the monetary value of the obligation to issue shares is based predominantly on a fixed monetary amount known at inception and the instrument should be classified as a liability.

ASC 480-10-55-53 through 55-61; ASC 460-10-60-6 Majority Owner's Accounting for a Transaction in the Shares of a Consolidated Subsidiary and a Derivative Indexed to the Noncontrolling Interest in That Subsidiary

> **OBSERVATION:** The guidance in ASC 810-10-65-1 which was issued in December 2007, establishes accounting and reporting standards for a *noncontrolling* interest in a subsidiary and changes the term *minority interest* to *noncontrolling interest*. It does not affect the guidance in this Issue.

BACKGROUND

This Issue addresses the accounting for a scenario in which a parent company has a controlling interest in 80% of a subsidiary's equity shares and an unrelated entity has a noncontrolling interest in 20% of the equity shares. At acquisition of its 20% noncontrolling interest, the noncontrolling interest holder and the holder of the controlling interest in the subsidiary enter into a derivative contract that is indexed to the subsidiary's equity shares. The form of the derivative may be structured as follows:

- *Derivative 1* The parent has a forward contract to *purchase* the 20% noncontrolling interest at a fixed price at a specified future date.
- *Derivative 2* The parent has a call option to *purchase* the 20% noncontrolling interest at a fixed price at a specified future date and the holder of the noncontrolling interest has a put option to *sell* its 20% interest to the parent at the fixed price of the call option.
- *Derivative 3* The parent and the holder of the noncontrolling interest enter into an arrangement referred to as a *total return swap*, which has the following characteristics:
  — The parent agrees to pay the owner of the noncontrolling interest an amount based on the London Interbank Offered Rate (LIBOR) plus an agreed spread and, at the termination date, an amount equal to the net depreciation, if any, of the fair value of the 20% interest since the inception of the swap.

The holder of the noncontrolling interest will pay the parent an amount equal to the dividends received on its 20% interest and, at the termination date, an amount equal to the net appreciation, if any, of the 20% interest since the inception of the swap. The net change in the fair value of the 20% noncontrolling interest at the termination date may be determined based on an appraisal or based on the sales price of the stock. The following guidance applies only to the derivatives discussed above. Further, at the inception of the derivative instrument, the parent company must be the holder of the majority interest of the subsidiary's outstanding common stock and the subsidiary must be consolidated in the parent's financial statements.

ACCOUNTING ISSUES

- How should an entity that is the holder of an 80% controlling interest in a subsidiary account for an arrangement in which it enters separately into a derivative transaction with the holder of the 20% noncontrolling interest in the subsidiary at the time the noncontrolling interest holder purchases its interest in the subsidiary?
- How should an entity that acquires an 80% controlling interest in a subsidiary account for an arrangement in which it enters separately into a derivative with the seller (the 20% noncontrolling interest holder) at the same time as it acquires a controlling interest in the entity?
- How should an entity that sells a 20% noncontrolling interest in its 100% owned subsidiary to an unrelated party account for an arrangement in which the majority owner and the holder of the noncontrolling interest enter into the type of derivative transaction described above?

ACCOUNTING GUIDANCE

1. ASC 480-10 provides guidance for issuers on the classification and measurement of financial instruments with the characteristics of both liabilities and equity. Financial instruments under the scope of ASC 480

must be classified as liabilities, or as assets in some situations. Freestanding financial instruments under the scope of ASC 480 are *not* permitted to be combined with other freestanding derivatives unless the combination is required under the guidance in ASC 815 and its related guidance. A parent of a subsidiary that has entered into a forward purchase contract with the terms of Derivative 1 is required to account for the transaction as a financing and to consolidate 100% of the subsidiary. Because the parent must settle the contract by a physical repurchase of the noncontrolling interest's shares in exchange for cash, the parent should recognize the forward purchase contract as a liability that is initially measured at its present value. The amount of the noncontrolling interest should be reduced by a corresponding amount. Subsequent accruals to the amount of the contract and amounts paid or to be paid to the contract holders, if any, should be accounted for as interest cost.

2. A financial instrument with the terms of Derivative 2 should be accounted for based on one of the following three methods, subject to how the contract was issued:

— *Issued as a single freestanding instrument.* Account for the entire contract initially as a liability, or as an asset under some circumstances, and measure initially and subsequently at fair value.

— *Issued as two separate freestanding instruments—a written put option and a purchased call option.* Initially classify (a) a written put option as a liability that is measured at fair value under the guidance in ASC 480, and (b) the purchased call option under the guidance in ASC 815-40-25-4 and ASC 815-40-55-13, as (1) a liability or as an asset if the contract requires net cash settlement or the *counterparty* can choose to settle the contract in net cash, net shares, or a physical settlement in shares; or (2) as equity if physical settlement in shares or net share settlement is required, or the *entity* can choose settlement in either net cash, physical shares, or net share settlement in its own shares, assuming all the criteria in ASC 815-10-25-7 through 25-35 and ASC 815-40-55-2 through 55-6 have been met.

3. Regardless of how Derivative 2 was issued, the noncontrolling interest should be accounted for separately from the derivative instrument. If, however, the written put option and the purchased call option are embedded in the noncontrolling interest's shares and they are not mandatorily redeemable, the freestanding instrument should be accounted for as a financing in accordance with the guidance in ASC 480-10-55-59 and the parent should consolidate 100% of the subsidiary. In that case, the stated yield earned under the combined derivative instrument and the noncontrolling interest would be allocated to interest expense. That is, the financing would be accreted to the strike price of the forward or option until settlement. The parent would not recognize a gain or loss on the sale of the noncontrolling interest at the inception of the derivative instrument. A total return swap with the terms of Derivative 3 above should be indexed to an obligation to repurchase the

issuer's shares. Because the issuer may be required to transfer assets to settle the obligation, the total return swap should be accounted for as a liability, or as an asset under some circumstances, that is measured initially and subsequently at fair value. The noncontrolling interest should be accounted for separately from the total return swap.

4. Under the guidance in ASC 480-10, a freestanding financial instrument is not permitted to be combined with another freestanding financial instrument, unless the combination is required under the guidance in ASC 815. Therefore, freestanding derivatives under the guidance in ASC 480-10 should not be combined with a noncontrolling interest.

5. The parent retains the risks and rewards of ownership in the noncontrolling interest during the period in which the derivative instrument is in effect, even though another party is the noncontrolling interest's legal owner.

6. The counterparty to the derivative is financing the noncontrolling interest. Therefore, the requirement that the parent account for a purchased noncontrolling interest and a related derivative on a combined basis as a financing results in a presentation of the substance of the transaction.

OBSERVATION: The combined instrument is *not* a derivative under the scope of ASC 815. The FASB's Derivatives Implementation Group reached a similar conclusion on the combination of two instruments that meet the following criteria:

a. The transactions are entered into intentionally at the same time,
b. The transactions are with the same counterparty (or structured through an intermediary),
c. The transactions are related to the same risk, and
d. No economic reason or business purpose exists to induce the parties to structure the transactions separately rather than as a single transaction.

ASC 480-10-S99-3A Classification and Measurement of Redeemable Securities

The SEC Observer stated the views of the SEC staff about the application of Accounting Series Release (ASR) No. 268, *Presentation in Financial Statements of "Redeemable Preferred Stocks."*

SCOPE

Under the guidance in ASR 268, SEC registrants are required to classify outside permanent equity redeemable preferred securities that can be redeemed (*a*) at a fixed or determinable price on a fixed or determinable date, (*b*) at the holder's option, or (*c*) when an event occurs that is not completely under the issuer's control. The SEC staff believes that the above guidance can be applied by analogy to other equity instruments, such as common stock, derivatives instruments, noncontrolling interests if the redemption feature is not considered to be a freestanding option under the scope of ASC 480-10, equity securities held by and employee stock ownership plan with terms allowing an employee to put the securities to the sponsor for cash or other assets, and redeemable instruments classified in equity granted under a share-based payment arrangement with employees as discussed in ASC 718-10-S99.

The guidance in ASR 268 does *not* apply to the following instruments:

- Freestanding financial instruments that are classified as assets or liabilities under the guidance in ASC 480-10 or other GAAP;
- Freestanding derivative instruments classified in stockholders' equity under the guidance in ASC 815-40, which applies to embedded derivatives indexed to, and potentially settled in, a company's own stock.
- Equity instruments subject to registration payment arrangements as defined in ASC 825-20-15-3;
- Share-based payment awards;
- Convertible debt instruments that contain an equity component that is classified separately. A convertible debt instrument may be required to be separated into a liability and an equity component under other GAAP. A convertible debt instrument that is not redeemable at the balance sheet date, but that may become redeemable based on the passage of time or the occurrence of an event is not considered to be redeemable at the balance sheet date;
- Certain redemptions that occur as a result of a liquidation event. However, deemed liquidation events under which a holder is required or permitted to redeem only one or more equity instruments of a specific class for cash or other assets would require the application of ASR 268;
- Certain redemptions covered by proceeds from insurance, for example, an equity instrument that becomes redeemable on the holder's or disability;

CLASSIFICATION

OBSERVATION: ASC 480 provides guidance for issuers on the classification and measurement of financial instruments with the characteristics of both liabilities and equity. Financial instruments under the scope of ASC 480 must be classified as liabilities, or as assets in some situations, because they represent an issuer's obligations.

The SEC Observer clarified the SEC staff's position regarding the interaction of the staff's guidance on this announcement with the guidance in ASC 480 when accounting for *conditionally* redeemable preferred shares. The guidance in ASC 480 does *not* apply to the accounting for such shares if they are conditionally redeemable at a holder's option or when an uncertain event *not* under the issuer's control occurs, because there is no unconditional obligation to redeem the shares by a transfer of assets at a specified or determinable date or when a certain event occurs. The condition is resolved when an uncertain event occurs. Once it becomes certain that such an event will occur, the shares should be accounted for under the provisions of ASC 480, which requires that the shares be measured at fair value and reclassified as a liability. As a result, stockholders' equity would be reduced by an equivalent amount with no gain or loss recognition. The reclassification is similar to a redemption of shares by issuing debt. As in the redemption of preferred shares discussed in ASC 260-10-99S-2 ("The

Effect on the Calculation of Earnings per Share for the Redemption or Induced Conversion of Preferred Stock"), when calculating earnings per share, the difference between the fair value of the liability and the carrying amount of the preferred debt at reclassification should be deducted from or added to net earnings available to common shareholders.

The SEC staff believes that an issuer of a redeemable equity security should evaluate separately all the events that could trigger redemption if some of the security's redemption features are not under the issuer's control. A security should be classified outside of permanent equity if *any* event not under the issuer's sole control, regardless of the probability of occurrence, could trigger its redemption. Although a change in classification is not required if an event occurs that would cause a potential ordinary liquidation that would require cash payment only if the company is totally liquidated, the occurrence of events that could cause the redemption of one or more particular classes or types of equity securities would require that those securities be classified outside of permanent equity. The classification of equity securities whose redemption is not solely under the issuer's control should be based on the individual facts and circumstances.

For example, the SEC Observer noted that a redeemable security with a provision that requires the issuer to obtain the approval of the board of directors to call the security may not necessarily be under the issuer's control, because the board of directors may be controlled by the holders of the particular redeemable security. In contrast, classification in permanent equity would continue to be appropriate in a situation in which a preferred stock agreement includes a provision stating that the issuer's decision to sell all or substantially all of the company's assets and a subsequent distribution to common stockholders triggers redemption of the preferred equity security, because the decision to sell all or substantially all of the issuer's assets is solely under the issuer's control. That is, a distribution to common stockholders cannot be *triggered* or required by the preferred stock holders as a result of their representation on the board of directors.

One exception to the requirement in this announcement that should *not* be analogized to other transactions occurs when there is a provision that the equity securities become redeemable as a result of the holder's death or disability. Under that circumstance, the redemption of the securities would be funded by the proceeds of an insurance policy that is in force and that the issuer intends to and is able to maintain in force. Consequently, the securities continue to be classified in permanent equity.

MEASUREMENT

The SEC staff believes the *initial* amount of a redeemable equity security included in temporary equity in accordance with the guidance in ASR 268 should be its fair value on the issue date, except in the following circumstances:

- *Share-based payment arrangements with employees.* Measure the initial amount recognized in temporary equity based on the instrument's redemption provisions and the proportion of consideration received as employee services.

- *Employee stock ownership plans.* If the cash redemption option is related only to a market value guarantee feature, a registrant's accounting policy for temporary equity may be to present (a) the amount of the total guaranteed market value of the equity securities, or (b) the maximum cash obligation based on the fair value of the underlying equity securities at the balance sheet date.
- *Noncontrolling interests.* Present in temporary equity the initial carrying amount of a noncontrolling interest in accordance with the guidance in ASC 805-20-30.
- *Convertible debt instruments that include a separately classified equity component.* Present an amount in temporary equity only if the instrument is currently redeemable or convertible at the issuance date for cash or other assets. If a portion of a component classified as equity is included in temporary equity, present the amount of cash or other assets that would be paid to a holder on conversion or redemption at the issuance date in excess of the component classified as a liability on the issuance date.
- *Host equity contracts.* Present in temporary equity the initial carrying amount of the host contract in accordance with the guidance in ASC 815-15-30.
- *Preferred stock with a beneficial conversion feature or that is issued with other instruments.* Include in temporary equity the total amount allocated to the instrument in accordance with the guidance in ASC 470-20 *less* the amount of the beneficial conversion feature recognized at the issuance date.

The following are the views of the SEC staff about the *subsequent measurement* of a redeemable equity instrument subject to the requirements of ASR 268:

- The amount of securities currently redeemable at a holder's option should be adjusted to their maximum redemption amount at each balance sheet date. If the maximum amount is contingent on an index or similar variable, the amount in temporary equity should be calculated based on the existing conditions at the balance sheet date, such as the instrument's current fair value. At each balance sheet date, the amount of dividends *not* currently declared or paid but that will be paid under the redemption features or if their ultimate payment is *not* under the registrant's control should be included. If an instrument is not currently redeemable, an adjustment is unnecessary if it is not probable that the instrument will become redeemable, such as when redemption will occur only based on the passage of time.
- If it is probable that an equity instrument will become redeemable, the SEC staff will not object if either of the following accounting methods are applied consistently for securities that will become redeemable at a future *determinable* date but whose redemption amount is *variable* (e.g., they are redeemable at fair value):

a. Accrete changes in the redemption value from the date of issuance or when redemption becomes probable (if later) to the security's earliest redemption date using an appropriate method, usually the interest method. Changes in redemption value are considered to be changes in accounting estimates and accounted for, and disclosed, in accordance with the guidance in ASC 250.

b. Recognize changes in the redemption value (for example, fair value) immediately as they occur and adjust the security's carrying amount to equal the redemption value at the end of each reporting period. Under this method, the end of the reporting period would be viewed as if it were also the security's redemption date.

The following is additional guidance provided by the SEC staff on subsequent measurement under the following circumstances:

- *Share based payment arrangements with employees.* At each balance sheet date, base the amount included in temporary equity on the instrument's redemption provisions considering the proportion of consideration received in the form of employee services (the pattern of recognition of compensation cost in accordance with the guidance in ASC 718).

- *Employee stock ownership plans.* If a cash redemption obligation is related only to a market value guarantee feature, a registrant's accounting policy for temporary equity may be to present (a) the amount of the total guaranteed market value of the equity securities, or (b) the maximum cash obligation based on the fair value of the underlying equity securities at the balance sheet date.

- *Noncontrolling interests.* Determine the adjustment of the carrying amount in temporary equity after attributing the subsidiary's net income or a loss according to the guidance in ASC 810-10.

- *Convertible debt instruments that include a separately classified equity component.* Present an amount in temporary equity only if the instrument is currently redeemable or convertible at the issuance date for cash or other assets. If a portion of a component classified as equity is included in temporary equity, present the amount of cash or other assets that would be paid to a holder on conversion or redemption at the issuance date in excess of the component classified as a liability on the issuance date.

- *Fair value option.* Redeemable equity instruments included in temporary equity in accordance with the requirements in ASR 268 should not be measured at fair value through earnings instead of applying the SEC staff's measurement guidance. Also see the guidance in ASC 825-10-50-8, which prohibits the use of the fair value option for financial instruments that are wholly or partially classified in stockholder's equity, including temporary equity.

The SEC staff believes that regardless of which of the above accounting methods is used to account for a redeemable equity security, that security's carrying amount should be reduced only to the extent that the registrant had previously increased the security's carrying amount as a result of the application of the guidance in this Topic.

The SEC staff expects registrants to apply the accounting method selected consistently and to disclose the selected policy in the notes to the financial statements. In addition, registrants that elect to accrete changes in redemption value over the period from the date of issuance to the earliest redemption date should disclose the security's redemption value as if it were redeemable.

RECLASSIFICATION INTO PERMANENT EQUITY

If temporary classification of a redeemable equity security is no longer required, its carrying amount should be reclassified from temporary to permanent equity at the date of the occurrence of the event causing reclassification. Prior financial statements should *not* be adjusted. The SEC staff also believes that reversal of previously recorded adjustments to the security's carrying amount would be inappropriate when a reclassification occurs.

DECONSOLIDATION OF A SUBSIDIARY

An entity that deconsolidates a subsidiary recognizes a gain or loss on that transaction in net income based on the measurement guidance in ASC 810-10-40-5. The carrying amount of a noncontrolling interest, if any, in the former subsidiary affects that gain or loss calculation. The SEC staff believes that because adjustments to a noncontrolling interest's carrying amount from the application of the guidance in this SEC staff announcement have not entered into the determination of the entity's net income, the noncontrolling interest's carrying amount should likewise *not* include any adjustments made to the noncontrolling interest as a result of the application of the guidance in this SEC staff announcement. Previous adjustments to the noncontrolling interest's carrying amount from the application of the guidance in this SEC staff announcement should be eliminated by recording a credit to the parent entity's equity.

EARNINGS PER SHARE

Preferred Securities Issued by a Parent or Single Reporting Entity

Increases or decreases in the carrying amount of a redeemable security should be treated like dividends on nonredeemable stock by charging retained earnings, or if no retained earnings exist, by charging paid-in capital, regardless of the method used to account for the security or whether the security is redeemable at a fixed price or at fair value. In calculating earnings per share and the ratio of earnings to combined fixed charges and preferred stock dividends, income available to common stockholders should be reduced or increased as a result of increases or decreases in a preferred security's carrying amount. Guidance related to the accounting at the date of a redemption or induced conversion of a preferred equity security may be found in ASC 260-10-S99-2 ("The Effect on the Calculation of Earnings per Share for the Redemption or Induced Conversion of Preferred Stock")

Common Securities Issued by a Parent or a Single Reporting Entity

Increases or decreases in the carrying amount of a redeemable security should be treated like dividends on nonredeemable stock by charging retained earnings, or if no retained earnings exist, by charging paid-in capital, regardless of the method used to account for the security or whether the security is redeemable at a fixed price or at fair value. But those increases or decreases in a redeemable common stock's carrying amount should *not* affect income available for common stock holders. The SEC staff believes that in so far as a common shareholder has a contractual right to receive an amount other than the fair value of those shares at redemption, a common shareholder has, in substance, received a different distribution than the other common shareholders. Entities whose capital structures include a class of common stock with dividend rates that differ from those of another class of common shareholders but without senior rights, are required to calculate their earnings per share based on the two-class method discussed in ASC 260-10-45-59A. As a result, increases or decreases in the carrying amount of a class of common stock that is redeemable at other than fair value should be considered in the calculation of earnings per share using the two-class method. In footnote 8 of this Topic, the SEC staff states that if a common security is redeemable at other than fair value, it is acceptable to allocate earnings under the two-class method using one of the following two methods:

- Treat the total periodic adjustment to the security's carrying amount as a result of the application of the guidance in this Topic like an actual dividend, or
- Treat like an actual dividend only the portion of the periodic adjustment to the security's carrying amount as a result of the application of the guidance in this Topic that represents a redemption in excess of fair value.

The SEC staff does not expect the two-class method to be used in the calculation of earnings per share if a class of common stock is redeemable at fair value, because the dividend distribution to those shareholders does not differ from that made to other common shareholders. The SEC staff believe that common stock redeemable based on a specified formula is considered redeemable at fair value if the formula is intended to equal or reasonably approximate fair value. However, a formula based only on a fixed multiple of earnings or a similar measure would *not* qualify.

The SEC staff also believe that likewise, the two-class method need *not* be used if share-based payment awards in the form of common shares or options or common shares granted to employees are redeemable at fair value. However, the two-class method may still apply to such share-based payment awards under the guidance in ASC 260-10-45-59A and ASC 260-10-45-60, 45-60A through 45-68, 55-24 through 55-30, 55-71 through 55-75 (*Participating Securities and the Two-Class Method under Statement No. 128*).

Noncontrolling Interests

In accordance with the guidance in ASC 810-10-45-23, (a) changes in a parent's ownership interest accounted for by the equity method while a parent retains control of the subsidiary and (b) an adjustment to a noncontrolling interest as a result of the application of the guidance in this SEC staff announcement, have no effect on net income or comprehensive income in the consolidated financial statements. Instead, such adjustments are accounted for like a repurchase of a noncontrolling interest, although they may be recognized in retained earnings rather than in paid-in capital. The SEC staff requires that the above earnings per share guidance for preferred securities and common shares issued by a parent should be applied to noncontrolling interests as follows:

- *Noncontrolling interest in the form of preferred securities.* If a redemption feature of a noncontrolling interest in the form of preferred securities was issued or guaranteed by a parent, an adjustment to the security's carrying amount reduces or increases income available to common stockholders. If not, the adjustment is attributed to the parent and the noncontrolling interest in accordance with the guidance in ASC 260-10-55-64 through 55-67.

- *Noncontrolling interest in the form of common securities.* Adjustments to the carrying amount of a noncontrolling interest issued in the form of common stock to represent a fair value redemption feature do *not* affect earnings per share. However, if a noncontrolling interest was issued in the form of common stock to represent a non-fair value redemption feature, adjustments to the noncontrolling interest's carrying amount affect earnings per share, but the way those adjustments reduce or increase income available to common stockholders may differ. Application of the two-class method is unnecessary if the terms of the redemption feature are fully considered when net income is attributed under the guidance in ASC 810-10-45-21. But if they are not fully considered, the two-class method must be applied at the level of the subsidiary to determine net income available to the parent's common stockholders.

Convertible Debt Instruments that Include a Separately Classified Equity Component

There should be no incremental earnings per share accounting from the application of the SEC staff's guidance in this announcement for convertible debt instruments to the requirements of ASR 268. The earnings per share accounting is addressed in ASC 260-10.

DISCLOSURES

Certain disclosures about redeemable equity instruments are required under the guidance in ASC 268 and SEC Regulation S-X. The SEC staff expects registrants to provide the following additional disclosures in the notes to the financial statements:

- The accounting method used to adjust the amount to be redeemed on a redeemable equity instrument.

- The redeemable amount of an equity instrument as if it were currently redeemable if a registrant chooses to accrete changes immediately in the amount at which a redeemable equity instrument would be redeemed (method b. discussed for equity instruments if it is probable that the equity instrument would be redeemed.)

- If a redeemable equity instrument is not adjusted to the amount at which it would be redeemed, the reasons why it is not probable that the instrument will be redeemed.

ASC 480—Distinguishing Liabilities from Equity

- A reconciliation between net income and income available to common stockholders if charges or credits related to preferred stock instruments issued by a parent and those related to a noncontrolling interest in the form of a preferred stock instrument, as discussed above, are material.
- The amount credited to a parent's equity when a subsidiary is deconsolidated, as discussed above.

ASC 480-10-65-1 Effective Date and Transition for Mandatorily Redeemable Financial Instruments of Certain Nonpublic Entities of FASB Statement No. 150, *Accounting for Certain Financial Instruments with Characteristics of both Liabilities and Equity*

The FASB directed the staff to issue this FSP to defer the effective date of ASC 480-10 as it applies to:

- Mandatorily redeemable financial instruments of certain nonpublic entities.
- Certain mandatorily redeemable *noncontrolling* interests.

The FASB also directed the staff to provide guidance on disclosure and transition for those entities.

BACKGROUND

The guidance in ASC 480 states that it is effective for mandatorily redeemable financial instruments of nonpublic entities in the first fiscal period beginning after December 15, 2003. Under the guidance in ASC 480-10-25-4, 25-6, liability classification of mandatorily redeemable financial instruments is required "unless the redemption is required to occur only upon the liquidation or termination of the reporting entity." However, that exception does *not* apply when a subsidiary's financial statements are consolidated with those of its parent. Many entities were concerned about the effect of liability classification and asked that this requirement be changed or delayed in order to give companies time to adapt to the provisions of ASC 480-10 and to educate users of their financial statements. Other entities were concerned about whether step acquisition accounting should be applied when mandatorily redeemable *noncontrolling* interests acquired in a purchase business combination are reclassified as liabilities or when they are redeemed. Still others requested a change or delay in the effective date of ASC 480 (FAS-150) because of concern that some implementation issues have not been resolved in time for the adoption of the guidance in ASC 480 (FAS-150) while financial reports are being completed.

ACCOUNTING GUIDANCE

- For *nonpublic* entities that are *not* SEC registrants, that is, entities that (*a*) have *not* or will *not* issue debt or equity securities traded in a public market, (*b*) are *not* required to file financial statements with the SEC, or (*c*) do *not* provide financial statements for the purpose of issuing any class of securities in a public market, the guidance in ASC 480 (FAS-150) is effective as follows:
    - *Instruments mandatorily redeemable on fixed dates for fixed amounts or determined by reference to an interest rate index, currency index, or another*

external index The classification, measurement, and disclosure provisions of FAS-150 are effective for fiscal periods beginning after December 15, 2004.

— *All other mandatorily redeemable financial instruments* The classification, measurement, and disclosure provisions of ASC 480 (FAS-150) are deferred *indefinitely* for those instruments until the FASB takes action. During that period, the FASB will reconsider the implementation issues and possibly reconsider the classification and measurement guidance for those instruments concurrently with its ongoing project on liabilities and equity.

Those deferrals do *not* apply to mandatorily redeemable financial instruments issued by SEC registrants, even if they meet the definition for a nonpublic entity in ASC 480 (FAS-150). Registrants should follow the Statement's effective dates and related guidance, which includes the deferral for certain mandatorily *noncontrolling* interests, as applicable.

If an entity is a *nonpublic* entity and *not* an SEC registrant, the deferral in this FSP *does* apply to shares required to be redeemed under related agreements that are issued with a redemption agreement for specific underlying shares that are consequently mandatorily redeemable. However, the requirements in ASC 505-10-15-1, 50-3 through 50-5, 50-11; ASC 470-10-50-5 continue to apply to such entities. Specifically, disclosure is required about the information in ASC 505-10-50-3, regarding pertinent rights and privileges of various securities outstanding, and the information in ASC 505-10-50-11, regarding the amount of redemption requirements for all issues of stock redeemable at fixed or determinable prices on fixed or determinable dates in each of the next five years.

- The effective date of the guidance in ASC 480 for certain mandatorily redeemable noncontrolling interests of public and nonpublic entities is deferred as follows:
  — For mandatorily redeemable *noncontrolling* interests, the classification and measurement provisions of ASC 480 (FAS-150) are deferred indefinitely until the FASB takes further action if a subsidiary would *not* be required to classify those interests as liabilities under the exception in ASC 480-10-25-4, 25-6, but the parent would have to classify them as liabilities in consolidation.

For other mandatorily redeemable *noncontrolling* interests issued before November 5, 2003, the *measurement* provisions of ASC 480, but not the provision related to classification, are deferred *indefinitely* for a parent in consolidated financial statements and for its subsidiary that issues those instruments until the FASB takes further action. The measurement guidance for redeemable shares and *noncontrolling* interests in ASC 480-10-S99-3, S45-2 through S45-3, S35-2, S55-1, S55-4, S30-1 through S30-2 ("Classification and Measurement of Redeemable Securities") should be followed while the deferral of the guidance in ASC 480 applies. During that time, the FASB will reconsider the implementation issues and possibly reconsider the classification and measurement guidance for those instruments concurrently with its ongoing project on liabilities and equity. During the deferral period, public and nonpublic entities that are SEC registrants should follow the Statement's disclosure requirement in ASC 480-10-50-1 through 50-3 and disclosures required in other applicable pronouncements.

CHAPTER 35
ASC 505—EQUITY

CONTENTS

Part I: General Guidance	35,002
Overview	35,002
ASC 505-10: Overall	35,003
Background	35,003
Illustration of Balance Sheet Presentation of Stockholders' Equity December 31, 20X5	35,003
Stockholders' Equity Terminology and Relationships	35,003
Illustration of Capital Stock Relationships	35,004
Disclosure of Information about Stockholders' Equity	35,005
Information about Securities	35,005
Liquidation Preference of Preferred Stock	35,006
Redeemable Stock	35,006
Illustration of Capital Structure Disclosures	35,006
Additional Paid-In Capital	35,007
Noncontrolling Interests	35,008
ASC 505-20: Cash Dividends, Stock Dividends, and Stock Splits	35,008
Cash Dividends	35,008
Stock Dividends	35,008
Illustration of Stock Dividends	35,009
Stock Splits	35,009
Figure 35-1: Accounting for Stock Dividends and Stock Splits	35,011
Stock Rights	35,011
ASC 505-30: Treasury Stock	35,011
Treasury Stock	35,011
Accounting and Reporting	35,011
Purchase Price of Treasury Stock	35,013
ASC 505-50: Equity-Based Payments to Nonemployees	35,013
Equity-Based Payments to Nonemployees	35,013
Recognition and Measurement Principles	35,014
Part II: Interpretive Guidance	35,015
ASC 505-10: Overall	35,015
ASC 505-10-15-2, 50-6, 50-8A, 50-9 through 50-10; ASC 470-10-60-2	
Disclosure Requirements under FASB Statement No. 129, Disclosure of Information about Capital Structure, Relating to Contingently Convertible Securities	35,015
ASC 310-10-45-14; ASC 505-10-45-1 through 45-2; ASC 850-10-60-4	
Classifying Notes Received for Capital Stock	35,016
ASC 505-20: Stock Dividends and Stock Splits	35,017
ASC 505-20-15-3A	
Accounting for Distributions to Shareholders with Components of Stock and Cash	35,017

35,002 ASC 505—Equity

ASC 505-30: Treasury Stock	35,018
ASC 505-30-25-3 through 25-4, 30-2, 30-4, 50-3 through 50-4, 60-1; ASC 225-20-55-4	
Accounting for a Purchase of Treasury Shares at a Price Significantly in Excess of the Current Market Price of the Shares and the Income Statement Classification of Costs Incurred in Defending against a Takeover Attempt	35,018
Illustration of the Accounting for "Greenmail" Payments	35,019
ASC 505-30-25-5 through 25-6, 55-1, 55-3, 55-5 through 55-6, 60-2; ASC 260-10-55-89	
Accounting for an Accelerated Share Repurchase Program	35,019
ASC 505-50: Equity-Based Payments to Nonemployees	35,020
ASC 505-50-05-1, 05-4 through 05-5, 25-5, 30-18 through 30-19, 30-29, 35-13 through 35-15, 50-2, 55-25 through 55-27; ASC 845-10-50-2	
Accounting by a Grantee for an Equity Instrument to Be Received in Conjunction with Providing Goods or Services	35,020
ASC 505-50-05-3, 05-8, 15-2 through 15-3, 25-2, 25-4, 25-9, 30-2 through 30-7, 30-11 through 30-14, 30-21 through 30-23, 30-25 through 30-28, 30-30 through 30-31, 35-3, 35-5 through 35-10, 55-2 through 55-11, 55-13 through 55-17, 55-20 through 55-24, 55-28, 55-31 through 55-40; ASC 440-10-60-4	
Accounting for Equity Instruments That Are Issued to Other Than Employees for Acquiring, or in Conjunction with Selling, Goods or Services	35,022
Illustration of Accounting for Nonemployee Stock Options with Variable Terms	35,027
ASC 505-50-05-6 through 05-7, 25-7 through 25-8, 30-15 through 30-16, 35-11 through 35-12, S25-2, S99-2, 45-1	
Accounting Recognition for Certain Transactions Involving Equity Instruments Granted to Other Than Employees	35,028
ASC 505-50-S25-1; S99-1	
Grantor Balance Sheet Presentation of Unvested, Forfeitable Equity Instruments Granted to a Nonemployee	35,030
ASC 505-60: Spinoffs and Reverser Spinoffs	35,031
ASC 505-60-05-2 through 05-4, 15-2, 25-2, 25-4 through 25-5, 25-7 through 25-8, 45-1, 55-2, 55-5, 55-7 through 55-12	
Accounting for Reverse Spinoffs	35,031

PART I: GENERAL GUIDANCE

OVERVIEW

The various elements constituting stockholders' equity in the statement of financial position are classified according to source. Stockholders' equity may be classified broadly into four categories: (1) legal capital, (2) additional paid-in capital, (3) noncontrolling interests in subsidiaries, and (4) retained earnings. Detailed information is presented in the body of the statement, in related notes, or in some combination thereof.

ASC 505-10: OVERALL

BACKGROUND

Stockholders' equity represents the interest of the owners of a corporation in the corporation's assets. It represents the residual interest in the enterprise's assets, after liabilities have been subtracted, arising from the investment of owners and the retention of earnings over time.

In the balance sheet, stockholders' equity usually is displayed in two broad categories—*paid-in* or *contributed capital* and *retained earnings*. Paid-in or contributed capital represents the amount provided by stockholders in the original purchase of shares of stock or resulting from subsequent transactions with owners, such as treasury stock transactions. Retained earnings represent the amount of previous income of the corporation that has not been distributed to owners as dividends or transferred to paid-in or contributed capital.

PRACTICE POINTER: A business may be able to eliminate an accumulated deficit in retained earnings in situations where the business has been struggling but reaches a turnaround point where profitable operations seem likely by going through a quasi-reorganization. For guidance as to when a quasi-reorganization would be appropriate and coverage of the accounting and reporting for a quasi-reorganization, see the Chapter 57, *ASC 852—Reorganizations*.

Illustration of Balance Sheet Presentation of Stockholders' Equity
December 31, 20X5

Preferred stock, $50 par value, 10,000 shares authorized, 7,000 shares authorized and outstanding	$ 350,000
Common stock, $25 par value, 100,000 shares authorized, 75,000 shares issued	1,875,000
Paid-in capital in excess of par value on common stock	500,000
Common stock dividend to be distributed	262,500
Total paid-in capital	$2,987,500
Retained earnings	1,000,000
Total paid-in capital and retained earnings	$3,987,500
Treasury stock, 10,000 shares of common stock at cost	(300,000)
Total stockholders' equity	$3,687,500

STOCKHOLDERS' EQUITY TERMINOLOGY AND RELATIONSHIPS

Legal (or *stated*) *capital* usually is defined by state law. It refers to the amount of capital that must be maintained by a corporation for the protection of its creditors. Legal capital may consist of common or preferred shares. Preferred shares may be participating or nonparticipating as to the earnings of the corporation, may be cumulative or noncumulative as to the payment of dividends, may have a preference claim on assets upon liquidation of the business, and may be callable for redemption at a specified price. Usually, preferred stock does not have voting rights.

Common stock usually has the right to vote, the right to share in earnings, a preemptive right to a proportionate share of any additional common stock issued, and the right to share in assets on liquidation.

Stock is usually issued with a par value. No-par value stock may or may not have a stated value. *Par* or *stated value* is the amount that is established in the stock account at the time the stock is issued. When stock is issued above or below par value, a premium or discount on the stock is recorded, respectively. A discount reduces paid-in or contributed capital; a premium increases paid-in or contributed capital. A premium on stock is often referred to as "paid-in capital in excess of par value." Because the issuance of stock at a discount is not legal in many jurisdictions, discounts on stock are not frequently encountered.

A corporation's charter contains the types and amounts of stock that it can legally issue, which is called the *authorized capital stock*. When part or all of the authorized capital stock is issued, it is called *issued capital stock*. Since a corporation may purchase its own capital stock in the form of treasury stock, the amount of issued capital stock in the hands of stockholders is called *outstanding capital stock*.

A corporation may sell its capital stock by subscriptions. An individual subscriber becomes a stockholder upon subscribing to the capital stock. Upon full payment of the subscription, a stock certificate evidencing ownership in the corporation is issued. When the subscription method is used to sell capital stock, a subscription receivable account is debited and a capital stock subscribed account is credited. On payment of the subscription, the subscription receivable account is credited and cash or other assets are debited. On the actual issuance of the stock certificates, the capital stock subscribed account is eliminated and the regular capital stock account is increased.

Illustration of Capital Stock Relationships

A company has the following capital stock structure: The numbers below represent shares of a particular class of stock (e.g., common stock) and indicate the relationships among the various components of authorized stock. The number of shares authorized is 10,000, of which 8,000 have been issued and 2,000 are unissued. Of the 8,000 issued shares, 7,000 are outstanding (i.e., in the hands of investors) and 1,000 represent treasury shares (i.e., shares that were issued and outstanding at one time, but have been reacquired by the company). Of the 2,000 unissued shares, 500 have been subscribed and 1,500 are unsubscribed. The 500 subscribed shares have been partially paid and are considered unissued until they are fully paid, at which time they will be issued and thereafter are outstanding shares.

Following are examples of how the numbers of shares change for several independent common capital stock transactions:

1. *Sale of 700 shares of previously unissued stock*—Unsubscribed stock declines by 700 shares, as does the number of unissued shares. Outstanding shares and issued shares both increase by 700. As a

result, unissued shares number 1,300 (2,000 − 700) and issued shares number 8,700 (8,000 + 700), of which 7,700 (7,000 + 700) are outstanding.

2. *Sale of 100 shares of treasury stock*—Treasury stock declines to 900 (1,000 − 100) shares and outstanding increases to 7,100 (7,000 + 100) shares. The total number of unissued and issued shares remains unchanged.

3. *Subscribed shares (500) are paid in full*—Subscribed shares become zero (500 − 500), reducing unissued shares to 1,500 (2,000 − 500). Outstanding and issued shares increase to 7,500 and 8,500, respectively.

DISCLOSURE OF INFORMATION ABOUT STOCKHOLDERS' EQUITY

When financial statements are prepared in conformity with GAAP, capital changes must be disclosed in a separate statement(s) or note(s) to the financial statement. This requirement is in addition to disclosure of the changes in retained earnings, although all capital changes may be included in one statement. Capital accounts may have to be disclosed because of changes during the year in capital stock, additional paid-in capital accounts, retained earnings, treasury stock, and other capital accounts (ASC 505-10-50-2).

ASC 505 establishes standards for disclosing information about an entity's capital structure. Three terms are particularly important in understanding and applying ASC 505—securities, participating rights, and preferred stock (ASC Glossary). These terms are defined as follows:

- **Securities**—evidence of debt or ownership or a related right, including options and warrants as well as debt and stock
- **Participating rights**—contractual rights of security holders to receive dividends or returns from the issuer's profits, cash flows, or returns on investments
- **Preferred stock**—a security that has preferential rights over common stock

ASC 505 requires information about capital structure to be disclosed in three separate categories—information about securities, liquidation preference of preferred stock, and redeemable stock.

Information about Securities

The entity shall provide within its financial statements a summary explanation of the pertinent rights and privileges of the various securities that are outstanding (ASC 505-10-50-3). Information that is to be disclosed includes:

- Dividend and liquidation preferences
- Participating rights
- Call prices and dates
- Conversion or exercise prices or rates and dates
- Sinking-fund requirements

- Unusual voting rights
- Significant terms of contracts to issue additional shares

In addition to the information about rights and privileges associated with securities, the number of shares issued upon conversion, exercise, or satisfaction of required conditions during the most recent annual fiscal period and any subsequent interim period shall be disclosed.

Liquidation Preference of Preferred Stock

Preferred stock or other senior securities may have a preference in involuntary liquidation that is in excess of the security's par or stated value. In this situation, the issuing entity shall disclose the liquidation preference of the stock (i.e., the relationship of the liquidation preference and the par or stated value of the shares). Under the following guidelines, this disclosure should be (ASC 505-10-50-4):

- Presented within the equity section, either parenthetically or "in short" (i.e., included in the body of the financial statement, but not added in the total of stockholders' equity).
- Presented as an aggregate amount.

PRACTICE POINTER: Take care not to overlook the requirement that the liquidation preference of preferred stock must be presented in the aggregate and *in the body of the equity section of the balance sheet* rather than in notes to the financial statements. This is an unusual requirement and could be easily overlooked.

Other disclosures, which may be made either in the financial statements or in related notes, are:

- The aggregate *or* per share amounts at which preferred stock may be called or are subject to redemption through sinking fund operations or otherwise
- The aggregate *and* per share amounts of cumulative preferred dividends in arrears

Redeemable Stock

Redeemable stock *must be repurchased* by the issuing entity. In this situation, the issuing entity is required to disclose the amount of redemption requirements, separately by issue or combined, for all issues of stock for which the redemption prices and dates are fixed or determinable. This information is required for each of the next five years following the date of the latest statement of financial position that is presented (ASC 505-10-50-11).

Illustration of Capital Structure Disclosures

Following are examples of the disclosures required by ASC 505. Disclosures of information about securities, the liquidation preference of preferred stock, and redeemable stock are the direct result of specific circumstances that exist within the reporting entity. No example can include all possible information that may require disclosure. Care should be taken in relying on these or other examples because of differences that may exist among reporting entities.

Information about Securities

ABC Company's capital structure includes common and preferred stock that is described as follows in its statement of financial position and in a note to the financial statements:

Statement of financial position:

> Convertible preferred stock—$40 par value, 5 million shares authorized, 4 million shares and 3.8 million shares issued and outstanding in 20X6 and 20X5, respectively
>
> Common stock—$10 par value, 10 million shares authorized, 6 million shares issued and outstanding in 20X6 and 20X5

Note to the financial statements:

> Each share of ABC preferred stock is convertible into four shares of ABC common stock at any time through December 31, 20X9. The preferred stock is entitled to a cumulative annual dividend of $2.50.

Liquidation Preference of Preferred Stock

DEF Company has preferred stock outstanding, as described below in the body of the statement of financial position:

> Preferred stock—$10 per share par value, 1 million shares authorized, issued and outstanding: 20X6 and 20X5—.8 million and .75 million shares, respectively. Aggregate liquidation preference: 20X6 and 20X5—$12 million and $11.25 million, respectively.

Redeemable Stock

GHI Company has redeemable preferred stock outstanding, as described below in notes to the financial statements:

> Preferred stock—Each share of GHI preferred stock is convertible into four shares of GHI common stock. On December 31, 20X8, the preferred shares are redeemable at the company's option at $50 per share. Based on the current market price of the stock, the company expects the majority of the preferred shares to be converted into common stock prior to December 31, 20X8.

ADDITIONAL PAID-IN CAPITAL

All stockholders' equity that is not classified as legal capital, noncontrolling interests in subsidiaries, or retained earnings usually is designated as additional paid-in capital. The common sources of additional paid-in capital are:

- Excess of par or stated value paid for capital stock
- Sale of treasury stock
- The issuance of detachable stock purchase warrants (ASC 470-20-25-2)
- Donated assets
- Capital created by a corporate readjustment or quasi-reorganization

If capital stock is issued for the acquisition of property and it appears that, at about the same time and pursuant to a previous agreement or understanding, some portion of the stock so issued is donated to the corporation, the par value of the stock is not an appropriate basis for valuing the property. Generally, donated stock should be recorded at fair value at the time it is received. Fair value may be determined by the value of the stock or the value of the asset, services, or other consideration received.

Charges that are properly chargeable to income accounts of the current or future years should not be made to paid-in capital (ASC 505-10-25-1).

NONCONTROLLING INTERESTS

In the presentation of consolidated financial statements, a noncontrolling interest (formerly referred to as *minority interest*) is that portion of equity (net assets) in a subsidiary company that is not attributable, directly or indirectly, to the parent company. The noncontrolling interest in the subsidiary is part of the equity of the consolidated group (ASC 810-10-45-15).

A noncontrolling interest is reported in the consolidated statement of financial position within equity, clearly labeled as being separate from the parent's equity. For example, the following title might be used: *Noncontrolling interest in subsidiary*. An entity with noncontrolling interests in more than one subsidiary may present those interests in the aggregate in the consolidated statement of financial position (ASC 810-10-45-16).

ASC 505-20: CASH DIVIDENDS, STOCK DIVIDENDS AND STOCK SPLITS

A *dividend* is a pro rata distribution by a corporation, based on shares of a particular class, and usually represents a distribution based on earnings.

CASH DIVIDENDS

Cash dividends are the most common type of dividend distribution. Preferred stock usually pays a fixed dividend, expressed in dollars or a percentage of par or stated value. Three dates usually are involved in a dividend distribution:

1. *Date of declaration*: The date the board of directors formally declares the dividend to the stockholders
2. *Date of record*: The date the board of directors specifies that stockholders of record on that date are entitled to the dividend payment
3. *Date of payment*: The date the dividend is actually disbursed by the corporation or its paying agent

Cash dividends are recorded on the books of the corporation as a liability (dividends payable) on the date of declaration. Dividends are paid only on authorized, issued, and outstanding shares, thereby eliminating any dividend payment on treasury stock.

STOCK DIVIDENDS

Stock dividends are distributions of a company's own capital stock to its existing stockholders in lieu of cash. Stock dividends are accounted for by transferring an amount equal to the fair market value of the stock from retained earnings to paid-in capital. The dividend is recorded at the date of declaration by reducing retained earnings and establishing a temporary account, such as "Stock Dividend to Be Distributed." Because no asset distribution is required for a stock dividend, that account is part of stockholders' equity, in contrast to a cash dividend payable account, which is a liability. When the stock is distributed, the stock dividend account is eliminated and permanent capital accounts (e.g., common stock and paid-in capital in excess of par [stated] value) are increased (ASC 505-20-30-3).

Illustration of Stock Dividends

LPS Corporation declares a 5% stock dividend on its 1,000,000 shares of outstanding $10 par common stock (5,000,000 authorized). On the date of declaration, LPS stock is selling for $25 per share.

Total stock dividend (5% of 1,000,000)		50,000 shares
Value of 50,000 shares @ $25 per share (market)		$1,250,000
Entry or date of declaration:		
Retained earnings	1,250,000	
Stock dividend to be distributed		1,250,000
Entry or date of distribution:		
Stock dividend to be distributed	1,250,000	
Common stock (50,000 × $10)		500,000
Paid-in capital in excess of par value		750,000

STOCK SPLITS

When a stock distribution is more than 20% to 25% of the outstanding shares immediately before the distribution, it is considered a stock split, sometimes referred to as a "stock split-up" (ASC 505-20-25-3). A stock split increases the number of shares of capital stock outstanding, and a reverse stock split decreases the number of shares of capital stock outstanding.

In both straight and reverse stock splits, the total dollar amount of stockholders' equity does not change. The par or stated value per share of capital stock, however, decreases or increases in proportion with the increase or decrease in the number of shares outstanding. For example, in a stock split of 4 for 1 of $40 par value capital stock, the new stock has a par value of $10 ($40 ÷ 4) and the number of shares outstanding increases to four shares for each share of stock previously outstanding. In a reverse stock split of 1 for 4 of $40 par value capital stock, the new stock has a par value of $160 per share ($40 × 4) and the number of shares outstanding decreases to one share for each four shares of stock previously outstanding.

A stock split is used by a corporation to reduce the market price of its capital stock to make the market price of the stock more attractive to buyers (ASC Glossary). Thus, in a 4 for 1 straight stock split, the new shares would probably sell for about one-fourth of the previous market price of the old shares prior to the split. Reverse stock splits are unusual and are used to increase the market price of a corporation's stock. For example, a reverse stock split of 1 for 4 of stock selling for $3 would be expected to increase the market price of the new shares to about $12 per share.

No journal entry is required to record a stock split except a memorandum entry in the capital stock account to indicate the new par or stated value of the stock and the number of new shares outstanding after the split. Stock splits should not be referred to as dividends (ASC 505-20-25-2; 505-20-30-6; 505-20-50-1).

A stock split may, however, be accomplished in the form of a stock dividend. In this case, the distribution of stock is called *a stock split issued in the form of a stock dividend*, and the percentage distribution is large enough (i.e., in excess of 20% to 25% of the outstanding stock) that the market value of the stock reacts accordingly. Accounting in this situation is similar to a stock dividend, except that only the par or stated value of the stock, rather than the market value, is transferred from retained earnings to paid-in capital.

PRACTICE NOTE: Stock dividends and stock splits are similar in that they result in increased numbers of outstanding shares of stock for which existing stockholders make no payment. They differ, however, in size, in their impact on the stock's market price, and, most important, in managerial intent. In the case of a stock dividend, management intent usually is to make a distribution to owners while preserving present cash; in the case of a stock split, management intent is to affect (reduce) market price. Accounting for stock dividends and stock splits is summarized in Figure 35-1. A key point in this illustration is that the accounting is driven by the impact on the market price of the stock.

Figure 35-1: Accounting for Stock Dividends and Stock Splits

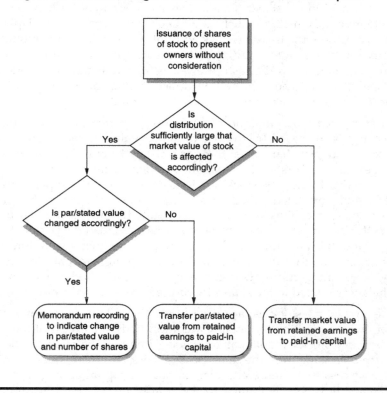

STOCK RIGHTS

No accounting entry is necessary for an entity issuing the stock right or warrant, except for detachable stock purchase warrants or similar rights, which are accounted for separately and assigned a value.

ASC 505-30: TREASURY STOCK

TREASURY STOCK

Treasury stock is a company's own capital stock that has been issued and subsequently reacquired. It is ordinarily presented as a reduction in the amount of stockholders' equity. Treasury stock is not considered an asset, because it is widely held that a corporation cannot own part of itself. The status of treasury stock is similar to that of authorized but unissued capital stock. Restrictions on the availability of retained earnings for the payment of dividends or any other restrictions required by state law are disclosed in the financial statements.

Accounting and Reporting

Under GAAP, both the cost method and the par value method of accounting for treasury stock are acceptable. Under the cost method, each acquisition of treasury stock is accounted for at cost. In addition, separate records are maintained to reflect the date of purchase of the treasury stock, the number of shares acquired, and the reacquisition cost per share. Treasury stock may be kept based on an acceptable inventory method, such as FIFO or average cost basis. Upon the sale or other disposition, the treasury stock account is credited for an amount equal to the number of shares sold, multiplied by the cost per share and the difference between this amount and the cash received is treated as paid-in capital in excess of par (stated) value. The cost method of accounting for treasury stock is more commonly used in practice than the par value method.

Under the par value method of accounting for treasury stock, the treasury stock account is increased by the par or stated value of each share reacquired. Any excess paid per share over the par or stated value is debited to paid-in capital in excess of par (stated) value, but only for the amount per share that was originally credited when the stock was issued. Any excess cost per share remaining over the par or stated value per share and the amount per share originally credited to paid-in capital in excess of par (stated) value is charged to retained earnings. If the cost per share of treasury stock is less than the par or stated value per share and the amount per share originally credited to paid-in capital in excess of par (stated) value the difference is credited to paid-in capital from treasury stock transactions. Under the par value method, all of the original capital balances related to the shares reacquired are removed from the books.

When treasury stock is acquired with the intent of retiring the stock (whether or not retirement is actually accomplished), the excess of the price paid for the treasury stock over its par or stated value may be allocated between (*a*) paid-in capital arising from the same class of stock and (*b*) retained earnings. The amount of excess that can be allocated to paid-in capital arising from the same class of stock, however, is limited to the sum of (*a*) any paid-in capital arising from previous retirements and net gains on sales of the same class of treasury stock and (*b*) the pro rata portion of paid-in capital, voluntary transfers of retained earnings, capitalization of stock dividends, etc., on the same class of stock. For this purpose, any paid-in capital arising from issues of capital stock that are fully retired (formal or constructive) is deemed to be applicable on a pro rata basis to all shares of common stock. As an alternative, the excess of the price paid for the treasury stock over its par or stated value may be charged entirely to retained earnings, based on the fact that a corporation can always capitalize or allocate retained earnings for such a purpose.

When the price paid for the acquired treasury stock is less than its par or stated value, the difference is credited to paid-in capital.

When treasury stock is acquired for purposes other than retirement, it is disclosed separately in the balance sheet as a deduction from stockholders' equity.

A gain on the sale of treasury stock acquired for purposes other than retirement is credited to paid-in capital from the sale of treasury stock. Losses are charged to paid-in capital, but only to the extent of available net gains from previous sales or retirements of the same class of stock; otherwise, losses are charged to retained earnings (ASC 505-30-30-8).

If treasury stock is donated to a corporation and then subsequently sold, the entire proceeds shall be credited to paid-in capital from the sale of donated treasury stock.

PRACTICE POINTER: Under the cost and par value methods, adjustments to paid-in capital from treasury stock transactions are recognized at different times and determined in different ways. Under the cost method, base adjustments to paid-in capital on the relationship between the purchase price and the subsequent selling price; they are recognized at the time of the sale of the treasury stock is sold. Under the par value method, base adjustments to paid-in capital on the relationship between the original selling price of the stock and the purchase price; they are recognized at the time the treasury stock is purchased.

These relationships are summarized as follows:

	Cost Method	Par Value Method
Timing of adjustment to paid-in capital	Point of sale	Point of purchase
Paid-in capital increased	Selling price greater than purchase price	Purchase price less than original selling price
Paid-in capital decreased	Selling price less than purchase price	Purchase price greater than original selling price
Retained earnings decreased	Loss on sale greater than paid-in capital from previous treasury stock transactions	Purchase price is so high that all paid-in capital from previous treasury stock transactions is eliminated

The cost method is much more widely used in practice than the par value method.

Purchase Price of Treasury Stock

If treasury shares are reacquired for a purchase price significantly in excess of their current market price, it is *presumed* that the total purchase price includes amounts for stated or unstated rights or privileges. Under this circumstance, the total purchase price is allocated between the treasury shares and the rights or privileges that are identified with the purchase of the treasury shares based on the fair value of the rights or privileges, or the fair value of the treasury shares, whichever is more clearly evident.

ASC 505-50: EQUITY-BASED PAYMENTS TO NONEMPLOYEES

EQUITY-BASED PAYMENTS TO NONEMPLOYEES

ASC 505-50 applies to all share-based payment transactions in which an entity acquires goods or services by issuing its shares, share options, or other equity instruments or by issuing liabilities to a nonemployee in amounts based, at least in part, on the price of the entity's shares or other equity instruments or that require or may require settlement by issuing the entity's equity shares or other equity instruments (ASC 505-50-15-2). For coverage of share-based payment transactions with employees, see the discussion in the Chapter 41, *ASC 718—Compensation—Stock Compensation*.

> **PRACTICE POINTER:** The SEC issued Staff Accounting Bulletin No. 107 (SAB 107), *Share-Based Payment*, in March 2005. SAB 107 is designed to provide guidance to public companies in applying GAAP related to share-based payments to employees and nonemployees. Although SEC pronouncements typically are not covered in the *GAAP Guide*, this edition is covering selected excerpts of SAB 107 because of the complexity of GAAP related to the accounting for share-based payments and because SAB 107 provides detailed and specific guidance in accounting for these types of payments.
>
> The SEC indicates that it is appropriate to apply ASC 718 to share-based payment transactions with nonemployees unless (1) another authoritative accounting pronouncement more clearly applies to the transaction or (2) applying ASC 718 would be inconsistent with the instrument issued to the nonemployees. For example, the expected term of an employee share option often is shorter than the option's contractual term because the option is not transferable, it is not hedgeable, and the option's term is truncated if an employee terminates employment after the vesting date but before the end of the contractual term of the option. If an option issued to a nonemployee does not have these restrictions (nontransferability, nonhedgeability, and truncation of the contractual term), it would be inappropriate to value the option using an expected term that is shorter than the contractual term.

Recognition and Measurement Principles

An entity shall recognize the services received or goods acquired in a share-based payment transaction as services are received or when it obtains the goods. The entity shall recognize an increase in equity or a liability, depending on whether the instruments granted satisfy the equity or liability classification criteria (ASC 505-50-25-6, 10).

A share-based payment transaction with nonemployees shall be measured based on the fair value (or, in some cases, a calculated or intrinsic value) of the equity instrument issued. If the fair value of goods or services received in a share-based payment with nonemployees is more reliably measurable than the fair value of the equity instrument issued, the fair value of the goods or services received shall be used to measure the transaction. Conversely, if the fair value of the equity instruments issued in a share-based payment transaction with nonemployees is more reliably measurable than the fair value of the consideration received, the transaction shall be measured at the fair value of the equity instruments issued (ASC 505-50-30-6).

PART II: INTERPRETIVE GUIDANCE

ASC 505-10: OVERALL

ASC 505-10-15-2, 50-6, 50-8A, 50-9 through 50-10; ASC 470-10-60-2 Disclosure Requirements under FASB Statement No. 129, *Disclosure of Information about Capital Structure*, **Relating to Contingently Convertible Securities**

Question: How do the disclosure requirements in ASC 505-10-50-3, which requires entities to explain the significant rights and privileges of their outstanding securities, including (a) conversion or exercise prices and rates and relevant dates, (b) sinking-fund requirements, (c) unusual voting rights, and (d) significant terms of contracts to issue additional shares, apply to contingently convertible securities, such as instruments with contingent conversion requirements that have not been met and that are not otherwise required to be included in computing diluted earnings per share (EPS)?

Answer: The FASB staff believes that the provisions of ASC 505 apply to all contingently convertible securities, including those with contingent conversion requirements that have not been met and that otherwise would not be included in the computation of EPS under the provisions of ASC 260, Earnings per Share. To help users of financial statements understand the conditions of a contingency, entities should disclose the significant terms of the conversion features of contingently convertible securities and the possible effect of conversion in accordance with the guidance in ASC 505-10-50-3. Disclosing the following quantitative and qualitative terms of contingently convertible securities would be useful to users:

- A description of (i) events or changes in circumstances under which a contingency causing conversion would be met and (ii) significant features of a security necessary to understand the conversion rights and their timing, for example, the periods in which a contingency might be met and in which securities might be converted

- The conversion price and the number of shares into which the security might be converted

- A description of events or changes in circumstances, if any, that might result in an adjustment or change in a contingency, the conversion price, or the number of shares, including the significant terms of those changes

- The manner in which a transaction will be settled when conversion occurs or alternative settlement methods, such as settlement in cash, shares, or a combination of the two

The following disclosures also may be useful to users:

- Whether a diluted EPS calculation includes shares that would be issued if contingently convertible securities were to be converted if the contingency is met, and if it does not, why

- As required under the guidance in ASC 460-10-60-14; ASC 480-10-55-63; ASC 505-10-60-5; ASC 815-10-15-78, 55-52, 15-25-15; ASC 815-40-05-1 through 05-4, 05-10 through 05-12, 25-1 through 25-5, 25-7 through 25-20, 25-22 through 25-24, 25-26 through 25-35, 25-37 through 25-40, 30-1 35-1 through 35-2, 35-6, 35-8 through 35-13, 40-1 through 40-2, 50-1 through 50-5, 55-1 through 55-18 (Accounting for Derivative Financial Instruments Indexed to, and Potentially Settled in, a Company's Own Stock), information about derivative transactions entered into as a result of the issuance of contingently convertible securities, such as the terms of derivative transactions, including the settlement terms, how the transactions are related to contingently convertible securities, the number of shares underlying the derivatives, and the possible effect of the issuance of contingently convertible securities. A purchase of a call option with terms that presumably would substantially offset changes in the value of a written call option embedded in a convertible security is an example of such a transaction.

ASC 310-10-45-14; ASC 505-10-45-1 through 45-2; ASC 850-10-60-4 Classifying Notes Received for Capital Stock

BACKGROUND

A contribution to an entity's equity is made by a noncontrolling shareholder(s), controlling majority shareholder(s), or an entity's majority or sole owner in the form of a note, rather than in cash. The transaction may occur because a new company is being formed, a company needs additional capital for credit or other purposes, or a parent company wants to make its wholly owned subsidiary more self-sufficient by increasing its equity. Such transactions may be in the form of a sale of stock or a contribution to paid-in capital.

ACCOUNTING ISSUE

Should the note always be classified as a reduction of equity, or are there any circumstances under which it can be classified as an asset?

ACCOUNTING GUIDANCE

Recognizing such a note receivable as an asset, even though generally inappropriate, would be permitted only in the following very limited circumstances:

- There is substantial evidence of intent and ability to pay.
- The note will be repaid within a reasonably short period of time.
- The note must be collected in cash before the financial statements are available or issued as discussed in ASC 855-10-25.

SEC STAFF COMMENT

The SEC Observer reiterated that exceptions from the SEC's rule would be very rare for registrants.

DISCUSSION

This Issue is one of the rare instances in which an issue that would apply only to privately held companies was discussed. Although there is no guidance on this matter in GAAP, the SEC has developed guidance for its registrants. Rule 5-02.30 of SEC Regulation S-X requires registrants to deduct from equity notes receivable when common stock transactions involve the company's common stock. This rule is restated in SEC Staff Accounting Bulletins, Topics 4E and 4G (ASC

310-10-S99-2, S99-3). In all cases, the presumption is that such notes are seldom paid.

Proponents of asset recognition suggested that a note should meet the following criteria to qualify as an asset:
- A scheduled repayment date
- Collection within a short period of time (five years suggested as the maximum)
- A market interest rate
- Collateralization by tangible assets with an adequate margin or a letter of credit
- The debtor's representation of intent to pay.

ASC 505-20: STOCK DIVIDENDS AND STOCK SPLITS

ASC 505-20-15-3A Accounting for Distributions to Shareholders with Components of Stock and Cash

BACKGROUND

Real estate investment trusts (REITs) are required by the Internal Revenue Service (IRS) to distribute at least 90 percent of their taxable income. REITS occasionally issue a "special" dividend distribution above the REIT's recurring quarterly dividend in periods in which a REIT has had large nonrecurring earnings. Frequently, those special dividends have been issued in cash and stock subject to IRS approval in a private letter ruling. In 2008, the IRS issued a ruling that permits REITS to make their annual required distributions in cash and stock if shareholders are permitted to elect to receive their total distribution in cash or in stock equal to the amount of the cash distribution. If too many shareholders elect to receive their distribution in cash, those electing to receive cash must receive a pro rata amount of cash that corresponds to their proportionate interest in the distribution. However, shareholders making that election cannot receive less than 10 percent of their total distribution in cash. The guidance in that ruling has also been extended to closed-end investment funds, which also must distribute at least 90 percent of their taxable income. Entities that want to declare regular or special dividends in cash and stock must obtain a private letter ruling from the IRS.

As a result of this IRS ruling, the following diversity in practice developed:
1. Some entities were accounting for the portion of a dividend issued in stock as a new stock issuance, which is included in earnings per share (EPS) *prospectively*. Others who considered it to be a stock dividend followed the guidance in ASC 260-10-55-12, and *retrospectively* restated shares outstanding and EPS.
2. Some believed that a stock dividend should be included in EPS on the date the dividend is declared, while others believed that a stock dividend should be included in EPS when the shares' trading price has been adjusted to include the effects of the stock dividend or when a dividend is settled.

ACCOUNTING GUIDANCE

The stock portion of a distribution to shareholders that contains components of cash and stock and allows shareholders to select their preferred form of distribution should be considered to be an issuance of stock in applying the EPS provisions of ASC 260. This guidance is based on the view that under this type of distribution a shareholder's ownership position changes unlike in the case of a stock dividend in which a shareholder is left in the same ownership position as before the transaction had occurred. Such a distribution should be classified as a liability when an entity becomes obligated to make the distribution in accordance with the guidance in ASC 480-10-25-14. Further, a distribution classified as a liability would be included in diluted EPS in accordance with the guidance in ASC 260-10-45-45 through 45-47 for contracts that may be settled in stock or in cash.

DISCLOSURE

In accordance with the guidance in ASC 260-10-50-2, an entity should disclose any transaction that occurs *after* the end of the most recent period but *before* the financial statements are issued or are available to be issued that would cause a material change in the number of common shares or potential common shares outstanding at the end of the period had that transaction occurred *before* the end of the period.

ASC 505-30: TREASURY STOCK

ASC 505-30-25-3 through 25-4, 30-2, 30-4, 50-3 through 50-4, 60-1; ASC 225-20-55-4 Accounting for a Purchase of Treasury Shares at a Price Significantly in Excess of the Current Market Price of the Shares and the Income Statement Classification of Costs Incurred in Defending against a Takeover Attempt

BACKGROUND

Most treasury stock transactions engaged in by an enterprise are solely capital transactions and do not involve recognition of revenue and expense. In some cases, however, treasury stock transactions may involve the receipt or payment of consideration in exchange for rights or privileges, which may require recognition of revenue or expense. The following guidance was issued to clarify this and other issues that may arise in a takeover attempt.

ACCOUNTING GUIDANCE

Purchase Price in Excess of Market Price

Question 1: How should a company account for a purchase of treasury shares at a price that is significantly in excess of the current market price of the shares?

Answer: This situation creates an assumption that the purchase price includes amounts attributable to items other than the shares purchased. The price paid in excess of the current market price of the shares should be attributed to the other elements in the transaction. If the fair value of those other elements is more clearly evident than the market value of the stock, the former amount should be assigned to those elements and the difference should be recorded as the cost of the treasury shares. If no stated or unstated consideration in addition to the capital stock can be identified, the entire purchase price should be assigned to the treasury stock.

Illustration of the Accounting for "Greenmail" Payments

Saul Rainwood buys 1 million shares of Old Steel Inc. over a period of time at prices ranging from $10 to $19 per share. On May 29, 20X5, shares of Old Steel Inc. close at $15 per share. On May 30, 20X5, Old Steel reacquires all of Rainwood's shares at $30 per share, and Rainwood enters into an agreement to not reacquire more than 5% of Old Steel's common stock for a period of three years. As a result of this transaction, Old Steel would recognize treasury stock of $15 million and record a $15 million expense for the excess purchase price over the stock's closing market price on May 29th. The $15 million charged to expense is the consideration Rainwood received, over and above the stock's market price, for disposing of his shares and agreeing not to reacquire a substantial ownership stake for a period of time (i.e., a greenmail payment).

Agreements with a Shareholder or Former Shareholder Not to Purchase Additional Shares

Question 2: Should amounts that an entity pays to a shareholder (or former shareholder) that are attributed to an agreement precluding that shareholder (or former shareholder) from purchasing additional shares be capitalized as assets and amortized over the period of the agreement?

Answer: No, such payments should be expensed as incurred.

Costs of Defense and "Standstill" Agreement in a Takeover Attempt

Question 3: Should the costs a company incurs to defend itself in a takeover attempt or the costs of a "standstill" agreement be classified as extraordinary?

Answer: No. Neither meets the criteria for an *extraordinary* item discussed in ASC 225-20.

ASC 505-30-25-5 through 25-6, 55-1, 55-3, 55-5 through 55-6, 60-2; ASC 260-10-55-89 Accounting for an Accelerated Share Repurchase Program

BACKGROUND

In an accelerated share repurchase program, an entity purchases a specified number of shares immediately, but the purchase price for those shares is based on the average market price of the shares over a specified period of time. Such programs combine the benefits of an immediate share retirement of a tender offer with the price benefits of repurchases on the open market. They may be structured as a treasury stock purchase or a forward contract:

1. *Treasury stock purchase* An investment banker who is an unrelated third party borrows 1 million shares of Company A's common stock from investors, becomes the shares' owner of record, and sells the shares short to Company A on July 1, 20X9 at the fair value of $50 a share and is paid $50 million in cash on that date. Company A has legal title to the shares,

which are held as treasury stock, and no other party can vote those shares.

2. *Forward contract* Company A enters into a forward contract with an investment banker on 1 million shares of Company A's common stock. If the volume-weighted average daily market price during the contract period from July 1, 20X9, to October 1, 20X9, exceeds the $50 initial purchase price (net of the investment banker's commission), the Company has the option to deliver to the investment banker on October 1, 20X9, cash or shares of common stock equal to the price difference times 1 million. If the volume-weighted average daily market price during the contract period is less than the $50 purchase price, the investment banker delivers to Company A on October 1, 20X9, cash or shares of common stock equal to the price difference times 1 million.

ACCOUNTING ISSUE

How should accelerated share repurchase programs be accounted for?

ACCOUNTING GUIDANCE

Accelerated repurchase programs should be accounted for as two separate transactions as follows:

1. As a treasury stock transaction in which shares of the company's stock are acquired and recognized on the acquisition date (e.g., July 1, 20X9)
2. As a forward contract that is indexed to its own common stock

According to the guidance in ASC 815-40, the forward contract in the example discussed above would be classified as an equity instrument, because the entity would receive cash if there is a gain on the contract, but has the option to pay in cash or stock if there is a loss on the contract. Therefore, no fair value changes of the contract would be recognized and the contract's settlement would be recognized in equity.

In calculating basic and diluted earnings per share (EPS), the number of shares used to calculate the weighted-average common shares outstanding would be reduced by the shares repurchased as treasury stock. The guidance in ASC 260-10-55-88 should be used to measure the effect of the forward contract on EPS.

ASC 505-50: EQUITY-BASED PAYMENTS TO NONEMPLOYEES

ASC 505-50-05-1, 05-4 through 05-5, 25-5, 30-18 through 30-19, 30-29, 35-13 through 35-15, 50-2, 55-25 through 55-27; ASC 845-10-50-2 Accounting by a Grantee for an Equity Instrument to Be Received in Conjunction with Providing Goods or Services

BACKGROUND

The following is guidance for grantors regarding the accounting for equity instruments issued to other than employees in exchange for products or services. Previous guidance addressed the amount at which such equity instruments should be recognized and the date on which recognition should occur. However, a *grantee's* accounting for such transactions, which may span over more than one reporting period and may contain terms contingent on the grantee's performance, is currently not addressed in the authoritative literature.

ACCOUNTING ISSUES

1. On what date should a *grantee* measure the fair value of revenue received in the form of equity instruments in exchange for goods or services provided to a grantor?
2. If the terms of equity instruments received by a *grantee* for goods or services provided to a grantor can be adjusted after the measurement date based on the resolution of a contingency, such as performance above a level to which the grantee has committed, performance after the instrument was earned, or market conditions, how should a grantee account for an increase in the fair value of revenue received in the form of equity instruments after the contingency has been resolved?

ACCOUNTING GUIDANCE

1. A grantee should measure the fair value of equity instruments received in exchange for providing goods or services to a grantor based on the stock price and other measurement assumptions on either of the following dates, whichever is earlier (the measurement date):
    a. When the parties agree on the terms of the compensation arrangement in the form of equity instruments and on the grantee's performance commitment to earn the equity instruments
    b. When the grantee's performance required to earn the equity instruments is completed (i.e., the vesting date)
2. The accounting is as follows if on the measurement date, the quantity or any of the terms of the equity instruments depend on:
    a. **Achieving a market condition** Revenue is measured based on the fair value of the equity instruments, including the adjustment provisions. The fair value of the equity instruments is used without considering the market condition plus the fair value of the commitment to change the quantity or terms of the equity instruments if the market condition is met.
    b. **Additional grantee performance** Changes in fair value as a result of an adjustment to the instrument for a condition requiring additional grantee performance should be measured as additional revenue based on the guidance in ASC 718-20-35-3 through 35-4 for modification accounting. At the date on which the quantity or terms of the equity instrument are revised, the adjustment is measured as the difference between (*a*) the current fair value on the date of the revised equity instrument using the known quantity and terms, and (*b*) the current fair value on that date of the old equity instrument before the adjustment. If the fair value of the equity instruments changes after the measurement date for reasons that are unrelated to the achievement of performance conditions, those fair value changes should be accounted for in accordance with the relevant guidance on

accounting and reporting for investments in equity instruments, such as the guidance in ASC Topics 320, 323, 325, 825, and 855. For example, on July 1, 2000, the date on which the parties agreed on the grantee's performance commitment, the fair value of an equity instrument granting options to the contractor is $500,000. On July 1, 2001, the amount of the original instrument is adjusted because the grantee has met a condition for additional performance. The equity instrument's fair value is $1 million on that date. If the fair value of the *original* instrument is $650,000 on July 1, 2001, the increase in its fair value due to the performance condition is $350,000 ($1 million less $650,000). The $150,000 increase in the fair value of the original instrument from $500,000 to $650,000 is unrelated to the grantee's performance and should be accounted for based on other relevant literature.

It was noted that although the Issue does not address the timing of revenue recognition, a grantee would recognize deferred revenue or revenue in the same periods and in the same manner as cash, rather than equity instruments, received for goods or services.

DISCLOSURE REQUIREMENTS

In accordance with the guidance in ASC 845-10-50-1, the amount of gross operating revenue recognized as a result of the nonmonetary transactions discussed in this Issue should be disclosed in the financial statements of each reporting period. In addition, the SEC Observer reminded registrants about the requirements in Item 303(a)(3)(ii) of Regulation S-K under which an entity must disclose known trends or uncertainties that have had or that are reasonably expected to have a materially favorable or unfavorable effect on revenues.

ASC 505-50-05-3, 05-8, 15-2 through 15-3, 25-2, 25-4, 25-9, 30-2 through 30-7, 30-11 through 30-14, 30-21 through 30-23, 30-25 through 30-28, 30-30 through 30-31, 35-3, 35-5 through 35-10, 55-2 through 55-11, 55-13 through 55-17, 55-20 through 55-24, 55-28, 55-31 through 55-40; ASC 440-10-60-4 **Accounting for Equity Instruments That Are Issued to Other Than Employees for Acquiring, or in Conjunction with Selling, Goods or Services**

BACKGROUND

Before the issuance of ASC 505 (FAS-123(R)), there was no guidance on the *measurement date* for *nonemployee* stock options, nor whether the measurement date guidance established for employee stock options should be used as a model. Also, no guidance was provided for the issuance of nonemployee stock options involving the *sale* of goods and services, such as stock options used as sales incentives.

Compensation cost for equity instruments issued to *employees* was generally measured based on the fair value of the award at the grant date, but there was an exception for certain situations in which it would be impossible to "reasonably estimate" the fair value of a stock option or other equity instrument on that date, for example, if the option exercise price changes by a specified amount based on a change in the price of the underlying security. Under such circumstances, the award's fair value had to be measured based on the stock price and other relevant information on the "first date at which it is reasonably possible to estimate that value." However, it required using the intrinsic value of the award at the grant date to estimate compensation cost in those situations. ASC 505 which was issued in 2004 as a revision of FAS-123, also did not provide guidance on the accounting for share-based payment transactions with *nonemployees* but referred readers to this Issue for such guidance.

This Issue provides guidance on the measurement date and the recognition of *all* stock-option transactions with *nonemployees*. It does not apply, however, to equity instruments issued in a business combination or to equity instruments issued to lenders or investors providing financing to an issuer.

ACCOUNTING ISSUES

1. What date should an issuer use to measure the fair value of equity instruments in all transactions under the scope of this Issue?
2. In what period(s) and in what manner (capitalize or expense) should an issuer recognize the fair value of equity instruments in all transactions under the scope of this Issue?
3. How should the cost of equity instruments be recognized *before the measurement date* if the quantity and terms are all known in advance, because they do not depend on the counterparty's performance or market conditions?
4. If the quantity or terms of the equity instruments are not all known in advance, because they are based on the counterparty's performance or market conditions:
   a. How should the equity instruments be measured *at the measurement date*?
   b. How should the cost of the equity instruments be recognized *before the measurement date*?
   c. How should the equity instruments be accounted for *after the measurement date* if the quantity or terms of the equity instruments change as a result of the counterparty's performance or market conditions?

ACCOUNTING GUIDANCE

1. The fair value of equity instruments in all awards to nonemployees should be measured based on the stock price and other measurement assumptions on one of the following dates (the measurement date), whichever occurs first:
   a. The date on which an issuer and a counterparty reach a commitment for the counterparty's performance to earn the equity instruments. The counterparty's performance is considered probable (there is a performance commitment) because of a strong enough disincentive for nonperformance (in addition to forfeiture of the equity instruments) resulting from the relationship between the issuer and the counterparty. However, performance is not assured merely because

an issuer can sue the counterparty for nonperformance. That action was not considered to be a large enough disincentive, because the option to sue for nonperformance always exists. In addition, there may not be sufficient assurance that damages will be collected.

    b. The date on which the counterparty's performance is concluded, because the counterparty has delivered or purchased, as appropriate, the goods or services, even though on that date, the quantity and all the terms of the equity instruments may still depend on other events, such as a target stock price. (This date is used if the counterparty made no performance commitment.) In some cases, a counterparty may be required to perform over a period of time, such as over several years; the equity award is fully vested, cannot be forfeited, and can be exercised on the date the parties enter into the contract. It was noted that this fact pattern would be rare, because usually there is a required vesting period. However, there was agreement if that situation occurs, the fair value of an award could be measured on the date the parties enter into a contract even if the services are yet to be performed.

2. The period(s) in which an entity should recognize the fair value of instruments that will be issued or whether the amounts should be expensed or capitalized was not discussed. However, the following conclusions were reached on the period and manner of recognition for all transactions:

    a. An asset, expense, or sales discount should be recognized (or previous recognition reversed) in the same period(s) and in the same manner as if the issuer had paid for the goods or services in cash or used cash rebates as a sales discount instead of paying with equity instruments.

    b. An asset, expense, or sales discount that had been recognized should *not* be reversed, if a counterparty does not exercise a stock option and the option expires unexercised.

3. Equity instruments should be measured at their current fair values at each interim financial reporting date, if the quantity and terms of the transaction are known and it is appropriate under GAAP for an issuer to recognize costs related to that transaction during financial periods preceding the measurement date. The methods illustrated in ASC 505-50-55-28 should be used to ascribe the changes in fair values to interim reporting dates.

4. If the quantity or any of the transaction's terms are unknown initially, the equity instruments should be accounted for as follows:

    a. The fair value of the equity instruments should be recognized as follows at the measurement date:

        (1) The issuer should recognize the equity instruments at their fair value on the measurement date, if the quantity or any of the transaction's terms depend on the achievement of market condi-

tions, which are related to achieving a specified market target, such as a specified stock price or intrinsic value of a stock option. The fair value of the equity instruments should be computed without considering the market condition plus the fair value of the issuer's commitment to change the quantity or terms of the equity instruments, based on whether the market condition is met.

  (2) The issuer should recognize, on the measurement date, the lowest total amount (i.e., the variable terms multiplied by the applicable number of equity instruments) within a range of total fair values for the equity instruments based on different possible outcomes, if the quantity or any terms of the equity instruments on that date depend on the achievement of performance conditions by the counterparty, such as increasing market share for a specified product by a specified amount. The amount recognized may be zero.

  (3) The consensus in 4(a)(2) above applies, if the transaction requires the counterparty to meet performance conditions and market conditions.

b. If the quantity or the terms of a transaction are unknown and it is appropriate for the issuer to recognize the cost of the transaction in reporting periods *before* the measurement date, the equity instruments should be accounted for as follows:

  (1) The equity instruments should be recognized at their fair value on the date of recognition, as in the consensus on Issue 3 above, if the outcome of a transaction depends only on market conditions. (See ASC 505-50-30-28 for application guidance).

  (2) The equity instruments should be recognized at the lowest total fair value at each interim date, if the outcome depends only on the counterparty's performance. The method illustrated in ASC 505-50-55-28, and 55-33 through 40 should be used to ascribe the changes in fair values between interim reporting dates (ASC 505-50-30-25).

  (3) The guidance in 4(a)(2) above also applies, if the outcome of a transaction depends both on the counterparty's performance and on market conditions (ASC 505-50-30-26).

c. If the quantity or any of the terms of a transaction are unknown initially, the accounting after the measurement date should be as follows:

  (1) For transactions that depend only on market conditions, ASC 505-50-35-6 provide that after measuring the current fair value of the issuer's commitment related to a market condition, in accordance with 4(a)(1) above, the issuer should, if necessary, recognize and classify future changes in the fair value of the

commitment in accordance with accounting guidance on financial instruments, such as the guidance in ASC 815-40.

(2) For transactions that depend only on a counterparty's performance, the lowest total fair value measured, based on the guidance in 4(a)(2) above, should be adjusted to recognize the additional cost of the transaction using the method for modification accounting in ASC 718-20-35-3 through 35-4 as each quantity and term of the transaction becomes known and until all such information becomes known as a result of the counterparty's performance. Under that method, the adjustment is measured at the date the quantity or terms of the equity instruments are known as the difference between (*a*) the current fair value of the *revised* instruments, using the current known quantity or term, and (*b*) the fair value of the equity instruments before knowing the revised quantity or term. The current fair value is calculated using the assumptions that result in the lowest total fair value, if the quantity or any terms are still unknown (ASC 505-50-35-7).

(3) For transactions that depend on a counterparty's performance and on market conditions, an issuer should apply the method discussed in ASC 718-20-35-3 through 35-4 until the last condition related to the counterparty's performance has been met. The issuer should measure the current fair value of the commitment to issue additional equity instruments or change the terms of the equity instruments, based on whether the market condition is met, if the counterparty has met the last performance condition but one or more market conditions remain unresolved. This amount is an additional cost of the transaction. An issuer should, if necessary, recognize and classify future changes in the fair value of a commitment in accordance with accounting guidance on financial instruments, such as that in ASC 815-40, after measuring the current fair value of the issuer's commitment related to market conditions (ASC 505-50-35-8 through 35-10).

5. In accordance with the guidance in ASC 505-50-25-7, the measurement date is the date on which the two parties enter into a contract under which Company X grants to Company Y fully vested and nonforfeitable equity instruments, even though Company Y's performance will occur over a period of time (e.g., over several years).

EFFECT OF ASC 815

The terms of the stock options in this Issue should be analyzed to determine whether they meet the definition of a derivative in ASC 815. Although paragraph ASC 815-10-15-74 exempts *issuers* of contracts related to stock-based compensation arrangements under the provisions in ASC 718 from accounting for those contracts as derivatives the guidance in ASC 815-10-55-49 through 55-51, 55-53 through 55-55, 15-75 provides that the exception in ASC 815-10-15-74 does not apply to nonemployee *holders* of derivatives who receive the options as compensation for goods or services. Those parties are required to account for the options as derivatives under the guidance in ASC 815. However, all or a portion of the contract may be exempt if the underlying is a specified volume of sales or service revenue of one of the counterparties in the arrangement. The guidance in ASC 815-10-15-122, 15-125 through 15-127 and ASC 815-10-15-133 through 15-138 may also be relevant.

Illustration of Accounting for Nonemployee Stock Options with Variable Terms

1. In the following arrangement, the counterparty's commitment to perform is made before performance is completed. However, the quantity of the equity instruments to be issued is unknown. On 8/1/X7, Gary and Harry Real Estate Corp. (the Company) enters into an agreement with APEX Painters, Inc., under which APEX would paint five of the Company's office buildings beginning on 9/1/X7. The agreement provides that, in exchange for its services, the Company will pay APEX $50,000 and will issue to APEX 5,000 stock options that are exercisable over five years at an exercise price of $10, if APEX completes the project by 12/31/X7. No stock options will be issued if the project is completed after that date, and the contract price will be reduced by $10,000 for each week completion is delayed. The project is completed on time. Assuming the total fair value of the award on 8/1/X7—the date the agreement is reached—is $50,000, the Company should measure the fair value of the award on the commitment date—8/1/X7—in accordance with the consensus in 1(a), because it is probable that APEX will perform. In accordance with the consensus in paragraph 4(a)(ii), the Company should recognize a fair value of zero at the commitment date, because that is the lowest total fair value if the project is not completed by the deadline. The fair value of the award should be measured at the award's current fair value on 12/31/X7, when the project is completed.

2. In the following example, there is no commitment to perform until the counterparty has completed performance:

    A manufacturer of a new type of oven offers its customers 5,000 shares of its stock as an incentive to purchase a minimum of 500 ovens over the following two years. For every additional 100 ovens purchased, the manufacturer offers its customers an additional 1,000 shares. Customers have no performance commitment, because they are not required to purchase the ovens. The manufacturer will recognize the fair value of the 5,000 shares on the date the customer has purchased the minimum number of ovens as discussed in paragraph 4(a)(ii). The cost of the incentive should be adjusted for each additional 100 ovens purchased by a customer in accordance with paragraph 4(c)(ii) using modification accounting.

3. In the following example, the guidance on the measurement date is applied to a transaction that has a market condition:

    On 7/1/98, the XYZ Insurance Co. hires ABC Software Company to modify the company's software to comply with the requirements for the year 2000. XYZ will pay ABC $50,000 in cash and will issue 500 stock options if the modifications are completed by 6/30/99. There is a performance commitment, because ABC will incur a substantial penalty, which is considered to be a "sufficiently large disincentive for nonperformance," if the software modifications are not completed by that date. XYZ and ABC agreed on the quantity and terms of the stock options when the contract was signed on 7/1/98. The fair value of the stock options is $50,000 on the commitment date. However, if ABC completes the project by 6/30/99 and the fair value of XYZ's shares is less than $50,000 on 12/31/01, XYZ will issue an additional five stock options for each dollar that the stock price is below $100 per share, up to 125 stock options. Initially, XYZ will measure the 500 stock options (one option per share) at their fair value on 7/1/98, the day ABC made a commitment to perform. The fair value of the shares on that date is $40,000. In addition, XYZ would also recognize an additional $10,000 for the fair value of the additional stock options that could potentially be issued, regardless of whether the commitment is in-the-money. The total cost to be recognized for the options would be $50,000. After the initial recognition on the commitment date, XYZ would account for the 125 stock options that may be issued in accordance with existing authoritative guidance on financial instruments, including EITF Issue 96-13.

ASC 505-50-05-6 through 05-7, 25-7 through 25-8, 30-15 through 30-16, 35-11 through 35-12, S25-2, S99-2, 45-1 Accounting Recognition for Certain Transactions Involving Equity Instruments Granted to Other Than Employees

BACKGROUND

The guidance in ASC 505-50-05-3, 05-8, 15-2 through 15-3, 25-2, 25-4, 25-9, 30-2 through 30-7, 30-11 through 30-14, 30-21 through 30-23, 30-25 through 30-28, 30-30 through 30-31, 35-3, 35-5 through 35-10, 55-2 through 55-11, 55-13 through 55-17, 55-20 through 55-24, 55-28, 55-31 through 55-40; ASC 440-10-60-4 applies to a grantor's measurement of the fair value of equity instruments granted to other than employees. The guidance in ASC 505-50-05-1, 05-4 through 05-5, 25-5, 30-18 through 30-19, 30-29, 35-13 through 35-15, 50-2, 55-25 through 55-27; ASC 845-10-50-2 applies to a grantee's measurement of the fair value of such equity instruments for revenue recognition purposes. However, that guidance provides only that recognition should occur in the same period and in the same manner as if cash had been exchanged, but it does not provide guidance on the period or manner in which to recognize the fair value of a transaction.

Under that guidance, the measurement date occurs when a performance commitment is reached or if there is no performance commitment, on the vesting date when performance is complete, whichever occurs earlier. As a result, some grantors were structuring equity instruments as nonforfeitable instruments under which a grantee was fully vested at the date the parties entered into a contract, thereby establishing the measurement date. Those arrangements did not require a grantee to achieve a specific future performance to earn or retain the equity instruments. That is, a grantee could exercise the instruments immediately or at a specified future date whether or not future performance was met. Because instruments with such provisions were issued for accounting purposes under the guidance in ASC 718, a grantor recognized their issuance as a credit in equity at the fair value of the instrument measured in accordance with the guidance in ASC 505-50-05-3, 05-8, 15-2 through 15-3, 25-2, 25-4, 25-9, 30-2 through 30-7, 30-11 through 30-14, 30-21 through 30-23, 30-25 through 30-28, 30-30 through 30-31, 35-3, 35-5 through 35-10, 55-2 through 55-11, 55-13 through 55-17, 55-20 through 55-24, 55-28, 55-31 through 55-40; ASC 440-10-60-4.

Although the equity instruments could not be forfeited, under many arrangements, they could not be exercised until a future date. Instruments with such provisions provided, however, that they could be exercised if a grantee met certain performance requirements. Some questioned whether a grantee's rights under those instruments were truly vested before the grantee's performance, which accelerated exercisability. In addition, some equity instruments were structured with sufficiently large disincentives to nonperformance. That also raised the question whether it is appropriate for a grantee to recognize equity instruments with such provisions as assets at the measurement date.

ACCOUNTING ISSUES

1. In what period and manner should a *grantor* recognize the measured cost of a transaction if a grantor issues a fully vested, exercisable, nonforfeitable equity instrument at the date a grantor and a grantee enter into an agreement for goods or services and no specific performance is required of the grantee?

1a. When, if ever, should a grantor present an asset in the balance sheet as contra-equity, if the grantor believes that an asset (other than a note or a receivable) has been received in return for fully vested, nonforfeitable equity instruments issued at the date the grantor and grantee enter into an agreement for goods or services under which the grantee retains the equity instruments without a specific performance requirement?

2. How should a *grantor* that issues a fully vested, exercisable, nonforfeitable equity instrument that can be exercised only after a specific period of time, measure and recognize the equity instrument at the date of the arrangement, and thereafter, if the grantee achieves a performance condition that accelerates exercisability under the terms of the instrument?

ACCOUNTING GUIDANCE

1. No specific guidance was provided on the period and manner in which a grantor should recognize the measured cost of fully vested, nonforfeitable equity instruments issued at the date a grantor and grantee enter into an agreement for goods or services. However, the guidance in ASC 505-50-25-7 provides that a grantor may recognize a prepaid asset or an immediate expense for the issuance of such financial instruments based on the circumstances.

1a. A grantor that issues fully vested, nonforfeitable equity instruments in exchange for an asset (other than a note or a receivable) should *not* report the acquired asset as a contra-equity in the balance sheet. This conclusion applies only to a grantor that issues equity instruments to *nonemployees* in exchange for goods or services. (ASC 505-50-45-1)

2. For nonforfeitable equity instruments that can be exercised only after a specified time period, but that a grantee may exercise earlier if specified performance conditions are achieved:

   a. Measure the fair value of the equity instruments at the *grant* date and recognize the measured cost in the same period and manner as if it has been paid for in cash or the grantor had used cash rebates as sales discounts rather than granting equity instruments.

   b. At the acceleration date, account for the incremental cost, if any, of the equity instruments issued, as the difference between (i) the current fair value of the *revised* equity instruments at the date they are exercisable and (ii) the current fair value of the *old* equity instruments immediately before their exercisability is accelerated. If acceleration of a grantee's ability to exercise the option is the only change in terms, a significant additional charge will only occur if the expected dividend on the underlying instrument is greater than the sum of (i) the effect of discounting the exercise price and (ii) a loss in the time value of money, without the discounting, because the equity instrument has been exercised early.

SEC OBSERVER'S COMMENTS

The SEC Observer stated that grantees and grantors should use the same commitment date and similar values for such transactions, or the staff would challenge their accounting.

ASC 505-50-S25-1; S99-1 Grantor Balance Sheet Presentation of Unvested, Forfeitable Equity Instruments Granted to a Nonemployee

The SEC Observer discussed the following guidance, which addresses the balance sheet classification of unvested forfeitable equity instruments granted to nonemployees for future services instead of cash. Under such arrangements, a grantor has the right to recover the consideration paid as well as to impose a large penalty as damages for nonperformance. The guidance in ASC 505-50-05-3, 05-8, 15-2 through 15-3, 25-2, 25-4, 25-9, 30-2 through 30-7, 30-11 through 30-14, 30-21 through 30-23, 30-25 through 30-28, 30-30 through 30-31, 35-3, 35-5 through 35-10, 55-2 through 55-11, 55-13 through 55-17, 55-20 through 55-24, 55-28, 55-31 through 55-40; ASC 440-10-60-4 (Accounting for Equity Instruments That Are Issued to Other Than Employees for Acquiring, or in Conjunction with Selling, Goods or Services) provides that the commitment and measurement date for such instruments is the date that equity instruments were issued to a grantee if the grantee has a large enough disincentive for nonperformance.

Because practice is diverse as to the recognition of such transactions on the measurement date, the SEC staff will require registrants that receive a right to receive future services in exchange for unvested, forfeitable equity instruments to consider such instruments as *unissued* for accounting purposes until the instruments vest, which occurs when the future services have been received. Therefore, there is no recognition at the measurement date and the transaction is not recorded.

This announcement does not apply to arrangements under which fully vested, nonforfeitable, equity instruments are exchanged for future services, which are addressed in ASC 505-50-05-6 through 05-7, 25-7 through 25-8, 30-15 through 30-16, 35-11 through 35-12, S25-2, S99-2, 45-1 (Accounting Recognition for Certain Transaction Involving Equity Instruments Granted to Other Than Employees).

ASC 505-60: SPINOFFS AND REVERSER SPINOFFS

ASC 505-60-05-2 through 05-4, 15-2, 25-2, 25-4 through 25-5, 25-7 through 25-8, 45-1, 55-2, 55-5, 55-7 through 55-12 Accounting for Reverse Spinoffs

BACKGROUND

A *spinoff* is a transaction in which a company (a *spinnor*) transfers assets (usually a subsidiary) into a new legal entity (the *spinnee*) and distributes the shares in that entity to its shareholders, who do *not* give up any shares held in the spinnor. Spinoff transactions benefit companies in several ways. For example, neither the spinnor nor its shareholders recognize a gain on the distribution of shares if the spinoff qualifies as a nontaxable reorganization. A spinoff also avoids the double taxation that would result from a sale of a subsidiary and distribution of the proceeds to the company's shareholders.

ASC 845-10-30-10 provides guidance on accounting for spinoff transactions, which are nonreciprocal transfers to owners. It requires that a spinoff be accounted for based on the carrying value of the assets distributed to its shareholders. The transaction should *not* be accounted for as a sale of a spinnee followed by a distribution of the proceeds.

Some companies have been accounting for spinoffs based on the form of the transaction rather than on its substance—that is, the spinnee becomes the continuing entity. It is important to determine which entity will be treated as the spinnee for accounting purposes, because under the provisions of ASC 205, a spinnor must report a spinnee as a discontinued operation if the spinnee is a component of an entity and meets the conditions in ASC 205-20-45-1 for such reporting.

ACCOUNTING ISSUE

Should a spinoff that treats a spinnee as the continuing entity be accounted for as a *reverse* spinoff, in which the spinnee is treated as the spinnor for accounting purposes based on the substance rather than the form of the transaction?

ACCOUNTING GUIDANCE

1. A transaction should be accounted for as a *reverse* spinoff if the substance of the transaction is most accurately depicted for shareholders and other users of financial statements by treating a legal spinee as the accounting spinnor. Judgment based on an evaluation of the relevant facts and circumstances should be used to determine whether a transaction should be accounted for as a reverse spinoff.

2. Although it should be presumed that the *legal* spinnor is also the spinnor for *accounting* purposes, that presumption may be tested by considering

the following indicators, neither of which should be considered presumptive or determinative:

a. The accounting spinnor (legal spinnee) is larger than the accounting spinnee (legal spinnor) based on assets, revenues, and earnings.

b. The fair value of the accounting spinnor (legal spinnee) exceeds that of the accounting spinnee (legal spinnor).

c. The former combined entity's senior management remains with the accounting spinnor (legal spinnee).

d. The accounting spinnor (legal spinnee) has been held longer than the accounting spinnee (legal spinnor).

CHAPTER 36
ASC 605—REVENUE RECOGNITION

CONTENTS

Part I: General Guidance	36,003
Overview	36,003
Background	36,004
ASC 605-10: Overall	36,005
Installment Sales Method	36,005
Illustration of Installment Sales Method	36,005
Cost Recovery Method	36,006
Illustration of Cost Recovery Method	36,006
Deferred Income Taxes	36,007
Disclosure	36,007
ASC 605-15: Products	36,007
Revenue Recognition for Returnable Merchandise	36,007
Reasonable Estimates of Returns	36,008
Illustration of Reasonable Estimates of Returns	36,009
ASC 605-35: Construction-Type and Production-Type Contracts	36,010
Completed-Contract Method	36,010
Illustration of the Completed-Contract Method	36,010
Accounting for the Completed-Contract Method	36,011
Percentage-of-Completion Method	36,011
Accounting for the Percentage-of-Completion Method	36,012
Illustration of Accounting for the Completed-Contract and Percentage-of-Completion Method	36,013
ASC 605-40: Gains and Losses	36,014
Involuntary Conversion of Nonmonetary Assets to Monetary Assets	36,014
Important Notice for 2014	36,015
Part II: Interpretive Guidance	36,016
ASC 605-15: Products	36,016
ASC 605-15-05-6, 15-2, 25-5; ASC 840-10-60-3	
Products Sold and Subsequently Repurchased Subject to an Operating Lease	36,016
ASC 605-20: Services	36,017
ASC 605-20-25-1 through 25-6; ASC 460-10-15-9; 60-41	
Separately Priced Extended Warranty and Product Maintenance Contracts	36,017
Illustration of Recognition of Revenue and Costs on a Separately Priced Extended Warranty Contract—Warranty Costs Not Incurred on a Straight-Line Basis	36,018
ASC 605-20-15-3, 25-8 through 25-12; ASC 460-10-60-8; ASC 310-10-60-4	
Fees for Guaranteeing a Loan	36,018
ASC 605-20-25-13; S25-1, S99-2	
Services for Freight-in-Transit at the End of a Reporting Period	36,020

36,002 ASC 605—Revenue Recognition

Illustration of Revenue and Expense Recognition by Motor Carriers	36,021
ASC 605-20-25-14 through 25-18, 50-1	
Accounting for Advertising Barter Transactions	36,022
ASC 605-20-S25-2, S99-1	
Accounting for Management Fees Based on a Formula	36,024
ASC 605-25: Multiple-Element Arrangements	36,025
ASC 605-25-15-3A, 25-2, 30-2, 30-5, 30-6A through 30-6B, 30-7, 50-1 through 50-2, 55-1, 55-3, 55-7, 55-12, 55-25, 55-29, 55-32, 55-34, 55-36 through 55-47, 55-52, 55-54, 55-6A through 55-57, 55-61, 55-69, 55-75 through 55-6B, 55-93, 65-1 (ASU 2009-13)	
Revenue Arrangements with Multiple Deliverables	36,025
ASC 605-28: Milestone Method	36,029
ASC 605-10-05-1, 25-2A; ASC 605-25-15-2A; ASC 605-28-05-1, 15-1 through 15-4, 25-1 through 25-3, 50-1 through 50-2, 65-1 (ASU 2010-17)	
Milestone Method of Revenue Recognition	36,029
ASC 605-35: Construction-Type and Production-Type Contracts	36,031
ASC 605-35-05-1 through 05-13, 15-6, 25-1 through 25-50, 25-54 through 25-88, 25-90 through 25-98, 45-1 through 45-2, 50-1 through 50-10, 55-1; ASC 210-10-60-2; ASC 460-1-60-10; ASC 910-20-25-5; ASC 912-20-25-1	
Accounting for Performance of Construction-Type and Certain Production-Type Contracts	36,031
ASC 605-45: Principal Agent Considerations	36,037
ASC 605-45-05-1 through 05-2, 15-3 through 15-5, 45-1 through 45-18, 50-1, 55-2 through 55-3, 55-5 through 55-6, 55-8 through 55-9, 55-11 through 55-14, 55-16, 55-18, 55-20, 55-22, 55-24 through 55-25, 55-27 through 55-31, 55-33 through 55-34, 55-36 through 55-38, 55-40 through 55-45	
Reporting Revenue Gross as a Principal versus Net as an Agent	36,037
ASC 605-45-15-2, 15-4; 45-22, 45-23	
Reimbursements Received for "Out-of-Pocket" Expenses Incurred	36,040
ASC 605-45-15-2, 50-3 through 50-4	
Taxes Collected from Customers and Remitted to Governmental Authorities	36,041
ASC 605-45-05-2, 15-2, 15-4, 45-19 through 45-21, S45-1, 50-2, S99	
Shipping and Handling Fees and Costs	36,042
ASC 605-50: Customer Payments and Incentives	36,043
ASC 605-50-05-1, 15-2 through 15-3, 25-1 through 25-9, 45-1 through 45-11, S45-1, 55-1, 55-3, 55-5, 55-8 through 55-12, 55-14 through 55-15, 55-17 through 55-22, 55-24 through 55-25, 55-27 through 55-28, 55-30 through 55-31, 55-33 through 55-37, 55-40 through 55-44, 55-46 through 55-47, 55-49 through, 55-50, 55-52, through 55-53, 55-55 through 55-69, 55-71 through 55-72, 55-74 through 55-77, 55-79 through 55-95, 55-97 through 55-107, S99-1; ASC 330-10-35-13; ASC 908-360-55-1	
Vendor's Income Statement Characterization of Consideration Given to a Customer (Including a Reseller)	36,043
ASC 605-50-05-1,15-2, 25-10 through 25-12, 45-12 through 45-15, 55-116 through 55-117, 55-119 through 55-120, 55-122 through 55-123	
Customer's Characterization of Certain Consideration Received from a Vendor	36,048
ASC 605-50-15-2, 25-13 through 25-18, 50-1, 55-108, 55-110 through 55-114	

ASC 605—Revenue Recognition	**36,003**
Service Provider's Accounting for Consideration Given to a Manufacturer or Reseller of Equipment	36,050
ASC 605-50-45-16 through 45-20, 55-124 through 55-127	
Reseller's Characterization of Sales Incentives Offered to Consumers by Manufacturers	36,051

PART I: GENERAL GUIDANCE

OVERVIEW

GAAP, as well as recognized industry practices, generally call for revenue recognition at the point of sale. One aspect of a sale that complicates this generally simple rule is a right of return on the part of the buyer. Revenue from sales in which a right of return exists is recognized at the time of sale only if certain specified conditions are met. If those conditions are met, sales revenue and cost of sales are reduced to reflect estimated returns and costs of those returns. If they are not met, revenue recognition is postponed.

> **PRACTICE NOTE:** Much of existing GAAP is highly transaction specific (e.g., franchise fee revenue, revenue recognition when right of return exists). The most generic guidance on revenue recognition currently in force is the Securities and Exchange Commission's Staff Accounting Bulletins on revenue recognition (SAB 101, SAB 104). SAB 101 is largely modeled after the guidance in ASC 985 (Software). A reader interested in understanding GAAP for recognizing revenue is advised to consult the *GAAP* to read SAB 101 and SAB 104. SAB 104 is useful as conceptual guidance in areas where no other authoritative literature exists. See Important Notice for 2013 at the end of this chapter.

Long-term construction contracts present a difficult financial reporting problem, primarily because of their large dollar amounts and their relatively long duration (i.e., they span more than one accounting period, sometimes beginning and ending several years apart). GAAP, in the area of revenue recognition for long-term construction contracts, deal with this situation by permitting two methods—the *percentage-of-completion method* and the *completed-contract method*—although the two are not alternatives for the same situation. The percentage-of-completion method is required in situations in which reliable estimates of the degree of completion are possible, in which case a pro rata portion of the income from the contract is recognized in each accounting period covered by the contract. In those rare situations where reliable estimates are not possible, the completed-contract method is used, in which income is deferred until the end of the contract period.

The installment sales method of accounting defers the recognition of gross profit on installment sales until cash is collected. It is commonly used for income tax purposes, but is acceptable for purposes of financial reporting in limited situations.

ASC 605—Revenue Recognition

BACKGROUND

Generally the broad principle underlying revenue recognition is that revenue must be earned before it is recognized. Revenue usually is recognized when an exchange has taken place which signifies that the earning process is complete. The earning process is not complete until collection of the sales price is complete or is reasonably assured. The authoritative accounting literature to date reflects a series of pronouncements on specific situations related to revenue recognition but lacks a broad, over-arching standard upon which accounting for specific situations is based. Revenue recognition situations that are specifically covered in promulgated standards include installment sales (including alternatives to the installment sales method), right of return, contract income, and the involuntary conversation of assets.

The installment sales method is acceptable only under unusual circumstances in which collectibility cannot be reasonably estimated or assured. The doubtfulness of collectibility can be caused by the length of an extended collection period or because no basis for estimating the probability of collection can be established. In such cases, a company may consider using either the installment sales method or the even more conservative cost recovery method (ASC 605-10-25-3).

In some industries, dealers and distributors of personal property have the right to return unsold merchandise. The right to return merchandise usually is an industry practice but may also occur as a result of a contractual agreement. The return period can last for a few days, as in the perishable food industry, or it can extend for several years, which is not infrequent for some types of publishers. The rate of return of some companies may be high, while in other industries, such as perishable foods, the rate of return may be insignificant.

As long as a right of return exists and the returns could be significant, the seller is exposed to reacquiring the ownership of the property. The risks and rewards of ownership have not, in substance, been passed on to the buyer. Because the earning process is not complete until collection of the sales price is assured reasonably, certain accounting problems arise in recognizing revenue when the right to return exists.

Because of the length of time involved in long-term construction contracts, a problem exists as to when income should be recognized. The completed-contract method and the percentage-of-completion method generally are followed to account for these long-term contracts.

PRACTICE NOTE: The specialized accounting and auditing practices for construction contractors that previously appeared in the AICPA Industry Audit and Accounting Guide titled "Construction Contractors" is now codified in ASC 605.

Involuntary conversion occurs when an asset that is not intended for sale is involuntarily converted to a monetary asset, such as in the case of fire or other destruction, theft, or condemnation by a governmental authority. In these situations, gains or losses may occur that require recognition.

ASC 605-10: OVERALL

INSTALLMENT SALES METHOD

The installment sales method of accounting recognizes gross profit only to the extent that cash has been collected. Each payment collected consists of *part* recovery of cost and *part* gross profit, in the same ratio that these two elements existed in the original sale.

> **PRACTICE POINTER:** Because gross profit ratios are different for many products and departments and may vary from year to year, it is necessary to keep a separate record of sales by year, product line, and department. This requires keeping separate accounts and records for receivables, realized gross profit, unrealized gross profit, and repossessions for each category of product.

Generally, the seller protects its interest in an installment sale by retaining title to the goods through a conditional sales contract, lease, mortgage, or trustee. In the event of a default on an installment sales contract, the related account receivable and unrealized gross profit are written off. In many cases of default, the goods are repossessed by the seller. The loss (or gain) on a default of an installment sales contract is determined as follows:

When goods are repossessed, one of the major problems is determining the value of these inventory goods. Some of the methods of determining their value include:

- Fair market value
- Unrecovered cost (results in no gain or loss)
- Resale value less reconditioning costs plus a normal profit (net realizable value)
- No value—a good method when no other method is appropriate, particularly when the actual value is minor

---

> **PRACTICE POINTER:** Care should be taken in valuing repossessed goods at unrecovered cost because a loss that should be recorded may be overlooked.

Illustration of Installment Sales Method

A furniture dealer sells for $1,000 a chair that cost $700. The gross profit percentage for this sale is 30%. Under the installment sales method, the dealer would recognize 70% of each payment as a recovery of cost and 30% as realized gross profit.

The entries to record the initial sale, assuming the use of a perpetual inventory system and no down payment, are:

Accounts receivable—installment sales	1,000	
Installment sales		1,000
Cost of installment sales	700	
Inventory		700

At the end of the accounting period, the company closes out the installment sales account and the cost of installment sales to unrealized gross profit on installment sales account, which in this example is $300. The entry is:

Installment sales	1,000	
Cost of installment sales		700
Unrealized gross profit on installment sales		300

In the period that the company collects $400, the entries are:

Cash	400	
Accounts receivable—installment sales		400
Unrealized gross profit on installment sales	120	
Realized gross profit on installment sales		120

The $400 collected includes $280 recovery of cost and $120 of realized gross profit on installment sales (a 70%/30% relationship).

If the first payment of $400 was the only payment the company received and the goods were not repossessed, the journal entry to record the default and loss would be:

Unrealized gross profit	180	
Loss on installment sales	420	
Accounts receivable—installment sales		600

If the goods were repossessed and had an inventory value of $250, the journal entry would be:

Unrealized gross profit	180	
Loss on installment sales	170	
Inventory	250	
Accounts receivable—installment sales		600

COST RECOVERY METHOD

The cost recovery method is used in very unusual situations in which recovery of cost is undeterminable or extremely questionable. The procedure is simply that all cost is recovered before any profit is recognized. Once all cost has been recovered, any other collections are recognized as profit. The only expenses remaining to be charged against such revenue are those relating to the collection process.

Illustration of Cost Recovery Method

If a company sells for $100 an item that cost $40 and receives no down payment, the first $20 collected, regardless of the year collected, is considered recovery of half the cost. The next $20 collected is recovery of the balance of the cost, regardless of the year collected. The remaining $60 (all gross profit) is recognized as income when received. The only additional expenses that are charged against the remaining $60 are those directly related to the collection process.

DEFERRED INCOME TAXES

The installment sales method is generally acceptable for income tax purposes, because the government attempts to collect taxes when the taxpayer has the cash available rather than basing collection on a theoretical analysis of accounting principles. The use of installment accounting for tax purposes and the accrual method for financial reporting purposes often results in a temporary difference and creates a deferred tax liability.

DISCLOSURE

Accounts receivable on installment sales are shown separately in the balance sheet. They are classified as current assets in accordance with the normal operating cycle of the entity, which may extend for more than one year. The amounts maturing each period for each class of installment receivable should also be disclosed.

Unrealized gross profit is presented in the balance sheet as a separate caption, usually as a contra account to the related installment receivable.

ASC 605-15: PRODUCTS

REVENUE RECOGNITION FOR RETURNABLE MERCHANDISE

When a buyer has the right to return merchandise purchased, the seller may not recognize income from the sale, unless *all* of the following conditions are met (ASC 605-15-25-1):

- The price between the seller and the buyer is substantially fixed, or determinable.
- The seller has received full payment, or the buyer is indebted to the seller and the indebtedness is not contingent on the resale of the merchandise.
- Physical destruction, damage, or theft of the merchandise would not change the buyer's obligation to the seller.
- The buyer has economic substance and is not a front, straw party, or conduit, existing for the benefit of the seller.
- No significant obligations exist for the seller to help the buyer resell the merchandise.
- A reasonable estimate can be made of the amount of future returns.

If all of the above conditions are met, revenue is recognized on sales for which a right of return exists, provided that an appropriate provision is made for costs or losses that may occur in connection with the return of merchandise from the buyer (ASC 605-15-25-2).

PRACTICE NOTE: An exchange of one item for a similar item of the same quality and value is not considered a return for the purposes of ASC 605.

If all of the conditions of ASC 605 are met, an appropriate provision for costs or losses that may occur in connection with the return of merchandise from the buyer must be made by the seller. The provision for costs or losses must be in accordance with ASC 450 (Contingencies) (ASC 605-15-45-1). Under ASC 450, a provision for a loss contingency is accrued, by a charge to income, provided that both of the following conditions exist:

- It is *probable* that at the date of the financial statements, an asset has been impaired or a liability incurred, based on information available prior to the issuance of the financial statements.
- The amount of loss can be estimated reasonably.

The requirement for the accrual of a loss contingency is satisfied when all of the conditions of ASC 605-15-25 are met. Thus, if returns are *probable* and all of the conditions of GAAP are met, accrual of a loss is required. This accrual results in a reduction in sales revenue and the related cost of sales in the income statement.

> **PRACTICE POINTER:** If all of the conditions of ASC 605-15-25 are not met, the seller cannot recognize the sales revenue until the right of return privilege has substantially expired or the applicable provisions are subsequently met (ASC 605-15-25-1). The seller has several alternatives in accounting for these transactions: First, do not record the transaction on the books at all and maintain a **memorandum account** for these types of transactions. Second, record the transaction as a debit to a deferred receivable account and a credit to a deferred sales account. Last, handle the transaction as a consignment. In any event, maintain control for these types of transactions, particularly if they are a part of recurring business activities.

Reasonable Estimates of Returns

Reasonable estimates of returns depend on individual circumstances. An enterprise must take into consideration its individual customers and the types of merchandise involved in determining the estimated amount of returns that may occur. The following factors may impair the ability to make a reasonable estimate of returns (ASC 605-15-25-3):

- Possible technological obsolescence or changes in demand for the merchandise
- A long return period
- Little or no past experience in determining returns for similar types of sales of similar merchandise
- An inability to apply past experience due to changing circumstances
- A limited number of similar transactions

> **PRACTICE POINTER:** The above factors are to be considered in conjunction with the past experience with a specific customer and the individual product involved in the sale. One or more of these factors may or may not impair the ability of an enterprise to make a reasonable estimate of the amount of future returns.

Illustration of Reasonable Estimates of Returns

The right to return merchandise to a seller may apply to only a portion of a total sale. For example, X Company sells 100,000 widgets to Y Company on January 1 for $1 per widget (cost $0.65). In the sales agreement, X Company grants to Y Company the right to return up to a maximum of 30% of the widgets within six months from the date of sale. Under these circumstances, ASC 605 would only apply to the 30% of the widgets that can be returned by Y Company. Assuming that all of the conditions imposed by ASC 605 are met and it is probable that one-half (50%) of the widgets subject to return will actually be returned and the estimated cost that X Company expects to incur in connection with the returns is $1,000, the computations would be as follows:

Total sale	$100,000
Less: Portion of the sale not subject to ASC 605	70,000
Balance of the sale subject to ASC 605	$ 30,000
Less: Provision for estimated returns (50% of $30,000)	15,000
Balance of sale which is recognized	$ 15,000
Balance of sale not subject to ASC 605	70,000
Total revenue recognized at date of sale	$ 85,000

Under ASC 605, X Company reports $84,000 of revenue on the date the title to the widgets passes to Y Company. X Company also sets up a provision for returnable merchandise and related costs of $16,000. Sales and related cost of sales are reported at their gross amounts in the income statement and the sales and related cost of sales for the *probable* returns are deducted from the gross amounts. The journal entries to record the transactions on the books of X Company are as follows:

Accounts receivable	100,000	
Sales		100,000
(To record the gross sales to Y Company.)		
Cost of sales	65,000	
Inventory		65,000
(To record cost of sales for Y Company order.)		
Estimated sales returns	15,000	
Deferred cost of sales ($0.65 per widget)	9,750	
Cost of sales		9,750
Provision for estimated returns		15,000
(To defer sales of $15,000 and the related cost of sales of $9,750.)		

The provision for estimated returns is a contra accounts to accounts receivable. The deferred cost of sales represents the cost of inventory that is expected to be returned; it is most logically classified as inventory.

ASC 605-35: CONSTRUCTION-TYPE AND PRODUCTION-TYPE CONTRACTS

COMPLETED-CONTRACT METHOD

The completed-contract method recognizes income only on completion or substantial completion of the contract. *A contract is regarded as substantially complete if the remaining costs are insignificant* (ASC 605-35-25-88).

Any excess of accumulated costs over related billings is reflected in the balance sheet as a current asset; any excess of accumulated billings over related costs is reflected as a current liability. In the case of more than one contract, the accumulated costs or liabilities should be stated separately on the balance sheet. The preferred terminology for the balance sheet presentation is *(Costs) (Billings) of uncompleted contracts in excess of related (billings) (costs)* (ASC 605-35-45-4).

In some cases, it is preferable to allocate general and administrative expenses to contract costs rather than to period income. In years in which no contracts are completed, a better matching of costs and revenues is achieved by carrying general expense as a charge to the contract. If a contractor has many jobs, however, it is more appropriate to charge these expenses to current periods (ASC 605-35-25-99).

Although income is not recognized until completion of the contract, a provision for an expected loss should be recognized when it becomes evident that a loss will occur (ASC 605-35-25-89).

Illustration of the Completed-Contract Method

A construction company has a balance in its construction-in-progress account of $500,000, representing the costs incurred to date on a project. While the project was initially expected to be profitable, management now expects a loss on the project at completion of $75,000. At the time of this determination, the following entry should be made:

Estimated loss on construction project	75,000
Construction in progress	75,000

This entry reduces the construction (inventory) account by $75,000 and recognizes the loss in income of the period in which the determination of the loss is estimable. Assuming the estimate of the loss is accurate, future costs will be charged to the construction account as incurred and the balance in that account will equal the revenue on the contract.

The primary advantage of the completed-contract method is that it is based on final results rather than on estimates. The primary disadvantage of this method is that it does not reflect current performances when the period of the contract extends over more than one accounting period (ASC 605-35-05-12).

Accounting for the Completed-Contract Method

The following are important points in accounting for contracts under the completed-contract method:

1. Overhead and direct costs are charged to a construction-in-progress account (an asset).
2. Billings and/or cash received are charged to advances on the construction-in-progress account (a liability).
3. At completion of the contract, gross profit or loss is recognized as follows:

    Contract price – total costs = gross profit or loss

4. At balance sheet dates that occur during the contract period, the excess of either the construction-in-progress account or the advances account over the other is classified as a current asset or a current liability. It is a *current* asset or a *current* liability because of the *normal operating cycle concept*.
5. Expected losses are recognized in full in the year they are identified. An expected loss on the total contract is determined by:
    a. Adding estimated costs to complete to the recorded costs to date to arrive at total contract costs
    b. Adding to advances any additional revenue expected to arrive at total contract revenue
    c. Subtracting b from a to arrive at total estimated loss on contract

PERCENTAGE-OF-COMPLETION METHOD

Revenues generally are recognized when (*a*) the earning process is complete or virtually complete and (*b*) an exchange has taken place.

Accounting for long-term construction contracts by the percentage-of-completion method is a modification of the general practice of realization at the point of sale. Realization is based on the evidence that the ultimate proceeds are available and the consensus that the result is a better measure of periodic income (matching-of-revenue-and-cost principle).

The principal merits of the percentage-of-completion method are the reflection of the status of the uncompleted contracts and the periodic recognition of the income currently rather than irregularly as contracts are completed. The principal disadvantage of this method is the necessity of relying on estimates of the ultimate costs (ASC 605-35-05-7).

The percentage-of-completion method recognizes income as work progresses on the contract. The method is based on an estimate of the income earned to date, less income recognized in earlier periods. Estimates of the degree of completion usually are based on one of the following (ASC 605-35-25-52):

- The relationship of costs incurred to date to expected total costs for the contract

- Other measures of progress toward completion, such as engineering estimates

During the early stages of a contract, all or a portion of items such as material and subcontract costs may be excluded if it appears that the results would produce a more meaningful allocation of periodic income (ASC 605-35-25-53).

When current estimates of the total contract costs indicate a loss, a provision for the loss on the entire contract should be made. When a loss is indicated on a total contract that is part of a related group of contracts, however, the group may be treated as a unit in determining the necessity of providing for losses (ASC 605-35-25-5, 46).

PRACTICE POINTER: Income to be recognized under the percentage-of-completion method at various stages ordinarily should not be measured by interim billings.

Accounting for the Percentage-of-Completion Method

The following are important points in accounting for contracts under the percentage-of-completion method:

- Journal entries and balance sheet treatment are the same as for the completed-contract method, *except* that the amount of estimated gross profit earned in each period is recorded by charging the construction-in-progress account and crediting realized gross profit.

- Gross profit or loss is recognized in each period by the following formula:

$$\left[\begin{array}{c} \text{percentage} \\ \text{of} \\ \text{completion} \end{array} \times \begin{array}{c} \text{total estimated} \\ \text{gross profit or} \\ \text{loss} \end{array} \right] - \begin{array}{c} \text{gross profit} \\ \text{recognized to} \\ \text{date} \end{array} = \begin{array}{c} \text{current period} \\ \text{realized gross} \\ \text{profit} \end{array}$$

- An estimated loss on the total contract is recognized immediately in the year it is discovered. Any gross profit (or loss) reported in prior years, however, must be added (or deducted) from the total estimated loss.

PRACTICE POINTER: The completed-contract and percentage-of-completion methods are *not* intended to be alternative methods of accounting for the same contract. Each is appropriate in certain circumstances, but do *not* consider them *equally appropriate in the same circumstances.* Where reasonable estimates of the percentage of completion are possible, the percentage-of-completion method constitutes GAAP and should be used. On the other hand, if reasonable estimates of the percentage are *not* possible, the completed-contract method constitutes GAAP and should be used.

ASC 605—Revenue Recognition

Illustration of Accounting for the Completed-Contract and Percentage-of-Completion Method

The following data pertain to a $2,000,000 long-term construction contract:

	20X5	20X6	20X7
Costs incurred during the year	$500,000	$700,000	$300,000
Year-end estimated costs to complete	1,000,000	300,000	—
Billing during the year	400,000	700,000	900,000
Collections during the year	200,000	500,000	1,200,000

The journal entries for both the completed-contract method and the percentage-of-completion method for the three years are as follows, assuming the degree of completion is determined based on costs incurred:

20X5	Completed Contract		% of Completion	
Construction in progress	500,000		500,000	
Cash or liability		500,000		500,000
Accounts receivable	400,000		400,000	
Advance billings		400,000		400,000
Cash	200,000		200,000	
Accounts receivable		200,000		200,000
Construction in progress	no entry		166,667	
Realized gross profit (P&L)				166,667

20X6	Completed Contract		% of Completion	
Construction in progress	700,000		700,000	
Cash or liability		700,000		700,000
Accounts receivable	700,000		700,000	
Advance billings		700,000		700,000
Cash	500,000		500,000	
Accounts receivable		500,000		500,000
Construction in progress	no entry		233,333	
Realized gross profit (P&L)				233,333

20X7	Completed Contract		% of Completion	
Construction in progress		300,000		300,000
Cash or liability		300,000		300,000
Accounts receivable	900,000		900,000	
Advance billings		900,000		900,000
Cash	1,200,000		1,200,000	
Accounts receivable		1,200,000		1,200,000
Construction in progress	no entry		100,000	
Realized gross profit (P&L)				100,000
Advance billings	2,000,000		2,000,000	
Construction in progress		1,500,000		2,000,000
Realized gross profit (P&L)		500,000		—

At the end of each year during which the contract is in progress, the excess of the construction–in–progress account over the advance billings account is presented as a current asset:

20X5: ($500,000 + $166,667) − $400,000 = $266,667

20X6: ($500,00 + $166,667 + $700,00 + $233,333)

− ($400,000 + $700,00) = $500,000

In this illustration, the estimated gross profit of $500,000 was the actual gross profit on the contract. If changes in the estimated cost to complete the contract had been appropriate at the end of 20X5 and/or 20X6, or if the actual costs to complete had been determined to be different when the contract was completed in 20X7, those changes would have been incorporated into revised estimates during the contract period. For example, if at the end of 20X6 the costs to complete were estimated to be $400,000 instead of $300,000, the 20X6 gross profit of $133,333 would have been determined as follows:

$$\left(\frac{\$1,200,000}{\$1,600,000^*}\right) \times (2,000,000 - \$1,6000,000) = \$300,000$$

$$\$300,000 - \$166,667 = \$133,333$$

---

*$500,000 (20X5) + $700,000 (20X6) + $400,000 (20X6 estimated) = $1,600,000

ASC 605-40: GAINS AND LOSSES

INVOLUNTARY CONVERSION OF NONMONETARY ASSETS TO MONETARY ASSETS

When a nonmonetary asset is involuntarily converted to a monetary asset, a monetary transaction results, and ASC 605 requires that a gain or loss be recognized in the period of conversion (ASC 605-40-25-3). The gain or loss is the difference between the carrying amount of the nonmonetary asset and the proceeds from the conversion.

Examples of involuntary conversion are the total or partial destruction of property through fire or other catastrophe, theft of property, or condemnation of property by a governmental authority (eminent domain proceedings).

Gain or loss from an involuntary conversion of a nonmonetary asset to a monetary asset is classified as part of continuing operations, extraordinary items, disposal of a segment, etc., according to the particular circumstances (ASC 605-40-45-1). In addition, a gain or loss recognized for tax purposes in a period different from that for financial accounting purposes creates a temporary difference, for which recognition of deferred taxes may be necessary (ASC 740-10-55-66).

The involuntary conversion of a LIFO inventory layer at an interim date is not required if the proceeds from involuntary conversion are expected to be reinvested in replacement inventory by the end of the fiscal year (ASC 605-40-25-3).

PRACTICE NOTE: This is the same treatment afforded a temporary liquidation at interim dates of a LIFO inventory layer that is expected to be replaced by the end of the annual period.

In the event the proceeds from an involuntary conversion of a LIFO inventory layer are not reinvested in replacement inventory by the end of the fiscal year, gain for financial accounting purposes need not be recognized, providing the taxpayer does not recognize such gains for income tax reporting purposes and provided that replacement is intended but not yet made by year-end (ASC 605-40-25-3).

REVENUE RECOGNITION

IMPORTANT NOTICE FOR 2014

As CCH's 2014 *GAAP Guide* goes to press, the FASB has outstanding an Exposure Draft (ED) that will have far-reaching effects on revenue recognition. The ED indicates that revenue is a crucial number to users of financial statements in assessing an entity's financial performance and financial position. Revenue recognition requirements in U.S. GAAP and in International Financial Reporting Standards differ and both are in need of improvement. U.S. GAAP include broad recognition standards and numerous requirements for particular industries and transactions that result in different accounting for economically similar transactions. IFRS have fewer requirements on revenue recognition, can be difficult to understand, and provide limited guidance on important topics that have a material impact on the financial statements.

The current project, which is a joint effort of the FASB and the IASB, is intended to develop a common revenue standard with the following characteristics:

- Remove inconsistencies and weaknesses in existing revenue recognition requirements.
- Provide a more robust framework for addressing revenue issues.
- Improve comparability of revenue recognition practices across entities, industries, jurisdictions, and capital markets.
- Provide more useful information to users of financial statements with improved disclosure requirements.
- Simplify the preparation of financial statements by reducing the number of requirements to which an entity must refer.

The Exposure Draft would require companies to apply a five-step process in recognizing revenue:

1. Identify the contract with the customer.
2. Identify the separate performance obligations in the contract.
3. Determine the transaction price.
4. Allocate the transaction price.
5. Recognize revenue when the performance obligation is satisfied.

The FASB continues to gather input on the important project in an attempt to understand if its proposals are clear and can be applied in a way that effectively communicates the economic substance of transactions, to identify any unintended consequences, to ensure that the FASB staff is aware of significant changes in current practice that will result, and to educate constituents about the proposals and the basis for conclusions.

The current technical plan of the FASB calls for the issuance of a final standard in the third quarter of 2013.

PART II: INTERPRETIVE GUIDANCE

ASC 605-15: PRODUCTS

ASC 605-15-05-6, 15-2, 25-5; ASC 840-10-60-3 Products Sold and Subsequently Repurchased Subject to an Operating Lease

BACKGROUND

Finished products are sold by a manufacturer to an independent dealer that sells those products to customers, who may be individuals or other independent entities. Customers may purchase such products by (*a*) paying cash, (*b*) using their own financing sources, or (*c*) using traditional consumer financing or lease financing arranged by the dealer and provided by unrelated commercial banks, other finance companies, or by the manufacturer's wholly owned subsidiary.

ACCOUNTING ISSUE

Should a manufacturer recognize a sale on a product sold to an independent dealer if the dealer's customer subsequently enters into an operating lease with the manufacturer or its finance subsidiary, which acquires title to the product subject to the lease?

ACCOUNTING GUIDANCE

A manufacturer can recognize a sale when a product is transferred to a dealer if *all* of the following conditions exist:

- The dealer is a substantive and independent entity whose business with the manufacturer and retail customers is conducted separately.

- The manufacturer has delivered the product and passed the risks and rewards of ownership to the dealer, including responsibility for the ultimate sale of the product and for insurability, theft, or damage. The dealer cannot return the product to the manufacturer if the customer does not enter into a lease with the manufacturer or its finance subsidiary.

- At the time the product is delivered to the dealer, the manufacturer or its finance affiliate has no legal obligation to provide a lease to the dealer's potential customer.

- Other financing alternatives are available to the customer from sources that are not affiliated with the manufacturer, and the customer makes the selection from the financing alternatives.

DISCUSSION

The guidance is based on the following views:

- A manufacturer's sale of the product to the dealer is a legal sale. Because the manufacturer has no further obligation related to the product, other than warranty obligations, the dealer's transaction with the retail customer is a separate transaction.

- The sale to the dealer meets the criteria for revenue recognition in paragraph 83 of CON-5 (not included in the ASC), because revenue was earned when the manufacturer sold the product to the dealer. The manufacturer has no obligation related to future sales to retail customers.

- The manufacturer's involvement in financing alternatives is not a primary issue in the dealer's sales process as long as the customer can choose between financing from the manufacturer's subsidiary and alternative financing sources from unaffiliated parties.

- The manufacturer does not guarantee the dealer's recovery of its investment in the product.

- The economic substance of the operating lease is independent of the manufacturer's sale to the dealer, because title, risks, and rewards of ownership have been transferred to the dealer, including the product's ultimate sale and disposition in case of theft or damage.

ASC 605-20: SERVICES

ASC 605-20-25-1 through 25-6; ASC 460-10-15-9; 60-41 Separately Priced Extended Warranty and Product Maintenance Contracts

BACKGROUND

An *extended warranty* is an agreement to provide warranty protection in addition to that covered in the manufacturer's original warranty, if any, or to extend the period of coverage beyond that provided by the manufacturer's warranty. A *product maintenance contract* is an agreement to perform certain agreed-upon services to maintain a product for a specified period. Some contracts cover both an extended warranty and product maintenance. A *separately priced contract* is one in which a customer has the option to purchase the services provided under the contract for a stated amount that is separate from the price of the product.

ACCOUNTING GUIDANCE

Question: How should revenue and costs from a separately priced extended warranty or a product maintenance contract be recognized?

Answer: Revenue should be deferred and recognized over the contract period on a straight-line basis, except when sufficient historical evidence indicates that the costs of performing under the contract are incurred in a pattern other than straight-line. In those circumstances, revenue should be recognized over the contract period in proportion to the costs expected to be incurred in performing the services required under the contract.

36,018 ASC 605—Revenue Recognition

Costs that are directly related to the acquisition of a contract and that would not have been incurred if the contract had not existed should be deferred and charged to expense in proportion to the revenue recognized. All other costs should be charged to expense as incurred.

A loss exists if the total expected costs of providing services under the contract and unamortized acquisition costs exceed the related unearned revenue. A loss is recognized by (a) charging any unamortized acquisition costs to expense, and (b) recognizing a liability for excess costs, if any.

Illustration of Recognition of Revenue and Costs on a Separately Priced Extended Warranty Contract—Warranty Costs Not Incurred on a Straight-Line Basis

Dorf Motors sells a separately priced extended warranty contract for $1,200 on 1/1/20X4 in conjunction with the sale of its Spitfire model. The extended warranty contract extends the manufacturer's warranty (three years, 36,000 miles) by an additional three years and 36,000 miles. Dorf has sufficient warranty experience to predict claim costs under the extended warranty as follows: year 1: $0 (manufacturer's warranty in effect), year 2: $0, year 3: $0, year 4: $100, year 5: $200, and year 6: $300. Dorf incurred $200 of costs directly related to the sale of the extended warranty contract that would not have been incurred if the contract had not been sold.

On 1/1/X4, Dorf would record a liability for deferred revenue of $1,200. None of this deferred revenue would be recognized in X4, X5, and X6, since any warranty work performed by Dorf in those years falls under the manufacturer's warranty, not under the extended warranty. Revenue, and amortization of direct costs, would be recognized as follows during X7—X9:

	Revenue Recognized	Amortization of Direct Costs
X7	$200 [($100 / $600) × $1,200]	$33 [($200 / $1,200)] × $200
X8	$400 [($200 / $600) × $1,200]	$67 [($400 / $1,200)] × $200
X9	$600 [($300 / $600) × $1,200]	$100 [($600 / $1,200)] × $200

ASC 605-20-15-3, 25-8 through 25-12; ASC 460-10-60-8; ASC 310-10-60-4 Fees for Guaranteeing a Loan

BACKGROUND

An entity, usually a financial institution or insurance company, guarantees the debt of another entity and is paid a fee for doing so. The guarantee may be in the form of (a) a general guarantee to ensure that the funds will be repaid or (b) a pledge of assets that could be claimed by a lender if the borrower defaults. Such guarantees are usually used by entities that would otherwise be unable to borrow or would have to pay a very high interest rate.

The following are examples of such transactions:
- An entity issues three-to-six-year notes, which are guaranteed with a surety bond issued by an insurance company. The entity pays an annual premium to the insurance company based on the entity's annual debt service and pledges assets valued at 110% of the debt as collateral to the insurance company.
- A developer issues tax-exempt industrial bonds to finance a project. A financial institution guarantees the debt by pledging specific assets.
- A guarantor and an investment banker establish a special-purpose entity that issues commercial paper for borrowers who would be unable to do so themselves. The guarantor provides a surety bond for each borrower to guarantee repayment of the funds. The investment banker sells the commercial paper and lends the funds to the borrower at a spread above the commercial paper interest rate. The loan and the commercial paper have the same maturity dates.

ACCOUNTING ISSUES

How should a guarantor account for initial and continuing fees received?

ACCOUNTING GUIDANCE SCOPE

The following guidance does not apply to:
- Guarantees accounted for as derivatives under the guidance in ASC 815-10-15;
- Product warranties;
- Guarantees that must be accounted for as financial guarantee insurance contracts under the guidance in ASC 944.

RECOGNITION

A loan guarantee generally consists of two sets of fees—an initial fee when a transaction is consummated and an annual fee over the term of a loan. A guarantor should recognize income from such fees over the term of the guarantee. Direct costs associated with a guarantee should be accounted for in a manner related to the recognition of income from the fee.

Guarantee contracts that are only intended to reimburse a guaranteed party for a loss because a debtor defaults on a loan are excluded from the guidance in ASC 815-10-15-58. However, if a guarantee meets the definition of a derivative because it is triggered by changes in an underlying, such as a decrease in a borrower's creditworthiness, the guarantee should be accounted for under the guidance in ASC 815-10.

DISCUSSION

A guarantor of a loan usually receives two fees: (*a*) an initial fee, which is paid when the transaction is closed, and (*b*) an annual fee, which is paid over the term of the loan. This Issue addresses the accounting for the initial fee. The guidance is based on the notion that the initial fee cannot be separated from annual fees and should thus be recognized over the term of the loan. The guarantor does not earn the total initial fee when the transaction is closed, but rather over the period during which the guarantor will be at risk.

ASC 605-20-25-13; S25-1, S99-2 Services for Freight-in-Transit at the End of a Reporting Period

BACKGROUND

Motor carriers provide a variety of services to their customers. The services can be (*a*) limited, involving only pickup and delivery (usually of a full trailer loaded by a customer—known as "truckload carriers"), or (*b*) extensive, including pickup of small loads, consolidation of loads from different customers, transportation to the motor carrier's terminal, transfer at hub terminals, and final delivery.

Revenue is recognized when customers are billed, usually at the time freight is received from a customer (shipper). Direct expenses are incurred throughout the freight service process from pickup to delivery and completion.

This Issue addresses revenue and expense recognition at the balance sheet date for freight that has been received but has not yet been delivered.

At the time this Issue was discussed, the following five alternative methods of revenue recognition were used in practice:

1. Revenue was recognized when freight was received from the shipper (or when freight left the carrier's terminal), and expenses were recognized when incurred.

2. Revenue was recognized when freight was received from the shipper (or when freight left the carrier's terminal), and estimated costs to complete were accrued at the end of each reporting period.

3. Revenue and direct costs were recognized when a shipment was completed, and the expense was recognized as incurred.

4. Revenue was recognized when the shipment was completed, and an expense was recognized as incurred.

5. Revenue was allocated between reporting periods based on the relative transit time in each reporting period, and an expense was recognized as incurred.

ACCOUNTING ISSUE

How should motor carriers recognize revenue and expense for freight services in process at the balance sheet date?

ACCOUNTING GUIDANCE

Alternative 1 is not an acceptable method of revenue recognition for freight carriers. This guidance is not limited to motor carriers.

SEC OBSERVER COMMENT

The SEC Observer indicated that a change from Alternative 1 to Alternative 2 would not be acceptable, because under Alternative 2, revenue would be recognized before performance has occurred, and liabilities would be recognized before they have been incurred.

DISCUSSION

The following illustration shows the potential income statement effect of revenue and expense recognition under the five alternatives. However, because only one shipment in one reporting period is considered, the results are not as extreme as for companies that have a large number of shipments and report revenue and expense over a number of periods.

Illustration of Revenue and Expense Recognition by Motor Carriers

Assumptions

Amount billable for shipment A	$2,000
Total expected direct costs associated with shipment A	$1,400
Date freight is received from shipper	June 29, 20X1
Date of final delivery	July 2, 20X1
Reporting date	June 30, 20X1
Direct costs (expenses) incurred through June 30, 20X1	$800
Amount billable and billed at June 30, 20X1	$2,000

Revenue and expense recognition at June 30, 20X1

	Alternative				
	1	2	3	4	5
Revenue	$2,000	$2,000	$0	$0	$1,000
Expense	800	1,400	0	800	800
Gross profit (loss)	$1,200	$600	$0	$(800)	$200

When this Issue was discussed, predominant industry practice was to recognize revenue based on Alternative 1. The appeal of that method was its simplicity; other methods could involve extensive record keeping. Proponents believed that because of the short-term nature of the service (normally no more than five days), using Alternative 1 would not lead to abuse or distortion. Opponents argued that the earnings process is not complete when the shipment is picked up, because the carrier still must perform significant services, including final delivery.

Paragraph 83 of CON-5 (not included in ASC) refers to two factors for revenue recognition: (*a*) revenues must be realized and realizable and (*b*) revenues must be earned. Alternative 1 does not conform to that guidance.

Although Alternative 2 attempts to match expenses to revenues recognized, it is unacceptable because revenue is recognized before delivery of the shipment. Thus, it does not meet the revenue recognition criteria in CON-5 (not included in ASC). In addition, direct operating expenses are accrued before they have been incurred and the benefits consumed.

Proponents of Alternative 3 believed that the act of delivering the freight is significant because it indicates performance of the service. They believed that revenue is not earned until performance.

Alternative 4 is the most conservative method. Under this alternative, revenue is recognized the same as in Alternative 3, but there is no deferral (or matching) of expenses. There are also no onerous record-keeping requirements. Those who supported this alternative agreed with the revenue recognition criteria in Alternative 3, but believed that direct costs should not be deferred but treated as period costs. In addition, they argued that the cost of estimating and allocating direct costs to different periods is not warranted. Those who supported Alternative 3 argued that revenues and expenses would not be matched properly under Alternative 4.

Proponents of Alternative 5 argued that it provides the best measure of revenue earned during the period and is most faithful to the revenue recognition criteria in CON-5 (not included in ASC), because revenue recognized under that alternative is based on proportional performance, i.e., relative transit time in each reporting period. In addition, an attraction of this alternative was that direct costs are charged to expense as incurred and not allocated between reporting periods. Proponents believed that allocation of such costs would be too subjective. Opponents of the proportional performance alternative argued that there is no reliable way to estimate the degree of performance.

ASC 605-20-25-14 through 25-18, 50-1 Accounting for Advertising Barter Transactions

OVERVIEW

In the late 1990s, a number of internet companies were entering into barter transactions with other internet companies under which the two companies advertised each other's products or services on their respective web sites without additional compensation. The transactions had no effect on net income or cash flow from operations because the companies generally accounted for the transactions by recognizing equal amounts of barter advertising revenue and barter advertising expense in their income statements.

Some accountants were concerned that this accounting treatment does not conform with the guidance on the recognition of revenues and expenses in Statement of Financial Accounting Concepts No. 6 (not in ASC), guidance on accounting for nonmonetary transactions in ASC 845 (formerly, APB-29) and ASC 845-10-05-11 through 05-12, 15-12 through 15-15, 15-17, 15-20, 25-3, 25-6 through 25-11, 30-12 through 30-14, 30-21 through 30-27, 55-2, 55-28, 55-30 through 55-37, 60-3, S99-3; and ASC 810-10-55-1A (formerly, EITF Issue 01-2, Interpretations of APB 29, see Chapter 55, ASC 845, Nonmonetary Transactions). Further, some contended that recognition of barter advertising revenue that

ASC 605—Revenue Recognition

results in no income or cash flows may mislead investors who use information about revenues to evaluate companies that have net operating *losses* and net cash *outflows*. The scope of this Issue is *not* limited to internet companies.

ACCOUNTING ISSUE

Should revenues and expenses related to nonmonetary exchanges involving barter transactions of advertising be recognized at the readily determinable fair values of the advertising provided or received in the exchange?

ACCOUNTING GUIDANCE

The following guidance was provided:

- Revenues and expenses related to advertising barter transactions should be recognized at their fair value only if the fair value of the advertising provided to the counterparty can be determined based on the entity's own known amount of cash received for similar advertising from other buyers that are unrelated to the counterparty in the current barter transaction. A swap of offsetting consideration between the parties to the barter transaction, such as exchanging checks for the same amount, does not provide evidence of the fair value of a transaction. If the fair value of an advertising barter transaction cannot be determined based on the above, the transaction should be recognized based on the carrying amount of the advertising provided to the counterparty, which most likely will be zero.

- An entity's historical practice of receiving cash or marketable securities for similar advertising provided should be based on a period no longer than six months before the current barter transaction. A shorter and more representative period should be used if as a result of economic changes, similar transactions that occurred during the previous six months are not representative of the fair value of the advertising provided. Cash transactions that occur after advertising was provided in a barter transaction should not be used to determine the fair value of the advertising provided in the barter transaction (i.e., no look back is permitted to value previous barter transactions).

- Advertising provided for cash may be considered to be similar to advertising provided in a barter transaction if the cash transaction was in the same medium and used the same advertising vehicle, such as the same publication, same web site, or the same broadcast channel, as the barter transaction. Further, the characteristics of advertising provided for cash and that provided in a barter transaction should be reasonably similar in the following respects:

    — Circulation, exposure, or saturation in an intended market

    — Timing in terms of time of day, day of week, daily, weekly, 24 hours a day/7 days a week, and the season

    — Prominence in terms of page on web site, section of periodical, location on page, and size of advertisement

    — Demographics of readers, viewers, or customers

    — Length of time advertising will be shown

- The quantity or volume of advertising provided in a past cash or near-cash transaction that meets the criteria in this Issue can be used as evidence of fair value for a subsequent barter transaction only if the latter provides an equal quantity or volume of advertising. That is, a past cash transaction can be used as evidence for the recognition of revenue on a barter transaction only up to the dollar amount of the cash transaction. In addition, a cash transaction that has been used to support an equivalent quantity and dollar amount of barter revenue, within the limits of this Issue, cannot be used as evidence of fair value of other barter transactions.

- The amount of revenue and expense recognized from advertising barter transactions should be disclosed for each income statement period presented. Entities providing advertising in barter transactions that do not qualify for recognition at fair value should disclose for each income statement period presented the volume and type of advertising provided and received, such as the number of equivalent pages, number of minutes, or the overall percentage of advertising volume.

ASC 605-20-S25-2, S99-1 Accounting for Management Fees Based on a Formula

Certain fee-based arrangements, which are common in the investment advisory and real estate management businesses, include an incentive fee related to performance in addition to a base fee—for example, based on cost savings generated by a real estate management company. Under such arrangements, the amount of the fee generally is not confirmed until the end of a contractual time period. This announcement states the views of the SEC staff on the accounting for revenue from incentive fees at interim dates before the final amount has been confirmed. The SEC staff has been asked to address this Issue because sometimes performance that exceeds the required target in the early part of a measurement period may be reversed if the performance target is not achieved in a later measurement period. The SEC staff provided the following example:

> An investment advisor managing a mutual fund is paid a monthly base fee. However, the advisor is also paid an incentive fee equal to 20% of the Fund's returns that exceed the S&P 500's return for the year. The contract can be terminated by each party with reasonable notice at the end of each quarter. At termination, the Advisor's incentive fee will be calculated based on the Fund's returns to date compared to those of the S&P 500 during that period. If the Fund's return exceeds the S&P 500's returns by $200,000 in the first quarter, $100,000 in the second quarter, and $50,000 in the fourth quarter, but is $75,000 less than the S&P 500's returns in the third quarter, the Fund's total return for the year would exceed the S&P 500's return by $275,000. The Advisor's total incentive fee for the year would be $55,000 in the fourth quarter.

An informal survey conducted by the SEC staff indicated that a majority of investment advisors and property managers recognize no income from incentive fees until the end of the contract period. Under that method, $55,000 would be recognized as incentive fee revenue at the end of the fourth quarter. However, others recognize the amount of revenue from incentive fees that would be receivable at a point in time as if the contract were terminated at that date. Under this second method, the advisor would recognize $40,000 as an incentive fee at the end of the first quarter ($200,000 × .2) and $20,000 at the end of the second quarter ($100,000 × .2). At the end of the third quarter, the advisor would reduce previously recognized revenue by $15,000 ($75,000 × .2) and would recognize $10,000 ($50,000 × .2) at the end of the fourth quarter.

Although the SEC Staff prefers the first method, because it believes it is more consistent with the guidance in SEC Staff Accounting Bulletin (SAB) Topic 13A, the staff would not object if companies use the second method, which provides better information about a manager's actual performance during each interim period.

The SEC Staff objects, however, to the use of another method under which revenue recognized under the second method discussed above would be reduced by an amount that management believes will be lost as a result of future performance. The Staff believes that method is inconsistent with the guidance in SAB Topic 13A and the requirement that the fee be fixed or determinable.

The following are the views of the SEC Staff on some variations of the methods discussed above:

- Unless an arrangement has been terminated, revenue should not be recognized based on amounts that would be receivable at termination as a result of provisions for penalties or liquidated damages in addition to the amount payable under the incentive fee formula.
- Revenue recorded at an interim date should not exceed the amount a customer would be required to pay on termination if a customer can terminate an arrangement at will and thus avoid paying all or some of the fee due to the manager.
- Revenue should be recognized in interim periods under the second method for a *fixed* incentive fee (e.g., a fixed amount for exceeding the S&P 500) only if the target has been exceeded and should be limited to a proportionate amount of the fixed payment due.
- The SEC Staff's views apply even if a manager or adviser has no termination rights during the contract term.

The SEC Staff encourages registrants to submit to the Staff for preclearance any questions regarding revenue accounting for such arrangements.

DISCLOSURE

The accounting policy for such arrangements should be disclosed in accordance with ASC 235-10-50, SAB Topic 13. Disclosure is required about previously recognized revenue that may be lost due to future performance contingencies, as well as disclosure of the nature of the contracts causing the contingencies, and the amount of revenue that would be affected, if material.

ASC 605-25: MULTIPLE-ELEMENT ARRANGEMENTS

ASC 605-25-15-3A, 25-2, 30-2, 30-5, 30-6A through 30-6B, 30-7, 50-1 through 50-2, 55-1, 55-3, 55-7, 55-12, 55-25, 55-29, 55-32, 55-34, 55-36 through 55-47, 55-52, 55-54, 55-6A through 55-57, 55-61, 55-69, 55-75 through 55-6B, 55-93, 65-1 (ASU 2009-13) Revenue Arrangements with Multiple Deliverables

BACKGROUND

The following accounting guidance addresses practice issues related to: (1) the determination of the unit of accounting for arrangements under which a vendor performs multiple activities that generate revenue (e.g., the delivery of multiple products or the performance of multiple services under arrangements that consist of products that cannot function separately and for which evidence of the separate fair values of the deliverables is unavailable); and (2) issues related to allocation methods used in revenue recognition under the guidance in ASC 605, *Revenue Recognition*, ASC 605-25-05-1 and 05-02. Although paragraph 83 of Financial Accounting Standards Board (FASB) Concepts Statement No. 5, Recognition and Measurement in Financial Statements of Business Enterprises (CON-5) (not included in the ASC), provides guidance on the fundamental factors to consider regarding the timing of revenue recognition, many issues encountered by entities in practice are not addressed in the current accounting literature.

SCOPE

The following accounting guidance, which amends the guidance in ASC 605-25, Multiple-Element Arrangements, applies to all deliverables under contractually binding arrangements, regardless of their form (i.e., written, oral, or implied), in all industries, if a vendor will perform multiple revenue-generating activities unless it is stated otherwise in ASC 605-25-15-3A and 15-4, which is the scope section of ASC 605-25.

The guidance in another ASC Topic or the guidance in ASC 605-25 should be applied as follows in determining how to: (1) separate units of accounting; and (2) allocate consideration to each unit of accounting in an arrangement:

- If guidance on determining separation and allocation is provided under another ASC Topic, the arrangement should be accounted for under the guidance in that Topic. (ASC 605-25-15-3A(a))

- If guidance on determining separation but not allocation is provided in another ASC Topic, the allocation of consideration to separate units, some of which may be accounted for under the guidance in that other ASC Topic and others under the guidance in ASC 605-25, should be based on the relative selling price of a deliverables under the scope of the other ASC Topic and the selling prices of the deliverables not under the scope of that ASC Topic. To allocate consideration for deliverables accounted for under the guidance of another ASC Topic and those accounted for not under the guidance of that ASC Topic, the selling prices of the deliverables should be determined based on the guidance in ASC 605-25-30-6A and 30-6B. Thereafter, the guidance in ASC 605-25 would apply to the identification of separate units of accounting and the allocation of consideration under an arrangement should be allocated to deliverables not subject to the guidance in the other ASC Topic. (ASC 605-25-15-3A(b))

- If no guidance for determining separation or allocation exists under another ASC Topic, the guidance in ASC 605-25 should be followed to determine the separation of units of accounting and the allocation of consideration. However, if a deliverable subject to the guidance of another ASC Topic does not meet the criteria in ASC 605-25-25-5, as amended (criterion b., which required "objective and reliable evidence of the fair value of the undelivered item(s)" is superseded by the guidance in ASC 605-25) for a deliverable to be considered a separate unit of accounting, consideration allocated to that deliverable should be combined with the amount allocated to other undelivered items under the arrangement. Revenue for those combined deliverables should be recognized as one unit of accounting. (ASC 605-25-15-3A(c))

ACCOUNTING ISSUES

The following issues have been raised regarding the model of revenue recognition when there are multiple payment streams:
- How should an entity determine whether an arrangement with multiple deliverables consists of more than one unit of accounting?
- How should consideration be allocated among separate units of accounting in an arrangement that consists of more than one unit of accounting?

ACCOUNTING GUIDANCE

The following principles and application guidance should be used to determine: (1) how to measure consideration on an arrangement; (2) whether to divide an arrangement into separate units of accounting; and (3) how consideration on an arrangement should be allocated to separate units of accounting.

Units of Accounting

The following principles apply:
- Divide revenue arrangements with multiple deliverables into separate units of accounting if a deliverable meets the criteria ASC 605-25-25-5 to be considered a separate unit of accounting.
- Allocate consideration on an arrangement among separate units of accounting based on their relative selling prices, except as specified in ASC 605-25-30-4. However, the amount to be allocated to a delivered unit of accounting is limited under the guidance in ASC 605-25-30-5.
- Consider recognition criteria separately for each unit of accounting. (ASC 605-25-25-2)

At the inception of an arrangement and as each item is delivered, a vendor should evaluate all of the deliverables in an arrangement to determine whether they are separate units of accounting. For an arrangement with multiple deliverables, a delivered item should be considered to be a separate unit of accounting if it meets both of the following criteria, which should be applied consistently to arrangements with similar characteristics and in similar circumstances:

- A delivered item has value to the customer on its own (i.e., the item can be sold separately by any vendor or the customer can resell it on its own). An observable market for a deliverable is not required in the case of a customer's resale of a deliverable.
- If an arrangement includes a general right of return for a delivered item, the delivery or performance of an undelivered item is considered probable and substantially under the vendor's control. (ASC 605-25-25-5)

A delivered item under an arrangement that does not meet those two criteria should be combined with other applicable undelivered items under the arrangement. Revenue on such an arrangement should be allocated and recognized for the combined deliverables as a single unit of accounting. (ASC 605-25-25-6)

Measurement and Allocation of Consideration Received on an Arrangement

The total amount of consideration on an arrangement should be fixed and determinable, except for the effect of: (1) a customer's right to a refund, if any, or other concessions; or (2) performance bonuses to which a vendor may be entitled. (ASC 605-25-30-1)

At the inception of an arrangement, consideration should be allocated to all of the deliverables under an arrangement based on their relative selling prices, except as discussed in ASC 605-25-30-4 and 30-5. To apply the relative selling price method, it is necessary to determine the selling price for a deliverable by using vendor-specific objective evidence (VSOE) of the selling price, if available. Otherwise, evidence of a third party's selling price should be used, as discussed in ASC 605-25-30-6B. If information about neither of those selling prices exists, a vendor should use its best estimate of a deliverable's selling price when applying the relative selling price method as discussed in ASC 605-25-30-6C. When a vendor decides whether to use VSOE or third-party evidence of a deliverable's selling price, the vendor should not overlook information that is reasonably available without excessive cost or effort. (ASC 605-25-30-2)

If a separate unit of accounting in an arrangement must be recognized at fair value under the guidance in another ASC Topic and marked to market in each subsequent period, the amount allocated to that deliverable should be its fair value. In that case, all other consideration on an arrangement should be allocated to other units of accounting based on the guidance in ASC 605-25-30-2. (ASC 605-25-30-4)

The amount that may be allocated to a delivered unit(s) of accounting should not exceed an amount that is not contingent on: (1) the delivery of additional items; or (2) meeting other specified performance conditions. That is, the amount allocated to a delivered unit or units is the lesser of the amount that would be allocated under the guidance in ASC 605-25-30-2 and 605-25-30-4, or the noncontingent amount. Although the guidance in ASC 605-15, may affect the amount of revenue recognized, the allocated amount is not adjusted for the effect of a general right of return under. (ASC 605-25-30-5)

Revenue recognized in a period should not exceed an amount that has been measured based on the assumption that the arrangement will not be canceled. An asset recognized for amounts in excess of revenue that has been recognized under an arrangement for cash payments or other consideration that a vendor has received from a customer since the arrangement's inception should not exceed all of the consideration to which the vendor is legally entitled, including cancellation fees if a customer cancels the order. However, a vendor's intent to enforce its contractual right if a customer cancels an order should be considered in determining the amount of asset recognition. (ASC 605-25-30-6)

The VSOE of a selling price should not exceed the price charged for a deliverable: (1) sold separately; or (2) not yet sold separately if it is probable that the established price will not change before the product is introduced. (ASC 605-25-30-6A)

Third-party evidence of a selling price consists of the price the vendor or a competitor would charge for interchangeable products or services sold separately to customers under similar circumstances. (ASC 605-25-30-6B)

A vendor's best estimate of a selling price should be consistent with the objective of determining VSOE of a deliverable's selling price. Market conditions and factors specifically related to an entity should be considered in estimating a selling price. (ASC 605-25-30-6C)

It should not be presumed that prices for individual products or services under an arrangement with multiple deliverables that are stated in a contract represent VSOE or third-party evidence of a selling price or a vendor's best estimate of a selling price. (ASC 605-25-30-7)

ASC 605—Revenue Recognition **36,029**

Disclosure

The objective of the following disclosures is to provide financial statement users with qualitative and quantitative information about: (1) a vendor's revenue arrangements, and (2) significant judgments made in applying the guidance on revenue allocation and how changes in those judgments or in the application of the guidance may significantly affect the timing or amount of revenue recognized. Consequently, to comply with this requirement, a vendor should disclose other qualitative and quantitative information, as necessary, in addition to the required disclosures. (ASC 605-25-50-1)

The following information should be disclosed by similar types of arrangements:

1. The nature of a vendor's arrangements for multiple-deliverables;
2. All significant deliverables under the arrangements;
3. The general timing of delivery or performance of a service for deliverables under those arrangements;
4. Provisions related to performance, cancellation, and refunds;
5. A discussion of the significant factors, inputs, assumptions, and methods used to determine a selling price, based on VSOE, third-party evidence, or an estimated selling price, for significant deliverables;
6. Whether significant deliverables under an arrangement qualify as separate units of accounting, and, if applicable, the reasons why they do not qualify;
7. The general timing of revenue recognition for significant units of accounting; and
8. Separate information about the effect of changes in either the selling price or the method or assumptions used to determine the selling price of a specific unit of accounting if either one of those changes significantly affects the allocation of consideration for an arrangement. (ASC 605-25-50-2)

ASC 605-28: MILESTONE METHOD

ASC 605-10-05-1, 25-2A; ASC 605-25-15-2A; ASC 605-28-05-1, 15-1 through 15-4, 25-1 through 25-3, 50-1 through 50-2, 65-1 (ASU 2010-17) Milestone Method of Revenue Recognition

BACKGROUND

One of the practice issues raised during the discussion of the guidance in ASC 605-25, Multiple Element Arrangements, was the need for guidance for the application of the milestone method as a means of allocating contingent consideration when revenue becomes fixed or determinable.

SCOPE

The following guidance, which applies to all entities, may be applied to arrangements under which (1) a vendor's obligations to a customer are satisfied over a period of time; and (2) all or a portion of the consideration under an arrangement is contingent on the achievement of one or more milestones, unless this guidance conflicts with other guidance in ASC 605.

Guidance related to the milestone method of revenue recognition should be used to account for research or development arrangements under which a vendor satisfies its performance obligation to provide deliverables or units of accounting over a period of time and a portion or all of the consideration to the vendor is contingent on the achievement of uncertain future events and circumstances (i.e., milestones), such as the successful completion of phases in a drug study or a specific result from research or development endeavors, except if this guidance conflicts with other guidance in ASC 605. The milestone method is not the only acceptable method of accounting for a vendor's revenue that is contingent on the achievement of milestones. However, regardless of the method used to attribute revenue that depends on the achievement of milestones, a vendor's revenue recognition policy should be applied consistently to similar deliverables or units of accounting.

ACCOUNTING GUIDANCE

- The guidance in ASC 605-28 may be applied to arrangements under which: (1) a vendor's obligations to a customer are satisfied over a period of time; and (2) all or a portion of revenue under an arrangement is contingent on the achievement of one or more milestones, unless the guidance conflicts with other guidance in ASC 605.
- A milestone is an event: (1) for which, at the date an arrangement is entered into there is a substantive uncertainty that the event will be achieved; (2) that can only be achieved based in whole or in part as result of a vendor's performance or a specific outcome as a result of a vendor's performance; and (3) that if achieved, will result in additional payments being made to the vendor. Further, a milestone is *not* an event that is contingent only on the passage of time or on a counterparty's performance.

To recognize all of the revenue in the period in which a milestone has been achieved, a vendor should account for a deliverable or unit of accounting that depends on the complete achievement of a *substantive* milestone according to the guidance in ASC 605-28. A vendor may not elect to follow another accounting method under which the vendor would recognize all of the revenue on a milestone in the period in which the milestone has been achieved. However, a vendor that meets the requirements of that guidance is not prohibited from electing to apply a different accounting policy under which revenue related to a portion of the revenue for achieving a milestone would be deferred.

Although determining whether a milestone is *substantive* at the inception of an arrangement is based on judgment, for a milestone to be considered substantive, revenue earned by achieving a milestone must meet all of the following principles: (1) It corresponds with either (a) the vendor's performance to achieve the milestone, or (b) the value of the delivered item(s) has been improved by the vendor's performance to achieve the milestone; (2) it is related only to *past* performance; and (3) it is reasonable relative to all of the deliverables and payment terms under the arrangement, including revenue on other potential on milestones.

A milestone is *not* considered to be substantive if any portion of the revenue received for achieving a milestone does *not* apply exclusively to *past* performance but is related to the remaining deliverables in a unit of accounting under an arrangement. If so, not all of the consideration received for reaching a milestone should be recognized as revenue. Further, since recognition of all revenue earned when a milestone is achieved must be related to a *substantive* milestone; a milestone cannot be separated into substantive and nonsubstantive portions. Further, if a portion of revenue earned on achieving a milestone is subject to a refund or an adjustment based on a vendor's future performance through a penalty or clawback, that revenue also is *not* considered to be related to past performance and, therefore, the milestone would not be considered to be substantive. However, a vendor would *not* be precluded from applying the milestone method to other milestones under an arrangement if revenue from an individual milestone is *not* related exclusively to past performance.

The attribution model in ASC 605-28 for revenue recognition on an arrangement that is contingent on the achievement of a milestone is *not* the only acceptable, revenue recognition method regardless of whether the milestone is considered to be substantive. However, a vendor's revenue recognition policy for arrangements under which revenue recognition is contingent on a vendor's achievement of a milestone should be applied *consistently* to similar deliverables or units of accounting.

DISCLOSURE

Entities that elect to apply the guidance in ASC 605-28 should disclose the following information in the notes to their financial statements for each arrangement that includes a milestone payment:

- A description of the overall arrangement;
- A description of the individual milestones and related contingent consideration;
- Whether the milestones are considered to be substantive;
- The factors considered in determining whether a milestone is substantive; and
- The amount of revenue recognized on milestones during the period.

ASC 605-35: CONSTRUCTION-TYPE AND PRODUCTION-TYPE CONTRACTS

ASC 605-35-05-1 through 05-13, 15-6, 25-1 through 25-50, 25-54 through 25-88, 25-90 through 25-98, 45-1 through 45-2, 50-1 through 50-10, 55-1; ASC 210-10-60-2; ASC 460-1-60-10; ASC 910-20-25-5; ASC 912-20-25-1 **Accounting for Performance of Construction-Type and Certain Production-Type Contracts**

BACKGROUND

ASC 605-35 provides guidance on the application of GAAP in accounting for the performance of contracts for which a customer provides specifications for any of the following:

- Construction of facilities
- Production of goods
- Provision of related services

The basic accounting issue for contract accounting is the point(s) at which revenue should be recognized as earned and costs should be recognized as expenses. Accounting for contracts involves the measurement and the allocation of revenues and expenses of relatively long-term events over relatively short-term accounting periods. To deal with the uncertainties inherent in the performance of contracts, the allocation process often requires contractors to rely on estimates of revenues, costs, and the extent of progress to completion.

Guidance for the following two generally accepted methods of accounting for long-term construction contracts, which should be applied in specified circumstances and should not be used as alternatives, is provided in ASC 605-35:

- *Percentage-of-completion* Revenue is recognized as work progresses on a contract.

- *Completed-contract* Revenue is recognized only when work on a contract is complete.

Under the units-of-delivery method, which is a modification of the percentage-of-completion method, revenue is recognized on a contract as deliverable products are completed.

The following three key estimates are required to account for long-term construction contracts:

- The extent of progress toward completion
- Contract revenues
- Contract costs

PRACTICE POINTER: If estimates of costs to complete work on a contract and the extent of progress toward completion are reasonably dependable, using the percentage-of-completion method is preferable. If those estimates are unreliable, the completed-contract method should be used. The two methods are not considered alternatives for the same circumstances.

ACCOUNTING GUIDANCE

Scope

The guidance in ASC 605-35 applies to all contractors. It is not limited to long-term contracts, nor is it limited to construction contracts. Contracts covered are binding agreements between a buyer and a seller in which a seller agrees, to perform a service to a buyer's specifications for compensation under a contract, which is a legally enforceable agreement. Performance often will extend over long periods, and a seller's right to receive payment depends on performance in accordance with the agreement. Contracts that are under the scope of this guidance include the following:

- Construction industry contracts (e.g., general building and heavy earthmoving);
- Contracts to design and build ships and transport vessels;
- Contracts to design, develop, manufacture, or modify complex aerospace or electronic equipment;
- Contracts for construction consulting services;
- Contracts for services performed by architects, engineers, or architectural or engineering design firms
- Contracts to design and deliver computer software or a software system, either alone or with other products or services that require significant production, modification, or customization. (See the guidance in ASC 985-605-25-88 through 25-107 for additional guidance on the application of ASC 605-35 to software contracts.)

Contracts under the scope of ASC 605-35 may be classified into four broad types based on their pricing method:

1. *Fixed-price* An agreement to perform all activities under a contract for a stated price;
2. *Cost-type (including cost-plus)* An agreement to perform under a contract for a price to be determined on the basis of a defined relationship to the costs to be incurred, e.g., costs of all activities required plus a fixed fee or a fixed percentage of incurred costs;
3. *Time-and-material* An agreement to perform all activities required under a contract for a price based on fixed hourly rates for some measure of the labor hours required;
4. *Unit-price* An agreement to perform all activities required under a contract for a specified price for each unit of output.

Each of those types of contracts may include provisions for incentives, penalties, or other provisions to modify a contract's basic pricing terms.

The term *contractor* refers to a person or entity that enters into a contract to construct facilities, produce goods, or to render services based on a buyer's specifications by acting as a general or prime contractor, a subcontractor, or a construction manager. The term *profit center* refers to a measurement unit designated for the accumulation of revenues and costs and the measurement of income on a contract. Revenues, costs, and income are usually determined for a single contract, but under specified circumstances they may be determined for a combination of two or more contracts, a segment of a contract, or a group of combined contracts.

Basic Accounting Policy

The basic accounting policy decision made in contract accounting under GAAP is between the percentage-of-completion method and the completed-contract method. As stated previously, the determination of which is preferable depends on a careful evaluation of circumstances, because the two methods are not alternatives for the same situation. The basic policy followed should be disclosed in a note to the financial statements.

The use of the percentage-of-completion method depends on the ability to make reasonably dependable estimates of the extent of completion, contract revenues, and contract costs. Entities with significant contracting operations generally have the ability to produce reasonably reliable estimates and, accordingly, the percentage-of-completion method is preferable in most circumstances. If estimating the final outcome of a contract would be impractical, except to assure that no loss will be incurred, a contractor should use a zero estimate of profit, and equal amounts of revenues and costs should be recognized until results can be estimated more precisely.

Under the completed-contract method, income is recognized only when a contract is completed or substantially completed. During the period of performance, billings and costs are accumulated on the balance sheet as inventory, but no profit or income is recorded until the contract is complete or substantially complete. The completed-contract method is appropriate if reasonably dependable estimates of the extent of completion, contract revenues, and/or contract costs cannot be made, or if a contractor's financial position and results of operations would not vary materially if the percentage-of-completion method were used. If there is assurance that no loss will be incurred on a contract, the percentage-of-completion method based on a zero profit margin is preferable until more precise estimates can be made.

Profit Center

The basic assumption is that each contract is a profit center for revenue recognition, cost accumulation, and income measurement. However, if a group of contracts is so closely related, that they are effectively parts of a single project with an overall profit margin, combining the contracts for purposes of profit recognition should be considered.

Contracts may be combined for accounting purposes if the following criteria are met:

(1) Negotiated as a package in the same economic environment with an overall profit margin.

(2) Essentially, constitute an agreement to perform a single project.

(3) Require performance of closely interrelated construction activities with common costs.

(4) In substance, represent an agreement with a single customer.

A single contract or a group of contracts that otherwise meet the test for combining may include several elements or phases, each of which was negotiated separately without regard to performance on the others. A contract may be segmented for accounting purposes if the following steps were taken and are documented and verifiable:

- The contractor submitted bona fide proposals on the separate components of the project and on the entire project.

- The customer had the right to accept the proposals either on the separate components of the project or on the entire project.

- The aggregate amount of the proposal on the separate components approximated the amount of the proposal on the entire project.

Measuring Progress on Accounts

Progress toward completion may be measured in terms of costs, units of work, or value added. All are acceptable in appropriate circumstances. The method or methods selected should be applied consistently.

Several approaches can be described as based on input measures. Those methods are based on costs and on other efforts expended. An example is the efforts-expended approach, in which a measure of work, such as labor hours, machine hours, or materials quantities, is used as a measurement of the extent of progress. Output methods, on the other hand, measure progress in terms of results achieved. Estimating the extent of progress toward completion based on units completed is an example of an output method.

Income Determination—Revenue Elements

The major factors that must be considered in determining total estimated revenues are the basic contract price, contract options and additions, change orders, and claims.

Basic Contract Price

The estimated revenue from a contract is the total amount that a contractor expects to realize from a contract. It is determined primarily based on the terms of the contract. The contract may be relatively fixed or highly variable and, as a result, subject to a great deal of uncertainty. One problem peculiar to cost-type contracts is the determination of reimbursable costs that should be reflected as revenue.

Contract Options and Additions

An option or an addition to an existing contract is treated as a separate contract in any of the following circumstances:

- The product or service to be provided differs significantly from the product or service provided under the original contract.
- The price of the new product or service is negotiated without regard to the original contract and involves different economic judgments.
- The product or service to be provided under an exercised option or amendment is similar to that under the original contract, but the contract price and anticipated contract cost relationship are significantly different.

If none of these circumstances is present, the option or addition may be combined with the original contract for purposes of revenue recognition.

Change Orders

Change orders are modifications of an original contract that effectively change the provisions of the contract without adding new provisions. Change orders may have a significant effect on the amount of contract revenue to be recognized.

Claims

Claims are amounts in excess of the agreed contract price that a contractor seeks to collect from customers or others as a result of customer-caused delays, errors in specifications and designs, contract terminations, change orders in dispute, and other similar causes. Recognition of such claims is appropriate only if it is probable that the claim will result in additional contract revenue and if the amounts can be reliably estimated.

Income Determination—Cost Elements

At any point in the contract, estimated contract costs consist of two components: costs incurred to date and estimated costs to complete the contract. Costs incurred to date generally can be determined with reasonable certainty, depending on the adequacy and effectiveness of the cost accounting system. Estimating the costs to complete a contract generally involves greater uncertainty.

Contract costs are accumulated in the same manner as inventory and are charged to operations as the related revenue from the contract is recognized. General principles for accounting for production costs are as follows:

- All direct costs (e.g., materials, labor, subcontracting costs) are included in contract costs.
- Indirect costs, such as indirect labor, contract supervision, tools and equipment, and supplies, may be allocated to contracts as indirect costs if otherwise allowable under GAAP.
- General and administrative costs ordinarily should be charged to expense, but may be included as contract costs under certain circumstances.
- Selling costs are generally excluded from contract costs.
- Costs under cost-type contracts are charged to contract costs in conformity with GAAP in the same manner as costs under other types of contracts.

- In computing estimated gross profit or in providing for losses on contracts, estimates of costs to complete should reflect all the types of costs included in contract costs.
- Inventoriable costs should not be carried at amounts that, when added to the estimated costs to complete, are greater than the estimated realizable value of the contract.

Estimating the costs to complete a contract should result from the following:

- Systematic and consistent procedures that are correlated with the cost accounting system to provide a basis for periodically comparing actual and estimated amounts
- Quantities and prices of all significant elements of costs
- Estimation procedures that include the same elements of cost that are included in actual accumulated costs
- The effects of future wage and price escalations
- Periodic review and revision, as appropriate, to reflect new information

Revised Estimates

Adjustments to the original estimates of the total contract revenue, total contract cost, and extent of progress toward completion may be required as work progresses under the contract and as experience is gained. Such revisions should be accounted for by the cumulative catch-up method in accordance with the guidance in ASC 250, Accounting Changes and Error Corrections.

Provisions for Anticipated Losses

If current estimates indicate that the total contract revenues and costs will result in a loss, a provision of the entire loss on the contract should be made. This is true for both the percentage-of-completion method and the completed-contract method. A provision for loss should be made in the accounting period in which it becomes evident.

A provision for a loss on a contract should be shown separately as a liability on the balance sheet—unless related costs are accumulated in the balance sheet, in which case the loss provision may be offset against the related accumulated costs. In a classified balance sheet, a provision shown as a liability should be classified as a current liability.

ASC 605-45: PRINCIPAL AGENT CONSIDERATIONS

ASC 605-45-05-1 through 05-2, 15-3 through 15-5, 45-1 through 45-18, 50-1, 55-2 through 55-3, 55-5 through 55-6, 55-8 through 55-9, 55-11 through 55-14, 55-16, 55-18, 55-20, 55-22, 55-24 through 55-25, 55-27 through 55-31, 55-33 through 55-34, 55-36 through 55-38, 55-40 through 55-45 Reporting Revenue Gross as a Principal versus Net as an Agent

BACKGROUND

As a result of the proliferation of sales of goods and services over the Internet, the SEC staff noted diversity in registrants' revenue recognition practices. Frequently, a vendor that does not stock merchandise sold on its Internet site arranges for a supplier to ship the merchandise directly to a buyer. Similarly, services sold on an Internet site are frequently performed by a third party, not by the Internet vendor. In some cases, a vendor's profit on a transaction consists of a commission or fee for selling a third party's products or services. The importance of a company's revenue recognition method has increased in the current economic environment because some investors value Internet companies—especially start-ups that may show losses or very little net income in the early years—based on multiples of revenues instead of multiples of gross profit or earnings.

SEC Staff Accounting Bulletin (SAB) Topic 13 addresses the question whether Company A, which sells Company T's products on the Internet, should recognize (a) both the gross amount of a sale and the related costs or (b) the net revenue earned on a sale. In determining how a company should recognize revenue, the SEC staff considers whether an entity

1. Is acting as a principal in the transaction
2. Takes title to the merchandise
3. Has the risks and rewards of ownership, such as risks of loss for collection, delivery, or returns
4. Is acting as an agent or broker (including performing services as an agent or broker) and is compensated by a commission or fee

The SEC also requires an entity that performs as an agent or broker to report sales on a net basis if no risks and rewards of ownership of the goods are assumed.

Because the SEC staff believes that additional factors may exist, the staff asked the EITF to develop an accounting model that is consistent with the requirements of SAB Topic 13. The following guidance is not limited to Internet transactions, but also may apply to transactions with travel agents, magazine subscription brokers, and sales of products through catalogs, consignment sales, or special-order retail sales.

The following guidance does not address the timing of revenue recognition and whether revenue should be deferred if the earnings process is not complete.

ACCOUNTING ISSUE

Under what circumstances should an entity report revenue based on (a) the *gross* amount billed to a customer for the sale of a product or service on which the company earns revenue or (b) the *net* amount retained (the amount billed less the amount paid the supplier), because the supplier or service provider paid the company a commission or fee?

ACCOUNTING GUIDANCE

The decision whether to report revenue at (a) the *gross* amount billed to a customer, because an entity earned the revenue from a sale of goods or services, or (b) the *net* difference between the amount billed to a customer less the amount paid to the supplier, because an entity earned a commission or a fee, requires judgment based on the facts and circumstances. The following factors, which should not be considered to be presumptive or determinative, should be considered in that decision based on their strength:

- Indicators of Gross Revenue Reporting
  - *Acting as the primary obligor* The fact that an entity is responsible for fulfilling a customer's order, including whether the product or service is acceptable to the customer, is a strong indicator that an entity has the risks and rewards of a principal and should report revenue at the *gross* amount billed to the customer. An entity's marketing representations and the terms of a sales contract indicate whether the entity or a supplier is fulfilling the order.
  - *General inventory risk before the order is placed or on product return* If an entity (a) takes title to a product before it is ordered by a customer who has the right of return and (b) takes title to a product if it is returned, the company has general inventory risk, which indicates that it has the risk and rewards of a principal in the transaction and is a strong indicator that it should report revenue at the gross amount. The entity and the supplier should have no arrangement to reduce or mitigate inventory risk, for example, the right to return unsold products to a supplier.
  - *Latitude in establishing the price* An entity's ability, within economic constraints, to establish the price of a product or service charged to a customer may indicate that an entity is acting as a principal in the transaction.
  - *Addition of meaningful value to a product or service* The fact that an entity adds meaningful value (the selling price is greater because of the addition) to a product or provides a significant portion of a service ordered by a customer may indicate that the entity has primary responsibility for fulfillment, including customer satisfaction with the component of the product or portion of total services provided by the supplier.
  - *Discretion in selecting the supplier* The fact that an entity can select a supplier among several to provide a product or service ordered by a customer may indicate that the entity has primary responsibility for fulfillment.
  - *Involvement in determining product or service specifications* The requirement for an entity to determine the nature, type, characteristics, or specifications of a product or service ordered by a customer may indicate that it has primary responsibility for fulfillment.
  - *Retention of the risk of physical loss of inventory after a customer's order or during shipping* The risk of physical loss of inventory exists (a) from the time an entity takes title to a product at the point of shipment (e.g., the supplier's facilities) until the product is transferred to a customer on delivery or (b) from the time an entity takes title to a product after a customer's order has been received until the product is delivered to a carrier for shipment to the customer. This indicator provides less

persuasive evidence than general inventory risk that the gross amount of revenue should be reported.

— *Assumption of credit risk* An entity assumes credit risk if it is responsible for collecting the sales price from the customer and has to pay the supplier regardless of whether it collects the full sales price. An entity's assumption of credit risk for the amount billed to a customer may provide weak evidence that the entity has the risks and rewards of a principal in the transaction and should report revenue gross. No credit risk is assumed if an entity collects the full sales price before delivering a product or service to a customer.

- Indicators of Net Revenue Reporting

— *The supplier is the primary obligor* The fact that a supplier is responsible for fulfillment, including whether the product or services ordered or purchased by the customer are acceptable, may indicate that an entity does not have the risks and rewards as a principal in the transaction and should report revenue based on the amount retained after paying the supplier. An entity's representations while marketing a product and the sales contract generally provide evidence of whether the entity or a supplier is required to fulfill the order or service.

— *The entity earns a fixed amount* The fact that an entity earns a fixed amount on a transaction regardless of the amount billed for a product or service indicates that the entity is acting as an agent for a supplier.

— *The supplier assumes the credit risk* The fact that a supplier assumes the credit risk, because the full sales price has not been collected before a product or service is delivered to a customer, indicates that the entity is acting as an agent for the supplier.

Disclosure

Voluntary disclosures of an entity's gross volume of transactions that are reported may be useful to users of financial statements. The information could be disclosed parenthetically in the income statement or in the notes to the financial statements. Gross amounts disclosed on the face of the income statement should not be described as revenues and should not be reported in a column that is included in the sum of net income or loss. Such amounts may be described as gross billings.

ASC 605-45-15-2, 15-4, 45-22 through 45-23 Reimbursements Received for "Out-of-Pocket" Expenses Incurred

BACKGROUND

The following guidance applies to the accounting for reimbursements received from customers for a service provider's "out-of-pocket" expenses incurred, such as expenses related to mileage, airfare, hotel stays, out-of-town meals, photocopies, and telecommunication and facsimile charges. Reimbursements may be based on actual amounts incurred or are included in a negotiated flat fee for professional services provided and out-of-pocket expenses incurred.

This Issue does not apply to the following transactions for which other guidance already exists::

- Sales of financial assets, including debt and equity securities, loans, and receivables
- Lending transactions
- Insurance and reinsurance premiums
- Broker-dealer transactions under the scope of ASC 940, *Financial Services—Brokers and Dealers*, and reimbursements received for expenses incurred by entities that follow the guidance for other specialized industries, which provide accounting guidance for reimbursements.

ACCOUNTING GUIDANCE

Service providers should present reimbursements for out-of-pocket expenses incurred as revenue in the income statement.

ASC 605-45-15-2, 50-3 through 50-4 Taxes Collected from Customers and Remitted to Governmental Authorities

BACKGROUND

Entities are assessed for taxes by various governmental authorities on all kinds of transactions—from sales taxes on a broad range of goods and services to excise taxes on specific kinds of transactions. Because such taxes are calculated, remitted to the governmental authority, and administered differently, there is no one model to follow in accounting and reporting for them. In addition, some taxes (such as sales taxes) are collected from customers and transmitted by vendors to the appropriate governmental agencies, and other taxes (such as income taxes) are paid by the entity.

The SEC staff has received questions regarding the income tax presentation of various taxes. In response to questions regarding how changes in the party responsible for paying state and local sales taxes would affect a vendor's presentation on the income statement, the SEC staff has recommended that pass-through taxes be accounted for in accordance with the guidance in ASC 605-45. The SEC staff continues to hold that view.

ACCOUNTING ISSUES

1. Should the scope of this Issue include all nondiscretionary amounts assessed by governmental authorities in connection with a transaction with a customer, or only sales, use, and value-added taxes?

2. Should taxes assessed by a governmental authority under the scope of Issue 1 be presented in the income statement on a gross or net basis?

ACCOUNTING GUIDANCE

1. The scope of this guidance includes any tax assessed by a governmental authority that is both imposed on and that occurs at the same time as a specific revenue-producing transaction between a seller and a customer and may include, but is not limited to, sales, use, value added, and some

excise taxes. Tax schemes based on gross receipts and taxes imposed while acquiring inventory are *excluded* from the scope of this Issue.

2. An entity's decision to present taxes discussed under the scope of ASC 605-45 in revenues and costs (a gross basis) or to exclude them from revenues and costs (a net basis) should be disclosed as an accounting policy under the guidance in ASC 235-10-05-3 through 05-4; 50-1 through 50-6. However, existing policies related to taxes assessed by a governmental authority as a result of this guidance need *not* be reevaluated. If an entity reports its taxes on a gross basis, the amounts of those taxes should be disclosed in interim and annual financial statements for each period for which an income statement is presented, if the amounts are significant. Taxes reported on a gross basis may be disclosed as a total amount.

ASC 605-45-05-2, 15-2, 15-4, 45-19 through 45-21, S45-1, 50-2, S99 Shipping and Handling Fees and Costs

BACKGROUND

The income statement classification of amounts charged to customers for shipping and handling and related costs differs among companies. Some report charges to customers in revenue and report costs incurred as expenses, but others report only the net amount of costs and revenues. In addition, the costs included in the shipping and handling category also differ by entity. Some include only amounts paid to third-party shippers, but others may also include internal costs, such as salaries and overhead related to the preparation of the goods for shipment. Some charge customers for shipping costs incurred and direct incremental handling costs. Many charge amounts for shipping and handling that are not a direct reimbursement of costs incurred.

The following guidance applies only to shipping and handling fees and costs reported by companies that report revenue at the gross amount billed.

ACCOUNTING ISSUES

1. How should a seller of goods classify in the income statement amounts billed to a customer for shipping and handling?
2. How should a seller of goods classify in the income statement costs incurred for shipping and handling?

ACCOUNTING GUIDANCE

1. An entity that reports the gross amount of shipping and handling fees based on the indicators in ASC 605-45-45 through 45-18 for gross revenue reporting should classify as revenue all amounts billed to customers for shipping and handling fees in sales transactions.
2. Netting shipping and handling costs against shipping and handling revenues is prohibited.
3. Application of the consensus in 1 above is subject to the SEC Observer's comments, which are discussed below.

SEC OBSERVER COMMENT

The SEC Observer stated that registrants are expected to evaluate the significance of shipping and handling costs so that the accounting guidance above is applied based on the significance of such costs to (*a*) each line item on the income statement in which they are included and (*b*) the total gross margin.

ASC 605-50: CUSTOMER PAYMENTS AND INCENTIVES

ASC 605-50-05-1, 15-2 through 15-3, 25-1 through 25-9, 45-1 through 45-11, S45-1, 55-1, 55-3, 55-5, 55-8 through 55-12, 55-14 through 55-15, 55-17 through 55-22, 55-24 through 55-25, 55-27 through 55-28, 55-30 through 55-31, 55-33 through 55-37, 55-40 through 55-44, 55-46 through 55-47, 55-49 through, 55-50, 55-52, through 55-53, 55-55 through 55-69, 55-71 through 55-72, 55-74 through 55-77, 55-79 through 55-95, 55-97 through 55-107, S99-1 ASC 330-10-35-13; ASC 908-360-55-1 Vendor's Income Statement Characterization of Consideration Given to a Customer (Including a Reseller)

BACKGROUND

The objective of the following discussion is to provide guidance on how a vendor, which is a manufacturer or distributor, should report in its income statement consideration, including sales incentives, given to a customer, which may be a reseller or an entity that purchases the vendor's products from a reseller. Consideration from a vendor to a customer may be in the form of cash, but it can also be in the form of discounts, coupons, free products or services, or rebates that a customer can apply against amounts owed to the vendor. The guidance also applies to a service provider's consideration to a manufacturer or a reseller of equipment.

ACCOUNTING ISSUES

Income Statement Presentation

1. When an incentive or other consideration is given by a vendor to a customer (*a*) should an adjustment of the vendor's selling price for products sold be deducted from revenue in the vendor's income statement or (*b*) should costs a vendor incurs for assets or services that a customer provides to the vendor be accounted for as an expense in the vendor's income statement?

2. Should a vendor that has "negative revenue" as a result of a revenue deduction for consideration given to customers based on the guidance provided recharacterize that amount as an expense in the income statement?

Recognition and Measurement

3. When should a vendor recognize as an asset upfront nonrefundable consideration that the vendor gives to a customer instead of immediately recognizing a cost in the income statement?

4. When should a vendor recognize and how should the vendor measure the cost of sales incentives offered voluntarily to customers at no charge that customers can exercise in a single transaction if *no* loss is incurred on the sale of the product or service?

5. When should a vendor recognize and how should the vendor measure the cost of sales incentives discussed in Issue 4 if a loss is incurred on the sale of the product or service?
6. How should a vendor account for an offer to a customer to rebate or refund a specified amount of cash that may be redeemed only if the customer completes a specified cumulative level of revenue transactions or remains a customer for a specified period of time?

ACCOUNTING GUIDANCE

Scope

The guidance applies to the following kinds of arrangements:

1. Slotting fees, which are fees that a vendor pays to a customer for shelf space for the vendor's products and other product placement arrangements, such as brand development or new product introduction arrangements, for which a vendor pays fees for the right to display its products in favorable locations in a store, for end-cap placement, and for additional shelf space. A vendor may incur slotting fees (a) before selling any of the products to the customer, (b) on a regular schedule to maintain a shelf space allocation, or to continue being a regular vendor, or (c) periodically as negotiated. The vendor may or may not receive stated rights for those fees.

2. Cooperative advertising arrangements, in which a vendor reimburses a customer for a portion of the costs incurred to advertise the vendor's products. The vendor is generally required to participate in advertising costs based on the actual cost. The customer may be reimbursed for an amount limited to a specified percentage of its purchases from the vendor. In other arrangements, the amount of reimbursement is based on a percentage of the customer's purchases from the vendor during a specific time period, regardless of actual costs incurred by the customer to advertise the vendor's products.

3. Buydowns, which are arrangements under which a vendor agrees to reimburse a customer up to a specified amount for shortfalls in the sales price received by the customer for the vendor's products over a specified time period. Under such arrangements, the vendor reimburses, compensates, or issues credit memos to the customer for a decrease in revenue per product unit during a specified promotion period for a product. The customer is not required to make any expenditures for advertising or promotions. Other related arrangements in which a vendor reduces the net price paid by the customer for the vendor's products include factory incentives, dealer holdbacks, price protection, and factory-to-dealer incentives.

The scope of this Issue does *not* include the following:

- Coupons, rebates, and other forms of rights for free or significantly discounted products or services that a customer received in an earlier exchange transaction and that the vendor accounted for as a separate element of that transaction.

- Offers for free or significantly discounted products or services that a customer can exercise in the future without an additional exchange with the vendor as a result of a current revenue transaction.

Recognition and Measurement

The following guidance for the measurement and timing of cost recognition of sales incentives applies only to arrangements that meet *both* of the following conditions:

- An incentive is linked to a single sales transaction; multiple sales transactions are not required to exercise an incentive.
- A vendor does not receive a benefit that can be identified from the customer in exchange for a sales incentive.

Vendors should recognize the cost of sales incentives offered voluntarily and without charge to customers that can be used or exercised as a result of a single exchange transaction if such incentives do *not* result in a loss on a sale or service on either of the following dates, whichever occurs later:

a. The date on which the vendor recognizes the related revenue.
b. The date on which a sales incentive is offered. (That is, if a vendor offers the sales incentive after having recognized revenue on the sale, for example, if a manufacturer offers discount coupons to customers after the sale of the products.)

A liability or deferred revenue should be recognized at the later of the above dates based on an estimated amount of refunds or rebates that will be claimed if customers must submit a form to receive refunds or rebates of specific amounts for prior purchases. A maximum potential liability or deferred revenue should be recognized for refunds or rebates if it is not possible to make a reasonable and reliable estimate of the amount of *future* refunds or rebates. Although that estimate depends on many factors, a vendor's ability to make a reasonable and reliable estimate may be impaired as a result of the following:

(1) The period during which refunds or rebates can be claimed is relatively long.
(2) A vendor has no historical experience with similar types of sales incentives or is unable to apply that experience because circumstances have changed.
(3) The volume of relatively homogeneous transactions is insufficient.

A vendor that offers sales incentives voluntarily at no cost to its customers that can be used or exercised as a result of a single exchange transaction and that will result in a loss on the sale of the products or services should *not* recognize a liability for the sales incentives before the date on which revenue is recognized on the transactions.

A sales incentive that will result in a loss on the sale of a product may indicate that existing inventory is impaired under the guidance in ASC 330.

The above guidance also applies to the accounting for an excess of the fair value of a sales incentive a vendor has provided to a customer over the fair value of an identifiable benefit received by the vendor in exchange for the sales incentive.

A vendor should *reduce* revenue by the amount recognized as an obligation for a rebate or refund to a customer. The cost of honoring claims for rebates or refunds should be allocated on a rational and systematic basis to each underlying revenue transaction with a customer that will enable the customer to reach a cumulative level at which a rebate or refund will be earned. The total rebate or refund obligation should be measured based on an estimated number of customers that will earn and claim refunds under the offer. "Breakage" should be included if the amount of future rebates can be reasonably estimated. Otherwise, the vendor should recognize a liability for the maximum rebate or refund, without a reduction for breakage. Although the ability to make that estimate may vary on a case-by-case basis, a vendor's ability to make a reasonable estimate may be affected by the following factors:

a. The period during which a rebate or refund can be claimed is relatively long.

b. The vendor has no historical experience with similar types of sales incentives for similar products or is unable to use that experience because the circumstances differ.

c. The volume of homogenous transactions is not large enough to make a reasonable estimate.

Under some programs, the amount of a cash rebate or refund may increase, based on the customer's volume of purchases. If a vendor can reasonably estimate the volume of a customer's future purchases, a liability should be recognized for the *estimated* amount of the cash rebate or refund. Otherwise, the vendor should recognize a liability for the maximum potential refund or rebate under the program.

Changes in the estimated amounts of cash rebates or refunds from a previous offer, such as a retroactive increase or decrease in the amount of the rebate, should be recognized immediately as a cumulative catch-up adjustment to adjust the balance of the rebate obligation. Revenue on future sales should be reduced based on the *revised* rate of the refund

Income Statement Presentation

Vendors account for sales incentives or other consideration given to customers under the following methods:

- As a reduction of revenue in the vendor's income statement by adjusting the selling prices of the vendor's products or services;
- As a cost or expense in the vendor's income statement by accounting for a sales incentive or other compensation as a cost incurred.

It is presumed that a vendor's consideration to a customer in the form of cash or sales incentives related to the vendor's products is a reduction of the vendor's prices that results in a reduction of revenue in the income statement. However, that presumption may be overcome, and the vendor should account for the consideration as a cost if the vendor has received or will receive from the customer a benefit that meets the following two conditions:

   a. In return for the consideration, the vendor has received or will receive an identifiable benefit from the customer in the form of goods or services. The benefit should be one for which the vendor would have entered into an exchange transaction with a third party that is separate from the vendor's sales of goods or services to the customer.

   b. The fair value of the benefit can be reasonably estimated. Otherwise, an excess of consideration paid by the vendor over the fair value of the benefit, if any, should be deducted from revenue presented in the vendor's income statement.

A vendor should report as an *expense* in its income statement the cost of consideration consisting of a free product or service, such as a gift from a vendor or a free airline ticket to be honored by an unrelated entity, and other noncash consideration in the form of equity instruments, because the free item is a deliverable in the exchange transaction and *not* a refund or rebate of a portion of the sales price obligation.

The effect of the requirement for separability in (*a*) above would generally result in the recognition of slotting fees or similar fees related to product development or placement as a reduction of revenue. For example, a vendor's agreement to reimburse a customer for a reduction in a product's sales price would always be recognized as a revenue reduction. Buydowns, which would never meet criterion (*a*), should always be accounted for as reductions of revenue.

In addition, this guidance also applies to consideration from a vendor to a customer that resells the product in another format or uses the product as a component of another product, for example, a payment for cooperative advertising from a fabric manufacturer to a clothing manufacturer.

Revenue reductions that result in negative revenue. Negative revenue may result from the application of this guidance to cash consideration given by a vendor to a customer or from transactions or changes in estimates under the application of guidance in other topics of the ASC that require a reduction of revenue. Although it is presumed that no portion of amounts accounted for under this guidance as a reduction of revenue should be reclassified as an expense, a vendor may be permitted to reclassify a cumulative shortfall of revenue from doing business with a particular customer, as an expense if the vendor can demonstrate that accounting for amounts under this and other guidance in the ASC have resulted in negative revenue for the specific customer. To provide that information, a vendor that sells products directly to resellers, which subsequently sell the products to other resellers, such as retailers, down the distribution chain, must perform a customer analysis to identify the specific reseller or distributor from which retailers purchased the vendor's products.

Reclassification of negative revenue as an expense would be permitted if a vendor gives cash consideration to a *new* customer before the customer has purchased any products or placed or committed to place any orders and that consideration exceeds cumulative revenue from that customer at the time that consideration is recognized in the income statement. Reclassification as an expense would *not* be permitted if a vendor has an existing supply arrangement with a customer under which (a) the vendor is an exclusive supplier of a specific product for a certain period of time and it is probable that the customer will place an order, or (b) the customer is required to order a minimum amount of the vendor's products in the future.

Revenue earned by a vendor from a particular customer also may include revenue earned from other entities in a consolidated group that includes the customer. Also, the *inception of an overall relationship* with a customer may occur when a new relationship is established or when a relationship is reestablished with a customer with whom the vendor previously had a business relationship that had been terminated.

Each financial reporting period should stand on its own when applying this guidance on the recharacterization of "negative revenue." Amounts presented as an expense in one period should not be reclassified in a later period even if a credit to expense results. A credit up to the expense previously recognized should be presented in the income statement as a reduction of expense if a reduction in the measured fair value of consideration occurs due to changes in estimates or other factors. A remaining credit, if any, should be presented as an increase in revenue.

ASC 605-50-05-1, 15-2, 25-10 through 25-12, 45-12 through 45-15, 55-116 through 55-117, 55-119 through 55-120, 55-122 through 55-123 Customer's Characterization of Certain Consideration Received from a Vendor

BACKGROUND

In ASC 605-50, *Accounting for Consideration Given by a Vendor to a Customer (Including a Reseller of the Vendor's Products)*, guidance is provided on (a) how *vendors* should account for consideration given to customers that are resellers of their products and entities that purchase their products from a reseller, and (b) how to measure and when to recognize such consideration in the income statement. The following guidance addresses how *resellers* of a vendor's products should account for cash consideration received from vendors.

ACCOUNTING ISSUES

1. Under what circumstances should a reseller account for cash consideration received from a vendor as (a) an adjustment of the vendor's prices for its products or services and presented as a reduction of cost of sales in the reseller's income statement, (b) an adjustment of a cost incurred by the reseller and presented as a reduction of that cost in the reseller's income statement, or (c) a payment received for assets or services delivered to a vendor and presented as revenue in the reseller's income statement?

2. How should a reseller measure the amount of and when should a reseller recognize a vendor's offer of a rebate or refund of a specific amount of cash consideration payable only if the reseller makes a specified amount of purchases or remains a reseller for a specified time period?

ACCOUNTING GUIDANCE

Scope

The following guidance applies to a customer's accounting for:

- Cash consideration received from a vendor;
- Sales incentives offered to consumers by manufacturers.

Customer's Accounting for Consideration Received from a Vendor

If a vendor's rebate or refund for a specified amount of cash consideration payable under a binding arrangement will occur only if a reseller achieves a cumulative level of purchases or remains a customer for a specified time period, a reseller should reduce its cost of sales based on a systematic and rational allocation of the cash consideration related to each of the underlying transactions resulting in the reseller's progress toward earning the rebate or refund only if receipt of the rebate or refund is *probable* and reasonably estimable. Otherwise, the consideration should be recognized as milestones are achieved.

Although making a reasonable estimate of the amount of future cash rebates or refunds depends on many factors and circumstance that may vary on a case-by-case basis, the existence of the following factors may impair a customer's ability to determine the probability and to reasonably estimate the amount of a rebate or refund:

- The purchases will occur over a relatively long period.
- No historical experience with similar products exists or such experience cannot be applied because of changing circumstances.
- In the past, expected cash rebates or refunds needed significant adjustments.
- The product is affected by significant external factors, such as technological obsolescence or changes in demand.

Changes in estimates of cash rebates or refunds and a vendor's retroactive changes of a previous offer, such as a retroactive increase or decrease in a rebate's amount, are changes in estimates that should be accounted for with a cumulative catch-up adjustment. That is, the cumulative balance of rebates would be revised immediately. Entities should consider whether any portion of such an adjustment would affect inventory, thus requiring that only a portion of the adjustment be reported in the income statement.

It is presumed that cash consideration received by a customer from a vendor is a *reduction* of the vendor's prices for its products or services and should be reported as a reduction of cost of sales in the customer's income statement.

That presumption may be overcome, however, if a vendor's cash consideration to a customer is (*a*) a payment for assets or services delivered to the vendor that should be presented as revenue or other income in the customer's income statement, depending on the circumstances, or (*b*) a reimbursement of the customer's costs to sell the vendor's products or services that should be reported as a reduction of the customer's selling costs in the income statement.

Payment for assets or services. If a vendor receives or will receive in exchange for its cash consideration an identifiable benefit (e.g., goods or services) that is sufficiently separable from the customer's purchases of the vendor's products, the customer should report the payment as revenue in its income statement. Indicators supporting that treatment include (*a*) the fact that the reseller could have entered into an exchange transaction with another party to provide the benefit and (*b*) the fair value of the benefit provided can be reasonably estimated. A customer should reduce its cost of sales reported in the income statement if the vendor's cash consideration for the benefit received exceeds the benefit's estimated fair value.

Reimbursement of customer's costs. If cash consideration paid by a vendor to a reseller is a reimbursement of the customer's specific, incremental, identifiable costs incurred to sell the vendor's products or services, that amount should be reported in the customer's income statement as a reduction of that cost. Cash consideration in excess of a customer's cost, if any, should be reported in the customer's income statement as a reduction of cost of sales.

ASC 605-50-15-2, 25-13 through 25-18, 50-1, 55-108, 55-110 through 55-114 Service Provider's Accounting for Consideration Given to a Manufacturer or Reseller of Equipment

BACKGROUND

Frequently, the customers of a service provider must purchase equipment produced by a manufacturer and sold by a third-party reseller that distributes the equipment without having a direct involvement with the service provider. To increase demand for its service, a service provider, may induce third-party manufacturers or resellers to reduce the price of the equipment.

ACCOUNTING ISSUES

1. Should consideration given by a service provider to a third-party manufacturer or reseller of equipment (*not* the service provider's customer) that provides a benefit to a service provider's customer be described as "cash consideration" or as "other than cash" consideration?

2. If a customer needs certain equipment in order to receive a service from a service provider, is consideration given by the service provider to a third-party manufacturer or a reseller of equipment that benefits a customer of both the service provider and the equipment manufacturer or reseller, in substance, the same as if the service provider had given the consideration directly to the end-customer?

3. Should consideration given by a service provider to a manufacturer or a reseller of equipment (*not* the service provider's customer) be accounted for under the model in ASC 605-50-05-1, 15-2 through 15-3, 25-1 through 25-9, 45-1 through 45-11 if the customer needs the equipment in order to receive a service from a service provider and the consideration can be linked to the benefit received by the service provider's customer?

ACCOUNTING GUIDANCE

If consideration given by a service provider to a third-party manufacturer or reseller that is *no t* the service provider's customer can be linked contractually to the benefit that the service provider's customer receives, the service provider should account for that consideration under the ASC 605-50-45-2 through 45-3 as cash or as other than cash.

This guidance is based on the view that consideration given by a service provider to a third-party manufacturer or a reseller that can be linked contractually to the service provider's customer is in substance the same as if the service provider had given the consideration directly to its customer.

There is a presumption that cash consideration should be accounted for as a *reduction* of revenue unless *both* of the following two conditions are met: (*a*) the vendor receives or will receive an identifiable benefit in exchange for the consideration, and (*b*) the vendor can make a reasonable estimate of the fair value of the benefit in condition (*a*). Under the guidance ASC 605-50-45-3, "other than cash consideration" should be accounted for as an expense.

A service provider that gives consideration to a third-party manufacturer or a reseller that provides a benefit to the service provider's customer should describe that consideration based on the form in which the service provider has instructed the third-party manufacturer or reseller that it be given. That is, if a service provider requires that consideration given to its customer by a third-party manufacturer or reseller be in a form other than "cash consideration," as defined in 605-50-45-3, the service provider should describe that consideration as "other than cash" in its application of that guidance. A service provider also should describe such consideration as "other than cash" if the service provider does *not* control the form in which the consideration is given to its customer. If a reseller or third-party manufacturer uses the consideration to reduce a customer's price on equipment purchased, the service provider should describe the consideration given to the third-party manufacturer or reseller as "other than cash."

Disclosure

The following information should be disclosed about such incentive programs:

- The program's features, and
- Amounts recognized in the income statement for such incentive programs and how they were classified in each period presented, if significant.

ASC 605-50-45-16 through 45-20, 55-124 through 55-127 Reseller's Characterization of Sales Incentives Offered to Consumers by Manufacturers

BACKGROUND

The guidance in ASC 605-50-25-10 through 25-12 and 45-12 through 45-14, *Customer Accounting for Certain Consideration Received from a Vendor*, provides that a customer receiving cash from a vendor should reduce its cost of sales in the income statement based on the presumption that the vendor's price is reduced by the cash received. That presumption may be overcome, however, if the cash received is (a) a payment for assets or services received from the customer that should be accounted for as revenue or other income in the customer's income statement, or (b) a payment to reimburse the customer for costs incurred to sell the vendor's products that should be accounted for as a reduction of those costs in the customer's income statement.

The following guidance addresses a reseller's accounting for sales incentives, such as coupons, offered by manufacturers (vendors) directly to consumers for products that will be purchased from resellers. Depending on the form of the incentive, some are tendered by a consumer directly to a reseller for a reduction in the sales price of a product, while others are sent by the consumer to the manufacturer for a rebate after the product has been purchased from a reseller. In either case, the reseller's gross margin for the product is unaffected. A reseller that agrees to accept an incentive as partial payment of a product's sales price will be reimbursed by the vendor for the amount of the incentive.

ACCOUNTING ISSUE

Should consideration received by a reseller from a vendor as a reimbursement for honoring the vendor's sales incentives offered directly to consumers be recognized as a reduction of the cost of the reseller's purchases from the vendor and, therefore, be accounted for as a reduction of cost of sales under the guidance in ASC 60-50-45-12 through 45-14?

ACCOUNTING GUIDANCE

The term "vendors' sales incentives offered directly to consumers" is limited to a vendor's incentive that meets all of the following criteria (a) consumers can use the incentives at any reseller that accepts the manufacturer's incentive as partial payment of the reseller's price for the vendor's product, (b) the vendor reimburses resellers directly for the face amount of the incentive, (c) the terms governing a reseller's reimbursement for the vendor's sales incentive offered to consumers may be determined only based on the terms of that incentive and must not be influenced by or negotiated in connection with any other incentive arrangement between the vendor and the reseller, and (d) the reseller is subject to an expressed or implied agency relationship with the vendor regarding the sales incentive transaction between the vendor and the consumer.

Sales that meet all of the above criteria are *not* covered under the guidance in ASC 605-50-45-12 through 45-14. Sales incentives that do *not* meet all of those criteria should be accounted for under the guidance in (a) ASC 605-50-45-2 through 45-3, which provide that a sales incentive should be accounted for as a reduction of revenue (paragraph 45-2) or as an expense (paragraph 45-3), or under the guidance in ASC 605-50-45-12 through 45-14, that is, as a reduction of cost of sales (paragraphs 45-12 and 45-13(b)), or as revenue (paragraphs 45-13(a) and 45-14, as applicable).

The following example illustrates a transaction that meets the above criteria:

- A reseller that purchases a box of cereal from a manufacturer for $3 sells it for $4. The reseller recognizes $4 as revenue and $3 as a cost of the sale of a box of cereal.

- The cereal's manufacturer offers a $.50 coupon to consumers for a limited period of time. The consumer pays $3.50 in cash for the box of cereal and presents a $.50 coupon that the reseller remits to a clearinghouse, which reimburses the $.50 to the reseller.

- Since the guidance in ASC 605-50-45-12 through 45-14 does *not* apply to the transaction discussed in this Issue, the reseller is in the same position as if the consumer had purchased the box of cereal without the coupon. Therefore, the reseller would recognize revenue of $4 and a cost of $3 for the sale of a box of cereal.

CHAPTER 37
ASC 705—COST OF SALES AND SERVICES

ASC 705 does not provide any unique guidance but rather only provides a link to guidance on accounting for the cost of sales and services in other ASC subtopics.

CHAPTER 38
ASC 710—COMPENSATION—GENERAL

CONTENTS

Part I: General Guidance	38,001
ASC 710-10: Overall	38,001
Overview	38,001
Background	38,001
Accounting Standards	38,002
Illustration of Calculating Deferred Compensation	38,002
Compensated Absences	38,003
Part II: Interpretive Guidance	38,004
ASC 710-10: Overall	38,004
ASC 710-10-05-8 through 05-9, 15-8 through 15-10, 25-15 through 25-18; 35-2 through 35-4, 45-2 through 45-4; ASC 260-10-60-1; ASC-810-15-10	
Accounting for Deferred Compensation Arrangements Where Amounts Earned Are Held in a Rabbi Trust and Invested	38,004
ASC 710-10-15-3, 25-12 through 25-14, S15-1, S25-1, S99-1	
Lump-Sum Payments under Union Contracts	38,007
ASC 710-10-15-3, 25-5	
Accounting for Sabbatical Leave and Other Similar Benefits Pursuant to FASB Statement No. 43, *Accounting for Compensated Absences*	38,008

PART I: GENERAL GUIDANCE

ASC 710-10: OVERALL

OVERVIEW

Deferred compensation contracts are accounted for individually on an accrual basis. Such contracts ordinarily include certain requirements such as continued employment for a specified period of time, availability for consulting services, and agreements not to compete after retirement. The estimated amounts to be paid under each contract are accrued in a systematic and rational manner over the period of active employment from the initiation of the contract, unless it is evident that future services expected to be received by the employer are commensurate with the payments or a portion of the payments to be made. If elements of both current and future services are present, only the portion applicable to the current services is accrued.

BACKGROUND

The main source of GAAP for deferred compensation contracts is ASC 710 and ASC 715 (Compensation—Retirement Benefits). If individual deferred compensation contracts, as a group, are tantamount to a pension plan, they are accounted for in accordance with the GAAP for pension plans, discussed in ASC 715-30 (Defined Benefit Plans—Pension).

If individual deferred compensation contracts are, as a group, equivalent to a plan for postretirement benefits other than pensions, they are accounted for in accordance with the GAAP on postretirement benefits, discussed in ASC 715-60 (Defined Benefit Plans—Other Post-Retirement).

> **PRACTICE NOTE:** Professional judgment is required to determine whether individual contracts are equivalent to a pension or postretirement plan.

ACCOUNTING STANDARDS

According to ASC 710, deferred compensation contracts are accounted for on an individual basis for each employee. If a deferred compensation contract is based on current and future employment, only the amounts attributable to the current portion of employment are accrued (ASC 710-10-25-9, 10).

If a deferred compensation contract contains benefits payable for the life of a beneficiary, the total liability is based on the beneficiary's life expectancy or on the estimated cost of an annuity contract that would provide sufficient funds to pay the required benefits (ASC 710-10-30-1).

The total liability for deferred compensation contracts is determined by the terms of each individual contract. The amount of the periodic accrual, computed from the first day of the employment contract, must total no less than the then present value of the benefits provided for in the contract. The periodic accruals are made systematically over the active term of employment.

Illustration of Calculating Deferred Compensation

A deferred compensation contract provides for the payment of $50,000 per year for five years, beginning one year after the end of the employee's ten year contract. A 10% interest rate is appropriate.

The present value for the five $50,000 payments at the end of ten years is determined as follows:

Present value of $50,000 in five years	$ 31,045
Present value of $50,000 in four years	34,150
Present value of $50,000 in three years	37,565
Present value of $50,000 in two years	41,320
Present value of $50,000 in one year	45,455
Total present value of benefits at end of employment	$189,535

In order to have available the funds required to pay the benefits in accordance with the contract, $189,535 must be accumulated over ten years. To find the amount of the annual accrual that earning 10% interest will total $189,535 at the end of ten years, assuming that payments are made at the beginning of each year over the 10-year period, the following formula for the value of an annuity due may be used:

$189,535 \quad = \quad R\ (17.531^*)$

$R \quad = \quad \$10,811$

*Amount of an annuity due at 10% for 10 periods

COMPENSATED ABSENCES

Compensated absences arise from employees' absences from employment because of illness, holiday, vacation, or other reasons. ASC 420 establishes GAAP for employees' compensated absences. When an employer expects to pay an employee for compensated absences, a liability for the estimated probable future payments must be accrued if all the following conditions are met (ASC 710-10-25-1):

- The employee's right to receive compensation for the future absences is attributable to services already performed by the employee.
- The employee's right to receive the compensation for the future absences is vested, or accumulates.
- It is probable that the compensation will be paid.
- The amount of compensation is reasonably estimable.

If no accrual is made because the fourth criterion is not met, the fact that the employer meets the first three conditions and not the fourth condition must be disclosed in the financial statements.

Vested rights are those that have been earned by the employee for services already performed. They are not contingent on future services by the employee and are an obligation of the employer even if the employee leaves the employer. Rights that accumulate are nonvesting rights to compensated absences that are earned and can be carried forward to succeeding years. Rights that accumulate increase an employee's benefits in one or more years subsequent to the year in which they are earned. An employer does not have to accrue a liability for nonvesting rights to compensated absences that expire at the end of the year in which they are earned, because they do not accumulate (ASC 710-10-25-3).

Nonvesting sick pay benefits that accumulate and can be carried forward to succeeding years are given special treatment by ASC 710. If payment of nonvesting accumulating sick pay benefits depends on the future illness of the employee, an employer is not required to accrue a liability for such payments. The reasons cited in ASC 710 for this exception are (*a*) cost/benefit, (*b*) materiality, and (*c*) the reliability of estimating the days an employee will be sick in succeeding years. This exception does not apply in circumstances in which the employer pays the sick pay benefits even though the employee is not actually sick. An employer's general policy for the payment of nonvesting accumulating sick pay benefits should govern the accounting for such payments (ASC 710-10-25-7).

PRACTICE POINTER: One issue that must be resolved in recognizing the expense and liability for compensated absences is the rate of compensation to use—the current rate or the rate expected to apply when the compensated absence is taken by the employee. In situations in which the rate of compensation increases rapidly and/or a long period of time lapses between the time the compensated absence is earned and taken by the employee, the rate of compensation used may be significant. GAAP does not provide guidance on this issue. Other authoritative standards may provide some help in making this decision. For example, net periodic pension cost is determined based on the projected benefit obligation, which includes expected future increases in compensation. If the difference in the amount of liability for compensated absences, when measured by the current and expected future rates of compensation, is material, the latter more faithfully measures the obligation and expense of the employer.

Once a total amount of liability for compensated absences is determined, the amount expected to require the use of current assets should be classified as a current liability. The remaining balance should be presented as a noncurrent liability.

PART II: INTERPRETIVE GUIDANCE

ASC 710-10: OVERALL

ASC 710-10-05-8 through 05-9, 15-8 through 15-10, 25-15 through 25-18; 35-2 through 35-4, 45-2 through 45-4; ASC 260-10-60-1; ASC-810-15-10 Accounting for Deferred Compensation Arrangements Where Amounts Earned Are Held in a Rabbi Trust and Invested

OBSERVATIONS: Under the guidance in ASC 810-10-05-8 through 05-8A, 15-12 through 15-17, 25-37 through 25-44, 30-1 through 30-4, 30-7 through 30-9, 35-3 through 35-5, 45-25, 50-2AA through 50-7, 50-9 through 50-10, 55-16 through 55-49, 55-93 through 55-181, 55-183 through 55-205, 60-13; ASC 323-10-45-4; ASC 712-10-60-2; ASC 715-10-60-3, 60-7; ASC 860-10-60-2; ASC 954-810-15-3, 45-2; ASC 958-810-15-4, an entity is required to consolidate a variable interest entity if the entity has a controlling interest in the variable entity. ASC 810-10-25-38 through 25-38G provides guidance for determining whether an entity has a controlling financial interest in a variable interest entity.

BACKGROUND

Some employers have set up deferred compensation arrangements under which amounts—such as bonuses earned by a select group of management or highly compensated employees—are placed in a grantor trust, which is commonly referred to as a "rabbi trust." Amounts placed in a rabbi trust are *not* tax deductible to the employer, and the employee is *not* taxed on deferred amounts until that compensation is paid. A rabbi trust qualifies for income tax purposes only if its terms state explicitly that the employer can use assets held by the trust to satisfy the claims of its creditors in bankruptcy.

The following are the types of deferred compensation plans in which a Rabbi Trust may be held:

ASC 710—Compensation—General   **38,005**

- Plan A—Diversification of the trust's assets is *not* permitted. The funds must be invested in an employer's stock and settlement must be in a fixed number of shares of the employer's stock.
- Plans B—Diversification of the trust's assets is *not* permitted. The funds must be invested in an employer's stock and settlement may be in cash or shares of the employer's stock.
- Plan C—Diversification of the trust's assets into the securities of other entities is permitted after a certain time period (e.g., six months), but an employee has elected *not* to diversify the trust's assets, so the funds are invested only in the employer's stock and would be settled in cash, shares of the employer's stock, or diversified assets.
- Plan D—Diversification of the trust's assets is permitted after a certain time period (e.g., six months) and an employee *has* elected to diversify the trust's assets. Settlement may be in cash, shares of the employer's stock, or diversified assets.

The following accounting guidance does not apply to stock appreciation rights (SARs), even if they are funded through a rabbi trust.

ACCOUNTING ISSUES

- Should an employer be required to consolidate the accounts of a rabbi trust in its financial statements?
- How should an employer report investments in a rabbi trust?
- How does an employee's election to diversify the assets held by a rabbi trust into nonemployer securities affect the accounting for the trust's assets and for the deferred compensation obligation?

ACCOUNTING GUIDANCE

1. Employers should consolidate in their financial statements the accounts of rabbi trusts in all plans.
2. Assets held by a rabbi trust should be accounted for as a follows:
   a. Employer stock held in a rabbi trust under Plans A, B, and C should be classified in equity and accounted for similar to treasury stock and reported in an employer's consolidated financial statements at acquisition cost without adjustment for changes in the fair value of the employer's stock
   b. If diversification is prohibited and the obligation must be settled in a fixed number of an employer's shares, as under Plan A, the employer's deferred compensation obligation should be classified as an equity instrument without adjustment for changes in the fair value of the employer's stock. However, a deferred compensation obligation for a rabbi trust under Plans B and C, which can be settled in cash, should be classified as a liability that should be adjusted for changes in the fair value of the employer's stock by a corresponding charge (or credit) to compensation cost.
   c. Diversified assets held by a rabbi trust under Plan D should be accounted for in accordance with generally accepted accounting

principles appropriate for each specific asset; for example, marketable equity securities should be accounted for based on the guidance in ASC 320, Investments-Debt and Equity Securities.

    d. If diversification is permitted (Plans C and D) and the obligation is not required to be settled in a fixed number of the employer's shares, the deferred compensation obligation should be adjusted for changes in its fair value. Deferred compensation cost should be adjusted by a corresponding charge (or credit) to compensation cost. Changes in the fair value of the deferred compensation obligation should *not* be recognized in comprehensive income even if changes in the fair value of the assets held by the rabbi trust are recognized in comprehensive income in accordance with the guidance in ASC 320. Diversified assets held by a rabbi trust may be classified in the trading category at acquisition.

The following is guidance for *earnings per share* (EPS) calculations:

1. Treat employer shares held by a rabbi trust in the same manner as treasury stock in EPS calculations and exclude the amount from the denominator in the calculation of basic and diluted EPS.
2. Include the deferred compensation obligation in the denominator of the EPS calculation in accordance with the guidance in ASC 260-1-45.
3. Include employer shares in Plan A in the basic and diluted EPS calculations, because ASC 260-10-45-13 requires that treatment if an obligation must be settled by delivering the employer's shares.
4. Include employer shares in the diluted EPS calculation only for rabbi trusts held under Plans B, C, or D, because according to the guidance in ASC 260-10-45-30, and 45-45 through 45-46, that treatment is required if an obligation can be settled by delivery of cash, shares of employer stock, or diversified assets.

DISCUSSION

- A rabbi trust should be consolidated, because it is not bankruptcy proof. That is, an employer can use the trust's assets to settle the claims of general creditors in bankruptcy. Consolidation of rabbi trusts is common practice and is consistent with the treatment implied in the discussion in ASC 715-60-55-26; ASC 710-10-60-2, Plan Assets under FASB Statement 106.
- A consolidated entity holding a parent's stock must treat it as treasury stock in consolidation and subtract it from equity.
- The decision to classify a deferred compensation obligation as an equity instrument under plan A, which does not permit diversification and must be settled in the employer's shares, was made, because that treatment conforms to the framework established in ASC 815-10-15-78, 15-25-15, 55-52; ASC 815-40-05-1 through 05-4, 05-10 through 05-12, 25-1 through 25-5, 25-7 through 25-20, 25-22 through 25-24, 25-26 through 25-35, 25-37 through 25-40, 30-1, 35-1 through 35-2, 35-6, 35-8 through 35-13, 40-1 through 40-2; 50-1 through 50-5, 55-1 through 55-18; ASC 460-10-60-14;

ASC 480-10-55-63; ASC 505-10-60-5, Accounting for Derivative Financial Instruments Indexed to, and Potentially Settled in, a Company's Own Stock (See Chapter 48, *ASC 815—Derivatives and Hedging*). Subsequent changes in the fair value of an employer's stock are not recognized for the same reason.

- The decision to recognize changes in the fair value of the deferred compensation obligation in income by adjusting compensation cost even if the diversified assets are recognized as available-for-sale securities is based on the view of the FASB staff that the award is a stock-based compensation award and that authoritative literature, such as ASC 840-40-25-4 through 25-5, 35-4, 55-79 through 55-80, 55-82 through 55-84, 55-86 through 55-88, 55-90 through 55-92, and 55-94, requires that changes in the value of such awards subsequent to an employee's service period be recognized in income as an adjustment of compensation cost.

ASC 710-10-15-3, 25-12 through 25-14, S15-1, S25-1, S99-1 Lump-Sum Payments under Union Contracts

BACKGROUND

In connection with the signing of a new union contract, a company might give employees one or more lump-sum payments instead of, or in addition to, a base wage rate increase. Typically, employees are not required to refund any portion of such lump-sum payments if they leave the company before the contract period ends. In addition, employees who leave the company generally are replaced by other union members at the same base wage rate but replacements receive no lump-sum payments.

ACCOUNTING ISSUE

Should lump-sum payments made to employees in connection with the signing of a new union contract be (1) charged to expense immediately or (2) deferred and amortized over the contract period or some portion of the contract period?

ACCOUNTING GUIDANCE

Lump-sum payments made to employees in connection with the signing of a new union contract may be deferred provided that the payments clearly will benefit future periods in the form of lower base wage rates. The deferred charge should be amortized over periods clearly benefited, but not longer than the contract period.

It was noted that the terms and conditions of those types of arrangements vary and must be reviewed to determine how to account for the lump-sum payments.

DISCUSSION

Those who supported deferral argued that lump-sum payments that result in lower wage costs over the contract period provide a future economic benefit to the entity. They believed that such payments represent a cost of the contract, which will benefit the entity over the entire contract period and consequently should be deferred and recognized in the periods in which services are performed.

Proponents also referred to certain pronouncements that recommend recognition of compensation costs over the periods during which an employee performs services. For example, the goal of recognizing pension costs over the periods in which employees provide services are discussed in ASC 715, Compensation - Retirement Benefits. Under the guidance in ASC 710-10-15-4 through 15-5, 25-9 through 25-11, 30-1 through 30-2; ASC 310-10-45-4, 50-14; ASC 360-10-50-1, ASC 715-20-60-1; ASC 505-10-50-2; and ASC 835-30-35-3, employers are required to accrue and amortize amounts to be paid to employees under deferred compensation contracts for current services in a systematic and rational manner over the period of active employment beginning when the employer enters into the contract.

To refute the argument of those who compare lump-sum payments to bonuses for past services, proponents of deferral also argued that such payments had not been promised to the employees before the union contract negotiation; all contractually required payments have already been made to the employees; and the only reason for making those payments is to obtain a lower base wage rate over the contract period.

ASC 710-10-15-3, 25-5 Accounting for Sabbatical Leave and Other Similar Benefits Pursuant to FASB Statement No. 43, *Accounting for Compensated Absences*

BACKGROUND

Some entities, such as colleges and universities, provide a benefit to their employees, known as a sabbatical leave. Under sabbatical leave, employees are entitled to a compensated absence for a specified period of time, such as three months, after having worked for the employer for a specified period of time (e.g., seven years). An employee is compensated during a sabbatical but is not required to perform any duties for the employer. Employees are not entitled to compensation for unused sabbatical leave if their employment terminates before having worked for the full eligibility period. Further, employees that have worked for the specified period but did not avail themselves of the benefit are not entitled to the benefit if their employment is terminated.

The guidance in ASC 710-10-25-1 provides that employers should accrue a liability for employees' compensation for future absences if certain conditions are met. Condition 6b states that "the obligation relates to rights that vest or accumulate." In addition, the guidance in ASC 710-10-25-1(b) defines *accumulate* to mean "that earned but unused rights to compensated absences may be carried forward to one or more periods subsequent to that in which they are earned even though there may be a limit to the amount that can be carried forward." Based on that guidance, some question whether a sabbatical benefit should be accrued even though the benefit does not vest.

ACCOUNTING ISSUE

Does an employee's right to a compensated absence under a sabbatical or similar benefit accumulate in accordance with the guidance in ASC 710-10-25-1 if the employee must complete a minimum service period and if the benefit does not increase with additional years of service?

SCOPE

The following guidance is limited to sabbatical or similar arrangements under which an employee is *not* required to perform direct or indirect services for or on behalf the employer during that absence. It does *not* apply to public colleges or universities, even those that have adopted GASB-20, because the guidance in ASC 710 conflicts with that in GASB-16.

ACCOUNTING GUIDANCE

Compensation costs associated with an employee's right to a sabbatical or other similar arrangement should be accrued over the required service period if, under that arrangement, (a) the employee is required to complete a minimum period of service, and (b) the benefit does *not* increase with additional years of service accumulated in accordance with the guidance in ASC 710-10-25-1(b) for arrangements under which an employee is *not* required to perform duties for the employer during a compensated absence. All of the other conditions in ASC 710-10-25-1 also must be met.

CHAPTER 39
ASC 712—COMPENSATION—NONRETIREMENT POSTEMPLOYMENT BENEFITS

General Guidance	39,001
ASC 712-10: Overall	39,001
Overview	39,001
Termination Benefits	39,001
Postemployment Benefits	39,001

GENERAL GUIDANCE

ASC 712-10: OVERALL

OVERVIEW

The FASB has established accounting standards for employers that provide benefits for former or inactive employees after employment, but before retirement (*postemployment benefits*). Employers are required to recognize the obligation to provide postemployment benefits in accordance with ASC 712 if the criteria for accrual established in that pronouncement are met. If the ASC 712 criteria are not met, the employer must account for postemployment benefits when it is probable that a liability has been incurred and the amount of that liability can be reasonably estimated, in accordance with ASC 450 (Contingencies).

TERMINATION BENEFITS

Termination benefits are classified as either *special* or *contractual*. Special termination benefits are those that are offered to employees for a short period in connection with the termination of their employment. Contractual termination benefits are those that are required by the terms of an existing plan or agreement and that are provided only on the occurrence of a specified event, such as early retirement or the closing of a facility (ASC 712-10-05-2).

POSTEMPLOYMENT BENEFITS

Accrual is required for an obligation for postemployment benefits that meet the following criteria (ASC 712-10-25-4):

- The employer's obligation relating to employees' rights to receive compensation for future compensated absences is attributable to employees' services already rendered.
- The obligation relates to rights that vest or accumulate.

- Payment of the compensation is probable.
- The amount can be estimated reasonably.

If an obligation for postemployment benefits is not accrued in accordance with either ASC 712 or ASC 450 only because the amount cannot be estimated, the financial statements shall disclose that fact (ASC 712-10-50-2).

CHAPTER 40
ASC 715—COMPENSATION—RETIREMENT BENEFITS

CONTENTS

Part I: General Guidance	40,006
ASC 715-10: Overall	40,006
Overview	40,006
Background	40,008
Pension Plan Accounting	40,008
Deferred Compensation Plan	40,009
Postemployment Benefits	40,009
Illustrations of Accruals Required by ASC 715	40,010
ASC 715-20: Defined Benefit Plans—General	40,011
Financial Statement Disclosure	40,011
Disclosures about Pension Plans and Other Postretirement Plans	40,011
Disclosures by Employers with Two or More Plans	40,013
Multiemployer Plan Disclosures	40,014
Reduced Disclosures for Nonpublic Companies	40,014
Disclosures in Interim Financial Reports	40,015
ASC 715-30: Defined Benefit Plans—Pension	40,015
Overview of Pension Plan Accounting	40,015
Scope and Applicability	40,015
Actuarial Assumptions	40,016
Pension Plan Assets	40,017
Recording Pension Events	40,018
Illustration of Basic Entries to Record Pension Events	40,018
Pension Plan Terminology	40,019
Projected Benefit Obligation	40,019
Accumulated Benefit Obligation	40,019
Fair Value of Plan Assets	40,020
Funded Status of Plan	40,020
Prior Service Cost or Credit	40,020
Gain or Loss	40,021
Net Periodic Pension Cost	40,021
Illustration of Computing Net Periodic Pension Cost	40,022
Service Cost Component	40,024
Interest Cost Component	40,026
Actual Return on Plan Assets Component	40,026
Amortization of Prior Service Cost or Credit Component	40,027
Gains and Losses Component	40,028
Illustration of Computing Market-Related Value	40,029
Illustration of Gains and Losses Component of Net Periodic Pension Cost	40,031

Amortization of the Transition Obligation or Transition Asset (as of the Date of Initial Application of Pension Plan Accounting)	40,033
Recognition of Funded Status of Pension Plan	40,034
Miscellaneous Considerations	40,034
Measurement Dates	40,034
Employers with Two or More Pension Plans	40,035
Annuity Contracts	40,035
Other Contracts with Insurance Companies	40,036
Multiple-Employer Plans	40,036
Non-U.S. Pension Plans	40,036
Business Combinations	40,036
Defined Contribution Pension Plans	40,037
Settlements and Curtailments	40,037
Settlements of Defined Benefit Pension Plans	40,039
Reporting Gain or Loss on a Plan Settlement	40,040
Small Settlements for the Year	40,040
Curtailment of Defined Benefit Pension Plans	40,041
Decrease (Loss) in Prior Service Cost	40,041
Illustration of Computation of Expected Years of Future Service and Loss from the Decrease in Prior Service Cost Resulting from the Expected Years of Future Service That Are Significantly Reduced by a Plan Curtailment	40,043
Decrease (Gain) or Increase (Loss) in the Projected Benefit Obligation	40,043
Recognition of the Total Effects of a Plan Curtailment	40,045
Reporting Total Effects of a Plan Curtailment	40,045
Termination Benefits	40,045
Special Termination Benefits	40,045
Contractual Termination Benefits	40,045
Reporting a Loss on Termination Benefits	40,046
Financial Statement Disclosure	40,046
Illustration of Curtailment and Settlement of a Pension Plan	40,046
ASC 715-60: Defined Benefit Plans—Other Post-Retirement	40,048
GAAP Requirements	40,048
General Approach—Deferred Compensation	40,049
Comparison of Pension Accounting to Postretirement Benefit Accounting	40,049
Illustration of Basic Entries for Recording Postretirement Benefits	40,049
Use of Reasonable Approximations	40,050
Scope and Applicability	40,050
Types of Benefits	40,050
Types of Beneficiaries	40,050
General Rather Than Selective Coverage of Employees	40,051
Source and Form of Payment	40,051
Nature of the Employer's Undertaking	40,051
Single-Employer Defined Benefit Postretirement Plans	40,053
Accumulated Postretirement Benefit Obligation	40,053
Illustration of Relationship between Expected and Accumulated Postretirement Benefit Obligations	40,054
Measurement of Cost and Obligations	40,055

Accounting for the Substantive Plan	40,055
Cost Sharing	40,055
Benefit Changes	40,056
Plan Amendments	40,056
Assumptions	40,056
Time Value of Money (Discount Rates)	40,057
Expected Long-Term Rate of Return on Plan Assets	40,058
Future Compensation Levels	40,058
Other General Assumptions	40,058
Assumptions Unique to Postretirement Health Care Benefits	40,059
Per Capita Claims Cost	40,059
Assumptions about Trends in Health Care Cost Rates	40,060
Attribution	40,061
Illustration of Attribution Period	40,061
Illustration of Attribution under a Frontloaded Plan	40,061
Recognition of Net Periodic Postretirement Benefit Cost	40,062
Illustration of Basic Transactions and Adjustments	40,062
Basic Transactions and Adjustments	40,063
Service Cost Component	40,063
Interest Cost Component	40,064
Actual Return on Plan Assets Component	40,064
Illustration of Actual Return on Plan Assets	40,064
Amortization of Prior Service Cost or Credit Component	40,065
Initiation of a Plan, or Amendment that Improves Benefits in an Existing Plan	40,065
Methods of Amortizing Prior Service Cost	40,065
Illustration of Plan Amendment Increasing Benefits	40,065
Plan Amendments that Reduce Obligation	40,067
Gain or Loss Component	40,067
Elements of the Gain or Loss Component	40,068
Plan Asset Gains and Losses	40,068
Other Gains and Losses Immediately Realized	40,069
Illustration of Gains and Losses	40,071
Amortization of Transition Obligation/Asset Component	40,073
Recognition of Funded Status of Postretirement Benefit Plans	40,074
Measurement of Plan Assets	40,074
Insurance Contracts	40,075
Definition of Insurance Contracts	40,075
Participating Insurance Contracts	40,075
Cost of Insurance	40,076
Insurance Company Not Fully Bound	40,076
Measurement Date	40,076
Disclosures	40,077
Employers with Two or More Plans	40,077
Aggregate Measurement	40,077
Multiple-Employer Plans	40,077
Plans Outside the United States	40,079
Business Combinations	40,080

40,004 ASC 715—Compensation—Retirement Benefits

Settlement and Curtailment of a Postretirement Benefit Obligation	40,080
Accounting for a Plan Settlement	40,081
Maximum Gain or Loss	40,081
Settlement Gain or Loss When Entire Obligation Is Settled	40,081
Settlement Gain or Loss When Only Part of Obligation Is Settled	40,081
Participating Insurance	40,081
Settlements at Lower Cost Than Current Cost of Service and Interest	40,081
Accounting for a Plan Curtailment	40,082
Gain and Loss Recognition	40,082
Curtailment Resulting from Termination of Employees	40,082
Curtailment Resulting from Terminating Accrual of Additional Benefits for Future Services	40,083
Changes in Accumulated Postretirement Benefit Obligation	40,083
Illustration of Curtailment	40,084
Relationship of Settlements and Curtailments to Other Events	40,084
Illustration of Partial Settlement and Full Curtailment Resulting from Sale of Line of Business	40,085
Measurement of the Effects of Termination Benefits	40,086
ASC 715-70: Deferred Contribution Plans	40,087
Defined Contribution Plans	40,087
Accounting for Contributions	40,087
Disclosure	40,087
ASC 715-80: Multi-Employer Plans	40,087
Multiemployer Plans	40,087
Accounting for Multiemployer Plans	40,088
Withdrawal from Multiemployer Plans	40,088
Obligation under "Maintenance of Benefits" Clause	40,088
Part II: Interpretive Guidance	40,089
ASC 715-20: Defined Benefits Plans—General	40,089
ASC 715-20-S50-1, S99-2; ASC 715-30-35-40 through 35-41	
Determination of Vested Benefit Obligation for a Defined Benefit Pension Plan	40,089
ASC 715-20-S55-1, S99-1	
Selection of Discount Rates Used for Measuring Defined Benefit Pension Obligations and Obligations of Postretirement Plans Other Than Pensions	40,091
ASC 715-30: Defined Benefit Plans Pension	40,092
ASC 715-30-15-3, 35-71, 35-72	
Accounting for "Cash Balance" Pension Plans	40,092
ASC 715-20-50-1, 50-8; ASC 715-30-15-4, 35-5, 35-15 through 35-16, 35-20, 35-23, 35-31, 35-39, 35-42, 35-46 through 35-49, 35-61, 35-69, 35-84 through 35-85, 55-3 through 55-5, 55-8 through 55-15, 55-17 through 55-22, 55-24 through 55-33, 55-35 through 55-43, 55-46 through 55-51, 55-53 through 55-61, 55-63 through 55-64, 55-66 through 55-67, 55-88, 55-90, 55-108, 55-110 through 55-120, 55-122 through 55-127; ASC 715-50-60-2; ASC 740-10-60-1; ASC 958-715-55-2; ASC 980-715-55-2 through 55-8, 55-10 through 55-25; ASC 330-10-55-5 through 55-7	
A Guide to Implementation of ASC 715-30 on Employers' Accounting for Pensions: Questions and Answers	40,093

ASC 715—Compensation—Retirement Benefits   40,005

Illustration of Return on Asset Component of Net Periodic Pension Cost	40,096
Illustration of the Effect on Net Periodic Pension Cost of Using the Market-Related Value of Plan Assets	40,100
Illustration of Attribution with Multiple Formulas	40,102
Illustration of Attribution of the Projected Benefit Obligation to a Qualified Pension Plan and an Excess Benefit Pension Plan	40,104
Illustration of Combining Two Plans	40,110

ASC 715-20-45-4; ASC 715-30-15-7, 25-9, 25-11, 35-22, 35-75, 35-81 through 35-82, 35-84, 35-95; 55-52, 55-92, 55-130 through 55-137, 55-140, 55-142 through 55-168, 55-170 through 55-184, 55-186 through 55-197, 55-201, 55-208, 55-217 through 55-219, 55-221, 55-226 though 55-230, 55-237 through 55-238, 55-241 through 55-246, 55-248 through 55-249, 55-251 through 55-252, 60-5, 60-8; ASC 740-10-55-75; ASC 845-10-55-1, 55-3 through 55-9; ASC 205-20-60-5; ASC 712-2-10-05-2; 25-1

Guide to Implementation of ASC 715 on Employers' Accounting for Settlements and Curtailments of Defined Benefit Pension Plans and for Termination Benefits	40,115
Illustration of Substituting New Plan for Existing Plan	40,121
Illustration of Incorporation and Subsequent Spinoff of a Pension Plan	40,126
Illustration of Pension Plan Curtailment: Transition Asset Remaining in Accumulated Other Comprehensive Income Is Less Than Net Loss Included in Accumulated Other Comprehensive Income	40,131
Illustration of Pension Plan Curtailment: Transition Asset Remaining in Accumulation Other Comprehensive Income Exceeds Net/Loss Included in Other Comprehensive Income	40,132
Illustration of Curtailment: Termination Benefits Offered to Employees	40,134

ASC 715-30-35-73

Accounting for the Transfer of Excess Pension Assets to a Retiree Health Care Benefits Account	40,138

ASC 715-30-35-89 through 35-91

Accounting for Pension Benefits Paid by Employers after Insurance Companies Fail to Provide Annuity Benefits	40,139

ASC 715-20-50-10; ASC 715-30-55-70 through 55-78, 55-171

Accounting for the Transfer to the Japanese Government of the Substitutional Portion of Employee Pension Fund Liabilities	40,139

ASC 715-30-55-81 through 55-86

Accounting for Early Retirement or Postemployment Programs with Specific Features (Such as Terms Specified in Altersteilzeit Early Retirement Arrangements)	40,141
ASC 715-60: Defined Benefit Plans—Other Post-Retirement	40,142

ASC 715-60-05-8 through 05-11, 15-11 through 15-13, 35-133 through 35-148, 50-2B, 50-4, 50-6, 55-103; ASC 715-740-10-55 through 10-57, 10-166 through 10-167

Accounting and Disclosure Requirements Related to the Medicare Prescription Drug Improvement and Modernization Act of 2003	40,142

ASC 715-60-05-14 through 05-15, 15-20 through 15-21, 35-177 through 35-179, 55-176 through 55-177, 55-179

Accounting for Deferred Compensation and Postretirement Benefit Aspects of Endorsement Split-Dollar Life Insurance Arrangements	40,145
ASC 715-60-05-15, 35-180 through 35-185, 55-178, 55-180 through 55-181	
Accounting for Deferred Compensation and Postretirement Benefit Aspects of Collateral Assignment Split-Dollar Life Insurance Arrangements	40,147
ASC 715-20-55-1 through 55-2; ASC 715-60-15-5 through 15-6, 25-4, 35-21, 35-33, 35-64 through 35-65, 35-96, 35-111 35-113, 35-168, 55-1 through 55-25, 55-27 through 55-30, 55-32, 55-34, 55-106 through 55-111, 55-140, 55-142 through 55-175; ASC 715-70-55-2 through 55-3; ASC 715-80-55-3 through 55-5; ASC 710-10-55-2, 55-5 through 55-6, 60-3	
Guide to Implementation of ASC 715-60 on Employers' Accounting for Postretirement Benefits Other Than Pensions	40,149
Illustration of a Frontloaded Plan	40,154
Illustration of a Negative Plan Amendment and a Curtailment That Reduces the APBO	40,156
Illustration of Negative Plan Amendment—Curtailment Gain	40,157
Illustration of Negative Plan Amendment—Curtailment Loss	40,159
Illustration of Immediate Termination of Plan	40,164
ASC 715-60-55-26; ASC 710-10-60-2	
Plan Assets under ASC 715-60	40,165
ASC 715-70: Deferred Contribution Plans	40,166
ASC 715-70-55-4 through 55-9	
Measurement of Excess Contributions to a Defined Contribution Plan or Employee Stock Ownership Plan	40,166
ASC 715-80: Multiemployer Plans	40,170
ASC 715-80-55-2	
Accounting for Employers' Obligations for Future Contributions to a Multiemployer Pension Plan	40,170

PART I: GENERAL GUIDANCE

ASC 715-10: OVERALL

OVERVIEW

GAAP for employers' accounting for pension plans emphasizes the determination of annual pension expense (identified as net periodic pension cost) and the presentation of the funded status of the pension plan. Net periodic pension cost is made up of several components that reflect different aspects of the employer's financial arrangements, as well as the cost of benefits earned by employees.

ASC 715 requires the accrual of postretirement benefits other than pensions in a manner similar to the recognition of net periodic pension cost in accounting for pension plan costs. The accounting requirements for postemployment and postretirement benefit plans are similar to the accounting requirements for pension plans and differ only where there are compelling reasons for different treatments.

In applying principles of accrual accounting for pension plans and postretirement benefits, the FASB emphasizes three fundamental features:

1. *Delayed income statement recognition*—Changes in the pension and postretirement benefit obligations and changes in the value of pension and plan assets are recognized on the balance sheet as they occur, through changes in the pension and postretirement benefit assets and/or liabilities; however, on the income statement these changes are not recognized as they occur, but rather systematically and gradually over subsequent periods. Items recognized on the balance sheet immediately but deferred for income statement recognition are included in accumulated other comprehensive income.

2. *Net cost*—The recognized consequences of events and transactions affecting a pension or postretirement benefit plan are reported for each type of plan as a single net amount in the employer's financial statements. This approach results in the aggregation of items that would be presented separately for any other part of the employer's operations: the compensation cost of benefits, the interest cost resulting from deferred payment of those benefits, and the results of investing pension or plan assets.

3. *Offsetting*—Pension plan assets and liabilities are shown net in the employer's statement of financial position, even though the liability has not been settled. Also, the return on plan assets reduces postretirement benefit cost in the employer's statement of income. The assets may still be controlled and substantial risks and rewards associated with both are clearly borne by the employer.

Employers may cancel (settle) or reduce (curtail) a pension plan. A *settlement of a pension plan* is an irrevocable action that relieves the employer (or the plan) of primary responsibility for an obligation and eliminates significant risks related to the obligation and the assets used to effect the settlement. Examples of transactions that constitute a settlement include (*a*) making lump-sum cash payments to plan participants in exchange for their rights to receive specified pension benefits and (*b*) purchasing nonparticipating annuity contracts to cover vested benefits.

Curtailment is a significant reduction in, or an elimination of, defined benefit accruals for present employees' future services. Examples of curtailments are (*a*) termination of employees' services earlier than expected, which may or may not involve closing a facility or discontinuing a segment of a business, and (*b*) termination or suspension of a plan so that employees do not earn additional defined benefits for future services.

The FASB also has established accounting standards for employers that provide benefits for former or inactive employees after employment, but before retirement (*postemployment benefits*). Employers are required to recognize the obligation to provide postemployment benefits in accordance with ASC 712 (Compensation—Nonretirement Postemployment Benefits) if the criteria for accrual established in that pronouncement are met. If ASC 710 criteria are not met, the employer must account for postemployment benefits when it is probable that a liability has been incurred and the amount of that liability can be reasonably estimated, in accordance with ASC 450 (Contingencies).

BACKGROUND

Employment is based on an explicit or implicit exchange agreement. The employee agrees to provide services for the employer in exchange for a current wage, a pension benefit, and frequently other benefits such as death, dental, disability. Although pension benefits and some other benefits are not paid currently, they represent deferred compensation that must be accounted for as part of the employee's total compensation package.

Pension benefits usually are paid to retired employees or their survivors on a periodic basis, but may be paid in a single lump sum. Other benefits, such as death and disability, may also be provided through a pension plan. Most pension plans also provide benefits upon early retirement or termination of service.

A pension plan may be contributory or noncontributory; that is, the employees may be required to contribute to the plan (contributory), or the entire cost of the plan may be borne by the employer (noncontributory). A pension plan may be funded or unfunded; that is, the employees and/or the employer may make cash contributions to a pension plan trustee (funded), or the employer may make only credit entries on its books reflecting the pension liability under the plan (unfunded).

PRACTICE NOTE: A qualified pension plan under the Employee Retirement Income Security Act (ERISA) has to be funded. Every year the plan actuary must determine the minimum funding for the defined benefit pension plan. If the plan fails to meet the minimum funding requirement, a penalty tax is imposed on the employer on the funding deficiency.

Although interest cost on the pension liability and the expected return on a pension plan's assets increase or decrease net periodic pension cost, they are considered financial costs rather than employee compensation costs. Financial costs can be controlled by the manner in which the employer provides financing for the pension plan. An employer can eliminate interest cost by funding the plan completely or by purchasing annuity contracts to settle all pension obligations. The return on plan assets can be increased by the contribution of more assets to the pension fund.

Pension Plan Accounting

The assets of a pension plan usually are kept in a trust account, segregated from the assets of the employer. The employer makes periodic contributions to the pension trust account and, if the plan is contributory, so do employees. The plan assets are invested in stocks, bonds, real estate, and other types of investments. Plan assets are increased by contributions and earnings and gains on investments and are decreased by losses on investments, payment of pension benefits, and administrative expenses. The employer usually cannot withdraw plan assets placed in a trust account. An exception arises, however, when the plan assets exceed the pension obligation and the plan is terminated. In this event, the pension plan agreement may permit the employer to withdraw the excess amount of plan assets, providing that all other existing pension plan obligations have been satisfied by the employer. Under GAAP, pension plan assets that are not effectively restricted for the payment of pension benefits or segregated in a trust are not considered pension plan assets.

Accounting and reporting for a pension plan (defined benefit plan) as a separate reporting entity are covered by ASC 960 (Plan Accounting—Defined Benefit Pension Plans).

Deferred Compensation Plan

A deferred compensation plan is a contractual agreement that specifies that a portion of the employee's compensation will be set aside and paid in future periods as retirement benefits. ASC 715 covers deferred compensation plans that are in substance pension plans.

Postemployment and postretirement benefits generally are considered a form of deferred compensation to an employee because an employer provides these types of benefits in exchange for an employee's services. Thus, these benefits must be measured properly and recognized in the financial statements and, if the amount is material, financial statement disclosure may be required. For convenient discussion, this chapter uses the term *postretirement benefits* to mean postretirement benefits other than pensions. Practice sometimes uses the abbreviation "OPEB" (other postretirement employee benefits) with the same meaning.

POSTEMPLOYMENT BENEFITS

ASC 715 also specifies GAAP for postemployment benefits and generally applies to benefits provided to former or inactive employees, their beneficiaries, and covered dependents after employment, but before retirement. Benefits may be provided in cash or in kind and may be paid as a result of a disability, layoff, death, or other event. Benefits may be paid immediately upon cessation of active employment, or over a specified period of time.

Postemployment benefits that meet the following requirements are accounted for as follows (ASC 712-10-25-4):

- The employer's obligation relating to employees' rights to receive compensation for future compensated absences is attributable to employees' services already rendered.
- The obligation relates to rights that vest or accumulate.
- Payment of the compensation is probable.
- The amount can be estimated reasonably.

Postemployment benefits that are covered by ASC 715 but do not meet the above criteria are accounted for in accordance with ASC 450. ASC 450 requires recognition of a loss contingency, including a liability for postemployment benefits, when the following conditions are met (ASC 715-10-25-5):

- Information available prior to issuance of the financial statements indicates that it is probable that an asset has been impaired or a liability incurred at the date of the financial statements.
- The amount of loss can be reasonably estimated.

ASC 715—Compensation—Retirement Benefits

If an obligation for postemployment benefits is not accrued in accordance with either ASC 712 (Compensation—Nonretirement Postemployment Benefits) or ASC 450 only because the amount cannot be estimated, the financial statements shall disclose that fact (ASC 712-10-50-2).

Illustrations of Accruals Required by ASC 715

ASC 715 amends ASC 710 with regard to the method of accruing an employer's obligation under deferred compensation contracts that are not tantamount to a plan for pension or other postretirement benefits. ASC 715 requires the employer to make periodic accruals, so that the cost of the deferred compensation is attributed to the appropriate years of an employee's service, in accordance with the terms of the contract between the employer and that employee.

PRACTICE NOTE: The employer must make the attribution in a systematic and rational manner. By the time an employee becomes fully eligible for the deferred compensation specified in the contract, the accrued amount should equal the then present value of the expected future payments of deferred compensation.

Illustrations of Accruals Required by ASC 715

Example 1: Employee must remain in service for a number of years to be eligible for the deferred compensation.

A deferred compensation contract with a newly hired employee provides for a payment of $100,000 upon termination of employment, provided the employee remains in service for at least four years.

The employer makes annual accruals during each of the first four years of this employee's service, to recognize the portion of deferred compensation cost attributable to each of these years. To make these annual accruals, the employer starts by making reasonable assumptions about (a) the employee's anticipated retirement date and (b) the discount rate for making computations of present value.

If the employer assumes that the employee will remain in service for a total of nine years (including five years after becoming fully eligible for the deferred compensation), and the discount rate is 8%, the present value of the $100,000 deferred compensation at the end of the fourth year will be $68,058 (present value of $100,000 payable at the end of five years at 8% discount).

Accruals are made for each of the first four years, so that the balance in the accrued liability account at the end of the fourth year will be $68,058. The simplest way to accomplish this is on a straight-line basis, as follows:

Accrued amount anticipated at end of fourth year	$68,058
Annual accrual during each of first four years (1/4 of $68,058)	$17,015

This computation results in the recognition of $17,015 deferred compensation cost during each of the first four years of the employee's service. The balance in the accrued liability account at the end of the fourth year, when the employee is eligible to terminate and collect the deferred compensation, is

$68,058, the present value of the $100,000 deferred compensation payable five years later. (The five years represent the anticipated total service of nine years, less the four years already served.)

Next, assume the employee remains in service throughout the fifth year and is still expected to complete the nine-year term originally anticipated. The accrued liability is adjusted as of the end of the fifth year to reflect the present value of the deferred compensation, which is $73,503 (present value of $100,000 payable at the end of four years at 8% discount).

The cost recognized for the fifth year will therefore be $5,445, determined as follows:

Accrued amount at end of fifth year	$ 73,503
Accrued amount at end of fourth year	(68,058)
Cost recognized in fifth year	$ 5,445

Example 2: *Employee is eligible in the same year the contract is signed.*

An employee is hired on January 1, 20X8. The contract provides for a payment of $20,000 upon termination of employment, provided the employee remains in service for at least six months. The employer anticipates that the employee will remain in service for three years. The assumed discount rate is 8%.

The employee is still in service at the end of calendar year 20X8. Having completed at least six months of service, the employee is eligible to terminate and collect the deferred compensation. The accrual as of December 31, 20X8, is $17,147, the present value of $20,000 payable at the end of two years at 8% discount. (The two years represent the originally anticipated service of three years, less the one year of 20X8 already served.) The entire amount of the accrual is recognized as a deferred compensation cost in 20X8, since the employee achieved full eligibility by the end of the year.

If the employee remains in service throughout 20X9 and all assumptions remain unchanged, the amount of the accrued liability as of December 31, 20X9, is adjusted to $18,519, the present value of $20,000 at the end of one year at 8% discount.

The cost recognized in 20X9 is therefore $1,372, determined as follows:

Accrued amount at end of 20X9	$18,519
Accrued amount at end of 20X8	(17,147)
Cost recognized in 20X9	$1,372

ASC 715-20: DEFINED BENEFIT PLANS—GENERAL

FINANCIAL STATEMENT DISCLOSURE

Disclosures about Pension Plans and Other Postretirement Plans

ASC 715 requires the following information to be provided for each period for which an income statement is presented (ASC 715-20-50-1):

- Reconciliation of beginning and ending balances of the benefit obligation showing separately the effects of service cost, interest cost, contributions by plan participants, actuarial gains and losses, changes in foreign cur-

rency exchange rates, benefits paid, plan amendments, business combinations, divestitures, curtailments, settlements, and special termination benefits
- Reconciliation of beginning and ending balances of the fair value of plan assets, showing separately the effects of actual return on plan assets, changes in foreign currency exchange rates, contributions by the employer, contributions by plan participants, benefits paid, business combinations, divestitures, and settlements
- Funded status of the plan, and the amounts recognized in the statement of financial position, with separate disclosure of assets, current liabilities, and noncurrent liabilities
- Information about plan assets:
  - For each class of plan assets, the percentage of the fair value of total plan assets held as of the financial statement date
  - Narrative description of investment policies and strategies
  - Narrative description of the basis used to determine the overall expected long-term rate-of-return-on-asset assumption
  - Additional asset categories and additional information about specific assets within a category are encouraged if they are expected to be useful in understanding the risks associated with each asset category and its expected long-term rate of return
  - The amount and timing of any plan assets expected to be returned to the employer (plan sponsor) over the next year, or operating cycle if longer
- For defined benefit pension plans, the accumulated benefit obligation
- The benefits expected to be paid in each of the next five fiscal years and in the aggregate for the five fiscal years thereafter
- The employer's best estimate of contributions expected to be paid to the plan during the next fiscal year beginning after the date of the latest statement of financial position
- The amount of net periodic benefit cost recognized, showing separately the service cost component, the interest cost component, the expected return on plan assets, the transition asset or obligation component, the gain or loss component, the prior service cost or credit component, and amount of gains or losses recognized due to a plan settlement or curtailment
- The net gain or loss and prior service cost or credit included in other comprehensive income during the period
- The net gain or loss, prior service cost or credit, and transition asset or obligation included in net periodic benefit cost during the period and removed from accumulated other comprehensive income via an entry to other comprehensive income
- Amounts included in accumulated other comprehensive income and not yet recognized as a component of net periodic benefit cost, separately

showing the net gain or loss, net prior service cost or credit, and net transition asset or obligation

- Amounts included in accumulated other comprehensive income and expected to be included as a component of net periodic benefit cost in the next fiscal year, separately showing the net gain or loss, net prior service cost or credit, and net transition asset or liability to be recognized
- On a weighted-average basis, the following assumptions: assumed discount rates, rates of compensation increase, and expected long-term rates of return on plan assets
- Assumed health care cost trend rates for the next year used to determine expected cost of benefits covered by the plan, and a general description of the direction and pattern of change in the assumed trend rates thereafter
- The effect of a one-percentage increase and a one-percentage decrease in the assumed health care cost trend rates on the aggregate of the service and interest cost components of net periodic postretirement health care benefit costs and the accumulated postretirement benefit obligation for health care benefits
- Amounts and types of securities of the employer and related parties included in the plan assets, the approximate future annual benefits of plan participants covered by insurance contracts issued by the employer or related parties, and any significant transactions between the employer or related parties and the plan during the period
- Any alternative method used to amortize prior service amounts or net gains and losses
- Any substantive commitments used as the basis for accounting for the benefit obligation
- The cost of providing special or contractual termination benefits recognized during the period and a description of the nature of the event
- Explanation of any significant change in the benefit obligation or plan assets not otherwise apparent from the other disclosures required

Disclosures by Employers with Two or More Plans

Employers with two or more plans shall aggregate information for all defined benefit pension plans and for all other defined benefit postretirement plans unless disaggregating in groups is considered to provide more useful information. Disclosures about pension plans with assets in excess of the accumulated benefit obligation generally may be aggregated with disclosures about pension plans with accumulated obligations in excess of assets. The same is true for other postretirement benefit plans. If aggregate disclosures are presented, the following information is required:

- The aggregate benefit obligation and aggregate fair value of plan assets for plans with benefit obligations in excess of plan assets
- The aggregate pension accumulated benefit obligation and aggregate fair values of plan assets for pension plans with accumulated benefit obligations in excess of plan assets (ASC 715-20-50-3).

The liability presented is current to the extent that the actuarial present value of benefits to be paid within the next year, or operating cycle if longer, exceeds the fair value of plan assets. This determination is to be made on a plan-by-plan basis. Otherwise, the liability is noncurrent (ASC 715-20-45-3).

Multiemployer Plan Disclosures

[See the *Multiple-Employer Plans* main section in this chapter for the disclosure requirements related to their plans.]

Reduced Disclosures for Nonpublic Companies

A nonpublic entity is not required to present the complete set of information identified earlier as being required for public entities. The required disclosures for a nonpublic entity are as follows (ASC 715-20-50-5):

- The benefit obligation, fair value of plan assets, and funded status of the plan.
- Employer contributions, participant contributions, and benefits paid.
- Information about plan assets:
  - For each class of plan assets (e.g., equity securities, debt securities, real estate), the percentage of the fair value of total plan asset held as of the measurement date used for each statement of financial position presented.
  - A narrative description of investment policies and strategies.
  - A narrative description of the basis used to determine the overall expected long-term rate-of-return-on-assets assumption.
  - Disclosure of additional asset categories and additional information about specific assets within a category is encouraged if that information is expected to be useful in understanding the risks associated with each asset category and the overall expected long-term rate of return on assets.
- For defined benefit pension plans, the accumulated benefit obligation.
- The benefits expected to be paid in each of the next five fiscal years, and in the aggregate for the five fiscal years thereafter.
- The employer's best estimate of contributions expected to be paid to the plan during the next fiscal year.
- The amounts recognized in the statements of financial position.
- The amount of net periodic benefit cost recognized, showing separately the service cost component, the interest cost component, the expected return on plan assets, the gain or loss component, the prior service cost or credit component, the transition asset or obligation component, and gain and loss from settlements or curtailments.

- On a weighted-average basis, the following assumptions used in the accounting for the plan: discount rates, rates of compensation increase, and expected long-term rates of return on plan assets.
- The assumed health care trend rates for the year used to measure the expected cost of benefits covered by the plan, and a general description of the direction and pattern of change in the assumed trend rates thereafter, and the ultimate trend rates and when those rates are expected to be achieved.
- If applicable, the amounts and types of securities of the employer and related parties included in plan assets, the approximate amount of future annual benefits of plan participants covered by insurance contracts issued by the employer or related parties, and any significant transactions between the employers and related parties and the plan during the period.
- The nature and effect of significant nonroutine events, such as amendments, combinations, divestitures, curtailments, and settlements.

A nonpublic entity that has more than one defined benefit pension plan or more than one other defined benefit postretirement plan shall provide the required information separately for pension plans and other postretirement benefit plans.

Disclosures in Interim Financial Reports

A publicly traded entity shall disclose the following information in its financial statements that include an income statement:

- The amount of net periodic benefit cost recognized for each period for which an income statement is presented with separate disclosure of the components of net periodic benefit cost
- The total amount of the employee's contributions paid, or expected to be paid, during the current year if significantly different from amounts previously disclosed

A nonpublic entity is required to disclose its best estimate of its contributions expected to be paid to the plan during the next fiscal year beginning after the date of the latest statement of financial position presented. In addition, a nonpublic entity shall disclose in interim periods for which a complete set of financial statements are presented the total amount of the employer's contributions paid and expected to be paid if significantly different from its disclosure in the immediately preceding annual report.

ASC 715-30: DEFINED BENEFIT PLANS—PENSION

OVERVIEW OF PENSION PLAN ACCOUNTING

Scope and Applicability

Most of the provisions of ASC 715 address *defined benefit pension plans* of single employers. A defined benefit pension plan is one that contains a pension benefit formula, which generally describes the amount of pension benefit that each employee will receive for services performed during a specified period of employment (ASC 715-30-05-1). The amount of the employer's periodic contribution to a defined benefit pension plan is based on the total pension benefits (projected to employees' normal retirement dates) that could be earned by all eligible participants.

In contrast, a *defined contribution pension plan* does not contain a pension benefit formula, but generally specifies the periodic amount that the employer must contribute to the pension plan and how that amount will be allocated to the eligible employees who perform services during that same period. Each periodic employer contribution is allocated among separate accounts maintained for each employee, and pension benefits are based solely on the amount available in each employee's account at the time of his or her retirement.

For the purposes of ASC 715, any plan that is not a defined contribution pension plan is considered a defined benefit pension plan (see definition of *defined benefit pension plan* in ASC Glossary).

ASC 715 requires that its provisions be applied to any arrangement, expressed or implied, that is similar in substance to a pension plan, regardless of its form or method of financing. Thus, a pension plan arrangement does not have to be in writing if the existence of a pension plan is implied by company policy. A qualified plan, however, has to be in writing under ERISA, as well as for federal and state tax purposes. Frequently, defined contribution pension plans provide for some method of determining defined benefits for employees, as may be the case with some *target benefit* plans. A target benefit plan is a defined contribution plan. The benefit defined in the document is only for the purpose of determining the contribution to be allocated to each participant's account. It is not intended to promise any benefit in the future. If, in substance, a plan does provide defined benefits for employees, it is accounted for as a defined benefit pension plan.

Actuarial Assumptions

Actuarial assumptions are factors used to calculate the estimated cost of pension plan benefits. Employee mortality, employee turnover, retirement age, administrative expenses of the pension plan, interest earned on plan assets, and the date on which a benefit becomes fully vested are some of the more important actuarial assumptions (ASC Glossary).

Under ASC 715, each significant actuarial assumption must reflect the best estimate for that particular assumption. In the absence of evidence to the contrary, all actuarial assumptions are made on the basis that the pension plan will continue in existence (going-concern concept) (ASC 715-30-35-42).

Discount rates used in actuarial valuations reflect the rates at which the pension benefits could be settled effectively. In selecting appropriate interest rates, employers should refer to current information on rates used in annuity contracts that could be purchased to settle pension obligations, including annuity rates published by the Pension Benefit Guaranty Corporation (PBGC), or the rates of return on high-quality fixed-income investments that are expected to be available through the maturity dates of the pension benefits (ASC 715-30-35-43).

The chosen discount rate should produce a liability amount that would generate the necessary future cash flows to pay pension benefits as they become due, if such amount was invested at the financial statement date in a portfolio of high-quality fixed-income investments. This liability amount is theoretically equal to the market value of a portfolio of high-quality zero coupon bonds, where each bond matches the amount and maturity of future payments due under the pension plan. However, reinvestment risk exists to the extent that the pension plan's assets include interest-bearing debt instruments (rather than only zero coupon bonds) and to the extent that plan investments have a maturity date less than some of the anticipated pension payments. In such cases, the assumed discount (interest) rate needs to consider expected reinvestment rates extrapolated using the existing yield curve at the financial statement date. The discount rate should be reevaluated at each measurement (financial statement) date (ASC 715-30-35-44).

PRACTICE POINTER: The discount rate used to determine the pension liability and the interest cost component of net periodic pension cost should change in accordance with changes in market interest rates—if interest rates rise the discount rate should increase, if interest rates fall the discount rate should decline. In addition, the determination of the discount rate is separate from the determination of the expected return on plan assets.

An actuarial gain or loss is the difference between an actuarial assumption and actual experience. Under ASC 715, actuarial gains and losses that are not included in determining net periodic pension cost in the year in which they arise are included in other comprehensive income, and they may be included as a component of net periodic pension cost in subsequent periods if certain criteria are met (ASC 715-30-35-18, 19).

PRACTICE POINTER: In accounting for pension plans—particularly defined benefit plans—the CPA relies heavily on the expertise of actuaries. Actuaries are educated in mathematics, modeling, and other areas that permit them to deal with the many uncertainties required to make estimates related to an enterprise's pension plan that are necessary for both funding and financial reporting. Actuarial assumptions are one area where the CPA is particularly vulnerable, because of the significant impact that different actuarial assumptions may have on the elements of the financial statements. Essentially, the CPA's responsibility is to be generally familiar with the actuary's work and to approach the results of the actuary's work with the professional skepticism that is typical of the CPA's work in many areas. The guidance in CCH's *GAAS Guide* AU Section 336 "Using the Work of a Specialist" is particularly germane when the CPA needs to rely on the work of an actuary.

Pension Plan Assets

The resources of a pension plan may be converted into (a) plan assets that are invested to provide pension benefits for the participants of the plan, such as stocks, bonds, and other investments (ASC Glossary) or (b) plan assets that are used in the operation of the plan, such as real estate, furniture, and fixtures (ASC 715-30-35-52). Plan assets must be segregated in a trust or otherwise effectively restricted so that the employer cannot use them for other purposes. Under ASC 715, plan assets do not include amounts accrued by an employer as net periodic pension cost, but not yet paid to the pension plan. Plan assets may include securities of the employer if they are freely transferable (ASC Glossary).

Pension plan assets that are held as investments to provide pension benefits are measured at fair value (ASC Glossary). (Additional guidance on determining fair values can be found in Chapter 49, *ASC 820—Fair Value Measurement and Disclosure.*) Pension plan assets that are used in the operation of the plan are measured at cost, less accumulated depreciation or amortization (ASC 715-30-35-52). All plan assets are measured as of the date of the financial statements or, if used consistently from year to year, as of a date not more than three months prior to that date (ASC 715-30-35-62).

> **PRACTICE NOTE:** ASC 715 requires pension plan assets and liabilities to be measured as of the financial statement date.

For the purposes of ASC 715, plan liabilities that are incurred, other than for pension benefits, may be considered reductions of plan assets (ASC Glossary).

Recording Pension Events

Under ASC 715 an enterprise makes three primary types of entries in its records each accounting period:

1. To record net periodic pension cost
2. To record funding of the pension plan
3. To recognize the funded status of the pension plan

Illustration of Basic Entries to Record Pension Events

Maddux Co. determines its net periodic pension cost to be $10,000 for 20X7, its first year of operation. An equal amount is funded by transferring cash to the insurance company that administers the plan. The fair value of Maddux's pension plan assets equals the pension liability at year end. The applicable tax rate is 35%. The entries to record these events areas follow:

Net periodic pension cost	10,000	
Deferred tax asset	3,500	
Deferred tax benefit—net income		3,500
Liability for pension benefits		10,000
Liability for pension benefits	10,000	
Cash		10,000

In this case, the fair value of the pension plan assets and liabilities are equal so there is no need for a third journal entry, to recognize a pension plan asset (overfunded plan) or a pension plan liability (underfunded plan).

As this illustration shows, the transfer of cash to the plan administrator is treated as a retirement of the pension liability. Most of the provisions of ASC 715 pertain to the computation of the amount to be recorded in the first journal entry type in the above illustration as net periodic pension cost. This computation requires numerous worksheet calculations, which are illustrated throughout ASC 715.

Pension Plan Terminology

Key terms that are important for an understanding of accounting for pensions in accordance with ASC 715 are discussed below.

Projected Benefit Obligation

Projected benefit obligation is the actuarial present value, as of a specified date, of the total cost of all employees' vested and nonvested pension benefits that have been attributed by the pension benefit formula to services performed by employees to that date.

The projected benefit obligation includes the actuarial present value of all pension benefits (vested and nonvested) attributed by the pension benefit formula, *including consideration of future employee compensation levels* (ASC Glossary). Vested benefits are pension benefits that an employee has an irrevocable right to receive at a date specified in the pension agreement, even if the employee does not continue to work for the employer (ASC Glossary). In the event a pension plan is discontinued, a vested benefit obligation remains a liability of the employer.

Payments of pension benefits decrease both the projected benefit obligation and the fair value of plan assets, while contributions to a plan decrease cash and the financial statement liability.

The projected benefit obligation does not appear on the books of the employer, but the difference between the projected benefit obligation and the fair value of the pension plan's assets (i.e., the funded status of the plan) is recognized as a pension plan asset or liability. In addition, the employer maintains a record of the projected benefit obligation.

Accumulated Benefit Obligation

Accumulated benefit obligation is an alternative measure of the pension obligation; it is calculated like the projected benefit obligation, except that current or past compensation levels instead of projected future compensation levels are used to determine pension benefits (ASC Glossary). In the event a pension plan is discontinued, the balance of any unfunded accumulated benefit obligation remains a liability of the employer.

PRACTICE NOTE: Basically, there are two types of pension benefit formulas: pay-related benefit and non-pay-related benefit. For a non-pay-related benefit formula, the accumulated benefit obligation and the projected benefit obligation are the same.

Fair Value of Plan Assets

Fair value of plan assets is determined in accordance with the guidance in ASC 820 (Fair Value Measurements and Disclosures). (Additional guidance on determining fair values can be found in the chapter of this *Guide* that discusses ASC 820.) The fair value of pension plan investments should be reduced by brokerage commissions and other selling costs if these are likely to be significant (ASC 715-30-35-50). Plan assets that are used in the operation of the pension plan (building, equipment, furniture, fixtures, etc.) are valued at cost less accumulated depreciation or amortization (ASC 715-30-35-52).

Pension plan assets are recorded on the books of the pension plan. However, an employer maintains records of the cost and fair value of all pension plan assets.

Funded Status of Plan

For the employer's accounting purposes, *funded status of plan* is the difference between the projected benefit obligation and the fair value of plan assets as of a given date (ASC Glossary). If the projected benefit obligation exceeds the fair value of the plan assets, a pension plan liability exists. If the fair value of plan assets exceeds the projected benefit obligation, a pension plan asset exists. ASC 715 requires that the employer recognize a pension plan asset or liability in its statement of financial position.

Prior Service Cost or Credit

Unrecognized prior service cost is the cost of retroactive benefits granted in a plan amendment. Upon the initial adoption of a pension plan or through a plan amendment, certain employees may be granted pension benefits for services performed in prior periods. These retroactive pension benefits are referred to as *prior service costs*, and usually are granted by the employer with the expectation that they will produce future economic benefits, such as reducing employee turnover, improving employee productivity, and minimizing the need to increase future employee compensation. If retroactive benefits are granted in a plan amendment the employer debits other comprehensive income and credits the liability for pension benefits. In addition, an employer is required to amortize any prior service cost in equal amounts over the future periods of active employees who are expected to receive the benefits (ASC 715-30-35-10). The amortization of prior service cost is included as a component of net periodic pension cost.

An employer may amend a pension plan to reduce pension benefits. This results in a prior service credit and is recorded by reducing the liability for pension benefits and increasing other comprehensive income. Any prior service credit is first applied to reduce any prior service cost remaining in accumulated other comprehensive income. Any balance remaining is amortized as a component of net periodic pension cost in a similar manner to the amortization of prior service cost (ASC 715-30-35-17).

An employer does not establish a general ledger account for prior service cost—rather any increase in this amount directly affects other comprehensive income and the liability for pension benefits, but the employer does maintain worksheet records of such amounts.

Gain or Loss

Gain or loss results in a change in either plan assets or the projected benefit obligation as a result of actual results that differ from expectations or changes in actuarial assumptions. For example, gains or losses arise from the difference between (*a*) the actual and expected amount of projected benefit obligation at the end of a period and/or (*b*) the actual and expected amount of the fair value of pension plan assets at the end of the period. Gains and losses are recognized by adjusting other comprehensive income and the liability for pension benefits. In addition, gains and losses may be recognized as a component of net periodic benefit cost in subsequent periods if certain criteria are met (ASC 715-30-35-18, 19, 21).

A gain or loss that, as of the beginning of the year, exceeds 10% of the greater of (*a*) the projected benefit obligation or (*b*) the market-related value of plan assets is subject to recognition. Recognition for the year is equal to the amount of the gain or loss in excess of 10% of the greater of the projected benefit obligation or the value of plan assets, divided by the average remaining service period of active employees expected to receive benefits under the plan. This frequently is referred to as the *corridor test* in applying ASC 715 (ASC 715-30-35-24). The gain or loss that is subject to the corridor test is included in the balance of accumulated other comprehensive income and, if recognized, is removed from accumulated other comprehensive income (through recognition in other comprehensive income in the current period) with the offsetting entry affecting net periodic pension cost.

An employer does not establish general ledger accounts for pension gains and losses. Rather, any changes in these amounts directly affect other comprehensive income and the liability for pension benefits; however, the employer does maintain worksheet records of such amounts.

NET PERIODIC PENSION COST

The employer's *net periodic pension cost* represents the net amount of pension cost for a specified period that is charged against income. Under ASC 715, the components of net periodic pension cost are (*a*) service cost, (*b*) interest cost on the projected benefit obligation, (*c*) actual return on plan assets, (*d*) amortization of prior service cost or credit (if any), (*e*) recognition of gain or loss (if required by ASC 715), and (*f*) amortization of any transition obligation or asset that remains and that is included in accumulated other comprehensive income (ASC 715-30-35-4).

All of the components of net periodic pension cost are not necessarily recognized in determining income in the year when they arise. For example, the total prior service cost that results from a plan amendment is determined in the period in which it arises. Under the provisions of ASC 715, however, the employer recognizes cost in equal amounts over the future service periods of each active employee who is expected to receive the benefits of the plan amendment that gave rise to the prior service cost (ASC 715-30-35-10).

Net periodic pension cost is estimated in advance at the beginning of a period based on actuarial assumptions relating to (a) the discount rate on the projected benefit obligation, (b) the expected long-term rate of return on pension plan assets, and (c) the average remaining service periods of active employees covered by the pension plan. At the end of the period, adjustments are made to account for the differences (actuarial gains or losses), if any, between the estimated and actual amounts (ASC 715-30-35-4).

The actuarial assumptions used to calculate the previous year's net periodic pension cost are used to calculate that cost in subsequent interim financial statements, unless more current valuations of plan assets and obligations are available or a significant event has occurred, such as a plan amendment, which usually would require new valuations (ASC 715-30-35-68).

The following illustration shows how the different components of net periodic pension cost are estimated.

Illustration of Computing Net Periodic Pension Cost

Service cost component	$2,000
Interest cost component	3,000
Return on plan assets	(2,500)
Amortization of prior service cost	1,000
Amortization of (gain) or loss	1,000
Amortization of transition obligation (asset)	1,500
Total net periodic pension cost	$6,000

For simplicity, an assumption is made that there are no differences (actuarial gains or losses) between the estimated and actual amounts at the end of the period, and that the employer made no contributions to the pension fund during the period.

		Beginning of period	End of period
(a)	Projected benefit obligation	$(115,000)	$(120,000)
(b)	Fair value of plan assets	65,000	67,500
(c)	Funded status of plan	$ (50,000)	$ (52,500)
(d)	Prior service cost	10,000	9,000
(e)	(Gain) or loss	5,000	4,000
(f)	Transition obligation or asset at date of initial application of pension plan accounting	35,000	33,500
(g)	Balance in accumulated other comprehensive income related to the pension plan	$ 50,000	$ 46,500
(h)	Reduction in net income during the period related to the pension plan		$ (6,000)

ASC 715—Compensation—Retirement Benefits

The following journal entries are recorded to record the initial funded status of the pension plan and to recognize net periodic pension cost during the year (and to transfer amounts out of accumulated other comprehensive income) (tax effects are not considered):

Accumulated other comprehensive income	50,000	
Liability for pension benefits		50,000
Net periodic pension cost	2,500	
Liability for pension benefits		2,500
Net periodic benefit cost	3,500	
Other comprehensive income		3,500

The following explains the changes in the accounts that were affected by the net periodic pension cost accrual.

(a) *Projected benefit obligation* An increase in the projected benefit obligation of $5,000, representing the service cost component of $2,000 and interest cost component of $3,000 for the period. The projected benefit obligation is not recorded in the employer's books, but is important information in accounting for pension cost.

(b) *Fair value of plan assets* The $2,500 increase in the fair value of plan assets, between the beginning and end of the period, represents the increase in the fair value of plan assets for the period. The fair value of plan assets is not recorded in the employer's books, but is important information in accounting for pension cost.

(c) *Funded status of plan* The $2,500 decrease in the funded status of the plan, between the beginning and end of the period, is the difference between the $5,000 increase in the projected benefit obligation for the period and the $2,500 increase in the fair value of plan assets for the period.

(d) *Prior service cost* The $1,000 decrease in prior service cost, between the beginning and end of the period, is the amount of amortization of prior service cost that has been recognized by the employer as a component of net periodic pension cost.

Prior service cost is not recorded on the books of the employer, but records are maintained for such amounts. Thus, the employer reduces the balance of the unrecognized prior service cost by $1,000. However, prior service cost is included in accumulated other comprehensive income until it is recognized as a component of net periodic pension cost.

(e) *Gain or loss* The $1,000 decrease in the gain or loss (actuarial gain or loss), between the beginning and end of the period, is the amount of amortization that has been recognized by the employer as a component of net periodic pension cost.

Gain or loss (actuarial gain or loss) is not recorded on the books of the employer, but records are maintained for such amounts. Thus, the employer reduces the balance of the unrecognized net gain or loss by $1,000. As above, the gain or loss is included in accumulated other comprehensive income until it is recognized as a component of net periodic pension cost.

(f) *Transition obligation or transition asset at date of initial application of pension plan accounting* The $1,500 decrease in the transition obligation, between the beginning and the end of the period, is the amount of amortization that has been recognized by the employer as a component of net periodic pension cost for the period.

The transition obligation or asset is not recorded on the books of the employer, but records are maintained for such amounts. Thus, the employer reduces the balance of the unrecognized net obligation or net asset by $1,500. As above, the transition obligation or asset is included in accumulated other comprehensive income until it is recognized as a component of net periodic pension cost.

(g) *Balance in accumulated other comprehensive income related to the pension plan* At the beginning of the year, the entire unfunded status of the pension plan is due to amounts for prior service cost, gain or loss, and transition obligation that have not yet been recognized as a component of net periodic benefit cost. By the end of the year, the balance in accumulated other comprehensive income is reduced to $46,500 because $3,500 of these amounts were included in net periodic pension cost during the year.

(h) *Reduction in net income during the period related to the pension plan* Net income is reduced during the year by the amount of net periodic pension cost, $6,000. The unfunded status of the pension plan, $52,500, now comprises two components: amounts for prior service cost, gain or loss, and transition obligations that have not yet been recognized as a component of net periodic benefit cost equal $46,500. The remaining $6,000 represents the pension cost for the period, none of which has been funded (i.e., the employer made no contributions to the plan during the period).

Service Cost Component

In a defined benefit pension plan, ASC 715 requires that a pension benefit formula be used to determine the amount of pension benefit earned by each employee for services performed during a specified period. Under ASC 715, attribution is the process of assigning pension benefits or cost to periods of employee service, in accordance with the pension benefit formula (ASC Glossary).

The service cost component of net periodic pension cost is defined as the actuarial present value of pension benefits attributed by the pension benefit formula to employee service during a specified period (ASC Glossary). For example, a pension benefit formula may state that an employee shall receive, at the retirement age stated in the plan, a pension benefit of $20 per month for life, for each year of service. To compute the total future value of the pension benefit for the year, the monthly benefit is multiplied by the number of months in the employee's life expectancy at retirement age. This number of months is determined by reference to mortality tables. The actuarial present value of all employees' future pension benefits that are earned during a period is computed and included as the service cost component of the net periodic pension cost for the same period (ASC 715-30-35-36).

If the terms of the pension benefit formula provide for benefits based on estimated future compensation levels of employees, estimates of those future compensation levels are used to determine the service cost component of net periodic pension cost. For example, if the pension benefit formula states that an employee's benefit for a period is equal to 1% of his or her final pay, an estimate of the employee's final pay is used to calculate the benefit for the period. Assumed compensation levels should reflect the best estimate of the future compensation levels of the employee involved and be consistent with assumed discount rates to the extent that they both incorporate expectation of the same future economic conditions. Thus, future compensation levels in final-pay plans or career-average-pay plans are reflected in the service cost component of net periodic pension cost. Assumed compensation levels also shall reflect changes because of general price levels, productivity, seniority, promotion, and other factors (ASC 715-30-35-31).

Changes resulting from a plan amendment that has become effective and automatic benefit changes specified by the terms of the pension plan, such as cost-of-living increases, are included in the determination of service cost for a period (ASC 715-30-35-35).

An employer's substantive commitment to make future plan amendments in recognition of employees' prior services may indicate pension benefits in excess of those reflected in the existing pension benefit formula. Such a commitment may be evidenced by a history of regular increases in non-pay-related benefits, benefits under a career-average pay plan, or other evidence. In this event, ASC 715 requires that the pension plan be accounted for based on the employer's substantive commitment, and that appropriate disclosure be made in the employer's financial statements (ASC 715-30-35-34).

A plan's pension benefit formula might provide no benefits for the first 19 years of an employee's service and a vested benefit of $1,000 per month for life in the 20th year of an employee's service. This benefit pattern is no different than providing a benefit of $50 per month for 20 years and requiring 20 years before the benefits vest. If a pension plan benefit formula attributes all or a disproportionate portion of total pension benefits to later years, the employee's *total projected benefit* is calculated and used as the basis of assigning the total pension benefits under the plan. In this event, the employee's total projected benefit is assumed to accumulate in proportion to the ratio of the total completed years of service to date to the total completed years of service as of the date the benefit becomes fully vested (ASC 715-30-35-38). An employee's total projected benefit from a pension plan is the actuarial present value of the total cost of pension benefits that the employee is likely to receive under the plan. If the pension benefit formula is based on future compensation, future compensation is used in calculating the employee's total projected benefit.

PRACTICE NOTE: Under current pension law, the longest a single employer can make an employee wait before receiving vested benefits is five years. For a multiemployer plan, the longest period is ten years.

In the event a pension benefit formula does not indicate the manner in which a specific benefit relates to specific services performed by an employee, the benefit shall be assumed to accumulate as follows (ASC 715-30-35-38):

- *If the benefit is includable in vested benefits* The benefit is accumulated in proportion to the ratio of total completed years of service to date to the total completed years of service as of the date the benefit becomes fully vested. A vested benefit is a benefit that an employee has an irrevocable right to receive. For example, an employee is entitled to receive a vested benefit whether or not he or she continues to work for the employer.

- *If the benefit is not includable in vested benefits* The benefit is accumulated in proportion to the ratio of completed years of service to date to the total projected years of service. (An example of a benefit that is not includable in vested benefits is a death or disability benefit that is payable only if death or disability occurs during the employee's active service.)

Interest Cost Component

The two factors used to determine the actuarial present value of a future pension benefit are (1) the probability that the benefit will be paid to the employee (through the use of actuarial assumptions) and (2) the time value of money (through the use of discounts for interest cost). The probability that a pension benefit will be paid is based on actuarial assumptions such as employee mortality, employee turnover, and the date the benefits become vested. An employer's liability for a retirement fund of $56,520 that is due in ten years is not equal to a present liability of $56,520. At an 8% discount rate the $56,520 has a present value of only $26,179. The $26,179 increases each year by the employer's interest cost of 8%, and in ten years grows to $56,520, if the 8% interest rate does not change.

ASC 715 requires an employer to recognize, as a component of net periodic pension cost, the interest cost on the projected benefit obligation. The interest cost is equal to the increase in the amount of the projected benefit obligation because of the passage of time (ASC Glossary).

PRACTICE NOTE: ASC 715 specifies that the interest cost component of net periodic pension cost shall **not** be considered to be interest for the purposes of applying the provisions of ASC 835 (Interest).

Actual Return on Plan Assets Component

The actual return on plan assets is equal to the difference between the fair value of plan assets at the beginning and end of a period, adjusted for employer and employee contributions (if a contributory plan) and pension benefit payments made during the period (ASC Glossary). *Fair value* is the amount that a pension plan could reasonably be expected to receive from a current sale of an investment in an orderly, nonforced transaction (ASC Glossary). Plan assets that are used in the operation of the pension plan (building, equipment, furniture, fixtures, etc.) are valued at cost, less accumulated depreciation or amortization (ASC 715-30-35-52).

A return on plan assets decreases the employer's cost of providing pension benefits to its employees, while a loss increases pension cost. Net periodic pension income can result from a significantly high return on pension plan assets during a period.

ASC 715 requires an employer to recognize, as a component of net periodic pension cost, the actual return (or loss) on pension plan assets (ASC 715-30-35-4).

Amortization of Prior Service Cost or Credit Component

Upon the initial adoption of a pension plan or as the result of a plan amendment, employees may be granted pension benefits for services performed in prior periods. These retroactive pension benefits are assumed to have been granted by the employer in the expectation that they will produce future economic benefits, such as reducing employee turnover, improving employee productivity, and minimizing the need for increasing future employee compensation. The cost of pension benefits that are granted retroactively to employees for services performed in prior periods is referred to as *prior service cost* (ASC 715-30-35-10).

Under ASC 715, only a portion of the total amount of prior service cost arising in a period, including retroactive benefits that are granted to retirees, is included in net periodic pension cost. ASC 715 requires that the total prior service cost arising in a period from an adoption or amendment of a plan be amortized in equal amounts over the future service periods of *active* employees who are expected to receive the retroactive benefits (ASC 715-30-35-1).

> **PRACTICE POINTER:** Because retirees are not expected to render future services, the cost of their retroactive benefits cannot be recognized over their remaining service periods. ASC 715 requires that the total prior service cost arising from a plan adoption or amendment, including the cost attributed to the benefits of retirees, amortized in equal amounts over the future service periods of only the active employees who are expected to receive benefits.

If substantially all of the participants of a pension plan are inactive, the prior service cost attributed to the benefits of the inactive participants are amortized over the remaining life expectancy of those participants (ASC 715-30-35-1).

> **PRACTICE NOTE:** ASC 715 addresses the method of amortizing that portion of the cost of retroactive plan amendments that affect benefits of inactive participants of a plan composed of substantially all inactive participants, but does not address the method of amortizing the portion of the cost of the same retroactive plan amendments that affect benefits of the active participants of the same plan (ASC 715-30-35-11). Two alternatives appear to be available. The first is that the cost of the active participants' benefits is charged to income of the period of the plan amendment. The second is that the cost of the **active** participants' benefits is amortized in the same manner as if the plan were not composed of substantially all inactive participants. In this event, the cost attributed to the retroactive benefits of the **active** participants of a plan composed of substantially all **inactive** participants is amortized in equal amounts over the future service periods of each active employee who is expected to receive the retroactive benefits.

ASC 715 permits the consistent use of an alternative approach that more rapidly amortizes the amount of prior service cost. For example, straight-line amortization of prior service cost over the average future service period of active employees who are expected to receive benefits under the plan is acceptable. If an alternative method is used to amortize prior service cost, it must be disclosed in the financial statements (ASC 715-30-35-13).

Some companies have a history of increasing pension benefits through regular plan amendments. In these cases, the period in which an employer expects to realize the economic benefits from retroactive pension benefits that were previously granted is shorter than the entire remaining future service period of all active employees. Under this circumstance, ASC 715 requires that a more rapid rate of amortization be applied to the remaining balance of the prior service cost to reflect the earlier realization of the employer's economic benefits and to allocate properly the cost to the periods benefited (ASC 715-30-35-14).

An amendment to a pension plan usually increases the cost of employees' pension benefits and increases the amount of the projected benefit obligation. However, a pension plan amendment may decrease the cost of employees' pension benefits, which results in a decrease in the amount of the projected benefit obligation and is referred to as a prior service credit. Any decrease resulting from a pension plan amendment is applied to reduce the balance of any existing prior service cost in accumulated other comprehensive income and any excess is amortized on the same basis as increases in prior service cost (ASC 715-30-35-17).

Gains and Losses Component

Gains and losses are changes in the amount of either the projected benefit obligation or pension plan assets, resulting from the differences between estimates or assumptions used and actual experience. A gain or loss can result from the difference between (*a*) the expected and actual amounts of the projected benefit obligation at the end of a period and/or (*b*) the expected and actual amounts of the fair value of pension plan assets at the end of a period. Technically, both of these types of gains and losses are considered *actuarial gains and losses*. Under ASC 715, however, a gain or loss resulting from a change in the projected benefit obligation is referred to as an *actuarial gain or loss*, while a gain or loss resulting from a change in the fair value of pension plan assets is referred to as a *net asset gain or loss*. For the purposes of ASC 715, the sources of these gains and losses are not distinguished separately, and they include amounts that have been realized as well as amounts that are unrealized (ASC 715-30-35-18).

Under ASC 715, the gains and losses component of net periodic pension cost consists of (*a*) the difference between the expected and actual returns on pension plan assets (net asset gain or loss) and (*b*) if required, amortization of any net gain or loss from previous periods and included in accumulated other comprehensive income (ASC 715-30-35-26).

As discussed in a previous section, the actual return on pension plan assets is equal to the difference between the fair value of pension plan assets at the beginning and end of a period, adjusted for any contributions and pension benefit payments made during that period. Fair value is the amount that a pension plan could reasonably be expected to receive from a current sale of an investment in an orderly, nonforced transaction (ASC Glossary).

The expected return on pension plan assets during the period is computed by multiplying the *market-related value* of plan assets by the *expected long-term rate of return*. The expected long-term rate of return is an actuarial assumption of the expected long-term rate of return that will be earned on plan assets during the period. Under ASC 715, the current rate of return earned on plan assets and the likely reinvestment rate of return should be considered in estimating the long-term rate of return on plan assets. The expected long-term rate of return on plan assets should reflect the average rate of earnings expected on plan investments (ASC 715-30-35-47).

To reduce the volatility of changes in the fair value of pension plan assets and the resulting effect on net periodic pension cost, ASC 715 requires the use of a market-related value for plan assets to compute the expected return on such assets during a period. Market-related value is used only to compute the expected return on pension plan assets for the period (expected return = market-related value × expected long-term rate of return) (ASC Glossary).

Under ASC 715, the market-related value of a plan asset can be either (*a*) the actual fair value of the pension plan asset or (*b*) a calculated value that recognizes, in a systematic and rational manner, the changes in the actual fair value of the pension plan asset over a period of not more than five years (ASC Glossary). In computing the market-related value of a pension plan asset, an enterprise may use actual fair value or a calculated value based on a five-year moving average of the changes in the actual fair value of the pension plan asset. In this event, the calculated market-related value would include only 20% of the total changes in the actual fair value of the pension plan asset that have occurred during the past five years. For example, if the actual fair value of a plan asset at the end of each of the last six years was $8,000, $10,000, $12,000, $14,000, $16,000, and $13,000, the net gain for the most recent five years is $5,000 ($2,000 + $2,000 + $2,000 + $2,000 −$3,000 = $5,000). In this event, only 20% of the $5,000 gain ($1,000) is included in computing the calculated market-related value of the pension plan asset for the current year.

The difference between the actual fair value of a pension plan asset and its calculated market-related value is the amount of net gain or loss from previous years that has not yet been recognized in the calculated market-related value.

Market-related value may be computed differently for each class of plan assets, but the method of computing it must be applied consistently from year to year for each class of plan assets. For example, fair value may be used for bonds and other fixed income investments, and a calculated market-related value for stocks and other equities (ASC Glossary).

Illustration of Computing Market-Related Value

For computing the market-related value of a particular class of plan assets as of the end of each period, an employer uses a calculated value that includes 20% of the gains and losses on the plan assets that have occurred over the last five years. The total market-related value of this particular class of plan assets at the beginning of calendar year 20X5 was $100,000. The total fair value of the plan assets was $120,000 at the beginning of 20X5 and $130,000 at the end of 20X5. Actual gains and losses for the past five years as of the beginning of 20X5 were: 20X0 $10,000; 20X1 $(8,000); 20X2 $12,000; 20X3 $10,000; 20X4 $(4,000); the result is a net gain of $20,000 for these five years. Employer's contributions to the plan for 20X5 are estimated at $2,000 and benefit payments expected to be paid from the plan in 20X5 are also $2,000. The expected long-term rate of return on plan assets for 20X5 is 10%. The computation of the estimated market-related value as of December 31, 20X5, for this particular class of plan assets is determined as follows:

Market-related value at the beginning of period	$100,000
Add:	
Expected return on assets for 20X5 (market-related value, multiplied by expected long-term rate of return ($100,000 × 10%)	10,000
20% of the net gain or loss for the last five years (20% × $20,000)	4,000
Employer's contribution	2,000
Benefit payments made from plan	(2,000)
Estimated market-related value, Dec. 31, 20X5	$114,000

Note: The difference between the fair value ($130,000) and market-related value ($114,000) of plan assets at the end of 20X5 is $16,000. This difference represents the amount of net gain from the five years to the beginning of 20X5 that has not yet been recognized in the market-related value of plan assets.

The expected return on plan assets is based on market-related values, which do not include all of the net asset gains and losses from previous years (unless market-related values are equal to fair values). Thus, net asset gains and losses may include both (*a*) gains and losses of previous years that have been included in market-related value and (*b*) gains and losses of previous years that have not yet been included in market-related value (ASC 715-30-35-22).

As mentioned above, ASC 715 does not require the recognition of any gains and losses as components of net periodic pension cost of the period in which they arise, except to the extent that the net asset gain or loss for the period offsets or supplements the actual return of pension plan assets for the period. However, gains and losses are recognized as a component of other comprehensive income as they occur. In subsequent years, however, all gains and losses, except those which have not yet been recognized in the market-related values of pension plan assets, are subject to certain minimum amortization provisions of ASC 715. Gains and losses that are amortized as a component of net periodic pension cost are removed from the beginning balance of accumulated other comprehensive income.

ASC 715 requires recognition of net gains or losses based on beginning-of-the-year balances. A net gain or loss that, as of the beginning of the year, exceeds 10% of (*a*) the projected benefit obligation or (*b*) the market-related value of plan assets, whichever is greater, is subject to recognition. The minimum recognition for the year is calculated by dividing the average remaining service period of active employees who are expected to receive benefits under the plan into the amount of net gain or loss that, as of the beginning of the year, exceeds 10 % of (*a*) the projected benefit obligation or (*b*) the market-related value of plan assets, whichever is greater. If substantially all of a plan's participants are inactive, however, the average remaining life expectancy of the inactive participants is divided into the excess net gain or loss subject to amortization. The computation of the minimum amortization required by ASC 715 is made each year based on beginning-of-the-year balances of unrecognized net gains or losses (ASC 715-30-35-24).

In lieu of the minimum amortization of net gains and losses specified by ASC 715, an employer may use an alternative method provided that the method (*a*) is systematic and applied consistently, (*b*) is applied to both gains and losses similarly, (*c*) reduces the unamortized balance included in accumulated other comprehensive income by an amount greater than the amount that would result from the minimum amortization method provided by ASC 715, and (*d*) is disclosed in the financial statements (ASC 715-30-35-25).

Illustration of Gains and Losses Component of Net Periodic Pension Cost

ABC Corporation has a remaining transition obligation of $400 on January 1, 20X5. ABC Corp. amortized $40 of this transition obligation in 20X5. The net asset (gain) or loss for 20X5, resulting from changes in actuarial assumptions, was a loss of $400, which was recognized in other comprehensive income. The market-related value of pension plan assets at the beginning of 20X6 is $1,600 and the average remaining service life of active employees is ten years.

The expected net periodic pension cost for 20X6 is $340, determined as follows: the sum of service cost $200, interest cost $240 (10%), amortization of unrecognized net asset loss $20, and amortization of the transition obligation $40, less a 10% expected return on plan assets of $160 (expected return = market-related value of plan assets of $1,600 × expected long-term rate of return of 10%). No contributions were made to the pension plan in 20X6.

	Actual 12/31/X5	Expected 12/31/X6	Actual 12/31/X6
(a) Projected benefit obligation	$(2,400)	$(2,840)	$(2,900)
(b) Fair value of plan assets	1,640	1,800	1,750
Funded status of plan	$ (760)	$(1,040)	$(1,150)
Prior service cost	0	0	0
Net (gain) or loss	400	380	490
Transition obligation existing at 12/31/X5	360	320	320

(a) The difference between the actual projected benefit obligation for 20X5 and the expected projected benefit obligation for 20X6 is $440, which consists of the expected service cost of $200, and the expected interest cost of $240. However, the actual projected benefit for 20X6 increased $500 over the actual projected benefit for 20X5. The difference between the expected increase in the projected benefit obligation of $440 and the actual increase of $500 represents a $60 actuarial loss. The $60 loss occurred because the actuarial assumptions used were different from actual experience.

The $40 amortization of the transition obligation does not affect the projected benefit obligation because the full amount of the transition obligation was recognized in the projected benefit obligation as of the date of the initial application of pension plan accounting.

(b) The difference between the actual fair value of plan assets for 20X5 and the expected fair value of plan assets for 20X6 is $160, which represents the 10% expected return on plan assets (market-related value of plan assets of $1,600 × 10%). However, the actual fair value of plan assets for 20X6 of $1,750 increased only $110 over the actual fair value of plan assets of $1,640 for 20X5. The difference between the expected increase in the fair value of plan assets of $160 and the actual increase of $110 represents a $50 net asset loss for the period. The loss occurred because the actual rate of return on pension plan assets was less than the expected rate of return.

Cost Components of Net Periodic Pension Cost for 20X6

ASC 715 requires financial statement disclosure of the amount of net periodic pension cost for the period. The disclosure shall indicate separately the service cost component, the interest cost component, the expected return on plan assets for the period, the amortization of the transition obligation or asset, gains and losses recognized, prior service cost recognized, and gain or loss recognized due to a settlement or curtailment (ASC 715-20-50-1).

Service cost	$200
Interest cost	240
Expected return on plan assets	(160)
Amortization of transition obligation	40
Amortization of prior service cost	0
Recognized net actuarial loss	20
Net periodic pension cost	$340

Note: A net asset gain or loss is not recognized in income in the period in which it arises (ASC 715-30-35-19). In this case, the net asset loss is $50—the difference between the expected return on plan assets, $160, and the actual return on plan assets, $110. The expected return on plan assets is included as a component of net periodic pension cost. Recognition of the net asset loss is deferred to future periods. However, the net asset gain or loss is included as a component of other comprehensive income.

Computation of the Amortization of the Net Gain or Loss for 20X6

Net (gain) or loss 1/1/X6	$400
Add asset gain or subtract asset loss not yet recognized in market-related values at 1/1 [difference between fair value of plan assets ($1,640) and market-related value ($1,600)]	40
Net (gain) or loss subject to the minimum amortization provisions of ASC 715	440
10% of the greater of the projected benefit obligation or market-related value at 1/1	(240)

Net (gain) or loss subject to amortization	$200
Amortization for 20X6 (over the ten-year average remaining service life of active employees)	$ 20

> **Note:** The net (gain) or loss at 1/1 must be adjusted to exclude asset gains and losses not yet reflected in market-related values, because gains and losses are not required to be amortized (ASC 715-30-35-22).

> **Note:** The $60 loss that occurred in 20X6 as a result of the difference between the expected and actual projected benefit obligation for 20X6, and the $50 loss that occurred in 20X6 as a result of the difference between the expected and actual fair value of plan assets for 20X6, will become subject to the minimum amortization provisions of ASC 715 as of 1/1/X7. The computation of the amount of net (gain) or loss as of 1/1/X7, is as follows:

Net asset (gain) or loss 1/1/X6		$400
Less: Amortization for 20X6		20
Net asset (gain) or loss 12/31/X6		380
Add: Actuarial net (gain) or loss for 20X6	$60	
Net asset (gain) or loss for 20X6	50	110
Net (gain) or loss as of 1/1/X7		$ 490

Amortization of the Transition Obligation or Transition Asset (as of the Date of Initial Application of Pension Plan Accounting)

The *funded status* of a pension plan for employer accounting purposes is equal to the difference between the projected benefit obligation and the fair value of pension plan assets. The funded status indicates whether the employer has underfunded or overfunded the pension plan.

The transition obligation or transition asset of a pension plan is determined by the employer as of the date of its financial statements of the beginning of the year in which pension plan accounting is initially applied. The transition obligation or transition asset is equal to the difference between the projected benefit obligation and fair value of pension plan assets, plus previously recognized unfunded accrued pension cost or less previously recognized prepaid pension cost.

A transition obligation or asset is amortized by the employer on a straight-line basis over the average remaining service period of employees expected to receive benefits under the plan, as of the date of initial application of the guidance that preceded the adoption of the ASC (i.e., FAS-87), except under the following circumstances:

- If the amortization period is less than 15 years, an employer may elect to use 15 years.
- If the plan is composed of all or substantially all inactive participants, the employer shall use those participants' average remaining life expectancy as the amortization period.

The above amortization method is also used to recognize any unrecognized net obligation or net asset of a defined contribution pension plan.

RECOGNITION OF FUNDED STATUS OF PENSION PLAN

An employer is required to recognize the overfunded or underfunded status of a defined benefit pension plan as an asset or a liability in its statement of financial position. If the fair value of a pension plan's assets exceeds the plan's projected benefit obligation the plan is overfunded and an asset is recognized. If the plan's projected benefit obligation exceeds the fair value of the plan's assets the plan is underfunded and a liability is recognized (ASC 715-30-25-1). When the funded status of the pension plan is first recognized in the statement of financial position, the offsetting entry is to accumulated other comprehensive income (net of tax). The recognition of a pension plan asset or liability may result in temporary differences under ASC 740 (Income Taxes). Deferred tax effects are to be recognized for these temporary differences as a component of income tax expense or benefit in the year in which the differences arise, and allocated to various financial statement components (ASC 715-30-25-3).

Asset and liability gains and losses, and prior service costs or credits, that occur in periods after recognition of the funded status of the plan and that are not immediately included as a component of net periodic pension cost are included in other comprehensive income. As gains and losses, prior service costs and credits, and the transition asset or obligation are included in net periodic pension cost they are recognized as an adjustment to other comprehensive income (ASC 715-30-25-4).

All pension plans that are overfunded are aggregated and a noncurrent asset presented in the statement of financial position. All pension plans that are underfunded are aggregated and a liability presented in the statement of financial position. The liability is current to the extent that the actuarial present value of benefits to be paid within the next year, or operating cycle if longer, exceeds the fair value of plan assets. This determination is made on a plan-by-plan basis. Otherwise, the liability is noncurrent (ASC 715-30-25-2). The employer should not reduce a liability resulting from an underfunded pension plan because another pension plan is overfunded (ASC 715-30-25-6).

MISCELLANEOUS CONSIDERATIONS

Measurement Dates

All pension plan assets that are held as investments to provide pension benefits are measured generally at their fair values as of the date of the financial statements. There are two exceptions to this general rule. If a subsidiary sponsors a pension plan and the subsidiary has a different year end than its parent, the fair value of the subsidiary's pension plan assets is measured at the date of the subsidiary's financial statements. If an investee accounted for by the equity method sponsors a pension plan and the investee has a different year-end than the investor, the fair value of the investee's pension plan assets is measured at the date of the investee's financial statements (ASC 715-30-35-62).

Unless more current amounts are available for both the obligation and plan assets, the funded status of the pension plan reported in interim financial statements is the same amount as reported by the employer in its previous year-end statement of financial position, adjusted for subsequent accruals of service cost, interest cost, return on plan assets, contributions, and benefit payments (ASC 715-30-35-65).

The same assumptions used to calculate the previous year-end net periodic pension cost are used to calculate the net periodic pension cost in subsequent interim financial statements, unless more current valuations of plan assets and obligations are available or a significant event has occurred, such as a plan amendment that usually would require new valuations (ASC 715-30-35-68).

Employers with Two or More Pension Plans

If an employer sponsors more than one defined benefit pension plan, the provisions of ASC 715 are applied separately to each plan. An employer shall not apply the assets of one plan to reduce or eliminate the underfunding of another plan, unless the employer clearly has the right to do so (ASC 715-30-25-6).

Annuity Contracts

All or part of an employer's obligation to provide pension plan benefits to individuals may be transferred effectively to an insurance company by the purchase of annuity contracts. An annuity contract is an irrevocable agreement in which an insurance company unconditionally agrees to provide specific periodic payments, or a lump-sum payment to another party, in return for a specified premium. Thus, by use of an annuity contract, an employer can effectively transfer to an insurance company its legal obligation to provide specific employee pension plan benefits. For the purposes of ASC 715, a contract is not considered an annuity contract if the insurance company is a captive insurer or there is reasonable doubt that the insurance company will meet its obligation. A captive insurer is one that does business primarily with the employer and its related parties (ASC 715-30-35-54).

An annuity contract may be participating or nonparticipating. In a participating annuity contract, the insurance company's investing activities with the funds received for the annuity contract generally are shared, in the form of dividends, with the purchaser (the employer or the pension fund). An annuity contract is not considered an annuity contract, for the purposes of ASC 715, unless all the risks and rewards associated with the assets and obligations assumed by the insurance company are actually transferred to the insurance company by the employer (ASC 715-30-35-57).

The cost incurred for currently earned benefits under an annuity contract is the cost of those benefits, except for the cost of participating rights of participating annuity contracts, which must be accounted for separately (see below). The service cost component of net periodic pension cost for the current period is the cost incurred for nonparticipating annuity contracts that cover all currently earned benefits (ASC 715-30-35-53). Pension benefits not covered by annuity contracts are accounted for in accordance with the provisions of ASC 715 that address accounting for the cost of pension benefits not covered by annuity contracts (ASC 715-30-35-55).

The projected benefit obligation and the accumulated benefit obligation do not include the cost of benefits covered by annuity contracts. Except for the cost of participation rights (see below), pension plan assets do not include the cost of any annuity contracts (ASC 715-30-35-53).

The difference in cost between a nonparticipating annuity contract and a participating annuity contract usually is attributable to the cost of the participation right. The cost of a participation right, at the date of its purchase, is recognized as a pension plan asset. In subsequent periods, a participation right is included in plan assets at its fair value, if fair value is reasonably determinable. If fair value is not reasonably determinable, a participation right is included in plan assets at its amortized cost and systematically amortized over the expected dividend period stated in the contract. In this event, amortized cost may not exceed the net realizable value of the participation right (ASC 715-30-35-57, 58).

Other Contracts with Insurance Companies

The purchase of insurance contracts that are, in substance, annuity contracts, is accounted for in accordance with the provisions of ASC 715 (see previous section). The purchase of other types of insurance contracts shall be accounted for as pension plan assets and reported at fair value. The best evidence of fair value for some insurance contracts may be their contract values. Under ASC 715, the cash surrender value or conversion value of an insurance contract is presumed to be its fair value (ASC 715-30-35-60).

Multiple-Employer Plans

Some pension plans to which two or more unrelated employers contribute are not multiemployer plans, but are groups of single-employer plans combined to allow participating employers to pool assets for investment purposes and to reduce the cost of plan administration. Under ASC 715, multiple-employer plans are considered single-employer plans and each employer's accounting shall be based on its respective interest in the plan (ASC 715-30-35-70).

Non-U.S. Pension Plans

ASC 715 does not make any special provision for non-U.S. pension plans. In some foreign countries, it is customary or required for an employer to provide benefits for employees in the event of a voluntary or involuntary severance of employment. In this event, if the substance of the arrangement is a pension plan, it is subject to the provisions of ASC 715 (e.g., benefits are paid for substantially all terminations) (ASC 715-30-15-3).

Business Combinations

When a single-employer defined benefit pension plan is acquired as part of a business combination accounted for by the acquisition method, the acquirer shall recognize an asset or a liability representing the funded status of the plan. When determining the funded status of the plan, the acquirer shall exclude the effects of expected plan amendments, terminations, or curtailments that at the acquisition date it has no obligation to make. If an acquiree participates in a multiemployer plan, and it is probable that it will withdraw from that plan, the acquirer shall recognize as part of the business combination a withdrawal liability in accordance with ASC 450 (ASC 805-20-25-23).

DEFINED CONTRIBUTION PENSION PLANS

A defined contribution pension plan provides for employers' contributions that are defined in the plan, but does not contain any provision for defined pension benefits for employees. Based on the amount of the employer's defined contributions, however, pension benefits are provided in return for services performed by employees.

Under ASC 715, a defined contribution pension plan provides for individual accounts for each plan participant and contains the terms that specify how contributions are determined for each participant's individual account. Each periodic employer contribution is allocated to each participant's individual account in accordance with the terms of the plan, and pension benefits are based solely on the amount available in each participant's account at the time of his or her retirement. The amount available in each participant's account at the time of his or her retirement is the total of the amounts contributed by the employer, plus the returns earned on investments of those contributions, and forfeitures of other participants' benefits that have been allocated to the participant's account, less any allocated administrative expenses.

Under ASC 715, the net periodic pension cost of a defined contribution pension plan is the amount of contributions made or due in a period on behalf of participants who performed services during that same period. Contributions for periods after an individual retires or terminates shall be estimated and accrued during periods in which the individual performs services.

SETTLEMENTS AND CURTAILMENTS

In connection with the operation of a defined benefit pension plan, ASC 715 provides for the delayed recognition of actuarial gains and losses, prior service costs, and the net obligation or asset that arises at the date of the initial application of pension plan accounting. As a result, at any given date, an employer's pension plan records may reflect a balance of a (*a*) net gain or loss, (*b*) prior service cost, and/or (*c*) net transition obligation or net asset. These amounts are included in accumulated other comprehensive income until they are recognized as a component of net periodic pension cost. Part or all of these amounts may be recognized in a settlement or curtailment of a pension plan.

In a settlement of a defined benefit pension plan, the employer or the pension plan is released irrevocably from its primary responsibility for all or part of its pension plan obligation, and all significant risks relating to the settlement are eliminated. For example, through the purchase of nonparticipating annuity contracts or cash payments to some or all of the plan participants in exchange for their pension benefits, an employer may be released irrevocably from the pension plan obligation related to the benefits involved in the exchange. After the settlement of a pension plan, an employer may continue to provide pension benefits in the same pension plan or a new plan.

In a curtailment of a defined benefit pension plan, some of the future pension benefits for present employees are reduced, generally resulting in a net decrease (gain) or increase (loss) in the projected benefit obligation. For example, if employees are terminated as a result of a plan curtailment, some or all of their pension benefits based on future compensation levels may cease to be an obligation of the employer or pension plan. In this event, the projected benefit obligation is decreased (a gain) by the amount of the pension benefits that are no longer an obligation of the plan. On the other hand, if terminated employees who are eligible for subsidized early retirement benefits accept the benefits at a date earlier than expected, there is an increase (loss) in the projected benefit obligation. Gain or loss on a plan curtailment is based on the net decrease (gain) or increase (loss) in the projected benefit obligation.

An employer may have to recognize an additional loss that is not included in the gain or loss on a plan curtailment, but is recognized as part of the total effects of a plan curtailment. This loss is equal to the amount of decrease in the unrecognized prior service cost of the pension benefits that are reduced by the plan curtailment. A separate loss computation is necessary for the prior service cost of each plan amendment.

The pension benefits that are reduced or eliminated in a plan curtailment may have been granted to some or all of the employees who were working for the employer as of the date of the initial application of pension plan accounting. For this reason, any transition *net obligation* that arose at the date of the initial application of pension plan accounting and that remains unamortized at the date of the plan curtailment is also treated as a separate prior service cost.

A pension plan settlement and a pension plan curtailment may occur simultaneously or separately. If the expected years of future service for some employees are reduced but the pension plan continues in existence, a curtailment has occurred, but not a settlement. If an employer settles all or a portion of its pension obligation and continues to provide defined benefits to employees for future services, either in the same plan or in a successor plan, a settlement has occurred, but not a curtailment. If an employer terminates its defined benefit pension plan without replacing it with another defined benefit pension plan, and settles its present pension plan obligation in full, a curtailment and settlement has occurred. Under these circumstances, it makes no difference whether or not some or all of the employees continue to work for the employer.

Employers frequently offer termination benefits as part of an overall plan to reduce employment levels, to increase productivity, or generally to decrease payroll costs. To induce certain groups of employees to terminate employment, many employers offer attractive termination benefits. This is particularly true for those employees who are close to, or have reached, the early retirement age specified in the employer's existing pension plan. Termination benefits may consist of periodic future payments, lump-sum payments, or a combination of both. The payment of termination benefits may be made from a new or existing employee benefit plan, from the employer's existing assets, or from a combination of these sources.

Under ASC 715 termination benefits are classified either as *special* or *contractual*. Special termination benefits are those that are offered to employees for a short period of time in connection with their termination of employment. Contractual termination benefits are those that are required by the terms of an existing plan or agreement and are provided only on the occurrence of a specified event, such as early retirement or the closing of a facility.

The cost of termination benefits is recognized by an employer as a loss and a corresponding liability. The recognition date depends on whether the benefits are special or contractual.

SETTLEMENTS OF DEFINED BENEFIT PENSION PLANS

Under ASC 715, a settlement of a defined benefit pension plan is an irrevocable transaction that (*a*) releases the employer or the pension plan from its primary responsibility for the payment of all or a portion of the pension plan obligation and (*b*) eliminates all of the significant risks associated with the assets and obligations used to effectuate the settlement (ASC 715-30-15-6). A settlement of a defined benefit pension plan does not require that the plan be completely terminated.

All or a part of an employer's obligation to provide pension plan benefits to individuals may be transferred effectively to an insurance company by the purchase of annuity contracts. An annuity contract is an irrevocable agreement in which an insurance company unconditionally agrees to provide specific periodic payments or a lump sum payment to another party in return for a specified premium. For the purposes of ASC 715, this definition of an annuity contract is not met if the insurance company is a *captive insurer* or there is reasonable doubt that the insurance company will meet its obligation. A captive insurer is one that does business primarily with the employer and its related parties (ASC 715-30-35-54).

An annuity contract may be participating or nonparticipating. In a participating annuity contract, the insurance company's investing returns are shared generally, in the form of dividends, with the purchaser of the contract (the employer or the pension fund). An annuity contract is not considered an annuity contract unless all the risks and rewards associated with the assets and obligations assumed by the insurance company are actually transferred to the insurance company by the employer (ASC 715-30-35-57).

Gain or loss on a plan settlement is based on pension plan records that have been updated as of the day before the settlement. Under ASC 715, the maximum gain or loss on a settlement of a defined benefit pension plan is equal to the total balance of (*a*) any net gain or loss that remains in accumulated other comprehensive income the date of the plan settlement and (*b*) any transition asset that arose at the date of the initial application of pension plan accounting that remains in accumulated other comprehensive income (ASC 715-30-35-79).

If the total pension plan obligation is settled by the employer, the maximum gain or loss is recognized. If part of the pension benefit obligation is settled, the employer must recognize a pro rata portion of the maximum gain or loss, equal to the percentage reduction in the projected benefit obligation, unless the transaction qualifies as a "small settlement" (discussed below). Thus, if 40% of the pension plan obligation is settled, 40% of the maximum gain or loss on the settlement is recognized, and if 100% of the pension benefit obligation is settled, 100% of the maximum gain or loss is recognized (ASC 715-30-35-79).

If the employer purchases a participating annuity contract to settle a pension obligation, the cost of the contract must be allocated between the cost of the pure annuity feature and the cost of the participation right. The amount of cost allocated to the participation rights reduces gain (but not loss) that would otherwise be recognized on a plan settlement. However, the participation rights do not affect the determination of the amount of loss that is recognized on a plan settlement (ASC 715-30-35-79).

Reporting Gain or Loss on a Plan Settlement

Gain or loss on a plan settlement is reported as an ordinary gain or loss, unless it meets the criteria of an extraordinary item as specified in ASC 225 (Income Statement).

Small Settlements for the Year

Part or all of a pension plan's obligation to an employee may be settled by the payment of cash or the purchase of an annuity contract.

The cost of a cash settlement of a pension plan obligation is the amount of cash paid to the employee. The cost of a settlement of a pension plan obligation involving a nonparticipating annuity contract is the cost of the contract. The cost of a settlement involving a participating annuity contract is the cost of the contract less the amount attributed to the participation rights (ASC 715-30-35-83).

If the total cost of all plan settlements for the year is small or insignificant, gain or loss recognition may not be required. ASC 715 provides that an employer is not required, but is permitted, to recognize the gain or loss on all plan settlements for the year if the cost of all such settlements does not exceed the sum of the service cost and interest cost components of the net periodic pension cost for the current year. Once an accounting policy is adopted for small or insignificant settlements, it must be applied consistently from year to year. Thus, an employer that initially elects nonrecognition of gain or loss on all small settlements during a year must continue that same accounting policy from year to year (ASC 715-30-35-82).

PRACTICE POINTER: If the total cost of all plan settlements for the year is small or insignificant, the employer has discretion to decide whether or not to recognize gain or loss, provided only that the accounting policy is followed consistently from year to year.

CURTAILMENT OF DEFINED BENEFIT PENSION PLANS

Under ASC 715, a curtailment of a defined benefit pension plan results from an event in which (*a*) the expected years of future service arising from a prior plan amendment are *significantly* reduced for present employees who are entitled to receive pension benefits from that prior plan amendment or (*b*) the accrual of defined pension benefits is eliminated for some or all of the future services of a *significant* number of employees (ASC Glossary).

The total effects of a plan curtailment consist of (1) the decrease (loss) in the prior service cost (or unrecognized transition obligation) remaining in accumulated other comprehensive income that results from the significant reduction of the expected years of future service for present employees (see (*a*) above), and (2) the net decrease (gain) or increase (loss) in the projected benefit obligation that results from the elimination of the accrual of defined pension benefits for some or all of the future services of a significant number of employees (see (*b*) above). Each of these two components that comprise the total effects of a plan curtailment are discussed separately below (ASC 715-30-35-92, 93).

Decrease (Loss) in Prior Service Cost

Retroactive pension benefits are sometimes granted by an employer, upon adoption of a plan or through a plan amendment, based on employees' services in prior periods. The costs of these retroactive pension benefits are referred to as prior service costs. Retroactive pension benefits are granted by an employer in expectation of future economic benefits, such as reduced employee turnover and higher productivity. ASC 715 requires that the prior service cost relating to a specific plan amendment be amortized in equal amounts over the expected years of future service of each active employee who is expected to receive benefits from the plan amendment. Periodic amortization for each expected year of future service is calculated by dividing the total expected years of future service into the total amount of unrecognized prior service cost. The total amount of prior service cost represents the total cost of pension benefits that have been granted under the provisions of the plan amendment. If the expected years of future service are reduced as a result of a plan curtailment, the related prior service cost also must be reduced and recognized as a loss by the employer.

The expected years of future service for present employees may be reduced significantly by the termination or suspension of pension benefits for future services so that employees are no longer allowed to earn additional benefits. In addition, the termination of some of the present employees earlier than expected may also result in a significant reduction in their total expected years of future service. As a result of the significant reduction in the expected years of future service, a loss is incurred by the employer in the amount of the decrease in the balance of the related unamortized unrecognized prior service cost at the date of the plan curtailment. To compute the loss, the percentage reduction in the total remaining expected years of future service at the date of the plan curtailment first must be calculated (number of expected years of future service that are reduced, divided by the total number of remaining expected years of future service before reduction). To determine the amount of the loss, the balance of the related prior service cost amount at the date of the plan curtailment is multiplied by the percentage reduction in the total number of expected years of future service. For example, if the total remaining expected years of future service at the date of the plan curtailment is 1,000, and the number of years of future service that is reduced is 400, the percentage reduction is 40%. The balance of the related prior service cost at the date of the plan curtailment is reduced by 40%, which represents the loss that the employer must recognize as part of the total effects of the plan curtailment.

For the purposes of ASC 715, the balance of any transition *net obligation* that arose at the date of the initial application of pension plan accounting, which is included in accumulated other comprehensive income at the date of a subsequent plan curtailment, also is treated as a separate prior service cost amount (ASC 715-30-35-92). Thus, if the expected years of future service are reduced significantly for those employees employed at the date of the initial application of pension plan accounting, a separate loss must be calculated and recognized by the employer. This loss equals the amount by which the *transition obligation* included in accumulated other comprehensive income is reduced when multiplied by the percentage reduction resulting from the expected years of future service that are significantly reduced for those employees who were employed at the date of the initial application of pension plan accounting.

The total of all decreases (losses) in prior service costs and/or transition net obligation is included in the total effects of a plan curtailment, but is not included in the gain or loss on the plan curtailment.

The following steps are necessary to compute each decrease (loss) in the balance of the prior service cost amount at the date of a plan curtailment arising from a significant reduction in the expected years of employees' future service:

Step 1: Compute the percentage reduction in the total remaining expected years of future service, at the date of the plan curtailment, resulting from the expected years of future service that are significantly reduced. For example, if the expected years of future service that are reduced are 600 and the total remaining expected years of future service at the date of the plan curtailment is 1,000, the percentage reduction is 60%.

Step 2: Multiply the balance of the prior service cost included in accumulated comprehensive income (or transition obligation) of each plan amendment affected by the plan curtailment by the percentage calculated in Step 1. The result is the amount of loss that the employer must recognize as part of the total effects of the plan curtailment. The balance of the prior service cost amount (or transition obligation) is also reduced by the same amount. (From a practical standpoint, the dollar amount of amortization for each expected year of future service can be multiplied by the total number of expected years of future service that is reduced.)

Step 3: The amount of loss recognized on the decrease in the balance of the prior service cost amount (or transition obligation) is not part of the gain or loss on the plan curtailment, but is included in the total effects of the plan curtailment.

Illustration of Computation of Expected Years of Future Service and Loss from the Decrease in Prior Service Cost Resulting from the Expected Years of Future Service That Are Significantly Reduced by a Plan Curtailment

Company X had 50 employees who were expected to receive pension benefits under a new pension plan amendment, which became effective January 1, 20X5. In the computation of the expected years of future service for each employee who was entitled to receive benefits under the new plan amendment, the company assumed that five employees would either quit or retire each year during the next ten years. The total amount of prior service cost arising from the new pension plan amendment was $27,500.

Employee Number	Expected Years of Future Service	Year									
		X5	X6	X7	X8	X9	Y0	Y1	Y2	Y3	Y4
1-5	5	5									
6-10	10	5	5								
11-15	15	5	5	5							
16-20	20	5	5	5	5						
21-25	25	5	5	5	5	5					
26-30	30	5	5	5	5	5	5				
31-35	35	5	5	5	5	5	5	5			
36-40	40	5	5	5	5	5	5	5	5		
41-45	45	5	5	5	5	5	5	5	5	5	
46-50	50	5	5	5	5	5	5	5	5	5	5
Service years rendered	275	50	45	40	35	30	25	20	15	10	5
Amortization fraction		50/275	45/275	40/275	35/275	30/275	25/275	20/275	15/275	10/275	5/275

Amortization for each expected year of future service equals $100 ($27,500 prior service cost divided by 275 years of expected future service).

Assume, at the beginning of X7, that 15 employees are terminated, resulting in a reduction of 90 years (given) of expected future service. The percentage reduction of expected future service years is 50%, determined as follows:

Expected years of future service, beginning of X7, before terminations (275, less amortization of 50 for X5 and 45 for X6)	180
Reduction due to terminations (given)	90
Percentage reduction: 90/180	50%

The remaining balance of prior service cost relating to the new plan amendment at the beginning of year 3 was $18,000 (180 remaining years of expected future service multiplied by the $100 amortization rate per year). Thus, the pension plan curtailment, relating to the expected years of future service that were significantly reduced by the termination of 15 employees, results in a loss of $9,000 (50% of $18,000).

Decrease (Gain) or Increase (Loss) in the Projected Benefit Obligation

A plan curtailment may result in a net decrease (gain) or net increase (loss) in the projected benefit obligation. For example, if employees are terminated as a result of a plan curtailment, some or all of their pension benefits based on future compensation levels may cease to be an obligation of the employer or pension plan. In this event, the projected benefit obligation is decreased (a gain) by the amount of the benefits that are no longer an obligation of the plan. On the other hand, if terminated employees who are eligible for subsidized early retirement benefits accept those benefits at an earlier date than expected, there usually is an increase (loss) in the projected benefit obligation. Gain or loss on a plan curtailment is based on the net decrease (gain) or increase (loss) in the projected benefit obligation (ASC 715-30-35-93).

The following steps are necessary to compute the gain or loss on a plan curtailment:

Step 1: Determine the total net gain (decrease) or net loss (increase) in the projected benefit obligation resulting from the plan curtailment. Do not include any increase (loss) in the projected benefit obligation that arises in connection with termination benefits (ASC 715-30-35-93).

Step 2: Determine whether a net gain or net loss exists. Combine the remaining balance of any unrecognized *net obligation* that arose at the date of the initial application of pension plan accounting and remains in accumulated other comprehensive income at the date of the plan curtailment, with the balance of any unrecognized net gain or loss that arose after the initial application of pension plan accounting and also remains unamortized at the date of the plan curtailment. **(Note:** The remaining balance of any transition obligation that arose at the date of the initial application of pension plan accounting and remains in accumulated other comprehensive income at the date of the plan curtailment is treated as part of prior service cost.) (ASC 715-30-35-92).

The amount of gain or loss on the plan curtailment is recognized as follows:

1. *If the change in the projected benefit obligation is a net gain (Step 1) and there is a net gain included in accumulated other comprehensive income (Step 2)* Curtailment gain is recognized in the amount of the net gain in the projected benefit obligation. (The unrecognized net gain computed in Step 2 is not used.)

2. *If the change in the projected benefit obligation is a net gain (Step 1) and there is an unrecognized net loss (Step 2)* If the net gain in the projected benefit obligation does not exceed the net loss included in accumulated other comprehensive income, no curtailment gain or loss is recognized. If the net gain exceeds the net loss included in accumulated other comprehensive income, curtailment gain is recognized in the amount of the excess of the net gain in the projected benefit obligation over the net loss included in accumulated other comprehensive income.

3. *If the change in the projected benefit obligation is a net loss (Step 1) and there is a net gain included in accumulated other comprehensive income (Step 2)* If the net loss in the projected benefit obligation does not exceed the net gain, no curtailment gain or loss is recognized. If the net loss exceeds the net gain included in accumulated other comprehensive income, curtailment loss is recognized in the amount of the excess of the net loss in the projected benefit obligation over the net gain in accumulated other comprehensive income.

4. *If the change in the projected benefit obligation is a net loss (Step 1) and there is a net loss in accumulated other comprehensive income (Step 2)* Curtailment loss is recognized in the amount of the net loss in the projected benefit obligation. (The unrecognized net loss computed in Step 2 is not used.)

Recognition of the Total Effects of a Plan Curtailment

The total effects of a plan curtailment consist of (*a*) the decrease (loss) in the prior service cost amount and/or transition net obligation, resulting from the significant reduction of the expected years of future service for present employees, and (*b*) the net decrease (gain) or increase (loss) in the projected benefit obligation that results from the elimination of the accrual of defined pension benefits for some or all of the future services of a significant number of employees.

If the total effects of a plan curtailment result in a loss, the loss is recognized when it is *probable* that the curtailment will occur and the effects of the curtailment can be *reasonably estimated*. If the total effects of a plan curtailment result in a gain, the gain is recognized only when the related employees terminate or the plan suspension or amendment is adopted (ASC 715-30-35-94).

Reporting Total Effects of a Plan Curtailment

Gain or loss on the total effects of a pension plan curtailment is reported as an ordinary gain or loss, unless it meets the criteria of an extraordinary item as specified by ASC 225 (Income Statement).

TERMINATION BENEFITS

Under ASC 715, termination benefits are classified as either *special* or *contractual*. Special termination benefits are those that are offered to employees for a short period in connection with the termination of their employment. Contractual termination benefits are those that are required by the terms of an existing plan or agreement and that are provided only on the occurrence of a specified event, such as early retirement or the closing of a facility (ASC 712-10-05-2).

ASC 715 requires the recognition of the cost of termination benefits as a loss and corresponding liability. The recognition date depends on whether the benefits are special or contractual.

Special Termination Benefits

The recognition date on which the employer records the loss and corresponding liability for special termination benefits occurs when (*a*) the employees accept the offer of the special termination benefits and (*b*) the amount of the cost of the benefits can be reasonably estimated (ASC 715-30-25-10).

Contractual Termination Benefits

The recognition date on which the employer records the loss and corresponding liability for contractual termination benefits occurs when (*a*) it is probable that employees will be entitled to the benefits and (*b*) the amount of the cost of the benefits can be estimated reasonably (ASC 715-30-25-10).

Reporting a Loss on Termination Benefits

A loss on termination benefits is reported as an ordinary loss, unless it meets the criteria of an extraordinary item as specified in ASC 225 (ASC 225-20).

FINANCIAL STATEMENT DISCLOSURE

The disclosure requirements for settlements and curtailments of plans are incorporated into a general set of disclosure requirements for all pension and other postretirement plans. They are covered earlier in this chapter.

Illustration of Curtailment and Settlement of a Pension Plan

The updated records of a defined benefit pension plan reflect the following:

Vested benefits	$ (30,000)
Nonvested benefits	(50,000)
Accumulated benefit obligation	$ (80,000)
Effects on benefits as a result of considering future compensation levels	(20,000)
Projected benefit obligation	$(100,000)
Fair value of plan assets	95,000
Funded status of plan, recognized as a liability on the balance sheet	$ (5,000)
Prior service cost	1,000
Net (gain) or loss	(1,000)
Transition net obligation or (net asset) at date of initial application of pension plan accounting	2,000

Assume that the above plan is completely terminated without a successor plan. Under this circumstance, the effects on benefits as a result of considering future compensation levels are no longer an obligation of the employer or the plan, since all of the plan participants have been terminated. Assume also that the total projected benefit obligation was settled by the purchase of nonparticipating annuity contracts for $80,000, and the excess plan assets in the amount of $15,000 were withdrawn by the employer.

Computation of the total effects of a plan curtailment

The total effects of a plan curtailment consist of (a) the total loss resulting from the decreases in the balances of any unamortized unrecognized prior service costs and/or the transition net obligation included in accumulated other comprehensive income relating to the expected years of future service that were significantly reduced for present employees and (b) the net decrease (gain) or increase (loss) in the projected benefit obligation resulting from the elimination of the accrual of defined pension benefits for some or all of the future services of a significant number of employees.

The loss resulting from the decrease in the balance of any prior service costs (or transition net obligation) is computed as follows:

ASC 715—Compensation—Retirement Benefits 40,047

Step 1. The percentage reduction, if any, in the balances of any prior service cost and/or the transition net obligation must be calculated (each loss must be computed separately, unless the pension plan is completely terminated). In the above illustration, the percentage reduction resulting from the significant reduction in the expected years of future service is 100%, because the plan is completely terminated. As a result, no separate computation is necessary.

Step 2. Multiply the balance of the prior service cost and transition net obligation by its percentage reduction, if any. In the above illustration, the balance of the prior service cost of $1,000 is multiplied by 100%, and the balance of the transition net obligation of $2,000 is multiplied by 100%; the sum of the resulting amounts is a total loss of $3,000.

Step 3. The $3,000 computed in Step 2 is treated as an effect of the plan curtailment, not as part of the gain or loss on the plan curtailment.

The net decrease (gain) or increase (loss) in the projected benefit obligation is computed as follows:

Step 4. Calculate the net decrease (gain) or net increase (loss) in the projected benefit obligation resulting from the plan curtailment. Do not include any increase (loss) in the projected benefit obligation that arose in connection with termination benefits. In the above illustration, the effects on benefits as a result of considering future compensation levels of $20,000 are no longer an obligation of the employer or the plan. This results in a $20,000 net decrease (gain) in the projected benefit obligation, because there are no other decreases or increases.

Step 5. Compute the total of (*a*) the balance of any net gain or loss that remains in accumulated other comprehensive income at the date of the plan curtailment and (*b*) the balance of any transition net asset that remains in accumulated other comprehensive income at the date of the plan curtailment. In the above illustration, the total is a gain of $1,000 (net gain of $1,000 and no net asset).

Step 6. Compute the gain or loss on the plan curtailment, as follows:

- If Step 4 (projected benefit obligation) is a gain and Step 5 is also a gain, curtailment gain is recognized in the amount of Step 4 (the amount of gain in Step 5 is ignored).

- If Step 4 (projected benefit obligation) is a loss and Step 5 is also a loss, curtailment loss is recognized in the amount of Step 4 (the amount of loss in Step 5 is ignored).

- If Step 4 (projected benefit obligation) is a gain and Step 5 is a loss, curtailment gain is recognized in the amount by which the gain in Step 4 exceeds the loss in Step 5. If Step 5 exceeds Step 4, no gain or loss is recognized.

- If Step 4 (projected benefit obligation) is a loss and Step 5 is a gain, curtailment loss is recognized in the amount by which the loss in Step 4 exceeds the gain in Step 5. If Step 5 exceeds Step 4, no gain or loss is recognized.

In the above illustration, the net decrease (gain) in the projected benefit obligation was $20,000 (Step 4) and the total net gain or loss is a gain of $1,000 (Step 5). Since both steps result in a gain, a gain on the plan curtailment in the amount of Step 4 is recognized, which is $20,000.

Settlement gain or loss

As in Step 5 above, compute the total of (a) the balance of any net gain or loss that remains in accumulated other comprehensive income at the date of the plan settlement and (b) the balance of any transition net asset that remains in accumulated other comprehensive income at the date of the plan settlement.

If part of the pension obligation is settled, the employer must recognize a pro rata portion of the maximum gain or loss, equal to the total of the net gain or loss and/or the transition net asset multiplied by the percentage reduction in the projected benefit obligation. In the above illustration, there was a net gain of $1,000 and no transition net asset. Since the pension plan was terminated, the pension obligation completely settled, and the decrease in the projected benefit obligation was 100%, the pro rata portion that must be recognized is 100%, or $1,000. Thus, the gain on the settlement of the pension plan is $1,000.

Summary

The loss on the decrease in the prior service cost amount and transition net obligation is $3,000, which was computed in Step 3. This loss is reported as a "Loss on Effects of Curtailment of Pension Plan." The net gain on the decrease in the projected benefit obligation is $20,000, which was computed in Step 6. This gain is reported as a "Gain on the Curtailment of Pension Plan." The "Gain on the Settlement of Pension Plan" is $1,000, which was computed separately above. Thus, the net gain on the pension plan curtailment and settlement was $18,000 ($3,000 loss, $20,000 gain, and $1,000 gain).

Journal entry

The journal entry and suggested financial statement presentation of the net gain on pension plan curtailment and settlement of $18,000 is as follows:

Cash (excess plan assets)	15,000	
Liability for pension benefits	3,000	
Gain from termination of pension plan		18,000
Suggested financial statement presentation:		
Gain on curtailment of pension plan	$20,000	
Loss on effects of curtailment of pension plan	(3,000)	
Total effects of plan curtailment	$17,000	
Gain on settlement of pension plan	1,000	
Net gain on pension plan curtailment and settlement	$18,000	

ASC 715-60: DEFINED BENEFIT PLANS—OTHER POST-RETIREMENT

GAAP REQUIREMENTS

ASC 715 establishes *accounting* standards for employers with postretirement benefit plans. *Postretirement benefits* consist of all forms of benefits other than retirement income provided by an employer to retired workers, their beneficiaries, and their dependents (ASC 715-60-15-3). The term does not include benefits paid after employment but before retirement, such as layoff benefits.

Postemployment benefits are also covered by ASC 715, which is the subject of a later section in this chapter.

Postretirement benefit payments may begin immediately on employees' termination of service or may be deferred until retired employees reach a specified age. Benefits such as health care, tuition assistance, or legal services are provided to retirees as the need arises. Other benefits, such as life insurance, are provided on the occurrence of specified events (ASC 715-10-05-7).

A *postretirement benefit plan* is one in which an employer agrees to provide certain postretirement benefits to current and former employees after they retire. A postretirement benefit plan may be *contributory* (employees may be required to contribute to the plan) or *noncontributory* (the entire cost of the plan is borne by the employer).

A postretirement benefit plan may be *funded* or *unfunded*—that is, the employees and/or the employer may make cash contributions to a postretirement benefit plan trustee (i.e., funded), or the employer may make only credit entries on its books reflecting the postretirement benefit liability under the plan and pay all benefits from its general assets (i.e., unfunded).

General Approach—Deferred Compensation

According to ASC 715, postretirement benefits are a type of *deferred compensation* that is accounted for as part of an employee's total compensation package. A *deferred compensation plan* is an agreement specifying that a portion of an employee's compensation will be set aside and paid in future periods. ASC 715 requires employers to account for postretirement benefit plans on the accrual basis.

Comparison of Pension Accounting to Postretirement Benefit Accounting

Although there are some important differences, the accounting for postretirement benefits is very similar to the accounting for pension benefits.

In accounting for postretirement benefits under ASC 715, an employer makes at least two types of journal entries to record its cost of these benefits— one to record the annual expense and related liability and a second to record the payment or funding of the liability, if any.

Illustration of Basic Entries for Recording Postretirement Benefits

Assuming a company determines its annual expense for postretirement benefits is $10,000 and funds that amount, the following entries are made (assume a 30% tax rate):

1.	Net periodic postretirement benefit cost	10,000	
	Deferred tax asset	3,000	
	Deferred tax benefit—net income		3,000
	Liability for postretirement benefits		10,000
	(To accrue postretirement benefit cost of $10,000 for a specific period.)		

2. Liability for postretirement benefits   10,000
     Cash   10,000
     (To record cash contribution to
     postretirement plan trust or to pay benefits of
     $10,000.)

These entries are similar to those required for pension accounting, except for differences in the titles of the accounts.

Most of the provisions of ASC 715 pertain to the computation of the amount to be recorded in journal entry type (1) above. This computation requires numerous worksheet calculations, which are illustrated throughout ASC 715.

Use of Reasonable Approximations

ASC 715 allows an employer to use estimates, averages, or computational shortcuts, provided that the employer reasonably expects that the results will not be materially different from those which would have been reached by a fully detailed application of the requirements in ASC 715 (ASC 715-60-35-1).

Scope and Applicability

The requirements of ASC 715 related to postretirement benefits affect:

4. Types of benefits
5. Types of beneficiaries
6. General rather than selective coverage of employees
7. Source and form of payment
8. Nature of the employer's undertaking

Types of Benefits

ASC 715 applies to an employer's undertaking to provide various types of nonpension benefits to employees after they retire. The benefits may commence immediately upon termination of the employee's active service, or may be deferred until the retired employee reaches a specified age.

The benefits include health care, life insurance outside of a pension plan, tuition assistance, day care, legal services, housing subsidies, and other types of postretirement benefits (ASC 715-60-15-4). If an employer has established a plan to provide benefits to active employees as well as to retired employees, ASC 715 requires the employer to divide the plan into two parts for accounting purposes; one part covering benefits to active employees and the other part covering benefits to retired employees. The employer should use the accounting standards of ASC 715 only for the part covering benefits to retired employees (ASC 715-60-15-7).

Types of Beneficiaries

The beneficiaries may be retired employees, disabled employees, any other former employees who are expected to receive benefits, or retirees' beneficiaries and covered dependents, pursuant to the terms of an employer's undertaking to provide such benefits. The beneficiaries may also be individuals who (*a*) have ceased permanent active employment because of disability, (b) have not yet completed formal procedures for retirement, or (c) are carried on nonretired status under the disability provisions of the plan so that they can continue accumulating credit for pensions or other postretirement benefits (ASC 715-60-35-44).

General Rather Than Selective Coverage of Employees

The plan should cover employees in general, rather than selected individual employees. An employer's practice of providing postretirement benefits to selected employees under individual contracts with specific terms determined on an individual basis does not constitute a postretirement benefit plan under ASC 715. ASC 715 does apply to contracts with individual employees if these contracts, taken together, are equivalent to a plan covering employees in general (ASC 715-10-15-5).

> **PRACTICE NOTE:** An employer's commitment to selected individual employees is accrued in accordance with the terms of the individual contracts (see the section in the ASC 715-10 discussion titled *Illustrations of Accruals Required by ASC 715*). Professional judgment is required whenever contracts with individual employees may be equivalent to a general plan.

Source and Form of Payment

A plan is covered by ASC 715 if it provides reimbursement or direct payment to providers for the cost of specified services as the need for those services arises, or if it provides lump sum benefits, such as death benefits. The plan may be either funded or unfunded (ASC 715-10-15-2).

> **PRACTICE NOTE:** If the plan is funded, the assets of a postretirement benefit plan usually are kept in a trust account, segregated from the assets of the employer. Contributions to the postretirement benefit plan trust account are made periodically by the employer and, if the plan is contributory, by the employees. The plan assets may be invested in stocks, bonds, real estate, and other types of investments. Plan assets are increased by earnings, gains on investments, and contributions by the employer (and employees if the plan is contributory), and are decreased by losses on investments and the payment of benefits and any related administrative expenses.

Nature of the Employer's Undertaking

ASC 715 applies to any arrangement that is in substance a plan for providing postretirement benefits, regardless of its form (ASC 715-10-15-3).

> **PRACTICE NOTE:** When it is not clear that a plan exists, professional judgment is required in determining whether a plan exists "in substance." ASC 715 provides little guidance on this issue.

ASC 715—Compensation—Retirement Benefits

ASC 715 applies not only to written plans, but also to unwritten plans if the existence of these plans can be perceived based on (a) the employer's practice of paying benefits or (b) the employer's oral representations to current or former employees. Once an employer pays benefits or promises to pay benefits, ASC 715 presumes that the employer has undertaken to provide future benefits as indicated by the past payments or promises, unless there is evidence to the contrary (ASC 715-10-15-3).

> **PRACTICE NOTE:** To indicate the existence of a plan, it appears that the employer's oral representations (a) should refer to a plan that is general in its scope and (b) should be communicated to current or former employees in general, or to individual employees as representatives of the employees in general.

One issue is whether ASC 715 applies only to legally enforceable obligations, or to a broader range of commitments including those that cannot be legally enforced.

> **PRACTICE NOTE:** The Employee Retirement Income Security Act (ERISA) gives substantial legal protection to the expectations of employees under pension plans, but does not give the same level of protection to employee expectations of nonpension benefits. Courts have upheld the right of employers to terminate or curtail benefits under non-pension plans, unless the employers have entered into legally binding commitments to maintain benefits, such as collective bargaining agreements.

> **PRACTICE NOTE:**
>
> - Accountants should obtain expert advice before (a) advising employers on the applicability of ASC 715 to existing plans, (b) advising employers on the structuring of new plans or the restructuring of existing plans if the structure of the plan may determine whether the plan is within the scope of ASC 715, or (c) auditing the financial statements of an employer if there is a serious question as to whether the employer's plan is within the scope of ASC 715.
> - If a plan is covered by ASC 715, the next question is whether the plan is a defined benefit plan or a defined contribution plan. ASC 715 prescribes significantly different accounting and reporting requirements for these two types of plans. ASC 715 deals primarily with defined benefit plans. For the distinctive accounting and reporting requirements applicable to defined contribution plans, see the section titled "Defined Contribution Plans" in this chapter. When considering the structuring or restructuring of a plan, the employer and its advisors should consider whether the plan is covered by ASC 715 and, if so, whether the plan is governed by the accounting and reporting requirements for defined benefit plans or for defined contribution plans.

ASC 715—Compensation—Retirement Benefits **40,053**

SINGLE-EMPLOYER DEFINED BENEFIT POSTRETIREMENT PLANS

ASC 715 deals primarily with an employer's accounting for a single-employer plan that provides defined benefits. ASC 715 also briefly covers multiemployer plans, multiple-employer plans, and defined contribution plans. Each is discussed later in this chapter.

> **PRACTICE NOTE:** The accounting and reporting requirements for defined contribution plans differ significantly from those for defined benefit plans. If a plan has some characteristics of each type, ASC 715 calls for careful analysis of the substance of the plan. The difference in the accounting and reporting requirements, depending on whether the plan is a defined benefit plan or a defined contribution plan, may be a significant factor to be considered by employers attempting to structure or restructure their plans.

In a defined benefit plan, the benefit may be defined in terms of a specified monetary amount (such as a life insurance benefit), or a specified type of benefit (such as all or a percentage of the cost of specified surgical procedures). The benefits may be subject to a maximum (or *cap*), either per individual employee or for the plan as a whole, or the employer may agree to pay the full amount of benefits without regard to any maximum amount (ASC 715-60-15-8).

The employee's entitlement to benefits is expressed in the benefit formula, which specifies the years of service to be rendered, age to be attained while in service, or a combination of both, which must be met for an employee to be eligible to receive benefits under the plan. The benefit formula may also define the beginning of the period of service during which the employee earns credit toward eligibility, as well as the levels of benefits earned for specific periods of service (ASC 715-60-05-4, 5).

The total amount of benefits depends not only on the benefit formula but also on actuarial factors, such as the longevity of the retired employee (and the longevity of the retiree's beneficiaries and covered dependents), and the occurrence of specific events entitling the individuals to benefits (such as illnesses) (ASC 715-60-35-2).

Because of these factors, the employer cannot precisely calculate the amount of benefits to be paid in the future to any retired employee (or to the retiree's beneficiaries and covered dependents). The FASB is satisfied, however, that employers can make reasonable estimates useful for accounting purposes.

Accumulated Postretirement Benefit Obligation

ASC 715 requires the employer to accrue the accumulated postretirement benefit obligation. Once an employee has attained full eligibility, the amount of this obligation is the same as the employee's *expected* postretirement benefit obligation. Until then, the *accumulated* amount is the portion of the expected amount attributed to employee service rendered to a particular date (ASC Glossary).

The accumulated and the expected amounts represent the actuarial present value of the anticipated benefits. Measurement of these amounts is based on

40,054 ASC 715—Compensation—Retirement Benefits

assumptions regarding such items as the expected cost of providing future benefits and any cost-sharing provisions under which the employee, the government, or others will absorb part of these costs. If the benefits or cost-sharing provisions are related to the employee's salary progression, the calculation of benefits and cost-sharing reflects the anticipated impact of this progression (ASC 715-60-35-2).

> **PRACTICE NOTE:** The accounting for postretirement benefits differs from the accounting for pensions in this respect, because the accounting for pensions does not anticipate salary progression in determining the accumulated pension benefit obligation.

Illustration of Relationship between Expected and Accumulated Postretirement Benefit Obligations

A plan provides postretirement health care benefits to all employees who render at least ten years of service and attain age 65 while in service. A 60-year-old employee, hired at age 45, is expected to terminate employment at the end of the year in which the employee attains age 67 and is expected to live to age 77. A discount rate of 8% is assumed.

At December 31, 20X5, the employer estimates the expected amount and timing of benefit payments for that employee as follows:

Age	Expected Future Claims	Present Value at Age 60	Present Value at Age 65
68	$ 2,322	$ 1,255	$ 1,843
69	2,564	1,283	1,885
70	2,850	1,320	1,940
71	3,154	1,353	1,988
72	3,488	1,385	2,035
73	3,868	1,422	2,090
74	4,274	1,455	2,138
75	4,734	1,492	2,193
76	5,240	1,530	2,247
77	7,798	2,108	3,097
	$40,292	$14,603	$21,456

At December 31, 20X5, when the employee's age is 60, the *expected* postretirement benefit obligation is $14,603, and the *accumulated* postretirement benefit obligation is $10,952 (15/20 of $14,603 because the employee has worked 15 of the 20 years needed to attain age 65 while in service and thus become fully eligible for benefits).

Assuming no changes in health care costs or other circumstances, the obligations at later dates are as follows:

- December 31, 20Y0 (age 65), the expected and the accumulated postretirement benefit obligations are both $21,456. These amounts are the same, because the employee is fully eligible.

- December 31, 20Y1 (age 66), the expected and the accumulated postretirement benefit obligations are both $23,172 ($21,456 the previous year, plus interest at 8% for 1 year).

Measurement of Cost and Obligations

In discussing the measurement of cost and obligations of single-employer defined benefit plans, ASC 715 addresses the following issues:

- Accounting for the substantive plan
- Assumptions
- Attribution

Accounting for the Substantive Plan

According to ASC 715, the accounting and reporting should reflect the substantive plan; that is, the plan as understood by the employer and the employees. Generally, the substantive plan is accurately reflected in writing. The employer's past practice or communications of intended future changes, however, may indicate that the substantive plan differs from the written plan (ASC 715-60-35-48).

PRACTICE NOTE: If an independent auditor is faced with a situation in which the substantive plan appears to be different from the written plan, the auditor should (a) seek expert advice, (b) consult with the highest levels of the employer's management, and (c) fully document the matter in the audit files.

ASC 715 discusses the following areas in which the substantive plan may differ from the written plan:

- Cost sharing
- Benefit changes
- Plan amendments

Cost Sharing

In general, the employer's cost-sharing policy is regarded as part of the substantive plan if (a) the employer has maintained a consistent level of cost-sharing with retirees, (b) the employer consistently has increased or decreased the share of the cost contributed by employees or retirees, or (c) the employer has the ability to change the cost-sharing provisions at a specified time or when certain conditions exist, and has communicated to plan participants its intent to make such changes (ASC 715-60-35-51).

An employer's past practice regarding cost sharing, however, is not regarded as the substantive plan if (ASC 715-60-35-52):

- The cost sharing was accompanied by offsetting changes in other benefits or compensation.
- The employer was subjected to significant costs, such as work stoppages, to carry out that policy.

Along similar lines, an employer's communication of its intent to change the cost-sharing provisions is not regarded as the substantive plan if (ASC 715-60-35-54):

- The plan participants would be unwilling to accept the change without adverse results to the employer's operations.
- The plan participants would insist on other modifications of the plan that would offset the change in cost sharing, to accept the proposed change.

In estimating the amount of contributions to be received by the plan from active or retired employees, the employer should consider any relevant substantive plan provisions, such as the employer's past practice of consistently changing the contribution rates. If the employer is obliged to return contributions to employees who do not become eligible for benefits (together with interest, if applicable), the estimated amount of this obligation is (*a*) included in the employer's total benefit obligation and (*b*) factored into calculations of the contributions needed by the plan (ASC 715-60-35-57).

Benefit Changes

The measurement of the obligation under the plan includes automatic benefit changes specified by the plan. An example is a plan that promises to pay a benefit in kind, such as health care benefits, instead of a defined dollar amount. The obligation to pay the benefit automatically changes in amount when the cost of the benefit changes (ASC 715-60-35-58, 59).

Plan Amendments

Measurement also includes plan amendments as soon as they have been contractually agreed upon, even if some or all of the provisions become effective in later periods (ASC 715-60-35-60).

PRACTICE NOTE: Even if a plan amendment has not been contractually agreed upon, it appears that an employer should reflect the amendment if it can be regarded as a change in the substantive plan. In general, a substantive plan may differ from the written plan in either of two cases: (1) when the employer has communicated its intention to adopt the amendment and certain conditions are met or (2) when the employer has engaged in consistent past practice.

Assumptions

An employer has to make numerous assumptions to apply ASC 715. Each assumption should reflect the best estimate of the future event to which it relates, without regard to the estimates involved in making other assumptions. ASC 715 describes this as an explicit approach to assumptions (ASC 715-60-35-71).

> **PRACTICE NOTE:** The FASB finds the use of **explicit** assumptions preferable to **implicit** assumptions, under which the reliability of assumptions would be judged in the aggregate, not individually.

All assumptions should be based on the expectation that the plan will continue in the absence of evidence that it will not continue (ASC 715-60-35-72). Some of the assumptions discussed in ASC 715 apply generally to all types of benefits, while other assumptions are unique to health care benefits.

ASC 715 discusses the following general assumptions:

- Time value of money (discount rates)
- Expected long-term rate of return on plan assets
- Future compensation levels
- Other general assumptions

Time Value of Money (Discount Rates)

One of the essential assumptions relates to discount rates. Assumed discount rates are used in measuring the expected and accumulated postretirement benefit obligations and the service cost and interest cost components of net periodic postretirement benefit cost. Assumed discount rates should reflect the time value of money at the measurement date, as indicated by rates of return on high-quality fixed-income investments currently available with cash flows corresponding to the anticipated needs of the plan. If the employer could settle its obligation under the plan by purchasing insurance (for example, nonparticipating life insurance contracts to provide death benefits), the interest rates inherent in the potential settlement amount are relevant to the employer's determination of assumed discount rates (ASC 715-60-35-79).

The chosen discount rate should produce a liability amount that would generate the necessary future cash flows to pay postretirement benefits as they become due if such amount was invested at the financial statement date in a portfolio of high-quality fixed-income investments. This liability amount is theoretically equal to the market value of a portfolio of high-quality zero coupon bonds, where each bond matches the amount and maturity of future payments due under the postretirement benefit plan. However, reinvestment risk exists to the extent that the plan's assets include interest-bearing debt instruments (rather than only zero coupon bonds) and to the extent that plan investments have a maturity date that is sooner than some of the anticipated postretirement benefit payments. In such cases, the assumed discount (interest) rate needs to consider expected reinvestment rates extrapolated using the existing yield curve at the financial statement date. The discount rate should be reevaluated at each measurement (financial statement) date (ASC 715-60-35-80, 81).

> **PRACTICE POINTER:** The discount rate used to determine the postretirement benefit liability and the interest cost component of net periodic postretirement benefit cost should change in accordance with changes in market interest

rates: if interest rates rise, the discount rate should increase; if interest rates fall, the discount rate should decline. In addition, the determination of the discount rate is separate from the determination of the expected return on plan assets.

Expected Long-Term Rate of Return on Plan Assets

Assumptions are also required in determining the expected long-term rate of return on plan assets. In general, plan assets are investments that have been segregated and restricted, usually in a trust, for the exclusive purpose of paying postretirement benefits.

The expected long-term rate of return on plan assets should reflect the anticipated average rate of earnings on existing plan assets and those expected to be contributed during the period (ASC 715-60-35-84).

PRACTICE NOTE: This factor is used, together with the *market-related value* of plan assets, in computing the *expected return* on plan assets. The difference between the actual return and the expected return on plan assets is defined in ASC 715 as "plan asset gain or loss," discussed later.

If the return on plan assets is taxable to the trust or other fund under the plan, the expected long-term rate of return shall be reduced to reflect the related income taxes expected to be paid (ASC 715-60-35-86).

When estimating the rate of return on plan assets, the employer should consider the rate of return on (*a*) assets currently invested and (*b*) assets that will be reinvested. If the income from plan assets is taxable, the anticipated amount of taxes should be deducted to produce a net-of-tax rate of return. If a plan is unfunded or has no assets that qualify as plan assets under ASC 715, the employer has no basis or need to calculate an expected long-term rate of return on plan assets (ASC 715-60-35-84).

Future Compensation Levels

If the benefit formula provides for varying amounts of postretirement benefits based on the compensation levels of employees, the employer has to make further assumptions about the impact of anticipated future compensation levels on the cost of benefits and the obligation to pay them (ASC 715-60-35-75).

Estimates of future compensation are based on anticipated compensation of individual employees, including future changes arising from general price levels, productivity, seniority, promotion, and other factors. All assumptions should be consistent with regard to general factors such as future rates of inflation. The assumptions should also include any indirect effects related to salary progression, such as the impact of inflation-based adjustments to the maximum benefit provided under the plan (ASC 715-60-35-75, 88).

Other General Assumptions

Other general assumptions involved in applying ASC 715 include the following:

- Participation rates for contributory plans
- The probability of payment (such as turnover of employees, dependency status, and mortality)

PRACTICE POINTER: As is the case in pension accounting, the CPA is not expected to be an expert in actuarial science. In fact, accounting for pensions and other retirement benefits is an area where the CPA relies heavily on the expertise of actuaries. However, the CPA still must have a general understanding of the work of the actuary, including the reasonableness of the underlying assumptions the actuary is using to prepare information that may have a significant impact on an enterprise's funding of benefit plans, as well as its financial statements.

Assumptions Unique to Postretirement Health Care Benefits

Many postretirement benefit plans include health care benefits. Measurement of an employer's postretirement health care obligation requires the use of special types of assumptions that will affect the amount and timing of future benefit payments for postretirement health care, in addition to the general assumptions required by all postretirement benefit plans.

ASC 715 discusses the following assumptions unique to postretirement health care benefits:

- Per capita claims cost
- Assumptions about trends in health care costs

Per Capita Claims Cost

An employer should estimate the net incurred claims cost at each age at which a participant is expected to receive benefits. To estimate this net cost, the employer first estimates the assumed per capita gross claims cost at each age, and then subtracts the effects of (*a*) Medicare and other reimbursements from third parties and (*b*) cost-sharing provisions that cause the participant to collect less than 100% of the claim. If plan participants are required to make contributions to the plan during their active service, the actuarial present value of the participants' future contributions should be subtracted from the actuarial present value of the assumed net incurred claims costs (ASC 715-60-35-91).

The *assumed per capita claims cost* is the annual cost of benefits from the time at which an individual's coverage begins, for the remainder of that person's life (or until coverage ends, when sooner). The annual benefit cost is based on the best possible estimate of the expected future cost of benefits covered by the plan that reflects age and other appropriate factors such as gender and geographical location. If the employer incurs significant costs in administering the plan, these costs should also be considered part of the assumed per capita claims cost (ASC 715-60-35-92, 93).

If an employer does not have a reliable basis for estimating the assumed per capita claims cost by age, the employer may base its estimate on other reliable information. For example, the estimate may be based on the claims costs that have actually been incurred for employees of all ages, adjusted by factors to reflect health care cost trends, age of the covered population, and cost sharing (ASC 715-60-35-95).

A number of assumptions are based on the estimated effects of inflation. The employer should use consistent methods of estimating inflation, whether the assumption relates to discount rates, compensation levels, or health care cost trend rates.

If the history of the plan is reliable enough to provide a basis for future estimates, the past and present claims data of the plan are considered in calculating the assumed per capita claims cost. If the plan does not provide any reliable data, the employer may base its estimates on other employers' claims information, as assembled by insurance companies, actuarial firms, or employee benefits consulting firms (ASC 715-60-35-95).

PRACTICE NOTE: The independent auditor should verify that any outside information comes from reliable and independent sources, and that the audit files fully identify these sources.

The estimates derived from the experience of other employers should, however, be adjusted to reflect the demographics of the specific employer and the benefits available under its plan, to the extent they differ from those of the other employers. Relevant factors include, for example, health care utilization patterns, expected geographical locations of retirees and their dependents, and significant differences among the nature and types of benefits covered (ASC 715-60-35-95).

Assumptions about Trends in Health Care Cost Rates

Assumptions about the trend in health care cost rates represent the expected annual rate of change in the cost of health care benefits currently provided under the plan (because of factors other than changes in the demographics of participants) for each year from the measurement date until the payment of benefits. The trend rates are based on past and current cost trends, reflecting such factors as health care cost inflation, changes in utilization or delivery patterns, technological advances, and changes in the health status of plan participants. Examples include the possible future use of technology that is now being developed or the reduction of the need for benefits resulting from participation in wellness programs (ASC 715-60-35-99).

Different cost trend rates may be required for different types of services. For example, the cost trend rate for hospital care may differ from that for dental care. Further, the cost trend rates may fluctuate at different rates during different projected periods in the future. For example, there may be a rapid short-term increase, with a subsequent leveling off in the longer term.

Absent information to the contrary, the employer should assume that governmental benefits will continue as provided by existing law, and that benefits from other providers will continue in accordance with their existing plans. Future changes in the law are not anticipated (ASC 715-60-35-102).

Attribution

Once the expected postretirement benefit obligation for an employee has been determined, an equal amount of that obligation is attributed to each year of service in the attribution period, unless the benefit formula of the plan is frontloaded and thus necessitates attribution on a different basis (ASC 715-60-35-62).

The attribution period starts when the employee begins earning credit toward postretirement benefits. This generally occurs on the date of hire, but may be at a later date if the benefit formula requires a waiting period before the employee can earn credit. In any event, the attribution period ends when the employee reaches full eligibility for benefits. The cost of providing the benefits is attributed to the period during which the employee builds up full eligibility. The employer does not attribute any of the service cost to any period after the employee has achieved full eligibility (ASC 715-60-35-66, 68).

Illustration of Attribution Period

Under the postretirement benefit plan of Company Q, employees qualify by rendering at least five years of service and reaching age 65 while in service. The company hires an employee at age 61. Assume the expected postretirement benefit obligation for this employee is $10,000. The attribution period is five years. (Note that the employee will not become eligible at age 65, because the employee will not yet have completed five years of service.) For each of the first five years of service, the annual service cost will be $2,000 (1/5 of $10,000). No service cost will be attributed after the first five years, even if the employee remains in service.

Illustration of Attribution under a Frontloaded Plan

A "frontloaded" plan is one in which a disproportionate share of the benefit obligation is attributed to the early years of an employee's service.

A life insurance plan provides postretirement death benefits of $200,000 for 10 years of service after age 45 and additional death benefits of $10,000 for each year of service thereafter until age 65. (The maximum benefit is therefore $300,000, consisting of the basic $200,000 plus 10 additional years @ $10,000.)

In this situation, the benefit obligation is attributed to periods corresponding to the benefit formula, as follows:

- The actuarial present value of a death benefit of $20,000 (1/10 of $200,000) is attributed to each of the first 10 years of service after age 45.

- The actuarial present value of an additional $10,000 death benefit is attributed to each year of service thereafter until age 65.

RECOGNITION OF NET PERIODIC POSTRETIREMENT BENEFIT COST

The amount of net periodic postretirement benefit cost is derived from the net change in the amount of the accumulated postretirement benefit obligation, after ignoring those components of the net change that do not pertain to the cost of benefits (ASC 715-60-35-7).

The net periodic postretirement benefit cost recognized for a period consists of the following components (ASC 715-60-35-9):

- Service cost
- Interest cost
- Actual return on plan assets, if any
- Amortization of prior service cost or credit included in accumulated other comprehensive income
- Gain or loss (to the extent recognized)
- Amortization of the transition obligation or asset at the date of initial application of the accounting requirements for postretirement benefit plans (if the full amount was not immediately recognized upon initial adoption of these requirements) and still remaining in accumulated other comprehensive income

---

PRACTICE NOTE: The employer makes one entry to accrue the net periodic postretirement benefit cost, the amount of which is the total of the components listed above, determined by worksheet calculations.

Illustration of Basic Transactions and Adjustments

Company A's date of transition to the accounting requirements for postretirement benefit plans was the beginning of Year 1. At that time, the accumulated postretirement benefit obligation was $300,000. The plan was unfunded.

At the end of Year 1, Company A paid $65,000 of postretirement benefits. Service cost attributed to Year 1 was $60,000. The assumed discount rate was 10%.

Worksheets as of the end of Year 1 are as follows:

	Postretirement Benefit Cost	Accumulated Postretirement Benefit Obligation	Transition Obligation
Beginning of year	$NA	$(300,000)	$300,000
Recognition of components of net periodic postretirement benefit cost:			
Service cost	(60,000)	(60,000)	
Interest cost[a]	(30,000)	(30,000)	

	Postretirement Benefit Cost	Accumulated Postretirement Benefit Obligation	Transition Obligation
Amortization of transition obligation[b]	(15,000)		(15,000)
	$(105,000)	(90,000)	(15,000)
Benefit payments		65,000	
Net change		(25,000)	(15,000)
End of year		$(325,000)	$285,000

[a] 10% (assumed discount rate) of $300,000 (accumulated postretirement obligation at beginning of year)
[b] 20-year straight-line amortization of transition obligation (discussed later in this chapter)

The amounts on this worksheet are reflected in the reconciliation of the funded status of the plan with the amounts shown on the statement of financial position, as follows:

	Beginning of Year 1	Net Change	End of Year 1
Accumulated postretirement benefit obligation	$(300,000)	$(25,000)	$(325,000)
Plan assets at fair value	-0-		-0-
Funded status—Recognized as a liability on the balance sheet[a]	(300,000)	(25,000)	(325,000)
Transition obligation included in other comprehensive income	300,000	(15,000)	285,000

[a] The liability for postretirement benefits is $300,000 at the beginning of Year 1. It increases during Year 1 by the amount that service cost, interest cost, and expected return on plan assets exceed the cash contributions during the year ($90,000 − $65,000).

Basic Transactions and Adjustments

Service Cost Component

The *service cost component* of net periodic postretirement benefit cost is defined by ASC 715 as the portion of the expected postretirement benefit obligation attributed to employee service during a specified period, based on the actuarial present value of the expected obligation (ASC 715-60-35-10).

A *defined benefit* postretirement benefit plan contains a benefit formula that defines the benefit an employee will receive for services performed during a specified period (service cost). ASC 715 requires that the terms of the benefit formula be used to determine the amount of postretirement benefit earned by each employee for services performed during a specified period. Under ASC 715, attribution is the process of assigning postretirement benefits or cost to periods of employee service, in accordance with the postretirement benefit formula.

Interest Cost Component

ASC 715 requires an employer to recognize as a component of net periodic postretirement benefit cost the interest cost on the accumulated postretirement benefit obligation. The interest cost is equal to the increase in the amount of the obligation because of the passage of time, measured at a rate equal to the assumed discount rate. ASC 715 specifies that the interest cost component of net periodic postretirement benefit cost is not considered interest expense for purposes of capitalizing interest as required by ASC 835 (Interest) (ASC Glossary).

Actual Return on Plan Assets Component

If a plan is funded, a component of periodic postretirement benefit cost is the actual return on plan assets. The amount of the actual return on plan assets is equal to the difference between the fair value of plan assets at the beginning and end of a period, adjusted for employer contributions, employee contributions (if the plan is contributory) and postretirement benefits paid during the period.

Fair value is the amount that reasonably could be expected to result from a current sale of an investment between a willing buyer and a willing seller, that is, a sale other than a forced liquidation. Plan assets that are used in the operation of the postretirement benefit plan (e.g., building, equipment, furniture, fixtures) are valued at cost less accumulated depreciation or amortization. The actual return on plan assets is shown net of tax expense if the fund holding the plan assets is a taxable entity (ASC Glossary).

A return on plan assets decreases the employer's cost of providing postretirement benefits to its employees, while a loss on plan assets increases postretirement benefit cost. Net periodic postretirement benefit income can result from a significantly high return on plan assets during a period.

Illustration of Actual Return on Plan Assets

An employer may determine its actual gain or loss on plan assets as follows:

Plan assets, beginning of year, at fair value	$ 200,000
Add: Amounts contributed to plan	750,000
Less: Benefit payments from plan	(650,000)
	300,000
Less: Plan assets, end of year, at fair value	340,000
Actual (return) loss on plan assets	$ (40,000)

PRACTICE NOTE: Actual return on plan assets is one of the components of net periodic postretirement benefit cost. As discussed later in this chapter, ASC 715 requires this component to be disclosed in the notes to the financial statements. Another component of net postretirement benefit cost is gains and losses (discussed later in this chapter). The "gains and losses" component includes, among other items, "plan asset gains and losses," defined as the difference between the actual return and the expected return on plan assets.

The following example illustrates the combined effect on net periodic postretirement benefit cost of (a) actual return on plan assets and (b) plan asset gains and losses: If the actual return on plan assets is $1,000,000 and the expected return is $700,000, the plan asset gain is the $300,000 difference between the actual return and the expected return. This $300,000 plan asset gain is part of the "gains and losses" component of net periodic postretirement benefit cost, while the $1,000,000 actual return on plan assets is another component. The combined effect is a net decrease of $700,000 in net periodic postretirement benefit cost, the result of offsetting the $300,000 plan asset gain against the $1,000,000 actual return. This $700,000 is equal to the expected return on plan assets. The total amount of net periodic postretirement benefit cost includes the $700,000 as well as other components, including service cost, interest cost, etc. The $300,000 plan asset gain is taken into account in computing in future years (a) the expected return on plan assets and (b) amortization of deferred gains and losses. (See discussion and illustration later in this chapter.)

Amortization of Prior Service Cost or Credit Component

When a postretirement benefit plan is initially adopted or amended, employees may be granted benefits for services performed in prior periods. The cost of postretirement benefits that are granted retroactively to employees is referred to as *prior service cost* (ASC 715-60-35-13).

Under ASC 715, only a portion of the total amount of prior service cost arising in a period is included in net periodic postretirement benefit cost. ASC 715 requires that the total prior service cost arising in a period from the adoption or amendment of a plan be amortized in a systematic manner. *Amortization* of prior service cost is a component of net periodic postretirement benefit cost (ASC 715-60-35-14).

Initiation of a Plan, or Amendment that Improves Benefits in an Existing Plan

When an employer initiates a plan or adopts an amendment that improves the benefits in an existing plan, the amount of prior service cost is the amount of increase in the accumulated postretirement benefit obligation that can be attributed to service of employees in prior periods.

Methods of Amortizing Prior Service Cost

ASC 715 provides a number of rules regarding the amortization of prior service cost, as follows:

- General rule
- Special rule if all or most employees are fully eligible
- Simplified computation
- Accelerated amortization

Illustration of Plan Amendment Increasing Benefits

At the beginning of Year 2, Company A amended its plan, causing the accumulated postretirement benefit obligation to increase by $84,000. Active plan participants had an average of 12 remaining years of service before reaching full eligibility for benefits.

At the end of Year 2, the employer paid $60,000 in benefits. Service cost was $50,000.

The worksheets as of the end of Year 2 are as follows:

	Postretirement Benefit Cost	Accumulated Postretirement Benefit Obligation	Transition Obligation	Prior Service Cost
Beginning of year	NA	$(325,000)	$285,000	$ -0-
Plan amendment		(84,000)		84,000
Recognition of components of net periodic postretirement benefit cost:				
Service cost	(50,000)	(50,000)		
Interest cost(a)	(40,900)	(40,900)		
Amortization of transition obligation(b)	(15,000)		(15,000)	
Amortization of prior service cost(c)	(7,000)			(7,000)
	(112,900)	(174,900)	(15,000)	77,000
Benefit payments		60,000		
Net change		(114,900)	(15,000)	77,000
End of year(d)		$(439,900)	$270,000	$77,000

(a) 10% (assumed discount rate) of $325,000 (accumulated postretirement benefit obligation at beginning of year), plus 10% of $84,000 (increase in obligation by plan amendment)
(b) 20-year amortization of original $300,000 transition obligation
(c) Straight-line amortization of prior service cost, based on average remaining years of service (12 years) of active plan participants before reaching full eligibility
(d) The liability on the balance sheet at the end of year 2 ($439,900) equals the liability at the beginning of the year ($325,000) increased by the plan amendment ($84,000) and by the excess of service cost, interest cost, and expected return on plan assets ($90,900) over cash contributions ($60,000) during the year.

Analysis of postretirement benefit accounts:

	End of Year 1	Net Change	End of Year 2
Accumulated postretirement benefit obligation	$(325,000)	$(114,900)	$(439,900)
Plan assets at fair value	-0-		-0-
Funded status—Recognized as a liability on the balance sheet	(325,000)	(114,900)	(439,900)

	End of Year 1	Net Change	End of Year 2
Prior service cost	-0-	77,000	77,000
Transition obligation	285,000	(15,000)	270,000

- *General rule*: The general rule requires amortization of prior service cost in equal installments during each employee's remaining years of service until that employee reaches full eligibility under the new or amended plan (ASC 715-60-35-15).
- *Special rule if all or most employees are fully eligible*: If all or almost all employees are already fully eligible for benefits when the plan is initiated or amended, the employer amortizes prior service cost over the remaining life expectancy of those employees (ASC 715-60-35-17).
- *Simplified computation*: ASC 715 allows a simplified form of computation, provided it amortizes prior service cost more quickly than the methods described above. For example, instead of basing its amortization on the period during which each individual employee reaches full eligibility, an employer may amortize prior service cost over the *average* remaining years of service of all active plan participants until they reach full eligibility (ASC 715-60-35-18).
- *Accelerated amortization*: An enterprise uses an accelerated method of amortization if a history of plan amendments and other evidence indicates that the employer's economic benefits from the initiation or amendment of the plan will be exhausted before the employees reach full eligibility for postretirement benefits. In this situation, amortization should reflect the period during which the employer expects to receive economic benefits from the existence of the plan (ASC 715-60-35-19).

Plan Amendments that Reduce Obligation

If a plan amendment reduces the accumulated postretirement obligation, the reduction (a negative prior service cost) is recognized as a credit to other comprehensive income. The prior service credit is amortized in accordance with the above rules after it is applied (*a*) to reduce any existing (positive) prior service cost included in accumulated other comprehensive income and (*b*) to reduce any transition obligation included in accumulated other comprehensive income (ASC 715-60-35-20).

Gain or Loss Component

The approach to gains and losses in ASC 715 is similar to that required for pension plan accounting. Gains or losses consist of certain types of changes in (*a*) the accumulated postretirement benefit obligation and (*b*) the plan assets. The changes may result from either (*a*) experience different from that assumed or (*b*) changes in assumptions (ASC 715-60-35-23).

Gains and losses include amounts that have been realized (for example, the sale of a security) and amounts that have not been realized (for example, changes in the market value of plan assets) (ASC 715-60-35-23). Gains or losses that are not recognized immediately are included in other comprehensive income in the year they occur.

Elements of the Gain or Loss Component

The gain or loss component of net periodic postretirement benefit cost is the combination of three elements (ASC 715-60-35-36):

1. Plan asset gains and losses during the period
2. Other gains and losses immediately realized
3. Amortization of deferred gains and losses from previous periods and included in accumulated other comprehensive income

> **PRACTICE POINTER:** The gain or loss component of net postretirement benefit cost does not include the actual return on plan assets during the period, which is another component of net periodic postretirement benefit cost, discussed earlier in this chapter.
>
> The gain or loss component does include, among other items, the difference between the actual return and the expected return on plan assets, since this difference falls within the general concept of gains and losses according to ASC 715—changes resulting from experience different from that assumed or from changes in assumptions.

Plan Asset Gains and Losses

Plan asset gains and losses are the difference between the actual return (including earnings and holding gains/losses) and the expected return for the same period (ASC Glossary).

The computation of plan asset gains and losses starts with determining the expected return on plan assets, which is computed by multiplying the following two items: (1) the expected long-term rate of return on plan assets and (2) the market-related value of plan assets. Plan asset gains and losses include both changes reflected in the market-related value of plan assets and changes not yet reflected in the market-related value of plan assets (ASC 715-60-35-27).

The market-related value may be either fair market value or a calculation that recognizes changes in fair market value systematically over a period of five years or less. The employer may use different methods of calculating market-related value for different categories of assets, but each category must be treated consistently during successive periods (ASC Glossary). ASC 715 requires plan asset gains and losses during the period to be included as a component of net periodic postretirement benefit cost.

> **PRACTICE NOTE:** Plan asset gains and losses (excluding amounts not yet reflected in the market-related value of plan assets) are taken into account in computing the future expected return on plan assets. This year's plan asset gains and losses will therefore be reflected, in the computation of the expected return on plan assets, in future years' net periodic postretirement benefit cost. Plan asset gains and losses (excluding amounts not yet reflected in the market-

related value of plan assets) are also taken into account in computing amortization of net gains and losses included in accumulated other comprehensive income.

Other Gains and Losses Immediately Realized

Immediate recognition of other types of gains and losses is required in some situations and permitted in others.

An employer recognizes an immediate gain or loss if it decides to deviate temporarily from its substantive plan, either by (*a*) forgiving a retrospective adjustment of the current or prior years' cost-sharing provisions as they relate to benefit costs already incurred by retirees or (*b*) otherwise changing the employer's share of benefit costs incurred in the current or prior periods (ASC 715-60-35-34).

If immediate recognition of gains and losses is not required, an employer may elect to use a method that consistently recognizes gains and losses immediately, provided: (*a*) any gain that does not offset a loss previously recognized in income must first offset any transition obligation included in accumulated other comprehensive income and (*b*) any loss that does not offset a gain previously recognized in income must first offset any transition asset included in accumulated other comprehensive income (ASC 715-60-35-32).

ASC 715—Compensation—Retirement Benefits

	Postretirement Benefit Cost	Cash	Transition Obligation	Net Loss	Liability for Postretirement Benefit Plan	MEMO ACCT Accumulated Postretirement Benefit Obligation	MEMO ACCT Plan Assets
Beginning of year	NA	NA	$2,700,000	$302,500	($2,596,500)	($3,625,000)	($1,028,500)
Recognition of components of net periodic postretirement benefit cost:							
Service cost	180,000					(180,000)	
Interest cost	326,250					(326,250)	
Amortization of transition obligation	150,000		(150,000)				
Amortization of unrecognized net loss							
Expected return on plan assets[a]	(96,850)						96,850
Assets contributed to plan		(956,250)					956,250
Benefit payments from plan						450,000	(450,000)
Net expense or net change	559,400	(956,250)	(150,000)		(546,850)	(56,250)	603,100
End of year—projected	NA	NA	$2,550,000	$302,500	($2,049,650)	($3,681,250)	$1,631,600

[a] See Schedule 1.

Amortization of deferred gains and losses from previous periods Any gains and losses not recognized immediately as a component of net periodic benefit cost are immediately recognized in other comprehensive income. ASC 715 establishes a special formula to determine (*a*) whether an employer is required to amortize gains and losses included in accumulated other comprehensive income and (*b*) if amortization is required, the minimum amount of periodic amortization. ASC 715 allows other methods instead of those provided by the formula, if certain qualifications are met.

ASC 715 requires amortization of net gains and losses included in accumulated other comprehensive income if the beginning-of-year balance of net unrecognized gain or loss (with a modification noted below) is more than a base figure used for comparison purposes (ASC 715-60-35-29).

The base figure is 10% of the greater of the accumulated postretirement benefit obligation or the market-related value of plan assets as of the beginning of the year (ASC 715-60-35-29).

For purposes of this comparison, the gain or loss included in accumulated other comprehensive income is modified, so as to exclude any plan asset gains or losses that have not yet been reflected in market-related value.

PRACTICE POINTER: If gains or losses included in accumulated other comprehensive income are not greater than the base figure, they come within the 10% "corridor" and the employer need not recognize them. This procedure is similar to the corridor test for recognizing gains and losses on pensions.

If amortization is required under the formula, the amount to be amortized is the difference between the beginning-of-year balance of net gain or loss (adjusted to exclude any plan asset gains or losses that have not yet been reflected in the market-related value) and the base figure.

The minimum amortization is the amount to be amortized, determined as above, divided by the average remaining service period of active plan participants. If all or almost all of the plan's participants are inactive, divide instead by the average remaining life expectancy of the inactive participants (ASC 715-60-35-29).

Instead of using the minimum amortization method, an employer may use any other systematic method of amortization, provided that (*a*) the amortization for each period is at least as much as the amount determined by the minimum amortization method, (*b*) the method is used consistently, (*c*) the method applies consistently to gains and losses, and (*d*) the method is disclosed (ASC 715-60-35-31).

Illustration of Gains and Losses

At the beginning of 20X5, Company L prepared the following projection of changes during that year:

As of the end of 20X5, Company L prepared the following worksheet and supporting schedules to reflect actual changes during the year:

ASC 715—Compensation—Retirement Benefits

	Projected 12/31/X5	Net Gain (Loss)	Actual 12/31/X5
Accumulated postretirement benefit obligation	$(3,681,250)	$ 118,630[b]	$(3,562,620)
Plan assets at fair value	1,631,600	(110,180)[c]	1,521,420
Funded status—liability	(2,049,650)	8,450	(2,041,200)
Net (gain) loss	302,500	(8,450)	294,050
Transition obligation	2,550,000	—	2,550,000

[b] Liability at year-end was $118,630 less than projected, because of changes in assumptions not detailed here.
[c] See Schedule 1.

	Net Periodic Postretirement Benefit Cost
Service cost	$180,000
Interest cost	326,250
Expected return on plan assets[d]	(96,850)
Amortization of transition obligation	150,000
Net periodic postretirement benefit cost	$559,400

[d] See Schedule 3.

Schedule 1—Plan Assets

Expected long-term rate of return on plan assets	10%
Beginning balance, market-related value[f]	$968,500
Contributions to plan (end of year)	956,250
Benefits paid by plan	(450,000)
Expected return on plan assets	96,850
	1,571,600
20% of each of last five years' asset gains (losses)	(7,036)
Ending balance, market-related value	$ 1,564,564
Beginning balance, fair value of plan assets	$ 1,028,500
Contributions to plan	956,250
Benefits paid	(450,000)
Actual return (loss) on plan assets[g]	(13,330)
Ending balance, fair value of plan assets	$ 1,521,420
Deferred asset gain (loss) for year[h]	$ (110,180)
Gain (loss) not included in ending balance market-related value[i]	$ (43,144)

[f] This example adds 20% of each of the last five years' gains or losses.
[g] See Schedule 3.
[h] (Actual return on plan assets) − (expected return on plan assets).
   Note: The term *deferred asset gain (loss) for year* follows the terminology in the illustrations attached to ASC 715, although the text of ASC 715 refers to the same item as *plan asset gains and losses*.

(i) (Ending balance, fair value of plan assets) − (ending balance, market-related value of plan assets).
(j) See Schedule 1.

Schedule 2—Amortization of Unrecognized Net Gain or Loss

10% of beginning balance of accumulated postretirement benefit obligation	$ 362,500
10% of beginning balance of market-related value of plan assets(j)	96,850
Greater of the above	$ 362,500
Unrecognized net (gain) loss at beginning of year	$ 302,500
Asset gain (loss) not included in beginning balance of market-related value(k) ($1,028,500 − $968,500)	60,000
Amount subject to amortization	$ 362,500
Amount in excess of the corridor subject to amortization	None
Required amortization	None

(j) See Schedule 1.
(k) See Schedule 1.

Schedule 3—Actual Return or Loss on Plan Assets

Plan assets at fair value, beginning of year	$1,028,500
Plus: Assets contributed to plan	956,250
Less: Benefit payments from plan	(450,000)
	1,534,750
Less: Plan assets at fair value, end of year	(1,521,420)
Actual (return) loss on plan assets	$ 13,330

Amortization of Transition Obligation/Asset Component

The final component of net periodic postretirement benefit cost is amortization of the transition obligation or asset at the date of initial application of ASC 715 that remains in accumulated other comprehensive income. At the beginning of the fiscal year in which ASC 715 is first applied, the funded status of the plan was computed by comparing the difference between (1) the accumulated postretirement benefit obligation and (2) the fair value of plan assets plus any recognized accrued postretirement benefit cost less any recognized prepaid postretirement benefit cost. The resulting difference, either a transition asset or transition obligation, can either be recognized immediately in net income or on a delayed basis as a component of net periodic postretirement benefit cost.

If delayed recognition is chosen, the transition asset or obligation is generally recognized over the average remaining service period of active plan participants (ASC 715-60-35-39). However, there are a number of exceptions to this general requirement:

- If the average remaining service period of active plan participants is less than 20 years, the transition asset or obligation can be amortized over 20 years.

- If all or almost all of the plan's participants are inactive, the transition asset or obligation can be amortized over the average remaining life expectancy of these plan participants.

- Amortization of the transition obligation (not transition asset) must be accelerated if cumulative benefit payments subsequent to the transition date exceed cumulative postretirement benefit cost accrued subsequent to the transition date. Additional amortization of the transition obligation is recognized to the extent that cumulative benefit payments exceed cumulative accrued postretirement benefit cost. Cumulative benefit payments include any payments related to a plan settlement and cumulative benefit payments are to be reduced by: (1) plan assets and (2) any recognized accrued postretirement benefit obligation, both measured as of the transition date.

RECOGNITION OF FUNDED STATUS OF POSTRETIREMENT BENEFIT PLANS

An employer is required to recognize the overfunded or underfunded status of a defined postretirement benefit plan as an asset or a liability in its statement of financial position. If the fair value of a postretirement benefit plan's assets exceeds the plan's accumulated postretirement benefit obligation, the plan is overfunded and an asset is recognized. If the plan's accumulated postretirement benefit obligation exceeds the fair value of the plan's assets, the plan is underfunded and a liability is recognized (ASC 715-60-35-5). When the funded status of the postretirement benefit plan is first recognized in the statement of financial position, the offsetting entry is to accumulated other comprehensive income (net of tax). The recognition of a postretirement benefit plan asset or liability may result in temporary differences under ASC 740 (Income Taxes). Deferred tax effects are to be recognized for these temporary differences as a component of income tax expense or benefit in the year in which the differences arise, and allocated to various financial statement components.

Asset and liability gains and losses as well as prior service costs or credits that occur in periods after recognition of the funded status of the plan and that are not immediately included as a component of net periodic postretirement benefit cost are included in other comprehensive income. As gains and losses, prior service costs and credits, and the transition asset or obligation are included in net periodic postretirement benefit cost, they are recognized as an adjustment to other comprehensive income.

MEASUREMENT OF PLAN ASSETS

Plan assets generally are stocks, bonds, and other investments. Such assets may include the participation rights in participating insurance contracts, but not other rights in insurance contracts. The employer's own securities may be included as plan assets, but only if they are transferable and otherwise meet the conditions under ASC 715 (ASC Glossary).

Plan assets are increased by various means, including the employer's contributions, employees' contributions if the plan is contributory, and earnings from investing the contributed amounts. Plan assets are decreased by benefit payments, income taxes, and other expenses (ASC Glossary).

All plan assets should be segregated and restricted for paying postretirement benefits. Usually, the assets are in a trust. Plan assets may be withdrawn only for the stated purposes of the plan. In limited circumstances, the plan may permit withdrawal when the plan's assets exceed its obligations and the employer has taken appropriate steps to satisfy existing obligations (ASC Glossary).

If assets are not segregated or restricted effectively in some other way, they are not plan assets even though the employer intends to use them for paying postretirement benefits. Contributions that are accrued but not yet paid into the plan are not regarded as plan assets (ASC Glossary).

For purposes of disclosure, ASC 715 requires the employer to use fair value as the measurement for all plan investments, including equity or debt securities, real estate, and other items (ASC 715-60-35-107). Fair value is determined in accordance with the guidance in ASC 820 (Fair Value Measurements and Disclosures). (Additional guidance on determining fair values can be found in the chapter of this *Guide* that discusses ASC 820.)

Plan assets used in plan operations, such as buildings, equipment, furniture and fixtures, and leasehold improvements, are measured at cost less accumulated depreciation or amortization (ASC 715-60-35-107).

Insurance Contracts

Benefits covered by insurance contracts (defined below) are excluded from the accumulated postretirement benefit obligation. Insurance contracts are also excluded from plan assets, except for the amounts attributable to participation rights in participating insurance contracts.

Definition of Insurance Contracts

ASC 715 defines an *insurance contract* as a contract in which the insurance company unconditionally undertakes a legal obligation to provide specified benefits to specific individuals in return for a fixed premium. The contract must be irrevocable and must involve the transfer of significant risk from the employer (or the plan) to the insurance company. A contract does not qualify as an insurance contract if (*a*) the insurance company is a *captive insurer* doing business primarily with the employer and related parties or (*b*) there is any reasonable doubt that the insurance company will meet its obligations under the contract (ASC 715-60-35-110).

Participating Insurance Contracts

Some contracts are *participating insurance contracts*, in which the purchaser (either the plan or the employer) participates in the experience of the insurance company. The purchaser's participation generally takes the form of a dividend that effectively reduces the cost of the plan. If, however, the employer's participation is so great that the employer retains all or most of the risks and rewards of the plan, the contract is not regarded as an insurance contract for purposes of ASC 715 (ASC 715-60-35-114, 117).

The purchase price of a participating contract ordinarily is higher than the price of a similar contract without the participation right. The difference between the price with and without the participation right is considered to be the cost of the participation right. The employer should regard this cost as an asset when purchased. At subsequent dates, the employer measures the participation right at its fair value if fair value can be estimated reasonably. Otherwise, the participation right is measured at its amortized cost, but this amount should not exceed the participation right's net realizable value. The cost is amortized systematically over the expected dividend period (ASC 715-60-35-115, 116).

Cost of Insurance

Insurance contracts, such as life insurance contracts, may be purchased during a period to cover postretirement benefits attributed to service by employees in the same period. In this situation, the cost of the benefits equals the cost of purchasing the insurance (after adjusting for the cost of any participation rights included in the contract) (ASC 715-60-35-118).

Accordingly, if all postretirement benefits attributed to service by employees in the current period are covered by nonparticipating insurance contracts purchased during the same period, the cost of the benefits equals the cost of purchasing the insurance. If the benefits are only partially covered by nonparticipating insurance contracts, the uninsured portion of the benefits is accounted for in the same way as benefits under uninsured plans (ASC 715-60-35-118, 119).

Insurance Company Not Fully Bound

If the insurance company does not unconditionally undertake a legal obligation to pay specified benefits to specific individuals, the arrangement does not qualify as an insurance contract for purposes of ASC 715. The arrangement is accounted for as an investment at fair value (ASC 715-60-35-120).

Fair value is presumed to equal the cash surrender value or conversion value, if any. In some cases, the best estimate of fair value is the contract value.

MEASUREMENT DATE

All postretirement benefit plan assets that are held as investments to provide postretirement benefits are generally measured at their fair values as of the date of the financial statements. There are two exceptions to this general rule. First, if a subsidiary sponsors a postretirement benefit plan and the subsidiary has a different year-end than its parent, the fair value of the subsidiary's postretirement benefit plan assets is measured at the date of the subsidiary's financial statements. Second, if an investee, accounted for using the equity method, sponsors a postretirement benefit plan and the investee has a different year-end than the investor, the fair value of the investee's postretirement benefit plan assets is measured at the date of the investee's financial statements (ASC 715-60-35-121).

Unless more current amounts are available for both the obligation and plan assets, the funded status of the postretirement benefit plan reported in interim financial statements shall be the same amount as reported by the employer in its previous year-end statement of financial position, adjusted for subsequent accruals of service cost, interest cost, and return on plan assets, contributions, and benefit payments (ASC 715-60-35-125).

DISCLOSURES

The disclosure requirements relating to postretirement benefit plans are covered in the discussion of subtopic ASC 715-20.

EMPLOYERS WITH TWO OR MORE PLANS

ASC 715 deals with the questions of measurement and disclosure separately for an employer with two or more plans and for employers with one plan.

Aggregate Measurement

ASC 715 generally requires an employer with two or more plans to measure each plan separately. An employer may measure its plans as an aggregate rather than as separate plans, however, if the plans meet the following criteria (ASC 715-60-35-129, 130):

- The plans provide postretirement health care benefits
- The plans provide either of the following:
  — Different benefits to the same group of employees
  — The same benefits to different groups of employees
- The plans are unfunded (without any plan assets)
- The employer aggregates all of its plans that meet the preceding three tests.

An employer may make a separate aggregation of plans providing welfare benefits (that is, postretirement benefits other than health care), if requirements (2) through (4) above are met. However, a plan that has plan assets should not be aggregated with other plans, but should be measured separately (ASC 715-60-35-130).

MULTIPLE-EMPLOYER PLANS

A multiple-employer plan is distinct from a multiemployer plan. In a *multiple-employer* plan, individual employers combine their single-employer plans for pooling assets for investment purposes, or for reducing the costs of administration. The participating employers may have different benefit formulas; each employer's contributions to the plan are based on that employer's benefit formula. These plans generally are not the result of collective bargaining agreements.

An employer shall apply the provisions of ASC 450 to its participation in a multiemployer plan if it is probable or reasonably possible that either of the following would occur:

1. An employer would withdraw from the plan under circumstances that would give rise to an obligation.
2. An employer's contribution to the fund would be increased during the remainder of the contract period to make up for a shortfall in the funds necessary to maintain the negotiated level of benefit coverage. (ASC 715-80-50-2)

An employer that participates in a multiemployer plans that provide pension benefits shall disclosure information prescribed in ASC 715-80-50-4 through 715-80-50-10. The disclosures of the employer's contributions to the plan include all items recognized as net pension costs and are based on the most recently available information through the date at which the employer has evaluated subsequent events. (ASC 715-80-50-3)

- Narrative description of both the general nature of the multi-employer plans that provide pension benefits and the employer.
- The employer's participation in the plans that would indicate how the risks of participation are different from single-employer plans. (ASC 715-80-50-4)
- When feasible, present in a tabular form, supplemented with greater narrative outside the table (ASC 715-80-50-5):
    — Legal name of the plan.
    — The plan's Employer Identification Number and, if available, its plan number.
    — For each statement of financial position, the most recently available certified zone status provided by the plan, specifying the date of the plan's year-end and whether the plan has utilized any extended amortization provisions that affect the calculation of the zone status.
    — If the zone status is not available, as of the most recent date available, the total plan assets and accumulate benefit obligation and whether the plan was less than 65% funded, between 65% and 80% funded, at least 80% funded.
    — The expiration dates of the collective-bargaining agreements requiring contributions to the plan. If more than one collective-bargaining agreement applies, a range of the expiration dates, supplemented with a qualitative description that identifies the significant collective-bargaining agreements within that arrange as well as other information to help investors understand the significance of the agreements and when they expire.
    — For each period for which a statement of income (statement of activities for not-for-profits) is presented the employer's contributions to the plan, whether the contributions represent more than 5% of total contributions to the plan.
    — As of the most recent annual period, whether a funding improvement plan or rehabilitation plan has been implemented, whether the em-

ployer paid a surcharge to the plan, and a description of any minimum contributions required for future periods by the collective-bargaining agreement, statutory obligation, or other contractual obligations.

- A description of the nature and effect of any significant changes that affect comparability of total employer contributions from period to period, such as a business combination or divestiture, a change in the contractual employer contribution rate, and a change in the number of employees covered by the plan during each year. (ASC 715-80-50-6)
- If information is not available in the public domain, in addition to the above requirements:
    — A description of the nature of the plan benefits.
    — A qualitative description of the extent to which the employer could be responsible for the obligations of the plan, including benefits earned by employees during employment with another employer.
    — Other quantitative information as of the most recent date available to help users understand the financial information about the plan. (ASC 715-80-50-7)
- In a tabular form for each annual period for which a statement of income or statement of activities is presented, the total contributions made to all plans that are not individually significant and the total contributions to all plans. (ASC 715-80-50-9)

An employer that participates in multiemployer plans that provide postretirement benefits other than pensions shall disclose the amount of contributions to those plans for each annual period for which a statement of income (or statement of activities) is presented. This disclosure shall include a description of the nature and effect of any changes that affect comparability of total employer contributions from period to period, such as a business combination or divestiture, a change in the contractual employer contribution rate, and a change in the number of employees covered by the plan during each year. The disclosure shall include a description of the nature of the benefits and the types of employees covered by these benefits, such as medical benefits provided to active and employees and retirees. (ASC 715-80-50-11)

> **PRACTICE POINTER:** The above represents a highly summarized version of the information required to be disclosed regarding multiemployer plans from ASC 715. Entities subject to these requirements are encouraged to consult ASC 715-80-50-1 through ASC 715-80-55-8 for more detailed guidance and illustrations.

PLANS OUTSIDE THE UNITED STATES

ASC 715 applies to plans outside as well as inside the United States. If the accumulated postretirement obligation of the plans outside the United States is significant in proportion to the total of all the employer's postretirement benefit plans, the employer should make separate disclosure of the plans outside the United States. Otherwise, the employer may make combined disclosure of plans outside and inside the United States (ASC 715-10-15-6).

> **PRACTICE NOTE:** ASC 715 does not define *outside the United States*. The following factors, among others, may be relevant: (a) where all or most of the employees and beneficiaries are located and (b) which country's law governs the relationships among employees, beneficiaries, and the employer.

BUSINESS COMBINATIONS

When a single-employer defined benefit postretirement plan is acquired as part of a business combination accounted for by the acquisition method, the acquirer recognizes an asset or a liability representing the funded status of the plan. When determining the funded status of the plan, the acquirer shall exclude the effects of expected plan amendments, terminations, or curtailments that at the acquisition date it has no obligation to make. If an acquiree participates in a multiemployer plan, and it is probable that it will withdraw from that plan, the acquirer recognizes as part of the business combination a withdrawal liability in accordance with ASC 450 (ASC 805-20-25-25).

SETTLEMENT AND CURTAILMENT OF A POSTRETIREMENT BENEFIT OBLIGATION

According to ASC 715, a *settlement* is a transaction that has the following characteristics (ASC Glossary):

- Is an irrevocable action
- Relieves the employer (or the plan) of primary responsibility for the postretirement benefit obligation
- Eliminates significant risks related to the obligation and the assets used to put the settlement into effect

Settlements take place, for example, in the following situations (ASC 715-60-15-16):

- The employer makes lump-sum cash payments to plan participants, buying their rights to receive future specified postretirement benefits.
- The employer purchases long-term nonparticipating insurance contracts to cover the accumulated postretirement benefit obligation for some or all of the participants in the plan (but the insurance company cannot be under the employer's control).

Settlements do *not* take place, however, in the following situations (ASC 715-60-55-105):

- The employer purchases an insurance contract from an insurance company controlled by the employer. This does not qualify as a settlement because the employer is still exposed to risk through its relationship with the insurance company.
- The employer invests in high-quality fixed-income securities with principal and income payment dates similar to the estimated due dates of benefits. This does not qualify as a settlement because (a) the investment decision can be revoked, (b) the purchase of the securities does not relieve the employer or the plan of primary responsibility for the postretirement

benefit obligation, and (c) the purchase of the securities does not eliminate significant risks related to the postretirement benefit obligation.

Accounting for a Plan Settlement

Maximum Gain or Loss

When a postretirement benefit obligation is settled, the maximum gain or loss recognized in income is the gain or loss plus any transition asset included in accumulated other comprehensive income. This maximum gain or loss includes any gain or loss resulting from the remeasurement of plan assets and of the accumulated postretirement benefit obligation at the time of settlement (ASC 715-60-35-151).

Settlement Gain or Loss When Entire Obligation Is Settled

If an employer settles the entire accumulated postretirement benefit obligation, a further distinction is made depending on whether the maximum amount subject to recognition is a gain or a loss.

If the maximum amount is a gain, the amount of this gain first reduces any transition obligation remaining in accumulated other comprehensive income and any excess gain is recognized in income. If the maximum amount is a loss, the full amount of this loss is recognized in income (ASC 715-60-35-153).

Settlement Gain or Loss When Only Part of Obligation Is Settled

If an employer settles only part of the accumulated postretirement benefit obligation, the employer recognizes in income a pro rata portion of the amount of gain or loss that would have been recognized if the entire obligation had been settled. The pro rata portion equals the percentage by which the partial settlement reduces the accumulated postretirement benefit obligation (ASC 715-60-35-135).

Participating Insurance

If an employer settles the obligation by purchasing a participating insurance contract, the cost of the participation right is deducted from the maximum gain but not from the maximum loss, before the employer determines the amount to be recognized in income (ASC 715-60-35-156).

Settlements at Lower Cost Than Current Cost of Service and Interest

ASC 715 defines the *cost of a settlement* as follows (ASC 715-60-35-157).
- If the settlement is for cash, its cost is the amount of cash paid to plan participants.
- If the settlement uses nonparticipating insurance contracts, its cost is the cost of the contracts.
- If the settlement uses participating insurance contracts, its cost is the cost of the contracts, less the amount attributed to participation rights.

If the cost of all settlements during a year is no more than the combined amount of service cost and interest cost components of net postretirement benefit cost for the same year, ASC 715 permits but does not require the employer to recognize gain or loss for those settlements. The employer should apply a consistent policy each year (ASC 715-60-35-158).

Accounting for a Plan Curtailment

A *curtailment* is an event that either (*a*) significantly reduces the expected years of future service of active plan participants or (*b*) eliminates the accrual of defined benefits for some or all of the future services of a significant number of active plan participants. The following events are examples of curtailments (ASC Glossary; 715-60-15-17):

- Termination of employees' services earlier than anticipated. (This may or may not relate to the closing of a facility or the discontinuation of a segment of the employer's business.)

- Termination or suspension of a plan, so that employees no longer earn additional benefits for future service. (If the plan is suspended, future service may be counted toward eligibility for benefits accumulated based on past service.)

Gain and Loss Recognition

Under the general provisions of ASC 715 for plans that continue without curtailment, the employer should recognize prior service cost on an amortized basis, on the theory that the employer receives economic benefits from the future services of employees covered by the plan.

When a plan is curtailed, the employer's expectation of receiving benefits from future services of its employees is reduced. Accordingly, curtailment requires the employer to recognize as a loss all or part of the remaining balance of prior service cost included in accumulated other comprehensive income. In this context, prior service cost includes the cost of plan amendments and any transition obligation remaining in accumulated other comprehensive income (ASC 715-60-35-164).

Curtailment Resulting from Termination of Employees

If a curtailment occurs as the result of the termination of a significant number of employees who were plan participants, the curtailment loss consists of the following components (ASC 715-60-35-165):

- The portion of the remaining prior service cost included in accumulated other comprehensive income (relating to this and any prior plan amendment) attributable to the previously estimated number of remaining future years of service of all terminated employees, **plus**

- The portion of the remaining transition obligation included in accumulated other comprehensive income attributable to the previously estimated number of remaining future years of service, but only of the terminated employees who were participants in the plan at the date of the initial application of the accounting guidance on postretirement benefit plans.

Curtailment Resulting from Terminating Accrual of Additional Benefits for Future Services

If a curtailment results from terminating the accrual of additional benefits for the future services of a significant number of employees, the curtailment loss consists of the following components (ASC 715-60-35-166):

- *The **pro rata** amount of the remaining prior service cost included in accumulated other comprehensive income*—This amount is based on the portion of the remaining expected years of service in the amortization period that originally was attributable to the employees (a) who were plan participants at the date of the plan amendment and (b) whose future accrual of benefits has been terminated, **plus**

- *The **pro rata** amount of the remaining transition obligation included in accumulated other comprehensive income*—This amount is based on the portion of the remaining years of service of all participants who were active at the date of transition to the accounting requirements for postretirement benefit obligations, that originally was attributable to the remaining expected future years of service of the employees whose future accrual of benefits has been terminated.

Changes in Accumulated Postretirement Benefit Obligation

A curtailment may cause a gain by decreasing the accumulated postretirement benefit obligation, or a loss by increasing that obligation.

If a curtailment decreases the accumulated obligation, the gain from this decrease is first used to offset any net loss included in accumulated other comprehensive income and the excess is a curtailment gain. If a curtailment increases the accumulated obligation, the loss from this increase is first used to offset any net gain included in accumulated other comprehensive income and the excess is a curtailment loss. In this context, any remaining transition asset is regarded as a net gain, and is combined with the net gain or loss included in accumulated other comprehensive income (ASC 715-60-35-169).

If a curtailment produces a net loss as the combined effect of the above calculations regarding prior service cost and the accumulated postretirement benefit obligation, this combined net loss is recognized in income when it is *probable* that a curtailment will occur and the net effect of the curtailment is reasonably estimable. If the sum of these effects results in a net gain, however, the net gain is recognized in income when the affected employees terminate or the plan suspension or amendment is adopted (ASC 715-60-35-171).

Illustration of Curtailment

Company B reduced its workforce, including a significant number of employees who had accumulated benefits under the postretirement benefit plan. An analysis of the terminated employees revealed:

1. At the time of curtailment, the terminated employees represented 22% of the *remaining years of expected service* of all employees who had been plan participants at the employer's date of transition.

2. At the time of curtailment, the terminated employees represented 18% of the *remaining years of service prior to full eligibility* of all employees who had been plan participants at the date of a prior plan amendment.

Company B's worksheet computation of the curtailment gain or loss is as follows:

	Before Curtailment	Curtailment	After Curtailment
Accumulated postretirement benefit obligation	$(514,000)	$108,000	$(406,000)
Plan assets at fair value	146,000		146,000
Funded status	(368,000)	108,000	(260,000)
Net gain	(89,150)		(89,150)
Prior service cost(a)	66,000	(11,880)	54,120
Transition obligation(b)	390,000	(85,800)	304,200

(a) Effect of curtailment is 18% of $66,000 (prior service cost).
(b) Effect of curtailment is 22% of $390,000 (transition obligation).

Relationship of Settlements and Curtailments to Other Events

An event may be either a settlement, or a curtailment, or both at the same time (ASC 715-60-35-172).

A curtailment occurs, but not a settlement, if the expected future benefits are eliminated for some plan participants (for example, because their employment is terminated), but the plan continues to exist, to pay benefits, to invest assets, and to receive contributions.

A settlement occurs, but not a curtailment, if an employer purchases nonparticipating insurance contracts to cover the accumulated postretirement benefit obligation, while continuing to provide defined benefits for future service (either in the same plan or in a successor plan).

A termination, or in effect both a settlement and curtailment, occurs if an employer settles its obligation and terminates the plan without establishing a successor defined benefit plan to take its place. This occurs whether the employees continue to work for the employer or not.

ASC 715—Compensation—Retirement Benefits   40,085

Illustration of Partial Settlement and Full Curtailment Resulting from Sale of Line of Business

Company C sold a line of business to Company D. Company C has a separate postretirement benefit plan that provides benefits to retirees of the division that is sold. In connection with the sale:

1. Company C terminated all employees of the sold division (a full curtailment).

2. Company D hired most of the employees.

3. Company D assumed the accumulated postretirement benefit obligation of $160,000 for postretirement benefits related to the former employees of Company C hired by Company D, and Company C retained the obligation for its current retirees (a partial settlement).

4. The plan trustee transferred $200,000 of plan assets to Company D, consisting of $160,000 for the settlement of the accumulated postretirement benefit obligation and $40,000 as an excess contribution.

5. Company C determined that its gain on the sale of the division was $600,000, before considering any of the effects of the sale on the postretirement benefit plan.

Company C's accounting policy is to determine the effects of a curtailment before determining the effects of a settlement when both events occur simultaneously.

For Company C, the net loss from the curtailment is $456,000, which is recognized with the $600,000 gain resulting from the disposal of the division. The effect of the curtailment is determined as follows:

	Before Curtailment	Curtailment-Related Effects Resulting from Sale	After Curtailment
Accumulated postretirement benefit obligation	$(514,000)	$ (20,000)(a)	$(534,000)
Plan assets at fair value	220,000		220,000
Funded status	(294,000)	(20,000)	(314,000)
Net gain	(99,150)	20,000(a)	(79,150)
Prior service cost	66,000	(66,000)(b)	—
Transition obligation	390,000	(390,000)(c)	—

(a) Loss from earlier-than-expected retirement of fully eligible employees (not detailed here)
(b) 100% (reduction in remaining years for service to full eligibility) of the unrecognized prior service cost
(c) 100% (reduction in remaining years for service to full eligibility) of the unrecognized transition obligation

The $16,255 loss related to the settlement and transfer of plan assets that is recognized with the gain from the sale is determined as follows:

	After Curtailment	Settlement and Transfer of Plan Assets	After Settlement
Accumulated postretirement benefit obligation	$(534,000)	$160,000	$(374,000)
Plan assets at fair value	220,000	(200,000)	20,000
Funded status	(314,000)	(40,000)	(354,000)
Net gain	(79,150)	23,745[d]	(55,405)
Prior service cost	—	—	—
Transition obligation	—	—	—
Computation of loss on settlement and transfer	$(393,150)	$ (16,255)	$(409,405)

[d] The unrecognized net gain is computed as follows:
Step 1. Compute the percentage of the accumulated postretirement benefit obligation settled to the total accumulated postretirement benefit obligation ($160,000/$534,000 = 30%).
Step 2. Maximum gain is measured as the transition asset, plus any net gain included in other comprehensive income ($79,150 + $0 = $79,150).
Step 3. The settlement gain is 30% of $79,150 = $23,745.

MEASUREMENT OF THE EFFECTS OF TERMINATION BENEFITS

If an employer offers postretirement benefits as special termination benefits that are not required by any preexisting contract, the employer recognizes a liability and a loss when the employees accept the offer and the amount is reasonably estimable. If the employer is contractually obliged to provide postretirement benefits as termination benefits, the employer recognizes a liability and a loss when it is probable that benefits will be paid and the amount is reasonably estimable (ASC 715-60-25-4, 5).

If an employer offers special or contractual termination benefits and curtails the postretirement benefit plan at the same time, ASC 715 requires the employer to account separately for the termination benefits and the curtailment (ASC 715-60-25-4, 5).

The amount of the liability and loss to be recognized when employees accept an offer of termination benefits in the form of postretirement benefits is determined by taking the following steps (ASC 715-60-25-6):

Step 1. Determine the accumulated postretirement benefit obligation for those employees (without including any special termination benefits), on the assumption that (a) any of those employees who are not yet fully eligible for benefits will terminate as soon as they become fully eligible, and (b) any of those employees who are fully eligible will retire immediately.

Step 2. Adjust the accumulated postretirement benefit obligation as computed in Step 1 to reflect the special termination benefits.

Step 3. Subtract the amount in Step 1 from the amount in Step 2.

ASC 715-70: DEFERRED CONTRIBUTION PLANS

DEFINED CONTRIBUTION PLANS

A *defined contribution plan* provides an individual account for each participant, and specifies how to determine the amount to be contributed to each individual's account. The plan does not specify the amount of postretirement benefits to be received by any individual. This amount is determined by the amount of contributions, the return on the investment of the amount contributed, and any forfeitures of the benefits of other plan participants that are allocated to the individual's account (ASC 715-70-05-3).

Accounting for Contributions

A defined contribution plan may require the employer to contribute to the plan only for periods in which an employee renders services, or the employer may be required to continue making payments for periods after the employee retires or terminates employment. To the extent an employer's contribution is made in the same period as the employee renders services, the employer's net periodic postretirement benefit cost equals the amount of contributions required for that period. If the plan requires the employer to continue contributions after the employee retires or terminates, the employer should make accruals during the employee's service period of the estimated amount of contributions to be made after the employee's retirement or termination (ASC 715-70-35-1).

Disclosure

The disclosure requirements for defined contribution plans are consolidated with disclosure requirements for both pension and other postretirement plans in the discussion on subtopic ASC 715-20.

ASC 715-80: MULTI-EMPLOYER PLANS

MULTIEMPLOYER PLANS

A *multiemployer plan* is one to which two or more unrelated employers contribute. Multiemployer plans generally result from *collective bargaining agreements*, and are administered by a joint board of trustees representing management and labor of all contributing employers. Sometimes these plans are called *joint trusts*, *Taft-Hartley*, or *union plans*. An employer may participate in a number of plans; for example, the employees may belong to a number of unions. Numerous employers may participate in a multiemployer plan. Often the employers are in the same industry, but sometimes the employers are in different industries, and the only common element among the employers is that their employees belong to the same labor union (ASC Glossary).

The assets contributed by one employer may be used to provide benefits to employees of other employers, since the assets contributed by one employer are not segregated from those contributed by other employers (ASC 715-80-05-1). Even though the plan provides defined benefits to employees of all the employers, the plan typically requires a defined contribution from each participating employer, but the amount of an employer's obligation may be changed by events affecting other participating employers and their employees.

A multiemployer plan can exist even without the involvement of a labor union. For example, a national not-for-profit organization may organize a multiemployer plan for itself and its local chapters.

Accounting for Multiemployer Plans

Distinctive accounting requirements apply to an employer that participates in a multiemployer plan. The employer recognizes as net periodic pension cost or net postretirement benefit cost the contribution required for the period, including cash and the fair value of noncash contributions. The employer recognizes as a liability any unpaid contributions required for the period (ASC 715-80-35-1).

PRACTICE NOTE:

- This accounting resembles that required for the single employer that has a *defined contribution plan* (see section covering subtopic ASC 715-70 titled "Defined Contribution Plans").
- By participating in a multiemployer plan, an employer that has a *defined benefit plan* accounts for it essentially as if it were a *defined contribution plan*. The financing of the plan is, in effect, off-balance-sheet.

Withdrawal from Multiemployer Plans

When an employer withdraws from a multiemployer plan, the employer may be contractually liable to pay into the plan a portion of its unfunded accumulated postretirement benefit obligation.

PRACTICE NOTE: Contractual obligations are the only ones facing the employer that withdraws from a multiemployer *postretirement* benefit plan. In contrast, an employer that withdraws from a multiemployer *pension* plan is subject not only to contractual obligations, but also to statutory obligations under the Multiemployer Pension Plan Amendments Act of 1980.

An employer should apply ASC 450 if withdrawal from the plan is probable or reasonably possible, and the employer will incur an obligation as a result (ASC 715-70-50-1).

Obligation under "Maintenance of Benefits" Clause

An employer should also apply ASC 450 if it is probable or reasonably possible that the employer's contribution to the multiemployer plan will increase during the remainder of the contract period under a "maintenance of benefits" clause, to make up for a shortfall in the funding of the plan to assure the full level of benefits described in the plan.

PART II: INTERPRETIVE GUIDANCE

ASC 715-20: DEFINED BENEFITS PLANS—GENERAL

ASC 715-20-S50-1, S99-2; ASC 715-30-35-40 through 35-41 Determination of Vested Benefit Obligation for a Defined Benefit Pension Plan

BACKGROUND

A projected benefit obligation (PBO) is defined in the ASC *Glossary* as "the actuarial present value as of a date of all benefits attributed by the pension benefit formula to employee service rendered prior to that date." The only difference between a PBO and an accumulated benefit obligation (ABO) is that the PBO considers assumptions about future compensation levels. The PBO and the ABO are both affected by the vested benefit obligation (VBO), which is the actuarial present value of benefits for which an employee is entitled to receive a pension currently or in the future without the requirement for continued employment.

Under some defined benefit pension plans, such as foreign plans, most or all of the benefits to which an employee is entitled upon termination is based on service to date. If the employee is terminated, the vested benefit would be payable to the employee immediately or indexed for inflation, if it were payable at a future date. For example, the Italian severance pay statute usually requires that the accrued benefit paid to an employee on separation be based on service to date. The undiscounted value of the amount paid immediately would be greater than the actuarial present value of the benefits the employee has a right to receive based on service to date. Similarly, legislation in the United Kingdom requires that deferred vested benefits of terminated employees be revalued from the separation date to the normal retirement age. In that situation, the VBO based on termination at the measurement date could be greater than the ABO if the calculation of the ABO considers the statutory revaluation only after the employee's expected termination date.

The difficulty in applying the guidance in ASC 715-30 to such plans is in determining whether the VBO should be calculated based on the presumption that the employee is terminated immediately (Approach 1) or the employee continues to provide service to the termination or retirement date with the maximum amount discounted to its present value (Approach 2). If the VBO exceeds the PBO, the ABO, or both in Approach 1, those amounts would have to be adjusted.

ACCOUNTING ISSUE

Should the VBO be the actuarial present value of the vested benefits to which an employee is entitled, based on service to date as if the employee were separated immediately (Approach 1), or to which an employee is currently entitled, based on the employee's expected separation or retirement date (Approach 2)?

ACCOUNTING GUIDANCE

The VBO may be based on either approach for situations that are not specifically considered in ASC 715-30 if the facts and circumstances are analogous to those discussed above.

A FASB staff representative reported that when responding to technical inquiries, the FASB staff recommended that the VBO be determined using Approach 1, because the staff believes that the VBO is not contingent on future service under that approach. Some believe that Approach 2 is more consistent with the intent of ASC 715-30 (FAS-87), because pension obligations are measured based on actuarial expectations.

SEC STAFF COMMENT

The SEC Observer noted that registrants should disclose the method used.

DISCUSSION

The following is the rationale for the two approaches.

Approach 1 Vested benefits are defined in the ASC's *Glossary* as "benefits for which the employee's right to receive a *present* or future pension benefit is no longer contingent on remaining in the service of the employer." (Emphasis added.) Those who supported this approach argued that the *present* benefit that the employee is entitled to should be measured at the *present* time. They believed that the value of the vested benefit is the actuarial value at the present, which should not be discounted. Supporters also believed that the employer's liability for the VBO should be based on the concept that it is a measure of the employer's obligation if the plan were discontinued. Proponents believed that if the vested benefit is an obligation, it should not be discounted to a lesser amount than the employer's current obligation. Rather, it should be measured based on service to date using the plan's benefit formula. They argued further that discounting the obligation assumes that the employee will perform future services for the employer. That conflicts with the definition of vested benefits, which do not depend on future services. Others argued for measuring the obligation at its current value, because some plans permit employees to take advances against their vested benefits while still employed.

Approach 2 Proponents of this approach noted that the PBO, ABO, and VBO are defined in FAS-87 in terms of actuarial present value, which is based on estimates of death, disability, withdrawal, or retirement in determining the probability and timing of payment. That amount is discounted from the expected payment date to the present. Others argued that even if the VBO under Approach 1 were greater than the PBO or the ABO or both, those amounts need not be adjusted, because they believed that the VBO does not represent a minimum value for the ABO and the PBO.

Background papers discussed the application of the two approaches to the Italian Termination Indemnity Plan and the U.K. Plan as follows:

Italian Termination Indemnity Plan Under the Italian plan, an employee's benefit generally is paid on termination. The amount equals a total of the following: (*a*) the prior year's balance, (*b*) the prior year's balance times 75% of the increase in the consumer price index, plus 1.5%, and (c) one month service accrual for the current year.

Under Approach 1, the VBO must equal the balance payable to the employee on immediate separation. The VBO will usually be greater than the PBO, which discounts the benefits of expected payment. If so, the PBO is adjusted so the two amounts are equal. As a result, net periodic pension cost equals the change in the balance of the VBO and PBO from the beginning to the end of the year, adjusted for payments to employees actually terminated during the year. This method is the same as the method by which pension costs were measured before the issuance of ASC 715-30. If the PBO is greater than the VBO, net periodic pension cost is based on the PBO and the usual application of ASC 715.

Under Approach 2, the VBO is calculated by projecting out to the date when benefits to which the employee is currently entitled would be paid and discounting that amount to the present. The VBO would thus be the same as the usual calculation of the PBO. ASC 715 would be applied as for U.S. plans.

U.K. Plan Under government regulations in the U.K., an employee who reaches a certain age is entitled to a guaranteed minimum pension of a specified amount based on salary and service to date. Legislation enacted near the time this Issue was discussed required that benefits for an employee's services after the date of the legislation be revalued from the date of separation to the normal retirement date based on changes in price indices. Some plans were amended to provide such increases for all of an employee's service. Consequently, the VBO often would be greater than the ABO when vested benefits are revalued. Because the PBO includes salary escalation, it would still be greater than the VBO.

Under Approach 1, the ABO would have to be adjusted to equal the VBO, because the ABO should not be less than the benefit to which an employee is currently entitled.

Under Approach 2, the VBO would be measured based on the discounted value of the benefit receivable at the date of expected separation. It would not exceed the ABO and would not require adjustment.

Although periodic pension cost is unlikely to be affected by the different ABO amounts under the two approaches, the minimum liability as calculated under FAS-87 could be affected.

ASC 715-20-S55-1, S99-1 Selection of Discount Rates Used for Measuring Defined Benefit Pension Obligations and Obligations of Postretirement Plans Other Than Pensions

The SEC Observer announced that registrants should use the guidance in ASC 715-30-35-44 to select the discount rate for measuring the pension benefit obligation in a defined benefit pension plan and the guidance in ASC 715-60-35-80 for obligations of postretirement benefit plans other than pensions. That paragraph states in part that "the objective of selecting assumed discount rates to measure the single amount that, if invested at the measurement date in a portfolio of high-quality debt instruments, would provide the necessary future cash flows to pay the accumulated benefits. The SEC Observer stated that the staff expects that discount rates used by registrants at each measurement date to measure obligations for pension benefits and postretirement benefits other than pensions would reflect the current level of interest rates. He stated that the SEC staff suggests that high-quality, fixed-income debt securities are those that receive one of the two highest ratings from a recognized ratings agency, such as a rating of Aa or higher from Moody's Investors Service, Inc.

ASC 715-30: DEFINED BENEFIT PLANS PENSION

ASC 715-30-15-3, 35-71, 35-72 Accounting for "Cash Balance" Pension Plans

BACKGROUND

A survey conducted in 2002 indicated that 32 of the Fortune 100 companies have changed their traditional defined benefit plans to cash balance plans. The IRS defines a cash balance plan as follows:

> A defined benefit plan that defines benefits for each employee by reference to the employee's hypothetical account. An employee's hypothetical account is determined by reference to hypothetical allocations of contributions and earnings to an employee's account under a defined contribution plan.

The benefits in most cash balance plans are reported to employees as accumulated cash balances. Although most plans offer members the option to receive a lump-sum distribution of the account balance in settlement of the full obligation, to maintain a plan's tax-qualified status, such plans are required to offer members the option to receive their benefits in the form of a life annuity. The IRS requires that cash balance plans are funded similar to defined benefit plans, but employers report the benefits to employees as principal credits and interest credits as in 401(k) plans and other defined contribution plans. Nevertheless, cash balance plans have some features of defined benefit plans, such as the option of a life annuity, interest credits not based on plan assets' performance, joint and survivor options, and grandfathered or transitional defined benefit formulas. The existence of prior-service costs, deferred gains or losses, and an inability to divide the assets into defined contribution and defined benefit components makes it impractical to account for cash balance plans as defined contribution plans. Further, most employers classify cash balance plans as defined benefit plans, because (*a*) under the IRS definition of a defined contribution plan, employers are required to report individual funded account balances, and (*b*) according to ASC 715-30 (FAS-87), a plan is a defined benefit plan if it is *not* a defined contribution plan.

ACCOUNTING ISSUE

- Should a cash balance pension plan be considered a defined benefit plan or a defined contribution plan when applying the provisions of ASC 715-30?
- What is the appropriate pattern of accruals for defined benefit plans that are cash balance pension plans?

ACCOUNTING GUIDANCE

1. For the purpose of applying the guidance in ASC 715-30, cash balance pension plans, which provide a pension benefit in the form of an account

balance based on principal credits and interest credits over time, are considered to be *defined benefit pension plans*. That conclusion was reached based on the following characteristics of cash balance plans:

   a. The amount of the pension benefit to be received is defined as a function of principal credits based on salary and future interest credits at a stated rate.

   b. Over time, an employer must fund amounts that can accumulate to the actuarial present value of the benefit due at the time of distribution to each participant based on the plan's terms.

   c. Individual account balances are determined based on a hypothetical account rather than on specific assets, and the benefit depends on an employer's promised interest that will be credited, not based on an actual return on a plan's assets. Under the guidance in ASC 715-30, any plan that is not a defined contribution plan is considered to be a defined benefit plan.

   d. An employer's contributions to a cash balance plan trust and the earnings on the invested assets are *not* related to the principal and interest credited to the hypothetical accounts.

2. Because the benefit promise in a cash balance arrangement is not pay related, using the projected unit credit method is *not* appropriate and therefore *not* required in measuring the benefit obligation and annual cost of benefits under FAS 715-30. Cost attribution should be based on the traditional unit credit method.

Thos conclusions apply specifically to the plan discussed here. To determine whether *cash balance* plans with other characteristics or other types of defined benefit plans are pay related and the benefit attribution approach that should be used, the specific features of those benefit arrangements should be evaluated.

ASC 715-20-50-1, 50-8; ASC 715-30-15-4, 35-5, 35-15 through 35-16, 35-20, 35-23, 35-31, 35-39, 35-42, 35-46 through 35-49, 35-61, 35-69, 35-84 through 35-85, 55-3 through 55-5, 55-8 through 55-15, 55-17 through 55-22, 55-24 through 55-33, 55-35 through 55-43, 55-46 through 55-51, 55-53 through 55-61, 55-63 through 55-64, 55-66 through 55-67, 55-88, 55-90, 55-108, 55-110 through 55-120, 55-122 through 55-127; ASC 715-50-60-2; ASC 740-10-60-1; ASC 958-715-55-2; ASC 980-715-55-2 through 55-8, 55-10 through 55-25; ASC 330-10-55-5 through 55-7 A Guide to Implementation of ASC 715-30 on Employers' Accounting for Pensions: Questions and Answers

ACCOUNTING GUIDANCE

Question E1: This question has been deleted.

Question E2: Does this guidance apply to a non-U.S. pension plan that provides death and disability benefits that are greater than the incidental death and disability benefits allowed in U.S. tax-qualified pension plans?

Answer: Yes, if the non-U.S. pension plan is in substance similar to a U.S. plan.

Question E3: This question has been deleted.

Question E4: How should an employer with regulated operations account for the effects of applying this Statement for financial reporting purposes if another method of accounting for pensions is used for determining allowable pension cost for rate-making purposes?

Answer: This Statement applies to an employer with regulated operations. However, the guidance in ASC 980 may require that an asset or a liability be recorded for the difference between net periodic pension cost recognized under this Statement and pension cost allowed for rate-making purposes. If an entity is subject to the provisions of ASC 980, an asset is recognized if the provisions of ASC 980-320-25-1 are met. Also, a liability is recognized if the conditions of ASC 980-405-25-1 are met.

Exceptions to the General Rule

For entities subject to the guidance in ASC 980, an asset is generally recognized if net periodic pension cost exceeds pension cost allowable for rate-making purposes in ASC 980-320-25-1. However, the criteria of ASC 980-320-25-1 would not be met if (1) it is probable that the regulator will soon adopt this Statement for rate-making purposes and (2) it is *not* probable that the regulator will permit the entity to recover the difference between pension costs under the guidance in this Statement and pension costs allowable by the regulator, before the regulator adopts the approach in ASC 980.

For entities subject to the requirements in ASC 980, a liability generally is recognized when net periodic pension cost under the guidance in this Statement is less than pension cost allowable for rate-making purposes ASC 980-405-25-1. However, the criteria in ASC 980-405-25-1 would not be met if (1) it is probable that the regulator will soon adopt the guidance in this Statement for rate-making purposes, (2) the regulator will not hold the employer responsible for the costs that were intended to be recovered by the current rates and that have been deferred by the change in method, *and* (3) the regulator will provide revenue to cover these same costs when they are ultimately recognized under the provisions of this Statement.

A regulator cannot eliminate a liability even if it was *not* imposed by its actions. Therefore, regulation does not affect the need to recognize the underfunded status of a defined benefit pension plan under the guidance in ASC 980-470-40-1 through 40-2.

Question E5: If an employer has a pension plan that also provides postemployment health care benefits, should the guidance in this Statement apply to those benefits?

Answer: No. ASC 715-60 provides guidance in accounting for postemployment health care benefits.

Question E6: Does the guidance stating that the interest cost component of net periodic pension cost should not be considered to be interest for purposes of applying the guidance in ASC 835-20 proscribe the capitalization of the interest cost component of net periodic pension cost if employee compensation is capitalized as part of the cost of inventory or other assets?

Answer: No. Net periodic pension cost, including the interest element included in that amount, is viewed as an element of employee compensation. If it is appropriate to capitalize employee compensation as part of the cost of inventory or as part of a self-constructed asset, the entire amount of net periodic pension cost is included in making this computation.

Question E7: May an employer have net periodic pension cost that is a net credit (i.e., net periodic pension income)?

Answer: Yes. The computation of net periodic pension cost involves the combination of elements that are both expenses/losses and revenues/gains. The revenues/gains components (e.g., return on plan assets, amortization of a transition asset) of the pension cost computation may exceed the expense/loss portion of the computation of net periodic pension cost.

> **PRACTICE POINTER:** In an environment of low interest rates and high stock market returns, many employers with a defined benefit pension plan may report net periodic pension credits. Low interest rates correspond with a reduction in the interest cost component of net periodic pension cost, and high stock market returns often correspond with a high realized return on plan assets.

Question E8: If an employer has net periodic pension cost that is a net credit (i.e., net periodic pension income), how should that be treated if employee compensation is capitalized as part of the cost of inventory or other assets?

Answer: The portion of net periodic pension income that is capitalized as part of the cost of an asset would serve to reduce the applicable asset's cost.

Question E9: If an employer sponsoring a pension plan that is overfunded has net periodic pension cost that is a net credit (i.e., net periodic pension income) and the employer makes no contribution to the pension plan because it cannot currently deduct the amount for tax purposes, is the difference between net periodic pension income and the tax deductible amount a temporary difference as discussed in ASC 740-10-25-18 through 20? If it is a temporary difference, when and how will it reverse?

Answer: Yes. A difference between the net periodic pension income and the tax deductible expense would create a temporary difference (i.e., the financial reporting basis of the pension liability or asset would differ from its tax basis). The temporary difference may reverse in the future when net periodic pension cost exceeds amounts funded (the pension plan may not be overfunded indefinitely). Alternatively, if the pension plan continues to be overfunded for an extended period of time, the employer may terminate the plan and capture the excess assets. In this case, the gain for accounting purposes would be less than the taxable amount.

Question E10: If transferable securities issued by the employer are included in plan assets, should the measurement of plan assets also include the interest accrued but not yet received on those securities?

Answer: Yes. Amounts accrued by the employer but not yet paid to the plan (which are to be excluded from plan assets per ASC 980-605-50-1 are related to the recognized pension liability.

Question E11: If an employer has a nonqualified pension plan (for tax purposes) that is funded with life insurance policies owned by the employer, should the cash surrender value of those policies be considered plan assets for purposes of applying this Statement?

Answer: Not if the employer is the owner or beneficiary of the life insurance policies. The applicable accounting treatment for those policies is specified in ASC 325-30-15-3 through 15-3; 35-2 through 35-2; 25-1; 05-3 through 05-5.

Question E12: If the actual return on plan assets for a period is a component of net periodic pension cost, how does the expected return on plan assets affect the determination of net periodic pension cost?

Answer: When the current year's net periodic pension cost is computed, both the actual return on plan assets and any difference between this actual return and the expected return are considered. The difference (a net gain or loss) between the actual return on plan assets and the expected return on assets is recognized in other comprehensive income in the period in which it occurs. The net result of this treatment is that the expected return on plan assets is included in the computation of the current year's net periodic pension cost. The total of the amount recognized in other comprehensive income and the actual return on plan assets equals the expected return on plan assets. Future net periodic pension cost is affected through the amortization of the net gain or loss recognized in other comprehensive income.

Illustration of Return on Asset Component of Net Periodic Pension Cost

As of January 1, 20X8, GAF, Inc., has pension plan assets of $500,000. The expected return on plan assets for 20X4 is 10%. Contributions and benefit payments during the year were both $100,000. At December 31, 20X8, plan assets are $600,000. Service cost is $100,000 and interest cost is $80,000. GAF has no other components of net periodic pension cost. GAF would compute net periodic pension cost as follows:

Service cost	$100,000
Interest cost	80,000
Actual return on plan assets	(100,000)
Net gain recognized in other comprehensive income	50,000
Net periodic pension cost	$130,000

Question E13: If an employer has a substantive commitment to have a formula greater than the pension plan's written formula, how should the difference between the effects of a retroactive plan amendment that was anticipated as part of that substantive commitment and the effects of the actual retroactive plan amendment be accounted for?

Answer: The accounting depends on whether the difference results from an intended modification of the formula for which there is a substantive commitment. If it does, then the accounting should follow the guidance in ASD 980-250-55-1 for a retroactive plan amendment. If it does not, the difference is a gain or loss and should be accounted for in accordance with the provisions of ASC 980-350-35-1 through 35-2; ASC 980-250-55-3; ASC 980-340-55-2 through 55-3.

Question E14: Once a schedule of amortization of prior service cost from a specific retroactive plan amendment has been established, should that schedule remain the same or is it subject to revision on a periodic basis?

Answer: An amortization schedule of prior service cost should be revised only if one of three conditions occurs: (1) the pension plan is curtailed, (2) events indicate that the period for which the employer will receive benefits from a retroactive plan benefit is shorter than initially estimated, or (3) the future economic benefits have been impaired. The amortization schedule should not be revised because of variances in the expected service lives of employees. Finally, this Statement specifically proscribes reducing the length of such an amortization schedule (i.e., under no circumstances can prior service cost be recognized in net periodic pension cost more slowly than originally planned).

Question E15: In a business combination that is accounted for by the purchase method under the guidance in ASC 805, if the acquiring employer includes the employees of the acquired employer in its pension plan and grants them credit for prior service (the acquired employer did not have a pension plan), should the credit granted for prior service be treated as prior service cost and recognized in other comprehensive income or treated as part of the cost of the acquisition?

Answer: It depends. If the selling entity requires that prior service credit be granted as a condition of the acquisition, the prior service credit granted would be treated as part of the cost of the acquisition; the offsetting debit is an adjustment to goodwill. In all other cases, the granting of prior service credit is treated as a retroactive plan amendment. Prior service cost is recognized in other comprehensive income and amortized under the guidance in ASC 980-250-55-1.

Question E16: In determining the periods for (*a*) amortization of prior service cost included in accumulated other comprehensive income, (*b*) minimum amortization of net gain or loss included in accumulated other comprehensive income, or (*c*) amortization of the transition asset or obligation remaining in accumulated other comprehensive income ASC 715-30, is it necessary to include the service periods of employees who are expected to receive only a return of their contributions (plus interest, if applicable) to a contributory defined benefit pension plan in determining the future service periods of employees who are expected to receive benefits under that pension plan?

Answer: No. Only the expected future service periods of employees who are expected to receive a benefit provided by the employer need to be included.

Question E17: Are the service periods of employees who are expected to terminate before their benefits are vested included in the determination of the average remaining service period of employees who are expected to receive benefits under the pension plan?

Answer: No. Only the expected service periods of employees who are expected to receive benefits under the pension plan need to be included.

Question E18: Is there a specific threshold for determining if a pension plan has "almost all" inactive participants for purposes of selecting the amortization period for certain components of net periodic pension cost?

Answer: No. Judgment is required for determining whether "almost all" of a pension plan's participants are inactive.

Question E19: May an employer adopt an accounting policy to immediately recognize as a component of net periodic pension cost the cost of all plan amendments that grant increased benefits for services rendered in prior periods (prior service cost)?

Answer: No. Under the guidance in ASC 715-30, an entity is not permitted to adopt an accounting policy under which the cost of *all* plan amendments granting increased benefits for services performed in prior periods would be recognized immediately as a component of net periodic pension cost. Prior service cost should be recognized immediately in other comprehensive income, unless based on an evaluation of the facts and circumstances, an employer does *not* expect to receive a future economic benefit from the retroactive plan amendment.

Question E20: If an employer has a history of granting retroactive plan amendments every three years, should the resulting prior service costs be amortized over a three-year period?

Answer: This decision needs to be made on a case-by-case basis after the applicable facts and circumstances are considered. If it is determined that future economic benefits that result from a plan amendment will last for example, for only three years, it would be appropriate to amortize prior periodic cost included in accumulated comprehensive income over a three-year period. That is, if employees become accustomed to a retroactive increase in plan benefits every three years, the expected future economic benefits may not continue if this pattern is broken.

Question E21: If an employer grants a retroactive plan amendment that reduces the projected benefit obligation (a negative retroactive plan amendment), what method should be used to reduce prior service cost included in accumulated comprehensive income when several prior retroactive plan amendments in the aggregate have resulted in prior service costs in accumulated comprehensive income that exceed the effects of the negative retroactive plan amendment?

Answer: Unless a negative retroactive plan amendment can be specifically related to a prior retroactive plan amendment, it is acceptable to apply any systematic and rational method (e.g., last-in, first-out; first-in, first-out; pro rata) in a consistent manner.

Question E22: If an employer amends a pension plan to delete a provision that a percentage of the employee's accumulated benefits be paid to the employee's spouse if the employee dies before reaching a specified age, should the reduction in benefits be accounted for as a retroactive plan amendment?

Answer: Yes. This is an example of a negative retroactive plan amendment.

Question E23: This question has been deleted.

Question E24: Should the amount and timing of pension plan contributions and benefit payments expected to be made during the year be considered in determining the expected return on plan assets for that year?

Answer: Yes. The expected return on plan assets should consider the asset amounts that will be available for investment purposes during the year, including new contributions made.

Question E25: This question has been deleted.

Question E26: May an employer that has several pension plans with similar plan assets use different asset valuation methods to determine the market-related value of those plan assets?

Answer: Ordinarily not, especially since one objective of this Statement is to enhance the comparability of pension plan information. However, different asset valuation methods may be appropriate if they reflect underlying differences in the pension plans' inherent facts and circumstances.

Question E27: Is there a limitation on the number of classes into which plan assets may be divided for purposes of selecting asset valuation methods for determining the market-related value of plan assets?

Answer: No. However, the method selected for each asset class should be appropriate for recognizing changes in the fair value of assets in a systematic and rational manner over a period not to exceed five years. Asset valuation methods adopted should be applied consistently within each class, and the method used to divide assets into different classes should be applied consistently.

Question E28: Is the following an acceptable asset valuation method for determining the market-related value of plan assets? The market-related value of plan assets is determined with a total return-on-plan asset component consisting of three layers:

1. An expected return-on-plan asset component based on the beginning-of-year market-related value of plan assets, cash flow during the year, and the expected long-term rate of return on plan assets

2. An amount equal to the change in the accumulated benefit obligation that resulted from any change during the year in the assumed discount rates used to determine the accumulated benefit obligation (The amount is reduced pro rata if plan assets are less than the accumulated benefit obligation.)

3. A variance component equal to a percentage (e.g., 20% if a five-year averaging period is used) of the difference between the actual return on plan assets based on the fair values of those plan assets and the expected return on plan assets derived from components (1) and (2)

Answer: No. Factor (2), the change in the accumulated benefit obligation resulting from changes in the assumed discount rate, is unrelated to changes in the fair value of plan assets. Only changes in the fair value of plan assets between various dates can be considered in computing the market-related value of plan assets.

Question E29: How does the use of a market-related value of plan assets affect the determination of net periodic pension cost?

Answer: The use of a market-related value of plan assets affects the determination of net periodic pension cost in two ways. First, the expected return on plan assets is based on the market-related value of plan assets (not based on the fair value of plan assets). Second, to the extent that gains and losses based on the fair value of plan assets are not yet reflected in the market-related value of plan assets, such amounts are excluded from the net gain or loss included in accumulated other comprehensive income that is subject to amortization in the following period.

Illustration of the Effect on Net Periodic Pension Cost of Using the Market-Related Value of Plan Assets

Touchstone Enterprises has pension plan assets with a fair value and FAS-87 market-related value of $10 million on 1/1/20X4. Touchstone expects a 10% return on pension plan assets. The actual return during 20X4 was $2 million. Touchstone's pension contributions and benefit payments were both $800,000 during 20X4. Touchstone adjusts the market-related value of plan assets for differences between the expected and actual return on assets over 5 years. Therefore, the expected return on plan assets in 20X5 is $1,120,000, computed as follows:

Plan assets (both at fair value and market-related value) at 1/1/20X4		$10,000,000
Contributions		800,000
Benefit payments		(800,000)
Actual return on plan assets	$2,000,000	
Expected return on plan assets	(1,000,000)	1,000,000
Difference	$1,000,000	
Amortization of difference over 5 years		200,000
Plan assets at market-related value at 1/1/20X5		$11,200,000
Expected return on plan assets during 20X5 at 10%		$ 1,120,000

Question E30: This question has been deleted.

Question E31: If all or almost all of a pension plan's participants are inactive due to a temporary suspension of the pension plan (i.e., for a limited period of time, employees will not earn additional defined benefits), should the minimum amortization of net gain or loss included in accumulated other comprehensive income be determined based on the average remaining life expectancy of the temporarily inactive participants?

Answer: No. The amortization period should be based on the average remaining service period of temporarily inactive participants who are expected to receive benefits under the pension plan.

Question E32: If all employees covered by a pension plan are terminated but not retired, should the minimum amortization of a net gain or loss included in accumulated comprehensive income be determined based on the average remaining life expectancy of the inactive participants?

Answer: Yes.

Question E33: May an employer immediately recognize gains and losses as a component of net periodic pension cost instead of recognizing them in accumulated other comprehensive income?

Answer: Yes. However, the following three conditions must be met: (1) the method must be used consistently, (2) the method must be applied to *all* gains and losses (on both plan assets and pension plan obligations), and (3) the method used is disclosed based on the guidance in ASC 715-20-50-1.

Questions E34-E43: These questions have been deleted.

Question E44: If a career-average-pay pension plan has a formula that provides pension benefits equal to 1% of each year's salary for that year's service and if prospective (flat-benefit) plan amendments are granted every three years as part of union negotiations (e.g., a negotiated increase may provide that additional benefits of $360 per year are earned for each of the following three years of service), should the projected unit credit method be used for both the career-average-pay and the flat-benefit portions of the pension benefits provided under the pension plan?

Answer: No. The projected unit credit method should be used to apportion the career-average-pay portion of the plan to the expected service period of active employees. The unit credit method should be used for the flat-benefit portion of the plan.

Question E45: If an employer has a pension plan that provides a pension benefit of 1% of final pay for each year of service up to a maximum of 20 years of service and final pay is frozen at year 20, should the employer attribute the total projected benefits under the pension plan for an employee over the employee's expected service period even if that service period is anticipated to exceed the 20-year limitation?

Answer: No. If a pension plan attributes all of its prospective benefits over a 20-year time period, the service cost component should be recognized over this time period even if the employee is expected to work beyond 20 years. Note, however, that interest cost would continue to accrue on the projected benefit obligation beyond 20 years.

Question E46: Would the answer to the question in paragraph E45 be different if the pension plan's formula provided a pension benefit of 1% of final pay for each year of service up to a maximum of 20 years of service and final pay was not frozen at year 20?

Answer: No. The only difference is that a liability gain or loss will exist beyond year 20 if future experience regarding employee pay levels differs from that which was assumed.

ASC 715—Compensation—Retirement Benefits

Question E47: How should an employer determine the accumulated and projected benefit obligations if a pension plan has more than one formula and an employee's pension benefits are determined based on the formula that provides the greatest pension benefit at the time the employee terminates or retires (For example, if the employee terminates in year 10, the pension plan's flat-benefit formula provides a greater pension benefit than does the pension plan's pay-related formula; however, if the employee terminates in year 11, the pension plan provides that same employee with a greater benefit under its pay-related formula than under its flat-benefit formula.)

Answer: A pension plan that uses more than one formula may not assign the same benefit for each year of service. Therefore, the employer may need to use an attribution approach that does not assign the same level of benefits for each year of service. In calculating the accumulated benefit obligation, the employer should choose the formula that produces the greatest liability amount based on service rendered to date. Since the accumulated benefit obligation (ABO) cannot exceed the projected benefit obligation (PBO), the calculated PBO for service already rendered must equal or exceed the ABO. For service not yet rendered, the PBO should be calculated using the formula that results in the largest measure of the liability. A number of illustrations of those concepts are included in in this guidance. One illustration, which has been adapted from FIG-ASC 715-30, appears below.

Illustration of Attribution with Multiple Formulas

FRW, Inc., has a pension plan that uses two benefit formulas. The plan benefit that participants will receive is the larger of the amounts computed by each of the two formulas. Formula A provides a flat benefit of $900 for each of the first 20 years of an employee's service, with no pension benefits earned for service beyond 20 years. Formula B provides a benefit equal to 1% of final pay for each year of service.

An employee starts at a salary of $21,000 in year 1 and receives a $2,000 increase in salary for each year of service. (For purposes of simplicity, the accumulated and projected benefit obligations are expressed in terms of the annual pension benefits that begin when the employee retires.) This employee of FRW is expected to retire at the end of year 30 with a final salary of $79,000. Formula A would provide an annual pension benefit of $18,000 for 30 years of service ($900 in each of the first 20 years of service and no additional benefits for any service beyond 20 years). Formula B would provide a pension benefit of $23,700 for 30 years of service (30 × 1% ×$79,000, or $790 for each year of service). Under Formula A, $900 of service cost is attributed to each of the first 20 years of service; no service cost is attributed to employee service beyond 20 years. Under Formula B, $790 of service cost is attributed to each of the 30 expected years of employee service.

At the end of year 20, the ABO and the PBO under Formula A, both $18,000, exceed the comparable amounts computed under Formula B. For example, the PBO under Formula B at the end of 20 years is $15,800 (20 × 1% × $79,000). Therefore, at the end of year 20, both the ABO and the PBO are measured using Formula A. However, by the end of year 30, the benefit under Formula B, $23,700, will exceed the benefit under Formula A, still $18,000 because no benefits are earned under Formula A after 20 years. Therefore, additional pension benefits of $570 [($23,700 − $18,000) / 10] are attributed to years 21-30.

The accumulated and projected benefit obligations for years 1-30 are as follows:

Year	ABO	PBO
1-19	—(a)	—(a)
20	$18,000(a)	$18,000(a)
21	18,000(a)	18,570(b)
22	18,000(a)	19,140(b)
23	18,000(a)	19,710(b)
24	18,000(a)	20,280(b)
25	18,000(c)	20,850(b)
26	18,460(c)	21,420(b)
27	19,710(c)	21,990(b)
28	21,000(c)	22,560(b)
29	22,330(c)	23,130(b)
30	23,700(b)	23,700(b)

(a) $900 × years of service, not to exceed 20 years (Formula A)
(b) Formula A benefits earned through year 20 plus attribution of additional projected benefits under Formula B (for years 21-30 of employee service) in proportion to the number of completed years of service compared to the number of years of service that are expected to be completed for the period during which Formula B is applied. Although no additional pension benefits are "earned" in years 21 and 22, because the PBO in those years is less than $18,000 ($16,590 at end of year 21 and $17,380 at end of year 22), $570 of pension benefits is attributed to each of those years of service based on the total incremental pension benefits for years 21-30 ($5,700/10 years).
(c) Computed as 1% of the end-of-year salary times the number of years worked. For example, in year 29, 1% of $77,000 times 29 years is $22,330; in year 30, 1% of $79,000 times 30 years is $23,700.

Question E48: Can a pension plan have an accumulated benefit obligation that exceeds the projected benefit obligation?

Answer: No. The projected benefit obligation must always equal or exceed the accumulated benefit obligation.

Question E49: How is the projected benefit obligation attributed to a qualified pension plan (for tax purposes) and an excess benefit (top hat) pension plan during an employee's service period if the employee is expected to receive a pension benefit under the excess benefit pension plan (i.e., the employee's pension benefit at retirement is expected to exceed the Section 415 limitations of the U.S. Internal Revenue Code)?

Answer: The projected benefit obligation should be attributed to the qualified pension plan (for tax purposes) until the Section 415 limitations are reached. Thereafter, any incremental pension benefits are attributed to the excess benefit plan. The following example illustrates this computation.

Illustration of Attribution of the Projected Benefit Obligation to a Qualified Pension Plan and an Excess Benefit Pension Plan

The pension plan formula of SBS, Inc., provides for an annual pension benefit of 1.5% of final salary for each year of service. Employee Jones has a beginning salary of $400,000, receives increases of $30,000 per year, and retires at the end of 21 years at a salary of $1,000,000. Section 415 will permit annual pension benefit payments of $200,000 for all the years Jones will receive benefit payments.

Attribution of the accumulated and projected benefit obligations is shown in the following table. Rather than being calculated, the actuarial present value of the accumulated and projected benefit obligations are expressed in terms of the benefit that Jones is expected to receive upon retirement.

ASC 715—Compensation—Retirement Benefits **40,105**

Year of Service	Salary	Total ABO	Total PBO	Qualified Pension Plan ABO	Qualified Pension Plan PBO	Excess Benefit Pension Plan ABO	Excess Benefit Pension Plan PBO
1	$400,000	$ 6,000	$15,000	$ 6,000	$15,000		
2	430,000	12,900	30,000	12,900	30,000		
3	460,000	20,700	45,000	20,700	45,000		
4	490,000	29,400	60,000	29,400	60,000		
5	520,000	39,000	75,000	39,000	75,000		
6	550,000	49,500	90,000	49,500	90,000		
7	580,000	60,900	105,000	60,900	105,000		
8	610,000	73,200	120,000	73,200	120,000		
9	640,000	86,400	135,000	86,400	135,000		
10	670,000	100,500	150,000	100,500	150,000		
11	700,000	115,500	165,000	115,500	165,000		
12	730,000	131,400	180,000	131,400	180,000		
13	760,000	148,200	195,000	148,200	195,000		
14	790,000	165,900	210,000	165,900	200,000		$10,000
15	820,000	184,500	225,000	184,500	200,000		25,000
16	850,000	204,000	240,000	200,000	200,000	$ 4,000	40,000
17	880,000	224,400	255,000	200,000	200,000	24,400	55,000
18	910,000	245,700	270,000	200,000	200,000	45,700	70,000
19	940,000	267,900	285,000	200,000	200,000	67,900	85,000
20	970,000	291,000	300,000	200,000	200,000	91,000	100,000
21	1,000,000	315,000	315,000	200,000	200,000	115,000	115,000

Question E50: If a pension plan's formula provides an annual pension benefit equal to 1% of each year's salary (i.e., the formula does not base pension benefits for the current year on any future salary level), should the projected unit credit method be used to attribute the service cost component of net periodic pension cost over employees' service periods?

Answer: Yes. This pension plan benefit is based on the level of employee pay. As such, it is in essence a career-average-pay pension plan. This Statement requires the use of the projected unit credit method for pay-related pension plans.

Question E51 is not included in the ASC.

Question E52: What constitutes a substantive commitment requiring recognition of pension benefits beyond those defined in the pension plan's written formula?

Answer: The guidance in ASC 715-30-35-34 states, "[I]n some situations a history of regular increases in non-pay-related benefits or benefits under a career-average-pay plan and other evidence may indicate that an employer has a present commitment to make future amendments and that the substance of the plan is to provide benefits attributable to prior service that are greater than the benefits defined by the written terms of the plan." In the determination of whether such a "substantive commitment" exists, all the facts and circumstances surrounding the pension plan should be carefully considered. Actions of the employer, including communications to employees, should be considered. A history of regular plan amendments is not enough, by itself, to demonstrate a substantive commitment. However, if the employer has a history of regular plan amendments, prior service cost should be amortized more quickly than might normally be the case (see ASC 715-30-35-14).

Question E53: Should an employer's accounting for its pension plan anticipate a retroactive plan amendment that is not part of a series of retroactive plan amendments necessary to effect a substantive commitment to have a formula greater than its written form?

Answer: No.

Question E54: Is it always necessary for assumed compensation levels to change each time assumed discount rates (and expectations of future inflation rates inherently contained in the assumed discount rates) change?

Answer: No. This Statement requires that assumed discount rates and compensation levels consider the same future economic conditions. However, it does not suggest that these future economic conditions—for example, inflation—will affect discount rates and compensation levels in exactly the same way, or to the same extent.

Question E55: May an employer determine a range of discount rates each year based, for example, on the Pension Benefit Guaranty Corporation's interest rates and high-quality bond rates and continue to use the prior year's assumed discount rates as long as those rates fall within the range?

Answer: No. On a yearly basis the employer should make its best estimate of what discount rate most closely approximates the rate inherent in the price at which the pension benefit obligation could be effectively settled. For example, this rate might be the interest rate inherent in annuity contracts or the interest rate on high-quality bonds.

Question E56: May an employer determine a range of discount rates as described in the question in paragraph E55 and then arbitrarily select the assumed discount rates from within that range?

Answer: No. The employer should make its best estimate of the discount rate consistent with effectively settling the pension benefit obligation. This process should be performed yearly.

Question E57: If an employer changes its basis of estimating assumed discount rates, for example, by using high-quality bond rates for one year and annuity rates for the following year, is that a change in method of applying an accounting principle?

Answer: No. This type of change would be viewed as a change in estimate. The decision to use a particular methodology in one year (e.g., the interest rate on high-quality bonds versus the interest rate inherent in annuity contracts) does not obligate the entity to continue using that approach in future years. The objective is to use a method that produces a discount rate that most closely approximates the rate inherent in the price at which the pension obligation could be effectively settled. However, if the facts and circumstances have not changed from the prior year, it generally would be inappropriate to change the method of selecting the discount rate. For example, an entity may historically have determined the discount rate by reference to the high-quality bond rate. Absent a change in circumstances that suggests this method does not produce the most appropriate measure of the discount rate at which the pension benefit obligation could be effectively settled, it should be used consistently from one year to the next.

Question E58: If a pension plan has a bond portfolio that was dedicated at a yield significantly higher or lower than current interest rates, may the historical rates of return as of the dedication date be used in discounting the projected and accumulated benefit obligations to their present value?

Answer: No. It would be acceptable to consider current rates of return on high quality fixed-income investments. The use of historical rates of return is not permitted.

Question E59: May the assumed discount rates used to discount the vested, accumulated, and projected benefit obligations be different?

Answer: Yes, if the circumstances justify different discount rates. For example, different discount rates may be appropriate for active and retired employees because of differences in the maturity and duration of expected pension benefits. However, the discount rate used to value pension benefits maturing in any particular year should not differ, regardless of whether the obligation is presently classified as vested, accumulated, or projected.

Question E60: This question has been deleted.

Question E61: Because a current settlement of the portion of the projected benefit obligation that relates to future compensation levels is unlikely, may an employer use those interest rates implicit in current prices of annuity contracts to determine the accumulated benefit obligation, and use interest rates expected to be implicit in future prices of annuity contracts to determine the pension obligation in excess of the accumulated benefit obligation?

Answer: No. This Statement requires the selection of a discount rate consistent with the rate inherent in the price at which the pension obligation could be effectively settled currently. An employer would not purchase an annuity contract to cover pension benefits based on future compensation levels, and an insurance company would not write such a contract without charging for the additional risk it would be assuming. However, this fact is irrelevant for selecting the appropriate discount rate. When interest rates on annuity contracts are discussed in the Statement, one approach is presented for determining the appropriate discount rate for valuing the pension plan benefit obligation. (Another approach is the interest rate on high-quality fixed-income investments.) The objective is *not* to determine the price an insurance company would charge for assuming the employer's obligation. Rather, the rates implicit in the current prices of annuity contracts might serve as a useful measure of the appropriate discount rate for valuing the pension plan obligation.

Question E62: Should the expected return on future years' contributions to a pension plan be considered in determining the expected long-term rate of return on plan assets?

Answer: No. The expected long-term rate of return on plan assets should be limited to the return expected on existing plan assets and on contributions received during the current year.

Question E63: Should changes under existing law in benefit limitations (such as those currently imposed by Section 415 of the U.S. Internal Revenue Code) that would affect benefits provided by a pension plan be anticipated in measuring the service cost component of net periodic pension cost and the projected benefit obligation?

Answer: Yes. Changes in existing pension law that would affect benefits provided should be considered in measuring service cost and the projected benefit obligation if such changes in laws have already been enacted. Possible changes to law should not be anticipated.

Question E64: If Section 415 of the U.S. Internal Revenue Code is incorporated by reference into a pension plan's formula, thereby limiting certain participants' accumulated benefits, should determination of the pension plan's accumulated benefit obligation reflect the current limitation if (*a*) the pension plan's formula requires automatic increases in accumulated benefits as each change in the limitation under existing law occurs and (*b*) future service is not a prerequisite for participants to receive those increases?

Answer: No. The calculation of the accumulated benefit obligation should reflect those increases in the limitation under existing law that would be consistent with the pension plan's other assumptions. This result presupposes that the employee does not have to render any additional service to be eligible for these benefits. However, if an employee would not automatically receive these benefit increases upon retiring or terminating his or her service, the accumulated benefit obligation should be calculated based on the Section 415 limitation as it currently exists.

Question E65: If an actuarial valuation is made as of a pension plan's year-end and that date precedes the date of the employer's fiscal year-end statement of financial position, is it always necessary to have another actuarial valuation made as of that date?

Answer: No. This Statement requires that the projected benefit obligation reflect the actuarial present value of benefits attributed to employee service rendered before the date of the employer's year-end statement of financial position, with limited exceptions. Actuarial assumptions for turnover, mortality, discount rates, etc., should be appropriate for the date of the employer's fiscal year-end statement of financial position. However, it may be possible to measure the projected benefit obligation at the date of the employer's year-end statement of financial position, with limited exceptions, with a sufficient degree of reliability based on rolling forward the earlier actuarial valuation of the PBO. In such a case, a new actuarial valuation is not required. This situation is analogous to taking a physical inventory before year-end and rolling the inventory balance forward to the financial statement date.

Question E66: How should net periodic pension cost for the year be determined if it is necessary to have an actuarial valuation as of the date of the employer's fiscal year-end (e.g., December 31) in addition to the actuarial valuation as of the pension plan's preceding year-end (e.g., June 30)?

Answer: Measurement of net periodic pension cost should be based on the most recent measurements of plan assets and obligations. If two actuarial measurements are completed during the year, net periodic pension cost should be the sum of two separate six-month periods (in the case above, January 1-June 30 and July 1-December 31). Net periodic pension cost for the first six months (latter six months) would be determined as of the preceding December 31 (the preceding June 30).

Question E67: If an employer that has a December 31 financial report date and measures its plan assets and obligations as of an interim date during its fiscal year (e.g., because of a significant retroactive plan amendment), should net periodic pension cost for the subsequent interim periods be based on those measurements?

Answer: Yes. Net periodic pension cost should be based on the most recent measurement of plan assets and obligations that is available. The guidance in ASC 715-30-35-68 states that, "[M]easurements of net periodic pension cost for both interim and annual financial statements shall be based on the assumptions used for the previous year-end measurements unless more recent measurements of both plan assets and obligations are available . . . ."

Question E68: Under the circumstances described in Question 67, should net periodic pension cost for the preceding interim periods be adjusted?

Answer: No.

ASC 715—Compensation—Retirement Benefits

Question E69: If an employer uses a measurement date of December 31 but does not complete the actual measurements until some time later in the year—for example, in January—should the determination of the pension obligations be based on the assumed discount rates and other actuarial assumptions as of January?

Answer: No. The employer should use the actuarial assumptions that were appropriate as of the measurement date of December 31.

Questions E70-E72: These questions have been deleted.

Question E73: This question has been moved to paragraph E88A.

Questions E74-E78: These questions have been deleted.

Question E79: Should the assumptions disclosed be as of the beginning or ending measurement date?

Answer: They should be as of the year-end measurement date.

Question E80: If an employer combines several of its pension plans and the assets of each predecessor pension plan are available to satisfy the previously existing obligations of the other, how should the combined pension plan be accounted for?

Answer: Except for prior service costs included in accumulated other comprehensive income, the fair value of pension plan assets and the actuarial present value of pension plan obligations (vested, accumulated, and projected) should be combined and reported as a single amount. Net gain or loss included in accumulated other comprehensive income, transition assets and liabilities included in accumulated other comprehensive income, and unrecognized prior service cost included in accumulated other comprehensive income are treated as follows:

Item	Combination Treatment	Amortization Treatment
Aggregate net gain/loss included in accumulated other comprehensive income	Aggregate amounts from previously separate pension plans	Amortize using the average remaining service period of the combined employee group
Transition asset/liability of separate pension plans remaining in accumulated other comprehensive income	Aggregate amounts from previously remaining amortization	Amortize using a weighted average of periods previously used by the separate pension plans
Prior service cost included in accumulated other comprehensive income of each pension plan	Not aggregated	Amortize separately, as previously determined, based on specific employee groups covered

Illustration of Combining Two Plans

TELWIN, Inc., has two separate pension plans, Plan A and Plan B, that it plans to combine into one plan on December 31, 20X4. TELWIN adopted the provisions of FAS-87 for the year ended December 31, 20Y0. Relevant details about each separate pension plan and about how the combination would be effected follow.

Prior to Combination of Plan A and Plan B

	Plan A	Plan B
Assumptions:		
Weighted-average discount rate	11%	10.5%
Expected long-term rate of return on plan assets	12%	12%
Average remaining service period	20 years	13 years
Average remaining service period at date of initial application of FAS-87	20 years	13 years
Number of employees as of December 31, 20X4, expected to receive benefits under the pension plan	400	550
Amortization Method:		
Prior service cost	Straight-line amortization over average remaining service period of employees expected to receive benefits (20 years)	Straight-line amortization over average remaining service period of employees expected to receive benefits (13 years)
Projected benefit obligation	$(1,004)	$(1,280)
Plan assets at fair value	1,608	410
Funded status and recognized asset/liability	$ 604	$ (870)
Amounts recognized in accumulated other comprehensive income:		
Net (gain) loss	(228)	82
Prior service cost (credit)	240	642
Prepaid pension cost	$ 12	$ 724

After Combination of Plan A and Plan B

	Combined Plan AB
Assumptions:	
Weighted-average discount rate	10.6%[a]
Expected long-term rate of return on plan assets	12%[b]
Average remaining service period	15.95 years[c]
Number of employees as of December 31, 20X4, expected to receive benefits under the pension plan	950

ASC 715—Compensation—Retirement Benefits

	Combined Plan AB
Amortization method:	
Prior service cost	The existing prior service costs of Plan A and Plan B continue to be amortized separately. The amortization bases used prior to the combination continue to apply.
Net gain or loss	Minimum amortization specified in paragraph 32 (ASC 715-30-35-24) (average remaining service period is 15.95 years[d])

(a) The weighted-average assumed discount rate reflects the rate at which the pension obligation could be effectively settled. (This illustration assumes that 10.6% is the appropriate discount rate. The discount rate is calculated without reference to either of the discount rates on the previously separate plans.)

(b) There is no change in the expected long-term rate of return on plan assets, because both Plan A and Plan B assume the same rate of return.

(c) The average remaining service period of employees who are expected to receive benefits under the pension plan is weighted by the number of covered employees from each group. This calculation is performed as follows: (20 years × 400/950) + (13 years × 550/950) = 15.95 years. The remaining service period should be the same when a new calculation is made for the combined group.

(d) The amortization period for the remaining unrecognized net obligation existing at the date of initial application of FAS-87 is determined by weighting (1) the average *remaining* amortization period for each plan and (2) the *absolute value* of the remaining unrecognized net asset or net obligation existing at the date FAS-87 was adopted. In this example, the calculation is as follows: [(20 years − 5 years) × 40/540] + [(15 years − 5 years) × 500/540] = 10.4 years (rounded).

	Combined Plan AB
Projected benefit obligation	$(2,284)
Plan assets at fair value	$ 2,018
Funded status and recognized asset/liability	$ (266)
Amounts recognized in accumulated other comprehensive income:	
Net (gain) loss	(146)
Prior service cost (credit)	882
Prepaid pension cost	$ 736

Question E81: If an employer divides a pension plan into two or more separate pension plans after the date of initial application of this Statement, how should (*a*) the transition asset or obligation remaining in accumulated other comprehensive income, (*b*) net gain or loss, if any, included in accumulated other comprehensive income, and (*c*) prior service included in accumulated other comprehensive income cost, if any, allocated to each of the separate plans based on the applicable individuals included in the employee groups covered?

Answer: An employer should allocate the transition asset or obligation remaining in accumulated other comprehensive income and the net gain or loss included in accumulated other comprehensive income the respective pension plans in proportion to the projected benefit obligation of the surviving plans. Prior service costs included in accumulated other comprehensive income should be allocated to the surviving pension plans based on the applicable individuals in the employee groups covered.

Question E82: Are annuity contracts defined differently in this Statement and ASC 715-30? If so, how are the definitions different, and why?

Answer: Yes. Settlement accounting under the guidance in ASC 715-30 does not apply if annuity contracts are purchased from an enterprise that is controlled by the employer. Therefore, if an employer purchases annuity contracts from an enterprise that is controlled by the employer, no settlement gain or loss is recognized on the transaction. Under this statement, pension benefits covered by annuity contracts purchased from a non-captive insurer are to be excluded from the projected benefit obligation and from plan assets. The net effect of the above is that no settlement gain or loss is recognized if annuity contracts are purchased from an entity controlled by the employer; however, unless these annuity contracts are purchased from a captive insurer, the pension benefits covered by the contracts are excluded from the PBO and from plan assets. Disclosure is required of the appropriate amount of annual benefits covered by annuity contracts issued by an employer and related entities.

Question E83: Is a guaranteed investment contract (GIC) an annuity contract?

Answer: No. All a GIC does is transfer investment risk to the insurer. In an annuity contract, the insurer assumes an unconditional legal obligation to provide specified pension benefits to specific individuals.

Question E84: If a GIC is not considered an annuity contract, how should an employer value the contract if it has a specified maturity date and there is no intent to liquidate the contract before that date?

Answer: The GIC should still be valued at its fair value on a yearly basis even if the employer has no intent to liquidate the contract before its maturity date. The employer may estimate the fair value of the GIC by looking to current interest rates on similar debt securities of comparable risk and duration.

Question E85: Should the market value adjustment in an immediate participation GIC be considered in determining its fair value?

Answer: Yes. The contract value adjusted for any such market value adjustment represents the contract's cash surrender value. In some cases an immediate participation GIC can be converted into an annuity contract. In these cases the conversion value of the contract is relevant in estimating the contract's fair value.

Question E86: A not-for-profit organization has a defined benefit pension plan that covers employees at the national level and in all local chapters. If (*a*) each chapter is required to contribute to the pension plan based on a predetermined formula (e.g., on a percentage-of-salary basis), (*b*) plan assets are not segregated or restricted on a chapter-by-chapter basis, and (*c*) the pension obligations for a chapter's employees are retained by the pension plan if a chapter withdraws from the pension plan, as opposed to being allocated to the withdrawing chapter, should that arrangement be accounted for as a single-employer pension plan or as a multiemployer pension plan?

Answer: The not-for-profit organization should account for the pension plan as a single-employer plan in its consolidated financial statements. However, each of the separate chapters should account for the plan as a multiemployer plan in its individual financial statements. Each chapter should recognize its required yearly contribution, whether fully funded or not, as net periodic pension cost. If the yearly contribution is not fully funded, the local chapter would need to record a liability. Each local chapter must make the disclosures required in paragraph 69 of this Statement and the required related-party disclosures of ASC 850-10 (if applicable).

Question E87: Does the answer to the previous question also apply to a similar parent subsidiary arrangement if each subsidiary issues separate financial statements?

Answer: Yes. The parent would account for the pension plan as a single-employer plan in the consolidated financial statements. Each subsidiary would account for the plan as a multiemployer plan in its individual financial statements.

Question E88: Should the pension asset or pension liability recognized by the acquiring employer be separately amortized to income in periods subsequent to the acquisition?

Answer: No. Any such pension asset or liability should not be separately amortized. However, a pension asset or liability recognized by the acquiring employer will be affected by the accounting for the pension plan in future periods.

Question E88a: If an employer has (*a*) a qualified pension plan (for tax purposes) and (*b*) a nonqualified pension plan (which pays pension benefits in excess of the maximum allowed for the qualified pension plan by Section 415 of the U.S. Internal Revenue Code—an excess benefit [top-hat] pension plan) and the plans cover the same employees, may those pension plans be considered in substance a single pension plan under this Statement?

Answer: No. In most cases a qualified pension plan (for tax purposes) is legally prohibited from using its assets to pay benefits of an excess benefit pension plan. Therefore, in the situation described above, each plan would be accounted for separately. The fact that the employer could (*a*) contribute less to the qualified plan and use any savings to pay benefits under the excess benefit plan or (*b*) terminate the qualified plan and use the assets that revert to it to pay benefits under the excess plan does not, in itself, indicate that the two pension plans should be combined.

Questions E89-E106: These questions have been deleted.

Question E107: If a pension plan curtailment occurs that causes almost all of the pension plan's participants to become inactive, should the employer continue to amortize any transition asset or obligation remaining in accumulated other comprehensive income using the same amortization period determined at that date of initial application of this Statement?

Answer: An employer should continue amortizing a transition asset or obligation, if any, that remains in accumulated other comprehensive income, which is the amount that remains after the employer accounts for the curtailment as required under the guidance in ASC 715-30-35-92, 93, based on the same amortization period that was determined on the date that this Statement was initially applied.

ASC 715-20-45-4; ASC 715-30-15-7, 25-9, 25-11,35-22, 35-75, 35-81 through 35-82, 35-84, 35-95; 55-52, 55-92, 55-130 through 55-137, 55-140, 55-142 through 55-168, 55-170 through 55-184, 55-186 through 55-197, 55-201, 55-208, 55-217 through 55-219, 55-221, 55-226 though 55-230, 55-237 through 55-238, 55-241 through 55-246, 55-248 through 55-249, 55-251 through 55-252, 60-5, 60-8; ASC 740-10-55-75; ASC 845-10-55-1, 55-3 through 55-9; ASC 205-20-60-5; ASC 712-2-10-05-2; 25-1 Guide to Implementation of ASC 715 on Employers' Accounting for Settlements and Curtailments of Defined Benefit Pension Plans and for Termination Benefits

ACCOUNTING GUIDANCE

Question C1: Should an employer recognize a settlement gain or loss in the period in which all of the following occur: (*a*) the employer decides to terminate a defined benefit pension plan and establish a successor pension plan, (*b*) a nonparticipating annuity contract for the vested benefits of all plan participants is purchased but can be rescinded if certain regulatory approvals for the termination of the pension plan are not obtained, and (*c*) it is determined that the regulatory approvals are probable?

Answer: No. ASC 715-30 specifies three criteria that define when a pension plan settlement has occurred. A *settlement* is defined as a transaction that (1) is irrevocable, (2) relieves the employer (or the pension plan) of the primary responsibility for a pension plan obligation, and (3) eliminates significant risks related to the pension plan obligation and plan assets used to effect the settlement. In the situation described above, an irrevocable transaction has not occurred. The probability that an irrevocable action will be completed is not relevant.

Question C2: If an employer decides in 20X4 to terminate its pension plan, withdraw excess plan assets, and establish a successor pension plan but is unable to effect the transactions (which include the settlement of the vested benefit obligation) until regulatory approval is obtained, does the purchase of nonparticipating annuity contracts in January 20X5 (after regulatory approval has been obtained and before issuance of the 20X4 financial statements) require adjustment of the 20X4 financial statements?

Answer: No. As discussed in the answer to the question in paragraph C1, a *settlement* is defined as a transaction that (1) is irrevocable, (2) relieves the employer (or the pension plan) of the primary responsibility for a pension plan obligation, and (3) eliminates significant risks related to the pension plan obligation and plan assets used to effect the settlement. All three of these criteria are not met until January 20X5. However, the employer would need to disclose its plans to terminate the pension plan and its receipt of the required regulatory approvals in January 20X5.

Question C3: If plan participants have agreed to accept lump-sum cash payments in exchange for their rights to receive specified pension benefits and the amounts of the payments have been fixed, may a settlement gain or loss be recognized before the cash payments are made to plan participants?

Answer: It depends. If the cash payments have yet to be made, the agreement itself may be revocable. Moreover, if the pension plan assets have not been used to effect the settlement, the employer may still be subject to risks related to these assets. Either of these conditions would preclude the employer from recognizing a settlement gain or loss.

Question C4: If an employer withdraws excess plan assets (cash) from a pension plan but is not required to settle a pension benefit obligation as part of the asset reversion transaction, should any of the net gain or loss included in accumulated other comprehensive income be immediately recognized in earnings?

Answer: No. A settlement has not occurred. Therefore, any net gain or loss should not be recognized in earnings.

Question C5: What is the accounting for the transaction described in paragraph C4?

Answer: The employer's withdrawal of cash is considered a negative plan contribution. The employer should debit cash and should credit the net pension asset or liability, as appropriate.

Question C6: If individual nonparticipating annuity contracts are to be used to settle a pension benefit obligation, may a settlement gain or loss be recognized if the individual annuity contracts have not been issued?

Answer: It depends. The issuance of individual annuity contracts is not the critical event in determining whether a settlement gain or loss can be recognized. However, the failure to issue individual contracts, along with other evidence, may indicate that the pension benefit obligation has not been effectively settled. In order for a settlement gain or loss to be recognized, an irrevocable transaction that relieves the employer (or the pension plan) from primary responsibility for the pension benefit obligation and that eliminates significant risks associated with the pension obligation and pension assets must have occurred. A commitment to purchase annuity contracts is not sufficient for a settlement gain or loss to be recognized.

Question C7: If individual nonparticipating annuity contracts are to be used to settle a pension benefit obligation, may a settlement gain or loss be recognized if the premium for the purchase of the individual annuity contracts has not been paid?

Answer: It depends. As discussed previously, for a settlement gain or loss to be recognized, an irrevocable transaction that relieves the employer (or the pension plan) of primary responsibility for the pension benefit obligation and that eliminates significant risks associated with the pension obligation and pension assets must have occurred. The failure to pay the insurance premium may indicate that the transaction is revocable. In addition, if pension plan assets have not been transferred to effect the settlement, they may still be at risk. In order for a settlement gain or loss to be recognized, the insurance company must have unconditionally assumed the legal obligation to provide the promised pension benefits.

Question C8: If a contract is entered into that requires an insurance company to pay only a portion of specific participants' pension benefits—for example, payments due retirees for the next five years—has a settlement occurred?

Answer: No. A contract to provide pension benefits for a specified period of time is a limited-term annuity. As such, it does not eliminate the risks associated with the pension benefit obligation. For example, the risk related to employee life expectancy (i.e., the duration of the pension benefits) remains. For an annuity contract with a life insurance company to qualify for settlement accounting, the contract needs to be a life annuity and not a limited-term annuity.

Question C9: Does the following constitute a settlement?

1. An employer (or the pension plan) irrevocably purchases an insurance contract that guarantees payment of those pension benefits vested as of the date of the purchase.
2. The purchase price of the insurance contract significantly exceeds the purchase price of a nonparticipating annuity contract covering the same pension benefits.
3. As compensation for the risk of guaranteeing those pension benefits, the insurance company receives an annual fee based on a percentage of the actuarial present value of the covered pension benefits.
4. If a specified ratio of assets to the covered pension benefit obligation is maintained, the employer (or the pension plan) continues to manage the assets used to effect the purchase; however, the insurance contract requires that a certain percentage of the assets be invested in high quality bonds or a dedicated bond portfolio, depending on the ratio of assets to the covered pension benefit obligation.
5. Upon final satisfaction of all of the pension benefit obligation covered by the insurance contract and payment of all of the contract's administrative fees due to the insurance company, the insurance company will remit to the employer (or the pension plan) any amounts remaining in the insurance contract's account balance. The employer (or the pension plan) is also permitted to make interim withdrawals from the account with prior notification of the insurance company, unless a withdrawal causes the ratio of assets to the covered pension benefit obligation to drop below a specified percentage.

Answer: No. The employer has not effectively transferred the risks and rewards associated with the pension plan assets and obligations. The type of annuity contract described in this question is a participating annuity contract. Because the employer is still subject to the pension plan's risks and rewards, the criteria for settlement accounting in ASC 715-30-15-6 and ASC 715-30-35-86 through 35-87 have not been met.

ASC 715—Compensation—Retirement Benefits

Question C10: What is the rationale for requiring settlement accounting for only certain participating annuity contracts?

Answer: The FASB had two basic reasons for requiring settlement accounting for only certain participating annuity contracts. First, some contracts that are essentially nonparticipating annuity contracts could be structured as participating contracts by requiring the payment of a small additional premium for a *de minimis* participation feature. Employers might have attempted to structure the purchase of an annuity contract in this manner to avoid having to recognize a pension plan settlement. Therefore, settlement plan accounting is applied to a participating annuity contract if the contract is essentially equivalent to a nonparticipating contract. Second, in some cases it might make economic sense for the employer to purchase a participating contract. Assuming that the requisite risks and rewards are transferred under the terms of the participating contract, settlement accounting is required. However, if the employer's exposure to pension plan gains and losses is substantially the same both before and after the employer enters into the participating annuity contract, settlement accounting would not be permitted.

Question C11: Are there quantitative criteria that can be used to determine whether the purchase of a participating annuity contract qualifies for settlement accounting?

Answer: No. Whether the purchase of a participating annuity contract qualifies for settlement accounting depends on the facts and circumstances of the particular case.

Question C12: If a parent company's wholly owned subsidiaries, Subsidiaries A and B, have separate pension plans, and Subsidiary B purchases nonparticipating annuity contracts from Subsidiary A (which is an insurance company) to provide the vested benefits under Subsidiary B's pension plan, does that purchase constitute a settlement in the parent company's consolidated financial statements? Does the transaction constitute a settlement in the separately issued financial statements of Subsidiary B?

Answer: The above transaction does not constitute a settlement in the parent company's consolidated financial statements. This Statement specifically precludes settlement accounting if an annuity contract is purchased from an insurance company controlled by the employer. In this case, the parent company is still subject to the risks associated with the pension benefit obligation and plan assets (all that has happened is that they have been transferred within the consolidated group, from Subsidiary B to Subsidiary A). The settlement would be recognized in Subsidiary B's separate financial statements, assuming the other criteria for settlement accounting have been met. The related-party nature of the pension settlement must be disclosed in the notes to the financial statements.

Question C13: Is the relative cost of the participation right (10%) used in Illustration 2, Example 2C, of ASC 715-30 intended to be an indication of a criterion that could be used to determine whether the purchase of a participating annuity contract qualifies for settlement accounting?

Answer: No. The facts assumed in that example were chosen solely to illustrate the application of ASC 715-30-35-79.

Question C14: If an employer terminates its pension plan, settles a pension benefit obligation, withdraws excess plan assets, and establishes a successor pension plan that has the same pension benefit formula, have both a settlement and a curtailment occurred?

Answer: No. A settlement has occurred but not a curtailment. Although employees will no longer earn benefits for future service under the old plan, they will earn credit under the new plan. For accounting purposes, the old and new pension plans are viewed as essentially one plan. The settlement of the pension benefit obligation and the withdrawal of excess plan assets are recognized (i.e., the settlement). If the new pension plan provides increased (reduced) pension benefits for future service, a pension plan amendment (negative amendment) has occurred.

Question C15: If as part of the sale of a segment or a portion of a line of business (see the question in paragraph C37) there is a transfer of a pension benefit obligation to the purchaser (i.e., the purchaser assumes the pension benefit obligation for specific employees), have both a settlement and a curtailment occurred?

Answer: It depends. A settlement has occurred if the criteria in ASC 715-30-15-6 are met. However, if there is a reasonable chance that the purchaser may not provide the promised pension benefits and if the employer remains contingently liable for such benefits, a settlement has not occurred. A curtailment has occurred if the sale significantly reduces the expected future years of employee service of present employees covered by the employer's pension plan.

Question C16: Are *annuity contracts* defined differently in ASC 715-20 and ASC 715-30? If so, how are the definitions different, and why?

Answer: Yes. Under the guidance in ASC 715-30, annuity contracts purchased from an entity that is controlled by an employer are *not* eligible for settlement accounting. The FASB's rationale for this requirement is that pension plan risks are merely being shifted from one part of the entity to another part of the same entity. Under the guidance in ASC 715-20 pension benefits covered by annuity contracts are excluded from the measurement of the projected benefit obligation and from plan assets. However, if the annuity contract is purchased from a captive insurer (a more limited definition than an insurer controlled by the employer), the projected benefit obligation is not reduced and the annuity contract purchased from the captive insurer is included among plan assets. This treatment is largely justified on the basis of practical expediency.

Question C17: If nonparticipating annuity contracts are purchased from a less-than-majority-owned investee that is not controlled by the employer and the criteria for a settlement are satisfied, is the resulting settlement gain or loss subject to partial recognition (i.e., should it be reduced to reflect the employer's ownership)?

Answer: No. The entire settlement gain or loss should be recognized in earnings. This treatment represents a departure from the normal practice of eliminating the applicable portion (based on ownership) of gains or losses from intercompany transactions. However, this treatment does not establish a new precedent for the treatment of nonpension intercompany transactions.

Question C18: Is there a specific threshold for determining if an event results in (*a*) a *significant* reduction of expected years of future service of present employees covered by a pension plan or (*b*) an elimination of the accrual of pension benefits for some or all of the future services of a *significant* number of employees covered by a pension plan?

Answer: No. Judgment should be exercised based on the facts and circumstances that are unique to each case.

Question C19: If an employer has a pension plan covering employees in several divisions and the employer terminates employees in one of those divisions, does a curtailment occur if the expected years of future service of present employees in that division are reduced significantly but the reduction is not significant in relation to the expected years of future service of all employees covered by the pension plan?

Answer: No. This Statement should be applied on an overall basis for each individual pension plan. In the above example, the reduction in the expected years of future service is not significant for the pension plan as a whole. The above example would give rise to a pension plan gain or loss (see ASC 715-30-35-18 through 35-19, 35-21, and 35-24 through 35-25, for additional details).

Question C20: Can a curtailment occur if an employer either (*a*) temporarily lays off a significant number of present employees covered by a pension plan or (*b*) temporarily suspends a pension plan so that employees covered by the pension plan do not earn additional pension benefits for some or all of their future services?

Answer: Yes. A curtailment occurs if there is a significant reduction in pension benefits for some or all of the future services of employees covered by the pension plan. This result holds regardless of whether the cause is a temporary employee layoff or a temporary suspension of the pension plan.

Question C21: If unrelated, individually insignificant reductions of expected years of future service of employees covered by a pension plan accumulate to a significant reduction over a single year or more than one year, does that constitute a curtailment?

Answer: No. Each of these reductions leads to a pension plan gain or loss (see ASC 715-30-35-18 through 35-19, 35-21, and 35-24 through 35-25, for additional details).

Question C22: If individually insignificant reductions of expected years of future service of employees covered by a pension plan are (*a*) caused by one event, such as a strike, or (*b*) related to a single plan of reorganization and those reductions accumulate to a significant reduction during more than one fiscal year, does a curtailment occur?

Answer: Yes. The fact that the significant reduction occurs over a period of time does not change the fact that an event giving rise to curtailment accounting has occurred.

Question C23: Does a curtailment occur if an employer terminates a pension plan and establishes a successor pension plan that provides additional but reduced pension benefits for all years of employees' future service?

Answer: No. In this case the pension plan continues to provide benefits for future employee service, albeit at a reduced level. In accordance with the guidance in this Statement, a curtailment involves the elimination, for a significant number of employees, of pension credit for some or all of their expected future service. This situation represents a reduction of future benefits, not an elimination of such benefits. Under the guidance in ASC 715-30, a reduction in future pension benefits must be treated as a negative plan amendment.

Question C24: Can a curtailment occur if a pension plan is terminated and replaced by a successor pension plan?

Answer: Yes. A curtailment involves the elimination, for a significant number of employees, of the accrual of defined pension benefits for some or all of their expected future service. The substitution of a new pension plan for an existing pension plan would represent a curtailment if (*a*) a significant number of employees covered under the old pension plan are not covered under the new pension plan or (*b*) a significant number of years of future employee service do not result in the accrual of defined pension benefits.

Illustration of Substituting New Plan for Existing Plan

Rorer Industries offers a pension plan that provides employees a flat pension benefit of $1,000 for each year of service. At December 31, 20X4, Rorer terminates this plan and replaces it with a new pension plan. Under the new plan, employees will be provided with a pension benefit of $500 for each year of service. At December 31, 20X4, Employee A had worked for Rorer for five years. The typical Rorer employee has five years of service.

Given the above facts, Rorer needs to account for the substitution of a new pension plan for its existing plan as a curtailment. At December 31, 20X4, the accumulated pension benefit obligation for Employee A was $5,000. Given the terms of the new pension plan, Employee A will not earn additional defined pension benefits under the new plan until the year 20Y0 (the accumulated pension benefit obligation for Employee A under the new plan will not reach $5,000 until December 31, 20X9). Therefore, Employee A will provide five years of future service without accruing any additional defined pension benefits. Since Employee A is a typical Rorer employee, these facts are consistent with a significant reduction in the accrual of additional pension benefits for future years of employee service.

Question C25: If an employer disposes of a segment or a portion of a line of business (see the question in paragraph C37) that results in a termination of some employees' services earlier than expected but does not significantly reduce the expected years of future service of present employees covered by the pension plan, should the effects of the reduction in the workforce on the pension plan be measured in the same manner as a curtailment to determine the gain or loss on the disposal pursuant to ASC 205-20-45-3?

Answer: Yes. The above facts do not represent a curtailment, since the expected years of future service of present employees covered by the pension plan have not been significantly reduced. However, the effects of the reduction in the workforce should be treated in the same manner as a curtailment for the purpose of calculating the gain or loss on disposal.

Question C26: What is considered a successor pension plan for purposes of applying this Statement?

Answer: This question is relevant because if a pension obligation is settled and the pension plan is terminated without being replaced by a successor plan, a pension plan termination and curtailment have both occurred.

An employer that terminates a pension plan may establish a new plan, or it may amend one or more existing pension plans. The new plan or the amended plan may provide for the accrual of defined pension benefits for the future services of present employees who were covered by the previous (terminated) pension plan. In these cases, a successor plan would exist unless (*a*) the defined pension benefits provided by the new plan are significantly fewer than the pension benefits provided by the old plan or (*b*) the present employees covered by the new plan are significantly fewer than the employees covered by the old plan.

This Statement does not apply to an employer's withdrawal from a multiemployer pension plan. If an employer withdraws from a multiemployer plan and establishes a new pension plan for its employees, the new plan is not considered a successor plan. In some cases the employer may be responsible for a portion of the plan's unfunded pension obligation. If the requirements of ASC 450-FAS-5 (Accounting for Contingencies) are met, the employer should accrue a liability for its share of the unfunded obligation.

Question C27: If settlement of the pension benefit obligation as part of a pension plan termination occurs (and there is no successor pension plan) in a financial reporting period that differs from the period in which the effects of the curtailment resulting from the pension plan termination ordinarily would be recognized, should the effects of both the settlement and the curtailment be recognized in the same financial reporting period?

Answer: Generally not. The effects of a settlement should be recognized in accordance with the guidance in ASC 715-30-35-79 and the effects of a curtailment should be recognized in accordance with the guidance in ASC 715-30-35-94. This may result in the effects of the settlement and the curtailment being recognized in different financial reporting periods.

PRACTICE POINTER: The effects of a pension plan curtailment are recognized on the date of the pension plan amendment. The effects of a settlement are recognized when the employer is relieved of its obligation for providing the pension plan benefits.

Question C28: This question has been deleted.

Question C29: If, in terminating its pension plan (old assets), an employer settles the pension benefit obligation and withdraws excess plan assets and then contributes and allocates those assets to participants' accounts in a new defined contribution pension plan, may the employer combine any net gain or loss from the settlement and curtailment of the old plan with the net periodic pension cost from the contribution to the defined contribution pension plan and thereby report both on a net basis for purposes of classification in the income statement or disclosure in accompanying footnotes?

Answer: No. In the facts at hand, both a pension plan termination and a contribution to a defined contribution plan have taken place. These are two separate events and they need to be recognized in earnings as such. As a result of the pension plan termination, all net pension amounts included in accumulated other comprehensive income are recognized in earnings. Net periodic pension cost is recognized for the amount contributed to the defined contribution pension plan. Therefore, it is inappropriate to net the results of the separate events.

Question 30: If a market-related value of plan assets other than fair value is used for purposes of determining the expected return on plan assets, is that basis also to be used in determining the maximum gain or loss subject to pro rata recognition in earnings when a pension benefit obligation is settled?

Answer: No. The fair value of the plan assets on the date of settlement is to be used.

Question C31: As of what date should plan assets and the projected benefit obligation be measured in determining the accounting for a settlement?

Answer: Plan assets and the projected benefit obligation should be measured as of the date of the settlement, which is the date on which the FAS-88 criteria for settlement accounting have been met. The appropriate date for measuring plan assets and the projected benefit obligation is important because these amounts determine (*a*) the maximum gain or loss subject to pro rata recognition in earnings (e.g., if 100% of the projected benefit obligation is settled, then 100% of the maximum gain or loss is recognized in earnings) and (*b*) the percentage reduction in the projected benefit obligation.

Question C32: If the interest rates implicit in the purchase price of nonparticipating annuity contracts used to effect a settlement are different from the assumed discount rates used to determine net periodic pension cost, should the employer measure the portion of the projected benefit obligation being settled (and the remaining portion, if appropriate) using the implicit annuity interest rates and include any resulting gain or loss in the maximum gain or loss subject to pro rata recognition in earnings?

Answer: Yes. As discussed in the answer to the question in paragraph C31, plan assets and the projected benefit obligation are measured as of the settlement date. In measuring the portion of the projected benefit obligation being settled, the employer should use the purchase price of the nonparticipating annuity contracts. Any gain or loss resulting from remeasuring the plan assets and the projected benefit obligation as of the settlement date are included in computing the maximum gain or loss subject to pro rata recognition in earnings.

Question C33: If a settlement occurs in the circumstances described in the question in paragraph C32 and the interest rates implicit in the purchase price of nonparticipating annuity contracts used to effect the settlement are different from the assumed discount rates used to determine net periodic pension cost, is it appropriate to measure the unsettled portion of the projected benefit obligation using the implicit annuity interest rates?

Answer: Maybe. The employer should consider measuring the projected benefit obligation for the unsettled portion of the pension obligation using the interest rate implicit in the annuity contract under the following circumstances:

1. If the demographics of the participants for whom the PBO was settled are similar to the demographics of participants for whom the PBO was *not* settled (in particular, the length of time until pension payments will be made should be similar for each group)

2. If the interest rates implicit in the annuity contracts represent the best estimate of the interest rates at which the unsettled portion of the PBO could be effectively settled

Question C34: If an employer settles a pension benefit obligation and withdraws excess plan assets as part of terminating its pension plan, should the settlement gain or loss determined under the guidance in ASC 715-30-35-79 be adjusted to eliminate any gains or losses relating to securities issued by the employer if those securities are included in the plan assets withdrawn?

Answer: No. It is the settlement of the pension plan, not the withdrawal of plan assets, that precipitates the recognition in earnings of any net gain or loss included in accumulated other comprehensive income. The withdrawal of plan assets does not affect the recognition of the settlement gain or loss. In addition, the nature of the plan assets that are withdrawn does not affect the recognition of the settlement gain or loss.

Question C35: If the transition asset or obligation is reduced when a settlement gain is recognized, how is any balance of the transition asset or obligation remaining in accumulated other comprehensive income amortized in future periods?

Answer: The balance of the transition asset or obligation asset is amortized on a straight-line basis over the remainder of the amortization period established at transition.

Question C36: If a negative pension plan amendment adopted shortly before the date of initial application of the guidance in ASC 715-30 is the reason that a transition asset exists in accumulated other comprehensive income, should any portion of the transition asset remaining in accumulated other comprehensive income as of the date of a settlement be included in the maximum gain or loss subject to pro rata recognition in earnings?

Answer: Yes. Any transition asset or obligation remaining in accumulated comprehensive income at the time of a settlement is included in determining the maximum gain or loss subject to pro rata recognition in earnings.

Question C37: If an employer sells a segment of a component of an entity as defined in the ASC *Glossary* and the employer settles a pension benefit obligation related to the employees affected by the sale, should the settlement gain or loss recognized in accordance with the guidance in ASC 715-30-35-79, 35-82 through 35-83 be classified separately in discontinued operations?

Answer: According to the guidance in ASC 360, a settlement is directly related to a disposal transaction if a cause-and-effect relationship is established and the settlement occurs one year or less after a disposal transaction, unless the settlement is delayed by events not under the entity's control. A direct cause-and-effect relationship would exist if a condition of the sale of a component of an entity were to require settlement of the pension benefit obligation for employees affected by a sale. The timing of a settlement that occurs because of a disposal of a component of an entity may be at the employer's discretion. An employer's decision to settle a pension benefit obligation when a sale occurs may cause a coincidence of events that would not by itself signify that there is a cause-and-effect relationship between the transactions. In this case the guidance in ASC 715-30-35-79, and 35-82 through 35-83 would apply.

Question C38: This question has been deleted.

Question C39: How should an employer determine and report a gain or loss from a settlement or curtailment that occurs as a direct result of a disposal of a component of an entity?

Answer: Under the guidance in ASC 715-30-35-94, a curtailment loss should be recognized in earnings if it is probable that a curtailment will occur and the related amount is estimable. Consequently, if it is probable that a disposal of a component of an entity will occur and the disposal loss is estimable, a curtailment loss should be recognized even if the reporting entity has not yet met all of the criteria required in ASC 360 to classify the disposal group's operations as discontinued operations. Gain recognition on a curtailment gain also is required under the guidance in paragraph ASC 715-30-35-94 if the related employees are terminated or a suspension or amendment of a plan is adopted. A curtailment gain or loss should be classified in income from continuing operations until the reporting entity meets the criteria required in ASC 360 to report discounting operations. A gain or loss from the settlement of a pension benefits obligation should be recognized when a settlement occurs.

Question C40: If an employer incorporates a division of its operations and subsequently spins it off to owners of the enterprise and also transfers to the new entity's pension plan either (*a*) a pension benefit obligation related to the employees transferred as part of the spinoff or (*b*) plan assets, how should the employer and the new entity account for the transaction?

Answer: ASC 845 precludes the recognition of a gain or loss on the distribution of nonmonetary assets to owners of the enterprise spinoff. In a similar fashion, the recognition of a gain or loss resulting from the transfer of pension assets or of the pension plan obligation in a spinoff also is prohibited. Any (a) transition asset or obligation remaining in accumulated other comprehensive income, and (b) net gain or loss included in accumulated other comprehensive income should be allocated between the employer's existing pension plan and the pension plan of the spun-off new entity in proportion to the projected benefit obligation of each pension plan. Prior service costs included in accumulated other comprehensive income should be allocated between the two pension plans based on an analysis of the prior service of the individuals that will be covered under each of the pension plans. The accounting for a transfer of plan assets and the pension benefit obligation to a new entity established as a result of a spinoff is illustrated below.

Illustration of Incorporation and Subsequent Spinoff of a Pension Plan

XYZ, Inc., incorporated one of its divisions, ABC, Inc. ABC is later spun off to XYZ's shareholders. ABC assumes XYZ's pension obligation that relates to ABC's employees. The accumulated benefit obligation assumed by ABC (all of which is vested) is $60,000. ABC's projected benefit obligation is $12,000 higher than this amount based on the expected future salary levels of these employees. In addition, XYZ transfers to ABC $56,000 in plan assets. The appropriate accounting treatment for XYZ, Inc., and ABC, Inc., is illustrated below.

	Old Plan Before Spinoff	Old Plan After Spinoff	New Plan After Spinoff
Assets and obligations:			
Accumulated benefit obligation	$(144,000)	$(84,000)	$(60,000)
Effects of future compensation levels	(36,000)	(24,000)	(12,000)
Projected benefit obligation	(180,000)	(108,000)	(72,000)
Plan assets at fair value	320,000	264,000	56,000
Funded status and recognized asset/liability	$(140,000)	$156,000	$(16,000)
Amounts remaining in accumulated other comprehensive income:			
Transition asset	(80,000)	(48,000)	(32,000)
Prior service cost	50,000	35,000	15,000
Net gain	(110,000)	(66,000)	(44,000)
	$(140,000)	$79,000	$(61,000)

Spreadsheet Notes

- The allocation of the $180,000 projected benefit obligation between the two plans was based on an analysis of the individual employees covered by each plan.

- The allocation of the $320,000 of plan assets between the two plans was chosen by XYZ's management (we assume that no regulatory requirements apply).

- The allocation of the transition asset or obligation remaining in accumulated other comprehensive income and the net gain or loss included in accumulated other comprehensive income between the two plans was based on the percentage of the total projected benefit obligation assumed by each plan (60% for the old plan, 40% for the new plan).

- The allocation of prior service cost included in accumulated other comprehensive income between the two plans was based on an analysis of the individual employees covered by each plan (for illustrative purposes we have assumed that this allocation differs from the PBO assumed by each plan).

Journal Entries

XYZ, Inc.

Pension asset	16,000	
Accumulated other comprehensive income—transition asset	32,000	
Accumulated other comprehensive income—net gain	44,000	
Stockholders' equity		77,000
Accumulated other comprehensive income—prior service cost		15,000

To record the transfer of plan assets, a pension benefit obligation, and net deferred amounts from XYZ, Inc. to ABC, Inc. Note that the credit to stockholders' equity represents the net of all assets and liabilities transferred from XYZ, Inc. to ABC, Inc.

ABC, Inc.

Stockholders' equity	77,000	
Accumulated other comprehensive income—prior service cost	15,000	
Pension asset		16,000
Accumulated other comprehensive income—transition asset		32,000
Accumulated other comprehensive income—net gain		44,000

To record the receipt of plan assets, a pension benefit obligation, and net deferred amounts from XYZ, Inc. Note that the debit to stockholders' equity represents the net of all assets and liabilities received from XYZ, Inc.

Question C41: What is the proper sequence of events to follow in measuring the effects of a settlement and a curtailment that are to be recognized at the same time?

Answer: Although the method selected may affect the determination of the aggregate gain or loss recognized, management decides whether the effects of the settlement are recognized first or the effects of the curtailment. Once management has selected a method, however, that method must be followed in future years when a settlement and a curtailment occur simultaneously.

Question C42: Because the amount of the vested benefit obligation settled and the amount of plan assets used to purchase nonparticipating annuity contracts are equal in Illustrations 1 and 2 of this Statement, is it appropriate to conclude that no gains and losses occurred when the projected benefit obligation and the plan assets were measured as of the date of the settlement?

Answer: No. The "Before" columns in these illustrations reflect the measurement of the plan assets and the projected benefit obligation as of the settlement date. Any gains and losses arising from measuring these two accounts at the settlement date have already been recognized. (See Question 31 for additional discussion.)

Question C43: Is the method that allocates an amount equal to the settlement gain on a pro rata basis to the transition asset or obligation remaining in accumulated other comprehensive income and the net gain included in accumulated other comprehensive income the only method of allocation permitted under those circumstances under the guidance in ASC 715-30?

Answer: No. An amount equal to the settlement gain could first be applied to the transition asset or obligation remaining in accumulated other comprehensive income. If any settlement gain remains, it would be applied against the net gain included in accumulated comprehensive income. If this method is selected, it must be applied consistently across years. Although this alternative method is acceptable, allocating the settlement gain based on the projected benefit obligation is preferable because (a) it is a more unbiased method, and (b) the allocation method can affect the determination of net periodic pension cost in subsequent periods.

Question C44: Is the method in Illustration 2, Example 2C, of this Statement that determines the maximum gain subject to pro rata recognition in earnings by first reducing the net gain included in accumulated other comprehensive income by the cost of the participation right the only method of allocation permitted under those circumstances by this Statement?

Answer: No. In the determination of the maximum gain subject to pro rata recognition in earnings, the cost of the participation right could be allocated as follows:

- To the transition asset or obligation remaining in accumulated other comprehensive income
- To the net gain included in accumulated other comprehensive income
- On a pro rata basis between those two amounts based on their relative amounts.

Any one of the three methods is acceptable. The method illustrated in Example 2C of Illustration 2 allocates the cost of the participation right to the net gain included in accumulated other comprehensive income. However, the preferred method is to allocate the cost of the participation right on a pro rata basis between those two amounts for the same reasons discussed in the answer in paragraph C43. Whichever method is selected must be applied on a consistent basis from year to year.

ASC 715—Compensation—Retirement Benefits 40,129

Question C45: May an employer adopt an accounting policy that requires recognition in earnings of gains and losses from all settlements during the year for a pension plan if the cost of those settlements exceeds the service cost component of net periodic pension cost for that pension plan for the year?

Answer: Yes. Recognition in earnings of gains and losses from pension plan settlements is required if the cost of those settlements exceeds the sum of the service cost and interest cost components of net periodic pension cost for the year in question. However, recognition of settlement gains and losses is permitted, but *not* required, if the aggregate settlement cost is below the sum of service cost and interest cost. The accounting policy adopted for recognition in earnings gains and losses from settlements must be applied on a consistent basis from year to year.

Question C46: If an employer's accounting policy is not to recognize in earnings a gain or loss from a settlement if the cost of all settlements during the year does not exceed the sum of the service cost and interest cost components of net periodic pension cost for the pension plan for the year, how should the employer account for the following situation: (*a*) it is estimated at the beginning of the year that the cost of all settlements during the year will not exceed the threshold amount described above; (*b*) a pension benefit obligation is settled during the first quarter and a settlement gain or loss is not recognized; and (*c*) in the second quarter and subsequent to the issuance of the first quarter's interim report, it is determined that the cost of all settlements during the year will exceed the threshold amount?

Answer: In this case, the change in handling settlement gains and losses should be treated as a change in accounting estimate. The settlement gain or loss would be recognized in the second quarter.

Question C47: How should an employer determine the amount of prior service cost included in accumulated other comprehensive income that should be recognized in earnings in the event of a curtailment if the employer amortizes prior service cost on a straight-line basis over the average remaining service period of employees expected to receive the related pension benefits?

Answer: Under the guidance ASC 715-30-35-92, the prior service cost included in accumulated other comprehensive income associated with future years of employee service that is no longer expected to be rendered should be recognized in earnings as part of a curtailment. This basic approach applies even if an employer amortizes prior service cost included in accumulated other comprehensive income on a straight-line basis over the employees' average remaining service period. However, if the employer amortizes prior service cost included in accumulated other comprehensive income using this alternate approach, the determination of the prior service cost included in accumulated other comprehensive income associated with the curtailment may be less precise. As a practical matter, the prior service cost included in accumulated other comprehensive income associated with the curtailment may have to be determined by referring to the reduction in the (remaining) expected future years of service. For example, assume that as of January 1, 20X8, the remaining expected future years of service that pertain to prior service costs included in accumulated other comprehensive income is ten years. As the result of a curtailment during 20X8, the remaining expected years of future service is five years. In this case, 50% of the prior service cost included in accumulated other comprehensive income is associated with the curtailment. Consequently, the employer would recognize in earnings 50% of the prior service cost included in accumulated other comprehensive income.

Question C48: If a curtailment occurs because an employer terminates or suspends a pension plan (so that employees do not earn additional pension benefits for future service) but the employees continue to work for the employer, should any prior service cost included in accumulated other comprehensive income that is associated with the employees who are affected by the pension plan termination or suspension be included in determining the net gain or loss to be recognized for the curtailment?

Answer: Yes. One reason why recognition of prior service cost in net periodic pension cost as a result of a retroactive pension plan amendment is deferred is the likelihood that the employer will receive future benefits as a result of the plan amendment. These future benefits are associated with future employee service for those employees active at the date of the plan amendment who are expected to receive benefits under the plan. Any future economic benefits the employer was expecting to receive as a result of the retroactive plan amendment are in all likelihood dissipated by the suspension or termination of the pension plan. As such, some, or all, of the prior service cost included in accumulated other comprehensive income should no longer be deferred and recognized in earnings. Further, if the pension plan is terminated, all prior service cost included in accumulated other comprehensive income must be recognized in earnings.

Question C49: If a curtailment results from a pension plan suspension that may be only temporary (e.g., the pension plan suspension will end as soon as the employer's financial condition sufficiently improves), how is the net gain or loss from the curtailment determined?

Answer: The curtailment gain or loss should be determined based on the probable duration of the pension plan suspension. [The term *probable* is defined in accordance with ASC 450]. In some cases, it may be possible to determine only a range for the likely duration of the pension plan suspension. If no length of time estimated within that range is more likely than any other length of time, the expected duration of the pension plan suspension is to be calculated to produce minimum curtailment gain or loss.

Question C50: If the transition asset or obligation remaining in accumulated comprehensive income is reduced as part of the accounting for a curtailment, how is any remaining balance amortized in future periods?

Answer: The balance of the transition asset or obligation remaining in accumulated other comprehensive income should be amortized on a straight-line basis over the remainder of the amortization period determined at the time ASC 715 (FAS-87) was adopted. (See the question in paragraph C35 for additional discussion.)

Question C51: If a curtailment occurs that causes almost all of the pension plan's participants to become permanently inactive, should the employer continue to amortize any balance of the transition asset remaining in accumulated other comprehensive income using the amortization period determined at transition?

Answer: Yes. The transition asset remaining in accumulated other comprehensive income should continue to be amortized over the remainder of the amortization period determined at transition. (See the question in paragraph C35 for additional discussion.)

Question C52: If both a transition asset remaining in accumulated other comprehensive income and a larger (smaller) net loss included in accumulated other comprehensive income exist at the date of a curtailment that decreases (increases) the projected benefit obligation, how should the effects of the curtailment be applied to those pension amounts?

Answer: The appropriate accounting treatment is as follows:

- Any reduction in the projected benefit obligation that is not recognized as a curtailment gain should be offset against the net loss included in accumulated other comprehensive income.
- Any increase in the projected benefit obligation that is not recognized as a curtailment loss should be offset against the transition asset remaining in accumulated other comprehensive income.

No further offsetting of amounts is permitted.

The first illustration below presents the appropriate accounting treatment when the transition asset remaining in accumulated other comprehensive income is less than the net loss. The second illustration presents the appropriate accounting treatment when the transition asset remaining in accumulated other comprehensive income exceeds the net loss included in accumulated other comprehensive income.

Illustration of Pension Plan Curtailment: Transition Asset Remaining in Accumulated Other Comprehensive Income Is Less Than Net Loss Included in Accumulated Other Comprehensive Income

Herring's Haberdashery sponsors a defined benefit pension plan. Herring's terminates a significant number of employees in an attempt to lower manufacturing costs. Herring's management makes the termination decision on September 30, 20X8, and the effects of the terminations are reasonably estimable at that time. The termination date is November 30, 20X8. Herring's has a transition asset remaining in accumulated other comprehensive income. As a result of the plan curtailment, Herring's escapes a pension liability for employees whose benefits are not yet vested, and its pension obligation is reduced to the extent that future compensation levels are no longer relevant for the terminated employees. Herring's projected benefit obligation is reduced by $220,000 ($180,000 from the elimination of future compensation levels on pension benefits to be received and $40,000 from the elimination of nonvested accumulated benefits). The appropriate accounting for this curtailment is as follows:

Since the projected benefit obligation is reduced, Herring's will recognize a net gain on the curtailment. In accordance with the guidance in this Statement, if the effect of a curtailment is the recognition of a net gain, the gain is recognized in earnings on the date the employees terminate (November 30, 20X8). In the

40,132 ASC 715—Compensation—Retirement Benefits

following schedule, plan assets and the projected benefit obligation are also measured as of that date.

	11/30/X8		
	Before Curtailment	Effects of Curtailment	After Curtailment
Assets and obligations:			
Vested benefit obligation	$(3,100,000)		$(3,100,000)
Nonvested benefits	(500,000)	$ 40,000	(460,000)
Accumulated benefit obligation	(3,600,000)	40,000	(3,560,000)
Effects of future compensation levels	(800,000)	180,000	(620,000)
Projected benefit obligation	(4,400,000)	220,000	(4,180,000)
Plan assets at fair value	4,200,000		4,200,000
Funded status and recognized asset (liability)	$(200,000)	220,000	$20,000
Amounts recognized in accumulated other comprehensive income:			
Transition asset	(400,000)		(400,000)
Net loss	600,000	(200,000)	400,000
	$200,000	$(200,000)	-0-

Spreadsheet Notes

- Under the guidance in this Statement, the potential curtailment gain—the $220,000 decrease in the projected benefit obligation—first should be offset against any net loss included in accumulated other comprehensive income. In this case, there is a net loss of $200,000 (a $600,000 net loss, net of the $400,000 transition asset remaining in accumulated other comprehensive income). Therefore, the curtailment gain recorded by Herring's Haberdashery is $20,000.

Journal Entry

Pension asset	$20,000	
Pension liability	$200,000	
Gain from Curtailment		$20,000
Other comprehensive income—net loss		$200,000

Illustration of Pension Plan Curtailment: Transition Asset Remaining in Accumulation Other Comprehensive Income Exceeds Net/Loss Included in Other Comprehensive Income

The facts are the same as in the previous illustration except for the following:

- Herring's supplements the retirement benefits of the employees who are terminated. This increases the projected benefit obligation by $440,000.
- The net loss included in other comprehensive income is $200,000.

ASC 715—Compensation—Retirement Benefits 40,133

Since the projected benefit obligation is increased, Herring's will recognize a net loss on the curtailment. In accordance with the guidance in this Statement, if the effect of a curtailment is the recognition of a net loss, which is recognized in earnings when it is probable that the curtailment will occur and the effects are estimable (September 30, 20X8). In the following schedule, plan assets and the projected benefit obligation are also measured as of that date.

	9/30/X8		
	Before Curtailment	Effects of Curtailment	After Curtailment
Assets and obligations:			
Vested benefit obligation	$(3,100,000)	$(440,000)	$(3,540,000)
Nonvested benefits	(500,000)	40,000	(460,000)
Accumulated benefit obligation	(3,600,000)	(400,000)	(4,000,000)
Effects of future compensation levels	(800,000)	180,000	(620,000)
Projected benefit obligation	(4,400,000)	(220,000)	(4,620,000)
Plan assets at fair value	4,200,000		4,200,000
Funded status and recognized liability	$(200,000)	$(220,000)	$(420,000)
Amounts recognized in other comprehensive income:			
Transition asset	(400,000)	200,000	(200,000)
Net loss	200,000		200,000
	$(200,000)	$ 200,000	$ -0-

Spreadsheet Notes

- Under the guidance in this statement the potential curtailment loss—the $220,000 increase in the projected benefit obligation—first should be offset against any net gain included in accumulated other comprehensive income. In this case, there is a net gain of $200,000 ($400,000 transition asset in accumulated comprehensive income, net of the $200,000 of net loss included in accumulated other comprehensive income). After $220,000 increase in the projected benefit obligation is offset against the $200,000 gain included in other comprehensive income the curtailment loss recorded by Herring's Haberdashery is $20,000.

Journal Entry

Loss from curtailment	$20,000	
Other comprehensive income—transition asset		$200,000
Pension liability		$220,000

Question C53: If both a transition asset remaining in accumulated other comprehensive income and a net gain included in accumulated other comprehensive income exist at the date of a curtailment that increases the projected benefit obligation, should the effects of the curtailment be offset (*a*) initially against a transition asset remaining in accumulated other comprehensive income, (b) initially against a net gain included in accumulated other comprehensive income, or (c) against both on a pro rata basis?

Answer: Any one of those approaches is acceptable, as long as the approach selected is applied on a consistent basis. However, the preferable approach is to apply the curtailment loss against both on a pro rata basis. (See the question in paragraph C43 for additional discussion.)

Question C54: How should (a) the liability and the loss from employees' acceptance of an offer of special termination benefits and (b) the change in the projected benefit obligation due to the related curtailment be determined?

Answer: The liability and the loss from employees' acceptance of an offer of special termination benefits are computed as the difference between:

- The actuarial present value of the accumulated benefit obligation for those employees receiving special termination benefits before consideration of the effects on the accumulated benefit obligation of those benefits *and*

- The actuarial present value of the accumulated benefit obligation for those employees receiving special termination benefits after consideration of the effects on the accumulated benefit obligation of those benefits.

Those amounts are determined as of the date the employees accept the offer of special termination benefits.

The change in the projected benefit obligation due to the related curtailment is determined as the difference between:

- The projected benefit obligation for the affected employees before their acceptance of the special termination benefits *and*

- The projected benefit obligation for the affected employees determined by applying the normal pension plan formula and assuming no future service due to the termination.

The following illustration presents the applicable accounting treatment for this circumstance.

Illustration of Curtailment: Termination Benefits Offered to Employees

On July 1, 20X8, AHB, Inc., offers its employees special pension benefits in connection with their voluntary termination of employment. Employees who accept this offer will receive an additional ten years of credited service, and employees can retire at age 50 instead of at age 55. Employees must elect to receive these special benefits, in exchange for their voluntary termination of employment, by November 1, 20X8.

On November 1, 20X8, employees representing 20% of AHB's workforce accept the special termination benefits. The actuarial present value of the accumulated benefit obligation for these employees, before consideration of the special termination benefits, as of November 1, 20X8, is $1,050,000. After consideration of the special termination benefits, the actuarial present value of the accumulated benefit obligation is $1,250,000.

Future compensation levels are no longer relevant for the 20% of AHB's workforce who accept the special termination benefits and who voluntarily leave AHB. This has the effect of reducing AHB's projected benefit obligation by $160,000.

At the time the special termination benefits are accepted, the transition obligation remaining in other comprehensive income unrecognized net obligation at transition was $1,600,000. Of that amount, $300,000 was assigned to the future years of service of the 20% of employees who accepted AHB's special termination offer. The appropriate accounting is as follows:

On November 1, 20X8, AHB will recognize a loss of $340,000 in earnings (this includes the loss from issuing the special termination benefits and the loss on the curtailment). Note that the loss is recognized on November 1, 20X8, because it is not until this date that the number of employees accepting the special termination benefits is known. The following schedule analyzes the effects of the special termination benefits on the applicable pension-related accounts.

	Before Employee Terminations	11/1/X8 Effects of Terminations	After Employee Terminations
Assets and obligations:			
Vested benefit obligation			
Employees accepting offer	$(1,050,000)	$(200,000)	$(1,250,000)
Other employees	(1,550,000)		(1,550,000)
Nonvested benefits	(400,000)		(400,000)
Accumulated benefit obligation	(3,000,000)	(200,000)	(3,200,000)
Effects of future compensation levels	(1,000,000)	160,000	(840,000)
Projected benefit obligation	(4,000,000)	(40,000)	(4,040,000)
Plan assets at fair value	2,800,000		2,800,000
Funded status and recognized liability	$(1,200,000)	$(40,000)	$(1,240,000)
Amounts recognized in accumulated other comprehensive income:			
Transition obligation	1,600,000	(300,000)	1,300,000
Net Gain	(600,000)		(600,000)
	$ 1,000,000	$ (300,000)	$ 700,000

Spreadsheet Notes

- The loss from the issuance of the special termination benefits is $200,000 ($1,250,000 – $1,050,000).

- The $160,000 decrease in future compensation levels is a potential gain. Under the guidance in this Statement, this amount should first be offset against any net loss included in accumulated other comprehensive income. Because AHB has a net gain in accumulated other comprehensive income, the entire potential gain of $160,000 is recognized in earnings (this amount represents a curtailment gain).

- Under the guidance in this Statement, the transition obligation remaining in accumulated other comprehensive income must be treated as prior service cost included in accumulated other comprehensive income for the purpose of applying the guidance in FAS-88. The reduction in prior service cost associated with the years of future service the terminated employees had been expected to work is $300,000. This amount represents a curtailment loss.
- The total loss recognized in earnings is $340,000 (the $200,000 loss from issuing the special termination benefits, the $160,000 gain from the reduction in future compensation, and a $300,000 loss from the immediate recognition of a portion of the transition obligation remaining in accumulated other comprehensive income.

Journal Entry

Loss on Employee Terminations	$340,000	
Other comprehensive income—transition obligation		$300,000
Pension liability		$40,000

Question C55: If (*a*) an employer adopts a plan to terminate employees that will significantly reduce the expected years of future service of present employees covered by a pension plan and (*b*) the sum of the effects of the resulting curtailment identified in ASC 715-30-35-92, 35-93 is expected to be a net gain, should that gain be recognized in earnings when the related employees terminate or when the plan is adopted?

Answer: The curtailment gain should be measured and recognized when the employees terminate.

Question C56: If (*a*) an employer amends its pension plan to provide for the plan's termination (or suspension) and thereby eliminates for a significant number of employees the accrual of all (or some) of the pension benefits for their future services after a subsequent date (i.e., the effective date of the pension plan termination or suspension is subsequent to the amendment date) and (*b*) the sum of the effects of the resulting curtailment identified in ASC 715-30-35-92 through 35-93 is a net gain, should that gain be recognized in earnings when the employer amends its pension plan or when the pension plan termination (or suspension) is effective?

Answer: The curtailment gain should be measured and recognized when the pension plan is amended.

Question C57: If an employer's offer of special termination benefits results in a curtailment, is it possible that the offer of termination benefits could be recognized in a reporting period different from the period in which the curtailment is recognized?

Answer: Yes. These two events may be recorded in different reporting periods. A loss from a curtailment is recognized when the curtailment is probable and its effects are reasonably estimable. The costs of termination benefits are recorded when the employees elect to receive the special termination benefits and the cost of these benefits is reasonably estimable.

Question C58: This question has been deleted.

Question C59: If an employer sponsors a pension plan that provides supplemental early retirement benefits, should those pension benefits be accounted for as contractual termination benefits?

Answer: No. The provision of supplemental early retirement benefits should be included in the computation of net periodic pension cost. Contractual termination benefits arise from the occurrence of a specific event that results in involuntary employee termination.

Question C60: Should termination indemnities that are associated with preretirement termination of employment be accounted for as contractual termination benefits?

Answer: *Termination indemnities,* which are more common outside the United States, are amounts payable to employees, often as a lump sum, upon termination of employment. The payment of termination indemnities should be accounted for as contractual termination benefits if they are paid only as the result of a specific event that results in involuntary termination. In these cases, a liability and a loss should be accrued when it is probable that employees will receive this benefit and the amount can be reasonably estimated. If virtually all employees who terminate their employment receive these benefits, the payments are in substance a pension plan and they should be accounted for under the provisions of ASC 715-30.

Question C61: If an employer offers for a short period of time special termination benefits to employees, may the employer recognize a loss at the date the offer is made based on the estimated acceptance rate?

Answer: No. Before the employer can recognize a liability and a loss, employees must accept the offer and the amount of the special termination benefits must be reasonably estimable. However, if the offer of special termination benefits is directly related to the disposal of a segment or a portion of a line of business, these benefits should be accounted for in accordance with the guidance in ASC 225-20-45.

Question C62: This question has been deleted.

Question C63: Would a gain or loss from a settlement or curtailment or the cost of termination benefits normally be classified as an extraordinary item?

Answer: Not unless the requirements of ASC 225-20-45 for classification as an extraordinary item—i.e., unusual in nature and infrequent in occurrence—are met. In most cases, a pension plan settlement, curtailment, or offer of special termination benefits would not meet the requirements for classification as an extraordinary item.

Question C64: Do any of the following meet the "unusual nature and infrequency of occurrence criteria" of ASC 225-20-45, thereby causing any resulting gain or loss to be classified as extraordinary?

1. An employer terminates its only pension plan and does not establish a successor pension plan.
2. An employer terminates its only pension plan, withdraws excess plan assets, and establishes a successor pension plan, but because of current regulatory guidelines is not permitted to effect the same series of transactions again for 15 years.
3. An employer terminates one of its foreign pension plans, withdraws excess plan assets, and establishes a successor pension plan. The employer has never affected this series of transactions in the past and has no intention of repeating these actions in the future.
4. An employer terminates its underfunded pension plan, and a regulatory agency takes over the pension plan and initiates a lien against 30% of the employer's net worth.

Answer: No. The basic problem with Items 1 through 4, Above, is that although they may be infrequent in occurrence, they are not unusual in nature. Terminating a pension plan is a normal occurrence in the current business environment.

Question C65: This question has been deleted.

Question C66: If an employer withdraws excess plan assets from its pension plan and is subject to an excise tax, is the excise tax an expense in the period of the withdrawal or should it be accounted for under the guidance in ASC 740 as an income tax and deferred if related gains (such as a settlement gain) will be recognized for financial reporting purposes in subsequent periods?

Answer: An excise tax due to an employer's withdrawal of excess plan assets does not constitute an income tax. This excise tax follows a particular transaction, and the presence of taxable income is not a prerequisite for its imposition. Therefore, the excise tax should be recognized in the period the excess assets are withdrawn, and it should not be displayed as part of income tax expense on the income statement.

Questions 67-70: These questions have been deleted.

ASC 715-30-35-73 Accounting for the Transfer of Excess Pension Assets to a Retiree Health Care Benefits Account

Under the Revenue Reconciliation Act of 1990 (the Act), an employer can transfer excess pension assets of a defined benefit pension plan (other than a multiemployer plan) to a health care benefits account that is part of the pension plan without including that amount in gross taxable income and without incurring penalties. The Act provides that such transfers be made beginning after December 31, 1990, and before the employer's 1996 tax year, and that amounts transferred not exceed the amount reasonably expected to be paid for "qualified current retiree health liabilities." Transfers are limited to one per year.

The FASB staff announced that such transfers should be recognized as a negative contribution or withdrawal from the pension plan and a positive contribution to the retiree health care plan. The transfer does not result in a gain or loss.

ASC 715-30-35-89 through 35-91 Accounting for Pension Benefits Paid by Employers after Insurance Companies Fail to Provide Annuity Benefits

BACKGROUND

Based on the guidance in ASC 715-30, a company purchases annuity contracts from an insurance company to settle its obligation under a defined benefit pension plan; the company may or may not terminate the plan. The insurance company subsequently becomes insolvent and is unable to meet its obligation under the annuity contracts. The company decides to make up some or all of the shortfall in payments to the plan's retirees.

ACCOUNTING ISSUE

How should a company account for the cost of making up the shortfall of payments to retirees caused by an insurance company's failure to fulfill its obligation under annuity contracts?

ACCOUNTING GUIDANCE

An employer's assumption of the cost of making up a shortfall in payments to retirees as a result of an insurance company's failure to meet its obligations under annuity contracts should be recognized as a loss to the extent of a gain, if any, and recognized on the original settlement. The loss recognized would be the lesser of (*a*) a gain recognized on the original settlement and (*b*) the amount of the benefit obligation assumed by the employer. The excess of the obligation assumed by the employer over the loss recognized should be accounted for as a plan amendment or a plan initiation in accordance with the provisions of ASC 715-30-35-10 through 35-11, 35-13 through 35-14, and 35-17. Thereafter, the provisions of ASC 715-30 should be applied.

ASC 715-20-50-10; ASC 715- 30-55-70 through 55-78, 55-171 Accounting for the Transfer to the Japanese Government of the Substitutional Portion of Employee Pension Fund Liabilities

BACKGROUND

Many large Japanese corporations have Employee Pension Fund (EPF) plans that are defined benefit pension plans established under the Japanese Welfare Pension Insurance Law (JWPIL). Those plans consist of the following:

- A substitutional portion based on the part of the old-age pension benefits set by JWPIL based on pay (similar to social security benefits).
- A corporate portion based on a contributory defined benefit pension arrangement established by employers with benefits based on a formula determined by each employer and its EPF.

Corporations that have an EPF—and their employees—need not contribute to Japanese Pension Insurance (JPI), which would be required if the substitutional portion of the benefit were not funded through the EPF. As a result, the corporate and substitutional benefits are paid to retired beneficiaries out of the EPF's assets. All of an EPF's assets are invested and managed as a single portfolio and are not separately segregated to the substitutional and corporate portions. The percentage of the substitutional portion relative to the total EPF is not predetermined and varies by employer.

In June 2001, the JWPIL was amended to allow employers and their EPFs to separate the substitutional portions of their pension plans and transfer the obligations and related assets to the government. The separation process will be completed in four phases. After completion of that process, employers and their EPFs will be released from making further payments of the substitutional portion to beneficiaries. In addition, employers and their employees will be required to contribute periodically to the JPI; the Japanese government will be responsible for making all benefit payments earned under JWPIL. The remaining part of the EPF will be a corporate defined benefit plan (CDBP), which employers will be able to transfer to a defined contribution plan.

ACCOUNTING ISSUE

How should Japanese companies that report on U.S. securities exchanges and consequently account for EPFs as single-employer defined benefit plans using a single-plan approach account for (*a*) the separation of the substitutional portion of the benefit obligation of an EPF from the corporate portion and (*b*) the transfer of the substitutional portion and related assets to the Japanese government?

ACCOUNTING GUIDANCE

When the transfer of the substitutional portion of the pension benefit obligation and the related assets (phase 4) to the Japanese government has been completed, employers should account for that process as the conclusion of a single settlement transaction consisting of a series of steps. The following guidance applies only to this specific situation.

The guidance should be applied as follows:

- A transaction should be accounted for as a settlement when it is complete, that is, when the total substitutional portion of the benefit obligation has been eliminated because a sufficient amount of assets to complete the separation process have been transferred to the Japanese government.
- In accordance with the guidance in ASC 715-30, immediately before the separation, the total projected benefit obligation should be remeasured at fair value, including the effects of changes in actuarial assumptions (such as expected future salary increases), if any, and actual experience since the previous measurement date. This remeasurement should include only benefits earned under the substitutional arrangement *before* the government accepts responsibility for all substitutional payments.
- A settlement of the substitutional portion of the obligation should be accounted for as follows:
    — Recognize as a gain or loss on settlement a proportionate amount of the ASC 715-30 net gain or loss included in accumulated other comprehensive income related to the total EPF as a gain or loss on settlement.
    — Determine the proportionate amount of the net gain or loss that should be recognized based on the proportion of the projected benefit

obligation settled to the total projected benefit obligation, but exclude previously accrued salary progression from that calculation.

— After separation, continue accounting for the EPF's remaining assets and obligation as well as for both prior-service costs included in accumulated other comprehensive income and gains and losses, if any, in accordance with the guidance in ASC 715-30 and ASC 715-20.

— Account for and disclose the difference between the settled obligation and the assets transferred to the government, which were determined based on the government's formula, as a subsidy from the government separately in accordance with generally accepted accounting principles.

— In accordance with this consensus, account for and disclose the derecognition of previously accrued salary progression at the time of settlement *separately* from the government's subsidy.

OBSERVATION: Under the guidance in ASC 715-30, employers are required to recognize in the financial statements the full amount of obligations related to single-employer defined benefit pension plans, retiree health care, and other postretirement plans.

Minimum pension liability adjustments are eliminated under the Statement. Gains or losses, prior service costs or credits, and transition assets and obligations must be recognized in accumulated other comprehensive income if they have not yet been recognized as components of net periodic benefit cost.

ASC 715-30-55-81 through 55-86 Accounting for Early Retirement or Postemployment Programs with Specific Features (Such as Terms Specified in Altersteilzeit Early Retirement Arrangements)

BACKGROUND

The German government has established an early retirement program, referred to as the Altersteilzeit (ATZ) arrangement, under which employees that meet certain age and other requirements transition from full or part-time employment to retirement before their legal retirement age. The German government reimburses employers that participate in the program for bonuses paid to participating employees and for additional contributions paid into the German government's pension program under an ATZ arrangement for a maximum of six years. The program, which was developed in 1996, will expire in 2009.

Typical features of ATZ arrangements include the following:

- Type I: Participants work 50% of a normal full-time schedule during each year of the ATZ period and receive 50% of their salaries each year.
- Type II: Participants work full time for half of the ATZ period (the active period) and do not work for the other half of the ATZ period (the inactive period). They receive 50% of their salary each year of the ATZ period.
- For both Type I and Type II arrangements: The participants receive an annual bonus. Although the amount of the bonus may vary by employer,

it generally equals 10-15% of the employee's most recent regular pay before the ATZ period. Therefore, during the ATZ period, employees generally receive 60-65% of their regular pay before the ATZ period. Employers also make additional contributions for the participants into the German government's pension program.

ACCOUNTING ISSUES

- How should a termination/retirement benefit under a Type II ATZ arrangement be accounted for?
- How should a government subsidy under Type I and Type II ATZ arrangements be accounted for?

ACCOUNTING GUIDANCE

- For Type II ATZ arrangements, employers should account for the bonus feature and additional contributions into the German government's pension program as postemployment benefits under the guidance in ASC 712. Additional compensation should be recognized from the time an employee signs an ATZ contract until the end of the employee's active service period.
- Under Type I and Type II arrangements, employers should recognize the government's subsidy when they meet the necessary criteria and are entitled to receive it.

The FASB staff noted that employers should recognize the salary components of Type I and Type II ATZ arrangements, other than the bonus and additional contributions to the German government's pension arrangement, from the beginning of the ATZ period to the end of the active service period. Under Type II arrangements, the deferred portion of an employee's salary should be discounted if it is expected that the payment will be deferred for longer than a year. The EITF agreed with the FASB staff's view.

ASC 715-60: DEFINED BENEFIT PLANS—OTHER POST-RETIREMENT

ASC 715-60-05-8 through 05-11, 15-11 through 15-13, 35-133 through 35-148, 50-2B, 50-4, 50-6, 55-103; ASC 715-740-10-55 through 10-57, 10-166 through 10-167 Accounting and Disclosure Requirements Related to the Medicare Prescription Drug Improvement and Modernization Act of 2003

BACKGROUND

The Medicare Prescription Drug Improvement and Modernization Act (the Act) will provide Medicare participants with a prescription drug benefit under Medicare Part D. In addition, sponsors of retiree health care benefit plans providing prescription drug benefits that are at least "actuarially equivalent" to those provided under Medicare Part D will be entitled to receive a federal subsidy.

Under the guidance in ASC 715-60-35-91, plan sponsors are required to consider Medicare in measuring a plan's accumulated postretirement benefit obligation (APBO) and net periodic postretirement benefit cost.

New Features of Medicare under the Act

Two new features have been added to Medicare as a result of the Act: (1) plan sponsors will receive subsidies based on 28% of the annual prescription drug costs between $250 and $5,000 incurred by individual beneficiaries (subject to indexing and the Act's provisions regarding *allowable retiree costs*) and (2) retirees will have the option to decide whether to enroll in a prescription drug benefit under Medicare Part D.

The amount of a plan sponsor's subsidy will depend on how many of the plan's beneficiaries that are eligible for Medicare decide *not* to enroll in Medicare Part D, which is voluntary. The Secretary of Health and Human Services has not yet issued detailed regulations on how to implement the Act, including how to determine whether a plan's prescription drug benefit is "actuarially equivalent" to the benefit under Medicare Part D, the evidence needed to demonstrate actuarial equivalency, documentation requirements for the subsidy, and the manner in which the subsidy will be paid by the appropriate agency.

The per capita claims cost of a plan that has been providing a prescription drug benefit to retirees will depend on (*a*) the extent that current and future retirees will voluntarily enroll in Medicare Part D and pay a monthly premium, which initially will be $35, and (*b*) how the Act will affect the trend in health care costs and consumers' behavior.

Other Effects of the Act

Under the Act, plan sponsors will be able to exclude the federal subsidy from their taxable income for federal income tax purposes, which means that the temporary difference related to the APBO that results in a deferred tax asset under ASC 740 (FAS-109, Accounting for Income Taxes) will be affected, depending on how the subsidy is accounted for.

In addition, the Act provides for a two-year transition period during which plan sponsors may amend existing plans or establish new ones in response to the legislation in order to maximize the financial benefit to the entity or improve employee relations. Changes in the benefit formula as a result of plan amendments will affect the APBO.

ACCOUNTING GUIDANCE

Question 1: How should the effect of the subsidy on the following matters be accounted for?

1. Benefits attributable to past service
2. Current measures of net periodic postretirement benefit cost
3. Changes in estimates
4. Plan amendments
5. Income tax accounting

Answer: The subsidy's effect should be accounted for as follows:

- On initial application of the guidance in this FSP, the effect of the subsidy on the APBO should be accounted for as an actuarial experience gain in accordance with the guidance in ASC 715-60-35-23, 35-25, 35-29 through 35-30.
- The subsidy should be included in measuring the cost of benefits attributable to current service because it affects the sponsor's share of the plan's

costs. By including the subsidy in the calculation of net periodic postretirement benefit cost, the sponsor's service cost—which is defined in ASC 715-60-35-10—is reduced.

- A change in estimate is an actuarial experience gain in accordance with the guidance in ASC 715-60-35-23 through 35-25, if the amount of the estimated expected subsidy changes because of changes in regulations or legislation, changes in the underlying estimates of postretirement prescription drug costs, or other changes that are *not* plan amendments.

- Sponsors that amend a plan to make it actuarially equivalent to Medicare Part D should combine the direct effect on the APBO and the effect on the APBO from the subsidy that the sponsor expects to receive. If actuarial equivalency under the Act of a plan's prescription drug benefits is disqualified as the result of a subsequent plan amendment that *reduces* the coverage, there is *no* effect on an actuarial experience gain, if any, that was previously recognized. Nevertheless, the combined net effect on the APBO of the plan's loss of (i) actuarial equivalency under the Act as a result of the plan amendment reducing coverage and (ii) the subsidy's elimination should be accounted for as a prior service cost or credit as of the date on which the amendment is adopted.

- Because the subsidy is exempt from federal taxation, it has *no* effect on temporary differences, if any, under the guidance in ASC 740 that are related to the plan.

Question 2: What disclosures are required?

Answer: Sponsors that have not yet determined whether the prescription drug benefits are actuarially equivalent to Medicare Part D under the Act should disclose the following information in their interim or annual financial statements:

- The Act's existence

- The fact that a subsidy has not been considered in amounts presented for the APBO or net periodic postretirement benefit cost because it has not been determined whether the benefits under the plan are actuarially equivalent to Medicare Part D under the Act

The following disclosures should be made in the financial statements of the first interim or annual period in which the effects of the subsidy are included in measuring the APBO and in the first period in which the effects of the subsidy are included in measuring net periodic postretirement benefit cost:

- The amount by which the APBO is reduced for the subsidy related to benefits attributed to past service

- The subsidy's effect on the measurement of net periodic postretirement benefit cost in the current period, including the(i) amortization of the actual experience gain, if any, as a component of the net amortization under the guidance in ASC 715-60-35-29 through 35-30 (ii) reduction in current period service cost as a result of the subsidy; and (iii) consequent reduction in interest cost on the APBO due to the subsidy

- Other disclosures under the guidance in ASC 715-20-50-1, which requires an explanation of significant changes, if any, in a plan's benefit obligation or assets that would *not* be obvious in the Statement's other required disclosures

Question 3: After this guidance has been adopted, how should an employer determine a plan's actuarial equivalence without a plan amendment?

Answer: A sponsor that was unable to determine whether its plan is actuarially equivalent to Medicare Part D when this guidance was adopted may receive new information about the Act, such as regulations clarifying actuarial equivalency or interpretive information. If after reconsideration of actuarial equivalency of the plan's benefits the sponsor concludes that there is actuarial equivalence, that conclusion may be a significant event under the guidance in ASC 715-60-35-126. If the effects of the subsidy on the plan are significant, the plan's assets and obligations should be measured as of the date that actuarial equivalency was determined. The subsidy's effect on the APBO should be presented as an actuarial gain in accordance with the guidance in paragraph (a) of the answer to Question 1 of this FSP. The amount of net periodic postretirement benefit cost in later periods should include the effects of those measurements. However, prior financial statements should *not* be retroactively adjusted. A cumulative effect for prior periods also should *not* be recognized in income.

ASC 715-60-05-14 through 05-15, 15-20 through 15-21, 35-177 through 35-179, 55-176 through 55-177, 55-179 Accounting for Deferred Compensation and Postretirement Benefit Aspects of Endorsement Split-Dollar Life Insurance Arrangements

BACKGROUND

A company may purchase life insurance to protect against a loss of "key" employees, to fund deferred compensation and postretirement benefit obligations, and to provide investment return. Split-dollar life insurance, the structure of which may be complex and varied, is one type of life insurance that may be purchased by a company. The most common types of such arrangements are *endorsement split-dollar* life insurance (owned and controlled by the company) and *collateral assignment split-dollar* life insurance (owned and controlled by the employee).

There is diversity in practice in accounting for the deferred compensation and postretirement features of *endorsement* split-life insurance policies, the terms of which may be as follows:

- The employer pays a single premium at the inception of a policy to insure an employee's life.

- The insurer may charge or credit the policyholder based on negative or positive experience for a specific risk (e.g., mortality risk). The insurer usually realizes an additional premium by adjusting the policy's cash surrender value.

- The employer and an employee enter into a separate agreement whereby the policy's benefits are split between the employer and the employee with the employer endorsing a portion of the death benefits to the employee.
- The employer owns and controls the policy and may terminate the arrangement at will.
- Upon the death of an employee, the employee's beneficiary receives the portion of the death benefits designated to the employee and the employer keeps the remainder.
- An employee's beneficiary may receive the benefit directly from the insurance company or from the employer.

An employee's portion of the death benefits is commonly based on (*a*) the amount by which the employee's portion of the death benefits exceeds the gross premiums, (*b*) the amount by which the employee's portion of the death benefits exceeds the gross premiums plus an additional fixed or variable investment return on those premiums, (*c*) the face amount of the death benefit under the policy less the employee's portion of the policy's cash surrender value, or (*d*) an amount equal to a multiple of the employee's base salary at retirement or death (e.g., twice the employee's base salary).

SCOPE

This Issue applies only to the recognition of a liability and the related compensation costs for endorsement split-life insurance arrangements that are owned and controlled by an employer. It does *not* apply to split-dollar life insurance arrangements that provide a specific benefit to an employee only during the period that the employee is the employer's active employee. The question is how employers should account for the aspects of those policies that are related to deferred compensation, postretirement, or postemployment benefits.

ACCOUNTING ISSUE

When an employer and an employee enter into a split-dollar life insurance arrangement, should the postretirement benefit associated with the arrangement be accounted for in accordance with the guidance in ASC 715-60 or that in ASC 710?

ACCOUNTING GUIDANCE

An employer should recognize a liability for future benefits associated with an *endorsement* split-dollar life insurance arrangement that is based on a substantive agreement with an employee in accordance with the guidance in ASC 715-60 if a substantive postretirement benefit plan exists. If an arrangement is in substance an individual deferred compensation contract with an employee, the guidance in ASC 710 should be followed based on the substantive arrangement with an employee. The purchase of a standard endorsement split-dollar life insurance policy does *not* settle an employer's liability for a benefit obligation under the provisions of ASC 715 or ASC 710-10-25-9 through 25-11. For example, an employer that agrees to maintain a life insurance policy during an employee's retirement should accrue the cost of the insurance policy under the guidance in ASC 715-60 or ASC 710-10-25-9 through 25-11. Likewise, an employer that has agreed to provide an employee with a death benefit should accrue a liability in accordance with the guidance in ASC 715-60 or ASC 710-10-25-9 through 25-11 over the employee's service period for the actuarial present value of the future death benefit as of the employee's expected retirement date.

It was noted that the substance of an arrangement should be determined based on the available evidence, such as an arrangement's explicit written terms, communications from the employer to an employee, and the conclusion as to who is the primary obligor for the postretirement benefit, the employer or the insurance company. For example, an employer's promise to pay a postretirement death benefit even if the insurance company defaults on a payment indicates that the employer has promised to provide a postretirement benefit and is the primary obligor. In addition, if the amount of a death benefit is *not* explicitly related to the insurance policy, the amount of the postretirement benefit should be the amount of the death benefit promised to the employee. In contrast, if under the terms of an arrangement, an employer has *no* obligation to pay a death benefit if the insurance company defaults on a payment, it is an indication that the employer has promised to maintain a life insurance policy during the employee's retirement. Employers should follow the guidance in ASC 715-60 and ASC 710-10-25-9 through 25-11, as applicable, to determine how to measure and attribute their cost or obligation under an arrangement.

ASC 715-60-05-15, 35-180 through 35-185, 55-178, 55-180 through 55-181
Accounting for Deferred Compensation and Postretirement Benefit Aspects of Collateral Assignment Split-Dollar Life Insurance Arrangements

BACKGROUND

A company may purchase life insurance to protect against a loss of "key" employees, to fund deferred compensation and postretirement benefit obligations, or to provide an investment return. Two types of split-dollar life insurance arrangements exist: *endorsement* split-dollar life insurance, which is owned and controlled by the company, and *collateral assignment* split-dollar life insurance, which is owned and controlled by the employee.

Under existing guidance, an employer is required to recognize a liability for future benefits associated with an *endorsement* split-dollar life insurance arrangement that is based on a substantive agreement with the employee in accordance with the guidance in ASC 715-60 if a substantive postretirement benefit plan exists. If an arrangement is, in substance, an individual deferred compensation contract with an employee, the guidance in ASC 710 should be followed based on a substantive arrangement with an employee.

The following guidance addresses how an employer should account for *collateral assignment* split-dollar life insurance arrangements. Under this type of arrangement, although an employee owns and controls the policy, the employer usually pays all of the premiums and in turn, the employee irrevocably assigns all or a portion of the death benefits to the employer as collateral for the employer's payment of the premiums, which are considered to be a loan. Usually, the employer is entitled to receive a portion of the death benefits equal to the amount of premiums paid by the employer or that amount plus an additional fixed return on the premiums. An employee that retires may have the option or be required to transfer the policy to the employer to satisfy the outstanding loan. Under the Sarbanes Oxley Act of 2002, all public and private entities are required to account for such arrangements as employer loans in accordance with the provisions of ASC 835-30.

Interest on Receivables and Payables. The employer must recognize a receivable from the employee at a discounted amount for the premiums paid.

ACCOUNTING ISSUES

- Based on a substantive agreement with an employee, should an employer recognize a liability for a postretirement benefit related to a *collateral assignment* split-dollar life insurance arrangement in accordance with the guidance in ASC 715 (FAS-106), if, in substance, a postretirement benefit exists, or in accordance with the guidance in APB-12, if an arrangement is, in substance, an individual deferred compensation contract?
- How should an employer recognize and measure the asset in a *collateral assignment* split-dollar life insurance arrangement?

ACCOUNTING GUIDANCE

1. If a substantive postretirement benefit plan exists, an employer should recognize a liability for a postretirement benefit associated with a *collateral assignment* split-dollar life insurance arrangement in accordance with the guidance in ASC 715-60. The guidance in ASC 710-10-25-9 through 25-11 should be followed for an arrangement that is, in substance, an individual deferred compensation contract with an employee and if, based on that contract, the employer has agreed to maintain a life insurance policy during the employee's retirement or to provide the employee with a death benefit. If in the past an employer has had a stated or implied commitment to provide an employee with a loan to pay premiums on an insurance policy during an employee's retirement or is currently promising to provide loans in the future, it may be presumed that the employer has in effect agreed to maintain the life insurance policy, unless there is opposing evidence. An employer that has committed to maintain a life insurance policy or to provide a death benefit after an employee's retirement should account for those obligations as follows:

    - Accrue the estimated cost of maintaining the life insurance policy after an employee's retirement in accordance with the guidance in ASC 715-60, or
    - Accrue a liability for the actuarial present value of a future death benefit as of an employee's expected retirement date in accordance with the guidance in ASC 710-10-25-9 through 25-11.

    To determine whether an arrangement is substantive, all relevant information should be considered, such as the explicit written terms of an

ASC 715—Compensation—Retirement Benefits   40,149

arrangement, an employer's communications to the employee, an employer's past administrative procedures for the same or similar arrangements, and whether an employer has the primary obligation for an employee's postretirement benefit. For example, if under the terms of an arrangement, an employer has *no* stated or implied obligation to provide loans to an employee to pay for premiums on a life insurance policy, the employer may have *no* postretirement obligation. In contrast, if under a collateral assignment arrangement with an employee, an employer has a stated or implied obligation to provide an employee with loans to cover the insurance company's gains or losses, the employer may have a postretirement obligation. The guidance in ASC 715-60 or ASC 710-10-25-9 through 25-11, as applicable, should be consulted to determine how to measure and assign the cost of the obligation under an arrangement.

Collateral assignment split-dollar insurance arrangements should be reevaluated in periods after their inception based on the guidance in ASC 715-60 to determine whether the substance of an arrangement has changed as a result of a change in facts and circumstances, such as an amendment to an arrangement or a change from an employer's past practice, and may require that a liability be recognized or that a previously recognized liability for a postretirement obligation be adjusted.

2. An employer should recognize and measure an asset based on the nature and substance of a collateral assignment split-dollar life insurance arrangement. To determine the nature and substance of an arrangement, an employer should evaluate (*a*) future cash flows to which the employer is entitled, if any, and (*b*) an employee's obligation and ability to repay the employer. For example, at the balance sheet date, an employer's asset would be limited to the cash surrender value of an insurance policy, if the amount the employer could recover from an employee or retiree is limited to the amount of the insurance policy's cash surrender value, even if the employer's loan to the employee or retiree exceeds that amount. In contrast, an employer should recognize the value of a loan, including accrued interest, if applicable, based on the guidance in ASC 835-30, if under the arrangement, an employee or retiree is required to repay the employer regardless of the collateral assigned and the employer (*a*) has determined that the employee's or retiree's loan is collectible and (*b*) intends to try to recover the amount by which the loan exceeds the insurance policy's cash surrender value. To determine the nature and substance of a collateral assignment split-dollar life insurance arrangement, an employer should consider all the available information.

ASC 715-20-55-1 through 55-2; ASC 715-60-15-5 through 15-6, 25-4, 35-21, 35-33, 35-64 through 35-65, 35-96, 35-111 35-113, 35-168, 55-1 through 55-25, 55-27 through 55-30, 55-32 55-34, 55-106 through 55-111, 55-140, 55-142 through 55-175; ASC 715-70-55-2 through 55-3; ASC 715-80-55-3 through 55-5; ASC 710-10-55-2,

40,150 ASC 715—Compensation—Retirement Benefits

55-5 through 55-6, 60-3 Guide to Implementation of ASC 715-60 on Employers' Accounting for Postretirement Benefits Other Than Pensions

ACCOUNTING GUIDANCE

Scope

Question F1: Does this Statement apply to long-term disability benefits paid to former employees on disability retirement under an employer's postretirement benefit plan?

Answer: Yes, as long as the benefits provided are postretirement benefits. Disability benefits paid to former or inactive employees who are not on disability retirement should be accounted for in accordance with guidance in ASC 712. Similarly, if disability income benefits are paid pursuant to a pension plan, the applicable accounting guidance is found in ASC 715-30.

Question F2: If some employees, upon their retirement, voluntarily elect under the provisions of the Consolidated Omnibus Budget Reconciliation Act of 1985 (COBRA), as amended, to continue their health care coverage provided through the active employee health care plan and the cost to the employer of their continuing coverage exceeds the retirees' contributions, should the employer account for that cost under the guidance in ASC 715-60?

Answer: No. The right to continue health care coverage under COBRA is not based on employee retirement. This right generally is available to any terminated employee. Therefore, employers should follow the guidance in ASC 712 when the cost of continuing health care coverage under COBRA exceeds the former employees' contributions.

Question F3: A collectively bargained defined benefit postretirement health care plan of a single employer may stipulate that benefits will be provided for the duration of the collective-bargaining agreement, or the plan may imply or explicitly state that benefits are subject to renegotiation upon the expiration of the current collective-bargaining agreement. Past negotiations have resulted in the continuation of the plan, although the plan has been amended at various times. Should the accumulated postretirement benefit obligation (APBO) be measured based only on benefits expected to be paid during the period in which the current agreement will be in force?

Answer: No. The APBO should be measured assuming that the defined benefit postretirement health care plan will continue after the expiration of the existing collective-bargaining agreement. Unless there is evidence to the contrary, a postretirement benefit plan that currently exists is expected to continue in the future.

Contracts Involving Deferred Compensation

Question F4: How should an employer account for a deferred compensation contract that does not provide a vested benefit for the employee's prior service at the date the contract is entered into? For example, an employee must render 30 years of service to receive benefits under a deferred compensation contract and has rendered 16 years of service at the date of entering into the contract. Credit is granted for that prior service in determining eligibility for the benefit to be provided. Should the total obligation be accrued over the remaining 14 years of service, or should the employer immediately recognize the portion related to the 16 years of service already rendered?

Answer: The total obligation under the deferred compensation contract should be accrued over the remaining 14 years of service. An obligation related to the prior service would be accrued only if the employee was entitled to part of the benefit without regard to future service (i.e., if the credit for prior service results in a vested benefit).

Question F5: An employee becomes fully eligible for benefits under a deferred compensation contract five years after entering into the contract. The contract states, however, that if the employee dies or becomes disabled, benefits will be payable immediately. The contract is not one of a group of contracts that possess the characteristics of a pension plan. What is the attribution period?

Answer: If the employee is expected to provide service over the five-year period, the obligation should be accrued over this time period. If the employee dies or becomes disabled before the five-year period expires, any remaining unrecognized cost would be recognized in the period in which the death or disability occurred. No accrual is required if the employee is not expected to work for the employer for the next five years.

Substantive Plan

Question F6: Can future amendments to a written postretirement health care plan that change the amount of a defined dollar cap be anticipated as part of the substantive plan?

Answer: Yes, if the employer's past practices indicate that plan amendments are a common occurrence. For example, the employer may have a history of regularly increasing (or decreasing) the defined dollar cap under a postretirement health care plan.

Question F7: Is a postretirement health care plan with a defined dollar cap considered to be a plan that provides benefits defined in terms of monetary amounts as discussed in ASC 715-60-35-56?

Answer: No. In this scenario, the benefit is reimbursement of specified eligible medical claims. The fact that the employer's reimbursement of these claims is limited to a specific dollar amount (i.e., the dollar cap) does not indicate that the benefits are defined in monetary amounts.

Measurement

Question F8: Should the assumed discount rates used to measure an employer's postretirement benefit obligation be the same rates used to measure its pension obligation under the guidance in ASC 715-30?

Answer: Not necessarily. As under the guidance in ASC 715-30, the discount rate chosen to measure the liability for postretirement benefit obligations should reflect the interest rate on high-quality debt instruments of a duration comparable to that of the benefit obligation. However, a different discount rate may be appropriate, because the timing of expected payments under the postretirement benefit plan may differ from the expected timing of pension payments.

Question F9: An employer sponsors a health care plan that provides benefits to both active employees and retirees under age 65. The plan requires active employees and retirees to contribute to the plan. Can the contributions of active employees ever be used to reduce the employer's cost of providing benefits to retirees?

Answer: Yes, but only if contributions by active employees exceed the cost of providing health care benefits for this group over its working life and the employer has no obligation to refund the excess contributions. The cost of providing health care coverage for active employees should be measured on the assumption they are the only group covered by the plan (i.e., retirees would be excluded in this computation).

Question F10: An employer has a contributory health care plan covering active employees and retirees under which retirees pay 100% of the average cost of benefits determined based on the combined experience of active employees and retirees. The employer pays all of the remaining cost. The active employees do not contribute to the plan. Under this arrangement, does the employer have an obligation under this Statement?

Answer: Yes, if the actual cost of providing health care benefits to retirees exceeds their contributions. If this is the case, the employer is subsidizing the retirees' health care benefits. The employer has an obligation for the difference between the expected cost of the retirees' benefits and the expected contribution amounts.

Question F11: Are there any circumstances under which an employer may measure its postretirement health care benefit obligation by projecting the cost of premiums for purchased health care insurance?

Answer: Yes, if the postretirement benefit plan provides that the benefit to be received by retirees is a payment of their future health care insurance premiums.

Question F12: If an employer has measured its postretirement health care benefit obligation by projecting the cost of premiums for purchased health care insurance, does that reduce or eliminate the applicability of any provisions of this Statement, for example, the calculation and disclosure of service and interest cost?

Answer: No. All of the provisions in this Statement, including the disclosure of service and interest cost, still apply.

Question F13: Should employers assume a trend of decreasing (or increasing) Medicare reimbursement rates if Medicare has consistently reduced (or increased) the portion of benefits it will cover? For example, certain health care costs may have increased by 15% last year but Medicare may have covered only a smaller increase, which increased the employer's or retirees' share of the cost of benefits. When determining its postretirement benefit obligation, should an employer assume that such a reduction in Medicare coverage would continue?

Answer: Generally not. Changes in Medicare coverage should be projected only if they result from currently enacted legislation or regulations. Future changes in

Medicare legislation or regulations should not be anticipated even if past experience indicates that such changes are likely.

Attribution

Question F14: An employer modifies the eligibility requirements under its postretirement benefit plan by changing the plan's credited service period from "25 years of service after age 40" to "15 years of service after both (*a*) reaching age 50 and (*b*) rendering 10 years of service." What is the beginning of the attribution period?

Answer: The credited service period for this pension plan is undefined. Therefore, the attribution period begins on the date of hire. The net effect of the above change is to lengthen the attribution period for employees under age 40.

Question F15: An employer provides retiree health care and life insurance benefits under one plan. Employees are eligible for health care and death benefits upon attaining age 55 and having rendered 20 years of service; however, the life insurance benefits are based on final pay. Does basing the life insurance benefits on final pay extend the full eligibility date to a plan participant's expected retirement date? For example, if an employee is expected to fulfill the 20-year service requirement before age 55 and is expected to retire at age 62 with salary increases in all years of service, is the employee's full eligibility date the date he or she reaches age 62?

Answer: Yes, assuming the additional life insurance benefits earned between age 55 and the employee's expected retirement date are not trivial in relation to the total benefit to be received. This postretirement benefit plan has an indefinite credited service period. Therefore, the attribution period begins on the date of hire and ends on the full eligibility date. The full eligibility date is the date on which an employee has earned all of the benefits that he or she will receive under the postretirement benefit plan. In this case, the full amount of life insurance benefits to be received will not be known until the employee retires.

Question F16: Would the answer to the question in paragraph F15 be different if the benefits were provided and accounted for under two separate plans, one providing life insurance benefits and the other providing health care benefits?

Answer: Yes. If health care and life insurance benefits are provided under separate plans, the full eligibility date would be determined separately for each plan.

Question F17: If the terms of the plan in the question in paragraph F15 specified which 20-year service period constituted the credited service period—for example, the first 20 years after date of hire, or the first 20 years of service after age 35—would basing life insurance benefits on final pay still extend the full eligibility date to the expected date of retirement?

Answer: Yes, assuming the additional life insurance benefits earned between age 55 and the employee's expected retirement date are not trivial in relation to the total benefit to be received.

Question F18: Under what conditions would a plan be considered a frontloaded plan?

Answer: A plan is considered frontloaded if all, or a disproportionate portion of, expected benefits to be received under the plan are attributed to employees' early years of service. If a plan is frontloaded, the expected postretirement benefit obligation (EPBO) should not be attributed ratably to each year of credited service in the credited service period but should be attributed in accordance with the plan benefit formula. The employee group as a whole is evaluated in determining whether the plan is frontloaded.

Illustration of a Frontloaded Plan

TWR, Inc., offers a postretirement benefit plan that provides both health care and life insurance benefits. Employees are eligible for health care and death benefits upon attaining age 55 and after having completed 20 years of service. Life insurance benefits are based on final pay, and employees are expected to receive annual pay raises between age 55 and their expected retirement age, 62. An employee named Jane Doe is hired at age 20 at a starting salary of $30,000. TWR assumes annual pay increases of 4%, a life expectancy of 75 years, and a discount rate of 7%.

Assume that the EPBO for Jane Doe at age 40 is $43,091 ($28,500 for health care benefits and $14,591 for life insurance benefits). A ratable allocation of the EPBO over her expected working life, 42 years, would result in an accumulated postretirement benefit obligation (APBO) of $20,519 at the end of year 20 ($13,571 for health care benefits and $6,948 for life insurance benefits; both of these amounts are 20/42 of the applicable EPBO). Based on the respective benefit formulas, assume that the APBO at the end of 20 years is $28,500 for health care benefits and $6,157 for life insurance benefits. Because the APBO based on the benefit formulas of $34,657 is a significantly greater amount than a ratable allocation of the EPBO of $20,519, the postretirement plan is considered to be frontloaded. For frontloaded benefit plans, benefits should be attributed using the respective benefit formulas. Therefore, TWR would report an APBO of $34,657 for Jane Doe at the end of year 20.

Question F19: An employer has a retiree health care plan that bases benefits on length of service; to be eligible for any benefits under it, employees must render a minimum of ten years of service after they reach age 45. However, upon attaining age 45, employees receive credit for 3% of the maximum benefit for each year of service before age 45. For example, at age 45 an employee hired at age 25 receives credit for 60% (3% × 20 years) of the plan's postretirement health care benefits. When does the credited service period begin?

Answer: The credited service period begins at the date of hire. The total benefits to be received are a function of the total years of service, including service before age 45.

Question F20: An employer requires that, in order to be eligible to participate in its retiree health care plan, an employee must participate in its contributory active health care plan. An employee can join the active plan at any time before retirement but must have worked 10 years and attained age 55 while in service to be eligible for benefits under the retiree plan. When does the attribution period begin?

Answer: At the date of hire if the employee is expected to participate in the active health care plan. This is because the plan does not specify which ten years of service must be worked in order to qualify for benefits under the plan. If an employee is not expected to participate in the active health care plan, the employee would not be considered a plan participant for purposes of the postretirement benefit plan.

Question F21: Should an employer's annual accrual for the service cost component of net periodic postretirement benefit cost relate to only those employees who are in their credited service periods?

Answer: In most cases, yes. However, in some cases a plan will establish a nominal service period in relation to the employee's expected total years of service. For example, an employee is hired at age 25 and is expected to work until age 62. The plan may specify that the credited service period begins at age 55 and runs until retirement. In this case, the credited service period according to the plan would be nominal in relation to the total expected years of service. In such instances, the attribution period, and the recognition of service cost, would begin at the date of hire.

Question F22: In determining the attribution period, what is considered a nominal credited service period?

Answer: Judgment is required in determining what qualifies as a nominal credited service period. Generally the service period would be considered nominal if it is very short in relation to the total expected years of employee service before full eligibility for benefits.

Curtailments and Negative Plan Amendments

Question F23: An employer's previous accounting for postretirement benefits has considered the written plan to be the substantive plan. On July 1, 20X4, its Board of Directors approves a negative plan amendment (i.e., an amendment that reduces benefits attributable to prior service) that will be effective on January 1, 20X6. The employer intends to announce the negative plan amendment to plan participants on July 1, 20X5. When should the effects of the negative plan amendment be considered for accounting purposes?

Answer: July 1, 20X5, the date on which the negative plan amendment is communicated to employees. It would have been appropriate to account for the effects of the negative plan amendment on July 1, 20X4, the date the amendment was approved by the Board, if the amendment had been communicated to employees at that time or within a reasonable period of time thereafter. A reasonable period of time would be the time it would normally take to prepare information about the amendment and to distribute it to employees and retirees. A one-year period is excessive for this purpose.

Question F24: Is it important to distinguish between a reduction in the accumulated postretirement benefit obligation (APBO) caused by a negative plan amendment and a reduction caused by a curtailment?

Answer: Yes. A reduction in the APBO caused by a curtailment is potentially recognizable as a current component of income. Conversely, a reduction in the

APBO caused by a negative plan amendment that exceeds any prior service cost or transition obligation included in accumulated other comprehensive income is *not* immediately recognized as a reduction of current postretirement benefit costs.

Question F25: What is the difference between a negative plan amendment and a curtailment that reduces the APBO?

Answer: A negative plan amendment is a change in the terms of the plan that reduces or eliminates benefits for employee services already rendered. A curtailment reduces the APBO by reducing the number of employees covered under the plan and/or by eliminating the benefits attributable to future service for some or all plan participants.

Illustration of a Negative Plan Amendment and a Curtailment That Reduces the APBO

Company A sponsors a postretirement health care plan that previously was noncontributory. A plan amendment requiring current and future retirees to contribute $200 per month toward the cost of benefits provided would be a negative plan amendment because this change reduces the APBO for employee service already rendered.

Company B sponsors a postretirement life insurance plan. Life insurance benefits previously were defined based on final pay. Company B changes this plan on December 31, 20X4, to fix the life insurance benefits payable based on salaries in effect on that date. This change qualifies as a curtailment because the accrual of additional death benefits based on future employee service has been eliminated.

Question F26: Company B sponsors a postretirement life insurance plan. Life insurance benefits previously were defined based on final pay. Company B changes this plan on December 31, 20X4, to fix the life insurance benefits payable based on salaries in effect on that date. Before this change, the APBO at December 31, 20X4, included an amount—$400,000—based on projected future employee pay levels. Thus, the APBO at December 31, 20X4, decreases by $400,000 as a result of the plan amendment because increases in employees' future pay levels will no longer increase their death benefits under the plan. Why is the $400,000 a "potentially" currently recognizable curtailment gain?

Answer: Whether any or all of the $400,000 curtailment gain should be recognized currently as a component of net periodic postretirement benefit cost depends on the existence and amount of a net loss included in accumulated other comprehensive income for prior service cost, or a transition obligation included in accumulated other comprehensive income that must be offset before a curtailment gain can be recognized.

Question 27: Should the accounting for a curtailment always consider any prior service cost included in accumulated other comprehensive income or a transition obligation included in accumulated other comprehensive income?

Answer: Yes. The theoretical reason for not immediately recognizing prior service cost as a current component of postretirement benefit cost is that amendments of the postretirement benefit plan will result in a positive future economic benefit (e.g., a more motivated and committed workforce). A curtailment raises doubt about the existence of these future economic benefits. Therefore, this Statement requires recognition in net periodic postretirement benefit cost of any prior service cost included in accumulated other comprehensive income. In the case of a curtailment, any transition obligation remaining in accumulated other comprehensive income is considered to be a prior service cost.

Question F28: Does a curtailment result only from events that occur outside a postretirement benefit plan?

Answer: No. Although many curtailments result from events that occur outside the postretirement benefit plan—for example, (*a*) closing a plant, (*b*) selling a division or subsidiary, or (*c*) laying off a number of employees—a curtailment can also result from events that occur inside—for example, from a negative plan amendment that has the effect of eliminating the accrual of some or all of the future benefits for a significant number of plan participants.

Question F29: Does a gain result if, at the time of a curtailment, there exists negative prior service cost included in accumulated other comprehensive income due to a previous plan amendment that reduced benefits under the plan?

Answer: Yes. In accounting for a curtailment, a (negative) prior service cost included in accumulated other comprehensive income that results from a reduction in benefits (a negative plan amendment) is treated the same as a prior service cost that results from an increase in benefits. Therefore, any *negative* prior service cost included in accumulated other comprehensive income associated with future years of service that are affected by the curtailment is a gain. To the extent that this gain is not offset by any other curtailment losses, it is recognized currently as a component of income.

Question F30: What are examples of the accounting for a negative plan amendment that results in a curtailment?

Answer: The first illustration that follows is an example of a negative plan amendment that results in a curtailment gain. The second illustration is an example of a negative plan amendment that results in a curtailment loss.

Illustration of Negative Plan Amendment—Curtailment Gain

X, Inc., sponsors a defined benefit postretirement benefit plan. The only benefit provided under the plan is a life insurance benefit. The amount of life insurance provided under the plan is based on final pay levels. On December 31, 20X8, X, Inc., eliminates this benefit for employees who are not age 45 or older. This group constitutes a significant portion of the workforce of X, Inc. This change in the postretirement benefit plan results in two separate reductions in the APBO. First, benefits earned by employees under age 45, based on prior pay levels, are eliminated (resulting in a $300,000 reduction in the APBO). Second, the APBO had been calculated based on assumptions about the future of those employees' pay levels. Because employees under age 45 will no longer be plan participants, the future pay levels of those employees, which were considered in calculating the APBO, are no longer relevant (resulting in a $500,000 reduction in the APBO). This change in the postretirement benefit plan results in the elimination of future benefit accruals for that group of employees. As such, the $500,000 reduction in the APBO is potentially recognizable as a current curtailment gain. This curtailment would be accounted for in the following manner:

	Before Negative Plan Amendment	Negative Plan Amendment	December 31, 20X8 After Negative Plan Amendment	Curtailment	After Curtailment
(APBO)	$(1,500,000)	$ 300,000	$(1,200,000)	$ 500,000	$(700,000)
Recognized liability					
Prior service cost	100,000	(100,000)	-0-		
Transition obligation	140,000	(140,000)	-0-		
Net loss	200,000		200,000	(200,000)	
Negative prior service cost		(60,000)	(60,000)		(60,000)
	$ 440,000	$ (300,000)	$ 140,000	$ (200,000)	$ (60,000)

The journal entry to record the negative plan amendment is as follows:

Postretirement benefit liability	$300,000	
Other comprehensive income		$300,000

The journal entry to record a curtailment gain is as follows:

Postretirement benefit liability	$500,000	
Other comprehensive income		$200,000
Curtailment gain		$300,000

The following facts should be noted about the above accounting:

- Any decrease in the APBO as a result of a negative plan amendment is used first to reduce any existing prior service cost included in accumulated other comprehensive income and then to reduce any transition obligation included in accumulated other comprehensive income. Any amount that remains from the negative plan amendment is treated as "negative prior service cost." The negative prior service cost, $60,000, is recognized by amortization over future periods beginning January 1, 20X8. The negative prior service cost is amortized and recognized in net periodic postretirement benefit cost by assigning an equal amount to each remaining year of service up to the full eligibility date for each plan participant who was active at the date of the amendment but was not yet fully eligible for benefits at that date. Only participants who are over age 45 and who do not yet qualify for plan benefits qualify under this definition.

- The decrease in the APBO as a result of the curtailment is used first to reduce any net loss included in accumulated other comprehensive income on the curtailment date. Any remaining curtailment amount is recognized currently in income. The curtailment gain currently recognized is *not* a component of net periodic postretirement benefit cost and should be disclosed separately.

Illustration of Negative Plan Amendment—Curtailment Loss

Crown Color, Inc., sponsors an unfunded postretirement health care plan covering employees at three locations. On December 1, 20X8, Crown Color amends its benefit plan. Any employee of its Butte, Montana, plant who does not retire by December 31, 20X8, is not entitled to receive benefits under the plan. Employees of the Butte plant who retire by December 31, 20X8, will receive benefits under the terms of the postretirement health care plan. Crown Color's employees at its other two locations are not affected by this change in the postretirement benefit plan.

As a result of the above, Crown Color's accumulated postretirement benefit obligation is reduced by $200,000. This reflects an elimination of benefits attributed to years of service already rendered by employees who are not yet eligible to retire and to service rendered by eligible employees who choose not to retire (this reduction represents the results of the negative plan amendment). As a result of the early retirement of other (eligible) employees at the Butte plant, Crown Color's APBO increases by $100,000 (this represents a curtailment).

Before these changes, Crown Color's transition obligation included in accumulated other comprehensive income was $400,000. At the date of transition to this Statement, the remaining expected years of service of employees at the Butte location represented 35% of the total remaining expected years of service of all of Crown Color's employees. This will be accounted for in the following manner:

	Before Negative Plan Amendment	Negative Plan Amendment	December 31, 20X8 After Negative Plan Amendment	Curtailment	After Curtailment
(APBO) Recognized liability	$(475,000)	$200,000	$(275,000)	$(100,000)	$(375,000)
Amounts recognized in accumulated other comprehensive income:					
Prior service cost	50,000	(50,000)	-0-		
Transition obligation	400,000	(150,000)	250,000	(87,500)	162,500
Net gain	(75,000)				
	$375,000	$(200,000)	$175,000	$(12,500)	$162,500

The journal entry to record the negative plan amendment is:

Postretirement benefit liability	$200,000	
Other comprehensive income		$200,000

The journal entry to record the curtailment loss is:

Curtailment loss	$100,000	
Other comprehensive income	$12,500	
Postretirement benefit liability		$112,500

The following facts should be noted about the above accounting:

- The increase in the APBO as a result of the curtailment is used first to reduce any net gain recognized in accumulated other comprehensive income at the date of the curtailment.
- As a result of the plan amendment, 35% of the total expected remaining years of service, for all of Crown Color's locations, have been eliminated. Therefore, Crown Color should accelerate the recognition of 35% of the transition obligation remaining in accumulated other comprehensive income *after* the negative plan amendment is recorded (i.e., 35% of $250,000, the transition obligation remaining in accumulated other comprehensive income after the negative plan amendment becomes effective, is immediately recognized).
- The curtailment loss is not a component of net periodic postretirement benefit cost and therefore should be disclosed separately.

Question F31: An employer adopts an amendment to its postretirement health care plan that has the dual effect of expanding the plan's coverage and increasing the deductible. Should the increase in the deductible be measured and recognized separately from the benefit improvement?

Answer: No. It is not unusual for numerous plan changes to be made at the same time. Some of the changes may increase benefits; other changes may decrease benefits. All of the changes should be considered together to determine whether there has been a net increase in benefits (a positive plan amendment) or a net decrease in benefits (a negative plan amendment).

Gains and Losses

Question F32: In applying the provisions of ASC 715-60-35-29, 35-32 for the recognition of gains and losses as a component of net periodic postretirement benefit cost is it appropriate for an employer to elect annually a new method of amortization of gains and losses included in accumulated other comprehensive income?

Answer: No. The employer should choose a method of amortizing gains and losses and follow the chosen method consistently from period to period. Any change in the method of recognizing gains and losses would fall within the scope of ASC 250 and would need to meet the preferability requirement of ASC 250 for an accounting change. Although the employer has some discretion in choosing how to recognize gains and losses, the amortization of these items must equal or exceed the minimum amortization as set forth in ASC 715-60-35-29, 35-30.

Question F33: An employer sponsors a contributory postretirement health care plan that has an annual limitation on the dollar amount of the employer's share of the cost of benefits (a defined dollar-capped plan). The cap on the employer's share of annual costs and the retirees' contribution rates are increased 5% annually. Any amount by which incurred claims costs exceed the combined employer and retiree contributions is initially borne by the employer but is passed back to retirees in the subsequent year through supplemental retiree contributions for that year. In 20X8, incurred claims costs exceed the combined employer and retiree contributions, requiring a supplemental retiree contribution in 20X9. If the employer decides in 20X9 to absorb the excess that arose in 20X8 rather than pass it on to the retirees, when should the employer recognize as a component of net periodic postretirement benefit cost the loss due to that temporary deviation from the substantive plan?

Answer: The loss should be recognized as a component of net periodic postretirement benefit cost at the time the employer makes the decision to deviate from the substantive plan. In this case, the loss would be recognized in 20X9.

Question F34: If an employer previously projected that health care costs under a defined dollar capped plan would exceed the cap in 20X8, but actual claims in that year do not exceed the cap, should a gain be recognized immediately as a component of net periodic postretirement benefit cost in 20X8 in accordance the guidance in ASC 715-60-35-34 through 35-35?

Answer: No. The above situation represents a situation where the experience of the benefit plan is better than expected. This situation gives rise to an unrealized gain. Under the provisions of ASC 715-60-35-23 and 35-25, this type of gain should be recognized in accumulated other comprehensive income (see question in paragraph F59). A gain is recognized immediately as a component of net periodic postretirement benefit cost only when the employer deviates, on a temporary basis, from the provisions of the substantive plan and, as a result, there is a reduction in the APBO.

Question F35: What situation would result in a gain that would be recognized immediately as a component of net periodic postretirement benefit cost in accordance with ASC 715-60-35-34, 35-35?

Answer: A gain would be recognized immediately as a component of net periodic postretirement benefit cost if plan participants agreed to make a one-time voluntary contribution to the plan that exceeds the amount called for under the terms of the substantive plan, and future contributions by plan participants are expected to revert to the level specified by the substantive plan.

Plan Assets

Question F36: May an employer include in plan assets the assets of a "rabbi trust" (so named because the first grantor trust to receive a favorable ruling from the Internal Revenue Service was one formed for a rabbi)?

Answer: No. Plan assets held in a rabbi trust are *explicitly* available to an employer's creditors in the event of bankruptcy. Under the guidance in ASC 715-60, assets must be segregated and restricted (typically in a trust) to qualify as plan assets. The guidance in ASC 715-60-55-26; and ASC 710-10-60-2 states that a trust does not have to be "bankruptcy-proof" for the trust assets to qualify as plan assets under the guidance in ASC 715-60. However, the EITF believes that trust assets would *not* qualify as plan assets if such assets were *explicitly* available to the employer's general creditors in the event of bankruptcy.

Question F37: An insurance contract with a captive insurance company does not qualify as a plan asset. However, can an investment contract with a captive insurance company qualify as a plan asset if it meets the criteria in the ASC's *Glossary*?

Answer: Yes, assuming the investment contract with the captive insurance company is segregated and restricted for the payment of plan benefits (see ASC 944-20-15-16 through 15-19). An investment contract with a captive insurance company represents an obligation of the employer to pay cash to the benefit plan to be used for the purpose of providing postretirement benefits. Since an accrued liability of the employer to pay cash is not considered a plan asset, the investment contract should be considered a debt security of the employer. This debt security must be currently transferable to be included in plan assets.

Question F38: If an employer issues its own debt or equity securities directly to its postretirement benefit trust, may those securities be included in plan assets under the guidance in this Statement?

Answer: Yes, provided there are no restrictions on the transfer of these assets. The plan trustee must have the unilateral right to unconditionally sell, transfer, or otherwise dispose of the securities. Assets that are not currently transferable but that can be converted into transferable assets should not be considered plan assets. For example, nontransferable convertible preferred stock does not qualify as a plan asset even if it can be converted into transferable common stock.

Disclosures

Question F39: This question has been deleted.

Question F40: Should an employer's disclosure of the weighted average of the assumed discount rates for its postretirement benefit obligation be the same as its disclosure for its pension benefit obligation?

Answer: Not necessarily (see the answer to the question in paragraph F8 for additional discussion). Even if the assumed discount rates are the same, the weighted average of those rates may differ between the timing and pattern of benefits to be provided and may be different for a postretirement benefit plan than for a pension plan. A pension plan typically provides a fixed yearly benefit, which is not expected to change over time. However, a postretirement health care plan is likely to pay more of its benefits as retirees age (since health typically deteriorates with age). If the timing or pattern of postretirement benefits differs from the timing or pattern of pension benefits because of the expected cost of health care, the difference should be considered in the weighting of the assumed discount rates.

Multiple Plans—Employers

Question F41: An employer has two legally separate postretirement benefit plans. Both plans are unfunded (defined benefit) plans covering the same employees. One plan provides postretirement medical care and the other provides postretirement dental care. May the employer account for the two plans as one plan?

Answer: Yes. The guidance in ASC 715-60-35-130, allows an employer to combine unfunded (defined benefit) postretirement health care plans if either (*a*) different benefits are provided to the same group of employees or (*b*) the same benefits are provided to different groups of employees. However, if either of these plans were funded (i.e., if they held plan assets), they could not be combined but must be measured separately.

Question F42: When is it appropriate for the employer in the question in paragraph F4 to change from one-plan accounting to two-plan accounting—that is, to accounting for each plan separately?

Answer: The employer must move to two-plan accounting if the provisions of ASC 715-60-35-130 are no longer met. For example, two-plan accounting would become mandatory if either (*a*) different benefits were provided to different groups of employees or (*b*) one or both of the plans became funded (i.e., held plan assets). If the conditions of ASC 715-60-35-130 continue to be met, the employer would have to meet the preferability requirement of ASC 250 in order to support a voluntary change from one-plan accounting to two-plan accounting.

Multiemployer Plans

Question F43: An employer that has a single-employer postretirement benefit plan decides to provide health care benefits to its retirees by participating with several unrelated employers in a group postretirement health care benefit arrangement that does not result from collective bargaining. The arrangement is administered by an independent board of trustees and provides a uniform level of benefits to all retirees by utilizing group medical insurance contracts. Each participating employer is assessed an annual contribution for its share of insurance premiums, plus administrative costs. Employers may require their respective retirees to pay a portion of the annual assessment. Retirees whose former employer stops paying the annual assessment have the right to continue participation if they assume the cost of the annual premiums needed to maintain their existing benefits. Should the employer account for this arrangement as a multiemployer plan?

Answer: No. The key factor is that in a multiemployer plan the obligation to retirees does not depend on the former employer's continued participation. This feature is lacking from the above example.

Question F44: May a multiemployer plan be considered a substantially equivalent replacement plan (a successor plan) for an employer that terminates its single-employer defined benefit postretirement plan in such a way that acceleration of the recognition of prior service cost included in accumulated other comprehensive income as a component of net periodic postretirement benefit cost is not required?

Answer: No. Multiemployer plans and single-employer plans are sufficiently different from each other that either one is precluded from being a successor plan for the other. In a multiemployer plan, the employer promises to make a defined contribution. A single employer plan that gives rise to prior service cost is a defined benefit plan. The nature of the employer's promise—to make a defined contribution or to provide defined benefits—is fundamentally different between these two types of plans.

Question F45: This question has been deleted.

Plan Settlements

Question F46: An employer that immediately recognized its transition obligation in income upon adopting the guidance in this Statement subsequently amends its plan to eliminate its obligation for postretirement benefits and partially compensates affected participants by increasing their pension benefits. How should those events be accounted for?

Answer: In this case, the employer has terminated its postretirement benefit plan and has effectively settled its postretirement benefit obligation by increasing the pension benefits that it will provide. The cost to the employer in providing enhanced pension benefits is the cost of settling the postretirement benefit plan. This increase in pension benefits results in an increase in pension liability (or a decrease in pension assets). The obligation for the postretirement benefit plan should be eliminated. The difference between the reduction in the postretirement benefit liability and the increase in the pension liability benefits equals the gain on the plan termination that should be recognized in accordance with the guidance in ASC 715-60.

Illustration of Immediate Termination of Plan

GPP, Inc., sponsors a postretirement benefit plan and a pension plan. On December 31, 20X8, GPP terminates its postretirement benefit plan. As partial compensation to the employees who are affected, GPP amends its pension plan so that current and future retirees will receive a pension benefit equal to 2% of final salary for each year of employment (GPP's previous pension benefit formula was 2% of an employee's salary over the employee's last five years of service). GPP's postretirement benefit liability at December 30, 20X8, is $4,400,000; the expected benefit obligation on that date is $7,800,000. As a result of the change in the pension plan formula, GPP's pension liability increases by $750,000. GPP wants to determine the gain on the plan termination.

The gain on the plan termination is the difference between the reduction in the accumulated postretirement benefit obligation and the increase in the expected benefit obligation. Therefore, GPP would recognize a gain of $3,650,000 ($4,400,000 − $750,000).

Special Termination Benefits

Question F47: What is the intent of the guidance in ASC 715-60-25-6 on special termination benefits?

Answer: ASC 715-60-25-6 provides guidance for an employer's accounting for special termination benefits offered to employees in exchange for early retirement.

Question F48: How should an employer measure the postretirement benefit incentive that employees are to receive in exchange for their early termination of employment?

Answer: The termination incentive typically is measured as the difference between (1) the actuarial present value of the accumulated benefits for the terminating employees considering the enhanced benefits (it is assumed that the employees retire immediately) *and* (2) the actuarial present value, based on benefits attributable to prior service, of the accumulated benefits for the terminating employees without the enhanced benefits. (It is assumed that the employees retire at the earliest date on which they would be eligible for postretirement benefits.)

Defined Contribution Plans

Question F49: An employer has two legally separate postretirement benefit plans: (1) a defined benefit plan and (2) a defined contribution plan. The terms of the defined benefit plan specify that the employer's obligation under that plan is reduced to the extent that a participant's account balance in the defined contribution plan will be used to pay incurred health care costs covered by the defined benefit plan. For purposes of applying the guidance in this Statement, should those plans be considered a single plan or two plans?

Answer: Two plans. The nature of the promises under each plan, the manner in which those promises are satisfied, the availability of plan assets to pay benefits, and the respective accounting for each type of plan are all so dissimilar as to preclude accounting for a defined benefit and a defined contribution plan as a single plan for the purposes of applying the guidance in this Statement.

Question F50: If any assets of the defined contribution plan described in the question in paragraph F49 have not yet been allocated to participants' individual accounts, do they reduce the accumulated postretirement benefit obligation of the defined benefit plan?

Answer: No. The employer's intent to allocate these assets to the accounts of individual employees in the future is not sufficient to reduce the employer's present obligation under the defined benefit plan. Under such an arrangement, the assets of individual employees in the defined contribution plan would be used to pay health care costs incurred in the future (the employer's obligation under the defined benefit plan is limited to covering health care costs in excess of amounts held in individual defined contribution accounts). When unallocated assets are assigned to the accounts of individual employees, the employer's obligation under the defined benefit plan is reduced. This reduction is recognized immediately as a component of net periodic postretirement benefit cost.

ASC 715-60-55-26; ASC 710-10-60-2 Plan Assets under ASC 715-60

BACKGROUND

According to Title I of the Employee Retirement Income Security Act (ERISA), the assets of a pension, profit-sharing, or stock bonus plan must be held in a trust created or organized in the United States. ERISA specifically provides that plan assets held in a trust are protected from the claims of general creditors and are considered bankruptcy-proof. This protection does not appear to extend to assets held to fund other postretirement employee benefits (OPEBs), which are addressed in under the guidance in ASC 715-60.

The guidance in ASC 715-60 sets standards for accounting for other postretirement benefit costs, specifically health care benefit costs. It requires entities to report their obligations to provide postretirement benefits at the time employees render services necessary to earn benefits. For example, Company X has a policy that all employees with 20 years of service are guaranteed lifetime health insurance coverage. In accordance with the guidance in ASC 715-60, the company must currently accrue the expected cost of providing health insurance to match the cost to each employee's actual service period.

Accounting for OPEB plans is similar to accounting for pension plans. Like pension and profit-sharing plans, OPEB plans must maintain sufficient plan assets to fund the expected costs of a postretirement plan. According to the ASC's *Glossary*, a plan's assets include stocks, bonds, and other investments that are segregated in a trust and restricted for the purpose of providing postretirement benefits. In accordance with the guidance in ASC 715-60, many employers have established trusts to fund OPEB plans. However, some of those trusts are not protected from general creditors in the event of a bankruptcy. Therefore, some have questioned whether a trust established to fund postretirement plans must be bankruptcy-proof.

ACCOUNTING ISSUE

Does a trust established to pay postretirement benefits in accordance with the provisions of ASC 715-60 have to be protected from the claims of general creditors in bankruptcy for the trust's assets to qualify as plan assets?

ACCOUNTING GUIDANCE

- It is not necessary to determine that a trust is bankruptcy-proof for the trust's assets to qualify as plan assets under the guidance in ASC 715-60.
- Assets held by a trust that explicitly provides that its trust assets are available to the employer's general creditors if the employer declares bankruptcy would *not* qualify as plan assets under the guidance in ASC 715-60.

DISCUSSION

Even though the guidance in ASC 715 (FAS-106) is clear that plan assets must be restricted solely to the provision of postretirement benefits and to the payment of retirees' benefits, and that the requirement is consistent with pension accounting, the guidance above confirms the view that plan assets do not have to be maintained in a bankruptcy-proof trust to qualify as plan assets. Furthermore, proponents of this view argued that accounting is generally based on the "going concern" notion—the possibility of an employer's bankruptcy is remote and protection in bankruptcy is not relevant. Also, in the event of a bankruptcy, an employer would no longer control plan assets, so the issue of proper asset segregation and usage would no longer apply.

Nevertheless, even though an explicit protection of plan assets in bankruptcy is not required under the guidance, the second conclusion prohibits an explicit statement that plan assets are available to creditors.

ASC 715-70: DEFERRED CONTRIBUTION PLANS

ASC 715-70-55-4 through 55-9 Measurement of Excess Contributions to a Defined Contribution Plan or Employee Stock Ownership Plan

Note: The conclusions below in Issues 1d, 1e, and 2a to 2e relating to employers' accounting for unallocated shares contributed to an ESOP as a result of a pension reversion have been nullified by the guidance in ASC 718-40. However, under the transition provisions of that guidance, employers may elect not to apply the provisions of ASC 718-40 to shares purchased in a pension reversion that occurred before December 31, 1992. The guidance below continues to apply to such shares, if an employer so elects. In addition, the guidance related to employers' accounting for unallocated shares contributed to defined contribution plans are not affected by the guidance in ASC 718-40.

BACKGROUND

An employer terminates a defined benefit pension plan and contributes the withdrawn assets to a defined contribution plan or to an employee stock ownership plan (ESOP). If the amount contributed exceeds the employer's required (or maximum) annual contribution to the plan, the excess assets are held in a suspense account until they are allocated to plan participants. The employer retains the risks and rewards of ownership related to those assets while they are held in the suspense account. Excess contributions made to an ESOP must either be converted to the employer's stock within 90 days of the asset reversion or be used to retire debt incurred to acquire the employer's stock.

ACCOUNTING ISSUES

1. Contributions to a defined contribution plan
    a. How should an employer initially account for the excess contribution not allocated to individual participants?
    b. If an employer recognizes the unallocated amount as an asset, how should it be measured and classified in subsequent periods, until it is allocated to individual participants?
    c. How should an employer measure compensation expense?
    d. How should an employer account for its own common stock?
    e. How should an employer account for its own debt securities and third-party debt securities?
2. Contributions to an ESOP
    a. How should an employer initially account for the excess contribution not allocated to individual participants?
    b. How should an employer measure compensation expense?
    c. How should an employer account for its own common stock and debt securities and third-party debt securities?
    d. How should an employer account for dividends on unallocated shares?
    e. How should an employer treat its own unallocated common stock in determining EPS?

ACCOUNTING GUIDANCE

The following guidance applies to *defined contribution plans* only:

1a. Recognize an excess contribution as an asset regardless of whether the excess unallocated contribution results from a plan reversion or from another source.

1b. Account for unallocated contributions in subsequent periods as follows:
   a. Recognize an unallocated amount as an asset and treat it as if it were part of the employer's investment portfolio. For example, an unallocated amount that consists of marketable equity securities should be accounted for in accordance with the guidance in ASC 320. Employers such as investment companies and broker-dealers subject to specialized industry accounting rules are exempt from the provisions of ASC. They should recognize income from such securities, including dividends, interest, and realized gains and losses, the same as for similar items.

1c. Recognize compensation expense at the time of plan allocation based on the assets' fair market value at that time.

The following guidance applies to both *defined contribution plans* and *ESOPs:*

1d. In the employer's financial statements, recognize as treasury stock the portion of the plan's unallocated assets consisting of the employer's common stock.

1e. Account for unallocated assets consisting of employer debt securities as follows:
   a. Recognize the portion of the plan's unallocated assets consisting of the employer's debt securities as an asset, not as an extinguishment of debt.
   b. Measure employer debt securities or debt securities issued by a third party that are included in the plan's unallocated assets at fair value, and recognize unrealized gains or losses in a separate component of equity in accordance with ASC 320 (FAS-115).

The following guidance applies only to employer debt securities included in the unallocated assets of a defined contribution plan or an ESOP and does *not* apply in other circumstances in which an entity reacquires its own debt securities.

The following guidance applies to *ESOPs* only:

2a. Reduce shareholders' equity for unallocated shares in the employer's own stock, as if they were treasury stock.

2b. Recognize compensation expense at the date of allocation based on the then-current market price of the stock, and recognize the difference between the purchase price and the current market price as an increase or decrease to shareholders' equity.

2c. Same as Issues 1d and 1e above.

2d. Account for dividends on an employer's own common stock as follows:
   a. Increase treasury stock for dividends on employer common stock that are invested in additional employer common stock. Such dividends are not considered income and should not reduce retained earnings. In conformity with the 1986 Tax Reform Act, an ESOP's sponsor receives a tax deduction for cash dividends paid to participants within 90 days or that are used to repay the ESOP's loan in a leveraged ESOP.
   b. Charge compensation expense for dividends paid to participants on unallocated shares.

c. Charge dividends on allocated shares to retained earnings.

d. Charge prepayments on ESOP debt as compensation expense, and account for dividends on unallocated shares as treasury stock.

e. Follow the guidance in SOP 76-3 for other dividends (See Chapter 41, ASC 718).

> **OBSERVATION:** The guidance in SOP 76-3 is not included in the FASB Accounting Standards Codification™, but has been grandfathered for existing ESOPs and, therefore, is included in Chapter 41, *ASC 718—Compensation—Stock Compensation*

2e. Unallocated shares of employer common stock should not be considered outstanding in the earnings-per-share computation.

It was noted that this accounting differs from that required in paragraph 11 of SOP 76-3. The Task Force reached this conclusion because they believed that unallocated employer common stock resulting from a pension reversion differs sufficiently from unallocated employer shares contemplated in the discussion of leveraged ESOPs in SOP 76-3.

DISCUSSION

The guidance in this Issue applies to two vehicles used for a similar purpose to compensate employees. The generic term *defined contribution plan* is used to describe plans under which employers make regular periodic awards to participants' accounts, which are subject to vesting provisions. A defined contribution plan—as contemplated in this Issue—is a type of pension plan, which is accounted for under the guidance in ASC 715-30. While an ESOP meets the definition of a defined contribution plan, it may be established for a variety of reasons, such as to raise new capital, create a market for the employer's stock, or to replace benefits lost on the termination of a defined benefit plan. ESOPs differ from other defined contribution plans because they invest only in shares of the employer's stock, whereas defined contribution plans invest primarily in debt and equity securities of other entities. Special accounting applies to ESOPs because of their specialized nature; they were accounted for under SOP 76-3 until the issuance of the guidance in ASC 718-40. The differences between those plans are considered in the guidance above.

1a. Two alternative methods of accounting for the excess contribution to defined contribution plans were suggested. One was to recognize that amount as prepaid pension cost, consistent with the requirement in ASC 715-30-25-1 for a defined benefit pension plan. Another was to recognize the entire contribution as net periodic pension cost. The conclusion that the employer should recognize the unallocated contribution as an asset was based on the view that the employer retains the risks and benefits of the excess contribution until it is actually allocated to participants. Because the employer will use the excess contributions to make future contributions to the plan, a gain or loss on those funds will determine whether the employer has to contribute additional assets in future years.

1b. This conclusion is consistent with the EITF's conclusion on Issue 1a. If the excess contribution is recognized as the employer's asset, it should be accounted for the same as other such assets held by the employer.

1c. This conclusion is a further extension of the view that the employer retains the risks and rewards of the excess contribution, which ultimately should be reflected in compensation expense. That is, the difference between the carrying amount of the unallocated shares and their market value is recognized as a realized gain or loss.

1d. The guidance on this Issue is the same as that in Issue 2a for ESOPs, which hold shares only in the employer's own stock. The rationale for treating an ESOP's unallocated shares in the employer's own stock as treasury stock in the employer's financial statements was that the shares were under the employer's control and that such shares do not differ from treasury stock held for the purpose of meeting the requirements of other employee stock plans. Those who supported this view argued that although the plans may differ, the substance of the transaction is the same.

1e. The recognition of unallocated assets consisting of employer debt securities as assets was supported rather than as an extinguishment of debt, because of the view that the conditions for an extinguishment of debt have not been met. That is, a debtor/creditor relationship continues to exist because control over the debt instrument has not been returned to the debtor (employer); the ESOP's trustee continues to control the debt instrument.

ASC 715-80: MULTIEMPLOYER PLANS

ASC 715-80-55-2 Accounting for Employers' Obligations for Future Contributions to a Multiemployer Pension Plan

BACKGROUND

A multiemployer pension plan is a pension plan established by two or more unrelated entities to provide pension benefits to employees of those participating employers. To qualify as a multiemployer plan, assets contributed by employers are not segregated into separate accounts and may be used by the multiemployer plan to provide pension benefits to any employer's employees. All employers share in the plan's gains and losses.

When an employer enters a plan initially or elects to improve employees' pension benefits, the employer must sign a written agreement and make an unconditional promise to make certain future contributions to the plan. The contributions will be used to liquidate the past service cost associated with initiating the plan or increasing benefits. In return, the plan agrees unconditionally to pay pension benefits to the employer's employees covered under the plan.

ACCOUNTING ISSUE

Should an employer recognize a liability to a multiemployer plan for the total amount of future payments related to prior service cost, as required under an agreement executed when an employer begins participating in a multiemployer plan or increases benefits to employees under the plan?

ACCOUNTING GUIDANCE

An employer that agrees to make future contributions to a multiemployer plan to liquidate prior service cost associated with initiating a defined benefit pension plan or increasing its benefits is not required to recognize a liability for more than unpaid contributions that are due.

DISCUSSION

In discussing the accounting for single-employer defined benefit pension plans, ASC 715-30-35-10 provides guidance on how to account for prior service cost related to initiation of a plan and plan amendments that provide for increased benefits based on prior service. It states that related costs should be recognized over the future service periods of active employees when a plan is amended who are expected to benefit under the plan.

This Issue was discussed because of diversity in views on the timing of recognition of prior service costs under an agreement in a multiemployer defined benefit plan. Such agreements provide that an employer has an "unconditional obligation" to make future installment payments for past service costs, and the plan has an unconditional obligation to make future benefit payments to participants. The problem was that although ASC 715-30-35-10 provides for delayed recognition of prior service costs, the discussion of multiemployer plans in ASC 715-80-05-1, does not specifically address the recognition of such costs. Some believed that an employer participating in a multiemployer plan should recognize a liability for the total obligation under the employer's agreement with the multiemployer plan. Proponents of recognition argued that the delayed recognition concept in ASC 715-30 does not apply to multiemployer plans, because of the bilateral agreement between the parties.

Opponents of immediate recognition of the total liability for prior service costs at the date of the agreement argued that a multiemployer plan does not differ from other defined benefit pension plans and that the agreement provides for a bilateral unconditional obligation to comply with federal pension laws. In addition, they argued that ASC 715-30 did not intend to change previous practice for multiemployer pension plans under which a prior service liability was not accrued.